KEY TO WORLD MAP PAGES

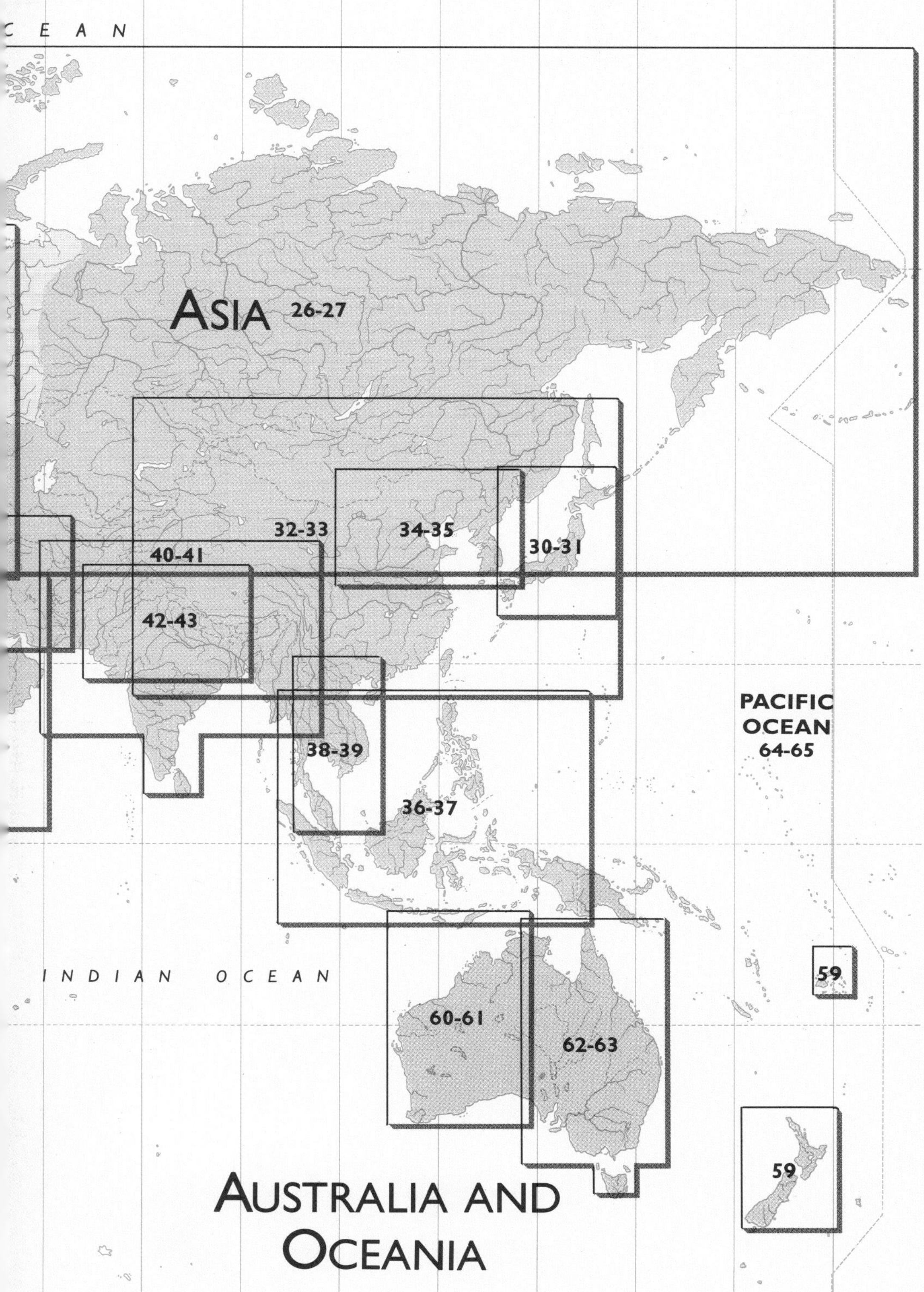

COUNTRY INDEX

ASIA 26-27

PACIFIC OCEAN 64-65

INDIAN OCEAN

32-33

34-35

30-31

40-41

42-43

38-39

36-37

60-61

62-63

59

59

AUSTRALIA AND OCEANIA

PHILIP'S

WORLD ATLAS
& GAZETTEER

CONSULTANTS

Philip's are grateful to the following people for acting as specialist geography consultants on '*The World in Focus*' front section:

Professor D. Brunsden, Kings College, University of London, UK
Dr C. Clarke, Oxford University, UK
Dr I. S. Evans, Durham University, UK
Professor P. Haggett, University of Bristol, UK
Professor K. McLachlan, University of London, UK
Professor M. Monmonier, Syracuse University, New York, USA
Professor M-L. Hsu, University of Minnesota, Minnesota, USA
Professor M. J. Tooley, University of St Andrews, UK
Dr T. Unwin, Royal Holloway, University of London, UK

THE GAZETTEER OF NATIONS
Text: Keith Lye

THE WORLD IN FOCUS
Cartography by Philip's

Picture Acknowledgements
Science Photo Library/NOAA page 14

Illustrations: Stefan Chabluk

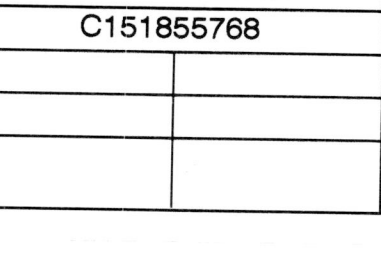
WORLD CITIES
Cartography by Philip's

Page 11, Dublin: The town plan of Dublin is based on Ordnance Survey Ireland by permission of the Government Permit Number 7516. © Ordnance Survey Ireland and Government of Ireland.

Page 11, Edinburgh, and page 15, London:
This product includes mapping data licensed from Ordnance Survey® with the permission of the Controller of Her Majesty's Stationery Office. © Crown copyright 2002. All rights reserved. Licence number 100011710.

Vector data: Courtesy of Gräfe and Unser Verlag GmbH, München, Germany
(city centre maps of Bangkok, Beijing, Cape Town, Jerusalem, Mexico City, Moscow, Singapore, Sydney, Tokyo and Washington D.C.)

All satellite images in this section courtesy of NPA Group Limited, Edenbridge, Kent (www.satmaps.com)

Published in Great Britain in 2002
by Philip's,
a division of Octopus Publishing Group Limited,
2–4 Heron Quays, London E14 4JP

Copyright © 2002 Philip's

Cartography by Philip's

ISBN 0–540–08234–1

A CIP catalogue record for this book is available from the British Library.

Printed in Hong Kong

Details of other Philip's titles and services can be found on our website at: www.philips-maps.co.uk

Philip's World Atlases are published in association with The Royal Geographical Society (with The Institute of British Geographers).

The Society was founded in 1830 and given a Royal Charter in 1859 for 'the advancement of geographical science'. It holds historical collections of national and international importance, many of which relate to the Society's association with and support for scientific exploration and research from the 19th century onwards. It was pivotal in establishing geography as a teaching and research discipline in British universities close to the turn of the century, and has played a key role in geographical and environmental education ever since.

Today the Society is a leading world centre for geographical learning – supporting education, teaching, research and expeditions, and promoting public understanding of the subject.

The Society welcomes those interested in geography as members. For further information, please visit the website at: www.rgs.org

PHILIP'S

WORLD ATLAS & GAZETTEER

TENTH EDITION

IN ASSOCIATION WITH
THE ROYAL GEOGRAPHICAL SOCIETY
WITH THE INSTITUTE OF BRITISH GEOGRAPHERS

Contents

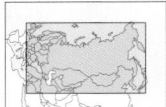

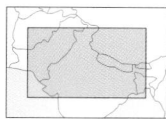
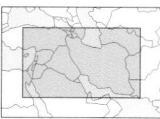

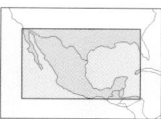

World Statistics: Countries

This alphabetical list includes all the countries and territories of the world. If a territory is not completely independent, the country it is associated with is named. The area figures give the total area of land, inland water and ice. The population figures are 2001 estimates. The annual income is the Gross Domestic Product per capita† in US dollars. The figures are the latest available, usually 2000 estimates.

Country/Territory	Area km² Thousands	Area miles² Thousands	Population Thousands	Capital	Annual Income US $
Afghanistan	652	252	26,813	Kabul	800
Albania	28.8	11.1	3,510	Tirana	3,000
Algeria	2,382	920	31,736	Algiers	5,500
American Samoa (US)	0.2	0.08	67	Pago Pago	8,000
Andorra	0.45	0.17	68	Andorra La Vella	18,000
Angola	1,247	481	10,366	Luanda	1,000
Anguilla (UK)	0.1	0.04	12	The Valley	8,200
Antigua & Barbuda	0.44	0.17	67	St John's	8,200
Argentina	2,767	1,068	37,385	Buenos Aires	12,900
Armenia	29.8	11.5	3,336	Yerevan	3,000
Aruba (Netherlands)	0.19	0.07	70	Oranjestad	28,000
Australia	7,687	2,968	19,358	Canberra	23,200
Austria	83.9	32.4	8,151	Vienna	25,000
Azerbaijan	86.6	33.4	7,771	Baku	3,000
Azores (Portugal)	2.2	0.87	243	Ponta Delgada	11,040
Bahamas	13.9	5.4	298	Nassau	15,000
Bahrain	0.68	0.26	645	Manama	15,900
Bangladesh	144	56	131,270	Dhaka	1,570
Barbados	0.43	0.17	275	Bridgetown	14,500
Belarus	207.6	80.1	10,350	Minsk	7,500
Belgium	30.5	11.8	10,259	Brussels	25,300
Belize	23	8.9	256	Belmopan	3,200
Benin	113	43	6,591	Porto-Novo	1,030
Bermuda (UK)	0.05	0.02	64	Hamilton	33,000
Bhutan	47	18.1	2,049	Thimphu	1,100
Bolivia	1,099	424	8,300	La Paz/Sucre	2,600
Bosnia-Herzegovina	51	20	3,922	Sarajevo	1,700
Botswana	582	225	1,586	Gaborone	6,600
Brazil	8,512	3,286	174,469	Brasília	6,500
Brunei	5.8	2.2	344	Bandar Seri Begawan	17,600
Bulgaria	111	43	7,707	Sofia	6,200
Burkina Faso	274	106	12,272	Ouagadougou	1,000
Burma (= Myanmar)	677	261	41,995	Rangoon	1,500
Burundi	27.8	10.7	6,224	Bujumbura	720
Cambodia	181	70	12,492	Phnom Penh	1,300
Cameroon	475	184	15,803	Yaoundé	1,700
Canada	9,976	3,852	31,593	Ottawa	24,800
Canary Is. (Spain)	7.3	2.8	1,577	Las Palmas/Santa Cruz	17,100
Cape Verde Is.	4	1.6	405	Praia	1,700
Cayman Is. (UK)	0.26	0.1	36	George Town	24,500
Central African Republic	623	241	3,577	Bangui	1,700
Chad	1,284	496	8,707	Ndjaména	1,000
Chile	757	292	15,328	Santiago	10,100
China	9,597	3,705	1,273,111	Beijing	3,600
Colombia	1,139	440	40,349	Bogotá	6,200
Comoros	2.2	0.86	596	Moroni	720
Congo	342	132	2,894	Brazzaville	1,100
Congo (Dem. Rep. of the)	2,345	905	53,625	Kinshasa	600
Cook Is. (NZ)	0.24	0.09	21	Avarua	5,000
Costa Rica	51.1	19.7	3,773	San José	6,700
Croatia	56.5	21.8	4,334	Zagreb	5,800
Cuba	111	43	11,184	Havana	1,700
Cyprus	9.3	3.6	763	Nicosia	13,800
Czech Republic	78.9	30.4	10,264	Prague	12,900
Denmark	43.1	16.6	5,353	Copenhagen	25,500
Djibouti	23.2	9	461	Djibouti	1,300
Dominica	0.75	0.29	71	Roseau	4,000
Dominican Republic	48.7	18.8	8,581	Santo Domingo	5,700
East Timor	14.9	5.7	737	Dili	N/A
Ecuador	284	109	13,184	Quito	2,900
Egypt	1,001	387	69,537	Cairo	3,600
El Salvador	21	8.1	6,238	San Salvador	4,000
Equatorial Guinea	28.1	10.8	486	Malabo	2,000
Eritrea	94	36	4,298	Asmara	710
Estonia	44.7	17.3	1,423	Tallinn	10,000
Ethiopia	1,128	436	65,892	Addis Ababa	600
Faroe Is. (Denmark)	1.4	0.54	46	Tórshavn	20,000
Fiji	18.3	7.1	844	Suva	7,300
Finland	338	131	5,176	Helsinki	22,900
France	552	213	59,551	Paris	24,400
French Guiana (France)	90	34.7	178	Cayenne	6,000
French Polynesia (France)	4	1.5	254	Papeete	10,800
Gabon	268	103	1,221	Libreville	6,300
Gambia, The	11.3	4.4	1,411	Banjul	1,100
Gaza Strip (OPT)*	0.36	0.14	1,178	–	1,000
Georgia	69.7	26.9	4,989	Tbilisi	4,600
Germany	357	138	83,030	Berlin	23,400
Ghana	239	92	19,894	Accra	1,900
Gibraltar (UK)	0.007	0.003	28	Gibraltar Town	17,500
Greece	132	51	10,624	Athens	17,200
Greenland (Denmark)	2,176	840	56	Nuuk (Godthåb)	20,000
Grenada	0.34	0.13	89	St George's	4,400
Guadeloupe (France)	1.7	0.66	431	Basse-Terre	9,000
Guam (US)	0.55	0.21	158	Agana	21,000
Guatemala	109	42	12,974	Guatemala City	3,700
Guinea	246	95	7,614	Conakry	1,300
Guinea-Bissau	36.1	13.9	1,316	Bissau	850
Guyana	215	83	697	Georgetown	4,800
Haiti	27.8	10.7	6,965	Port-au-Prince	1,800
Honduras	112	43	6,406	Tegucigalpa	2,700
Hong Kong (China)	1.1	0.4	7,211	–	25,400
Hungary	93	35.9	10,106	Budapest	11,200
Iceland	103	40	278	Reykjavik	24,800
India	3,288	1,269	1,029,991	New Delhi	2,200
Indonesia	1,890	730	227,701	Jakarta	2,900
Iran	1,648	636	66,129	Tehran	6,300
Iraq	438	169	23,332	Baghdad	2,500
Ireland	70.3	27.1	3,841	Dublin	21,600
Israel	20.6	7.96	5,938	Jerusalem	18,900
Italy	301	116	57,680	Rome	22,100
Ivory Coast (= Cote d'Ivoire)	322	125	16,393	Yamoussoukro	1,600
Jamaica	11	4.2	2,666	Kingston	3,700
Japan	378	146	126,772	Tokyo	24,900
Jordan	89.2	34.4	5,153	Amman	3,500
Kazakstan	2,717	1,049	16,731	Astana	5,000
Kenya	580	224	30,766	Nairobi	1,500
Kiribati	0.72	0.28	94	Tarawa	850
Korea, North	121	47	21,968	Pyŏngyang	1,000
Korea, South	99	38.2	47,904	Seoul	16,100
Kuwait	17.8	6.9	2,042	Kuwait City	15,000
Kyrgyzstan	198.5	76.6	4,753	Bishkek	2,700
Laos	237	91	5,636	Vientiane	1,700
Latvia	65	25	2,385	Riga	7,200
Lebanon	10.4	4	3,628	Beirut	5,000
Lesotho	30.4	11.7	2,177	Maseru	2,400
Liberia	111	43	3,226	Monrovia	1,100
Libya	1,760	679	5,241	Tripoli	8,900
Liechtenstein	0.16	0.06	33	Vaduz	23,000
Lithuania	65.2	25.2	3,611	Vilnius	7,300
Luxembourg	2.6	1	443	Luxembourg	36,400
Macau (China)	0.02	0.006	454	–	17,500
Macedonia (FYROM)	25.7	9.9	2,046	Skopje	4,400
Madagascar	587	227	15,983	Antananarivo	800
Madeira (Portugal)	0.81	0.31	259	Funchal	12,120
Malawi	118	46	10,548	Lilongwe	900
Malaysia	330	127	22,229	Kuala Lumpur	10,300
Maldives	0.3	0.12	311	Malé	2,000
Mali	1,240	479	11,009	Bamako	850
Malta	0.32	0.12	395	Valletta	14,300
Marshall Is.	0.18	0.07	71	Dalap-Uliga-Darrit	1,670
Martinique (France)	1.1	0.42	418	Fort-de-France	11,000
Mauritania	1,030	398	2,747	Nouakchott	2,000
Mauritius	2	0.72	1,190	Port Louis	10,400
Mayotte (France)	0.37	0.14	163	Mamoundzou	600
Mexico	1,958	756	101,879	Mexico City	9,100
Micronesia, Fed. States of	0.7	0.27	135	Palikir	2,000
Moldova	33.7	13	4,432	Chişinău	2,500
Monaco	0.002	0.001	32	Monaco	27,000
Mongolia	1,567	605	2,655	Ulan Bator	1,780
Montserrat (UK)	0.1	0.04	8	Plymouth	5,000
Morocco	447	172	30,645	Rabat	3,500
Mozambique	802	309	19,371	Maputo	1,000
Namibia	825	318	1,798	Windhoek	4,300
Nauru	0.02	0.008	12	Yaren District	5,000
Nepal	141	54	25,284	Katmandu	1,360
Netherlands	41.5	16	15,981	Amsterdam/The Hague	24,400
Netherlands Antilles (Neths)	0.99	0.38	212	Willemstad	11,400
New Caledonia (France)	18.6	7.2	205	Nouméa	15,000
New Zealand	269	104	3,864	Wellington	17,700
Nicaragua	130	50	4,918	Managua	2,700
Niger	1,267	489	10,355	Niamey	1,000
Nigeria	924	357	126,636	Abuja	950
Northern Mariana Is. (US)	0.48	0.18	75	Saipan	12,500
Norway	324	125	4,503	Oslo	27,700
Oman	212	82	2,622	Muscat	7,700
Pakistan	796	307	144,617	Islamabad	2,000
Palau	0.46	0.18	19	Koror	7,100
Panama	77.1	29.8	2,846	Panamá	6,000
Papua New Guinea	463	179	5,049	Port Moresby	2,500
Paraguay	407	157	5,734	Asunción	4,750
Peru	1,285	496	27,484	Lima	4,550
Philippines	300	116	82,842	Manila	3,800
Poland	313	121	38,634	Warsaw	8,500
Portugal	92.4	35.7	9,444	Lisbon	15,800
Puerto Rico (US)	9	3.5	3,939	San Juan	10,000
Qatar	11	4.2	769	Doha	20,300
Réunion (France)	2.5	0.97	733	St-Denis	4,800
Romania	238	92	22,364	Bucharest	5,900
Russia	17,075	6,592	145,470	Moscow	7,700
Rwanda	26.3	10.2	7,313	Kigali	900
St Kitts & Nevis	0.36	0.14	39	Basseterre	7,000
St Lucia	0.62	0.24	158	Castries	4,500
St Vincent & Grenadines	0.39	0.15	116	Kingstown	2,800
Samoa	2.8	1.1	179	Apia	3,200
San Marino	0.06	0.02	27	San Marino	32,000
São Tomé & Príncipe	0.96	0.37	165	São Tomé	1,100
Saudi Arabia	2,150	830	22,757	Riyadh	10,500
Senegal	197	76	10,285	Dakar	1,600
Seychelles	0.46	0.18	80	Victoria	7,700
Sierra Leone	71.7	27.7	5,427	Freetown	510
Singapore	0.62	0.24	4,300	Singapore	26,500
Slovak Republic	49	18.9	5,415	Bratislava	10,200
Slovenia	20.3	7.8	1,930	Ljubljana	12,000
Solomon Is.	28.9	11.2	480	Honiara	2,000
Somalia	638	246	7,489	Mogadishu	600
South Africa	1,220	471	43,586	C. Town/Pretoria/Bloem.	8,500
Spain	505	195	38,432	Madrid	18,000
Sri Lanka	65.6	25.3	19,409	Colombo	3,250
Sudan	2,506	967	36,080	Khartoum	1,000
Surinam	163	63	434	Paramaribo	3,400
Swaziland	17.4	6.7	1,104	Mbabane	4,000
Sweden	450	174	8,875	Stockholm	22,200
Switzerland	41.3	15.9	7,283	Bern	28,600
Syria	185	71	16,729	Damascus	3,100
Taiwan	36	13.9	22,370	Taipei	17,400
Tajikistan	143.1	55.2	6,579	Dushanbe	1,140
Tanzania	945	365	36,232	Dodoma	710
Thailand	513	198	61,798	Bangkok	6,700
Togo	56.8	21.9	5,153	Lomé	1,500
Tonga	0.75	0.29	104	Nuku'alofa	2,200
Trinidad & Tobago	5.1	2	1,170	Port of Spain	9,500
Tunisia	164	63	9,705	Tunis	6,500
Turkey	779	301	66,494	Ankara	6,800
Turkmenistan	488.1	188.5	4,603	Ashkhabad	4,300
Turks & Caicos Is. (UK)	0.43	0.17	18	Cockburn Town	7,300
Tuvalu	0.03	0.01	11	Fongafale	1,100
Uganda	236	91	23,986	Kampala	1,100
Ukraine	603.7	233.1	48,760	Kiev	3,850
United Arab Emirates	83.6	32.3	2,407	Abu Dhabi	22,800
United Kingdom	243.3	94	59,648	London	22,800
United States of America	9,373	3,619	278,059	Washington, DC	36,200
Uruguay	177	68	3,360	Montevideo	9,300
Uzbekistan	447.4	172.7	25,155	Tashkent	2,400
Vanuatu	12.2	4.7	193	Port-Vila	1,300
Vatican City	0.0004	0.0002	0.89	Vatican City	N/A
Venezuela	912	352	23,917	Caracas	6,200
Vietnam	332	127	79,939	Hanoi	1,950
Virgin Is. (UK)	0.15	0.06	21	Road Town	16,000
Virgin Is. (US)	0.34	0.13	122	Charlotte Amalie	15,000
Wallis & Futuna Is. (France)	0.2	0.08	15	Mata-Utu	2,000
West Bank (OPT)*	5.86	2.26	2,091	–	1,500
Western Sahara	266	103	251	El Aaiún	N/A
Yemen	528	204	18,078	Sana	820
Yugoslavia (Serbia & Montenegro)	102.3	39.5	10,677	Belgrade	2,300
Zambia	753	291	9,770	Lusaka	880
Zimbabwe	391	151	11,365	Harare	2,500

*OPT = Occupied Palestinian Territory N/A = Not Available

† Gross Domestic Product per capita has been measured using the purchasing power parity method. This enables comparisons to be made between countries through their purchasing power (in US dollars), showing real price levels of goods and services rather than using currency exchange rates.

World Statistics: Physical Dimensions

Each topic list is divided into continents and within a continent the items are listed in order of size. The bottom part of many of the lists is selective in order to give examples from as many different countries as possible. The order of the continents is the same as in the atlas, beginning with Europe and ending with South America. The figures are rounded as appropriate.

World, Continents, Oceans

	km²	miles²	%
The World	509,450,000	196,672,000	–
Land	149,450,000	57,688,000	29.3
Water	360,000,000	138,984,000	70.7
Asia	44,500,000	17,177,000	29.8
Africa	30,302,000	11,697,000	20.3
North America	24,241,000	9,357,000	16.2
South America	17,793,000	6,868,000	11.9
Antarctica	14,100,000	5,443,000	9.4
Europe	9,957,000	3,843,000	6.7
Australia & Oceania	8,557,000	3,303,000	5.7
Pacific Ocean	179,679,000	69,356,000	49.9
Atlantic Ocean	92,373,000	35,657,000	25.7
Indian Ocean	73,917,000	28,532,000	20.5
Arctic Ocean	14,090,000	5,439,000	3.9

Ocean Depths

Atlantic Ocean

	m	ft
Puerto Rico (Milwaukee) Deep	9,220	30,249
Cayman Trench	7,680	25,197
Gulf of Mexico	5,203	17,070
Mediterranean Sea	5,121	16,801
Black Sea	2,211	7,254
North Sea	660	2,165

Indian Ocean

	m	ft
Java Trench	7,450	24,442
Red Sea	2,635	8,454

Pacific Ocean

	m	ft
Mariana Trench	11,022	36,161
Tonga Trench	10,882	35,702
Japan Trench	10,554	34,626
Kuril Trench	10,542	34,587

Arctic Ocean

	m	ft
Molloy Deep	5,608	18,399

Mountains

Europe

		m	ft
Elbrus	Russia	5,642	18,510
Mont Blanc	France/Italy	4,807	15,771
Monte Rosa	Italy/Switzerland	4,634	15,203
Dom	Switzerland	4,545	14,911
Liskamm	Switzerland	4,527	14,852
Weisshorn	Switzerland	4,505	14,780
Taschorn	Switzerland	4,490	14,730
Matterhorn/Cervino	Italy/Switzerland	4,478	14,691
Mont Maudit	France/Italy	4,465	14,649
Dent Blanche	Switzerland	4,356	14,291
Nadelhorn	Switzerland	4,327	14,196
Grandes Jorasses	France/Italy	4,208	13,806
Jungfrau	Switzerland	4,158	13,642
Grossglockner	Austria	3,797	12,457
Mulhacén	Spain	3,478	11,411
Zugspitze	Germany	2,962	9,718
Olympus	Greece	2,917	9,570
Triglav	Slovenia	2,863	9,393
Gerlachovka	Slovak Republic	2,655	8,711
Galdhöpiggen	Norway	2,468	8,100
Kebnekaise	Sweden	2,117	6,946
Ben Nevis	UK	1,343	4,406

Asia

		m	ft
Everest	China/Nepal	8,850	29,035
K2 (Godwin Austen)	China/Kashmir	8,611	28,251
Kanchenjunga	India/Nepal	8,598	28,208
Lhotse	China/Nepal	8,516	27,939
Makalu	China/Nepal	8,481	27,824
Cho Oyu	China/Nepal	8,201	26,906
Dhaulagiri	Nepal	8,172	26,811
Manaslu	Nepal	8,156	26,758
Nanga Parbat	Kashmir	8,126	26,660
Annapurna	Nepal	8,078	26,502
Gasherbrum	China/Kashmir	8,068	26,469
Broad Peak	China/Kashmir	8,051	26,414
Xixabangma	China	8,012	26,286
Kangbachen	India/Nepal	7,902	25,925
Trivor	Pakistan	7,720	25,328
Pik Kommunizma	Tajikistan	7,495	24,590
Demavend	Iran	5,604	18,386
Ararat	Turkey	5,165	16,945
Gunong Kinabalu	Malaysia (Borneo)	4,101	13,455
Fuji-San	Japan	3,776	12,388

Africa

		m	ft
Kilimanjaro	Tanzania	5,895	19,340
Mt Kenya	Kenya	5,199	17,057
Ruwenzori (Margherita)	Ug./Congo (D.R.)	5,109	16,762
Ras Dashan	Ethiopia	4,620	15,157
Meru	Tanzania	4,565	14,977
Karisimbi	Rwanda/Congo (D.R.)	4,507	14,787
Mt Elgon	Kenya/Uganda	4,321	14,176
Batu	Ethiopia	4,307	14,130
Toubkal	Morocco	4,165	13,665
Mt Cameroon	Cameroon	4,070	13,353

Oceania

		m	ft
Puncak Jaya	Indonesia	5,029	16,499
Puncak Trikora	Indonesia	4,750	15,584
Puncak Mandala	Indonesia	4,702	15,427
Mt Wilhelm	Papua New Guinea	4,508	14,790
Mauna Kea	USA (Hawaii)	4,205	13,796
Mauna Loa	USA (Hawaii)	4,169	13,681
Mt Cook (Aoraki)	New Zealand	3,753	12,313
Mt Kosciuszko	Australia	2,237	7,339

North America

		m	ft
Mt McKinley (Denali)	USA (Alaska)	6,194	20,321
Mt Logan	Canada	5,959	19,551
Citlaltepetl	Mexico	5,700	18,701
Mt St Elias	USA/Canada	5,489	18,008
Popocatepetl	Mexico	5,452	17,887
Mt Foraker	USA (Alaska)	5,304	17,401
Ixtaccihuatl	Mexico	5,286	17,342
Lucania	Canada	5,227	17,149
Mt Steele	Canada	5,073	16,644
Mt Bona	USA (Alaska)	5,005	16,420
Mt Whitney	USA	4,418	14,495
Tajumulco	Guatemala	4,220	13,845
Chirripó Grande	Costa Rica	3,837	12,589
Pico Duarte	Dominican Rep.	3,175	10,417

South America

		m	ft
Aconcagua	Argentina	6,960	22,834
Bonete	Argentina	6,872	22,546
Ojos del Salado	Argentina/Chile	6,863	22,516
Pissis	Argentina	6,779	22,241
Mercedario	Argentina/Chile	6,770	22,211
Huascaran	Peru	6,768	22,204
Llullaillaco	Argentina/Chile	6,723	22,057
Nudo de Cachi	Argentina	6,720	22,047
Yerupaja	Peru	6,632	21,758
Sajama	Bolivia	6,542	21,463
Chimborazo	Ecuador	6,267	20,561
Pico Colon	Colombia	5,800	19,029
Pico Bolivar	Venezuela	5,007	16,427

Antarctica

		m	ft
Vinson Massif		4,897	16,066
Mt Kirkpatrick		4,528	14,855

Rivers

Europe

		km	miles
Volga	Caspian Sea	3,700	2,300
Danube	Black Sea	2,850	1,770
Ural	Caspian Sea	2,535	1,575
Dnepr (Dnipro)	Black Sea	2,285	1,420
Kama	Volga	2,030	1,260
Don	Black Sea	1,990	1,240
Petchora	Arctic Ocean	1,790	1,110
Oka	Volga	1,480	920
Dnister (Dniester)	Black Sea	1,400	870
Vyatka	Kama	1,370	850
Rhine	North Sea	1,320	820
N. Dvina	Arctic Ocean	1,290	800
Elbe	North Sea	1,145	710

Asia

		km	miles
Yangtze	Pacific Ocean	6,380	3,960
Yenisey–Angara	Arctic Ocean	5,550	3,445
Huang He	Pacific Ocean	5,464	3,395
Ob–Irtysh	Arctic Ocean	5,410	3,360
Mekong	Pacific Ocean	4,500	2,795
Amur	Pacific Ocean	4,400	2,730
Lena	Arctic Ocean	4,400	2,730
Irtysh	Ob	4,250	2,640
Yenisey	Arctic Ocean	4,090	2,540
Ob	Arctic Ocean	3,680	2,285
Indus	Indian Ocean	3,100	1,925
Brahmaputra	Indian Ocean	2,900	1,800
Syrdarya	Aral Sea	2,860	1,775
Salween	Indian Ocean	2,800	1,740
Euphrates	Indian Ocean	2,700	1,675
Amudarya	Aral Sea	2,540	1,575

Africa

		km	miles
Nile	Mediterranean	6,670	4,140
Congo	Atlantic Ocean	4,670	2,900
Niger	Atlantic Ocean	4,180	2,595
Zambezi	Indian Ocean	3,540	2,200
Oubangi/Uele	Congo (D.R.)	2,250	1,400
Kasai	Congo (D.R.)	1,950	1,210
Shaballe	Indian Ocean	1,930	1,200
Orange	Atlantic Ocean	1,860	1,155
Cubango	Okavango Swamps	1,800	1,120
Limpopo	Indian Ocean	1,600	995
Senegal	Atlantic Ocean	1,600	995

Australia

		km	miles
Murray–Darling	Indian Ocean	3,750	2,330
Darling	Murray	3,070	1,905
Murray	Indian Ocean	2,575	1,600
Murrumbidgee	Murray	1,690	1,050

North America

		km	miles
Mississippi–Missouri	Gulf of Mexico	6,020	3,740
Mackenzie	Arctic Ocean	4,240	2,630
Mississippi	Gulf of Mexico	3,780	2,350
Missouri	Mississippi	3,780	2,350
Yukon	Pacific Ocean	3,185	1,980
Rio Grande	Gulf of Mexico	3,030	1,880
Arkansas	Mississippi	2,340	1,450
Colorado	Pacific Ocean	2,330	1,445
Red	Mississippi	2,040	1,270
Columbia	Pacific Ocean	1,950	1,210
Saskatchewan	Lake Winnipeg	1,940	1,205

South America

		km	miles
Amazon	Atlantic Ocean	6,450	4,010
Paraná–Plate	Atlantic Ocean	4,500	2,800
Purus	Amazon	3,350	2,080
Madeira	Amazon	3,200	1,990
São Francisco	Atlantic Ocean	2,900	1,800
Paraná	Plate	2,800	1,740
Tocantins	Atlantic Ocean	2,750	1,710
Paraguay	Paraná	2,550	1,580
Orinoco	Atlantic Ocean	2,500	1,550
Pilcomayo	Paraná	2,500	1,550
Araguaia	Tocantins	2,250	1,400

Lakes

Europe

		km²	miles²
Lake Ladoga	Russia	17,700	6,800
Lake Onega	Russia	9,700	3,700
Saimaa system	Finland	8,000	3,100
Vänern	Sweden	5,500	2,100

Asia

		km²	miles²
Caspian Sea	Asia	371,800	143,550
Lake Baykal	Russia	30,500	11,780
Aral Sea	Kazakstan/Uzbekistan	28,687	11,086
Tonlé Sap	Cambodia	20,000	7,700
Lake Balqash	Kazakstan	18,500	7,100

Africa

		km²	miles²
Lake Victoria	East Africa	68,000	26,000
Lake Tanganyika	Central Africa	33,000	13,000
Lake Malawi/Nyasa	East Africa	29,600	11,430
Lake Chad	Central Africa	25,000	9,700
Lake Turkana	Ethiopia/Kenya	8,500	3,300
Lake Volta	Ghana	8,500	3,300

Australia

		km²	miles²
Lake Eyre	Australia	8,900	3,400
Lake Torrens	Australia	5,800	2,200
Lake Gairdner	Australia	4,800	1,900

North America

		km²	miles²
Lake Superior	Canada/USA	82,350	31,800
Lake Huron	Canada/USA	59,600	23,010
Lake Michigan	USA	58,000	22,400
Great Bear Lake	Canada	31,800	12,280
Great Slave Lake	Canada	28,500	11,000
Lake Erie	Canada/USA	25,700	9,900
Lake Winnipeg	Canada	24,400	9,400
Lake Ontario	Canada/USA	19,500	7,500
Lake Nicaragua	Nicaragua	8,200	3,200

South America

		km²	miles²
Lake Titicaca	Bolivia/Peru	8,300	3,200
Lake Poopo	Bolivia	2,800	1,100

Islands

Europe

		km²	miles²
Great Britain	UK	229,880	88,700
Iceland	Atlantic Ocean	103,000	39,800
Ireland	Ireland/UK	84,400	32,600
Novaya Zemlya (N.)	Russia	48,200	18,600
Sicily	Italy	25,500	9,800
Corsica	France	8,700	3,400

Asia

		km²	miles²
Borneo	South-east Asia	744,360	287,400
Sumatra	Indonesia	473,600	182,860
Honshu	Japan	230,500	88,980
Sulawesi (Celebes)	Indonesia	189,000	73,000
Java	Indonesia	126,700	48,900
Luzon	Philippines	104,700	40,400
Hokkaido	Japan	78,400	30,300

Africa

		km²	miles²
Madagascar	Indian Ocean	587,040	226,660
Socotra	Indian Ocean	3,600	1,400
Réunion	Indian Ocean	2,500	965

Oceania

		km²	miles²
New Guinea	Indonesia/Papua NG	821,030	317,000
New Zealand (S.)	Pacific Ocean	150,500	58,100
New Zealand (N.)	Pacific Ocean	114,700	44,300
Tasmania	Australia	67,800	26,200
Hawaii	Pacific Ocean	10,450	4,000

North America

		km²	miles²
Greenland	Atlantic Ocean	2,175,600	839,800
Baffin Is.	Canada	508,000	196,100
Victoria Is.	Canada	212,200	81,900
Ellesmere Is.	Canada	212,000	81,800
Cuba	Caribbean Sea	110,860	42,800
Hispaniola	Dominican Rep./Haiti	76,200	29,400
Jamaica	Caribbean Sea	11,400	4,400
Puerto Rico	Atlantic Ocean	8,900	3,400

South America

		km²	miles²
Tierra del Fuego	Argentina/Chile	47,000	18,100
Falkland Is. (E.)	Atlantic Ocean	6,800	2,600

Philip's World Maps

The reference maps which form the main body of this atlas have been prepared in accordance with the highest standards of international cartography to provide an accurate and detailed representation of the Earth. The scales and projections used have been carefully chosen to give balanced coverage of the world, while emphasizing the most densely populated and economically significant regions. A hallmark of Philip's mapping is the use of hill shading and relief colouring to create a graphic impression of landforms: this makes the maps exceptionally easy to read. However, knowledge of the key features employed in the construction and presentation of the maps will enable the reader to derive the fullest benefit from the atlas.

Map sequence

The atlas covers the Earth continent by continent: first Europe; then its land neighbour Asia (mapped north before south, in a clockwise sequence), then Africa, Australia and Oceania, North America and South America. This is the classic arrangement adopted by most cartographers since the 16th century. For each continent, there are maps at a variety of scales. First, physical relief and political maps of the whole continent; then a series of larger-scale maps of the regions within the continent, each followed, where required, by still larger-scale maps of the most important or densely populated areas. The governing principle is that by turning the pages of the atlas, the reader moves steadily from north to south through each continent, with each map overlapping its neighbours.

Map presentation

With very few exceptions (e.g. for the Arctic and Antarctica), the maps are drawn with north at the top, regardless of whether they are presented upright or sideways on the page. In the borders will be found the map title; a locator diagram showing the area covered and the page numbers for maps of adjacent areas; the scale; the projection used; the degrees of latitude and longitude; and the letters and figures used in the index for locating place names and geographical features. Physical relief maps also have a height reference panel identifying the colours used for each layer of contouring.

Map symbols

Each map contains a vast amount of detail which can only be conveyed clearly and accurately by the use of symbols. Points and circles of varying sizes locate and identify the relative importance of towns and cities; different styles of type are employed for administrative, geographical and regional place names. A variety of pictorial symbols denote features such as glaciers and marshes, as well as man-made structures including roads, railways, airports and canals.

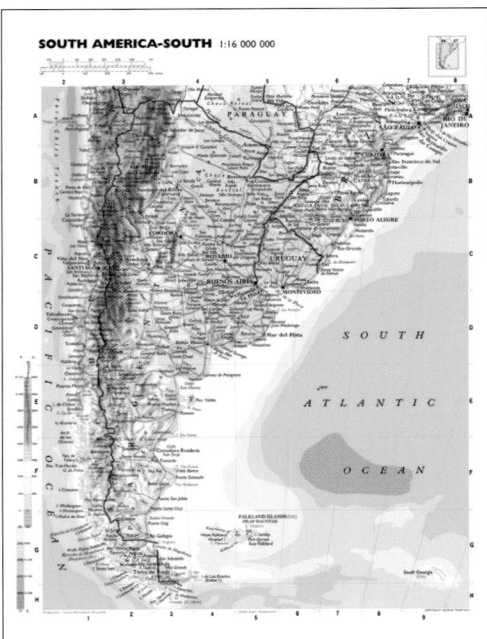

International borders are shown by red lines. Where neighbouring countries are in dispute, for example in the Middle East, the maps show the *de facto* boundary between nations, regardless of the legal or historical situation. The symbols are explained on the first page of the *World Maps* section of the atlas.

Map scales

The scale of each map is given in the numerical form known as the 'representative fraction'. The first figure is always one, signifying one unit of distance on the map; the second figure, usually in millions, is the number by which the map unit must be multiplied to give the equivalent distance on the Earth's surface. Calculations can easily be made in centimetres and kilometres, by dividing the Earth units figure by 100 000 (i.e. deleting the last five 0s). Thus 1:1 000 000 means 1 cm = 10 km. The calculation for inches and miles is more laborious, but 1 000 000 divided by 63 360 (the number of inches in a mile) shows that the ratio 1:1 000 000 means approximately 1 inch = 16 miles. The table below provides distance equivalents for scales down to 1:50 000 000.

LARGE SCALE		
1:1 000 000	1 cm = 10 km	1 inch = 16 miles
1:2 500 000	1 cm = 25 km	1 inch = 39.5 miles
1:5 000 000	1 cm = 50 km	1 inch = 79 miles
1:6 000 000	1 cm = 60 km	1 inch = 95 miles
1:8 000 000	1 cm = 80 km	1 inch = 126 miles
1:10 000 000	1 cm = 100 km	1 inch = 158 miles
1:15 000 000	1 cm = 150 km	1 inch = 237 miles
1:20 000 000	1 cm = 200 km	1 inch = 316 miles
1:50 000 000	1 cm = 500 km	1 inch = 790 miles
SMALL SCALE		

Measuring distances

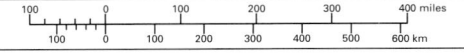

Although each map is accompanied by a scale bar, distances cannot always be measured with confidence because of the distortions involved in portraying the curved surface of the Earth on a flat page. As a general rule, the larger the map scale (i.e. the lower the number of Earth units in the representative fraction), the more accurate and reliable will be the distance measured. On small-scale maps such as those of the world and of entire continents, measurement may only be accurate along the 'standard parallels', or central axes, and should not be attempted without considering the map projection.

Latitude and longitude

Accurate positioning of individual points on the Earth's surface is made possible by reference to the geometrical system of latitude and longitude. Latitude *parallels* are drawn west-east around the Earth and numbered by degrees north and south of the Equator, which is designated 0° of latitude. Longitude *meridians* are drawn north–south and numbered by degrees east and west of the *prime meridian*, 0° of longitude, which passes through Greenwich in England. By referring to these co-ordinates and their subdivisions of minutes ($^1/_{60}$th of a degree) and seconds ($^1/_{60}$th of a minute), any place on Earth can be located to within a few hundred metres. Latitude and longitude are indicated by blue lines on the maps; they are straight or curved according to the projection employed. Reference to these lines is the easiest way of determining the relative positions of places on different maps, and for plotting compass directions.

Name forms

For ease of reference, both English and local name forms appear in the atlas. Oceans, seas and countries are shown in English throughout the atlas; country names may be abbreviated to their commonly accepted form (e.g. Germany, not The Federal Republic of Germany). Conventional English forms are also used for place names on the smaller-scale maps of the continents. However, local name forms are used on all large-scale and regional maps, with the English form given in brackets only for important cities – the large-scale map of Russia and Central Asia thus shows Moskva (Moscow). For countries which do not use a Roman script, place names have been transcribed according to the systems adopted by the British and US Geographic Names Authorities. For China, the Pin Yin system has been used, with some more widely known forms appearing in brackets, as with Beijing (Peking). Both English and local names appear in the index, the English form being cross-referenced to the local form.

THE GAZETTEER OF NATIONS

Index to Countries

Notes

The countries are arranged alphabetically, with Afghanistan as the first entry and Zimbabwe as the last. Information is given for all countries and territories, except for some of the smallest and near uninhabited islands. The form of names for all the countries follows the conventions used in all Philip's world atlases.

The statistical data is the latest available, usually for 2001. In the statistics boxes: Country area includes inland water and land areas covered in ice, as in Greenland and Canada, for example. City populations are usually those of the 'urban agglomerations' rather than within the legal city boundaries.

AFGHANISTAN

 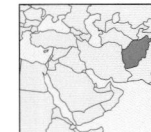

GEOGRAPHY The Republic of Afghanistan is a landlocked, mountainous country in southern Asia. The central highlands reach a height of more than 7,000 m [22,966 ft] in the east and make up nearly three-quarters of Afghanistan. The main range is the Hindu Kush, which is cut by deep, fertile valleys.

In winter, northerly winds bring cold, snowy weather to the mountains, but summers are hot and dry.

POLITICS & ECONOMY The modern history of Afghanistan began in 1747, when the various tribes in the area united for the first time. In the 19th century, Russia and Britain struggled for control of the country. Following Britain's withdrawal in 1919, Afghanistan became fully independent. Soviet troops invaded Afghanistan in 1979 to support a socialist regime in Kabul, but they withdrew in 1989. By the early 21st century, a group called the Taliban ('Islamic students') controlled 90% of the country. In 2001, following the refusal of the Taliban government to hand over the terrorist leader Osama bin Laden, an international force overthrew the Taliban regime and a coalition government was set up.

Afghanistan is one of the world's poorest countries. About 60% of the people live by farming. Many people are semi-nomadic herders. Natural gas is produced, together with some coal, copper, gold, precious stones and salt.

AREA 652,090 sq km [251,772 sq mi]
POPULATION 26,813,000
CAPITAL (POPULATION) Kabul (1,565,000)
GOVERNMENT Islamic state
ETHNIC GROUPS Pashtun ('Pathan') 38%, Tajik 25%, Hazara 19%, Uzbek 6%, others 12%
LANGUAGES Pashtu, Dari/Persian (both official), Uzbek
RELIGIONS Islam (Sunni Muslim 84%, Shiite Muslim 15%)
CURRENCY Afghani = 100 puls

ALBANIA

 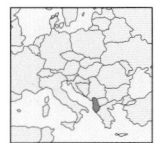

GEOGRAPHY The Republic of Albania lies in the Balkan peninsula, facing the Adriatic Sea. About 70% of the land is mountainous, but most Albanians live on the coastal lowlands. Albania's coastal areas have a typical Mediterranean climate, with fairly dry, sunny summers and cool, moist winters. The mountains have a severe climate, with heavy snowfalls in winter.

POLITICS & ECONOMY Albania is Europe's poorest country. Formerly a Communist regime, Albania introduced a multiparty system in the early 1990s. The change proved difficult. But, following elections in 1997, a socialist government committed to a market system took office. In 2001, the stability of the region was threatened when Albanian-speaking Kosovars and Macedonians, many of whom favoured the creation of a Greater Macedonia, fought with government forces in north-western Macedonia.

In the early 1990s, agriculture employed 56% of the people. The land was divided into large collective and state farms, but private ownership has been encouraged since 1991. Albania has some minerals and chromite, copper and nickel are exported.

AREA 28,750 sq km [11,100 sq mi]
POPULATION 3,510,000
CAPITAL (POPULATION) Tirana (251,000)
GOVERNMENT Multiparty republic
ETHNIC GROUPS Albanian 95%, Greek 3%, Macedonian, Vlachs, Gypsy
LANGUAGES Albanian (official)
RELIGIONS Many people say they are non-believers; of the believers, 65% follow Islam and 33% follow Christianity (Orthodox 20%, Roman Catholic 13%)
CURRENCY Lek = 100 qindars

ALGERIA

 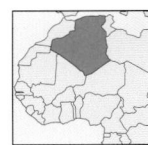

GEOGRAPHY The People's Democratic Republic of Algeria is Africa's second largest country after Sudan. Most Algerians live in the north, on the fertile coastal plains and hill country bordering the Mediterranean Sea. Four-fifths of Algeria is in the Sahara. The coast has a Mediterranean climate, but the arid Sahara is hot by day and cool at night.

POLITICS & ECONOMY France ruled Algeria from 1830 until 1962, when the socialist FLN (National Liberation Front) formed a one-party government. Following the recognition of opposition parties in 1989, a Muslim group, the FIS (Islamic Salvation Front), won an election in 1991. The FLN cancelled the elections and civil conflict broke out. About 100,000 people were killed in the 1990s. In 1999, following the withdrawal of the other candidates who alleged fraud, Abdelaziz Bouteflika, who was assumed to be favoured by the army, was elected president. Bouteflika's peace offensive reduced the violence, but sporadic killings continued into 2001.

Algeria is a developing country, whose chief resources are oil and natural gas. The natural gas reserves are among the world's largest, and gas and oil account for 90% of Algeria's exports. Cement, iron and steel, textiles and vehicles are manufactured.

AREA 2,381,740 sq km [919,590 sq mi]
POPULATION 31,736,000
CAPITAL (POPULATION) Algiers (1,722,000)
GOVERNMENT Socialist republic
ETHNIC GROUPS Arab-Berber 99%
LANGUAGES Arabic (official), Berber, French
RELIGIONS Sunni Muslim 99%
CURRENCY Algerian dinar = 100 centimes

AMERICAN SAMOA

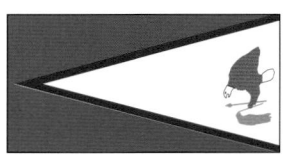 

An 'unincorporated territory' of the United States, American Samoa lies in the south-central Pacific Ocean. **AREA** 200 sq km [77 sq mi]; **POPULATION** 67,000; **CAPITAL** Pago Pago.

ANDORRA

 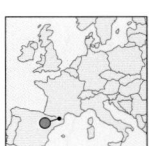

A mini-state situated in the Pyrenees Mountains, Andorra is a co-principality whose main activity is tourism. Most Andorrans live in the six valleys (the Valls) that drain into the River Valira. **AREA** 453 sq km [175 sq mi]; **POPULATION** 68,000; **CAPITAL** Andorra La Vella.

ANGOLA

 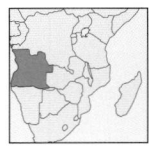

GEOGRAPHY The Republic of Angola is a large country in south-western Africa. Much of the country is part of the plateau that forms most of southern Africa, with a narrow coastal plain in the west.

Angola has a tropical climate, with temperatures of over 20°C [68°F] throughout the year, though the highest areas are cooler. The coastal regions are dry, but the rainfall increases to the north and east.

POLITICS & ECONOMY A former Portuguese colony, Angola gained its independence in 1975, after which rival nationalist forces began a struggle for power. A long-running civil war developed which, despite a cease-fire in the mid-1990s, continued until 2002, when the rebel leader, Jonas Savimbi, was killed in action and his successors negotiated peace.

Angola is a developing country, where 70% of the people are poor farmers. The main food crops are cassava and maize. Coffee is exported. Angola has much economic potential. It has oil reserves near Luanda and in the Cabinda enclave, which is separated from Angola by a strip of land belonging to Congo (Dem. Rep.). Oil is the leading export. Angola also produces diamonds and has reserves of copper, manganese and phosphates.

AREA 1,246,700 sq km [481,351 sq mi]
POPULATION 10,366,000
CAPITAL (POPULATION) Luanda (2,250,000)
GOVERNMENT Multiparty republic
ETHNIC GROUPS Ovimbundu 37%, Kimbundu 25%, Bakongo 13%, others 25%
LANGUAGES Portuguese (official), many others
RELIGIONS Traditional beliefs 47%, Roman Catholic 38%, Protestant 15%
CURRENCY Kwanza = 100 lwei

ANGUILLA

 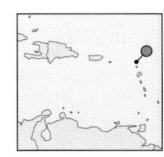

Formerly part of St Kitts and Nevis, Anguilla became a British dependency (now a British overseas territory) in 1980. The main source of revenue is now tourism, although lobster still accounts for half the island's exports. **AREA** 96 sq km [37 sq mi]; **POPULATION** 12,000; **CAPITAL** The Valley.

ANTIGUA AND BARBUDA

 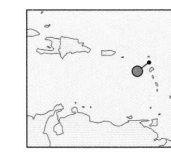

A former British dependency in the Caribbean, Antigua and Barbuda became independent in 1981. Tourism is the main industry. **AREA** 442 sq km [170 sq mi]; **POPULATION** 67,000; **CAPITAL** St John's.

ARGENTINA

GEOGRAPHY The Argentine Republic is South America's second largest and the world's eighth largest country. The Andes range in the west contains Mount Aconcagua, the highest peak in the Americas. In the south, the Andes overlook Patagonia, a plateau region. In east-central Argentina lies a fertile plain called the *pampas*.

The climate varies from subtropical to temperate. Rainfall is abundant in the north-east, but is lower to the west and south. Patagonia is arid.

POLITICS & ECONOMY Argentina became independent from Spain in the early 19th century, but it later suffered from instability and periods of military rule. In 1982, Argentina invaded the Falkland (Malvinas) Islands, but Britain regained the islands later in the year. Elections were held in 1983 and a new constitution was adopted in 1994.

According to the World Bank, Argentina is an 'upper-middle-income' developing country. Large areas are fertile and the main agricultural products are beef, maize and wheat. But about 87% of the people live in cities and towns. Industries include food processing and the manufacture of cars, electrical equipment and textiles. Oil is the chief natural resource. Major exports include meat, wheat, maize, vegetable oils, hides and skins, and wool. In 1991, Argentina, Brazil, Paraguay and Uruguay set up Mercosur, an alliance aimed to create a common market. However, in late 2001, a severe economic crisis forced the government to devalue the peso.

AREA 2,766,890 sq km [1,068,296 sq mi]
POPULATION 37,385,000
CAPITAL (POPULATION) Buenos Aires (10,990,000)
GOVERNMENT Federal republic
ETHNIC GROUPS European 97%, Mestizo, Amerindian
LANGUAGES Spanish (official)
RELIGIONS Roman Catholic 92%, Protestant 2%, Jewish 2%
CURRENCY Peso = 10,000 australs

ARMENIA

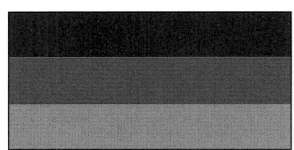 

GEOGRAPHY The Republic of Armenia is a landlocked country in south-western Asia. Most of Armenia consists of a rugged plateau, criss-crossed by long faults (cracks). Movements along the faults

cause earthquakes. The highest point is Mount Aragats, at 4,090 m [13,419 ft] above sea level.

The height of the land, which averages 1,500 m [4,920 ft] above sea level gives rise to severe winters and cool summers. The rainfall is generally low.

POLITICS & ECONOMY In 1920, Armenia became a Communist republic and, in 1922, it became, with Azerbaijan and Georgia, part of the Transcaucasian Republic within the Soviet Union. But the three territories became separate Soviet Socialist Republics in 1936. After the break-up of the Soviet Union in 1991, Armenia became an independent republic. Fighting broke out over Nagorno-Karabakh, an area enclosed by Azerbaijan where the majority of the people are Armenians. In 1992, Armenia occupied the territory between it and Nagorno-Karabakh. A cease-fire agreed in 1994 left Armenia in control of about 20% of Azerbaijan's land area. Talks aimed at settling the dispute failed in 2001.

The World Bank classifies Armenia as a 'lower-middle-income' economy. The conflict has badly damaged the economy, but the government has encouraged free enterprise, selling farmland and government-owned businesses.

AREA 29,800 sq km [11,506 sq mi]
POPULATION 3,336,000
CAPITAL (POPULATION) Yerevan (1,256,000)
GOVERNMENT Multiparty republic
ETHNIC GROUPS Armenian 93%, Azerbaijani 3%, Russian, Kurd
LANGUAGES Armenian (official)
RELIGIONS Armenian Orthodox
CURRENCY Dram = 100 couma

ARUBA

 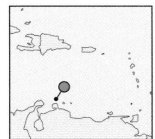

Formerly part of the Netherlands Antilles, Aruba became a separate self-governing Dutch territory in 1986. **AREA** 193 sq km [75 sq mi]; **POPULATION** 70,000; **CAPITAL** Oranjestad.

AUSTRALIA

GEOGRAPHY The Commonwealth of Australia, the world's sixth largest country, is also a continent. Australia is the flattest of the continents and the main highland area is in the east. Here the Great Dividing Range separates the eastern coastal plains from the Central Plains. This range extends from the Cape York Peninsula to Victoria in the far south. The longest rivers, the Murray and Darling, drain the south-eastern part of the Central Plains. The Western Plateau makes up two-thirds of Australia. A few mountain ranges break the monotony of the generally flat landscape.

Only 10% of Australia has an average yearly rainfall of more than 1,000 mm [39 in]. These areas include the tropical north, where Darwin is situated, the north-east coast, and the south-east, where Sydney is located. The interior is dry, and water is quickly evaporated in the heat.

POLITICS & ECONOMY The Aboriginal people of Australia entered the continent from South-east Asia more than 50,000 years ago. The first European explorers were Dutch in the 17th century, but they did not settle. In 1770, the British Captain Cook explored the east coast and, in 1788, the first British settlement was established for convicts on the site of what is now Sydney. Australia has strong ties with the British Isles. But in the last 50 years, people from other parts of Europe and, most recently, from Asia have settled in Australia. Ties with Britain were also weakened by Britain's membership of the European Union. Many Australians believe that they should become more involved with the nations of eastern Asia and the Americas rather than with Europe. In 1999, Australia held a referendum on whether the country should become a republic or remain a constitutional monarchy. By a majority of about 55 to 45, the country retained its status as a monarchy.

Australia is a prosperous country. Crops can be grown on only 6% of the land, but dry pasture covers another 58%. Yet the country remains a major producer and exporter of farm products, particularly cattle, wheat and wool. Grapes grown for wine-making are also important. The country is a major producer of minerals, including bauxite, coal, copper, diamonds, gold, iron ore, manganese, nickel, silver, tin, tungsten and zinc. Australia also produces oil and natural gas. Metals, minerals and farm products account for the bulk of exports. Australia's imports are mostly manufactured products, although the country makes many factory products, especially consumer goods, such as foods and household articles. Major imports include machinery.

AREA 7,686,850 sq km [2,967,893 sq mi]
POPULATION 19,358,000
CAPITAL (POPULATION) Canberra (325,000)
GOVERNMENT Federal constitutional monarchy
ETHNIC GROUPS Caucasian 92%, Asian 7.5%, Aboriginal 1.5%
LANGUAGES English (official)
RELIGIONS Roman Catholic 26%, Anglican 26%, other Christian 24%, non-Christian 24%
CURRENCY Australian dollar = 100 cents

AUSTRIA

 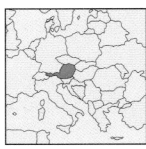

GEOGRAPHY Austria is a landlocked country in Europe. Northern Austria contains the valley of the River Danube, which flows from Germany to the Black Sea, and the Vienna basin. Southern Austria contains ranges of the Alps, their highest point at Grossglockner, 3,797 m [12,457 ft] above sea level.

The climate is influenced by westerly and easterly winds. Moist westerly winds bring rain and snow, and moderate temperatures. Dry easterly winds bring cold weather in winter and hot weather in summer.

POLITICS & ECONOMY Formerly part of the monarchy of Austria-Hungary, which collapsed in 1918, Austria was annexed by Germany in 1938. After World War II, the Allies partitioned and occupied the country. In 1955, Austria became a neutral federal republic. It joined the European Union on 1 January 1995, but was a focus of controversy when, in 2000, a coalition government was formed by the right-wing People's Party and the extreme right-wing Freedom Party.

Austria is a prosperous country. It has plenty of hydroelectric power, as well as some oil, gas and coal reserves. The country's leading economic activity is manufacturing metals and metal products. Crops are grown on 18% of the land, and another 24% is pasture. Dairy and livestock farming are the leading activities. Major crops include barley, potatoes, rye, sugar beet and wheat. Tourism is a major activity in this scenic country.

AREA 83,850 sq km [32,374 sq mi]
POPULATION 8,151,000
CAPITAL (POPULATION) Vienna (1,560,000)
GOVERNMENT Federal republic
ETHNIC GROUPS Austrian 93%, Croatian, Slovene, other
LANGUAGES German (official)
RELIGIONS Roman Catholic 78%, Protestant 5%, Islam and other
CURRENCY Euro = 100 cents

AZERBAIJAN

GEOGRAPHY The Azerbaijani Republic is a country in the south-west of Asia, facing the Caspian Sea to the east. It includes an area called the Naxçivan Autonomous Republic, which is completely cut off from the rest of Azerbaijan by Armenian territory. The Caucasus Mountains border Russia in the north.

Azerbaijan has hot summers and cool winters. The plains are fairly dry, but the mountains are rainy.
POLITICS & ECONOMY After the Russian Revolution of 1917, attempts were made to form a Transcaucasian Federation made up of Armenia, Azerbaijan and Georgia. When this failed, Azerbaijanis set up an independent state. But Russian forces occupied the area in 1920. In 1922, the Communists set up a Transcaucasian Republic consisting of Armenia, Azerbaijan and Georgia under Russian control. In 1936, the three areas became separate Soviet Socialist Republics within the Soviet Union. In 1991, following the break-up of the Soviet Union, Azerbaijan became an independent nation. After independence, the country's economic progress was slow, partly because of the conflict with Armenia over the enclave of Nagorno-Karabakh, a region in Azerbaijan where the majority of people are Armenians. A cease-fire in 1994 left Armenia in control of about 20% of Azerbaijan's area, including Nagorno-Karabakh. Attempts to resolve the problem failed in 2001.

In the mid-1990s, the World Bank classified Azerbaijan as a 'lower-middle-income' economy. Yet by the late 1990s, the enormous oil reserves in the Baku area, on the Caspian Sea and in the sea itself, held out great promise for the future. Oil extraction and manufacturing, including oil refining and the production of chemicals, machinery and textiles, are now the most valuable activities.

AREA 86,600 sq km [33,436 sq mi]
POPULATION 7,771,000
CAPITAL (POPULATION) Baku (1,713,000)
GOVERNMENT Federal multiparty republic
ETHNIC GROUPS Azeri 90%, Dagestani 3%, Russian, Armenian, other
LANGUAGES Azerbaijani (official)
RELIGIONS Islam 93%, Russian Orthodox 2%, Armenian Orthodox 2%
CURRENCY Manat = 100 gopik

BAHAMAS

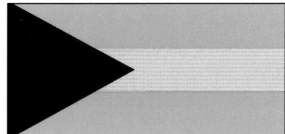 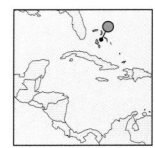

A coral-limestone archipelago off the coast of Florida, the Bahamas became independent from Britain in 1973, and has since developed strong ties with the United States. Tourism and banking are major activities. **AREA** 13,940 sq km [5,380 sq mi]; **POPULATION** 298,000; **CAPITAL** Nassau.

BAHRAIN

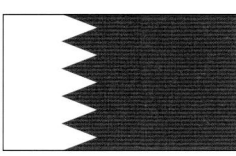 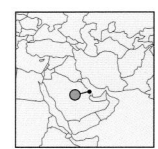

The Emirate of Bahrain, an island nation in the Gulf, became independent from the UK in 1971. Oil accounts for 80% of the country's exports. **AREA** 678 sq km [262 sq mi]; **POPULATION** 645,000; **CAPITAL** Manama.

BANGLADESH

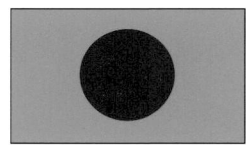 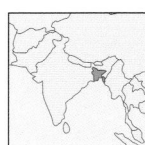

GEOGRAPHY The People's Republic of Bangladesh is one of the world's most densely populated countries. Apart from hilly regions in the far north-east and south-east, most of the land is flat and covered by fertile alluvium spread over the land by the Ganges, Brahmaputra and Meghna rivers. These rivers overflow when they are swollen by the annual monsoon rains. Floods also occur along the coast, 575 km [357 mi] long, when cyclones (hurricanes) drive sea-water inland.

Bangladesh has a tropical monsoon climate. Dry northerly winds blow in winter, but, in summer, moist winds from the south bring monsoon rains. Heavy monsoon rains cause floods. In 1998, about two-thirds of the entire country was submerged, causing great suffering.
POLITICS & ECONOMY In 1947, British India was partitioned between the mainly Hindu India and the Muslim Pakistan. Pakistan consisted of two parts, West and East Pakistan, which were separated by about 1,600 km [1,000 mi] of Indian territory. Differences developed between West and East Pakistan. In 1971, the East Pakistanis rebelled. After a nine-month civil war, they declared East Pakistan to be a separate nation named Bangladesh.

Bangladesh is one of the world's poorest countries. Its economy depends mainly on agriculture, which employs over half the population. Bangladesh is the world's fourth largest producer of rice.

AREA 144,000 sq km [55,598 sq mi]
POPULATION 131,270,000
CAPITAL (POPULATION) Dhaka (7,832,000)
GOVERNMENT Multiparty republic
ETHNIC GROUPS Bengali 98%, tribal groups
LANGUAGES Bengali, English (both official)
RELIGIONS Islam 83%, Hinduism 16%
CURRENCY Taka = 100 paisas

BARBADOS

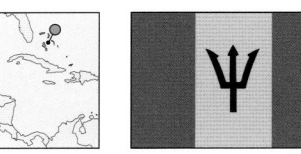 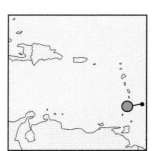

The most easterly Caribbean country, Barbados became independent from the UK in 1960. A densely populated island, Barbados is prosperous by comparison with most Caribbean countries. **AREA** 430 sq km [166 sq mi]; **POPULATION** 275,000; **CAPITAL** Bridgetown.

BELARUS

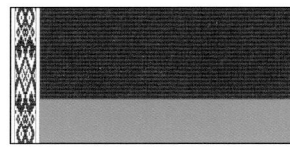 

GEOGRAPHY The Republic of Belarus is a landlocked country in Eastern Europe. The land is low-lying and mostly flat. In the south, much of the land is marshy and this area contains Europe's largest marsh and peat bog, the Pripet Marshes.

The climate of Belarus is affected by both the moderating influence of the Baltic Sea and continental conditions to the east. The winters are cold and the summers warm.
POLITICS & ECONOMY In 1918, Belarus (White Russia) became an independent republic, but Russia invaded the country and, in 1919, a Communist state was set up. In 1922, Belarus became a founder republic of the Soviet Union. In 1991, Belarus again became an independent republic, though Belarus continued to support reunification with Russia. In 1998, Belarus and Russia set up a 'union state', with plans to have a common currency, a customs union, and common foreign and defence policies. But any surrender of sovereignty was not anticipated. A union treaty aimed at a merger of the two countries, but in reality largely symbolic, was signed in 1999.

The World Bank classifies Belarus as an 'upper-middle-income' economy. Like other former republics of the Soviet Union, it faces many problems in turning from Communism to a free-market economy.

AREA 207,600 sq km [80,154 sq mi]
POPULATION 10,350,000
CAPITAL (POPULATION) Minsk (1,717,000)
GOVERNMENT Multiparty republic
ETHNIC GROUPS Belarussian 81%, Russian 11%, Polish, Ukrainian
LANGUAGES Belarussian, Russian (both official)
RELIGIONS Eastern Orthodox 80%, other 20%
CURRENCY Belarussian rouble = 100 kopecks

BELGIUM

GEOGRAPHY The Kingdom of Belgium is a densely populated country in western Europe. Behind the coastline on the North Sea, which is 63 km [39 mi] long, lie its coastal plains. Central Belgium consists of low plateaux and the only highland region is the Ardennes in the south-east.

Belgium has a cool, temperate climate. Moist winds from the Atlantic Ocean bring fairly heavy rain, especially in the Ardennes. In January and February much snow falls on the Ardennes.

POLITICS & ECONOMY In 1815, Belgium and the Netherlands united as the 'low countries', but Belgium became independent in 1830. Belgium's economy was weakened by the two World Wars, but, from 1945, the country recovered quickly, first through collaboration with the Netherlands and Luxembourg, which formed a customs union called Benelux, and later through its membership of the European Union.

A central political problem in Belgium has been the tension between the Dutch-speaking Flemings and the French-speaking Walloons. In the 1970s, the government divided the country into three economic regions: Dutch-speaking Flanders, French-speaking Wallonia and bilingual Brussels. In 1993, Belgium adopted a federal system of government. Each of the regions now has its own parliament, which is responsible for local matters. Elections under this system were held in 1995 and 1999.

Belgium is a major trading nation, with a highly developed economy. Its main products include chemicals, processed food and steel. The textile industry is also important and has existed since medieval times in the Belgian province of Flanders.

Agriculture employs only 3% of the people, but Belgian farmers produce most of the food needed by the people. Barley and wheat are the chief crops, followed by flax, hops, potatoes and sugar beet, but the most valuable activities are dairy farming and livestock rearing.

AREA 30,510 sq km [11,780 sq mi]
POPULATION 10,259,000
CAPITAL (POPULATION) Brussels (948,000)
GOVERNMENT Federal constitutional monarchy
ETHNIC GROUPS Belgian 91% (Fleming 58%, Walloon 31%), other 11%
LANGUAGES Dutch, French, German (all official)
RELIGIONS Roman Catholic 75%, other 25%
CURRENCY Euro = 100 cents

BELIZE

GEOGRAPHY Behind the swampy coastal plain in the south, the land rises to the low Maya Mountains, which reach a height of 1,120 m [3,674 ft] at Victoria Peak. The north is mostly low-lying and swampy.

Belize has a tropical, humid climate. Temperatures are high throughout the year and the average yearly rainfall ranges from 1,300 mm [51 in] in the north to over 3,800 mm [150 in] in the south.

POLITICS & ECONOMY From 1862, Belize (then called British Honduras) was a British colony. Full independence was achieved in 1981, but Guatemala, which had claimed the area since the early 19th century, opposed Belize's independence and British troops remained to prevent a possible invasion. In 1983, Guatemala reduced its claim to the southern fifth of Belize. Improved relations in the early 1990s led Guatemala to recognize Belize's independence and, in 1992, Britain agreed to withdraw its troops from the country.

The World Bank classifies Belize as a 'lower-middle-income' developing country. Its economy is based on agriculture and sugar cane is the chief commercial crop and export. Other crops include bananas, beans, citrus fruits, maize and rice. Forestry, fishing and tourism are other important activities.

AREA 22,960 sq km [8,865 sq mi]
POPULATION 256,000
CAPITAL (POPULATION) Belmopan (4,000)
GOVERNMENT Constitutional monarchy
ETHNIC GROUPS Mestizo (Spanish-Indian) 44%, Creole (mainly African American) 30%, Mayan Indian 11%, Garifuna (Black-Carib Indian) 7%, other 8%
LANGUAGES English (official), Creole, Spanish
RELIGIONS Roman Catholic 62%, Protestant 30%
CURRENCY Belize dollar = 100 cents

BENIN

GEOGRAPHY The Republic of Benin is one of Africa's smallest countries. It extends north–south for about 620 km [390 mi]. Lagoons line the short coastline, and the country has no natural harbours.

Benin has a hot, wet climate. The average annual temperature on the coast is about 25°C [77°F], and the average rainfall is about 1,330 mm [52 in]. The inland plains are wetter than the coast.

POLITICS & ECONOMY After slavery was ended in the 19th century, the French began to gain influence in the area. Benin became self-governing in 1958 and fully independent in 1960. After much instability and many changes of government, a military group took over in 1972. The country, renamed Benin in 1975, became a one-party socialist state. Socialism was abandoned in 1989, and multiparty elections were held in 1991, 1996, 1999 and 2001.

Benin is a developing country. About 70% of the people earn their living by farming, though many remain at subsistence level. The chief exports include cotton, petroleum and palm products.

AREA 112,620 sq km [43,483 sq mi]
POPULATION 6,591,000
CAPITAL (POPULATION) Porto-Novo (179,000)
GOVERNMENT Multiparty republic
ETHNIC GROUPS Fon, Adja, Bariba, Yoruba, Fulani
LANGUAGES French (official), Fon, Adja, Yoruba
RELIGIONS Traditional beliefs 50%, Christianity 30%, Islam 20%
CURRENCY CFA franc = 100 centimes

BERMUDA

 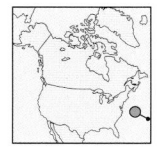

A group of about 150 small islands situated 920 km [570 mi] east of the USA. Bermuda remains Britain's oldest overseas territory, but it has a long tradition of self-government. **AREA** 53 sq km [20 sq mi]; **POPULATION** 64,000; **CAPITAL** Hamilton.

BHUTAN

 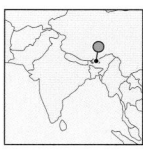

GEOGRAPHY A mountainous, isolated Himalayan country located between India and Tibet. The climate is similar to that of Nepal, being dependent on altitude and affected by monsoonal winds.

POLITICS & ECONOMY The monarch of Bhutan is head of both state and government and this predominantly Buddhist country remains, even in the Asian context, both conservative and poor. Bhutan is the world's most 'rural' country, with about 87% of the population dependent on agriculture and only 7% living in towns.

AREA 47,000 sq km [18,147 sq mi]
POPULATION 2,049,000
CAPITAL (POPULATION) Thimphu (30,000)
GOVERNMENT Constitutional monarchy
ETHNIC GROUPS Bhutanese 50%, Nepali 35%
LANGUAGES Dzongkha (official)
RELIGIONS Buddhism 75%, Hindu 25%
CURRENCY Ngultrum = 100 chetrum

BOLIVIA

GEOGRAPHY The Republic of Bolivia is a land-locked country which straddles the Andes Mountains in central South America. The Andes rise to a height of 6,542 m [21,464 ft] at Nevado Sajama in the west.

About 40% of Bolivians live on a high plateau called the Altiplano in the Andean region, while the sparsely populated east is essentially a vast lowland plain. The Andean peaks are permanently snow-covered, while the eastern plains are hot and humid.

POLITICS & ECONOMY American Indians have lived in Bolivia for at least 10,000 years. The main groups today are the Aymara and Quechua people.

In the last 50 years, Bolivia, an independent country since 1825, has been ruled by a succession of civilian and military governments, which violated human rights. Constitutional government was restored in 1982. From the 1980s, Bolivia has pursued economic reforms and free-market policies.

Bolivia is one of the poorest countries in South America. It has several natural resources, including tin, silver and natural gas, but the chief activity is agriculture, which employs 47% of the people. Coca, which is used to make cocaine, is exported illegally. In the early 2000s, the government was trying to stamp out the coca trade, while experts estimated that oil and gas were beginning to replace coca as the chief export.

AREA 1,098,580 sq km [424,162 sq mi]
POPULATION 8,300,000
CAPITAL (POPULATION) La Paz (1,126,000)
GOVERNMENT Multiparty republic
ETHNIC GROUPS Mestizo 30%, Quechua 30%, Aymara 25%, White 15%
LANGUAGES Spanish, Aymara, Quechua (all official)
RELIGIONS Roman Catholic 95%
CURRENCY Boliviano = 100 centavos

BOSNIA-HERZEGOVINA

GEOGRAPHY The Republic of Bosnia-Herzegovina is one of the five republics to emerge from the former Federal People's Republic of Yugoslavia. Much of the country is mountainous or hilly, with an arid limestone plateau in the south-west. The River Sava, which forms most of the northern border with Croatia, is a tributary of the River Danube. Because of the country's odd shape, the coastline is limited to a short stretch of 20 km [13 mi] on the Adriatic coast.

A Mediterranean climate, with dry, sunny summers and moist, mild winters, prevails only near the coast. Inland, the weather becomes more severe, with hot, dry summers and bitterly cold, snowy winters.

POLITICS & ECONOMY In 1918, Bosnia-Herzegovina became part of the Kingdom of the Serbs, Croats and Slovenes, which was renamed Yugoslavia in 1929. Germany occupied the area during World War II (1939–45). From 1945, Communist governments ruled Yugoslavia as a federation containing six republics, one of which was Bosnia-Herzegovina. In the 1980s, the country faced problems as Communist policies proved unsuccessful and differences arose between ethnic groups.

In 1990, free elections were held in Bosnia-Herzegovina and the non-Communists won a majority. A Muslim, Alija Izetbegovic, was elected president. In 1991, Croatia and Slovenia, other parts of the former Yugoslavia, declared themselves independent. In 1992, Bosnia-Herzegovina held a vote on independence. Most Bosnian Serbs boycotted the vote, while the Muslims and Bosnian Croats voted in favour. Many Bosnian Serbs, opposed to independence, started a war against the non-Serbs. They soon occupied more than two-thirds of the land. The Bosnian Serbs were accused of 'ethnic cleansing' – that is, the killing or expulsion of other ethnic groups from Serb-occupied areas. The war was later extended when Croat forces seized other parts of the country.

In 1995, the warring parties agreed to a solution to the conflict. This involved keeping the present boundaries of Bosnia-Herzegovina, but dividing it into two self-governing provinces, one Bosnian Serb and the other Muslim-Croat, under a central, unified, multi-ethnic government. Elections were held in 1996 and 1998 under this new arrangement.

The economy of Bosnia-Herzegovina, the least developed of the six republics of the former Yugoslavia apart from Macedonia, was shattered by the war in the early 1990s. Before the war, manufactures were the main exports, including electrical equipment, machinery and transport equipment, and textiles. Farm products include fruits, maize, tobacco, vegetables and wheat, but the country has to import food.

AREA 51,129 sq km [19,745 sq mi]
POPULATION 3,922,000
CAPITAL (POPULATION) Sarajevo (526,000)
GOVERNMENT Federal republic
ETHNIC GROUPS Bosnian 49%, Serb 31%, Croat 17%
LANGUAGES Serbo-Croatian
RELIGIONS Islam 40%, Serbian Orthodox 31%, Roman Catholic 15%, Protestant 4%
CURRENCY Convertible mark = 100 paras

BOTSWANA

 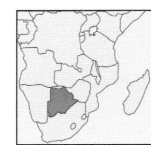

GEOGRAPHY The Republic of Botswana is a landlocked country in southern Africa. The Kalahari, a semi-desert area covered mostly by grasses and thorn scrub, covers much of the country. Most of the south has no permanent streams. But large depressions in the north are inland drainage basins. In one of them, the Okavango River, which rises in Angola, forms a large, swampy delta.

Temperatures are high in the summer months (October to April), but the winter months are much cooler. In winter, night-time temperatures sometimes drop below freezing point. The average annual rainfall ranges from over 400 mm [16 in] in the east to less than 200 mm [8 in] in the south-west.

POLITICS & ECONOMY The earliest inhabitants of the region were the San, who are also called Bushmen. They had a nomadic way of life, hunting wild animals and collecting wild plant foods.

Britain ruled the area as the Bechuanaland Protectorate between 1885 and 1966. When the country became independent, it was renamed Botswana. Since then, the country has been a stable, multiparty democracy. However, a major setback occurred in the early 21st century, when health officials announced that around 25% of the people were infected with HIV/AIDS. In 1966, Botswana was extremely poor, depending on meat and live cattle for its exports. But the discovery of minerals, including coal, cobalt, copper, diamonds and nickel, has boosted the economy. About 22% of the people now depend on agriculture, raising cattle and growing crops. Industries include the processing of farm products.

AREA 581,730 sq km [224,606 sq mi]
POPULATION 1,586,000
CAPITAL (POPULATION) Gaborone (133,000)
GOVERNMENT Multiparty republic
ETHNIC GROUPS Tswana 75%, Shona 12%, San (Bushmen) 3%
LANGUAGES English (official), Setswana
RELIGIONS Traditional beliefs 50%, Christianity 50%
CURRENCY Pula = 100 thebe

BRAZIL

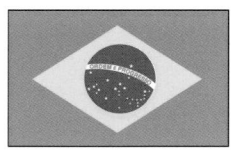 

GEOGRAPHY The Federative Republic of Brazil is the world's fifth largest country. It contains three main regions. The Amazon basin in the north covers more than half of Brazil. The Amazon, the world's second longest river, has a far greater volume than any other river. The second region, the north-east, consists of a coastal plain and the *sertão*, which is the name for the inland plateaux and hill country. The main river in this region is the São Francisco.

The third region is made up of the plateaux in the south-east. This region, which covers about a quarter of the country, is the most developed and densely populated part of Brazil. Its main river is the Paraná, which flows south through Argentina.

Manaus has high temperatures all through the year. The rainfall is heavy, though the period from June to September is drier than the rest of the year. The capital, Brasília, and the city Rio de Janeiro also have tropical climates, with much more marked dry seasons than Manaus. The far south has a temperate climate. The north-eastern interior is the driest region, with an average annual rainfall of only 250 mm [10 in] in places. The rainfall is also unreliable and severe droughts are common in this region.

POLITICS & ECONOMY The Portuguese explorer Pedro Alvarez Cabral claimed Brazil for Portugal in 1500. With Spain occupied in western South America, the Portuguese began to develop their colony, which was more than 90 times as big as Portugal. To do this, they enslaved many local Amerindian people and introduced about 4 million African slaves. Brazil declared itself an independent empire in 1822 and a republic in 1889. From the 1930s, Brazil faced periods of military rule and widespread corruption. Civilian rule was restored in 1985. Brazil adopted a new constitution in 1988, though it was amended in 1997 to allow presidents to serve for two four-year terms.

The United Nations has described Brazil as a 'Rapidly Industrializing Country', or RIC. Its total volume of production is one of the largest in the world. But many people, including poor farmers and residents of the *favelas* (city slums), do not share in the country's fast economic growth. Widespread poverty, together with high inflation and unemployment, cause political problems.

By the early 1990s, industry was the most valuable activity, employing 25% of the people. Brazil is among the world's top producers of bauxite, chrome, diamonds, gold, iron ore, manganese and tin. It is also a major manufacturing country. Its products include aircraft, cars, chemicals, processed food, including raw sugar, iron and steel, paper and textiles.

Brazil is one of the world's leading farming countries and agriculture employs 22% of the people. Coffee is a major export. Other leading products include bananas, citrus fruits, cocoa, maize, rice, soya beans and sugar cane. Brazil is also the top producer of eggs, meat and milk in South America.

Forestry is a major industry, though many people fear that the exploitation of the rainforests, with 1.5% to 4% of Brazil's forest being destroyed every year, is a disaster for the entire world.

AREA 8,511,970 sq km [3,286,472 sq mi]
POPULATION 174,469,000
CAPITAL (POPULATION) Brasília (2,051,000)
GOVERNMENT Federal republic
ETHNIC GROUPS White 55%, Mulatto 38%, African American 6%, other 1%
LANGUAGES Portuguese (official)
RELIGIONS Roman Catholic 80%
CURRENCY Real = 100 centavos

BRUNEI

 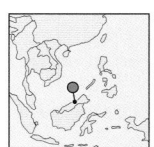

The Islamic Sultanate of Brunei, a British protectorate until 1984, lies on the north coast of Borneo. The climate is tropical and rainforests cover large areas. Brunei is a prosperous country because of its oil and natural gas production, and the Sultan is said to be among the world's richest men. **AREA** 5,770 sq km [2,228 sq mi]; **POPULATION** 344,000; **CAPITAL** Bandar Seri Begawan.

BULGARIA

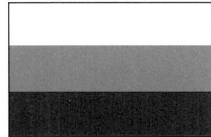 

GEOGRAPHY The Republic of Bulgaria is a country in the Balkan peninsula, facing the Black Sea in the east. The heart of Bulgaria is mountainous. The main ranges are the Balkan Mountains in the centre and the Rhodope (or Rhodopi) Mountains in the south.

Summers are hot and winters are cold, though seldom severe. The rainfall is moderate.

POLITICS & ECONOMY Ottoman Turks ruled Bulgaria from 1396 and ethnic Turks still form a sizeable minority in the country. In 1879, Bulgaria became a monarchy, and in 1908 it became fully independent. Bulgaria was an ally of Germany in World War I (1914–18) and again in World War II (1939–45). In 1944, Soviet troops invaded Bulgaria and, after the war, the monarchy was abolished and the country became a Communist ally of the Soviet Union. In the late 1980s, reforms in the Soviet Union led Bulgaria's government to introduce a multiparty system in 1990. A non-Communist government was elected in 1991, the first free elections in 44 years. Throughout the 1990s, Bulgaria faced many problems. In 2001, a coalition led by the former King Siméon, who had left Bulgaria in 1948, won the elections. Siméon became prime minister.

According to the World Bank, Bulgaria in the 1990s was a 'lower-middle-income' developing country. Bulgaria has some deposits of minerals, including brown coal, manganese and iron ore. But manufacturing is the leading economic activity, though problems arose in the early 1990s, because much industrial technology is outdated. The main products are chemicals, processed foods, metal products, machinery and textiles. Manufactures are the leading exports. Bulgaria trades mainly with countries in Eastern Europe.

AREA 110,910 sq km [42,822 sq mi]
POPULATION 7,707,000
CAPITAL (POPULATION) Sofia (1,139,000)
GOVERNMENT Multiparty republic
ETHNIC GROUPS Bulgarian 83%, Turkish 8%, Gypsy 3%, Macedonian, Armenian, other
LANGUAGES Bulgarian (official), Turkish
RELIGIONS Christianity (Eastern Orthodox 87%), Islam 13%
CURRENCY Lev = 100 stotinki

BURKINA FASO

GEOGRAPHY The Democratic People's Republic of Burkina Faso is a landlocked country, a little larger than the United Kingdom, in West Africa. But Burkina Faso has only one-sixth of the population of the UK. The country consists of a plateau, between about 300 m and 700 m [650 ft to 2,300 ft] above sea level. The plateau is cut by several rivers.

The capital city, Ouagadougou, in central Burkina Faso, has high temperatures throughout the year. Most of the rain falls between May and September, but the rainfall is erratic and droughts are common.

POLITICS & ECONOMY The people of Burkina Faso are divided into two main groups. The Voltaic group includes the Mossi, who form the largest single group, and the Bobo. The French conquered the Mossi capital of Ouagadougou in 1897 and they made the area a protectorate. In 1919, the area became a French colony called Upper Volta. After independence in 1960, Upper Volta became a one-party state. But it was unstable – military groups seized power several times and political killings took place. In 1984, the country's name was changed to Burkina Faso. In 1991 and 1998, the former military leader, Captain Blaise Compaoré, was elected president, but the military continued to play an important part in the government.

Burkina Faso is one of the world's 20 poorest countries and has become very dependent on foreign aid. Most of Burkina Faso is dry with thin soils. The country's main food crops are beans, maize, millet, rice and sorghum. Cotton, groundnuts and shea nuts, whose seeds produce a fat used to make cooking oil and soap, are grown for sale abroad. Livestock are also an important export.

The country has few resources and manufacturing is on a small scale. There are some deposits of manganese, zinc, lead and nickel in the north of the country, but there is not yet a good enough transport system there. Many young men seek jobs abroad in Ghana and Ivory Coast. The money they send home to their families is important to the country's economy.

AREA 274,200 sq km [105,869 sq mi]
POPULATION 12,272,000
CAPITAL (POPULATION) Ouagadougou (690,000)
GOVERNMENT Multiparty republic
ETHNIC GROUPS Mossi 48%, Gurunsi, Senufo, Lobi, Bobo, Mande, Fulani
LANGUAGES French (official), Mossi, Fulani
RELIGIONS Islam 50%, traditional beliefs 40%, Christianity 10%
CURRENCY CFA franc = 100 centimes

BURMA (MYANMAR)

 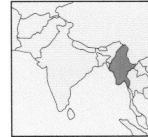

GEOGRAPHY The Union of Burma is now officially known as the Union of Myanmar; its name was changed in 1989. Mountains border the country in the east and west, with the highest mountains in the north. Burma's highest mountain is Hkakabo Razi, which is 5,881 m [19,294 ft] high. Between these ranges is central Burma, which contains the fertile valleys of the Irrawaddy and Sittang rivers. The Irrawaddy delta on the Bay of Bengal is one of the world's leading rice-growing areas. Burma also includes the long Tenasserim coast in the south-east.

Burma has a tropical monsoon climate. There are three seasons. The rainy season runs from late May to mid-October. A cool, dry season follows, between late October and the middle part of February. The hot season lasts from late February to mid-May, though temperatures remain high during the humid rainy season.

POLITICS & ECONOMY Many groups settled in Burma in ancient times. Some, called the hill peoples, live in remote mountain areas where they have retained their own cultures. The ancestors of the country's main ethnic group today, the Burmese, arrived in the 9th century AD.

Britain conquered Burma in the 19th century and made it a province of British India. But, in 1937, the British granted Burma limited self-government. Japan conquered Burma in 1942, but the Japanese were driven out in 1945. Burma became a fully independent country in 1948.

Revolts by Communists and various hill people led to instability in the 1950s. In 1962, Burma became a military dictatorship and, in 1974, a one-party state. Attempts to control minority liberation movements and the opium trade led to repressive rule. The National League for Democracy led by Aung San Suu Kyi won the elections in 1990, but the military continued their repressive rule throughout the 1990s, earning Burma the reputation for having one of the world's worst human rights records. Burma's internal political problems have helped to make it one of the world's poorest countries. Its admission to ASEAN (Association of South-east Asian Nations) in 1997 may have implied regional recognition of the regime, but the European Union continues to voice its concern over human rights abuses.

Agriculture is the main activity, employing 64% of the people. The chief crop is rice. Maize, pulses, oilseeds and sugar cane are other major products. Forestry is important. Teak and rice together make up about two-thirds of the total value of the exports. Burma has many mineral resources, though they are mostly undeveloped, but the country is famous for its precious stones, especially rubies. Manufacturing is mostly on a small scale.

AREA 676,577 sq km [261,228 sq mi]
POPULATION 41,995,000
CAPITAL (POPULATION) Rangoon (2,513,000)
GOVERNMENT Military regime
ETHNIC GROUPS Burman 69%, Shan 9%, Karen 6%, Rakhine 5%, Mon 2%, Kachin 1%
LANGUAGES Burmese (official), Shan, Karen, Rakhine, Mon, Kachin, English, Chin
RELIGIONS Buddhism 89%, Christianity, Islam
CURRENCY Kyat = 100 pyas

BURUNDI

 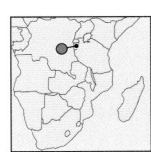

GEOGRAPHY The Republic of Burundi is the fifth smallest country in mainland Africa. It is also the second most densely populated after its northern neighbour, Rwanda. Part of the Great African Rift Valley, which runs throughout eastern Africa into south-western Asia, lies in western Burundi. It includes part of Lake Tanganyika.

Bujumbura, the capital city, lies on the shore of Lake Tanganyika. It has a warm climate. A dry season occurs from June to September, but the other months are fairly rainy. The mountains and plateaux to the east are cooler and wetter, but the rainfall generally decreases to the east.

POLITICS & ECONOMY The Twa, a pygmy people, were the first known inhabitants of Burundi. About 1,000 years ago, the Hutu, a people who speak a Bantu language, gradually began to settle the area, pushing the Twa into remote areas.

From the 15th century, the Tutsi, a cattle-owning people from the north-east, gradually took over the country. The Hutu, although greatly outnumbering the Tutsi, were forced to serve the Tutsi overlords.

Germany conquered the area that is now Burundi and Rwanda in the late 1890s. The area, called

Ruanda-Urundi, was taken by Belgium during World War I (1914–18). In 1961, the people of Urundi voted to become a monarchy, while the people of Ruanda voted to become a republic. The two territories became fully independent as Burundi and Rwanda in 1962. After 1962, the rivalries between the Hutu and Tutsi led to periodic outbreaks of fighting. The Tutsi monarchy was ended in 1966 and Burundi became a republic. Instability continued with frequent coups and massacres of thousands of people as Tutsis and Hutus fought for power. In 2001, leaders signed a power-sharing agreement.

Burundi is one of the world's ten poorest countries. About 92% of the people are farmers, who mostly grow little more than they need to feed their own families. The main food crops are beans, cassava, maize and sweet potatoes. Cattle, goats and sheep are raised, while fish are an important supplement to people's diets. However, Burundi has to import food.

AREA 27,830 sq km [10,745 sq mi]
POPULATION 6,224,000
CAPITAL (POPULATION) Bujumbura (300,000)
GOVERNMENT Republic
ETHNIC GROUPS Hutu 85%, Tutsi 14%, Twa (pygmy) 1%
LANGUAGES French and Kirundi (both official)
RELIGIONS Roman Catholic 62%, traditional beliefs 23%, Islam 10%, Protestant 5%
CURRENCY Burundi franc = 100 centimes

CAMBODIA

 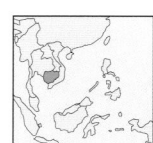

GEOGRAPHY The Kingdom of Cambodia is a country in South-east Asia. Low mountains border the country except in the south-east. But most of Cambodia consists of plains drained by the River Mekong, which enters Cambodia from Laos in the north and exits through Vietnam in the south-east. The north-west contains Tonlé Sap (or Great Lake). In the dry season, this lake drains into the River Mekong. But in the wet season, the level of the Mekong rises and water flows in the opposite direction from the river into Tonlé Sap – the lake then becomes the largest freshwater lake in Asia.

Cambodia has a tropical monsoon climate, with high temperatures all through the year. The dry season, when winds blow from the north or north-east, runs from November to April. During the rainy season, from May to October, moist winds blow from the south or south-east. The high humidity and heat often make conditions unpleasant. The rainfall is heaviest near the coast, and rather lower inland.

POLITICS & ECONOMY From 802 to 1432, the Khmer people ruled a great empire, which reached its peak in the 12th century. The Khmer capital was at Angkor. The Hindu stone temples built there and at nearby Angkor Wat form the world's largest group of religious buildings. France ruled the country between 1863 and 1954, when the country became an independent monarchy. But the monarchy was abolished in 1970 and Cambodia became a republic.

In 1970, US and South Vietnamese troops entered Cambodia but left after destroying North Vietnamese Communist camps in the east. The country became involved in the Vietnamese War, and then in a civil war as Cambodian Communists of the Khmer Rouge organization fought for power. The Khmer Rouge took over Cambodia in 1975 and launched a reign of

terror in which between 1 million and 2.5 million people were killed. In 1979, Vietnamese and Cambodian troops overthrew the Khmer Rouge government. But fighting continued between several factions. Vietnam withdrew in 1989, and in 1991 Prince Sihanouk was recognized as head of state. Elections were held in May 1993, and in September 1993 the monarchy was restored. Sihanouk again became king. In 1997, the prime minister, Prince Norodom Ranariddh, was deposed, so ending four years of democratic rule. Further elections were held in 1998 and, in 2001, the government set up courts to try leaders of the Khmer Rouge.

Cambodia is a poor country whose economy has been wrecked by war. Until the 1970s, the country's farmers produced most of the food needed by the people. But by 1986, it was only able to supply 80% of its needs. Farming is the main activity and rice, rubber and maize are major products. Manufacturing is almost non-existent, apart from rubber processing and a few factories producing items for sale in Cambodia.

AREA 181,040 sq km [69,900 sq mi]
POPULATION 12,492,000
CAPITAL (POPULATION) Phnom Penh (570,000)
GOVERNMENT Constitutional monarchy
ETHNIC GROUPS Khmer 90%, Vietnamese 5%, Chinese 1%, other 5%
LANGUAGES Khmer (official)
RELIGIONS Buddhism 95%, other 5%
CURRENCY Riel = 100 sen

CAMEROON

 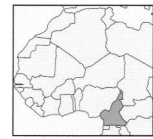

GEOGRAPHY The Republic of Cameroon in West Africa got its name from the Portuguese word *camarões*, or prawns. This name was used by Portuguese explorers who fished for prawns along the coast. Behind the narrow coastal plains on the Gulf of Guinea, the land rises to a series of plateaux, with a mountainous region in the south-west where the volcano Mount Cameroon is situated. In the north, the land slopes down towards the Lake Chad basin.

The rainfall is heavy, especially in the highlands. The rainiest months near the coast are June to September. The rainfall decreases to the north and the far north has a hot, dry climate. Temperatures are high on the coast, whereas the inland plateaux are cooler.

POLITICS & ECONOMY Germany lost Cameroon during World War I (1914–18). The country was then divided into two parts, one ruled by Britain and the other by France. In 1960, French Cameroon became the independent Cameroon Republic. In 1961, after a vote in British Cameroon, part of the territory joined the Cameroon Republic to become the Federal Republic of Cameroon. The other part joined Nigeria. In 1972, Cameroon became a unitary state called the United Republic of Cameroon. It adopted the name Republic of Cameroon in 1984, but the country had two official languages. In 1995, partly to placate English-speaking people, Cameroon became the 52nd member of the Commonwealth.

Like most countries in tropical Africa, Cameroon's economy is based on agriculture, which employs 73% of the people. The chief food crops include cassava, maize, millet, sweet potatoes and yams. The country also has plantations to produce such crops as cocoa and coffee for export.

Cameroon is fortunate in having some oil, the country's chief export, and bauxite. Although it has few manufacturing and processing industries, its mineral exports and self-sufficiency in food production make it one of the better-off countries in tropical Africa.

AREA 475,440 sq km [183,567 sq mi]
POPULATION 15,803,000
CAPITAL (POPULATION) Yaoundé (800,000)
GOVERNMENT Multiparty republic
ETHNIC GROUPS Fang 20%, Bamileke and Bamum 19%, Duala, Luanda and Basa 15%, Fulani 10%
LANGUAGES French and English (both official), many others
RELIGIONS Christianity 40%, traditional beliefs 40%, Islam 20%
CURRENCY CFA franc = 100 centimes

CANADA

GEOGRAPHY Canada is the world's second largest country after Russia. It is thinly populated, however, with much of the land too cold or too mountainous for human settlement. Most Canadians live within 300 km [186 mi] of the southern border.

Western Canada is rugged. It includes the Pacific ranges and the mighty Rocky Mountains. East of the Rockies are the interior plains. In the north lie the bleak Arctic islands, while to the south lie the densely populated lowlands around lakes Erie and Ontario and in the St Lawrence River valley.

Canada has a cold climate. In winter, temperatures fall below freezing point throughout most of Canada. But the south-western coast has a relatively mild climate. Along the Arctic Circle, mean temperatures are below freezing for seven months a year.

Western and south-eastern Canada experience high rainfall, but the prairies are dry with 250 mm to 500 mm [10 in to 20 in] of rain every year.

POLITICS & ECONOMY Canada's first people, the ancestors of the Native Americans, or Indians, arrived in North America from Asia around 40,000 years ago. Later arrivals were the Inuit (Eskimos), who also came from Asia. Europeans reached the Canadian coast in 1497 and a race began between Britain and France for control of the territory.

France gained an initial advantage, and the French founded Québec in 1608. But the British later occupied eastern Canada. In 1867, Britain passed the British North America Act, which set up the Dominion of Canada, which was made up of Québec, Ontario, Nova Scotia and New Brunswick. Other areas were added, the last being Newfoundland in 1949. Canada fought alongside Britain in both World Wars and many Canadians feel close ties with Britain. Canada is a constitutional monarchy, and the British monarch is Canada's head of state.

Rivalries between French- and English-speaking Canadians continue. In 1995, Québeckers voted against a move to make Québec a sovereign state. The majority was less than 1% and this issue seems unlikely to disappear. Another problem concerns the rights of the Aboriginal minorities, who would like to have more say in the running of their own affairs. To this end, in 1999, Canada created a new territory called Nunavut for the Inuit population in the north. Nunavut covers approximately 64% of what was formerly the eastern part of Northwest Territories.

Canada is a highly developed and prosperous country. Although farmland covers only 8% of the country, Canadian farms are highly productive. Canada is one of the world's leading producers of barley, wheat, meat and milk. Forestry and fishing are other important industries. It is rich in natural resources, especially oil and natural gas, and is a major exporter of minerals. The country also produces copper, gold, iron ore, uranium and zinc. Manufacturing is highly developed, especially in the cities where 78% of the people live. Canada has many factories that process farm and mineral products. It also produces cars, chemicals, electronic goods, machinery, paper and timber products.

AREA 9,976,140 sq km [3,851,788 sq mi]
POPULATION 31,593,000
CAPITAL (POPULATION) Ottawa (1,107,000)
GOVERNMENT Federal multiparty constitutional monarchy
ETHNIC GROUPS British 28%, French 23%, other European 15%, Native American (Amerindian/Inuit) 2%, other 32%
LANGUAGES English and French (both official)
RELIGIONS Roman Catholic 42%, Protestant 40%, Judaism, Islam, Hinduism
CURRENCY Canadian dollar = 100 cents

CAPE VERDE

 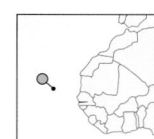

Cape Verde consists of ten large and five small islands, and is situated 560 km [350 mi] west of Dakar in Senegal. The islands have a tropical climate, with high temperatures all year round. Cape Verde became independent from Portugal in 1975 and is rated as a 'low-income' developing country by the World Bank. **AREA** 4,030 sq km [1,556 sq mi]; **POPULATION** 405,000; **CAPITAL** Praia.

CAYMAN ISLANDS

The Cayman Islands are an overseas territory of the UK, consisting of three low-lying islands. Financial services are the main economic activity and the islands offer a secret tax haven to many companies and banks. **AREA** 259 sq km [100 sq mi]; **POPULATION** 36,000; **CAPITAL** George Town.

CENTRAL AFRICAN REPUBLIC

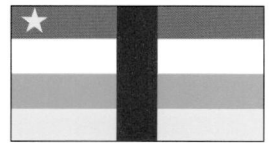 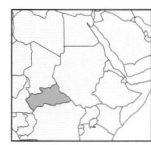

GEOGRAPHY The Central African Republic is a remote, landlocked country in the heart of Africa. It consists mostly of a plateau lying between 600 m and 800 m [1,970 ft to 2,620 ft] above sea level. The Ubangi drains the south, while the Chari (or Shari)

River flows from the north to the Lake Chad basin.

Bangui, the capital, lies in the south-west of the country on the Ubangi River. The climate is warm throughout the year, with average yearly rainfall totalling 1,574 mm [62 in]. The north is drier, with an average yearly rainfall of about 800 mm [31 in].
POLITICS & ECONOMY France set up an outpost at Bangui in 1899 and ruled the country as a colony from 1894. Known as Ubangi-Shari, the country was ruled by France as part of French Equatorial Africa until it gained independence in 1960.

Central African Republic became a one-party state in 1962, but army officers seized power in 1966. The head of the army, Jean-Bedel Bokassa, made himself emperor in 1976. The country was renamed the Central African Empire, but after a brutal reign, the tyrannical Bokassa was overthrown in a military coup in 1979. The country again became a republic.

The country adopted a new, multiparty constitution in 1991. Multiparty elections were held in 1993 and 1998. An army rebellion in 1996 was put down in 1977 with French help. Another unsuccessful coup, put down with Libyan help, occurred in 2001.

The World Bank classifies Central African Republic as a 'low-income' developing country. Over 80% of the people are farmers, and most of them produce little more than they need to feed their families. The main crops are bananas, maize, manioc, millet and yams. Coffee, cotton, timber and tobacco are produced for export, mainly on commercial plantations. The country's development has been impeded by its remote position, its poor transport system and its untrained workforce. The country depends heavily on aid, especially from France.

AREA 622,980 sq km [240,533 sq mi]
POPULATION 3,577,000
CAPITAL (POPULATION) Bangui (553,000)
GOVERNMENT Multiparty republic
ETHNIC GROUPS Baya 34%, Banda 27%, Mandjia 21%, Sara 10%, Mbaka 4%, Mboum 4%
LANGUAGES French (official), Sangho
RELIGIONS Traditional beliefs 57%, Christianity 35%, Islam 8%
CURRENCY CFA franc = 100 centimes

CHAD

GEOGRAPHY The Republic of Chad is a landlocked country in north-central Africa. It is Africa's fifth largest country and is over twice the size of France, the country which once ruled it as a colony.

Ndjamena in central Chad has a hot, tropical climate, with a dry season from November to April. The south of the country is wetter, with an average yearly rainfall of around 1,000 mm [39 in]. The hot desert in the north has an average yearly rainfall of less than 130 mm [5 in].
POLITICS & ECONOMY Chad straddles two worlds. The north is populated by Muslim Arab and Berber peoples, while black Africans, who follow traditional beliefs or who have converted to Christianity, live in the south.

French explorers were active in the area in the late 19th century. France finally made Chad a colony in 1902. Since becoming independent in 1960, Chad has been hit by ethnic conflict. The 1970s were marked by civil war and coups. Chad and Libya agreed a truce in 1987 and, in 1994, the International Court of Justice ruled against Libya's claim on the

Aozou Strip. Chad enjoyed more stability in the 1990s. A new constitution was adopted in 1997.

Hit by drought and civil war, Chad is one of the world's poorest countries. Farming, fishing and livestock raising employ 83% of the people. Groundnuts, millet, rice and sorghum are major food crops in the wetter south, but the most valuable crop in export terms is cotton. The country has few natural resources and very few manufacturing industries.

AREA 1,284,000 sq km [495,752 sq mi]
POPULATION 8,707,000
CAPITAL (POPULATION) Ndjamena (530,000)
GOVERNMENT Multiparty republic
ETHNIC GROUPS Bagirmi, Kreish and Sara 31%, Sudanic Arab 26%, Teda 7%, Mbum 6%
LANGUAGES French and Arabic (both official), many others
RELIGIONS Islam 50%, Christianity 25%, traditional beliefs 25%
CURRENCY CFA franc = 100 centimes

CHILE

GEOGRAPHY The Republic of Chile stretches about 4,260 km [2,650 mi] from north to south, although the maximum east–west distance is only about 430 km [267 mi]. The high Andes Mountains form Chile's eastern borders with Argentina and Bolivia. To the west are basins and valleys, with coastal uplands overlooking the shore. Most people live in the central valley, where Santiago is situated.

Santiago has a Mediterranean climate, with hot, dry summers and mild, moist winters. The Atacama Desert in the north is one of the world's driest places, while southern Chile is cold and stormy.
POLITICS & ECONOMY Amerindian people reached the southern tip of South America 8,000 years ago. In 1520, Portuguese navigator Ferdinand Magellan was the first European to sight Chile. The country became a Spanish colony in the 1540s. Chile became independent in 1818. During a war (1879–83), it gained mineral-rich areas from Peru and Bolivia.

In 1970, Salvador Allende became the first Communist leader to be elected democratically. He was overthrown in 1973 by army officers, who were supported by the CIA. General Augusto Pinochet then ruled as a dictator. A new constitution was introduced in 1981 and elections were held in 1989. In 2000, a socialist, Ricardo Lagos, was elected president. Pinochet, who had been charged with presiding over acts of torture, was found to be too ill to stand trial in 2001.

The World Bank classifies Chile as a 'lower-middle-income' developing country. Mining is important, especially copper production. Minerals dominate exports. The most valuable activity is manufacturing; products include processed foods, metals, iron and steel, transport equipment and textiles.

AREA 756,950 sq km [292,258 sq mi]
POPULATION 15,328,000
CAPITAL (POPULATION) Santiago (4,691,000)
GOVERNMENT Multiparty republic
ETHNIC GROUPS Mestizo 95%, Amerindian 3%
LANGUAGES Spanish (official)
RELIGIONS Roman Catholic 89%, Protestant 11%
CURRENCY Peso = 100 centavos

CHINA

CHINA

GEOGRAPHY The People's Republic of China is the world's third largest country. Most people live in the east – on the coastal plains or in the fertile valleys of the Huang He (Hwang Ho or Yellow River), the Chang Jiang (Yangtze Kiang), which is Asia's longest river at 6,380 km [3,960 mi], and the Xi Jiang (Si Kiang).

Western China is thinly populated. It includes the bleak Tibetan plateau which is bounded by the Himalaya, the world's highest mountain range. Other ranges include the Kunlun Shan, the Altun Shan and the Tian Shan. Deserts include the Gobi Desert along the Mongolian border and the Taklimakan Desert in the far west.

Beijing in north-eastern China has cold winters and warm summers, with a moderate rainfall. Shanghai, in the east-central region of China, has milder winters and more rain. The south-east has a wet, subtropical climate. In the west, the climate is severe. Lhasa has very cold winters and a low rainfall.

POLITICS & ECONOMY China is one of the world's oldest civilizations, going back 3,500 years. Under the Han dynasty (202 BC to AD 220), the Chinese empire was as large as the Roman empire. Mongols conquered China in the 13th century, but Chinese rule was restored in 1368. The Manchu people of Mongolia ruled the country from 1644 to 1912, when the country became a republic.

War with Japan (1937–45) was followed by civil war between the nationalists and the Communists. The Communists triumphed in 1949, setting up the People's Republic of China. In the 1980s, following the death of the revolutionary leader Mao Zedong (Mao Tse-tung) in 1976, China encouraged formerly forbidden policies, namely private enterprise and foreign investment. But the Communist leaders have not permitted political freedom. Opponents are still harshly treated, while attempts to negotiate some degree of autonomy for Tibet were rejected in 1998.

China's economy, which is one of the world's largest, has expanded rapidly since the late 1970s. This is partly the result of the gradual abandonment of some fundamental Communist policies, including the setting up of many private manufacturing industries in the east. China's sheer size, combined with its rapid economic growth, led to predictions in the 1990s that China would become the world's biggest economy 'within a generation'. This was made more likely by the return of Hong Kong in 1997 and the admission of China into the World Trade Organization (WTO) in 2001. China would like to regain the prosperous island of Taiwan, which was admitted to the WTO on 1 January 2002, but this seemed unlikely in the early 21st century.

In the early 1990s, agriculture employed about 70% of the people, although only 10% of the land is used for crops. Major products include rice, sweet potatoes, tea and wheat, together with many fruits and vegetables. Livestock farming is also important. Pork is a popular meat and China has more than a third of the world's pigs.

China's resources include coal, oil, iron ore and various other metals. China has huge steel industries and manufactures include cement, chemicals, fertilizers, machinery, telecommunications and recording equipment, and textiles. Consumer goods, such as bicycles and radios, are becoming increasingly important.

AREA 9,596,960 sq km [3,705,386 sq mi]
POPULATION 1,273,111,000
CAPITAL (POPULATION) Beijing (12,362,000)
GOVERNMENT Single-party Communist republic
ETHNIC GROUPS Han Chinese 92%, 55 minority groups
LANGUAGES Mandarin Chinese (official)
RELIGIONS Atheist (official)
CURRENCY Renminbi yuan = 10 jiao = 100 fen

COLOMBIA

GEOGRAPHY The Republic of Colombia, in north-eastern South America, is the only country in the continent to have coastlines on both the Pacific and the Caribbean Sea. Colombia also contains the northernmost ranges of the Andes Mountains.

There is a tropical climate in the lowlands. But the altitude greatly affects the climate of the Andes. The capital, Bogotá, which stands on a plateau in the eastern Andes at about 2,800 m [9,200 ft] above sea level, has mild temperatures throughout the year. The rainfall is heavy, especially on the Pacific coast

POLITICS & ECONOMY Amerindian people have lived in Colombia for thousands of years. But today, only a small proportion of the people are of unmixed Amerindian ancestry. Mestizos (people of mixed white and Amerindian ancestry) form the largest group, followed by whites and mulattos (people of mixed European and African ancestry).

Spaniards opened up the area in the early 16th century. They set up a territory known as the Viceroyalty of the New Kingdom of Granada, including Colombia, Ecuador, Panama and Venezuela. In 1819, the area became independent, but Ecuador and Venezuela soon split away, followed by Panama in 1903. Recent history has been unstable. Rivalries between main political parties led to civil wars in 1899–1902 and 1949–57, when the parties agreed to form a coalition. The coalition government ended in 1986 when the Liberal Party was elected. Colombia faces economic problems, as well as the difficulty of controlling a large illicit drug industry run by violent dealers. In 2000, the United States began to provide military aid to help Colombia fight drug-trafficking. Colombia exports oil, coffee and chemicals.

AREA 1,138,910 sq km [439,733 sq mi]
POPULATION 40,349,000
CAPITAL (POPULATION) Bogotá (6,005,000)
GOVERNMENT Multiparty republic
ETHNIC GROUPS Mestizo 58%, White 20%, Mulatto 14%, Black 4%
LANGUAGES Spanish (official)
RELIGIONS Roman Catholic 90%
CURRENCY Peso = 100 centavos

COMOROS

 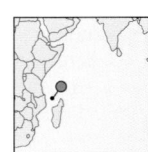

The Federal Islamic Republic of the Comoros consists of three large islands and some smaller ones,

lying at the north end of the Mozambique Channel in the Indian Ocean. The country became independent from France in 1974, but the people on a fourth island, Mayotte, voted to remain French. In 1997, secessionists on the island of Anjouan, who favoured a return to French rule, defeated forces from Grand Comore and, in 1998, they voted overwhelmingly to break away from the Comoros. Most people are subsistence farmers, although cash crops such as coconuts, coffee, cocoa and spices are also produced. The main exports are cloves, perfume oils and vanilla. **AREA** 2,230 sq km [861 sq mi]; **POPULATION** 596,000; **CAPITAL** Moroni.

CONGO

GEOGRAPHY The Republic of Congo is a country on the River Congo in west-central Africa. The Equator runs through the centre of the country. Congo has a narrow coastal plain on which its main port, Pointe Noire, stands. Behind the plain are uplands through which the River Niari has carved a fertile valley. Central Congo consists of high plains. The north contains large swampy areas in the valleys of the tributaries of the River Congo.

Congo has a hot, wet equatorial climate. Brazzaville has a dry season between June and September. The coast is drier and cooler than the rest of Congo, because of the cold offshore Benguela ocean current.

POLITICS & ECONOMY Part of the huge Kongo kingdom between the 15th and 18th centuries, the coast of the Congo later became a centre of the European slave trade. The area came under French protection in 1880. It was later governed as part of a larger region called French Equatorial Africa. The country remained under French control until 1960.

Congo became a one-party state in 1964 and a military group took over the government in 1968. In 1970, Congo declared itself a Communist country, though it continued to seek aid from Western countries. The government officially abandoned its Communist policies in 1990. Multiparty elections were held in 1992, but the elected president, Pascal Lissouba, was overthrown in 1997 by former president Denis Sassou-Nguesso. Civil war again occurred in January 1999, but peace was restored. In 2002, Sassou-Nguesso was elected president.

The World Bank classifies Congo as a 'lower-middle-income' developing country. Agriculture is the most important activity, employing more than 60% of the people. But many farmers produce little more than they need to feed their families. Major food crops include bananas, cassava, maize and rice, while the leading cash crops are coffee and cocoa. Congo's main exports are oil (which makes up 70% of the total) and timber. Manufacturing is relatively unimportant at the moment, still hampered by poor transport links, but it is gradually being developed.

AREA 342,000 sq km [132,046 sq mi]
POPULATION 2,894,000
CAPITAL (POPULATION) Brazzaville (938,000)
GOVERNMENT Military regime
ETHNIC GROUPS Kongo 48%, Sangha 20%, Teke 17%, M'bochi 12%
LANGUAGES French (official), many others
RELIGIONS Christianity 50%, Animist 48%, Islam 2%
CURRENCY CFA franc = 100 centimes

CONGO (DEM. REP. OF THE)

GEOGRAPHY The Democratic Republic of the Congo, formerly known as Zaïre, is the world's 12th largest country. Much of the country lies within the drainage basin of the huge River Congo. The river reaches the sea along the country's coastline, which is 40 km [25 mi] long. Mountains rise in the east, where the country's borders run through lakes Tanganyika, Kivu, Edward and Albert.

The equatorial region has high temperatures and heavy rainfall throughout the year.

POLITICS & ECONOMY Pygmies were the first inhabitants of the region, with Portuguese navigators not reaching the coast until 1482, but the interior was not explored until the late 19th century. In 1885, the country, called Congo Free State, became the personal property of King Léopold II of Belgium. In 1908, the country became a Belgian colony.

The Belgian Congo became independent in 1960 and was renamed Zaïre in 1971. Ethnic rivalries caused instability until 1965, when the country became a one-party state, ruled by President Mobutu. The government allowed the formation of political parties in 1990, but elections were repeatedly postponed. In 1996, fighting broke out in eastern Zaïre, as the Tutsi–Hutu conflict in Burundi and Rwanda spilled over. The rebel leader Laurent Kabila took power in 1997, ousting Mobutu and renaming the country. A rebellion against Kabila broke out in 1998. Rwanda and Uganda supported the rebels, while Angola, Chad, Namibia and Zimbabwe assisted Kabila. A peace treaty was signed in 1999, but the fighting continued. However, hopes for peace were rekindled when Kabila was assassinated in 2001 and succeeded by his son, Major-General Joseph Kabila.

The World Bank classifies the Democratic Republic of the Congo as a 'low-income' developing country, despite its reserves of copper, the main export, and other minerals. Agriculture, mainly at subsistence level, employs 71% of the people.

AREA 2,344,885 sq km [905,365 sq mi]
POPULATION 53,625,000
CAPITAL (POPULATION) Kinshasa (2,664,000)
GOVERNMENT Single-party republic
ETHNIC GROUPS Over 200; the largest are Mongo, Luba, Kongo, Mangbetu-Azande
LANGUAGES French (official), tribal languages
RELIGIONS Roman Catholic 50%, Protestant 20%, Islam 10%, others 20%
CURRENCY Congolese franc

COSTA RICA

GEOGRAPHY The Republic of Costa Rica in Central America has coastlines on both the Pacific Ocean and also on the Caribbean Sea. Central Costa Rica consists of mountain ranges and plateaux with many volcanoes.

The coolest months are December and January. The north-east trade winds bring heavy rain to the Caribbean coast. There is less rainfall in the highlands and on the Pacific coastlands.

POLITICS & ECONOMY Christopher Columbus reached the Caribbean coast in 1502 and rumours of treasure soon attracted many Spaniards to settle in the country. Spain ruled the country until 1821, when Spain's Central American colonies broke away to join Mexico in 1822. In 1823, the Central American states broke with Mexico and set up the Central American Federation. Later, this large union broke up and Costa Rica became fully independent in 1838. From the late 19th century, Costa Rica experienced a number of revolutions, with periods of dictatorship and periods of democracy. In 1948, following a revolt, the armed forces were abolished. Since 1948, Costa Rica has enjoyed a long period of stable democracy, which many in Latin America admire and envy.

Costa Rica is classified by the World Bank as a 'lower-middle-income' developing country and one of the most prosperous countries in Central America. There are high educational standards and a high life expectancy (to an average of 73.5 years). Agriculture employs 20% of the people.

The country's resources include its forests, but it lacks minerals apart from some bauxite and manganese. Manufacturing is increasing. The United States is Costa Rica's chief trading partner. Tourism is a growing industry.

AREA 51,100 sq km [19,730 sq mi]
POPULATION 3,773,000
CAPITAL (POPULATION) San José (1,220,000)
GOVERNMENT Multiparty republic
ETHNIC GROUPS White 85%, Mestizo 8%, Black and Mulatto 3%, East Asian (mostly Chinese) 1%
LANGUAGES Spanish (official)
RELIGIONS Roman Catholic 76%, Evangelical 14%
CURRENCY Colón = 100 céntimos

CROATIA

GEOGRAPHY The Republic of Croatia was one of the six republics that made up the former Communist country of Yugoslavia until it became independent in 1991. The region bordering the Adriatic Sea is called Dalmatia. It includes the coastal ranges, which contain large areas of bare limestone. Most of the rest of the country consists of the fertile Pannonian plains.

The coastal area has a typical Mediterranean climate, with hot, dry summers and mild, moist winters. Inland, the climate becomes more continental. Winters are cold, while temperatures often soar to 38°C [100°F] in the summer months.

POLITICS & ECONOMY Slav people settled in the area around 1,400 years ago. In 803, Croatia became part of the Holy Roman empire and the Croats soon adopted Christianity. Croatia was an independent kingdom in the 10th and 11th centuries. In 1102, the king of Hungary also became king of Croatia, creating a union that lasted 800 years. In 1526, part of Croatia came under the Turkish Ottoman empire, while the rest came under the Austrian Habsburgs.

After Austria–Hungary was defeated in World War I (1914–18), Croatia became part of the new Kingdom of the Serbs, Croats and Slovenes. This kingdom was renamed Yugoslavia in 1929. Germany occupied

Yugoslavia during World War II (1939–45). Croatia was proclaimed independent, but it was really ruled by the invaders.

After the war, Communists took power with Josip Broz Tito as the country's leader. Despite ethnic differences between the people, Tito held Yugoslavia together until his death in 1980. In the 1980s, economic and ethnic problems, including a deterioration in relations with Serbia, threatened stability. In the 1990s, Yugoslavia split into five nations, one of which was Croatia, which declared itself independent in 1991.

After Serbia supplied arms to Serbs living in Croatia, war broke out between the two republics, causing great damage. Croatia lost more than 30% of its territory. But in 1992, the United Nations sent a peacekeeping force to Croatia, which effectively ended the war with Serbia.

In 1992, when war broke out in Bosnia-Herzegovina, Bosnian Croats occupied parts of the country. But in 1994, Croatia helped to end Croat–Muslim conflict in Bosnia-Herzegovina and, in 1995, after retaking some areas occupied by Serbs, it helped to draw up the Dayton Peace Accord which ended the civil war there.

The wars of the early 1990s disrupted Croatia's economy, though the election of a pro-democratic coalition government in 2000 held out hope for the future, including a revival of the valuable tourist industry. The country has many manufacturing industries and manufactures are the main exports.

AREA 56,538 sq km [21,824 sq mi]
POPULATION 4,334,000
CAPITAL (POPULATION) Zagreb (868,000)
GOVERNMENT Multiparty republic
ETHNIC GROUPS Croat 78%, Serb 12%
LANGUAGES Serbo-Croatian
RELIGIONS Roman Catholic 77%, Eastern Orthodox 11%, Islam 1%
CURRENCY Kuna = 100 lipas

CUBA

GEOGRAPHY The Republic of Cuba is the largest island country in the Caribbean Sea. It consists of one large island, Cuba, the Isle of Youth (Isla de la Juventud) and about 1,600 small islets. Mountains and hills cover about a quarter of Cuba. The highest mountain range, the Sierra Maestra in the south-east, reaches 2,000 m [6,562 ft] above sea level. The rest of the land consists of gently rolling country or coastal plains, crossed by fertile valleys carved by the short, mostly shallow and narrow rivers.

Cuba lies in the tropics. But sea breezes moderate the temperature, warming the land in winter and cooling it in summer.

POLITICS & ECONOMY Christopher Columbus discovered the island in 1492 and Spaniards began to settle there from 1511. Spanish rule ended in 1898, when the United States defeated Spain in the Spanish–American War. American influence in Cuba remained strong until 1959, when revolutionary forces under Fidel Castro overthrew the dictatorial government of Fulgencio Batista.

The United States opposed Castro's policies, when he turned to the Soviet Union for assistance. In 1961, Cuban exiles attempting an invasion were defeated. In 1962, the US learned that nuclear missile bases

armed by the Soviet Union had been established in Cuba. The US ordered the Soviet Union to remove the missiles and bases and, after a few days, when many people feared that a world war might break out, the Soviet Union agreed to the American demands.

Cuba's relations with the Soviet Union remained strong until 1991, when the Soviet Union was broken up. The loss of Soviet aid greatly damaged Cuba's economy, but Castro continued the country's left-wing policies. In 2000, the United States lifted its food embargo on Cuba. The ban on travel was also liberalized, though the ban on tourists remained.

The government runs Cuba's economy and owns 70% of the farmland. Agriculture is important and sugar is the chief export, followed by refined nickel ore. Other exports include cigars, citrus fruits, fish, medical products and rum.

Before 1959, US companies owned most of Cuba's manufacturing industries. But under Fidel Castro, they became government property. After the collapse of Communist governments in the Soviet Union and its allies, Cuba worked to increase its trade with Latin America and China.

AREA 110,860 sq km [42,803 sq mi]
POPULATION 11,184,000
CAPITAL (POPULATION) Havana (2,204,000)
GOVERNMENT Socialist republic
ETHNIC GROUPS White 37%, Mulatto 51%, Black 11%
LANGUAGES Spanish (official)
RELIGIONS Roman Catholic 40%, Protestant 3%
CURRENCY Cuban peso = 100 centavos

CYPRUS

 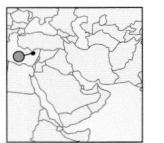

GEOGRAPHY The Republic of Cyprus is an island nation in the north-eastern Mediterranean Sea. Geographers regard it as part of Asia, but it resembles southern Europe in many ways.

Cyprus has scenic mountain ranges, including the Kyrenia range in the north and the Troodos Mountains in the south, which rise to 1,951 m [6,401 ft] at Mount Olympus. The island also contains several fertile lowlands, including the broad Mesaoria plain between the Kyrenia and Troodos mountains.

Cyprus has a Mediterranean climate, with hot, dry summers and mild, moist winters. But the summers are hotter than in the western Mediterranean lands; this is because Cyprus lies close to the hot mainland of south-western Asia.

POLITICS & ECONOMY Greeks settled on Cyprus around 3,200 years ago. From AD 330, the island was part of the Byzantine empire. In the 1570s, Cyprus became part of the Turkish Ottoman empire. Turkish rule continued until 1878 when Cyprus was leased to Britain. Britain annexed the island in 1914 and proclaimed it a colony in 1925.

In the 1950s, Greek Cypriots, who made up four-fifths of the population, began a campaign for enosis (union) with Greece. Their leader was the Greek Orthodox Archbishop Makarios. A secret guerrilla force called EOKA attacked the British, who exiled Makarios. Cyprus became an independent country in 1960, although Britain retained two military bases. Independent Cyprus had a constitution which provided for power-sharing between the Greek and Turkish Cypriots. But the constitution proved unworkable and fighting broke out. In 1964,

the United Nations sent in a peace-keeping force, but communal clashes recurred in 1967.

In 1974, Cypriot forces led by Greek officers overthrew Makarios. This led Turkey to invade northern Cyprus, a territory occupying about 40% of the island. Many Greek Cypriots fled from the north which, in 1979, was proclaimed an independent state called the Turkish Republic of Northern Cyprus. But the United Nations still regarded Cyprus as a single nation under the Greek-Cypriot government in the south. In 2002, new talks were opened to resolve the conflict as negotiations for Cyprus's entry to the European Union reached an advanced stage.

Cyprus got its name from the Greek word *kypros*, meaning copper. But little copper remains and the chief minerals today are asbestos and chromium. However, the most valuable activity in Cyprus is tourism. In the early 1990s, the United Nations reclassified Cyprus as a developed rather than a developing country. But the economy of the Turkish-Cypriot north lags behind that of the more prosperous Greek-Cypriot south.

AREA 9,250 sq km [3,571 sq mi]
POPULATION 763,000
CAPITAL (POPULATION) Nicosia (189,000)
GOVERNMENT Multiparty republic
ETHNIC GROUPS Greek Cypriot 78%, Turkish Cypriot 18%
LANGUAGES Greek and Turkish (both official), English
RELIGIONS Greek Orthodox 78%, Islam 18%
CURRENCY Cyprus pound = 100 cents

CZECH REPUBLIC

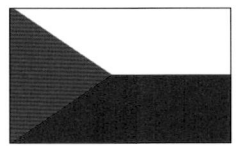 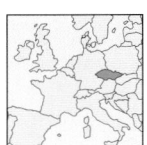

GEOGRAPHY The Czech Republic is the western three-fifths of the former country of Czechoslovakia. It contains two regions: Bohemia in the west and Moravia in the east. Mountains border much of the country in the west. The Bohemian basin in the north-centre is a fertile lowland region, with Prague, the capital city, as its main centre. Highlands cover much of the centre of the country, with lowlands in the south-east.

The climate is influenced by its landlocked position in central Europe. Prague has warm, sunny summers and cold winters. The average rainfall is moderate, with 500 mm to 750 mm [20 in to 30 in] every year in lowland areas.

POLITICS & ECONOMY After World War I (1914–18), Czechoslovakia was created. Germany seized the country in World War II (1939–45). In 1948, Communist leaders took power and Czechoslovakia was allied to the Soviet Union. When democratic reforms were introduced in the Soviet Union in the late 1980s, the Czechs also demanded reforms. Free elections were held in 1990, but differences between the Czechs and Slovaks and a resurgence of Slovak nationalism led the government to agree in 1992 to the partitioning of the country on 1 January 1993. The break was peaceful. In 1999, the Czech Republic became a member of NATO.

Under Communist rule the Czech Republic became one of the most industrialized parts of Eastern Europe. The country has deposits of coal, uranium, iron ore, magnesite, tin and zinc. Manufacturing employs about 40% of the Czech Republic's entire

workforce. Farming is also important. Under Communism, the government owned the land, but private ownership is now being restored. The country was admitted into the OECD in 1995.

AREA 78,864 sq km [30,449 sq mi]
POPULATION 10,264,000
CAPITAL (POPULATION) Prague (1,203,000)
GOVERNMENT Multiparty republic
ETHNIC GROUPS Czech 81%, Moravian 13%, Slovak 3%, Polish, German, Silesian, Gypsy, Hungarian, Ukrainian
LANGUAGES Czech (official)
RELIGIONS Atheist 40%, Roman Catholic 39%, Protestant 4%
CURRENCY Czech koruna = 100 haler

DENMARK

 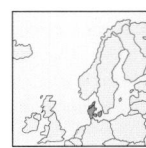

GEOGRAPHY The Kingdom of Denmark is the smallest country in Scandinavia. It consists of a peninsula, called Jutland (or Jylland), which is joined to Germany, and more than 400 islands, 89 of which are inhabited.

The land is flat and mostly covered by rocks dropped there by huge ice-sheets during the last Ice Age. The highest point in Denmark is on Jutland. It is only 173 m [568 ft] above sea level.

Denmark has a cool but pleasant climate, except during cold spells in the winter when The Sound between Sjælland and Sweden may freeze over. Summers are warm. Rainfall occurs all through the year.

POLITICS & ECONOMY Danish Vikings terrorized much of Western Europe for about 300 years after AD 800. Danish kings ruled England in the 11th century. In the late 14th century, Denmark formed a union with Norway and Sweden (which included Finland). Sweden broke away in 1523, while Denmark lost Norway to Sweden in 1814.

After 1945, Denmark played an important part in European affairs, becoming a member of the North Atlantic Treaty Organization (NATO). In 1973, Denmark joined the European Union, although it rejected the adoption of the euro in 2000. The Danes now enjoy some of the world's highest living standards, although the extensive social welfare provisions exert a considerable cost.

Denmark has few natural resources apart from some oil and gas from wells deep under the North Sea. But the economy is highly developed. Manufacturing industries, which employ about 17% of all workers, produce a wide variety of products, including furniture, processed food, machinery, television sets and textiles. Farms cover about three-quarters of the land. Farming employs only 4% of the workers, but it is highly scientific and productive. Meat and dairy farming are the chief activities.

AREA 43,070 sq km [16,629 sq mi]
POPULATION 5,353,000
CAPITAL (POPULATION) Copenhagen (1,362,000)
GOVERNMENT Parliamentary monarchy
ETHNIC GROUPS Danish 97%
LANGUAGES Danish (official)
RELIGIONS Lutheran 95%, Roman Catholic 1%
CURRENCY Krone = 100 øre

DJIBOUTI

 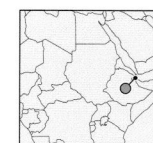

GEOGRAPHY The Republic of Djibouti in eastern Africa occupies a strategic position where the Red Sea meets the Gulf of Aden. Djibouti has one of the world's hottest and driest climates.

POLITICS & ECONOMY France set up a territory called French Somaliland in 1888. Its capital, Djibouti, became important when a railway was built to Addis Ababa and Djibouti became the main outlet for Ethiopian trade.

In 1967, France renamed the dependency the French Territory of the Afars and Issas, but it was renamed Djibouti when it became independent in 1977. Djibouti became a one-party state in 1981, but a new constitution (1992) permitted four parties which had to maintain a balance between the country's ethnic groups. Conflict flared up between the Afars and Issas in 1992 and 1993, but a peace agreement was signed in 1994. Djibouti is a poor country. Its economy is based largely on the revenue it gets from its port and the railway to Addis Ababa.

AREA 23,200 sq km [8,958 sq mi]
POPULATION 461,000
CAPITAL (POPULATION) Djibouti (383,000)
GOVERNMENT Multiparty republic
ETHNIC GROUPS Somali 60%, Afar 35%
LANGUAGES Arabic and French (both official)
RELIGIONS Islam 94%, Christianity 6%
CURRENCY Djibouti franc = 100 centimes

DOMINICA

 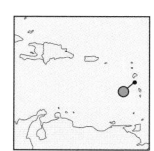

The Commonwealth of Dominica, a former British colony, became independent in 1978. The island has a mountainous spine and less than 10% of the land is cultivated. Yet agriculture employs more than 60% of the people. Manufacturing, mining and tourism are other minor activities. **AREA** 751 sq km [290 sq mi]; **POPULATION** 71,000; **CAPITAL** Roseau.

DOMINICAN REPUBLIC

GEOGRAPHY Second largest of the Caribbean nations in both area and population, the Dominican Republic shares the island of Hispaniola with Haiti. The country is mountainous, and the generally hot and humid climate eases with altitude.

POLITICS & ECONOMY The Dominican Republic has chaotic origins, having been held by Spain, France, Haiti and the USA at various times. Civil war broke out in 1966 but soon ended after US intervention. Joaquín Balaguer, elected president in 1966 under a new constitution, stood down in 1996 and was replaced by Leonel Fernández Reyna.

AREA 48,730 sq km [18,815 sq mi]
POPULATION 8,581,000
CAPITAL (POPULATION) Santo Domingo (2,135,000)
GOVERNMENT Multiparty republic
ETHNIC GROUPS Mulatto 73%, White 16%, Black 11%
LANGUAGES Spanish (official)
RELIGIONS Roman Catholic 95%
CURRENCY Peso = 100 centavos

EAST TIMOR

 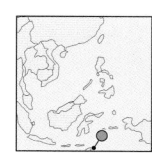

The Republic of East Timor became fully independent and the world's newest country on 20 May 2002. The land is mainly rugged. Temperatures are generally high and the rainfall is moderate. Portugal ruled the area from the late 19th century, when it was called Portuguese Timor. Portugal withdrew in 1975 and Indonesia seized the area. Guerrilla activity mounted under Indonesian rule and, in 1999, the people voted for independence. Agriculture is the main activity. East Timor is heavily dependent on foreign aid, but its offshore deposits of oil and natural gas are due to come on line in 2004. **AREA** 14,870 sq km [5,731 sq mi]; **POPULATION** 737,000; **CAPITAL** Dili.

ECUADOR

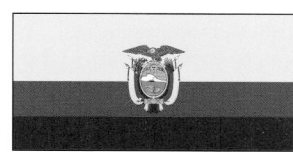 

GEOGRAPHY The Republic of Ecuador straddles the Equator on the west coast of South America. Three ranges of the high Andes Mountains form the backbone of the country. Between the towering, snow-capped peaks of the mountains, some of which are volcanoes, lie a series of high plateaux, or basins. Nearly half of Ecuador's population lives on these plateaux.

The climate in Ecuador depends on the height above sea level. Though the coastline is cooled by the cold Peruvian Current, temperatures are between 23°C and 25°C [73°F to 77°F] all through the year. In Quito, at 2,500 m [8,200 ft] above sea level, temperatures are 14°C to 15°C [57°F to 59°F], though the city is just south of the Equator.

POLITICS & ECONOMY The Inca people of Peru conquered much of what is now Ecuador in the late 15th century. They introduced their language, Quechua, which is widely spoken today. Spanish forces defeated the Incas in 1533 and took control of Ecuador. The country became independent in 1822, following the defeat of a Spanish force in a battle near Quito. In the 19th and 20th centuries, Ecuador suffered from political instability, while successive governments failed to tackle the country's social and economic problems. A war with Peru in 1941 led to a loss of territory. Disputes continued until 1995, but a border agreement was signed in January 1998. Economic crises in the early 21st century led the government to abolish the sucre, its official currency, and replace it with the US dollar.

The World Bank classifies Ecuador as a 'lower-middle-income' developing country. Agriculture employs 30% of the people and bananas, cocoa and coffee are all important crops. Fishing, forestry, mining and manufacturing are other activities.

AREA 283,560 sq km [109,483 sq mi]
POPULATION 13,184,000
CAPITAL (POPULATION) Quito (1,574,000)
GOVERNMENT Multiparty republic
ETHNIC GROUPS Mestizo (mixed White and Amerindian) 40%, Amerindian 40%, White 15%, Black 5%
LANGUAGES Spanish (official), Quechua
RELIGIONS Christianity (Roman Catholic 92%)
CURRENCY US dollar = 100 cents

EGYPT

GEOGRAPHY The Arab Republic of Egypt is Africa's second largest country by population after Nigeria, though it ranks 13th in area. Most of Egypt is desert. Almost all the people live either in the Nile Valley and its fertile delta or along the Suez Canal, the artificial waterway between the Mediterranean and Red seas. This canal shortens the sea journey between the United Kingdom and India by 9,700 km [6,027 mi]. Recent attempts have been made to irrigate parts of the western desert and thus redistribute the rapidly growing Egyptian population into previously uninhabited regions.

Apart from the Nile Valley, Egypt has three other main regions. The Western and Eastern deserts are parts of the Sahara. The Sinai peninsula (Es Sina), to the east of the Suez Canal, is a mountainous desert region, geographically within Asia. It contains Egypt's highest peak, Gebel Katherina (2,637 m [8,650 ft]); few people live in this area.

Egypt is a dry country. The low rainfall occurs, if at all, in winter and the country is one of the sunniest places on Earth.

POLITICS & ECONOMY Ancient Egypt, which was founded about 5,000 years ago, was one of the great early civilizations. Throughout the country, pyramids, temples and richly decorated tombs are memorials to its great achievements.

After Ancient Egypt declined, the country came under successive foreign rulers. Arabs occupied Egypt in AD 639–42. They introduced the Arabic language and Islam. Their influence was so great that most Egyptians now regard themselves as Arabs.

Egypt came under British rule in 1882, but it gained partial independence in 1922, becoming a monarchy. The monarchy was abolished in 1952, when Egypt became a republic. The creation of Israel in 1948 led Egypt into a series of wars in 1948–9, 1956, 1967 and 1973. Since the late 1970s, Egypt has sought for peace. In 1979, Egypt signed a peace treaty with Israel and regained the Sinai region which it had lost in a war in 1967. Extremists opposed contacts with Israel and, in 1981, President Sadat, who had signed the treaty, was assassinated.

While Egypt plays a major part in Arab affairs, most of its people are poor. Some Islamic fundamentalists, who dislike Western influences on their way of life, have resorted to violence. In the 1990s, attacks on foreign visitors caused a decline in the valuable tourist industry. In 1999, Hosni Mubarak, president since 1981, was himself attacked by extremists, but he was re-elected to a fourth term in office.

Egypt is Africa's second most industrialized country after South Africa, but it remains a developing country and income levels remain low for the vast majority of Egyptian people. Oil and textiles are the chief exports.

EL SALVADOR

EL SALVADOR

AREA 1,001,450 sq km [386,660 sq mi]
POPULATION 69,537,000
CAPITAL (POPULATION) Cairo (6,800,000)
GOVERNMENT Republic
ETHNIC GROUPS Egyptian 99%
LANGUAGES Arabic (official), French, English
RELIGIONS Islam (Sunni Muslim 94%), Christianity (mainly Coptic Christian 6%)
CURRENCY Pound = 100 piastres

EL SALVADOR

GEOGRAPHY The Republic of El Salvador is the only country in Central America which does not have a coast on the Caribbean Sea. El Salvador has a narrow coastal plain along the Pacific Ocean. Behind the coastal plain, the coastal range is a zone of rugged mountains, including volcanoes, which overlooks a densely populated inland plateau. Beyond the plateau, the land rises to the sparsely populated interior highlands.

The coast has a hot, tropical climate. Inland, the climate is moderated by the altitude. Rain falls on practically every afternoon between May and October.

POLITICS & ECONOMY Amerindians have lived in El Salvador for thousands of years. The ruins of Mayan pyramids built between AD 100 and 1000 are still found in the western part of the country. Spanish soldiers conquered the area in 1524 and 1525, and Spain ruled until 1821. In 1823, all the Central American countries, except for Panama, set up a Central American Federation. But El Salvador withdrew in 1840 and declared its independence in 1841. El Salvador suffered from instability throughout the 19th century. The 20th century saw a more stable government, but from 1931 military dictatorships alternated with elected governments and the country remained poor.

In the 1970s, El Salvador was plagued by conflict as protesters demanded that the government introduce reforms to help the poor. Kidnappings and murders committed by left- and right-wing groups caused instability. A civil war broke out in 1979 between the US-backed, right-wing government forces and left-wing guerrillas in the FMLN (Farabundo Marti National Liberation Front). In 12 years, more than 750,000 people died and hundreds of thousands were made homeless. A cease-fire was agreed on 1 February 1992 and elections were held in 1993 and 1999. With its economy shattered by war, El Salvador remains a 'lower-middle-income' economy, according to the World Bank. Farmland and pasture cover about three-quarters of the country. Coffee, grown in the highlands, is the main export, followed by sugar and cotton, which grow on the coastal lowlands. Fishing for lobsters and shrimps is important, but manufacturing is on a small scale.

AREA 21,040 sq km [8,124 sq mi]
POPULATION 6,238,000
CAPITAL (POPULATION) San Salvador (1,522,000)
GOVERNMENT Republic
ETHNIC GROUPS Mestizo (mixed White and Amerindian) 89%, White 10%, Amerindian 1%
LANGUAGES Spanish (official)
RELIGIONS Roman Catholic 86%
CURRENCY US dollar; Colón = 100 centavos

EQUATORIAL GUINEA

 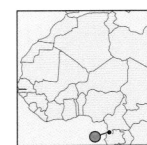

GEOGRAPHY The Republic of Equatorial Guinea is a small republic in west-central Africa. It consists of a mainland territory which makes up 90% of the land area, called Mbini (or Rio Muni), between Cameroon and Gabon, and five offshore islands in the Bight of Bonny, the largest of which is Bioko. The island of Annobon lies 560 km [350 mi] south-west of Mbini. Mbini consists mainly of hills and plateaux behind the coastal plains.

The climate is hot and humid. Bioko is mountainous, with the land rising to 3,008 m [9,869 ft], and hence it is particularly rainy. However, there is a marked dry season between the months of December and February. Mainland Mbini has a similar climate, though the rainfall diminishes inland.

POLITICS & ECONOMY Portuguese navigators reached the area in 1471. In 1778, Portugal granted Bioko, together with rights over Mbini, to Spain.

In 1959, Spain made Bioko and Mbini provinces of overseas Spain and, in 1963, it gave the provinces a degree of self-government. Equatorial Guinea became independent in 1968.

The first president of Equatorial Guinea, Francisco Macias Nguema, proved to be a tyrant. He was overthrown in 1979 and a group of officers, led by Lt.-Col. Teodoro Obiang Nguema Mbasogo, set up a Supreme Military Council to rule the country. In 1991, the people voted to set up a multiparty democracy. Elections were held in the 1990s, but accusations of human rights abuses continued.

Equatorial Guinea is a poor country. Agriculture employs up to 66% of the people. The main food crops are bananas, cassava and sweet potatoes, but the most valuable crop is cocoa, grown on Bioko.

AREA 28,050 sq km [10,830 sq mi]
POPULATION 486,000
CAPITAL (POPULATION) Malabo (35,000)
GOVERNMENT Multiparty republic (transitional)
ETHNIC GROUPS Fang 83%, Bubi 10%, Ndowe 4%
LANGUAGES Spanish and French (both official)
RELIGIONS Roman Catholic 89%
CURRENCY CFA franc = 100 centimes

ERITREA

 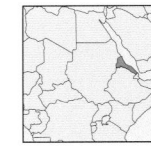

GEOGRAPHY The State of Eritrea consists of a hot, dry coastal plain facing the Red Sea, with a fairly mountainous area in the centre. Most people live in the cooler highland area.

POLITICS & ECONOMY Eritrea, which was an Italian colony from the 1880s, was part of Ethiopia from 1952 until 1993, when it became a fully independent nation. National reconstruction was hampered by conflict with Yemen over three islands in the Red Sea, while in 1998–9, border clashes with Ethiopia caused loss of life. However, a peace agreement was signed in 2000. Farming and livestock-rearing are the main activities in this war-ravaged territory. Eritrea has few manufacturing industries, based mainly in Asmara.

AREA 94,000 sq km [36,293 sq mi]
POPULATION 4,298,000
CAPITAL (POPULATION) Asmara (367,500)
GOVERNMENT Transitional government
ETHNIC GROUPS Tigrinya 49%, Tigre 32%, Afar 4%, Beja 3%, Saho 3%, Kunama 3%, Nara 2%
LANGUAGES Afar, Amharic, Arabic, Tigrinya
RELIGIONS Coptic Christian 50%, Islam 50%
CURRENCY Nakfa

ESTONIA

GEOGRAPHY The Republic of Estonia is the smallest of the three states on the Baltic Sea, which were formerly part of the Soviet Union, but which became independent in the early 1990s. Estonia consists of a generally flat plain which was covered by ice-sheets during the Ice Age. The land is strewn with moraine (rocks deposited by the ice).

The country is dotted with more than 1,500 small lakes, and water, including the large Lake Peipus (Chudskoye Ozero) and the River Narva makes up much of Estonia's eastern border with Russia. Estonia has more than 800 islands, which together make up about a tenth of the country. The largest island is Saaremaa (Sarema).

Despite its northerly position, Estonia has a fairly mild climate because of its nearness to the sea. This is because sea winds tend to warm the land in winter and cool it in summer.

POLITICS & ECONOMY The ancestors of the Estonians, who are related to the Finns, settled in the area several thousand years ago. German crusaders, known as the Teutonic Knights, introduced Christianity in the early 13th century. By the 16th century, German noblemen owned much of the land in Estonia. In 1561, Sweden took the northern part of the country and Poland the south. From 1625, Sweden controlled the entire country until Sweden handed it over to Russia in 1721.

Estonian nationalists campaigned for their independence from around the mid-19th century. Finally, Estonia was proclaimed independent in 1918. In 1919, the government began to break up the large estates and distribute land among the peasants.

In 1939, Germany and the Soviet Union agreed to take over parts of Eastern Europe. In 1940, Soviet forces occupied Estonia, but they were driven out by the Germans in 1941. Soviet troops returned in 1944 and Estonia became one of the 15 Soviet Socialist Republics of the Soviet Union. The Estonians strongly opposed Soviet rule. Many of them were deported to Siberia.

Political changes in the Soviet Union in the late 1980s led to renewed demands for freedom. In 1990, the Estonian government declared the country independent and, finally, the Soviet Union recognized this act in September 1991, shortly before the Soviet Union was dissolved. Estonia adopted a new constitution in 1992, when multiparty elections were held for a new national assembly. In 1993, Estonia negotiated an agreement with Russia to withdraw its troops.

Under Soviet rule, Estonia was the most prosperous of the three Baltic states. Since 1988, Estonia has begun to change its government-dominated economy to one based on private enterprise, and the country has started to strengthen its links with the rest of Europe. Estonia's resources include oil shale and its

forests. Industries produce fertilizers, machinery, petrochemical products, processed food, wood products and textiles. Agriculture and fishing are also important.

AREA 44,700 sq km [17,300 sq mi]
POPULATION 1,423,000
CAPITAL (POPULATION) Tallinn (435,000)
GOVERNMENT Multiparty republic
ETHNIC GROUPS Estonian 65%, Russian 28%, Ukrainian 3%, Belarussian 2%, Finnish 1%
LANGUAGES Estonian (official), Russian
RELIGIONS Lutheran, Russian and Estonian Orthodox, Methodist, Baptist, Roman Catholic
CURRENCY Kroon = 100 sents

ETHIOPIA

 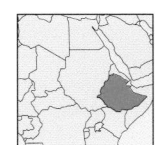

GEOGRAPHY Ethiopia is a landlocked country in north-eastern Africa. The land is mainly mountainous, though there are extensive plains in the east, bordering southern Eritrea, and in the south, bordering Somalia. The highlands are divided into two blocks by an arm of the Great Rift Valley which runs throughout eastern Africa. North of the Rift Valley, the land is especially rugged, rising to 4,620 m [15,157 ft] at Ras Dashen. South-east of Ras Dashen is Lake Tana, source of the River Abay (Blue Nile).

The climate in Ethiopia is greatly affected by the altitude. Addis Ababa, at 2,450 m [8,000 ft], has an average yearly temperature of 20°C [68°F]. The rainfall is generally more than 1,000 mm [39 in]. But the lowlands bordering the Eritrean coast are hot.

POLITICS & ECONOMY Ethiopia was the home of an ancient monarchy, which became Christian in the 4th century. In the 7th century, Muslims gained control of the lowlands, but Christianity survived in the highlands. In the 19th century, Ethiopia resisted attempts to colonize it. Italy invaded Ethiopia in 1935, but Ethiopian and British troops defeated the Italians in 1941.

In 1952, Eritrea, on the Red Sea coast, was federated with Ethiopia. But in 1961, Eritrean nationalists demanded their freedom and began a struggle that ended in their independence in 1993. Clashes along the border with Eritrea occurred in 1998 and 1999, but a peace agreement was signed in 2000. Ethnic diversity in Ethiopia has led to demands by some minorities for self-government. As a result, the government divided Ethiopia into nine provinces in 1995. Each province has its own regional assembly.

Ethiopia is one of the world's poorest countries, particularly in the 1970s and 1980s when it was plagued by civil war and famine caused partly by long droughts. Many richer countries have sent aid (money and food) to help the Ethiopian people. Agriculture remains the leading activity.

AREA 1,128,000 sq km [435,521 sq mi]
POPULATION 65,892,000
CAPITAL (POPULATION) Addis Ababa (2,316,000)
GOVERNMENT Federation of nine provinces
ETHNIC GROUPS Oromo 40%, Amharic 32%, Sidamo 9%, Shankella 6%, Somali 6%
LANGUAGES Amharic (official), 280 others
RELIGIONS Islam 47%, Ethiopian Orthodox 40%, traditional beliefs 11%
CURRENCY Birr = 100 cents

FALKLAND ISLANDS

 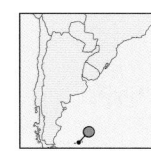

Comprising two main islands and over 200 small islands, the Falkland Islands lie 480 km [300 mi] from South America. Sheep farming is the main activity, though the search for oil and diamonds holds out hope for the future of this harsh and virtually treeless environment. **AREA** 12,170 sq km [4,699 sq mi]; **POPULATION** 2,895; **CAPITAL** Stanley.

FAROE ISLANDS

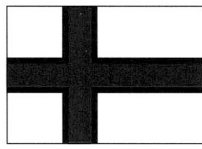 

The Faroe Islands are a group of 18 volcanic islands and some reefs in the North Atlantic Ocean. The islands have been Danish since the 1380s, but they became largely self-governing in 1948. In 1998, the government of the Faroes announced its intention to become independent of Denmark. **AREA** 1,400 sq km [541 sq mi]; **POPULATION** 46,000; **CAPITAL** Torshávn.

FIJI

 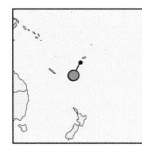

The Republic of Fiji comprises more than 800 Melanesian islands, the biggest being Viti Levu and Vanua Levu. The climate is tropical, with south-east trade winds blowing throughout the year. A former British colony, Fiji became independent in 1970. Its recent history has been marred by efforts by ethnic Fijians to impose their rule, stopping members of the ethnic Indian community from holding senior cabinet posts. Their actions have provoked international criticism. **AREA** 18,270 sq km [7,054 sq mi]; **POPULATION** 844,000; **CAPITAL** Suva.

FINLAND

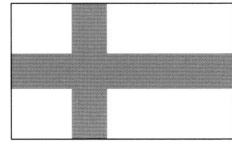 

GEOGRAPHY The Republic of Finland is a beautiful country in northern Europe. In the south, behind the coastal lowlands where most Finns live, lies a region of sparkling lakes worn out by ice-sheets in the Ice Age. The thinly populated northern uplands cover about two-fifths of the country.

Helsinki, the capital city, has warm summers, but the average temperatures between the months of December and March are below freezing point. Snow covers the land in winter. The north has less precipitation than the south, but it is much colder.

POLITICS & ECONOMY Between 1150 and 1809, Finland was under Swedish rule. The close links between the countries continue today. Swedish

remains an official language in Finland and many towns have Swedish as well as Finnish names.

In 1809, Finland became a grand duchy of the Russian empire. It finally declared itself independent in 1917, after the Russian Revolution and the collapse of the Russian empire. But during World War II (1939–45), the Soviet Union declared war on Finland and took part of Finland's territory. Finland allied itself with Germany, but it lost more land to the Soviet Union at the end of the war.

After World War II, Finland became a neutral country and negotiated peace treaties with the Soviet Union. Finland also strengthened its relations with other northern European countries and became an associate member of the European Free Trade Association (EFTA) in 1961. Finland became a full member of EFTA in 1986, but in 1992, along with most of its fellow EFTA members, it applied for membership of the European Union, which it finally achieved on 1 January 1995. On 1 January 2002, the euro became Finland's sole official unit of currency.

Forests are Finland's most valuable resource, and forestry accounts for about 35% of the country's exports. The chief manufactures are wood products, pulp and paper. Since World War II, Finland has set up many other industries, producing such things as machinery and transport equipment. Its economy has expanded rapidly, but there has been a large increase in the number of unemployed people.

AREA 338,130 sq km [130,552 sq mi]
POPULATION 5,176,000
CAPITAL (POPULATION) Helsinki (532,000)
GOVERNMENT Multiparty republic
ETHNIC GROUPS Finnish 93%, Swedish 6%
LANGUAGES Finnish and Swedish (both official)
RELIGIONS Evangelical Lutheran 88%
CURRENCY Euro = 100 cents

FRANCE

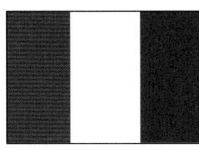 

GEOGRAPHY The Republic of France is the largest country in Western Europe. The scenery is extremely varied. The Vosges Mountains overlook the Rhine valley in the north-east, the Jura Mountains and the Alps form the borders with Switzerland and Italy in the south-east, while the Pyrenees straddle France's border with Spain. The only large highland area entirely within France is the Massif Central in southern France.

Brittany (Bretagne) and Normandy (Normande) form a scenic hill region. Fertile lowlands cover most of northern France, including the densely populated Paris basin. Another major lowland area, the Aquitanian basin, is in the south-west, while the Rhône-Saône valley and the Mediterranean lowlands are in the south-east.

The climate of France varies from west to east and from north to south. The west comes under the moderating influence of the Atlantic Ocean, giving generally mild weather. To the east, summers are warmer and winters colder. The climate also becomes warmer as one travels from north to south. The Mediterranean Sea coast has hot, dry summers and mild, moist winters. The Alps, Jura and Pyrenees mountains have snowy winters. Winter sports centres are found in all three areas. Large glaciers occupy high valleys in the Alps.

FRANCE

POLITICS & ECONOMY The Romans conquered France (then called Gaul) in the 50s BC. Roman rule began to decline in the fifth century AD and, in 486, the Frankish realm (as France was called) became independent under a Christian king, Clovis. In 800, Charlemagne, who had been king since 768, became emperor of the Romans. He extended France's boundaries, but, in 843, his empire was divided into three parts and the area of France contracted. After the Norman invasion of England in 1066, large areas of France came under English rule, but this was finally ended in 1453.

France later became a powerful monarchy. But the French Revolution (1789–99) ended absolute rule by French kings. In 1799, Napoleon Bonaparte took power and fought a series of brilliant military campaigns before his final defeat in 1815. The monarchy was restored until 1848, when the Second Republic was founded. In 1852, Napoleon's nephew became Napoleon III, but the Third Republic was established in 1875. France was the scene of much fighting during World War I (1914–18) and World War II (1939–45), causing great loss of life and much damage to the economy.

In 1946, France adopted a new constitution, establishing the Fourth Republic. But political instability and costly colonial wars slowed France's post-war recovery. In 1958, Charles de Gaulle was elected president and he introduced a new constitution, giving the president extra powers and inaugurating the Fifth Republic.

Since the 1960s, France has made rapid economic progress, becoming one of the most prosperous nations in the European Union. But France's government faced a number of problems, including unemployment, pollution and the growing number of elderly people, who find it difficult to live when inflation rates are high. One social problem concerns the presence in France of large numbers of immigrants from Africa and southern Europe, many of whom live in poor areas.

A socialist government under Lionel Jospin was elected in June 1997. Under Jospin, France adopted the euro, the single European currency, and shortened the working week. The French system of high social security taxes seemed likely to continue, although the economy continued to thrive. In the early 21st century, French politicians were plagued by allegations of corruption and illegal party funding.

France is one of the world's most developed countries. Its natural resources include its fertile soil, together with deposits of bauxite, coal, iron ore, oil and natural gas, and potash. France is also one of the world's top manufacturing nations, and it has often innovated in bold and imaginative ways. The TGV, Concorde and hypermarkets are all typical examples. Paris is a world centre of fashion industries, but France has many other industrial towns and cities. Major manufactures include aircraft, cars, chemicals, electronic products, machinery, metal products, processed food, steel and textiles.

Agriculture employs about 7% of the people, but France is the largest producer of farm products in Western Europe, producing most of the food it needs. Wheat is the leading crop and livestock farming is of major importance. Fishing and forestry are leading industries, while tourism is a major activity.

AREA 551,500 sq km [212,934 sq mi]
POPULATION 59,551,000
CAPITAL (POPULATION) Paris (11,175,000)
GOVERNMENT Multiparty republic
ETHNIC GROUPS Celtic, Latin, Arab, Teutonic, Slavic
LANGUAGES French (official), Breton, Occitan
RELIGIONS Roman Catholic 90%, Islam 3%
CURRENCY Euro = 100 cents

FRENCH GUIANA

GEOGRAPHY French Guiana is the smallest country in mainland South America. The coastal plain is swampy in places, but some dry areas are cultivated. Inland lies a plateau, with the low Tumachumac Mountains in the south. Most of the rivers run north towards the Atlantic Ocean.

French Guiana has a hot, equatorial climate, with high temperatures throughout the year. The rainfall is heavy, especially between December and June, but it is dry between August and October. The north-east trade winds blow constantly across the country.

POLITICS & ECONOMY The first people to live in what is now French Guiana were Amerindians. Today, only a few of them survive in the interior. The first Europeans to explore the coast arrived in 1500, and they were followed by adventurers seeking El Dorado, the mythical city of gold. Cayenne was founded in 1637 by a group of French merchants. The area became a French colony in the late 17th century.

France used the colony as a penal settlement for political prisoners from the times of the French Revolution in the 1790s. From the 1850s to 1945, the country became notorious as a place where prisoners were harshly treated. Many of them died, unable to survive in the tropical conditions.

In 1946, French Guiana became an overseas department of France, and in 1974 it also became an administrative region. An independence movement developed in the 1980s, but most people want to retain their links with France and continue to obtain financial aid to develop their territory.

Although it has rich forest and mineral resources, such as bauxite (aluminium ore), French Guiana is a developing country. It depends greatly on France for money to run its services and the government is the country's biggest employer. Since 1968, Kourou in French Guiana, the European Space Agency's rocket-launching site, has earned money for France by sending communications satellites into space.

AREA 90,000 sq km [34,749 sq mi]
POPULATION 178,000
CAPITAL (POPULATION) Cayenne (42,000)
GOVERNMENT Overseas department of France
ETHNIC GROUPS Mulatto 66%, Chinese and Amerindian 12%, White 10%
LANGUAGES French (official)
RELIGIONS Christianity (Roman Catholic 80%, Protestant 4%)
CURRENCY French franc = 100 centimes

FRENCH POLYNESIA

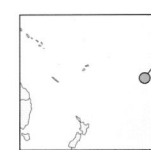

French Polynesia consists of 130 islands, scattered over 4 million sq km [1.5 million sq mi] of the Pacific Ocean. Tribal chiefs in the area agreed to a French protectorate in 1843. They gained increased autonomy in 1984, but the links with France ensure a high standard of living. **AREA** 3,941 sq km [1,520 sq mi]; **POPULATION** 254,000; **CAPITAL** Papeete.

GABON

GEOGRAPHY The Gabonese Republic lies on the Equator in west-central Africa. In area, it is a little larger than the United Kingdom, with a coastline 800 km [500 mi] long. Behind the narrow, partly lagoon-lined coastal plain, the land rises to hills, plateaux and mountains divided by deep valleys carved by the River Ogooué and its tributaries.

Most of Gabon has an equatorial climate, with high temperatures and humidity throughout the year. The rainfall is heavy and the skies are often cloudy.

POLITICS & ECONOMY Gabon became a French colony in the 1880s, but it achieved full independence in 1960. In 1964, an attempted coup was put down when French troops intervened and crushed the revolt. In 1967, Bernard-Albert Bongo, who later renamed himself El Hadj Omar Bongo, became president. He declared Gabon a one-party state in 1968. Opposition parties were legalized in 1991, but Bongo was re-elected president in 1993 and 1998.

Gabon's abundant natural resources include its forests, oil and gas deposits near Port Gentil, together with manganese and uranium. These mineral deposits make Gabon one of Africa's better-off countries. But agriculture still employs about 75% of the population and many farmers produce little more than they need to support their families.

AREA 267,670 sq km [103,347 sq mi]
POPULATION 1,221,000
CAPITAL (POPULATION) Libreville (418,000)
GOVERNMENT Multiparty republic
ETHNIC GROUPS Four major Bantu tribes: Fang, Eshira, Bapounou and Bateke
LANGUAGES French (official), Bantu languages
RELIGIONS Roman Catholic 65%, Protestant 19%, African churches 12%, traditional beliefs 3%, Islam 2%
CURRENCY CFA franc = 100 centimes

GAMBIA, THE

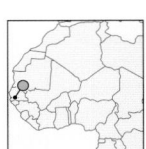

GEOGRAPHY The Republic of The Gambia is the smallest country in mainland Africa. It consists of a narrow strip of land bordering the River Gambia. The Gambia is almost entirely enclosed by Senegal, except along the short Atlantic coastline.

The Gambia has hot and humid summers, but the winter temperatures (November to May) drop to around 16°C [61°F]. In the summer, moist south-westerlies bring rain, which is heaviest on the coast.

POLITICS & ECONOMY English traders bought rights to trade on the River Gambia in 1588, and in 1664 the English established a settlement on an island in the river estuary. In 1765, the British founded a colony called Senegambia, which included parts of The Gambia and Senegal. In 1783, Britain handed this colony over to France.

In the 1860s and 1870s, Britain and France discussed the exchange of The Gambia for some other French territory. But no agreement was reached and Britain made The Gambia a British

colony in 1888. It remained under British rule until it achieved full independence in 1965. In 1970, The Gambia became a republic. Relations between the English-speaking Gambians and the French-speaking Senegalese form a major political issue. In 1981, an attempted coup in The Gambia was put down with the help of Senegalese troops. In 1982, The Gambia and Senegal set up a defence alliance, called the Confederation of Senegambia. But this alliance was dissolved in 1989. In July 1994, a military group overthrew the president, Sir Dawda Jawara, who fled into exile. Captain Yahya Jammeh, who took power, was elected president in 1996.

Agriculture employs more than 80% of the people. The main food crops include cassava, millet and sorghum, but groundnuts and groundnut products are the chief exports. Tourism is a growing industry.

AREA 11,300 sq km [4,363 sq mi]
POPULATION 1,411,000
CAPITAL (POPULATION) Banjul (171,000)
GOVERNMENT Military regime
ETHNIC GROUPS Mandinka 42%, Fula 18%, Wolof 16%, Jola 10%, Serahuli 9%
LANGUAGES English (official), Mandinka, Wolof, Fula
RELIGIONS Islam 90%, Christianity 9%, traditional beliefs 1%
CURRENCY Dalasi = 100 butut

GEORGIA

GEOGRAPHY Georgia is a country on the borders of Europe and Asia, facing the Black Sea. The land is rugged with the Caucasus Mountains forming its northern border. The highest mountain in this range, Mount Elbrus (5,633 m [18,481 ft]), lies over the border with Russia.

The Black Sea plains have hot summers and mild winters, when temperatures seldom drop below freezing point. The rainfall is heavy, but inland areas are much drier.

POLITICS & ECONOMY The first Georgian state was set up nearly 2,500 years ago. But for much of its history, the area was ruled by various conquerors. Christianity was introduced in AD 330. Georgia freed itself of foreign rule in the 11th and 12th centuries, but Mongol armies attacked in the 13th century. From the 16th to the 18th centuries, Iran and the Turkish Ottoman empire struggled for control of the area, and in the late 18th century Georgia sought the protection of Russia and, by the early 19th century, Georgia was part of the Russian empire. After the Russian Revolution of 1917, Georgia declared its independence, but Russia invaded, making the country part of the Soviet regime. Georgia declared itself independent in 1991. It became a separate country when the Soviet Union was dissolved in December 1991.

Georgia contains three regions containing minority peoples: Abkhazia in the north-west, South Ossetia in north-central Georgia, and Adjaria (also spelled Adzharia) in the south-west. Civil war broke out in South Ossetia in the early 1990s, while fierce fighting continued in Abkhazia until the late 1990s. In 2000, Georgia agreed to recognize Adjaria's autonomy in the country's constitution. In 2002, Russia stated that Chechen rebels were taking refuge in eastern Georgia, while the US alleged that terrorists from Afghanistan and elsewhere were moving into the area.

Georgia is a developing country. Agriculture is important. Major products include barley, citrus fruits, grapes for wine-making, vegetables, maize, tobacco and tea. Food processing and silk and perfume-making are other important activities. Sheep and cattle are reared.

AREA 69,700 sq km [26,910 sq mi]
POPULATION 4,989,000
CAPITAL (POPULATION) Tbilisi (1,253,000)
GOVERNMENT Multiparty republic
ETHNIC GROUPS Georgian 70%, Armenian 8%, Russian 6%, Azeri 6%, Ossetian 3%, Greek 2%, Abkhaz 2%, others 3%
LANGUAGES Georgian (official), Russian
RELIGIONS Georgian Orthodox 65%, Islam 11%, Russian Orthodox 10%, Armenian Apostolic 8%
CURRENCY Lari = 100 tetri

GERMANY

GEOGRAPHY The Federal Republic of Germany is the fourth largest country in Western Europe, after France, Spain and Sweden. The North German plain borders the North Sea in the north-west and the Baltic Sea in the north-east. Major rivers draining the plain include the Weser, Elbe and Oder.

The central highlands contain plateaux and highlands, including the Harz Mountains, the Thuringian Forest (Thüringer Wald), the Ore Mountains (Erzgebirge), and the Bohemian Forest (Böhmerwald) on the Czech border. South Germany is largely hilly, but the land rises in the south to the Bavarian Alps, which contain Germany's highest peak, Zugspitze, at 2,963 m [9,721 ft] above sea level. The scenic Black Forest (Scharzwald) overlooks the River Rhine, which flows through a rift valley in the south-west. The Black Forest contains the source of the River Danube.

North-western Germany has a mild climate, but the Baltic coastlands are cooler. To the south, the climate becomes more continental, especially in the highlands. The precipitation is greatest on the uplands, many of which are snow-capped in winter.

POLITICS & ECONOMY Germany and its allies were defeated in World War I (1914–18) and the country became a republic. Adolf Hitler came to power in 1933 and ruled as a dictator. His order to invade Poland led to the start of World War II (1939–45), which ended with Germany in ruins.

In 1945, Germany was divided into four military zones. In 1949, the American, British and French zones were amalgamated to form the Federal Republic of Germany (West Germany), while the Soviet zone became the German Democratic Republic (East Germany), a Communist state. Berlin, which had also been partitioned, became a divided city. West Berlin was part of West Germany, while East Berlin became the capital of East Germany. Bonn was the capital of West Germany.

Tension between East and West mounted during the Cold War, but West Germany rebuilt its economy quickly. In East Germany, the recovery was less rapid. In the late 1980s, reforms in the Soviet Union led to unrest in East Germany. Free elections were held in East Germany in 1990 and, on 3 October 1990, Germany was reunited.

The united Germany adopted West Germany's official name, the Federal Republic of Germany. Elections in December 1990 returned Helmut Kohl, West Germany's Chancellor (head of government) since 1982, to power. His government faced many problems, especially the restructuring of the economy of the former East Germany. Kohl was defeated in elections in 1998 and was succeeded as Chancellor by Social Democrat Gerhard Schröder. In 1999, Germany's parliament moved from Bonn to the reconstructed Reichstag building in Berlin.

West Germany's 'economic miracle' after the destruction of World War II was greatly helped by foreign aid. Today, despite all the problems caused by reunification, Germany is one of the world's greatest economic and trading nations.

Manufacturing is the most valuable part of Germany's economy and manufactured goods make up the bulk of the country's exports. Cars and other vehicles, cement, chemicals, computers, electrical equipment, processed food, machinery, scientific instruments, ships, steel, textiles and tools are among the leading manufactures. Germany has some coal, lignite, potash and rock salt deposits. But it imports many of the raw materials needed by its industries.

Germany also imports food. Major agricultural products include fruits, grapes for wine-making, potatoes, sugar beet and vegetables. Beef and dairy cattle are raised, together with many other livestock.

AREA 356,910 sq km [137,803 sq mi]
POPULATION 83,030,000
CAPITAL (POPULATION) Berlin (3,426,000)
GOVERNMENT Federal multiparty republic
ETHNIC GROUPS German 93%, Turkish 2%, Serbo-Croat 1%, Italian 1%, Greek, Polish, Spanish
LANGUAGES German (official)
RELIGIONS Protestant (mainly Lutheran) 38%, Roman Catholic 34%, Islam 2%
CURRENCY Euro = 100 cents

GHANA

GEOGRAPHY The Republic of Ghana faces the Gulf of Guinea in West Africa. This hot country, just north of the Equator, was formerly called the Gold Coast. Behind the thickly populated southern coastal plains, which are lined with lagoons, lies a plateau region in the south-west.

Accra has a hot, tropical climate. Rain occurs all through the year, though Accra is drier than areas inland.

POLITICS & ECONOMY Portuguese explorers reached the area in 1471 and named it the Gold Coast. The area became a centre of the slave trade in the 17th century. The slave trade was ended in the 1860s and, gradually, the British took control of the area. After independence in 1957, attempts were made to develop the economy by creating large state-owned manufacturing industries. But debt and corruption, together with falls in the price of cocoa, the chief export, caused economic problems. This led to instability and frequent coups. In 1981, power was invested in a Provisional National Defence Council, led by Flight-Lieutenant Jerry Rawlings.

The government steadied the economy and introduced several new policies, including the relaxation of government controls. In 1992, the

government introduced a new constitution, which allowed for multiparty elections. Rawlings was elected president in 1992 and 1996, but he retired in 2002. The World Bank classifies Ghana as a 'low-income' developing country. Most people are poor and farming employs 59% of the population.

AREA 238,540 sq km [92,100 sq mi]
POPULATION 19,894,000
CAPITAL (POPULATION) Accra (1,781,000)
GOVERNMENT Republic
ETHNIC GROUPS Akan 44%, Moshi-Dagombe 16%, Ewe 12%, Ga 8%
LANGUAGES English (official), Akan, Moshi-Dagombe
RELIGIONS Traditional beliefs 38%, Islam 30%, Christianity 24%
CURRENCY Cedi = 100 pesewas

GIBRALTAR

 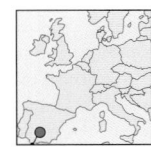

Gibraltar occupies a strategic position on the south coast of Spain where the Mediterranean meets the Atlantic. It was recognized as a British possession in 1713 and, despite Spanish claims, its population has consistently voted to retain its contacts with Britain. **AREA** 6.5 sq km [2.5 sq mi]; **POPULATION** 28,000; **CAPITAL** Gibraltar Town.

GREECE

GEOGRAPHY The Hellenic Republic, as Greece is officially called, is a rugged country situated at the southern end of the Balkan peninsula. Olympus, at 2,917 m [9,570 ft], is the highest peak. Islands make up about a fifth of the land.

Low-lying areas in Greece have mild, moist winters and hot, dry summers. The east coast has more than 2,700 hours of sunshine a year and only about half of the rainfall of the west. The mountains have a more severe climate, with snow on the higher slopes in winter.
POLITICS & ECONOMY After World War II (1939–45), when Germany had occupied Greece, a civil war broke out between Communist and nationalist forces. This war ended in 1949. A military dictatorship took power in 1967. The monarchy was abolished in 1973 and democratic government was restored in 1974. Greece joined the European Community (now the EU) in 1981. Despite efforts to develop the economy, Greece remains one of the EU's poorest nations. On 1 January 2002, the euro became Greece's sole official unit of currency.

Manufacturing is important. Products include processed food, cement, chemicals, metal products, textiles and tobacco. Greece also mines lignite (brown coal), bauxite and chromite.

Farmland covers about a third of the country, and grazing land another 40%. Major crops include barley, grapes for wine-making, dried fruits, olives, potatoes, sugar beet and wheat. Poultry, sheep, goats, pigs and cattle are raised. Greece's beaches and ancient ruins make it a major tourist destination.

AREA 131,990 sq km [50,961 sq mi]
POPULATION 10,624,000
CAPITAL (POPULATION) Athens (3,097,000)
GOVERNMENT Multiparty republic
ETHNIC GROUPS Greek 98%
LANGUAGES Greek (official)
RELIGIONS Greek Orthodox 98%
CURRENCY Euro = 100 cents

GREENLAND

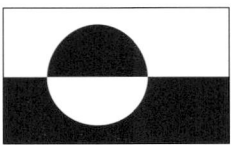 

Greenland is the world's largest island. Settlements are confined to the coast, because an ice-sheet covers four-fifths of the land. Greenland became a Danish possession in 1380. Full internal self-government was granted in 1981 and, in 1997, Danish place names were superseded by Inuit name forms. However, Greenland remains heavily dependent on Danish subsidies. **AREA** 2,175,600 sq km [838,999 sq mi]; **POPULATION** 56,000; **CAPITAL** Nuuk (Godthaab).

GRENADA

 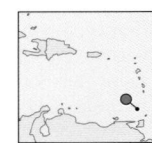

The most southerly of the Windward Islands in the Caribbean Sea, Grenada became independent from the UK in 1974. A military group seized power in 1983, when the prime minister was killed. US troops intervened and restored order and constitutional government. **AREA** 340 sq km [131 sq mi]; **POPULATION** 89,000; **CAPITAL** St George's.

GUADELOUPE

 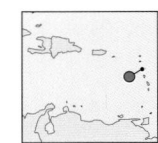

Guadeloupe is a French overseas department which includes seven Caribbean islands, the largest of which is Basse-Terre. French aid has helped to mantain a reasonable standard of living for the people. **AREA** 1,706 sq km [658 sq mi]; **POPULATION** 431,000; **CAPITAL** Basse-Terre.

GUAM

Guam, a strategically important 'unincorporated territory' of the USA, is the largest of the Mariana Islands in the Pacific Ocean. It is composed of a coralline limestone plateau. **AREA** 549 sq km [212 sq mi]; **POPULATION** 158,000; **CAPITAL** Agana.

GUATEMALA

GEOGRAPHY The Republic of Guatemala in Central America contains a thickly populated mountain region, with fertile soils. The mountains, which run in an east–west direction, contain many volcanoes, some of which are active. Volcanic eruptions and earthquakes are common in the highlands. South of the mountains lie the thinly populated Pacific coastlands, while a large inland plain occupies the north.

Guatemala lies in the tropics. The lowlands are hot and rainy. But the central mountain region is cooler and drier. Guatemala City, at about 1,500 m [5,000 ft] above sea level, has a pleasant, warm climate, with a marked dry season between November and April.
POLITICS & ECONOMY In 1823, Guatemala joined the Central American Federation. But it became fully independent in 1839. Since independence, Guatemala has been plagued by instability and periodic violence.

Guatemala has a long-standing claim over Belize, but this was reduced in 1983 to the southern fifth of the country. Violence became widespread in Guatemala from the early 1960s, because of the conflict between left-wing groups, including many Amerindians, and government forces. A peace accord was signed in 1996, ending a war that had lasted 36 years and claimed perhaps 200,000 lives.

The World Bank classifies Guatemala as a 'lower-middle-income' developing country. Agriculture employs nearly half of the population and coffee, sugar, bananas and beef are the leading exports. Other important crops include the spice cardamom and cotton, while maize is the chief food crop. But Guatemala still has to import food to feed the people.

AREA 108,890 sq km [42,042 sq mi]
POPULATION 12,974,000
CAPITAL (POPULATION) Guatemala City (1,167,000)
GOVERNMENT Republic
ETHNIC GROUPS Ladino (mixed Hispanic and Amerindian) 55%, Amerindian 43%, other 2%
LANGUAGES Spanish (official), Amerindian languages
RELIGIONS Roman Catholic 75%, Protestant 25%
CURRENCY US dollar; Quetzal = 100 centavos

GUINEA

 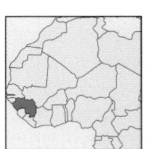

GEOGRAPHY The Republic of Guinea faces the Atlantic Ocean in West Africa. A flat, swampy plain borders the coast. Behind this plain, the land rises to a plateau region called Fouta Djalon. The Upper Niger plains, named after one of Africa's longest rivers, the Niger, which rises there, are in the north-east.

Guinea has a tropical climate and Conakry, on the coast, has heavy rains between May and November. This is also the coolest period in the year. During the dry season, hot, dry harmattan winds blow south-westwards from the Sahara Desert.

POLITICS & ECONOMY Guinea became independent in 1958. Its president, Sékou Touré, pursued socialist policies, though he had to resort to repressive policies to hold on to power. After his death in 1984, a military government, under President Lansana Conté, introduced free enterprise policies. In the late 1990s and early 2000s, Guinea was drawn into the civil conflicts which were taking place in neighbouring Liberia and Sierra Leone.

The World Bank classifies Guinea as a 'low-income' developing country. It has several natural resources, including bauxite (aluminium ore), diamonds, gold, iron ore and uranium. Bauxite and alumina (processed bauxite) account for 90% of the value of the exports. Agriculture, however, employs 78% of the people, many of whom produce little more than they need for their own families. Guinea has some manufacturing industries. Products include alumina, processed food and textiles.

AREA 245,860 sq km [94,927 sq mi]
POPULATION 7,614,000
CAPITAL (POPULATION) Conakry (1,508,000)
GOVERNMENT Multiparty republic
ETHNIC GROUPS Peuml 40%, Malinke 30%, Soussou 20%, other 10%
LANGUAGES French (official)
RELIGIONS Islam 85%, Christianity 8%, traditional beliefs 7%
CURRENCY Guinean franc = 100 cauris

GUINEA-BISSAU

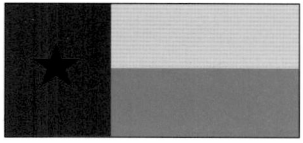

GEOGRAPHY The Republic of Guinea-Bissau, formerly known as Portuguese Guinea, is a small country in West Africa. The land is mostly low-lying, with a broad, swampy coastal plain and many flat offshore islands, including the Bijagós Archipelago.

The country has a tropical climate, with one dry season (December to May) and a rainy season from June to November.

POLITICS & ECONOMY Portugal appointed a governor to administer Guinea-Bissau and the Cape Verde Islands in 1836, but in 1879 the two territories were separated and Guinea-Bissau became a colony, then called Portuguese Guinea. But development was slow, partly because the territory did not attract settlers on the same scale as Portugal's much healthier African colonies of Angola and Mozambique.

In 1956, African nationalists in Portuguese Guinea and Cape Verde founded the African Party for the Independence of Guinea and Cape Verde (PAIGC). Because Portugal seemed determined to hang on to its overseas territories, the PAIGC began a guerrilla war in 1963. By 1968, it held two-thirds of the country. In 1972, a rebel National Assembly, elected by the people in the PAIGC-controlled area, voted to make the country independent as Guinea-Bissau.

In 1974, newly independent Guinea-Bissau faced many problems arising from its under-developed economy and its lack of trained people to work in the administration. One objective of the leaders of Guinea-Bissau was to unite their country with Cape Verde. But, in 1980, army leaders overthrew Guinea-Bissau's government. The Revolutionary Council, which took over, opposed unification with Cape Verde. Guinea-Bissau ceased to be a one-party state in 1991 and multiparty elections were held in 1994. Civil war broke out in 1998 and a military coup occurred in May 1999. In elections in 1999 and 2000, Kumba Ialá was elected president.

Guinea-Bissau is a poor country. Agriculture employs more than 80% of the people, but most farming is at subsistence level. Major crops include beans, coconuts, groundnuts, maize and rice.

AREA 36,120 sq km [13,946 sq mi]
POPULATION 1,316,000
CAPITAL (POPULATION) Bissau (145,000)
GOVERNMENT 'Interim' government
ETHNIC GROUPS Balanta 30%, Fula 20%, Manjaca 14%, Mandinga 13%, Papel 7%
LANGUAGES Portuguese (official), Crioulo
RELIGIONS Traditional beliefs 50%, Islam 45%, Christianity 5%
CURRENCY CFA franc = 100 centimes

GUYANA

GEOGRAPHY The Co-operative Republic of Guyana is a country facing the Atlantic Ocean in north-eastern South America. The coastal plain is flat and much of it is below sea level.

The climate is hot and humid, though the interior highlands are cooler than the coast. The rainfall is heavy, occurring on more than 200 days a year.

POLITICS & ECONOMY British Guiana became independent in 1966. A black lawyer, Forbes Burnham, became the first prime minister. Under a new constitution adopted in 1980, the president's powers were increased. Burnham became president until his death in 1985. He was succeeded by Hugh Desmond Hoyte. Hoyte was defeated in elections in 1993 by an ethnic Indian, Cheddi Jagan. Jagan died in 1997 and was succeeded by his wife, Janet. In 1999, Bharrat Jagdeo was elected president.

Guyana is a poor country. Its resources include gold, bauxite (aluminium ore) and other minerals, forests and fertile soils. Sugar cane and rice are leading crops. Electric power is in short supply, although the country has great potential for producing hydroelectricity from its many rivers.

AREA 214,970 sq km [83,000 sq mi]
POPULATION 697,000
CAPITAL (POPULATION) Georgetown (200,000)
GOVERNMENT Multiparty republic
ETHNIC GROUPS East Indian 49%, Black 32%, Mixed 12%, Amerindian 6%, Portuguese, Chinese
LANGUAGES English (official), Creole, Hindi, Urdu
RELIGIONS Protestant 34%, Roman Catholic 18%, Hinduism 34%, Islam 9%
CURRENCY Guyana dollar = 100 cents

HAITI

GEOGRAPHY The Republic of Haiti occupies the western third of Hispaniola in the Caribbean. The land is mainly mountainous. The climate is hot and humid, though the northern highlands, with about 200 mm [79 in], have more than twice as much rainfall as the southern coast.

POLITICS & ECONOMY Visited by Christopher Columbus in 1492, Haiti was later developed by the French. The African slaves revolted in 1791 and the country became independent in 1804. Since independence, Haiti has suffered from instability, violence and dictatorial rule. Elections in 1990 returned Jean-Bertrand Aristide as president, but he was overthrown in 1991. Following US intervention, he returned in 1994. In 1995, René Préval was elected president, but Aristide was again elected president in 2000 amid accusations of vote-rigging.

AREA 27,750 sq km [10,714 sq mi]
POPULATION 6,965,000
CAPITAL (POPULATION) Port-au-Prince (885,000)
GOVERNMENT Multiparty republic
ETHNIC GROUPS Black 95%, Mulatto 5%
LANGUAGES French and Creole (both official)
RELIGIONS Roman Catholic 80%, Voodoo
CURRENCY Gourde = 100 centimes

HONDURAS

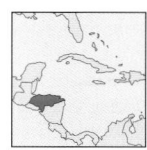

GEOGRAPHY The Republic of Honduras is the second largest country in Central America. The northern coast on the Caribbean Sea extends more than 600 km [373 mi], but the Pacific coast in the south-east is only about 80 km [50 mi] long.

Honduras has a tropical climate, but the highlands, where the capital Tegucigalpa is situated, have a cooler climate than the hot coastal plains. The months between May and November are the rainiest. The north coast is often hit by hurricanes. In 1998, Hurricane Mitch caused the worst destruction in the area in modern times.

POLITICS & ECONOMY In the 1890s, American companies developed plantations in Honduras to grow bananas, which soon became the country's chief source of income. The companies exerted great political influence in Honduras and the country became known as a 'banana republic', a name that was later applied to several other Latin American nations. Instability has continued to mar the country's progress. In 1969, Honduras fought the short 'Soccer War' with El Salvador. The war was sparked off by the treatment of fans during a World Cup soccer series. But the real reason was that Honduras had forced Salvadoreans in Honduras to give up land. A peace agreement was signed in 1980.

Honduras is a developing country – one of the poorest in the Americas and the least industrialized in Central America. It has few resources besides some silver, lead and zinc, and agriculture dominates the economy. Bananas and coffee are the leading exports, and maize is the main food crop. Manufactures include processed food, textiles, and a variety of wood products.

AREA 112,090 sq km [43,278 sq mi]
POPULATION 6,406,000
CAPITAL (POPULATION) Tegucigalpa (814,000)
GOVERNMENT Republic
ETHNIC GROUPS Mestizo 90%, Amerindian 7%, Black (including Black Carib) 2%, White 1%
LANGUAGES Spanish (official)
RELIGIONS Roman Catholic 85%
CURRENCY Honduran lempira = 100 centavos

HUNGARY

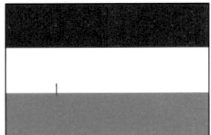 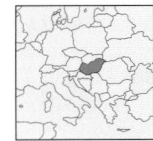

GEOGRAPHY The Hungarian Republic is a land-locked country in central Europe. The land is mostly low-lying and drained by the Danube (Duna) and its tributary, the Tisza. Most of the land east of the Danube belongs to a region called the Great Plain (Nagyalföld), which covers about half of Hungary.

Hungary lies far from the moderating influence of the sea. As a result, summers are warmer and sunnier, and the winters colder than in Western Europe.
POLITICS & ECONOMY Hungary entered World War II (1939–45) in 1941, as an ally of Germany, but the Germans occupied the country in 1944. The Soviet Union invaded Hungary in 1944 and, in 1946, the country became a republic. The Communists gradually took over the government, taking complete control in 1949. From 1949, Hungary was an ally of the Soviet Union. In 1956, Soviet troops crushed an anti-Communist revolt. But in the 1980s, reforms in the Soviet Union led to the growth of anti-Communist groups in Hungary.

In 1989, Hungary adopted a new constitution making it a multiparty state. Elections held in 1990 led to a victory for the non-Communist Democratic Forum. However, in 2002, the Hungarian Socialist Party, in alliance with the liberal Free Democrats, won a majority in parliament, defeating the Fidesz-Hungarian Civic Party.

Before World War II, Hungary's economy was based mainly on agriculture. But the Communists set up many manufacturing industries. The new factories were owned by the government, as also was most of the land. However, from the late 1980s, the government has worked to increase private ownership. This change of policy caused many problems, including inflation and high rates of unemployment. Manufacturing is the chief activity. Major products include aluminium, chemicals, and electrical and electronic goods.

AREA 93,030 sq km [35,919 sq mi]
POPULATION 10,106,000
CAPITAL (POPULATION) Budapest (1,885,000)
GOVERNMENT Multiparty republic
ETHNIC GROUPS Magyar 90%, Gypsy, German, Croat, Romanian, Slovak
LANGUAGES Hungarian (official)
RELIGIONS Roman Catholic 64%, Protestant 23%, Orthodox 1%, Judaism 1%
CURRENCY Forint = 100 fillér

ICELAND

GEOGRAPHY The Republic of Iceland, in the North Atlantic Ocean, is closer to Greenland than Scotland. Iceland sits astride the Mid-Atlantic Ridge. It is slowly getting wider as the ocean is being stretched apart by continental drift.

Iceland has around 200 volcanoes, and eruptions are frequent. An eruption under the Vatnajökull ice-cap in 1996 created a subglacial lake which subsequently burst, causing severe flooding. Geysers and hot springs are other common volcanic features. Ice-caps and glaciers cover about an eighth of the land. The only habitable regions are the coastal lowlands.

Although it lies far to the north, Iceland's climate is moderated by the warm waters of the Gulf Stream. The port of Reykjavik is ice-free all the year round.
POLITICS & ECONOMY Norwegian Vikings colonized Iceland in AD 874, and in 930 the settlers founded the world's oldest parliament, the Althing.

Iceland united with Norway in 1262. But when Norway united with Denmark in 1380, Iceland came under Danish rule. Iceland became a self-governing kingdom, united with Denmark, in 1918. It became a fully independent republic in 1944, following a referendum in which 97% of the people voted to break their country's ties with Denmark.

Iceland has played an important part in European affairs and is a member of the North Atlantic Treaty Organization. Conflict with Britain over fishing rights have occurred since Iceland extended its territorial waters in the 1970s. Other fishing disputes with Norway, Russia and others continued in the 1990s.

Iceland has few resources besides the fishing grounds which surround it. Fishing and fish processing are major industries which dominate Iceland's overseas trade. Barely 1% of the land is used to grow crops, mainly root vegetables and fodder for livestock. But 23% of the country is used for grazing sheep and cattle.

AREA 103,000 sq km [39,768 sq mi]
POPULATION 278,000
CAPITAL (POPULATION) Reykjavik (103,000)
GOVERNMENT Multiparty republic
ETHNIC GROUPS Icelandic 97%, Danish 1%
LANGUAGES Icelandic (official)
RELIGIONS Evangelical Lutheran 92%, other Lutheran 3%, Roman Catholic 1%
CURRENCY Króna = 100 aurar

INDIA

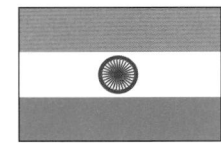 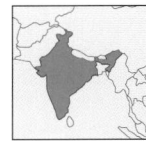

GEOGRAPHY The Republic of India is the world's seventh largest country. In population, it ranks second only to China. The north is mountainous, with mountains and foothills of the Himalayan range. Rivers, such as the Brahmaputra and Ganges (Ganga), rise in the Himalaya and flow across the fertile northern plains. Southern India consists of a large plateau, called the Deccan. The Deccan is bordered by two mountain ranges, the Western Ghats and the Eastern Ghats.

India has three main seasons. The cool season runs from October to February. The hot season runs from March to June. The rainy monsoon season starts in the middle of June and continues into September. Delhi has a moderate rainfall, with about 640 mm [25 in] a year. The south-western coast and the north-east have far more rain. Darjeeling in the north-east has an average annual rainfall of 3,040 mm [120 in]. But parts of the Thar Desert in the north-west have only 50 mm [2 in] of rain per year.
POLITICS & ECONOMY In southern India, most of the people are descendants of the dark-skinned Dravidians, who were among India's earliest people. Most northerners are descendants of lighter-skinned Aryans who arrived around 3,500 years ago.

India was the birthplace of several major religions, including Hinduism, Buddhism and Sikhism. Islam was introduced from about AD 1000. The Muslim Mughal empire was founded in 1526. From the 17th century, Britain began to gain influence. From 1858 to 1947, India was ruled as part of the British empire. An independence movement began after the Sepoy Rebellion (1857–9) and, in 1885, the Indian National Congress was formed. In 1920, Mohandas K. Gandhi became its leader and it soon became a mass movement. When independence was finally achieved in 1947, British India was divided into modern India and Muslim Pakistan. Partition was marred by mass slaughter as Hindus and Sikhs fled from Pakistan, and Indian Muslims poured into Pakistan. In the ensuing disputes, some 1 million people were killed.

Although India has 15 major languages and hundreds of minor ones, together with many religions, the country remains the world's largest democracy. It has faced many problems, especially with Pakistan, over the disputed territory of Jammu and Kashmir. Two wars in 1965 and 1972 failed to alter greatly the 1948 cease-fire lines. In the late 1980s, Kashmiri nationalists in the Indian-controlled area waged a campaign, demanding either integration into Pakistan or independence. India sent in troops and accused Pakistan of intervention. In the 1990s, Pakistani-backed guerrillas fought to break India's hold on the Srinigar valley, Kashmir's most populous region. The tense situation was further aggravated by the testing of nuclear devices by both India and Pakistan in 1998. Between 2000 and 2002, attempts were made to achieve a lasting cease-fire in the region, but the negotiations were unsuccessful.

Economic development has been a major problem and, according to the World Bank, India is a 'low-income' developing country. After socialist policies failed to raise the living standards of the poor, the government introduced private enterprise. Farming employs 64% of the people. The main crops are rice, wheat, millet, sorghum, peas and beans. India has more cattle than any other country. Milk is produced but Hindus do not eat beef. India has reserves of coal, iron ore and oil, and manufacturing has expanded greatly since 1947. Iron and steel, machinery, refined petroleum, textiles, jewellery and transport equipment are major products.

AREA 3,287,590 sq km [1,269,338 sq mi]
POPULATION 1,029,991,000
CAPITAL (POPULATION) New Delhi (7,207,000)
GOVERNMENT Multiparty federal republic
ETHNIC GROUPS Indo-Aryan (Caucasoid) 72%, Dravidian (Aboriginal) 25%, other (mainly Mongoloid) 3%
LANGUAGES Hindi, English, Telugu, Bengali, Marati, Urdu, Gujarati, Malayalam, Kannada, Oriya, Punjabi, Assamese, Kashmiri, Sindhi and Sanskrit are all official languages
RELIGIONS Hinduism 83%, Islam (Sunni Muslim) 11%, Christianity 2%, Sikhism 2%, Buddhism 1%
CURRENCY Rupee = 100 paisa

INDONESIA

GEOGRAPHY The Republic of Indonesia is an island nation in South-east Asia. In all, Indonesia contains about 13,600 islands, less than 6,000 of which are inhabited. Three-quarters of the country is made up of five main areas: the islands of Sumatra, Java and Sulawesi (Celebes), together with

Kalimantan (southern Borneo) and Irian Jaya (western New Guinea). The islands are generally mountainous, with many volcanoes. The larger islands have extensive coastal lowlands. Indonesia has a hot and humid equatorial climate, with a high rainfall. Only Java and the Sunda Islands have a relatively dry season.

POLITICS & ECONOMY Indonesia is the world's most populous Muslim nation, though Islam was introduced as recently as the 15th century. The Dutch became active in the area in the early 17th century and Indonesia became a Dutch colony in 1799. After a long struggle, the Netherlands recognized Indonesia's independence in 1949. The economy has expanded, but ethnic and religious conflict have slowed down economic progress. In the early 21st century, Indonesia was facing many problems, arising from widespread corruption in the government and the army. Separatists were operating in Aceh province in northern Sumatra and in West Papua (formerly Irian Jaya), Christian-Muslim clashes led to loss of life in the Moluccas, and East (formerly Portuguese) Timor seceded from Indonesia, becoming an independent country, in May 2002.

Indonesia is a developing country. Its resources include oil, natural gas, tin and other minerals, its fertile volcanic soils and its forests. Oil and gas are major exports. Timber, textiles, rubber, coffee and tea are also exported. The principal food crop is rice. Manufacturing is increasing, particularly on Java.

AREA 1,889,700 sq km [729,613 sq mi]
POPULATION 227,701,000
CAPITAL (POPULATION) Jakarta (11,500,000)
GOVERNMENT Multiparty republic
ETHNIC GROUPS Javanese 45%, Sundanese 14%, Madurese 7%, Coastal Malays 7%, more than 300 others
LANGUAGES Bahasa Indonesian (official), others
RELIGIONS Islam 88%, Roman Catholic 3%, Hinduism 2%, Buddhism 1%
CURRENCY Indonesian rupiah = 100 sen

IRAN

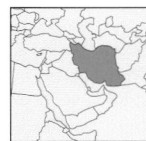

GEOGRAPHY The Republic of Iran contains a barren central plateau which covers about half of the country. It includes the Dasht-e-Kavir (Great Salt Desert) and the Dasht-e-Lut (Great Sand Desert). The Elburz Mountains north of the plateau contain Iran's highest peak, Damavand, while narrow lowlands lie between the mountains and the Caspian Sea. West of the plateau are the Zagros Mountains, beyond which the land descends to the plains bordering the Gulf.

Much of Iran has a severe, dry climate, with hot summers and cold winters. In Tehran, rain falls on only about 30 days in the year and the annual temperature range is more than 25°C [45°F]. The climate in the lowlands, however, is generally milder.

POLITICS & ECONOMY Iran was called Persia until 1935. The empire of Ancient Persia flourished between 550 and 350 BC, when it fell to Alexander the Great. Islam was introduced in AD 641.

Britain and Russia competed for influence in the area in the 19th century, and in the early 20th century the British began to develop the country's oil resources. In 1925, the Pahlavi family took power.

Reza Khan became shah (king) and worked to modernize the country. The Pahlavi dynasty was ended in 1979 when a religious leader, Ayatollah Ruhollah Khomeini, made Iran an Islamic republic. In 1980–8, Iran and Iraq fought a war over disputed borders. Khomeini died in 1989, but his fundamentalist views and anti-Western attitudes continued to dominate politics. In 1997, Mohammad Khatami, a liberal, was elected president. His reform policies won support in elections in 2000, but the conservative clerics made actual reform difficult.

Iran's prosperity is based on its oil production and oil accounts for 95% of the country's exports. However, the economy was severely damaged by the Iran–Iraq war in the 1980s. Oil revenues have been used to develop a growing manufacturing sector. Agriculture is important even though farms cover only a tenth of the land. The main crops are wheat and barley. Livestock farming and fishing are other important activities, although Iran has to import much of the food it needs.

AREA 1,648,000 sq km [636,293 sq mi]
POPULATION 66,129,000
CAPITAL (POPULATION) Tehran (6,759,000)
GOVERNMENT Islamic republic
ETHNIC GROUPS Persian 51%, Azeri 24%, Gilaki and Mazandarani 8%, Kurd 7%, Arab 3%, Lur 2%, Baluchi 2%, Turkmen 2%
LANGUAGES Persian 58%, Turkic 26%, Kurdish
RELIGIONS Islam 99%
CURRENCY Rial = 100 dinars

IRAQ

GEOGRAPHY The Republic of Iraq is a south-west Asian country at the head of the Gulf. Rolling deserts cover western and south-western Iraq, with mountains in the north-east. The northern plains, across which flow the rivers Euphrates (Nahr al Furat) and Tigris (Nahr Dijlah), are dry. But the southern plains, including Mesopotamia, and the delta of the Shatt al Arab, the river formed south of Al Qurnah by the combined Euphrates and Tigris, contain irrigated farmland, together with marshes. The climate of Iraq ranges from temperate in the north to subtropical in the south.

POLITICS & ECONOMY Mesopotamia was the home of several great civilizations, including Sumer, Babylon and Assyria. It later became part of the Persian empire. Islam was introduced in AD 637 and Baghdad became the brilliant capital of the powerful Arab empire. But Mesopotamia declined after the Mongols invaded it in 1258. From 1534, Mesopotamia became part of the Turkish Ottoman empire. Britain invaded the area in 1916. In 1921, Britain renamed the country Iraq and set up an Arab monarchy. Iraq finally became independent in 1932.

By the 1950s, oil dominated Iraq's economy. In 1952, Iraq agreed to take 50% of the profits of the foreign oil companies. This revenue enabled the government to pay for welfare services and development projects. But many Iraqis felt that they should benefit more from their oil.

Since 1958, when army officers killed the king and made Iraq a republic, the country has undergone turbulent times. In the 1960s, the Kurds, who live in northern Iraq and also in Iran, Turkey, Syria and Armenia, asked for self-rule. The government

rejected their demands and war broke out. A peace treaty was signed in 1975, but conflict has continued.

In 1979, Saddam Hussein became Iraq's president. Under his leadership, Iraq invaded Iran in 1980, starting an eight-year war. During this war, Iraqi Kurds supported Iran and the Iraqi government attacked Kurdish villages with poison gas.

In 1990, Iraqi troops occupied Kuwait but an international force drove them out in 1991. Since 1991, Iraqi troops have attacked Shiite Marsh Arabs and Kurds. In 1998, Iraq's failure to permit UNSCOM, the United Nations body charged with disposing of Iraq's deadliest weapons, access to all suspect sites, led to Western bombardment of military sites in Iraq. Another major Western offensive against strategic sites was launched in February 2001, while threats of war again mounted following the terrorist attacks on the United States on 11 September 2001.

Civil war, war damage, UN sanctions and economic mismanagement have all contributed to economic chaos in the 1990s. Oil remains Iraq's main resource, but a UN trade embargo in 1990 halted oil exports. Farmland, including pasture, covers about a fifth of the land. Products include barley, cotton, dates, fruit, livestock, wheat and wool, but Iraq still has to import food. Industries include oil refining and the manufacture of petrochemicals and consumer goods.

AREA 438,320 sq km [169,235 sq mi]
POPULATION 23,332,000
CAPITAL (POPULATION) Baghdad (3,841,000)
GOVERNMENT Republic
ETHNIC GROUPS Arab 77%, Kurdish 19%, Turkmen, Persian, Assyrian
LANGUAGES Arabic (official), Kurdish (official in Kurdish areas)
RELIGIONS Islam 96%, Christianity 4%
CURRENCY Iraqi dinar = 20 dirhams = 1,000 fils

IRELAND

GEOGRAPHY The Republic of Ireland occupies five-sixths of the island of Ireland. The country consists of a large lowland region surrounded by a broken rim of low mountains. The uplands include the Mountains of Kerry where Carrauntoohill, Ireland's highest peak at 1,041 m [3,415 ft], is situated. The River Shannon is the longest in the British Isles. It flows through three large lakes, loughs Allen, Ree and Derg.

Ireland has a mild, damp climate greatly influenced by the warm Gulf Stream current that washes its shores. The effects of the Gulf Stream are greatest in the west. Dublin in the east is cooler than places on the west coast. Rain occurs throughout the year.

POLITICS & ECONOMY In 1801, the Act of Union created the United Kingdom of Great Britain and Ireland. But Irish discontent intensified in the 1840s when a potato blight caused a famine in which a million people died and nearly a million emigrated. Britain was blamed for not having done enough to help. In 1916, an uprising in Dublin was crushed, but between 1919 and 1922 civil war occurred. In 1922, the Irish Free State was created as a Dominion in the British Commonwealth. But Northern Ireland remained part of the UK.

Ireland became a republic in 1949. Since then, Irish governments have sought to develop the economy,

ISRAEL

and it was for this reason that Ireland joined the European Community in 1973. In 1998, Ireland took part in the negotiations to produce a constitutional settlement in Northern Ireland. As part of the agreement, Ireland agreed to give up its constitutional claim on Northern Ireland.

Major farm products in Ireland include barley, cattle and dairy products, pigs, potatoes, poultry, sheep, sugar beet and wheat, while fishing provides another valuable source of food. Farming is now profitable, aided by European Union grants, but manufacturing is the leading economic sector. Many factories produce food and beverages. Chemicals and pharmaceuticals, electronic equipment, machinery, paper and textiles are also important.

AREA 70,280 sq km [27,135 sq mi]
POPULATION 3,841,000
CAPITAL (POPULATION) Dublin (1,024,000)
GOVERNMENT Multiparty republic
ETHNIC GROUPS Irish 94%
LANGUAGES Irish and English (both official)
RELIGIONS Roman Catholic 93%,
Protestant 3%
CURRENCY Euro = 100 cents

ISRAEL

 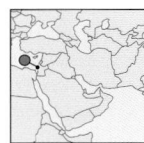

GEOGRAPHY The State of Israel is a small country in the eastern Mediterranean. It includes a fertile coastal plain, where Israel's main industrial cities, Haifa (Hefa) and Tel Aviv-Jaffa are situated. Inland lie the Judaeo-Galilean highlands, which run from northern Israel to the northern tip of the Negev Desert. To the east lies part of the Great Rift Valley which contains the River Jordan, the Sea of Galilee and the Dead Sea.

Summers are hot and dry. Winters on the coast are mild and moist, but the rainfall decreases from west to east and from north to south.

POLITICS & ECONOMY Israel is part of a region called Palestine. Some Jews have always lived in the area, though most modern Israelis are descendants of immigrants who began to settle there from the 1880s. Britain ruled Palestine from 1917. Large numbers of Jews escaping Nazi persecution arrived in the 1930s, provoking an Arab uprising against British rule. In 1947, the UN agreed to partition Palestine into an Arab and a Jewish state. Fighting broke out after Arabs rejected the plan. The State of Israel came into being in May 1948, but fighting continued into 1949. Other Arab–Israeli wars in 1956, 1967 and 1973 led to land gains for Israel.

In 1978, Israel signed a treaty with Egypt which led to the return of the occupied Sinai peninsula to Egypt in 1979. But conflict continued between Israel and the PLO (Palestine Liberation Organization). In 1993, the PLO and Israel agreed to establish Palestinian self-rule in two areas: the occupied Gaza Strip, and in the town of Jericho in the occupied West Bank. The agreement was extended in 1995 to include more than 30% of the West Bank. Israel's prime minister, Yitzhak Rabin, was assassinated in 1995. In 1996, his successor, Simon Peres, was defeated by the right-wing Benjamin Netanyahu, under whom the peace process stalled. In 1999, the left-wing Ehud Barak defeated Netanyahu and revived the peace process. But, following violence between the Palestinians and Israeli forces, Barak resigned. In 2001, Barak was defeated by the right-

wing Ariel Sharon, who adopted a hardline policy against the Palestinians. In early 2002, the violence mounted and the killing of Israelis by Arab suicide bombers brought the region close to war.

Israel's most valuable activity is manufacturing and the country's products include chemicals, electronic equipment, fertilizers, military equipment, plastics, processed food, scientific instruments and textiles. Fruits and vegetables are leading exports.

AREA 20,600 sq km [7,960 sq mi]
POPULATION 5,938,000
CAPITAL (POPULATION) Jerusalem (591,000)
GOVERNMENT Multiparty republic
ETHNIC GROUPS Jewish 82%, Arab and others 18%
LANGUAGES Hebrew and Arabic (both official)
RELIGIONS Judaism 80%, Islam (mostly Sunni) 14%, Christianity 2%, Druze and others 2%
CURRENCY New Israeli sheqel = 100 agorat

ITALY

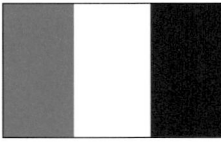 

GEOGRAPHY The Republic of Italy is famous for its history and traditions, its art and culture, and its beautiful scenery. Northern Italy is bordered in the north by the high Alps, with their many climbing and skiing resorts. The Alps overlook the northern plains – Italy's most fertile and densely populated region – drained by the River Po. The rugged Apennines form the backbone of southern Italy. Bordering the range are scenic hilly areas and coastal plains. Southern Italy contains a string of volcanoes, stretching from Vesuvius, through the Lipari Islands, to Etna on Sicily, the largest Mediterranean island.

Northern Italy has cold, often snowy, winters, but the summer months are warm and sunny, with brief summer thunderstorms. Rainfall is abundant. The south has mild, moist winters and warm, dry summers.

POLITICS & ECONOMY Magnificent ruins throughout Italy testify to the glories of the ancient Roman Empire, which was founded, according to legend, in 753 BC. It reached its peak in the AD 100s. It finally collapsed in the 400s, although the Eastern Roman empire, also called the Byzantine empire, survived for another 1,000 years.

In the Middle Ages, Italy was split into many tiny states. These states made a great contribution to the revival of art and learning, called the Renaissance, in the 14th to 16th centuries. Beautiful cities, such as Florence (Firenze) and Venice (Venézia), testify to the artistic achievements of this period.

Italy finally became a united kingdom in 1861, although the Papal Territories (a large area ruled by the Roman Catholic Church) was not added until 1870. The Pope and his successors disputed the takeover of the Papal Territories. The dispute was finally resolved in 1929, when the Vatican City was set up in Rome as a fully independent state.

Italy fought in World War I (1914–18) alongside the Allies – Britain, France and Russia. In 1922, the dictator Benito Mussolini, leader of the Fascist party, took power. Under Mussolini, Italy conquered Ethiopia. During World War II (1939–45), Italy at first fought on Germany's side against the Allies. But in late 1943, Italy declared war on Germany. Italy became a republic in 1946. It has played an important part in European affairs. It was a founder member of the North Atlantic Treaty Organization

(NATO) in 1949 and also of what has now become the European Union in 1958.

After the setting up of the European Union, Italy's economy developed quickly. But the country faced many problems. For example, much of the economic development was in the north. This forced many people to leave the poor south to find jobs in the north or abroad. Social problems, corruption at high levels of society, and a succession of weak coalition governments all contributed to instability. Elections in 1996 were won by the left-wing Olive Tree alliance led by Romano Prodi, who was replaced in 1998 by an ex-Communist, Massimo d'Alema, who tried but failed to introduce a two-party system. In 2001, a centre-right coalition won a substantial majority in parliament and its leader, media tycoon Silvio Berlusconi, became prime minister.

Only 50 years ago, Italy was a mainly agricultural society – today it is a leading industrial power. It lacks mineral resources, and imports most of the raw materials used in industry. Manufactures include textiles, processed food, machinery, cars and chemicals. The chief industrial region is in the north-west.

Farmland covers around 42% of the land, pasture 17%, and forest and woodland 22%. Major crops include citrus fruits, grapes which are used to make wine, olive oil, sugar beet and vegetables. Livestock farming is important, though meat is imported.

AREA 301,270 sq km [116,320 sq mi]
POPULATION 57,680,000
CAPITAL (POPULATION) Rome (2,654,000)
GOVERNMENT Multiparty republic
ETHNIC GROUPS Italian 94%, German, French, Albanian, Ladino, Slovene, Greek
LANGUAGES Italian 94% (official), German, French, Slovene
RELIGIONS Roman Catholic 83%
CURRENCY Euro = 100 cents

IVORY COAST

 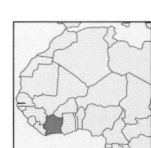

GEOGRAPHY The Republic of the Ivory Coast, in West Africa, is officially known as Côte d'Ivoire. The south-east coast is bordered by sand bars that enclose lagoons. The south-west coast is lined by rocky cliffs.

Ivory Coast has a hot and humid tropical climate, with high temperatures all year. The south has two rainy seasons: between May and July, and from October to November. Inland, the rainfall decreases and the north has one dry and one rainy season.

POLITICS & ECONOMY From 1895, Ivory Coast was governed as part of French West Africa, a massive union which also included what are now Benin, Burkina Faso, Guinea, Mali, Mauritania, Niger and Senegal. In 1946, Ivory Coast became a territory in the French Union.

Ivory Coast became fully independent in 1960. Its first president, Félix Houphouët-Boigny, became the longest serving head of state in Africa with an uninterrupted period in office which ended with his death in 1993. Houphouët-Boigny was a paternalistic, pro-Western leader, who made his country a one-party state. In 1983, the National Assembly agreed to make Yamoussoukro, the president's birthplace, the new capital. In 1993, Henri Konan Bédié became president. In 1999, he was overthrown by a military coup led by General Robert Guei. However, in presidential elections in 2000, Guei was defeated by a veteran politician, Laurent Gbagbo.

Agriculture employs about two-thirds of the people, and farm products make up nearly half the value of the exports. Manufacturing has grown in importance since 1960; products include fertilizers, processed food, refined oil, textiles and timber.

AREA 322,460 sq km [124,502 sq mi]
POPULATION 16,393,000
CAPITAL (POPULATION) Yamoussoukro (120,000)
GOVERNMENT Multiparty republic
ETHNIC GROUPS Akan 42%, Voltaic 18%, Northern Mande 16%, Kru 11%, Southern Mande 10%
LANGUAGES French (official), Akan, Voltaic
RELIGIONS Christianity 34%, Islam 27%, traditional beliefs 17%
CURRENCY CFA franc = 100 centimes

JAMAICA

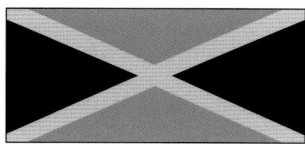 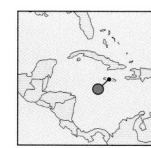

GEOGRAPHY Third largest of the Caribbean islands, half of Jamaica lies above 300 m [1,000 ft] and moist south-east trade winds bring rain to the central mountain range.

The 'cockpit country' in the north-west of the island is an inaccessible limestone area of steep broken ridges and isolated basins.

POLITICS & ECONOMY Britain took Jamaica from Spain in the 17th century, and the island did not gain its independence until 1962. Some economic progress was made by the socialist government in the 1980s, but migration and unemployment remain high. Farming is the leading activity and sugar cane is the main crop, though bauxite production provides much of the country's income. Jamaica has some industries and tourism is a major industry.

AREA 10,990 sq km [4,243 sq mi]
POPULATION 2,666,000
CAPITAL (POPULATION) Kingston (644,000)
GOVERNMENT Constitutional monarchy
ETHNIC GROUPS Black 91%, Mixed 7%, East Indian 1%
LANGUAGES English (official), Creole
RELIGIONS Protestant 61%, Roman Catholic 4%
CURRENCY Dollar = 100 cents

JAPAN

 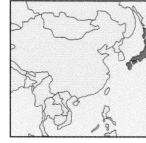

GEOGRAPHY Japan's four largest islands – Honshu, Hokkaido, Kyushu and Shikoku – make up 98% of the country. But Japan contains thousands of small islands. The four largest islands are mainly mountainous, while many of the small islands are the tips of volcanoes. Japan has more than 150 volcanoes, about 60 of which are active. Volcanic eruptions, earthquakes and tsunamis (destructive sea waves triggered by underwater earthquakes and eruptions) are common because the islands lie in an unstable part of our planet, where continental plates are always on the move. One powerful recent earthquake

killed more than 5,000 people in Kobe in 1995.

The climate of Japan varies greatly from north to south. Hokkaido in the north has cold, snowy winters. At Sapporo, temperatures below –20°C [4°F] have been recorded between December and March. But summers are warm, with temperatures sometimes exceeding 30°C [86°F]. Rain falls throughout the year, though Hokkaido is one of the driest parts of Japan.

Tokyo has higher rainfall and temperatures, though frosts may occur as late as April when north-westerly winds are blowing. The southern islands of Shikoku and Kyushu have warm temperate climates. Summers are long and hot. Winters are mild.

POLITICS & ECONOMY In the late 19th century, Japan began a programme of modernization. Under its new imperial leaders, it began to look for lands to conquer. In 1894–5, it fought a war with China and, in 1904–5, it defeated Russia. Soon its overseas empire included Korea and Taiwan. In 1930, Japan invaded Manchuria (north-east China) and, in 1937, it began a war against China. In 1941, Japan launched an attack on the US base at Pearl Harbor in Hawaii. This drew both Japan and the United States into World War II.

Japan surrendered in 1945 when the Americans dropped atomic bombs on two cities, Hiroshima and Nagasaki. The United States occupied Japan until 1952. During this period, Japan adopted a democratic constitution. The emperor, who had previously been regarded as a god, became a constitutional monarch. Power was vested in the prime minister and cabinet, who are chosen from the Diet (elected parliament).

From the 1960s, Japan experienced many changes as the country rapidly built up new industries. By the early 1990s, Japan had become the world's second richest economic power after the US. But economic success has brought problems. For example, the rapid growth of cities has led to housing shortages and pollution. Another problem is that the proportion of people over 65 years of age is steadily increasing.

Japan has the world's second highest gross domestic product (GDP) after the United States. [The GDP is the total value of all goods and services produced in a country in one year.] The most important sector of the economy is industry. Yet Japan has to import most of the raw materials and fuels it needs for its industries. Its success is based on its use of the latest technology, its skilled and hard-working labour force, its vigorous export policies and its comparatively small government spending on defence. Manufactures dominate its exports, which include machinery, electrical and electronic equipment, vehicles and transport equipment, iron and steel, chemicals, textiles and ships.

Japan is one of the world's top fishing nations and fish is an important source of protein. Because the land is so rugged, only 15% of the country can be farmed. Yet Japan produces about 70% of the food it needs. Rice is the chief crop, taking up about half of the total farmland. Other major products include fruits, sugar beet, tea and vegetables. Livestock farming has increased since the 1950s.

AREA 377,800 sq km [145,869 sq mi]
POPULATION 126,772,000
CAPITAL (POPULATION) Tokyo (17,950,000)
GOVERNMENT Constitutional monarchy
ETHNIC GROUPS Japanese 99%, Chinese, Korean, Ainu
LANGUAGES Japanese (official)
RELIGIONS Shintoism and Buddhism 84% (most Japanese consider themselves to be both Shinto and Buddhist)
CURRENCY Yen = 100 sen

JORDAN

 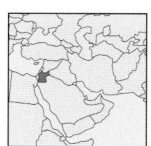

GEOGRAPHY The Hashemite Kingdom of Jordan is an Arab country in south-western Asia. The Great Rift Valley in the west contains the River Jordan and the Dead Sea, which Jordan shares with Israel. East of the Rift Valley is the Transjordan plateau, where most Jordanians live. To the east and south lie vast areas of desert.

Amman has a much lower rainfall and longer dry season than the Mediterranean lands to the west. The Transjordan plateau, on which Amman stands, is a transition zone between the Mediterranean climate zone to the west and the desert climate to the east.

POLITICS & ECONOMY In 1921, Britain created a territory called Transjordan east of the River Jordan. In 1923, Transjordan became self-governing, but Britain retained control of its defences, finances and foreign affairs. This territory became fully independent as Jordan in 1946.

Jordan has suffered from instability arising from the Arab–Israeli conflict since the creation of the State of Israel in 1948. After the first Arab–Israeli War in 1948–9, Jordan acquired East Jerusalem and a fertile area called the West Bank. In 1967, Israel occupied this area. In Jordan, the presence of Palestinian refugees led to civil war in 1970–1.

In 1974, Arab leaders declared that the PLO (Palestine Liberation Organization) was the sole representative of the Palestinian people. In 1988, King Hussein of Jordan renounced Jordan's claims to the West Bank and passed responsibility for it to the PLO. Opposition parties were legalized in 1991 and elections were held in 1993. In October 1994, Jordan and Israel signed a peace treaty, ending a state of war that had lasted more than 40 years. Jordan's King Hussein commanded respect for his role in Middle Eastern affairs until his death in 1999. He was succeeded by his eldest son who became Abdullah II.

Jordan lacks natural resources, apart from phosphates and potash, and the economy depends substantially on aid. The World Bank classifies Jordan as a 'lower-middle-income' developing country. Less than 6% of the land is farmed or used as pasture. Jordan has an oil refinery and manufactures include cement, pharmaceuticals, processed food, fertilizers and textiles.

AREA 89,210 sq km [34,444 sq mi]
POPULATION 5,153,000
CAPITAL (POPULATION) Amman (1,752,000)
GOVERNMENT Constitutional monarchy
ETHNIC GROUPS Arab 99%, of which Palestinians make up roughly half
LANGUAGES Arabic (official)
RELIGIONS Islam (mostly Sunni) 93%, Christianity (mostly Greek Orthodox) 5%
CURRENCY Jordan dinar = 1,000 fils

KAZAKSTAN

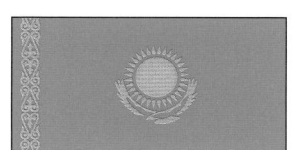 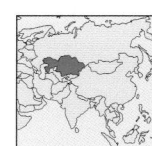

GEOGRAPHY Kazakstan is a large country in west-central Asia. In the west, the Caspian Sea lowlands include the Karagiye depression, which

reaches 132 m [433 ft] below sea level. The lowlands extend eastwards through the Aral Sea area. The north contains high plains, but the highest land is along the eastern and southern borders. These areas include parts of the Altai and Tian Shan mountain ranges.

Eastern Kazakstan contains several freshwater lakes, the largest of which is Lake Balkhash. The water in the rivers has been used for irrigation, causing ecological problems. For example, the Aral Sea, deprived of water, shrank from 66,900 sq km [25,830 sq mi] in 1960 to 33,642 sq km [12,989 sq mi] in 1993. Areas which once provided fish have dried up and are now barren desert.

The climate reflects Kazakstan's position in the heart of Asia, far from the moderating influence of the oceans. Winters are cold and snow covers the land for about 100 days, on average, at Almaty. The rainfall is generally low.

POLITICS & ECONOMY After the Russian Revolution of 1917, many Kazaks wanted to make their country independent. But the Communists prevailed and in 1936 Kazakstan became a republic of the Soviet Union, called the Kazak Soviet Socialist Republic. During World War II and also after the war, the Soviet government moved many people from the west into Kazakstan. From the 1950s, people were encouraged to work on a 'Virgin Lands' project, which involved bringing large areas of grassland under cultivation.

Reforms in the Soviet Union in the 1980s led to the break-up of the country in December 1991. Kazakstan kept contacts with Russia and most of the other republics in the former Soviet Union by joining the Commonwealth of Independent States (CIS), and in 1995 Kazakstan announced that its army would unite with that of Russia. In December 1997, the government moved the capital from Almaty to Aqmola (later renamed Astana), a town in the Russian-dominated north. It was hoped that this move would bring some Kazak identity to the area.

The World Bank classifies Kazakstan as a 'lower-middle-income' developing country. Livestock farming, especially sheep and cattle, is an important activity, and major crops include barley, cotton, rice and wheat. The country is rich in mineral resources, including coal and oil reserves, together with bauxite, copper, lead, tungsten and zinc. Manufactures include chemicals, food products, machinery and textiles. Oil is exported via a pipeline through Russia, though, to reduce dependence on Russia, Kazakstan signed an agreement in 1997 to build a new pipeline to China. Other exports include metals, chemicals, grain, wool and meat.

AREA 2,717,300 sq km [1,049,150 sq mi]
POPULATION 16,731,000
CAPITAL (POPULATION) Astana (280,000)
GOVERNMENT Multiparty republic
ETHNIC GROUPS Kazak 53%, Russian 30%, Ukrainian 4%, German 2%, Uzbek 2%
LANGUAGES Kazak (official); Russian, the former official language, is widely spoken
RELIGIONS Islam 47%, Russian Orthodox 44%
CURRENCY Tenge

KENYA

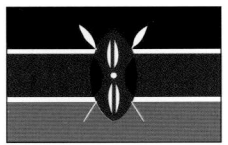
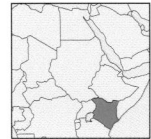

GEOGRAPHY The Republic of Kenya is a country in East Africa which straddles the Equator. It is slightly larger in area than France. Behind the narrow coastal plain on the Indian Ocean, the land rises to high plains and highlands, broken by volcanic mountains, including Mount Kenya, the country's highest peak at 5,199 m [17,057 ft]. Crossing the country is an arm of the Great Rift Valley, on the floor of which are several lakes, including Baringo, Magadi, Naivasha, Nakuru and, on the northern frontier, Lake Turkana (formerly Lake Rudolf).

Mombasa on the coast is hot and humid. But inland, the climate is moderated by the height of the land. As a result, Nairobi, in the thickly populated south-western highlands, has summer temperatures which are 10°C [18°F] lower than Mombasa. Nights can be cool, but temperatures do not fall below freezing. Nairobi's main rainy season is from April to May, with 'little rains' in November and December. However, only about 15% of the country has a reliable rainfall of 800 mm [31 in].

POLITICS & ECONOMY The Kenyan coast has been a trading centre for more than 2,000 years. Britain took over the coast in 1895 and soon extended its influence inland. In the 1950s, a secret movement, called Mau Mau, launched an armed struggle against British rule. Although Mau Mau was eventually defeated, Kenya became independent in 1963.

Many Kenyans felt that Kenya should have a strong central government, and Kenya was a one-party state for much of the time since 1963. But democracy was restored in the early 1990s and elections were held in 1992 and 1997. In 1999, Kenya, with Tanzania and Uganda, set up an East African Community, which aimed to create a customs union, a common market, a monetary union, and, ultimately a political union.

According to the United Nations, Kenya is a 'low-income' developing country. Agriculture employs about 80% of the people, but many Kenyans are subsistence farmers, growing little more than they need to support their families. The chief food crop is maize. The main cash crops and leading exports are coffee and tea. Manufactures include chemicals, leather and footwear, processed food, petroleum products and textiles.

AREA 580,370 sq km [224,081 sq mi]
POPULATION 30,766,000
CAPITAL (POPULATION) Nairobi (2,000,000)
GOVERNMENT Multiparty republic
ETHNIC GROUPS Kikuyu 21%, Luhya 14%, Luo 13%, Kalenjin 12%, Kamba 11%
LANGUAGES Kiswahili and English (both official)
RELIGIONS Protestant 38%, Roman Catholic 28%, other Christian 27%, traditional beliefs 26%, Islam 7%
CURRENCY Kenya shilling = 100 cents

KIRIBATI

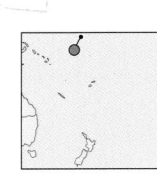

The Republic of Kiribati comprises three groups of corall atolls scattered over about 5 million sq km [2 million sq mi]. Kiribati straddles the equator and temperatures are high and the rainfall is abundant.

Formerly part of the British Gilbert and Ellice Islands, Kiribati became independent in 1979. The main export is copra and the country depends heavily on foreign aid. **AREA** 728 sq km [281 sq mi]; **POPULATION** 94,000; **CAPITAL** Tarawa.

KOREA, NORTH

GEOGRAPHY The Democratic People's Republic of Korea occupies the northern part of the Korean peninsula which extends south from north-eastern China. Mountains form the heart of the country, with the highest peak, Paektu-san, reaching 2,744 m [9,003 ft] on the northern border.

North Korea has a fairly severe climate, with bitterly cold winters when winds blow from across central Asia, bringing snow and freezing conditions. In summer, moist winds from the oceans bring rain.

POLITICS & ECONOMY North Korea was created in 1945, when the peninsula, a Japanese colony since 1910, was divided into two parts. Soviet forces occupied the north, with US forces in the south. Soviet occupation led to a Communist government being established in 1948 under the leadership of Kim Il Sung. He initiated a Stalinist regime in which he assumed the role of dictator, and a personality cult developed around him. He was to become the world's most durable Communist leader.

The Korean War began in June 1950 when North Korean troops invaded the south. North Korea, aided by China and the Soviet Union, fought with South Korea, which was supported by troops from the United States and other UN members. The war ended in July 1953. An armistice was signed but no permanent peace treaty was agreed. After the war, North Korea adopted a hostile policy towards South Korea in pursuit of its policy of reunification.

The ending of the Cold War in the late 1980s eased the situation and both North and South Korea joined the United Nations in 1991. The two countries made several agreements, including one in which they agreed not to use force against each other. However, North Korea remained as isolated as ever.

In 1993, North Korea began a new international crisis by announcing that it was withdrawing from the Nuclear Non-Proliferation Treaty. This led to suspicions that North Korea, which had signed the Treaty in 1985, was developing its own nuclear weapons. Kim Il Sung, who had ruled as a virtual dictator from 1948 until his death in 1994, was succeeded by his son, Kim Jong Il.

In the early 2000s, attempts were made to reconcile the two Koreas, though the prospect of reunification seemed remote, especially after the United States accused North Korea of supporting international terrorism in 2002.

North Korea has considerable resources, including coal, copper, iron ore, lead, tin, tungsten and zinc. Under Communism, North Korea has concentrated on developing heavy, state-owned industries. Manufactures include chemicals, iron and steel, machinery, processed food and textiles. Agriculture employs about a third of the people of North Korea and rice is the leading crop. Economic decline and mismanagement, aggravated by three successive crop failures caused by floods in 1995 and 1996 and a drought in 1997, led to famine on a large scale.

AREA 120,540 sq km [46,540 sq mi]
POPULATION 21,968,000
CAPITAL (POPULATION) Pyŏngyang (2,741,000)
GOVERNMENT Single-party people's republic
ETHNIC GROUPS Korean 99%
LANGUAGES Korean (official)
RELIGIONS Buddhism and Confucianism
CURRENCY North Korean won = 100 chon

KOREA, SOUTH

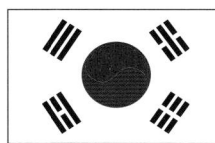 

GEOGRAPHY The Republic of Korea, as South Korea is officially known, occupies the southern part of the Korean peninsula. Mountains cover much of the country. The southern and western coasts are major farming regions. Many islands are found along the west and south coasts. The largest is Cheju-do, which contains South Korea's highest peak, which rises to 1,950 m [6,398 ft].

Like North Korea, South Korea is chilled in winter by cold, dry winds blowing from central Asia. Snow often covers the mountains in the east. The summers are hot and wet, especially in July and August.

POLITICS & ECONOMY After Japan's defeat in World War II (1939–45), North Korea was occupied by troops from the Soviet Union, while South Korea was occupied by United States forces. Attempts to reunify Korea failed and, in 1948, a National Assembly was elected in South Korea. This Assembly created the Republic of Korea, while North Korea became a Communist state. North Korean troops invaded the South in June 1950, sparking off the Korean War (1950–3).

In the 1950s, South Korea had a weak economy, which had been further damaged by the destruction caused by the Korean War. From the 1960s to the 1980s, South Korean governments worked to industrialize the economy. The governments were dominated by military leaders, who often used authoritarian methods and flouted human rights. In 1987, a new constitution was approved, enabling presidential elections to be held every five years. In 1991, South and North Korea became members of the United Nations and they signed agreements, including one in which they agreed not to use force against each other. Tensions continued, though hopes were raised when negotiations between the two countries took place in the early 21st century.

The World Bank classifies South Korea as an 'upper-middle-income' developing country. It is also one of the world's fastest growing industrial economies. The country's resources include coal and tungsten, and its main manufactures are processed food and textiles. Since partition, heavy industries have been built up, making chemicals, fertilizers, iron and steel, and ships. South Korea has also developed the production of such things as computers, cars and television sets. In late 1997, however, the dramatic expansion of the economy was halted by a market crash which affected many of the booming economies of Asia. In an effort to negate the economic and social turmoil that resulted, tough reforms were demanded by the International Monetary Fund and an agreement was reached to restructure much of the short-term debt faced by the government.

Farming remains important in South Korea. Rice is the chief crop, together with fruit, grains and vegetables, while fishing provides a major source of protein.

AREA 99,020 sq km [38,232 sq mi]
POPULATION 47,904,000
CAPITAL (POPULATION) Seoul (10,231,000)
GOVERNMENT Multiparty republic
ETHNIC GROUPS Korean 99%
LANGUAGES Korean (official)
RELIGIONS Christianity 49%, Buddhism 47%, Confucianism 3%
CURRENCY South Korean won = 100 chon

KUWAIT

 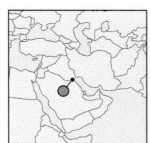

The State of Kuwait at the north end of the Gulf is largely made up of desert. Temperatures are high and the rainfall low. Kuwait became independent from Britain in 1961 and revenues from its oil wells have made it highly prosperous. Iraq invaded Kuwait in 1990 and much damage was inflicted in the ensuing conflict in 1991 when Kuwait was liberated.

AREA 17,820 sq km [6,880 sq mi]; **POPULATION** 2,042,000; **CAPITAL** Kuwait City.

KYRGYZSTAN

 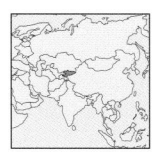

GEOGRAPHY The Republic of Kyrgyzstan is a landlocked country between China, Tajikistan, Uzbekistan and Kazakstan. The country is mountainous, with spectacular scenery. The highest mountain, Pik Pobedy in the Tian Shan range, reaches 7,439 m [24,406 ft] in the east. The lowlands have warm summers and cold winters. But January temperatures in the mountains plummet to −28°C [−18°F]. Kyrgyzstan has a low annual rainfall.

POLITICS & ECONOMY In 1876, Kyrgyzstan became a province of Russia and Russian settlement in the area began. In 1916, Russia crushed a rebellion among the Kyrgyz, and many subsequently fled to China. In 1922, the area became an autonomous *oblast* (self-governing region) of the newly formed Soviet Union but, in 1936, it became one of the Soviet Socialist Republics. Under Communist rule, nomads were forced to work on government-run farms, while local customs and religious worship were suppressed. However, there were concurrent improvements in education and health.

In 1991, Kyrgyzstan became an independent country following the break-up of the Soviet Union. The Communist party was dissolved, but the country maintained ties with Russia through an organization called the Commonwealth of Independent States. Kyrgyzstan adopted a new constitution in 1994 and parliamentary elections were held in 1995. However, in the late 1990s, the government increased presidential powers and curbed press freedoms.

In the early 1990s, when Kyrgyzstan was working to reform its economy, the World Bank classified it as a 'lower-middle-income' developing country. Agriculture, especially livestock rearing, is the chief activity. The chief products include cotton, eggs, fruits, grain, tobacco, vegetables and wool. But food must be imported. Industries are mainly concentrated around the capital Bishkek.

AREA 198,500 sq km [76,640 sq mi]
POPULATION 4,753,000
CAPITAL (POPULATION) Bishkek (589,000)
GOVERNMENT Multiparty republic
ETHNIC GROUPS Kyrgyz 52%, Russian 18%, Uzbek 13%, Ukrainian 3%, German, Tatar
LANGUAGES Kyrgyz and Russian (both official), Uzbek
RELIGIONS Islam
CURRENCY Som = 100 tyiyn

LAOS

GEOGRAPHY The Lao People's Democratic Republic is a landlocked country in South-east Asia. Mountains and plateaux cover much of the country.

Most people live on the plains bordering the River Mekong and its tributaries. This river, one of Asia's longest, forms much of the country's north-western and south-western borders.

Laos has a tropical monsoon climate. Winters are dry and sunny, with winds blowing in from the north-east. The temperatures rise until April, when the wind directions are reversed and moist south-westerly winds reach Laos, heralding the start of the wet monsoon season.

POLITICS & ECONOMY France made Laos a protectorate in the late 19th century and ruled it as part of French Indo-China, a region which also included Cambodia and Vietnam. Laos became a member of the French Union in 1948 and an independent kingdom in 1954.

After independence, Laos suffered from instability caused by a long power struggle between royalist government forces and a pro-Communist group called the Pathet Lao. A civil war broke out in 1960 and continued into the 1970s. The Pathet Lao took control in 1975 and the king abdicated. Laos then came under the influence of Communist Vietnam, which had used Laos as a supply base during the Vietnam War (1957–75). From the early 1980s, the economy deteriorated and opposition appeared when bombings occurred in Vientiane in 2000. They were attributed to rebels in the minority Hmong tribe or to politicians who wanted faster economic reforms.

Laos is one of the world's poorest countries. Agriculture employs about 76% of the people, as compared with 7% in industry and 17% in services. Rice is the main crop, and timber and coffee are both exported. But the most valuable export is electricity, which is produced at hydroelectric power stations on the River Mekong and is exported to Thailand. Laos also produces opium.

AREA 236,800 sq km [91,428 sq mi]
POPULATION 5,636,000
CAPITAL (POPULATION) Vientiane (532,000)
GOVERNMENT Single-party republic
ETHNIC GROUPS Lao Loum 68%, Lao Theung 22%, Lao Soung 9%
LANGUAGES Lao (official), Khmer, Tai, Miao
RELIGIONS Buddhism 58%, traditional beliefs 34%, Christianity 2%, Islam 1%
CURRENCY Kip = 100 at

LATVIA

GEOGRAPHY The Republic of Latvia is one of three states on the south-eastern corner of the Baltic Sea which were ruled as parts of the Soviet Union between 1940 and 1991. Latvia consists mainly of flat plains separated by low hills, composed of moraine (ice-worn rocks).

Riga has warm summers, but the winter months

LEBANON

(from December to March) are subzero. In the winter, the sea often freezes over. The rainfall is moderate and it occurs throughout the year, with light snow in winter.

POLITICS & ECONOMY In 1800, Russia was in control of Latvia, but Latvians declared their independence after World War I. In 1940, under a German-Soviet pact, Soviet troops occupied Latvia, but they were driven out by the Germans in 1941. Soviet troops returned in 1944 and Latvia became part of the Soviet Union. Under Soviet rule, many Russian immigrants settled in Latvia and many Latvians feared that the Russians would become the dominant ethnic group.

In the late 1980s, when reforms were being introduced in the Soviet Union, Latvia's government ended absolute Communist rule and made Latvian the official language. In 1990, it declared the country to be independent, an act which was finally recognized by the Soviet Union in September 1991.

Latvia held its first free elections to its parliament (the Saeima) in 1993. Voting was limited only to citizens of Latvia on 17 June 1940 and their descendants. This meant that about 34% of Latvian residents were unable to vote. In 1994, Latvia restricted the naturalization of non-Latvians, including many Russian settlers, who were not allowed to vote or own land. However, in 1998, the government agreed that all children born since independence should have automatic citizenship regardless of the status of their parents.

The World Bank classifies Latvia as a 'lower-middle-income' country and, in the 1990s, it faced many problems in turning its economy into a free-market system. Products include electronic goods, farm machinery, fertilizers, processed food, plastics, radios and vehicles. Latvia produces only about a tenth of the electricity it needs. It imports the rest from Belarus, Russia and Ukraine.

AREA 64,589 sq km [24,938 sq mi]
POPULATION 2,385,000
CAPITAL (POPULATION) Riga (811,000)
GOVERNMENT Multiparty republic
ETHNIC GROUPS Latvian 56%, Russian 30%, Belarussian 4%, Ukrainian 3%, Polish 2%, Lithuanian, Jewish
LANGUAGES Latvian (official), Russian
RELIGIONS Lutheran, Russian Orthodox and Roman Catholic
CURRENCY Lats = 10 santimi

LEBANON

 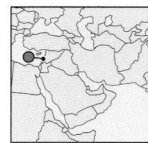

GEOGRAPHY The Republic of Lebanon is a country on the eastern shores of the Mediterranean Sea. Behind the coastal plain are the rugged Lebanon Mountains (Jabal Lubnan), which rise to 3,088 m [10,131 ft]. Another range, the Anti-Lebanon Mountains (Al Jabal Ash Sharqi), form the eastern border with Syria. Between the two ranges is the Bekaa (Beqaa) Valley, a fertile farming region.

The Lebanese coast has the hot, dry summers and mild, wet winters that are typical of many Mediterranean lands. Inland, onshore winds bring heavy rain to the western slopes of the mountains in the winter months, with snow at the higher altitudes.

POLITICS & ECONOMY Lebanon was ruled by Turkey from 1516 until World War I. France ruled the country from 1923, but Lebanon became independent in 1946. After independence, the Muslims and Christians agreed to share power, and Lebanon made rapid economic progress. But from the late 1950s, development was slowed by periodic conflict between Sunni and Shia Muslims, Druze and Christians. The situation was further complicated by the presence of Palestinian refugees who used bases in Lebanon to attack Israel.

In 1975, civil war broke out as private armies representing the many factions struggled for power. This led to intervention by Israel in the south and Syria in the north. UN peacekeeping forces arrived in 1978, but bombings, assassinations and kidnappings became almost everyday events in the 1980s. From 1991, Lebanon enjoyed an uneasy peace. But, Israel continued to occupy an area in the south. In the 1990s, Israel launched several attacks on pro-Iranian Hezbollah guerrillas in Lebanon, but all Israeli troops were withdrawn in May 2000.

Lebanon's civil war almost destroyed valuable trade and financial services that had been Lebanon's chief source of income, together with tourism. Manufacturing, which had formerly been a major activity, was badly hit.

AREA 10,400 sq km [4,015 sq mi]
POPULATION 3,628,000
CAPITAL (POPULATION) Beirut (1,500,000)
GOVERNMENT Multiparty republic
ETHNIC GROUPS Lebanese 80%, Palestinian 12%, Armenian 5%, Syrian, Kurdish
LANGUAGES Arabic (official)
RELIGIONS Islam 70%, Christianity 30%
CURRENCY Lebanese pound = 100 piastres

LESOTHO

 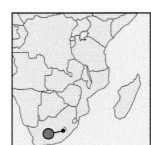

GEOGRAPHY The Kingdom of Lesotho is a landlocked country, completely enclosed by South Africa. The land is mountainous, rising to 3,482 m [11,424 ft] on the north-eastern border. The Drakensberg range covers most of the country.

The climate of Lesotho is greatly affected by the altitude, because most of the country lies above 1,500 m [4,921 ft]. Maseru has warm summers, but the temperatures fall below freezing in the winter. The mountains are colder. The rainfall varies, averaging around 700 mm [28 in].

POLITICS & ECONOMY The Basotho nation was founded in the 1820s by King Moshoeshoe I, who united various groups fleeing from tribal wars in southern Africa. Britain made the area a protectorate in 1868 and, in 1871, placed it under the British Cape Colony in South Africa. But in 1884, Basutoland, as the area was called, was reconstituted as a British protectorate, where whites were not allowed to own land.

The country finally became independent in 1966 as the Kingdom of Lesotho, with Moshoeshoe II, great-grandson of Moshoeshoe I, as its king. Since independence, Lesotho has suffered instability. The military seized power in 1986 and stripped Moshoeshoe II of his powers in 1990, installing his son, Letsie III, as monarch. After elections in 1993, Moshoeshoe II was restored to office in 1995. But after his death in a car crash in 1996, Letsie III again became king. In 1998, an army revolt, following an election in which the ruling party won 79 out of the

80 seats, caused much damage to the economy, despite the intervention of a South African force intended to maintain order.

Lesotho is a 'low-income' developing country. It lacks natural resources. Agriculture, mainly at subsistence level, light manufacturing and money sent home by Basotho working abroad are the main sources of income.

AREA 30,350 sq km [11,718 sq mi]
POPULATION 2,177,000
CAPITAL (POPULATION) Maseru (130,000)
GOVERNMENT Constitutional monarchy
ETHNIC GROUPS Sotho 99%
LANGUAGES Sotho and English (both official)
RELIGIONS Christianity 80%, traditional beliefs 20%
CURRENCY Loti = 100 lisente

LIBERIA

 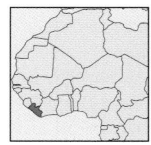

GEOGRAPHY The Republic of Liberia is a country in West Africa. Behind the coastline, 500 km [311 mi] long, lies a narrow coastal plain. Beyond, the land rises to a plateau region, with the highest land along the border with Guinea.

Liberia has a tropical climate with high temperatures and high humidity all through the year. The rainfall is abundant all year round, but there is a particularly wet period from June to November. The rainfall generally increases from east to west.

POLITICS & ECONOMY In the late 18th century, some white Americans in the United States wanted to help freed black slaves to return to Africa. In 1816, they set up the American Colonization Society, which bought land in what is now Liberia.

In 1822, the Society landed former slaves at a settlement on the coast which they named Monrovia. In 1847, Liberia became a fully independent republic with a constitution much like that of the United States. For many years, the Americo-Liberians controlled the country's government. US influence remained strong and the American Firestone Company, which ran Liberia's rubber plantations, was especially influential. Foreign companies were also involved in exploiting Liberia's mineral resources, including its huge iron-ore deposits.

In 1980, a military group composed of people from the local population killed the Americo-Liberian president, William R. Tolbert. An army sergeant, Samuel K. Doe, was made president of Liberia. Elections held in 1985 resulted in victory for Doe.

From 1989, the country was plunged into civil war between various ethnic groups. Doe was assassinated in 1990 and the struggle with rebel groups continued. West African peacekeeping forces arrived in Liberia and, in 1995, a cease-fire was agreed. A council of state, composed of former warlords, was set up and, in 1997, one of the warlords, Charles Taylor, was elected president. A cease-fire in 1998 led to the withdrawal of the peacekeeping forces. But unrest continued and, in 2002, a state of emergency was declared.

Liberia's civil war devastated its economy. Three out of every four people depend on agriculture, though many of them grow little more than they need to feed their families. Major food crops include cassava, rice and sugar cane, while rubber, cocoa and coffee are exported. But the most valuable export is iron ore.

Liberia also obtains revenue from its 'flag of

convenience', which is used by about one-sixth of the world's commercial shipping, exploiting low taxes.

AREA 111,370 sq km [43,000 sq mi]
POPULATION 3,226,000
CAPITAL (POPULATION) Monrovia (962,000)
GOVERNMENT Multiparty republic
ETHNIC GROUPS Kpelle 19%, Bassa 14%, Grebo 9%, Gio 8%, Kru 7%, Mano 7%
LANGUAGES English (official), Mande, Mel, Kwa
RELIGIONS Christianity 40%, Islam 20%, traditional beliefs and others 40%
CURRENCY Liberian dollar = 100 cents

LIBYA

GEOGRAPHY The Socialist People's Libyan Arab Jamahiriya, as Libya is officially called, is a large country in North Africa. Most people live on the coastal plains in the north-east and north-west. The Sahara, which occupies 95% of Libya, reaches the Mediterranean coast along the Gulf of Sidra (Khalij Surt).

The north-eastern and north-western coastal plains have Mediterranean climates, with hot, dry summers and mild, moist winters. Inland, the average annual rainfall drops to 100 mm [4 in] or less.
POLITICS & ECONOMY Italy took over Libya in 1911, but lost it during World War II. Britain and France then jointly ruled Libya until 1951, when the country became an independent kingdom.

In 1969, a military group headed by Colonel Muammar Gaddafi deposed the king and set up a military government. Under Gaddafi, the government took control of the economy and used money from oil exports to finance welfare services and development projects. Gaddafi was criticized for supporting terrorist groups around the world, and Libya became isolated from the mid-1980s. In 1998, he tried to restore Libya's reputation by surrendering for trial two Libyans suspected of planting a bomb on a PanAm plane which exploded over the Scottish town of Lockerbie in 1988. In 2001, one of the Libyans was found guilty and the other acquitted of the bombing. Gaddafi also compensated the family of a British policewoman killed in 1984 in London. However, in 2002, Libya remained on the US blacklist for its alleged support for international terrorism.

The discovery of oil and natural gas in 1959 led to the transformation of Libya's economy. Once one of the world's poorest countries, it has become Africa's richest in terms of its per capita income. It remains a developing country because of its dependence on oil, which accounts for nearly all of its export revenues.

Agriculture is important, although Libya has to import food. Crops include barley, citrus fruits, dates, olives, potatoes and wheat. Cattle, sheep and poultry are raised. Libya has oil refineries and petrochemical plants. Other manufactures include cement and steel.

AREA 1,759,540 sq km [679,358 sq mi]
POPULATION 5,241,000
CAPITAL (POPULATION) Tripoli (960,000)
GOVERNMENT Single-party socialist state
ETHNIC GROUPS Libyan Arab and Berber 97%
LANGUAGES Arabic (official), Berber
RELIGIONS Islam (Sunni)
CURRENCY Libyan dinar = 1,000 dirhams

LIECHTENSTEIN

 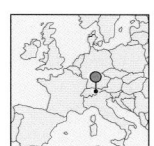

The tiny Principality of Liechtenstein is sandwiched between Switzerland and Austria. The River Rhine flows along its western border, while Alpine peaks rise in the east and south. The climate is relatively mild. Since 1924, Liechtenstein has been in a customs union with Switzerland and, like its neighbour, it is extremely prosperous. Taxation is low and, as a result, the country has become a haven for international companies. **AREA** 157 sq km [61 sq mi]; **POPULATION** 33,000; **CAPITAL** Vaduz.

LITHUANIA

GEOGRAPHY The Republic of Lithuania is the southernmost of the three Baltic states which were ruled as part of the Soviet Union between 1940 and 1991. Much of the land is flat or gently rolling, with the highest land in the south-east.

Winters are cold. January's temperatures average –3°C [27°F] in the west and –6°C [21°F] in the east. Summers are warm, with average temperatures in July of 17°C [63°F]. The average rainfall in the west is about 630 mm [25 in]. Inland areas are drier.
POLITICS & ECONOMY The Lithuanian people were united into a single nation in the 12th century, and later joined a union with Poland. In 1795, Lithuania came under Russian rule. After World War I (1914–18), Lithuania declared itself independent, and in 1920 it signed a peace treaty with the Russians, though Poland held Vilnius until 1939. In 1940, the Soviet Union occupied Lithuania, but the Germans invaded in 1941. Soviet forces returned in 1944, and Lithuania was integrated into the Soviet Union. In 1988, when the Soviet Union was introducing reforms, the Lithuanians demanded independence. Their language is one of the oldest in the world, and the country was always the most homogenous of the Baltic states, staunchly Catholic and resistant of attempts to suppress their culture. Pro-independence groups won the national elections in 1990 and, in 1991, the Soviet Union recognized Lithuania's independence.

After independence, Lithuania faced many problems as it sought to reform its economy and introduce a private enterprise system. In 1998, Valdas Adamkus, a Lithuanian-American who had fled the country in 1944, was elected president.

The World Bank classifies Lithuania as a 'lower-middle-income' developing country. Lithuania lacks natural resources, but manufacturing, based on imported materials, is the most valuable activity.

AREA 65,200 sq km [25,200 sq mi]
POPULATION 3,611,000
CAPITAL (POPULATION) Vilnius (580,000)
GOVERNMENT Multiparty republic
ETHNIC GROUPS Lithuanian 80%, Russian 9%, Polish 7%, Belarussian 2%
LANGUAGES Lithuanian (official), Russian, Polish
RELIGIONS Mainly Roman Catholic
CURRENCY Litas = 100 centai

LUXEMBOURG

 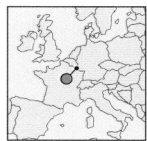

GEOGRAPHY The Grand Duchy of Luxembourg is one of the smallest and oldest countries in Europe. The north belongs to an upland region which includes the Ardenne in Belgium and Luxembourg, and the Eifel highlands in Germany.

Luxembourg has a temperate climate. The south has warm summers and autumns, when grapes ripen in sheltered south-eastern valleys. Winters are sometimes severe, especially in upland areas.
POLITICS & ECONOMY Germany occupied Luxembourg in World Wars I and II. In 1944–5, northern Luxembourg was the scene of the famous Battle of the Bulge. In 1948, Luxembourg joined Belgium and the Netherlands in a union called Benelux and, in the 1950s, it was one of the six founders of what is now the European Union. Luxembourg has played a major role in Europe. Its capital contains the headquarters of several international agencies, including the European Coal and Steel Community and the European Court of Justice. The city is also a major financial centre.

Luxembourg has iron-ore reserves and is a major steel producer. It also has many high-technology industries, producing electronic goods and computers. Steel and other manufactures, including chemicals, rubber products, glass and aluminium, dominate the country's exports. Other major activities include tourism and financial services.

AREA 2,590 sq km [1,000 sq mi]
POPULATION 443,000
CAPITAL (POPULATION) Luxembourg (76,000)
GOVERNMENT Constitutional monarchy (Grand Duchy)
ETHNIC GROUPS Luxembourger 71%, Portuguese 10%, Italian 5%, French 3%, Belgian 3%
LANGUAGES Luxembourgish (official), French, German
RELIGIONS Roman Catholic 95%
CURRENCY Euro = 100 cents

MACEDONIA (FYROM)

GEOGRAPHY The Republic of Macedonia is a country in south-eastern Europe, which was once one of the six republics that made up the former Federal People's Republic of Yugoslavia. This landlocked country is largely mountainous or hilly.

Macedonia has hot summers, though highland areas are cooler. Winters are cold and snowfalls are often heavy. The climate is fairly continental in character and rain occurs throughout the year.
POLITICS & ECONOMY Until the 20th century, Macedonia's history was closely tied to a larger area, also called Macedonia, which included parts of northern Greece and south-western Bulgaria. This region reached its peak in power at the time of Philip II (382–336 BC) and his son Alexander the Great (336–323 BC). After Alexander's death, his empire was split up and it gradually declined. The area became a Roman province in the 140s BC and part of

the Byzantine Empire from AD 395. In the 6th century, Slavs from eastern Europe settled in the area, followed by the Bulgars from central Asia in the 9th century. The Byzantine Empire regained control in 1018, but Serbia took Macedonia in the early 14th century. In 1371, the Ottoman Turks conquered the area and ruled it for more than 500 years. The Ottoman Empire began to collapse in the late 19th century. In 1913, at the end of the Balkan Wars, the area was divided between Serbia, Bulgaria and Greece. At the end of World War I, Serbian Macedonia became part of the Kingdom of the Serbs. Croats and Slovenes, which was renamed Yugoslavia in 1929. After World War II, Yugoslavia became a Communist country under ex-partisan leader Josip Broz Tito.

Tito died in 1980 and, in the early 1990s, the country broke up into five separate republics. Macedonia declared its independence in September 1991. Greece objected to this territory using the name Macedonia, which it considered to be a Greek name. It also objected to a symbol on Macedonia's flag and a reference in the constitution to the desire to reunite the three parts of the old Macedonia.

Macedonia adopted a new clause in its constitution rejecting any Macedonian claims on Greek territory and, in 1993, the United Nations accepted the new republic as a member under the name of The Former Yugoslav Republic of Macedonia (FYROM).

By the end of 1993, all the countries of the EU, except Greece, were establishing diplomatic relations with the FYROM. In 1995, Greece lifted its trade ban, when Macedonia agreed to redesign its flag and remove territorial claims from its constitution. In 2001, fighting along the Kosovo border spilled over into north-western Macedonia. It was attributed to nationalists who wanted to create a Great Albania, including part of Macedonia. The uprising ended when the Macedonian government gave its Albanian-speakers increased rights.

The World Bank describes Macedonia as a 'lower-middle-income' developing country. Manufactures dominate the country's exports. Macedonia mines coal, but imports all its oil and natural gas. The country is self-sufficient in its basic food needs.

AREA 25,710 sq km [9,927 sq mi]
POPULATION 2,046,000
CAPITAL (POPULATION) Skopje (541,000)
GOVERNMENT Multiparty republic
ETHNIC GROUPS Macedonian 67%, Albanian 23%, Turkish 4%, Romanian 2%, Serb 2%
LANGUAGES Macedonian (official), Albanian
RELIGIONS Macedonian Orthodox, Islam
CURRENCY Dinar = 100 paras

MADAGASCAR

GEOGRAPHY The Democratic Republic of Madagascar, in south-eastern Africa, is an island nation, which has a larger area than France. Behind the narrow coastal plains in the east lies a highland zone, mostly between 610 m and 1,220 m [2,000 ft to 4,000 ft] above sea level. Broad plains border the Mozambique Channel in the west.

Temperatures in the highlands are moderated by the altitude. The winters (from April to September) are dry, but heavy rains occur in summer. The eastern coastlands are warm and humid. The west is drier and the south and south-west are hot and dry.

POLITICS & ECONOMY People from South-east Asia began to settle on Madagascar around 2,000 years ago. Subsequent influxes from Africa and Arabia added to the island's diverse heritage, culture and language.

French troops defeated a Malagasy army in 1895 and Madagascar became a French colony. In 1960, it achieved full independence as the Malagasy Republic. In 1972, army officers seized control and, in 1975, under the leadership of Lt-Commander Didier Ratsiraka, the country was renamed Madagascar. Parliamentary elections were held in 1977, but Ratsiraka remained president of a one-party socialist state. The government resigned in 1991, following huge demonstrations. In 2002, the country came close to civil war when Ratsiraka and his opponent, Marc Ravalomanana, both claimed victory in presidential elections.

Madagascar is one of the world's poorest countries. The land has been badly eroded because of the cutting down of the forests and overgrazing of the grasslands. Farming, fishing and forestry employ about 80% of the people. The country's food crops include bananas, cassava, rice and sweet potatoes. Coffee is the leading export.

AREA 587,040 sq km [226,656 sq mi]
POPULATION 15,983,000
CAPITAL (POPULATION) Antananarivo (1,053,000)
GOVERNMENT Republic
ETHNIC GROUPS Merina 27%, Betsimisaraka 15%, Betsileo 11%, Tsimihety 7%, Sakalava 6%
LANGUAGES Malagasy, French (both official)
RELIGIONS Traditional beliefs 52%, Christianity 41%, Islam 7%
CURRENCY Malagasy franc = 100 centimes

MALAWI

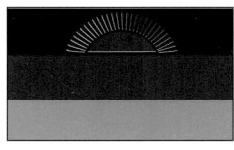 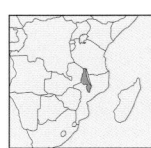

GEOGRAPHY The Republic of Malawi includes part of Lake Malawi, which is drained by the River Shire, a tributary of the River Zambezi. The land is mostly mountainous. The highest peak, Mulanje, reaches 3,000 m [9,843 ft] in the south-east.

While the low-lying areas of Malawi are hot and humid all year round, the uplands have a pleasant climate. Lilongwe, at about 1,100 m [3,609 ft] above sea level, has a warm and sunny climate. Frosts sometimes occur in July and August, in the middle of the long dry season.

POLITICS & ECONOMY Malawi, then called Nyasaland, became a British protectorate in 1891. In 1953, Britain established the Federation of Rhodesia and Nyasaland, which also included what are now Zambia and Zimbabwe. Black African opposition, led in Nyasaland by Dr Hastings Kamuzu Banda, led to the dissolution of the federation in 1963. In 1964, Nyasaland became independent as Malawi, with Banda as prime minister. Banda became president when the country became a republic in 1966 and, in 1971, he was made president for life. Banda ruled autocratically through the only party, the Malawi Congress Party. A multiparty system was restored in 1993. Banda and his party were defeated in elections in 1993. Bakili Muluzi became president and was re-elected in 1999. Banda died in 1997.

Malawi is one of the world's poorest countries. More than 80% of the people are farmers, but many grow little more than they need to feed their families.

AREA 118,480 sq km [45,745 sq mi]
POPULATION 10,548,000
CAPITAL (POPULATION) Lilongwe (395,000)
GOVERNMENT Multiparty republic
ETHNIC GROUPS Maravi (Chewa, Nyanja, Tonga, Tumbuka) 58%, Lomwe 18%, Yao 13%, Ngoni 7%
LANGUAGES Chichewa and English (both official)
RELIGIONS Protestant 55%, Roman Catholic 20%, Islam 20%
CURRENCY Kwacha = 100 tambala

MALAYSIA

 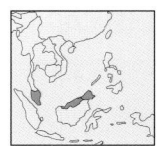

GEOGRAPHY The Federation of Malaysia consists of two main parts. Peninsular Malaysia, which is joined to mainland Asia, contains about 80% of the population. The other main regions, Sabah and Sarawak, are in northern Borneo, an island which Malaysia shares with Indonesia. Much of the land is mountainous, with coastal lowlands bordering the rugged interior. The highest peak, Kinabalu, reaches 4,101 m [13,455 ft] in Sabah.

Malaysia has a hot equatorial climate. The temperatures are high all through the year, though the mountains are much cooler than the lowland areas. The rainfall is heavy throughout the year.

POLITICS & ECONOMY Japan occupied what is now Malaysia during World War II, but British rule was re-established in 1945. In the 1940s and 1950s, British troops fought a war against Communist guerrillas, but Peninsular Malaysia (then called Malaya) became independent in 1957. Malaysia was created in 1963, when Malaya, Singapore, Sabah and Sarawak agreed to unite, but Singapore withdrew in 1965.

From the 1970s, Malaysia achieved rapid economic progress and, by the mid-1990s, it was playing a major part in regional affairs, especially through its membership of ASEAN (Association of South-east Asian Nations). However, together with several other countries in eastern Asia, Malaysia was hit by economic recession in 1997, including a major fall in stock market values. In response to the crisis, the government ordered the repatriation of many temporary foreign workers and initiated a series of austerity measures aimed at restoring confidence and avoiding the chronic debt problems affecting some other Asian countries.

The World Bank classifies Malaysia as an 'upper-middle-income' developing country. Malaysia is a leading producer of palm oil, rubber and tin.

Manufacturing now plays a major part in the economy. Manufactures are diverse, including cars, chemicals, a wide range of electronic goods, plastics, textiles, rubber and wood products.

AREA 329,750 sq km [127,316 sq mi]
POPULATION 22,229,000
CAPITAL (POPULATION) Kuala Lumpur (1,145,000)
GOVERNMENT Federal constitutional monarchy
ETHNIC GROUPS Malay and other indigenous groups 58%, Chinese 27%, Indian 8%
LANGUAGES Malay (official), Chinese, English
RELIGIONS Islam 53%, Buddhism 17%, Chinese folk religionist 12%, Hinduism 7%, Christianity 6%
CURRENCY Ringgit (Malaysian dollar) = 100 cents

MALDIVES

 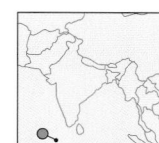

The Republic of the Maldives consists of about 1,200 low-lying coral islands, south of India. The highest point is 24 m [79 ft], but most of the land is only 1.8 m [6 ft] above sea level. The islands became a British territory in 1887 and independence was achieved in 1965. Tourism and fishing are the main industries. **AREA** 298 sq km [115 sq mi]; **POPULATION** 311,000; **CAPITAL** Malé.

MALI

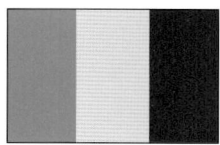 

GEOGRAPHY The Republic of Mali is a landlocked country in northern Africa. The land is generally flat, with the highest land in the Adrar des Iforhas on the border with Algeria.

Northern Mali is part of the Sahara, with a hot, practically rainless climate. But the south has enough rain for farming.

POLITICS & ECONOMY France ruled the area, then known as French Sudan, from 1893 until the country became independent as Mali in 1960.

The first socialist government was overthrown in 1968 by an army group led by Moussa Traoré, but he was ousted in 1991. Multiparty democracy was restored in 1992 and Alpha Oumar Konaré was elected president. The new government agreed a pact providing for a special administration for the Tuareg minority in the north.

Mali is one of the world's poorest countries and 70% of the land is desert or semi-desert. Only about 2% of the land is used for growing crops, while 25% is used for grazing animals. Despite this, agriculture employs more than 80% of the people, many of whom still subsist by nomadic livestock rearing.

AREA 1,240,190 sq km [478,837 sq mi]
POPULATION 11,009,000
CAPITAL (POPULATION) Bamako (810,000)
GOVERNMENT Multiparty republic
ETHNIC GROUPS Bambara 32%, Fulani (or Peul) 14%, Senufo 12%, Soninke 9%, Tuareg 7%, Songhai 7%, Malinke (Mandingo or Mandinke) 7%
LANGUAGES French (official), Voltaic languages
RELIGIONS Islam 90%, traditional beliefs 9%, Christianity 1%
CURRENCY CFA franc = 100 centimes

MALTA

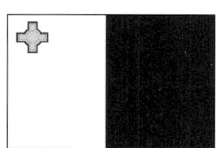 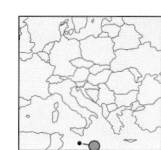

GEOGRAPHY The Republic of Malta consists of two main islands, Malta and Gozo, a third, much smaller island called Comino lying between the two large islands, and two tiny islets.

Malta's climate is typically Mediterranean, with hot and dry summers and mild and wet winters. The sirocco, a hot wind from North Africa, may raise temperatures considerably during the spring.

POLITICS & ECONOMY During World War I (1914–18) Malta was an important naval base. In World War II (1939–45), Italian and German aircraft bombed the islands. In recognition of the bravery of the Maltese, the British King George VI awarded the George Cross to Malta in 1942. In 1953, Malta became a base for NATO (North Atlantic Treaty Organization). Malta became independent in 1964, and in 1974 it became a republic. In 1979, Britain's military agreement with Malta expired, and Malta ceased to be a military base when all the British forces withdrew. In the 1980s, the people declared Malta a neutral country. In the 1990s, Malta applied to join the European Union. The application was scrapped when the Labour Party won the elections in 1996, but, in 2000, after the Labour Party's defeat in 1998, Malta formally reopened negotiations for its entry into the EU.

The World Bank classifies Malta as an 'upper-middle-income' developing country. It lacks natural resources, and most people work in the former naval dockyards, which are now used for commercial shipbuilding and repair, in manufacturing industries and in the tourist industry.

Manufactures include chemicals, processed food and chemicals. Farming is difficult, because of the rocky soils. Crops include barley, fruits, potatoes and wheat. Malta also has a small fishing industry.

AREA 316 sq km [122 sq mi]
POPULATION 395,000
CAPITAL (POPULATION) Valletta (102,000)
GOVERNMENT Multiparty republic
ETHNIC GROUPS Maltese 96%, British 2%
LANGUAGES Maltese and English (both official)
RELIGIONS Roman Catholic 91%
CURRENCY Maltese lira = 100 cents

MARSHALL ISLANDS

 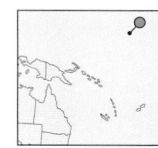

The Republic of the Marshall Islands, a former US territory, became fully independent in 1991. This island nation, lying north of Kiribati in a region known as Micronesia, is heavily dependent on US aid. The main activities are agriculture and tourism. **AREA** 181 sq km [70 sq mi]; **POPULATION** 71,000; **CAPITAL** Dalap-Uliga-Darrit, on Majuro island.

MARTINIQUE

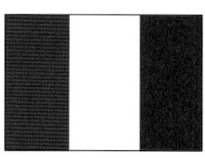 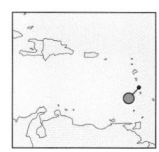

Martinique, a volcanic island nation in the Caribbean, was colonized by France in 1635. It became a French overseas department in 1946. Tourism and agriculture are major activities. About 70% of Martinique's gross domestic product is provided by the French government, allowing for a good standard of living. **AREA** 1,100 sq km [425 sq mi]; **POPULATION** 418,000; **CAPITAL** Fort-de-France.

MAURITANIA

 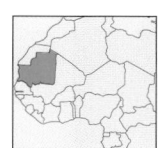

GEOGRAPHY The Islamic Republic of Mauritania in north-western Africa is nearly twice the size of France. But France has more than 28 times as many people. Part of the world's largest desert, the Sahara, covers northern Mauritania and most Mauritanians live in the south-west.

The amount of rainfall and the length of the rainy season increase from north to south. Much of the land is desert, with dry north-east and easterly winds throughout the year. But south-westerly winds bring summer rain to the south.

POLITICS & ECONOMY Originally part of the great African empires of Ghana and Mali, France set up a protectorate in Mauritania in 1903, attempting to exploit the trade in gum arabic. The country became a territory of French West Africa and a French colony in 1920. French West Africa was a huge territory, which included present-day Benin, Burkina Faso, Guinea, Ivory Coast, Mali, Niger and Senegal, as well as Mauritania. In 1958, Mauritania became a self-governing territory in the French Union and it became fully independent in 1960.

In 1976, Spain withdrew from Spanish (now Western) Sahara, a territory bordering Mauritania to the north. Morocco occupied the northern two-thirds of this territory, while Mauritania took the rest. But Saharan guerrillas belonging to POLISARIO (the Popular Front for the Liberation of Saharan Territories) began an armed struggle for independence. In 1979, Mauritania withdrew from the southern part of Western Sahara, which was then occupied by Morocco. In 1991, the country adopted a new constitution when the people voted to create a multiparty government. Multiparty elections were held in 1992 and 1996–7.

The World Bank classifies Mauritania as a 'low-income' developing country. Agriculture employs 40% of the people. Some are herders who move around with herds of cattle and sheep, though recent droughts forced many farmers to seek aid in the cities.

AREA 1,030,700 sq km [397,953 sq mi]
POPULATION 2,747,000
CAPITAL (POPULATION) Nouakchott (735,000)
GOVERNMENT Multiparty Islamic republic
ETHNIC GROUPS Moor (Arab-Berber) 70%, Wolof 7%, Tukulor 5%, Soninke 3%, Fulani 1%
LANGUAGES Arabic and Wolof (both official), French
RELIGIONS Islam 99%
CURRENCY Ouguiya = 5 khoums

MAURITIUS

 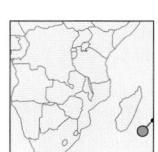

The Republic of Mauritius, an Indian Ocean nation lying east of Madagascar, was previously ruled by France and Britain until it achieved independence in 1968. It became a republic in 1992. Sugar production is in decline but tourism is vital to the economy. **AREA** 1,860 sq km [718 sq mi]; **POPULATION** 1,190,000; **CAPITAL** Port Louis.

MEXICO

GEOGRAPHY The United Mexican States, as Mexico is officially named, is the world's most populous Spanish-speaking country. Much of the land is mountainous, although most people live on the central plateau. Mexico contains two large peninsulas, Lower (or Baja) California in the north-west and the flat Yucatán peninsula in the south-east.

The climate varies according to the altitude. The resort of Acapulco on the south-west coast has a dry and sunny climate. Mexico City, at about 2,300 m [7,546 ft] above sea level, is much cooler. Most rain occurs between June and September. The rainfall decreases north of Mexico City and northern Mexico is mainly arid.

POLITICS & ECONOMY In the mid-19th century, Mexico lost land to the United States, and between 1910 and 1921 violent revolutions created chaos.

Reforms were introduced in the 1920s and, in 1929, the Institutional Revolutionary Party (PRI) was formed. The PRI ruled Mexico effectively as a one-party state until it was finally defeated in 2001. The new president, Vicente Fox, faced many problems, including unemployment and rapid urbanization especially around Mexico City, demands for indigenous rights by Amerindian groups, and illegal emigration to the United States.

The World Bank classifies Mexico as an 'upper-middle-income' developing country. Agriculture is important. Food crops include beans, maize, rice and wheat, while cash crops include coffee, cotton, fruits and vegetables. Beef cattle, dairy cattle and other livestock are raised and fishing is also important.

But oil and oil products are the chief exports, while manufacturing is the most valuable activity. Many factories near the northern border assemble goods, such as car parts and electrical products, for US companies. These factories are called *maquiladoras*. Hope for the future lies in increasing economic co-operation with the USA and Canada through NAFTA (North American Free Trade Association), which came into being on 1 January 1994.

AREA 1,958,200 sq km [756,061 sq mi]
POPULATION 101,879,000
CAPITAL (POPULATION) Mexico City (15,643,000)
GOVERNMENT Federal republic
ETHNIC GROUPS Mestizo 60%, Amerindian 30%, White 9%
LANGUAGES Spanish (official)
RELIGIONS Roman Catholic 90%, Protestant 5%
CURRENCY New peso = 100 centavos

MICRONESIA

 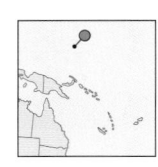

The Federated States of Micronesia, a former US territory covering a vast area in the western Pacific Ocean, became fully independent in 1991. The main export is copra. Fishing and tourism are also important. **AREA** 705 sq km [272 sq mi]; **POPULATION** 135,000; **CAPITAL** Palikir.

MOLDOVA

GEOGRAPHY The Republic of Moldova is a small country sandwiched between Ukraine and Romania. It was formerly one of the 15 republics that made up the Soviet Union. Much of the land is hilly and the highest areas are near the centre of the country.

Moldova has a moderately continental climate, with warm summers and fairly cold winters. Most of the rain comes in the warmer months.

POLITICS & ECONOMY In the 14th century, the Moldavians formed a state called Moldavia. It included part of Romania and Bessarabia (now the modern country of Moldova). The Ottoman Turks took the area in the 16th century, but in 1812 Russia took over Bessarabia. In 1861, Moldavia and Walachia united to form Romania. Russia retook southern Bessarabia in 1878.

After World War I (1914–18), all of Bessarabia was returned to Romania, but the Soviet Union did not recognize this act. From 1944, the Moldovan Soviet Socialist Republic was part of the Soviet Union.

In 1989, the Moldovans asserted their independence and ethnicity by making Romanian the official language and, at the end of 1991, Moldova became an independent country. In 1992, fighting occurred between Moldovans and Russians in Trans-Dniester, a mainly Russian-speaking area east of the River Dniester. The first multiparty elections were held in 1994, when a proposal to unite with Romania was rejected. Economic problems made the government unpopular and, in 2001, Moldova became the first former Soviet state to return the Communist party to power in a general election.

Moldova is a fertile country in which agriculture remains central to the economy. Major products include fruits, maize, tobacco and wine. Moldova has few natural resources and the country imports materials and fuels for its industries. Light industries, such as food processing and household appliance factories, are gradually increasing.

AREA 33,700 sq km [13,010 sq mi]
POPULATION 4,432,000
CAPITAL (POPULATION) Chişinău (658,000)
GOVERNMENT Multiparty republic
ETHNIC GROUPS Moldovan 65%, Ukrainian 14%, Russian 13%, Gagauz 4%, Jewish 2%, Bulgarian
LANGUAGES Moldovan/Romanian (official)
RELIGIONS Eastern Orthodox
CURRENCY Leu = 100 bani

MONACO

The tiny Principality of Monaco consists of a narrow strip of coastline and a rocky peninsula on the French Riviera. Its considerable wealth is derived largely from banking, finance, gambling and tourism. Monaco's citizens do not pay any state tax. Its attractions include the Monte Carlo casino and such sporting events as the Monte Carlo Rally and the Monaco Grand Prix. **AREA** 1.5 sq km [0.6 sq mi]; **POPULATION** 32,000; **CAPITAL** Monaco.

MONGOLIA

GEOGRAPHY The State of Mongolia is the world's largest landlocked country. It consists mainly of high plateaux, with the Gobi Desert in the south-east.

Ulan Bator lies on the northern edge of a desert plateau. It has bitterly cold winters. Summer temperatures are moderated by the altitude.

POLITICS & ECONOMY In the 13th century, Genghis Khan united the Mongolian peoples and built up a great empire. Under his grandson, Kublai Khan, the Mongol empire extended from Korea and China to eastern Europe and present-day Iraq.

The Mongol empire broke up in the late 14th century. In the early 17th century, Inner Mongolia came under Chinese control, and by the late 17th century Outer Mongolia had become a Chinese province. In 1911, the Mongolians drove the Chinese out of Outer Mongolia and made the area a Buddhist kingdom. But in 1924, under Russian influence, the Communist Mongolian People's Republic was set up. From the 1950s, Mongolia supported the Soviet Union in its disputes with China. In 1990, the people demonstrated for more freedom, and free elections in June 1990 resulted in victory for the Mongolian People's Revolutionary Party, which was composed of Communists. Communist rule ended in 1996, when the Democratic Union coalition won power. But the Communists regained power in 2000, though they were expected to continue free-market policies.

The World Bank classifies Mongolia as a 'lower-middle-income' developing country. Most people were once nomads, who moved around with their herds of sheep, cattle, goats and horses. Under Communist rule, most people were moved into permanent homes on government-owned farms. But livestock and animal products remain leading exports. The Communists also developed industry, especially the mining of coal, copper, gold, molybdenum, tin and tungsten, and manufacturing. Minerals and fuels now account for around half of Mongolia's exports.

AREA 1,566,500 sq km [604,826 sq mi]
POPULATION 2,655,000
CAPITAL (POPULATION) Ulan Bator (673,000)
GOVERNMENT Multiparty republic
ETHNIC GROUPS Khalkha Mongol 85%, Kazak 6%
LANGUAGES Khalkha Mongolian (official), Turkic, Russian
RELIGIONS Tibetan Buddhist (Lamaist)
CURRENCY Tugrik = 100 möngös

MONTSERRAT

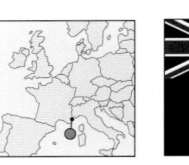 

Monserrat is a British overseas territory in the Caribbean Sea. The climate is tropical and hurricanes often cause much damage. Intermittent eruptions of the Soufrière Hills volcano between 1995 and 1998 led to the emigration of many of the inhabitants and the virtual destruction of Plymouth, the capital, in the southern part of the island. **AREA** 1,100 sq km [39 sq mi]; **POPULATION** (prior to the volcanic activity) 8,000; **CAPITAL** Plymouth.

MOROCCO

GEOGRAPHY The Kingdom of Morocco lies in north-western Africa. Its name comes from the Arabic Maghreb-el-Aksa, meaning 'the farthest west'. Behind the western coastal plain the land rises to a broad plateau and ranges of the Atlas Mountains. The High (Haut) Atlas contains the highest peak, Djebel Toubkal, at 4,165 m [13,665 ft]. East of the mountains, the land descends to the arid Sahara.

The Atlantic coast of Morocco is cooled by the Canaries Current. Inland, summers are hot and dry. The winters are mild. In winter, between October and April, south-westerly winds from the Atlantic Ocean bring moderate rainfall, and snow often falls on the High Atlas Mountains.

POLITICS & ECONOMY The original people of Morocco were the Berbers. But in the 680s, Arab invaders introduced Islam and the Arabic language. By the early 20th century, France and Spain controlled Morocco, which became an independent kingdom in 1956. Although Morocco is a constitutional monarchy, King Hassan II ruled the country in a generally authoritarian way since his accession to the throne in 1961 to his death in 1999. His son and successor Mohamed VI faced several problems, including the future of Western Sahara which Hassan II had vigorously claimed for Morocco.

Morocco is classified as a 'lower-middle-income' developing country. It is the world's third largest producer of phosphate rock, which is used to make fertilizer. One of the reasons why Morocco wants to keep Western Sahara is that it, too, has large phosphate reserves. Farming employs 44% of Moroccans. Crops include barley, beans, citrus fruits, maize and wheat. Tourism is also important.

AREA 446,550 sq km [172,413 sq mi]
POPULATION 30,645,000
CAPITAL (POPULATION) Rabat (1,220,000)
GOVERNMENT Constitutional monarchy
ETHNIC GROUPS Arab 70%, Berber 30%
LANGUAGES Arabic (official), Berber, French
RELIGIONS Islam 99%, Christianity 1%
CURRENCY Moroccan dirham = 100 centimes

MOZAMBIQUE

 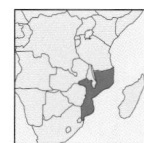

GEOGRAPHY The Republic of Mozambique borders the Indian Ocean in south-eastern Africa. The coastal plains are narrow in the north but broaden in the south. Inland lie plateaux and hills, which make up another two-fifths of Mozambique.

Mozambique has a mostly tropical climate. The capital Maputo, which lies outside the tropics, has hot and humid summers, though the winters are mild and fairly dry.

POLITICS & ECONOMY In 1885, when the European powers divided Africa, Mozambique was recognized as a Portuguese colony. But black African opposition to European rule gradually increased. In 1961, the Front for the Liberation of Mozambique (FRELIMO) was founded to oppose Portuguese rule.

In 1964, FRELIMO launched a guerrilla war, which continued for ten years. Mozambique became independent in 1975.

After independence, Mozambique became a one-party state. Its government aided African nationalists in Rhodesia (now Zimbabwe) and South Africa. But the white governments of these countries helped an opposition group, the Mozambique National Resistance Movement (RENAMO) to lead an armed struggle against Mozambique's government. Civil war, combined with droughts, caused much suffering in the 1980s. In 1989, FRELIMO declared that it had dropped its Communist policies and ended one-party rule. The war ended in 1992 and multiparty elections in 1994 heralded more stable conditions. In 1995 Mozambique became the 53rd member of the Commonwealth.

In the early 1990s, the UN rated Mozambique as one of the world's poorest countries. The second half of the 1990s saw a surge in economic growth, but huge floods in 2000 and 2001 proved to be a major setback. About 80% of the people are poor and agriculture is the main activity. Crops include cassava, cotton, maize, rice and tea.

AREA 801,590 sq km [309,494 sq mi]
POPULATION 19,371,000
CAPITAL (POPULATION) Maputo (2,000,000)
GOVERNMENT Multiparty republic
ETHNIC GROUPS Indigenous tribal groups (Shangaan, Chokwe, Manyika, Sena, Makua, others) 99%
LANGUAGES Portuguese (official), many others
RELIGIONS Traditional beliefs 48%, Roman Catholic 31%, Islam 20%
CURRENCY Metical = 100 centavos

NAMIBIA

 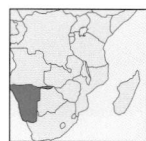

GEOGRAPHY The Republic of Namibia was formerly ruled by South Africa, which called it South West Africa. The country became independent in 1990. The coastal region contains the arid Namib Desert, which is virtually uninhabited. Inland is a central plateau, bordered by a rugged spine of mountains stretching north–south. Eastern Namibia contains part of the Kalahari Desert.

Namibia is a warm and arid country. Lying at 1,700 m [5,500 ft] above sea level, Windhoek has an average annual rainfall of about 370 mm [15 in], often occurring during thunderstorms in the hot summer months.

POLITICS & ECONOMY During World War I, South African troops defeated the Germans who ruled what is now Namibia. After World War II, many people challenged South Africa's right to govern the territory and a civil war began in the 1960s between African guerrillas and South African troops. A cease-fire was agreed in 1989 and Namibia became independent in 1990. In the 1990s, the government pursued a policy of 'national reconciliation'. An enclave on the coast, called Walvis Bay (Walvisbaai), remained part of South Africa until 1994, when it was transferred to Namibia. In 1999, a secessionist group staged an unsuccessful uprising in the Caprivi Strip.

Namibia is rich in mineral reserves, including diamonds, uranium, zinc and copper. Minerals make up 90% of the exports. But farming employs about two out of every five Namibians. Sea fishing is also important, though overfishing has reduced the yields of the country's fishing fleet. The country has few industries, but tourism is increasing.

AREA 825,414 sq km [318,434 sq mi]
POPULATION 1,798,000
CAPITAL (POPULATION) Windhoek (126,000)
GOVERNMENT Multiparty republic
ETHNIC GROUPS Ovambo 50%, Kavango 9%, Herero 7%, Damara 7%, White 6%, Nama 5%
LANGUAGES English (official), Ovambo, Afrikaans, German
RELIGIONS Christianity 90% (Lutheran 51%)
CURRENCY Namibian dollar = 100 cents

NAURU

 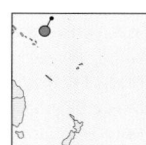

Nauru is the world's smallest republic, located in the western Pacific Ocean, close to the equator. Independent since 1968, Nauru's prosperity is based on phosphate mining, but the reserves are running out. **AREA** 21 sq km [8 sq mi]; **POPULATION** 12,000; **CAPITAL** Yaren.

NEPAL

 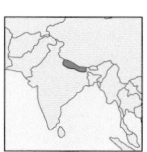

GEOGRAPHY Over three-quarters of Nepal lies in the Himalayan region, culminating in the world's highest peak (Mount Everest, or Chomolongma in Nepali) at 8,850 m [29,035 ft]. As a result, climatic conditions vary widely according to the altitude.

POLITICS & ECONOMY Nepal was united in the late 18th century, although its complex topography has ensured that it remains a diverse patchwork of peoples. From the mid-19th century to 1951, power was held by the royal Rana family. Attempts to introduce a democratic system in the 1950s failed. The first democratic elections in 32 years were held in 1991, but, by the early 21st century, Nepal faced many problems, including the activities of Maoist guerrillas and corruption. In 2001, King Birendra and other members of the royal family were shot dead by his heir, Crown Prince Dipendra, who was upset that his mother refused to accept his choice of a bride.

Agriculture remains the chief activity in this overwhelmingly rural country and the government is heavily dependent on aid. Tourism, centred around the high Himalaya, grows in importance each year, although Nepal was closed to foreigners until 1951. There are also plans to exploit the hydroelectric potential offered by the Himalayan rivers.

AREA 140,800 sq km [54,363 sq mi]
POPULATION 25,284,000
CAPITAL (POPULATION) Katmandu (535,000)
GOVERNMENT Constitutional monarchy
ETHNIC GROUPS Nepalese 53%, Bihari 18%, Tharu 5%, Tamang 5%, Newar 3%
LANGUAGES Nepali (official), local languages
RELIGIONS Hindu 86%, Buddhist 8%, Islam 4%
CURRENCY Nepalese rupee = 100 paisa

NETHERLANDS

GEOGRAPHY The Netherlands lies at the western end of the North European Plain, which extends to the Ural Mountains in Russia. Except for the far south-eastern corner, the Netherlands is flat and about 40% lies below sea level at high tide. To prevent flooding, the Dutch have built dykes (sea walls) to hold back the waves. Large areas which were once under the sea, but which have been reclaimed, are called polders.

Because of its position on the North Sea, the Netherlands has a temperate climate. The winters are mild, with rain coming from the Atlantic depressions which pass over the country.

POLITICS & ECONOMY Before the 16th century, the area that is now the Netherlands was under a succession of foreign rulers, including the Romans, the Germanic Franks, the French and the Spanish. The Dutch declared their independence from Spain in 1581 and their status was finally recognized by Spain in 1648. In the 17th century, the Dutch built up a great overseas empire, especially in South-east Asia. But in the early 18th century, the Dutch lost control of the seas to England.

France controlled the Netherlands from 1795 to 1813. In 1815, the Netherlands, then containing Belgium and Luxembourg, became an independent kingdom. Belgium broke away in 1830 and Luxembourg followed in 1890.

The Netherlands was neutral in World War I (1914–18), but was occupied by Germany in World War II (1939–45). After the war, the Netherlands Indies became independent as Indonesia. The Netherlands became active in West European affairs. With Belgium and Luxembourg, it formed a customs union called Benelux in 1948. In 1949, it joined NATO (the North Atlantic Treaty Organization), and the European Coal and Steel Community (ECSC) in 1953. In 1957, it became a founder member of the European Economic Community (now the European Union), and its economy prospered. On 1 January 2002, the Netherlands became one of the 12 EU countries to adopt the euro as its sole official unit of currency.

The Netherlands is a highly industrialized country and industry and commerce are the most valuable activities. Its resources include natural gas, some oil, salt and china clay. But the Netherlands imports many of the materials needed by its industries and it is, therefore, a major trading country. Industrial products are wide-ranging, including aircraft, chemicals, electronic equipment, machinery, textiles and vehicles. Agriculture employs only 5% of the people, but scientific methods are used and yields are high. Dairy farming is the leading farming activity. Major products include barley, flowers and bulbs, potatoes, sugar beet and wheat.

AREA 41,526 sq km [16,033 sq mi]
POPULATION 15,981,000
CAPITAL (POPULATION) Amsterdam (1,115,000); The Hague (seat of government, 700,000)
GOVERNMENT Constitutional monarchy
ETHNIC GROUPS Dutch 95%, Indonesian, Turkish, Moroccan
LANGUAGES Dutch (official), Frisian
RELIGIONS Roman Catholic 34%, Protestant 21%, Islam 4%
CURRENCY Euro = 100 cents

NETHERLANDS ANTILLES

 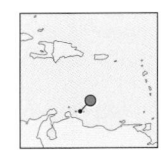

The Netherlands Antilles consists of two different island groups; one off the coast of Venezuela, and the other at the northern end of the Leeward Islands, some 800 km [500 mi] away. They remain a self-governing Dutch territory. The island of Aruba was once part of the territory, but it broke away in 1986. Oil refining and tourism are important activities.
AREA 993 sq km [383 sq mi]; **POPULATION** 212,000; **CAPITAL** Willemstad.

NEW CALEDONIA

 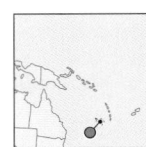

New Caledonia is the most southerly of the Melanesian countries in the Pacific. A French possession since 1853 and an Overseas Territory since 1958. In 1998, France announced an agreement with local Melanesians that a vote on independence would be postponed until 2014. The country is rich in mineral resources, especially nickel.
AREA 18,580 sq km [7,174 sq mi]; **POPULATION** 205,000; **CAPITAL** Nouméa.

NEW ZEALAND

 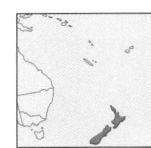

GEOGRAPHY New Zealand lies about 1,600 km [994 mi] south-east of Australia. It consists of two main islands and several other small ones. Much of North Island is volcanic. Active volcanoes include Ngauruhoe and Ruapehu. Hot springs and geysers are common, and steam from the ground is used to produce electricity. The Southern Alps, which contain the country's highest peak Mount Cook (Aoraki), at 3,753 m [12,313 ft] form the backbone of South Island. The island also has some large, fertile plains.

Auckland in the north has a warm, humid climate throughout the year. Wellington has cooler summers, while in Dunedin, in the south-east, temperatures sometimes dip below freezing in winter. The rainfall is heaviest on the western highlands.
POLITICS & ECONOMY Evidence suggests that early Maori settlers arrived in New Zealand more than 1,000 years ago. The Dutch navigator Abel Tasman reached New Zealand in 1642, but his discovery was not followed up. In 1769, the British Captain James Cook rediscovered the islands. In the early 19th century, British settlers arrived and, in 1840, under the Treaty of Waitangi, Britain took possession of the islands. Clashes occurred with the Maoris in the 1860s but, from the 1870s, the Maoris were gradually integrated into society.

In 1907, New Zealand became a self-governing dominion in the British Commonwealth. The country's economy developed quickly and the people became increasingly prosperous. However, after

Britain joined the European Economic Community in 1973, New Zealand's exports to Britain shrank and the country had to reassess its economic and defence strategies and seek new markets. The world economic recession also led the government to cut back on its spending on welfare services in the 1990s. Maori rights and the preservation of Maori culture are other major political issues.

New Zealand's economy has traditionally depended on agriculture, but manufacturing now employs twice as many people as agriculture. Meat and dairy products are the most valuable items produced on farms. The country has more than 44 million sheep, 4 million dairy cattle and 4 million beef cattle.

AREA 268,680 sq km [103,737 sq mi]
POPULATION 3,864,000
CAPITAL (POPULATION) Wellington (329,000)
GOVERNMENT Constitutional monarchy
ETHNIC GROUPS New Zealand European 74%, New Zealand Maori 10%, Polynesian 4%
LANGUAGES English and Maori (both official)
RELIGIONS Anglican 24%, Presbyterian 18%, Roman Catholic 15%
CURRENCY New Zealand dollar = 100 cents

NICARAGUA

GEOGRAPHY The Republic of Nicaragua is a large country in Central America. In the east is a broad plain bordering the Caribbean Sea. The plain is drained by rivers that flow from the Central Highlands. The fertile western Pacific region contains about 40 volcanoes, many of which are active, and earthquakes are common.

Nicaragua has a tropical climate. Managua is hot throughout the year and there is a marked rainy season from May to October. The Central Highlands and Caribbean region are cooler and wetter. The wettest region is the humid Caribbean plain.
POLITICS & ECONOMY In 1502, Christopher Columbus claimed the area for Spain, which ruled Nicaragua until 1821. By the early 20th century, the United States had considerable influence in the country and, in 1912, US forces entered Nicaragua to protect US interests. From 1927 to 1933, rebels under General Augusto César Sandino, tried to drive US forces out of the country. In 1933, US marines set up a Nicaraguan army, the National Guard, to help to defeat the rebels. Its leader, Anastasio Somoza Garcia, had Sandino murdered in 1934 and, from 1937, Somoza ruled as a dictator.

In the mid-1970s, many people began to protest against Somoza's rule. Many joined a guerrilla force, called the Sandinista National Liberation Front, named after General Sandino. The rebels defeated the Somoza regime in 1979. In the 1980s, the US-supported forces, called the 'Contras', launched a campaign against the Sandinista government. The US government opposed the Sandinista regime, under Daniel José Ortega Saavedra, claiming that it was a Communist dictatorship. A coalition, the National Opposition Union, defeated the Sandinistas in elections in 1990. In 1996 and again in 2001, the Sandinista candidate Daniel Ortega was defeated in presidential elections.

In the early 1990s, Nicaragua faced many problems in rebuilding its shattered economy. Agriculture is the main activity, employing nearly half of the people.

Coffee, cotton, sugar and bananas are grown for export, while rice is the main food crop.

AREA 130,000 sq km [50,193 sq mi]
POPULATION 4,918,000
CAPITAL (POPULATION) Managua (864,000)
GOVERNMENT Multiparty republic
ETHNIC GROUPS Mestizo 69%, White 17%, Black 9%, Amerindian 5%
LANGUAGES Spanish (official), Misumalpan
RELIGIONS Roman Catholic 85%
CURRENCY Córdoba oro (gold córdoba) = 100 centavos

NIGER

GEOGRAPHY The Republic of Niger is a landlocked nation in north-central Africa. The northern plateaux lie in the Sahara Desert, while Central Niger contains the rugged Aïr Mountains. The most fertile, densely populated region is the Niger valley in the south-west.

Niger has a tropical climate and the south has a rainy season between June and September. The north is practically rainless.

POLITICS & ECONOMY Since independence in 1960, Niger, a French territory from 1900, has suffered severe droughts. Food shortages and the collapse of the traditional nomadic way of life of some of Niger's people have caused political instability. After a period of military rule, a multiparty constitution was adopted in 1992, but the military again seized power in 1996. Later that year, the coup leader, Col. Ibrahim Barre Mainassara, was elected president. He was assassinated in 1999, but parliamentary rule was rapidly restored and Tandja Mamadou was elected president in November.

Niger's chief resource is uranium and it is the fourth largest producer in the world. Some tin and tungsten are also mined, although other mineral resources are largely untouched.

Despite its resources, Niger is one of the world's poorest countries. Farming employs 85% of the population, but only 3% of the land can be used for crops and 7% for grazing.

AREA 1,267,000 sq km [489,189 sq mi]
POPULATION 10,355,000
CAPITAL (POPULATION) Niamey (398,000)
GOVERNMENT Multiparty republic
ETHNIC GROUPS Hausa 56%, Djerma 22%, Tuareg 8%, Fula 8%
LANGUAGES French (official), Hausa, Djerma
RELIGIONS Islam 98%
CURRENCY CFA franc = 100 centimes

NIGERIA

GEOGRAPHY The Federal Republic of Nigeria is the most populous nation in Africa. The country's main rivers are the Niger and Benue, which meet in central Nigeria. North of the two river valleys are high plains and plateaux. The Lake Chad basin is in the north-east, with the Sokoto plains in the north-west. The south contains hilly uplands and coastal plains.

The south has high temperatures and rain throughout the year. The north is drier and often hotter than the south.

POLITICS & ECONOMY Nigeria has a long artistic tradition. Major cultures include the Nok (500 BC to AD 200), Ife, which developed about 1,000 years ago, and Benin, which flourished between the 15th and 17th centuries. Britain gradually extended its influence over the area in the second half of the 19th century. Nigeria became independent in 1960 and a federal republic in 1963. A federal constitution dividing the country into regions was necessary because Nigeria contains more than 250 ethnic and linguistic groups, as well as several religious ones. Local rivalries have long been a threat to national unity, and six new states were created in 1996 in an attempt to overcome this. Civil war occurred between 1967 and 1970, when the people of the south-east attempted unsuccessfully to secede during the Biafran War. Between 1960 and 1998, Nigeria had only nine years of civilian government. However, in 1988–9, Nigeria held elections restoring civilian rule. A former general, Olusegun Obasanjo, was elected president. The new regime faced many problems. In 2000, Muslim–Christian clashes occurred in the north when several states adopted *sharia* (Islamic law).

Nigeria is a developing country with great potential. Its chief natural resource is oil, which accounts for most of its exports. Agriculture employs 43% of the people and the country is a major producer of cocoa, palm oil and palm kernels, groundnuts and rubber.

AREA 923,770 sq km [356,668 sq mi]
POPULATION 126,636,000
CAPITAL (POPULATION) Abuja (339,000)
GOVERNMENT Federal multiparty republic
ETHNIC GROUPS Hausa and Fulani 29%, Yoruba 21%, Ibo (or Igbo) 18%, Ijaw 10%, Kanuri 4%
LANGUAGES English (official), Hausa, Yoruba, Ibo
RELIGIONS Islam 50%, Christianity 40%, traditional religions 10%
CURRENCY Naira = 100 kobo

NORTHERN MARIANA ISLANDS

The Commonwealth of the Northern Mariana Islands contains 16 mountainous islands north of Guam in the western Pacific Ocean. In a 1975 plebiscite, the islanders voted for Commonwealth status in union with the USA and, in 1986, they were granted US citizenship. **AREA** 477 sq km [184 sq mi]; **POPULATION** 75,000; **CAPITAL** Saipan.

NORWAY

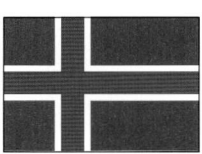 

GEOGRAPHY The Kingdom of Norway forms the western part of the rugged Scandinavian peninsula. The deep inlets along the highly indented coastline were worn out by glaciers during the Ice Age.

The warm North Atlantic Drift off the coast of Norway moderates the climate, with mild winters and cool summers. Nearly all the ports are ice-free throughout the year. Inland, winters are colder and snow cover lasts for at least three months a year.

POLITICS & ECONOMY Under a treaty in 1814, Denmark handed Norway over to Sweden, but it kept Norway's colonies – Greenland, Iceland and the Faroe Islands. Norway briefly became independent, but Swedish forces defeated the Norwegians and Norway had to accept Sweden's king as its ruler.

The union between Norway and Sweden ended in 1903. During World War II (1939–45), Germany occupied Norway. Norway's economy developed quickly after the war and the country now enjoys one of the world's highest standards of living. In 1960, Norway, together with six other countries, formed the European Free Trade Association (EFTA). In 1994, the Norwegians voted against joining the EU.

Norway's chief resources and exports are oil and natural gas which come from wells under the North Sea. Farmland covers only 3% of the land. Dairy farming and meat production are important, but Norway has to import food. Norway has many industries powered by cheap hydroelectricity.

AREA 323,900 sq km [125,050 sq mi]
POPULATION 4,503,000
CAPITAL (POPULATION) Oslo (502,000)
GOVERNMENT Constitutional monarchy
ETHNIC GROUPS Norwegian 97%
LANGUAGES Norwegian (official)
RELIGIONS Lutheran 88%
CURRENCY Krone = 100 ore

OMAN

 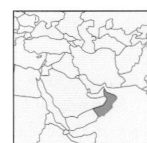

GEOGRAPHY The Sultanate of Oman in the south-eastern Arabian peninsula also includes the tip of the Musandam peninsula. Oman has a hot tropical climate. In Muscat, temperatures may reach 47°C [117°F] in summer.

POLITICS & ECONOMY British influence in Oman dates back to the end of the 18th century, but the country became fully independent in 1971. Since then, using revenue from oil, which was discovered in 1964, the absolute ruler, Qaboos ibn Said, and his government have sought to modernize the country. In 2000, Oman held its first direct elections to its consultative parliament. Unusually for the Gulf region, two women were returned.

The World Bank classifies Oman as an 'upper-middle-income' country. Oil accounts for the bulk of the exports, but agriculture remains important. Major crops include alfalfa, bananas, coconuts, dates, limes, tobacco, vegetables and wheat. Some cattle are raised and fishing, especially for sardines, is important. But Oman still has to import food.

AREA 212,460 sq km [82,031 sq mi]
POPULATION 2,622,000
CAPITAL (POPULATION) Muscat (350,000)
GOVERNMENT Monarchy with consultative council
ETHNIC GROUPS Omani Arab 74%, Pakistani 21%
LANGUAGES Arabic (official), Baluchi, English
RELIGIONS Islam (Ibadiyah), Hinduism
CURRENCY Omani rial = 100 baizas

PAKISTAN

 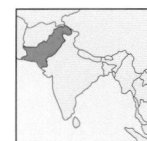

GEOGRAPHY The Islamic Republic of Pakistan contains high mountains, fertile plains and rocky deserts. The Karakoram range, which contains K2, the world's second highest peak, lies in the northern part of Jammu and Kashmir, which is occupied by Pakistan but claimed by India. Other mountains rise in the west. Plains, drained by the River Indus and its tributaries, occupy much of eastern Pakistan. Arid areas include the Thar Desert and the Baluchistan plateau. Most of Pakistan has hot summers and mild winters, though the mountains have cold winters. The rainfall is generally sparse. Most of it occurs between July and September.

POLITICS & ECONOMY Pakistan was the site of the Indus Valley civilization which developed about 4,500 years ago. But Pakistan's modern history dates from 1947, when British India was divided into India and Pakistan. Muslim Pakistan was divided into two parts: East and West Pakistan, but East Pakistan broke away in 1971 to become Bangladesh. In 1948–9, 1965 and 1971, Pakistan and India clashed over the disputed territory of Kashmir. In 1998, Pakistan responded in kind to a series of Indian nuclear weapon tests, provoking global controversy.

Pakistan has been subject to several periods of military rule, but elections in 1988 led to Benazir Bhutto becoming prime minister. She was removed from office in 1990, but she returned as prime minister between 1993 and 1996. In 1997, Narwaz Sharif was elected prime minister, but he was overthrown in 1999 by a military coup led by General Pervez Musharraf. In 2001, Pakistan supported the Western attacks on the Taliban forces in Afghanistan. The United States responded by lifting sanctions on Pakistan and promising more aid.

According to the World Bank, Pakistan is a 'low-income' developing country. The economy is based on farming or rearing goats and sheep. Agriculture employs nearly half the people. Major crops include cotton, fruits, rice, sugar cane and wheat.

AREA 796,100 sq km [307,374 sq mi]
POPULATION 144,617,000
CAPITAL (POPULATION) Islamabad (525,000)
GOVERNMENT Military regime
ETHNIC GROUPS Punjabi 60%, Sindhi 12%, Pashtun 13%, Baluch, Muhajir
LANGUAGES Urdu (official), many others
RELIGIONS Islam 97%, Christianity, Hinduism
CURRENCY Pakistan rupee = 100 paisa

PALAU

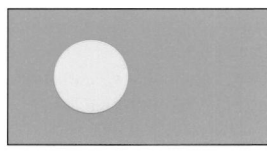 

The Republic of Palau became fully independent in 1994, after the USA refused to accede to a 1979 referendum that declared this island nation a nuclear-free zone. The economy relies on US aid, tourism, fishing and subsistence agriculture. The main crops include cassava, coconuts and copra. **AREA** 458 sq km [177 sq mi]; **POPULATION** 19,000; **CAPITAL** Koror.

PANAMA

GEOGRAPHY The Republic of Panama forms an isthmus linking Central America to South America. The Panama Canal, which is 81.6 km [50.7 mi] long, cuts across the isthmus. It has made the country a major transport centre.

Panama has a tropical climate. Temperatures are high, though the mountains are much cooler than the coastal plains. The main rainy season is between May and December.

POLITICS & ECONOMY Christopher Columbus landed in Panama in 1502 and Spain soon took control of the area. In 1821, Panama became independent from Spain and a province of Colombia.

In 1903, Colombia refused a request by the United States to build a canal. Panama then revolted against Colombia, and became independent. The United States then began to build the canal, which was opened in 1914. The United States administered the Panama Canal Zone, a strip of land along the canal. But many Panamanians resented US influence and, in 1979, the Canal Zone was returned to Panama. Control of the canal itself was handed over by the USA to Panama on 31 December 1999.

Panama's government has changed many times since independence, and there have been periods of military dictatorships. In 1983, General Manuel Antonio Noriega became Panama's leader. In 1988, two US grand juries in Florida indicted Noriega on charges of drug trafficking. In 1989, Noriega apparently defeated in a presidential election, but the government declared the election invalid. After the killing of a US marine, US troops entered Panama and arrested Noriega, who was convicted by a Miami court of drug offences in 1992. However, Panama held national elections in 1994. In 1999, Mireya Moscoso became Panama's first woman president.

The World Bank classifies Panama as a 'lower-middle-income' developing country. The Panama Canal is an important source of revenue and it generates many jobs in commerce, trade, manufacturing and transport. Away from the Canal, the main activity is agriculture, which employs 27% of the people.

AREA 77,080 sq km [29,761 sq mi]
POPULATION 2,846,000
CAPITAL (POPULATION) Panama City (452,000)
GOVERNMENT Multiparty republic
ETHNIC GROUPS Mestizo 70%, Black and Mulatto 14%, White 10%, Amerindian 6%
LANGUAGES Spanish (official)
RELIGIONS Roman Catholic 84%, Protestant 5%
CURRENCY US dollar; Balboa = 100 centésimos

PAPUA NEW GUINEA

GEOGRAPHY Papua New Guinea is an independent country in the Pacific Ocean, north of Australia. It is part of a Pacific island region called Melanesia. Papua New Guinea includes the eastern part of New Guinea, the Bismarck Archipelago, the northern Solomon Islands, the D'Entrecasteaux Islands and the Louisiade Archipelago. The land is largely mountainous.

Papua New Guinea has a tropical climate, with high temperatures throughout the year. Most of the rain occurs during the monsoon season (from December to April), when the north-westerly winds blow. Winds blow from the south-east during the dry season.

POLITICS & ECONOMY The Dutch took western New Guinea (now part of Indonesia) in 1828, but it was not until 1884 that Germany took north-eastern New Guinea and Britain took the south-east. In 1906, Britain handed the south-east over to Australia. It then became known as the Territory of Papua. When World War I broke out in 1914, Australia took German New Guinea and, in 1921, the League of Nations gave Australia a mandate to rule the area, which was named the Territory of New Guinea.

Japan invaded New Guinea in 1942, but the Allies reconquered the area in 1944. In 1949, Papua and New Guinea were combined into the Territory of Papua and New Guinea. Papua New Guinea became fully independent in 1975.

Since independence, the government has worked to develop its mineral reserves. One of the most valuable mines was on Bougainville, in the northern Solomon Islands. But the people of Bougainville demanded a larger share in the profits of the mine. Conflict broke out, the mine was closed and the Bougainville Revolutionary Army proclaimed the island independent. But their attempted secession was not recognized internationally. An agreement to end the conflict was signed in 1998 and the island was granted local autonomy in 2000.

The World Bank classifies Papua New Guinea as a 'lower-middle-income' developing country. Agriculture employs three out of every four people, many of whom produce little more than they need to feed their families. Minerals, notably copper and gold, are the most valuable exports.

AREA 462,840 sq km [178,703 sq mi]
POPULATION 5,049,000
CAPITAL (POPULATION) Port Moresby (174,000)
GOVERNMENT Constitutional monarchy
ETHNIC GROUPS Papuan, Melanesian
LANGUAGES English (official), Pidgin English, about 800 others
RELIGIONS Traditional beliefs 34%, Roman Catholic 22%, Lutheran 16%
CURRENCY Kina = 100 toea

PARAGUAY

GEOGRAPHY The Republic of Paraguay is a landlocked country and rivers, notably the Paraná, Pilcomayo (Brazo Sur) and Paraguay, form most of its borders. A flat region called the Gran Chaco lies in the north-west, while the south-east contains plains, hills and plateaux.

Northern Paraguay lies in the tropics, while the south is subtropical. Most of the country has a warm, humid climate.

POLITICS & ECONOMY In 1776, Paraguay became part of a large colony called the Vice-royalty of La Plata, with Buenos Aires as the capital. Paraguayans opposed this move and the country declared its independence in 1811.

For many years, Paraguay was torn by internal strife and conflict with its neighbours. A war against Brazil, Argentina and Uruguay (1865–70) led to the deaths of more than half of Paraguay's population, and a great loss of territory.

General Alfredo Stroessner took power in 1954 and ruled as a dictator. His government imprisoned many opponents. Stroessner was overthrown in 1989. Free multiparty elections were held in 1993 and 1998. However, the return of democracy frequently seemed precarious because of rivalries between politicians and army leaders.

The World Bank classifies Paraguay as a 'lower-middle-income' developing country. Agriculture and forestry are the leading activities, employing 48% of the population. The country has abundant hydroelectricity and it exports power to Argentina and Brazil.

AREA 406,750 sq km [157,046 sq mi]
POPULATION 5,734,000
CAPITAL (POPULATION) Asunción (945,000)
GOVERNMENT Multiparty republic
ETHNIC GROUPS Mestizo 90%, Amerindian 3%
LANGUAGES Spanish and Guaraní (both official)
RELIGIONS Roman Catholic 96%, Protestant 2%
CURRENCY Guaraní = 100 céntimos

PERU

GEOGRAPHY The Republic of Peru lies in the tropics in western South America. A narrow coastal plain borders the Pacific Ocean in the west. Inland are ranges of the Andes Mountains, which rise to 6,768 m [22,205 ft] at Mount Huascarán, an extinct volcano. East of the Andes lies the Amazon basin.

Lima, on the coastal plain, has an arid climate. The coastal region is chilled by the cold, offshore Humboldt Current. The rainfall increases inland and many mountains in the high Andes are snow-capped.

POLITICS & ECONOMY Spanish conquistadors conquered Peru in the 1530s. In 1820, an Argentinian, José de San Martín, led an army into Peru and declared it independent. But Spain still held large areas. In 1823, the Venezuelan Simon Bolívar led another army into Peru and, in 1824, one of his generals defeated the Spaniards at Ayacucho. The Spaniards surrendered in 1826. Peru suffered much instability throughout the 19th century.

Instability continued in the 20th century. In 1980, when civilian rule was restored, a left-wing group called the Sendero Luminoso, or the 'Shining Path', began guerrilla warfare against the government. In 1990, Alberto Fujimori, son of Japanese immigrants, became president. In 1992, he suspended the constitution and dismissed the legislature. The guerrilla leader, Abimael Guzmán, was arrested in 1992, but instability continued. Following his victory in disputed presidential elections in 2000, Fujimori resigned and sought sanctuary in Japan. In 2001, Alejandro Toledo became the first Peruvian of Amerindian descent to be elected president.

The World Bank classifies Peru as a 'lower-middle-income' developing country. Agriculture employs 35% of the people and major food crops include beans, maize, potatoes and rice. Fish products are exported, but the most valuable export is copper. Peru also produces lead, silver, zinc and iron ore.

AREA 1,285,220 sq km [496,223 sq mi]
POPULATION 27,484,000
CAPITAL (POPULATION) Lima (Lima-Callao, 6,601,000)
GOVERNMENT Transitional republic
ETHNIC GROUPS Quechua 45%, Mestizo 37%, White 15%
LANGUAGES Spanish and Quechua (both official), Aymara
RELIGIONS Roman Catholic 90%
CURRENCY New sol = 100 centavos

PHILIPPINES

 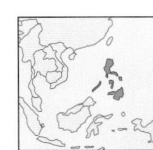

GEOGRAPHY The Republic of the Philippines is an island country in south-eastern Asia. It includes about 7,100 islands, of which 2,770 are named and about 1,000 are inhabited. Luzon and Mindanao, the two largest islands, make up more than two-thirds of the country. The land is mainly mountainous.

The country has a tropical climate, with high temperatures all through the year. The dry season runs from December to April. The rest of the year is wet. The high rainfall is associated with typhoons which periodically strike the east coast.

POLITICS & ECONOMY The first European to reach the Philippines was the Portuguese navigator Ferdinand Magellan in 1521. Spanish explorers claimed the region in 1565 when they established a settlement on Cebu. The Spaniards ruled the country until 1898, when the United States took over at the end of the Spanish–American War. Japan invaded the Philippines in 1941, but US forces returned in 1944. The country became fully independent as the Republic of the Philippines in 1946.

Since independence, the country's problems have included armed uprisings by left-wing guerrillas demanding land reform, and Muslim separatist groups, crime, corruption and unemployment. The dominant figure in recent times was Ferdinand Marcos, who ruled in a dictatorial manner from 1965 to 1986. His successors were Corazon Aquino (1986–92), Fidel Ramos (1992–8), and Joseph Estrada, who resigned after massive public protests against his alleged corruption in 2001. He was succeeded by the vice-president, Gloria Macapagal Arroyo.

The Philippines is a developing country which has a 'lower-middle-income' economy. Agriculture employs 45% of the people. The main foods are rice and maize, while such crops as bananas, cocoa, coconuts, coffee, sugar cane and tobacco are all grown commercially. Manufacturing now plays an increasingly important role in the economy.

AREA 300,000 sq km [115,300 sq mi]
POPULATION 82,842,000
CAPITAL (POPULATION) Manila (8,594,000)
GOVERNMENT Multiparty republic
ETHNIC GROUPS Tagalog 30%, Cebuano 24%, Ilocano 10%, Hiligaynon Ilongo 9%, Bicol 6%
LANGUAGES Pilipino (Tagalog) and English (both official), Spanish, many others
RELIGIONS Roman Catholic 83%, Protestant 9%, Islam 5%
CURRENCY Philippine peso = 100 centavos

PITCAIRN ISLANDS

 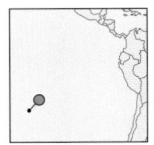

Pitcairn Island is a British overseas territory in the Pacific Ocean. Its inhabitants are descendants of the original settlers – nine mutineers from HMS *Bounty* and 18 Tahitians who arrived in 1790. **AREA** 48 sq km [19 sq mi]; **POPULATION** 47; **CAPITAL** Adamstown.

POLAND

GEOGRAPHY The Republic of Poland faces the Baltic Sea and, behind its lagoon-fringed coast, lies a broad plain. A plateau lies in the south-east, while the Sudeten Highlands straddle part of the border with the Czech Republic. Part of the Carpathian Range (the Tatra) lies in the south-east.

Poland's climate is influenced by its position in Europe. Warm, moist air masses come from the west, while cold air masses come from the north and east. Summers are warm, but winters are cold and snowy.

POLITICS & ECONOMY Poland's boundaries have changed several times in the last 200 years, partly as a result of its geographical location between the powers of Germany and Russia. It disappeared from the map in the late 18th century, when a Polish state called the Grand Duchy of Warsaw was set up. But in 1815, the country was partitioned, between Austria, Prussia and Russia. Poland became independent in 1918, but in 1939 it was divided between Germany and the Soviet Union. The country again became independent in 1945, when it lost land to Russia but gained some from Germany. Communists took power in 1948, but opposition mounted and eventually became focused through an organization called Solidarity.

Solidarity was led by a trade unionist, Lech Walesa. A coalition government was formed between Solidarity and the Communists in 1989. In 1990, the Communist party was dissolved and Walesa became president. But Walesa faced many problems in turning Poland towards a market economy. In presidential elections in 1995, Walesa was defeated by ex-Communist Aleksander Kwasniewski. However, Kwasniewski continued to follow westward-looking policies and he was re-elected president in 2000. Poland joined NATO in 1999 and seemed likely to be among the first eastern European countries to join an expanded European Union.

Poland has large reserves of coal and deposits of various minerals which are used in its factories. Manufactures include chemicals, processed food, machinery, ships, steel and textiles.

AREA 312,680 sq km [120,726 sq mi]
POPULATION 38,634,000
CAPITAL (POPULATION) Warsaw (1,626,000)
GOVERNMENT Multiparty republic
ETHNIC GROUPS Polish 98%, Ukrainian 1%, German 1%
LANGUAGES Polish (official)
RELIGIONS Roman Catholic 94%, Orthodox 2%
CURRENCY Zloty = 100 groszy

PORTUGAL

GEOGRAPHY The Republic of Portugal is the most westerly of Europe's mainland countries. The land rises from the coastal plains on the Atlantic Ocean to the western edge of the huge plateau, or Meseta, which occupies most of the Iberian peninsula. Portugal also contains two autonomous regions, the Azores and Madeira island groups.

The climate is moderated by winds blowing from the Atlantic Ocean. Summers are cooler and winters are milder than in other Mediterranean lands.

POLITICS & ECONOMY Portugal became a separate country, independent of Spain, in 1143. In the 15th century, Portugal led the 'Age of European Exploration'. This led to the growth of a large Portuguese empire, with colonies in Africa, Asia and, most valuable of all, Brazil in South America. Portuguese power began to decline in the 16th century and, between 1580 and 1640, Portugal was ruled by Spain. Portugal lost Brazil in 1822 and, in 1910, Portugal became a republic. Instability hampered progress and army officers seized power in 1926. In 1928, they chose Antonio de Salazar to be minister of finance. He became prime minister in 1932 and ruled as a dictator from 1933.

Salazar ruled until 1968, but his successor, Marcello Caetano, was overthrown in 1974 by a group of army officers. The new government made most of Portugal's remaining colonies independent. Free elections were held in 1978. Portugal joined the European Community (now the European Union) in 1986 and, on 1 January 2002, the euro replaced the escudo as Portugal's sole official unit of currency.

Agriculture and fishing were the mainstays of the economy until the mid-20th century. However, manufacturing is now the most valuable sector.

AREA 92,390 sq km [35,670 sq mi]
POPULATION 9,444,000
CAPITAL (POPULATION) Lisbon (2,561,000)
GOVERNMENT Multiparty republic
ETHNIC GROUPS Portuguese 99%
LANGUAGES Portuguese (official)
RELIGIONS Roman Catholic 95%, other Christians 2%
CURRENCY Euro = 100 cents

PUERTO RICO

 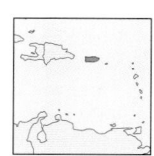

The Commonwealth of Puerto Rico, a mainly mountainous island, is the easternmost of the Greater Antilles chain. The climate is hot and wet. Puerto Rico is a dependent territory of the USA and the people are US citizens. In 1998, 50.2% of the population voted in a referendum on possible statehood to maintain the status quo. Puerto Rico is the most industrialized country in the Caribbean. Tax exemptions attract US companies to the island and manufacturing is expanding. **AREA** 8,900 sq km [3,436 sq mi]; **POPULATION** 3,939,000; **CAPITAL** San Juan.

QATAR

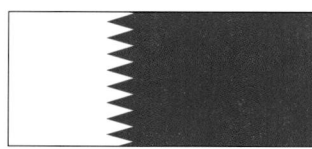 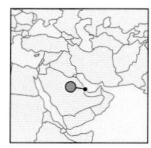

The State of Qatar occupies a low, barren peninsula that extends northwards from the Arabian peninsula into the Gulf. The climate is hot and dry. Qatar became a British protectorate in 1916, but it became fully independent in 1971. Oil, first discovered in 1939, is the mainstay of the economy of this prosperous nation. **AREA** 11,000 sq km [4,247 sq mi]; **POPULATION** 769,000; **CAPITAL** Doha.

RÉUNION

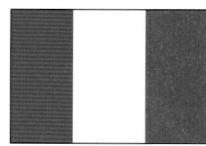 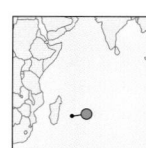

Réunion is a French overseas department in the Indian Ocean. The land is mainly mountainous, though the lowlands are intensely cultivated. Sugar and sugar products are the main exports, but French aid, given to the island in return for its use as a military base, is important to the economy. **AREA** 2,510 sq km [969 sq mi]; **POPULATION** 733,000; **CAPITAL** Saint-Denis.

ROMANIA

GEOGRAPHY Romania is a country on the Black Sea in eastern Europe. Eastern and southern Romania form part of the Danube river basin. The delta region, near the mouths of the Danube, where the river flows into the Black Sea, is one of Europe's finest wetlands. The southern part of the coast contains several resorts. The heart of the country is called Transylvania. It is ringed in the east, south and west by scenic mountains which are part of the Carpathian mountain system.

Romania has hot summers and cold winters. The rainfall is heaviest in spring and early summer, when thundery showers are common.

POLITICS & ECONOMY From the late 18th century, the Turkish empire began to break up. The modern history of Romania began in 1861 when Walachia and Moldavia united. After World War I (1914–18), Romania, which had fought on the side of the victorious Allies, obtained large areas, including Transylvania, where most people were Romanians. This almost doubled the country's size and population. In 1939, Romania lost territory to Bulgaria, Hungary and the Soviet Union. Romania fought alongside Germany in World War II, and Soviet troops occupied the country in 1944. Hungary returned northern Transylvania to Romania in 1945, but Bulgaria and the Soviet Union kept former Romanian territory. In 1947, Romania officially became a Communist country.

In 1990, Romania held its first free elections since the end of World War II. The National Salvation Front, led by Ion Iliescu and containing many former Communist leaders, won a large majority. A new

constitution, approved in 1991, made the country a democratic republic. Elections held under this constitution in 1992 again resulted in victory for Ion Iliescu, whose party was renamed the Party of Social Democracy (PDSR) in 1993. But the government faced many problems. In 1996, the centre-right Democratic Convention defeated the PDSR, led by Emil Constantinescu, who became president. But Iliescu was re-elected president in 2000.

According to the World Bank, Romania is a 'lower-middle-income' economy. Under Communist rule, industry, including mining and manufacturing, became more important than agriculture.

AREA 237,500 sq km [91,699 sq mi]
POPULATION 22,364,000
CAPITAL (POPULATION) Bucharest (2,028,000)
GOVERNMENT Multiparty republic
ETHNIC GROUPS Romanian 89%, Hungarian 7%, Roma 2%
LANGUAGES Romanian (official), Hungarian, German
RELIGIONS Romanian Orthodox 70%, Protestant 6%, Roman Catholic 3%
CURRENCY Romanian leu = 100 bani

RUSSIA

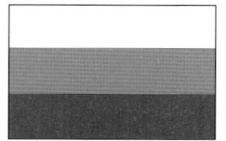 

GEOGRAPHY Russia is the world's largest country. About 25% lies west of the Ural Mountains in European Russia, where 80% of the population lives. It is mostly flat or undulating, but the land rises to the Caucasus Mountains in the south, where Russia's highest peak, Elbrus, at 5,633 m [18,481 ft], is found. Asian Russia, or Siberia, contains vast plains and plateaux, with mountains in the east and south. The Kamchatka peninsula in the far east has many active volcanoes. Russia contains many of the world's longest rivers, including the Yenisey-Angara and the Ob-Irtysh. It also includes part of the world's largest inland body of water, the Caspian Sea, and Lake Baikal, the world's deepest lake.

Moscow has a continental climate with cold and snowy winters and warm summers. Krasnoyarsk in south-central Siberia has a harsher, drier climate, but it is not as severe as parts of northern Siberia.

POLITICS & ECONOMY In the 9th century AD, a state called Kievan Rus was formed by a group of people called the East Slavs. Kiev, now capital of Ukraine, became a major trading centre, but, in 1237, Mongol armies conquered Russia and destroyed Kiev. Russia was part of the Mongol empire until the late 15th century. Under Mongol rule, Moscow became the leading Russian city.

In the 16th century, Moscow's grand prince was retitled 'tsar'. The first tsar, Ivan the Terrible, expanded Russian territory. In 1613, after a period of civil war, Michael Romanov became tsar, founding a dynasty which ruled until 1917. In the early 18th century, Tsar Peter the Great began to westernize Russia and, by 1812, when Napoleon failed to conquer the country, Russia was a major European power. But during the 19th century, many Russians demanded reforms and discontent was widespread.

In World War I (1914–18), the Russian people suffered great hardships and, in 1917, Tsar Nicholas II was forced to abdicate. In November 1917, the Bolsheviks seized power under Vladimir Lenin. In 1922, the Bolsheviks set up a new nation, the Union

of Soviet Socialist Republics (also called the USSR or the Soviet Union).

From 1924, Joseph Stalin introduced a socialist economic programme, suppressing all opposition. In 1939, the Soviet Union and Germany signed a non-aggression pact, but Germany invaded the Soviet Union in 1941. Soviet forces pushed the Germans back, occupying eastern Europe. They reached Berlin in May 1945. From the late 1940s, tension between the Soviet Union and its allies and Western nations developed into a 'Cold War'. This continued until 1991, when the Soviet Union was dissolved.

The Soviet Union collapsed because of the failure of its economic policies. From 1991, President Boris Yeltsin introduced democratic and economic reforms. Yeltsin retired in 1999 and, in 2000, was succeeded by Vladimir Putin. Russia maintains contacts with 11 of the republics in the former Soviet Union through the Commonwealth of Independent States. However, fighting in Chechenia in the 1990s and early 21st century showed that Russia's sheer size and diverse population makes national unity difficult to achieve.

Russia's economy was thrown into disarray after the collapse of the Soviet Union, and in the early 1990s the World Bank described Russia as a 'lower-middle-income' economy. Russia was admitted to the Council of Europe in 1997, essentially to discourage instability in the Caucasus. More significantly still, Boris Yeltsin was invited to attend the G7 summit in Denver in 1997. The summit became known as 'the Summit of the Eight' and it appeared that Russia will now be included in future meetings of the world's most power-ful economies. Industry is the most valuable activity, though, under Communist rule, manufacturing was less efficient than in the West, and the emphasis was on heavy industry. Today, light industries producing consumer goods are becoming important. Russia's adundant resources include oil and natural gas, coal, timber, metal ores and hydroelectric power.

Most farmland is still government-owned or run as collectives. Russia is a major producer of farm products, though it imports grains. Major crops include barley, flax, fruits, oats, rye, potatoes, sugar beet, sunflower seeds, vegetables and wheat.

AREA 17,075,000 sq km [6,592,800 sq mi]
POPULATION 145,470,000
CAPITAL (POPULATION) Moscow (8,405,000)
GOVERNMENT Federal multiparty republic
ETHNIC GROUPS Russian 82%, Tatar 4%, Ukrainian 3%, Chuvash 1%, more than 100 other nationalities
LANGUAGES Russian (official), many others
RELIGIONS Mainly Russian Orthodox, Islam, Judaism
CURRENCY Russian rouble = 100 kopeks

RWANDA

 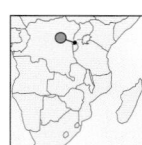

GEOGRAPHY The Republic of Rwanda is a small, landlocked country in east-central Africa. Lake Kivu and the River Ruzizi in the Great African Rift Valley form the country's western border.

Kigali stands on the central plateau of Rwanda. Here, temperatures are moderated by the altitude. The rainfall is abundant, but much heavier rain falls on the western mountains.

POLITICS & ECONOMY Germany conquered the

area, called Ruanda-Urundi, in the 1890s. However, Belgium occupied the region during World War I (1914–18) and ruled it until 1961, when the people of Ruanda voted for their country to become a republic, called Rwanda. This decision followed a rebellion by the majority Hutu people against the Tutsi monarchy. About 150,000 deaths resulted from this conflict. Many Tutsis fled to Uganda, where they formed a rebel army. Burundi became independent as a monarchy, though it became a republic in 1966. Relations between Hutus and Tutsis continued to cause friction. Civil war broke out in 1994 and in 1996 the conflict spilled over into Congo (then Zaïre), where Zaïrean Tutsis staged a rebellion. This led to political instability.

According to the World Bank, Rwanda is a 'low-income' developing country. Most people are poor farmers. Food crops include bananas, beans, cassava and sorghum. Some cattle are raised.

AREA 26,340 sq km [10,170 sq mi]
POPULATION 7,313,000
CAPITAL (POPULATION) Kigali (235,000)
GOVERNMENT Republic
ETHNIC GROUPS Hutu 84%, Tutsi 15%, Twa 1%
LANGUAGES French, English and Kinyarwanda (all official)
RELIGIONS Roman Catholic 53%, Protestant 24%, Adventist 10%
CURRENCY Rwanda franc = 100 centimes

ST HELENA

 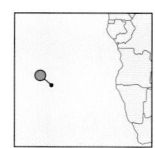

St Helena, which became a British colony in 1834, is an isolated volcanic island in the south Atlantic Ocean. Now a British overseas territory, it is also the administrative centre of Ascension and Tristan da Cunha. **AREA** 122 sq km [47 sq mi]; **POPULATION** 7,266; **CAPITAL** Jamestown.

ST KITTS AND NEVIS

 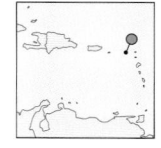

The Federation of St Kitts and Nevis became independent from Britain in 1983. In 1998, a vote for the secession of Nevis fell short of the two-thirds required. **AREA** 360 sq km [139 sq mi]; **POPULATION** 39,000; **CAPITAL** Basseterre.

ST LUCIA

 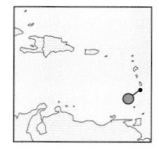

St Lucia, which became independent from Britain in 1979, is a mountainous, forested island of extinct volcanoes. It exports bananas and coconuts, and now attracts many tourists. **AREA** 610 sq km [236 sq mi]; **POPULATION** 158,000; **CAPITAL** Castries.

ST VINCENT AND THE GRENADINES

 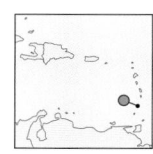

St Vincent and the Grenadines achieved its indepen-dence from Britain in 1979. Tourism is growing, but the territory is less prosperous than its neighbours. **AREA** 388 sq km [150 sq mi]; **POPULATION** 116,000; **CAPITAL** Kingstown.

SAMOA

 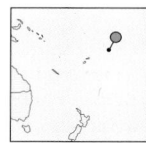

The Independent State of Samoa (formerly Western Samoa) comprises two islands in the South Pacific Ocean. Governed by New Zealand from 1920, the territory became independent in 1962. Exports include coconut cream and beer. **AREA** 2,840 sq km [1,097 sq mi]; **POPULATION** 179,000; **CAPITAL** Apia.

SAN MARINO

 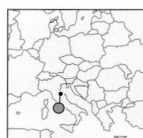

San Marino in northern Italy has been independent since 885 and a republic since the 14th century. It is the world's oldest republic. **AREA** 61 sq km [24 sq mi]; **POPULATION** 27,000; **CAPITAL** San Marino

SÃO TOMÉ AND PRÍNCIPE

 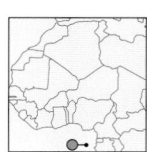

The Democratic Republic of São Tomé and Príncipe, a mountainous island territory west of Gabon, became a Portuguese colony in 1522. Following independence in 1975, the islands became a one-party Marxist state, but multiparty elections were held in 1991. **AREA** 964 sq km [372 sq mi]; **POPULATION** 165,000; **CAPITAL** São Tomé.

SAUDI ARABIA

GEOGRAPHY The Kingdom of Saudi Arabia occupies about three-quarters of the Arabian peninsula in south-west Asia. Deserts cover most of the land. Mountains border the Red Sea plains in the west. In the north is the sandy Nafud Desert (An Nafud). In the south is the Rub' al Khali (the 'Empty Quarter'), one of the world's bleakest deserts.

SENEGAL

Saudi Arabia has a hot, dry climate. In the summer months, the temperatures in Riyadh often exceed 40°C [104°F], though the nights are cool.

POLITICS & ECONOMY Saudi Arabia contains the two holiest places in Islam – Mecca (or Makka), the birthplace of the Prophet Muhammad in AD 570, and Medina (Al Madinah) where Muhammad went in 622. These places are visited by many pilgrims.

Saudi Arabia was poor until the oil industry began to operate on the eastern plains in 1933. Oil revenues have been used to develop the country and Saudi Arabia has given aid to poorer Arab nations. The monarch has supreme authority and Saudi Arabia has no formal constitution. In the first Gulf War (1980–8), Saudi Arabia supported Iraq against Iran. But when Iraq invaded Kuwait in 1990, it joined the international alliance to drive Iraq's forces out of Kuwait in 1991. In 2001, relations with the US became strained after the terrorist attacks on 11 September 2001, partly because many alleged terrorists were Saudi nationals. However, Saudi Arabia denounced the attacks.

Saudi Arabia has about 25% of the world's known oil reserves, and oil and oil products make up 85% of its exports. But agriculture still employs 48% of the people. Irrigation and desalination schemes have increased crop production, while the government continues to diversify the country's economy.

AREA 2,149,690 sq km [829,995 sq mi]
POPULATION 22,757,000
CAPITAL (POPULATION) Riyadh (1,800,000)
GOVERNMENT Absolute monarchy with consultative assembly
ETHNIC GROUPS Arab 90%, Afro-Asian 10%
LANGUAGES Arabic (official)
RELIGIONS Islam 100%
CURRENCY Saudi riyal = 100 halalas

SENEGAL

GEOGRAPHY The Republic of Senegal is on the north-west coast of Africa. The volcanic Cape Verde (Cap Vert), on which Dakar stands, is the most westerly point in Africa. Plains cover most of Senegal, though the land rises gently in the south-east.

Dakar has a tropical climate, with a short rainy season between July and October.

POLITICS & ECONOMY In 1882, Senegal became a French colony, and from 1895 it was ruled as part of French West Africa, the capital of which, Dakar, developed as a major port and city.

In 1959, Senegal joined French Sudan (now Mali) to form the Federation of Mali. But Senegal withdrew in 1960 and became the separate Republic of Senegal. Its first president, Léopold Sédar Senghor, served until 1981, when he was succeeded by Abdou Diouf, who was later made 'president for life'. However, in 2000, Diouf was defeated in presidential elections by Abdoulaye Wade.

Senegal and The Gambia have always enjoyed close relations despite their differing French and British traditions. In 1981, Senegalese troops put down an attempted coup in The Gambia and, in 1982, the two countries set up a defence alliance, called the Confederation of Senegambia. But this confederation was dissolved in 1989.

According to the World Bank, Senegal is a 'lower-

middle-income' developing country. It was badly hit in the 1960s and 1970s by droughts, which caused starvation. Agriculture still employs 81% of the population though many farmers produce little more than they need to feed their families. Food crops include groundnuts, millet and rice. Phosphates are the country's chief resource, but Senegal also refines oil which it imports from Gabon and Nigeria. Dakar is a busy port and has many industries.

AREA 196,720 sq km [75,954 sq mi]
POPULATION 10,285,000
CAPITAL (POPULATION) Dakar (1,905,000)
GOVERNMENT Multiparty republic
ETHNIC GROUPS Wolof 44%, Pular 24%, Serer 15%
LANGUAGES French (official), tribal languages
RELIGIONS Islam 92%, traditional beliefs and others 6%, Christianity (mainly Roman Catholic) 2%
CURRENCY CFA franc = 100 centimes

SEYCHELLES

 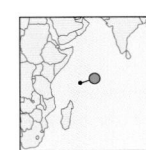

The Republic of Seychelles in the western Indian Ocean achieved independence from Britain in 1976. Coconuts are the main cash crop and fishing and tourism are important. **AREA** 455 sq km [176 sq mi]; **POPULATION** 80,000; **CAPITAL** Victoria.

SIERRA LEONE

GEOGRAPHY The Republic of Sierra Leone in West Africa is about the same size as the Republic of Ireland. The coast contains several deep estuaries in the north, with lagoons in the south. The most prominent feature is the mountainous Freetown (or Sierra Leone) peninsula. Sierra Leone has a tropical climate, with heavy rainfall between April and November.

POLITICS & ECONOMY A former British territory, Sierra Leone became independent in 1961 and a republic in 1971. It became a one-party state in 1978, but, in 1991, the people voted for the restoration of democracy. The military seized power in 1992 and a civil war caused much destruction in 1994–5. Elections in 1996 were followed by another military coup. In 1998, the West African Peace Force restored the deposed President Ahmed Tejan Kabbah. In 1999, a peace agreement followed further conflict. As part of this agreement, Foday Sankoh, one of the rebel leaders, became vice-president. However, he was arrested in 2000 and charged with war crimes. Conflict resumed, but another cease-fire was agreed. Disarmament continued through 2001 and, in 2002, the war seemed to be over.

The World Bank classifies Sierra Leone among the 'low-income' economies. Agriculture provides a living for 70% of the people, though farming is mainly at subsistence level. The most valuable exports are minerals, including diamonds, bauxite and rutile (titanium ore). The country has few manufacturing industries.

AREA 71,740 sq km [27,699 sq mi]
POPULATION 5,427,000
CAPITAL (POPULATION) Freetown (505,000)
GOVERNMENT Single-party republic
ETHNIC GROUPS Mende 35%, Temne 30%, Creole
LANGUAGES English (official), Mende, Temne, Krio
RELIGIONS Islam 60%, traditional beliefs 30%, Christianity 10%
CURRENCY Leone = 100 cents

SINGAPORE

 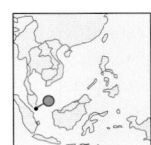

GEOGRAPHY The Republic of Singapore is an island country at the southern tip of the Malay peninsula. It consists of the large Singapore Island and 58 small islands, 20 of which are inhabited.

Singapore has a hot, humid climate. Temperatures are high and rainfall is heavy throughout the year.

POLITICS & ECONOMY In 1819, Sir Thomas Stamford Raffles (1781–1826), agent of the British East India Company, made a treaty with the Sultan of Johor allowing the British to build a settlement on Singapore Island. Singapore soon became the leading British trading centre in South-east Asia and it later became a naval base. Japanese forces seized the island in 1942, but British rule was restored in 1945.

In 1963, Singapore became part of the Federation of Malaysia, which also included Malaya and the territories of Sabah and Sarawak on Borneo. In 1965, Singapore broke away and became independent.

The People's Action Party (PAP) has ruled Singapore since 1959. Its leader, Lee Kuan Yew, served as prime minister from 1959 until 1990, when he resigned and was succeeded by Goh Chok Tong. Under the PAP, the economy has expanded rapidly though some consider its rule rather dictatorial.

The World Bank classifies Singapore as a 'high-income' economy. A skilled workforce has created a fast growing economy, but the recession in 1997–8 was a setback. Trade and finance are leading activities. Manufactures include electronic products, machinery, scientific instruments, textiles and ships. Singapore has a large oil refinery. Petroleum products and manufactures are the main exports.

AREA 618 sq km [239 sq mi]
POPULATION 4,300,000
CAPITAL (POPULATION) Singapore City (3,866,000)
GOVERNMENT Multiparty republic
ETHNIC GROUPS Chinese 77%, Malay 14%, Indian 8%
LANGUAGES Chinese, Malay, Tamil and English (all official)
RELIGIONS Buddhism, Islam, Christianity, Hinduism
CURRENCY Singapore dollar = 100 cents

SLOVAK REPUBLIC

GEOGRAPHY The Slovak Republic is a predominantly mountainous country, consisting of part

of the Carpathian range. The highest peak is Gerlachovka in the Tatra Mountains, which reaches 2,655 m [8,711 ft]. The south is a fertile lowland.

The Slovak Republic has cold winters and warm summers. Kosice, in the east, has average temperatures ranging from –3°C [27°F] in January to 20°C [68°F] in July. The highland areas are much colder. Snow or rain falls throughout the year. Kosice has an average annual rainfall of 600 mm [24 in], the wettest months being July and August.

POLITICS & ECONOMY Slavic peoples settled in the region in the 5th century AD. They were subsequently conquered by Hungary, beginning a millennium of Hungarian rule and suppression of Slovak culture.

In 1867, Hungary and Austria united to form Austria–Hungary, of which the present-day Slovak Republic was a part. Austria–Hungary collapsed at the end of World War I (1914–18). The Czech and Slovak people then united to form a new nation, Czechoslovakia. But Czech domination led to resentment by many Slovaks. In 1939, the Slovak Republic declared itself independent, but Germany occupied the country. At the end of World War II, the Slovak Republic again became part of Czechoslovakia.

The Communist party took control in 1948. In the 1960s, many people sought reform, but they were crushed by the Russians. In the late 1980s, demands for democracy mounted and a non-Communist government took office in 1990. Elections in 1992 led to victory for the Movement for a Democratic Slovakia headed by a former Communist and nationalist, Vladimir Meciar, and the independent Slovak Republic came into existence on 1 January 1993.

Independence raised national aspirations among Slovakia's Magyar-speaking community, but relations with Hungary deteriorated when the Magyars felt that administrative changes under-represented them politically. The government also made Slovak the only official language. The government's autocratic rule and human rights record provoked international criticism. In 1998, Meciar's party was defeated and Mikulas Dzurinda replaced Meciar as prime minister. In 2001, the parliament approved changes to the constitution that would enable Slovakia to become a member of NATO and the European Union.

Before 1948, the Slovak Republic's economy was based on farming, but Communist governments developed manufacturing industries, producing such things as chemicals, machinery, steel and weapons. Since the late 1980s, many state-run businesses have been handed over to private owners.

AREA 49,035 sq km [18,932 sq mi]
POPULATION 5,415,000
CAPITAL (POPULATION) Bratislava (451,000)
GOVERNMENT Multiparty republic
ETHNIC GROUPS Slovak 86%, Hungarian 11%, Roma 2%
LANGUAGES Slovak (official), Hungarian
RELIGIONS Roman Catholic 60%, Protestant 8%, Orthodox 4%
CURRENCY Koruna = 100 halierov

SLOVENIA

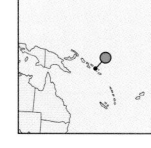

GEOGRAPHY The Republic of Slovenia was one of the six republics which made up the former Yugoslavia. Much of the land is mountainous, rising to 2,863 m [9,393 ft] at Mount Triglav in the Julian Alps (Julijske Alpe) in the north-west. Central Slovenia contains the limestone Karst region. The Postojna caves near Ljubljana are among the largest in Europe.

The coast has a mild Mediterranean climate, but inland the climate is more continental. The mountains are snow-capped in winter.

POLITICS & ECONOMY In the last 2,000 years, the Slovene people have been independent as a nation for less than 50 years. The Austrian Habsburgs ruled over the region from the 13th century until World War I. Slovenia became part of the Kingdom of the Serbs, Croats and Slovenes (later called Yugoslavia) in 1918. During World War II, Slovenia was invaded and partitioned between Italy, Germany and Hungary but, after the war, Slovenia again became part of Yugoslavia.

From the late 1960s, some Slovenes demanded independence, but the central government opposed the break-up of the country. In 1990, when Communist governments had collapsed throughout Eastern Europe, elections were held and a non-Communist coalition government was set up. Slovenia then declared itself independent. This led to fighting between Slovenes and the federal army, but Slovenia did not become a battlefield like other parts of the former Yugoslavia. The European Community recognized Slovenia's independence in 1992. The electors returned a coalition led by the Liberal Democrats in 1992, 1996 and again in 2000.

The reform of the economy, formerly run by the government, and the fighting in areas to the south have caused problems for Slovenia, although it remains one of the fastest growing economies in Europe. In 1992, the World Bank classified Slovenia as an 'upper-middle-income' developing country, and it is expected to be among the first countries to join an expanded European Union.

Manufacturing is the leading activity and manufactures are the main exports. Manufactures include chemicals, machinery and transport equipment, metal goods and textiles. Agriculture employs 8% of the people. Fruits, maize, potatoes and wheat are major crops, and many farmers raise animals.

AREA 20,251 sq km [7,817 sq mi]
POPULATION 1,930,000
CAPITAL (POPULATION) Ljubljana (280,000)
GOVERNMENT Multiparty republic
ETHNIC GROUPS Slovene 88%, Croat 3%, Serb 2%, Bosnian 1%
LANGUAGES Slovene (official), Serbo-Croat
RELIGIONS Mainly Roman Catholic
CURRENCY Tolar = 100 stotin

SOLOMON ISLANDS

The Solomon Islands, a chain of mainly volcanic islands in the Pacific Ocean, were a British territory between 1893 and 1978. The chain extends for some 2,250 km [1,400 mi]. They were the scene of fierce fighting during World War II. Most people are Melanesians, and the islands have a young population profile, with half the people aged under 20. Fish, coconuts and cocoa are leading products, though development is hampered by mountainous, forested terrain. **AREA** 28,370 sq km [10,954 sq mi]; **POPULATION** 480,000; **CAPITAL** Honiara.

SOMALIA

GEOGRAPHY The Somali Democratic Republic, or Somalia, is in a region known as the 'Horn of Africa'. It is more than twice the size of Italy, the country which once ruled the southern part of Somalia. The most mountainous part of the country is in the north, behind the narrow coastal plains that border the Gulf of Aden.

Rainfall is light throughout Somalia. The wettest regions are the south and the northern mountains, but droughts often occur. Temperatures are high on the low plateaux and plains.

POLITICS & ECONOMY European powers became interested in the Horn of Africa in the 19th century. In 1884, Britain made the northern part of what is now Somalia a protectorate, while Italy took the south in 1905. The new boundaries divided the Somalis into five areas: the two Somalilands, Djibouti (which was taken by France in the 1880s), Ethiopia and Kenya. Since then, many Somalis have longed for reunification in a Greater Somalia.

Italy entered World War II in 1940 and invaded British Somaliland. But British forces conquered the region in 1941 and ruled both Somalilands until 1950, when the United Nations asked Italy to take over the former Italian Somaliland for ten years. In 1960, both Somalilands became independent and united to become Somalia.

Somalia has faced many problems since independence. Economic problems led a military group to seize power in 1969. In the 1970s, Somalia supported an uprising of Somali-speaking people in the Ogaden region of Ethiopia. But Ethiopian forces prevailed and, in 1988, Somalia signed a peace treaty with Ethiopia. The cost of the fighting weakened Somalia's economy. In the 1990s, Somalia gradually broke apart. In 1991, the people in what was formerly British Somaliland set up the 'Somaliland Republic', although it never received international recognition. The north-east, which was called Puntland, also seceded from Somalia, while civil war, based on clan rivalry, raged in the south. US troops sent into the south by the UN in 1993 were forced to withdraw in 1994 and the clan warfare continued. However, hopes of reunification were raised in 2000, when a three-year transitional Assembly was set up in the south, following a peace conference held in Djibouti.

Somalia is a developing country, whose economy has been shattered by drought and war. Catastrophic flooding in late 1997 displaced tens of thousands of people, further damaging the country's infrastructure and destroying hopes of economic recovery.

Many Somalis are nomads who raise livestock. Live animals, meat and hides and skins are major exports, followed by bananas grown in the wetter south. Other crops include citrus fruits, cotton, maize and sugar cane. Mining and manufacturing remain relatively unimportant in the economy.

AREA 637,660 sq km [246,201 sq mi]
POPULATION 7,489,000
CAPITAL (POPULATION) Mogadishu (997,000)
GOVERNMENT Single-party republic, military dominated
ETHNIC GROUPS Somali 85%, Arab 1%
LANGUAGES Somali and Arabic (both official), English, Italian
RELIGIONS Islam (mainly Sunni) 99%
CURRENCY Somali shilling = 100 cents

SOUTH AFRICA

GEOGRAPHY The Republic of South Africa is made up largely of the southern part of the huge plateau which makes up most of southern Africa. The highest peaks are in the Drakensberg range, which is formed by the uplifted rim of the plateau. The coastal plains include part of the Namib Desert in the north-west.

Most of South Africa has a mild, sunny climate. Much of the coastal strip, including the city of Cape Town, has warm, dry summers and mild, rainy winters. Inland, large areas are arid.

POLITICS & ECONOMY Early inhabitants in South Africa were the Khoisan. In the last 2,000 years, Bantu-speaking people moved into the area. Their descendants include the Zulu, Xhosa, Sotho and Tswana. The Dutch founded a settlement at the Cape in 1652, but Britain took over in the early 19th century, making the area a colony. The Dutch, called Boers or Afrikaners, resented British rule and moved inland. Rivalry between the groups led to Anglo-Boer Wars in 1880–1 and 1899–1902.

In 1910, the country was united as the Union of South Africa. In 1948, the National Party won power and introduced a policy known as apartheid, under which non-whites had no votes and their human rights were strictly limited. In 1990, Nelson Mandela, leader of the African National Congress (ANC), was released from prison. Multiracial elections were held in 1994 and Mandela became president. After Mandela's retirement in 1999, his successor, Thabo Mbeki, led the ANC to an emphatic victory in the elections. Mbeki faces many problems, including a health crisis arising from a government estimate in the early 21st century that one in five South Africans is infected with the HIV virus.

South Africa is Africa's most developed country. However, most of the black people are poor, with low standards of living. Natural resources include diamonds, gold and many other metals. Mining and manufacturing are the most valuable activities.

AREA 1,219,916 sq km [470,566 sq mi]
POPULATION 43,586,000
CAPITAL (POPULATION) Cape Town (legislative, 2,350,000); Pretoria (administrative, 1,080,000); Bloemfontein (judiciary, 300,000)
GOVERNMENT Multiparty republic
ETHNIC GROUPS Black 76%, White 13%, Coloured 9%, Asian 2%
LANGUAGES Afrikaans, English, Ndebele, North Sotho, South Sotho, Swazi, Tsonga, Tswana, Venda, Xhosa, Zulu (all official)
RELIGIONS Christianity 68%, Islam 2%, Hinduism 1%
CURRENCY Rand = 100 cents

SPAIN

GEOGRAPHY The Kingdom of Spain is the second largest country in Western Europe after France. It shares the Iberian peninsula with Portugal. A large plateau, called the Meseta, covers most of Spain.

Much of the Meseta is flat, but it is crossed by several mountain ranges, called sierras.

The northern highlands include the Cantabrian Mountains (Cordillera Cantabrica) and the high Pyrenees, which form Spain's border with France. But Mulhacén, the highest peak on the Spanish mainland, is in the Sierra Nevada in the south-east. Spain also contains fertile coastal plains. Other major lowlands are the Ebro river basin in the north-east and the Guadalquivir river basin in the south-west. Spain also includes the Balearic Islands in the Mediterranean Sea and the Canary Islands off the north-west coast of Africa.

The Meseta has a continental climate, with hot summers and cold winters, when temperatures often fall below freezing point. Snow frequently covers the mountain ranges on the Meseta. The Mediterranean coastal regions also have hot, dry summers, but the winters are mild.

POLITICS & ECONOMY In the 16th century, Spain became a world power. At its peak, it controlled much of Central and South America, parts of Africa and the Philippines in Asia. Spain began to decline in the late 16th century. Its sea power was destroyed by a British fleet in the Battle of Trafalgar (1805). By the 20th century, it was a poor country.

Spain became a republic in 1931, but the republicans were defeated in the Spanish Civil War (1936–9). General Francisco Franco (1892–1975) became the country's dictator, though, technically, it was a monarchy. When Franco died, the monarchy was restored. Prince Juan Carlos became king.

Spain has several groups with their own languages and cultures. Some of these people want to run their own regional affairs. In the northern Basque region, some nationalists have waged a terrorist campaign. A truce in 1998 was ended in 1999 when talks failed to produce results.

Since the late 1970s, a regional parliament with a considerable degree of autonomy has been set up in the Basque Country (called Euskadi in the indigenous tongue and Pais Vasco in Spanish). Similar parliaments have been initiated in Catalonia in the north-east and Galicia in the north-west. All these regions have their own languages.

The revival of Spain's economy, which was shattered by the Civil War, began in the 1950s and 1960s, especially through the growth of tourism and manufacturing. Since the 1950s, Spain has changed from a poor country, dependent on agriculture, to a fairly prosperous industrial nation.

By the early 1990s, agriculture employed 10% of the people, as compared with industry 35% and services, including tourism, 55%. Farmland, including pasture, makes up about two-thirds of the land, with forest making up most of the rest. Major crops include barley, citrus fruits, grapes for wine-making, olives, potatoes and wheat.

Spain has some high-grade iron ore in the north, though otherwise it lacks natural resources. But it has many manufacturing industries. Manufactures include cars, chemicals, clothing, electronics, processed food, metal goods, steel and textiles. The leading manufacturing centres are Barcelona, Bilbao and Madrid.

AREA 504,780 sq km [194,896 sq mi]
POPULATION 38,432,000
CAPITAL (POPULATION) Madrid (3,030,000)
GOVERNMENT Constitutional monarchy
ETHNIC GROUPS Castilian Spanish 72%, Catalan 16%, Galician 8%, Basque 2%
LANGUAGES Castilian Spanish (official) 74%, Catalan 17%, Galician 7%, Basque 2%
RELIGIONS Roman Catholic 99%
CURRENCY Euro = 100 cents

SRI LANKA

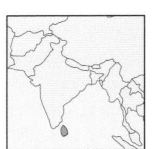

GEOGRAPHY The Democratic Socialist Republic of Sri Lanka is an island nation, separated from the south-east coast of India by the Palk Strait. The land is mostly low-lying, surrounding mountains in the south-centre. Western Sri Lanka has a wet equatorial climate. Temperatures are high and the rainfall is heavy. The east is drier than the west.

POLITICS & ECONOMY From the early 16th century, Ceylon (as Sri Lanka was then known) was ruled successively by the Portuguese, Dutch and British. Independence was achieved in 1948 and the country was renamed Sri Lanka in 1972.

After independence, rivalries between the two main ethnic groups, the Sinhalese and Tamils, marred progress. In the 1950s, the government made Sinhala the official language. Following protests, the prime minister made provisions for Tamil to be used in some areas. In 1959, the prime minister was assassinated by a Sinhalese extremist and he was succeeded by Sirimavo Bandanaraike, who became the world's first woman prime minister.

Conflict between Tamils and Sinhalese continued in the 1970s and 1980s. In 1987, India helped to engineer a cease-fire. Indian troops arrived to enforce the agreement, but withdrew in 1990 after failing to subdue the main guerrilla group, the Tamil Tigers, who wanted to set up an independent Tamil home-land in northern Sri Lanka. In 1993, the country's president was assassinated by a suspected Tamil separatist. Offensives against the Tamil Tigers continued until hopes of peace were raised in 2002, with the signing of a long-term cease-fire.

The World Bank classifies Sri Lanka as a 'low-income' developing country. Agriculture employs half of the workforce, and coconuts, rubber and tea are exported.

AREA 65,610 sq km [25,332 sq mi]
POPULATION 19,409,000
CAPITAL (POPULATION) Colombo (1,863,000)
GOVERNMENT Multiparty republic
ETHNIC GROUPS Sinhalese 74%, Tamil 18%, Sri Lankan Moor 7%
LANGUAGES Sinhala and Tamil (both official)
RELIGIONS Buddhism 69%, Hinduism 16%, Christianity 8%, Islam 7%
CURRENCY Sri Lankan rupee = 100 cents

SUDAN

GEOGRAPHY The Republic of Sudan is the largest country in Africa. From north to south, it spans a vast area extending from the arid Sahara in the north to the wet equatorial region in the south. The land is mostly flat, with the highest mountains in the far south. The main physical feature is the River Nile.

The climate of Khartoum represents a transition between the virtually rainless northern deserts and the equatorial lands in the south. Some rain falls in Khartoum in summer.

POLITICS & ECONOMY In the 19th century, Egypt

gradually took over Sudan. In 1881, a Muslim religious teacher, the Mahdi ('divinely appointed guide'), led an uprising. Britain and Egypt put the rebellion down in 1898. In 1899, they agreed to rule Sudan jointly as a condominium.

After independence in 1952, the black Africans in the south, who were either Christians or followers of traditional beliefs, feared domination by the Muslim northerners. For example, they objected to the government declaring that Arabic was the only official language. In 1964, civil war broke out and continued until 1972, when the south was given regional self-government, though executive power was still vested in the military government in Khartoum.

In 1983, the government established Islamic law throughout the country. This sparked off further conflict when the Sudan People's Liberation Army in the south launched attacks on government installations. Despite attempts to restore order, the fighting continued into the 21st century. In 1998, the government announced that it accepted the idea of a referendum on the secession of the south, though definitions of the 'south' varied. Widespread famine in southern Sudan in 1998 attracted global attention and humanitarian aid.

AREA 2,505,810 sq km [967,493 sq mi]
POPULATION 36,080,000
CAPITAL (POPULATION) Khartoum (925,000)
GOVERNMENT Military regime
ETHNIC GROUPS Sudanese Arab 49%, Dinka 12%, Nuba 8%, Beja 6%, Nuer 5%, Azande 3%
LANGUAGES Arabic (official), Nubian, Dinka
RELIGIONS Islam (mainly Sunni) 70%, traditional beliefs 25%, Christianity 5%
CURRENCY Dinar = 10 Sudanese pounds

SURINAM

GEOGRAPHY The Republic of Surinam is sandwiched between French Guiana and Guyana in north-eastern South America. The narrow coastal plain was once swampy, but it has been drained and now consists mainly of farmland. Inland lie hills and low mountains, which rise to 1,280 m [4,199 ft].

Surinam has a hot, wet and humid climate. Temperatures are high throughout the year.
POLITICS & ECONOMY In 1667, the British handed Surinam to the Dutch in return for New Amsterdam, an area that is now the state of New York. Slave revolts and Dutch neglect hampered development. In the early 19th century, Britain and the Netherlands disputed the ownership of the area. The British gave up their claims in 1813. Slavery was abolished in 1863 and, soon afterwards, Indian and Indonesian labourers were introduced to work on the plantations. Surinam became fully independent in 1975, but the economy was weakened when thousands of skilled people emigrated from Surinam to the Netherlands. Following a coup in 1980, Surinam was ruled by a military dictator, Dési Bouterse. The adoption of a new constitution led to the restoration of democracy in 1988, though another military coup occurred in 1990. Elections were held in 1996, but instability, deteriorating relations with the Netherlands and economic problems continued. In 1999, Bouterse was convicted in absentia in the Netherlands of having led a cocaine-trafficking ring during and after his tenure in office.

The World Bank classifies Surinam as an 'upper-middle-income' developing country. Its economy is based on mining and metal processing. Surinam is a leading producer of bauxite, from which the metal aluminium is made.

AREA 163,270 sq km [63,039 sq mi]
POPULATION 434,000
CAPITAL (POPULATION) Paramaribo (201,000)
GOVERNMENT Multiparty republic
ETHNIC GROUPS Asian Indian 37%, Creole (mixed White and Black) 31%, Indonesian 14%, Black 9%, Amerindian 3%, Chinese 3%, Dutch 1%
LANGUAGES Dutch (official), Sranantonga
RELIGIONS Hinduism 27%, Roman Catholic 23%, Islam 20%, Protestant 19%
CURRENCY Surinam guilder = 100 cents

SWAZILAND

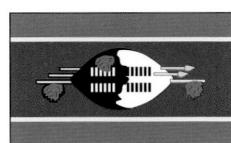 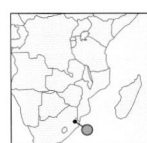

GEOGRAPHY The Kingdom of Swaziland is a small, landlocked country in southern Africa. The country has four regions which run north–south. In the west, the Highveld, with an average height of 1,200 m [3,937 ft], makes up 30% of Swaziland. The Middleveld, between 350 m and 1,000 m [1,148 ft to 3,281 ft], covers 28% of the country. The Lowveld, with an average height of 270 m [886 ft], covers another 33%. Finally, the Lebombo Mountains reach 800 m [2,600 ft] along the eastern border.

The Lowveld is almost tropical, with an average temperature of 22°C [72°F] and low rainfall. The altitude moderates the climate in the west.
POLITICS & ECONOMY In 1894, Britain and the Boers of South Africa agreed to put Swaziland under the control of the South African Republic (the Transvaal). But at the end of the Anglo–Boer War (1899–1902), Britain took control of the country. In 1968, when Swaziland became fully independent as a constitutional monarchy, the head of state was King Sobhuza II. Sobhuza died in 1982 and was succeeded by one of his sons, Prince Makhosetive, who, in 1986, was installed as King Mswati III. Elections in 1993 and 1998, in which political parties were banned, failed to satisfy protesters who opposed the absolute monarchy. But Mswati continued to rule by decree and freedom of speech was severely restricted.

The World Bank classifies Swaziland as a 'lower-middle-income' developing country. Agriculture employs 74% of the people, and farm products and processed foods, including soft drink concentrates, sugar, wood pulp, citrus fruits and canned fruit, are the leading exports. Many farmers live at subsistence level, producing little more than they need to feed their own families. Swaziland is heavily dependent on South Africa and the two countries are linked through a customs union.

AREA 17,360 sq km [6,703 sq mi]
POPULATION 1,104,000
CAPITAL (POPULATION) Mbabane (42,000)
GOVERNMENT Monarchy
ETHNIC GROUPS Swazi 84%, Zulu 10%, Tsonga
LANGUAGES Siswati and English (both official)
RELIGIONS Protestant 55%, Islam 10%, Roman Catholic 5%
CURRENCY Lilangeni = 100 cents

SWEDEN

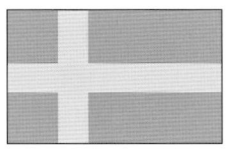 

GEOGRAPHY The Kingdom of Sweden is the largest of the countries of Scandinavia in both area and population. It shares the Scandinavian peninsula with Norway. The western part of the country, along the border with Norway, is mountainous. The highest point is Kebnekaise, which reaches 2,117 m [6,946 ft] in the north-west.

The climate of Sweden becomes more severe from south to north. Stockholm has cold winters and cool summers. The far south is much milder.
POLITICS & ECONOMY Swedish Vikings plundered areas to the south and east between the 9th and 11th centuries. Sweden, Denmark and Norway were united in 1397, but Sweden regained its independence in 1523. In 1809, Sweden lost Finland to Russia, but, in 1814, it gained Norway from Denmark. The union between Sweden and Norway was dissolved in 1905. Sweden was neutral in World Wars I and II. Since 1945, Sweden has become a prosperous country. In 1995, it joined the European Union. However, many people were sceptical about the advantages of EU membership and Sweden did not adopt the euro, the single EU currency, in 1999.

Sweden has wide-ranging welfare services. But many people are concerned about the high cost of these services and the high taxes they must pay. In 1991, the Social Democrats, who had built up the welfare state, were defeated. They were re-elected in 1994 and 1998, but they tried to control public spending and expand the economy.

Sweden is a highly developed industrial country. Major products include steel and steel goods. Steel is used in the engineering industry to manufacture aircraft, cars, machinery and ships. Sweden has some of the world's richest iron ore deposits. They are located near Kiruna in the far north. But most of this ore is exported, and Sweden imports most of the materials needed by its industries. In 1996, a decision was taken to decommission all of Sweden's nuclear power stations. This is said to be one of the boldest and most expensive environmental pledges ever made by a government.

AREA 449,960 sq km [173,730 sq mi]
POPULATION 8,875,000
CAPITAL (POPULATION) Stockholm (727,000)
GOVERNMENT Constitutional monarchy
ETHNIC GROUPS Swedish 91%, Finnish 3%
LANGUAGES Swedish (official), Finnish
RELIGIONS Lutheran 89%, Roman Catholic 2%
CURRENCY Swedish krona = 100 öre

SWITZERLAND

GEOGRAPHY The Swiss Confederation is a landlocked country in Western Europe. Much of the land is mountainous. The Jura Mountains lie along Switzerland's western border with France, while the Swiss Alps make up about 60% of the country in the south and east. Four-fifths of the people of

Switzerland live on the fertile Swiss plateau, which contains most of Switzerland's large cities.

The climate varies according to the height of the land. The plateau region has warm summers and cold, snowy winters. Rain occurs throughout the year.

POLITICS & ECONOMY In 1291, three small cantons (states) united to defend their freedom against the Habsburg rulers of the Holy Roman Empire. They were Schwyz, Uri and Unterwalden, and they called the confederation they formed 'Switzerland'. Switzerland expanded and, in the 14th century, defeated Austria in three wars of independence. After a defeat by the French in 1515, the Swiss adopted a policy of neutrality, which they still follow. In 1815, the Congress of Vienna expanded Switzerland to 22 cantons and guaranteed its neutrality. Switzerland's 23rd canton, Jura, was created in 1979 from part of Bern. Neutrality combined with the vigour and independence of its people have made Switzerland prosperous. In 1993 and again in 2001, the Swiss people voted against starting negotiations to join the European Union. However, in 2002, the Swiss voted by a narrow majority to join the United Nations.

Although lacking in natural resources, Switzerland is a wealthy, industrialized country. Many workers are highly skilled. Major products include chemicals, electrical equipment, machinery and machine tools, precision instruments, processed food, watches and textiles. Farmers produce about three-fifths of the country's food – the rest is imported. Livestock raising, especially dairy farming, is the chief agricultural activity. Crops include fruits, potatoes and wheat. Tourism and banking are also important. Swiss banks attract investors from all over the world.

AREA 41,290 sq km [15,942 sq mi]
POPULATION 7,283,000
CAPITAL (POPULATION) Bern (942,000)
GOVERNMENT Federal republic
ETHNIC GROUPS German 64%, French 19%, Italian 10%, Yugoslav 3%, Spanish 2%, Romansch 1%
LANGUAGES French, German, Italian, Romansch (all official)
RELIGIONS Roman Catholic 46%, Protestant 40%
CURRENCY Swiss franc = 100 centimes

SYRIA

 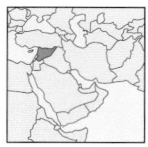

GEOGRAPHY The Syrian Arab Republic is a country in south-western Asia. The narrow coastal plain is overlooked by a low mountain range which runs north–south. Another range, the Jabal ash Sharqi, runs along the border with Lebanon. South of this range is the Golan Heights, which Israel has occupied since 1967.

The coast has a Mediterranean climate, with dry, warm summers and wet, mild winters. The low mountains cut off Damascus from the sea. It has less rainfall than the coastal areas. To the east, the land becomes drier.

POLITICS & ECONOMY After the collapse of the Turkish Ottoman empire in World War I, Syria was ruled by France. Since independence in 1946, Syria has been involved in the Arab–Israeli wars and, in 1967, it lost a strategic border area, the Golan Heights, to Israel. In 1970, Lieutenant-General

Hafez al-Assad took power, establishing a stable but repressive regime. In 1999, Syria had talks with Israel concerning the future of the Golan Heights. These talks formed part of an attempt to establish a peace settlement for the entire east Mediterranean region. Following the death of Assad in 2000, his son, Bashar Assad, succeeded him.

The World Bank classifies Syria as a 'lower-middle-income' developing country. But it has great potential for development. Its main resources are oil, hydro-electricity from the dam at Lake Assad, and fertile land. Oil is the main export; farm products, textiles and phosphates are also important. Agriculture employs about 26% of the workforce.

AREA 185,180 sq km [71,498 sq mi]
POPULATION 16,729,000
CAPITAL (POPULATION) Damascus (1,394,000)
GOVERNMENT Multiparty republic
ETHNIC GROUPS Arab 90%, Kurdish, Armenian, others
LANGUAGES Arabic (official)
RELIGIONS Islam 90%, Christianity 9%
CURRENCY Syrian pound = 100 piastres

TAIWAN

GEOGRAPHY High mountain ranges run down the length of the island, with dense forest in many areas. The climate is warm, moist and suitable for agriculture.

POLITICS & ECONOMY Chinese settlers occupied Taiwan from the 7th century. In 1895, Japan seized the territory from the Portuguese, who had named it Isla Formosa, or 'beautiful island'. China regained the island after World War II. In 1949, it became the refuge of the Nationalists who had been driven out of China by the Communists. They set up the Republic of China, which, with US help, launched an ambitious programme of economic development. Today, it produces a wide range of manufactured goods. Mainland China regards Taiwan as one of its provinces, though reunification seems unlikely in the foreseeable future.

AREA 36,000 sq km [13,900 sq mi]
POPULATION 22,370,000
CAPITAL (population) Taipei (2,596,000)
GOVERNMENT Unitary multiparty republic
ETHNIC GROUPS Taiwanese (Han Chinese) 84%, mainland Chinese 14%
LANGUAGES Mandarin (official), Min, Hakka
RELIGIONS Buddhism 43%, Taoism and Confucianism 49%
CURRENCY New Taiwan dollar = 100 cents

TAJIKISTAN

 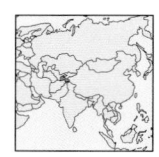

GEOGRAPHY The Republic of Tajikistan is one of the five central Asian republics that formed part of the former Soviet Union. Only 7% of the land is below 1,000 m [3,280 ft], while almost all of eastern

Tajikistan is above 3,000 m [9,840 ft]. The highest point is Communism Peak (Pik Kommunizma), which reaches 7,495 m [24,590 ft].

Tajikistan has a severe continental climate. Summers are hot and dry in the lower valleys, and winters are long and bitterly cold in the mountains.

POLITICS & ECONOMY Russia conquered parts of Tajikistan in the late 19th century and, by 1920, Russia took complete control. In 1924, Tajikistan became part of the Uzbek Soviet Socialist Republic, but, in 1929, it was expanded, taking in some areas populated by Uzbeks, becoming the Tajik Soviet Socialist Republic.

While the Soviet Union began to introduce reforms during the 1980s, many Tajiks demanded freedom. In 1989, the Tajik government made Tajik the official language instead of Russian and, in 1990, it stated that its local laws overruled Soviet laws. Tajikistan became fully independent in 1991, following the break-up of the Soviet Union. As the poorest of the ex-Soviet republics, Tajikistan faced many problems in trying to introduce a free-market system.

In 1992, civil war broke out between the government, which was run by former Communists, and an alliance of democrats and Islamic forces. A cease-fire was agreed in 1996, and in 1997 representatives of the opposition were brought into the government. Presidential elections were held in 1999, followed by parliamentary elections in 2000.

The World Bank classifies Tajikistan as a 'low-income' developing country. Agriculture, mainly on irrigated land, is the main activity and cotton is the chief product. Other crops include fruits, grains and vegetables. The country has large hydroelectric power resources and it produces aluminium.

AREA 143,100 sq km [55,520 sq mi]
POPULATION 6,579,000
CAPITAL (POPULATION) Dushanbe (524,000)
GOVERNMENT Transitional democracy
ETHNIC GROUPS Tajik 65%, Uzbek 25%, Russian 3%, Tatar, Kyrgyz, Ukrainian, German
LANGUAGES Tajik (official), Uzbek, Russian
RELIGIONS Islam (mainly Sunni) 80%
CURRENCY Somoni = 100 dirams

TANZANIA

 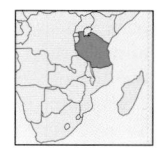

GEOGRAPHY The United Republic of Tanzania consists of the former mainland country of Tanganyika and the island nation of Zanzibar, which also includes the island of Pemba. Behind a narrow coastal plain, most of Tanzania is a plateau, which is broken by arms of the Great African Rift Valley. In the west, this valley contains lakes Nyasa and Tanganyika. The highest peak is Kilimanjaro, Africa's tallest mountain.

The coast has a hot and humid climate, with the greatest rainfall in April and May. The inland plateaux and mountains are cooler and less humid.

POLITICS & ECONOMY Mainland Tanganyika became a German territory in the 1880s, while Zanzibar and Pemba became a British protectorate in 1890. Following Germany's defeat in World War I, Britain took over Tanganyika, which remained a British territory until its independence in 1961. In 1964, Tanganyika and Zanzibar united to form the United Republic of Tanzania. The country's president, Julius Nyerere, pursued socialist policies of

self-help (*ujamaa*) and egalitarianism. Many of its social reforms were successful, though the country failed to make economic progress. Nyerere resigned as president in 1985, although he retained much influence until his death in 1999. His successors, Ali Hassan Mwinyi and, from 1995, Benjamin Mkapa, introduced more liberal economic policies.

Tanzania is one of the world's poorest countries. Crops are grown on only 5% of the land, yet agriculture employs 85% of the people. Food crops include bananas, cassava, maize, millet and rice.

AREA 945,090 sq km [364,899 sq mi]
POPULATION 36,232,000
CAPITAL (POPULATION) Dodoma (204,000)
GOVERNMENT Multiparty republic
ETHNIC GROUPS Nyamwezi and Sukuma 21%, Swahili 9%, Hehet and Bena 7%, Makonde 6%, Haya 6%
LANGUAGES Swahili and English (both official)
RELIGIONS Christianity (mostly Roman Catholic) 45%, Islam 35% (99% in Zanzibar), traditional beliefs and others 20%
CURRENCY Tanzanian shilling = 100 cents

THAILAND

 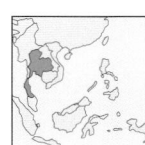

GEOGRAPHY The Kingdom of Thailand is one of the ten countries in South-east Asia. The highest land is in the north, where Doi Inthanon, the highest peak, reaches 2,595 m [8,514 ft]. The Khorat plateau, in the north-east, makes up about 30% of the country and is the most heavily populated part of Thailand. In the south, Thailand shares the finger-like Malay peninsula with Burma and Malaysia.

Thailand has a tropical climate. Monsoon winds from the south-west bring heavy rains between the months of May and October. The rainfall in Bangkok is lower than in many other parts of South-east Asia, because mountains shelter the central plains from the rain-bearing winds.

POLITICS & ECONOMY The first Thai state was set up in the 13th century. By 1350, it included most of what is now Thailand. European contact began in the early 16th century. But, in the late 17th century, the Thais, fearing interference in their affairs, forced all Europeans to leave. This policy continued for 150 years. In 1782, a Thai General, Chao Phraya Chakkri, became king, founding a dynasty which continues today. The country became known as Siam, and Bangkok became its capital. From the mid-19th century, contacts with the West were restored. In World War I, Siam supported the Allies against Germany and Austria-Hungary. But in 1941, the country was conquered by Japan and became its ally. However, after the end of World War II, it became an ally of the United States.

Since 1967, when Thailand became a member of ASEAN (the Association of South-east Asian Nations), its economy has grown, especially its manufacturing and service industries. However, in 1997, it suffered recession along with other fast-developing countries in eastern Asia, and its economic policies had to be modified. The economy still depends on agriculture, which employs more than two-fifths of the people. Rice is the chief crop. Cassava, cotton, maize, rubber, sugar cane and tobacco are also grown. Thailand also mines tin and other minerals. However, the chief exports are manufactures, including food products, machinery, timber products and textiles. Tourism is another major source of income.

AREA 513,120 sq km [198,116 sq mi]
POPULATION 61,798,000
CAPITAL (POPULATION) Bangkok (7,507,000)
GOVERNMENT Constitutional monarchy
ETHNIC GROUPS Thai 75%, Chinese 14%, Malay 4%, Khmer 3%
LANGUAGES Thai (official), Chinese, Malay, English
RELIGIONS Buddhism 94%, Islam 4%, Christianity 1%
CURRENCY Thai baht = 100 satang

TOGO

GEOGRAPHY The Republic of Togo is a long, narrow country in West Africa. From north to south, it extends about 500 km [311 mi]. Its coastline on the Gulf of Guinea is only 64 km [40 mi] long and it is only 145 km [90 mi] at its widest point.

Togo has high temperatures all through the year. The main wet season is from March to July, with a minor wet season in October and November.
POLITICS & ECONOMY Togo became a German protectorate in 1884 but, in 1919, Britain took over the western third of the territory, while France took over the eastern two-thirds. In 1956, the people of British Togoland voted to join Ghana, while French Togoland became an independent republic in 1960.

A military regime took power in 1963. In 1967, General Gnassingbe Eyadema became head of state and suspended the constitution. Under a new constitution adopted in 1992, multiparty elections were held in 1994. However, in 1998, paramilitary policies stopped the count in the presidential elections when it became clear that Eyadema had been defeated. As a result, the leading opposition parties boycotted the general elections in 1999.

Togo is a poor, developing country. Farming employs 65% of the people and major food crops include cassava, maize, millet and yams. The leading export is phosphate rock, which is used to make fertilizers.

AREA 56,790 sq km [21,927 sq mi]
POPULATION 5,153,000
CAPITAL (POPULATION) Lomé (590,000)
GOVERNMENT Multiparty republic
ETHNIC GROUPS Ewe-Adja 43%, Tem-Kabre 26%, Gurma 16%
LANGUAGES French (official), Ewe, Kabiye
RELIGIONS Traditional beliefs 50%, Christianity 35%, Islam 15%
CURRENCY CFA franc = 100 centimes

TONGA

The Kingdom of Tonga, a former British protectorate, became independent in 1970. Situated in the South Pacific Ocean, it contains more than 170 islands, 36 of which are inhabited. Agriculture is the main activity; coconuts, copra, fruits and fish are leading products. **AREA** 750 sq km [290 sq mi]; **POPULATION** 104,000; **CAPITAL** Nuku'alofa.

TRINIDAD AND TOBAGO

 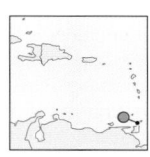

The Republic of Trinidad and Tobago became independent from Britain in 1962. These tropical islands, populated by people of African, Asian (mainly Indian) and European origin, are hilly and forested, though there are some fertile plains. Oil production is the main sector of the economy. **AREA** 5,130 sq km [1,981 sq mi]; **POPULATION** 1,170,000; **CAPITAL** Port-of-Spain.

TUNISIA

GEOGRAPHY The Republic of Tunisia is the smallest country in North Africa. The mountains in the north are an eastwards and comparatively low extension of the Atlas Mountains. To the north and east of the mountains lie fertile plains, especially between Sfax, Tunis and Bizerte. In the south, low-lying regions contain a vast salt pan, called the Chott Djerid, and part of the Sahara Desert.

Northern Tunisia has a Mediterranean climate, with dry, sunny summers, and mild winters with a moderate rainfall. The average yearly rainfall decreases towards the south.
POLITICS & ECONOMY In 1881, France established a protectorate over Tunisia and ruled the country until 1956. The new parliament abolished the monarchy and declared Tunisia to be a republic in 1957, with the nationalist leader, Habib Bourguiba, as president. His government introduced many reforms, including votes for women, but various problems arose, including unemployment among the middle class and fears that Western values introduced by tourists might undermine Muslim values. In 1987, the prime minister Zine el Abidine Ben Ali removed Bourguiba from office and succeeded him as president. He was elected in 1989 and re-elected in 1994 and 1999.

The World Bank classifies Tunisia as a 'middle-income' developing country. The main resources and chief exports are phosphates and oil. Most industries are concerned with food processing. Agriculture employs 22% of the people; major crops being barley, dates, grapes, olives and wheat. Fishing is important, as is tourism. Almost 4 million tourists visited Tunisia in 1994.

AREA 163,610 sq km [63,170 sq mi]
POPULATION 9,705,000
CAPITAL (POPULATION) Tunis (1,827,000)
GOVERNMENT Multiparty republic
ETHNIC GROUPS Arab 98%, Berber 1%, French
LANGUAGES Arabic (official), French
RELIGIONS Islam 99%
CURRENCY Dinar = 1,000 millimes

TURKEY

 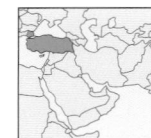

GEOGRAPHY The Republic of Turkey lies in two continents. European Turkey, also called Thrace, lies west of a waterway linking the Mediterranean and Black seas. Most of Asian Turkey consists of plateaux and mountains, which rise to 5,165 m [16,945 ft] at Mount Ararat (Agri Dagi) near the border with Armenia. Earthquakes are common.

Central Turkey has a dry climate, with hot, sunny summers and cold winters. The driest part of the central plateau lies south of the city of Ankara, around Lake Tuz. The west has a Mediterranean climate, but the Black Sea coast has cooler summers.

POLITICS & ECONOMY In AD 330, the Roman empire moved its capital to Byzantium, which it renamed Constantinople. Constantinople became capital of the East Roman (or Byzantine) empire in 395. Muslim Seljuk Turks from central Asia invaded Anatolia in the 11th century. In the 14th century, another group of Turks, the Ottomans, conquered the area. In 1435, the Ottoman Turks took Constantinople, which they called Istanbul.

The Ottoman Turks built up a large empire which finally collapsed during World War I (1914–18). In 1923, Turkey became a republic. Its leader Mustafa Kemal, or Atatürk ('father of the Turks'), launched policies to modernize and secularize the country.

Since the 1940s, Turkey has sought to strengthen its ties with Western powers. It joined NATO (North Atlantic Treaty Organization) in 1951 and it applied to join the European Economic Community in 1987. But Turkey's conflict with Greece, together with its invasion of northern Cyprus in 1974, have led many Europeans to treat Turkey's aspirations with caution. Political instability, military coups, conflict with Kurdish nationalists in eastern Turkey and concern about the country's record on human rights are other problems.

Turkey has enjoyed democracy since 1983, though, in 1998, the government banned the Islamist Welfare Party, which it accused of violating secular principles. In 1999, the Muslim Virtue Party (successor to Islamist Welfare Party) lost ground. The largest numbers of parliamentary seats were won by the ruling Democratic Left Party and the far-right National Action Party. In 2001, the government introduced a package of reforms, including one that recognized men and women as equals. The reforms were apparently intended to ease Turkey's entry into the European Union.

The World Bank classifies Turkey as a 'lower-middle-income' developing country. Agriculture employs 37% of the people, and barley, cotton, fruits, maize, tobacco and wheat are major crops. Livestock farming is important and wool is a leading product.

Turkey produces chromium, but manufacturing is the chief activity. Manufactures include processed farm products and textiles, cars, fertilizers, iron and steel, machinery, metal products and paper products. Over 9 million tourists visited Turkey in 1998.

AREA 779,450 sq km [300,946 sq mi]
POPULATION 66,494,000
CAPITAL (POPULATION) Ankara (3,294,000)
GOVERNMENT Multiparty republic
ETHNIC GROUPS Turkish 80%, Kurdish 20%
LANGUAGES Turkish (official), Kurdish
RELIGIONS Islam 99%
CURRENCY Turkish lira = 100 kurus

TURKMENISTAN

 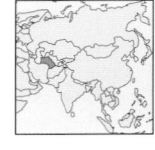

GEOGRAPHY The Republic of Turkmenistan is one of the five central Asian republics which once formed part of the former Soviet Union. Most of the land is low-lying, with mountains lying on the southern and south-western borders. In the west lies the salty Caspian Sea. Most of Turkmenistan is arid and the Garagum, Asia's largest sand desert, covers about 80% of the country. Turkmenistan has a continental climate, with average annual rainfall varying from 80 mm [3 in] in the desert to 300 mm [12 in] in the mountains. Summer months are hot but winter temperatures drop well below freezing point.

POLITICS & ECONOMY Just over 1,000 years ago, Turkic people settled in the lands east of the Caspian Sea and the name 'Turkmen' comes from this time. Mongol armies conquered the area in the 13th century and Islam was introduced in the 14th century. Russia took over the area in the 1870s and 1880s. After the Russian Revolution of 1917, the area came under Communist rule and, in 1924, it became the Turkmen Soviet Socialist Republic. The Communists strictly controlled all aspects of life and discouraged religion. But they improved such services as education, health, housing and transport.

In the 1980s, when the Soviet Union began to introduce reforms, the Turkmen began to demand more freedom. In 1990, the Turkmen government stated that its laws overruled Soviet laws. In 1991, Turkmenistan became fully independent after the break-up of the Soviet Union. But the country kept ties with Russia through the Commonwealth of Independent States (CIS).

In 1992, Turkmenistan adopted a new constitution, allowing for the setting up of political parties, providing that they were not ethnic or religious in character. But, effectively, Turkmenistan remained a one-party state and, in 1992, Saparmurad Niyazov, the former Communist and now Democratic Party leader, was the only candidate. In 1994, a referendum prolonged Niyazov's term of office to 2002, while, in 1999, the parliament declared him president for life, though he later said that he would retire before 2010.

Faced with many economic problems, Turkmenistan began to look south rather than to the CIS for support. As part of this policy, it joined the Economic Co-operation Organization which had been set up in 1985 by Iran, Pakistan and Turkey. In 1996, the completion of a rail link from Turkmenistan to the Iranian coast was seen as a highly significant step for the future economic development of Central Asia.

Turkmenistan's chief resources are oil and natural gas, but the main activity is agriculture, with cotton, grown on irrigated land, as the main crop. Grain and vegetables are also important. Manufactures include cement, glass, petrochemicals and textiles.

AREA 488,100 sq km [188,450 sq mi]
POPULATION 4,603,000
CAPITAL (POPULATION) Ashkhabad (536,000)
GOVERNMENT Single-party republic
ETHNIC GROUPS Turkmen 77%, Russian 17%, Uzbek 9%, Kazak 2%, Tatar
LANGUAGES Turkmen (official), Russian, Uzbek, Kazak
RELIGIONS Islam
CURRENCY Manat = 100 tenesi

TURKS AND CAICOS ISLANDS

 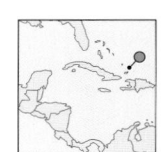

The Turks and Caicos Islands, a British territory in the Caribbean since 1776, are a group of about 30 islands. Fishing and tourism are major activities. **AREA** 430 sq km [166 sq mi]; **POPULATION** 18,000; **CAPITAL** Cockburn Town.

TUVALU

 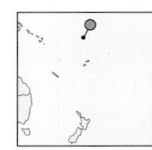

Tuvalu, formerly called the Ellice Islands, was a British territory from the 1890s until it became independent in 1978. It consists of nine low-lying coral atolls in the southern Pacific Ocean. Copra is the chief export. **AREA** 24 sq km [9 sq mi]; **POPULATION** 11,000; **CAPITAL** Fongafale.

UGANDA

 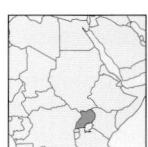

GEOGRAPHY The Republic of Uganda is a land-locked country on the East African plateau. It contains part of Lake Victoria, Africa's largest lake and a source of the River Nile, which occupies a shallow depression in the plateau.

The equator runs through Uganda and the country is warm throughout the year, though the high altitude moderates the temperature. The wettest regions are the lands to the north of Lake Victoria, where Kampala is situated, and the western mountains, especially the high Ruwenzori range.

POLITICS & ECONOMY Little is known of the early history of Uganda. When Europeans first reached the area in the 19th century, many of the people were organized in kingdoms, the most powerful of which was Buganda, the home of the Baganda people. Britain took over the country between 1894 and 1914, and ruled it until independence in 1962.

In 1967, Uganda became a republic and Buganda's Kabaka (king), Sir Edward Mutesa II, was made president. But tensions between the Kabaka and the prime minister, Apollo Milton Obote, led to the dismissal of the Kabaka in 1966. Obote also abolished the traditional kingdoms, including Buganda. Obote was overthrown in 1971 by an army group led by General Idi Amin Dada. Amin ruled as a dictator. He forced most of the Asians who lived in Uganda to leave the country and had many of his opponents killed.

In 1978, a border dispute between Uganda and Tanzania led Tanzanian troops to enter Uganda. With help from Ugandan opponents of Amin, they overthrew Amin's government. In 1980, Obote led his party to victory in national elections. But after charges of fraud, Obote's opponents began guerrilla warfare. A military group overthrew Obote in 1985, though strife continued until 1986, when Yoweri

Museveni's National Resistance Movement seized power. In 1993, Museveni restored the traditional kingdoms, including Buganda where a new Kabaka was crowned. Museveni also held elections in 1994 but political parties were not permitted. Museveni was elected president in 1996 and re-elected in 2001.

The strife since the 1960s has greatly damaged the economy, but the economy grew during a period of stability in the 1990s. The situation worsened when Uganda intervened militarily in Congo (then Zaïre) in 1998. Agriculture dominates the economy, employing 86% of the people. The chief export is coffee.

AREA 235,880 sq km [91,073 sq mi]
POPULATION 23,986,000
CAPITAL (POPULATION) Kampala (954,000)
GOVERNMENT Republic in transition
ETHNIC GROUPS Baganda 17%, Karamojong 12%, Basogo 8%, Iteso 8%, Langi 6%, Rwanda 6%, Bagisu 5%, Acholi 4%, Lugbara 4%
LANGUAGES English & Swahili (both official), Ganda
RELIGIONS Roman Catholic 33%, Protestant 33%, traditional beliefs 18%, Islam 16%
CURRENCY Uganda shilling = 100 cents

UKRAINE

GEOGRAPHY Ukraine is the second largest country in Europe after Russia. It was formerly part of the Soviet Union, which split apart in 1991. This mostly flat country faces the Black Sea in the south. The Crimean peninsula includes a highland region overlooking Yalta. Summers are warm, but winters are cold, becoming more severe from west to east. In summer, eastern Ukraine is often warmer than the west. The heaviest rainfall occurs in the summer.

POLITICS & ECONOMY Kiev was the original capital of the early Slavic civilization known as Kievan Rus. In the 17th and 18th centuries, parts of Ukraine came under Polish and Russian rule. But Russia gained most of Ukraine in the late 18th century. In 1918, Ukraine became independent, but in 1922 it became part of the Soviet Union. Millions of people died in the 1930s as a result of Soviet policies, while millions more died during the Nazi occupation (1941–4).

In the 1980s, Ukrainian people demanded more say over their affairs. The country finally became independent when the Soviet Union broke up in 1991. Ukraine continued to work with Russia through the Commonwealth of Independent States. But Ukraine differed with Russia on some issues, including control over Crimea. In 1999, a treaty ratifying Ukraine's present boundaries failed to get the approval of Russia's upper house.

The World Bank classifies Ukraine as a 'lower-middle-income' economy. Agriculture is important. Crops include wheat and sugar beet, which are the major exports, together with barley, maize, potatoes, sunflowers and tobacco. Livestock rearing and fishing are also important industries.

Manufacturing is the chief economic activity. Major manufactures include iron and steel, machinery and vehicles. Ukraine has large coalfields. The country imports oil and natural gas, but it has hydroelectric and nuclear power stations. In 1986, an accident at the Chernobyl (Chornobyl) nuclear power plant caused widespread nuclear radiation. The plant was finally closed in 2001.

AREA 603,700 sq km [233,100 sq mi]
POPULATION 48,760,000
CAPITAL (POPULATION) Kiev (2,621,000)
GOVERNMENT Multiparty republic
ETHNIC GROUPS Ukrainian 73%, Russian 22%, Jewish 1%, Belarussian 1%, Moldovan, Bulgarian, Polish
LANGUAGES Ukrainian (official), Russian
RELIGIONS Mostly Ukrainian Orthodox
CURRENCY Hryvnia = 100 kopiykas

UNITED ARAB EMIRATES

 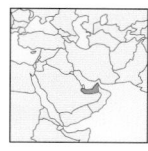

The United Arab Emirates were formed in 1971 when the seven Trucial States of the Gulf (Abu Dhabi, Dubai, Sharjah, Ajman, Umm al Qawayn, Ra's al Khaymah and Al Fujayrah) opted to join together and form an independent country. The economy of this hot and dry country depends on oil production, and oil revenues give the United Arab Emirates one of the highest per capita GNPs in Asia.
AREA 83,600 sq km [32,278 sq mi]; **POPULATION** 2,407,000; **CAPITAL** Abu Dhabi.

UNITED KINGDOM

GEOGRAPHY The United Kingdom (or UK) is a union of four countries. Three of them – England, Scotland and Wales – make up Great Britain. The fourth country is Northern Ireland. The Isle of Man and the Channel Islands, including Jersey and Guernsey, are not part of the UK. They are self-governing British dependencies.

The land is highly varied. Much of Scotland and Wales is mountainous, and the highest peak is Scotland's Ben Nevis at 1,343 m [4,406 ft]. England has some highland areas, including the Cumbrian Mountains (or Lake District) and the Pennine range in the north. But England also has large areas of fertile lowland. Northern Ireland is also a mixture of lowlands and uplands. It contains the UK's largest lake, Lough Neagh.

The UK has a mild climate, influenced by the warm Gulf Stream which flows across the Atlantic from the Gulf of Mexico, then past the British Isles. Moist winds from the south-west bring rain, but the rainfall decreases from west to east. Winds from the east and north bring cold weather in winter.

POLITICS & ECONOMY In ancient times, Britain was invaded by many peoples, including Iberians, Celts, Romans, Angles, Saxons, Jutes, Norsemen, Danes, and Normans, who arrived in 1066. The evolution of the United Kingdom spanned hundreds of years. The Normans finally overcame Welsh resistance in 1282, when King Edward I annexed Wales and united it with England. Union with Scotland was achieved by the Act of Union of 1707. This created a country known as the United Kingdom of Great Britain.

Ireland came under Norman rule in the 11th century, and much of its later history was concerned with a struggle against English domination. In 1801,

Ireland became part of the United Kingdom of Great Britain and Ireland. But in 1921, southern Ireland broke away to become the Irish Free State. Most of the people in the Irish Free State were Roman Catholics. In Northern Ireland, where the majority of the people were Protestants, most people wanted to remain citizens of the United Kingdom. As a result, the country's official name changed to the United Kingdom of Great Britain and Northern Ireland.

The modern history of the UK began in the 18th century when the British empire began to develop, despite the loss in 1783 of its 13 North American colonies which became the core of the modern United States. The other major event occurred in the late 18th century, when the UK became the first country to industrialize its economy.

The British empire broke up after World War II (1939–45), though the UK still administers many small, mainly island, territories around the world. The empire was transformed into the Commonwealth of Nations, a free association of independent countries which numbered 54 in 2001.

The UK retained an important world role through the Commonwealth and the United Nations, both diplomatically and militarily. For example, in 2001, it played a prominent role in creating the broad alliance to counter international terrorism following the attacks on the United States. However, it recognized that its economic future lay within Europe. As a result, it became a member of the European Economic Community (now the European Union) in 1973. In the early 2000s, most people accepted the importance of the EU to the UK's economic future. But some feared a loss of British identity should the EU ever evolve into a political federation.

The UK is a major industrial and trading nation. It lacks natural resources apart from coal, iron ore, oil and natural gas, and has to import most of the materials it needs for its industries. The UK also has to import food, because it produces only about two-thirds of the food it needs. In the first half of the 20th century, Britain was a major exporter of cars, ships, steel and textiles. But many industries have suffered from competition from other countries, with lower labour costs. Today, industries have to use high-technology in order to compete on the world market.

The UK is one of the world's most urbanized countries, and agriculture employs only 1% of the people. Production is high because of the use of scientific methods and modern machinery. However, in the early 21st century, especially following the outbreak of foot-and-mouth disease in 2001, questions were raised about the future of rural industries. Major crops include barley, potatoes, sugar beet and wheat. Sheep are the leading livestock, but beef and dairy cattle, pigs and poultry are also important. Fishing is another major activity.

Service industries play a major part in the UK's economy. Financial and insurance services bring in much-needed foreign exchange, while tourism has become a major earner.

AREA 243,368 sq km [94,202 sq mi]
POPULATION 59,648,000
CAPITAL (POPULATION) London (8,089,000)
GOVERNMENT Constitutional monarchy
ETHNIC GROUPS White 94%, Asian Indian 1%, Pakistani 1%, West Indian 1%
LANGUAGES English (official), Welsh, Gaelic
RELIGIONS Anglican 57%, Roman Catholic 13%, Presbyterian 7%, Methodist 4%, Baptist 1%, Islam 1%, Judaism, Hinduism, Sikhism
CURRENCY Pound sterling = 100 pence

UNITED STATES OF AMERICA

UNITED STATES OF AMERICA

GEOGRAPHY The United States of America is the world's fourth largest country in area and the third largest in population. It contains 50 states, 48 of which lie between Canada and Mexico, plus Alaska in north-western North America, and Hawaii, a group of volcanic islands in the North Pacific Ocean. Densely populated coastal plains lie to the east and south of the Appalachian Mountains. The central lowlands drained by the Mississippi–Missouri rivers stretch from the Appalachians to the Rocky Mountains in the west. The Pacific region contains fertile valleys, separated by mountain ranges.

The climate varies greatly, ranging from the Arctic cold of Alaska to the intense heat of Death Valley, California. Of the 48 states between Canada and Mexico, winters are cold and snowy in the north, but mild in the south.

POLITICS & ECONOMY The first people in North America, the ancestors of the Native Americans (or American Indians) arrived perhaps 40,000 years ago from Asia. Although Vikings probably reached North America 1,000 years ago, European exploration proper did not begin until the late 15th century.

The first Europeans to settle in large numbers were the British, who founded settlements on the eastern coast in the early 17th century. British rule ended in the War of Independence (1775–83). The country expanded in 1803 when a vast territory in the south and west was acquired through the Louisiana Purchase, while the border with Mexico was fixed in the mid-19th century. The Civil War (1861–5) ended slavery and the serious threat that the nation might split into two parts. In the late 19th century, the West was opened up, while immigrants flooded in from Europe and elsewhere.

During the late 19th and early 20th centuries, industrialization led to the United States becoming the world's leading economic superpower and a pioneer in science and technology. Because of its economic strength, it took on the mantle of the champion of Western democracy. The fall of Communism and the break-up of the Soviet Union left the US as the world's only real superpower. But the attacks on New York City and Washington, D.C., on 11 September 2001 demonstrated the vulnerability of the country to the threat of terrorists or rogue states. The response of the government was vigorous, in creating an international alliance to combat terrorism and any nation that aids terrorists.

The United States has the world's largest economy in terms of the total value of its production. Although agriculture employs only 2% of the people, farming is highly mechanized and scientific, and the United States leads the world in farm production. Major products include beef and dairy cattle, together with such crops as cotton, fruits, groundnuts, maize, potatoes, soya beans, tobacco and wheat.

The country's natural resources include oil, natural gas and coal. There are also a wide range of metal ores which are used in manufacturing industries, together with timber, especially from the forests of the Pacific north-west. Manufacturing is the single most important activity, employing about 17% of the population. Major products include vehicles, food products, chemicals, machinery, printed goods, metal products and scientific instruments. California is now the leading manufacturing state. Many southern states, petroleum rich and climatically favoured, have also become highly prosperous in recent years.

AREA 9,372,610 sq km [3,618,765 sq mi]
POPULATION 278,059,000
CAPITAL (POPULATION) Washington, D.C. (4,466,000)
GOVERNMENT Federal republic
ETHNIC GROUPS White 83%, African American 12%, Asian 3%, other races 2%
LANGUAGES English (official), Spanish, more than 30 others
RELIGIONS Protestant 56%, Roman Catholic 28%, Islam 2%, Judaism 2%
CURRENCY US dollar = 100 cents

URUGUAY

GEOGRAPHY Uruguay is South America's second smallest independent country after Surinam. The land consists mainly of flat plains and hills. The River Uruguay, which forms the country's western border, flows into the Río de la Plata, a large estuary which leads into the South Atlantic Ocean.

Uruguay has a mild climate, with rain in every month, though droughts sometimes occur. Summers are pleasantly warm, especially near the coast. The weather remains relatively mild throughout the winter.

POLITICS & ECONOMY In 1726, Spanish settlers founded Montevideo in order to halt the Portuguese gaining influence in the area. By the late 18th century, Spaniards had settled in most of the country. Uruguay became part of a colony called the Viceroyalty of La Plata, which also included Argentina, Paraguay, and parts of Bolivia, Brazil and Chile. In 1820 Brazil annexed Uruguay, ending Spanish rule. In 1825, Uruguayans, supported by Argentina, began a struggle for independence. Finally, in 1828, Brazil and Argentina recognized Uruguay as an independent republic. Social and economic developments were slow in the 19th century, but, from 1903, Uruguay became stable and democratic.

From the 1950s, economic problems caused unrest. Terrorist groups, notably the Tupumaros, carried out murders and kidnappings. The army crushed the Tupumaros in 1972, but the army took over the government in 1973. Military rule continued until 1984 when elections were held. Julio Maria Sanguinetti, who led Uruguay back to civilian rule, was re-elected president in 1994. He was succeeded in 2000 by Jorge Batlle of the incumbent Colorado Party.

The World Bank classifies Uruguay as an 'upper-middle-income' developing country. Agriculture employs only 5% of the people, but farm products, notably hides and leather goods, beef and wool, are the leading exports, while the leading manufacturing industries process farm products. The main crops include maize, potatoes, wheat and sugar beet.

AREA 177,410 sq km [68,498 sq mi]
POPULATION 3,360,000
CAPITAL (POPULATION) Montevideo (1,379,000)
GOVERNMENT Multiparty republic
ETHNIC GROUPS White 88%, Mestizo 8%, Mulatto or Black 4%
LANGUAGES Spanish (official)
RELIGIONS Roman Catholic 66%, Protestant 2%, Judaism 1%
CURRENCY Uruguay peso = 100 centésimos

UZBEKISTAN

GEOGRAPHY The Republic of Uzbekistan is one of the five republics in Central Asia which were once part of the Soviet Union. Plains cover most of western Uzbekistan, with highlands in the east. The main rivers, the Amu (or Amu Darya) and Syr (or Syr Darya), drain into the Aral Sea. So much water has been taken from these rivers to irrigate the land that the Aral Sea shrank from 66,900 sq km [25,830 sq mi] in 1960 to 33,642 sq km [12,989 sq mi] in 1993. The dried-up lake area has become desert. The climate is continental, with warm summers and cold winters. The west is extremely arid, with an average annual rainfall of about 200 mm [8 in].

POLITICS & ECONOMY Russia took the area in the 19th century. After the Russian Revolution of 1917, the Communists took over and, in 1924, they set up the Uzbek Soviet Socialist Republic. Under Communism, all aspects of Uzbek life were controlled and religious worship was discouraged. But education, health, housing and transport were improved. In the late 1980s, the people demanded more freedom and, in 1990, the government stated that its laws overruled those of the Soviet Union. Uzbekistan became independent in 1991 when the Soviet Union broke up, but it retained links with Russia through the Commonwealth of Independent States. Islam Karimov, leader of the People's Democratic Party (formerly the Communist Party), was elected president in December 1991. In 1992–3, many opposition leaders were arrested because the government said that they threatened national stability. In 1994–5, the PDP was victorious in national elections and, in 1995, a referendum extended Karimov's term in office until 2000, when he was again re-elected. In 2001, Karimov declared his support for the United States in its campaign against terrorist bases in Afghanistan.

The World Bank classifies Uzbekistan as a 'lower-middle-income' developing country and the government still controls most economic activity. The country produces coal, copper, gold, oil and natural gas.

AREA 447,400 sq km [172,740 sq mi]
POPULATION 25,155,000
CAPITAL (POPULATION) Tashkent (2,118,000)
GOVERNMENT Socialist republic
ETHNIC GROUPS Uzbek 80%, Russian 5%, Tajik 5%, Kazak 3%, Tatar 2%, Kara-Kalpak 2%
LANGUAGES Uzbek (official), Russian
RELIGIONS Islam 88%, Eastern Orthodox 9%
CURRENCY Som = 100 tyiyn

VANUATU

 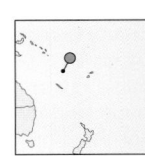

The Republic of Vanuatu, formerly the Anglo-French Condominium of the New Hebrides, became independent in 1980. It consists of a chain of 80 islands in the South Pacific Ocean. Its economy is based on agriculture and it exports copra, beef and veal, timber and cocoa. **AREA** 12,190 sq km [4,707 sq mi]; **POPULATION** 193,000; **CAPITAL** Port-Vila.

VATICAN CITY

 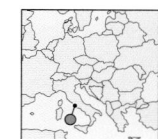

Vatican City State, the world's smallest independent nation, is an enclave on the west bank of the River Tiber in Rome. It forms an independent base for the Holy See, the governing body of the Roman Catholic Church. **AREA** 0.44 sq km [0.17 sq mi]; **POPULATION** 890.

VENEZUELA

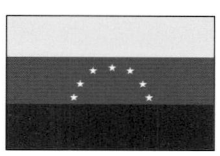 

GEOGRAPHY The Bolivarian Republic of Venezuela, in northern South America, contains the Maracaibo lowlands around the oil-rich Lake Maracaibo in the west. Andean ranges enclose the lowlands and extend across most of northern Venezuela. The Orinoco river basin, containing tropical grasslands called *llanos*, lies between the northern highlands and the Guiana Highlands in the south-east.

Venezuela has a tropical climate. Temperatures are high throughout the year on the lowlands, though the mountains are much cooler. The rainfall is heaviest in the mountains. But much of the country has a marked dry season between December and April.

POLITICS & ECONOMY In the early 19th century, Venezuelans, such as Simón Bolívar and Francisco de Miranda, began a struggle against Spanish rule. Venezuela declared its independence in 1811. But it only became truly independent in 1821, when the Spanish were defeated in a battle near Valencia.

The development of Venezuela in the 19th and the first half of the 20th centuries was marred by instability, violence and periods of harsh dictatorial rule. But Venezuela has had elected governments since 1958. The country has greatly benefited from its oil resources which were first exploited in 1917. In 1960, Venezuela helped to form OPEC (the Organization of Petroleum Exporting Countries) and, in 1976, the government of Venezuela took control of the entire oil industry. In 1999, Hugo Chavez, who had staged an unsuccessful coup in 1992, was elected president and a new constitution, giving the president considerably more power, was adopted. In April 2002, Chavez survived an attempted coup.

The World Bank classifies Venezuela as an 'upper-middle-income' developing country. Oil accounts for 80% of the exports. Other exports include bauxite and aluminium, iron ore and farm products. Agriculture employs 13% of people and cattle ranching is important. The chief industry is petroleum refining. Other manufactures include aluminium, cement, processed food, steel and textiles.

AREA 912,050 sq km [352,143 sq mi]
POPULATION 23,917,000
CAPITAL (POPULATION) Caracas (1,975,000)
GOVERNMENT Federal republic
ETHNIC GROUPS Mestizo 67%, White 21%, Black 10%, Amerindian 2%
LANGUAGES Spanish (official), Goajiro
RELIGIONS Roman Catholic 96%
CURRENCY Bolívar = 100 céntimos

VIETNAM

GEOGRAPHY The Socialist Republic of Vietnam occupies an S-shaped strip of land facing the South China Sea in South-east Asia. The coastal plains include two densely populated, fertile delta regions: the Red (Hong) delta facing the Gulf of Tonkin in the north, and the Mekong delta in the south.

Vietnam has a tropical climate, though the driest months of January to March are a little cooler than the wet, hot summer months, when monsoon winds blow from the south-west. Typhoons (cyclones) sometimes hit the coast, causing much damage.

POLITICS & ECONOMY China dominated Vietnam for a thousand years before AD 939, when a Vietnamese state was founded. The French took over the area between the 1850s and 1880s. They ruled Vietnam as part of French Indo-China, which also included Cambodia and Laos.

Japan conquered Vietnam during World War II (1939–45). In 1946, war broke out between a nationalist group, called the Vietminh, and the French colonial government. France withdrew in 1954 and Vietnam was divided into a Communist North Vietnam, led by the Vietminh leader, Ho Chi Minh, and a non-Communist South.

A force called the Viet Cong rebelled against South Vietnam's government in 1957 and a war began, which gradually increased in intensity. The United States aided the South, but after it withdrew in 1975, South Vietnam surrendered. In 1976, the united Vietnam became a Socialist Republic.

Vietnamese troops intervened in Cambodia in 1978 to defeat the Communist Khmer Rouge government, but it withdrew its troops in 1989. In the 1990s, Vietnam began to introduce reforms. In 1995, the United States opened an embassy in Hanoi and, in 2000, a major trade pact was agreed by the countries.

The World Bank classifies Vietnam as a 'low-income' developing country and agriculture employs 67% of the population. The main food crop is rice. The country also produces chromium, oil (which was discovered off the south coast in 1986), phosphates and tin.

AREA 331,689 sq km [128,065 sq mi]
POPULATION 79,939,000
CAPITAL (POPULATION) Hanoi (3,056,000)
GOVERNMENT Socialist republic
ETHNIC GROUPS Vietnamese 87%, Tho (Tay), Chinese (Hoa), Tai, Khmer, Muong, Nung
LANGUAGES Vietnamese (official), Chinese
RELIGIONS Buddhism 55%, Roman Catholic 7%
CURRENCY Dong = 10 hao = 100 xu

VIRGIN ISLANDS, BRITISH

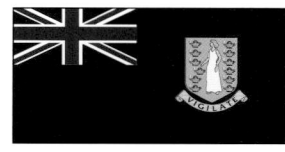 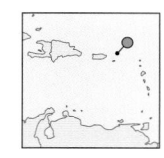

The British Virgin Islands, the most northerly of the Lesser Antilles, are a British overseas territory, with a substantial measure of self-government. **AREA** 153 sq km [59 sq mi]; **POPULATION** 21,000; **CAPITAL** Road Town.

VIRGIN ISLANDS, US

 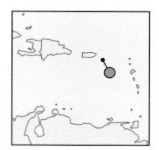

The Virgin Islands of the United States, a group of three islands and 65 small islets, are a self-governing US territory. Purchased from Denmark in 1917, its residents are US citizens and they elect a non-voting delegate to the US House of Representatives. **AREA** 340 sq km [130 sq mi]; **POPULATION** 122,000; **CAPITAL** Charlotte Amalie.

WALLIS AND FUTUNA

Wallis and Futuna, in the South Pacific Ocean, is the smallest and the poorest of France's overseas territories. **AREA** 200 sq km [77 sq mi]; **POPULATION** 15,000; **CAPITAL** Mata-Utu.

YEMEN

 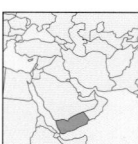

GEOGRAPHY The Republic of Yemen faces the Red Sea and the Gulf of Aden in the south-western corner of the Arabian peninsula. Behind the narrow coastal plain along the Red Sea, the land rises to a mountain region called High Yemen.

The climate ranges from hot and often humid conditions on the coast to the cooler highlands. Most of the country is arid. The south coasts are hot and humid, especially from June to September.

POLITICS & ECONOMY After World War I, northern Yemen, which had been ruled by Turkey, began to evolve into a separate state from the south, where Britain was in control. Britain withdrew in 1967 and a left-wing government took power in the south. North Yemen became a republic in 1962, when the monarchy was abolished.

Clashes occurred between the traditionalist Yemen Arab Republic in the north and the formerly British Marxist People's Democratic Republic of Yemen but, in 1990, the two Yemens merged to form a single country. Further conflict occurred in 1994, when southern secessionist forces were defeated. In 1998 and 1999, militants in the Aden-Abyan Islamic army sought to destabilize the country. In 2000, suicide bombers, thought to be part of the al Qaida network, steered a craft into a US destroyer in Aden harbour, killing 17 sailors.

The World Bank classifies Yemen as a 'low-income' developing country. Agriculture employs up to 63% of the people. Herders raise sheep and other animals, while farmers grow such crops as barley, fruits, wheat and vegetables in highland valleys and around oases. Cash crops include coffee and cotton.

Imported oil is refined at Aden and petroleum extraction began in the north-west in the 1980s. Handicrafts, leather goods and textiles are manufactured. Remittances from Yemenis abroad are a major source of revenue.

YUGOSLAVIA

AREA 527,970 sq km [203,849 sq mi]
POPULATION 18,078,000
CAPITAL (POPULATION) Sana' (972,000)
GOVERNMENT Multiparty republic
ETHNIC GROUPS Arab 96%, Somali 1%
LANGUAGES Arabic (official)
RELIGIONS Islam
CURRENCY Rial = 100 fils

YUGOSLAVIA

GEOGRAPHY The Federal Republic of Yugoslavia consists of Serbia and Montenegro, two of the six republics which made up the former country of Yugoslavia until it broke up in the early 1990s. In 2002, the government announced plans to give both republics semi-independence under the name of the Union of Serbia and Montenegro.

Behind the coastline on the Adriatic Sea lies an upland region, including the Dinaric Alps and part of the Balkan Mountains. The Pannonian plains, which are drained by the River Danube, are in the north. The coast has a Mediterranean climate. The interior highlands have bitterly cold winters and cool summers. The wettest season is the summer.

POLITICS & ECONOMY People who became known as the South Slavs began to move into the region around 1,500 years ago. Each group, including the Serbs and Croats, founded its own state. But, by the 15th century, foreign countries controlled the region. Serbia and Montenegro were under the Turkish Ottoman empire.

In the 19th century, many Slavs worked for independence and Slavic unity. In 1914, Austria-Hungary declared war on Serbia, blaming it for the assassination of Archduke Francis Ferdinand of Austria–Hungary. This led to World War I and the defeat of Austria–Hungary. In 1918, the South Slavs united in the Kingdom of the Serbs, Croats and Slovenes, which consisted of Bosnia-Herzegovina, Croatia, Dalmatia, Montenegro, Serbia and Slovenia. The country was renamed Yugoslavia in 1929. Germany occupied Yugoslavia during World War II, but partisans, including a Communist force led by Josip Broz Tito, fought the invaders.

From 1945, the Communists controlled the country, which was called the Federal People's Republic of Yugoslavia. But after Tito's death in 1980, the country faced many problems. In 1990, non-Communist parties were permitted and non-Communists won majorities in elections in all but Serbia and Montenegro, where Socialists (former Communists) won control. Yugoslavia split apart in 1991–2 with Bosnia-Herzegovina, Croatia, Macedonia and Slovenia proclaiming their independence. The two remaining republics of Serbia and Montenegro became the new Yugoslavia.

Fighting broke out in Croatia and Bosnia-Herzegovina as rival groups struggled for power. In 1992, the United Nations withdrew recognition of Yugoslavia because of its failure to halt atrocities committed by Serbs living in Croatia and Bosnia. In 1995, Yugoslavia was involved in the talks that led to the Dayton Peace Accord, which brought peace to Bosnia-Herzegovina. But the issue of Yugoslav repression of minorities flared up again in 1998 in Kosovo, a province where the majority are ethnic Albanians. In response to Serb ethnic cleansing, NATO forces began an offensive against Yugoslavia.

A Serb withdrawal was agreed in June 1999. Elections in 2000 resulted in defeat for Slobodan Milosevic, who was succeeded by Vojislav Kostunica. In 2002, Milosevic, whom many regarded as responsible for much of the conflict in the 1990s, faced charges of crimes against humanity at the UN War Crimes Tribunal in The Hague.

Under Communist rule, manufacturing became increasingly important in Yugoslavia. But in the early 1990s, the World Bank classified Yugoslavia as a 'lower-middle-income' economy. Its resources include bauxite, coal, copper and other metals, together with oil and natural gas. Manufactures include aluminium, machinery, plastics, steel, textiles and vehicles. Chief exports are manufactures, but agriculture remains important. Crops include fruits, maize, potatoes, tobacco and wheat. Cattle, pigs and sheep are reared.

AREA 102,170 sq km [39,449 sq mi]
POPULATION 10,677,000
CAPITAL (POPULATION) Belgrade (1,598,000)
GOVERNMENT Federal republic
ETHNIC GROUPS Serb 62%, Albanian 17%, Montenegrin 5%, Hungarian, Muslim, Croat
LANGUAGES Serbo-Croat (official), Albanian
RELIGIONS Christianity (mainly Serbian Orthodox), Islam
CURRENCY Yugoslav new dinar = 100 paras

ZAMBIA

 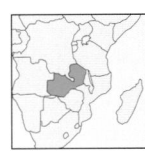

GEOGRAPHY The Republic of Zambia is a land-locked country in southern Africa. Zambia lies on the plateau that makes up most of southern Africa. Much of the land is between 900 m and 1,500 m [2,950 ft to 4,920 ft] above sea level. The Muchinga Mountains in the north-east rise above this flat land.

Lakes include Bangweulu, which is entirely within Zambia, together with parts of lakes Mweru and Tanganyika in the north.

Zambia lies in the tropics, but temperatures are moderated by the altitude. The rainy season runs from November to March.

POLITICS & ECONOMY European contact with Zambia began in the 19th century, when the explorer David Livingstone crossed the River Zambezi. In the 1890s, the British South Africa Company, set up by Cecil Rhodes (1853–1902), the British financier and statesman, made treaties with local chiefs and gradually took over the area. In 1911, the Company named the area Northern Rhodesia. In 1924, Britain took over the government of the country.

In 1953, Britain formed a federation of Northern Rhodesia, Southern Rhodesia (now Zimbabwe) and Nyasaland (now Malawi). Because of African opposition, the federation was dissolved in 1963 and Northern Rhodesia became independent as Zambia in 1964. Kenneth Kaunda became president and one-party rule was introduced in 1972. However, a new constitution was adopted in 1990 and, in 1991, Kaunda's party was defeated and Frederick Chiluba became president. Chiluba was re-elected in 1996, but stood down in 2001, and his party's candidate, Levy Mwanawasa, was elected president.

Copper is the main resource, accounting for 80% of Zambia's exports in 1997. Zambia also produces cobalt, lead, zinc and gemstones. Agriculture employs 69% of workers, as compared with 4% in industry and mining. Maize is the chief crop.

AREA 752,614 sq km [290,586 sq mi]
POPULATION 9,770,000
CAPITAL (POPULATION) Lusaka (982,000)
GOVERNMENT Multiparty republic
ETHNIC GROUPS Bemba 36%, Maravi (Nyanja) 18%, Tonga 15%
LANGUAGES English (official), Bemba, Nyanja, and about 70 others
RELIGIONS Christianity 68%, Islam, Hinduism
CURRENCY Kwacha = 100 ngwee

ZIMBABWE

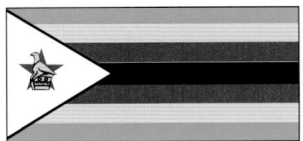 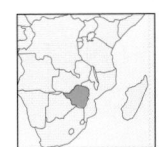

GEOGRAPHY The Republic of Zimbabwe is a landlocked country in southern Africa. Most of the country lies on a high plateau between the Zambezi and Limpopo rivers between 900 m to 1,500 m [2,950 ft to 4,920 ft] above sea level. From October to March, the weather is hot and wet. But daily temperatures may vary greatly in the winter. Frosts have been recorded between June and August.

POLITICS & ECONOMY The Shona people became dominant in the region about 1,000 years ago. The British South Africa Company, under the statesman Cecil Rhodes (1853–1902), occupied the area in the 1890s, after obtaining mineral rights from local chiefs. The area was named Rhodesia and later Southern Rhodesia. It became a self-governing British colony in 1923. Between 1953 and 1963, Southern and Northern Rhodesia (now Zambia) were joined to Nyasaland (Malawi) in the Central African Federation.

In 1965, the European government of Southern Rhodesia (then called Rhodesia) declared their country independent but Britain refused to accept this. Finally, after a civil war, the country became legally independent in 1980, though rivalries between the Shona and Ndebele people threatened stability. Order was restored when the Shona prime minister, Robert Mugabe, brought his Ndebele rivals into his government. In 1987, Mugabe became the country's executive president and, in 1991, the government renounced its Marxist ideology. Mugabe was re-elected president in 1990 and 1996. During the late 1990s, Mugabe threatened to seize white-owned farms without paying compensation to the owners. Despite international pressure, landless 'war veterans' began to occupy white farms. The situation worsened in the early 2000s, resulting in violence and murder. In 2002, Mugabe was re-elected president amid accusations of electoral irregularities. As a result, the Commonwealth suspended Zimbabwe's membership for 12 months.

The World Bank classifies Zimbabwe as a 'low-income' developing country. The country has valuable mineral resources and mining accounts for a fifth of the country's exports. Agriculture employs 27% of working people. Maize is the chief food crop.

AREA 390,579 sq km [150,873 sq mi]
POPULATION 11,365,000
CAPITAL (POPULATION) Harare (1,189,000)
GOVERNMENT Multiparty republic
ETHNIC GROUPS Shona 71%, Ndebele 16%, other Bantu-speaking Africans 11%, White 1%, Asian 1%
LANGUAGES English (official), Shona, Ndebele
RELIGIONS Christianity 45%, traditional beliefs 40%
CURRENCY Zimbabwe dollar = 100 cents

THE WORLD IN FOCUS

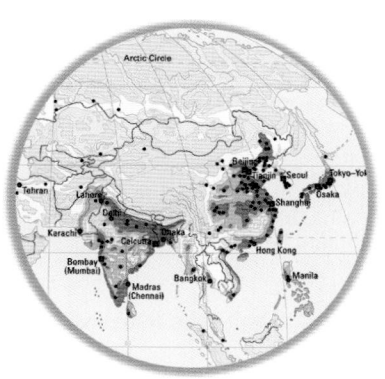

Planet Earth

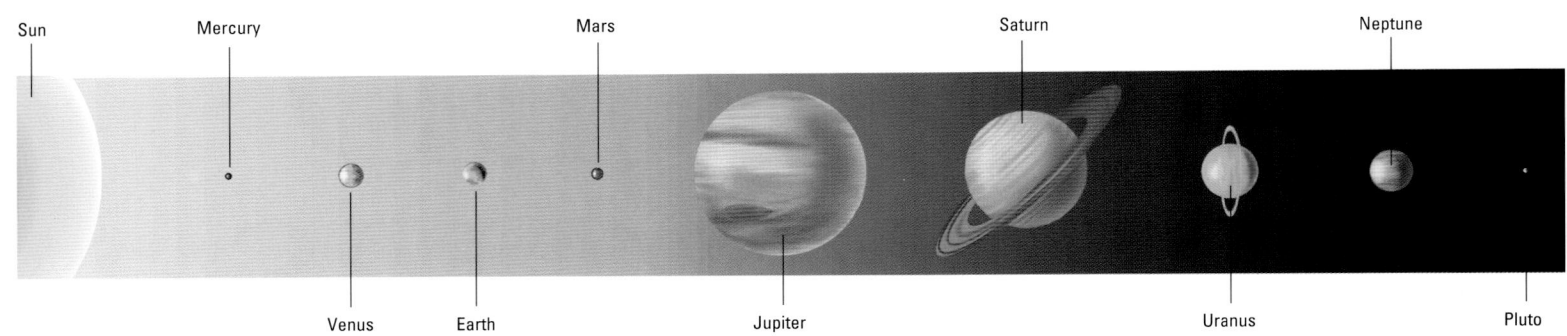

Sun — Mercury — Mars — Saturn — Neptune — Venus — Earth — Jupiter — Uranus — Pluto

The Solar System

A minute part of one of the billions of galaxies (collections of stars) that comprises the Universe, the Solar System lies some 27,000 light-years from the centre of our own galaxy, the 'Milky Way'. Thought to be about 4,600 million years old, it consists of a central sun with nine planets and their moons revolving around it, attracted by its gravitational pull. The planets orbit the Sun in the same direction – anti-clockwise when viewed from the Northern Heavens – and almost in the same plane. Their orbital paths, however, vary enormously.

The Sun's diameter is 109 times that of Earth, and the temperature at its core – caused by continuous thermonuclear fusions of hydrogen into helium – is estimated to be 15 million degrees Celsius. It is the Solar System's only source of light and heat.

Profile of the Planets

	Mean distance from Sun (million km)	Mass (Earth = 1)	Period of orbit (Earth years)	Period of rotation (Earth days)	Equatorial diameter (km)	Number of known satellites
Mercury	57.9	0.055	0.24 years	58.67	4,878	0
Venus	108.2	0.815	0.62 years	243.00	12,104	0
Earth	149.6	1.0	1.00 years	1.00	12,756	1
Mars	227.9	0.107	1.88 years	1.03	6,787	2
Jupiter	778.3	317.8	11.86 years	0.41	142,800	27
Saturn	1,427	95.2	29.46 years	0.43	120,000	30
Uranus	2,871	14.5	84.01 years	0.75	51,118	21
Neptune	4,497	17.1	164.80 years	0.80	49,528	8
Pluto	5,914	0.002	248.50 years	6.39	2,320	1

All planetary orbits are elliptical in form, but only Pluto and Mercury follow paths that deviate noticeably from a circular one. Near perihelion – its closest approach to the Sun – Pluto actually passes inside the orbit of Neptune, an event that last occurred in 1983. Pluto did not regain its station as outermost planet until February 1999.

The Seasons

Seasons occur because the Earth's axis is tilted at a constant angle of 23½°. When the northern hemisphere is tilted to a maximum extent towards the Sun, on 21 June, the Sun is overhead at the Tropic of Cancer (latitude 23½° North). This is midsummer, or the summer solstice, in the northern hemisphere.

On 22 or 23 September, the Sun is overhead at the Equator, and day and night are of equal length throughout the world. This is the autumn equinox in the northern hemisphere. On 21 or 22 December, the Sun is overhead at the Tropic of Capricorn (23½° South), the winter solstice in the northern hemisphere. The overhead Sun then tracks north until, on 21 March, it is overhead at the Equator. This is the spring (vernal) equinox in the northern hemisphere.

In the southern hemisphere, the seasons are the reverse of those in the north.

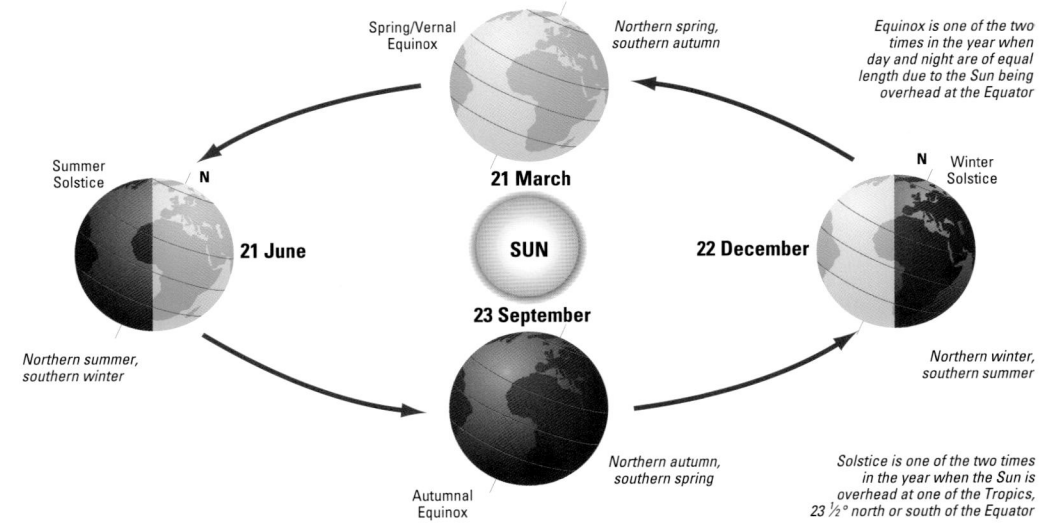

Equinox is one of the two times in the year when day and night are of equal length due to the Sun being overhead at the Equator

Solstice is one of the two times in the year when the Sun is overhead at one of the Tropics, 23½° north or south of the Equator

Day and Night

The Sun appears to rise in the east, reach its highest point at noon, and then set in the west, to be followed by night. In reality, it is not the Sun that is moving but the Earth rotating from west to east. The moment when the Sun's upper limb first appears above the horizon is termed sunrise; the moment when the Sun's upper limb disappears below the horizon is sunset.

At the summer solstice in the northern hemisphere (21 June), the Arctic has total daylight and the Antarctic total darkness. The opposite occurs at the winter solstice (21 or 22 December). At the Equator, the length of day and night are almost equal all year.

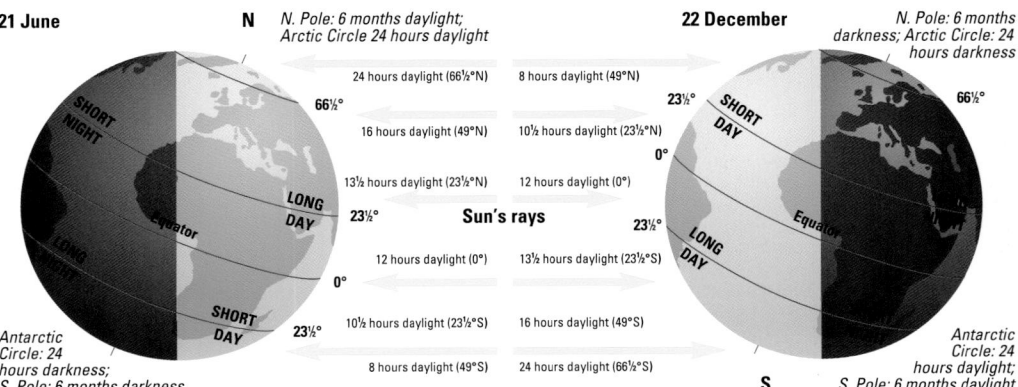

Time

Year: The time taken by the Earth to revolve around the Sun, or 365.24 days.

Leap Year: A calendar year of 366 days, 29 February being the additional day. It offsets the difference between the calendar and the solar year.

Month: The approximate time taken by the Moon to revolve around the Earth. The 12 months of the year in fact vary from 28 (29 in a Leap Year) to 31 days.

Week: An artificial period of 7 days, not based on astronomical time.

Day: The time taken by the Earth to complete one rotation on its axis.

Hour: 24 hours make one day. Usually the day is divided into hours AM (ante meridiem or before noon) and PM (post meridiem or after noon), although most timetables now use the 24-hour system, from midnight to midnight.

Sunrise

Spring Equinox   Autumnal Equinox

Hours AM

Latitude: 60°N, 40°N, 20°N, 0°(Equator), 20°S, 40°S, 60°S

Months of the year: J F M A M J J A S O N D

Sunset

Spring Equinox   Autumnal Equinox

Hours PM

Latitude: 60°S, 40°S, 20°S, 0°(Equator), 20°N, 40°N, 60°N

Months of the year: J F M A M J J A S O N D

The Moon

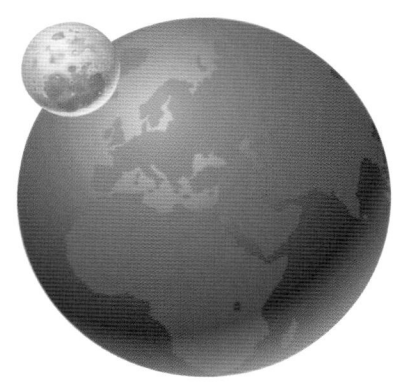

The Moon rotates more slowly than the Earth, making one complete turn on its axis in just over 27 days. Since this corresponds to its period of revolution around the Earth, the Moon always presents the same hemisphere or face to us, and we never see 'the dark side'. The interval between one full Moon and the next (and between new Moons) is about 29½ days – a lunar month. The apparent changes in the shape of the Moon are caused by its changing position in relation to the Earth; like the planets, it produces no light of its own and shines only by reflecting the rays of the Sun.

Phases of the Moon

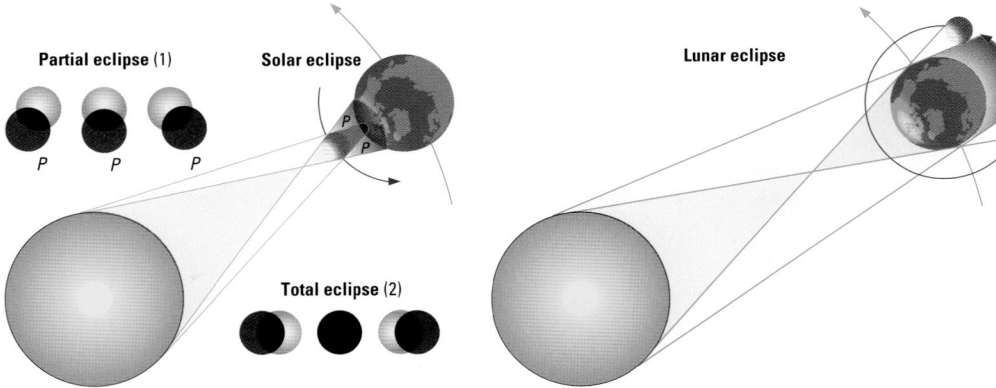

Distance from Earth: 356,410 km – 406,685 km; Mean diameter: 3,475.1 km; Mass: approx. 1/81 that of Earth; Surface gravity: one-sixth of Earth's; Daily range of temperature at lunar equator: 200°C; Average orbital speed: 3,683 km/h

New Moon | Crescent | First quarter | Gibbous | Full Moon | Gibbous | Last quarter | Crescent | New Moon

Eclipses

When the Moon passes between the Sun and the Earth it causes a partial eclipse of the Sun (1) if the Earth passes through the Moon's outer shadow (P), or a total eclipse (2) if the inner cone shadow crosses the Earth's surface. In a lunar eclipse, the Earth's shadow crosses the Moon and, again, provides either a partial or total eclipse.

Eclipses of the Sun and the Moon do not occur every month because of the 5° difference between the plane of the Moon's orbit and the plane in which the Earth moves. In the 1990s only 14 lunar eclipses were possible, for example, seven partial and seven total; each was visible only from certain, and variable, parts of the world. The same period witnessed 13 solar eclipses – six partial (or annular) and seven total.

Partial eclipse (1)   Solar eclipse   Lunar eclipse

Total eclipse (2)

Tides

The daily rise and fall of the ocean's tides are the result of the gravitational pull of the Moon and that of the Sun, though the effect of the latter is only 46.6% as strong as that of the Moon. This effect is greatest on the hemisphere facing the Moon and causes a tidal 'bulge'. When the Sun, Earth and Moon are in line, tide-raising forces are at a maximum and Spring tides occur: high tide reaches the highest values, and low tide falls to low levels. When lunar and solar forces are least coincidental with the Sun and Moon at an angle (near the Moon's first and third quarters), Neap tides occur, which have a small tidal range.

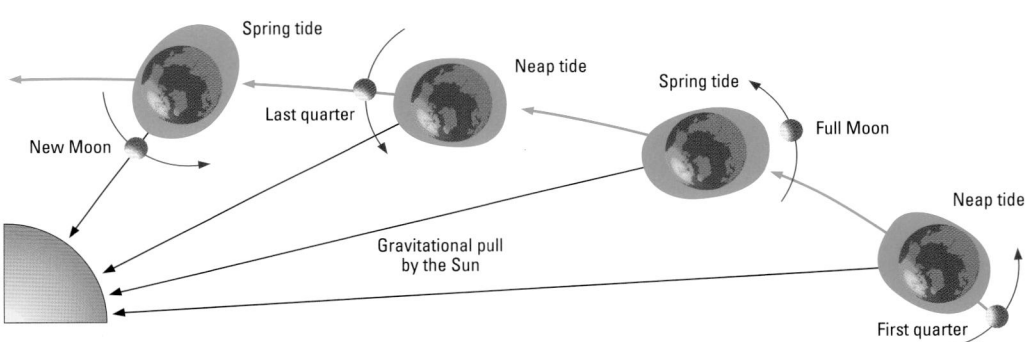

Spring tide   Neap tide   Spring tide

New Moon   Last quarter   Full Moon

Gravitational pull by the Sun

First quarter   Neap tide

Restless Earth

The Earth's Structure

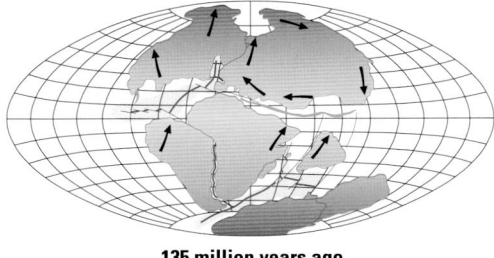

Crust (average 5–50 km)
Upper mantle (c. 370 km)
Transitional zone (600 km)
Outer core (2,100 km)
Lower mantle (1,700 km)
Inner core (1,350 km)

Continental Drift

About 200 million years ago the original Pangaea landmass began to split into two continental groups, which further separated over time to produce the present-day configuration.

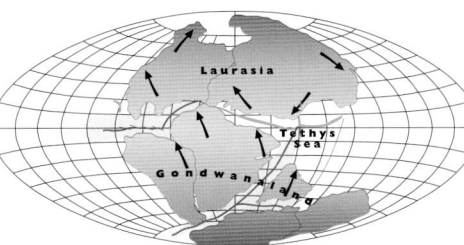

180 million years ago

Laurasia
Tethys Sea
Gondwanaland

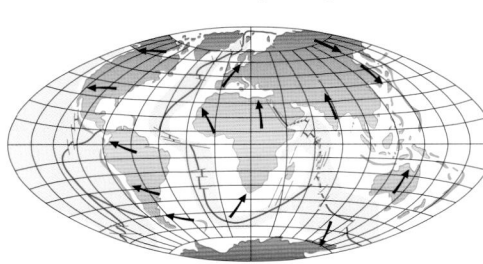

135 million years ago

Present day

— Trench
— Rift
New ocean floor
— Zones of slippage

Notable Earthquakes Since 1900

Year	Location	Richter Scale	Deaths
1906	San Francisco, USA	8.3	503
1906	Valparaiso, Chile	8.6	22,000
1906	San Francisco, USA	7.7	3,000
1906	Valparaiso, Chile	8.6	22,000
1908	Messina, Italy	7.5	83,000
1915	Avezzano, Italy	7.5	30,000
1920	Gansu (Kansu), China	8.6	180,000
1923	Yokohama, Japan	8.3	143,000
1927	Nan Shan, China	8.3	200,000
1932	Gansu (Kansu), China	7.6	70,000
1933	Sanriku, Japan	8.9	2,990
1934	Bihar, India/Nepal	8.4	10,700
1935	Quetta, India (now Pakistan)	7.5	60,000
1939	Chillan, Chile	8.3	28,000
1939	Erzincan, Turkey	7.9	30,000
1960	S. W. Chile	9.5	2,200
1960	Agadir, Morocco	5.8	12,000
1962	Khorasan, Iran	7.1	12,230
1964	Anchorage, USA	9.2	125
1968	N. E. Iran	7.4	12,000
1970	N. Peru	7.7	66,794
1972	Managua, Nicaragua	6.2	5,000
1974	N. Pakistan	6.3	5,200
1976	Guatemala	7.5	22,778
1976	Tangshan, China	8.2	255,000
1978	Tabas, Iran	7.7	25,000
1980	El Asnam, Algeria	7.3	20,000
1980	S. Italy	7.2	4,800
1985	Mexico City, Mexico	8.1	4,200
1988	N.W. Armenia	6.8	55,000
1990	N. Iran	7.7	36,000
1992	Flores, Indonesia	6.8	1,895
1993	Maharashtra, India	6.4	30,000
1994	Los Angeles, USA	6.6	51
1995	Kobe, Japan	7.2	5,000
1995	Sakhalin Is., Russia	7.5	2,000
1996	Yunnan, China	7.0	240
1997	N. E. Iran	7.1	2,400
1998	Takhar, Afghanistan	6.1	4,200
1998	Rostaq, Afghanistan	7.0	5,000
1999	Izmit, Turkey	7.4	15,000
1999	Taipei, Taiwan	7.6	1,700
2001	Gujarat, India	7.7	14,000
2002	Afyon, Turkey	6.5	44
2002	Baghlan, Afghanistan	6.1	1,000

Earthquakes

Earthquake magnitude is usually rated according to either the Richter or the Modified Mercalli scale, both devised by seismologists in the 1930s. The Richter scale measures absolute earthquake power with mathematical precision: each step upwards represents a tenfold increase in shockwave amplitude. Theoretically, there is no upper limit, but the largest earthquakes measured have been rated at between 8.8 and 8.9. The 12–point Mercalli scale, based on observed effects, is often more meaningful, ranging from I (earthquakes noticed only by seismographs) to XII (total destruction); intermediate points include V (people awakened at night; unstable objects overturned), VII (collapse of ordinary buildings; chimneys and monuments fall) and IX (conspicuous cracks in ground; serious damage to reservoirs).

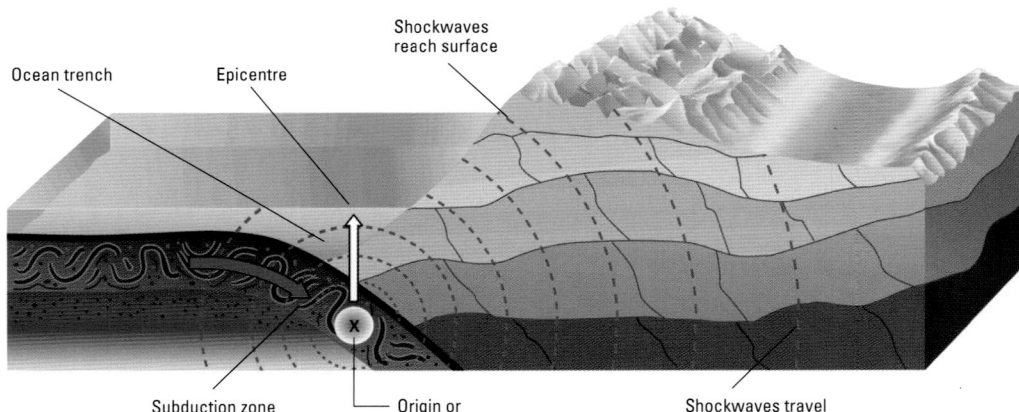

Shockwaves reach surface
Ocean trench
Epicentre
Subduction zone
Origin or focus
Shockwaves travel away from focus

Structure and Earthquakes

Mobile land areas
Submarine zones of mobile land areas
Stable land platforms
Submarine extensions of stable land platforms
Mid-oceanic volcanic ridges
Oceanic platforms

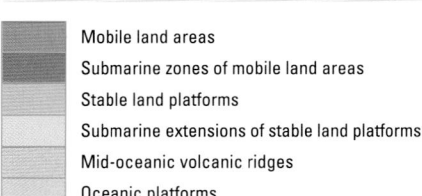

1976 ○   Principal earthquakes and dates (since 1900)

Earthquakes are a series of rapid vibrations originating from the slipping or faulting of parts of the Earth's crust when stresses within build up to breaking point. They usually happen at depths varying from 8 km to 30 km. Severe earthquakes cause extensive damage when they take place in populated areas, destroying structures and severing communications. Most initial loss of life occurs due to secondary causes such as falling masonry, fires and flooding.

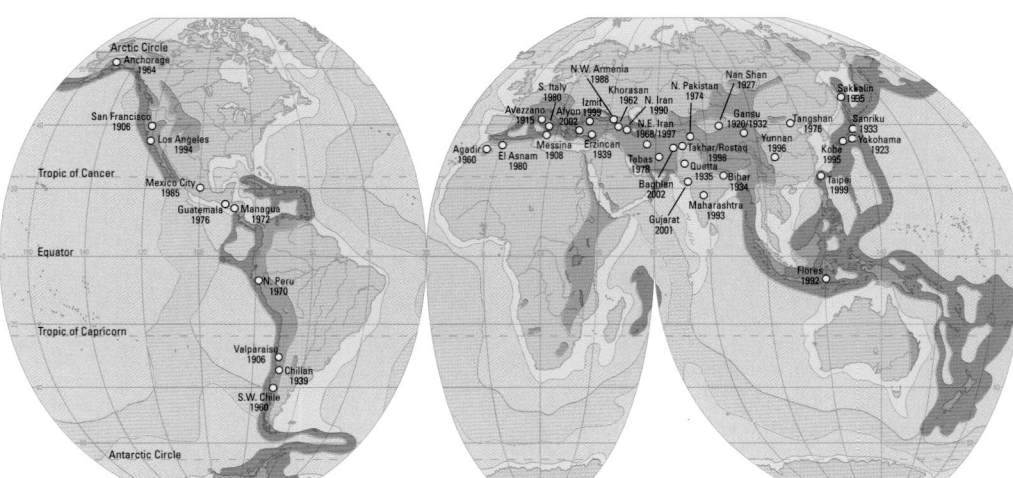

Projection: Interrupted Mollweide

Plate Tectonics

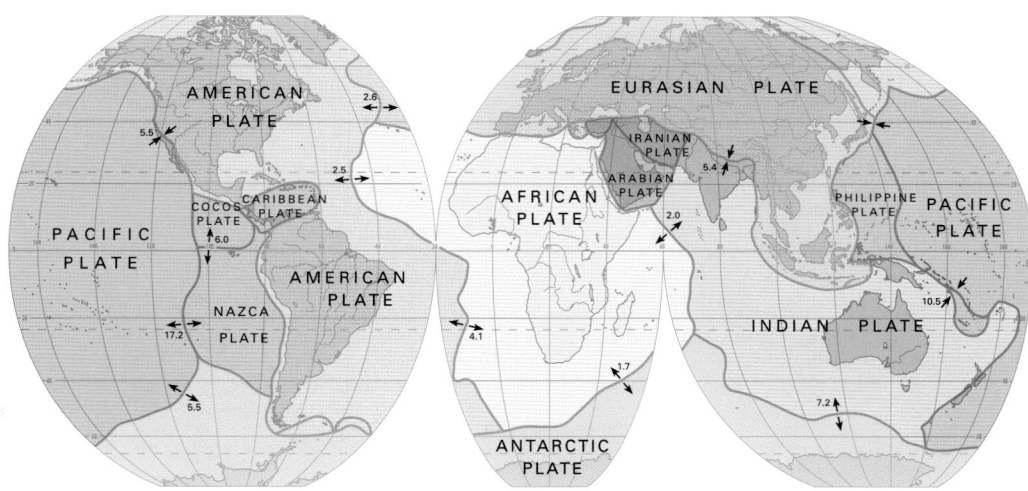

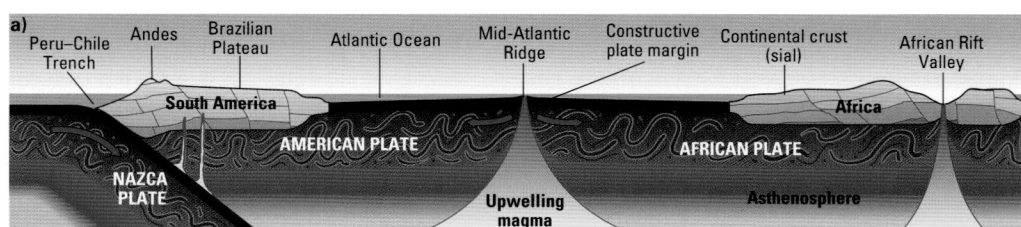

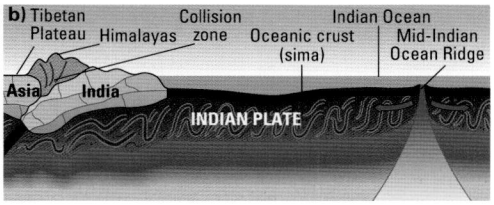

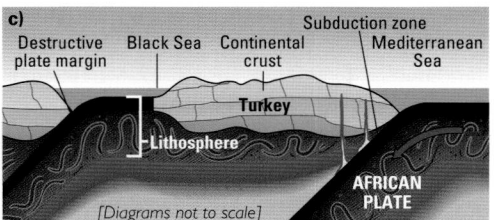

The drifting of the continents is a feature that is unique to Planet Earth. The complementary, almost jigsaw-puzzle fit of the coastlines on each side of the Atlantic Ocean inspired Alfred Wegener's theory of continental drift in 1915. The theory suggested that the ancient super-continent, which Wegener named Pangaea, incorporated all of the Earth's landmasses and gradually split up to form today's continents.

The original debate about continental drift was a prelude to a more radical idea: plate tectonics. The basic theory is that the Earth's crust is made up of a series of rigid plates which float on a soft layer of the mantle and are moved about by continental convection currents within the Earth's interior. These plates diverge and converge along margins marked by seismic activity. Plates diverge from mid-ocean ridges where molten lava pushes upwards and forces the plates apart at rates of up to 40 mm [1.6 in] a year.

The three diagrams, left, give some examples of plate boundaries from around the world. Diagram (a) shows sea-floor spreading at the Mid-Atlantic Ridge as the American and African plates slowly diverge. The same thing is happening in (b) where sea-floor spreading at the Mid-Indian Ocean Ridge is forcing the Indian plate to collide into the Eurasian plate. In (c) oceanic crust (sima) is being subducted beneath lighter continental crust (sial).

Volcanoes

Volcanoes occur when hot liquefied rock beneath the Earth's crust is pushed up by pressure to the surface as molten lava. Some volcanoes erupt in an explosive way, throwing out rocks and ash, whilst others are effusive and lava flows out of the vent. There are volcanoes which are both, such as Mount Fuji. An accumulation of lava and cinders creates cones of variable size and shape. As a result of many eruptions over centuries, Mount Etna in Sicily has a circumference of more than 120 km [75 miles].

Climatologists believe that volcanic ash, if ejected high into the atmosphere, can influence temperature and weather for several years afterwards. The 1991 eruption of Mount Pinatubo in the Philippines ejected more than 20 million tonnes of dust and ash 32 km [20 miles] into the atmosphere and is believed to have accelerated ozone depletion over a large part of the globe.

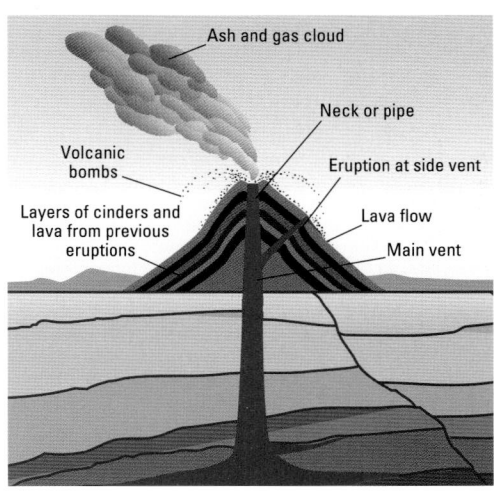

Distribution of Volcanoes

Volcanoes today may be the subject of considerable scientific study but they remain both dramatic and unpredictable: in 1991 Mount Pinatubo, 100 km [62 miles] north of the Philippines capital Manila, suddenly burst into life after lying dormant for more than six centuries. Most of the world's active volcanoes occur in a belt around the Pacific Ocean, on the edge of the Pacific plate, called the 'ring of fire'. Indonesia has the greatest concentration with 90 volcanoes, 12 of which are active. The most famous, Krakatoa, erupted in 1883 with such force that the resulting tidal wave killed 36,000 people and tremors were felt as far away as Australia.

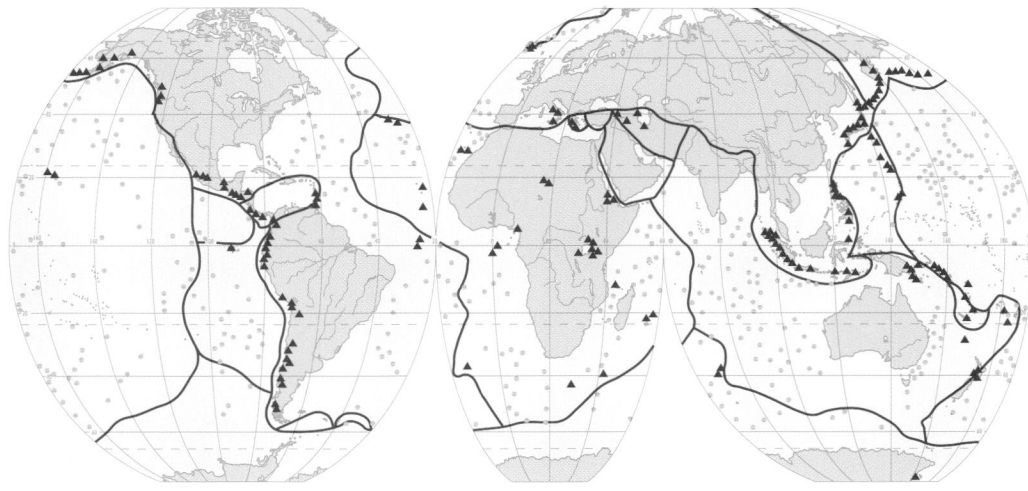

- Submarine volcanoes

▲ Land volcanoes active since 1700

—— Boundaries of tectonic plates

Landforms

The Rock Cycle

James Hutton first proposed the rock cycle in the late 1700s after he observed the slow but steady effects of erosion.

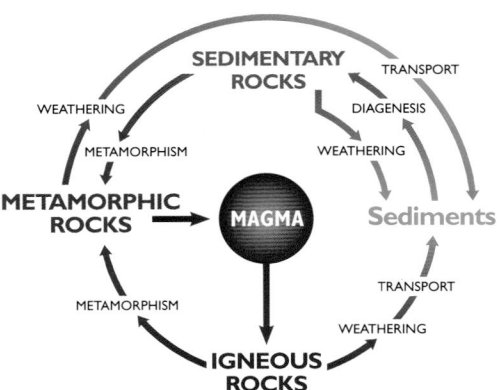

Above and below the surface of the oceans, the features of the Earth's crust are constantly changing. The phenomenal forces generated by convection currents in the molten core of our planet carry the vast segments or 'plates' of the crust across the globe in an endless cycle of creation and destruction. A continent may travel little more than 25 mm [1 in] per year, yet in the vast span of geological time this process throws up giant mountain ranges and creates new land.

Destruction of the landscape, however, begins as soon as it is formed. Wind, water, ice and sea, the main agents of erosion, mount a constant assault that even the most resistant rocks cannot withstand. Mountain peaks may dwindle by as little as a few millimetres each year, but if they are not uplifted by further movements of the crust they will eventually be reduced to rubble and transported away.

Water is the most powerful agent of erosion – it has been estimated that 100 billion tonnes of sediment are washed into the oceans every year. Three

Asian rivers account for 20% of this total, the Huang He, in China, and the Brahmaputra and Ganges in Bangladesh.

Rivers and glaciers, like the sea itself, generate much of their effect through abrasion – pounding the land with the debris they carry with them. But as well as destroying they also create new landforms, many of them spectacular: vast deltas like those of the Mississippi and the Nile, or the deep fjords cut by glaciers in British Columbia, Norway and New Zealand.

Geologists once considered that landscapes evolved from 'young', newly uplifted mountainous areas, through a 'mature' hilly stage, to an 'old age' stage when the land was reduced to an almost flat plain, or peneplain. This theory, called the 'cycle of erosion', fell into disuse when it became evident that so many factors, including the effects of plate tectonics and climatic change, constantly interrupt the cycle, which takes no account of the highly complex interactions that shape the surface of our planet.

Mountain Building

Mountains are formed when pressures on the Earth's crust caused by continental drift become so intense that the surface buckles or cracks. This happens where oceanic crust is subducted by continental crust or, more dramatically, where two tectonic plates collide: the Rockies, Andes, Alps, Urals and Himalayas resulted from such impacts. These are all known as fold mountains because they were formed by the compression of the rocks, forcing the surface to bend and fold like a crumpled rug. The Himalayas are formed from the folded former sediments of the Tethys Sea which was trapped in the collision zone between the Indian and Eurasian plates.

The other main mountain-building process occurs when the crust fractures to create faults, allowing rock to be forced upwards in large blocks; or when the pressure of magma within the crust forces the surface to bulge into a dome, or erupts to form a volcano. Large mountain ranges may reveal a combination of those features; the Alps, for example, have been compressed so violently that the folds are fragmented by numerous faults and intrusions of molten igneous rock.

Over millions of years, even the greatest mountain ranges can be reduced by the agents of erosion (most notably rivers) to a low rugged landscape known as a peneplain.

Types of faults: Faults occur where the crust is being stretched or compressed so violently that the rock strata break in a horizontal or vertical movement. They are classified by the direction in which the blocks of rock have moved. A normal fault results when a vertical movement causes the surface to break apart; compression causes a reverse fault. Horizontal movement causes shearing, known as a strike-slip fault. When the rock breaks in two places, the central block may be pushed up in a horst fault, or sink (creating a rift valley) in a graben fault.

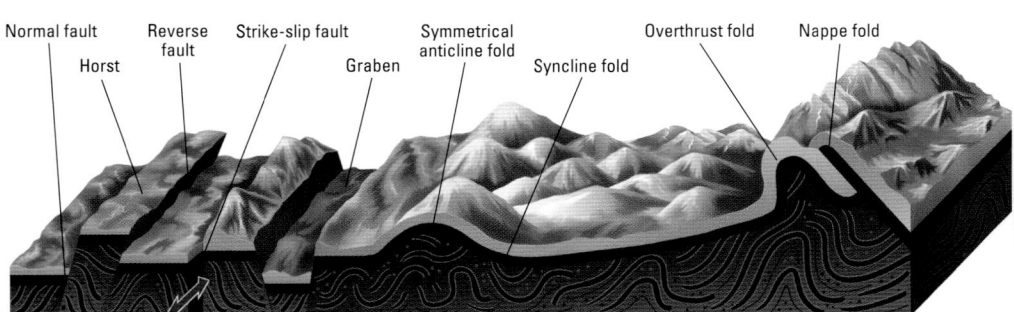

Types of fold: Folds occur when rock strata are squeezed and compressed. They are common therefore at destructive plate margins and where plates have collided, forcing the rocks to buckle into mountain ranges. Geographers give different names to the degrees of fold that result from continuing pressure on the rock. A simple fold may be symmetric, with even slopes on either side, but as the pressure builds up, one slope becomes steeper and the fold becomes asymmetric. Later, the ridge or 'anticline' at the top of the fold may slide over the lower ground or 'syncline' to form a recumbent fold. Eventually, the rock strata may break under the pressure to form an overthrust and finally a nappe fold.

Continental Glaciation

Ice sheets were at their greatest extent about 200,000 years ago. The maximum advance of the last Ice Age was about 18,000 years ago, when ice covered virtually all of Canada and reached as far south as the Bristol Channel in Britain.

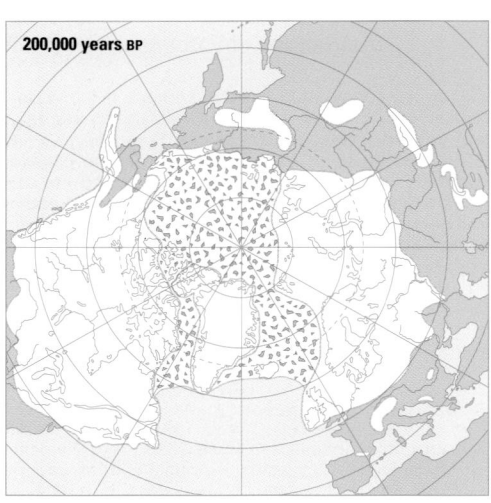

200,000 years BP

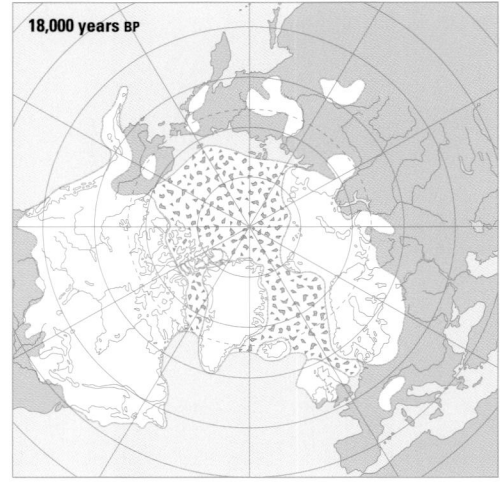

18,000 years BP

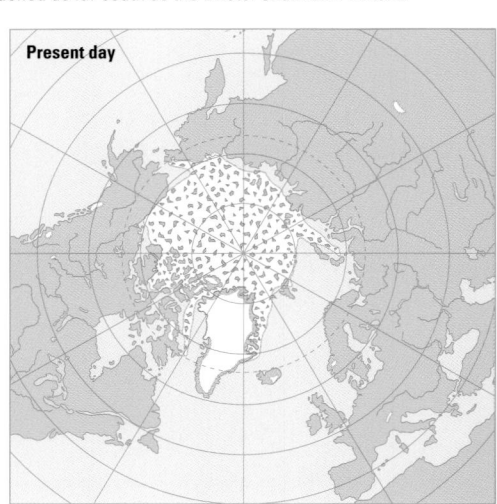

Present day

Natural Landforms

A stylized diagram to show a selection of landforms found in the mid-latitudes.

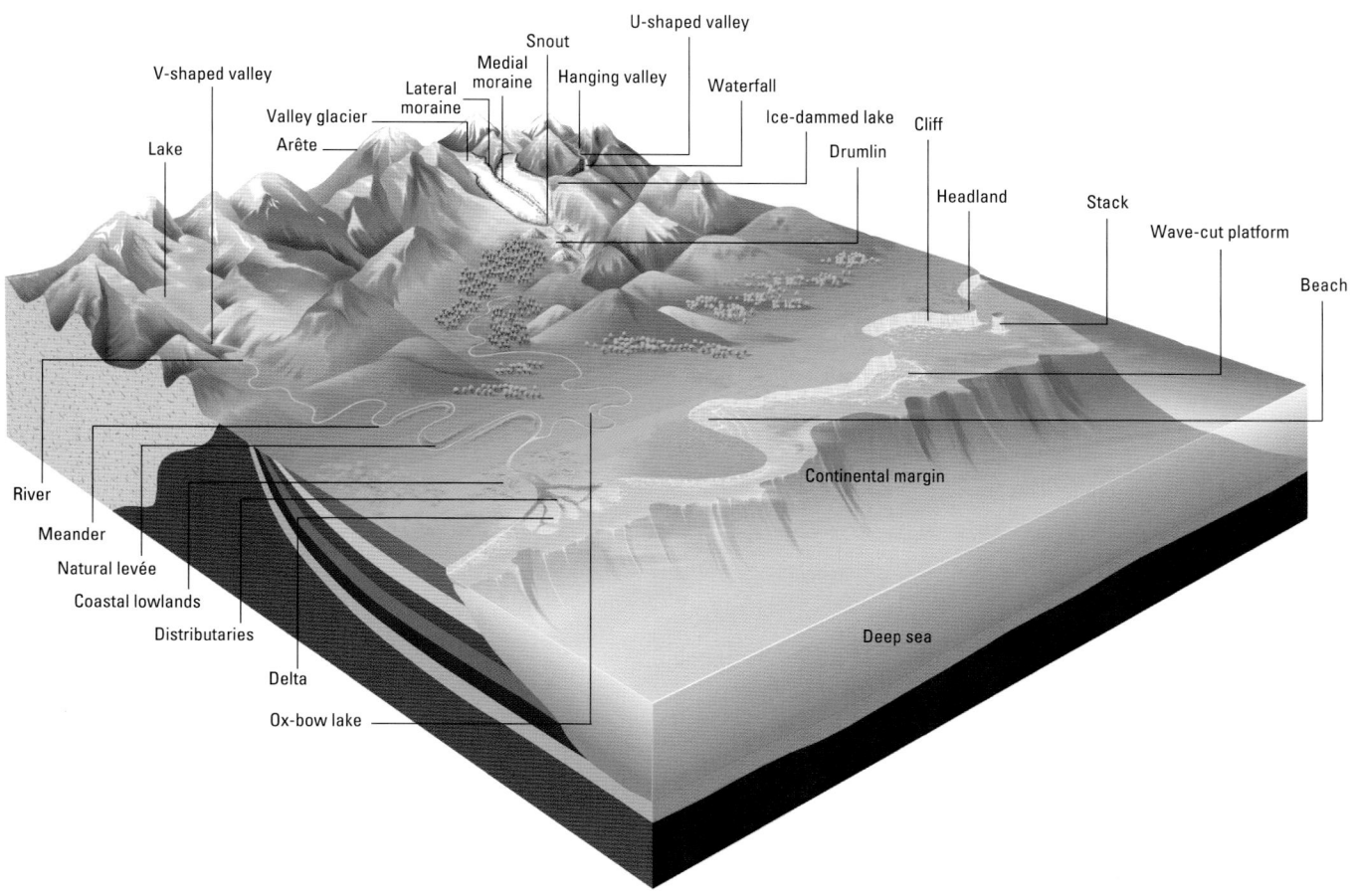

V-shaped valley

Snout

U-shaped valley

Medial moraine

Lateral moraine

Hanging valley

Waterfall

Valley glacier

Arête

Ice-dammed lake

Cliff

Lake

Drumlin

Headland

Stack

Wave-cut platform

Beach

River

Meander

Natural levée

Coastal lowlands

Distributaries

Continental margin

Delta

Deep sea

Ox-bow lake

Desert Landscapes

The popular image that deserts are all huge expanses of sand is wrong. Despite harsh conditions, deserts contain some of the most varied and interesting landscapes in the world. They are also one of the most extensive environments – the hot and cold deserts together cover almost 40% of the Earth's surface.

The three types of hot desert are known by their Arabic names: sand desert, called *erg*, covers only about one-fifth of the world's desert; the rest is divided between *hammada* (areas of bare rock) and *reg* (broad plains covered by loose gravel or pebbles).

In areas of *erg*, such as the Namib Desert, the shape of the dunes reflects the character of local winds. Where winds are constant in direction, crescent-shaped *barchan* dunes form. In areas of bare rock, wind-blown sand is a major agent of erosion. The erosion is mainly confined to within 2 m [6.5 ft] of the surface, producing characteristic, mushroom-shaped rocks.

Erg

Hammada

Reg

Surface Processes

Catastrophic changes to natural landforms are periodically caused by such phenomena as avalanches, landslides and volcanic eruptions, but most of the processes that shape the Earth's surface operate extremely slowly in human terms. One estimate, based on a study in the United States, suggested that 1 m [3 ft] of land was removed from the entire surface of the country, on average, every 29,500 years. However, the time-scale varies from 1,300 years to 154,200 years depending on the terrain and climate.

In hot, dry climates, mechanical weathering, a result of rapid temperature changes, causes the outer layers of rock to peel away, while in cold mountainous regions, boulders are prised apart when water freezes in cracks in rocks. Chemical weathering, at its greatest in warm, humid regions, is responsible for hollowing out limestone caves and decomposing granites.

The erosion of soil and rock is greatest on sloping land and the steeper the slope, the greater the tendency for mass wasting – the movement of soil and rock downhill under the influence of gravity. The mechanisms of mass wasting (ranging from very slow to very rapid) vary with the type of material, but the presence of water as a lubricant is usually an important factor.

Running water is the world's leading agent of erosion and transportation. The energy of a river depends on several factors, including its velocity and volume, and its erosive power is at its peak when it is in full flood. Sea waves also exert tremendous erosive power during storms when they hurl pebbles against the shore, undercutting cliffs and hollowing out caves.

Glacier ice forms in mountain hollows and spills out to form valley glaciers, which transport rocks shattered by frost action. As glaciers move, rocks embedded into the ice erode steep-sided, U-shaped valleys. Evidence of glaciation in mountain regions includes cirques, knife-edged ridges, or arêtes, and pyramidal peaks.

Oceans

The Great Oceans

Relative sizes of the world's oceans

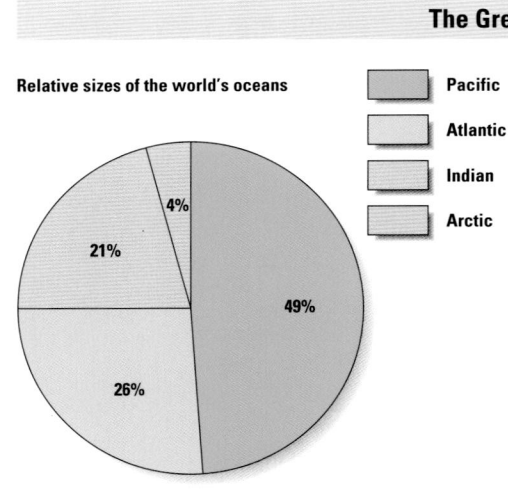

- Pacific
- Atlantic
- Indian
- Arctic

In a strict geographical sense there are only three true oceans – the Atlantic, Indian and Pacific. The legendary 'Seven Seas' would require these to be divided at the Equator and the addition of the Arctic Ocean – which accounts for less than 4% of the total sea area. The International Hydrographic Bureau does not recognize the Antarctic Ocean (even less the 'Southern Ocean') as a separate entity.

The Earth is a watery planet: more than 70% of its surface – over 360,000,000 sq km [140,000,000 sq miles] – is covered by the oceans and seas. The mighty Pacific alone accounts for nearly 36% of the total, and 49% of the sea area. Gravity holds in around 1,400 million cu. km [320 million cu. miles] of water, of which over 97% is saline.

The vast underwater world starts in the shallows of the seaside and plunges to depths of more than 11,000 m [36,000 ft]. The continental shelf, part of the landmass, drops gently to around 200 m [650 ft]; here the seabed falls away suddenly at an angle of 3° to 6° – the continental slope. The third stage, called the continental rise, is more gradual with gradients varying from 1 in 100 to 1 in 700. At an average depth of 5,000 m [16,500 ft] there begins the aptly-named abyssal plain – massive submarine depths where sunlight fails to penetrate and few creatures can survive.

From these plains rise volcanoes which, taken from base to top, rival and even surpass the tallest continental mountains in height. Mount Kea, on Hawaii, reaches a total of 10,203 m [33,400 ft], some 1,355 m [4,500 ft] more than Mount Everest, though scarcely 40% is visible above sea level.

In addition, there are underwater mountain chains up to 1,000 km [600 miles] across, whose peaks sometimes appear above sea level as islands such as Iceland and Tristan da Cunha.

The Ocean Depths

Average and maximum depths of the world's great oceans, in metres

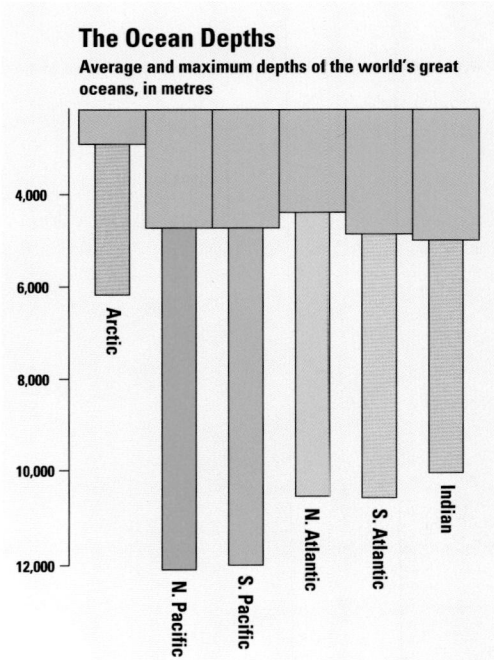

Ocean Currents

January temperatures and ocean currents

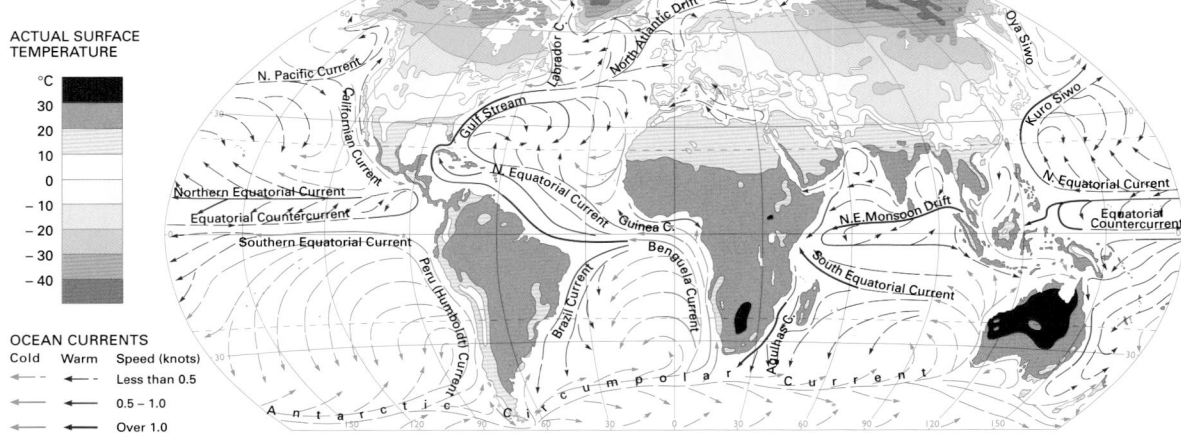

ACTUAL SURFACE TEMPERATURE

°C
- 30
- 20
- 10
- 0
- −10
- −20
- −30
- −40

OCEAN CURRENTS

Cold	Warm	Speed (knots)
		Less than 0.5
		0.5 – 1.0
		Over 1.0

July temperatures and ocean currents

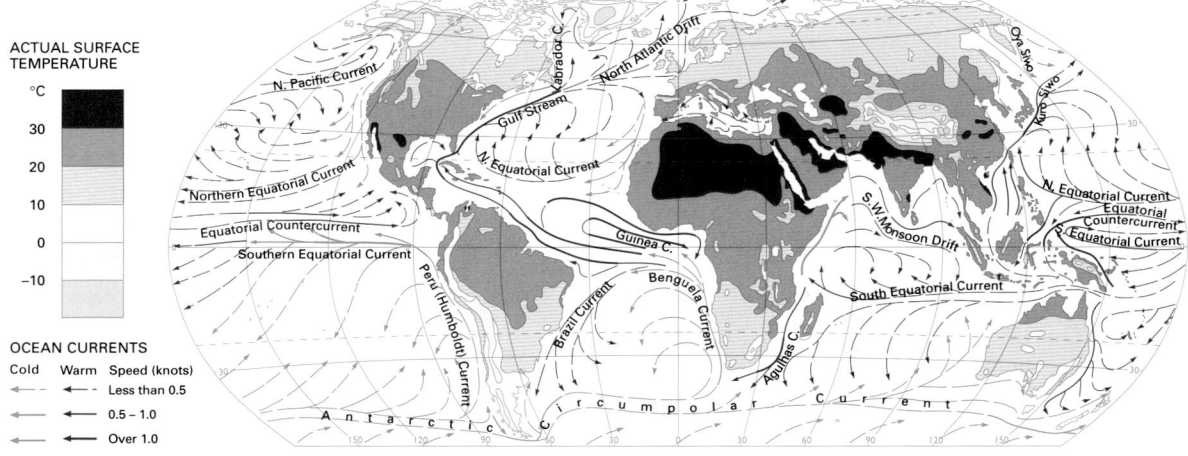

ACTUAL SURFACE TEMPERATURE

°C
- 30
- 20
- 10
- 0
- −10

OCEAN CURRENTS

Cold	Warm	Speed (knots)
		Less than 0.5
		0.5 – 1.0
		Over 1.0

Moving immense quantities of energy as well as billions of tonnes of water every hour, the ocean currents are a vital part of the great heat engine that drives the Earth's climate. They themselves are produced by a twofold mechanism. At the surface, winds push huge masses of water before them; in the deep ocean, below an abrupt temperature gradient that separates the churning surface waters from the still depths, density variations cause slow vertical movements.

The pattern of circulation of the great surface currents is determined by the displacement known as the Coriolis effect. As the Earth turns beneath a moving object – whether it is a tennis ball or a vast mass of water – it appears to be deflected to one side. The deflection is most obvious near the Equator, where the Earth's surface is spinning eastwards at 1,700 km/h [1,050 mph]; currents moving polewards are curved clockwise in the northern hemisphere and anti-clockwise in the southern.

The result is a system of spinning circles known as gyres. The Coriolis effect piles up water on the left of each gyre, creating a narrow, fast-moving stream that is matched by a slower, broader returning current on the right. North and south of the Equator, the fastest currents are located in the west and in the east respectively. In each case, warm water moves from the Equator and cold water returns to it. Cold currents often bring an upwelling of nutrients with them, supporting the world's most economically important fisheries.

Depending on the prevailing winds, some currents on or near the Equator may reverse their direction in the course of the year – a seasonal variation on which Asian monsoon rains depend, and whose occasional failure can bring disaster to millions.

World Fishing Areas

Main commercial fishing areas (numbered FAO regions)

Catch by top marine fishing areas, thousand tonnes (1997)

1.	Pacific, NW	[61]	26,785	28.7%
2.	Pacific, SE	[87]	15,717	16.8%
3.	Atlantic, NE	[27]	12,721	13.6%
4.	Pacific, WC	[71]	9,753	10.5%
5.	Indian, W	[51]	4,461	4.8%
6.	Indian, E	[57]	4,228	4.5%
7.	Atlantic, EC	[34]	3,873	4.2%
8.	Pacific, NE	[67]	3,042	3.3%

 Principal fishing areas

Leading fishing nations

China 16.8% Peru 8.4% Japan 6.3% Chile 6.2% U.S.A. 5.4% Russia 5.0% India 3.9% Indonesia 3.9%

World total catch (1997): 93,329,200 tonnes
(Marine catch 91.7% Inland catch 8.3%)

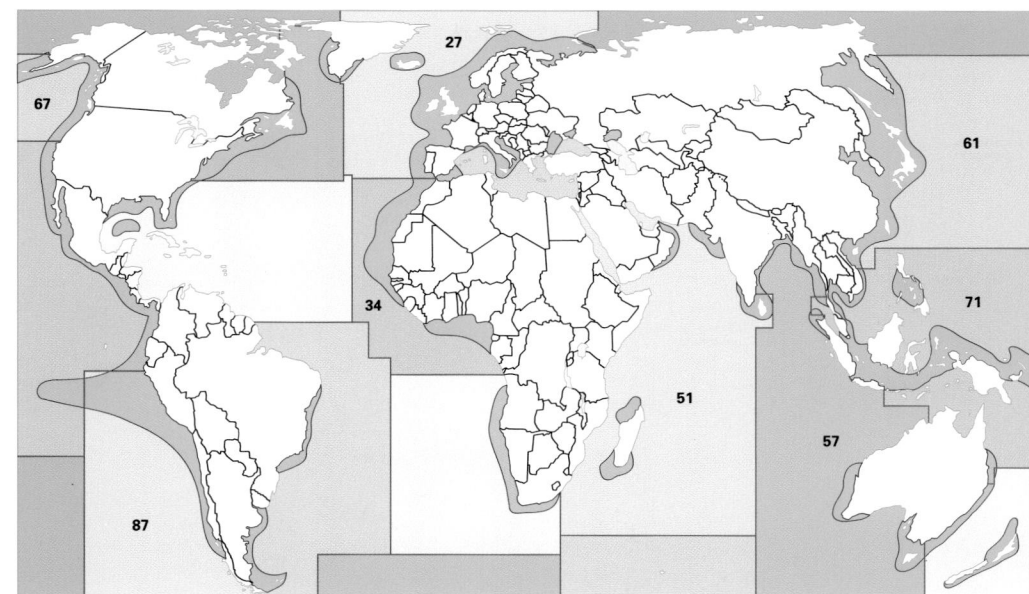

Marine Pollution

Sources of marine oil pollution (latest available year)

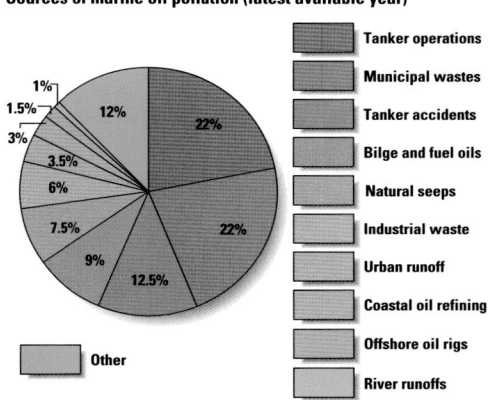

- Tanker operations
- Municipal wastes
- Tanker accidents
- Bilge and fuel oils
- Natural seeps
- Industrial waste
- Urban runoff
- Coastal oil refining
- Offshore oil rigs
- River runoffs
- Other

Oil Spills

Major oil spills from tankers and combined carriers

Year	Vessel	Location	Spill (barrels)**	Cause
1979	Atlantic Empress	West Indies	1,890,000	collision
1983	Castillo De Bellver	South Africa	1,760,000	fire
1978	Amoco Cadiz	France	1,628,000	grounding
1991	Haven	Italy	1,029,000	explosion
1988	Odyssey	Canada	1,000,000	fire
1967	Torrey Canyon	UK	909,000	grounding
1972	Sea Star	Gulf of Oman	902,250	collision
1977	Hawaiian Patriot	Hawaiian Is.	742,500	fire
1979	Independenta	Turkey	696,350	collision
1993	Braer	UK	625,000	grounding
1996	Sea Empress	UK	515,000	grounding

Other sources of major oil spills

Year	Vessel	Location	Spill (barrels)**	Cause
1983	Nowruz oilfield	The Gulf	4,250,000†	war
1979	Ixtoc 1 oilwell	Gulf of Mexico	4,200,000	blow-out
1991	Kuwait	The Gulf	2,500,000†	war

** 1 barrel = 0.136 tonnes/159 lit./35 Imperial gal./42 US gal. † estimated

River Pollution

Sources of river pollution, USA (latest available year)

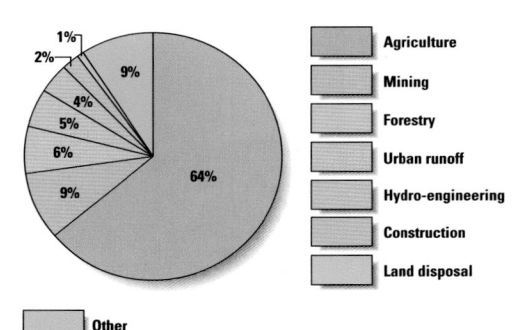

- Agriculture
- Mining
- Forestry
- Urban runoff
- Hydro-engineering
- Construction
- Land disposal
- Other

Water Pollution

 Severely polluted sea areas and lakes

 Polluted sea areas and lakes

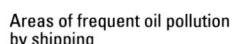 Areas of frequent oil pollution by shipping

▶ Major oil tanker spills

▲ Major oil rig blow-outs

▼ Offshore dumpsites for industrial and municipal waste

—— Severely polluted rivers and estuaries

The most notorious tanker spillage of the 1980s occurred when the *Exxon Valdez* ran aground in Prince William Sound, Alaska, in 1989, spilling 267,000 barrels of crude oil close to shore in a sensitive ecological area. This rates as the world's 28th worst spill in terms of volume.

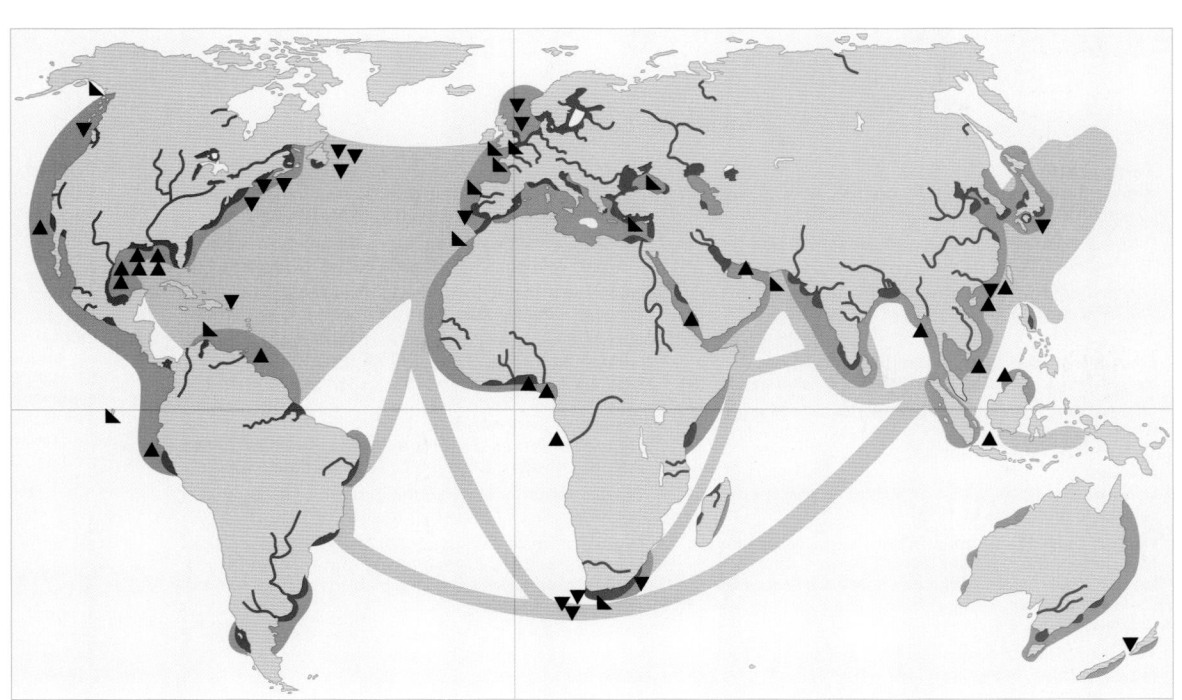

Climate

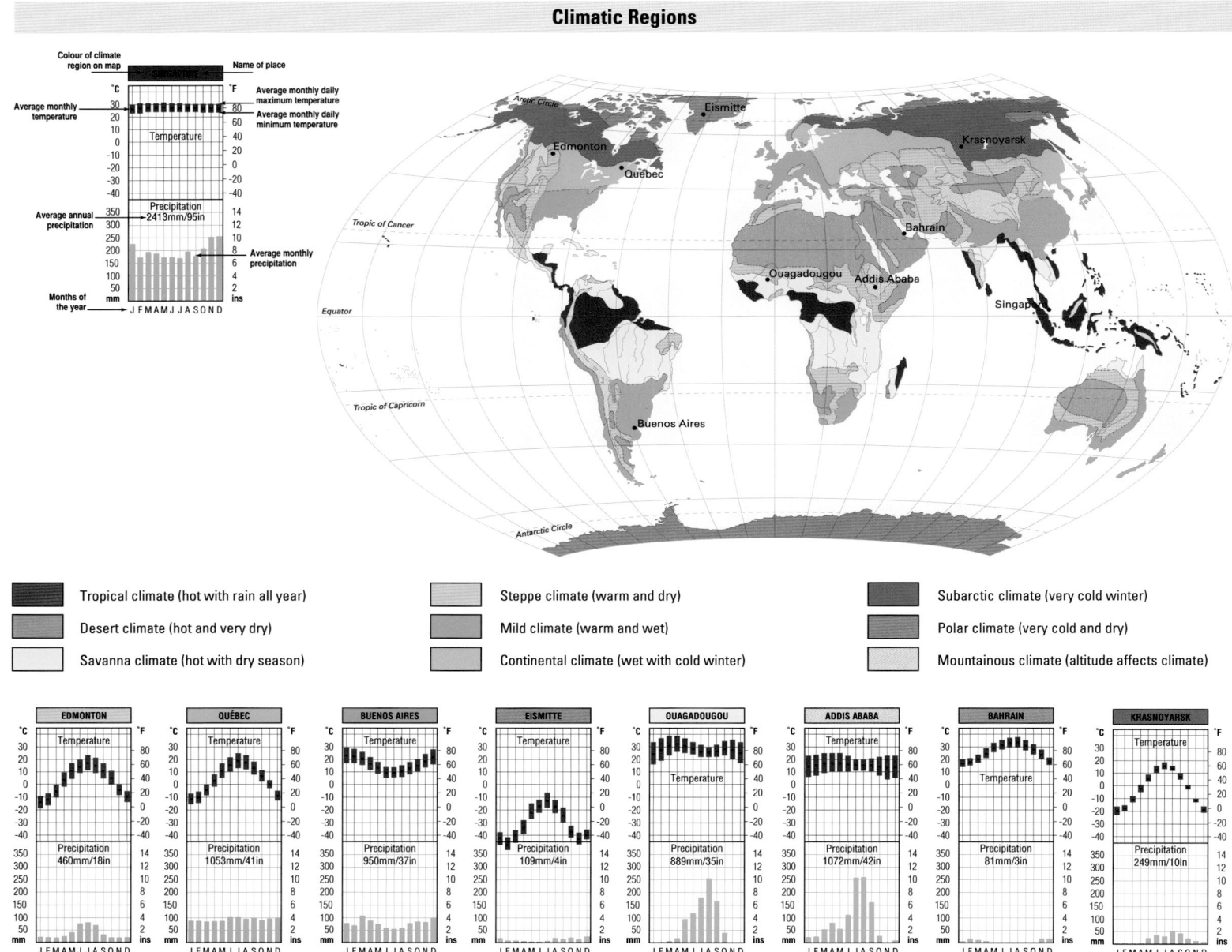

Tropical climate (hot with rain all year)

Desert climate (hot and very dry)

Savanna climate (hot with dry season)

Steppe climate (warm and dry)

Mild climate (warm and wet)

Continental climate (wet with cold winter)

Subarctic climate (very cold winter)

Polar climate (very cold and dry)

Mountainous climate (altitude affects climate)

Climate Records

Temperature

Highest recorded shade temperature: Al Aziziyah, Libya, 58°C [136.4°F], 13 September 1922.

Highest mean annual temperature: Dallol, Ethiopia, 34.4°C [94°F], 1960–66.

Longest heatwave: Marble Bar, W. Australia, 162 days over 38°C [100°F], 23 October 1923 to 7 April 1924.

Lowest recorded temperature (outside poles): Verkhoyansk, Siberia, –68°C [–90°F], 6 February 1933.

Lowest mean annual temperature: Plateau Station, Antarctica, –56.6°C [–72.0°F]

Pressure

Longest drought: Calama, N. Chile, no recorded rainfall in 400 years to 1971.

Wettest place (12 months): Cherrapunji, Meghalaya, N. E. India, 26,470 mm [1,040 in], August 1860 to August 1861. Cherrapunji also holds the record for the most rainfall in one month: 2,930 mm [115 in], July 1861.

Wettest place (average): Mawsynram, India, mean annual rainfall 11,873 mm [467.4 in].

Wettest place (24 hours): Cilaos, Réunion, Indian Ocean, 1,870 mm [73.6 in], 15–16 March 1952.

Heaviest hailstones: Gopalganj, Bangladesh, up to 1.02 kg [2.25 lb], 14 April 1986 (killed 92 people).

Heaviest snowfall (continuous): Bessans, Savoie, France, 1,730 mm [68 in] in 19 hours, 5–6 April 1969.

Heaviest snowfall (season/year): Paradise Ranger Station, Mt Rainier, Washington, USA, 31,102 mm [1,224.5 in], 19 February 1971 to 18 February 1972.

Pressure and winds

Highest barometric pressure: Agata, Siberia (at 262 m [862 ft] altitude), 1,083.8 mb, 31 December 1968.

Lowest barometric pressure: Typhoon Tip, Guam, Pacific Ocean, 870 mb, 12 October 1979.

Highest recorded wind speed: Mt Washington, New Hampshire, USA, 371 km/h [231 mph], 12 April 1934. This is three times as strong as hurricane force on the Beaufort Scale.

Windiest place: Commonwealth Bay, Antarctica, where gales frequently reach over 320 km/h [200 mph].

Climate

Climate is weather in the long term: the seasonal pattern of hot and cold, wet and dry, averaged over time (usually 30 years). At the simplest level, it is caused by the uneven heating of the Earth. Surplus heat at the Equator passes towards the poles, levelling out the energy differential. Its passage is marked by a ceaseless churning of the atmosphere and the oceans, further agitated by the Earth's diurnal spin and the motion it imparts to moving air and water. The heat's means of transport – by winds and ocean currents, by the continual evaporation and recondensation of water molecules – is the weather itself. There are four basic types of climate, each of which can be further subdivided: tropical, desert (dry), temperate and polar.

Composition of Dry Air

Nitrogen	78.09%	Sulphur dioxide	trace
Oxygen	20.95%	Nitrogen oxide	trace
Argon	0.93%	Methane	trace
Water vapour	0.2–4.0%	Dust	trace
Carbon dioxide	0.03%	Helium	trace
Ozone	0.00006%	Neon	trace

El Niño

In a normal year, south-easterly trade winds drive surface waters westwards off the coast of South America, drawing cold, nutrient-rich water up from below. In an El Niño year (which occurs every 2–7 years), warm water from the west Pacific suppresses upwelling in the east, depriving the region of nutrients. The water is warmed by as much as 7°C [12°F], disturbing the tropical atmospheric circulation. During an intense El Niño, the south-east trade winds change direction and become equatorial westerlies, resulting in climatic extremes in many regions of the world, such as drought in parts of Australia and India, and heavy rainfall in south-eastern USA. An intense El Niño occurred in 1997–8, with resultant freak weather conditions across the entire Pacific region.

Normal year

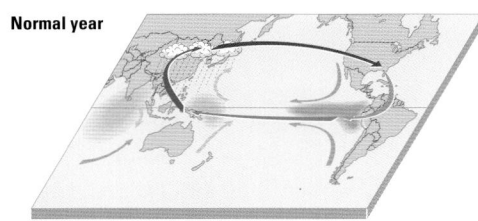

El Niño event

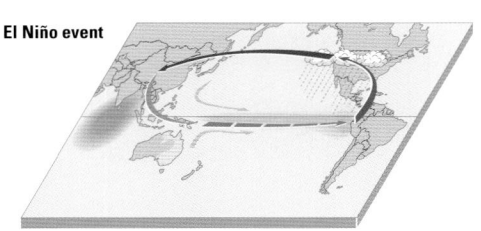

Beaufort Wind Scale

Named after the 19th-century British naval officer who devised it, the Beaufort Scale assesses wind speed according to its effects. It was originally designed as an aid for sailors, but has since been adapted for use on the land.

Scale	Wind speed km/h	mph	Effect
0	0–1	0–1	**Calm** Smoke rises vertically
1	1–5	1–3	**Light air** Wind direction shown only by smoke drift
2	6–11	4–7	**Light breeze** Wind felt on face; leaves rustle; vanes moved by wind
3	12–19	8–12	**Gentle breeze** Leaves and small twigs in constant motion; wind extends small flag
4	20–28	13–18	**Moderate** Raises dust and loose paper; small branches move
5	29–38	19–24	**Fresh** Small trees in leaf sway; wavelets on inland waters
6	39–49	25–31	**Strong** Large branches move; difficult to use umbrellas
7	50–61	32–38	**Near gale** Whole trees in motion; difficult to walk against wind
8	62–74	39–46	**Gale** Twigs break from trees; walking very difficult
9	75–88	47–54	**Strong gale** Slight structural damage
10	89–102	55–63	**Storm** Trees uprooted; serious structural damage
11	103–117	64–72	**Violent storm** Widespread damage
12	118+	73+	**Hurricane**

Conversions
°C = (°F − 32) × 5/9; °F = (°C × 9/5) + 32; 0°C = 32°F
1 in = 25.4 mm; 1 mm = 0.0394 in; 100 mm = 3.94 in

Temperature

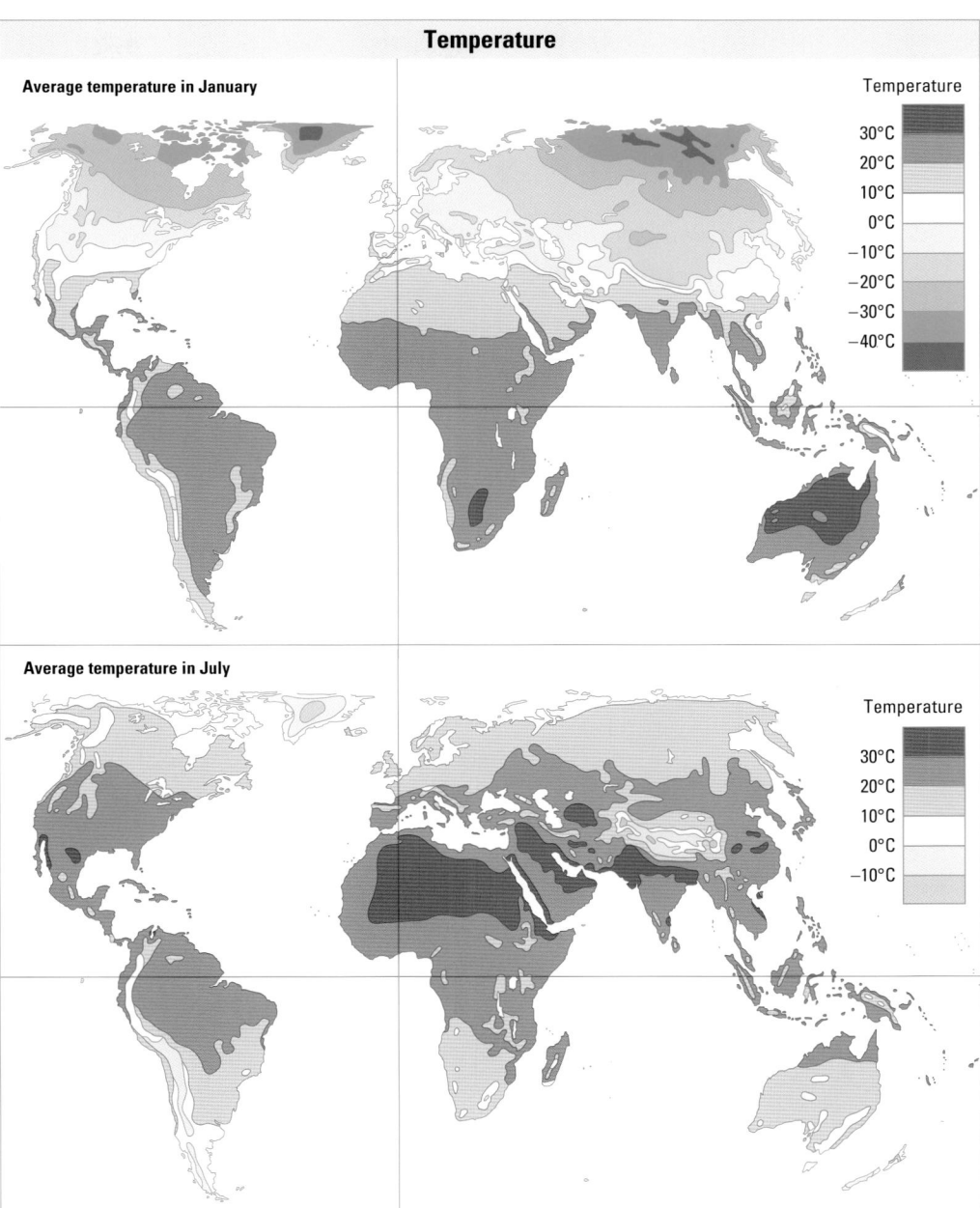

Average temperature in January

Temperature
- 30°C
- 20°C
- 10°C
- 0°C
- −10°C
- −20°C
- −30°C
- −40°C

Average temperature in July

Temperature
- 30°C
- 20°C
- 10°C
- 0°C
- −10°C

Precipitation

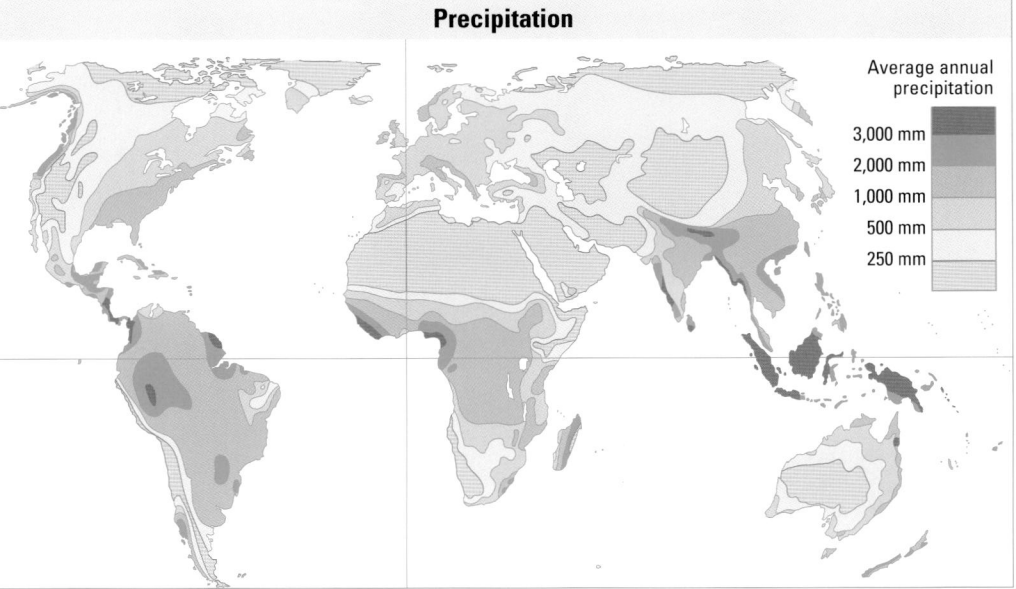

Average annual precipitation
- 3,000 mm
- 2,000 mm
- 1,000 mm
- 500 mm
- 250 mm

Water and Vegetation

The Hydrological Cycle

The world's water balance is regulated by the constant recycling of water between the oceans, atmosphere and land. The movement of water between these three reservoirs is known as the hydrological cycle. The oceans play a vital role in the hydrological cycle: 74% of the total precipitation falls over the oceans and 84% of the total evaporation comes from the oceans.

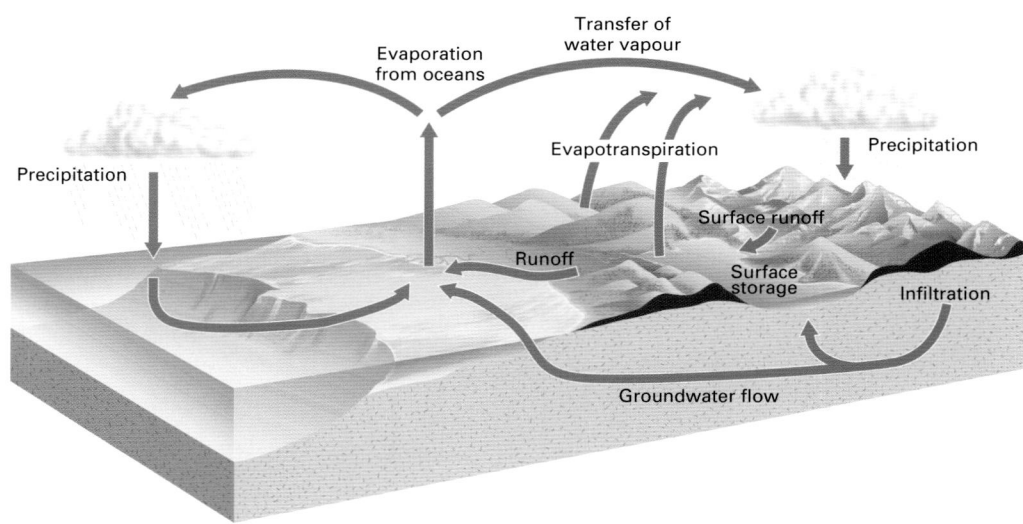

Water Distribution

The distribution of planetary water, by percentage. Oceans and ice caps together account for more than 99% of the total; the breakdown of the remainder is estimated.

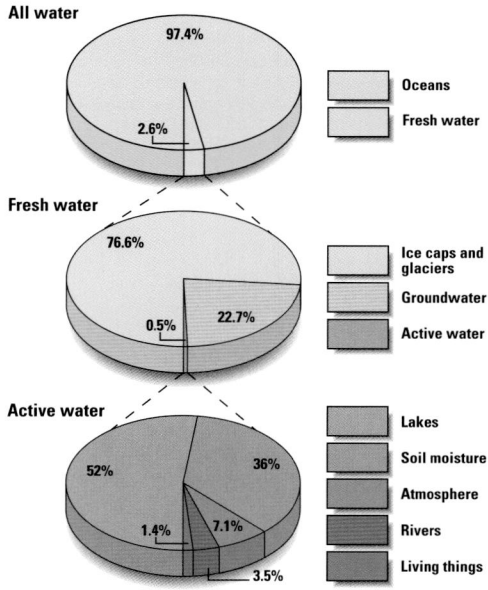

All water
- Oceans 97.4%
- Fresh water 2.6%

Fresh water
- Ice caps and glaciers 76.6%
- Groundwater 22.7%
- Active water 0.5%

Active water
- Lakes 52%
- Soil moisture 36%
- Atmosphere 7.1%
- Rivers 1.4%
- Living things 3.5%

Water Utilization

Domestic | Industrial | Agriculture

The percentage breakdown of water usage by sector, selected countries (1996)

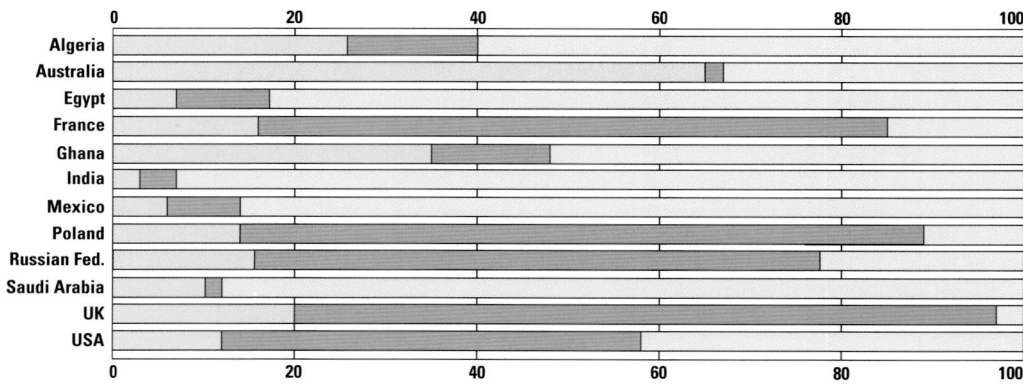

Algeria, Australia, Egypt, France, Ghana, India, Mexico, Poland, Russian Fed., Saudi Arabia, UK, USA

Water Usage

Almost all the world's water is 3,000 million years old, and all of it cycles endlessly through the hydrosphere, though at different rates. Water vapour circulates over days, even hours, deep ocean water circulates over millennia, and ice-cap water remains solid for millions of years.

Fresh water is essential to all terrestrial life. Humans cannot survive more than a few days without it, and even the hardiest desert plants and animals could not exist without some water. Agriculture requires huge quantities of fresh water: without large-scale irrigation most of the world's people would starve. In the USA, agriculture uses 42% and industry 45% of all water withdrawals.

The United States is one of the heaviest users of water in the world. According to the latest figures the average American uses 380 litres a day and the average household uses 415,000 litres a year. This is two to four times more than in Western Europe.

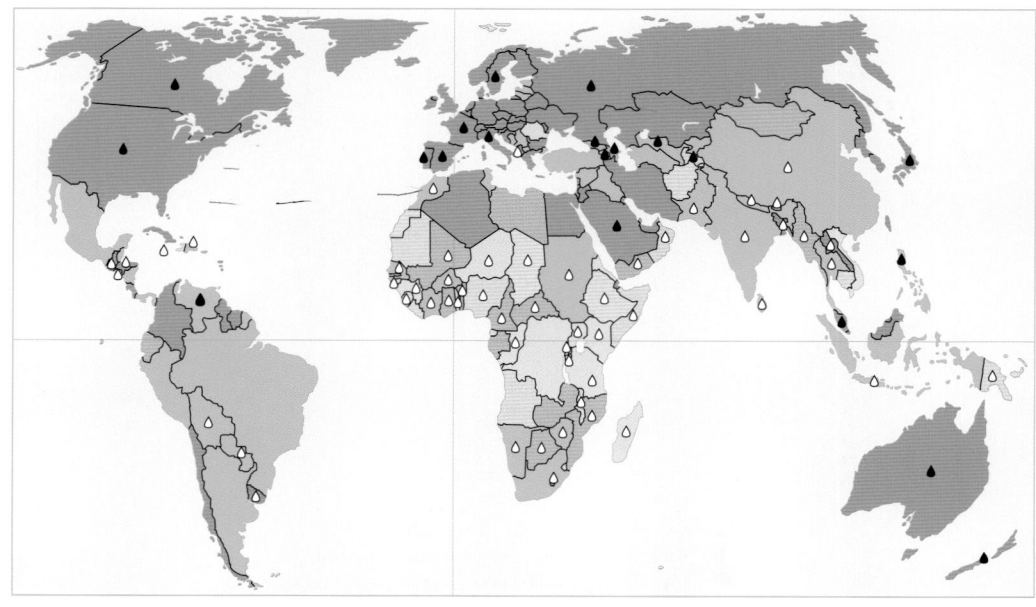

Water Supply

Percentage of total population with access to safe drinking water (2000)

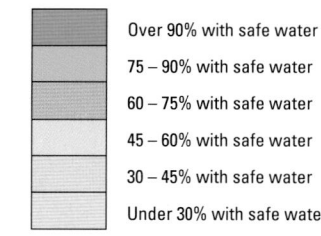

- Over 90% with safe water
- 75 – 90% with safe water
- 60 – 75% with safe water
- 45 – 60% with safe water
- 30 – 45% with safe water
- Under 30% with safe water

△ Under 80 litres per person per day domestic water consumption

▲ Over 320 litres per person per day domestic water consumption

NB: 80 litres of water a day is considered necessary for a reasonable quality of life.

Least well-provided countries

Afghanistan	13%	Sierra Leone	28%
Ethiopia	24%	Cambodia	30%
Chad	27%	Mauritania	37%

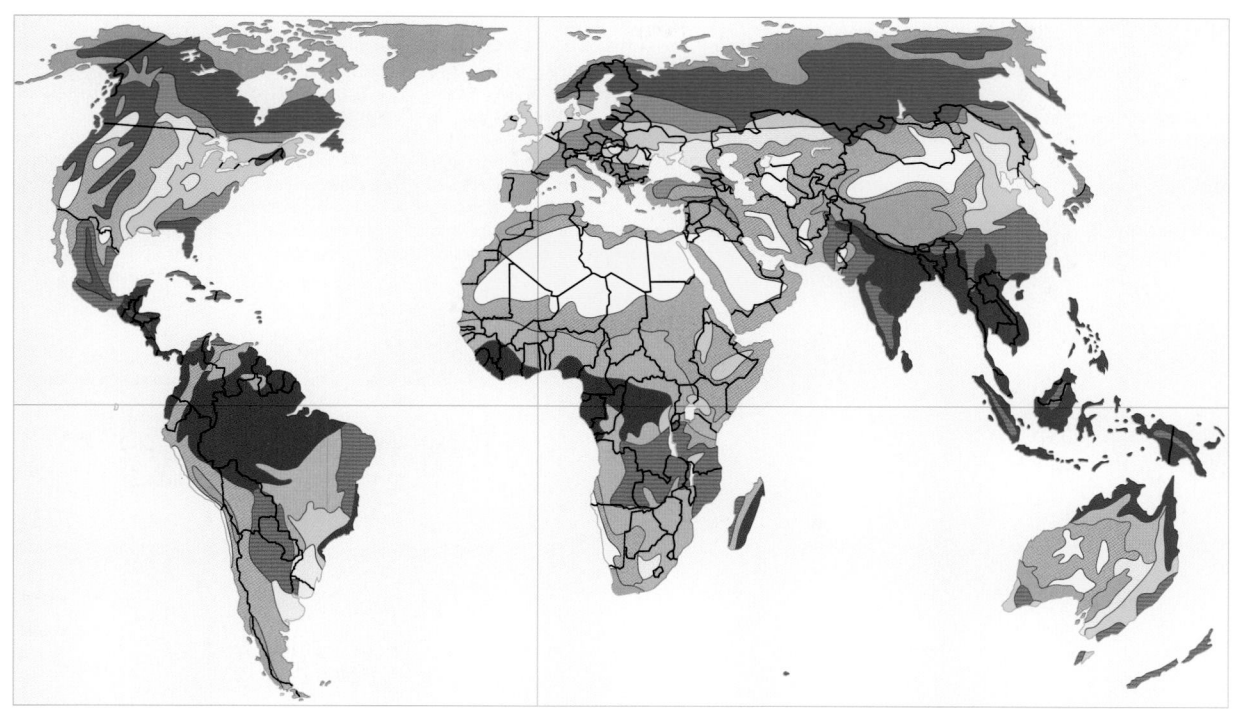

Natural Vegetation

Regional variation in vegetation

- Tundra and mountain vegetation
- Needleleaf evergreen forest
- Mixed needleleaf evergreen & broadleaf deciduous trees
- Broadleaf deciduous woodland
- Mid-latitude grassland
- Evergreen broadleaf and deciduous trees & shrubs
- Semi-desert scrub
- Desert
- Tropical grassland (savanna)
- Tropical broadleaf rainforest and monsoon forest
- Subtropical broadleaf and needleleaf forest

The map shows the natural 'climax vegetation' of regions, as dictated by climate and topography. In most cases, however, agricultural activity has drastically altered the vegetation pattern. Western Europe, for example, lost most of its broadleaf forest many centuries ago, while irrigation has turned some natural semi-desert into productive land.

Land Use by Continent

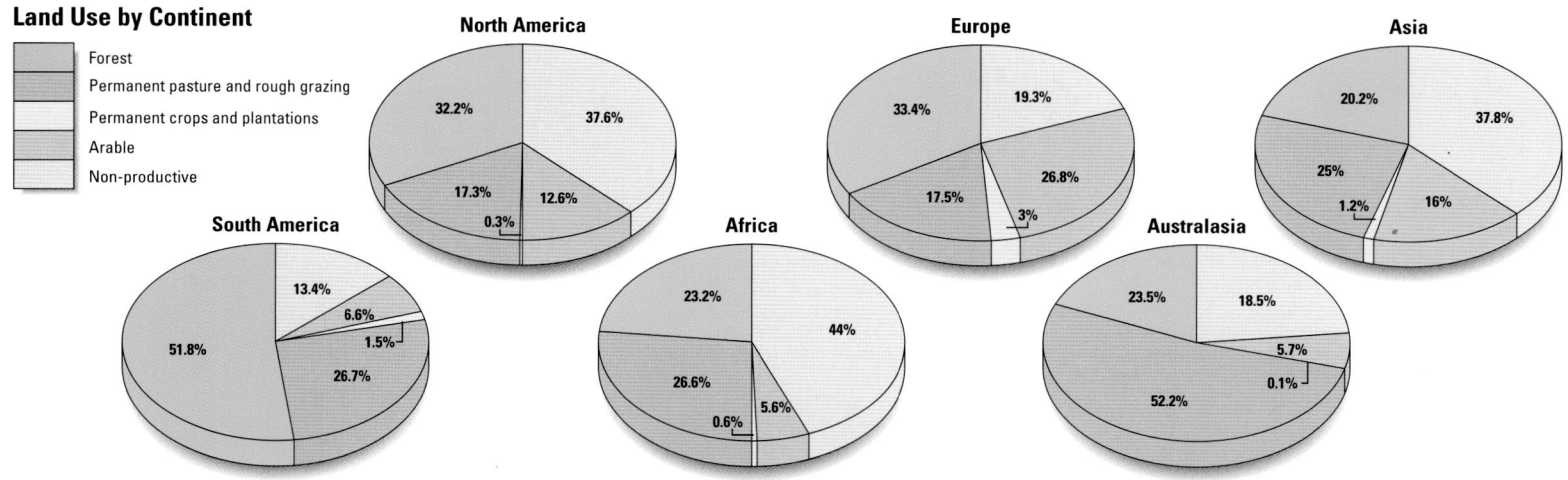

- Forest
- Permanent pasture and rough grazing
- Permanent crops and plantations
- Arable
- Non-productive

North America
37.6%, 12.6%, 0.3%, 17.3%, 32.2%

Europe
19.3%, 26.8%, 3%, 17.5%, 33.4%

Asia
37.8%, 16%, 1.2%, 25%, 20.2%

South America
13.4%, 6.6%, 1.5%, 26.7%, 51.8%

Africa
44%, 5.6%, 0.6%, 26.6%, 23.2%

Australasia
18.5%, 5.7%, 0.1%, 52.2%, 23.5%

Forestry: Production

Forest and woodland (million hectares)	Annual production (1996, million cubic metres)	
	Fuelwood and charcoal	Industrial roundwood*
World **3,987.9**	**1,864.8**	**1,489.5**
S. America 829.3	193.0	129.9
N. & C. America 709.8	155.4	600.4
Africa 684.6	519.9	67.9
Asia 131.8	905.2	280.2
Europe 157.3	82.4	369.7
Australasia 157.2	8.7	41.5

Paper and Board

Top producers (1996)**		Top exporters (1996)**	
USA	85,173	Canada	13,393
China	30,253	USA	9,113
Japan	30,014	Finland	8,529
Canada	18,414	Sweden	7,483
Germany	14,733	Germany	6,319

* roundwood is timber as it is felled
** in thousand tonnes

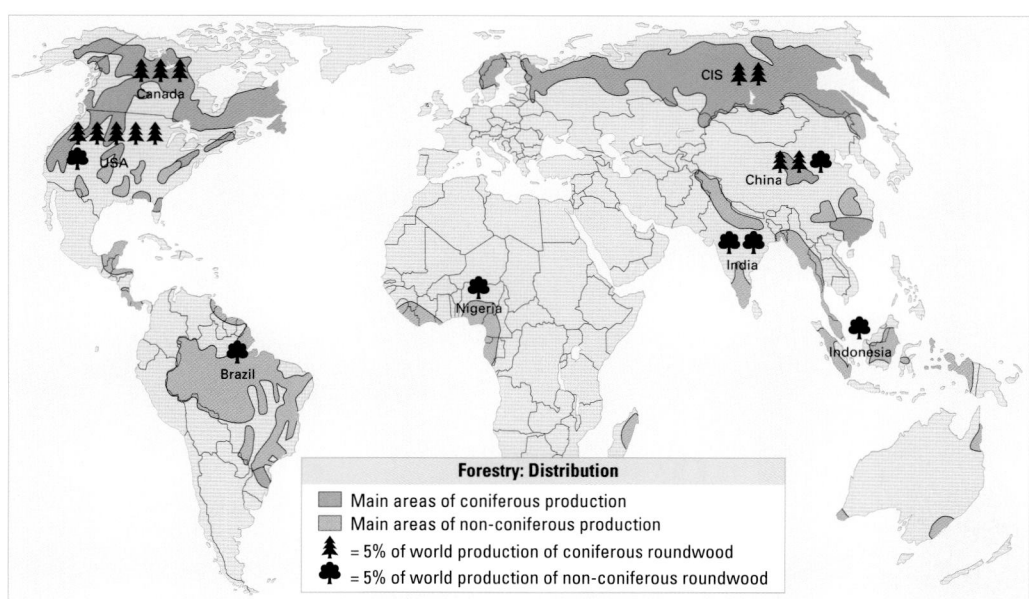

Forestry: Distribution

- Main areas of coniferous production
- Main areas of non-coniferous production
- 🌲 = 5% of world production of coniferous roundwood
- 🌳 = 5% of world production of non-coniferous roundwood

Environment

Humans have always had a dramatic effect on their environment, at least since the development of agriculture almost 10,000 years ago. Generally, the Earth has accepted human interference without obvious ill effects: the complex systems that regulate the global environment have been able to absorb substantial damage while maintaining a stable and comfortable home for the planet's trillions of lifeforms. But advancing human technology and the rapidly-expanding populations it supports are now threatening to overwhelm the Earth's ability to compensate.

Industrial wastes, acid rainfall, desertification and large-scale deforestation all combine to create environmental change at a rate far faster than the great slow cycles of planetary evolution can accommodate. As a result of overcultivation, overgrazing and overcutting of groundcover for firewood, desertification is affecting as much as 60% of the world's croplands. In addition, with fire and chain-saws, humans are destroying more forest in a day than their ancestors could have done in a century, upsetting the balance between plant and animal, carbon dioxide and oxygen, on which all life ultimately depends.

The fossil fuels that power industrial civilization have pumped enough carbon dioxide and other so-called greenhouse gases into the atmosphere to make climatic change a near-certainty. As a result of the combination of these factors, the Earth's average temperature has risen by approximately 0.5°C [1°F] since the beginning of the 20th century, and it is still rising.

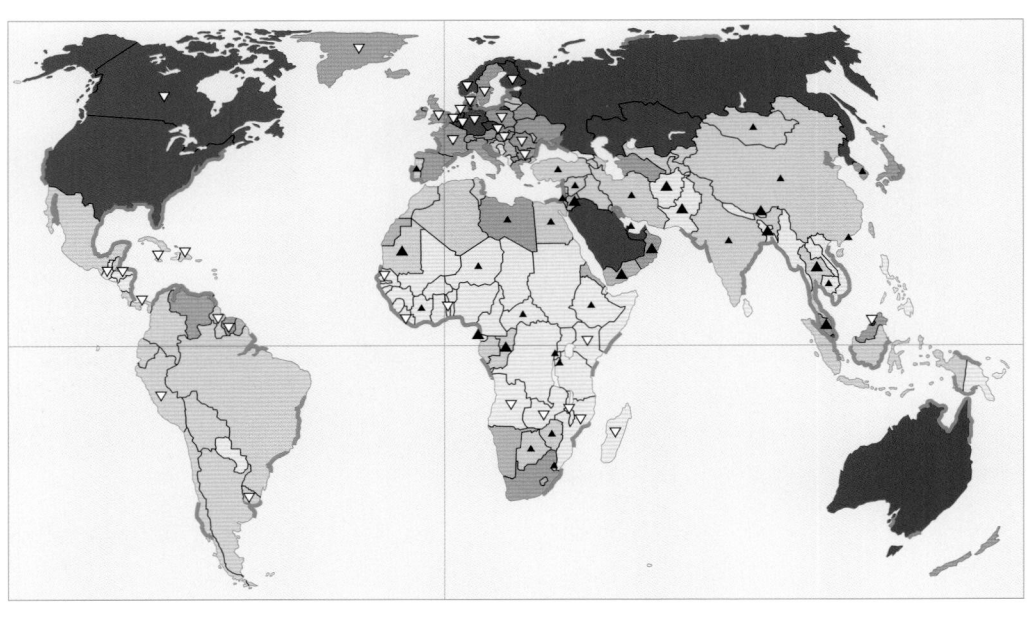

Global Warming

Carbon dioxide emissions in tonnes per person per year (latest available year)

- Over 10 tonnes of CO_2
- 5 – 10 tonnes of CO_2
- 1 – 5 tonnes of CO_2
- Under 1 tonne of CO_2
- No data available

Changes in CO_2 emissions 1980–90

- ▲ Over 100% increase in emissions
- ▲ 50–100% increase in emissions
- ▽ Reduction in emissions
- ─── Coastal areas in danger of flooding from rising sea levels caused by global warming

High atmospheric concentrations of heat-absorbing gases appear to be causing a rise in average temperatures worldwide – up to 1.5°C [3°F] by the year 2020, according to some estimates. Global warming is likely to bring about a rise in sea levels that may flood some of the world's densely populated coastal areas.

Greenhouse Power

Relative contributions to the Greenhouse Effect by the major heat-absorbing gases in the atmosphere.

The chart combines greenhouse potency and volume. Carbon dioxide has a greenhouse potential of only 1, but its concentration of 350 parts per million makes it predominate. CFC 12, with 25,000 times the absorption capacity of CO_2, is present only as 0.00044 ppm.

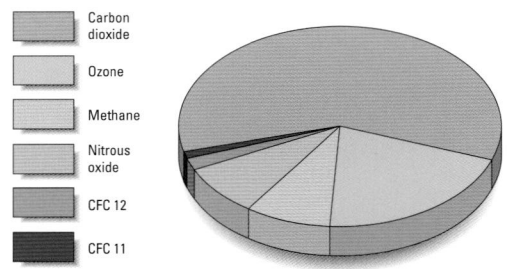

- Carbon dioxide
- Ozone
- Methane
- Nitrous oxide
- CFC 12
- CFC 11

Ozone Layer

The ozone 'hole' over the northern hemisphere on 12 March 1995.

The colours represent Dobson Units (DU). The ozone 'hole' is seen as the dark blue and purple patch in the centre, where ozone values are around 120 DU or lower. Normal levels are around 280 DU. The ozone 'hole' over Antarctica is much larger.

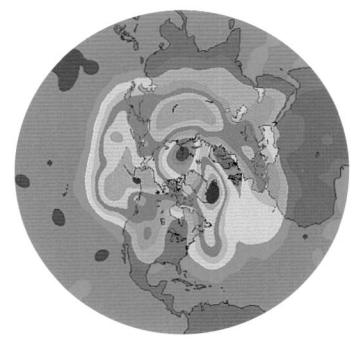

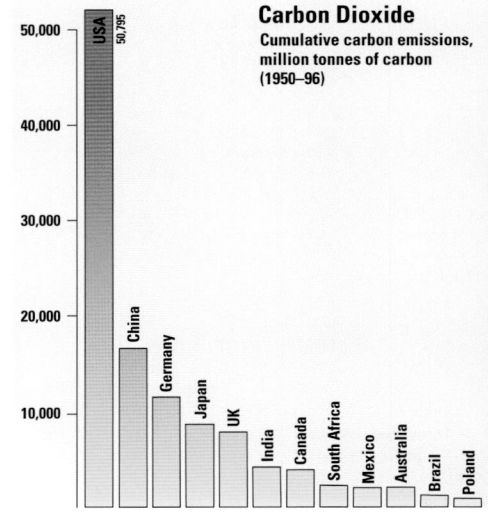

Carbon Dioxide

Cumulative carbon emissions, million tonnes of carbon (1950–96)

USA 50,795

China, Germany, Japan, UK, India, Canada, South Africa, Mexico, Australia, Brazil, Poland

The Greenhouse Effect

Carbon dioxide is increased by burning fossil fuels and cutting forests

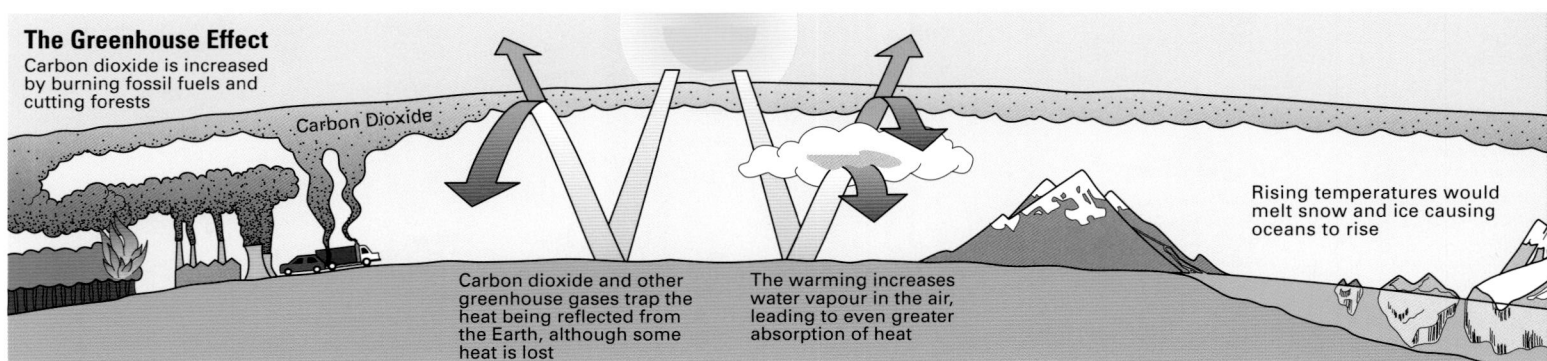

Carbon Dioxide

Carbon dioxide and other greenhouse gases trap the heat being reflected from the Earth, although some heat is lost

The warming increases water vapour in the air, leading to even greater absorption of heat

Rising temperatures would melt snow and ice causing oceans to rise

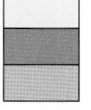

Existing deserts

Areas with a high risk of desertification

Areas with a moderate risk of desertification

Former areas of rainforest

Existing rainforest

Forest Clearance

Thousands of hectares of forest cleared annually, tropical countries surveyed 1981–85, 1987–90 and 1990–5. Loss as a percentage of remaining stocks is shown in figures on each column.

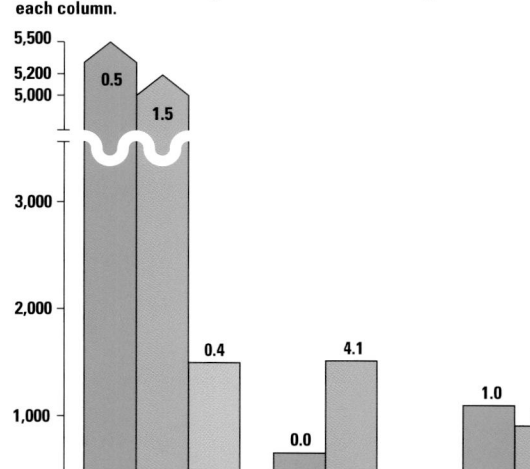

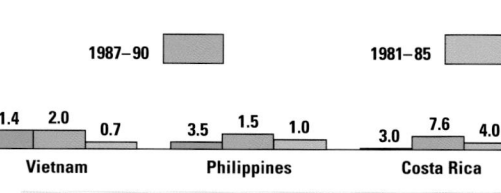

Deforestation

The Earth's remaining forests are under attack from three directions: expanding agriculture, logging, and growing consumption of fuelwood, often in combination. Sometimes deforestation is the direct result of government policy, as in the efforts made to resettle the urban poor in some parts of Brazil; just as often, it comes about despite state attempts at conservation. Loggers, licensed or unlicensed, blaze a trail into virgin forest, often destroying twice as many trees as they harvest. Landless farmers follow, burning away most of what remains to plant their crops, completing the destruction.

Ozone Depletion

The ozone layer, 25–30 km [15–18 miles] above sea level, acts as a barrier to most of the Sun's harmful ultra-violet radiation, protecting us from the ionizing radiation that can cause skin cancer and cataracts. In recent years, however, two holes in the ozone layer have been observed during winter: one over the Arctic and the other, the size of the USA, over Antarctica. By 1996, ozone had been reduced to around a half of its 1970 amount. The ozone (O_3) is broken down by chlorine released into the atmosphere as CFCs (chlorofluorocarbons) – chemicals used in refrigerators, packaging and aerosols.

Air Pollution

Sulphur dioxide is the main pollutant associated with industrial cities. According to the World Health Organization, at least 600 million people live in urban areas where sulphur dioxide concentrations regularly reach damaging levels. One of the world's most dangerously polluted urban areas is Mexico City, due to a combination of its enclosed valley location, 3 million cars and 60,000 factories. In May 1998, this lethal cocktail was added to by nearby forest fires and the resultant air pollution led to over 20% of the population (3 million people) complaining of respiratory problems.

Acid Rain

Killing trees, poisoning lakes and rivers and eating away buildings, acid rain is mostly produced by sulphur dioxide emissions from industry and volcanic eruptions. By the mid 1990s, acid rain had sterilized 4,000 or more of Sweden's lakes and left 45% of Switzerland's alpine conifers dead or dying, while the monuments of Greece were dissolving in Athens' smog. Prevailing wind patterns mean that the acids often fall many hundred kilometres from where the original pollutants were discharged. In parts of Europe acid deposition has slightly decreased, following reductions in emissions, but not by enough.

World Pollution

Acid rain and sources of acidic emissions (latest available year)

Acid rain is caused by high levels of sulphur and nitrogen in the atmosphere. They combine with water vapour and oxygen to form acids (H_2SO_4 and HNO_3) which fall as precipitation.

Regions where sulphur and nitrogen oxides are released in high concentrations, mainly from fossil fuel combustion

• Major cities with high levels of air pollution (including nitrogen and sulphur emissions)

Areas of heavy acid deposition

pH numbers indicate acidity, decreasing from a neutral 7. Normal rain, slightly acid from dissolved carbon dioxide, never exceeds a pH of 5.6.

pH less than 4.0 (most acidic)

pH 4.0 to 4.5

pH 4.5 to 5.0

Areas where acid rain is a potential problem

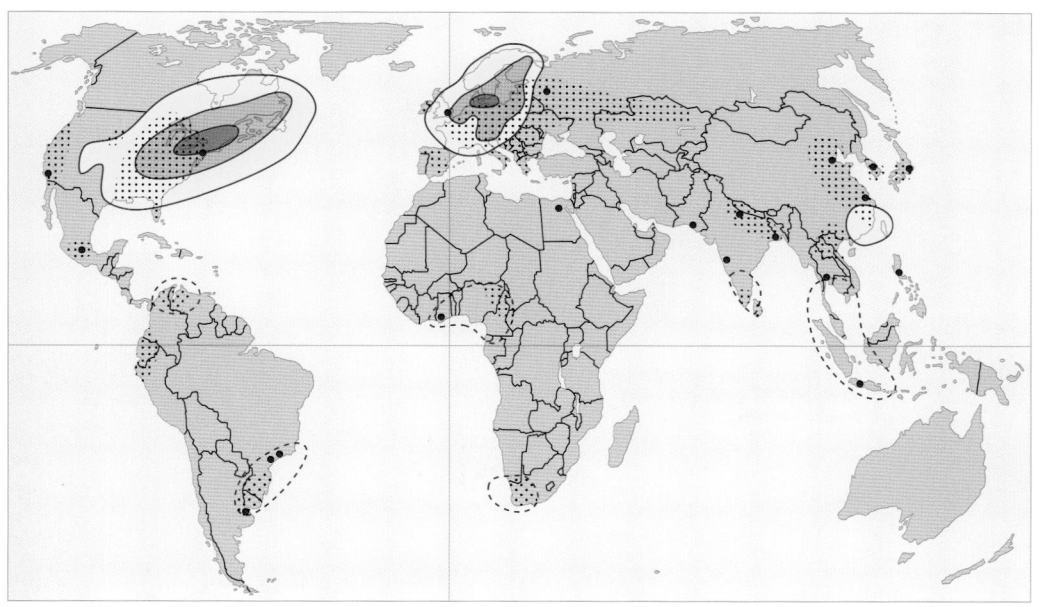

Population

CARTOGRAPHY BY PHILIP'S. COPYRIGHT PHILIP'S

Demographic Profiles

Developed nations such as the UK have populations evenly spread across the age groups and, usually, a growing proportion of elderly people. The great majority of the people in developing nations, however, are in the younger age groups, about to enter their most fertile years. In time, these population profiles should resemble the world profile (even Kenya has made recent progress with reducing its birth rate), but the transition will come about only after a few more generations of rapid population growth.

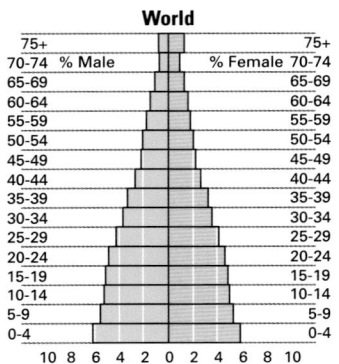

World

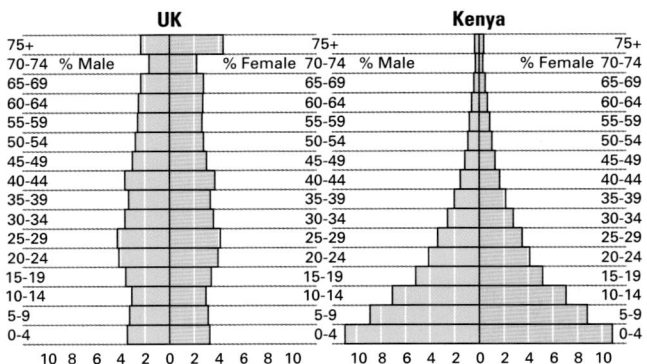

UK

Kenya

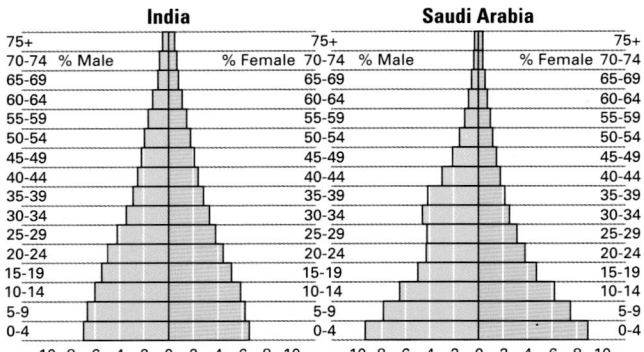

India

Saudi Arabia

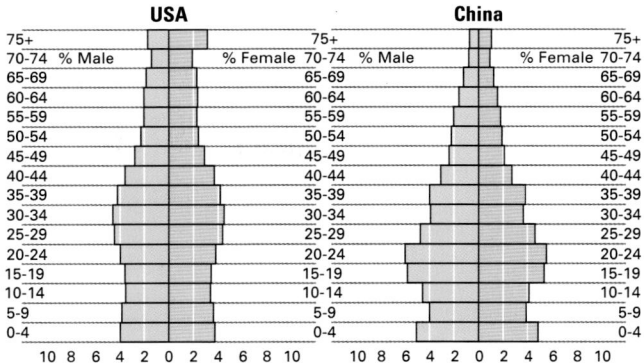

USA

China

Most Populous Nations [in millions (2001 estimates)]

1.	China	1,273	9. Japan	127	17. Iran	66
2.	India	1,003	10. Nigeria	127	18. Ethiopia	66
3.	USA	278	11. Mexico	102	19. Thailand	62
4.	Indonesia	228	12. Germany	83	20. UK	60
5.	Brazil	174	13. Philippines	83	21. France	60
6.	Russia	145	14. Vietnam	80	22. Italy	58
7.	Pakistan	145	15. Egypt	70	23. Congo (Dem. Rep.)	54
8.	Bangladesh	131	16. Turkey	66	24. Ukraine	49

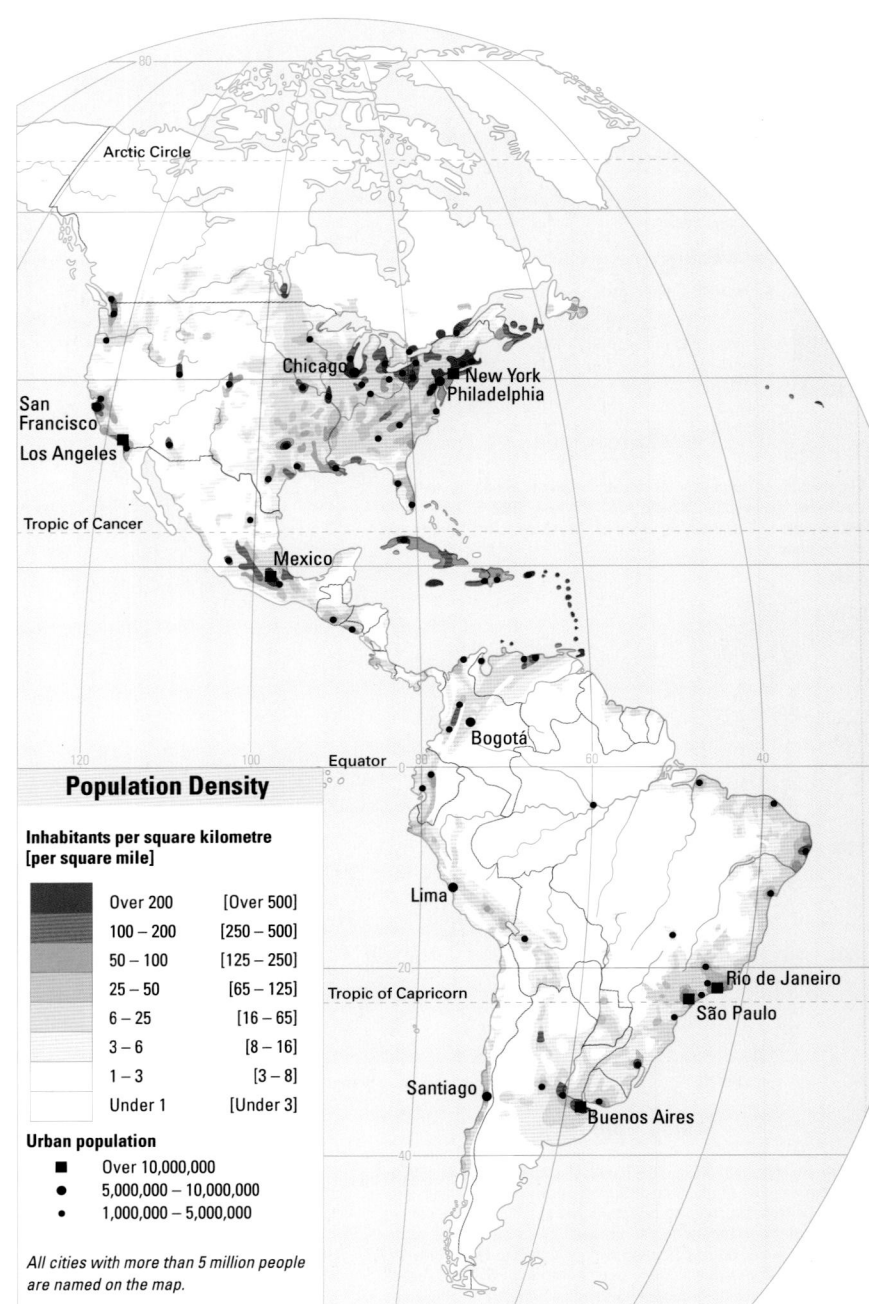

Population Density

Inhabitants per square kilometre
[per square mile]

	Over 200	[Over 500]
	100 – 200	[250 – 500]
	50 – 100	[125 – 250]
	25 – 50	[65 – 125]
	6 – 25	[16 – 65]
	3 – 6	[8 – 16]
	1 – 3	[3 – 8]
	Under 1	[Under 3]

Urban population

- ■ Over 10,000,000
- ● 5,000,000 – 10,000,000
- • 1,000,000 – 5,000,000

All cities with more than 5 million people are named on the map.

Continental Comparisons

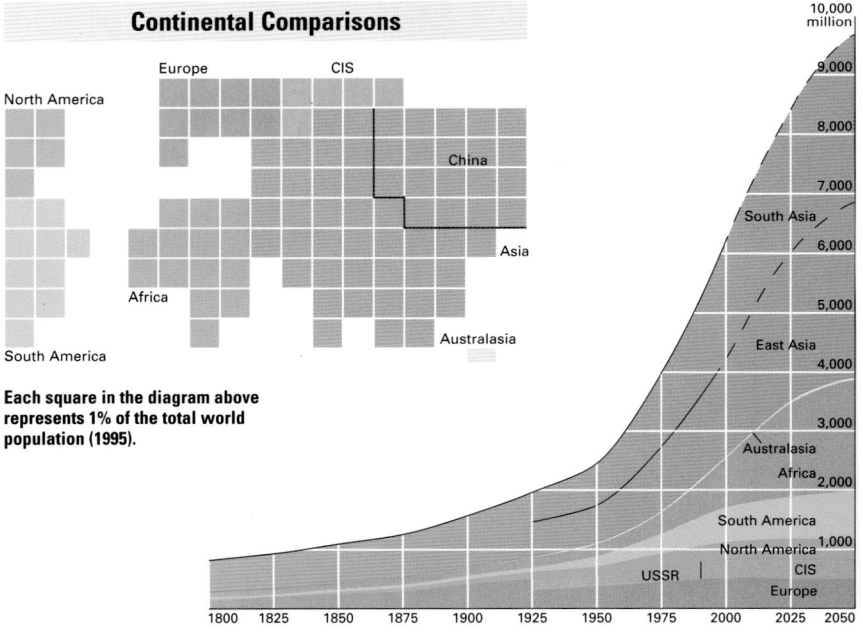

Each square in the diagram above represents 1% of the total world population (1995).

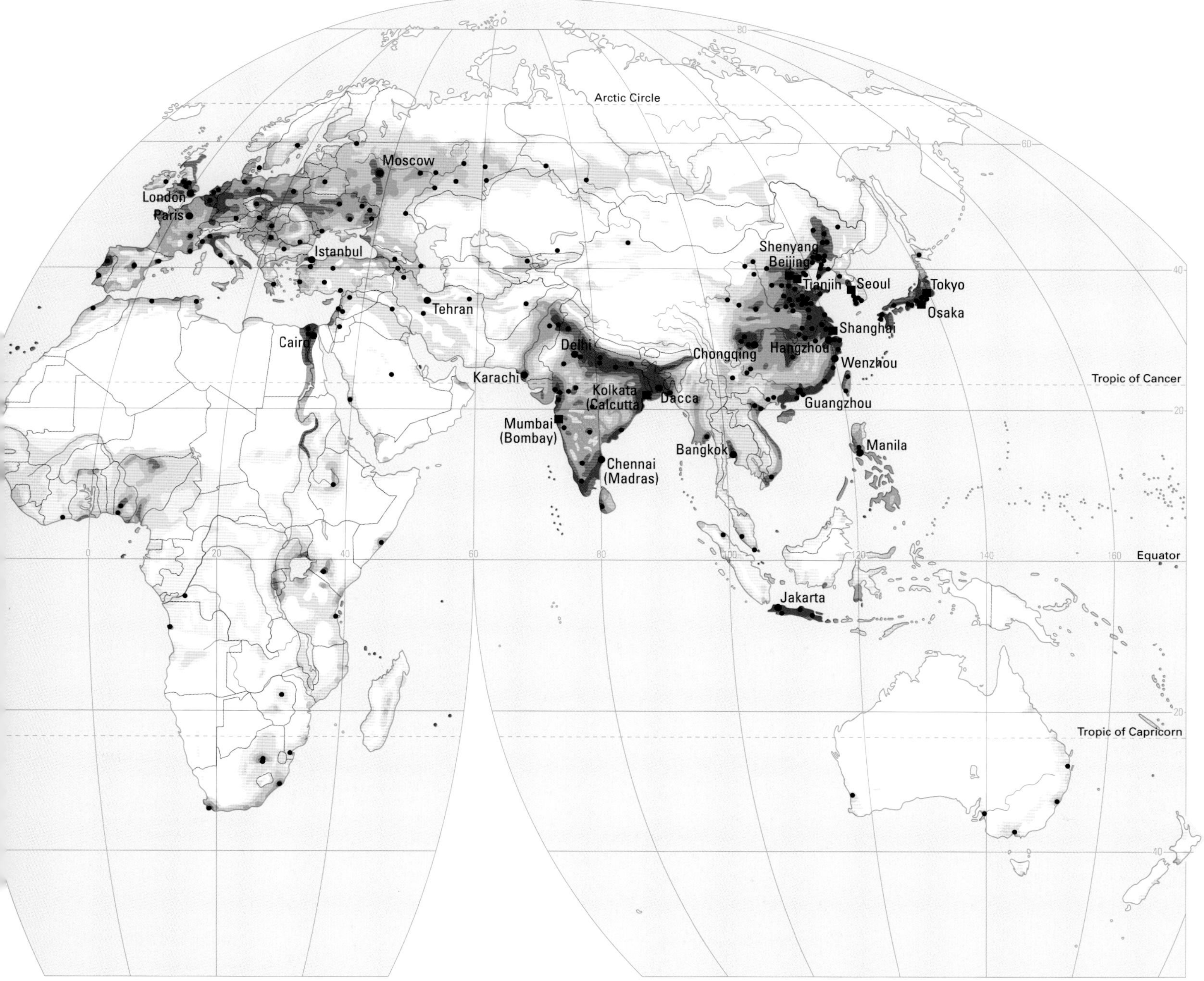

Arctic Circle

Moscow

London
Paris

Istanbul

Tehran

Cairo

Karachi

Delhi

Mumbai
(Bombay)

Kolkata
(Calcutta)

Dacca

Chennai
(Madras)

Bangkok

Shenyang
Beijing

Tianjin   Seoul   Tokyo

Osaka

Shanghai

Chongqing   Hangzhou

Wenzhou

Guangzhou

Manila

Jakarta

Tropic of Cancer

Equator

Tropic of Capricorn

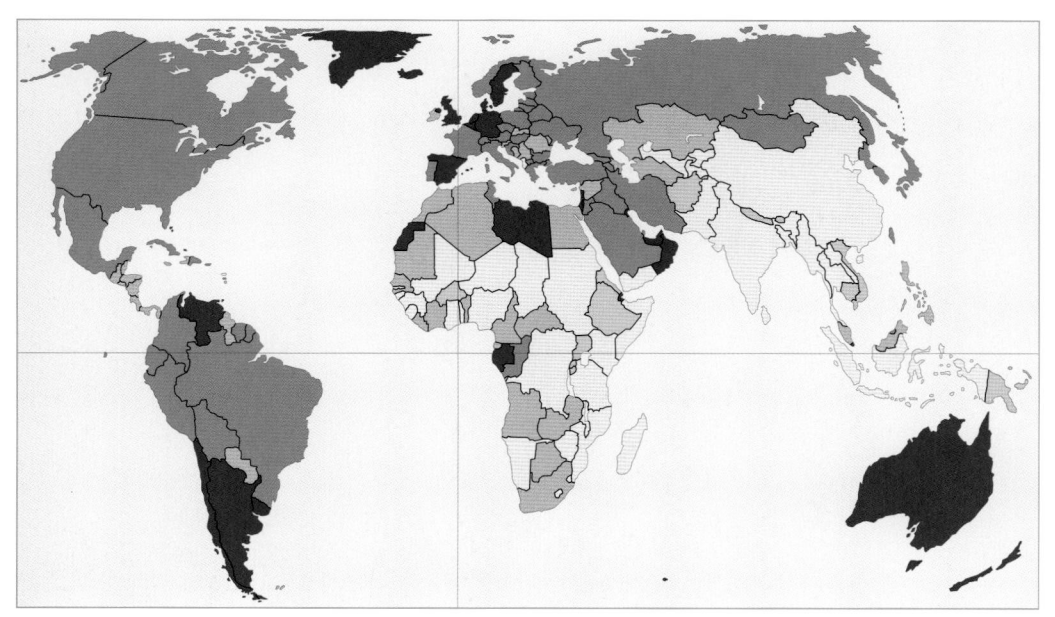

Urban Population

Percentage of total population living in towns and cities (2000)

	Over 80%
	60 – 80%
	40 – 60%
	20 – 40%
	Under 20%

Most urbanized		Least urbanized	
Belgium	97%	Rwanda	6%
W. Sahara	96%	Bhutan	7%
Singapore	93%	East Timor	7%
UAE	93%	Burunda	9%
Iceland	93%	Nepal	11%

[UK 89%]

The Human Family

Predominant Languages

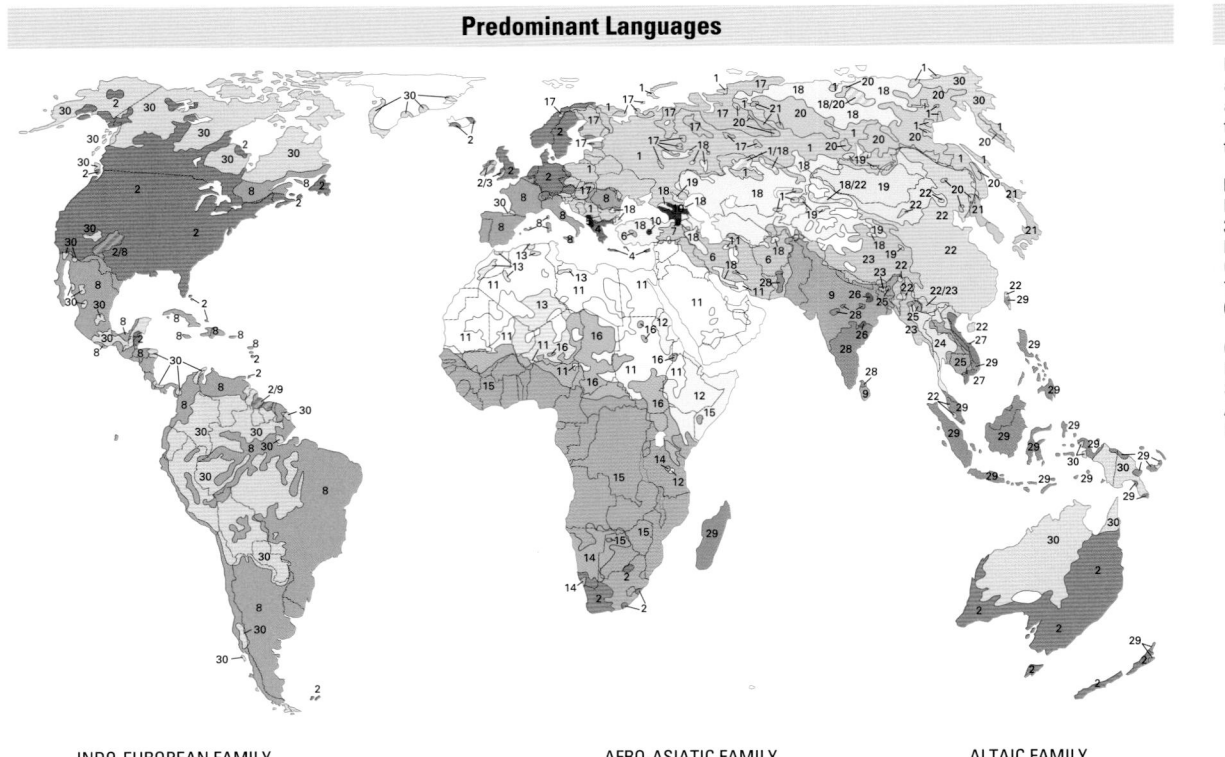

Languages of the World

Language can be classified by ancestry and structure. For example, the Romance and Germanic groups are both derived from an Indo-European language believed to have been spoken 5,000 years ago.

First-language speakers, 1999 (in millions)
Mandarin Chinese 835, Spanish 332, English 322, Bengali 189, Hindi 182, Portuguese 170, Russian 170, Japanese 125, German 98, Wu Chinese 77, Javanese 76, Korean 75, French 72, Vietnamese 68, Yue Chinese 66, Marathi 65, Tamil 63, Turkish 59, Urdu 58.

Official languages (% of total population)
English 27%, Chinese 19%, Hindi 13.5%, Spanish 5.4%, Russian 5.2%, French 4.2%, Arabic 3.3%, Portuguese 3%, Malay 3%, Bengali 2.9%, Japanese 2.3%.

INDO-EUROPEAN FAMILY

1	Balto-Slavic group (incl. Russian, Ukrainian)
2	Germanic group (incl. English, German)
3	Celtic group
4	Greek
	Albanian
6	Iranian group
	Armenian
8	Romance group (incl. Spanish, Portuguese, French, Italian)
9	Indo-Aryan group (incl. Hindi, Bengali, Urdu, Punjabi, Marathi)
	CAUCASIAN FAMILY

AFRO-ASIATIC FAMILY

11	Semitic group (incl. Arabic)
12	Kushitic group
13	Berber group
14	KHOISAN FAMILY
15	NIGER-CONGO FAMILY
16	NILO-SAHARAN FAMILY
17	URALIC FAMILY

ALTAIC FAMILY

18	Turkic group (incl. Turkish)
19	Mongolian group
20	Tungus-Manchu group
21	Japanese and Korean

SINO-TIBETAN FAMILY

22	Sinitic (Chinese) languages (incl. Mandarin, Wu, Yue)
23	Tibetic-Burmic languages
24	TAI FAMILY

AUSTRO-ASIATIC FAMILY

25	Mon-Khmer group
26	Munda group
27	Vietnamese
28	DRAVIDIAN FAMILY (incl. Telugu, Tamil)
29	AUSTRONESIAN FAMILY (incl. Malay-Indonesian, Javanese)
30	OTHER LANGUAGES

Predominant Religions

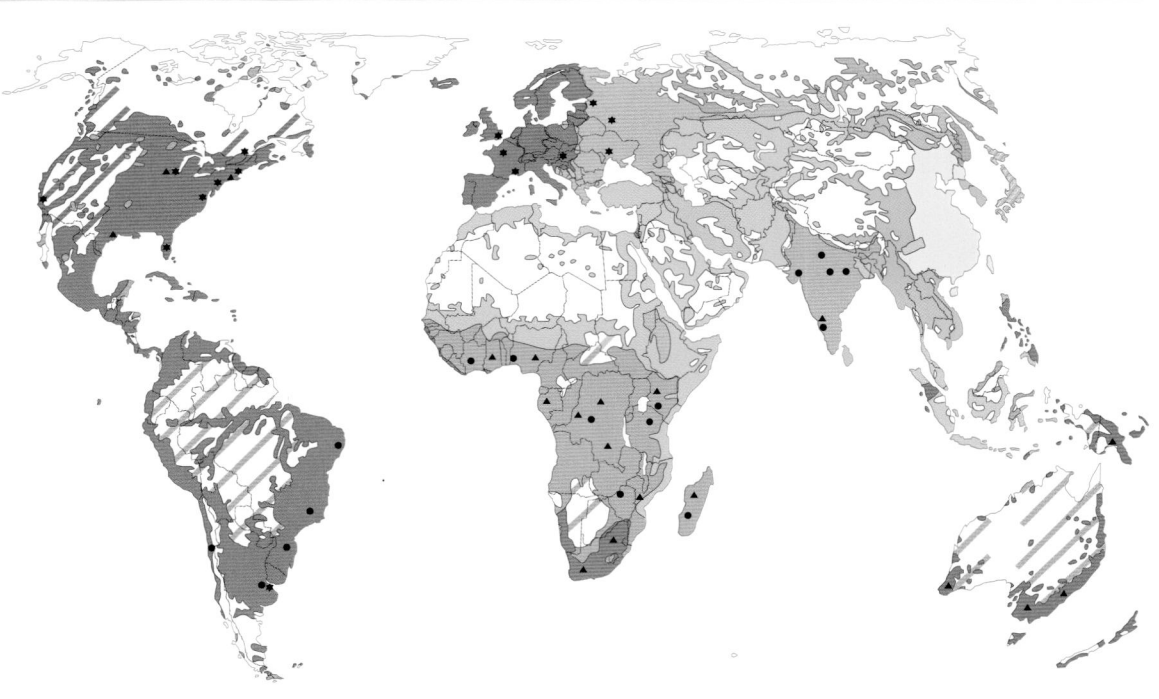

Religious Adherents

Religious adherents in millions (1998)

Christianity	1,980	Buddhist	360
Roman Catholic	1,300	Chinese Trad.	225
Orthodox	240	Indigenous	190
African sects	110	Sikh	23
Pentecostal	105	Yoruba	20
Others	225	Juche	19
Islam	1,300	Spiritism	14
Sunni	940	Judaism	14
Shiite	120	Baha'i	6
Others	240	Jainism	4
Hindu	900	Shinto	4
Secular	850		

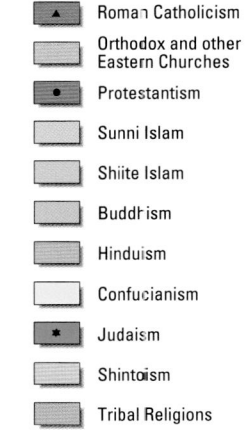

- Roman Catholicism
- Orthodox and other Eastern Churches
- Protestantism
- Sunni Islam
- Shiite Islam
- Buddhism
- Hinduism
- Confucianism
- Judaism
- Shintoism
- Tribal Religions

United Nations

Created in 1945 to promote peace and co-operation and based in New York, the United Nations is the world's largest international organization, with 188 members and an annual budget of US \$1.3 billion (2002). Each member of the General Assembly has one vote, while the five permanent members of the 15-nation Security Council – China, France, Russia, UK and USA – hold a veto. The Secretariat is the UN's principal administrative arm. The 54 members of the Economic and Social Council are responsible for economic, social, cultural, educational, health and related matters. The UN has 16 specialized agencies – based in Canada, France, Switzerland and Italy, as well as the USA – which help members in fields such as education (UNESCO), agriculture (FAO), medicine (WHO) and finance (IFC). By the end of 1994, all the original 11 trust territories of the Trusteeship Council had become independent.

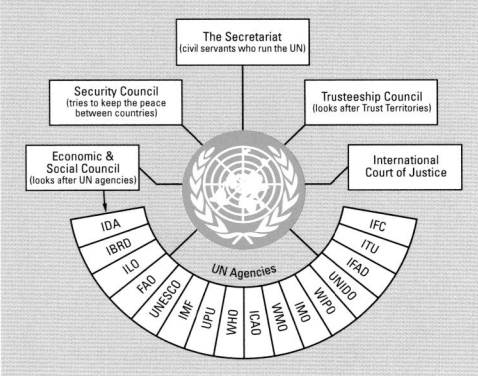

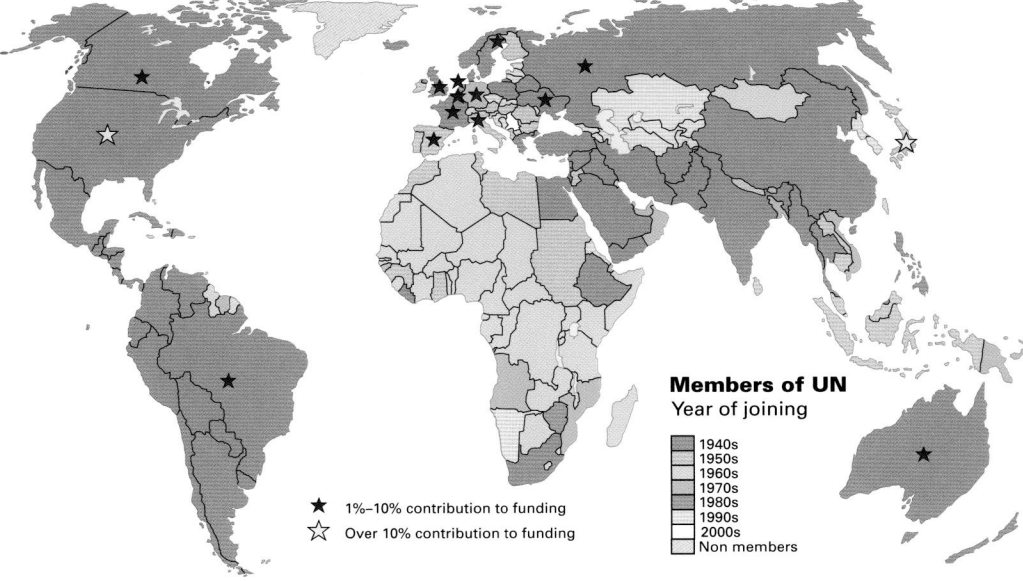

Members of UN
Year of joining

★ 1%–10% contribution to funding
☆ Over 10% contribution to funding

- 1940s
- 1950s
- 1960s
- 1970s
- 1980s
- 1990s
- 2000s
- Non members

MEMBERSHIP OF THE UN In 1945 there were 51 members; by 2000 membership had increased to 188 following the admission of Kiribati, Nauru and Tonga. There are 3 independent states which are not members of the UN – Switzerland, Taiwan and the Vatican City. All the successor states of the former USSR had joined by the end of 1992. The official languages of the UN are Chinese, English, French, Russian, Spanish and Arabic.

FUNDING The UN regular budget for 2000 was US \$1.3 billion. Contributions are assessed by the members' ability to pay, with the maximum 22% of the total (USA's share), the minimum 0.01%. The 15-country European Union pays over 37% of the budget.

PEACEKEEPING The UN has been involved in 54 peacekeeping operations worldwide since 1948.

International Organizations

ACP African-Caribbean-Pacific (formed in 1963). Members have economic ties with the EU.
ARAB LEAGUE (formed in 1945). The League's aim is to promote economic, social, political and military co-operation. There are 21 member nations.
ASEAN Association of South-east Asian Nations (formed in 1967). Cambodia joined in 1999.
CIS The Commonwealth of Independent States (formed in 1991) comprises the countries of the former Soviet Union except for Estonia, Latvia and Lithuania.
COLOMBO PLAN (formed in 1951). Its 26 members aim to promote economic and social development in Asia and the Pacific.
COMMONWEALTH The Commonwealth of Nations evolved from the British Empire; it comprises 16 Queen's realms, 32 republics and 5 indigenous monarchies, giving a total of 53. Nigeria was suspended in 1995, but reinstated in 1999.
EFTA European Free Trade Association (formed in 1960). Portugal left the original 'Seven' in 1989 to join what was then the EC, followed by Austria, Finland and Sweden in 1995. Only 4 members remain: Norway, Iceland, Switzerland and Liechtenstein.
EU European Union (evolved from the European Community in 1993). The 15 members – Austria, Belgium, Denmark, Finland, France, Germany, Greece, Ireland, Italy, Luxembourg, Netherlands, Portugal, Spain, Sweden and the UK – aim to integrate economies, co-ordinate social developments and bring about political union. These members, of what is now the world's biggest market, share agricultural and industrial policies and tariffs on trade. The original body, the European Coal and Steel Community (ECSC), was created in 1951 following the signing of the Treaty of Paris.
LAIA Latin American Integration Association (1980). Its aim is to promote freer regional trade.
NATO North Atlantic Treaty Organization (formed in 1949). It continues after 1991 despite the winding up of the Warsaw Pact. The Czech Republic, Hungary and Poland were the latest members to join in 1999.
OAS Organization of American States (formed in 1948). It aims to promote social and economic co-operation between developed countries of North America and developing nations of Latin America.
OAU Organization of African Unity (formed in 1963). Its 53 members represent over 94% of Africa's population. Arabic, French, Portuguese and English are recognized as working languages.

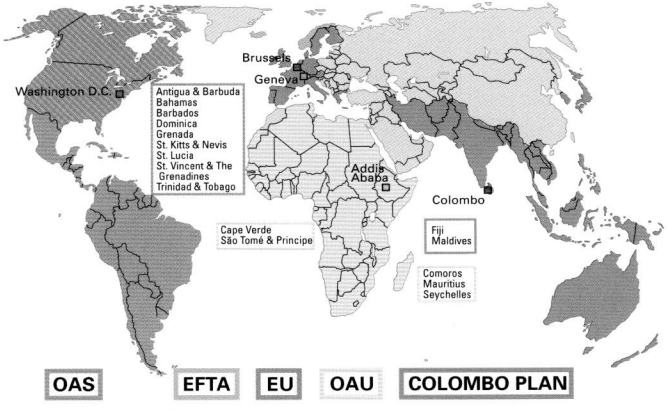

| OAS | EFTA | EU | OAU | COLOMBO PLAN |

OECD Organization for Economic Co-operation and Development (formed in 1961). It comprises 29 major free-market economies. Poland, Hungary and South Korea joined in 1996. 'G8' is its 'inner group' of leading industrial nations, comprising Canada, France, Germany, Italy, Japan, Russia, UK and USA.
OPEC Organization of Petroleum Exporting Countries (formed in 1960). It controls about three-quarters of the world's oil supply. Gabon left the organization in 1996.

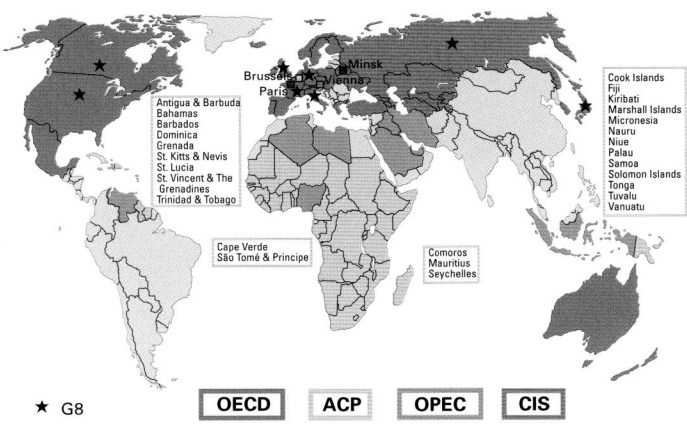

★ G8

| OECD | ACP | OPEC | CIS |

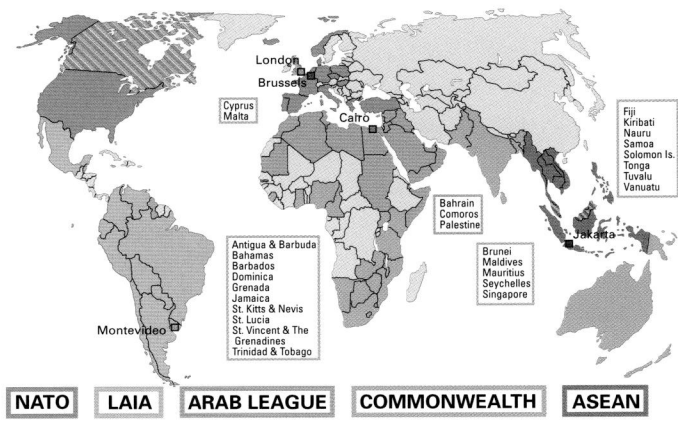

| NATO | LAIA | ARAB LEAGUE | COMMONWEALTH | ASEAN |

Wealth

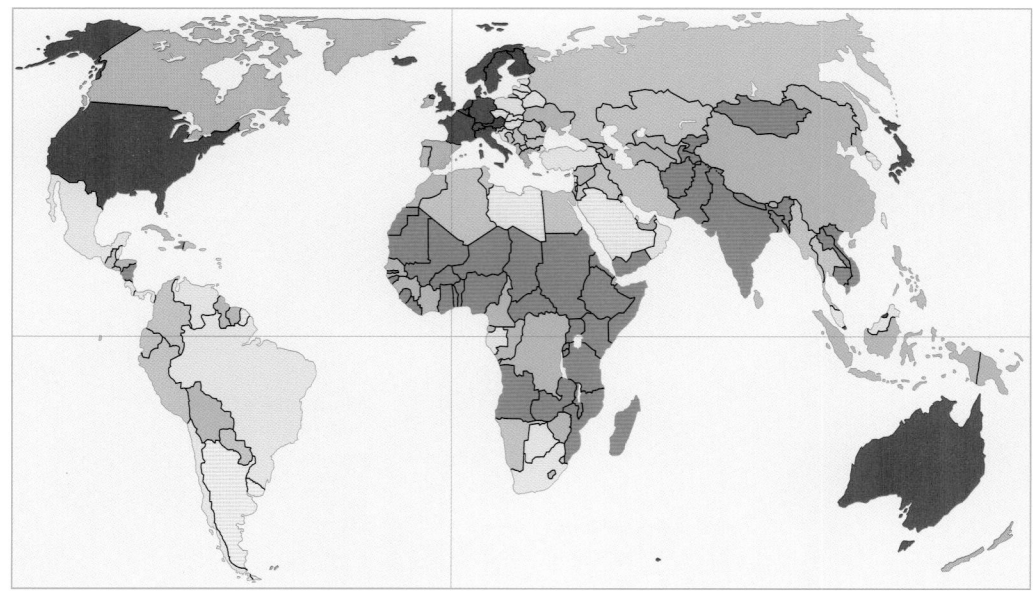

Gross National Product per capita: the value of total production divided by the population (1999)

	Over 400% of world average
	200 – 400% of world average
	100 – 200% of world average

[World average wealth per person US $4,390]

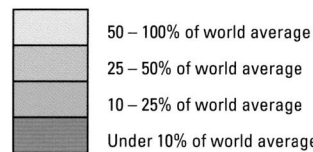

	50 – 100% of world average
	25 – 50% of world average
	10 – 25% of world average
	Under 10% of world average

Top 5 countries

Luxembourg	$44,640
Switzerland	$38,350
Bermuda	$35,590
Norway	$32,880
Japan	$32,230

Bottom 5 countries

Ethiopia	$100
Burundi	$120
Sierra Leone	$130
Guinea-Bissau	$160
Niger	$190

Wealth Creation

The Gross National Product (GNP) of the world's largest economies, US $ million (1998)

1.	USA	7,922,651	23.	Saudi Arabia	186,000
2.	Japan	4,089,910	24.	Denmark	176,374
3.	Germany	2,122,673	25.	Hong Kong	158,286
4.	Italy	1,666,178	26.	Norway	152,082
5.	France	1,466,014	27.	Poland	150,798
6.	UK	1,263,777	28.	Indonesia	138,501
7.	China	928,950	29.	Thailand	134,433
8.	Brazil	758,043	30.	Finland	124,293
9.	Canada	612,332	31.	Greece	122,880
10.	Spain	553,690	32.	South Africa	119,001
11.	India	421,259	33.	Iran	109,645
12.	Netherlands	388,682	34.	Portugal	106,376
13.	Mexico	380,917	35.	Colombia	106,090
14.	Australia	380,625	36.	Israel	95,179
15.	South Korea	369,890	37.	Singapore	95,095
16.	Russia	337,914	38.	Venezuela	81,347
17.	Argentina	324,084	39.	Malaysia	79,848
18.	Switzerland	284,808	40.	Egypt	79,208
19.	Belgium	259,045	41.	Philippines	78,896
20.	Sweden	226,861	42.	Chile	71,294
21.	Austria	217,163	43.	Ireland	67,491
22.	Turkey	200,505	44.	Pakistan	63,159

The Wealth Gap

The world's richest and poorest countries, by Gross National Product per capita in US $ (1999 estimates)

1.	Liechtenstein	50,000	1.	Ethiopia	100
2.	Luxembourg	44,640	2.	Congo (D. Rep.)	110
3.	Switzerland	38,350	3.	Burundi	120
4.	Bermuda	35,590	4.	Sierra Leone	130
5.	Norway	32,880	5.	Guinea-Bissau	160
6.	Japan	32,230	6.	Niger	190
7.	Denmark	32,030	7.	Malawi	190
8.	USA	30,600	8.	Eritrea	200
9.	Singapore	29,610	9.	Chad	200
10.	Iceland	29,280	10.	Nepal	220
11.	Austria	25,970	11.	Angola	220
12.	Germany	25,350	12.	Mozambique	230
13.	Sweden	25,040	13.	Tanzania	240
14.	Monaco	25,000	14.	Burkina Faso	240
15.	Belgium	24,510	15.	Mali	240
16.	Brunei	24,630	16.	Rwanda	250
17.	Netherlands	24,320	17.	Madagascar	250
18.	Finland	23,780	18.	Cambodia	260
19.	Hong Kong	23,520	19.	São Tomé & Príncipe	270
20.	France	23,480	20.	Laos	280

GNP per capita is calculated by dividing a country's Gross National Product by its total population.

Continental Shares

Shares of population and of wealth (GNP) by continent

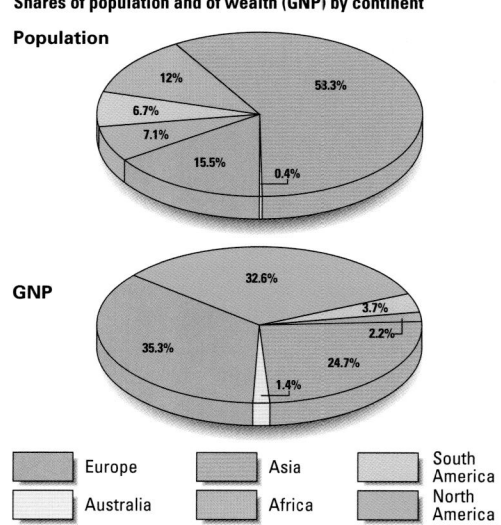

Population

GNP

Europe	Asia	South America
Australia	Africa	North America

Inflation

Average annual rate of inflation (2000 est.)

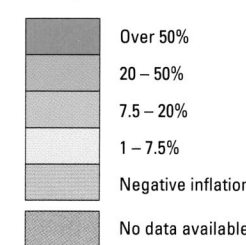

	Over 50%
	20 – 50%
	7.5 – 20%
	1 – 7.5%
	Negative inflation
	No data available

Highest average inflation

Congo (Dem. Rep.)	540%
Angola	325%
Belarus	200%
Iraq	100%
Ecuador	96%

Lowest average inflation

Nauru	–3.6%
Macau (China)	–1.8%
Argentina*	–0.9%
Oman	–0.8%
Japan	–0.7%

* During 2002, Argentina experienced a sharp rise in inflation which is not reflected on this map.

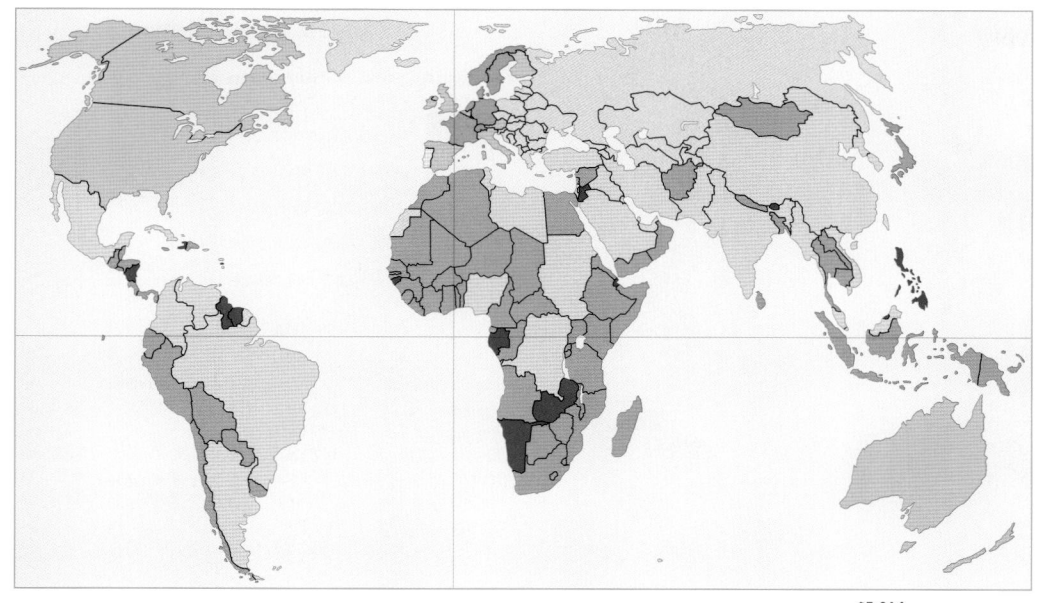

Aid provided or received, divided by the total population, in US $ (1995)

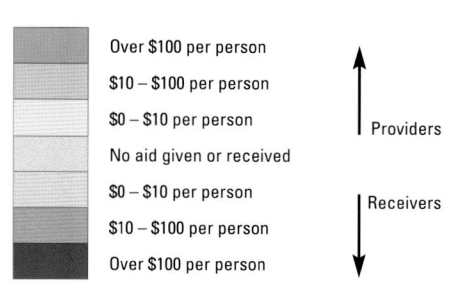

Over $100 per person
$10 – $100 per person
$0 – $10 per person
No aid given or received — Providers
$0 – $10 per person
$10 – $100 per person
Over $100 per person — Receivers

Top 5 providers per capita (1994)		Top 5 receivers per capita (1994)	
France	$279	São Tomé & P.	$378
Denmark	$260	Cape Verde	$314
Norway	$247	Djibouti	$235
Sweden	$201	Surinam	$198
Germany	$166	Mauritania	$153

Debt and Aid

International debtors and the aid they receive (1996)

Although aid grants make a vital contribution to many of the world's poorer countries, they are usually dwarfed by the burden of debt that the developing economies are expected to repay. In 1992, they had to pay US $160,000 million in debt service charges alone – more than two and a half times the amount of Official Development Assistance (ODA) the developing countries were receiving, and US $60,000 million more than total private flows of aid in the same year. In 1990, the debts of Mozambique, one of the world's poorest countries, were estimated to be 75 times its entire earnings from exports.

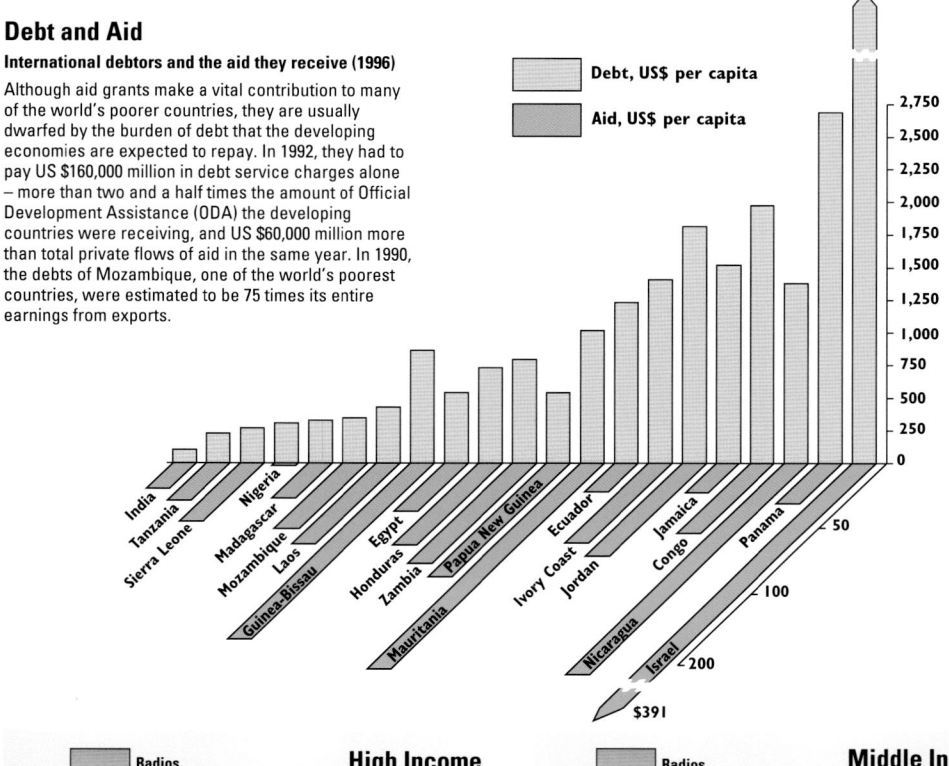

Debt, US$ per capita
Aid, US$ per capita

Distribution of Spending

Percentage share of household spending, selected countries

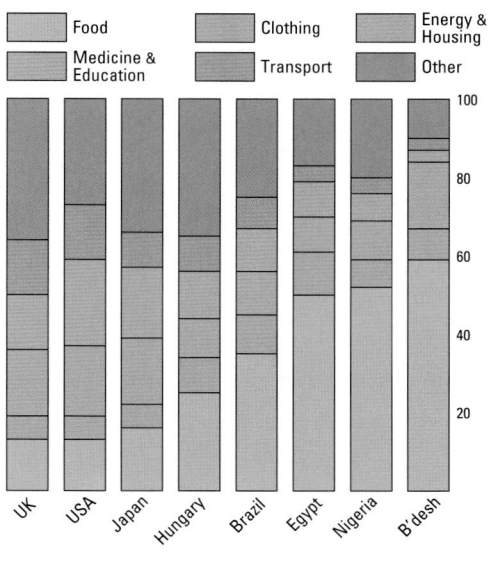

Food | Clothing | Energy & Housing
Medicine & Education | Transport | Other

UK USA Japan Hungary Brazil Egypt Nigeria B'desh

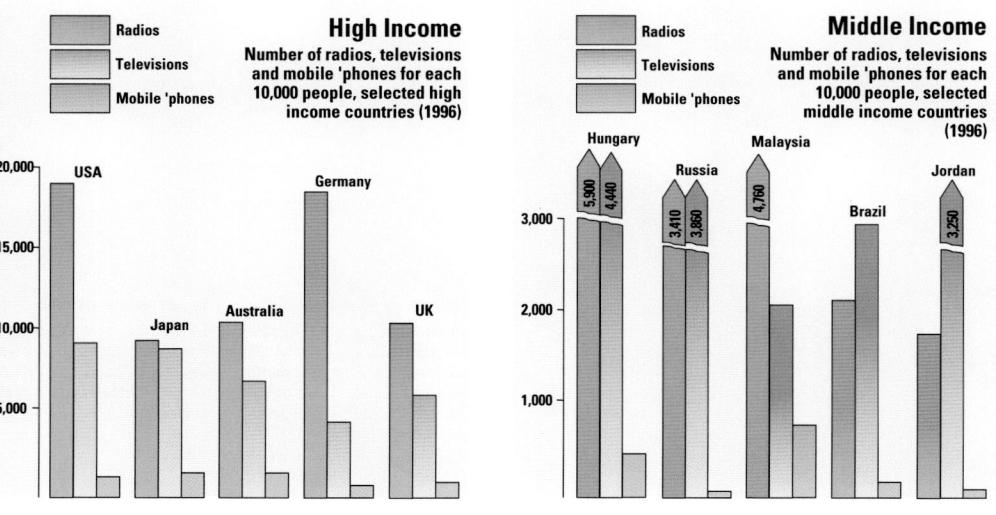

High Income

Radios
Televisions
Mobile 'phones

Number of radios, televisions and mobile 'phones for each 10,000 people, selected high income countries (1996)

Middle Income

Radios
Televisions
Mobile 'phones

Number of radios, televisions and mobile 'phones for each 10,000 people, selected middle income countries (1996)

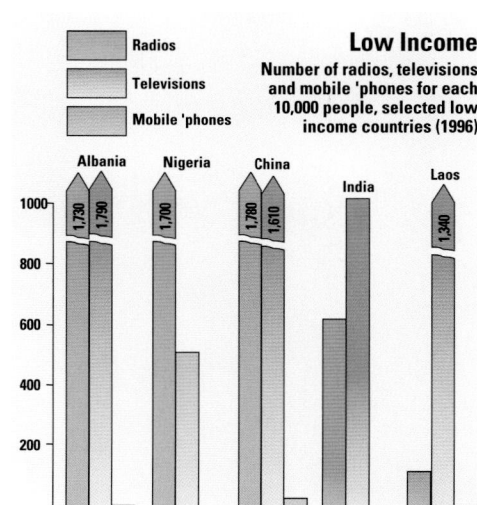

Low Income

Radios
Televisions
Mobile 'phones

Number of radios, televisions and mobile 'phones for each 10,000 people, selected low income countries (1996)

Quality of Life

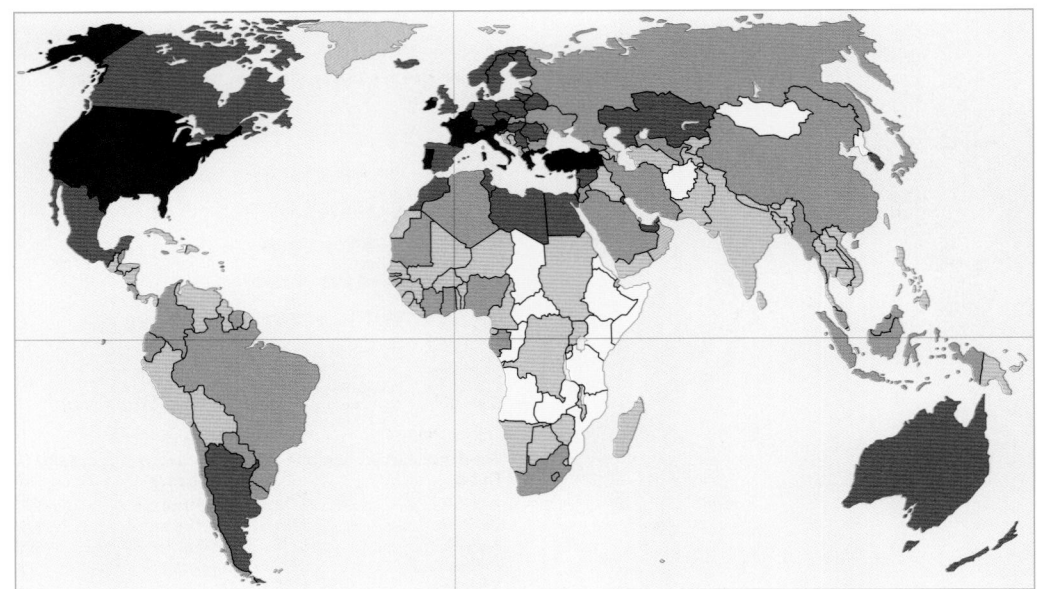

Daily Food Consumption

Average daily food intake in calories per person (1997)

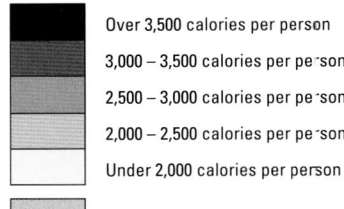

Over 3,500 calories per person

3,000 – 3,500 calories per person

2,500 – 3,000 calories per person

2,000 – 2,500 calories per person

Under 2,000 calories per person

No available data

Top 5 countries		Bottom 5 countries	
Portugal	3,654 cal.	Somalia	1,573 cal.
Greece	3,617 cal.	Eritrea	1,627 cal.
Belgium	3,602 cal.	Burundi	1,687 cal.
Ireland	3,557 cal.	Afghanistan	1,732 cal.
Austria	3,555 cal.	Mozambique	1,782 cal.

[UK 3,211 calories]

Hospital Capacity

Hospital beds available for each 1,000 people (1996)

Highest capacity		Lowest capacity	
Switzerland	20.8	Benin	0.2
Japan	16.2	Nepal	0.2
Tajikistan	16.0	Afghanistan	0.3
Norway	13.5	Bangladesh	0.3
Belarus	12.4	Ethiopia	0.3
Kazakstan	12.2	Mali	0.4
Moldova	12.2	Burkina Faso	0.5
Ukraine	12.2	Niger	0.5
Latvia	11.9	Guinea	0.6
Russia	11.8	India	0.6

[UK 4.9] [USA 4.2]

Although the ratio of people to hospital beds gives a good approximation of a country's health provision, it is not an absolute indicator. Raw numbers may mask inefficiency and other weaknesses: the high availability of beds in Kazakstan, for example, has not prevented infant mortality rates over three times as high as in the United Kingdom and the United States.

Life Expectancy

Years of life expectancy at birth, selected countries (1997)

The chart shows combined data for both sexes. On average, women live longer than men worldwide, even in developing countries with high maternal mortality rates. Overall, life expectancy is steadily rising, though the difference between rich and poor nations remains dramatic.

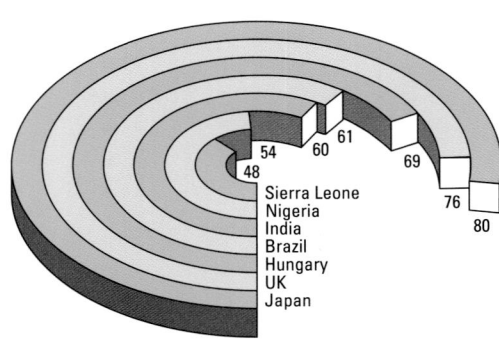

54 – Sierra Leone
48
60 – Nigeria
61 – India
69 – Brazil
76 – Hungary
80 – UK
Japan

Causes of Death

Causes of death for selected countries by percentage

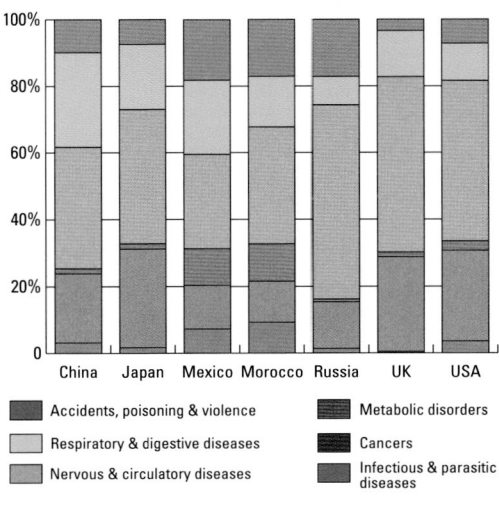

China Japan Mexico Morocco Russia UK USA

- Accidents, poisoning & violence
- Respiratory & digestive diseases
- Nervous & circulatory diseases
- Metabolic disorders
- Cancers
- Infectious & parasitic diseases

Infant Mortality

Number of babies who died under the age of one, per 1,000 births (2000)

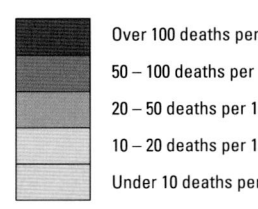

Over 100 deaths per 1,000 births

50 – 100 deaths per 1,000 births

20 – 50 deaths per 1,000 births

10 – 20 deaths per 1,000 births

Under 10 deaths per 1,000 births

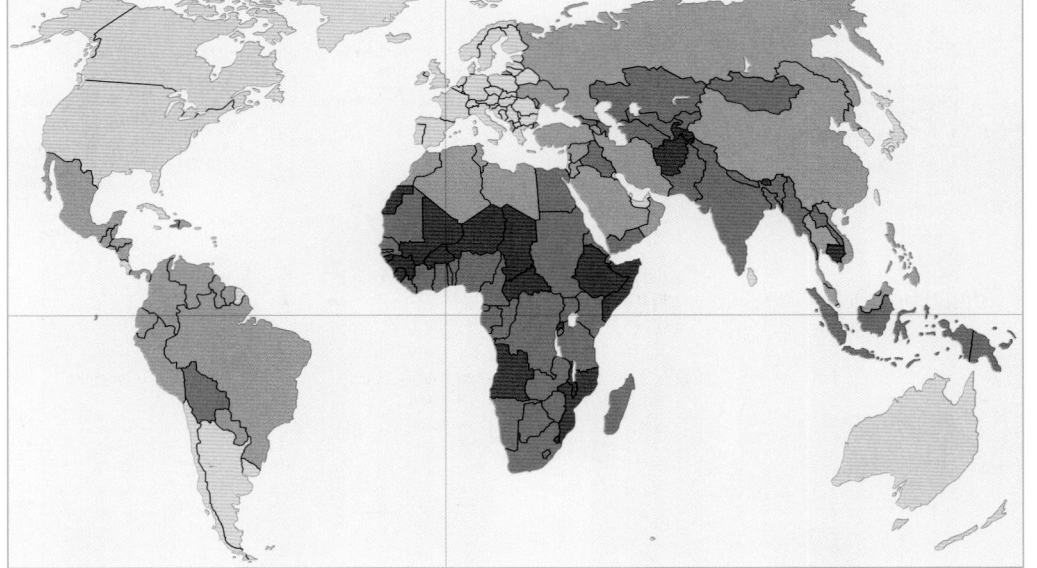

Highest infant mortality		Lowest infant mortality	
Afghanistan	137 deaths	Iceland	5 deaths
W. Sahara	134 deaths	Finland	4 deaths
Malawi	131 deaths	Japan	4 deaths
Angola	126 deaths	Macau (China)	4 deaths
Somalia	126 deaths	Andorra	4 deaths

[UK 6 deaths]

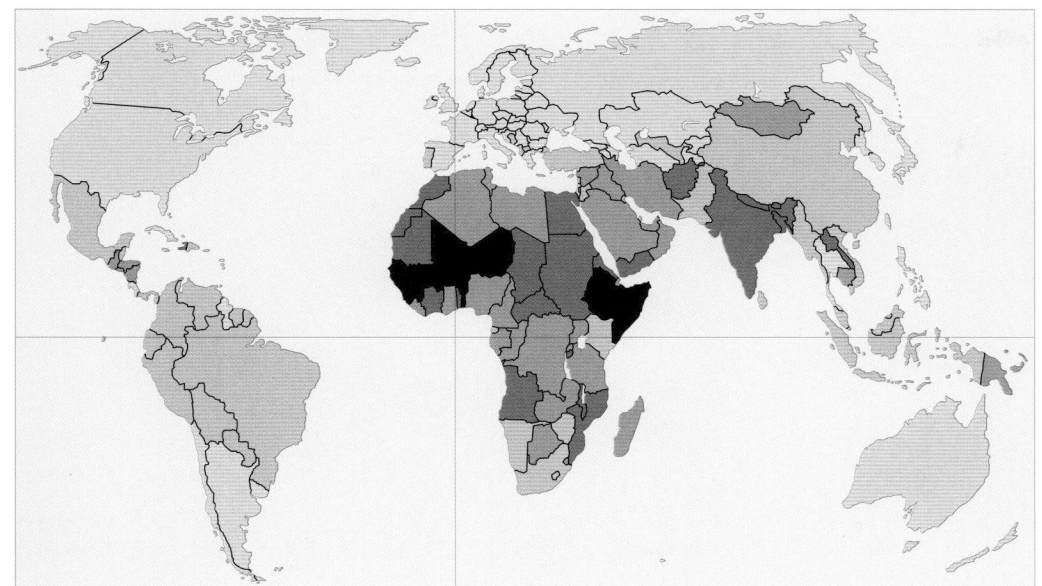

Illiteracy

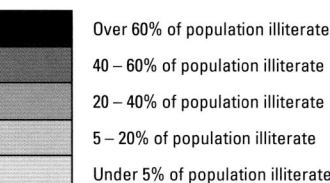

Percentage of the total population unable to read or write (1999)

⬛	Over 60% of population illiterate
▨	40 – 60% of population illiterate
▨	20 – 40% of population illiterate
▨	5 – 20% of population illiterate
☐	Under 5% of population illiterate

Educational expenditure per person (latest available year)

Top 5 countries		Bottom 5 countries	
Sweden	$997	Chad	$2
Qatar	$989	Bangladesh	$3
Canada	$983	Ethiopia	$3
Norway	$971	Nepal	$4
Switzerland	$796	Somalia	$4

[UK $447]

Fertility and Education

Fertility rates compared with female education, selected countries (1992–95)

▨ Percentage of females aged 12–17 in secondary education   ▨ Fertility rate: average number of children borne per woman

Denmark, Austria, France, Canada, Belgium, Switzerland, UK, Poland, Australia, Sri Lanka, Malaysia, Turkey, Saudi Arabia, Thailand, Bolivia, Nigeria, Sierra Leone, Niger

Living Standards

At first sight, most international contrasts in living standards are swamped by differences in wealth. The rich not only have more money, they have more of everything, including years of life. Those with only a little money are obliged to spend most of it on food and clothing, the basic maintenance costs of their existence; air travel and tourism are unlikely to feature on their expenditure lists. However, poverty and wealth are both relative: slum dwellers living on social security payments in an affluent industrial country have far more resources at their disposal than an average African peasant, but feel their own poverty nonetheless. A middle-class Indian lawyer cannot command a fraction of the earnings of a counterpart living in New York, London or Rome; nevertheless, he rightly sees himself as prosperous.

The rich not only live longer, on average, than the poor, they also die from different causes. Infectious and parasitic diseases, all but eliminated in the developed world, remain a scourge in the developing nations. On the other hand, more than two-thirds of the populations of OECD nations eventually succumb to cancer or circulatory disease.

Women in the Workforce

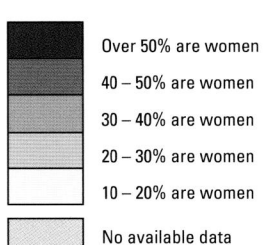

Women in paid employment as a percentage of the total workforce (1997)

⬛	Over 50% are women
▨	40 – 50% are women
▨	30 – 40% are women
▨	20 – 30% are women
☐	10 – 20% are women
▨	No available data

Most women in the workforce		Fewest women in the workforce	
Rwanda	56%	Oman	14%
Cambodia	53%	Saudi Arabia	13%
Ghana	51%	UAE	13%
Ukraine	50%	Qatar	13%
Vietnam	49%	Pakistan	13%

[USA 45%] [UK 44%]

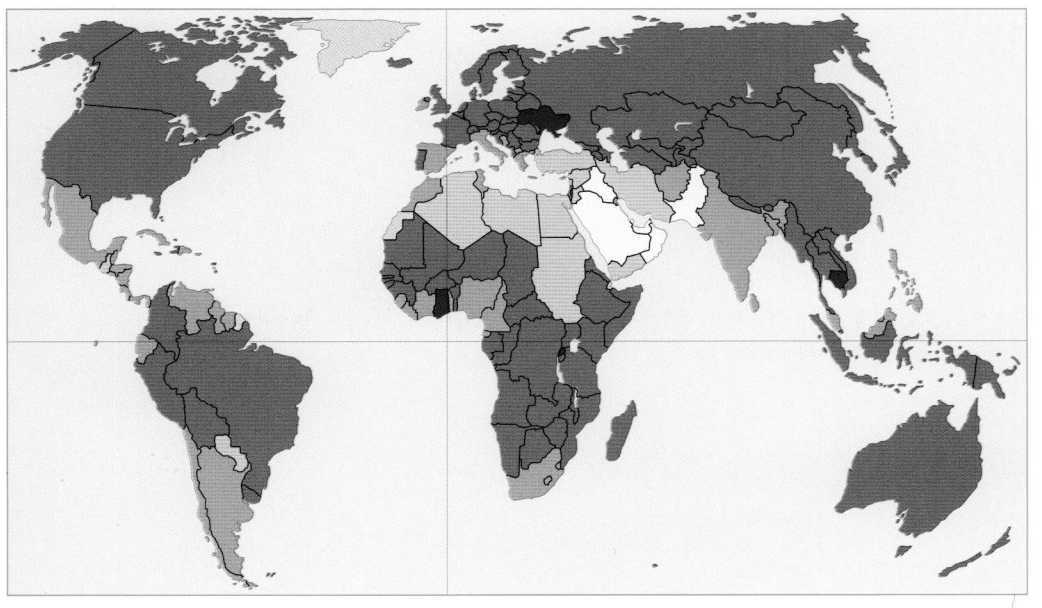

Energy

Production

[Each square represents 1% of world energy production]

North America   Europe   CIS

Middle East   Japan

Africa   Asia

South America   Australasia

Consumption

[Each square represents 1% of world energy consumption]

North America   Europe   CIS

Middle East

Africa   Asia

Japan

South America   Australasia

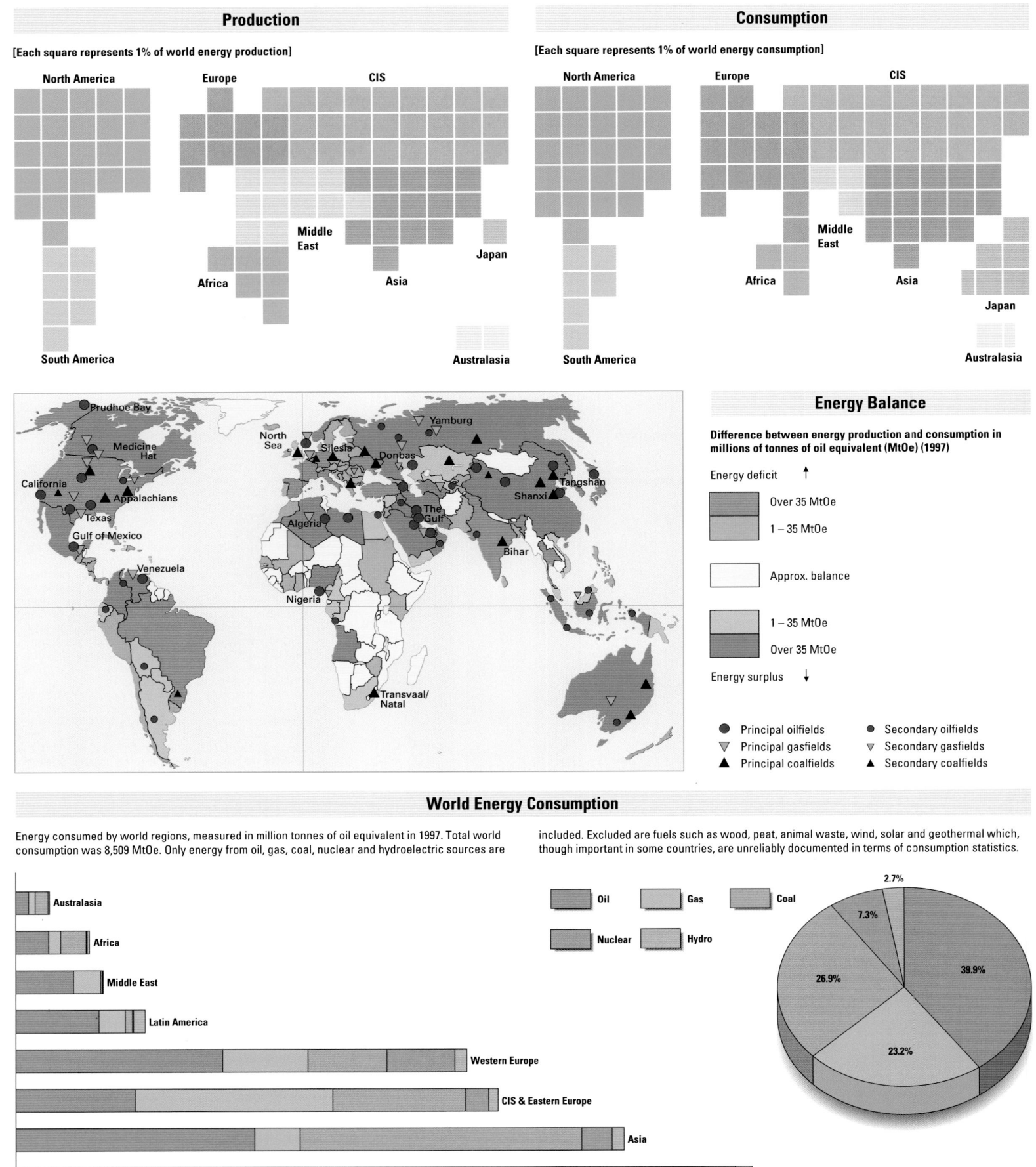

Prudhoe Bay

Medicine Hat

California

Appalachians

Texas

Gulf of Mexico

Venezuela

Nigeria

North Sea   Yamburg

Silesia   Donbas

Algeria

The Gulf

Shanxi   Tangshan

Bihar

Transvaal/Natal

Energy Balance

Difference between energy production and consumption in millions of tonnes of oil equivalent (MtOe) (1997)

Energy deficit ↑

Over 35 MtOe

1 – 35 MtOe

Approx. balance

1 – 35 MtOe

Over 35 MtOe

Energy surplus ↓

● Principal oilfields   ● Secondary oilfields
▽ Principal gasfields   ▽ Secondary gasfields
▲ Principal coalfields   ▲ Secondary coalfields

World Energy Consumption

Energy consumed by world regions, measured in million tonnes of oil equivalent in 1997. Total world consumption was 8,509 MtOe. Only energy from oil, gas, coal, nuclear and hydroelectric sources are included. Excluded are fuels such as wood, peat, animal waste, wind, solar and geothermal which, though important in some countries, are unreliably documented in terms of consumption statistics.

Australasia

Africa

Middle East

Latin America

Western Europe

CIS & Eastern Europe

Asia

North America

Oil   Gas   Coal

Nuclear   Hydro

2.7%
7.3%
26.9%
39.9%
23.2%

5   10   15   20   25 million tonnes of oil equivalent

24 CARTOGRAPHY BY PHILIP'S. COPYRIGHT PHILIP'S

Energy

Energy is used to keep us warm or cool, fuel our industries and our transport systems, and even feed us; high-intensity agriculture, with its use of fertilizers, pesticides and machinery, is heavily energy-dependent. Although we live in a high-energy society, there are vast discrepancies between rich and poor; for example, a North American consumes 13 times as much energy as a Chinese person. But even developing nations have more power at their disposal than was imaginable a century ago.

The distribution of energy supplies, most importantly fossil fuels (coal, oil and natural gas), is very uneven. In addition, the diagrams and map opposite show that the largest producers of energy are not necessarily the largest consumers. The movement of energy supplies around the world is therefore an important component of international trade. In 1999, total world movements in oil amounted to 2,025 million tonnes.

As the finite reserves of fossil fuels are depleted, renewable energy sources, such as solar, hydro-thermal, wind, tidal and biomass, will become increasingly important around the world.

Nuclear Power

Major producers by percentage of world total and by percentage of domestic electricity generation (1998)

Country	% of world total production	Country	% of nuclear as proportion of domestic electricity
1. USA	29.2%	1. France	77%
2. France	15.9%	2. Sweden	47%
3. Japan	13.6%	3. Ukraine	44%
4. Germany	6.6%	4. South Korea	38%
5. Russia	4.3%	5. Japan	32%
6. UK	4.1%	6. Germany	29%
7. South Korea	3.7%	7. UK	28%
8. Ukraine	3.1%	8. USA	19%
9. Sweden	3.0%	9. Canada	13%
10. Canada	2.9%	10. Russia	13%

Although the 1980s were a bad time for the nuclear power industry (major projects ran over budget and fears of long-term environmental damage were heavily reinforced by the 1986 disaster at Chernobyl), the industry picked up in the early 1990s. Whilst the number of reactors is still increasing, however, orders for new plants have shrunk. In 1997, the Swedish government began to decommission the country's 12 nuclear power plants.

Hydroelectricity

Major producers by percentage of world total and by percentage of domestic electricity generation (1998)

Country	% of world total production	Country	% of hydroelectric as proportion of domestic electricity
1. Canada	12.6%	1. Norway	99.4%
2. USA	12.2%	2. Brazil	90.6%
3. Brazil	11.0%	3. Canada	59.1%
4. China	7.9%	4. Sweden	47.0%
5. Russia	6.0%	5. Russia	19.3%
6. Norway	4.4%	6. China	17.4%
7. Japan	3.9%	7. India	16.8%
8. India	3.1%	8. France	12.9%
9. Sweden	2.8%	9. Japan	9.8%
10. France	2.5%	10. USA	8.4%

Countries heavily reliant on hydroelectricity are usually small and non-industrial: a high proportion of hydroelectric power more often reflects a modest energy budget than vast hydroelectric resources. The USA, for instance, produces only 8% of power requirements from hydroelectricity; yet that 8% amounts to more than three times the hydropower generated by the whole of Africa.

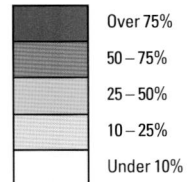

Fuel Exports

Fuels as a percentage of total value of exports (1999)

- Over 75%
- 50 – 75%
- 25 – 50%
- 10 – 25%
- Under 10%

In the 1970s, oil exports became a political issue when OPEC sought to increase the influence of developing countries in world affairs by raising oil prices and restricting production. But its power was short-lived, following a fall in demand for oil in the 1980s, due to an increase in energy efficiency and development of alternative resources.

Conversion Rates

1 barrel = 0.136 tonnes or 159 litres or 35 Imperial gallons or 42 US gallons

1 tonne = 7.33 barrels or 1,185 litres or 256 Imperial gallons or 261 US gallons

1 tonne oil = 1.5 tonnes hard coal or 3.0 tonnes lignite or 12,000 kWh

1 Imperial gallon = 1.201 US gallons or 4.546 litres or 277.4 cubic inches

Measurements
For historical reasons, oil is traded in 'barrels'. The weight and volume equivalents (shown right) are all based on average-density 'Arabian light' crude oil.

The energy equivalents given for a tonne of oil are also somewhat imprecise: oil and coal of different qualities will have varying energy contents, a fact usually reflected in their price on world markets.

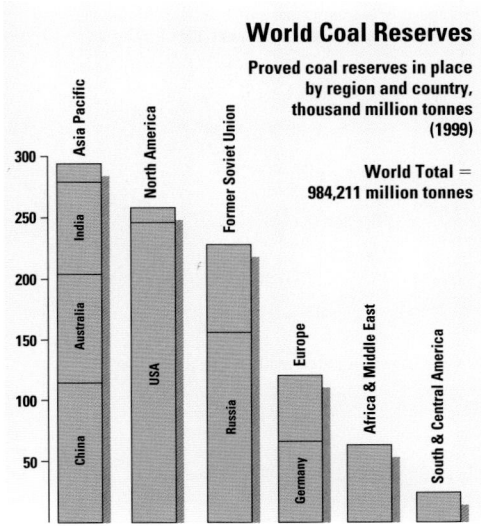

World Coal Reserves

Proved coal reserves in place by region and country, thousand million tonnes (1999)

World Total = 984,211 million tonnes

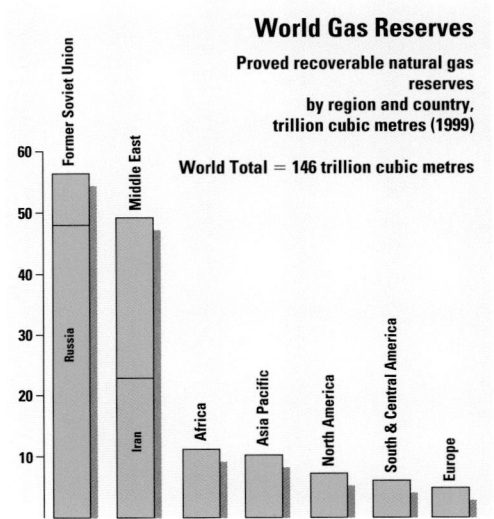

World Gas Reserves

Proved recoverable natural gas reserves by region and country, trillion cubic metres (1999)

World Total = 146 trillion cubic metres

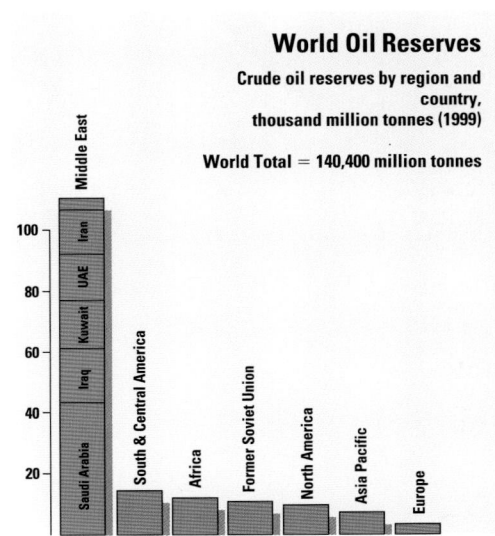

World Oil Reserves

Crude oil reserves by region and country, thousand million tonnes (1999)

World Total = 140,400 million tonnes

Production

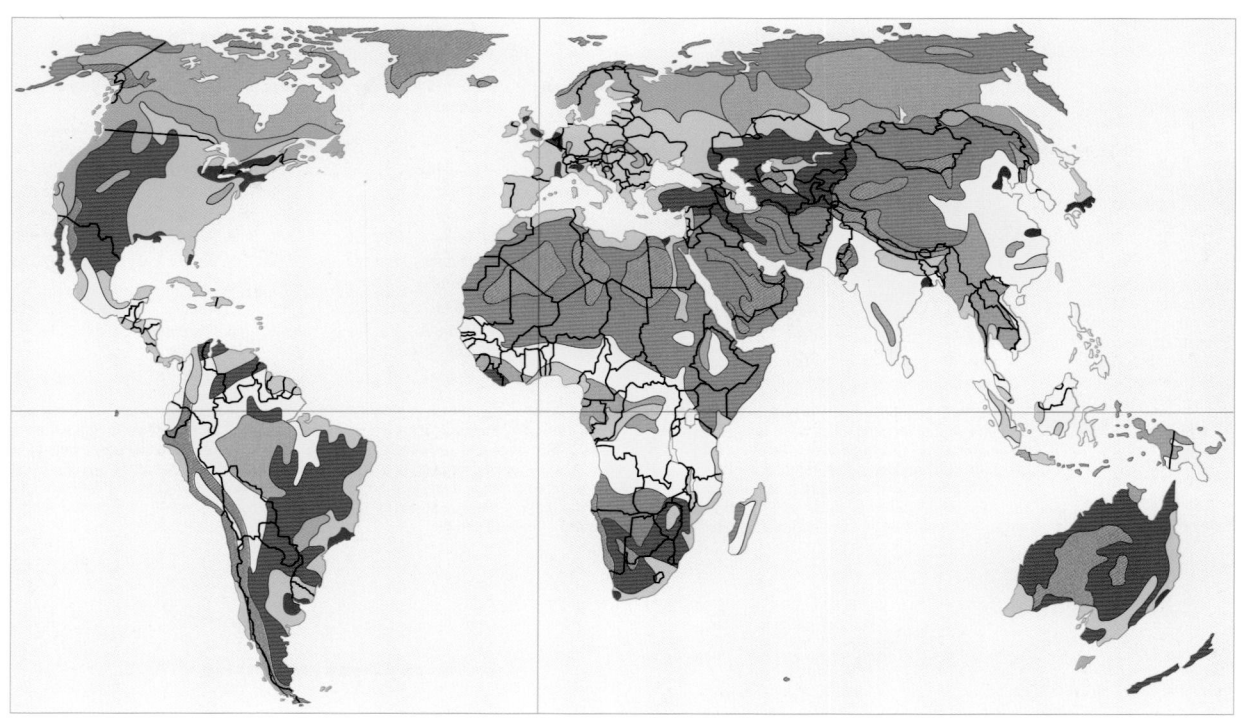

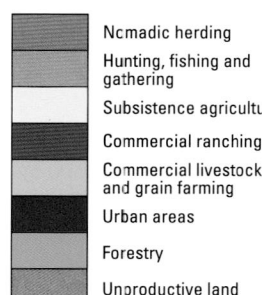
The development of agriculture has transformed human existence more than any other. The whole business of farming is constantly developing: due mainly to the new varieties of rice and wheat, world grain production has increased by over 70% since 1965. New machinery and modern agricultural techniques enable relatively few farmers to produce enough food for the world's 6 billion or so people.

Staple Crops

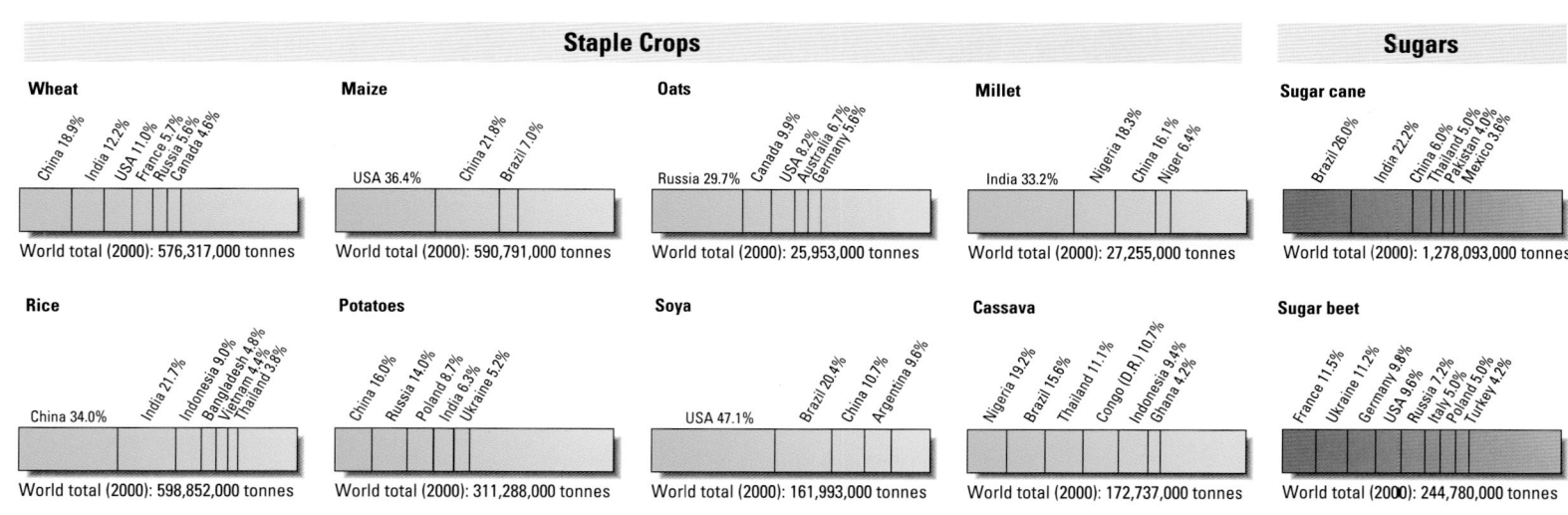

Wheat
- China 18.9%
- India 12.2%
- USA 11.0%
- France 5.7%
- Russia 5.0%
- Canada 4.6%

World total (2000): 576,317,000 tonnes

Maize
- USA 36.4%
- China 21.9%
- Brazil 7.0%

World total (2000): 590,791,000 tonnes

Oats
- Russia 29.7%
- Canada 9.9%
- USA 8.2%
- Australia 6.7%
- Germany 5.6%

World total (2000): 25,953,000 tonnes

Millet
- India 33.2%
- Nigeria 18.3%
- China 16.1%
- Niger 6.4%

World total (2000): 27,255,000 tonnes

Rice
- China 34.0%
- India 21.7%
- Indonesia 9.0%
- Bangladesh 4.8%
- Vietnam 4.4%
- Thailand 3.8%

World total (2000): 598,852,000 tonnes

Potatoes
- China 16.0%
- Russia 14.0%
- Poland 8.7%
- India 6.3%
- Ukraine 5.2%

World total (2000): 311,288,000 tonnes

Soya
- USA 47.1%
- Brazil 20.4%
- China 10.7%
- Argentina 9.6%

World total (2000): 161,993,000 tonnes

Cassava
- Nigeria 19.2%
- Brazil 15.6%
- Thailand 11.1%
- Congo (D.R.) 10.7%
- Indonesia 9.4%
- Ghana 4.2%

World total (2000): 172,737,000 tonnes

Sugars

Sugar cane
- Brazil 26.0%
- India 22.2%
- China 6.0%
- Thailand 5.0%
- Pakistan 4.0%
- Mexico 3.6%

World total (2000): 1,278,093,000 tonnes

Sugar beet
- France 11.5%
- Ukraine 11.2%
- Germany 9.8%
- USA 9.6%
- Russia 7.2%
- Italy 5.0%
- Poland 5.0%
- Turkey 4.2%

World total (2000): 244,780,000 tonnes

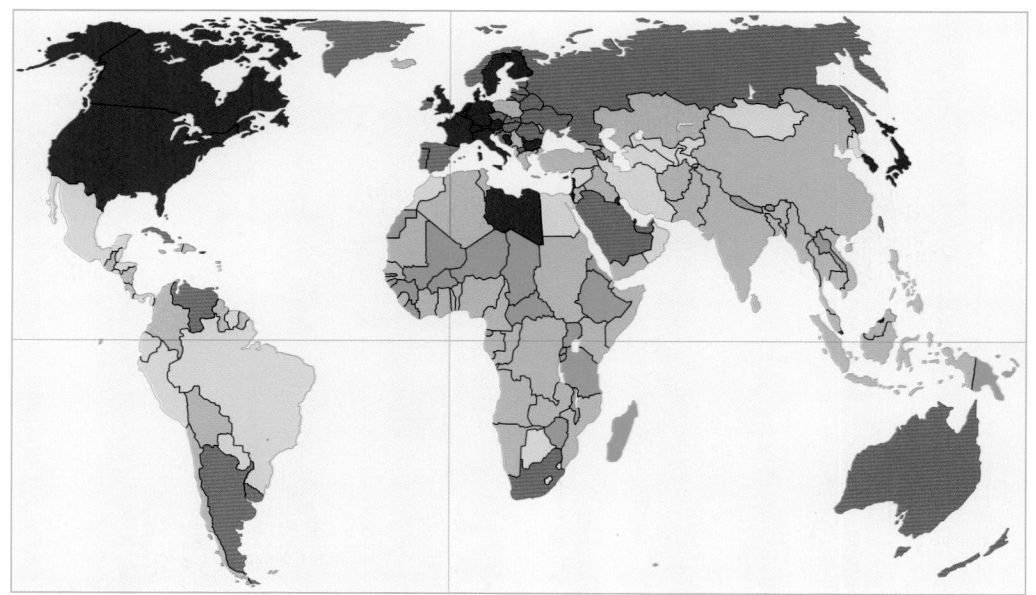

Employment

The number of workers employed in manufacturing for every 100 workers engaged in agriculture (1997)

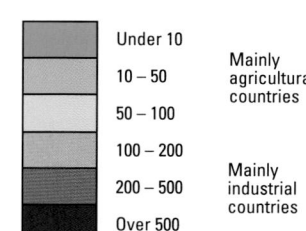

- Under 10 — Mainly agricultural countries
- 10 – 50
- 50 – 100
- 100 – 200
- 200 – 500 — Mainly industrial countries
- Over 500

Selected countries (latest available year)

Singapore	8,860	Germany	800
Hong Kong	3,532	Kuwait	767
UK	1,270	Bahrain	660
Belgium	820	USA	657
Yugoslavia	809	Israel	633

Mineral Production

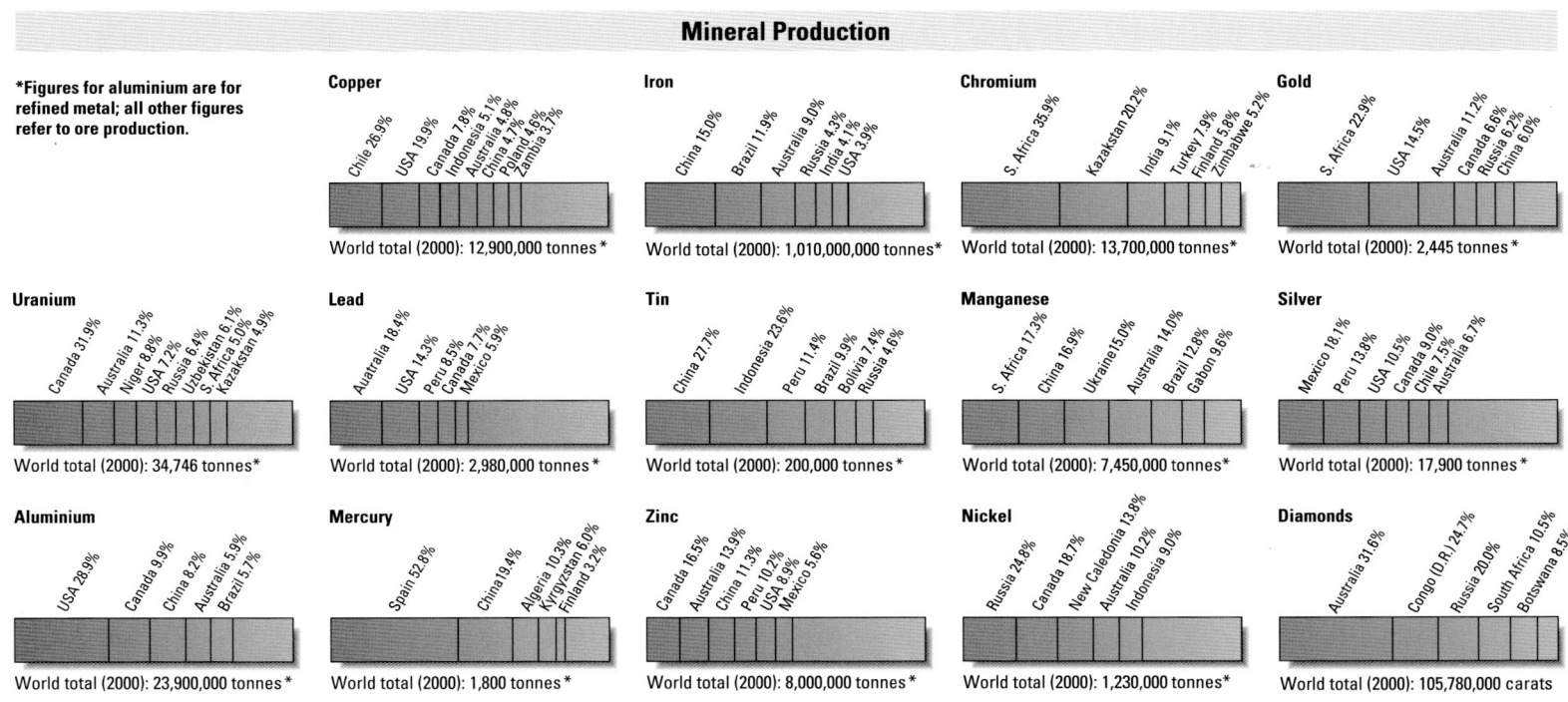

*Figures for aluminium are for refined metal; all other figures refer to ore production.

Copper
Chile 26.9% | USA 19.9% | Canada 7.8% | Indonesia 5.1% | Australia 4.8% | China 4.7% | Poland 4.6% | Zambia 3.7%
World total (2000): 12,900,000 tonnes *

Iron
China 15.0% | Brazil 11.9% | Australia 9.0% | Russia 4.3% | India 4.1% | USA 3.9%
World total (2000): 1,010,000,000 tonnes*

Chromium
S. Africa 35.9% | Kazakstan 20.2% | India 9.1% | Turkey 7.9% | Finland 5.8% | Zimbabwe 5.2%
World total (2000): 13,700,000 tonnes*

Gold
S. Africa 22.9% | USA 14.5% | Australia 11.2% | Canada 6.6% | Russia 6.2% | China 6.0%
World total (2000): 2,445 tonnes *

Uranium
Canada 31.9% | Australia 11.3% | Niger 8.8% | USA 7.2% | Russia 6.4% | Uzbekistan 6.1% | S. Africa 5.0% | Kazakstan 4.9%
World total (2000): 34,746 tonnes*

Lead
Australia 18.4% | USA 14.3% | Peru 8.5% | Canada 7.7% | Mexico 5.9%
World total (2000): 2,980,000 tonnes *

Tin
China 27.7% | Indonesia 23.6% | Peru 11.4% | Brazil 9.9% | Bolivia 7.4% | Russia 4.6%
World total (2000): 200,000 tonnes *

Manganese
S. Africa 17.3% | China 16.9% | Ukraine 15.0% | Australia 14.0% | Brazil 12.8% | Gabon 9.6%
World total (2000): 7,450,000 tonnes*

Silver
Mexico 18.1% | Peru 13.8% | USA 10.5% | Canada 7.5% | Chile 7.5% | Australia 6.7%
World total (2000): 17,900 tonnes *

Aluminium
USA 28.9% | Canada 9.9% | China 8.2% | Australia 5.9% | Brazil 5.7%
World total (2000): 23,900,000 tonnes *

Mercury
Spain 52.8% | China 19.4% | Algeria 10.3% | Kyrgyzstan 6.0% | Finland 3.2%
World total (2000): 1,800 tonnes *

Zinc
Canada 16.5% | Australia 13.9% | China 11.3% | Peru 10.2% | USA 8.9% | Mexico 5.6%
World total (2000): 8,000,000 tonnes *

Nickel
Russia 24.8% | Canada 18.7% | New Caledonia 13.8% | Australia 10.2% | Indonesia 9.0%
World total (2000): 1,230,000 tonnes*

Diamonds
Australia 31.6% | Congo (D.R.) 24.7% | Russia 20.0% | South Africa 10.5% | Botswana 8.5%
World total (2000): 105,780,000 carats

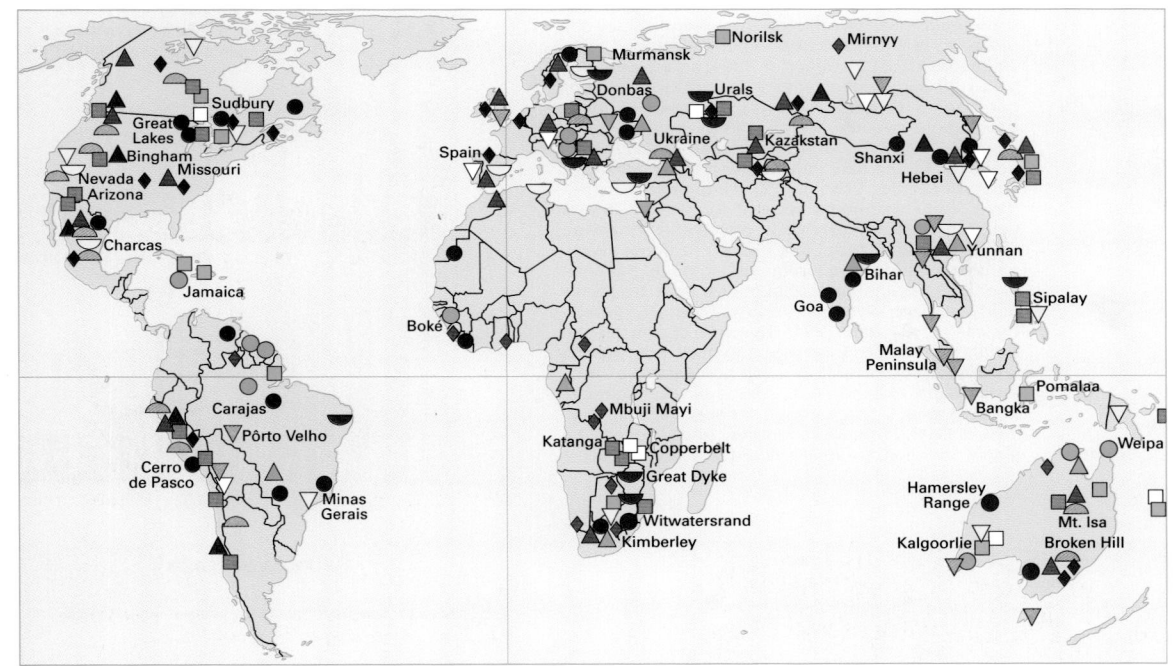

Mineral Distribution

The map shows the richest sources of the most important minerals. Major mineral locations are named.

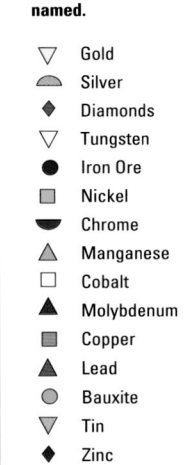

- ▽ Gold
- ◗ Silver
- ◆ Diamonds
- ▽ Tungsten
- ● Iron Ore
- ▢ Nickel
- ◖ Chrome
- △ Manganese
- □ Cobalt
- ▲ Molybdenum
- ▢ Copper
- ▲ Lead
- ● Bauxite
- ▽ Tin
- ◆ Zinc
- ◡ Mercury

The map does not show undersea deposits, most of which are considered inaccessible.

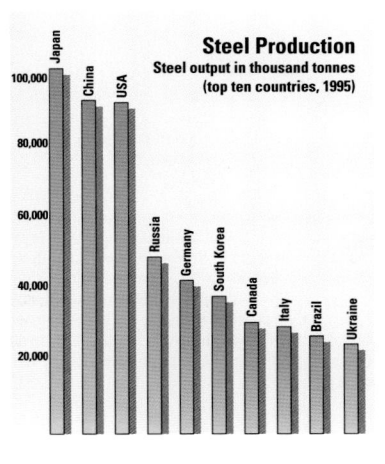

Steel Production
Steel output in thousand tonnes (top ten countries, 1995)

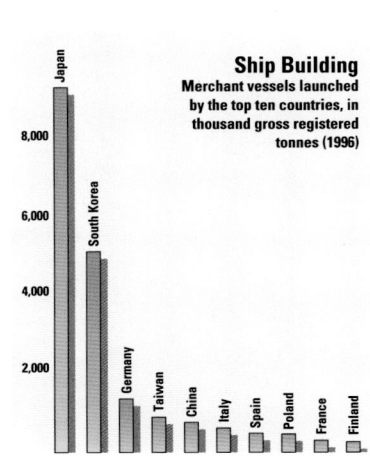

Ship Building
Merchant vessels launched by the top ten countries, in thousand gross registered tonnes (1996)

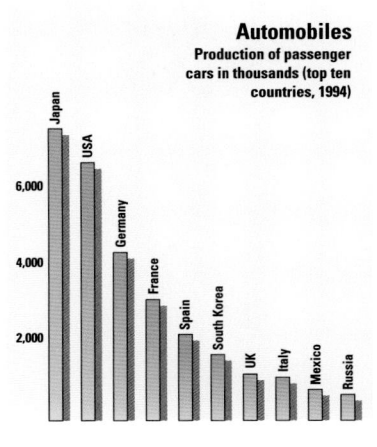

Automobiles
Production of passenger cars in thousands (top ten countries, 1994)

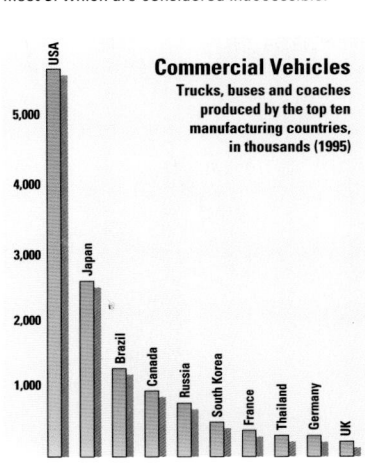

Commercial Vehicles
Trucks, buses and coaches produced by the top ten manufacturing countries, in thousands (1995)

Trade

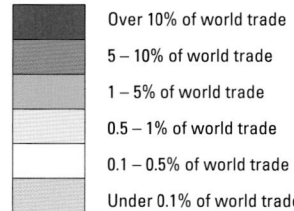

Share of World Trade

Percentage share of total world exports by value (1999)

- Over 10% of world trade
- 5 – 10% of world trade
- 1 – 5% of world trade
- 0.5 – 1% of world trade
- 0.1 – 0.5% of world trade
- Under 0.1% of world trade

International trade is dominated by a handful of powerful maritime nations. The members of 'G8', the inner circle of OECD (see page 19), and the top seven countries listed in the diagram below, account for more than half the total. The majority of nations – including all but four in Africa – contribute less than one quarter of 1% to the worldwide total of exports; the EU countries account for 40%, the Pacific Rim nations over 35%.

The Main Trading Nations

The imports and exports of the top ten trading nations as a percentage of world trade (1999). Each country's trade in manufactured goods is shown in dark blue.

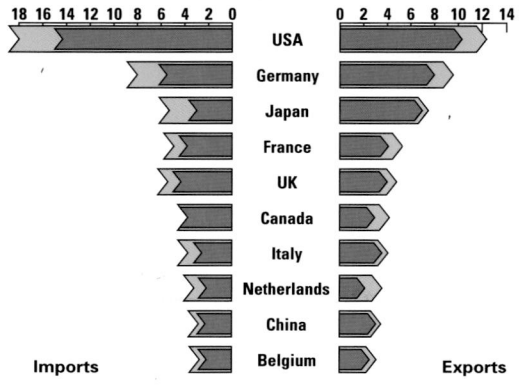

18 16 14 12 10 8 6 4 2 0   0 2 4 6 8 10 12 14

- USA
- Germany
- Japan
- France
- UK
- Canada
- Italy
- Netherlands
- China
- Belgium

Imports   Exports

Patterns of Trade

Thriving international trade is the outward sign of a healthy world economy, the obvious indicator that some countries have goods to sell and others the means to buy them. Global exports expanded to an estimated US $3.92 trillion in 1994, an increase due partly to economic recovery in industrial nations but also to export-led growth strategies in many developing nations and lowered regional trade barriers. International trade remains dominated, however, by the rich, industrialized countries of the Organization for Economic Development: between them, OECD members account for almost 75% of world imports and exports in most years. However, continued rapid economic growth in some developing countries is altering global trade patterns. The 'tiger economies' of South-east Asia are particularly vibrant, averaging more than 8% growth between 1992 and 1994. The size of the largest trading economies means that imports and exports usually represent only a small percentage of their total wealth. In export-concious Japan, for example, trade in goods and services amounts to less than 18% of GDP. In poorer countries, trade – often in a single commodity – may amount to 50% of GDP.

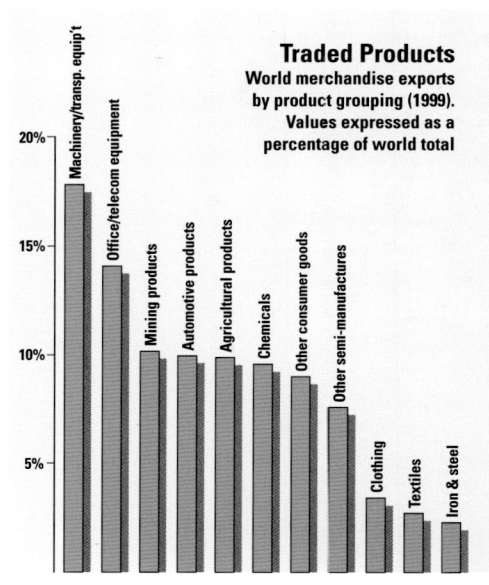

Traded Products

World merchandise exports by product grouping (1999). Values expressed as a percentage of world total

- Machinery/transp. equip't
- Office/telecom equipment
- Mining products
- Automotive products
- Agricultural products
- Chemicals
- Other consumer goods
- Other semi-manufactures
- Clothing
- Textiles
- Iron & steel

Balance of Trade

Value of exports in proportion to the value of imports (1999)

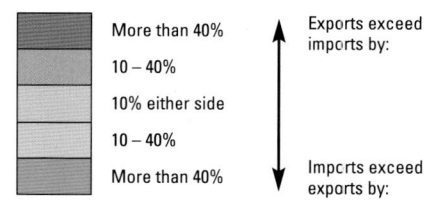

- More than 40%
- 10 – 40%
- 10% either side
- 10 – 40%
- More than 40%

Exports exceed imports by:

Imports exceed exports by:

The total world trade balance should amount to zero, since exports must equal imports on a global scale. In practice, at least $100 billion in exports go unrecorded, leaving the world with an apparent deficit and many countries in a better position than public accounting reveals. However, a favourable trade balance is not necessarily a sign of prosperity: many poorer countries must maintain a high surplus in order to service debts, and do so by restricting imports below the levels needed to sustain successful economies.

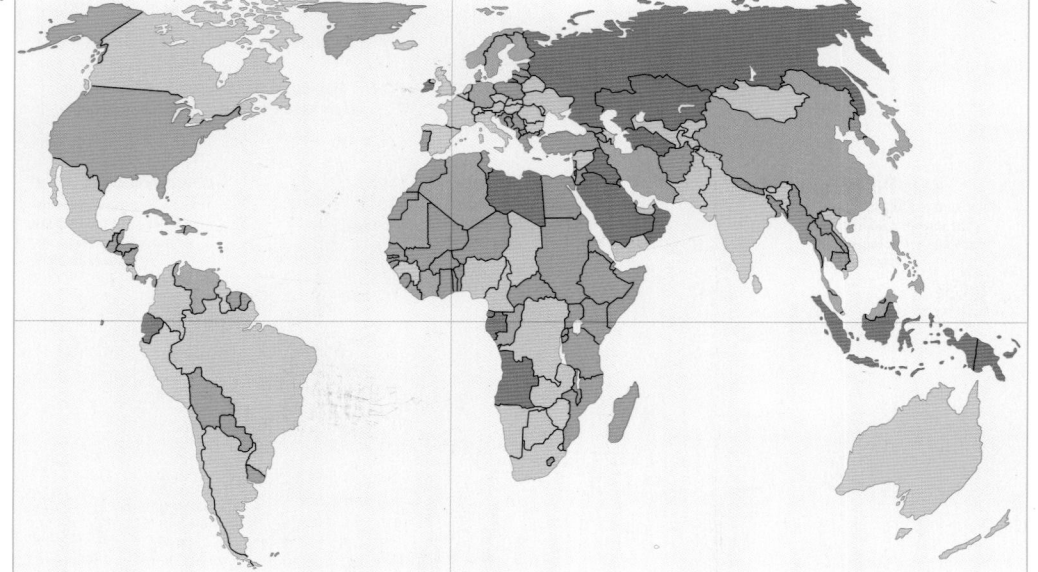

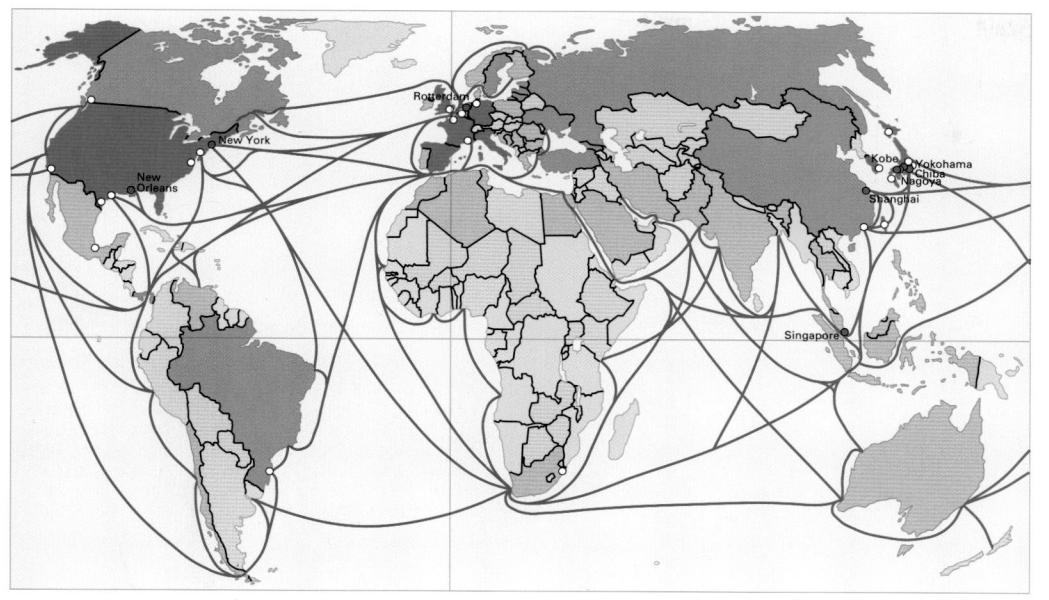

Seaborne Freight

Freight unloaded in millions of tonnes (latest available year)

- Over 100
- 50 – 100
- 10 – 50
- 5 – 10
- Under 5
- Landlocked countries

Major seaports

- ● Over 100 million tonnes per year
- ○ 50–100 million tonnes per year
- — Major shipping routes

Cargoes

Type of seaborne freight

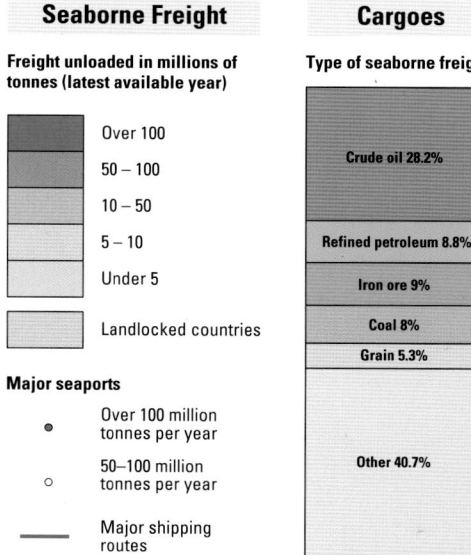

- Crude oil 28.2%
- Refined petroleum 8.8%
- Iron ore 9%
- Coal 8%
- Grain 5.3%
- Other 40.7%

Merchant Fleets

Merchant fleets in thousand gross tonnage (1999). A large number of vessels are registered in Liberia and Panama but they are not part of the national fleet.

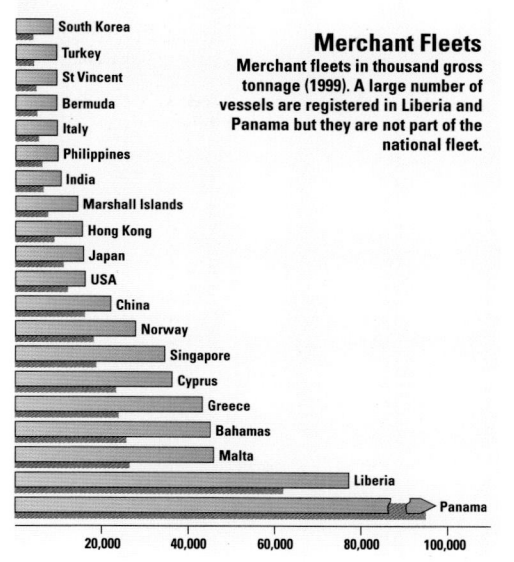

South Korea, Turkey, St Vincent, Bermuda, Italy, Philippines, India, Marshall Islands, Hong Kong, Japan, USA, China, Norway, Singapore, Cyprus, Greece, Bahamas, Malta, Liberia, Panama

20,000 40,000 60,000 80,000 100,000

The Great Ports

Total cargo traffic, in thousand tonnes (latest available year)

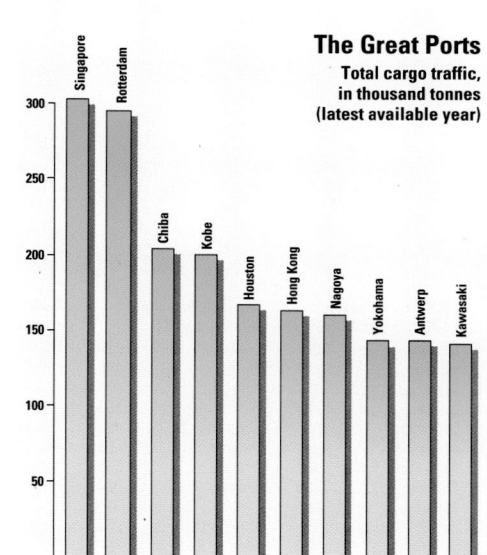

Singapore, Rotterdam, Chiba, Kobe, Houston, Hong Kong, Nagoya, Yokohama, Antwerp, Kawasaki

World Shipping

World merchant fleet by type of vessel and deadweight tonnage (latest available year)

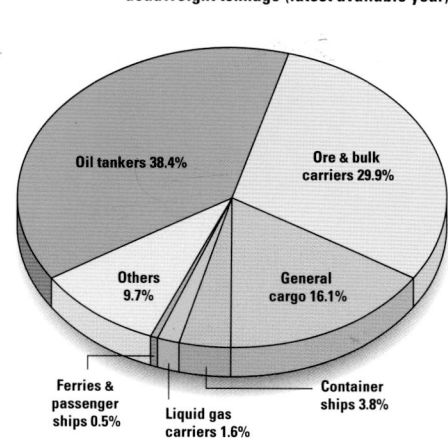

- Oil tankers 38.4%
- Ore & bulk carriers 29.9%
- General cargo 16.1%
- Container ships 3.8%
- Others 9.7%
- Ferries & passenger ships 0.5%
- Liquid gas carriers 1.6%

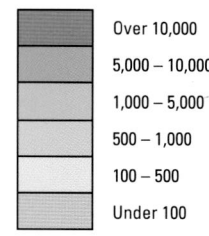

Exports Per Capita

Value of exports in US $, divided by total population (2000)

- Over 10,000
- 5,000 – 10,000
- 1,000 – 5,000
- 500 – 1,000
- 100 – 500
- Under 100

[UK 4,728] [USA 2,791]

Highest per capita

Kuwait	113,614
Liechtenstein	78,848
Singapore	31,860
Aruba (Neths)	31,429
Hong Kong (China)	28,290
Ireland	19,136

Travel and Tourism

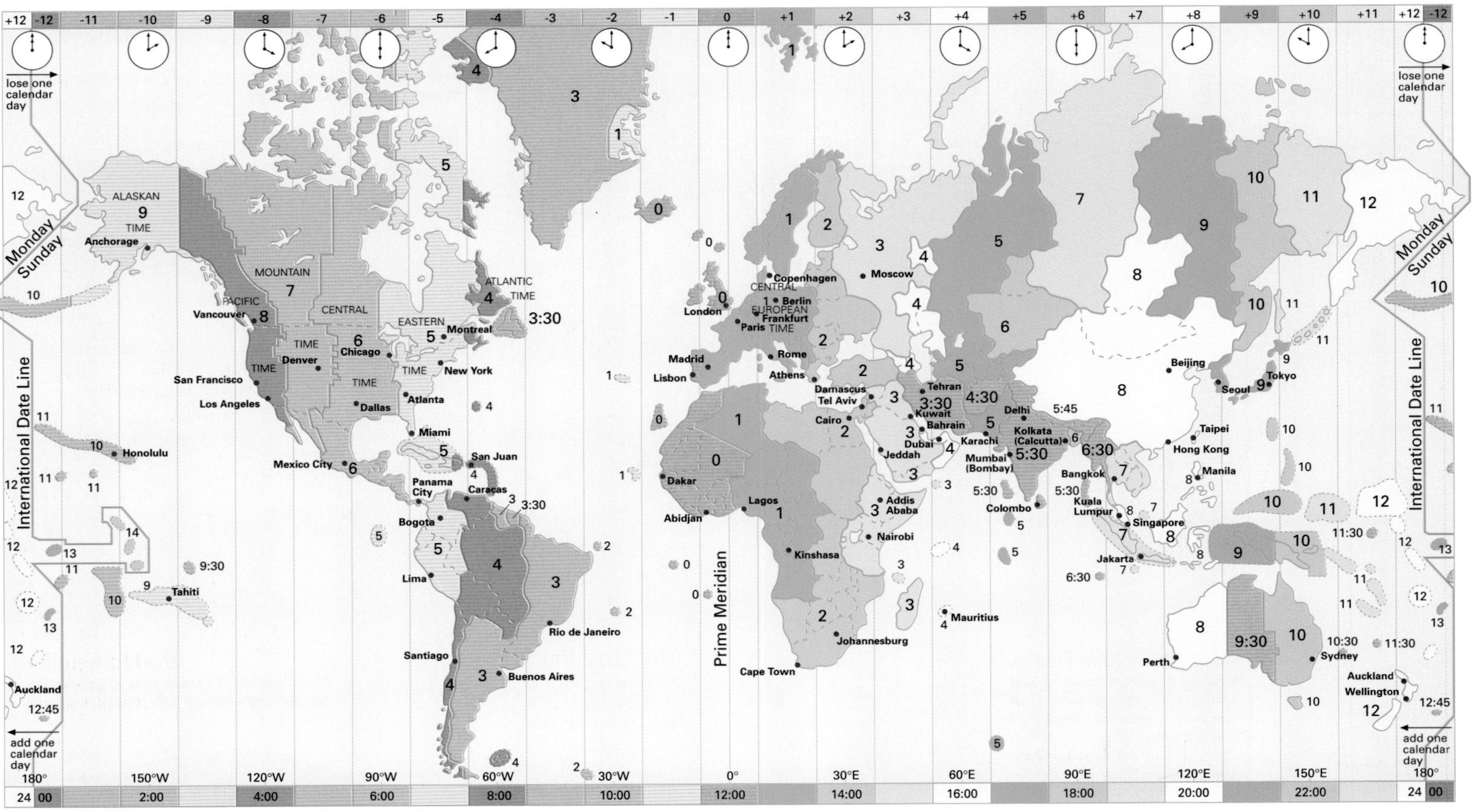

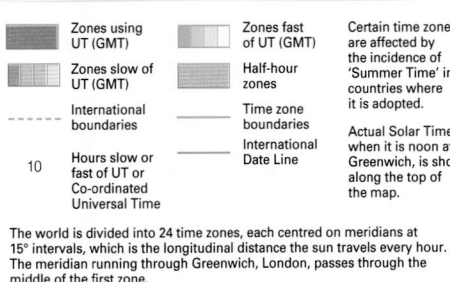

Projection: Mercator

Time Zones

Zones using UT (GMT)	Zones fast of UT (GMT)
Zones slow of UT (GMT)	Half-hour zones

- - - - International boundaries
—— Time zone boundaries
—— International Date Line

10 Hours slow or fast of UT or Co-ordinated Universal Time

Certain time zones are affected by the incidence of 'Summer Time' in countries where it is adopted.

Actual Solar Time, when it is noon at Greenwich, is shown along the top of the map.

The world is divided into 24 time zones, each centred on meridians at 15° intervals, which is the longitudinal distance the sun travels every hour. The meridian running through Greenwich, London, passes through the middle of the first zone.

Rail and Road: The Leading Nations

Total rail network ('000 km) (1995)		Passenger km per head per year		Total road network ('000 km)		Vehicle km per head per year		Number of vehicles per km of roads	
1. USA	235.7	Japan	2,017	USA	6,277.9	USA	12,505	Hong Kong	284
2. Russia	87.4	Belarus	1,880	India	2,962.5	Luxembourg	7,989	Taiwan	211
3. India	62.7	Russia	1,826	Brazil	1,824.4	Kuwait	7,251	Singapore	152
4. China	54.6	Switzerland	1,769	Japan	1,130.9	France	7,142	Kuwait	140
5. Germany	41.7	Ukraine	1,456	China	1,041.1	Sweden	6,991	Brunei	96
6. Australia	35.8	Austria	1,168	Russia	884.0	Germany	6,806	Italy	91
7. Argentina	34.2	France	1,011	Canada	849.4	Denmark	6,764	Israel	87
8. France	31.9	Netherlands	994	France	811.6	Austria	6,518	Thailand	73
9. Mexico	26.5	Latvia	918	Australia	810.3	Netherlands	5,984	Ukraine	73
10. South Africa	26.3	Denmark	884	Germany	636.3	UK	5,738	UK	67
11. Poland	24.9	Slovak Rep.	862	Romania	461.9	Canada	5,493	Netherlands	66
12. Ukraine	22.6	Romania	851	Turkey	388.1	Italy	4,852	Germany	62

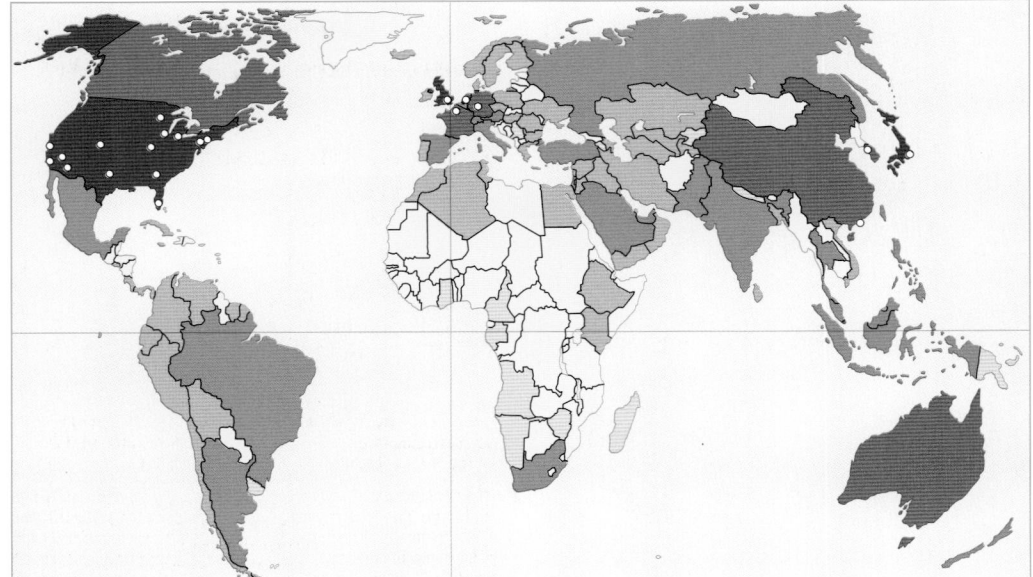

Air Travel

Passenger kilometres flown (the number of passengers – international and domestic – multiplied by the distance flown by each passenger from the airport of origin) (1997)

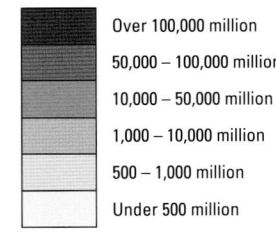

- Over 100,000 million
- 50,000 – 100,000 million
- 10,000 – 50,000 million
- 1,000 – 10,000 million
- 500 – 1,000 million
- Under 500 million

o Major airports (handling over 25 million passengers in 2000)

World's busiest airports (total passengers)
1. Atlanta (Hartsfield)
2. Chicago (O'Hare)
3. Los Angeles (Intern'l)
4. London (Heathrow)
5. Dallas (Dallas/Ft Worth)

World's busiest airports (international passengers)
1. London (Heathrow)
2. Tokyo (Haneda)
3. Frankfurt (International)
4. Paris (De Gaulle)
5. Amsterdam (Schipol)

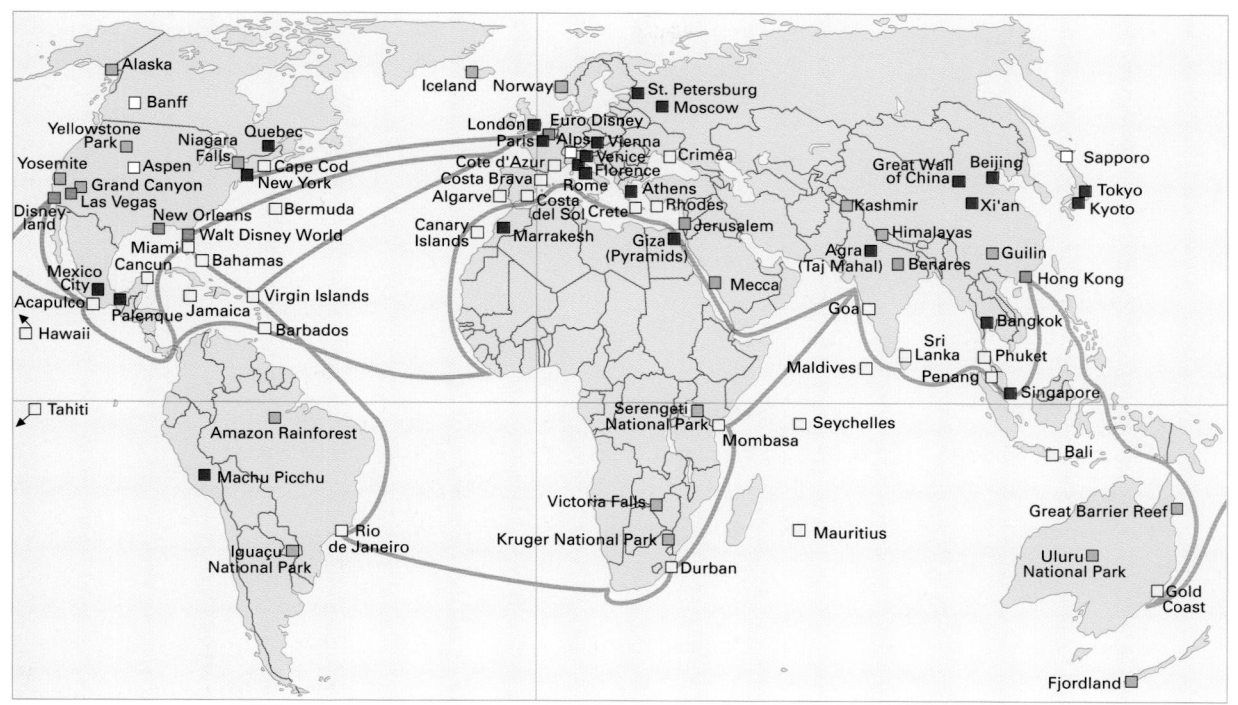

Destinations

- Cultural and historical centres
- Coastal resorts
- Ski resorts
- Centres of entertainment
- Places of pilgrimage
- Places of great natural beauty
- Popular holiday cruise routes

Visitors to the USA

Overseas travellers to the USA, thousands (1997 estimates)

1.	Canada	13,900
2.	Mexico	12,370
3.	Japan	4,640
4.	UK	3,350
5.	Germany	1,990
6.	France	1,030
7.	Taiwan	885
8.	Venezuela	860
9.	South Korea	800
10.	Brazil	785

In 1996, the USA earned the most from tourism, with receipts of more than US $75 billion.

Tourist Spending

Countries spending the most on overseas tourism, US $ million (1996)

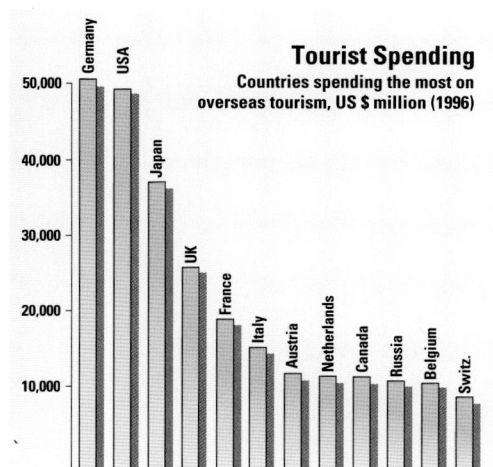

Importance of Tourism

		Arrivals from abroad (1996)	% of world total (1996)
1.	France	66,800,000	10.2%
2.	USA	49,038,000	7.5%
3.	Spain	43,403,000	6.6%
4.	Italy	34,087,000	5.2%
5.	UK	25,960,000	3.9%
6.	China	23,770,000	3.6%
7.	Poland	19,514,000	3.0%
8.	Mexico	18,667,000	2.9%
9.	Canada	17,610,000	2.7%
10.	Czech Republic	17,400,000	2.7%
11.	Hungary	17,248,000	2.6%
12.	Austria	16,642,000	2.5%

In 1996, there was a 4.6% rise, to 593 million, in the total number of people travelling abroad. Small economies in attractive areas are often completely dominated by tourism: in some West Indian islands, for example, tourist spending provides over 90% of total income.

Tourist Earning

Countries receiving the most from overseas tourism, US $ million (1996)

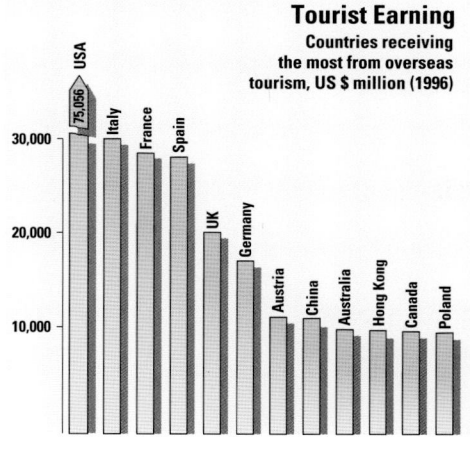

Tourism

Tourism receipts as a percentage of Gross National Product (1996)

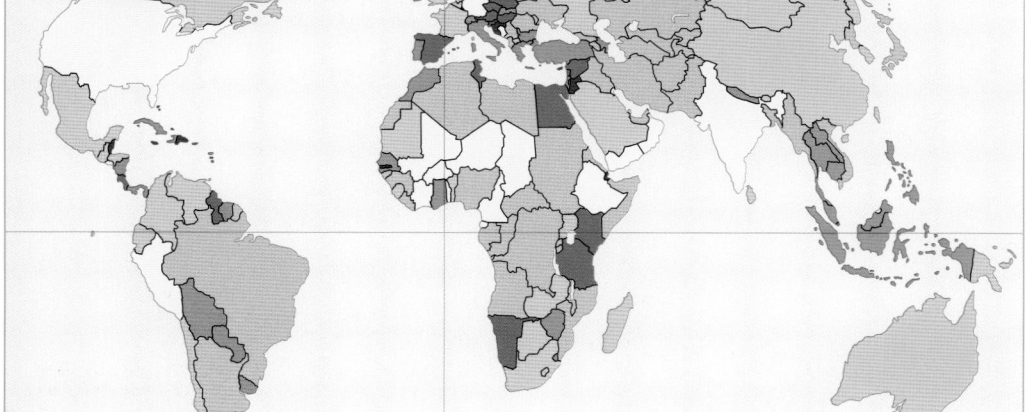

- Over 10% of GNP from tourism
- 5 – 10% of GNP from tourism
- 2.5 – 5% of GNP from tourism
- 1 – 2.5% of GNP from tourism
- 0.5 – 1% of GNP from tourism
- Under 0.5% of GNP from tourism

Countries spending the most on promoting tourism, millions of US $ (1996)

Germany	51
USA	49
Japan	37
UK	25
France	18

Countries with largest tourism receipts, millions of US $ (1996)

USA	75
Italy	30
France	28
Spain	27
UK	21

The World In Focus: **Index**

WORLD CITIES

CITY MAPS

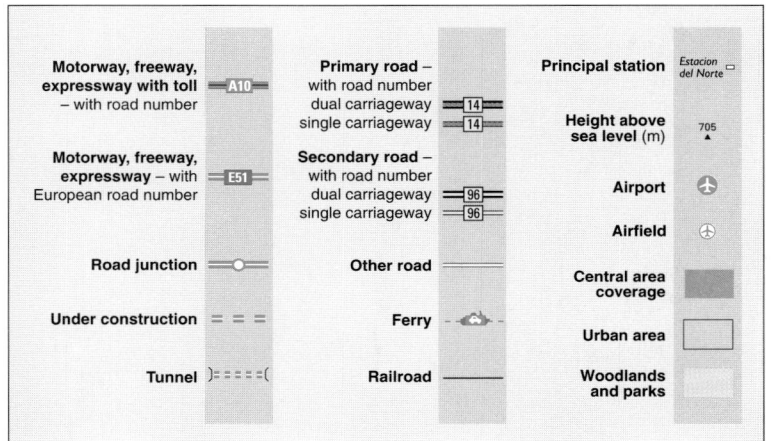

CENTRAL AREA MAPS

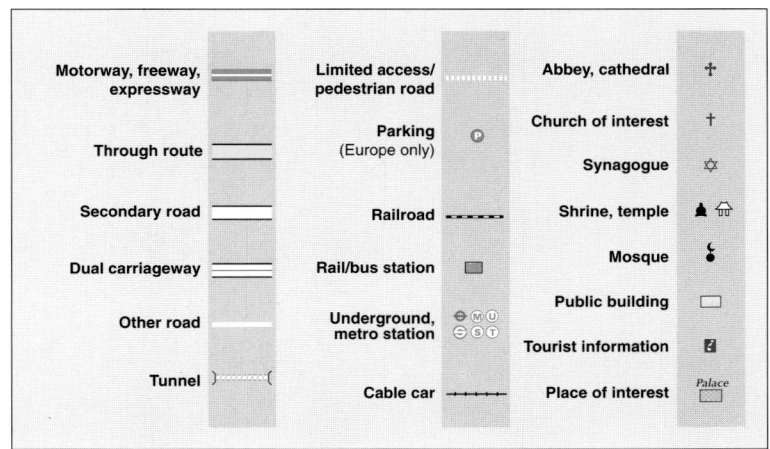

AMSTERDAM

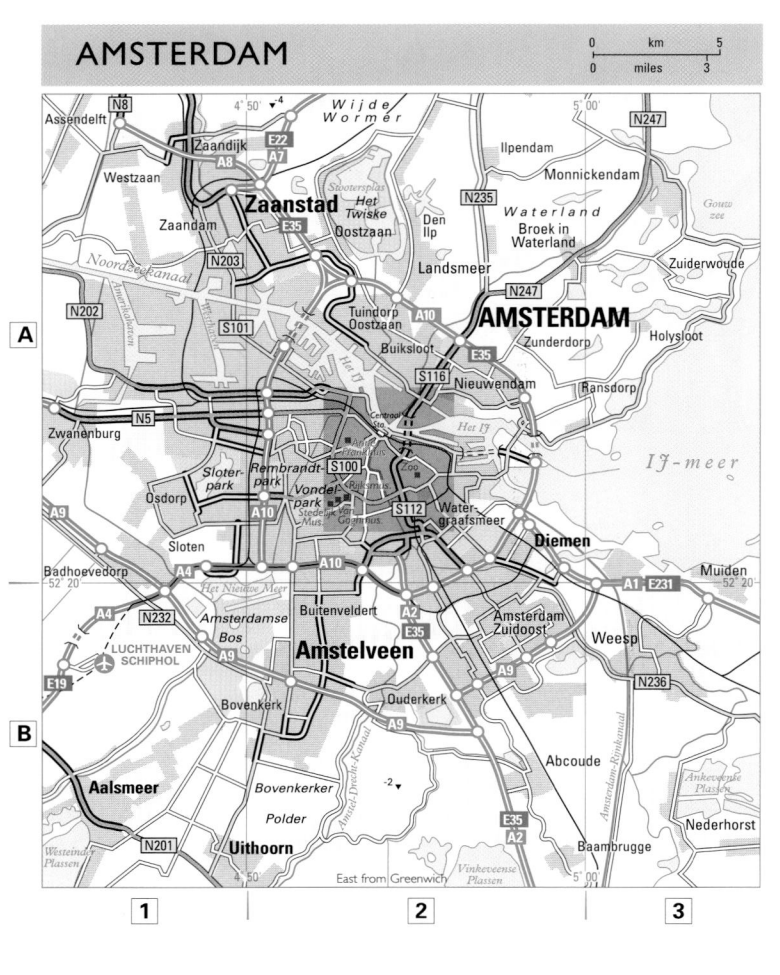

CENTRAL AMSTERDAM

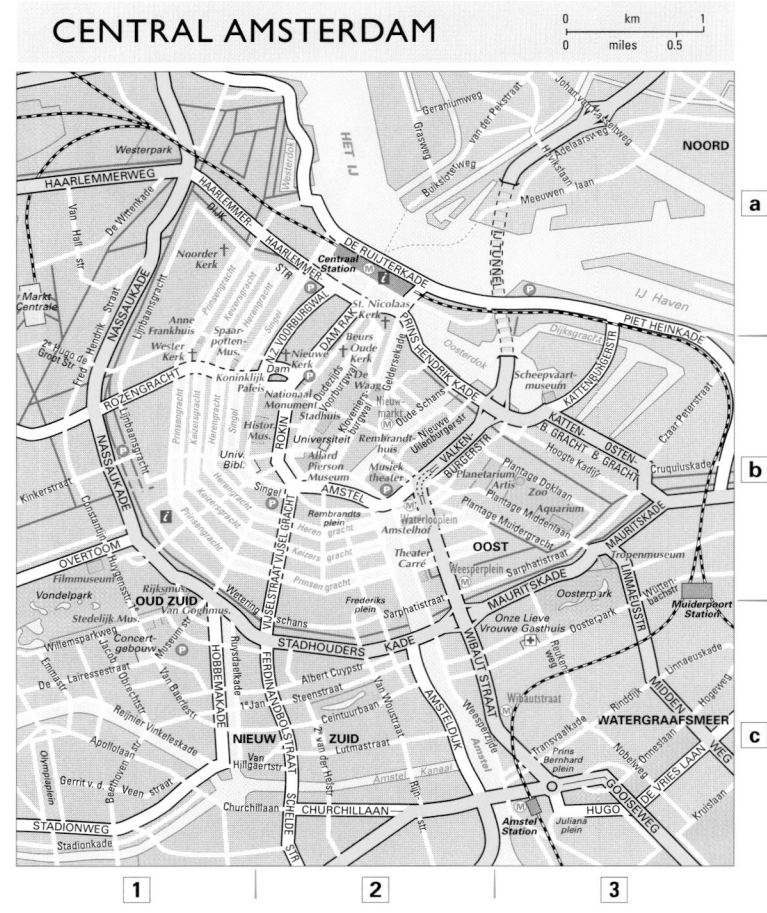

ATHENS

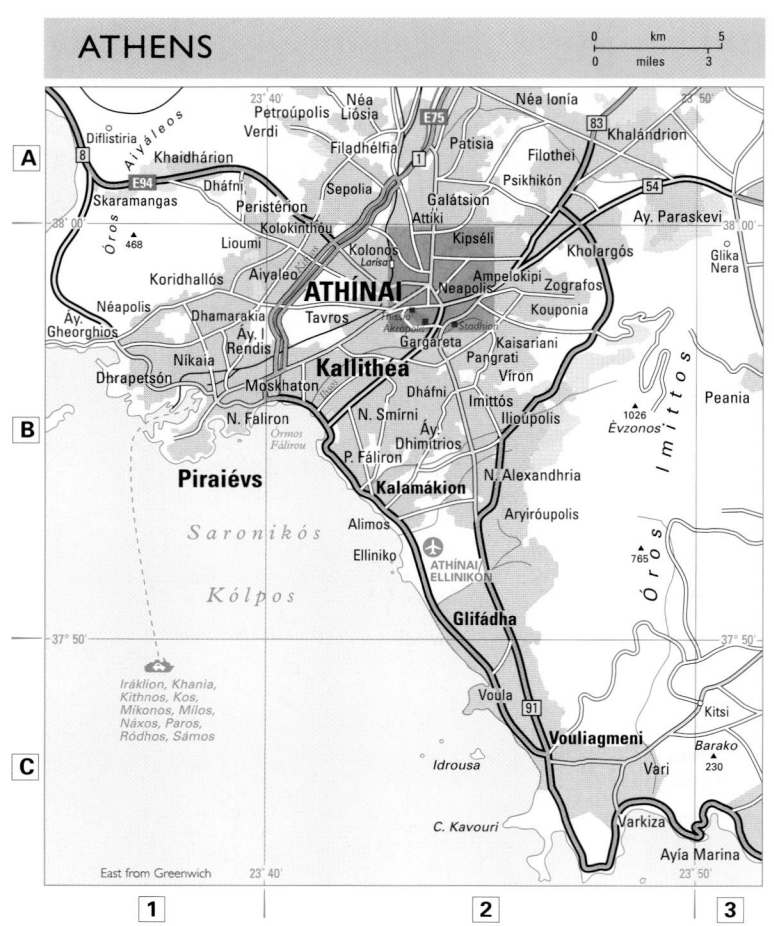

CENTRAL ATHENS

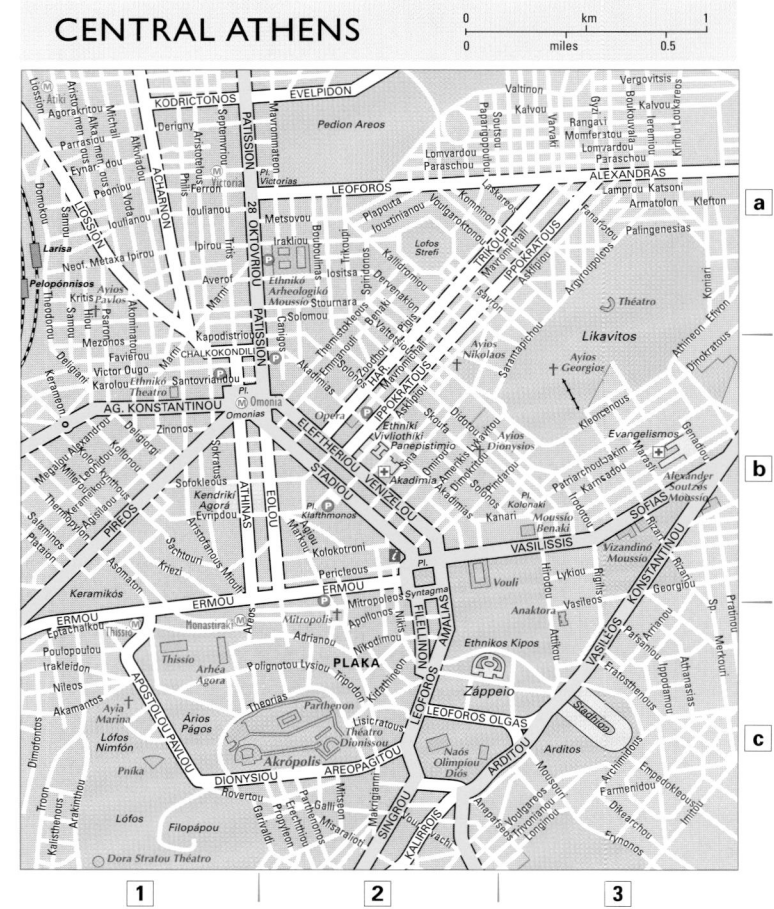

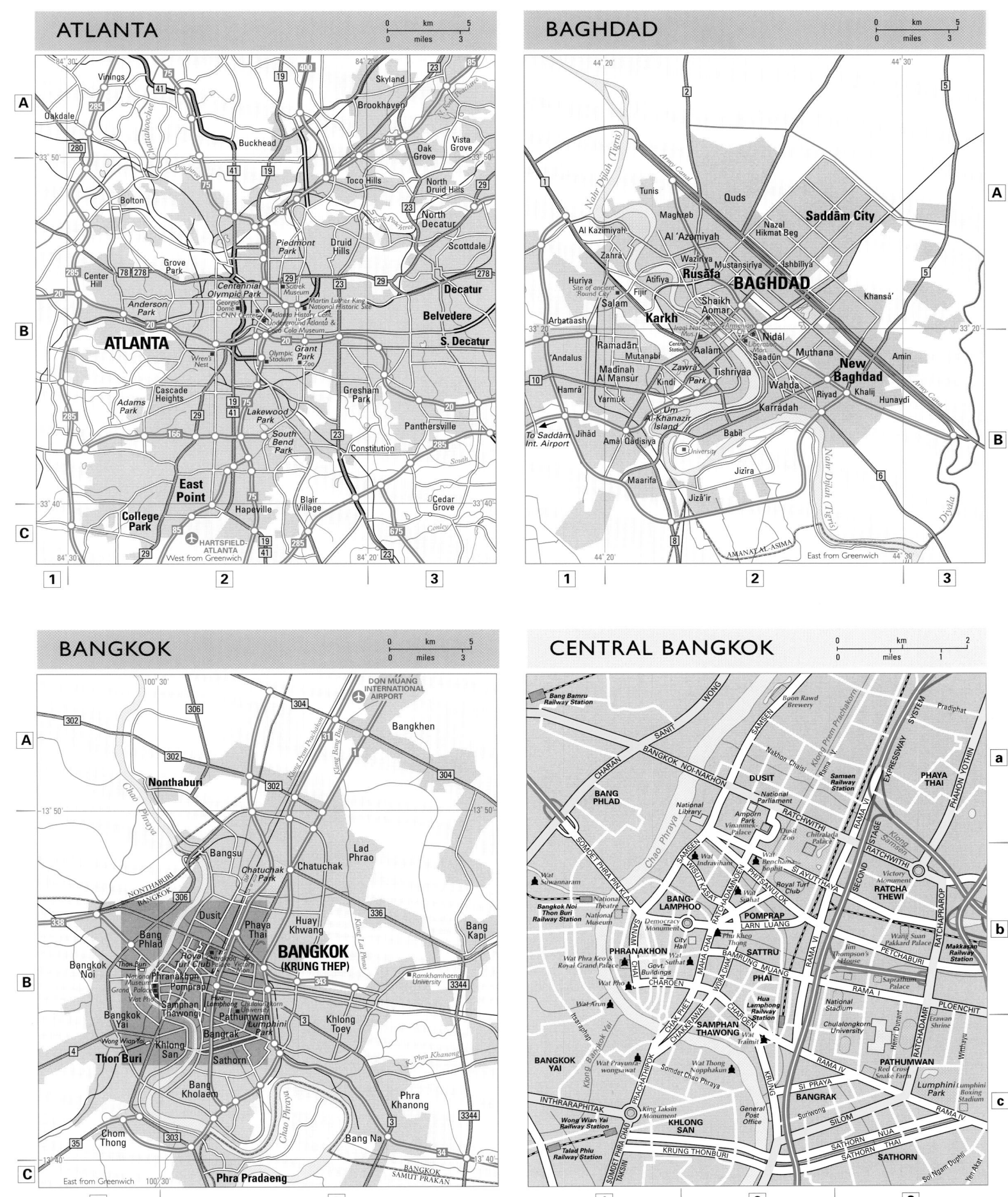

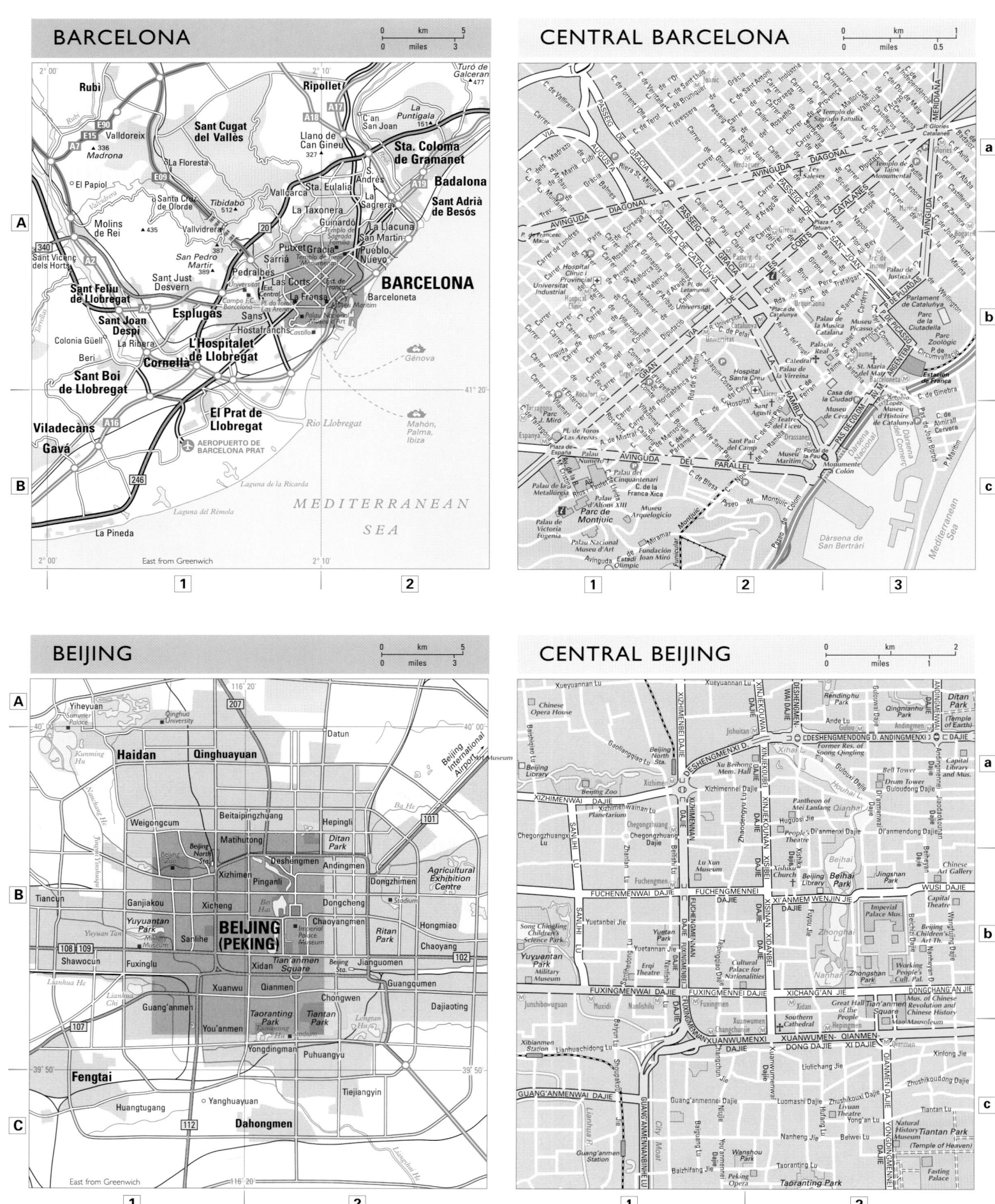

BARCELONA

km 5 / miles 3

Turó de Galceran ▲477

Rubi
Ripollet
La Puntigala 151▲

Sant Cugat del Vallès
C'an San Joan
Llano de Can Gineu 327▲

E90
E15
A7
340
Valldoreix
▲336 Madrona
La Floresta
Sta. Coloma de Gramanet

El Papiol
E09
Santa Cruz de Olorde
Tibidabo 512▲
Vallcarca
Sta. Eulalia
S. Andrés
La Sagrera
Badalona

Molins de Rei
Talandrera
▲435
San Pedro Martir 389▲
387
Vallvidrera
La Táxonera
Guinardó
La Llacuna
San Martin
Sant Adrià de Besós

Sant Vicenç dels Horts
A2
Pedralbes
Sant Just Desvern
Putxet Gracia
Sarrià
Temple de la Sagrada Familia
Pueblo Nuevo

Sant Feliu de Llobregat
A2
Campo F.C. Barcelona
Universit.
Est. Central
Las Corts
La Fransa
Est. de Francia
BARCELONA

Sant Joan Despi
Colonia Güell
La Ribera
Sans
Pl. do Toros
Barceloneta

Esplugas
Hostafranchs
Palau Nacional Museu d'Art

Beri
Cornella
L'Hospitalet de Llobregat
Castillo

Sant Boi de Llobregat
Génova

Viladecans
Gavá
A16
246
El Prat de Llobregat
Rio Llobregat
Mahón, Palma, Ibiza

340
Laguna de la Ricarda
AEROPUERTO DE BARCELONA PRAT
41° 20'

La Pineda
Laguna del Rémola
MEDITERRANEAN SEA

2° 00'   East from Greenwich   2° 10'

1   **2**

CENTRAL BARCELONA

km 1 / miles 0.5

(street map of central Barcelona)

1   **2**   **3**

BEIJING

km 5 / miles 3

Yiheyuan Summer Palace
Qinghua University
116° 20'
207
Datun
40° 00'
Beijing International Airport
Museum

Haidan
Qinghuayuan
Kunming Hu

Weigongcum
Beitaipingzhuang
Hepingli
Ba He
101

Nanhua Lu
Beijing Zoo
Beijing North Sta.
Matihutong
Ditan Park

Tiancun
Ganjiakou
Xicheng
Xizhimen
Pinganli
Deshengmen
Andingmen
Dongzhimen

Yeyuan Tan
Yuyuantan Park
Bei Hai
Dongcheng
Agricultural Exhibition Centre

108 109
Sanlihe
BEIJING (PEKING)
Imperial Palace Museum
Chaoyangmen
Ritan Park
Hongmiao

Shawocun
Fuxinglu
Xidan
Tian'anmen Square
Beijing Sta.
Chaoyang
102
107

Xuanwu
Qianmen
Jianguomen
Guangqumen

Guang'anmen
You'anmen
Taoranting Park
Chongwen
Tiantan Park
Dajiaoting

Lianhua He
Lianhua Chi
Changchunjie
Taoranting Hu
Longtan Hu

Yongdingmen
Puhuangyu

Fengtai
39° 50'
39° 50'

Huangtugang
Yanghuayuan
Tiejiangyin

112
Dahongmen
116° 20'

East from Greenwich

1   **2**

CENTRAL BEIJING

km 2 / miles 1

(street map of central Beijing)

1   **2**

BERLIN

km 0 — 5
miles 0 — 3

Wansdorf Hennigsdorf Hermsdorf Lübars Blankenfelde Schwanebeck Birkholzaue Löhme Werneuchen
Nieder Neuendorf Schulzendorf Waidmannslust Bucholz Neu Buch Birkholz Seefeld Rudolfshöhe
Alter Finkenkrug Heiligensee Tegel Niederschönhausen Karow Neu Lindenberg Lindenberg Blumberg Krummensee Wegendorf
Waldheim Falkensee Johannesstift Tegelort Scharfenberg Rosenthal Blankenburg Ahrensfelde Paulshof Neuhönow
Falkenhagen Siedlung Schönwalde FLUGHAFEN BERLIN-TEGEL Reinickendorf Pankow Heinersdorf Malchow Wartenberg Mehrow Eiche Trappenfelde Altlandsberg Nord
Finkenkrug Seegefeld Haselhorst Wedding Weissensee Falkenburg Hohenschönhausen Eiche Süd Hönow Seeberg Altlandsberg
Döberitz Spandau Volkspark Jungfernheide Siemensstadt Prenzlauerberg Marzahn Friedrichslust
Dallgow Staaken Charlottenburg Tiergarten Mitte Volkspark Friedrichshain Lichtenburg Hellersdorf Neuenhagen Fredersdorf Nord
Seeburg Schlossgarten BERLIN Friedrichshain Biesdorf Wuhlgarten Fredersdorf
Olympia Stadion Teufelsberg Kreuzberg Friedrichsfelde Kaulsdorf Mahlsdorf Dahlwitz-Hoppegarten Birkenstein Bollensdorf
Gatow Grunewald Rathaus Schöneberg Treptow Karlshorst Münchehofe Vogelsdorf
Gross Glienicke Schmargendorf Neukölln FLUGHAFEN BERLIN-TEMPELHOF Heidemühle Kleinschönebeck Schöneiche Gratzwalde
Krampnitz Dahlem Friedenau Tempelhof Oberschöneweide Waldesruh Schönblick
Neu Fahrland Steglitz Niederschöneweide Fichtenau Friedrichshagen Woltersdorf
Nedlitz Schwanenwerder Zehlendorf Britz Köpenick Grosse Müggelsee Wilmshagen Springeberg
Sacrow Nikolassee Lichterfelde Lankwitz Mariendorf Johannisthal Aldershof Rahnsdorf Erkner
Schloss Cecilienhof Wannsee Buckow Rudow Grünau Müggelberge Müggelheim Neu Buchhorst
Potsdam Dreilinden Kleinmachnow Seehof Marienfelde Altglienicke Wendenschloss Gosen
Teltow Grossziethen Bohnsdorf Karolinenhof
FLUGHAFEN BERLIN-SCHÖNEFELD
East from Greenwich

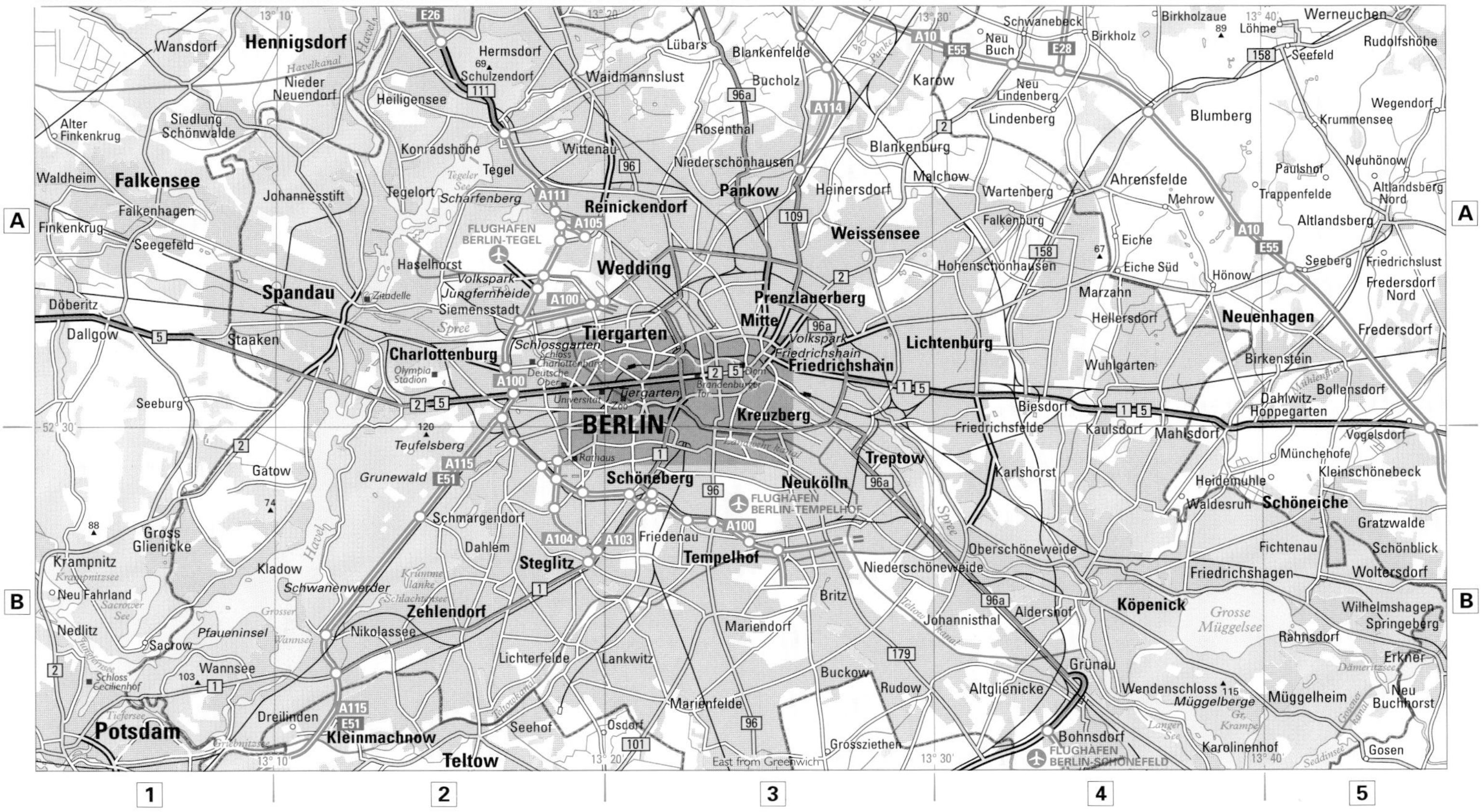

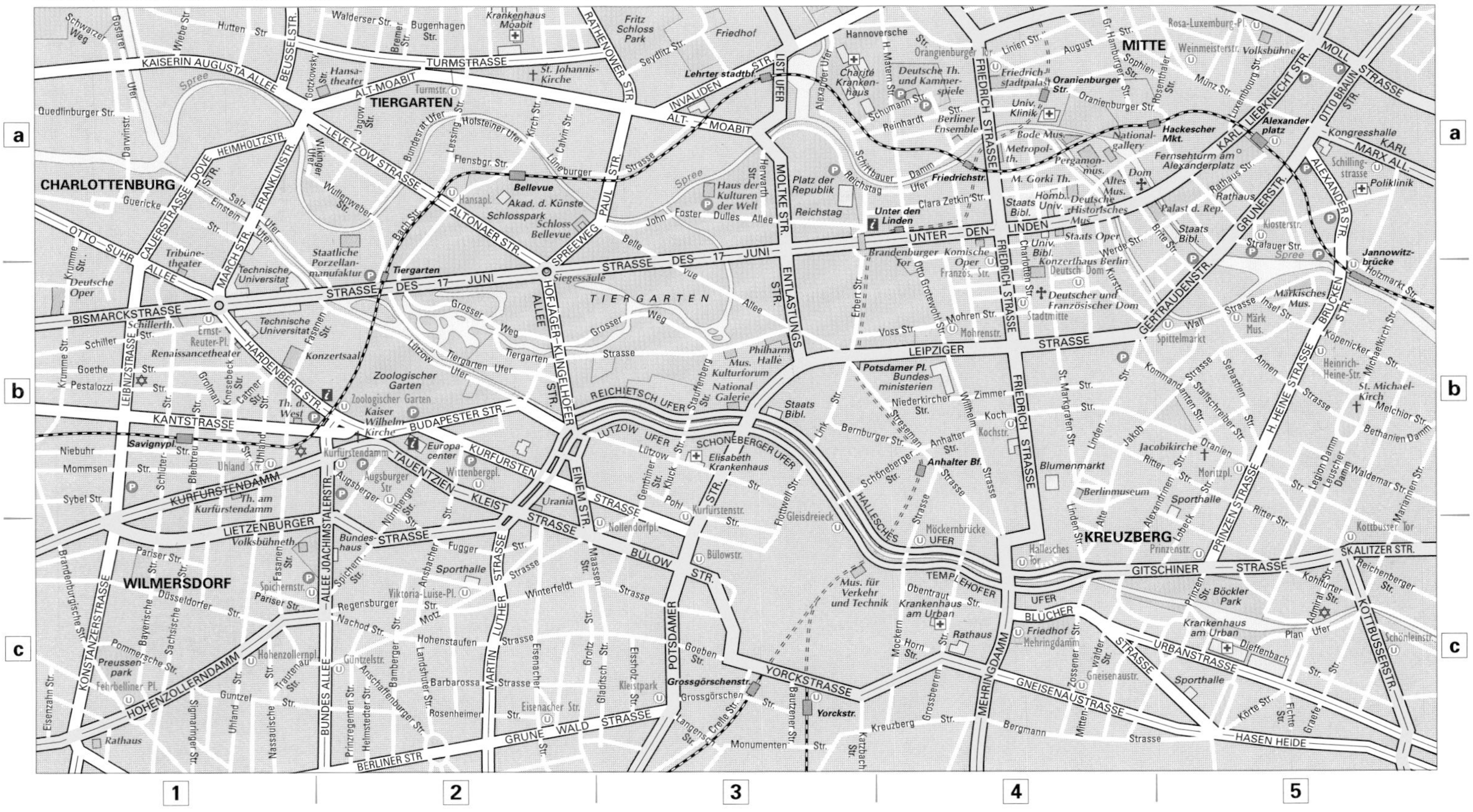

CENTRAL BERLIN

km 0 — 1
miles 0 — 0.5

TIERGARTEN CHARLOTTENBURG MITTE
WILMERSDORF KREUZBERG

Kurfürstendamm Unter den Linden Alexanderplatz
Tiergarten Brandenburger Tor Potsdamer Pl.
Zoologischer Garten Reichstag

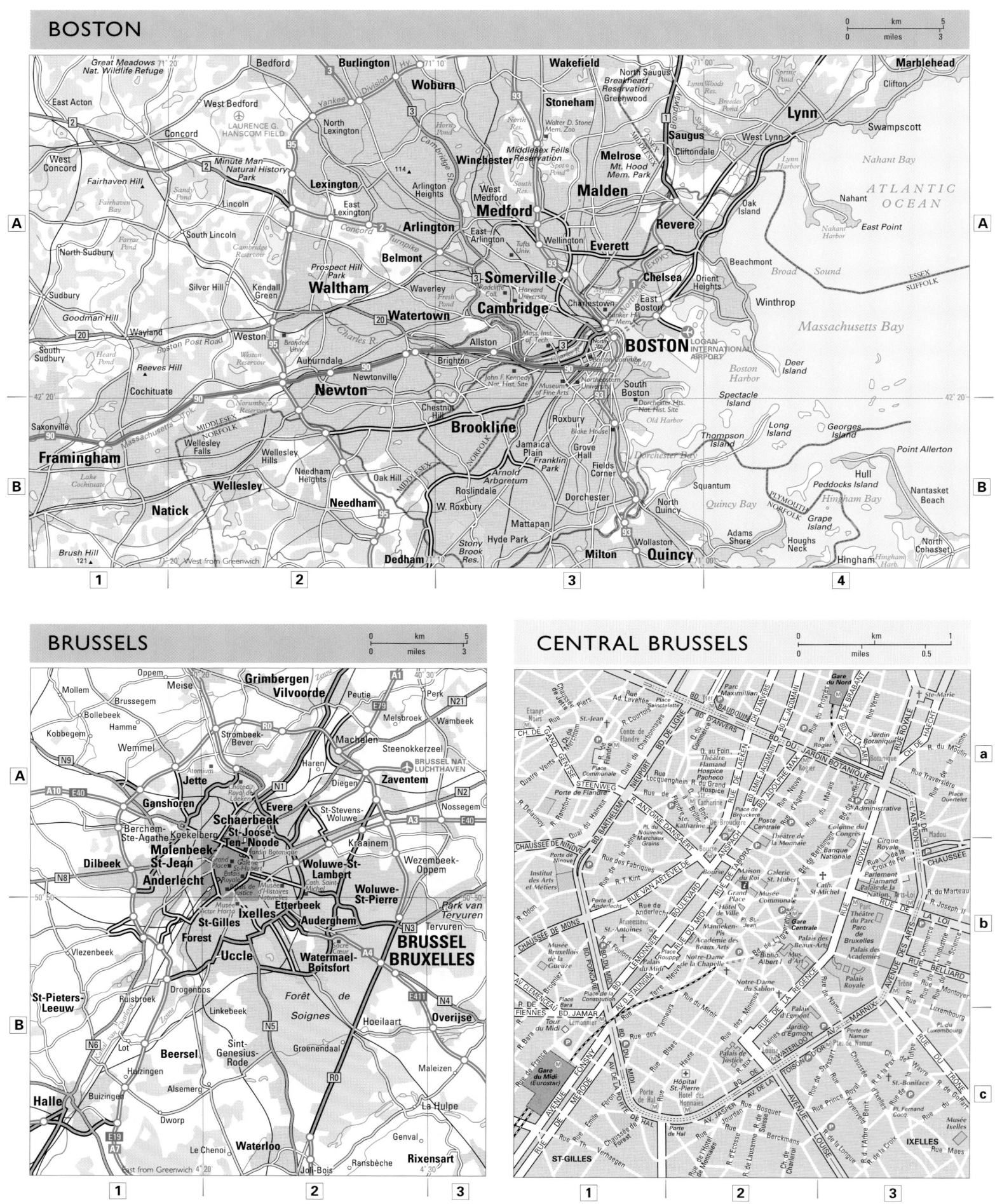

BOSTON

BRUSSELS

CENTRAL BRUSSELS

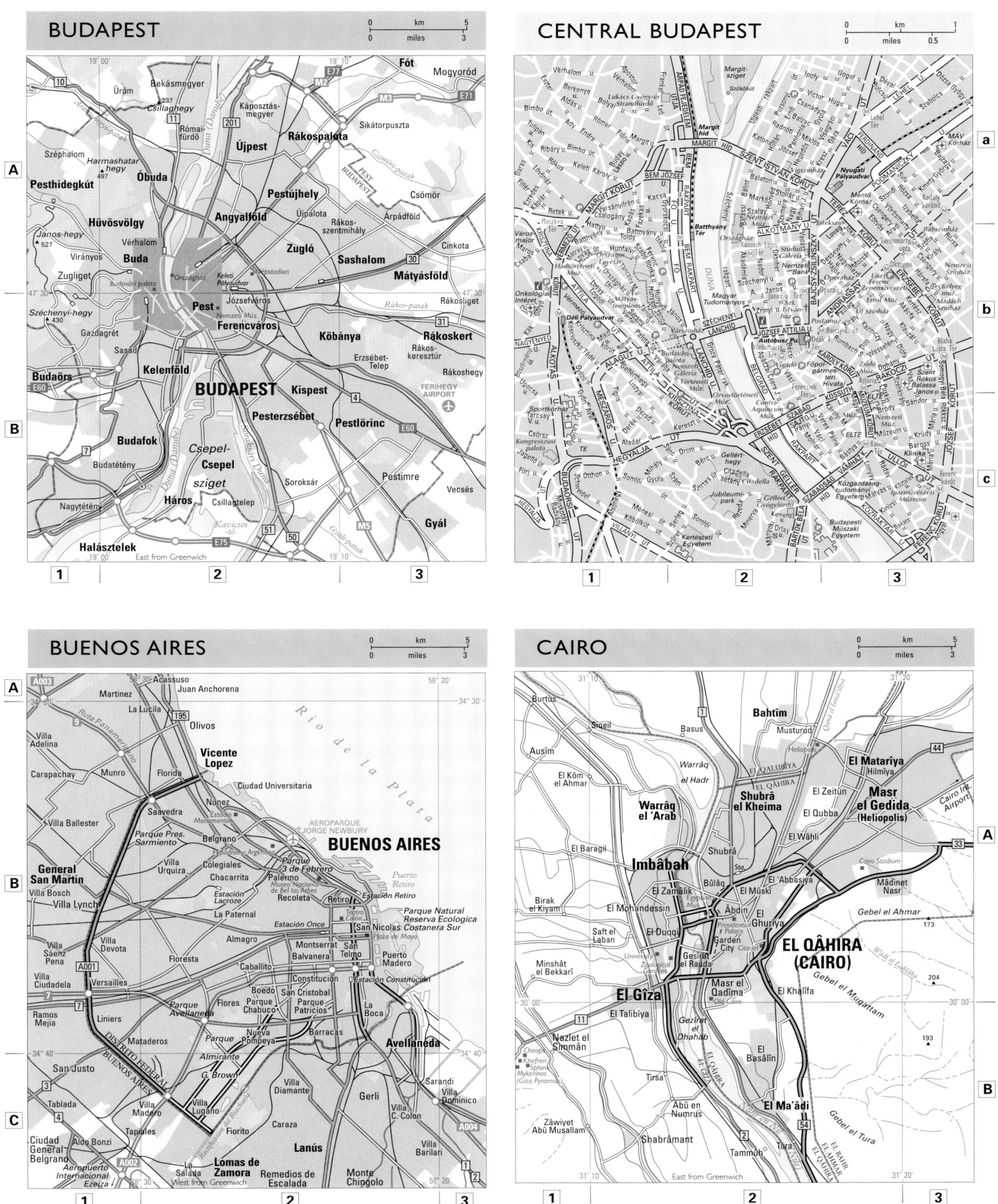

CALCUTTA

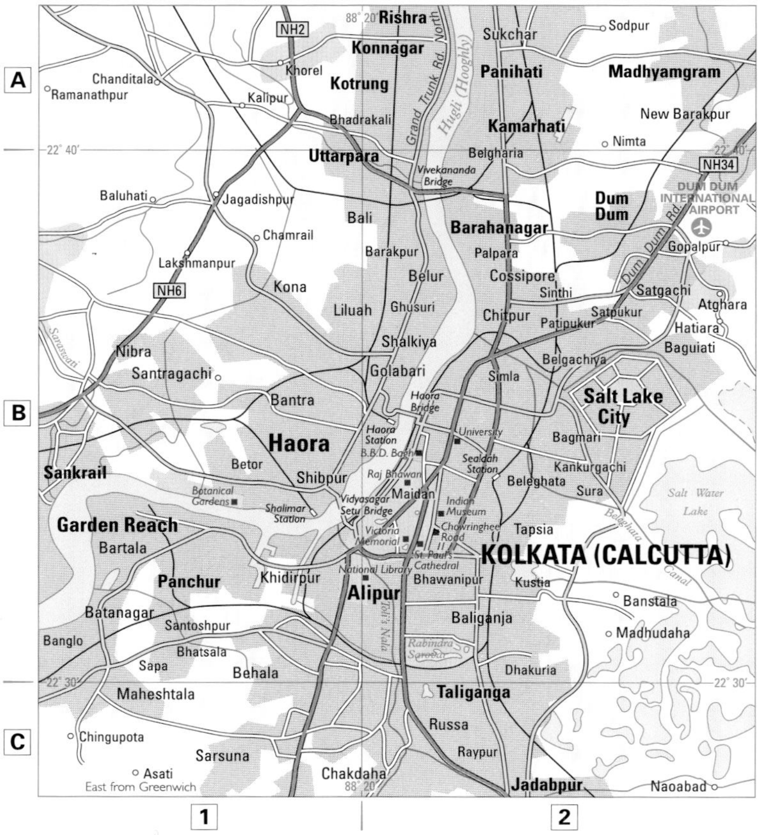

0 km 5
0 miles 3
Rishra
Konnagar
Khorel
Kotrung
Sukchar
Sodpur
Panihati
Madhyamgram
Chanditala
Ramanathpur
Kalipur
Bhadrakali
Kamarhati
New Barakpur
Nimta
Uttarpara
Belgharia
Grand Trunk Rd. North
Hugli (Hooghly)
Vivekananda Bridge
NH2
NH34
NH6
Baluhati
Jagadishpur
Chamrail
Bali
Dum Dum
DUM DUM INTERNATIONAL AIRPORT
Barahanagar
Palpara
Gopalpur
Lakshmanpur
Barakpur
Belur
Cossipore
Sinthi
Satgachi
Atghara
Kona
Liluah
Ghusuri
Chitpur
Satpukur
Patipukur
Hatiara
Baguiati
Shalkiya
Nibra
Santragachi
Golabari
Belgachiya
Simla
Salt Lake City
Bantra
Haora Bridge
Haora
Haora Station
B.B.D. Bagh
University
Bagmari
Sankrail
Betor
Shibpur
Raj Bhawan
Sealdah Station
Kankurgachi
Beleghata
Botanical Gardens
Shalimar Station
Maidan
Vidyasagar Setu Bridge
Indian Museum
Sura
Salt Water Lake
Garden Reach
Victoria Memorial
Chowringhee Road
Tapsia
Bartala
St. Paul's Cathedral
KOLKATA (CALCUTTA)
Panchur
Khidirpur
National Library
Bhawanipur
Kustia
Alipur
Banstala
Batanagar
Tolly's Nala
Baliganja
Santoshpur
Madhudaha
Banglo
Bhatsala
Rabindra Sarobar
Sapa
Behala
Dhakuria
Maheshtala
Taliganga
Chingupota
Russa
Raypur
Sarsuna
Asati
Chakdaha
Jadabpur
Naoabad
East from Greenwich
88° 20'
22° 40'
22° 30'
A
B
C
1
2

CANTON

0 km 5
0 miles 3
113° 10'
113° 20'
Gangtou
Xiaoping
107
Lishui
Yuanxiatian
Chienzui
Chantian
BAIYUN AIRPORT
Baiyun Hill Scenic Spot
Zhushadi
205
106
Zhoucun
Shuikou
23° 10'
Hengsha
Shahe
Sanyuanli
Guangzhou Zhan (Railway Station)
Exhibition Hall
Guangzhou Museum
Xichang
Huanghuagang Mausoleum of the 72 Martyrs
Yongfucun
Guangzhou Zoo
Lieshi
Lingyuan
Xiasha chong
Baisha
Datansha
Liurong Temple
Nongminyundong
Jiangxisuo
Shipai
Beitsun
Haizhu
Guangchang
Nan Zhan (Railway Station)
GUANGZHOU (CANTON)
Dongshanhu Park
Ershatou
324
Shiweitang
Shamian
Nandang
Xiaogang Park
Zhu Jiang (Pearl)
Fangcun
Zhongshan University
Yanbu
Shayuan
Luojiang
Hedong
Gangwei
Dongjiao
Nanbiancun
Guanshuo
Lichiao
Zhu Jiang (Pearl)
Pingzhou
Dashi
Zhicun
105
East from Greenwich
A
B
1
2
3

CAPE TOWN

0 km 5
0 miles 3
ATLANTIC OCEAN
Table Bay
Milnerton
18° 30'
R27
Tijgerhof
N7
N1
CAPE TOWN
YSTERPLAAT AERODROME
Goodwood
Green Point
WINGFIELD AERODROME
Parow
Vasco
Sea Point
Brooklyn
Windermere
Signal Hill 350
St. George's Cathedral
Maitland
R102
Elsies-rivier
Tamboers-kloof
Woodstock
Salt River
Thornton
Zonnebloem
699
Vredehoek
M3
N2
M4
Royal Observatory
Pinelands
Groote Schuur Hospital
Langa
Bishop Lavis
Camps Bay
Devil's Peak 1000
Bonteheuwel
University of Cape Town
Bridge-town
D.F. MALAN AIRPORT
Table Mountain 1086
Rondebosch
Athlone
M18
Heideveld
Twelve Apostles
M6
Claremont
M5
Crawford
M7
Manenberg
M17
Kirstenbosch Botanical Gardens
Bishops-court
Lansdowne
M18
Nyanga
M63
Kenilworth
725
Wynberg
Wetton
34° 00'
M63
Constantia
Youngsfield
Ottery
R300
Plumstead
M41
Hout Bay
Diep-rivier
Parkwood
Grassy Park
Mitchell's Plain
Bergvliet
Heathfield
Cape Flats
M6
Tokai Plantation
M17
Hout Bay
Retreat
Rondevlei
Zeekoevlei
Strandfontein
Westlake
R310
593
Lakeside
Sandvlei
Silvermine Nature Reserve
R310
M6
M64
Kalkbaaiberg 516
Muizenberg
False Bay
INDIAN OCEAN
East from Greenwich
A
B
1
2

CENTRAL CAPE TOWN

0 km 0.5
0 miles 0.25
Green Point Common
Fritz Sonnenberg Rd.
Fort Wynyard Museum
GREEN POINT
Beach Road
Victoria Wharf
Robben Island Trips
Victoria Basin
IMAX
Market Sq.
V & A Waterfront
Bill Peters Drive
Vlei Rd.
Green Point Stadium
Fort Wynyard Rd.
Portswood Road
Dock Road Theatre
Old Port Captain's Bldg.
Berties Landing
SA Maritime Museum
Clock Tower
Alfred Basin
South Arm
Fish Market
Western Boulevard
Main Drive
Two Oceans Aquarium
Antrim Rd.
St. George's Rd.
Clydebank Rd.
Pine Rd.
Dysart Rd.
Wigtown Rd.
Cheviot
Cavalcade
FORESHORE
Duncan Dock
High Level Road
Thornhill
Joubert Rd.
Ocean View Dr.
Springbok Rd.
Vesperdene Rd.
Wessels Rd.
Hillside
Dock Road
Duncan Rd.
Chepstow
Ocean View Dr.
Carreg
Ebenezer Rd.
Port Rd.
Merriman Rd.
Old Malay Cemetery
Somerset Road
Strand Street
Prestwich St.
Alfred Rd.
Dock Rd.
Waterkant Loader
Alfred St.
Chiappini St.
Hans Strijdom Ave
Coen Steytler Ave.
CENTRAL
Signal Hill 350 m
Noon Gun
Signal Hill Rd.
SCHOTSCHE KLOOF
Longmarket St.
Jamai Mosque
Vos Hudson
Rose St.
Bree St.
Riebeek St.
Waterkant St.
Nico Theatre Centre
Heerengracht Boulevard
Military Rd.
Voetboog Rd.
Yusuf
Church St.
Chiappini St.
Berg St.
Shortmarket St.
Van Riebeeck Statue
Pentz Rd.
Wale St.
Rose St.
Pan African Market
Civic Centre
MALAY QUARTER
Bo-Kaap Museum
Koopmans de Wet Hse.
Old Marine Dr.
Cape Town Railway Station
Upr. Bloem St.
Leeuwen
Tudor Hse.
Old Town Hse.
Greenmarket Sq.
Main Post Office
Strand
Adderley
Buitengracht
Loop
Long
Wale St.
Groote Kerk
Bus Station
Street
Military Rd.
Bryant St.
Lion St.
Peace Jordaan
St. George's Cath.
Old Slave Lodge
Castle of Good Hope, Military Museum, W. Fehr Collection
Leekloof
Poyser Rd.
Milner
Devonport Rd.
Queens Rd.
Brownlow Rd.
Parliament
City Hall
Company's Gardens
Plein St.
Barrack St.
Darling St.
Burnside Rd.
Leeuwenvoet
Tamboerskloof
Upper Buitengracht
Buitensingel
Queen Victoria St.
Parliament
District Six Mus.
South African Mus.
De Tuynhuys
Boeland St.
Albert Rd.
Gilmour Hills
Woodside
New Church St.
Park Rd.
Orange St.
Government Ave.
National Art Gallery
Canterbury St.
Hanover Rd.
a
b
c
1
2
3

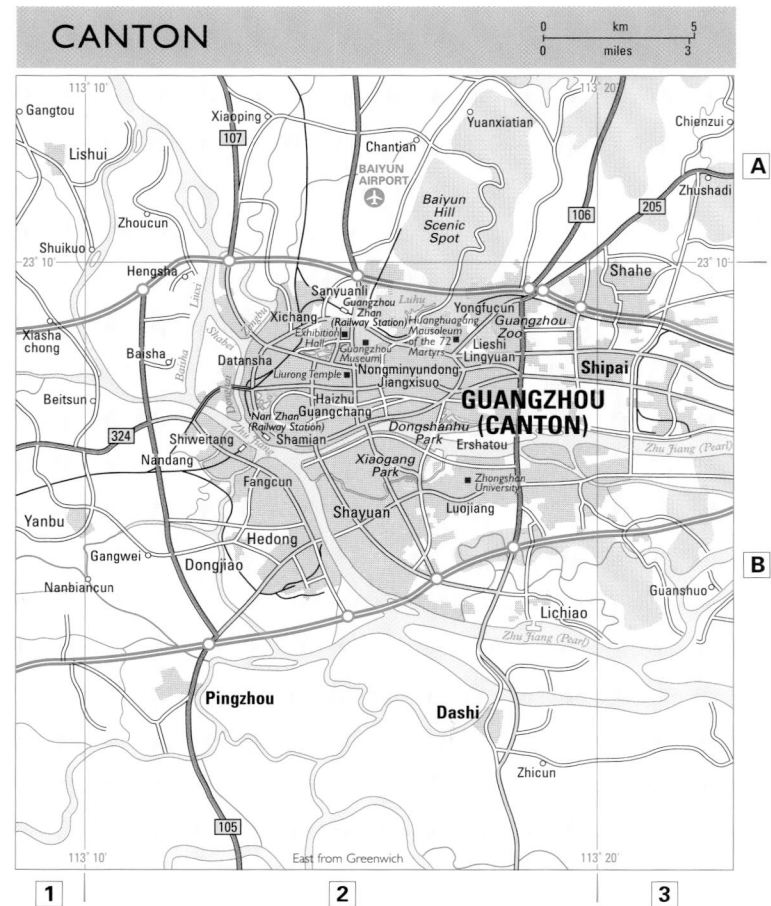

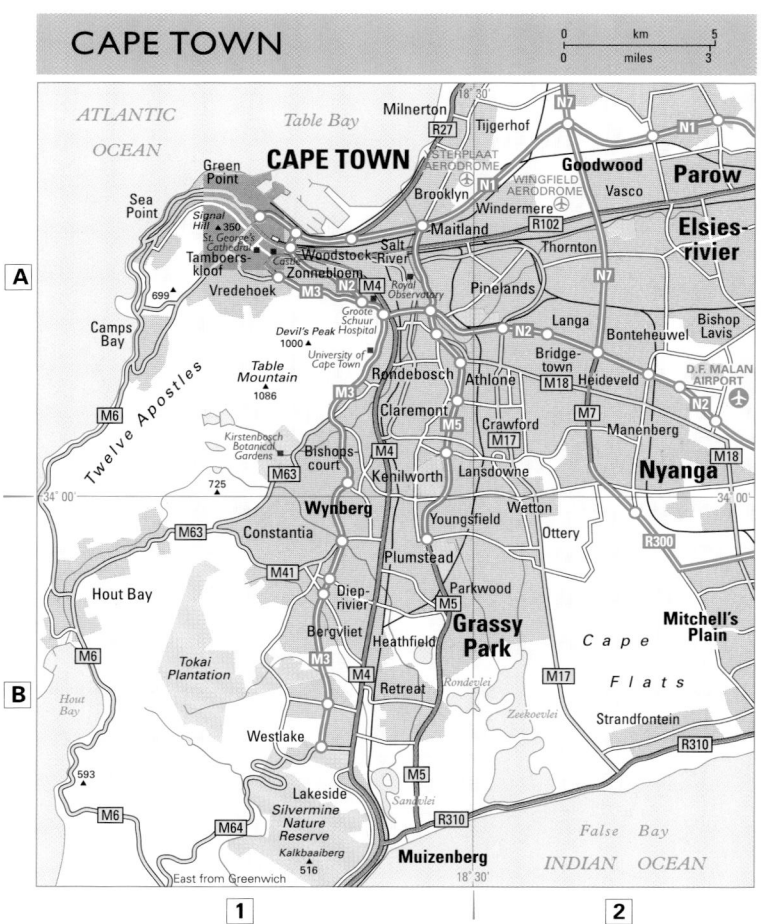

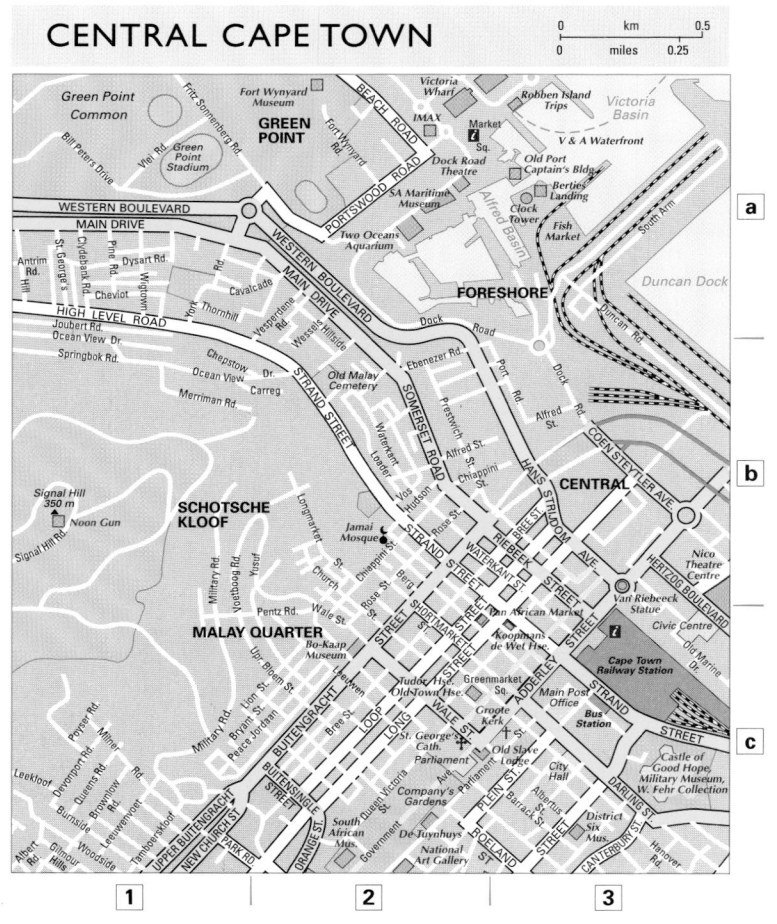

CHICAGO

0 km 5
0 miles 3

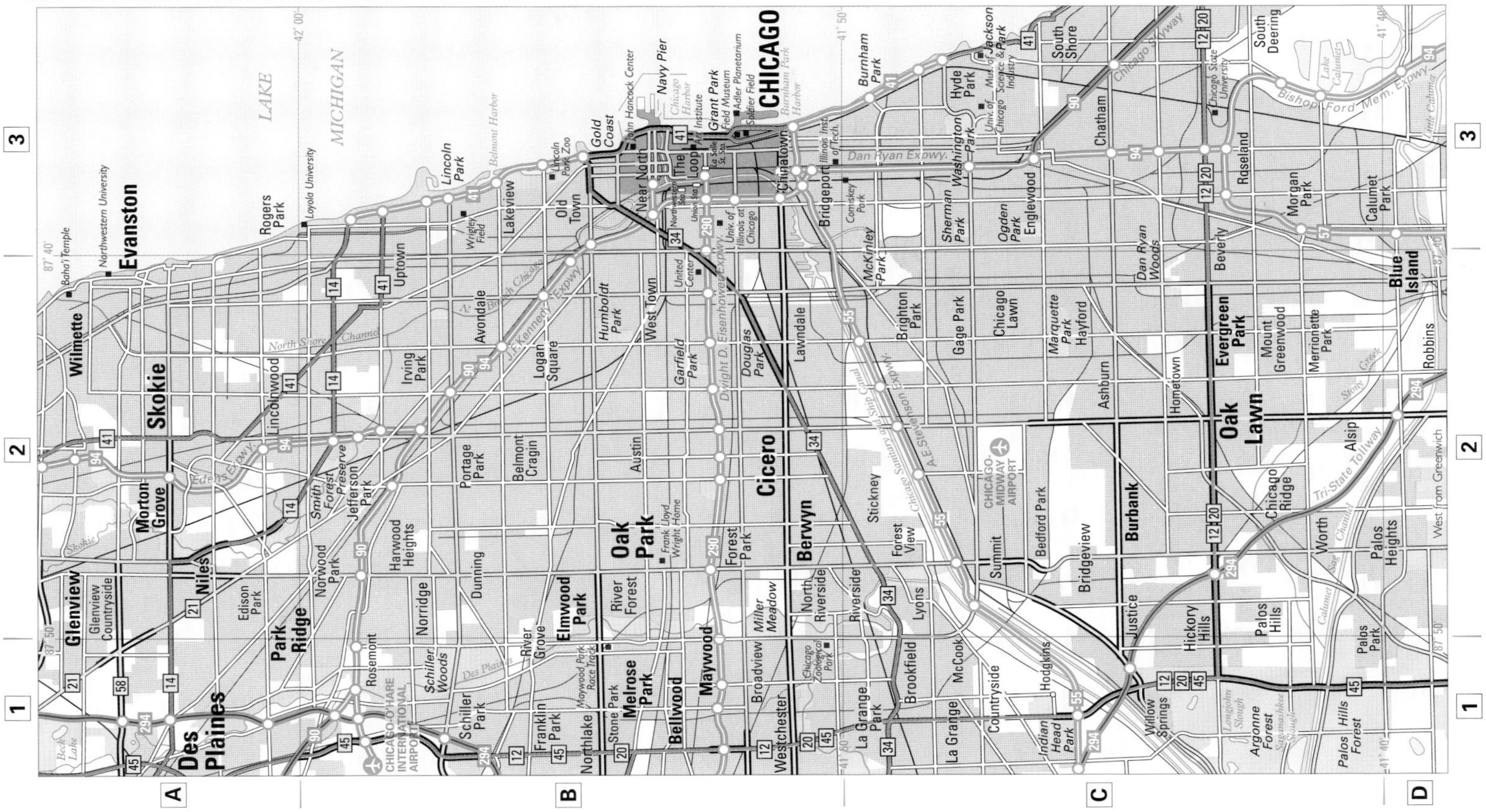

LAKE MICHIGAN

Northwestern University
Baha'i Temple
Evanston
Loyola University
Rogers Park
Wilmette
Skokie
Morton Grove
Glenview
Glenview Countryside
Niles
Park Ridge
Edison Park
Norridge
Rosemont
Schiller Woods
Des Plaines
CHICAGO O'HARE INTERNATIONAL AIRPORT
Harwood Heights
Norwood Park
Dunning
Schiller Park
Franklin Park
Northlake
Melrose Park
Bellwood
Maywood
River Grove
Elmwood Park
River Forest
Oak Park
Stone Park
Broadview
Westchester
La Grange Park
La Grange
Brookfield
Chicago Zoological Park
Riverside
North Riverside
Forest View
Stickney
Berwyn
Cicero
Countryside
Indian Head Park
Willow Springs
Lincolnwood
Lincolnshire
Uptown
Lakeview
Wrigley Field
Old Town
Lincoln Park
Lincoln Park Zoo
Gold Coast
John Hancock Center
Navy Pier
Near North
The Loop
CHICAGO
Grant Park
Art Institute
Adler Planetarium
Shedd Field Museum
Soldier Field
Burnham Park
Avondale
Logan Square
Humboldt Park
West Town
United Center
Univ. of Illinois at Chicago
Garfield Park
Douglas Park
Lawndale
Chinatown
Bridgeport
Illinois Tech.
Comiskey Park
McKinley Park
Portage Park
Belmont Cragin
Austin
Brighton Park
Gage Park
Chicago Lawn
Marquette Park
Hayford
Ashburn
Hometown
Oak Lawn
Evergreen Park
Mount Greenwood
Merrionette Park
Robbins
Blue Island
Palos Heights
Palos Park
Palos Hills
Hickory Hills
Justice
Burbank
Chicago Ridge
Worth
Bridgeview
Bedford Park
Summit
Lyons
McCook
Hodgkins
CHICAGO MIDWAY AIRPORT
Sherman Park
Ogden Park
Englewood
Washington Park
Hyde Park
Univ. of Chicago
Museum of Science & Industry
Chatham
South Shore
Jackson Park
Beverly
Morgan Park
Roseland
Calumet Park
South Deering
Dan Ryan Expwy
Bishop Ford Mem. Expwy
Tri-State Tollway

CENTRAL CHICAGO

0 km 1
0 miles 0.5

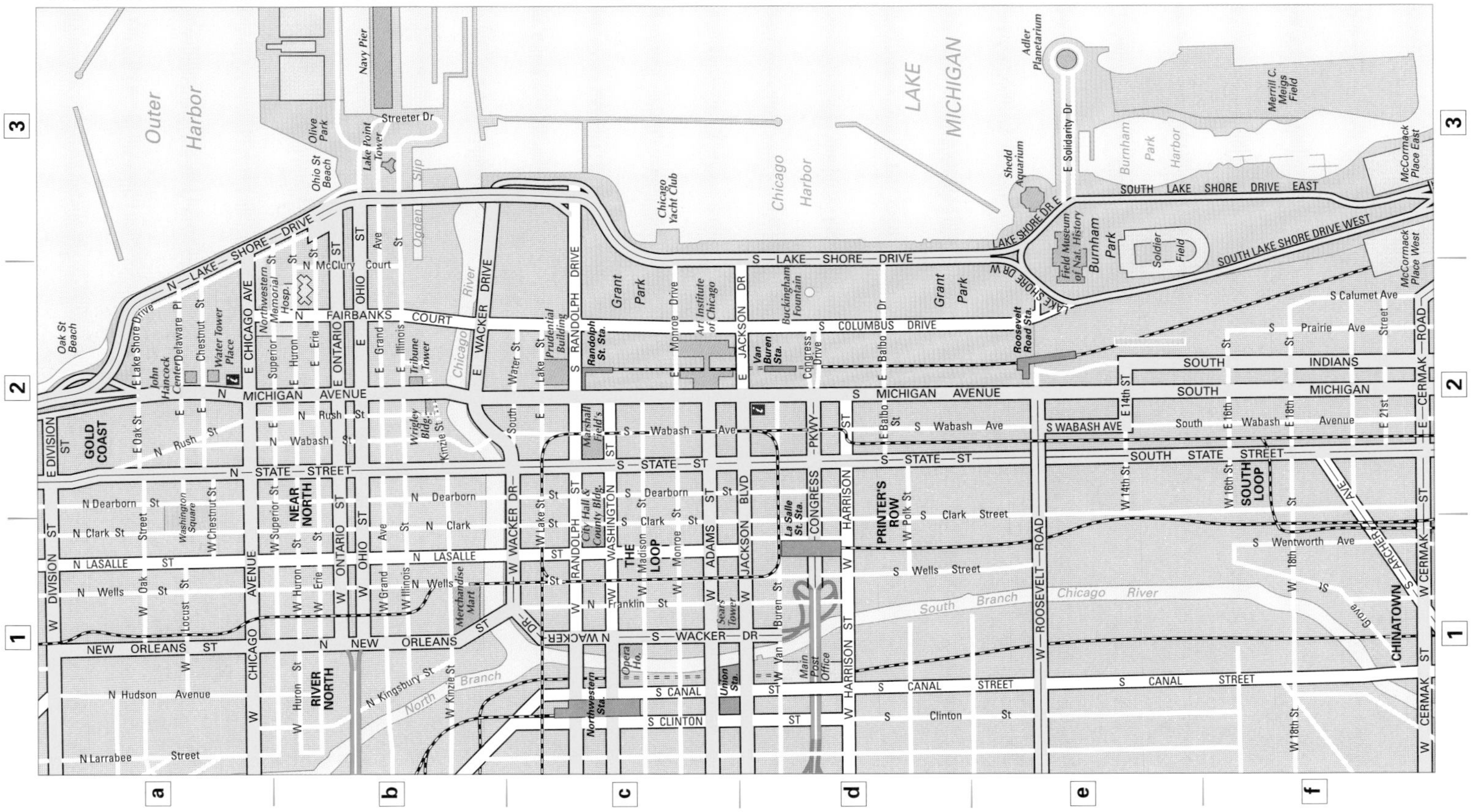

Outer Harbor
Navy Pier
Olive Park
Lake Point Tower
Ohio St Beach
Streeter Dr
LAKE MICHIGAN
Chicago Harbor
Adler Planetarium
Shedd Aquarium
Merrill C. Meigs Field
Burnham Park Harbor
McCormick Place East
McCormick Place West
Field Museum of Nat. History
Soldier Field
Burnham Park
Oak St Beach
Gold Coast
John Hancock Center
Water Tower Place
Near North
River North
Chicago Yacht Club
Grant Park
Art Institute of Chicago
Buckingham Fountain
Prudential Building
Tribune Tower
Wrigley Bldg.
Marshall Field's
The Loop
City Hall County Bldg.
La Salle St. Sta.
Printer's Row
Randolph St. Sta.
Van Buren St. Sta.
Roosevelt Road Sta.
Union Sta.
Northwestern Sta.
Opera Ho.
Sears Tower
Main Post Office
South Loop
Chinatown
Chicago River
South Branch
North Branch

N Lake Shore Drive
E Lake Shore Drive
N Michigan Avenue
S Michigan Avenue
S Lake Shore Drive
S Wabash Ave
State Street
S State Street
E Wacker Drive
S Wacker Drive
E Randolph St
W Randolph St
E Washington St
W Washington St
E Madison St
W Madison St
E Monroe St
W Monroe St
E Adams St
W Adams St
W Jackson Blvd
E Jackson Dr
Congress Pkwy
E Balbo Ave
W Harrison St
W Roosevelt Road
W Cermak Rd
E Solidarity Dr
South Lake Shore Drive East
South Lake Shore Drive West
S Columbus Drive
Columbus Drive
Monroe Drive
Jackson Drive
Van Buren Drive
Grant Park
New Orleans St
N Canal St
S Canal Street
S Clinton St
N LaSalle St
N Clark St
N Dearborn St
N Wells St
N Franklin St
E Division St
E Oak St
E Cedar St
E Bellevue Pl
E Delaware Pl
E Chestnut St
E Pearson St
E Chicago Ave
E Superior St
E Huron St
E Erie St
E Ontario St
E Ohio St
E Grand Ave
E Illinois St
N Rush St
N St Clair St
N McClurg Ct
N Fairbanks Court
E Prairie Ave
S Calumet Ave
S Indiana Ave
E 14th St
E 18th St
E 21st St
N Larrabee Street
N Hudson Avenue
N Kingsbury St

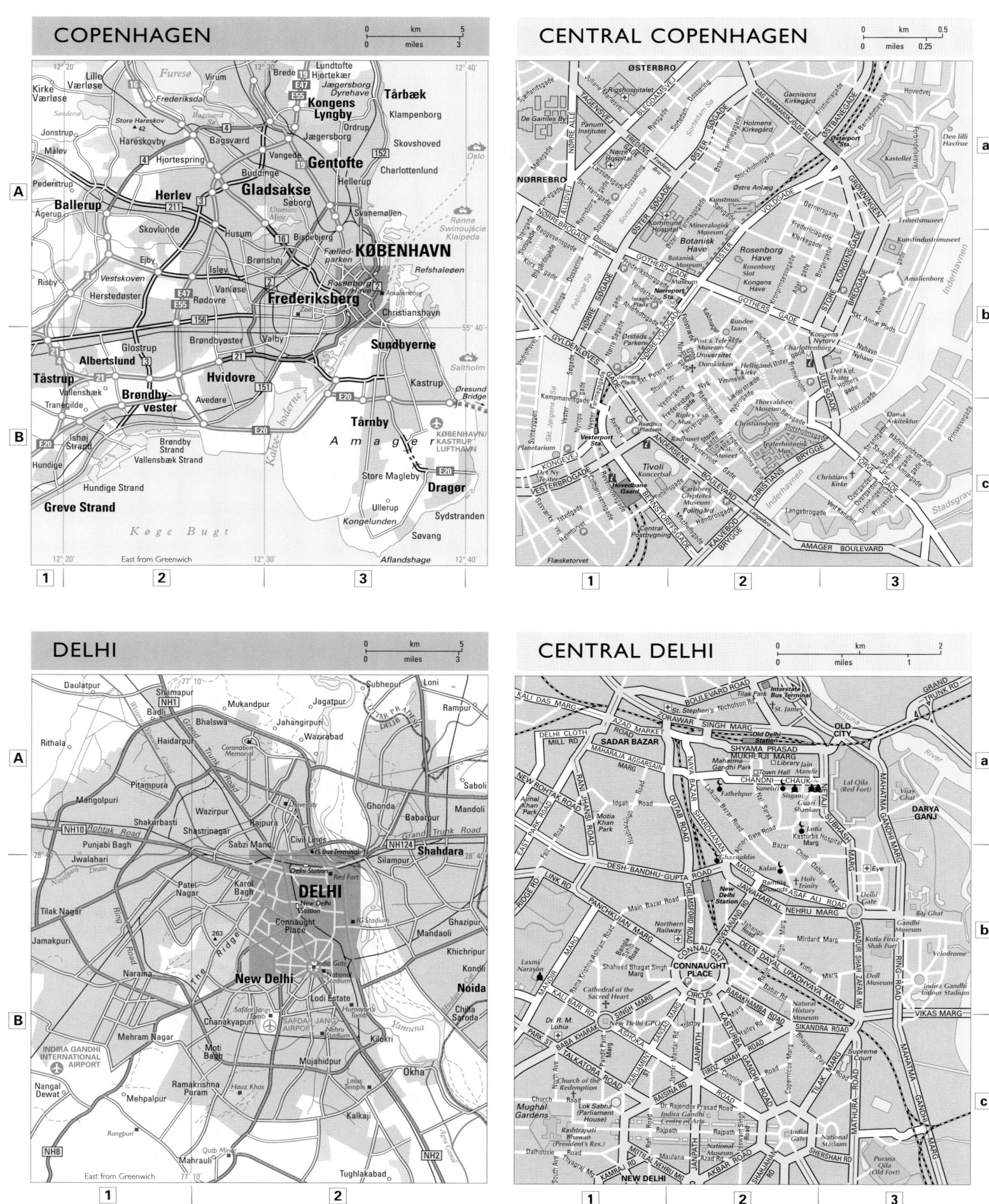

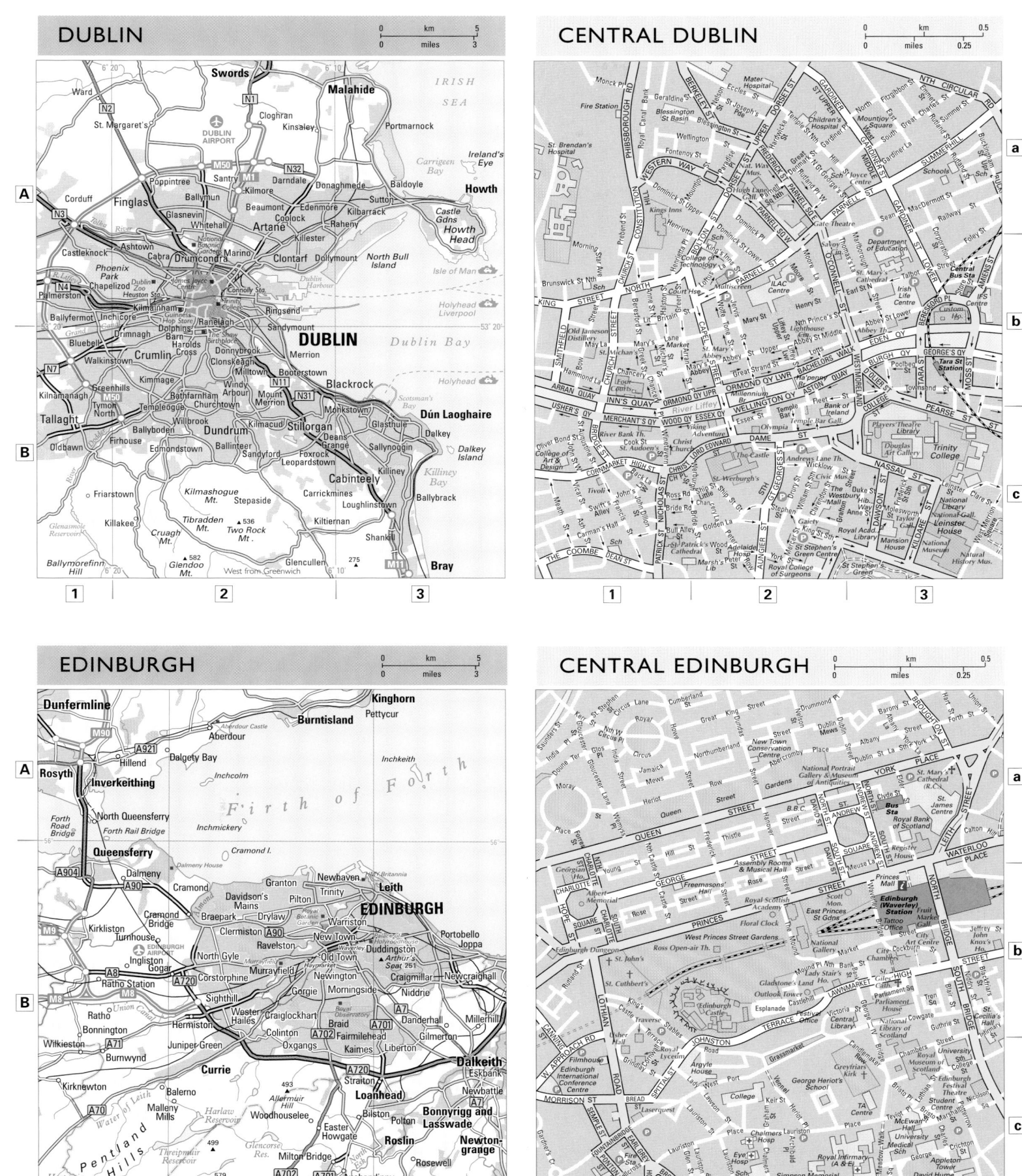

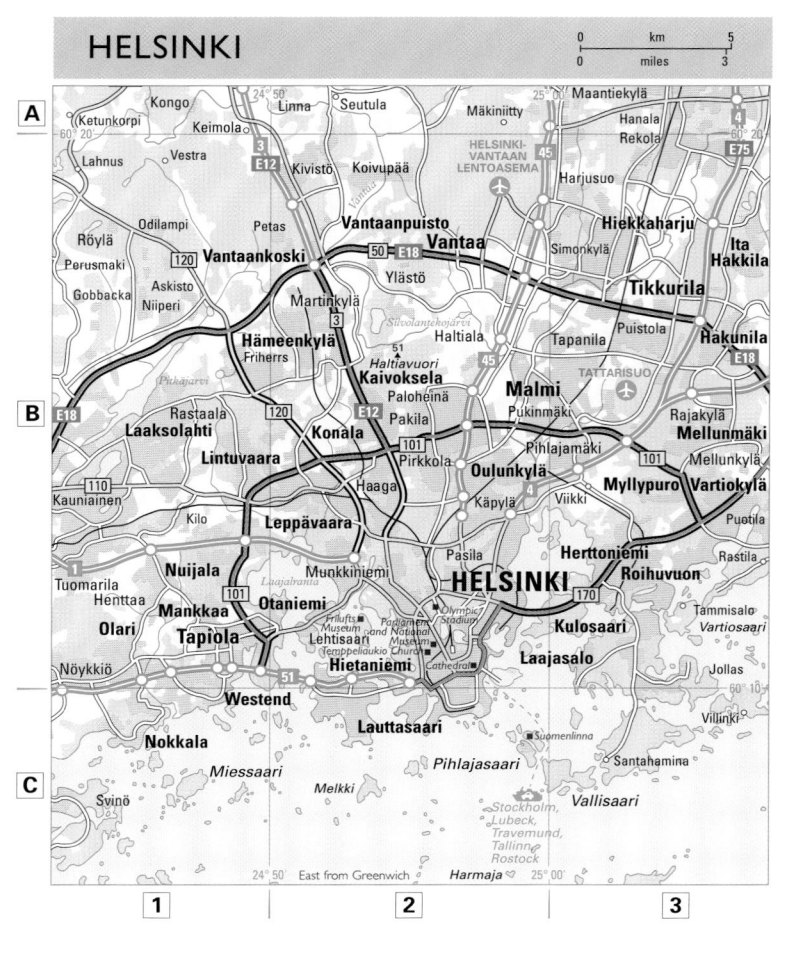

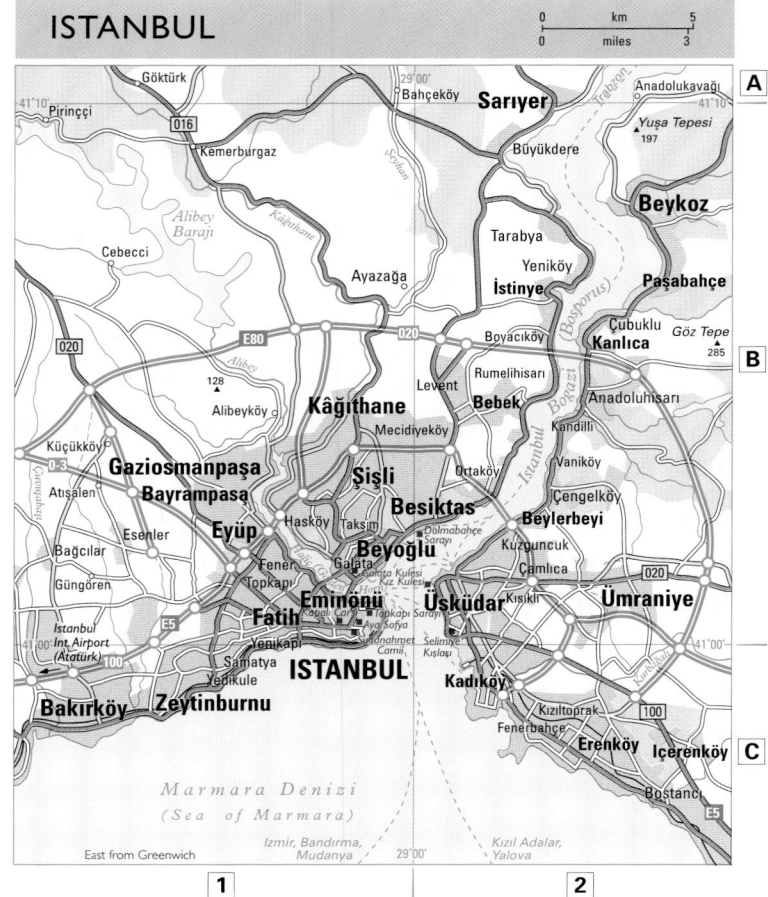

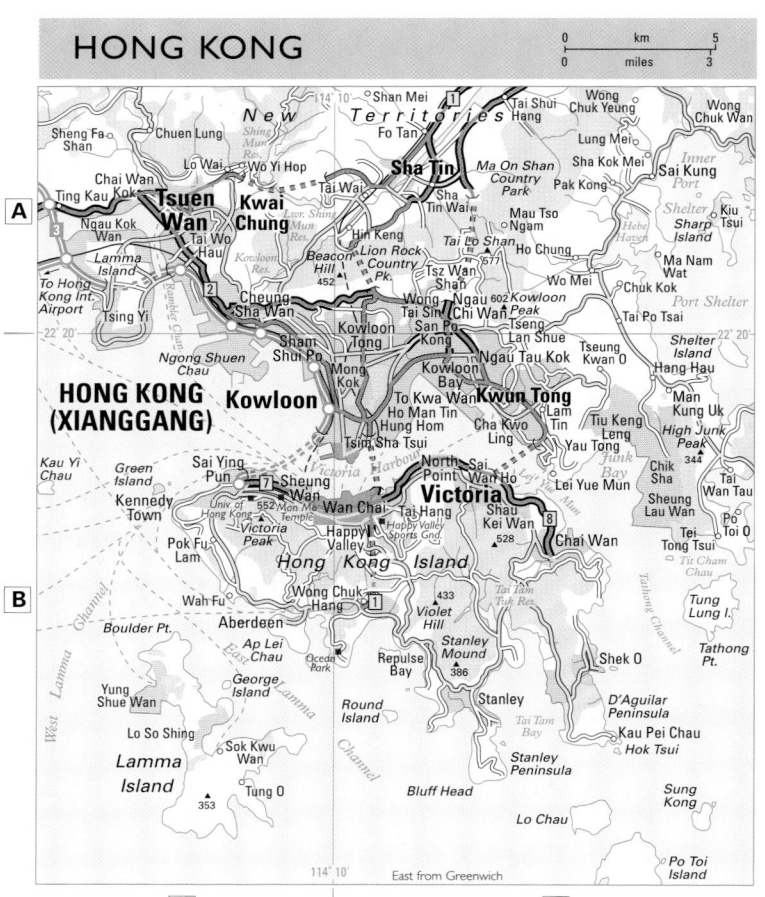

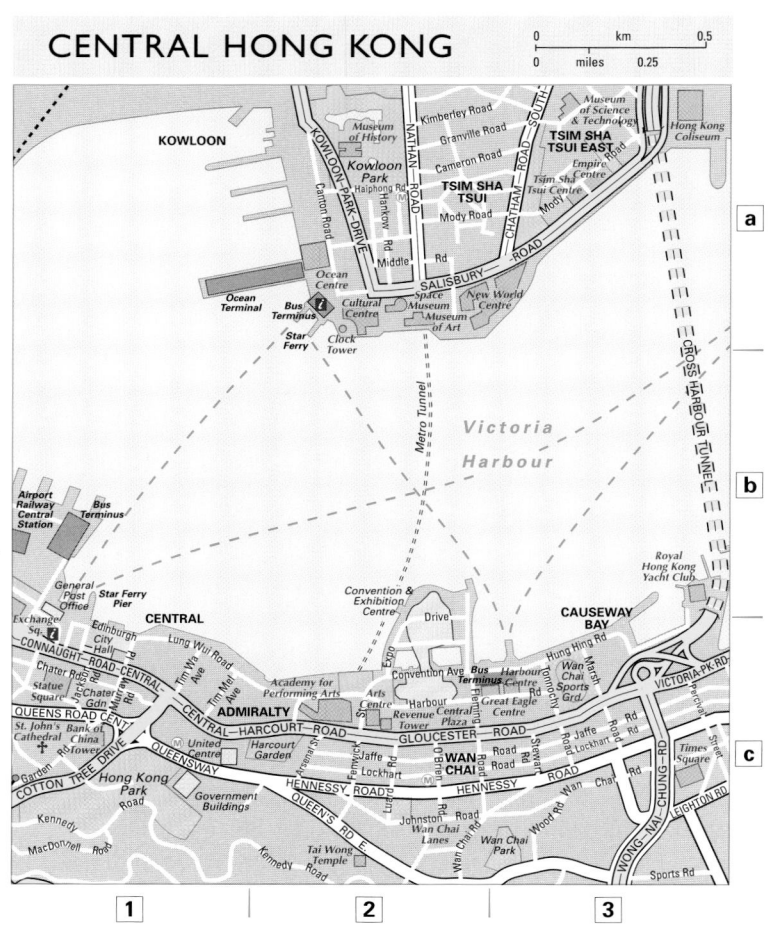

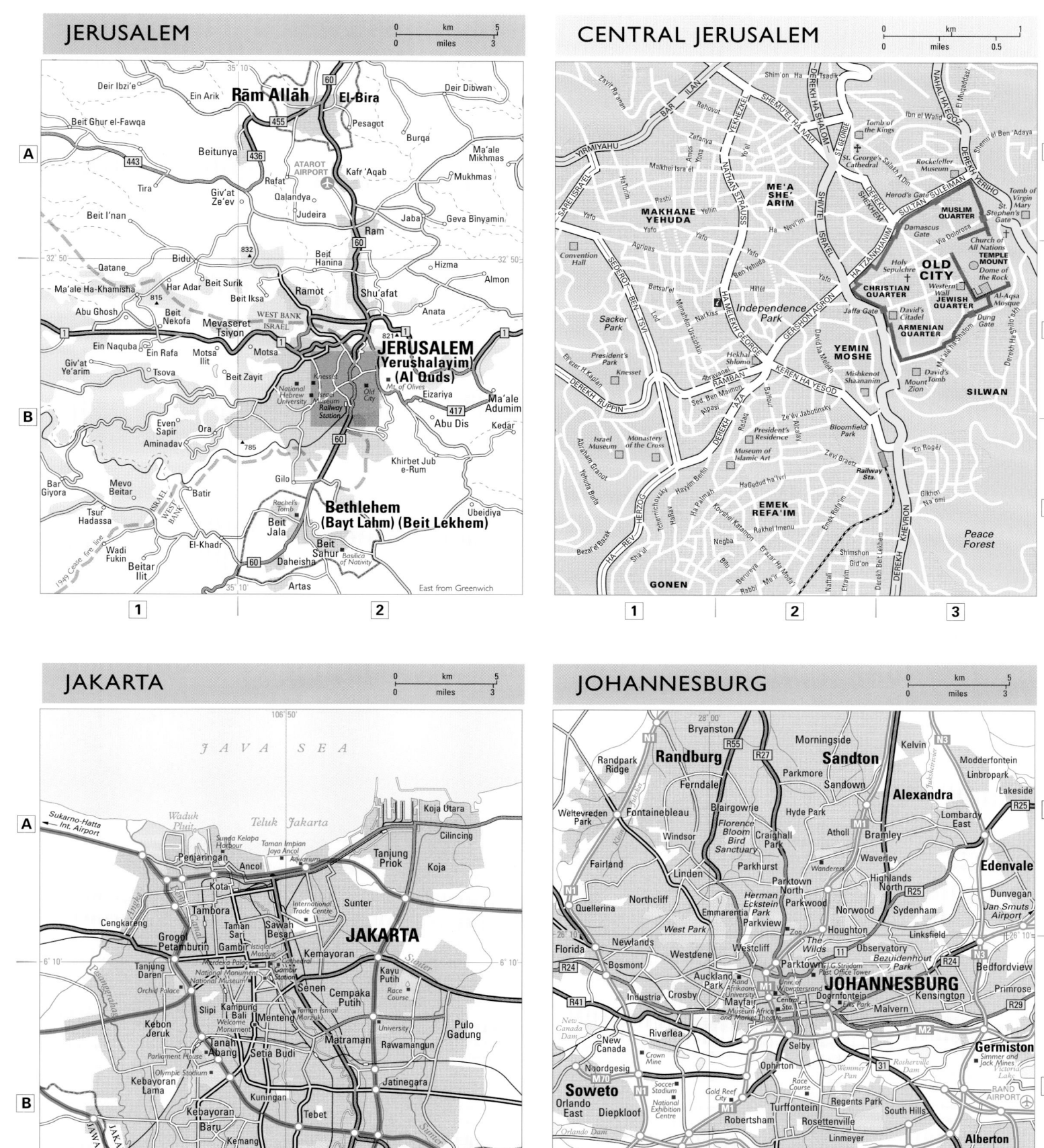

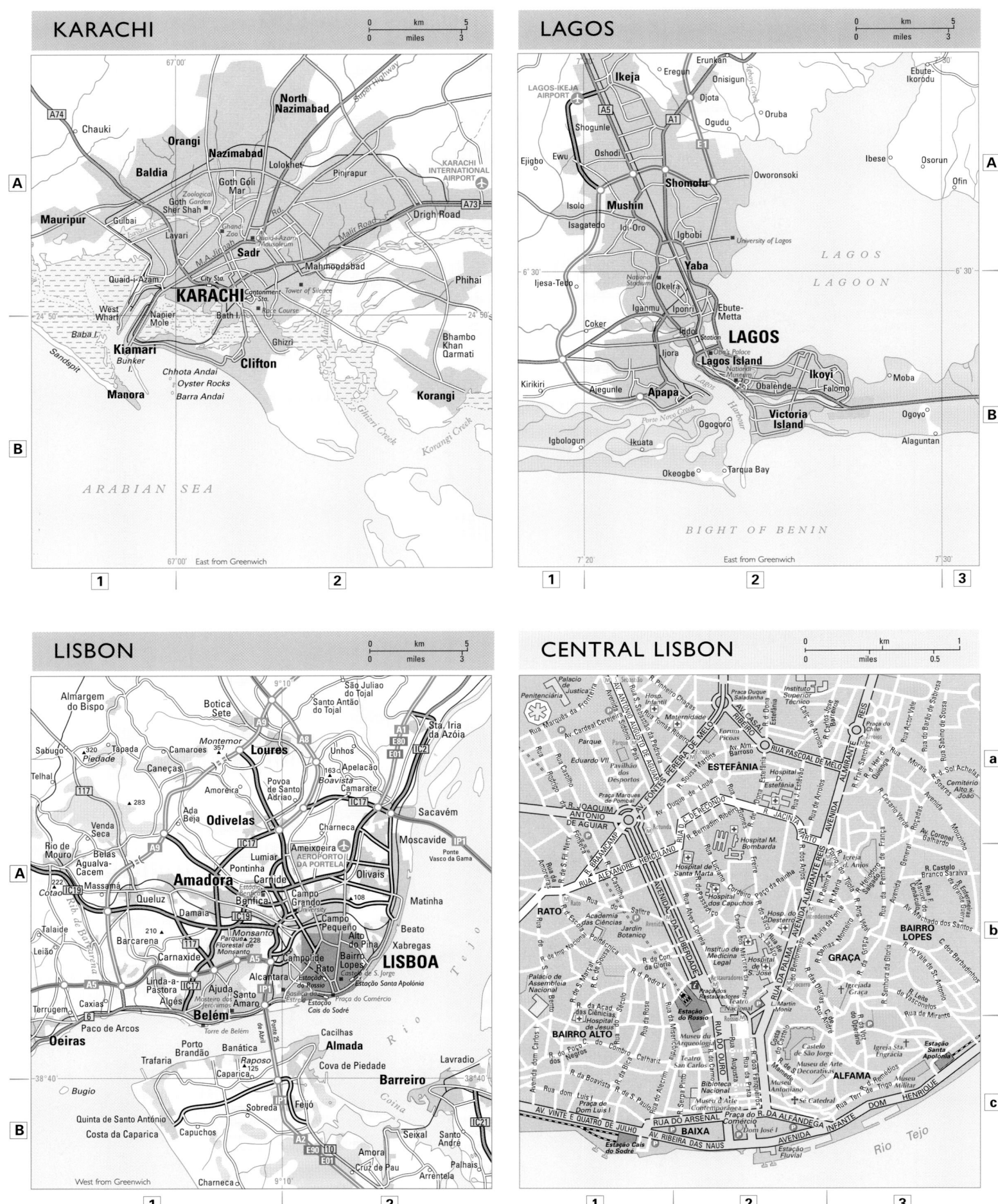

LONDON

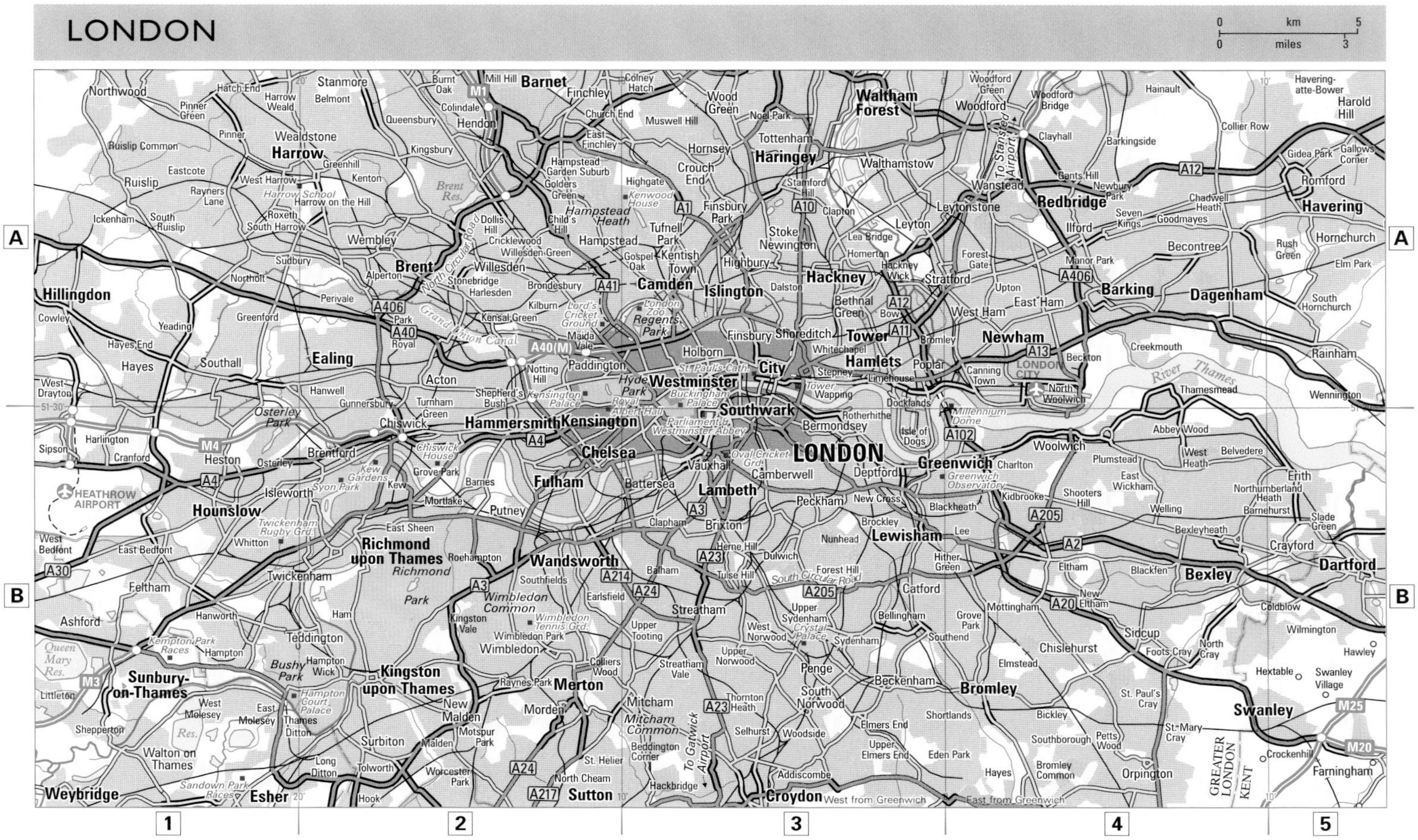

0 km 5
0 miles 3

A · B

1 · 2 · 3 · 4 · 5

Northwood · Stanmore · Burnt Oak · Mill Hill · Barnet · Finchley · Colney Hatch · Wood Green · Noel Park · Woodford Green · Woodford Bridge · Hainault · Havering-atte-Bower · Harold Hill

Pinner Green · Hatch End · Harrow Weald · Belmont · Queensbury · Colindale · Hendon · Church End · East Finchley · Muswell Hill · Tottenham · Clayhall · Barkingside · Collier Row · Gidea Park · Gallows Corner

Harrow · Wealdstone · Greenhill · Kingsbury · Hampstead Garden Suburb · Golders Green · Crouch End · Hornsey · Walthamstow · Wanstead · Redbridge · Chadwell Heath · Goodmayes · Romford · Havering · Hornchurch

Ruislip Common · Eastcote · West Harrow · Harrow School · Harrow on the Hill · Kenton · Dollis Hill · Cricklewood · Child's Hill · Hampstead · Tufnell Park · Kentish Town · Highbury · Stoke Newington · Clapton · Leyton · Leytonstone · Forest Gate · Upton · East Ham · Manor Park · Seven Kings · Rush Green · Elm Park

Ickenham · Rayners Lane · Roxeth · South Harrow · Wembley · Willesden Green · Harlesden · Kensal Green · Maida Vale · Lord's Cricket Ground · Regent's Park · Holborn · Finsbury · Shoreditch · Bethnal Green · Bow · West Ham · Canning Town · Beckton · LONDON CITY AIRPORT · North Woolwich

Hillingdon · Cowley · Perivale · Greenford · Alperton · Brent · Acton · Shepherd's Bush · Paddington · Westminster · City · Stepney · Poplar · Limehouse · Rotherhithe · Isle of Dogs · Millennium Dome · North Woolwich · Wennington

West Drayton · Hayes End · Yeading · Southall · Ealing · Hanwell · Gunnersbury · Turnham Green · Chiswick · Kensington · Hyde Park · Buckingham Palace · Southwark · Wapping · Docklands · Creekmouth · Rainham

Harlington · Cranford · Heston · Osterley · Osterley Park · Brentford · Kew Gardens · Kew · Hammersmith · Kensington · Chelsea · Vauxhall · Oval Cricket Grd · Camberwell · Deptford · Greenwich · Charlton · Woolwich · Plumstead · West Heath · Belvedere · Erith

HEATHROW AIRPORT · Sipson · Hounslow · Isleworth · Syon Park · Grove Park · Barnes · Mortlake · Putney · Fulham · Battersea · Lambeth · LONDON · Greenwich Observatory · Blackheath · Kidbrooke · Shooters Hill · Welling · Northumberland Heath · Bexleyheath · Crayford · Dartford

West Bedfont · Twickenham Rugby Grd · East Sheen · Roehampton · Clapham · Brixton · Peckham · New Cross · Brockley · Lewisham · Lee · Eltham · Bexley · Coldblow

Ashford · Feltham · Hanworth · Teddington · Richmond Park · Southfields · Earlsfield · Tooting · Streatham · Dulwich · Forest Hill · South Circular Road · Hither Green · Blackfen · Wilmington

Queen Mary Res. · Littleton · Hampton Park Races · Ham · Richmond upon Thames · Richmond · Wimbledon Common · Wimbledon Tennis Grd · Wimbledon Park · Upper Tooting · West Norwood · Crystal Palace · Sydenham · Grove Park · Mottingham · Chislehurst · Sidcup · St. Paul's Cray · Hextable · Swanley Village

Shepperton · Sunbury-on-Thames · West Molesey · Bushy Park · Hampton Court Palace · Kingston Vale · Wimbledon · Streatham Vale · Upper Norwood · South Norwood · Penge · Beckenham · Shortlands · Bickley · Petts Wood · St Mary Cray · Swanley · M25

Walton on Thames · East Molesey · Thames Ditton · Kingston upon Thames · New Malden · Morden · Mitcham Common · Thornton Heath · Elmers End · Woodside · Bromley · Bromley Common · Orpington · Crockenhill · Farningham · M20

Weybridge · Sandown Park Races · Esher · Long Ditton · Tolworth · Surbiton · Malden · Motspur Park · Merton · Raynes Park · Beddington Corner · Beddington · Addiscombe · Hayes · GREATER LONDON KENT

1 · 2 · 3 · 4 · 5

CENTRAL LONDON

0 km 2
0 miles 1

a · b · c

1 · 2 · 3 · 4 · 5

KENSAL RISE · WEST KILBURN · ST. JOHN'S WOOD · King's Cross · HOXTON · SHOREDITCH

MAIDA VALE · WESTBOURNE GREEN · Regent's Park · Euston · St Pancras · CLERKENWELL · Old Street

PADDINGTON · BAYSWATER · NOTTING HILL · MARYLEBONE · BLOOMSBURY · HOLBORN · Barbican · CITY · Liverpool St

KENSINGTON GARDENS · HYDE PARK · MAYFAIR · SOHO · Covent Garden · Fleet St · St Paul's · Bank · Fenchurch St

KENSINGTON · HOLLAND PARK · KNIGHTSBRIDGE · Hyde Park Corner · ST. JAMES'S · Buckingham Palace · Charing Cross · Trafalgar Sq · Tate Modern · SOUTHWARK · London Bridge · Tower of London

OLYMPIA · WEST KENSINGTON · SOUTH KENSINGTON · BROMPTON · BELGRAVIA · Victoria · Houses of Parliament · Westminster Abbey · LAMBETH · NEWINGTON · BERMONDSEY

CHELSEA · PIMLICO · Tate Britain · Vauxhall · KENNINGTON · Kennington Oval · WALWORTH · River Thames

1 · 2 · 3 · 4 · 5

LOS ANGELES

0 km 5
0 miles 3

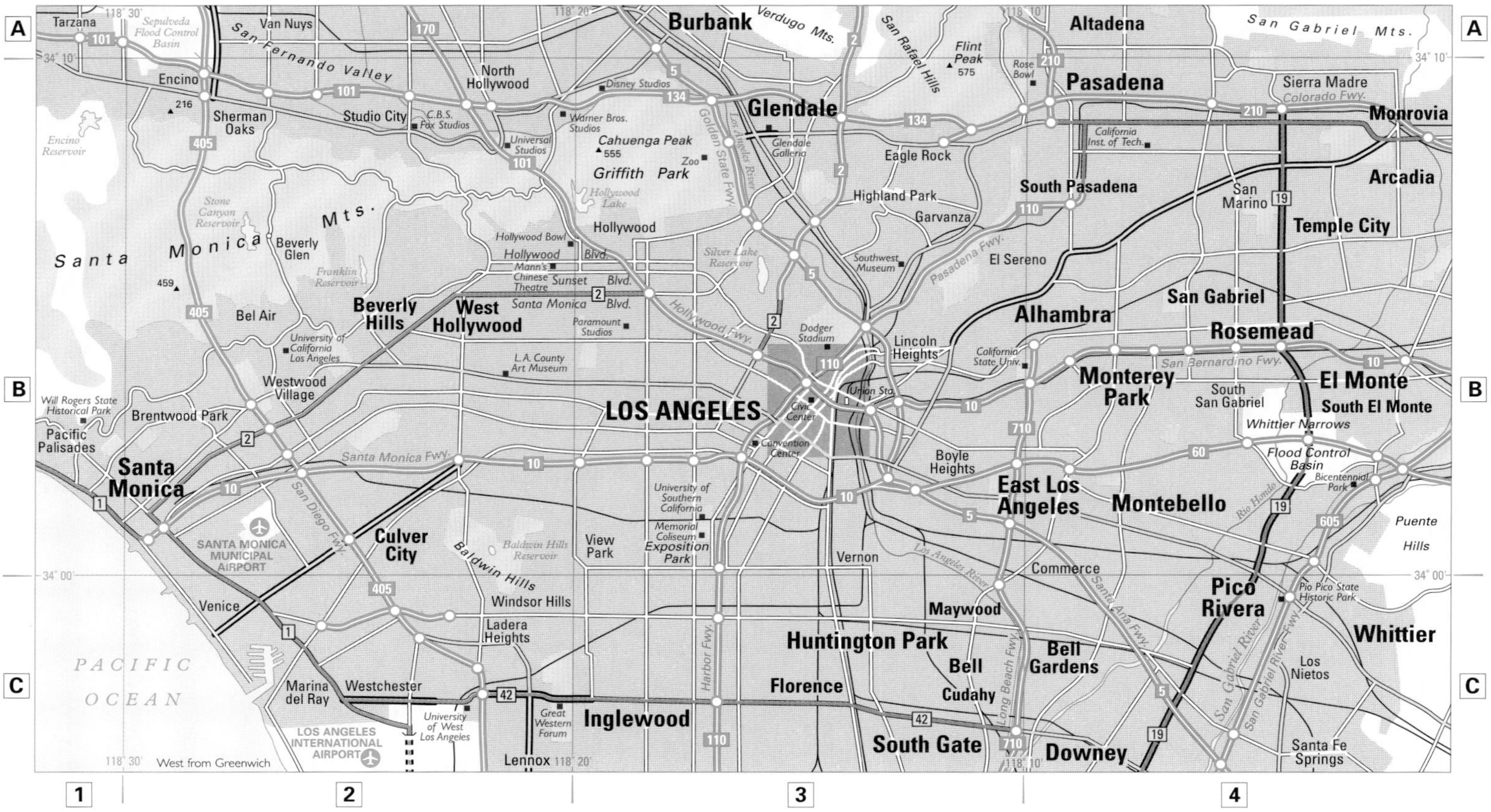

Tarzana · 118° 30' · Sepulveda Flood Control Basin · Van Nuys · San Fernando Valley · **Burbank** · Verdugo Mts. · **Altadena** · San Gabriel Mts. · A · 34° 10'

101 · 170 · 2 · Flint Peak 575 · Rose Bowl · 210

Encino · 216 · North Hollywood · Disney Studios · 5 · **Pasadena** · Sierra Madre · Colorado Fwy. · **Monrovia**

Sherman Oaks · Studio City · 101 · Warner Bros. Studios · 134 · **Glendale** · Glendale Galleria · 134 · Eagle Rock · California Inst. of Tech. · San Marino · 19 · **Arcadia**

405 · C.B.S. Fox Studios · Universal Studios · Cahuenga Peak 555 · Zoo · 101 · Griffith Park · 2 · Highland Park · Garvanza · **South Pasadena** · 110 · Pasadena Fwy. · El Sereno · 210 · **Temple City**

Santa Monica Mts. · 459 · Beverly Glen · Hollywood Lake · Hollywood Bowl · Hollywood Blvd. · Hollywood · Silver Lake Reservoir · Southwest Museum · **Alhambra** · **San Gabriel** · **Rosemead** · 10

Stone Canyon Reservoir · Franklin Reservoir · Mann's Chinese Theatre · Sunset Blvd. · 2 · Dodger Stadium · Lincoln Heights · California State Univ. · San Bernardino Fwy. · **Monterey Park** · South San Gabriel · **El Monte** · B

Bel Air · Santa Monica Blvd. · Paramount Studios · Hollywood Fwy. · 110 · Union Sta. · 10 · **South El Monte** · 710 · Whittier Narrows

University of California Los Angeles · **Beverly Hills** · **West Hollywood** · L.A. County Art Museum · **LOS ANGELES** · City Center · Convention Center · Boyle Heights · 60 · Flood Control Basin · Bicentennial Park · 605

Westwood Village · 2 · Santa Monica Fwy. · 10 · University of Southern California · **East Los Angeles** · **Montebello** · Rio Hondo · Puente Hills

Will Rogers State Historical Park · Brentwood Park · San Diego Fwy. · Baldwin Hills Reservoir · Memorial Coliseum · Exposition Park · Vernon · Commerce · 19 · 34° 00'

Pacific Palisades · 405 · **Santa Monica** · 10 · **Culver City** · View Park · Los Angeles River · **Pico Rivera** · Pío Pico State Historic Park · **Whittier**

Venice · 1 · Windsor Hills · Baldwin Hills · Harbor Fwy. · Long Beach Fwy. · Maywood · Bell Gardens · San Gabriel River · Los Nietos

Santa Monica Municipal Airport · Ladera Heights · **Huntington Park** · Bell · Cudahy · C

PACIFIC OCEAN · Marina del Ray · Westchester · 42 · **Inglewood** · Great Western Forum · **Florence** · **South Gate** · **Downey** · Santa Fe Springs

Los Angeles International Airport · University of West Los Angeles · 110 · 710 · 19

118° 30' · West from Greenwich · Lennox · 118° 20'

1 · 2 · 3 · 4

LIMA

0 km 5
0 miles 3

Bocanegra · Los Olivos · **Independencia** · Huascar · 77° · A · 12°

LIMA CALLAO · Chavarria · 755 · Cerro San Jeronimo · San Juan de Lurigancho · 12°

AEROPUERTO INTERNACIONAL JORGE CHAVEZ · Cerro La Milla · 242 · San Martín de Porras · Cerro Observatorio 465 · Rimac

Terminal Maritimo · Rimac · Carmen de la Legua · El Agustino · Cerro El Agustino 482

Callao · Edificio Desamparados · El Congreso · **LIMA**

Fuerte Real Felipe · Bellavista · Breña · La Victoria · Museo de Arte · B

La Punta · La Perla · Campo de Marte · Estadio Nacional · Parque de la Reserva · San Luis

Isla Frontón · San Miguel · Pueblo Libre · Museo Nacional · Museo de la Nación · San Borja

Parque de las Leyendas · Univ. Católica · Jesús Maria · Lince · Huaca Juliana · Hipódromo de Monterrico

Magdalena · San Isidro · Surquillo

Miraflores · Vista Alegre

PACIFIC OCEAN · Santiago de Surco · 12° 10'

Barranco · La Campiña

Cerro Morro Solar 273 · Chorrillos · C

Punta La Chira · La Encantada

77° 10' · West from Greenwich · 77°

1 · 2 · 3

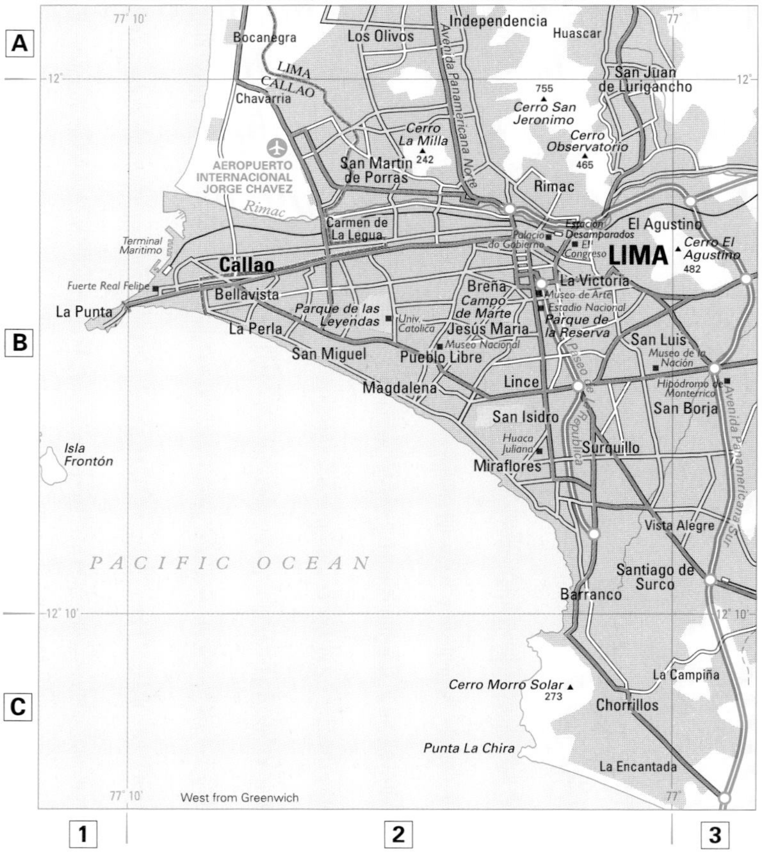

CENTRAL LOS ANGELES

0 km 1
0 miles 0.5

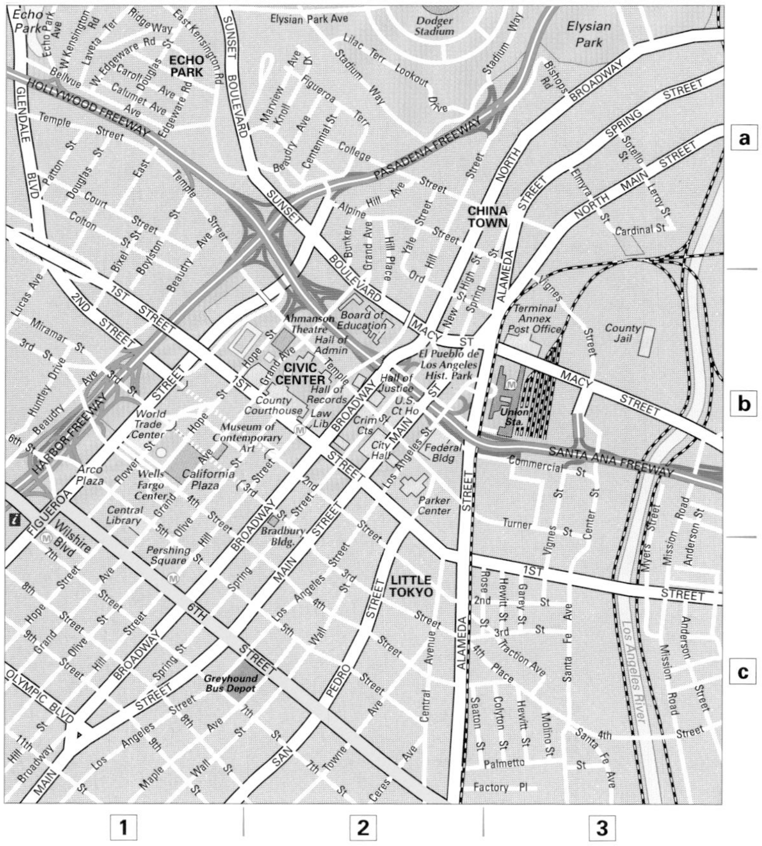

Echo Park Ave · Elysian Park Ave · Dodger Stadium · Elysian Park · a

ECHO PARK · SUNSET BOULEVARD · BROADWAY · SPRING STREET

HOLLYWOOD FREEWAY · GLENDALE BLVD · Temple · PASADENA FREEWAY · NORTH MAIN STREET · CHINA TOWN · Cardinal St

Ahmanson Theatre · Board of Education · Terminal Annex Post Office · County Jail · b

CIVIC CENTER · Hall of Admin · El Pueblo de Los Angeles Hist. Park · Union Sta. · MACY ST · SANTA ANA FREEWAY

HARBOR FREEWAY · World Trade Center · County Courthouse · Hall of Records · Law Library · Parker Center · Commercial St

Arco Plaza · Wells Fargo Center · Museum of Contemporary Art · California Plaza · Federal Bldg · City Hall

FIGUEROA · Wilshire Blvd · Central Library · Pershing Square · Bradbury Bldg. · LITTLE TOKYO · ALAMEDA · LOS ANGELES RIVER · c

OLYMPIC BLVD · BROADWAY · Greyhound Bus Depot · SAN PEDRO · Factory Pl

MAIN · 11th Street

1 · 2 · 3

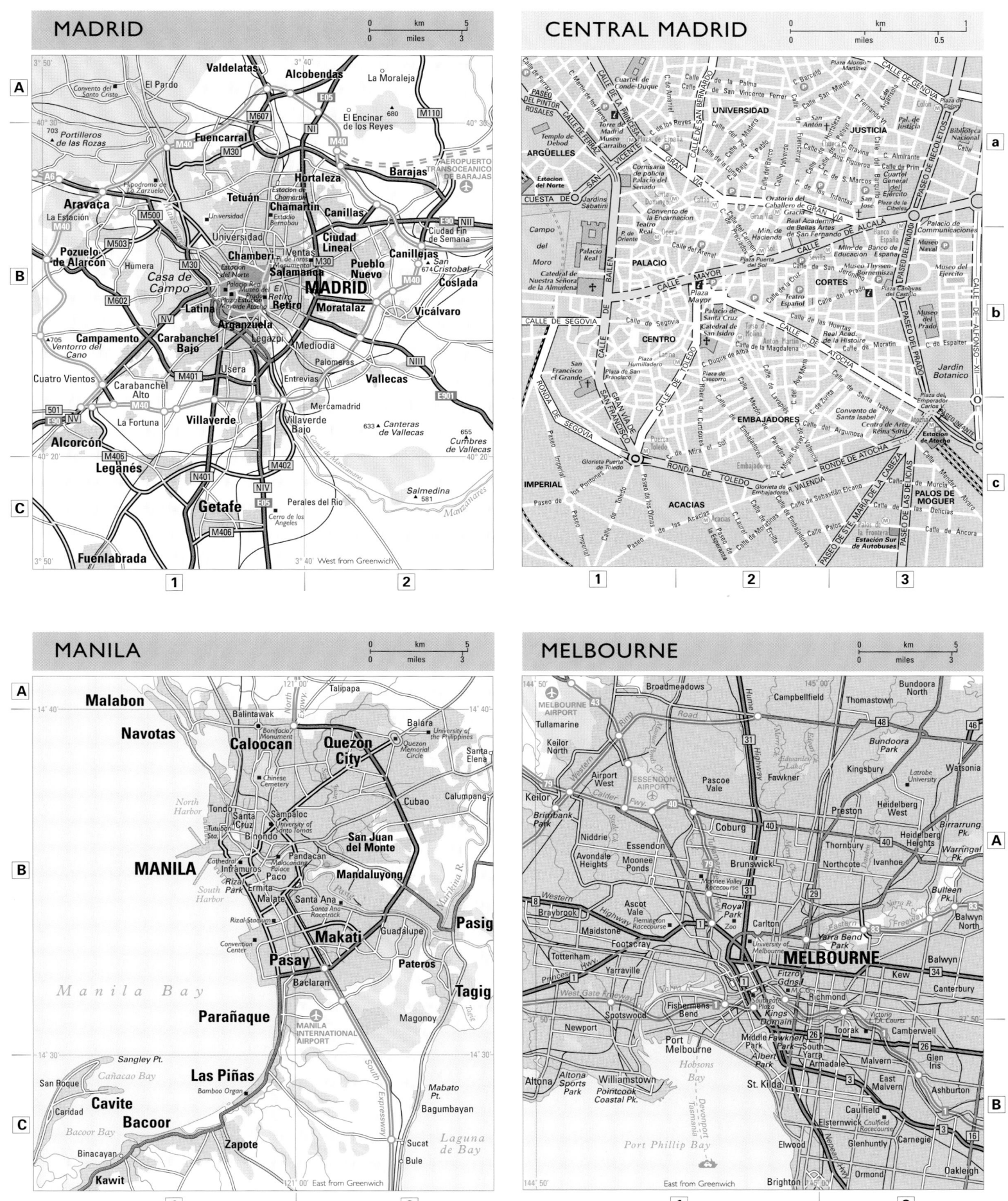

MEXICO CITY

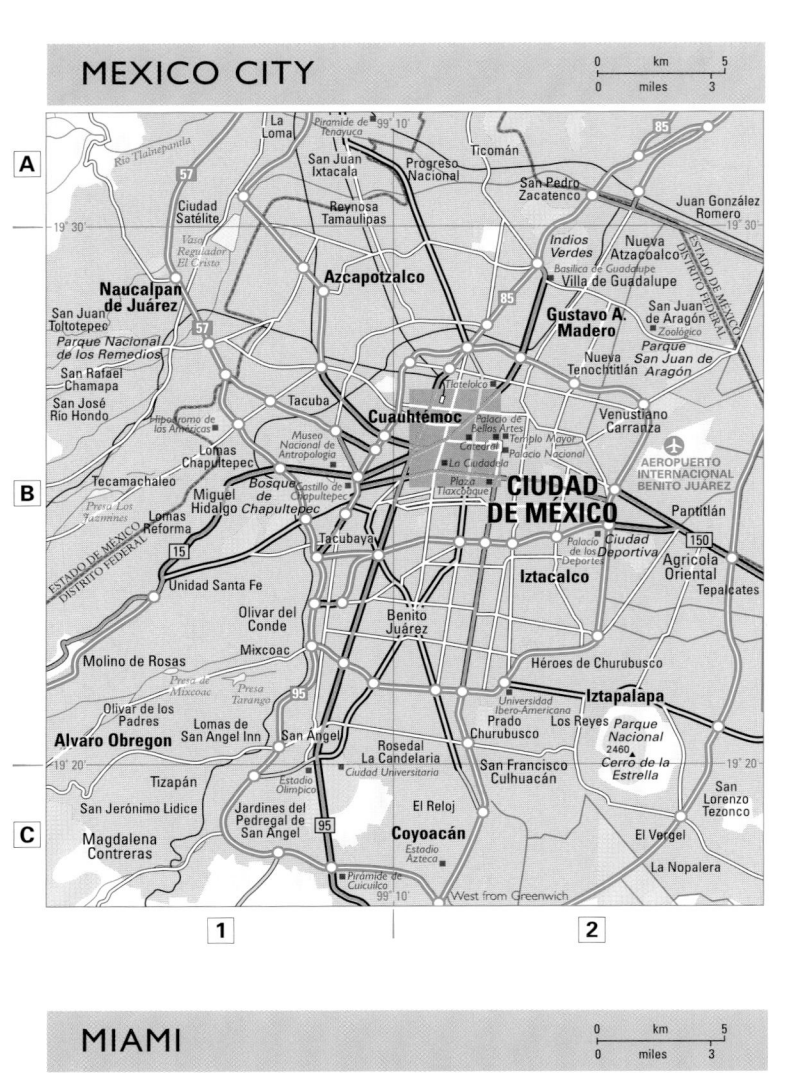

CENTRAL MEXICO CITY

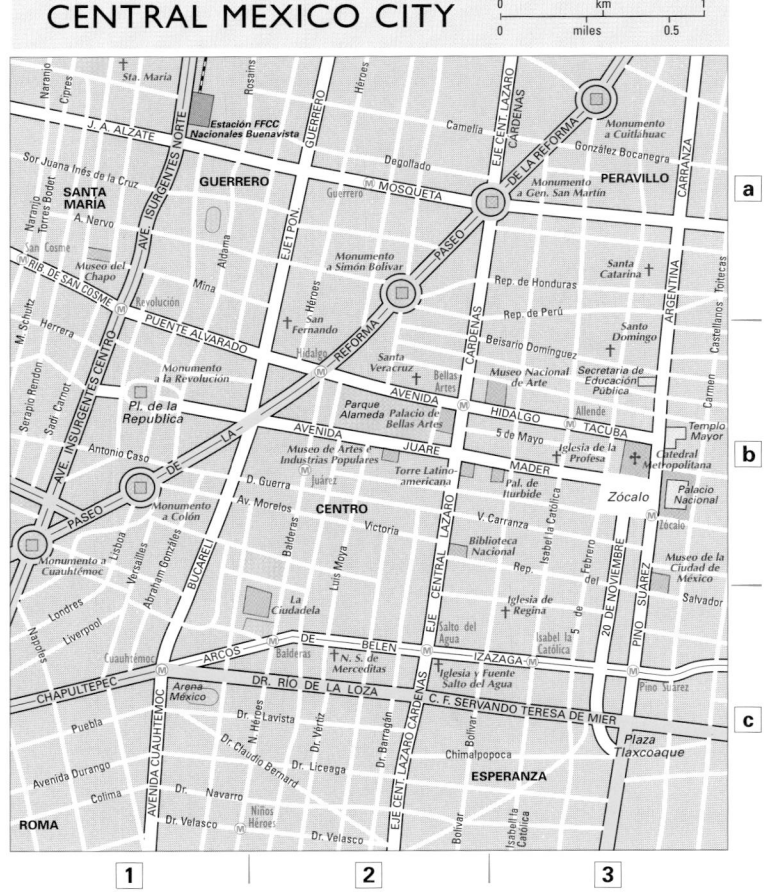

MIAMI

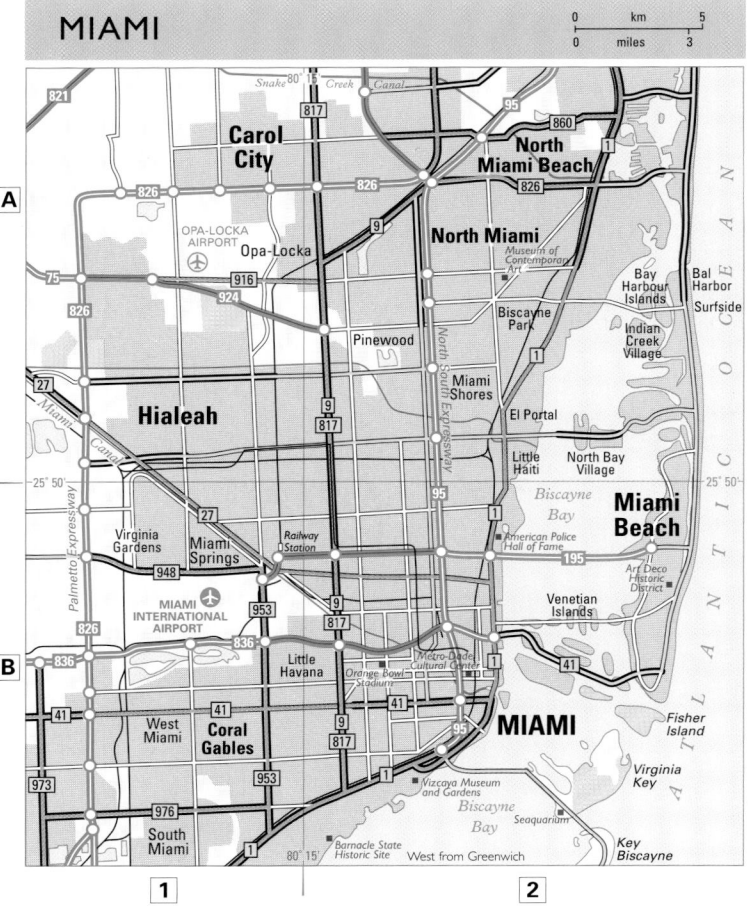

MILAN

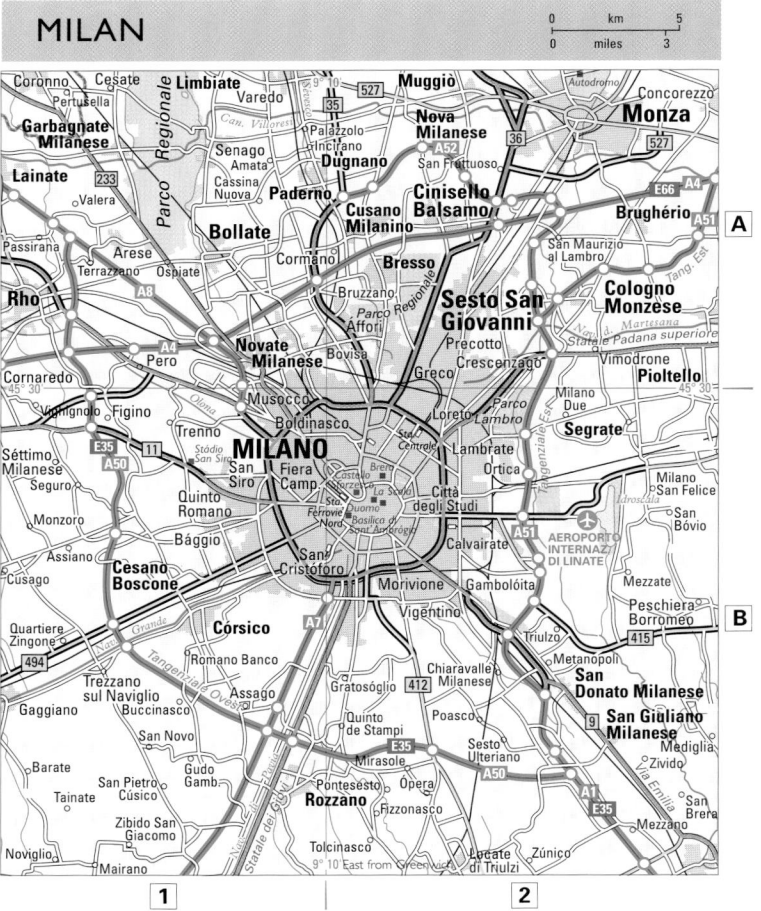

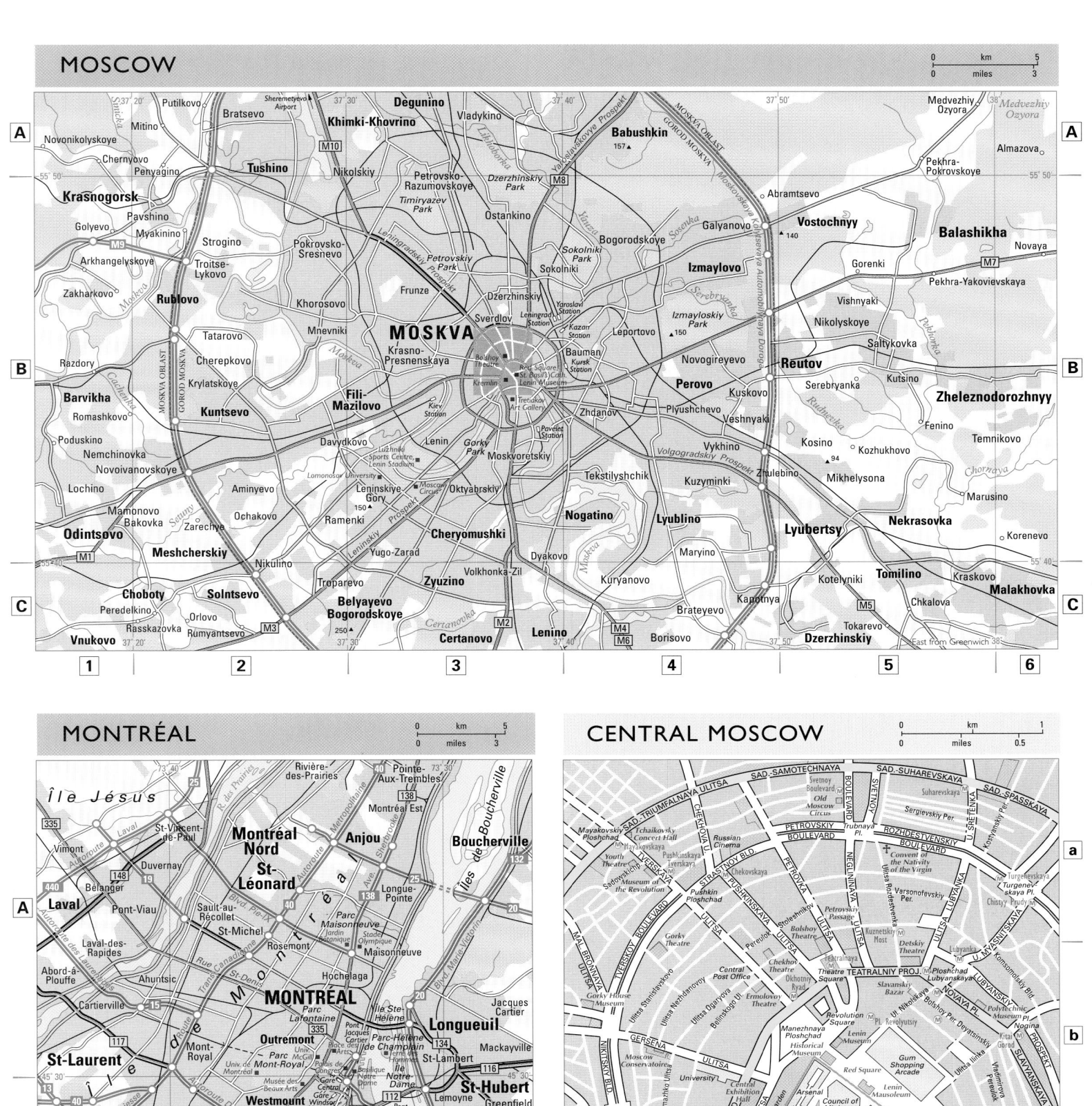

MOSCOW

	km	5
0	miles	3

Novonikolyskoye · Putilkovo · Sheremetyevo Airport · Bratsevo · **Degunino** · Vladykino · **Babushkin** 157▲ · Medvezhiy Ozyora · *Medvezhiy Ozyora* 38

A Mitino · Nikolskiy · **Khimki-Khovrino** · M10 · M8 · Dzerzhinskiy Park · GOROD MOSKVA · MOSKVA OBLAST · 37° 50' · Pekhra-Pokrovskoye · Almazova **A**

55° 50' · Chernyovo · Penyaging · **Tushino** · Petrovsko-Razumovskoye · Timiryazev Park · Ostankino · Abramtsevo · 55° 50'

Krasnogorsk · Pavshino · Strogino · Pokrovsko-Sresnevo · Petrovskiy Park · Frunze · Bogorodskoye · Galyanovo · **Vostochnyy** ▲ 140 · Gorenki · **Balashikha** Novaya

Golyevo · Myakinino · Troitse-Lykovo · Khorosovo · Sverdlov · Leningrad Station · Sokolniki Park · Sokolniki · **Izmaylovo** · Izmaylosky Park 150 · Vishnyaki · Pekhra-Yakovievskaya · M7

M9 · Arkhangelskoye · Zakharkovo · **Rublovo** · Tatarovo · Cherepkovo · Mnevniki · **MOSKVA** · Kazan Station · Krasno-Presnenskaya · Bolshoy Theatre · Leportovo · Nikolyskoye · Saltykovka

B Razdory · Krylatskoye · **Fili-Mazilovo** · Kiev Station · Kremlin · Red Square, St. Basil's Cath. Lenin Museum · Bauman Kursk Station · **Perovo** · **Reutov** · Kutsino · Serebryanka · **B**

Barvikha · Romashkovo · **Kuntsevo** · Zhdanov · Kuskovo · Plyushchevo · **Zheleznodorozhnyy**

Poduskino · Nemchinovka · Davydkovo · Lenin · Gorky Park · Moskvoretskiy · Pavelet Station · Tekstilyshchik · Vykhino · Kosino · Fenino · Temnikovo

Novoivanovskoye · Lomonosov University · Luzhniki Sports Centre Lenin Stadium · Moscow Circus · Oktyabrskiy · Kuzyminki · Zhulebino ▲ 94 · Kozhukhovo · Marusino

Lochino · Mamonovo · Bakovka · Zarechye · Aminyevo · Ochakovo · Ramenki · Leninskiye Gory · **Nogatino** · **Lyublino** · **Lyubertsy** · **Nekrasovka** · Korenevo

Odintsovo · **Meshcherskiy** · Nikulino · Yugo-Zarad · **Cheryomushki** · Dyakovo · Maryino · **Tomilino** · Kraskovo

55° 40' · M1 · Troparevo · Volkhonka-Zil · Kuryanovo · Kotelniki · M5 · 55° 40'

C **Choboty** · **Solntsevo** · **Belyayevo Bogorodskoye** · **Zyuzino** · Kapotnya · Chkalova · **Malakhovka** **C**

Peredelkino · Orlovo · M3 · 250▲ · Brateyevo · Tokarevo

Vnukovo · 37° 20' · Rasskazovka · Rumyantsevo · **Certanovo** · Certanovka · M2 · **Lenino** · M4 · M6 · Borisovo · **Dzerzhinskiy** · 37° 50' · East from Greenwich 38°

1 **2** **3** **4** **5** **6**

MONTRÉAL

	km	5
0	miles	3

Île Jésus · 25 · Rivière-des-Prairies · Pointe-Aux-Trembles · Boucherville

335 · Laval · St-Vincent-de-Paul · **Montréal Nord** · **Anjou** · **Boucherville**

Vimont · 148 · Duvernay · **St-Léonard** · Longue-Pointe · 132

A **Laval** · 440 · 19 · Bélanger · Pont-Viau · Sault-au-Récollet · 40 · Parc Maisonneuve Jardin botanique · Stade Olympique · Maisonneuve **A**

Laval-des-Rapides · St-Michel · Rosemont · Hochelaga

Abord-à-Plouffe · Ahuntsic · **MONTRÉAL** · St-Denis · Jacques Cartier

45° 30' · 15 · Cartierville · Parc Lafontaine · Île Ste Hélène · **Longueuil** · Mackayville

117 · **St-Laurent** · Mont-Royal · Outremont · Parc Champlain · 134 · St-Lambert · 116

13 · 40 · Univ. de Mont-Royal · Palais des · Pont Jacques Cartier · Île Notre-Dame · **St-Hubert** · Lemoyne · Greenfield Park

Hampstead · Musée des Beaux Arts · Place Ville Marie · Central Gare Windsor · Basilique Notre Dame · Île Notre-Dame · Préville · Notre-Dame-de-l'Île

AÉROPORT DE DORVAL · Côte-St-Luc · **Westmount** · Forum de Montréal · Pont Victoria · 112 · Pont Champlain · **Brossard**

Notre-Dame-de-Grâce · Montréal Ouest · 10 15 20 · 10

St-Pierre · Île des Soeurs · 15 · 134

B 20 · **Lachine** · **Verdun** · **Lasalle** · 20 · St. Lawrence (St-Laurent) · Île aux Herons · 15 · La Prairie **B**

Pont Honoré Mercier · Kahnawake · 138 · 132 · West from Greenwich · 73° 30' · Ste-Catherine · 30 · Candiac · 104

1 **2** **3**

CENTRAL MOSCOW

	km	1
0	miles	0.5

SAD-SAMOTECHNAYA · SAD-SUHAREVSKAYA · SAD-SPASSKAYA

Svetnoy Boulevard · Old Moscow Circus · Sergievsky Per. · Sukharevskaya

Mayakovsky Ploshchad · Tchaikovsky Concert Hall · Russian Cinema · PETROVSKIY BOULEVARD · Trubnaya Pl. · ROZHDESTVENSKY BOULEVARD · U. SRETENKA

a Youth Theatre · Pushkinskaya · Chekovskaya · Convent of the Nativity of the Virgin · Turgenev Turgenevskaya Pl. · Chisty Prudy **a**

Museum of the Revolution · Pushkin Ploshchad · Petrovsky Passage · Varsonofevsky Per.

Gorky Theatre · Stoleshnikov · Bolshoi Theatre · Kuznetsky Most · Detsky Theatre · Lubyanka · Komsomolskaya Pl.

Chekhov Theatre · Teatralnaya · **Theatre** TEATRALNIY PROJ. · Ploshchad Lubyanskaya · LUBYANSKY Bld. · NOVAYA PL. · Polytechnic Museum

b Gorky House Museum · Central Post Office · Okhotny Ryad · Ermolovoy Theatre · Revolution Square · Slavanskiy Bazar · Gum Shopping Arcade · Kitai Gorod · Nogina **b**

Moscow Conservatoire · GERSENA · ULITSA · Belinskogo Ul. · Manezhnaya Ploshchad Historical Museum · Lenin Museum · Red Square · Lenin Mausoleum

Arbatskaya Ploshchad · VOZDVIZHENKA U. · Museum of Russian Architecture · Alexandrovsky Sad · Arsenal · Council of Ministers · St. Basil's Cathedral · ULITSA VARVARKA · Central Concert Hall

c ULITSA ARBAT · Lenin State Library · Alexander Garden · Ivan Square · Presidium of the Supreme Soviet · Kremlin · Borovitskaya Ploshchad · Terem Cathedral Square · Archangel Cathedral **c**

GOGOLEVSKY BOULEVARD · Armoury Palace · Kremlin Palace · KREMLEVSKAYA NABEREZHNAYA · Moskva · MOSKVORETS. NAB. · RAUSHSKAYA NAB.

Pushkin Fine Arts Museum · SOFIYSKAYA NABEREZHNAYA · Bolotnaya NAB. · SADOVNICHESKAYA · OVCHINNIKOVSKAYA

Ryleyev Ulitsa · Kropotkinskaya · Moscow Swimming Pool · BOLOTNAYA NAB. · KADASHEVSKAYA NAB.

1 **2** **3**

MUMBAI

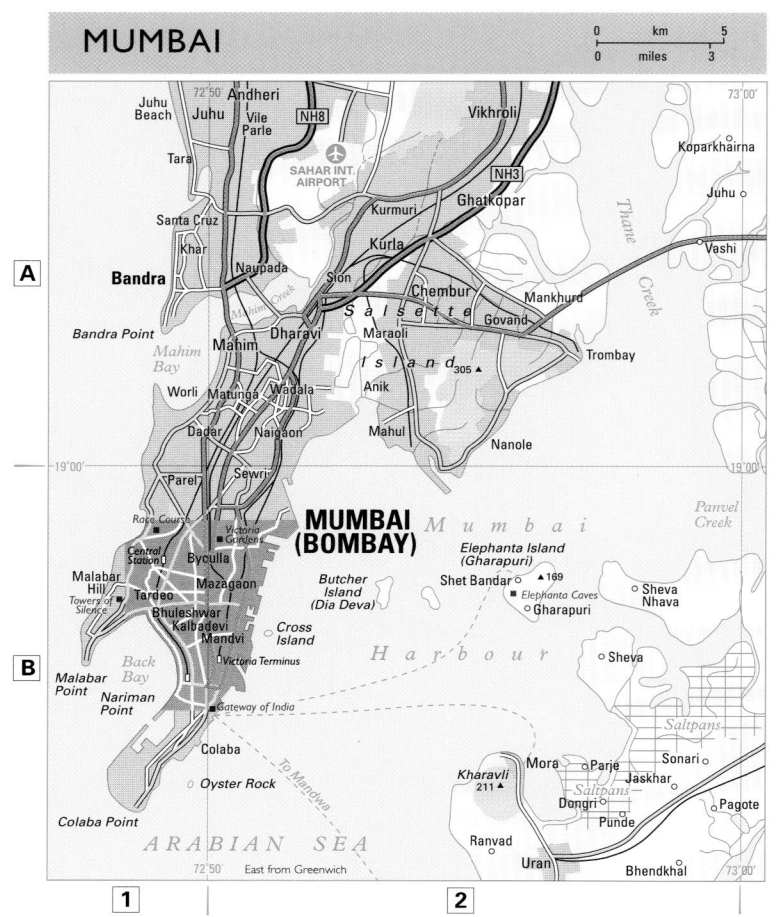

CENTRAL MUMBAI

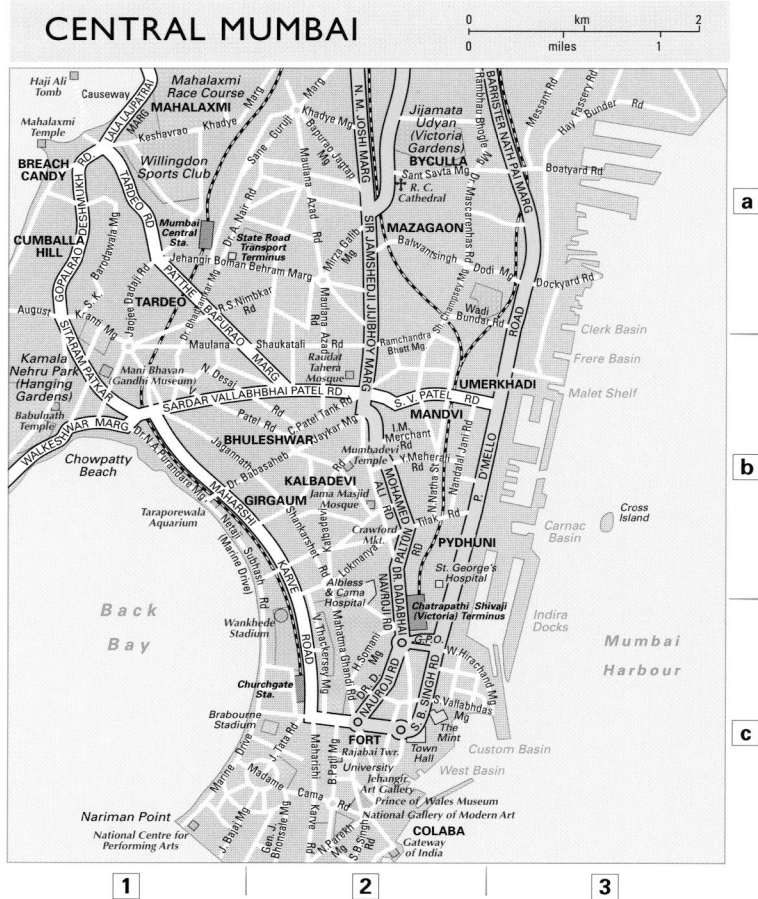

MUNICH

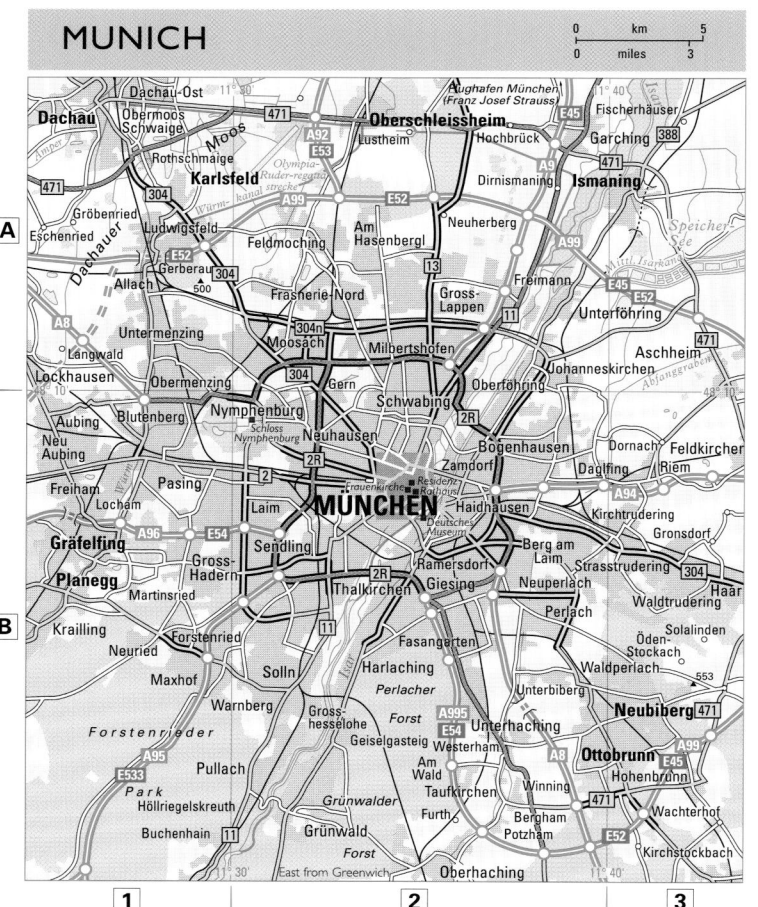

CENTRAL MUNICH

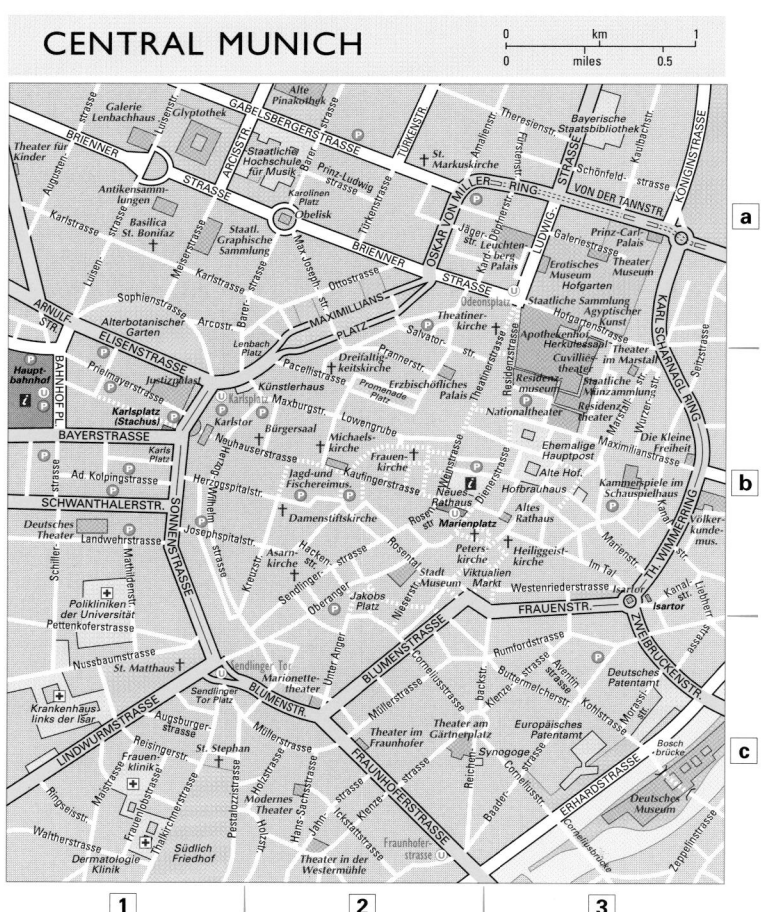

NEW YORK

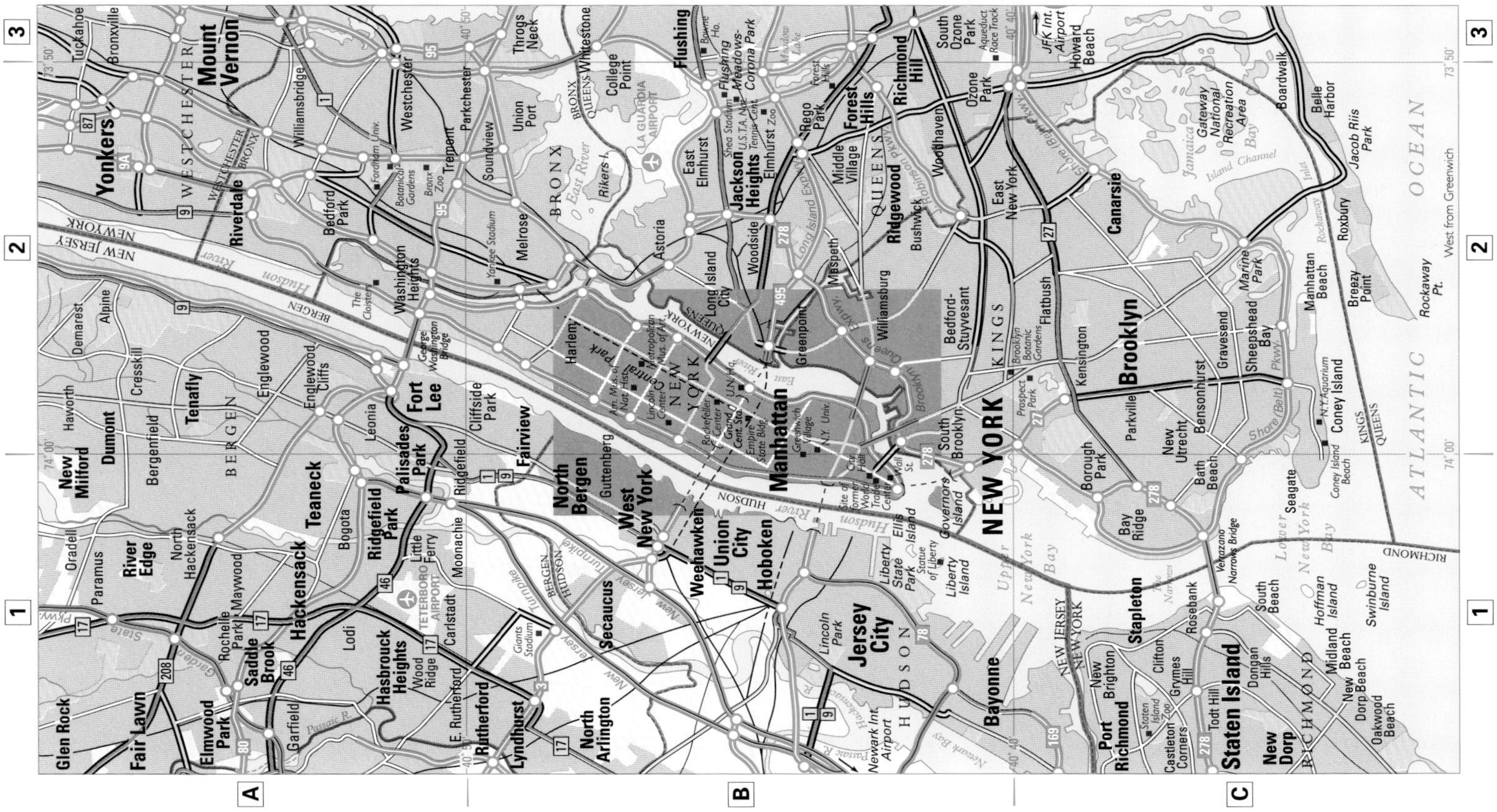

km 5
miles 3

3

Tuckahoe
Bronxville
Yonkers
87
9A
WESTCHESTER
Mount Vernon
Williamsbridge
Westchester
Parkchester
Trepnt
Union Port
Soundview
Throgs Neck
BRONX
College Point
Flushing
Flushing Meadows Corona Park
Whitestone
QUEENS
Astoria
Shea Stadium
U.S.T.A.
LA GUARDIA AIRPORT
Rego Park
Forest Hills
Richmond Hill
Ozone Park
South Ozone Park
Aqueduct Race Track
JFK Int. Airport
Howard Beach
Belle Harbor
Boardwalk
ATLANTIC OCEAN

2
NEW YORK
NEW JERSEY
BERGEN
Riverdale
Bedford Park
Fordham Univ.
Yankee Stadium
Melrose
Washington Heights
Long Island City
Woodside
Elmhurst
Jackson Heights
East Elmhurst
Maspeth
Ridgewood
Bushwick
Williamsburg
Bedford-Stuyvesant
East New York
Canarsie
Flatbush
Gravesend
Sheepshead Bay
Manhattan Beach
Breezy Point
Rockaway Pt.
West from Greenwich
73° 50'

1
New Milford
Dumont
Demarest
Alpine
Crosskill
Tenafly
Englewood
Englewood Cliffs
Leonia
Cliffside Park
Ridgefield
Fort Lee
George Washington Bridge
Fairview
North Bergen
Guttenberg
West New York
Weehawken
Union City
Hoboken
9
HUDSON
Liberty State Park
Liberty Island
Ellis Island
Governors Island
NEW YORK
Manhattan
South Brooklyn
Brooklyn
Borough Park
Bath Beach
Bay Ridge
Verrazano Bridge
Fort Hamilton
Staten Island
Stapleton
Rosebank
South Beach
Swinburne Island
Hoffman Island
Midland Beach
New Dorp Beach
Oakwood Beach
RICHMOND
KINGS
New Dorp
Port Richmond
New Brighton
Clifton
Grymes Hill
Todt Hill
Dongan Hills
Castleton Corners
Jersey City
Lincoln Park
Bayonne
78
Newark Int. Airport
NEW JERSEY
9
169

Glen Rock
Fair Lawn
Elmwood Park
Garfield
Paterson
Saddle Brook
Hackensack
Lodi
Wood Ridge
Carlstadt
E. Rutherford
Rutherford
Lyndhurst
North Arlington
Hasbrouck Heights
TETERBORO AIRPORT
Giants Stadium
Secaucus
River Edge
Paramus
New Rochelle
208
17
46
46

A   B   C

CENTRAL NEW YORK

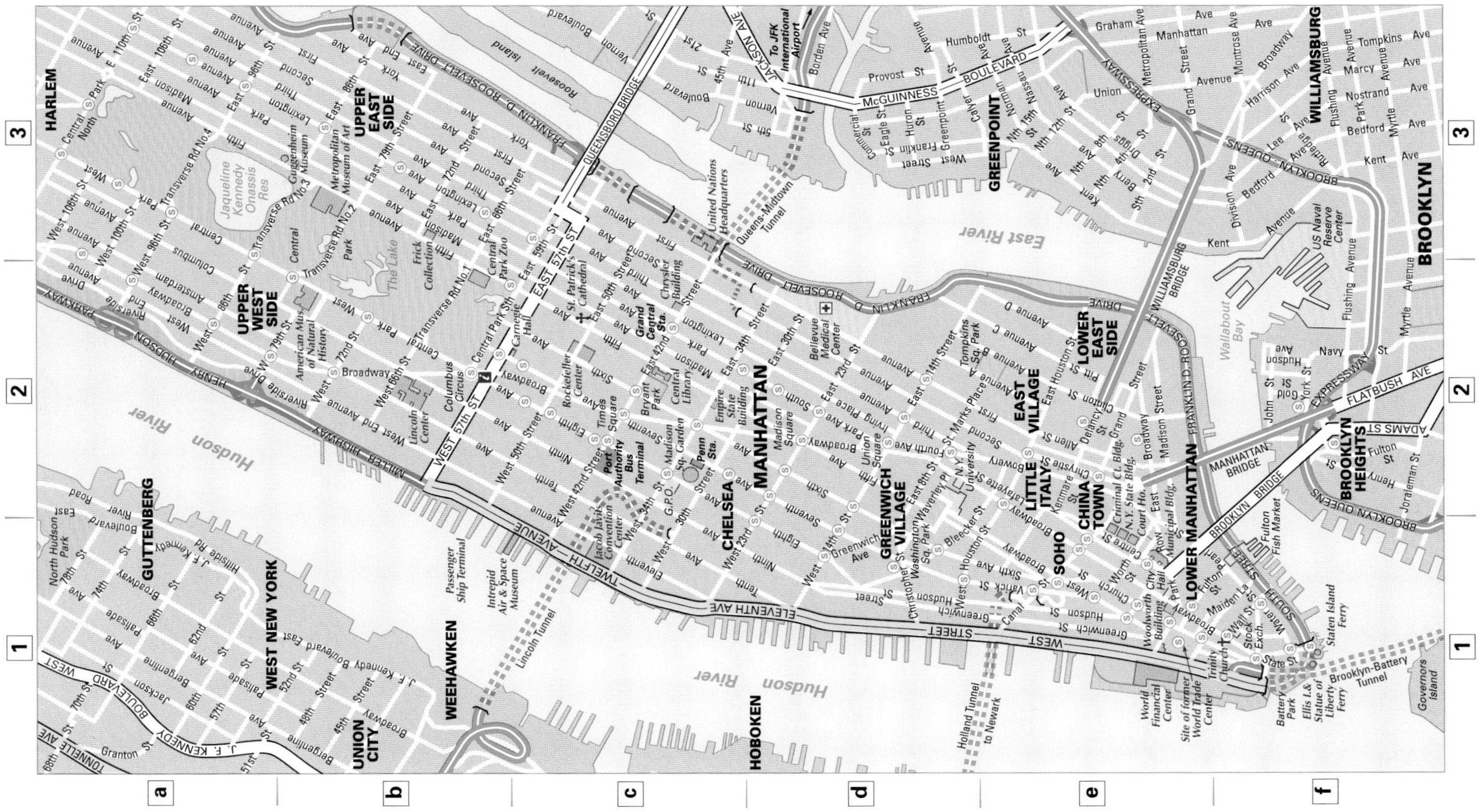

km 2
miles 1

HARLEM
UPPER WEST SIDE
UPPER EAST SIDE
Jacqueline Kennedy Onassis Res.
Central Park
The Lake
Central Park Zoo
Metropolitan Museum of Art
Guggenheim Museum
Frick Collection
American Mus. of Natural History
Columbus Circle
Lincoln Center
MANHATTAN
Rockefeller Center
Times Square
Grand Central Sta.
Chrysler Building
United Nations Headquarters
St. Patrick's Cathedral
Bryant Park
Empire State Building
Madison Square
Port Authority Bus Terminal
Penn Sta.
G.P.O.
Jacob Javits Convention Center
Intrepid Air & Space Museum
Passenger Ship Terminal
CHELSEA
GREENWICH VILLAGE
EAST VILLAGE
LOWER EAST SIDE
Tompkins Sq. Park
Washington Square
SOHO
LITTLE ITALY
CHINA TOWN
LOWER MANHATTAN
World Trade Center
Battery Park
Ellis I. & Statue of Liberty Ferry
Staten Island Ferry
Brooklyn-Battery Tunnel
Governors Island

Hudson River
East River
Roosevelt Island
QUEENSBORO BRIDGE
FRANKLIN D. ROOSEVELT DRIVE
GREENPOINT
McGUINNESS BOULEVARD
Queens Midtown Tunnel
WILLIAMSBURG
WILLIAMSBURG BRIDGE
BROOKLYN
US Naval Reserve Center
Wallabout Bay
MANHATTAN BRIDGE
BROOKLYN BRIDGE
BROOKLYN HEIGHTS
FLATBUSH AVE.
BROOKLYN-QUEENS EXPRESSWAY

WEST NEW YORK
GUTTENBERG
WEEHAWKEN
UNION CITY
HOBOKEN
Hudson River
J.F. KENNEDY BOULEVARD
Lincoln Tunnel
Holland Tunnel
to Newark

a   b   c   d   e   f

OSAKA

km 0 5
miles 0 3

509 · Funasaka · Takarazuka · Yamada · Senriyama · Hirakata · Kori
Karato · Arima · 462 · Settsu · Toyonaka · Kwansei Gakuin University · Itami · OSAKA INTERNATIONAL AIRPORT · Suita · Neyagawa
598 · 722 · Rokkō-Zan · 932 · Higashiyodogawa · Kadoma · Shijonawate · 170
428 · Obu-tôge · 365 · Maya-Zan · 699 · Rokkō Tunnel · Iwazono · Hirota · Nishinomiya · Asahi · Moriguchi
A · Nada · Okamoto · Ashiaya · 43 · Naruo · Amagasaki · Jūsō · Oyodo · Miyakojima · Jōto · Daitō · A
Ōbu · Fukiai · Higashinada · Umeda · Kita · Higashi · Minami · Ōsaka Castle · Higashinari · Kōnoike
403 · Ikuta · KŌBE · Rokkō Island · Nishiyodogawa · Yodo · Fukushima · Higashi · 308 · Ishikiri
Nagata · 2 · Kōbe Harbour · Port Island · Konohana · Aji · Nishi · Ikuno · Naniwa · Stadium · Higashiōsaka
Suma · Minato · Ōsaka Harbour · Tennoji · Shitennoji Temple · ŌSAKA · Kizuri · Yamamoto
Ōsaka Aquarium Suntory Museum · Taishō · Liberty Ōsaka Museum · Zoo Abeno · Kyūhōji · Yao
Nishinari · Higashisumiyoshi · Sumiyoshi Shrine · Sumiyoshi · Tainaka · 25 · Onchi
B · Sakai Harbour · YAO AIRPORT · Ikeuchi · Kashiwara · B
26 · Matsubara · Fujidera
Osaka Bay · Sakai

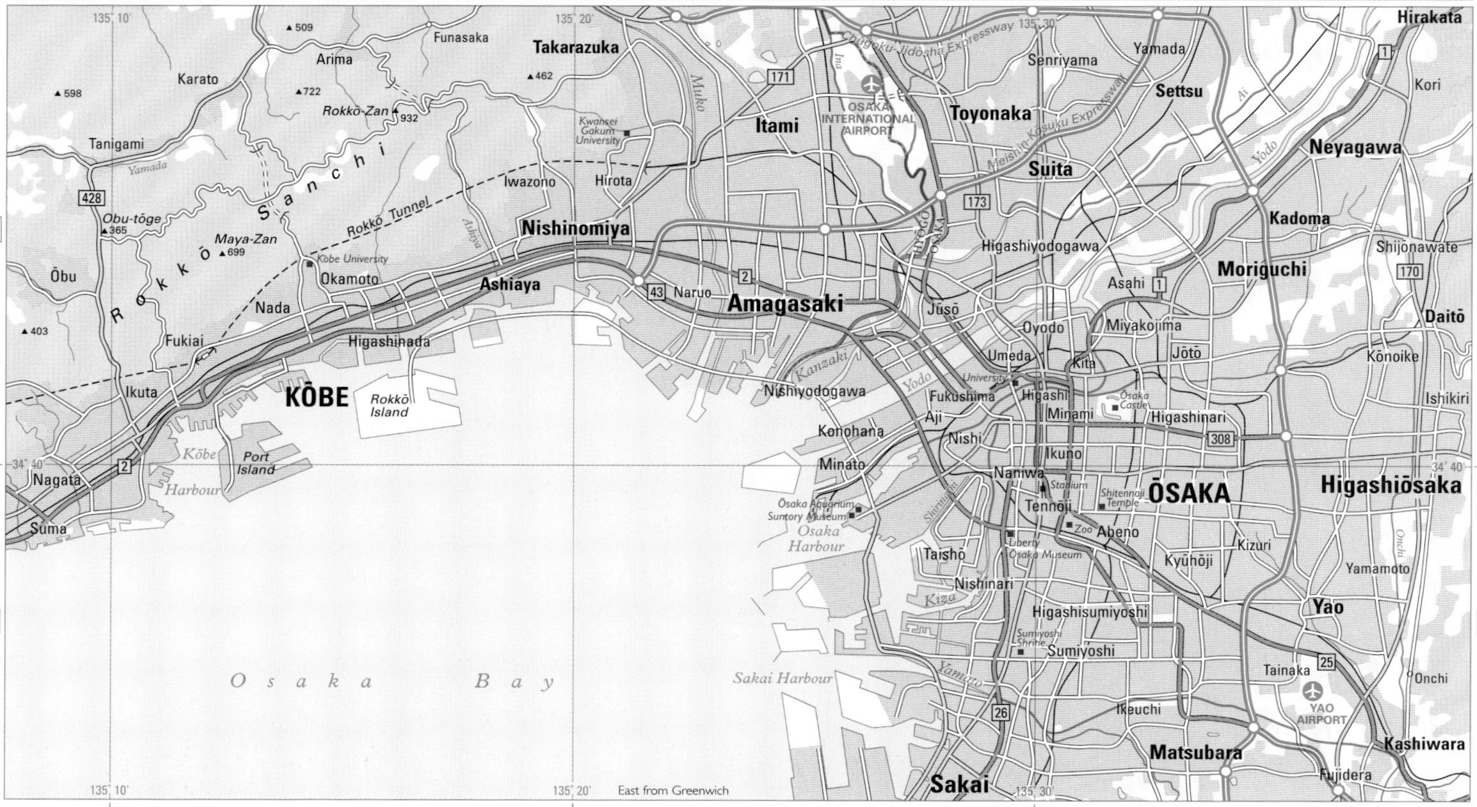

East from Greenwich

135° 10' · 135° 20' · 135° 30'
1 · 2 · 3 · 4

OSLO

km 0 5
miles 0 3

Byo · OSLO AKERSHUS · Tryvannshøgda 531 · Maridalen · Maridalsvatnet · Alnsjøen
Bogstadvannet · Burudvann · 418 · Holmenkollen · Kjelsås · Gorud · Rødtvet
Bærums Verk · Ila · Røa · Ris · RING 3 · Ulleväl · 163 · 4
168 · Lijordet · OSLO · RING 2 · Sinsen · E6
A · Bryn · 379 · Haslum · Ullern · Skøyen · Alna · A
Kolsås · 160 · Stabekk · Lysaker · Universitet Vestbane · Sentrum · Tøyen · Bryn
E16 · 164 · Bærum · Hovik · Norsk Folke Museum · Akershus Slott · Hovedøya · Ryen · Oppsal · Bøler
Tanum · 166 · Bygdøy · Lindøya · E18 · Bekkelaget · Lambertseter · Østmark-kapellet
Sandvika · Snarøya · Fornebu · Ormøya · Nordstrand · 155
Slependen · Nesøya · Ostøya · Frederikshavn Helsingborg København Hirtshals, Kiel · Nesoddtangen · Malmøya · Ljabru · Hauketo
Hvalstad Nesbru · Brønnøya · Oksval · Skoklefall · Bunnefjorden · 155
Asker · 165 · Flaskebekk
E18 · Konglungen · Ingierstrand · Klemetsrud
167 · Blakstad · 157 · 215 · Torvvik · Kolbotn
Vollen · Nesodden · E6
B · Slemmestad · Fjellstrand · 156 · Oppegård · Myrvoll · B
157 · Svestad · Hasle · Blylaget · 152
E18 · 134 · Oppegård
Nærsnes · Garder

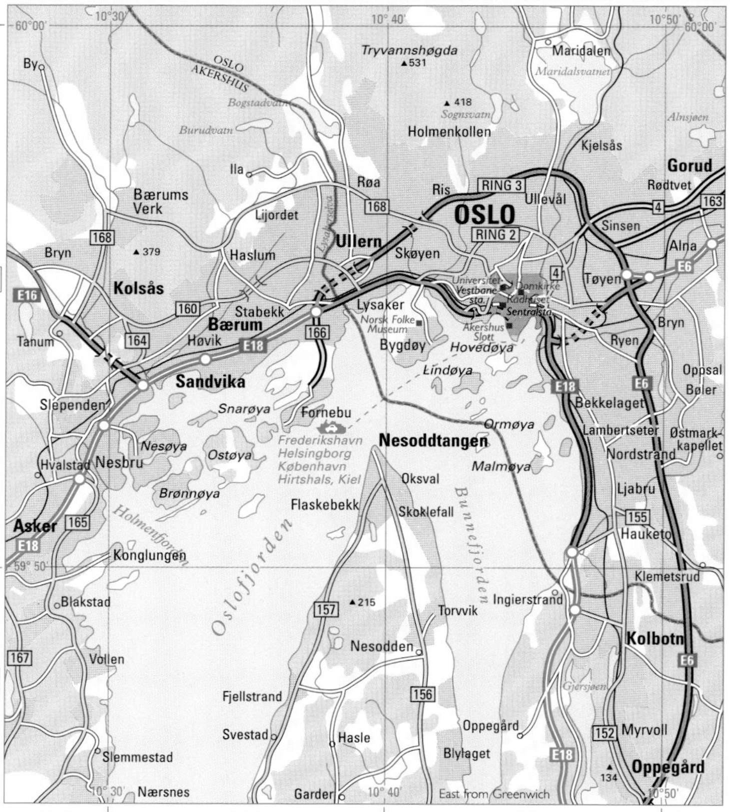

Holmenfjorden · Oslofjorden

East from Greenwich

10° 30' · 10° 40' · 10° 50'
1 · 2 · 3 · 4

CENTRAL OSLO

km 0 0.5
miles 0 0.25

Stensberg · Rikshospitalet · Vår Frelsers Gravlund · Westye Egebergs gate · Nordre gate
Welhavens gate · PARKVEIEN · Hegdehaugsveien · WERGELANDSVEIEN · Wessels gate · Vor Frue hospitalet · Damstredet · Brenneveien · Korsgata · Markveien
a · St. Olavs-kirke · Rosteds gate · Akerselva · a
Slotts parken · ST. OLAVS GATE · Historisk museum · HAMMERSBORG TUNNELEN · MØLLERGATA · Torggata
Det Kongelige Slottet · KRISTIAN IV GATE · FREDERIKS GATE · Nasjonal galleriet · Keysers gate · Deichmanske bibliotek
Dronningparken · DRAMMENSVEIEN · PILESTREDET · Universitet · Det Norske Teater · Youngs Torget · TEATER GATA · Christian Krohgs gate
A · Ibsen-museet · National theatret · GRENSEN · Operaen · STENERSGATA · A
Stenersmuseet · Konserthuset · Stortinget · Karl Johans gate · Domkirke · Oslo Spektrum
MUNKEDAMSVEIEN · Rådhuset · Stortinget · Jernbane-torget · Sentralstasjon · Buss-terminalen
b · Vestbane stasjonen · Hovedpost kontor · b
Dokkveien · OSLO TUNNELEN · Christiania torv · Havnegata
Teater-museet · Arkitekt-museet · Børsen · DRONNINGENSVEIEN
Piervika · Museet for samtidskunst · Astrup Fearnley-museet
Hjemmefront-museet · Akershus Slott og festning · BISPEGATA
c · Forsvars-museet · Bjørvika · Bispevika · c
Frederikshavn, Helsingborg, København · Havnevein

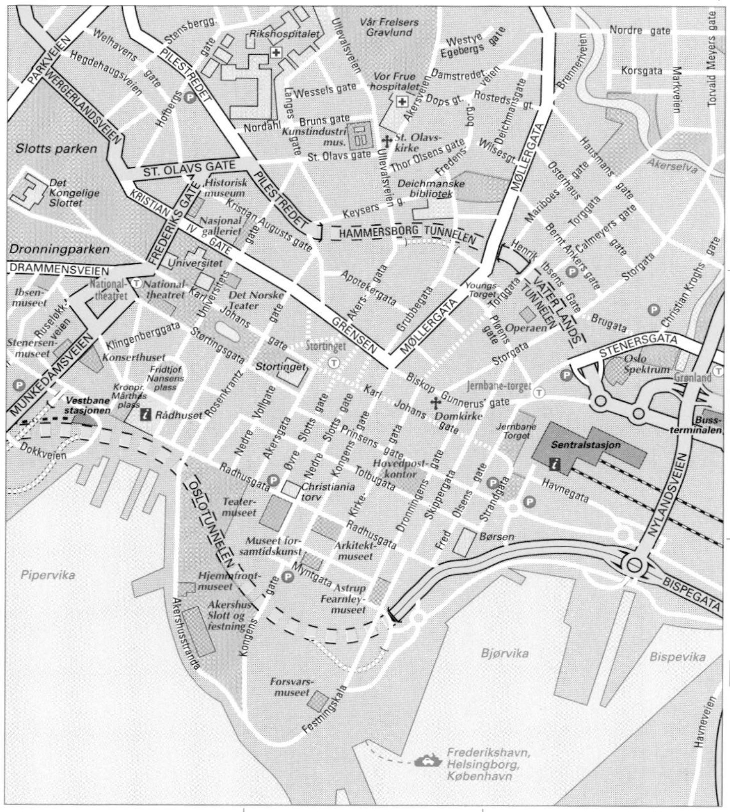

1 · 2 · 3

PARIS

km 0 — 5
miles 0 — 3

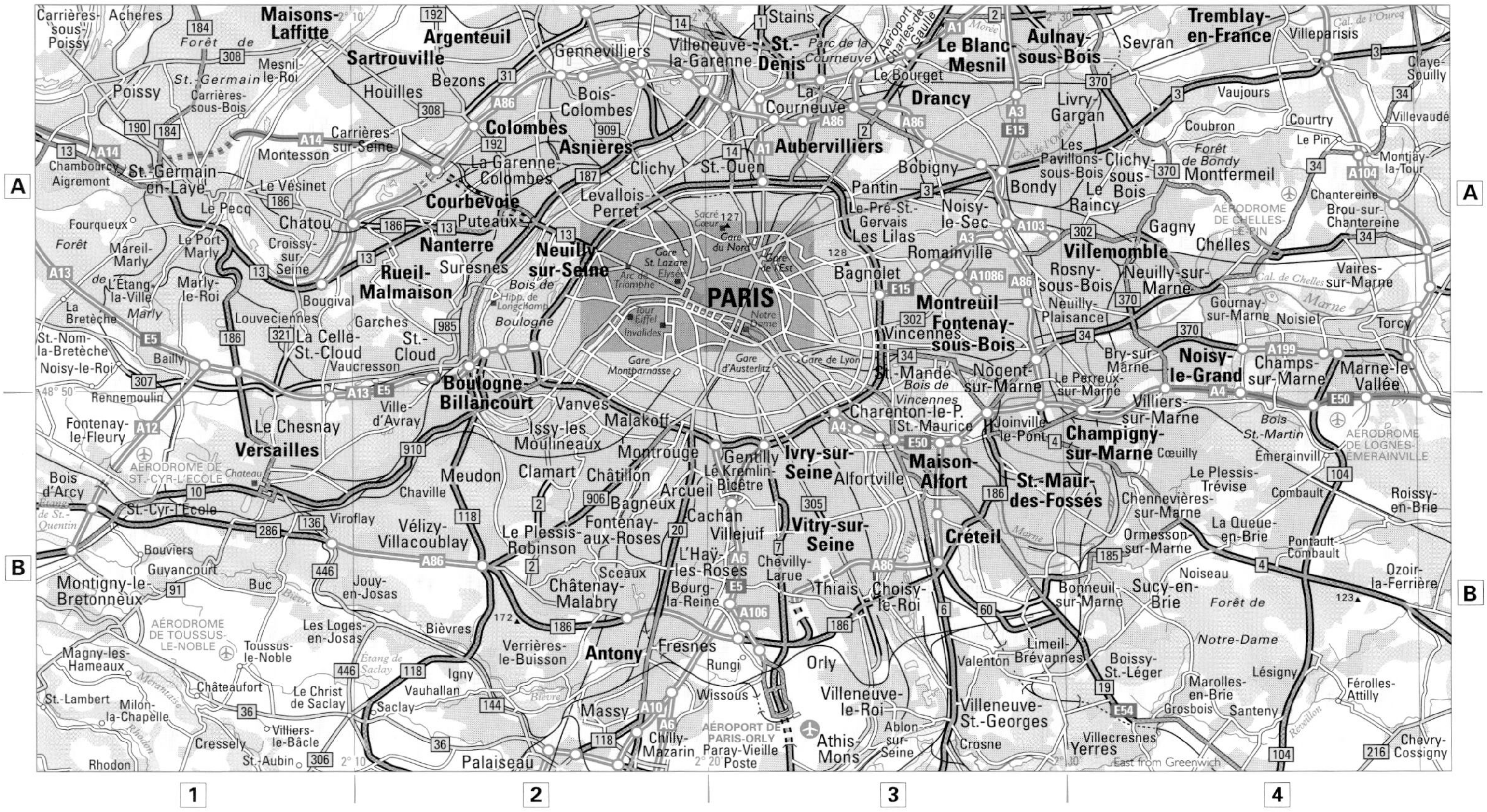

Carrières-sous-Poissy · Achères · Maisons-Laffitte · 184 · 192 · 10 · Stains · Parc de la Courneuve · A1 · Tremblay-en-France · Villeparisis · Cal. de l'Ourcq · Claye-Souilly · 34
Mesnil-le-Roi · Argenteuil · Gennevilliers · Villeneuve-la-Garenne · St.-Denis · Le Bourget · Le Blanc-Mesnil · Aulnay-sous-Bois · Sevran · Vaujours
St.-Germain · Sartrouville · Bezons · 31 · Bois-Colombes · Drancy · A3 · E15 · Livry-Gargan · 370 · Coubron · Le Pin · Montjay-la-Tour
Poissy · Houilles · A86 · Colombes · 909 · La Courneuve · A86 · Les Pavillons-sous-Bois · Clichy-sous-Bois · Forêt de Bondy · Courtry · Villevaudé
190 · 184 · 308 · Carrières-sur-Seine · 308 · Asnières · 187 · Aubervilliers · A86 · Pantin · Bobigny · Le Bois · A104 · Montjay
13 · A14 · Chambourcy · Montesson · La Garenne-Colombes · Clichy · St.-Ouen · Le Pré-St.-Gervais · Les Lilas · Noisy-le-Sec · Bondy · 370 · Montfermeil · Chanteraine
Aigremont · St.-Germain-en-Laye · Le Vésinet · Courbevoie · Levallois-Perret · Sacré-Cœur 127 · Gare du Nord · A103 · 302 · Gagny · Chelles · Aérodrome de Chelles-le-Pin · Brou-sur-Chantereine
Fourqueux · Le Pecq · Chatou · 186 · Puteaux · Gare St. Lazare · Gare de l'Est · 128 · Romainville · A1086 · Villemomble · Rosny-sous-Bois · Neuilly-sur-Marne · Cal. de Chelles · Vaires-sur-Marne
Mareil-Marly · Le Port-Marly · Croissy-sur-Seine · Nanterre · Neuilly-sur-Seine · Arc de Triomphe · Champs Élysées · A86 · E50 · Bagnolet · Montreuil · Gournay-sur-Marne · Marne · Noisiel · Torcy
Étang-la-Ville · Marly-le-Roi · 13 · Suresnes · Rueil-Malmaison · Bois de Boulogne · Tour Eiffel · **PARIS** · Notre Dame · 302 · Fontenay-sous-Bois · Vincennes · Neuilly-Plaisance · Bry-sur-Marne · Champs-sur-Marne · Marne-la-Vallée
La Bretèche · Louveciennes · Garches · St.-Cloud · 985 · Invalides · Gare de Lyon · Gare d'Austerlitz · Charenton-le-P. · Vincennes · Noisy-le-Grand · A199
St.-Nom-la-Bretèche · Bailly · 186 · 321 · La Celle-St.-Cloud · Vaucresson · Gare Montparnasse · Bois de Vincennes · Nogent-sur-Marne · Le Perreux-sur-Marne · Villiers-sur-Marne · A4 · E50
Noisy-le-Roi · E5 · Vaucresson · Ville d'Avray · Boulogne-Billancourt · A4 · St.-Mandé · St.-Maurice · Joinville-le-Pont · Champigny-sur-Marne · Émerainville · Aérodrome de Lognes-Émerainville
Rennemoulin · 307 · Fontenay-le-Fleury · A12 · Le Chesnay · Vanves · Malakoff · Ivry-sur-Seine · Maison-Alfort · St.-Maur-des-Fossés · Chennevières-sur-Marne · 104 · Roissy-en-Brie
Bois d'Arcy · Versailles · A13 · Issy-les-Moulineaux · Montrouge · Gentilly · Le Kremlin-Bicêtre · Alfortville · 186 · Le Plessis-Trévise · Combault
Aérodrome de St.-Cyr-l'École · Château · 910 · Meudon · Clamart · Châtillon · Arcueil · Cachan · Vitry-sur-Seine · Créteil · Ormesson-sur-Marne · La Queue-en-Brie
St.-Cyr-l'École · Viroflay · 136 · 118 · Bagneux · 906 · Fontenay-aux-Roses · Villejuif · A6 · Cœuilly · Noiseau · 185 · Pontault-Combault · Ozoir-la-Ferrière
Montigny-le-Bretonneux · 286 · Vélizy-Villacoublay · A86 · Le Plessis-Robinson · 2 · Sceaux · Châtenay-Malabry · L'Haÿ-les-Roses · Chevilly-Larue · Bonneuil-sur-Marne · Sucy-en-Brie · Forêt de Notre-Dame · 123 · 91 · Buc · Jouy-en-Josas · Bourg-la-Reine · E5 · Thiais · Choisy-le-Roi · Valenton · Limeil-Brévannes · Boissy-St.-Léger · Lésigny
Guyancourt · Aérodrome de Toussus-le-Noble · Les Loges-en-Josas · Bièvres · 172 · 186 · A106 · 60 · 19 · E54 · Marolles-en-Brie · Grosbois · Santeny · Férolles-Attilly
Magny-les-Hameaux · 446 · 118 · Igny · Verrières-le-Buisson · Antony · Fresnes · 936 · Rungis · Orly · Villeneuve-le-Roi · Crosne · Villecresnes · Yerres · Chevry-Cossigny
Cressely · Châteaufort · Le Christ de Saclay · Saclay · Vauhallan · Wissous · Aéroport de Paris-Orly · Ablon-sur-Seine · 104 · 216
Milon-la-Chapelle · 36 · 446 · 144 · Massy · A10 · Chilly-Mazarin · Paray-Vieille-Poste · Athis-Mons · St.-Lambert · St.-Aubin · 306 · Palaiseau · A6 · 118

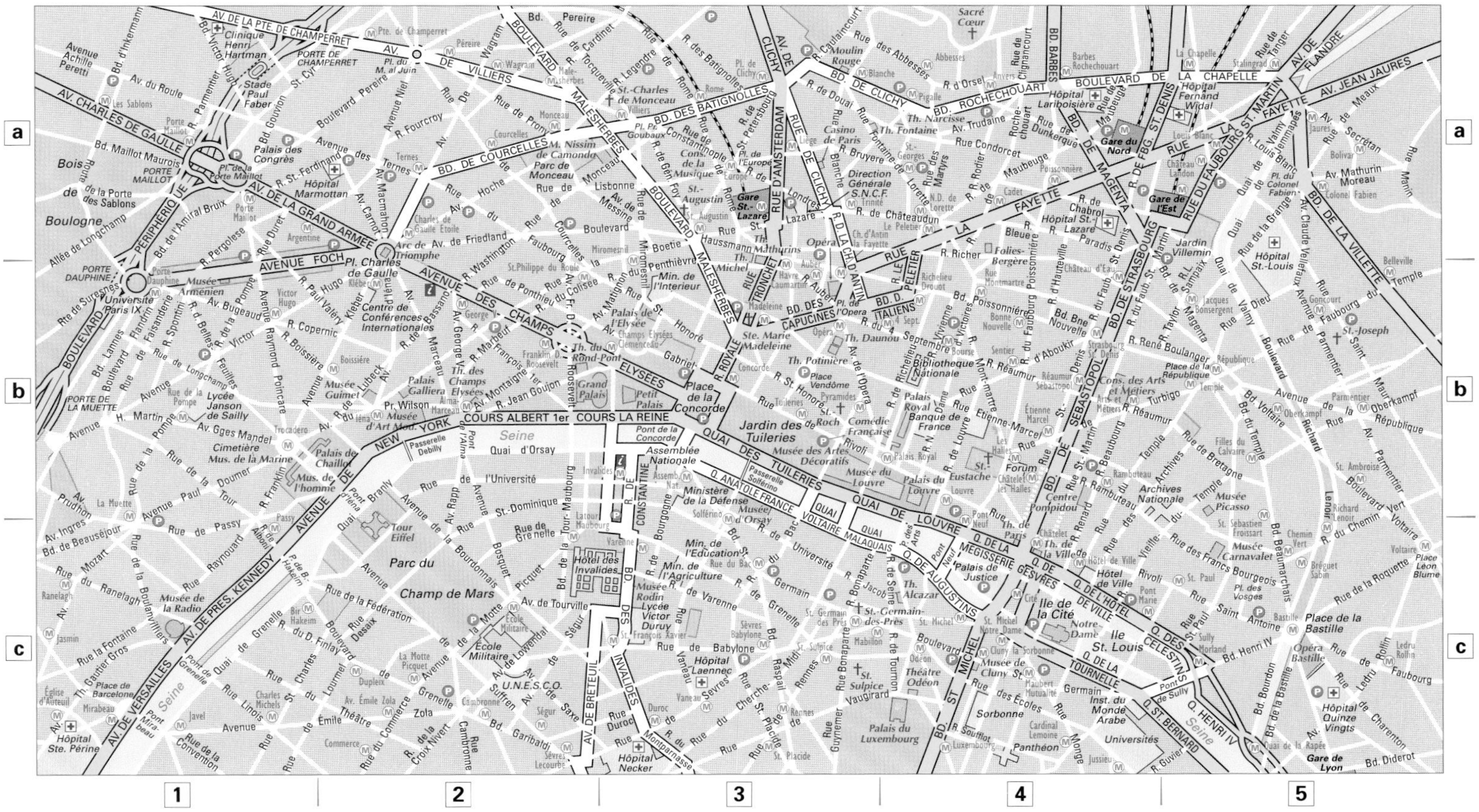

1 2 3 4

CENTRAL PARIS

km 0 — miles — 0.5

a b c — a b c
1 2 3 4 5

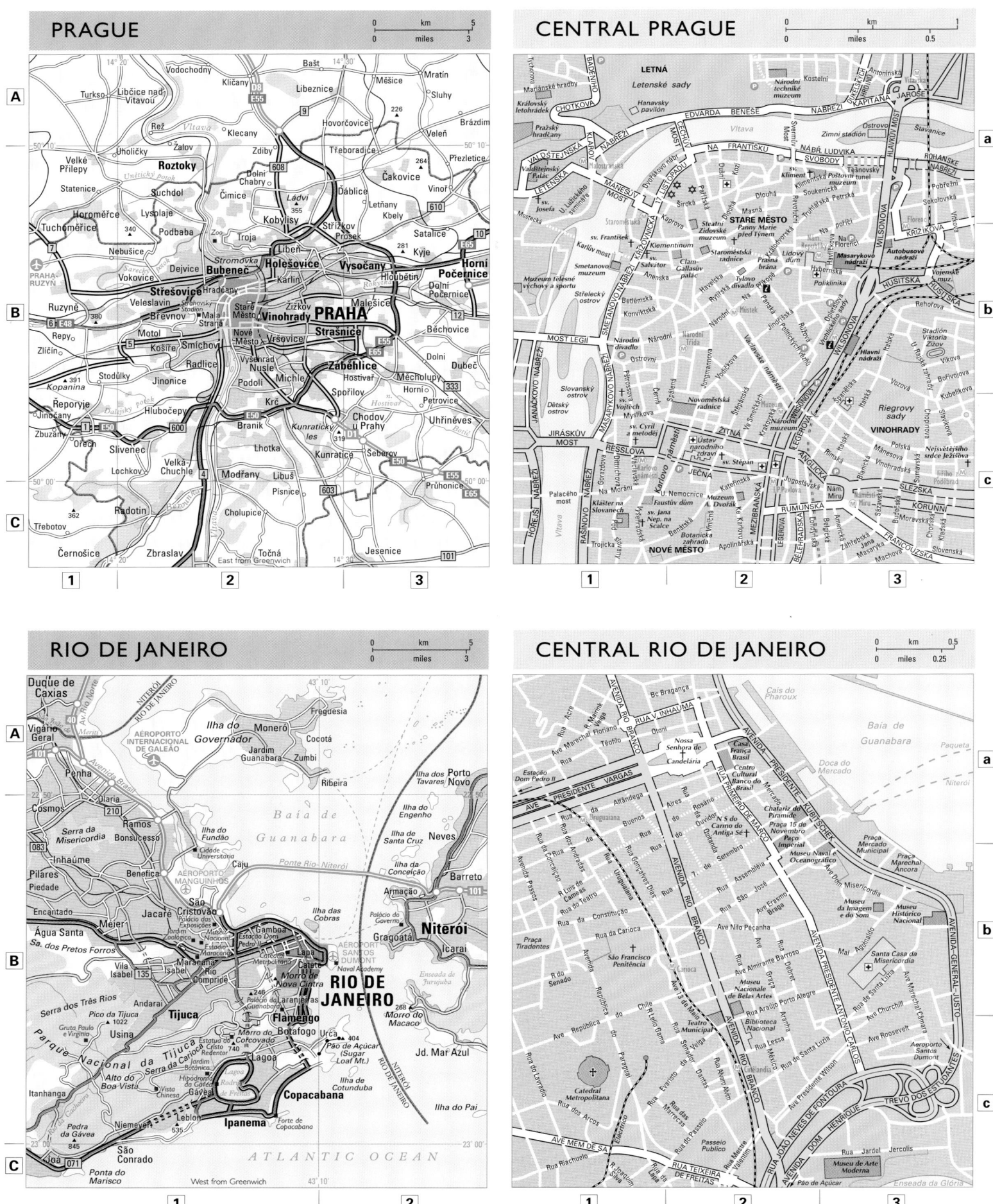

ROME

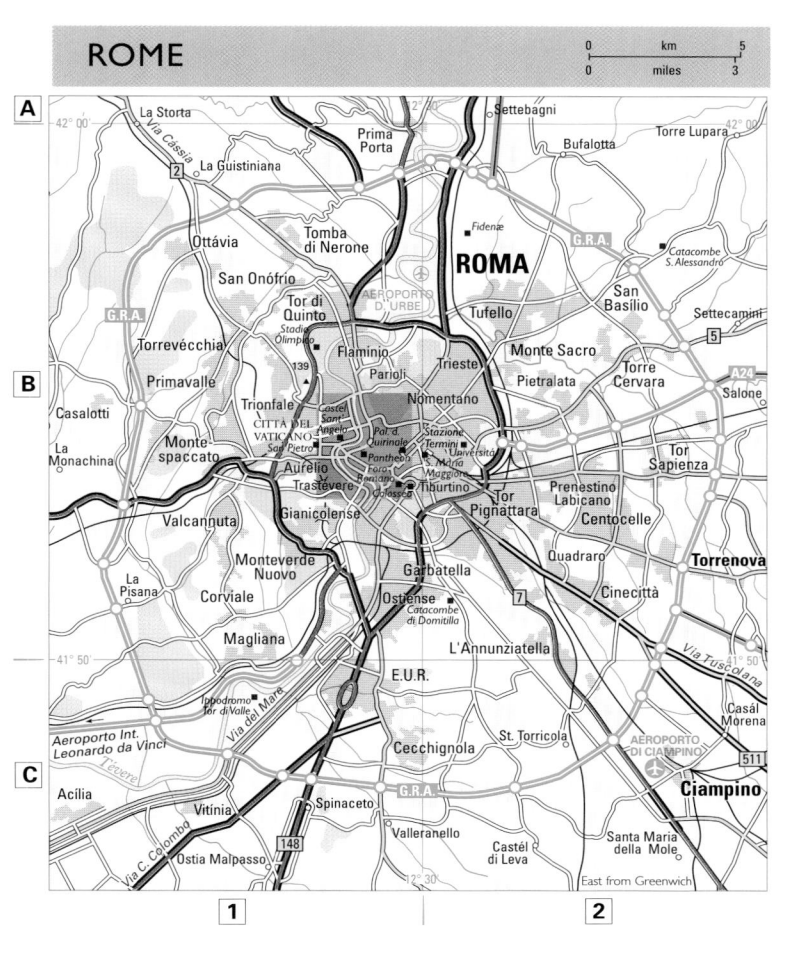

CENTRAL ROME

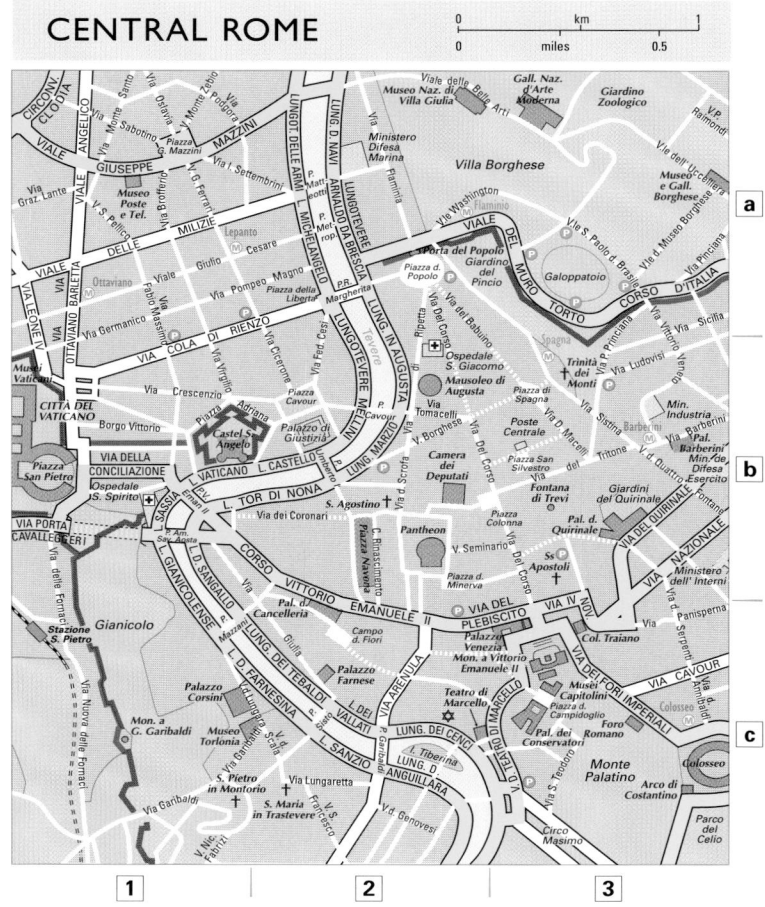

SAN FRANCISCO

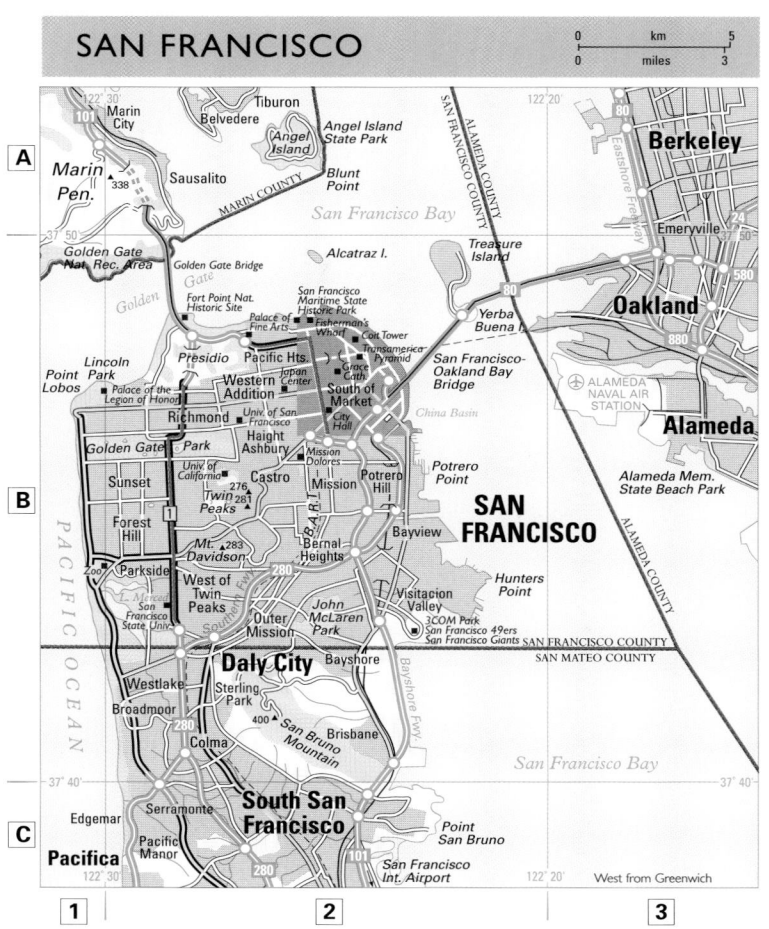

CENTRAL SAN FRANCISCO

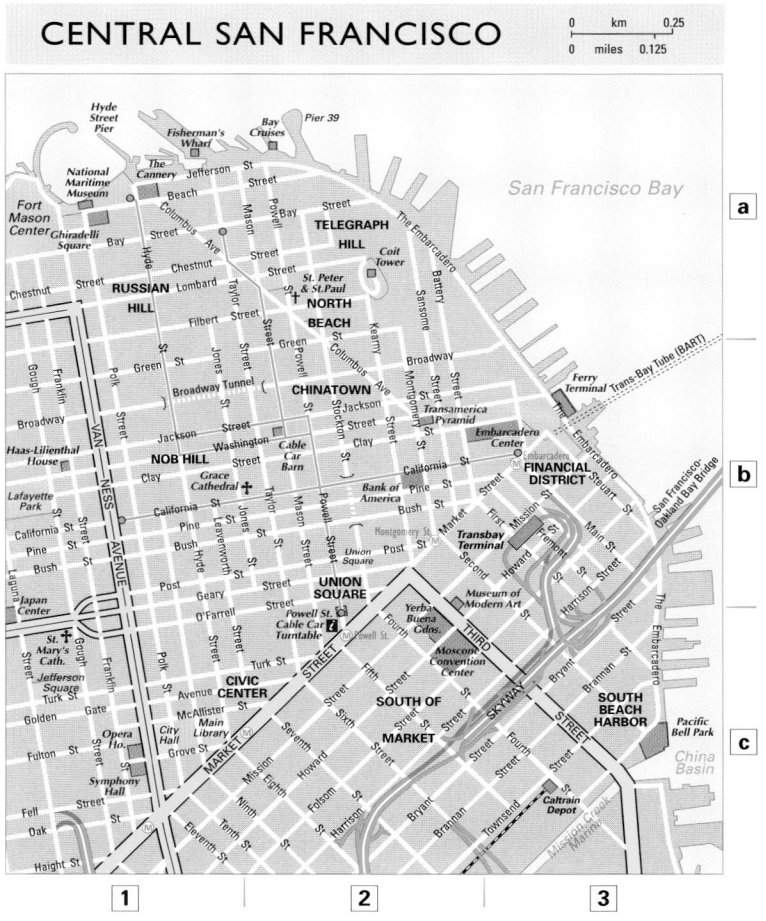

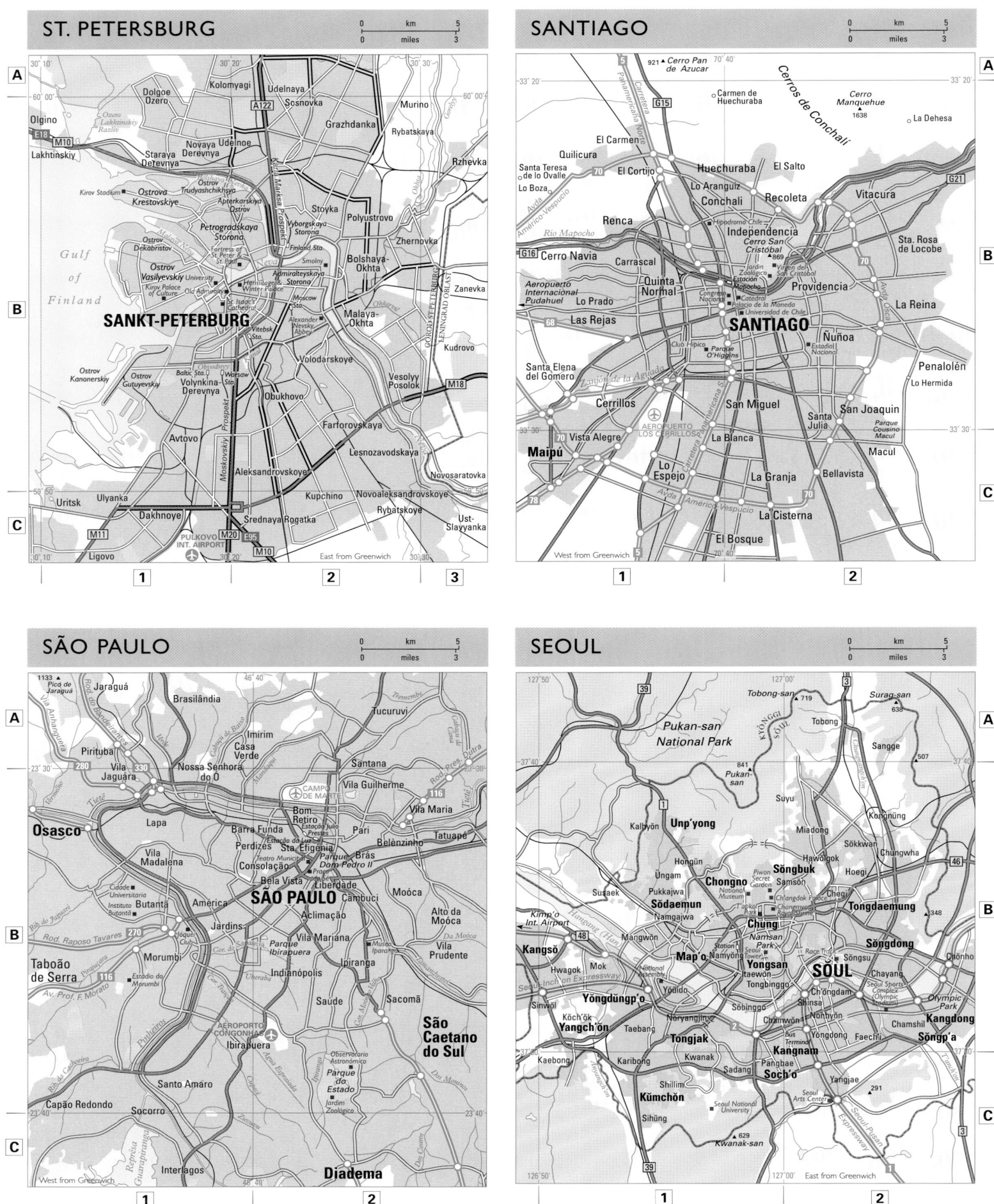

ST. PETERSBURG

km 0 — 5
miles 0 — 3

Olgino
Lakhtinskiy
Dolgoe Ozero
Kolomyagi
Udelnaya
Sosnovka
Murino
Grazhdanka
Rybatskaya
Rzhevka
Staraya Derevnya
Novaya Udelnoe
Novaya Derevnya
Ostrova Krestovskiye
Kirov Stadium
Apterkarskiy Ostrov
Ostrov Trudyashchikhsya
Stoyka
Polyustrovo
Zhernovka
Petrogradskaya Storona
Vyborgskaya Storona
Finland Sta.
Ostrov Dekabristov
Fortress of St. Peter & St. Paul
Smolny
Bolshaya-Okhta
Zanevka
Ostrov Vasilyevskiy University
Hermitage & Winter Palace
Admiralteyskaya Storona
Moscow Sta.
Kirov Palace of Culture
Old Admiralty
St. Isaac's Cathedral
Alexander Nevsky Abbey
Malaya-Okhta
Kudrovo
Gulf of Finland
SANKT-PETERBURG
Vitebsk Sta.
Volodarskoye
Ostrov Kanonerskiy
Ostrov Gutuyevskiy
Baltic Sta.
Warsaw Sta.
Obukhovo
Vesolyy Posolok
Volynkina-Derevnya
Farforovskaya
Avtovo
Moskovskiy Prospekt
Lesnozavodskaya
Novosaratovka
Aleksandrovskoye
Uritsk
Ulyanka
Kupchino
Novoaleksandrovskoye
Rybatskoye
Dakhnoye
Srednaya Rogatka
Ust-Slavyanka
PULKOVO INT. AIRPORT
Ligovo

SANTIAGO

km 0 — 5
miles 0 — 3

Cerro Pan de Azucar
Cerros de Conchali
Cerro Manquehue
La Dehesa
Carmen de Huechuraba
El Carmen
Quilicura
Santa Teresa de lo Ovalle
Lo Boza
El Cortijo
Huechuraba
El Salto
Lo Aranguiz
Recoleta
Vitacura
Renca
Conchali
Hipodromo Chile
Independencia
Cerro San Cristóbal
Sta. Rosa de Locobe
Cerro Navia
Carrascal
Jardin Zoológico
Estación Mapocho
Virgen del San Cristóbal
Providencia
Quinta Normal
Catedral
Palacio de la Moneda
La Reina
Las Rejas
Congreso Nacional
Universidad de Chile
SANTIAGO
Ñuñoa
Santa Elena del Gómero
Club Hípico
Parque O'Higgins
Estadio Nacional
Penalolén
Lo Hermida
Cerrillos
San Miguel
Santa Julia
San Joaquin
Parque Cousino Macul
Maipú
AEROPUERTO LOS CERRILLOS
Vista Alegre
La Blanca
Macul
Lo Espejo
La Granja
Bellavista
La Cisterna
El Bosque

SÃO PAULO

km 0 — 5
miles 0 — 3

Pica de Jaraguá
Jaraguá
Brasilândia
Tucuruvi
Pirituba
Imirim
Casa Verde
Santana
Vila Jaguára
Nossa Senhora do Ó
Vila Guilherme
Osasco
Lapa
CAMPO DE MARTE
Vila Maria
Bom Retiro
Pari
Vila Maria
Barra Funda
Tatuapé
Perdizes
Sta. Efigenia
Brás
Belènzinho
Vila Madalena
Teatro Municipal
Consolação
Parque Dom Pedro II
Moóca
Cidade Universitaria
Butantã
América
Bela Vista
Liberdade
SÃO PAULO
Cambuci
Alto da Moóca
Instituto Butantã
Jardins
Aclimação
Da Moóca
Jóquei Club
Parque Ibirapuera
Vila Mariana
Vila Prudente
Taboão de Serra
Morumbi
Ipiranga
Estádio do Morumbi
Indianópolis
Saúde
Sacomã
AEROPORTO CONGONHAS
São Caetano do Sul
Ibirapuera
Observatorio Astronómico
Parque do Estado
Santo Amáro
Jardim Zoológico
Capão Redondo
Socorro
Interlagos
Diadema

SEOUL

km 0 — 5
miles 0 — 3

Tobong-san
Surag-san
Pukan-san National Park
Tobong
Sangge
Pukan-san
Suyu
Konününg
Kalbyön
Unp'yong
Miadong
Sökkwan
Chungwha
Hongün
Hawölgok
Hoegi
Susaek
Pukkajwa
Piwon Secret Garden
Songbuk
Chegi
Chongno
Samsöh
Södaemun
National Museum
Ch'angdok Palace
Tongdaemung
Namgajwa
Chongmyo
Chung
Kimp'o Int. Airport
Mangwön
Namsan Park
Songdong
Kangsö
Station
Namsan Tower
Race Trk
Songsu
Ohonho
Mok
National Assembly
Yongsan
Seoul Sports Complex
Hwagok
Namyöng
Chayang
Yöuido
Map'o
itaewon
Tongbinggo
SOUL
Olympic Park
Yöngdüngp'o
Sinsa
Ch'öngdam
Sinwöl
Söbinggo
Nonhyön
Yöngdong
Chamshil
Noryangjin
Chamwön
Kangdong
Yangch'ön
Taebang
Faechi
Songp'a
Tongjak
Kangnam
Kaebong
Karibong
Kwanak
Sadang
Pangbae
Soch'o
Yangjae
Shillim
Kümchön
Seoul National University
Seoul Arts Center
Sihüng
Kwanak-san

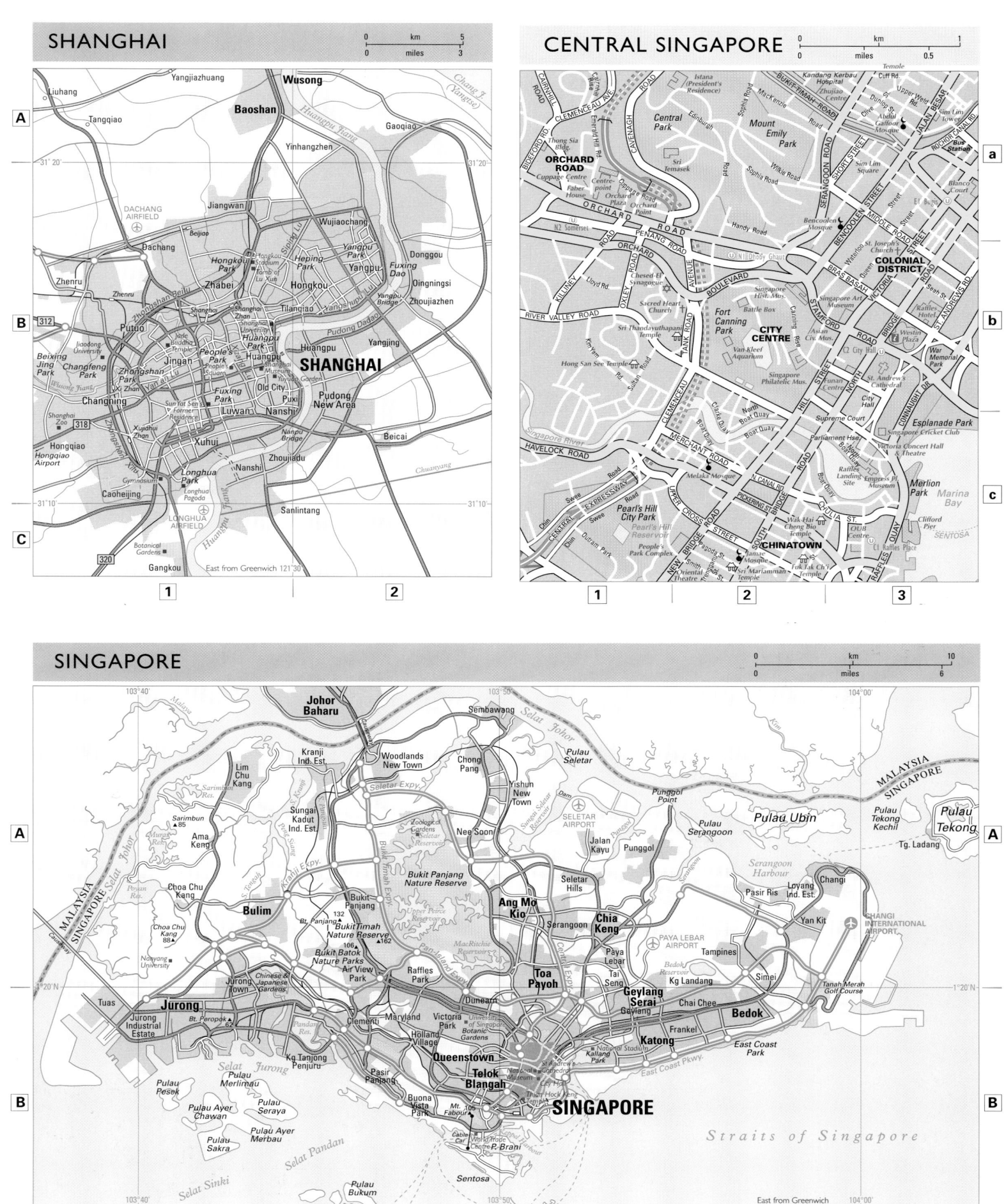

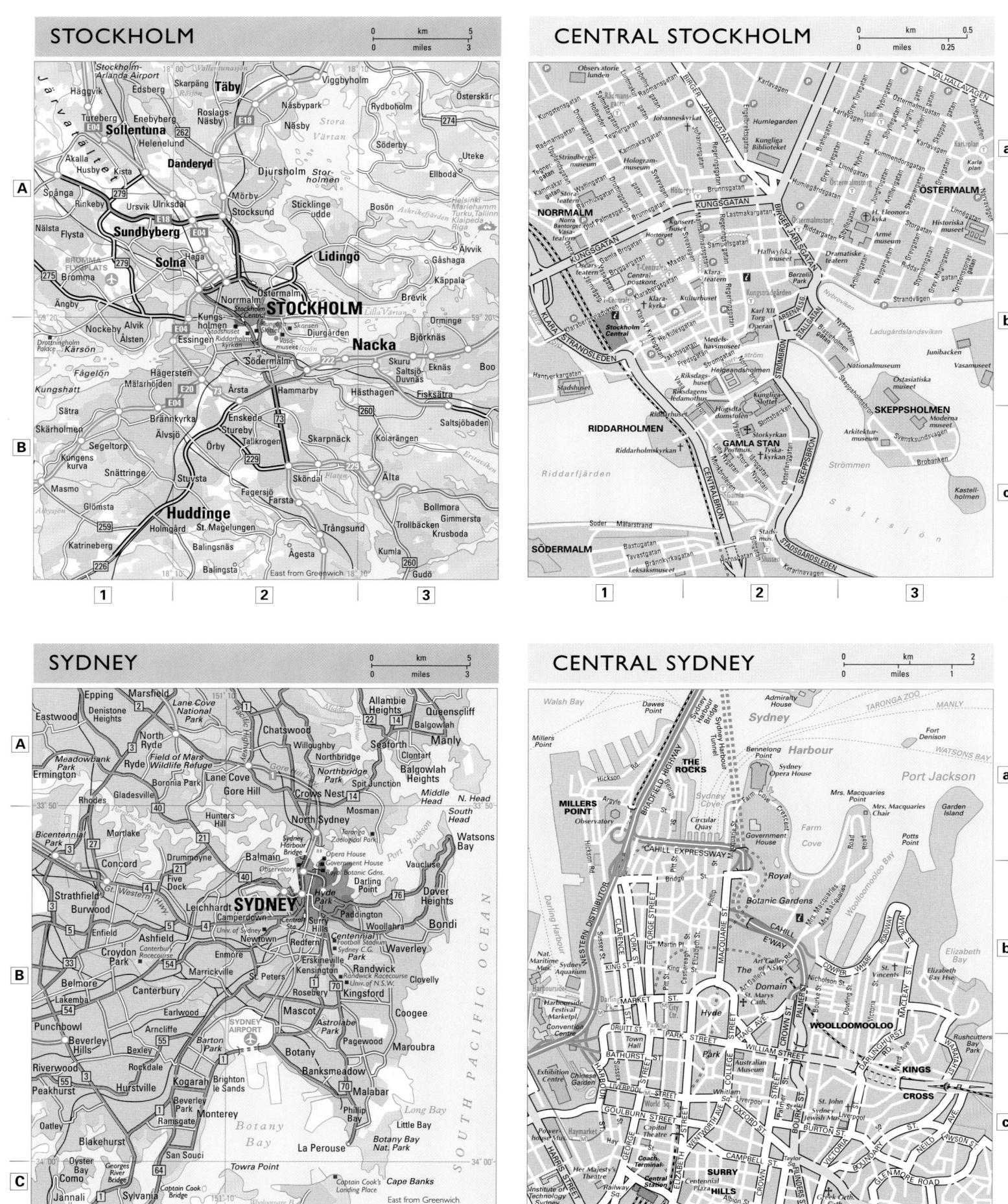

TOKYO

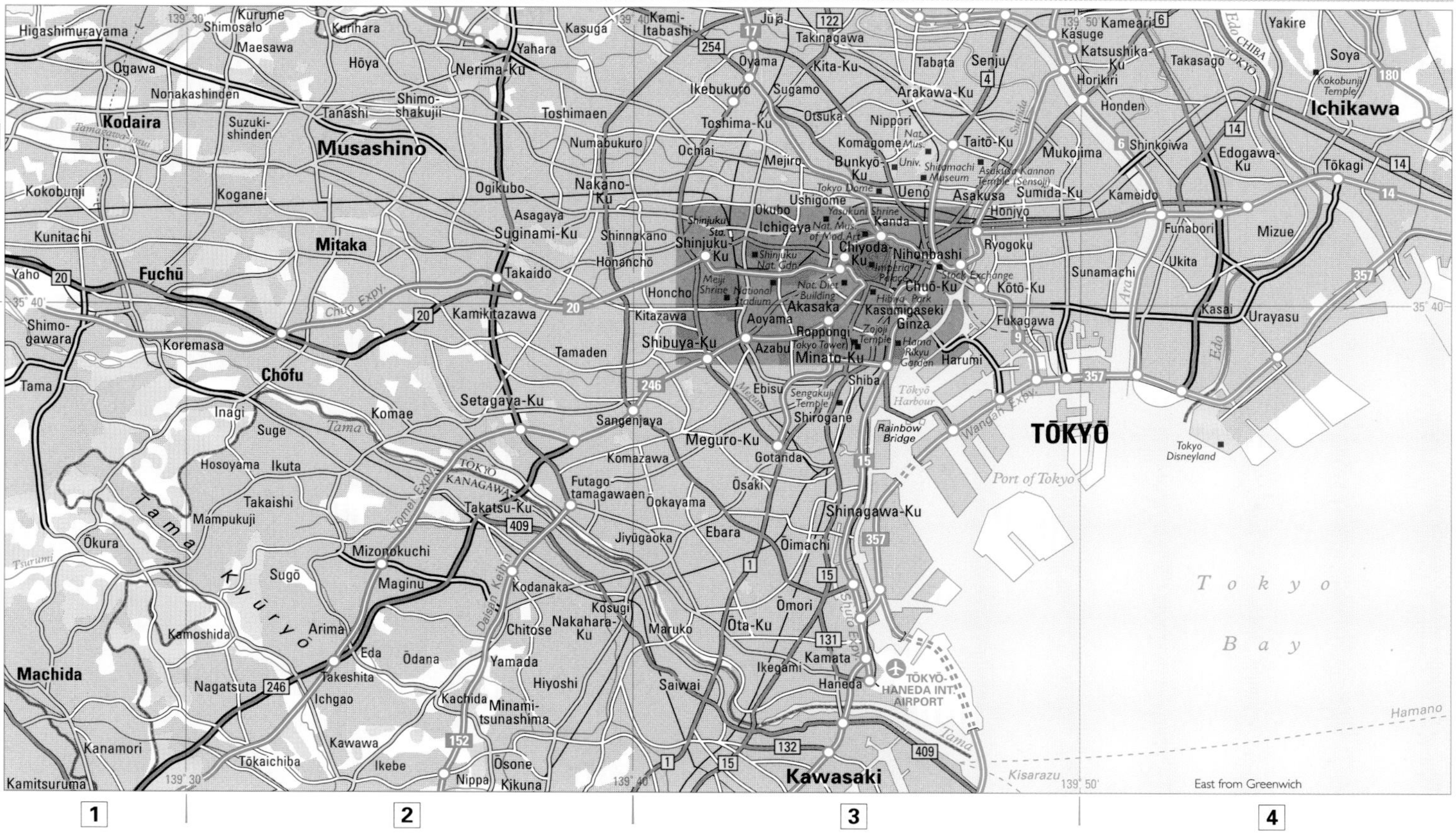

km 0 — 5
miles 0 — 3

Higashimurayama · Kurume · Shimosato · Kasuga · Kami-Itabashi · Jūjō · Takinegawa · Kameari · Yakire · Soya

Kodaira · Ogawa · Nonakashinden · Maesawa · Hōya · Shimo-shakujii · Nerima-Ku · Yahara · Ōyama · Kita-Ku · Arakawa-Ku · Tabata · Senju · Kasuge · Katsushika-Ku · Takasago · Horikiri · Kōkunji Temple · Ichikawa

Kokubunji · Kunitachi · Suzuki-shinden · Tanashi · Shimo-Ogikubo · Nakano-Ku · Ikebukuro · Toshima-Ku · Ōtsuka · Komagome · Nippori · Taitō-Ku · Mukojima · Shinkoiwa · Edogawa-Ku · Tōkagi

Musashino · Koganei · Asagaya · Suginami-Ku · Ochiai · Mejiro · Bunkyō-Ku · Ueno · Asakusa · Sumida-Ku · Kameido · Mizue

Mitaka · Takaido · Shimmakano · Honanchō · Shinjuku-Ku · Chiyoda-Ku · Nihonbashi · Chūō-Ku · Kōtō-Ku · Funabori

Fuchū · Kamikitazawa · Honchō · Kitazawa · Akasaka · Kasumigaseki · Ginza · Fukagawa · Kasai · Urayasu

Shimo-gawara · Koremasa · Chōfu · Tamaden · Shibuya-Ku · Aoyama · Roppongi · Minato-Ku · Harumi

Tama · Inagi · Suge · Komae · Setagaya-Ku · Sangenjaya · Ebisu · Shiba · Rainbow Bridge · Port of Tokyo · Tokyo Disneyland

Hosoyama · Ikuta · Takaishi · Futago-tamagawaen · Meguro-Ku · Komazawa · Gotanda · Shirogane · **TŌKYŌ**

Machida · Mizonokuchi · Maginu · Takatsu-Ku · Kodanaka · Ōkayama · Ōsaki · Jiyūgaoka · Ebara · Ōimachi · Shinagawa-Ku

Ōkura · Sugō · Arima · Eda · Chitose · Yamada · Maruko · Ōta-Ku · Ōmori

Kanamori · Nagatsuta · Ichgao · Takeshita · Kachida · Minami-tsunashima · Hiyoshi · Saiwai · Ikegami · Kamata · Haneda

Kamitsuruma · Tōkaichiba · Ikebe · Ōsone · Nippa · Kikuna · **Kawasaki** · TŌKYŌ-HANEDA INT. AIRPORT

Tokyo Bay · Kisarazu · Hamano · East from Greenwich

1 2 3 4

CENTRAL TOKYO

km 0 — 1
miles 0 — 0.5

SHINJUKU-KU · ŌKUBO · KUDANKITA · **AKIHABARA** · **ASAKUSABASHI**

ICHIGAYA · JIMBŌCHŌ · KANDA · KODENMACHO

YOTSUYA · SANBANCHO · Fukiage Imperial Garden · East Garden · MARUNŌUCHI · NIHONBASHI

Shinjuku National Garden · **CHIYODA-KU** · Imperial Palace · Tōkyō Station · **CHŪŌ-KU**

Meiji Shrine Inner Garden · Yoyogi Park · National Stadium · Jingū Outer Garden · Akasaka Palace · National Diet Building · Hibiya · **GINZA**

Harajuku Sta. · **AOYAMA** · **AKASAKA** · **KASUMIGASEKI** · **SHIMBASHI** · **TSUKIJI**

SHIBUYA-KU · Aoyama Cemetery · **TORANOMON** · Tokyo Tower · Hama Rikyū Garden

ROPPONGI · **MINATO-KU** · Shiba Park · Zōjōji Temple · **SHIBA** · **HARUMI**

AZABU · Sumida-Gawa

1 2 3 4 5

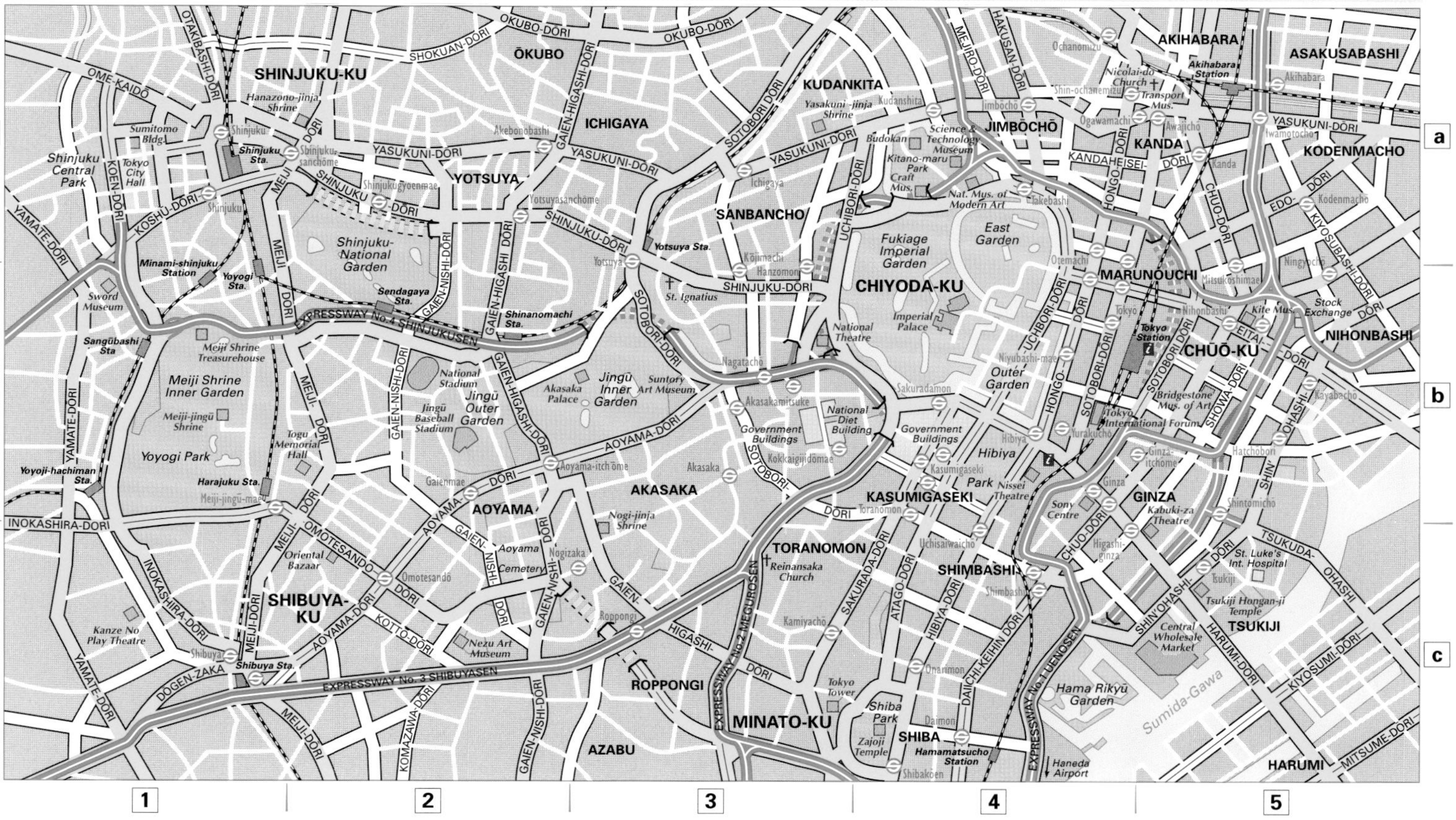

COPYRIGHT GEORGE PHILIP LTD

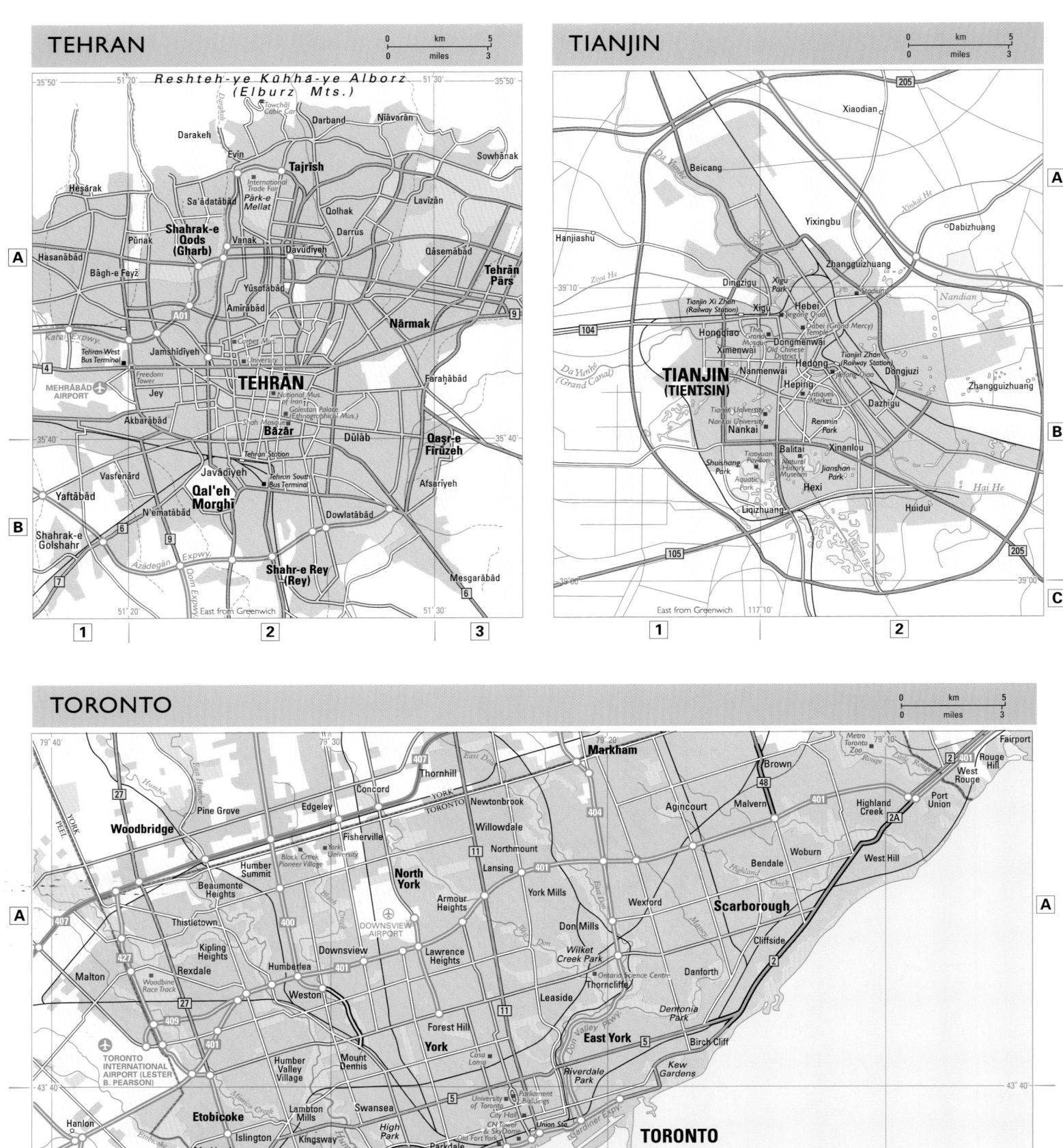

TEHRAN

Reshteh-ye Kūhhā-ye Alborz
(*Elburz Mts.*)

Darakeh · Darband · Nīāvarān · Sowhānak
Hesārak · Evīn · **Tajrīsh** · Lavīzān
Saʻādatābād · Pārk-e Mellat · Qolhak
Shahrak-e Qods (Gharb) · Vanak · Darrūs
Pūnak · Dāvūdīyeh · Qāsemābād
Hasanābād · **Tehrān Pārs**
Bāgh-e Feyż · Yūsofābād
Amīrābād · **Nārmak**
Corbet Hill · Tehran University
Jamshīdīyeh · Farahābād
Freedom Tower · Jey
MEHRĀBĀD AIRPORT
Karaj Expwy · Tehran West Bus Terminal
TEHRĀN · National Mus. of Iran · Golestan Palace · Ethnographical Mus.
Akbarābād · Shah Mosque · **Bāzār** · Dūlāb · **Qaşr-e Fīrūzeh**
Vasfenārd · Tehran Station · Tehran South Bus Terminal · Afsarīyeh
Yaftābād · Javādīyeh · **Qalʻeh Morghī** · Nʻematābād
Shahrak-e Golshahr · Dowlatābād
Āzādegān Expwy · Don Expwy · **Shahr-e Rey (Rey)** · Mesgarābād
East from Greenwich

TIANJIN

Xiaodian
Beicang · Da Yunhe · Xinkai He
Hanjiashū · Yixingbu · Dabizhuang
Zhangguizhuang
Dingzigu · Xigu Park · Hebei · Nandian
Tianjin Xi Zhan (Railway Station) · Xigu · Dabei (Grand Mercy) · Old Chinese Temple
Hongqiao · The Grand Mosque · Ximenwai · Dongmenwai · Dongjuzi
Da Yunhe (Grand Canal) · Nanmenwai · Hedong · Tianjin Zhan (Railway Station)
TIANJIN (TIENTSIN) · Heping · Antiques Market · Dazhigu · Zhangguizhuang
Tianjin University · Nankai University · Renmin Park
Nankai · Balitai · Xinanlou · Hai He
Shuishang Park · Tiaoyuan Pavilion · Natural History Museum · Jianshan Park
Aquatic Park · Hexi · Huidui
Liqizhuang
East from Greenwich

TORONTO

Fairport
Markham · Brown · Metro Toronto Zoo · Rouge Hill · West Rouge
Thornhill · Concord · East Don · Port Union
Pine Grove · Edgeley · Newtonbrook · Agincourt · Malvern · Highland Creek · 2A
Woodbridge · Fisherville · Willowdale · Northmount · Bendale · Woburn · West Hill
Humber Summit · Black Creek Pioneer Village · York University · Lansing · York Mills · Wexford · Scarborough
Beaumonte Heights · **North York** · Armour Heights · Don Mills · Cliffside
Thistletown · Downsview Airport · Wilket Creek Park
Kipling Heights · Downsview · Lawrence Heights · Ontario Science Centre · Danforth
Rexdale · Humberlea · Thorncliffe · Demoina Park
Malton · Woodbine Race Track · Weston · Leaside · East York · Birch Cliff
TORONTO INTERNATIONAL AIRPORT (LESTER B. PEARSON) · Forest Hill · Riverdale Park · Kew Gardens
Humber Valley Village · Mount Dennis · **York** · Casa Loma
Hanlon · Lambton Mills · Swansea · University of Toronto · Parliament Buildings · City Hall
Etobicoke · Islington · Kingsway · High Park · CN Tower & SkyDome · Old Fort York · Union Sta. · Gardiner Expwy
Markland Wood · Humber Bay · Parkdale · Exhibition Place · TORONTO CITY CENTRE AIRPORT · **TORONTO**
Burnhamthorpe · Summerville · Humber Bay · Ontario Place · Island Park · Toronto Harbour
LAKE ONTARIO
Mimico · Toronto Islands · Gibraltar Point
Mississauga · Cooksville · New Toronto · Long Branch

COPYRIGHT PHILIPS

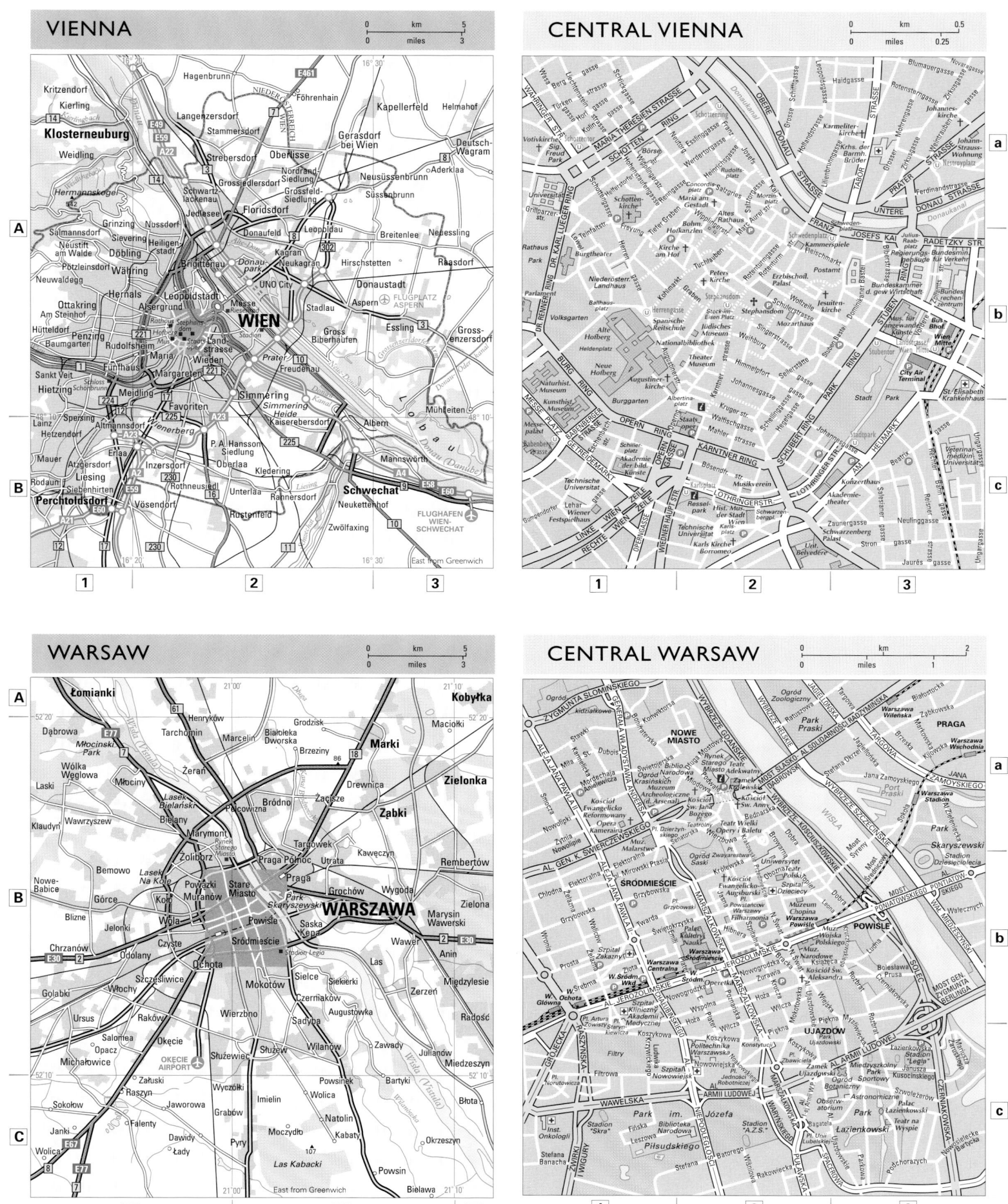

VIENNA

CENTRAL VIENNA

WARSAW

CENTRAL WARSAW

WASHINGTON

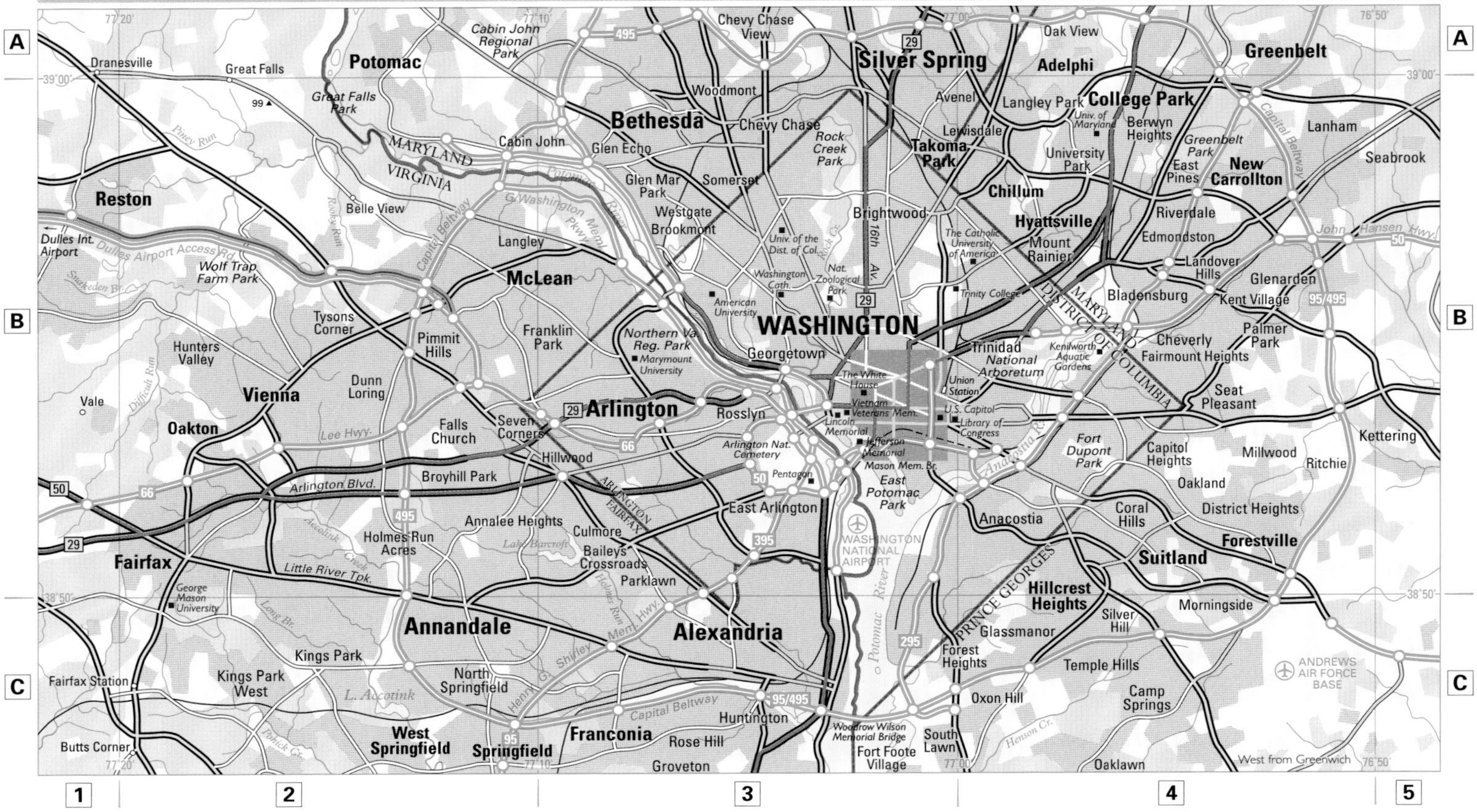

CENTRAL WASHINGTON

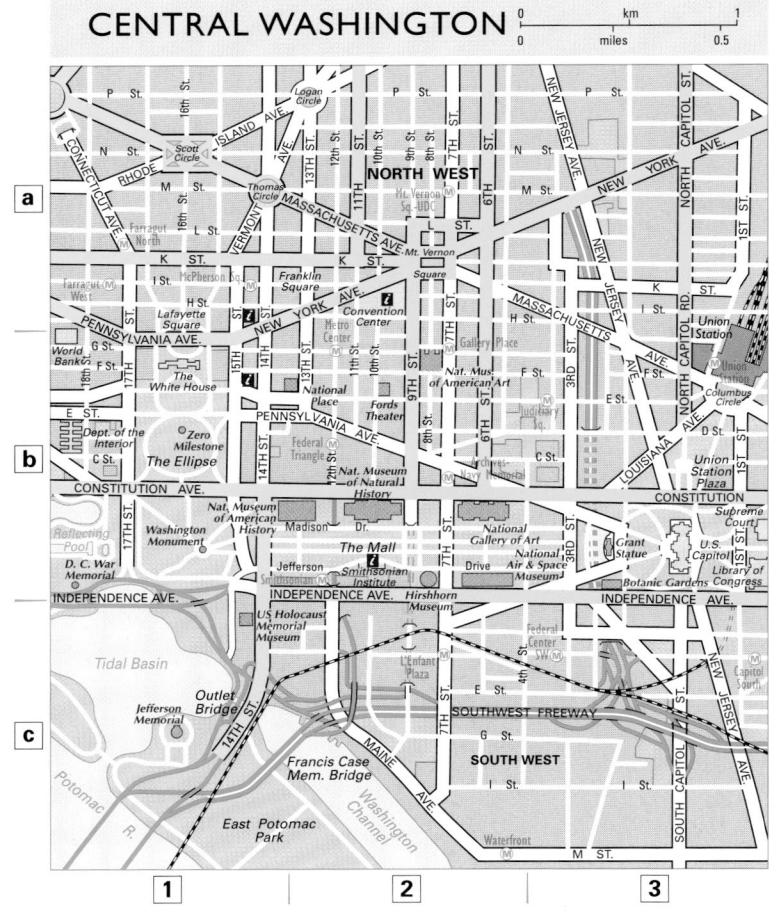

WELLINGTON

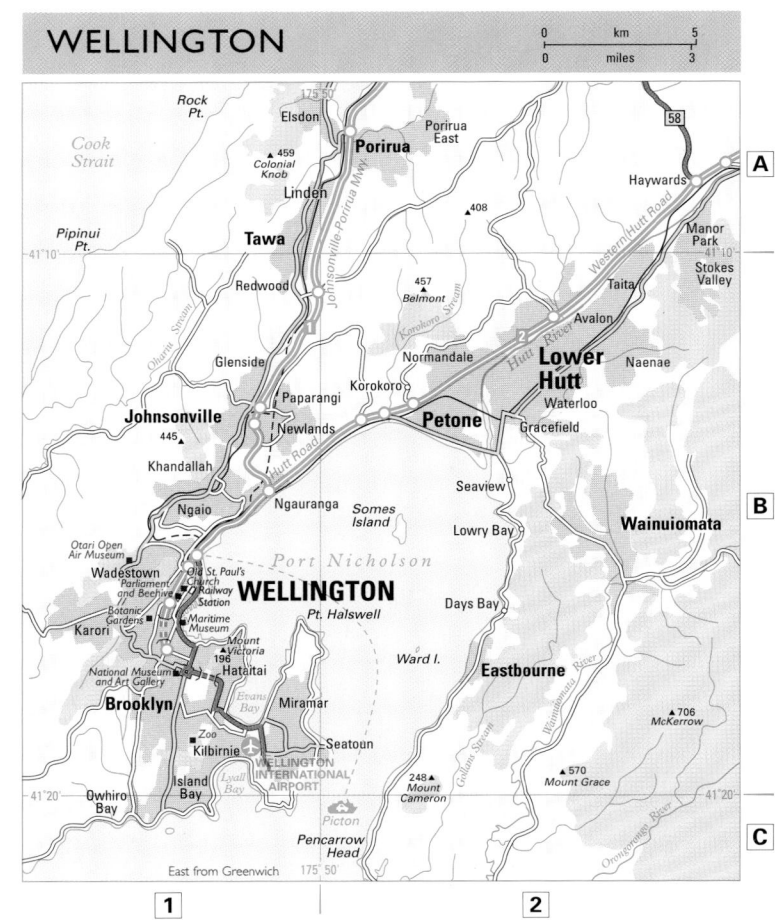

INDEX TO CITY MAPS

The index contains the names of all the principal places and features shown on the City Maps. Each name is followed by an additional entry in italics giving the name of the City Map within which it is located.

The number in bold type which follows each name refers to the number of the City Map page where that feature or place will be found.

The letter and figure which are immediately after the page number give the grid square on the map within which the feature or place is situated. The letter represents the latitude and the figure the longitude. Upper case letters refer to the City Maps, lower case letters to the Central Area Maps. The full geographic reference is provided in the border of the City Maps.

The location given is the centre of the city, suburb or feature and is not necessarily the name. Rivers, canals and roads are indexed to their name. Rivers carry the symbol → after their name.

An explanation of the alphabetical order rules and a list of the abbreviations used are to be found at the beginning of the World Map Index.

A

Aalām, *Baghdad* **3** B2
Aalsmeer, *Amsterdam* **2** B1
Abbey Wood, *London* **15** B4
Abcoude, *Amsterdam* **2** B2
Âbdin, *Cairo* **7** A2
Abeno, *Osaka* **22** B4
Aberdeen, *Hong Kong* **12** B2
Aberdour, *Edinburgh* **11** A2
Aberdour Castle, *Edinburgh* **11** A2
Abfanggraben →, *Munich* **20** A3
Ablon-sur-Seine, *Paris* **23** B3
Abord-à-Plouffe, *Montreal* **19** A1
Abramtsevo, *Moscow* **19** B4
Abu Dis, *Jerusalem* **13** B2
Abû en Numrus, *Cairo* **7** B2
Abu Ghosh, *Jerusalem* **13** B1
Acacias, *Madrid* **17** c2
Acassuso, *Buenos Aires* **7** A1
Accotink Cr. →, *Washington* **32** B2
Acheres, *Paris* **23** A1
Acília, *Rome* **25** C1
Aclimação, *São Paulo* **26** B2
Acton, *London* **15** A2
Açúcar, Pão de, *Rio de Janeiro* **24** B2
Ada Beja, *Lisbon* **14** A1
Adams Park, *Atlanta* **3** B2
Adams Shore, *Boston* **6** B4
Addiscombe, *London* **15** B3
Adelphi, *Washington* **32** A4
Aderklaa, *Vienna* **31** A3
Admiralteyskaya Storona, *St. Petersburg* **26** B2
Áffori, *Milan* **18** A2
Aflandshage, *Copenhagen* **10** B3
Afsarīyeh, *Tehran* **30** B2
Agboyi Cr. →, *Lagos* **14** A2
Ågerup, *Copenhagen* **10** A1
Ågesta, *Stockholm* **28** B2
Agincourt, *Toronto* **30** A3
Agora, Arhéa, *Athens* **2** c1
Agra Canal, *Delhi* **10** B2
Agricola Oriental, *Mexico City* **18** B2
Agua Espraiada →, *São Paulo* **26** B2
Agualva-Cacem, *Lisbon* **14** A1
Agustino, Cerro El, *Lima* **16** B2
Ahrensfelde, *Berlin* **5** A4
Ahuntsic, *Montreal* **19** A1
Ai →, *Osaka* **22** A4
Aigremont, *Paris* **23** A1
Air View Park, *Singapore* **27** A2
Airport West, *Melbourne* **17** A1
Aiyaleo, *Athens* **2** B2
Aiyáleos, Óros, *Athens* **2** B1
Ajegunle, *Lagos* **14** B2
Aji, *Osaka* **22** A3
Ajuda, *Lisbon* **14** A1
Akalla, *Stockholm* **28** A1
Akasaka, *Tokyo* **29** b3
Akbarābād, *Tehran* **30** A2
Akershus Slott, *Oslo* **22** A3
Akihabara, *Tokyo* **29** a5
Akrópolis, *Athens* **2** c2
Al 'Azamiyah, *Baghdad* **3** A2
Al Quds = Jerusalem, *Jerusalem* **13** B2
Alaguntan, *Lagos* **14** B2
Alameda, *San Francisco* **25** B3
Alameda, Parque, *Mexico City* **18** b2
Alameda Memorial State Beach Park, *San Francisco* **25** B3
Albern, *Vienna* **31** B2
Albert Park, *Melbourne* **17** B1
Alberton, *Johannesburg* **13** B2
Albertslund, *Copenhagen* **10** B2
Albysjön, *Stockholm* **28** B1
Alcantara, *Lisbon* **14** A1
Alcatraz I., *San Francisco* **25** B2
Alcobendas, *Madrid* **17** A2
Alcorcón, *Madrid* **17** B1
Aldershof, *Berlin* **5** B4
Aldo Bonzi, *Buenos Aires* **7** C1
Aleksandrovskoye, *St. Petersburg* **26** B2
Alexander Nevsky Abbey, *St. Petersburg* **26** B2
Alexander Soutzos Moussío, *Athens* **2** b3
Alexandra, *Johannesburg* **13** A2
Alexandra, *Singapore* **27** B2
Alexandria, *Washington* **32** C3
Alfama, *Lisbon* **14** c3
Alfortville, *Paris* **23** B3
Algés, *Lisbon* **14** A1
Alhambra, *Los Angeles* **16** B4
Alibey →, *Istanbul* **12** B1
Alibey Barajı, *Istanbul* **12** B1
Alibeyköy, *Istanbul* **12** B1
Alimos, *Athens* **2** B2
Alipur, *Calcutta* **8** B1
Allach, *Munich* **20** A1
Allambie Heights, *Sydney* **28** A2
Allard Pierson Museum, *Amsterdam* **2** b2
Allermuir Hill, *Edinburgh* **11** B2
Allerton, Pt., *Boston* **6** B4
Allston, *Boston* **6** A3
Almada, *Lisbon* **14** A2
Almagro, *Buenos Aires* **7** B2
Almargem do Bispo, *Lisbon* **14** A1
Almazovo, *Moscow* **19** A6
Almirante G. Brown, Parque, *Buenos Aires* **7** C2
Almon, *Jerusalem* **13** B2
Almond →, *Edinburgh* **11** B2
Alnabru, *Oslo* **22** A4
Alnsjøen, *Oslo* **22** A4
Alperton, *London* **15** A2
Alpine, *New York* **21** A2
Alrode, *Johannesburg* **13** B2
Alsemerg, *Brussels* **6** B1
Alsergrund, *Vienna* **31** A2
Alsip, *Chicago* **9** C2
Ålsten, *Stockholm* **28** B1
Älta, *Stockholm* **28** B3
Altadena, *Los Angeles* **16** A4
Alte-Donau →, *Vienna* **31** A2
Alte Hofburg, *Vienna* **31** b1
Alter Finkenkrug, *Berlin* **5** A1
Altes Rathaus, *Munich* **20** b3
Altglienicke, *Berlin* **5** B4
Altlandsberg, *Berlin* **5** A5
Altlandsberg Nord, *Berlin* **5** A5
Altmannsdorf, *Vienna* **31** B1
Alto da Moóca, *São Paulo* **26** B2
Alto do Pina, *Lisbon* **14** A2
Altona, *Melbourne* **17** B1
Alvaro Obregon, *Mexico City* **18** B1
Alvik, *Stockholm* **28** B1
Älvsjo, *Stockholm* **28** B2
Älvvik, *Stockholm* **28** A3
Am Hasenbergl, *Munich* **20** A2
Am Steinhof, *Vienna* **31** A1
Am Wald, *Munich* **20** B2
Ama Keng, *Singapore* **27** A2
Amadora, *Lisbon* **14** A1
Amagasaki, *Osaka* **22** A3
Amager, *Copenhagen* **10** B3
Amāl Qādisiya, *Baghdad* **3** B2
Amalienborg, *Copenhagen* **10** b3
Amata, *Milan* **18** A1
Ameixoeira, *Lisbon* **14** A2
América, *São Paulo* **26** B1
Amin, *Baghdad* **3** B2
Aminadov, *Jerusalem* **13** B1
Aminyevo, *Moscow* **19** B2
Amīrābād, *Tehran* **30** A2
Amora, *Lisbon* **14** B2
Amoreira, *Lisbon* **14** A1
Ampelokipi, *Athens* **2** B2
Amper →, *Munich* **20** A1
Amstel, *Amsterdam* **2** b2
Amstel →, *Amsterdam* **2** c2
Amstel-Drecht-Kanaal, *Amsterdam* **2** B2
Amstel Station, *Amsterdam* **2** c3
Amstelhof, *Amsterdam* **2** b2
Amstelveen, *Amsterdam* **2** B2
Amsterdam, *Amsterdam* **2** A2
Amsterdam-Rijnkanaal, *Amsterdam* **2** B3
Amsterdam Zoo, *Amsterdam* **2** b3
Amsterdam Zuidoost, *Amsterdam* **2** B2
Amsterdamse Bos, *Amsterdam* **2** B1
Anacostia, *Washington* **32** B4
Anadoluhisarı, *Istanbul* **12** B2
Anadolukavağı, *Istanbul* **12** A2
Anata, *Jerusalem* **13** B2
Ancol, *Jakarta* **13** A1
'Andalus, *Baghdad* **3** B1
Andarai, *Rio de Janeiro* **24** B1
Anderlecht, *Brussels* **6** A1
Anderson Park, *Atlanta* **3** B2
Andingmen, *Beijing* **4** B2
Andrews Air Force Base, *Washington* **32** C4
Ang Mo Kio, *Singapore* **27** A3
Ängby, *Stockholm* **28** A1
Angel I., *San Francisco* **25** A2
Angel Island State Park, *San Francisco* **25** A2
Angke, Kali →, *Jakarta* **13** A1
Angyalföld, *Budapest* **7** A2
Anik, *Mumbai* **20** A2
Anin, *Warsaw* **31** B2
Anjou, *Montreal* **19** A2
Annalee Heights, *Washington* **32** B2
Annandale, *Washington* **32** C2
Anne Frankhuis, *Amsterdam* **2** a1
Antony, *Paris* **23** B2
Anyangch'on, *Seoul* **26** C1
Aoyama, *Tokyo* **29** b2
Ap Lei Chau, *Hong Kong* **12** B1
Apapa, *Lagos* **14** B2
Apelacão, *Lisbon* **14** A2
Apterkarskiy Ostrov, *St. Petersburg* **26** B2
Ar Kazimiyah, *Baghdad* **3** B1
Ara →, *Tokyo* **29** A4
Arakawa-Ku, *Tokyo* **29** A3
Arany-hegyi-patak →, *Budapest* **7** A2
Aravaca, *Madrid* **17** B1
Arbataash, *Baghdad* **3** A1
Arc de Triomphe, *Paris* **23** a2
Arcadia, *Los Angeles* **16** B4
Arceuil, *Paris* **23** B2
Arco Plaza, *Los Angeles* **16** b1
Arese, *Milan* **18** A1
Arganzuela, *Madrid* **17** B1
Argenteuil, *Paris* **23** A2
Argonne Forest, *Chicago* **9** C1
Argüelles, *Madrid* **17** a1
Arima, *Osaka* **22** A2
Arima, *Tokyo* **29** B2
Ários Págos, *Athens* **2** c1
Arkhangelskoye, *Moscow* **19** B1
Arlington, *Boston* **6** A2
Arlington, *Washington* **32** B3
Arlington Heights, *Boston* **6** A2
Arlington Nat. Cemetery, *Washington* **32** B3
Armação, *Rio de Janeiro* **24** B2
Armadale, *Melbourne* **17** B2
Armenian Quarter, *Jerusalem* **13** b3
Armour Heights, *Toronto* **30** A2
Arncliffe, *Sydney* **28** B1
Arnold Arboretum, *Boston* **6** B3
Árpádföld, *Budapest* **7** A3
Arrentela, *Lisbon* **14** B2
Årsta, *Stockholm* **28** B2
Art Institute, *Chicago* **9** c2
Artane, *Dublin* **11** A2
Artas, *Jerusalem* **13** B2
Arthur's Seat, *Edinburgh* **11** B3
Aryiróupolis, *Athens* **2** B2
Asagaya, *Tokyo* **29** A2
Asahi, *Osaka* **22** A4
Asakusa, *Tokyo* **29** A3
Asakusabashi, *Tokyo* **29** a5
Asati, *Calcutta* **8** C1
Aschheim, *Munich* **20** A3
Ascot Vale, *Melbourne* **17** A1
Ashburn, *Chicago* **9** C2
Ashburton, *Melbourne* **17** B2
Ashfield, *Sydney* **28** B1
Ashford, *London* **15** B1
Ashiya, *Osaka* **22** A2
Ashiya →, *Osaka* **22** A2
Ashtown, *Dublin* **11** A2
Askisto, *Helsinki* **12** B1
Askrikefjärden, *Stockholm* **28** A3
Asnières, *Paris* **23** A2
Aspern, *Vienna* **31** A2
Aspern, Flugplatz, *Vienna* **31** A3
Assago, *Milan* **18** B1
Assemblée Nationale, *Paris* **23** b3
Assendelft, *Amsterdam* **2** A1
Assiano, *Milan* **18** B1
Astoria, *New York* **21** B2
Astrolabe Park, *Sydney* **28** B2
Atarot Airport, *Jerusalem* **13** A2
Atghara, *Calcutta* **8** B2
Athens = Athínai, *Athens* **2** B2
Athínai, *Athens* **2** B2
Athinai-Ellinikón Airport, *Athens* **2** B2
Athis-Mons, *Paris* **23** B3
Athlone, *Cape Town* **8** A2
Atholl, *Johannesburg* **13** A2
Atīfīya, *Baghdad* **3** A2
Atişalen, *Istanbul* **12** B1
Atlanta, *Atlanta* **3** B2
Atlanta History Center, *Atlanta* **3** B2
Atomium, *Brussels* **6** A2
Attiki, *Athens* **2** A2
Atzgersdorf, *Vienna* **31** B1
Aubervilliers, *Paris* **23** A3
Aubing, *Munich* **20** B1
Auburndale, *Boston* **6** A2
Aucherdinny, *Edinburgh* **11** B2
Auckland Park, *Johannesburg* **13** B2
Auderghem, *Brussels* **6** B2
Augusta, Mausoleo di, *Rome* **25** b2
Augustówka, *Warsaw* **31** B2
Aulnay-sous-Bois, *Paris* **23** A3
Aurelio, *Rome* **25** B1
Ausîm, *Cairo* **7** A1
Austerlitz, Gare d', *Paris* **23** A3
Austin, *Chicago* **9** B2
Avalon, *Wellington* **32** B2
Avedøre, *Copenhagen* **10** B2
Avellaneda, *Buenos Aires* **7** C2
Avenel, *Washington* **32** B4
Avondale, *Chicago* **9** B2
Avondale Heights, *Melbourne* **17** A1
Avtovo, *St. Petersburg* **26** B1
Ayazağa, *Istanbul* **12** B1
Ayer Chawan, P., *Singapore* **27** B2
Ayer Merbau, P., *Singapore* **27** B2
Ayía Marina, *Athens* **2** C3
Ayía Paraskevi, *Athens* **2** A2
Áyios Dhimitrios, *Athens* **2** B2
Áyios Ioánnis Rendis, *Athens* **2** B1
Azabu, *Tokyo* **29** c3
Azcapotzalco, *Mexico City* **18** B1
Azteca, Estadia, *Mexico City* **18** C2
Azucar, Cerro Pan de, *Santiago* **26** A1

B

Baambrugge, *Amsterdam* **2** B2
Baba I., *Karachi* **14** B1
Babarpur, *Delhi* **10** A2
Babushkin, *Moscow* **19** A4
Back B., *Mumbai* **20** B1
Baclaran, *Manila* **17** B2
Bacoor, *Manila* **17** C1
Bacoor B., *Manila* **17** C1
Badalona, *Barcelona* **4** A2
Badhoevedorp, *Amsterdam* **2** A1
Badli, *Delhi* **10** A1
Bærum, *Oslo* **22** A2
Bağcılar, *Istanbul* **12** B1
Bággio, *Milan* **18** B1
Bāgh-e-Feyz, *Tehran* **30** A1
Baghdād, *Baghdad* **3** A2
Bagmari, *Calcutta* **8** B2
Bagneux, *Paris* **23** B2
Bagnolet, *Paris* **23** A3
Bagsværd, *Copenhagen* **10** A2
Bagsværd Sø, *Copenhagen* **10** A2
Baguiati, *Calcutta* **8** B2
Bagumbayan, *Manila* **17** C2
Bahçeköy, *Istanbul* **12** A1
Bahtîm, *Cairo* **7** A2
Baileys Crossroads, *Washington* **32** B3
Bailly, *Paris* **23** A1
Bairro Alto, *Lisbon* **14** c1
Bairro Lopes, *Lisbon* **14** b3
Baisha, *Canton* **8** B2
Baisha →, *Canton* **8** B2
Baixa, *Lisbon* **14** c2
Baiyun Airport, *Canton* **8** A2
Baiyun Hill Scenic Spot, *Canton* **8** B2
Bakırköy, *Istanbul* **12** C1
Bakovka, *Moscow* **19** B2
Bal Harbor, *Miami* **18** A2
Balara, *Manila* **17** B2
Balashikha, *Moscow* **19** B5
Baldia, *Karachi* **14** A1
Baldoyle, *Dublin* **11** A3
Baldwin Hills, *Los Angeles* **16** B2
Baldwin Hills Res., *Los Angeles* **16** B2
Balgowlah, *Sydney* **28** A2
Balgowlah Heights, *Sydney* **28** A2
Balham, *London* **15** B3
Bali, *Calcutta* **8** B1
Baliganja, *Calcutta* **8** B2
Balingsnäs, *Stockholm* **28** B2
Balingsta, *Stockholm* **28** B2
Balintawak, *Manila* **17** B1
Balitai, *Tianjin* **30** B2
Ballerup, *Copenhagen* **10** A2
Ballinteer, *Dublin* **11** B2
Ballyboden, *Dublin* **11** B2
Ballybrack, *Dublin* **11** B3
Ballyfermot, *Dublin* **11** A1
Ballymorefinn Hill, *Dublin* **11** B1
Ballymun, *Dublin* **11** A2
Balmain, *Sydney* **28** B2
Baluhati, *Calcutta* **8** B1
Balvanera, *Buenos Aires* **7** B2
Balwyn, *Melbourne* **17** A2
Balwyn North, *Melbourne* **17** A2
Banática, *Lisbon* **14** A1
Banco do Brasil, Centro Cultural, *Rio de Janeiro* **24** a2
Bandra, *Mumbai* **20** A1
Bandra Pt., *Mumbai* **20** A1
Bang Kapi, *Bangkok* **3** B2
Bang Kholaem, *Bangkok* **3** A2
Bang Na, *Bangkok* **3** B2
Bang Phlad, *Bangkok* **3** a1
Bangkhen, *Bangkok* **3** A2
Bangkok = Krung Thep, *Bangkok* **3** B2
Bangkok Noi, *Bangkok* **3** B1
Bangkok Yai, *Bangkok* **3** B1
Banglamphoo, *Bangkok* **3** b2
Banglo, *Calcutta* **8** B1
Bangrak, *Bangkok* **3** B2
Bangsu, *Bangkok* **3** B2
Bank, *London* **15** b5
Bank of America, *San Francisco* **25** b2
Bank of China Tower, *Hong Kong* **12** c1
Banks, C., *Sydney* **28** C2
Banksmeadow, *Sydney* **28** B2
Banstala, *Calcutta* **8** B2
Bantra, *Calcutta* **8** B1
Baoshan, *Shanghai* **27** A1
Bar Giyora, *Jerusalem* **13** B1
Barahanagar, *Calcutta* **8** B2
Barajas, *Madrid* **17** B2
Barajas, Aeropuerto Transoceanico de, *Madrid* **17** B2
Barakpur, *Calcutta* **8** A2
Barberini, Palazzo, *Rome* **25** b3
Barbican, *London* **15** a4
Barcarena, *Lisbon* **14** A1
Barcarena, Rib. de →, *Lisbon* **14** A1
Barcelona, *Barcelona* **4** A2
Barcelona-Prat, Aeropuerta de, *Barcelona* **4** B1
Barceloneta, *Barcelona* **4** A2
Barking, *London* **15** A4
Barkingside, *London* **15** A4
Barnes, *London* **15** B2
Barnet, *London* **15** A2
Barra Andai, *Karachi* **14** B2
Barra Funda, *São Paulo* **26** B2
Barracas, *Buenos Aires* **7** B2
Barranco, *Lima* **16** B2
Barreiro, *Lisbon* **14** B2
Barreto, *Rio de Janeiro* **24** B2
Bartala, *Calcutta* **8** B1
Barton Park, *Sydney* **28** B1
Bartyki, *Warsaw* **31** C2
Barvikha, *Moscow* **19** B1
Bastille, Place de la, *Paris* **23** c5
Basus, *Cairo* **7** A2
Batanagar, *Calcutta* **8** B1
Bath Beach, *New York* **21** C1
Bath I., *Karachi* **14** B2
Batir, *Jerusalem* **13** B1
Batok, Bukit, *Singapore* **27** A2
Battersea, *London* **15** B3
Battery Park, *New York* **21** f1
Bauman, *Moscow* **19** B4
Baumgarten, *Vienna* **31** A1
Bay Harbour Islands, *Miami* **18** A2
Bay Ridge, *New York* **21** C1
Bayonne, *New York* **21** B1
Bayshore, *San Francisco* **25** B3
Bayswater, *London* **15** b2
Bayt Lahm = Bethlehem, *Jerusalem* **13** B2
Bayview, *San Francisco* **25** B2
Bāzār, *Tehran* **30** A2
Beachmont, *Boston* **6** A4
Beacon Hill, *Hong Kong* **12** A2
Beato, *Lisbon* **14** A2
Beaumont, *Dublin* **11** A2
Beaumonte Heights, *Toronto* **30** A1
Bebek, *Istanbul* **12** B2
Běchovice, *Prague* **24** B3
Beck L., *Chicago* **9** A1
Beckenham, *London* **15** B3
Beckton, *London* **15** A4
Becontree, *London* **15** A4
Beddington Corner, *London* **15** B3
Bedford, *Boston* **6** A2
Bedford Park, *Chicago* **9** C2
Bedford Park, *New York* **21** A2
Bedford Stuyvesant, *New York* **21** B2
Bedford View, *Johannesburg* **13** B2
Bedok, *Singapore* **27** B3
Bedok, Res., *Singapore* **27** A3
Beersel, *Brussels* **6** B1
Behala, *Calcutta* **8** B1
Bei Hai, *Beijing* **4** B2
Beicai, *Shanghai* **27** B2
Beicang, *Tianjin* **30** A1
Beihai Park, *Beijing* **4** b2
Beijing, *Beijing* **4** B1
Beit Ghur el-Fawqa, *Jerusalem* **13** A1
Beit Hanina, *Jerusalem* **13** B2
Beit Iksa, *Jerusalem* **13** B2
Beit I'nan, *Jerusalem* **13** A1
Beit Jala, *Jerusalem* **13** B2
Beit Lekhem = Bethlehem, *Jerusalem* **13** B2
Beit Nekofa, *Jerusalem* **13** B1
Beit Sahur, *Jerusalem* **13** B2
Beit Surik, *Jerusalem* **13** B1
Beit Zayit, *Jerusalem* **13** B1
Beitaipingzhuan, *Beijing* **4** B1
Beitar Ilit, *Jerusalem* **13** B1
Beitsun, *Canton* **8** B2
Beitunya, *Jerusalem* **13** A2
Beixing Jing Park, *Shanghai* **27** B1
Békásmegyer, *Budapest* **7** A2
Bekkelaget, *Oslo* **22** A3
Bel Air, *Los Angeles* **16** B2
Bela Vista, *São Paulo* **26** B2
Bélanger, *Montreal* **19** A1
Belas, *Lisbon* **14** A1
Belas Artes, Museu Nacionale de, *Rio de Janeiro* **24** b2
Beleghata, *Calcutta* **8** B2
Belém, *Lisbon* **14** A1
Belém, Torre de, *Lisbon* **14** A1
Belènzinho, *São Paulo* **26** B2
Belgachiya, *Calcutta* **8** B2
Belgharia, *Calcutta* **8** B2
Belgrano, *Buenos Aires* **7** B2
Belgravia, *London* **15** c3
Bell, *Los Angeles* **16** C3
Bell Gardens, *Los Angeles* **16** C4
Bell Tower, *Beijing* **4** a2
Bellavista, *Lima* **16** B2
Bellavista, *Santiago* **26** C2
Belle Harbor, *New York* **21** C2
Belle View, *Washington* **32** B2
Bellevue, Schloss, *Berlin* **5** a2
Bellingham, *London* **15** B3
Bellwood, *Chicago* **9** B1
Belmont, *Boston* **6** A2
Belmont, *London* **15** A2
Belmont, *Wellington* **32** B2
Belmont Harbor, *Chicago* **9** B3
Belmore, *Sydney* **28** B1
Belur, *Calcutta* **8** B2
Belvedere, *Atlanta* **3** B3
Belvedere, *London* **15** B4
Belvedere, *San Francisco* **25** A2
Belyayevo Bogorodskoye, *Moscow* **19** C3
Bemowo, *Warsaw* **31** B1
Benaki, Moussío, *Athens* **2** b3
Bendale, *Toronto* **30** A3
Bendkhal, *Mumbai* **20** B2
Benefica, *Rio de Janeiro* **24** B1
Benfica, *Lisbon* **14** A1
Benito Juárez, *Mexico City* **18** B2
Benito Juárez, Aeropuerto Int., *Mexico City* **18** B2
Bensonhurst, *New York* **21** C2
Berchem-Sainte-Agathe, *Brussels* **6** A1
Berg am Laim, *Munich* **20** B2
Bergenfield, *New York* **21** A2
Bergham, *Munich* **20** B2
Bergvliet, *Cape Town* **8** B1
Beri, *Barcelona* **4** A1
Berkeley, *San Francisco* **25** A3
Berlin, *Berlin* **5** A3
Bermondsey, *London* **15** B3
Bernabeu, Estadio, *Madrid* **17** B1
Bernal Heights, *San Francisco* **25** B2
Berwyn, *Chicago* **9** B2
Berwyn Heights, *Washington* **32** B4
Besiktas, *Istanbul* **12** B2
Besós →, *Barcelona* **4** A2
Bethesda, *Washington* **32** B3
Bethlehem, *Jerusalem* **13** B2
Bethnal Green, *London* **15** A3
Betor, *Calcutta* **8** B1
Beurs, *Amsterdam* **2** b2
Beverley Hills, *Sydney* **28** B1
Beverley Park, *Sydney* **28** B1
Beverly, *Chicago* **9** C3
Beverly Glen, *Los Angeles* **16** B2
Beverly Hills, *Los Angeles* **16** B2
Bexley, *London* **15** B4
Bexley, *Sydney* **28** B1
Bexleyheath, *London* **15** B4
Beykoz, *Istanbul* **12** B2
Beylerbeyi, *Istanbul* **12** B2
Beyoğlu, *Istanbul* **12** B1
Bezons, *Paris* **23** A2
Bezuidenhout Park, *Johannesburg* **13** B2
Bhadrakali, *Calcutta* **8** A2
Bhalswa, *Delhi* **10** A2
Bhambo Khan Qarmati, *Karachi* **14** B2
Bhatsala, *Calcutta* **8** B1
Bhawanipur, *Calcutta* **8** B2
Bhuleshwar, *Mumbai* **20** b2
Białołeka Dworska, *Warsaw* **31** B2
Biblioteca Nacional, *Rio de Janeiro* **24** c2
Bicentennial Park, *Sydney* **28** B1
Bickley, *London* **15** B4
Bidu, *Jerusalem* **13** B1
Bielany, *Warsaw* **31** B1
Bielawa, *Warsaw* **31** C2
Biesdorf, *Berlin* **5** A4
Bièvre →, *Paris* **23** B1
Bièvres, *Paris* **23** B2
Bilston, *Edinburgh* **11** B2
Binacayan, *Manila* **17** C1
Binondo, *Manila* **17** B1
Birak el Kiyam, *Cairo* **7** A1
Birch Cliff, *Toronto* **30** A3
Birkenstein, *Berlin* **5** A5
Birkholz, *Berlin* **5** A4
Birkholzaue, *Berlin* **5** A4
Birrarrung Park, *Melbourne* **17** A2
Biscayne Bay, *Miami* **18** B2
Biscayne Park, *Miami* **18** A2
Bishop Lavis, *Cape Town* **8** A2
Bishopscourt, *Cape Town* **8** A1
Bispebjerg, *Copenhagen* **10** A3
Biwon Secret Garden, *Seoul* **26** B1
Björknas, *Stockholm* **28** B3
Black Cr. →, *Toronto* **30** A2
Blackfen, *London* **15** B4
Blackheath, *London* **15** B4
Blackrock, *Dublin* **11** B2
Bladensburg, *Washington* **32** B4
Blair Village, *Atlanta* **3** C2
Blairgowrie, *Johannesburg* **13** A2
Blakehurst, *Sydney* **28** B1
Blakstad, *Oslo* **22** B1
Blankenburg, *Berlin* **5** A3
Blankenfelde, *Berlin* **5** A3
Blizne, *Warsaw* **31** B1
Bloomsbury, *London* **15** a3
Błota, *Warsaw* **31** C3
Blue Island, *Chicago* **9** C2
Bluebell, *Dublin* **11** B1
Bluff Hd., *Hong Kong* **12** B2
Blumberg, *Berlin* **5** A4
Blunt Pt., *San Francisco* **25** A2
Blutenberg, *Munich* **20** B1
Blylaget, *Oslo* **22** B3
Bo-Kaap Museum, *Cape Town* **8** c2
Boa Vista, Alto do, *Rio de Janeiro* **24** B1
Boardwalk, *New York* **21** C3
Boavista, *Lisbon* **14** A2
Bobigny, *Paris* **23** A3
Bocanegra, *Lima* **16** A2
Boedo, *Buenos Aires* **7** B2
Bogenhausen, *Munich* **20** B2
Bogorodskoye, *Moscow* **19** B4
Bogota, *New York* **21** A1
Bogstadvatnet, *Oslo* **22** A2
Bohnsdorf, *Berlin* **5** B4
Bois-Colombes, *Paris* **23** A2
Bois-d'Arcy, *Paris* **23** B1
Boissy-St.-Léger, *Paris* **23** B4
Boldinasco, *Milan* **18** B1
Bøler, *Oslo* **22** A4
Bollate, *Milan* **18** A1
Bollebeek, *Brussels* **6** A1
Bollensdorf, *Berlin* **5** A5
Bollmora, *Stockholm* **28** B3
Bolshaya-Okhta, *St. Petersburg* **26** B2
Bolton, *Atlanta* **3** B2
Bom Retiro, *São Paulo* **26** B2
Bombay = Mumbai, *Mumbai* **20** B2
Bondi, *Sydney* **28** B2
Bondy, *Paris* **23** A3
Bondy, Forêt de, *Paris* **23** A4
Bonifacio Monument, *Manila* **17** B1
Bonneuil-sur-Marne, *Paris* **23** B4
Bonnington, *Edinburgh* **11** B1
Bonnyrig and Lasswade, *Edinburgh* **11** B3
Bonsucesso, *Rio de Janeiro* **24** B1
Bonteheuwel, *Cape Town* **8** A2
Boo, *Stockholm* **28** A3
Booterstown, *Dublin* **11** B2
Borisovo, *Moscow* **19** C4
Borle, *Mumbai* **20** A2
Boronia Park, *Sydney* **28** A1
Borough Park, *New York* **21** C2
Bosmont, *Johannesburg* **13** B1
Bosön, *Stockholm* **28** A3
Bosporus = Istanbul Boğazi, *Istanbul* **12** B2
Bostancı, *Istanbul* **12** C2
Boston Harbor, *Boston* **6** A4
Botafogo, *Rio de Janeiro* **24** B1
Botanisk Have, *Copenhagen* **10** b2
Botany, *Sydney* **28** B2
Botany B., *Sydney* **28** B2
Botany Bay Nat. Park, *Sydney* **28** B2
Botič →, *Prague* **24** B3
Botica Sete, *Lisbon* **14** A1
Boucherville, *Montreal* **19** A3
Boucherville, Îs. de, *Montreal* **19** A3
Bougival, *Paris* **23** A1
Boulder Pt., *Hong Kong* **12** B1
Boulogne, Bois de, *Paris* **23** A2
Boulogne-Billancourt, *Paris* **23** A2
Bourg-la-Reine, *Paris* **23** B2
Bouviers, *Paris* **23** B1
Bovenkerk, *Amsterdam* **2** B2
Bovenkerker Polder, *Amsterdam* **2** B2
Bovisa, *Milan* **18** A2
Bow, *London* **15** A3
Bowery, *New York* **21** e2
Boyacıköy, *Istanbul* **12** B2
Boyle Heights, *Los Angeles* **16** B3
Bradbury Building, *Los Angeles* **16** b2
Braepark, *Edinburgh* **11** B2
Braid, *Edinburgh* **11** B2
Bramley, *Johannesburg* **13** A2
Brandenburger Tor, *Berlin* **5** A3
Brani, P., *Singapore* **27** B3
Branik, *Prague* **24** B2
Brännkyrka, *Stockholm* **28** B2
Brás, *São Paulo* **26** B2
Brasilândia, *São Paulo* **26** A1
Brateyevo, *Moscow* **19** C4
Bratsevo, *Moscow* **19** A2
Bray, *Dublin* **11** B3
Braybrook, *Melbourne* **17** A1
Brázdim, *Prague* **24** A3
Breach Candy, *Mumbai* **20** a1
Breakheart Reservation, *Boston* **6** A3
Brede, *Copenhagen* **10** A3
Breeds Pond, *Boston* **6** A4
Breezy Point, *New York* **21** C2
Breitenlee, *Vienna* **31** A3
Breña, *Lima* **16** B2
Brent, *London* **15** A2
Brent Res., *London* **15** A2
Brentford, *London* **15** B2
Brentwood Park, *Los Angeles* **16** B2
Brera, *Milan* **18** B2
Bresso, *Milan* **18** A2
Brevik, *Stockholm* **28** A3
Břevnov, *Prague* **24** B2
Bridgeport, *Chicago* **9** B3
Bridgetown, *Cape Town* **8** A2
Bridgeview, *Chicago* **9** C2
Brighton, *Boston* **6** A3
Brighton, *Melbourne* **17** B1
Brighton le Sands, *Sydney* **28** B1
Brighton Park, *Chicago* **9** C2
Brightwood, *Washington* **32** B3
Brigittenau, *Vienna* **31** A2
Brimbank Park, *Melbourne* **17** A1
Brisbane, *San Francisco* **25** B2
British Museum, *London* **15** a3
Britz, *Berlin* **5** B3
Brixton, *London* **15** B3
Broad Sd., *Boston* **6** A4
Broadmeadows, *Melbourne* **17** A1
Broadmoor, *San Francisco* **25** B2
Broadview, *Chicago* **9** B1
Broadway, *New York* **21** e1
Brockley, *London* **15** B3
Bródno, *Warsaw* **31** B2
Bródnowski, Kanal, *Warsaw* **31** B2
Broek in Waterland, *Amsterdam* **2** A2
Bromley, *London* **15** B4
Bromley Common, *London* **15** B4
Bromma, *Stockholm* **28** A1
Bromma flygplats, *Stockholm* **28** A1
Brompton, *London* **15** c2
Brøndby Strand, *Copenhagen* **10** B2
Brøndbyøster, *Copenhagen* **10** B2
Brøndbyvester, *Copenhagen* **10** B2
Brondesbury, *London* **15** A2
Brønnøya, *Oslo* **22** A2
Brønshøj, *Copenhagen* **10** A2

KAPELLERFELD

Fawkner Park, *Melbourne* 17 B1
Feijó, *Lisbon* 14 B2
Feldkirchen, *Munich* 20 B3
Feldmoching, *Munich* 20 A2
Feltham, *London* 15 B1
Fener, *Istanbul* 12 B1
Fenerbahçe, *Istanbul* 12 C2
Fengtai, *Beijing* 4 C1
Fenino, *Moscow* 19 B5
Ferencváros, *Budapest* 7 B2
Ferihegyi Airport, *Budapest* 7 B3
Ferndale, *Johannesburg* 13 A2
Férolles-Attilly, *Paris* 23 B4
Fichtenau, *Berlin* 5 B5
Fields Corner, *Boston* 6 B3
Fiera Camp, *Milan* 18 B1
Fifth Avenue, *New York* 21 b3
Figino, *Milan* 18 B1
Fijir, *Baghdad* 3 A2
Filadhélfia, *Athens* 2 A2
Fili-Mazilovo, *Moscow* 19 B2
Filothei, *Athens* 2 A2
Finchley, *London* 15 A2
Finglas, *Dublin* 11 A2
Finsbury, *London* 15 A3
Finsbury Park, *London* 15 A3
Fiorito, *Buenos Aires* 7 C2
Firhouse, *Dublin* 11 B2
Fischerhäuser, *Munich* 20 A3
Fisher Island, *Miami* 18 B2
Fishermans Bend, *Melbourne* 17 A1
Fisherman's Wharf, *San Francisco* 25 a1
Fisherville, *Toronto* 30 A2
Fisksätra, *Stockholm* 28 B3
Fitzroy Gardens, *Melbourne* 17 A1
Five Dock, *Sydney* 28 B1
Fjellstrand, *Oslo* 22 B2
Flamengo, *Rio de Janeiro* 24 B1
Flaminio, *Rome* 25 B1
Flaskebekk, *Oslo* 22 A2
Flatbush, *New York* 21 C2
Flaten, *Stockholm* 28 B2
Flemington Racecourse, *Melbourne* 17 A1
Flint Pk., *Los Angeles* 16 B3
Florence, *Los Angeles* 16 C3
Florence Bloom Bird Sanctuary, *Johannesburg* 13 A2
Florentia, *Johannesburg* 13 B2
Flores, *Buenos Aires* 7 B2
Floresta, *Buenos Aires* 7 B2
Florida, *Buenos Aires* 7 B2
Florida, *Johannesburg* 13 B1
Floridsdorf, *Vienna* 31 A2
Flushing, *New York* 21 B3
Flushing Meadows Corona Park, *New York* 21 B2
Flysta, *Stockholm* 28 A1
Fo Tan, *Hong Kong* 12 A2
Föhrenhain, *Vienna* 31 A2
Fontainebleau, *Johannesburg* 13 A1
Fontenay-aux-Roses, *Paris* 23 B2
Fontenay-le-Fleury, *Paris* 23 B1
Fontenay-sous-Bois, *Paris* 23 A3
Foots Cray, *London* 15 B4
Footscray, *Melbourne* 17 A1
Foreshore, *Cape Town* 8 a3
Forest, *Brussels* 6 B1
Forest Gate, *London* 15 A4
Forest Heights, *Washington* 32 C3
Forest Hill, *London* 15 B3
Forest Hill, *Toronto* 30 A2
Forest Hills, *New York* 21 B2
Forest Park, *Chicago* 9 B2
Forest View, *Chicago* 9 C2
Forestville, *Washington* 32 B4
Fornebu, *Oslo* 22 A2
Fornebu Airport, *Oslo* 22 A2
Foro Romano, *Rome* 25 c3
Forstenried, *Munich* 20 B1
Forstenrieder Park, *Munich* 20 B1
Fort, *Mumbai* 20 c2
Fort Canning Park, *Singapore* 27 b2
Fort Dupont Park, *Washington* 32 B4
Fort Foote Village, *Washington* 32 C3
Fort Lee, *New York* 21 A2
Fort Mason Center, *San Francisco* 25 a1
Forth, Firth of, *Edinburgh* 11 A2
Forth Rail Bridge, *Edinburgh* 11 A1
Forth Road Bridge, *Edinburgh* 11 A1
Fót, *Budapest* 7 A3
Fourqueux, *Paris* 23 A1
Foxrock, *Dublin* 11 B2
Framingham, *Boston* 6 B1
Franconia, *Washington* 32 C3
Frankel, *Singapore* 27 B3
Franklin Park, *Boston* 6 B3
Franklin Park, *Chicago* 9 B1
Franklin Park, *Washington* 32 B3
Franklin Res., *Los Angeles* 16 B2
Frauenkirche, *Munich* 20 b2
Frederiksberg, *Copenhagen* 10 A3
Frederiksdal, *Copenhagen* 10 A2
Fredersdorf, *Berlin* 5 A5
Freguesia, *Rio de Janeiro* 24 A1
Freidrichshain, Volkspark, *Berlin* 5 A3
Freiham, *Munich* 20 B1
Freimann, *Munich* 20 A2
Fresh Pond, *Boston* 6 A3
Fresnes, *Paris* 23 B2
Freudenau, *Vienna* 31 A2
Friarstown, *Dublin* 11 B1
Frick Collection, *New York* 21 b3
Friedenau, *Berlin* 5 B3
Friedrichsfelde, *Berlin* 5 B4
Friedrichshagen, *Berlin* 5 B4
Friedrichshain, *Berlin* 5 A3
Friedrichslust, *Berlin* 5 A5
Friherrs, *Helsinki* 12 B1
Frontón, I., *Lima* 16 B1
Frunze, *Moscow* 19 B3
Fuchū, *Tokyo* 29 A1
Fuencarral, *Madrid* 17 B1
Fuenlabrada, *Madrid* 17 C1
Fujidera, *Osaka* 22 B4
Fukagawa, *Tokyo* 29 B3
Fukiage Imperial Garden, *Tokyo* 29 a4
Fukiai, *Osaka* 22 A2
Fukushima, *Osaka* 22 A3
Fulham, *London* 15 B2
Funabori, *Tokyo* 29 A4
Funasaka, *Osaka* 22 A2
Fundão, I. do, *Rio de Janeiro* 24 B1
Fünfhaus, *Vienna* 31 A2
Furesø, *Copenhagen* 10 A2
Furth, *Munich* 20 B2
Futago-tamagawaen, *Tokyo* 29 B2
Fuxing Dao, *Shanghai* 27 B2
Fuxing Park, *Shanghai* 27 B1
Fuxinglu, *Beijing* 4 B1

G

Gage Park, *Chicago* 9 C2
Gagny, *Paris* 23 A4
Galata, *Istanbul* 12 B1
Galátsion, *Athens* 2 A2
Galeão, Aéroporto Int. de, *Rio de Janeiro* 24 A1
Galyanovo, *Moscow* 19 B4
Gambir, *Jakarta* 13 A1
Gamboa, *Rio de Janeiro* 24 B1
Gambolóita, *Milan* 18 B2
Gamla Stan , *Stockholm* 28 c2
Gamlebyen, *Oslo* 22 A3
Gangtou, *Canton* 8 A1
Gangwei, *Canton* 8 B2
Ganjiakou, *Beijing* 4 B1
Ganshoren, *Brussels* 6 A1
Gants Hill, *London* 15 A4
Gaoqiao, *Shanghai* 27 A2
Garbagnate Milanese, *Milan* 18 A1
Garbatella, *Rome* 25 B2
Garches, *Paris* 23 A2
Garching, *Munich* 20 A3
Garden City, *Cairo* 7 A2
Garden Reach, *Calcutta* 8 B1
Garder, *Oslo* 22 B2
Garfield, *New York* 21 A1
Garfield Park, *Chicago* 9 B2
Gargareta, *Athens* 2 B2
Garvanza, *Los Angeles* 16 B3
Gåshaga, *Stockholm* 28 A3
Gateway National Recreation Area, *New York* 21 C2
Gateway of India, *Mumbai* 20 B2
Gatow, *Berlin* 5 B1
Gávea, *Rio de Janeiro* 24 B1
Gávea, Pedra da, *Rio de Janeiro* 24 B1
Gazdagrét, *Budapest* 7 B1
Gebel el Ahmar, *Cairo* 7 A2
Gebel el Muqattam, *Cairo* 7 A2
Gebel el Tura, *Cairo* 7 B2
Geiselgasteig, *Munich* 20 B2
General San Martin, *Buenos Aires* 7 B1
Gennevilliers, *Paris* 23 A2
Gentilly, *Paris* 23 B3
Gentofte, *Copenhagen* 10 A3
Genval, *Brussels* 6 B2
George I., *Hong Kong* 12 B1
Georges I., *Boston* 6 B4
Georges River Bridge, *Sydney* 28 C1
Georgetown, *Washington* 32 B3
Georgia Dome, *Atlanta* 3 B2
Gerasdorf bei Wien, *Vienna* 31 A2
Gerberau, *Munich* 20 A1
Gerli, *Buenos Aires* 7 C2
Germiston, *Johannesburg* 13 B2
Gern, *Munich* 20 B2
Gesîrat el Rauda, *Cairo* 7 A2
Getafe, *Madrid* 17 C1
Geva Binyamin, *Jerusalem* 13 A2
Geylang Serai, *Singapore* 27 B3
Gezîrat el Dhahab, *Cairo* 7 B2
Gharapuri, *Mumbai* 20 B2
Ghatkopar, *Mumbai* 20 A2
Ghazipur, *Delhi* 10 B2
Ghizri, *Karachi* 14 B2
Ghizri Cr. →, *Karachi* 14 B2
Ghonda, *Delhi* 10 A2
Ghusuri, *Calcutta* 8 B2
Gianicolense, *Rome* 25 B1
Gianicolo, *Rome* 25 c1
Gibraltar Pt., *Toronto* 30 B2
Gidea Park, *London* 15 A5
Giesing, *Munich* 20 B2
Gilmerton, *Edinburgh* 11 B3
Gilo, *Jerusalem* 13 B2
Gimmersta, *Stockholm* 28 B3
Ginza, *Tokyo* 29 b5
Girgaum, *Mumbai* 20 b2
Giv'at Ye'arim, *Jerusalem* 13 B1
Giv'at Ze'ev, *Jerusalem* 13 A2
Giza Pyramids = Pyramids, *Cairo* 7 B1
Gjersjøen, *Oslo* 22 B3
Gladesville, *Sydney* 28 B1
Gladsakse, *Copenhagen* 10 A2
Glasnevin, *Dublin* 11 A2
Glassmanor, *Washington* 32 C3
Glasthule, *Dublin* 11 B3
Glen Iris, *Melbourne* 17 B2
Glen Mar Park, *Washington* 32 B3
Glen Rock, *New York* 21 A1
Glenarden, *Washington* 32 B4
Glenasmole Reservoirs, *Dublin* 11 B1
Glencorse Res., *Edinburgh* 11 B2
Glencullen, *Dublin* 11 B2
Glendale, *Los Angeles* 16 B3
Glendoo Mt., *Dublin* 11 B2
Glenhuntly, *Melbourne* 17 B2
Glenside, *Wellington* 32 B1
Glenview, *Chicago* 9 A2
Glenview Countryside, *Chicago* 9 A2
Glenvista, *Johannesburg* 13 B2
Glifádha, *Athens* 2 B2
Glömsta, *Stockholm* 28 B1
Glostrup, *Copenhagen* 10 B2
Gogar, *Edinburgh* 11 B2
Göktürk, *Istanbul* 12 A1
Golabari, *Calcutta* 8 B2
Golabki, *Warsaw* 31 B1
Gold Coast, *Chicago* 9 a2
Golden Gate, *San Francisco* 25 B2
Golden Gate Bridge, *San Francisco* 25 B2
Golden Gate Park, *San Francisco* 25 B2
Golden Horn, *Istanbul* 12 B1
Golders Green, *London* 15 A2
Gollans Stream →, *Wellington* 32 B2
Golyevo, *Moscow* 19 B1
Goodman Hill, *Boston* 6 A1
Goodmayes, *London* 15 A4
Goodwood, *Cape Town* 8 A2
Gopalpur, *Calcutta* 8 B2
Górce, *Warsaw* 31 B1
Gore Hill, *Sydney* 28 A2
Gorelyy →, *St. Petersburg* 26 A3
Gorenki, *Moscow* 19 B5
Gorgie, *Edinburgh* 11 B2
Gorky Park, *Moscow* 19 B3
Gosen, *Berlin* 5 B5
Gosener kanal, *Berlin* 5 B5
Gospel Oak, *London* 15 A3
Gotanda, *Tokyo* 29 B3
Goth Goli Mar, *Karachi* 14 A2
Goth Sher Shah, *Karachi* 14 A1
Gournay-sur-Marne, *Paris* 23 A4
Governador, I. do, *Rio de Janeiro* 24 A1
Governor's I., *New York* 21 B1
Graben, *Vienna* 31 b2
Grabów, *Warsaw* 31 C1
Graça, *Lisbon* 14 b3
Grace, Mt., *Wellington* 32 B2
Grace Cathedral, *San Francisco* 25 b1
Gracefield, *Wellington* 32 B2
Gracia, *Barcelona* 4 A2
Gräfelfing, *Munich* 20 B1
Gragoatá, *Rio de Janeiro* 24 B2
Grand Cemtral Station, *New York* 21 c2
Grand Union Canal, *London* 15 A2
Grande Place, *Brussels* 6 b2
Grant Park, *Atlanta* 3 B2
Grant Park, *Chicago* 9 c2
Granton, *Edinburgh* 11 B2
Grape I., *Boston* 6 B4
Grassy Park, *Cape Town* 8 B2
Gratosóglio, *Milan* 18 B2
Gratzwalde, *Berlin* 5 B5
Gravesend, *New York* 21 C2
Grazhdanka, *St. Petersburg* 26 B2
Great Falls, *Washington* 32 B2
Great Falls Park, *Washington* 32 B2
Great Hall of the People, *Beijing* 4 b2
Great Meadows National Wildlife Refuge, *Boston* 6 A1
Greco, *Milan* 18 A2
Green I., *Hong Kong* 12 B1
Green Point, *Cape Town* 8 A1
Greenbelt, *Washington* 32 A4
Greenbelt Park, *Washington* 32 B4
Greenfield Park, *Montreal* 19 B3
Greenford, *London* 15 A1
Greenhill, *London* 15 A2
Greenhills, *Dublin* 11 B1
Greenmarket Square, *Cape Town* 8 c2
Greenpoint, *New York* 21 B2
Greenwich, *London* 15 B3
Greenwich Observatory, *London* 15 B3
Greenwich Village, *New York* 21 B2
Greenwood, *Boston* 6 A3
Grefsen, *Oslo* 22 A3
Gresham Park, *Atlanta* 3 B2
Greve Strand, *Copenhagen* 10 B1
Greyfriars Kirk, *Edinburgh* 11 c2
Griebnitzsee, *Berlin* 5 B1
Griffen Park, *Los Angeles* 16 B3
Grimbergen, *Brussels* 6 A2
Grinzing, *Vienna* 31 A2
Gröbenried, *Munich* 20 A1
Grochów, *Warsaw* 31 B2
Grodzisk, *Warsaw* 31 B2
Groenendaal, *Brussels* 6 B2
Grogol Petamburin, *Jakarta* 13 A1
Gronsdorf, *Munich* 20 B3
Grorud, *Oslo* 22 A4
Gross Glienicke, *Berlin* 5 B1
Gross-Hadern, *Munich* 20 B1
Gross-Lappen, *Munich* 20 A2
Grosse Krampe, *Berlin* 5 B5
Grosse Müggelsee, *Berlin* 5 B4
Grossenzersdorf, *Vienna* 31 A3
Grossenzersdorfer Arm →, *Vienna* 31 A3
Grosser Biberhaufen, *Vienna* 31 A2
Grosser Wannsee, *Berlin* 5 B2
Grossfeld-Siedlung, *Vienna* 31 A2
Grosshesselohe, *Munich* 20 B2
Grossjedlersdorf, *Vienna* 31 A2
Grossziethen, *Berlin* 5 B3
Grove Hall, *Boston* 6 B3
Grove Park, *Atlanta* 3 B2
Grove Park, *London* 15 B4
Grove Park, *London* 15 B2
Groveton, *Washington* 32 C3
Grünau, *Berlin* 5 B4
Grunewald, *Berlin* 5 B2
Grünwald, *Munich* 20 B2
Grünwalder Forst, *Munich* 20 B2
Grymes Hill, *New York* 21 C1
Guadalupe, *Manila* 17 B2
Guadalupe, Basilica de, *Mexico City* 18 B2
Guanabara, B. de, *Rio de Janeiro* 24 B1
Guanabara, Jardim, *Rio de Janeiro* 24 A1
Guanabara, Palácio da, *Rio de Janeiro* 24 B1
Guang'anmen, *Beijing* 4 B1
Guangqumen, *Beijing* 4 B2
Guangzhou, *Canton* 8 B2
Guanshuo, *Canton* 8 B3
Gudö, *Stockholm* 28 B3
Güell, Parque de, *Barcelona* 4 A2
Guerrero, *Mexico City* 18 a1
Guggenheim Museum, *New York* 21 b3
Guinardó, *Barcelona* 4 A2
Gulbai, *Karachi* 14 A1
Güngören, *Istanbul* 12 B1
Gunnersbury, *London* 15 B2
Gustavo A. Madero, *Mexico City* 18 B2
Guttenberg, *New York* 21 B1
Gutuyevskiy, Ostrov, *St. Petersburg* 26 B1
Guyancourt, *Paris* 23 B1
Gyál, *Budapest* 7 B3
Gyáli-patak →, *Budapest* 7 B2

H

Haaga, *Helsinki* 12 B2
Haar, *Munich* 20 B3
Hackbridge, *London* 15 B3
Hackensack, *New York* 21 A1
Hackensack →, *New York* 21 B1
Hackney, *London* 15 A3
Hackney Wick, *London* 15 A3
Haga, *Stockholm* 28 A2
Hagenbrunn, *Vienna* 31 A2
Hägersten, *Stockholm* 28 B1
Häggvik, *Stockholm* 28 A1
Hai He →, *Tianjin* 30 B2
Haidan, *Beijing* 4 B1
Haidarpur, *Delhi* 10 A1
Haidhausen, *Munich* 20 B2
Haight-Ashbury, *San Francisco* 25 B2
Hainault, *London* 15 A4
Haizhu Guangchang, *Canton* 8 B2
Hakunila, *Helsinki* 12 B3
Halásztelek, *Budapest* 7 B1
Haliç = Golden Horn, *Istanbul* 12 B1
Halim Perdanakusuma International Airport, *Jakarta* 13 B2
Halle, *Brussels* 6 B1
Haltiala, *Helsinki* 12 B2
Haltiavuori, *Helsinki* 12 B2
Ham, *London* 15 B2
Hämeenkylä, *Helsinki* 12 B1
Hammarby, *Stockholm* 28 B2
Hamme, *Brussels* 6 A1
Hammersmith, *London* 15 B2
Hampstead, *London* 15 A2
Hampstead, *Montreal* 19 B2
Hampstead Garden Suburb, *London* 15 A2
Hampstead Heath, *London* 15 A2
Hampton, *London* 15 B1
Hampton Court Palace, *London* 15 B1
Hampton Wick, *London* 15 B2
Hamrā', *Baghdad* 3 B1
Hanala, *Helsinki* 12 A3
Haneda, *Tokyo* 29 B3
Hang Hau, *Hong Kong* 12 B2
Hanging Gardens, *Mumbai* 20 b1
Hanjiashu, *Tianjin* 30 A1
Hanlon, *Toronto* 30 B1
Hanwell, *London* 15 A1
Hanworth, *London* 15 B1
Haora, *Calcutta* 8 B1
Hapeville, *Atlanta* 3 C2
Happy Valley, *Hong Kong* 12 B2
Har Adar, *Jerusalem* 13 B1
Haren, *Brussels* 6 A2
Hareskovby, *Copenhagen* 10 A2
Haringey, *London* 15 A3
Harjusuo, *Helsinki* 12 B3
Harlaching, *Munich* 20 B2
Harlaw Res., *Edinburgh* 11 B2
Harlem, *New York* 21 B2
Harlesden, *London* 15 A2
Harlington, *London* 15 B1
Harmaja, *Helsinki* 12 C2
Harmashatar hegy, *Budapest* 7 A2
Harolds Cross, *Dublin* 11 B2
Háros, *Budapest* 7 B2
Harperrig Reservoir, *Edinburgh* 11 B1
Harrow, *London* 15 A1
Harrow on the Hill, *London* 15 A1
Harrow School, *London* 15 A1
Harrow Weald, *London* 15 A1
Hartsfield-Atlanta International Airport, *Atlanta* 3 C2
Harumi, *Tokyo* 29 c5
Harvard Univ., *Boston* 6 A3
Harwood Heights, *Chicago* 9 B2
Hasanābād, *Tehran* 30 A1
Hasbrouck Heights, *New York* 21 A1
Haselhorst, *Berlin* 5 A2
Hasköy, *Istanbul* 12 B1
Hasle, *Oslo* 22 B2
Haslum, *Oslo* 22 A2
Hästhagen, *Stockholm* 28 B2
Hataitai, *Wellington* 32 B1
Hatch End, *London* 15 A1
Hatiara, *Calcutta* 8 B2
Hauketo, *Oslo* 22 A3
Havel →, *Berlin* 5 A2
Havelkanal, *Berlin* 5 A2
Havering, *London* 15 A5
Havering-atte-Bower, *London* 15 A5
Hawŏlgok, *Seoul* 26 B2
Haworth, *New York* 21 A2
Hayes, *London* 15 B4
Hayes, *London* 15 A1
Hayes End, *London* 15 A1
Hayford, *Chicago* 9 C2
Haywards, *Wellington* 32 A2
Heard Pond, *Boston* 6 A1
Heathfield, *Cape Town* 8 B1
Heathrow Airport, *London* 15 B1
Hebe Haven, *Hong Kong* 12 A2
Hebei, *Tianjin* 30 B2
Hedong, *Canton* 8 B2
Hedong, *Tianjin* 30 B2
Heidelberg Heights, *Melbourne* 17 A2
Heidelberg West, *Melbourne* 17 A2
Heidemühle, *Berlin* 5 B5
Heideveld, *Cape Town* 8 A2
Heiligensee, *Berlin* 5 A2
Heiligenstadt, *Vienna* 31 A2
Heinersdorf, *Berlin* 5 A3
Heldenplatz, *Vienna* 31 b1
Hélène Champlain, Parc, *Montreal* 19 A2
Helenelund, *Stockholm* 28 A1
Heliopolis = Masr el Gedida, *Cairo* 7 A2
Hellersdorf, *Berlin* 5 A4
Hellerup, *Copenhagen* 10 A3
Helmahof, *Vienna* 31 A3
Helsingfors = Helsinki, *Helsinki* 12 B2
Helsinki, *Helsinki* 12 B2
Helsinki Airport, *Helsinki* 12 B2
Hendon, *London* 15 A2
Hengsha, *Canton* 8 B2
Hennigsdorf, *Berlin* 5 A2
Henryków, *Warsaw* 31 B1
Henson Cr. →, *Washington* 32 C4
Henttaa, *Helsinki* 12 B1
Heping, *Tianjin* 30 B2
Heping Park, *Shanghai* 27 B2
Hepingli, *Beijing* 4 B2
Herlev, *Copenhagen* 10 A2
Herman Eckstein Park, *Johannesburg* 13 A2
Hermannskogel, *Vienna* 31 A1
Hermiston, *Edinburgh* 11 B2
Hermitage and Winter Palace, *St. Petersburg* 26 B1
Hermsdorf, *Berlin* 5 A2
Hernals, *Vienna* 31 A2
Herne Hill, *London* 15 B3
Héroes de Churubusco, *Mexico City* 18 B2
Herons, Î. aux, *Montreal* 19 B2
Herstedøster, *Copenhagen* 10 A2
Herttoniemi, *Helsinki* 12 B3
Ḥeşārak, *Tehran* 30 A1
Heston, *London* 15 B1
Hetzendorf, *Vienna* 31 B1
Hexi, *Tianjin* 30 B2
Hextable, *London* 15 B5
Hialeah, *Miami* 18 A1
Hickory Hills, *Chicago* 9 C2
Hiekkaharju, *Helsinki* 12 B3
Hietaniemi, *Helsinki* 12 B2
Hietzing, *Vienna* 31 A1
Higashi, *Osaka* 22 A4
Higashimurayama, *Tokyo* 29 A1
Higashinada, *Osaka* 22 A2
Higashinari, *Osaka* 22 A4
Higashiōsaka, *Osaka* 22 B4
Higashisumiyoshi, *Osaka* 22 B4
Higashiyodogawa, *Osaka* 22 A3
High Park, *Toronto* 30 B2
Highbury, *London* 15 A3
Highgate, *London* 15 A3
Highland Cr. →, *Toronto* 30 A3
Highland Creek, *Toronto* 30 A3
Highland Park, *Los Angeles* 16 B3
Highlands North, *Johannesburg* 13 A2
Hillcrest Heights, *Washington* 32 C4
Hillend, *Edinburgh* 11 A1
Hillingdon, *London* 15 A1
Hillwood, *Washington* 32 B3
Hilmîya, *Cairo* 7 A2
Hin Keng, *Hong Kong* 12 A2
Hingham, *Boston* 6 B4
Hingham B., *Boston* 6 B4
Hingham Harbor, *Boston* 6 B4
Hirakata, *Osaka* 22 A4
Hirota, *Osaka* 22 A3
Hirschstetten, *Vienna* 31 A2
Histórico Nacional, Museu, *Rio de Janeiro* 24 b3
Hither Green, *London* 15 B3
Hiyoshi, *Tokyo* 29 B2
Hizma, *Jerusalem* 13 B2
Hjortekær, *Copenhagen* 10 A3
Hjortespring, *Copenhagen* 10 A2
Hlubočepy, *Prague* 24 B2
Ho Chung, *Hong Kong* 12 A2
Ho Man Tin, *Hong Kong* 12 B2
Hoboken, *New York* 21 B1
Hobsons B., *Melbourne* 17 B1
Hochbrück, *Munich* 20 A2
Hochelaga, *Montreal* 19 A2
Hodgkins, *Chicago* 9 C1
Hoegi, *Seoul* 26 B2
Hoeilaart, *Brussels* 6 B2
Hofberg, *Vienna* 31 A2
Hoffman I., *New York* 21 C1
Hofgarten, *Munich* 20 a3
Högsdtadomstolen, *Stockholm* 28 c2
Hohenbrunn, *Munich* 20 B3
Hohenschönhausen, *Berlin* 5 A4
Holborn, *London* 15 a4
Holešovice, *Prague* 24 B2
Holland Village, *Singapore* 27 B2
Höllriegelskreuth, *Munich* 20 B1
Hollywood, *Los Angeles* 16 B3
Holmenkollen, *Oslo* 22 A3
Holmes Run Acres, *Washington* 32 B2
Holmgård, *Stockholm* 28 B1
Holysloot, *Amsterdam* 2 A3
Homerton, *London* 15 A3
Hometown, *Chicago* 9 C2
Hōnanchō, *Tokyo* 29 A2
Honcho, *Tokyo* 29 A3
Honden, *Tokyo* 29 A4
Hondo, Rio →, *Los Angeles* 16 B4
Hong Kong, *Hong Kong* 12 B1
Hong Kong, Univ. of, *Hong Kong* 12 B1
Hong Kong I., *Hong Kong* 12 B2
Hong Kong Park, *Hong Kong* 12 c1
Hongkou, *Shanghai* 27 B1
Hongkou Park, *Shanghai* 27 B1
Hongmiao, *Beijing* 4 B2
Hongqiao, *Shanghai* 27 B1
Hongqiao, *Tianjin* 30 B1
Hongqiao Airport, *Shanghai* 27 B1
Hongŭn, *Seoul* 26 B1
Honjyo, *Tokyo* 29 A3
Honoré Mercier, Pont, *Montreal* 19 B1
Hönow, *Berlin* 5 A4
Hooghly = Hugli →, *Calcutta* 8 A2
Hook, *London* 15 B2
Horikiri, *Tokyo* 29 A4
Horn Pond, *Boston* 6 A2
Hornchurch, *London* 15 A5
Horni, *Prague* 24 B3
Horni Počernice, *Prague* 24 B3
Hornsey, *London* 15 A3
Horoměřice, *Prague* 24 B1
Hortaleza, *Madrid* 17 B2
Hosoyama, *Tokyo* 29 B2
Hostafranchs, *Barcelona* 4 A1
Hostivař, *Prague* 24 B3
Hôtel des Invalides, *Paris* 23 c2
Houbětin, *Prague* 24 B3
Houghs Neck, *Boston* 6 B4
Houghton, *Johannesburg* 13 B2
Houilles, *Paris* 23 A2
Hounslow, *London* 15 B1
Houses of Parliament, *London* 15 c3
Hout Bay, *Cape Town* 8 B1
Hove Å →, *Copenhagen* 10 A1
Hovedøya, *Oslo* 22 A3
Høvik, *Oslo* 22 A2
Hovorčovice, *Prague* 24 A3
Howard Beach, *New York* 21 C2
Howth, *Dublin* 11 A3
Howth Head, *Dublin* 11 A3
Hoxton, *London* 15 a5
Hōya, *Tokyo* 29 A2
Hradčany, *Prague* 24 B2
Huanghuagang Mausoleum of the 72 Martyrs, *Canton* 8 B2
Huangpu, *Shanghai* 27 B2
Huangpu Jiang →, *Shanghai* 27 B1
Huangpu Park, *Shanghai* 27 B1
Huangtugang, *Beijing* 4 C1
Huascar, *Lima* 16 A2
Huay Khwang, *Bangkok* 3 B2
Huddinge, *Stockholm* 28 B2
Hudson →, *New York* 21 A2
Huechuraba, *Santiago* 26 B1
Huertas de San Beltran, *Barcelona* 4 A1
Hugli →, *Calcutta* 8 A2
Huidui, *Tianjin* 30 B2
Huizingen, *Brussels* 6 B1
Hull, *Boston* 6 B4
Humber →, *Toronto* 30 A1
Humber B., *Toronto* 30 B2
Humber Bay, *Toronto* 30 B2
Humber Summit, *Toronto* 30 A1
Humber Valley Village, *Toronto* 30 A1
Humberlea, *Toronto* 30 A1
Humboldt Park, *Chicago* 9 B2
Humera, *Madrid* 17 B1
Hunaydī, *Baghdad* 3 B2
Hundige, *Copenhagen* 10 B1
Hundige Strand, *Copenhagen* 10 B2
Hung Hom, *Hong Kong* 12 B2
Hunters Hill, *Sydney* 28 B1
Hunters Pt., *San Francisco* 25 B2
Hunters Valley, *Washington* 32 B2
Huntington, *Washington* 32 C3
Huntington Park, *Los Angeles* 16 C3
Hurīya, *Baghdad* 3 A1
Hurstville, *Sydney* 28 B1
Husby, *Stockholm* 28 A1
Husum, *Copenhagen* 10 A2
Hutt R. →, *Wellington* 32 B2
Hütteldorf, *Vienna* 31 A1
Hüvösvölgy, *Budapest* 7 A2
Hvalstad, *Oslo* 22 A1
Hvalstrand, *Oslo* 22 A2
Hvidovre, *Copenhagen* 10 B2
Hwagok, *Seoul* 26 B1
Hyattsville, *Washington* 32 B4
Hyde Park, *Boston* 6 B3
Hyde Park, *Chicago* 9 C3
Hyde Park, *Johannesburg* 13 A2
Hyde Park, *London* 15 A2
Hyde Park, *Sydney* 28 B2

I

Ibese, *Lagos* 14 A2
Ibirapuera, *São Paulo* 26 B1
Ibirapuera, Parque, *São Paulo* 26 B2
Icarai, *Rio de Janeiro* 24 B2
Içerenköy, *Istanbul* 12 C2
Ichgao, *Tokyo* 29 B2
Ichigaya, *Tokyo* 29 a3
Ichikawa, *Tokyo* 29 A4
Ickenham, *London* 15 A1
Iddo, *Lagos* 14 B2
Idi-Oro, *Lagos* 14 A2
Iganmu, *Lagos* 14 B2
Igbobi, *Lagos* 14 A2
Igbologun, *Lagos* 14 B1
Igny, *Paris* 23 B2
IJ, Het →, *Amsterdam* 2 A2
IJ-meer, *Amsterdam* 2 A3
Ijesa-Tedo, *Lagos* 14 B1
Ijora, *Lagos* 14 B2
IJtunnel, *Amsterdam* 2 a3
Ikebe, *Tokyo* 29 B2
Ikebukuro, *Tokyo* 29 A3
Ikegami, *Tokyo* 29 B3
Ikeja, *Lagos* 14 A2
Ikeuchi, *Osaka* 22 B4
Ikoyi, *Lagos* 14 B2
Ikuata, *Lagos* 14 B2
Ikuno, *Osaka* 22 A4
Ikuta, *Osaka* 22 A2
Ikuta, *Tokyo* 29 B2
Ila, *Oslo* 22 A2
Ilford, *London* 15 A4
Ilioúpolis, *Athens* 2 B2
Ilpendam, *Amsterdam* 2 A2
Ilsós →, *Athens* 2 B2
Imagem e do Som, Museu da, *Rio de Janeiro* 24 b3
Imbâbah, *Cairo* 7 A2
Imielin, *Warsaw* 31 C2
Imirim, *São Paulo* 26 A2
Imittós, *Athens* 2 B2
Imittoś, Óros, *Athens* 2 B2
Imperial Palace Museum, *Beijing* 4 b2
Inagi, *Tokyo* 29 B2
Inchcolm, *Edinburgh* 11 A2
Inchicore, *Dublin* 11 A1
Inchkeith, *Edinburgh* 11 A3
Inchmickery, *Edinburgh* 11 A2
Incirano, *Milan* 18 A1
Independencia, *Lima* 16 A2
Independencia, *Santiago* 26 B2
India Gate, *Delhi* 1 c2
Indian Creek Village, *Miami* 18 A2
Indian Head Park, *Chicago* 9 C1
Indianópolis, *São Paulo* 26 B2
Indios Verdes, *Mexico City* 18 B2
Indira Ghandi International Airport, *Delhi* 10 B1
Industria, *Johannesburg* 13 B1
Ingierstrand, *Oslo* 22 B3
Inglewood, *Los Angeles* 16 C3
Ingliston, *Edinburgh* 11 B1
Inhaúme, *Rio de Janeiro* 24 B1
Inner Port Shelter, *Hong Kong* 12 A2
Interlagos, *São Paulo* 26 C1
Intramuros, *Manila* 17 B1
Invalides, *Paris* 23 A2
Inverkeithing, *Edinburgh* 11 A1
Inzersdorf, *Vienna* 31 B2
Ipanema, *Rio de Janeiro* 24 B1
Ipiranga, *São Paulo* 26 B2
Ipiranga →, *São Paulo* 26 B2
Iponri, *Lagos* 14 B2
Ireland's Eye, *Dublin* 11 A3
Irving Park, *Chicago* 9 B2
Isabel, *Rio de Janeiro* 24 B1
Isagatedo, *Lagos* 14 A1
Isar →, *Munich* 20 A3
Ishbīlīya, *Baghdad* 3 A2
Ishikiri, *Osaka* 22 A4
Ishøj Strand, *Copenhagen* 10 B2
Island Bay, *Wellington* 32 B1
Island Park, *Toronto* 30 B2
Isle of Dogs, *London* 15 B3
Islev, *Copenhagen* 10 A2
Isleworth, *London* 15 B2
Islington, *London* 15 A3
Islington, *Toronto* 30 B1
Ismaning, *Munich* 20 A3
Ismayloskiy Park, *Moscow* 19 B4
Isolo, *Lagos* 14 A1
Issy-les-Moulineaux, *Paris* 23 B2
Istanbul, *Istanbul* 12 C1
Istanbul Boğazi, *Istanbul* 12 B2
Istinye, *Istanbul* 12 B2
Itä Hakkila, *Helsinki* 12 B3
Itaewŏn, *Seoul* 26 B1
Itahanga, *Rio de Janeiro* 24 B1
Itami, *Osaka* 22 A3
Ivanhoe, *Melbourne* 17 A2
Ivry-sur-Seine, *Paris* 23 B3
Iwazono, *Osaka* 22 A2
Ixelles, *Brussels* 6 B2
Izmaylovo, *Moscow* 19 B4
Iztacalco, *Mexico City* 18 B2
Iztapalapa, *Mexico City* 18 B2

J

Jaba, *Jerusalem* 13 A2
Jababpur, *Calcutta* 8 C2
Jacaré, *Rio de Janeiro* 24 B1
Jackson Heights, *New York* 21 B2
Jackson Park, *Chicago* 9 C3
Jacques Cartier, *Montreal* 19 A3
Jacques Cartier, Pont, *Montreal* 19 A2
Jade Buddha Temple, *Shanghai* 27 B1
Jægersborg, *Copenhagen* 10 A3
Jægersborg Dyrehave, *Copenhagen* 10 A3
Jagadishpur, *Calcutta* 8 B1
Jagatpur, *Delhi* 10 A2
Jaguaré, Rib. do →, *São Paulo* 26 B1
Jahangirpur, *Delhi* 10 A2
Jakarta, *Jakarta* 13 A2
Jakarta, Teluk, *Jakarta* 13 A1
Jalan Kayu, *Singapore* 27 A3
Jamaica B., *New York* 21 C3
Jamaica Plain, *Boston* 6 B3
Jamakpuri, *Delhi* 10 B1
Jamshīdīyeh, *Tehran* 30 A2
Janki, *Warsaw* 31 C1
Jannali, *Sydney* 28 C1
Japan Center, *San Francisco* 25 c1
Jaraguá, *São Paulo* 26 A1
Jaraguá, Pico de, *São Paulo* 26 A1
Jardim Paulista, *São Paulo* 26 B1
Jardin Botanique, *Brussels* 6 a3
Järvatältet, *Stockholm* 28 A1
Jaskhar, *Mumbai* 20 B2
Jatinegara, *Jakarta* 13 B2
Javādīyeh, *Tehran* 30 B2
Jaworowa, *Warsaw* 31 C1
Jedlesee, *Vienna* 31 A2
Jefferson Memorial, *Washington* 32 c1
Jefferson Park, *Chicago* 9 B2
Jelonki, *Warsaw* 31 B1
Jerónimos, Mosteiro dos, *Lisbon* 14 A1
Jersey City, *New York* 21 B1
Jerusalem, *Jerusalem* 13 B2
Jésus, Î., *Montreal* 19 A1
Jesús Maria, *Lima* 16 B2
Jette, *Brussels* 6 A1
Jewish Quarter, *Jerusalem* 13 b3
Jey, *Tehran* 30 B2
Jianguomen, *Beijing* 4 B2
Jiangwan, *Shanghai* 27 B1
Jianshan Park, *Tianjin* 30 B2
Jihād, *Baghdad* 3 B1
Jim Thompson's House, *Bangkok* 3 b3
Jimbōchō, *Tokyo* 29 a4
Jingan, *Shanghai* 27 B1
Jingu Outer Garden, *Tokyo* 29 b2
Jinočany, *Prague* 24 B1
Jinonice, *Prague* 24 B2
Jiyūgaoka, *Tokyo* 29 B3
Jizā'ir, *Baghdad* 3 B2
Jizīra, *Baghdad* 3 B2
Johannesburg, *Johannesburg* 13 B2
Johanneskirchen, *Munich* 20 A2
Johannesstift, *Berlin* 5 A2
Johannisthal, *Berlin* 5 B4
John Hancock Center, *Chicago* 9 a2
John McLaren Park, *San Francisco* 25 B2
Johnsonville, *Wellington* 32 B1
Joinville-le-Pont, *Paris* 23 B3
Joli-Bois, *Brussels* 6 B2
Jollas, *Helsinki* 12 B3
Jonstrup, *Copenhagen* 10 A2
Joppa, *Edinburgh* 11 B3
Jorge Chavez, Aeropuerto Int., *Lima* 16 B2
Jorge Newbury, Aeroparque, *Buenos Aires* 7 B2
Jósefa Piłsudskiego Park, *Warsaw* 31 B1
Jōtō, *Osaka* 22 A4
Jouy-en-Josas, *Paris* 23 B2
Juan Anchorena, *Buenos Aires* 7 A2
Juan González Romero, *Mexico City* 18 A2
Judeira, *Jerusalem* 13 A2
Juhu, *Mumbai* 20 A2
Jūjā, *Tokyo* 29 A3
Jukskeirivier →, *Johannesburg* 13 A2
Julianów, *Warsaw* 31 B2
Jungfernheide, Volkspark, *Berlin* 5 A2
Jungfernsee, *Berlin* 5 B1
Juniper Green, *Edinburgh* 11 B2
Junk B., *Hong Kong* 12 B2
Jurong, *Singapore* 27 B2
Jurong, Selat, *Singapore* 27 B2
Jurong Industrial Estate, *Singapore* 27 B1
Jurujuba, Enseada de, *Rio de Janeiro* 24 B2
Jūsō, *Osaka* 22 A3
Justice, *Chicago* 9 C2
Justicia, *Madrid* 17 a3
Jwalahari, *Delhi* 10 B1

K

Kabaty, *Warsaw* 31 C2
Kadıköy, *Istanbul* 12 C2
Kadoma, *Osaka* 22 A4
Kaebong, *Seoul* 26 C1
Kafr 'Aqab, *Jerusalem* 13 A2
Kâğıthane, *Istanbul* 12 B1
Kâğıthane →, *Istanbul* 12 B1
Kagran, *Vienna* 31 A2
Kahnawake, *Montreal* 19 B1
Kaimes, *Edinburgh* 11 B2
Kaisariani, *Athens* 2 B2
Kaiser Wilhelm Kirche, *Berlin* 5 b2
Kaiserebersdorf, *Vienna* 31 B2
Kaivoksela, *Helsinki* 12 B2
Kalamákion, *Athens* 2 B2
Kalbadevi, *Mumbai* 20 b2
Kalhyŏn, *Seoul* 26 B1
Kalipur, *Calcutta* 8 A1
Kalkaji, *Delhi* 10 B2
Kallithéa, *Athens* 2 B2
Kalveboderne, *Copenhagen* 10 B3
Kamarhati, *Calcutta* 8 A2
Kamata, *Tokyo* 29 B3
Kameari, *Tokyo* 29 A4
Kameido, *Tokyo* 29 A4
Kami-Itabashi, *Tokyo* 29 A3
Kamikitazawa, *Tokyo* 29 B2
Kamitsuruma, *Tokyo* 29 B1
Kamoshida, *Tokyo* 29 B2
Kampong Landang, *Singapore* 27 A3
Kampong Tanjong Penjuru, *Singapore* 27 B2
Kampung Bali, *Jakarta* 13 B1
Kanamori, *Tokyo* 29 B1
Kanda, *Tokyo* 29 a5
Kandilli, *Istanbul* 12 B2
Kangdong, *Seoul* 26 B2
Kangnam, *Seoul* 26 B1
Kangsŏ, *Seoul* 26 B1
Kankurgachi, *Calcutta* 8 B2
Kanlıca, *Istanbul* 12 B2
Kanonerskiy, Ostrov, *St. Petersburg* 26 B1
Kanzaki →, *Osaka* 22 A3
Kapellerfeld, *Vienna* 31 A2

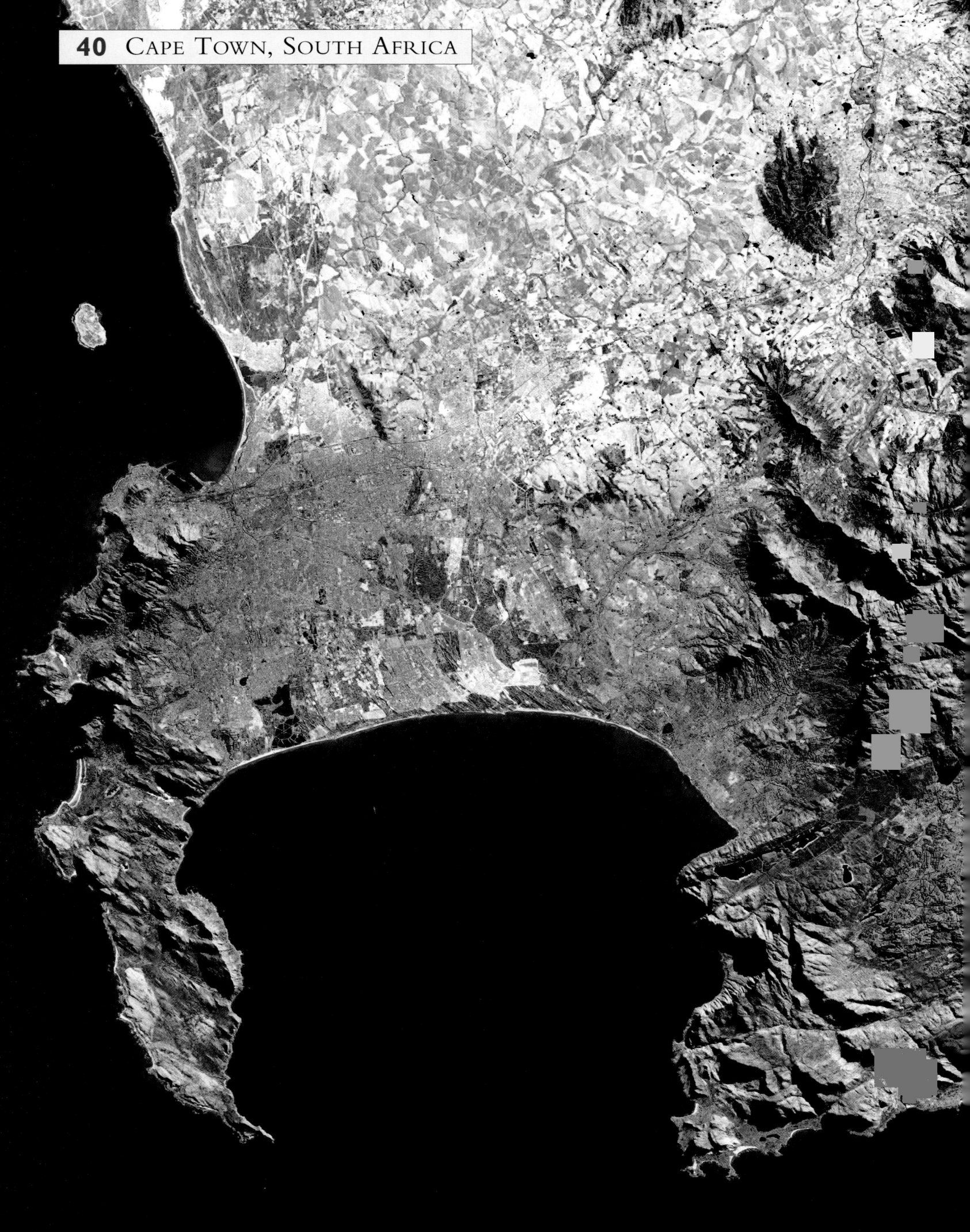

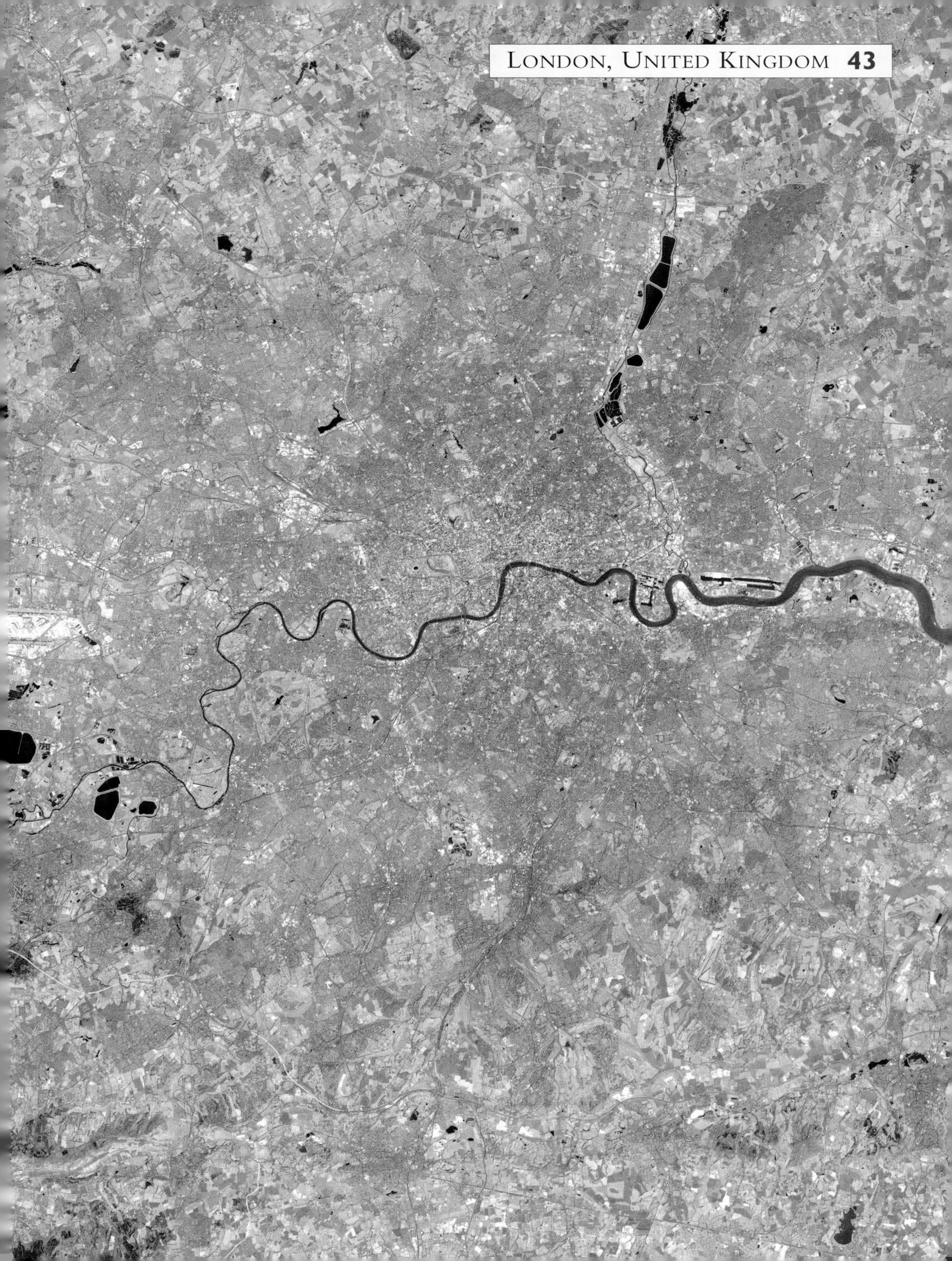

WORLD MAPS

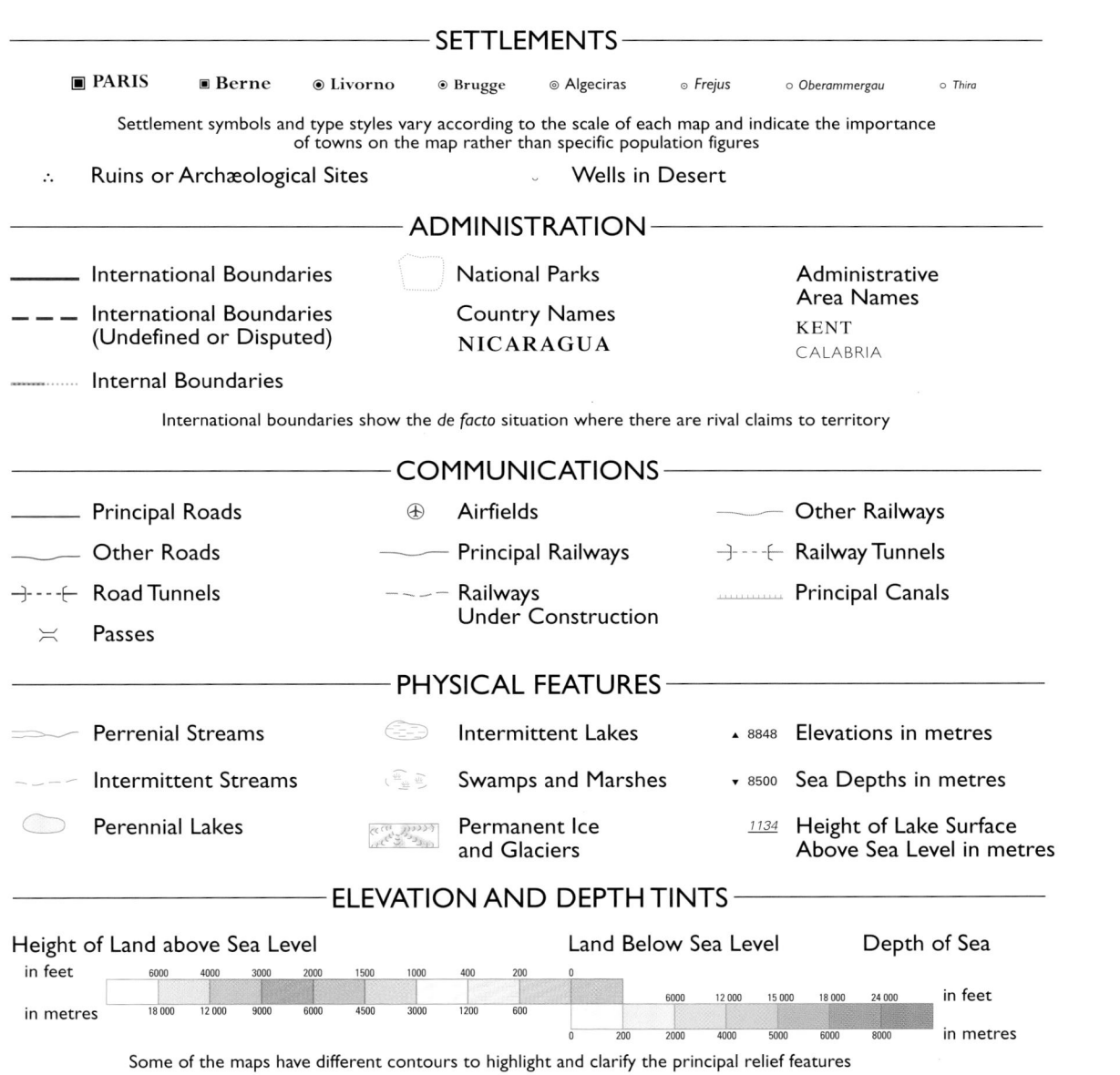

SETTLEMENTS

■ PARIS   ■ Berne   ◉ Livorno   ◎ Brugge   ◎ Algeciras   ○ Frejus   ○ Oberammergau   ○ Thira

Settlement symbols and type styles vary according to the scale of each map and indicate the importance
of towns on the map rather than specific population figures

∴ Ruins or Archæological Sites   ᵕ Wells in Desert

ADMINISTRATION

———— International Boundaries

– – – International Boundaries
(Undefined or Disputed)

········· Internal Boundaries

National Parks

Country Names
NICARAGUA

Administrative
Area Names

KENT

CALABRIA

International boundaries show the *de facto* situation where there are rival claims to territory

COMMUNICATIONS

———— Principal Roads

——— Other Roads

✛--⊦ Road Tunnels

⌇ Passes

⊕ Airfields

——— Principal Railways

– ⌇ – Railways
Under Construction

——— Other Railways

✛--⊦ Railway Tunnels

········· Principal Canals

PHYSICAL FEATURES

——— Perrenial Streams

– ⌐ – Intermittent Streams

◯ Perennial Lakes

Intermittent Lakes

Swamps and Marshes

Permanent Ice
and Glaciers

▲ 8848   Elevations in metres

▼ 8500   Sea Depths in metres

1134   Height of Lake Surface
Above Sea Level in metres

ELEVATION AND DEPTH TINTS

Height of Land above Sea Level   Land Below Sea Level   Depth of Sea

in feet	6000	4000	3000	2000	1500	1000	400	200	0					
in metres	18 000	12 000	9000	6000	4500	3000	1200	600		6000	12 000	15 000	18 000	24 000	in feet
										0	200	2000	4000	5000	6000	8000	in metres

Some of the maps have different contours to highlight and clarify the principal relief features

Projection : Hammer Equal Area

ARCTIC OCEAN

Svalbard *(Norw.)*

Barents Sea Novaya Zemlya *Kara Sea*

Severnaya Zemlya *Laptev Sea* *East Siberian* New Siberian Is. Wrangel I.

Sea

A

NORWAY Oslo SWEDEN FINLAND Helsinki
Murmansk
Arkhangelsk
Norilsk
Verkhoyansk
Yakutsk
Magadan
Arctic Circle

Stockholm EST. ST.PETERSBURG
Copenhagen LATVIA
DENMARK LITH.
Hamburg Berlin POLAND Minsk BELARUS Kiev
Amsterdam NETH.
Brussels GERMANY Prague Warsaw
LUX. Vienna CZECH SLOVAK
PARIS AUSTRIA HUNG. UKRAINE
Lyons SW. Budapest ROMANIA
Milan CRO. YUG. Bucharest
Marseilles ITALY BULGARIA
Barcelona Rome YUG. Sofia
Naples ALB. MAC.
Algiers Sicily Athens GREECE

MOSCOW
Perm
Yekaterinburg
Salekhard
Ob
Volga
Kazan
Samara
Chelyabinsk
Omsk
Tomsk Krasnoyarsk
Novosibirsk
Astana
Qaraghandy
Barnaul
Irkutsk
L. Baikal
Ulan Ude

Okhotsk
Sea of Okhotsk

Petropavlovsk-Kamchatskiy

Bering Sea

B

Sakhalin
Komsomolsk
Khabarovsk
Amur

International Date Line

RUSSIA

Saratov
Volgograd
Astrakhan
KAZAKSTAN
Aral Sea
L. Balkhash
Almaty
Bishkek KYRGYZSTAN
UZBEKISTAN
Caspian Sea
Baku
Tbilisi GEORGIA ARM. AZER.
TURKMENISTAN Ashkhabad
Samarkand Tashkent
Dushanbe TAJIKISTAN

Ulan Bator
MONGOLIA
Ürümqi

Harbin
Changchun
SHENYANG
BEIJING TIANJIN
Lanzhou Taiyuan
Xi'an

Vladivostok
NORTH KOREA
P'yongyang
SOUTH KOREA
SEOUL
Dalian

Sapporo
JAPAN
TŌKYŌ
Ōsaka
Kitakyūshū

Kuril

PACIFIC

C

40

TURKEY
Ankara
İSTANBUL
İzmir
Yerevan
CYPRUS
Beirut SYRIA
Crete LEB. Damascus
Jerusalem ISRAEL Ammān JORDAN
Alexandria
CAIRO
Tabriz
Mashhad
TEHRAN
Esfahān
Baghdād
IRAQ IRAN
Shīrāz
KUWAIT
Kābul
AFGHANISTAN
Islamabad
Lahore
JAMMU & KASHMIR
DELHI
New Delhi
Kanpur

Hwang
Nanjing
Chengdu
Wuhan
CHONGQING
SHANGHAI
East China Sea
Fuzhou

Zhengzhou
Ryukyus

OCEAN

Bonin Is. *(Japan)*
Tropic of Cancer

Volcano Is. *(Japan)*
Marcus I. *(Japan)*
Wake I. *(U.S.A.)*

20

Mediterranean Sea
Tripoli
Benghazi
MALTA
TUNISIA

LIBYA
EGYPT
Aswân

Riyadh
SAUDI
QATAR BAHRAIN
U.A.E. Abu Dhabi
Muscat OMAN

The Gulf
PAKISTAN
KARACHI
Ahmadabad
MUMBAI *(Bombay)*

NEPAL
Katmandu
BHU.
Lhasa
TIBET

INDIA
Nagpur

KOLKATA *(Calcutta)*
DACCA
BANGLA-DESH
BURMA
MYANMAR
Hyderabad
Bay of Bengal
Rangoon
Kunming
GUANGZHOU
HONG KONG
Taipei
TAIWAN

Mecca
Omdurmân
Khartoum
Asmara
Sana
NIGER
CHAD
L. Chad
ERITREA
YEMEN
Aden
Socotra *(Yemen)*

CHENNAI *(Madras)*
Bangalore
Lakshadweep Is. *(India)*
Andaman Is. *(India)*

THAILAND
BANGKOK
VIET-NAM
Hanoi
Hainan

Vientiane
CAMBODIA
MANILA
PHILIPPINES

South China Sea

NORTHERN MARIANAS *(U.S.A.)*

GUAM *(U.S.A.)*

MARSHALL IS.

D

Niamey
Kano
NIGERIA Abuja
BENIN Ibadan
Lagos
CAMEROON Douala
EQUATORIAL GUINEA Yaoundé
SÃO TOMÉ & PRÍNCIPE
GABON Libreville
CONGO
Brazzaville Kinshasa
CABINDA *(Angola)*

SUDAN
CENTRAL AFRICAN REP.
Bangui
Kisangani
DEM. REP. OF THE CONGO
Kananga
Lubumbashi

White Nile
Blue Nile
DJIBOUTI
Addis Ababa
ETHIOPIA
SOMALI REP.
UGANDA Kampala
KENYA
Nairobi
RWANDA Kigali
BURUNDI Bujumbura
Dodoma
TANZANIA
Zanzibar
Dar es Salaam

L. Turkana
L. Victoria
Mombasa
Tanganyika
Mogadishu

Colombo
SRI LANKA
Nicobar Is. *(India)*

MALDIVES

Equator

Phnom Penh
Ho Chi Minh City
MALAYSIA
Kuala Lumpur
PEN. MALAYSIA
SABAH
BRUNEI
SARAWAK
SINGAPORE
Medan
Palembang
Sumatra

Borneo
Banjarmasin

IRIAN JAYA

Yap
PALAU
Truk
Caroline Is.
Pohnpei
FEDERATED STATES OF MICRONESIA

Gilbert Is.
NAURU KIRIBATI

INDIAN

OCEAN

SEYCHELLES
Amirante Is.
Aldabra Is.
COMOROS
Mayotte *(Fr.)*

Diego Garcia
Chagos Arch. *(U.K.)*
Agalega Is.

Cocos Is. *(Austral.)*
Christmas I. *(Austral.)*

INDONESIA
JAKARTA
Bandung
Java
Surabaya
Ujung Pandang
Timor
EAST TIMOR
Arafura Sea

PAPUA NEW GUINEA
Port Moresby
C. York

New Ireland
New Britain

SOLOMON IS.
Santa Cruz Is.

TUVALU

E

Luanda
ANGOLA
Benguela
ZAMBIA
Lusaka
Lubumbashi
Malawi
Lilongwe
MALAWI
ZIMBABWE MOZAMBIQUE
Harare
Bulawayo
NAMIBIA
Windhoek
BOTSWANA
Gaborone
Pretoria
Johannesburg
SOUTH
Maputo
AFRICA
SWAZILAND
LESOTHO
Durban
Cape Town
C. of Good Hope
Port Elizabeth

Mozambique Channel
MADAGASCAR
Antananarivo
RÉUNION *(Fr.)*
MAURITIUS
Rodriguez *(Mauritius)*
Cargados Carajos

Amsterdam I. *(Fr.)*
St. Paul *(Fr.)*

Tropic of Capricorn

Port Hedland
Alice Springs
AUSTRALIA
Darwin
Cairns
Townsville

Geraldton
Perth
Fremantle
Kalgoorlie-Boulder
Great Australian Bight
Adelaide
Darling
Rockhampton
Brisbane

Newcastle
Sydney
Canberra
Melbourne
Tasman Sea
Tasmania
Hobart

VANUATU

FIJI
Suva

NEW CALEDONIA *(Fr.)*

Lord Howe I. *(Austral.)*
Norfolk I. *(Austral.)*

20

F

Prince Edward Is. *(S.Africa)*
Crozet Is. *(Fr.)*
Kerguelen *(Fr.)*

McDonald Is. *(Austral.)* Heard I. *(Austral.)*

Bouvet I. *(Norw.)*

Auckland
North I.
NEW ZEALAND
Wellington
Christchurch
South I.
Stewart I.
Dunedin
Antipodes Is. *(N.Z.)*
Bounty Is. *(N.Z.)*

40

G

SOUTHERN OCEAN

Campbell I. *(N.Z.)* Auckland Is. *(N.Z.)*
Macquarie Is. *(Austral.)*

Antarctic Circle

60

Ross Sea

H

Hanoi ● Capital Cities

Projection: Zenithal Equidistant

West from Greenwich   East from Greenwich

COPYRIGHT GEORGE PHILIP LTD

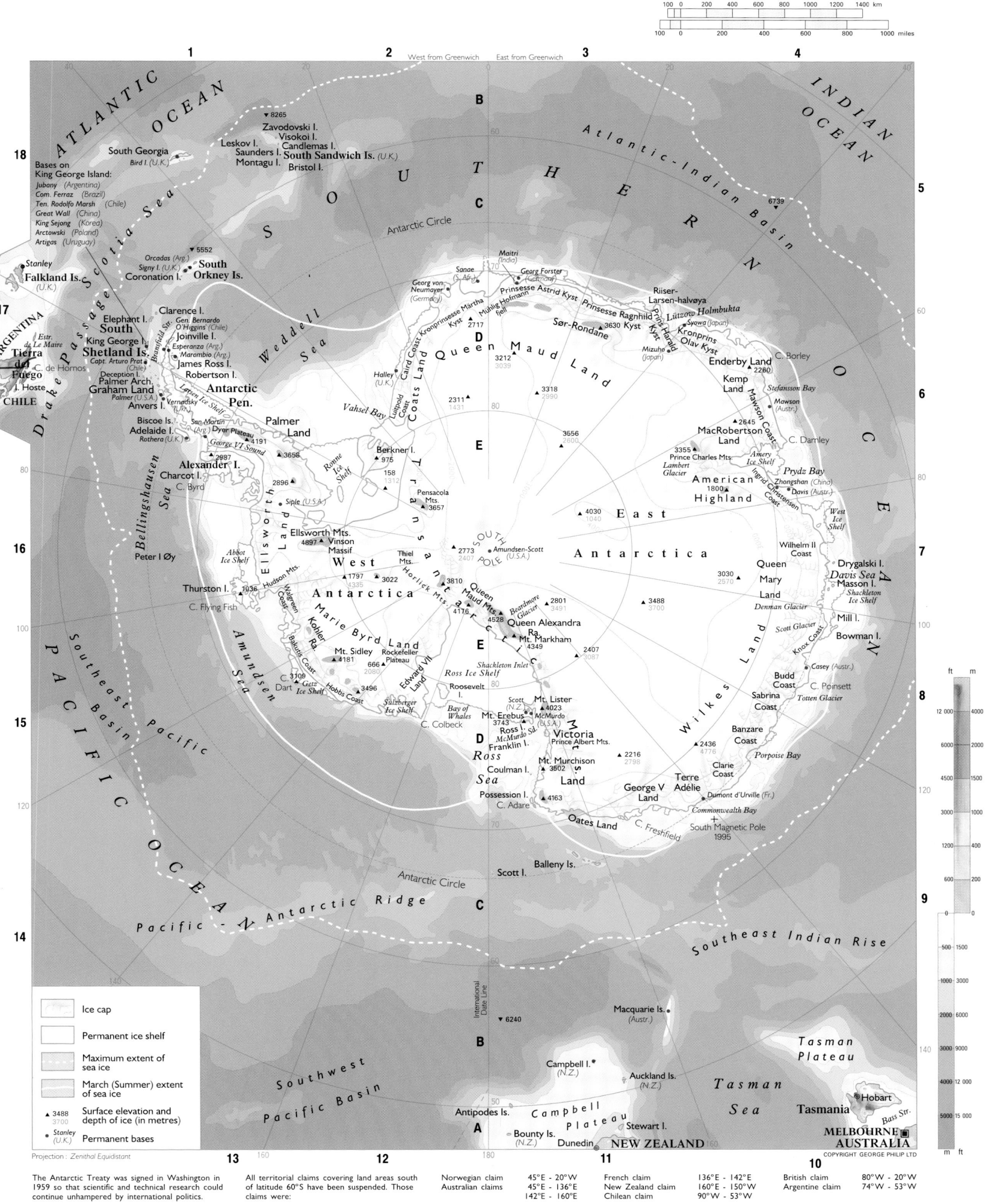

100 0 200 400 600 800 1000 1200 1400 km
100 0 200 400 600 800 1000 miles

ft *m*

12 000 — 4000
6000 — 2000
4500 — 1500
3000 — 1000
1200 — 400
600 — 200
0 — 0
500 — 1500
1000 — 3000
2000 — 6000
3000 — 9000
4000 — 12 000
5000 — 15 000
m *ft*

COPYRIGHT GEORGE PHILIP LTD

Projection : Zenithal Equidistant

Legend

| Ice cap |
| Permanent ice shelf |
| Maximum extent of sea ice |
| March (Summer) extent of sea ice |
| ▲ 3488 / 3700 Surface elevation and depth of ice (in metres) |
| • Stanley (U.K.) Permanent bases |

The Antarctic Treaty was signed in Washington in 1959 so that scientific and technical research could continue unhampered by international politics.

All territorial claims covering land areas south of latitude 60°S have been suspended. Those claims were:

Norwegian claim	45°E - 20°W
Australian claims	45°E - 136°E
	142°E - 160°E
French claim	136°E - 142°E
New Zealand claim	160°E - 150°W
Chilean claim	90°W - 53°W
British claim	80°W - 20°W
Argentine claim	74°W - 53°W

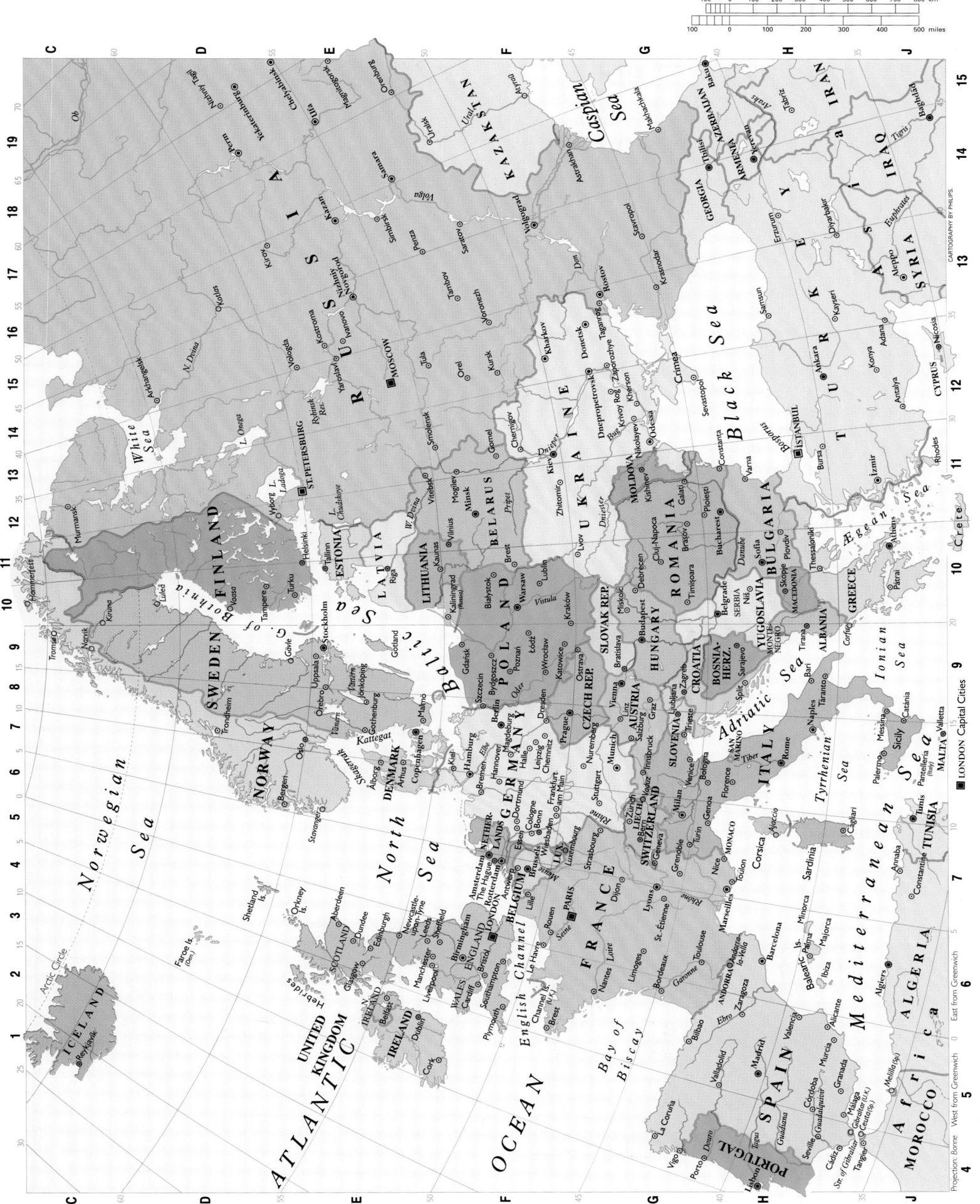

SCANDINAVIA 1:5 000 000

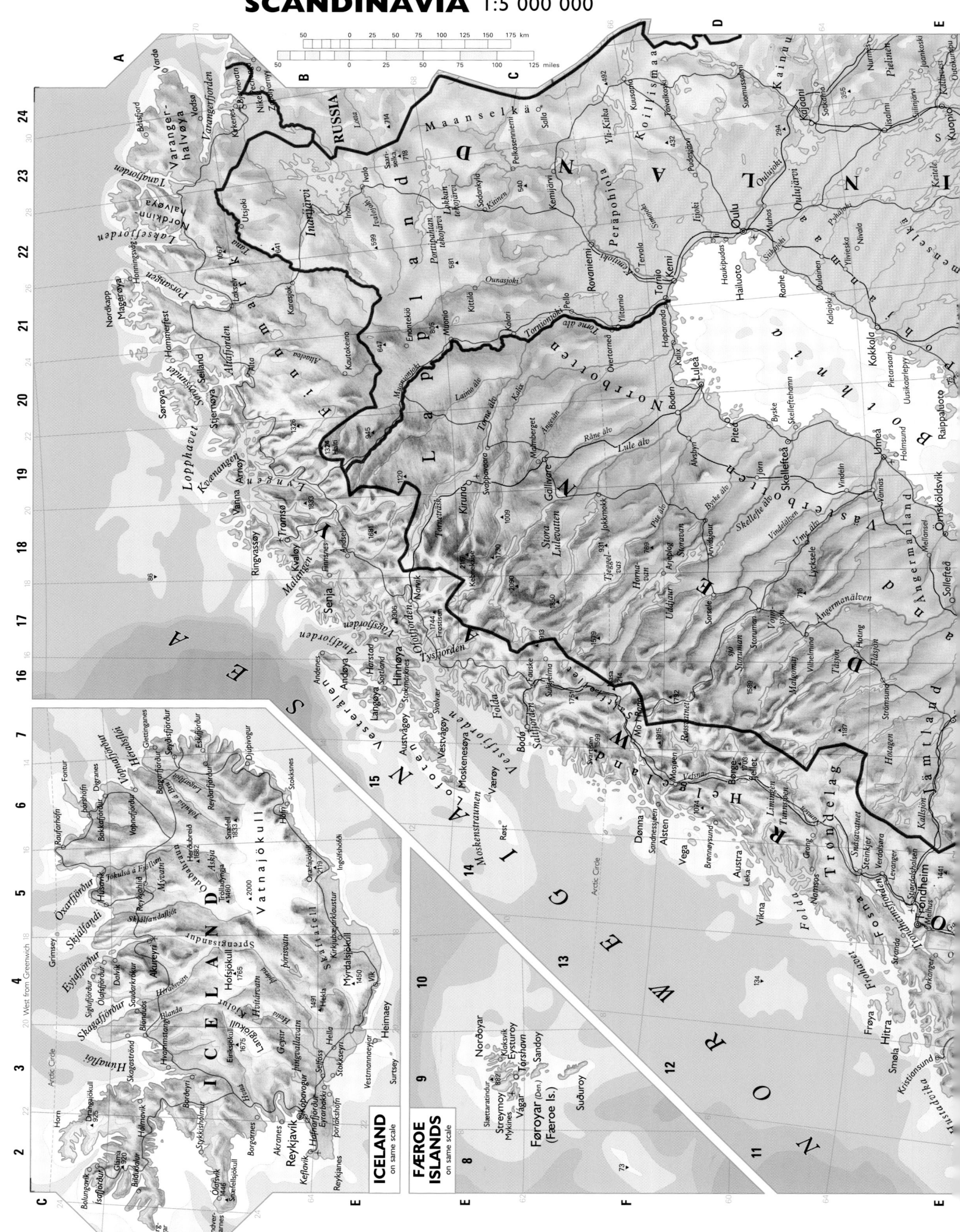

50   0   25   50   75   100 125 150 175 km

50   0   25   50   75   100   125 miles

ICELAND
on same scale

FÆROE
ISLANDS
on same scale

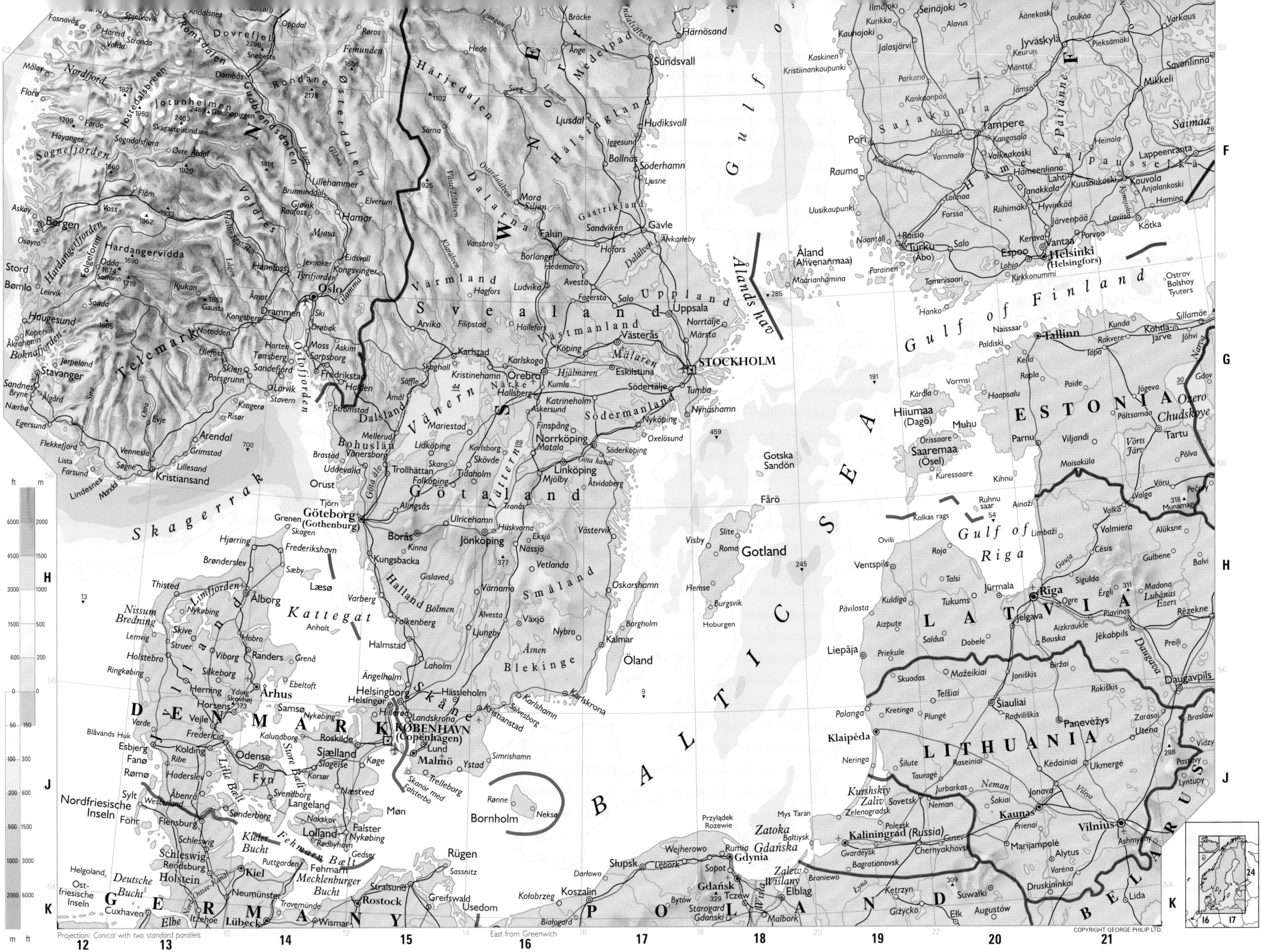

FINLAND

Mikkeli · Lappeenranta · Savonlinna · Kouvola · Kotka · Hamina · Kymijoki · Lahti · Hyvinkää · Porvoo · Helsinki (Helsingfors) · Espoo · Tampere · Nokia · Salo · Turku (Åbo) · Pori · Rauma · Uusikaupunki

Saimaa · Gulf of Finland

ESTONIA

Tallinn · Narva · Tartu · Pärnu · Viljandi · Haapsalu · Hiiumaa (Dagö) · Saaremaa (Ösel) · Kuressaare · Lake Peipus · Chudskoye Ozero

RUSSIA · Pskov · Ostrov

Gulf of Riga · Ruhnu saar

LATVIA

Riga · Jūrmala · Ventspils · Liepāja · Valmiera · Cēsis · Sigulda · Jelgava · Bauska · Daugava · Daugavpils · Rēzekne

LITHUANIA

Vilnius · Kaunas · Panevėžys · Šiauliai · Klaipėda · Palanga · Telšiai · Mažeikiai · Marijampolė · Alytus

BELARUS · Lida

Kaliningrad (Russia) · Gusev · Sovetsk · Chernyakhovsk

POLAND

Gdańsk · Gdynia · Sopot · Elbląg · Malbork · Słupsk · Koszalin · Kołobrzeg · Gdańska Zatoka

SWEDEN

Stockholm · Uppsala · Västerås · Eskilstuna · Södertälje · Norrköping · Linköping · Örebro · Karlstad · Gävle · Falun · Borlänge · Mora · Sundsvall · Härnösand · Hudiksvall · Söderhamn · Jönköping · Växjö · Kalmar · Karlskrona · Kristianstad · Halmstad · Helsingborg · Malmö · Göteborg (Gothenburg) · Borås · Trollhättan · Uddevalla · Varberg · Karlshamn

Vänern · Vättern · Mälaren · Hjälmaren

Dalarna · Värmland · Svealand · Västmanland · Uppland · Södermanland · Östergötland · Götaland · Småland · Halland · Skåne · Blekinge · Bohuslän · Dalsland · Härjedalen · Medelpad · Hälsingland · Gästrikland

Gotland · Visby · Öland · Gotska Sandön

Gulf of Bothnia · Ålands hav · Åland (Ahvenanmaa) · Mariehamn

NORWAY

Oslo · Drammen · Hamar · Lillehammer · Kongsberg · Hønefoss · Moss · Fredrikstad · Sarpsborg · Halden · Tønsberg · Sandefjord · Larvik · Skien · Porsgrunn · Arendal · Kristiansand · Grimstad · Flekkefjord · Egersund · Sandnes · Stavanger · Haugesund · Bergen · Voss · Odda

Dovrefjell · Jotunheimen · Galdhøpiggen · Gudbrandsdalen · Østerdalen · Rondane · Hardangervidda · Telemark · Valdres · Hallingdal · Sognefjorden · Nordfjord · Romsdalen

Oslofjorden · Skagerrak

DENMARK

København (Copenhagen) · Helsingør · Roskilde · Køge · Næstved · Slagelse · Korsør · Nykøbing · Odense · Svendborg · Nyborg · Kolding · Vejle · Fredericia · Horsens · Århus · Randers · Viborg · Herning · Silkeborg · Esbjerg · Ribe · Ålborg · Hjørring · Frederikshavn · Thisted · Sønderborg · Åbenrå · Haderslev

Jylland · Sjælland · Fyn · Lolland · Falster · Møn · Langeland · Bornholm · Rønne

Kattegat · Lille Bælt · Store Bælt · Limfjorden

GERMANY

Kiel · Lübeck · Rostock · Wismar · Flensburg · Schleswig · Rendsburg · Neumünster · Husum · Greifswald · Stralsund · Usedom · Rügen · Fehmarn · Mecklenburger Bucht · Deutsche Bucht · Nordfriesische Inseln · Sylt · Föhr · Helgoland · Elbe · Cuxhaven

Baltic Sea · Ostsee

Projection: Conical with two standard parallels

East from Greenwich

Projection: Conical with two standard parallels

m · ft

1:4 000 000

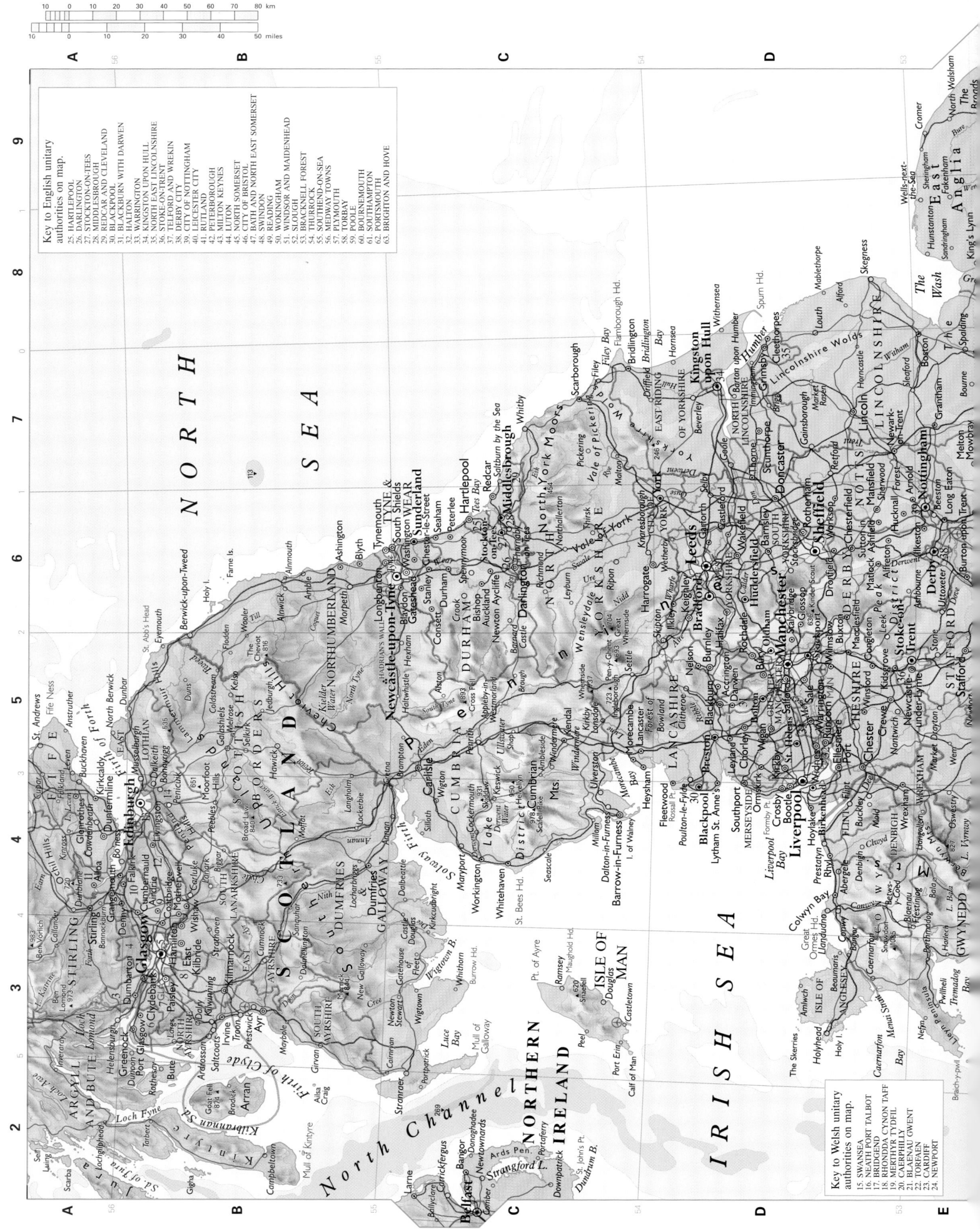

Key to English unitary authorities on map.

25. HARTLEPOOL
26. DARLINGTON
27. STOCKTON-ON-TEES
28. MIDDLESBROUGH
29. REDCAR AND CLEVELAND
30. BLACKPOOL
31. BLACKBURN WITH DARWEN
32. HALTON
33. WARRINGTON
34. KINGSTON UPON HULL
35. NORTH EAST LINCOLNSHIRE
36. STOKE-ON-TRENT
37. TELFORD AND WREKIN
38. DERBY CITY
39. CITY OF NOTTINGHAM
40. LEICESTER CITY
41. RUTLAND
42. PETERBOROUGH
43. MILTON KEYNES
44. LUTON
45. NORTH SOMERSET
46. CITY OF BRISTOL
47. BATH AND NORTH EAST SOMERSET
48. SWINDON
49. READING
50. WOKINGHAM
51. WINDSOR AND MAIDENHEAD
52. SLOUGH
53. BRACKNELL FOREST
54. THURROCK
55. SOUTHEND-ON-SEA
56. MEDWAY TOWNS
57. PLYMOUTH
58. TORBAY
59. POOLE
60. BOURNEMOUTH
61. SOUTHAMPTON
62. PORTSMOUTH
63. BRIGHTON AND HOVE

Key to Welsh unitary authorities on map.

15. SWANSEA
16. NEATH PORT TALBOT
17. BRIDGEND
18. RHONDDA CYNON TAFF
19. MERTHYR TYDFIL
20. CAERPHILLY
21. BLAENAU GWENT
22. TORFAEN
23. CARDIFF
24. NEWPORT

ENGLAND

WALES

FRANCE

NORMANDIE

SEINE-MARITIME

HAUTE-

CALVADOS

MANCHE

Cotentin

ENGLISH CHANNEL

Strait of Dover

Bristol Channel

Cardigan Bay

Carmarthen Bay

Baie de la Seine

Baie de la Somme

LONDON

BIRMINGHAM

Cardiff

Swansea

Bristol

Plymouth

Exeter

Portsmouth

Southampton

Bournemouth

Brighton

Hove

Worthing

Le Havre

Rouen

Caen

Cherbourg

Calais

Boulogne-sur-Mer

Dieppe

Évreux

Lisieux

Bayeux

St-Lô

Coutances

NORFOLK

SUFFOLK

ESSEX

CAMBRIDGE

SHIRE

BEDFORD

HERTS

BUCKS

BERKSHIRE

HANTS

WILTSHIRE

DORSET

SOMERSET

DEVON

CORNWALL

SURREY

WEST SUSSEX

EAST SUSSEX

KENT

GLOUCS

WEST

MONMOUTHSHIRE

HEREFORD

SHROPSHIRE

WORCESTER

WARWICK

NORTHAMPTON

SHIRE

POWYS

CEREDIGION

PEMBROKESHIRE

CARMARTHENSHIRE

VALE OF GLAMORGAN

ISLE OF WIGHT

Newport

Ryde

Cowes

CHANNEL ISLANDS (U.K.)

Jersey

Guernsey

Alderney

Sark

Herm

St. Peter Port

St. Helier

Isles of Scilly
On same scale

St. Mary's
Tresco

Land's End

Penzance

Newlyn

St. Ives

Camborne

Redruth

Truro

Falmouth

Helston

Newquay

Padstow

Wadebridge

Bodmin

Bodmin Moor

Launceston

Bude

Barnstaple

Bideford

Ilfracombe

Lynton

Minehead

Exmoor

Dartmoor

Torquay

Paignton

Brixham

Dartmouth

Kingsbridge

Salcombe

Start Pt.

Bolt Head

Teignmouth

Dawlish

Exmouth

Sidmouth

Lyme Regis

Bridport

Weymouth

Portland Bill

I. of Portland

Dorchester

Swanage

Poole

Lyme Bay

Chesil Beach

Yeovil

Taunton

Wellington

Bridgwater

Wells

Glastonbury

Bath

Trowbridge

Warminster

Salisbury

Salisbury Plain

Andover

Winchester

Basingstoke

Reading

Newbury

Swindon

Cirencester

Cheltenham

Gloucester

Stroud

Chepstow

Newport

Monmouth

Hereford

Ross-on-Wye

Worcester

Kidderminster

Wolverhampton

Walsall

Dudley

Coventry

Warwick

Royal Leamington Spa

Stratford-upon-Avon

Banbury

Oxford

Bicester

Aylesbury

High Wycombe

Maidenhead

Windsor

Slough

Guildford

Dorking

Reigate

Crawley

Horsham

Chichester

Bognor Regis

Littlehampton

Selsey Bill

Gosport

Fareham

Eastleigh

Petersfield

Haslemere

Aldershot

Bracknell

Croydon

Epsom

Leatherhead

Sutton

Kingston

Watford

St. Albans

Hemel Hempstead

Hertford

Harlow

Bishop's Stortford

Stevenage

Hitchin

Letchworth

Luton

Dunstable

Milton Keynes

Bedford

Biggleswade

Northampton

Kettering

Wellingborough

Rushden

Corby

Market Harborough

Huntingdon

St. Neots

Cambridge

Newmarket

Bury St. Edmunds

Sudbury

Colchester

Clacton-on-Sea

Harwich

Ipswich

Felixstowe

Woodbridge

Stowmarket

Aldeburgh

Orford Ness

Saxmundham

Beccles

Lowestoft

Southwold

Diss

Wymondham

Thetford

Brandon

Mildenhall

Ely

March

Peterborough

Oundle

Stamford

Rutland Water

Chelmsford

Brentwood

Basildon

Southend-on-Sea

Gravesend

Dartford

Rochester

Chatham

Gillingham

Sheerness

Sittingbourne

Maidstone

Royal Tunbridge Wells

Tonbridge

Sevenoaks

Canterbury

Whitstable

Herne Bay

Margate

Ramsgate

Deal

Dover

Folkestone

Hythe

Ashford

Tenterden

Rye

Hastings

Bexhill

Eastbourne

Beachy Head

Seaford

Newhaven

Lewes

Haywards Heath

East Grinstead

Caterham

North Foreland

South Foreland

Dungeness

Rye Bay

Romney Marsh

Thames Estuary

The Naze

Mersea I.

Foulness I.

Canvey Island

Rayleigh

Wickford

Braintree

Witham

Halstead

Saffron Walden

Hadleigh

Haverhill

Marlborough

Devizes

Calne

Chippenham

Malmesbury

Shepton Mallet

Frome

Wincanton

Sherborne

Shaftesbury

Blandford Forum

Wimborne Minster

Christchurch

Ringwood

New Forest

Lymington

Portland

St. Alban's Head

Isle of Purbeck

Weymouth Bay

Chard

Honiton

Axminster

Crediton

Tiverton

Okehampton

Tavistock

Saltash

Looe

Fowey

St. Austell

St. Blazey

Liskeard

Brown Willy

FRANCE

Étaples

Berck

Le Touquet-Paris-Plage

Marquise

Wimereux

C. Gris-Nez

Wissant

Sangatte

Ault

Cayeux-sur-Mer

St-Valery-en-Caux

Fécamp

Étretat

Yport

C. d'Antifer

Ste-Adresse

Honfleur

Deauville

Trouville

Cabourg

Ouistreham

Courseulles-sur-Mer

Arromanches-les-Bains

Port-en-Bessin

Grandcamp

Carentan

Valognes

Montebourg

Ste-Mère-Église

St-Vaast-la-Hougue

Barfleur

Pte. de Barfleur

Les Pieux

Octeville

Tourlaville

Querqueville

Bricquebec

Carteret

La Haye-du-Puits

Lessay

Périers

Coutances

Agon-Coutainville

Granville

Nez de Jobourg

Cap de la Hague

Pont-Audemer

Bernay

Elbeuf

Louviers

Gisors

Les Andelys

Beaumont-le-Roger

Bolbec

Lillebonne

Yvetot

Doudeville

Bacqueville-en-Caux

Neufchâtel-en-Bray

Forges-les-Eaux

Gournay-en-Bray

Bréauté

Goderville

Criquetot-l'Esneval

Montivilliers

Pavilly

Mont-St-Aignan

St-Étienne-du-Rouvray

Gaillon

Vernon

Pacy-sur-Eure

Conches-en-Ouche

Breteuil

Verneuil-sur-Avre

Argences

Mézidon-Canon

Villers-sur-Mer

Dives-sur-Mer

Houlgate

Troarn

Bourg-Achard

Brionne

East from Greenwich

West from Greenwich

Projection: Lambert's Conformal Conic

COPYRIGHT GEORGE PHILIP LTD.

10 0 10 20 30 40 50 60 70 80 km
10 0 10 20 30 40 50 miles

Key to Scottish unitary authorities on map
1. CITY OF ABERDEEN
2. DUNDEE CITY
3. WEST DUNBARTONSHIRE
4. EAST DUNBARTONSHIRE
5. CITY OF GLASGOW
6. INVERCLYDE
7. RENFREWSHIRE
8. EAST RENFREWSHIRE
9. NORTH LANARKSHIRE
10. FALKIRK
11. CLACKMANNANSHIRE
12. WEST LOTHIAN
13. CITY OF EDINBURGH
14. MIDLOTHIAN

ORKNEY IS.
On same scale

ORKNEY

SHETLAND IS.
On same scale

SHETLAND

ATLANTIC OCEAN

NORTH SEA

WESTERN ISLES

Outer Hebrides

Inner Hebrides

SCOTLAND

ENGLAND

NORTHERN IRELAND

North Channel

Projection : Lambert's Conformal Conic

West from Greenwich

COPYRIGHT GEORGE PHILIP LTD.

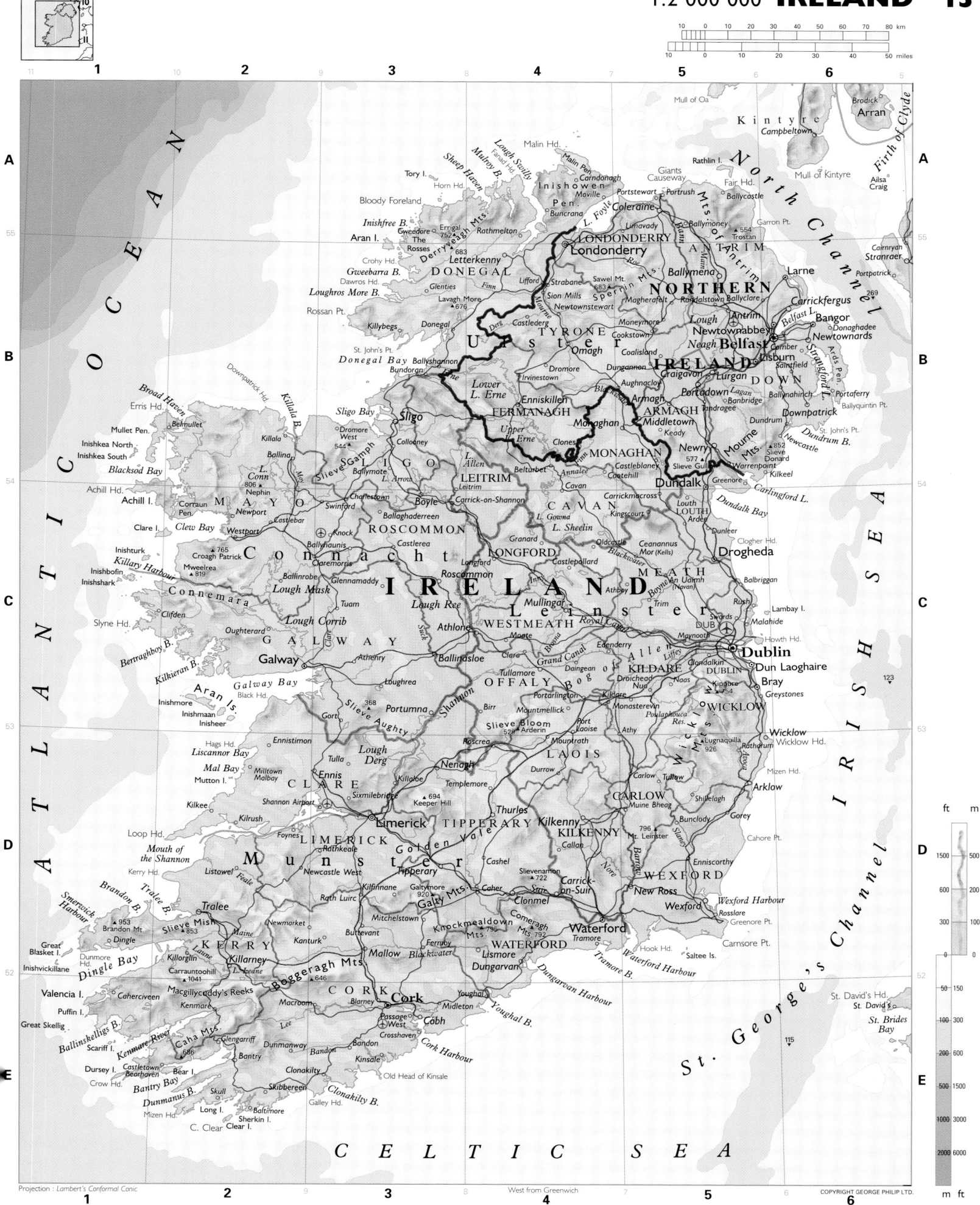

Projection: Conical with two standard parallels

East from Greenwich
COPYRIGHT GEORGE PHILIP LTD.

West from Greenwich

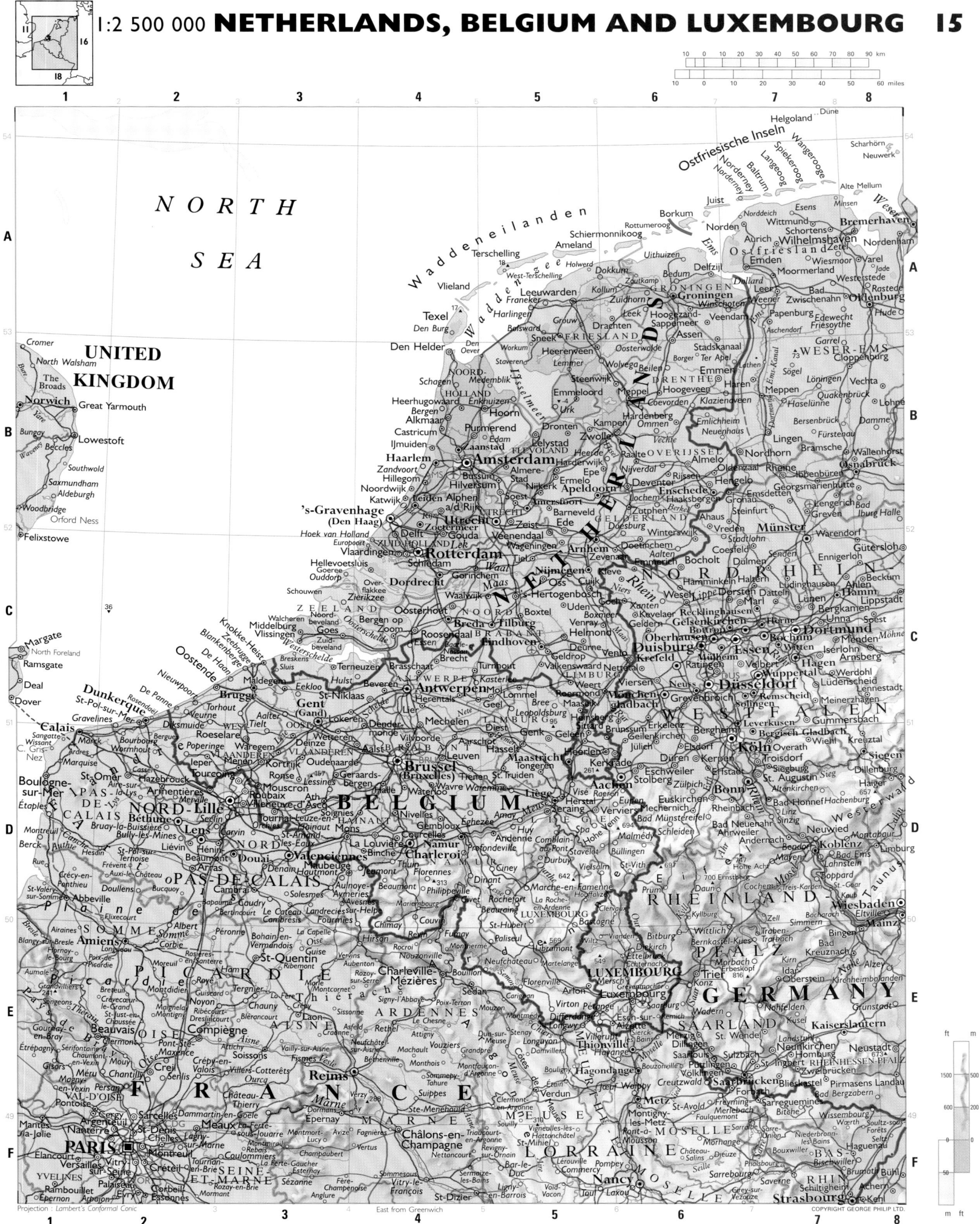

NORTH

SEA

UNITED
KINGDOM

Waddeneilanden

NETHERLANDS

BELGIUM

GERMANY

LUXEMBOURG

FRANCE

PARIS

Projection : Lambert's Conformal Conic

East from Greenwich

COPYRIGHT GEORGE PHILIP LTD.

Underlined towns give their name to the
administrative area in which they stand.

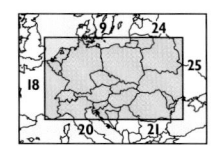

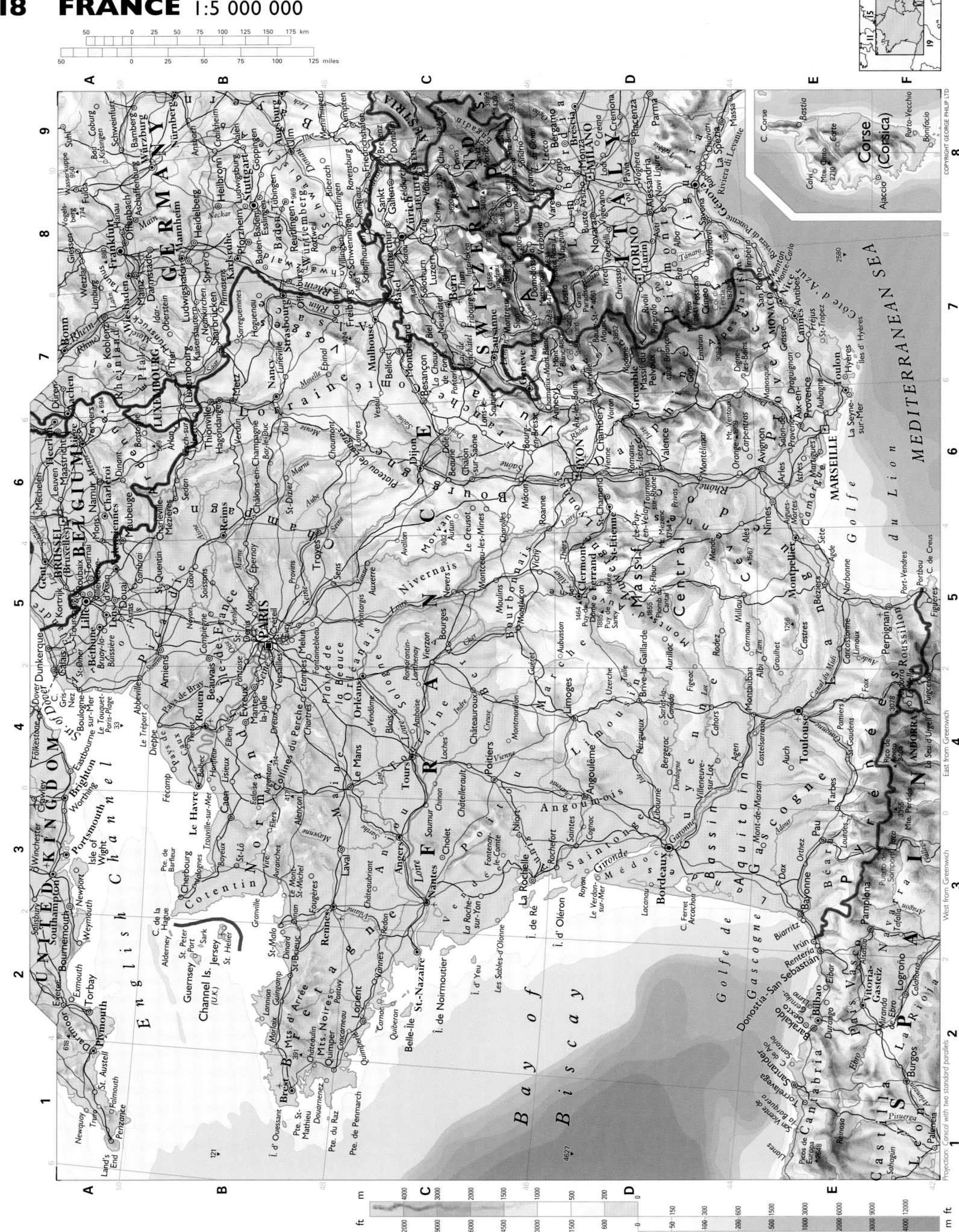

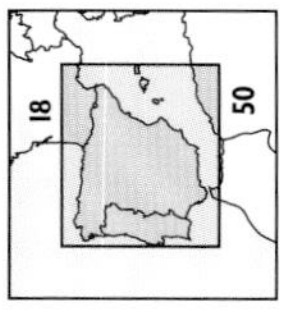

50 0 25 50 75 100 125 150 175 km

50 0 25 50 75 100 125 miles

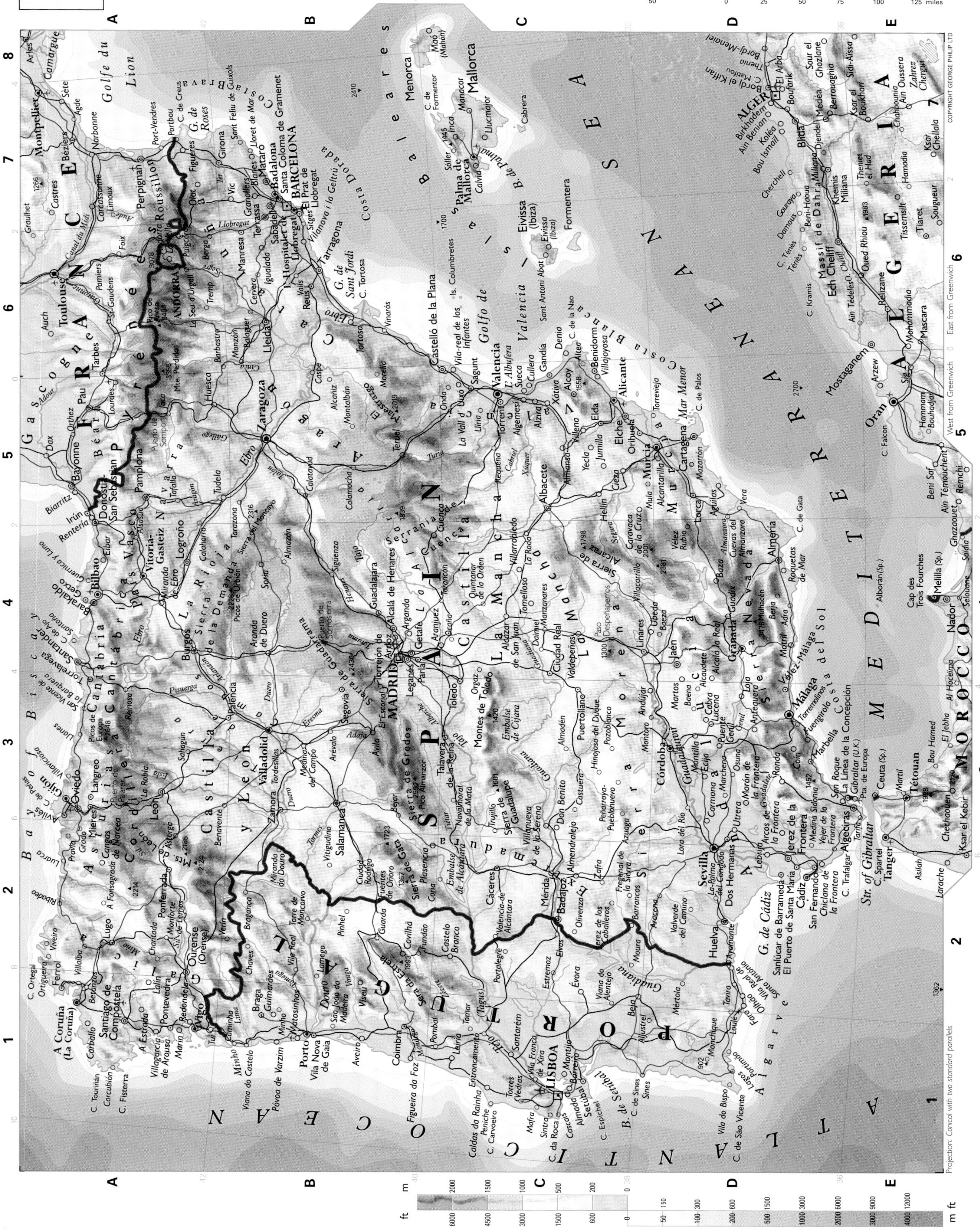

Projection: Conical with two standard parallels

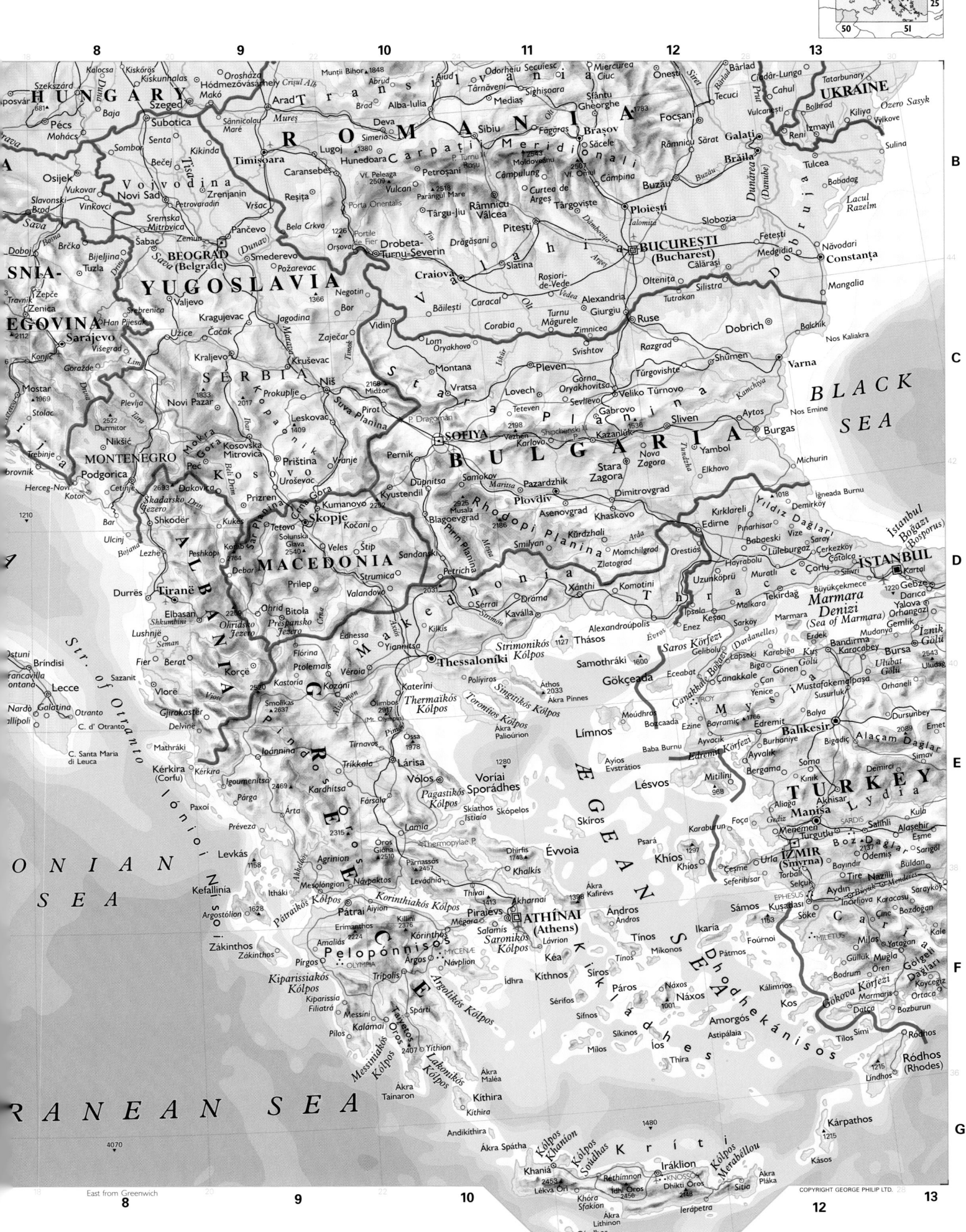

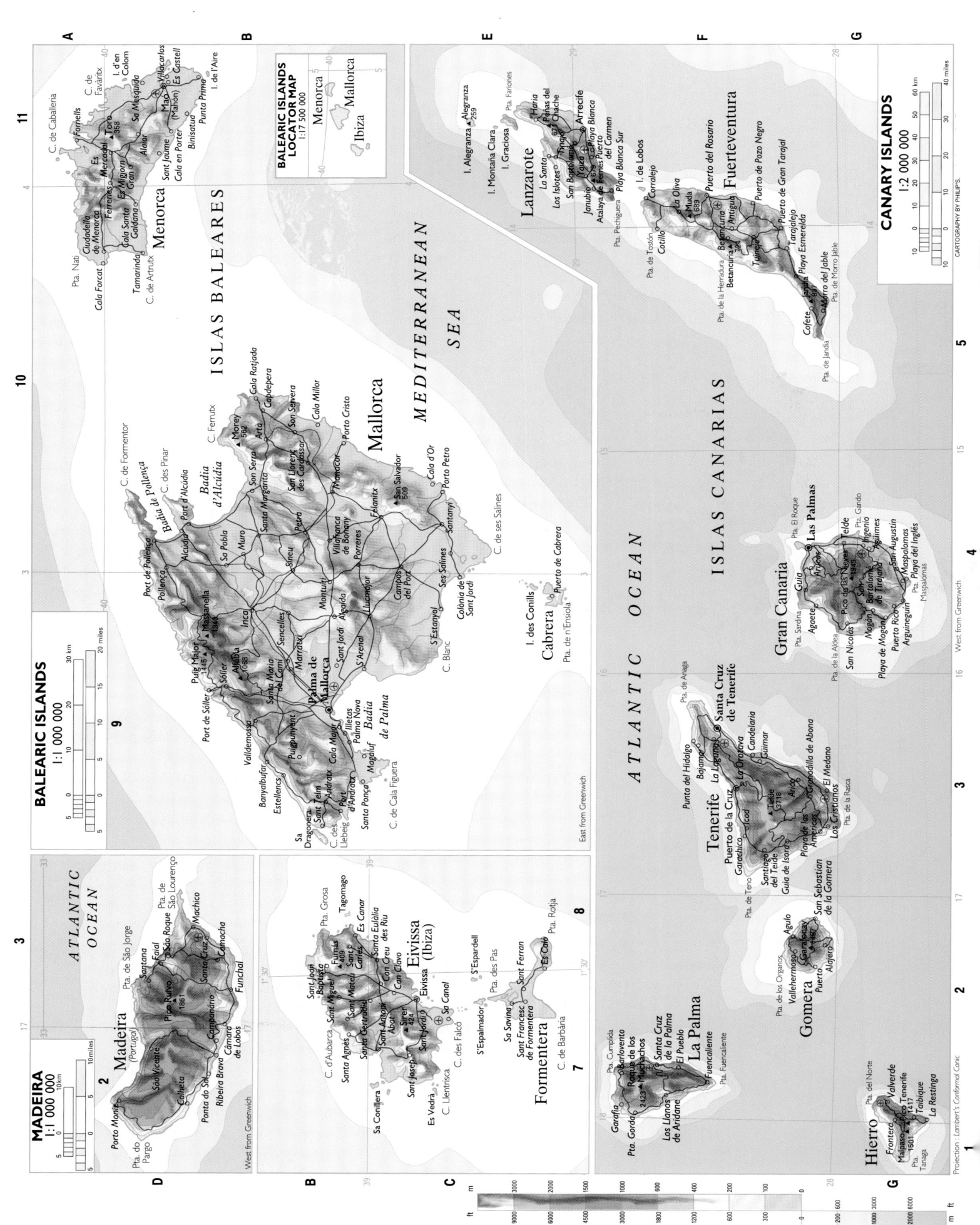

BALEARIC ISLANDS LOCATOR MAP
1:17 500 000

Menorca

Mallorca

Ibiza

ISLAS BALEARES

MEDITERRANEAN SEA

Menorca

Mallorca

BALEARIC ISLANDS
1:1 000 000

MADEIRA
1:1 000 000

Madeira
(Portugal)

ATLANTIC OCEAN

Eivissa (Ibiza)

Formentera

CANARY ISLANDS
1:2 000 000

CARTOGRAPHY BY PHILIP'S.

Lanzarote

Fuerteventura

ISLAS CANARIAS

Gran Canaria

ATLANTIC OCEAN

Tenerife

Gomera

La Palma

Hierro

Las Palmas

Santa Cruz de Tenerife

Projection: Lambert's Conformal Conic.

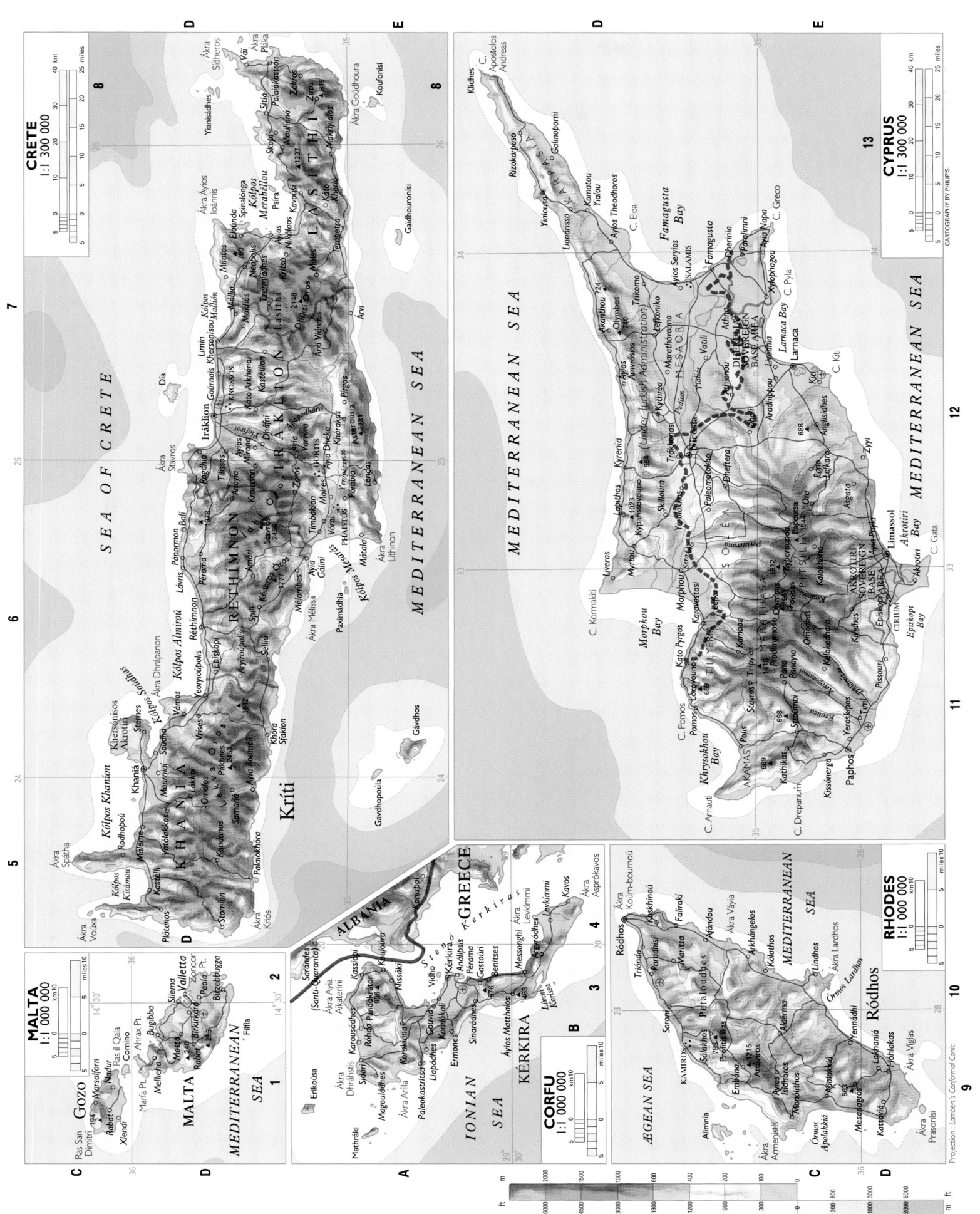

CARTOGRAPHY BY PHILIP'S

CRETE
1:1 300 000

CYPRUS
1:1 300 000

MALTA
1:1 000 000

CORFU
1:1 000 000

RHODES
1:1 000 000

Projection: Lambert's Conformal Conic

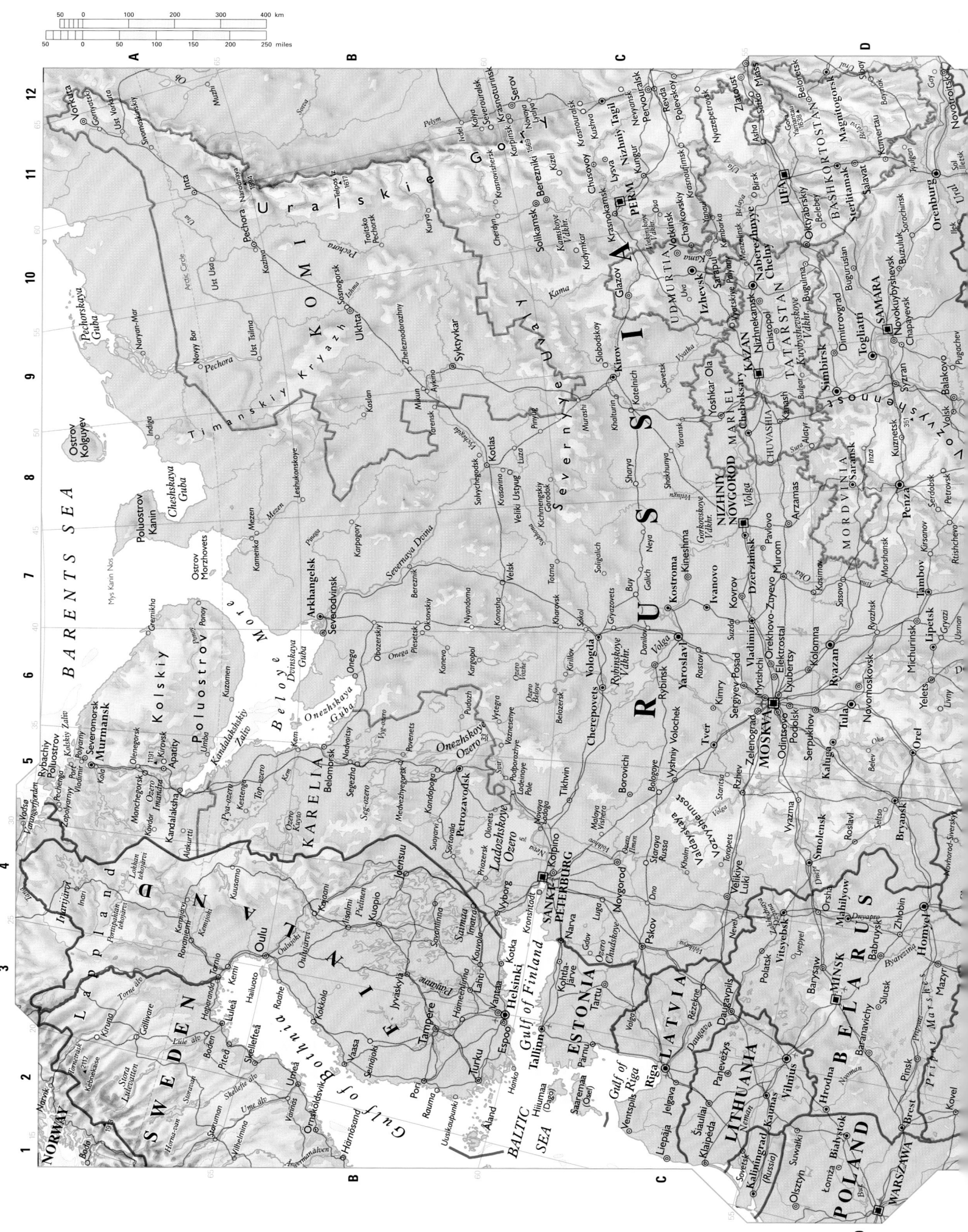

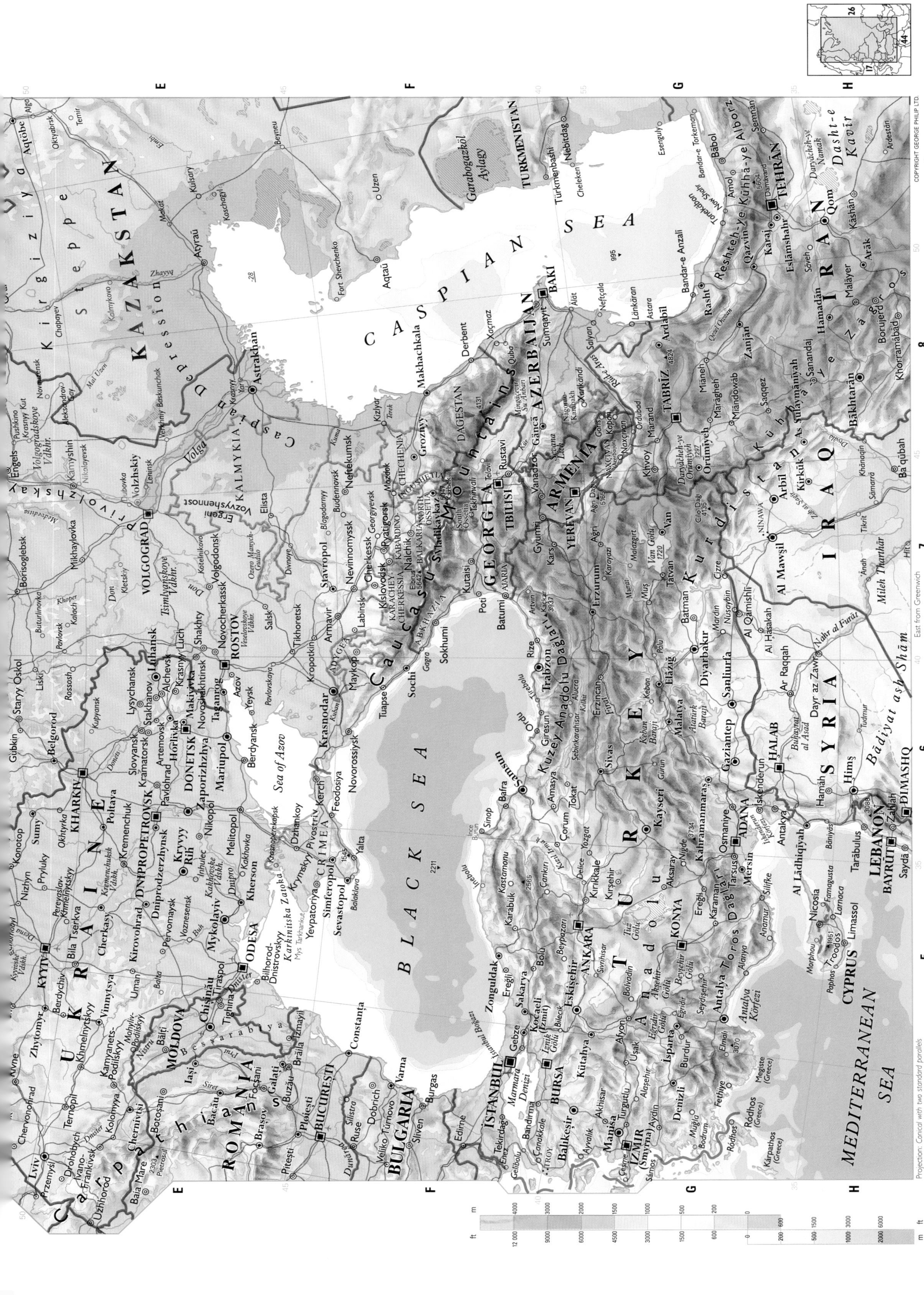

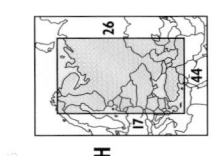

RUSSIA	
1	Adygea
2	Karachey-Cherkessia
3	Kabardino-Balkaria
4	North Ossetia
5	Ingushetia
6	Chechenia
7	Dagestan
8	Mordvinia
9	Chuvashia
10	Mari El
11	Tatarstan
12	Udmurtia
13	Khakassia
AZERBAIJAN	
14	Naxçivan
GEORGIA	UKRAINE
15 Ajaria	17 Crimea
16 Abkhazia	

Projection: Conical Orthomorphic with two standard parallels

East from Greenwich

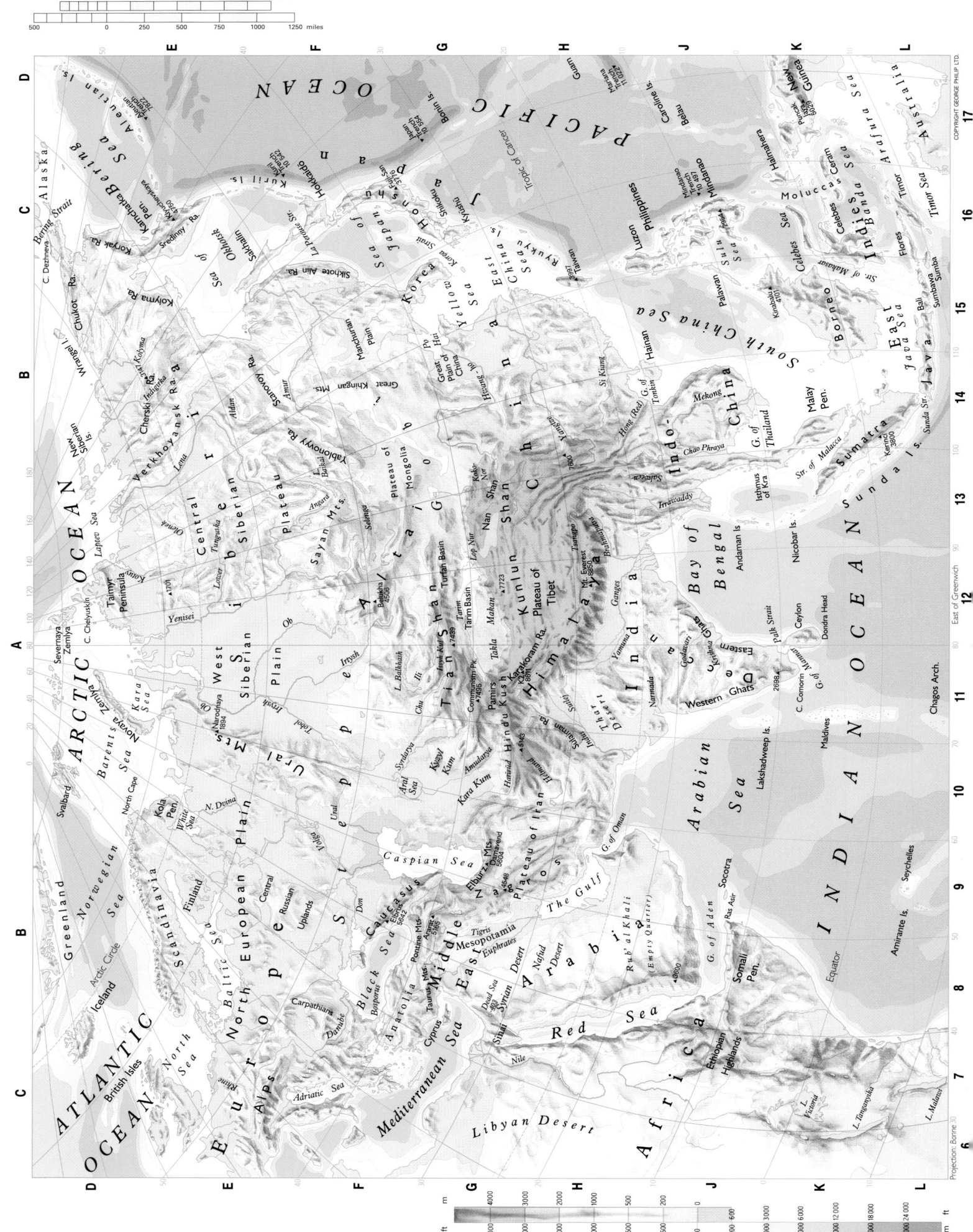

JAPAN 1:5 000 000

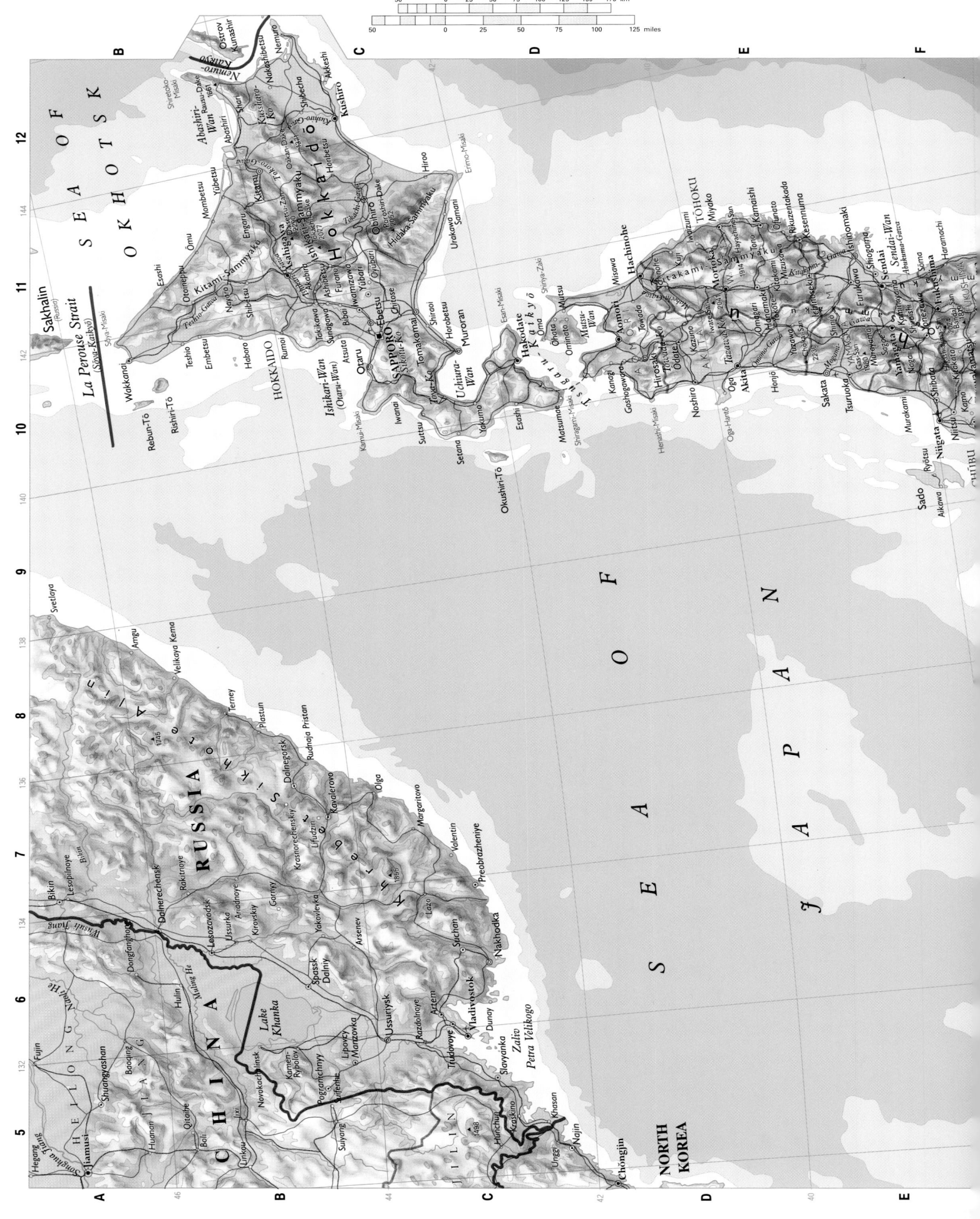

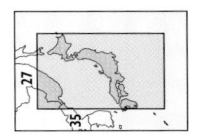

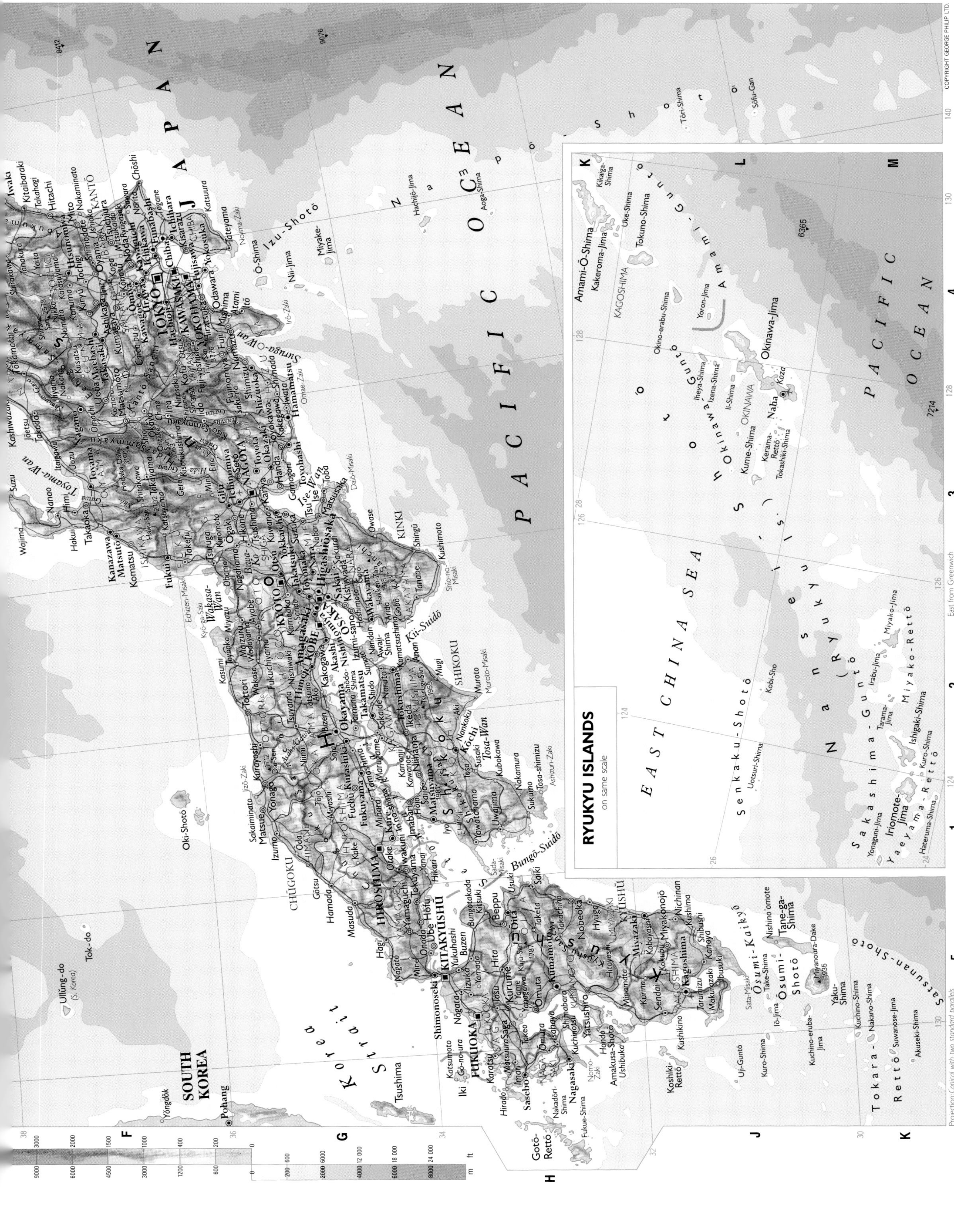

JAPAN

SOUTH KOREA

PACIFIC OCEAN

EAST CHINA SEA

RYUKYU ISLANDS
on same scale

Nansei-shotō (RYUKYU)

Amami-Guntō

Okinawa-Guntō

Sakishima-Guntō

Senkaku-Shotō

KAGOSHIMA

OKINAWA

Naha

Amami-Ō-Shima

Okinawa-Jima

Projection: Conical with two standard parallels

East from Greenwich

TŌKYŌ

YOKOHAMA

KAWASAKI

NAGOYA

KYŌTO

ŌSAKA

KŌBE

HIROSHIMA

KITAKYŪSHŪ

FUKUOKA

KAGOSHIMA

KINKI

CHŪGOKU

SHIKOKU

KYŪSHŪ

KANTŌ

Tosa-Wan

Bungō-Suidō

Kii-Suidō

Korea Strait

Tsushima

Tok-do

Ullŭng-do (S. Korea)

Pohang

 Ōsumi-Shotō

Tokara-Rettō

Satsunan-Shotō

Izu-Shotō

Projection: Bonne

East from Greenwich

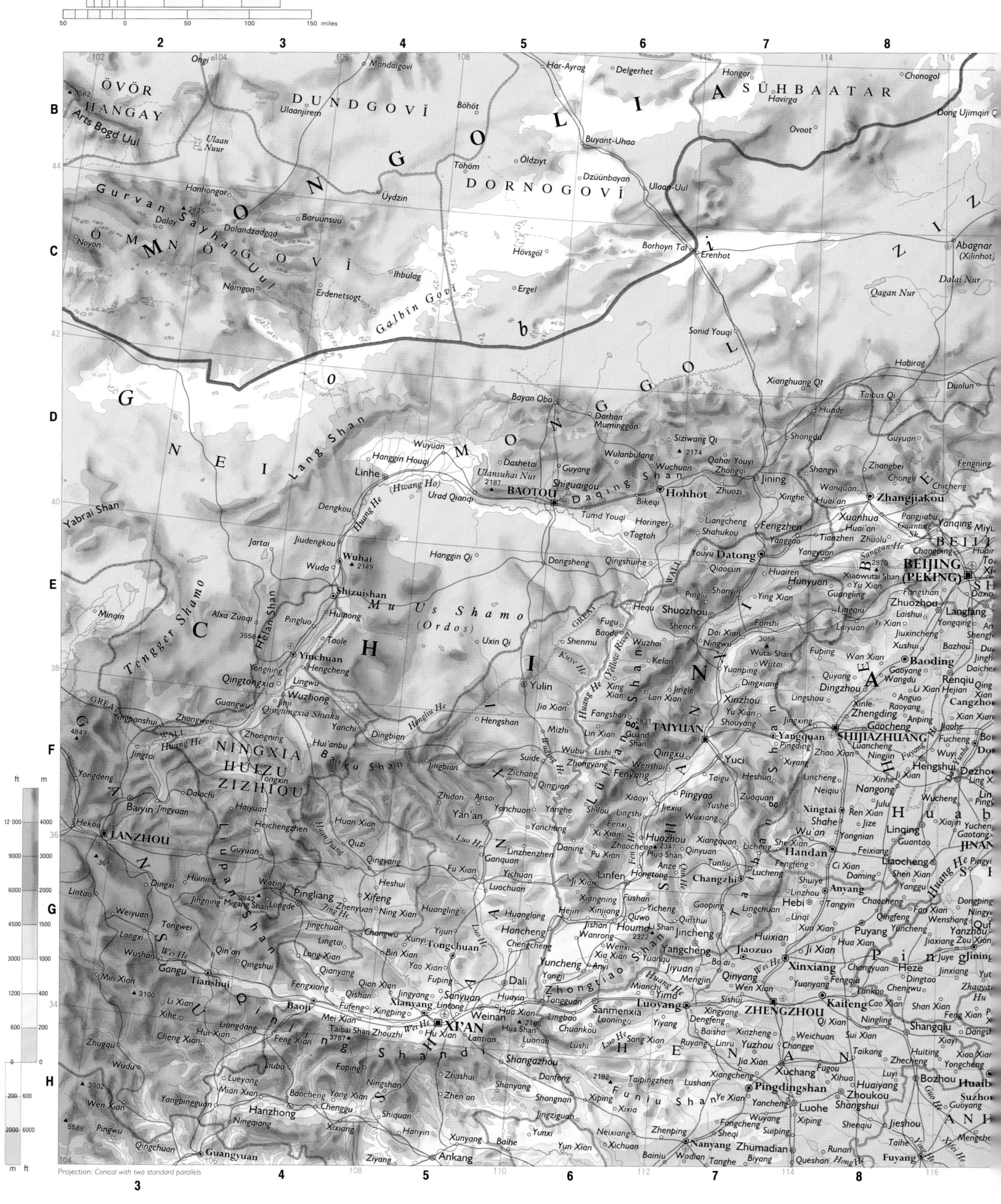

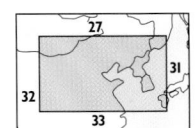

Projection: Mercator

East from Greenwich

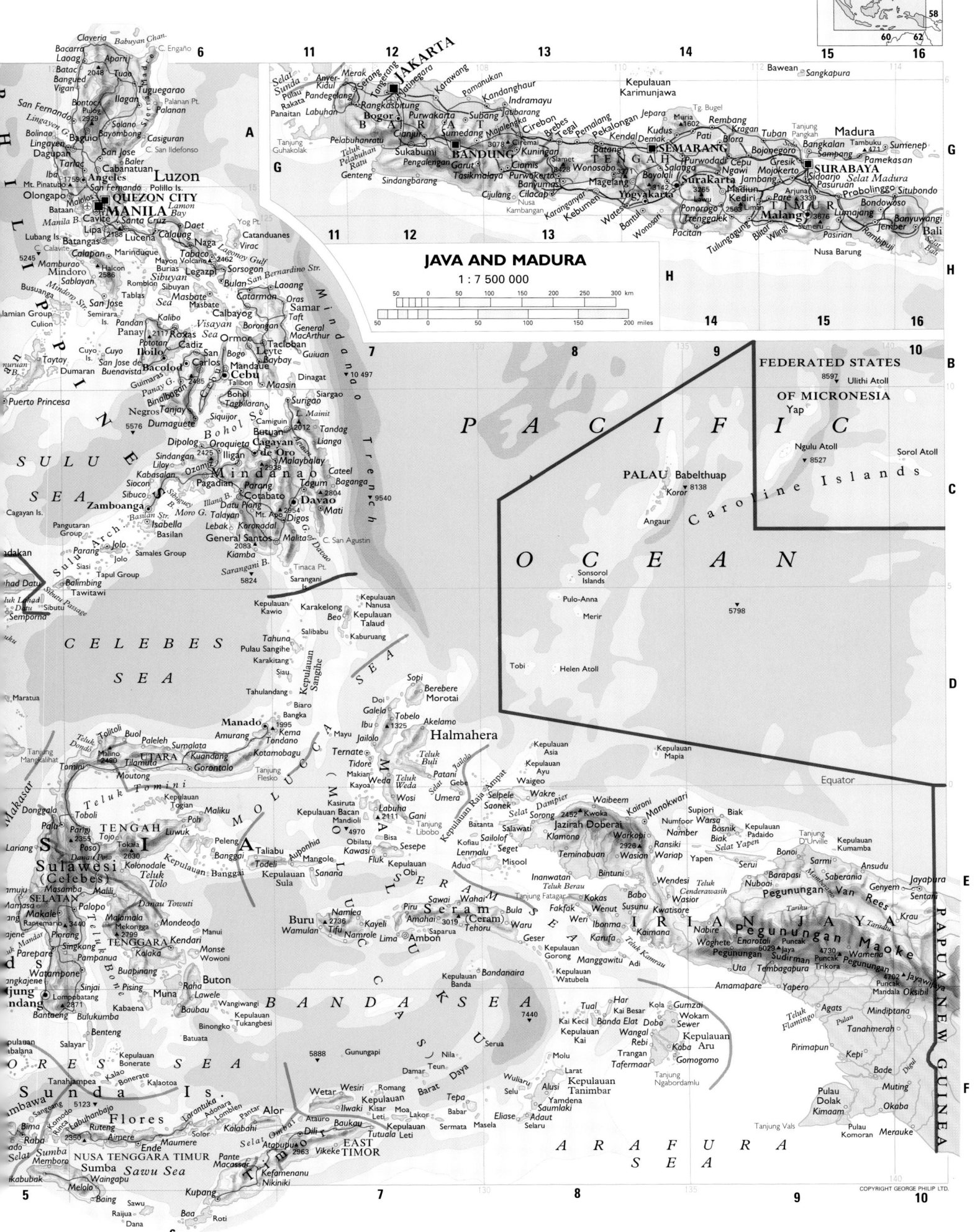

JAVA AND MADURA
1 : 7 500 000

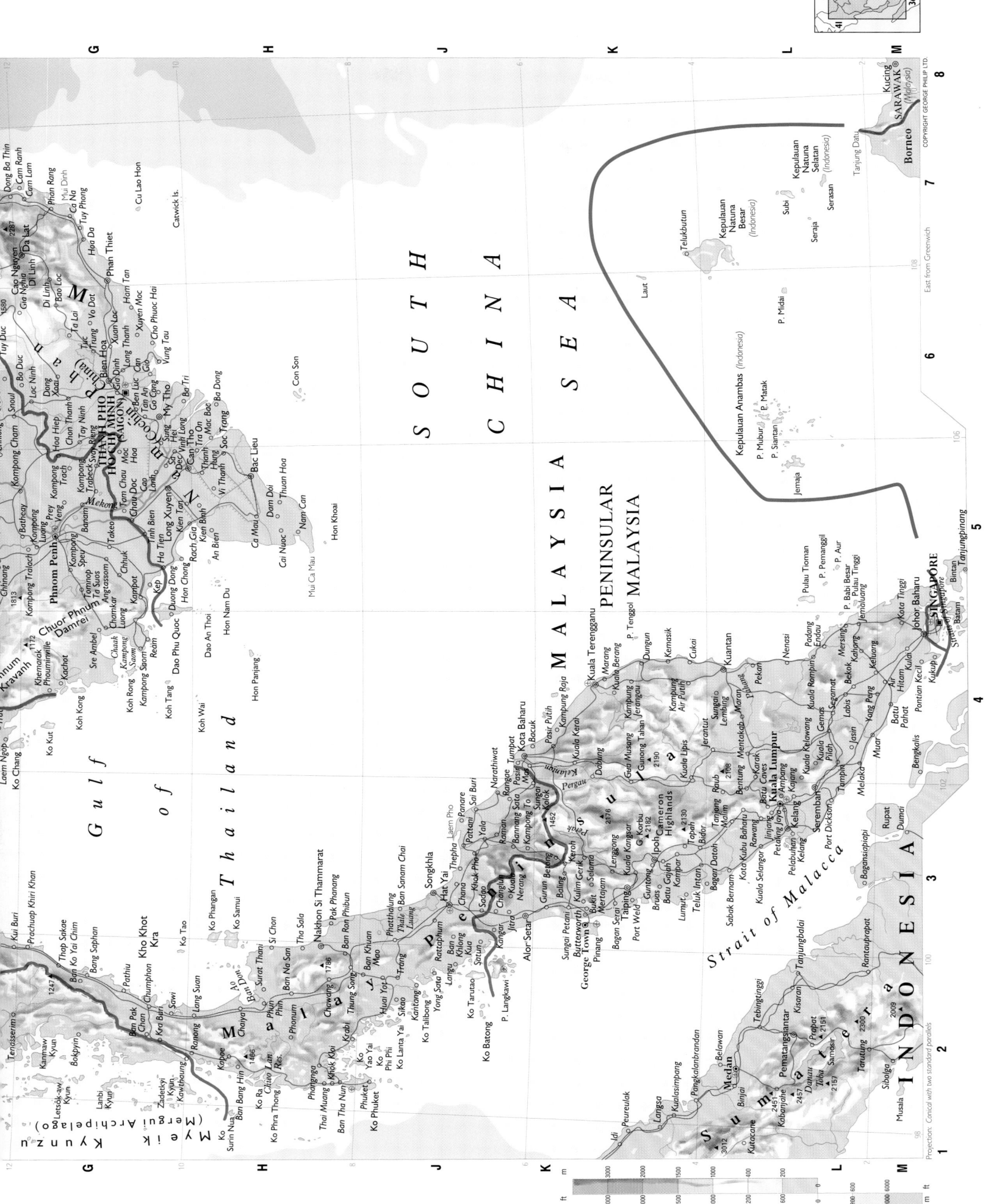

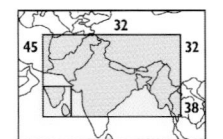

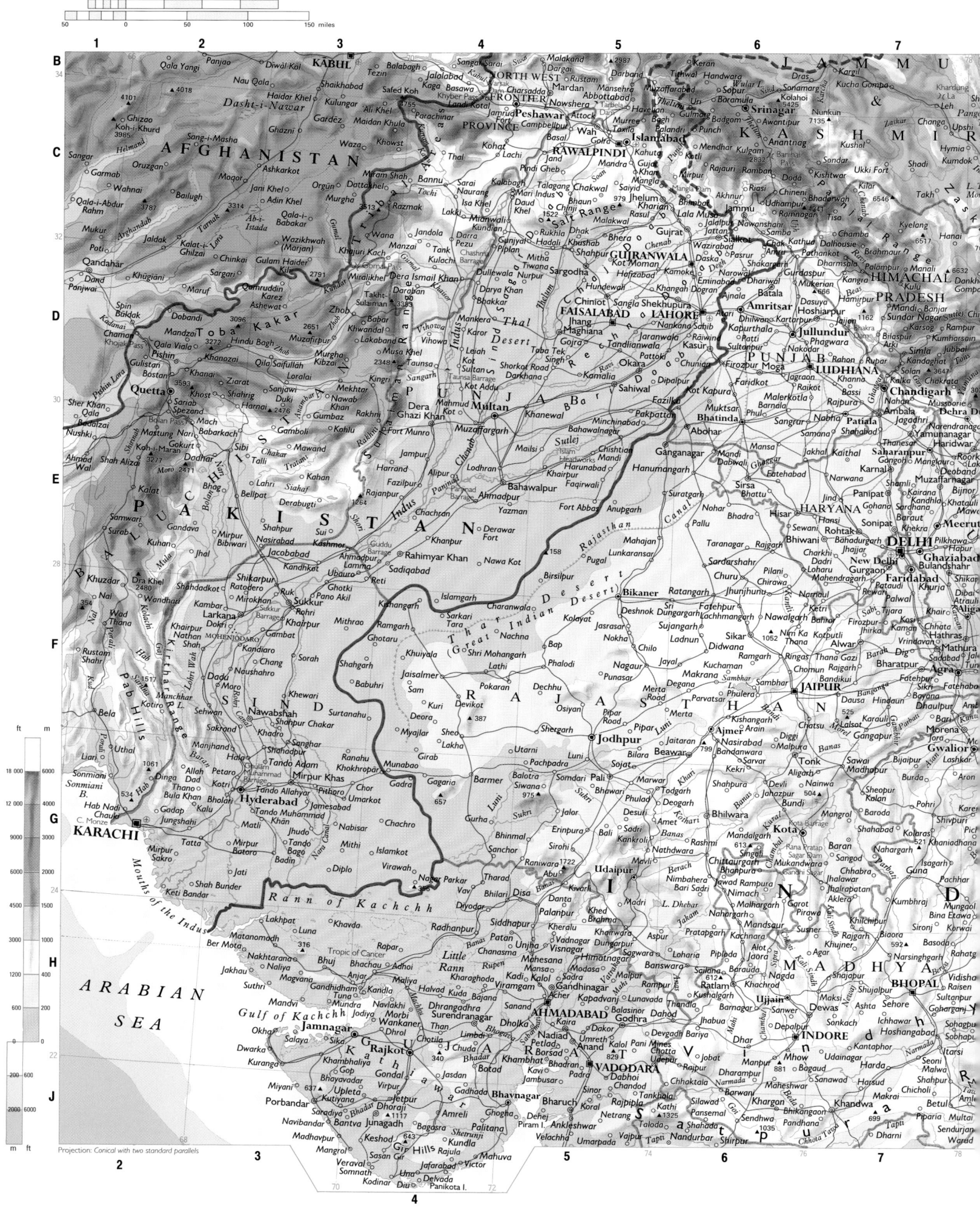

32
40
41
40

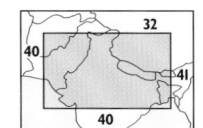

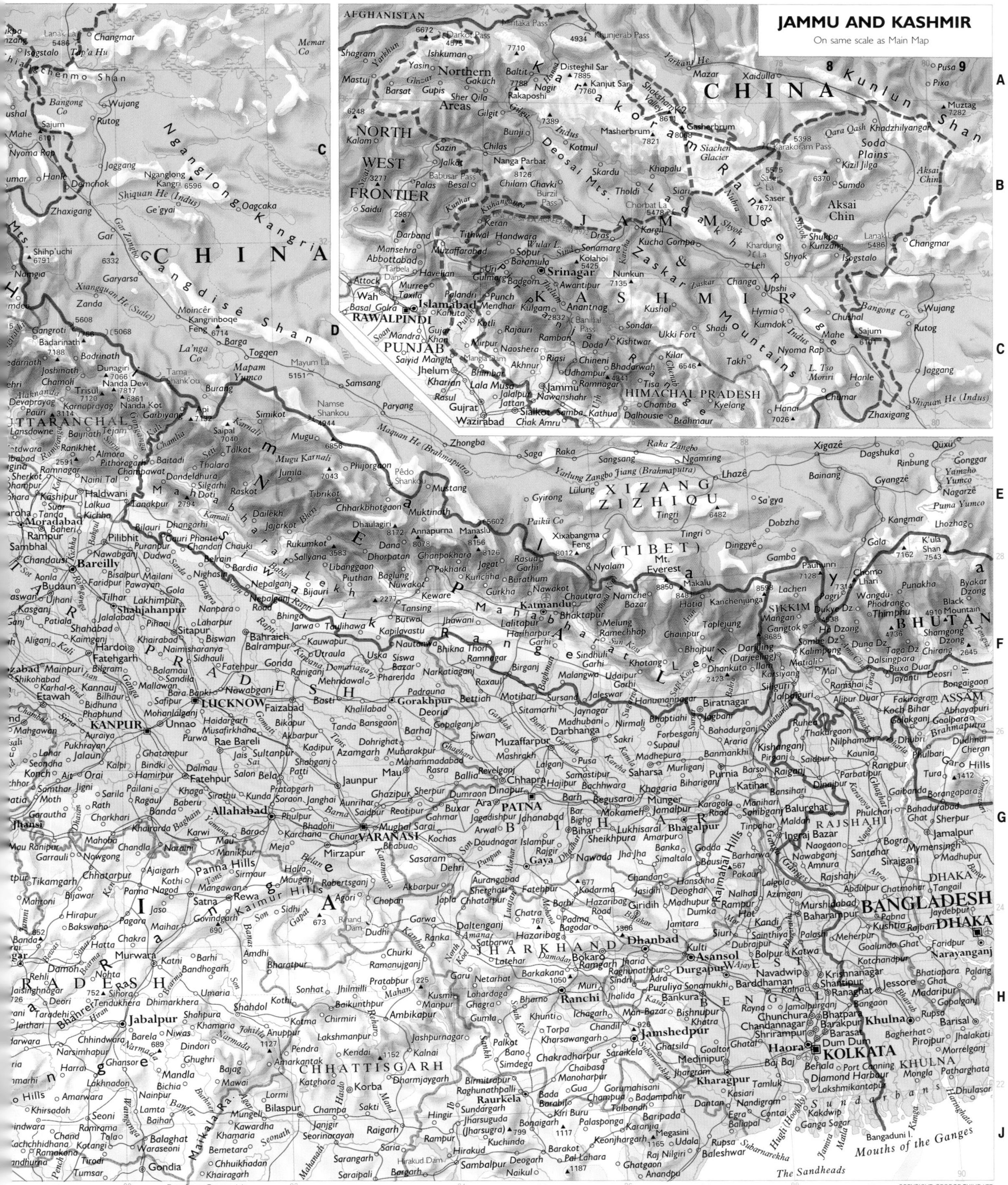

JAMMU AND KASHMIR
On same scale as Main Map
AFGHANISTAN
CHINA
Northern Areas
NORTH WEST FRONTIER
Karakoram Range
Deosai Mts.
Ladakh Range
Zaskar Mountains
JAMMU & KASHMIR
Srinagar
Islamabad
RAWALPINDI
PUNJAB
HIMACHAL PRADESH
Gilgit
Leh
Kargil
Jammu
Aksai Chin
Kunlun Shan
Gasherbrum
Siachen Glacier
Karakoram Pass
CHINA
Nganglong Kangri
Gangdisê Shan
UTTARANCHAL
NEPAL
XIZANG ZIZHIQU (TIBET)
Mt. Everest
Kathmandu
SIKKIM
BHUTAN
Thimphu
ASSAM
UTTAR PRADESH
LUCKNOW
KANPUR
Allahabad
VARANASI
BIHAR
PATNA
JHARKHAND
Ranchi
Dhanbad
Jamshedpur
WEST BENGAL
KOLKATA
Haora
BANGLADESH
DHAKA
Khulna
RAJSHAHI
Rajmahal Hills
Kaimur Hills
MADHYA PRADESH
Jabalpur
CHHATTISGARH
Bilaspur
Mouths of the Ganges
The Sandheads
Sundarbans
Yarlung Zangbo Jiang (Brahmaputra)
Ganga
Mahabharat Lekh
Siwalik Range
Jhansi
Bareilly
Moradabad
Gorakhpur
Darjeeling
Siliguri
Rewa
Satna
Gondia
East from Greenwich
8 9 10 5 6 7 8 9 10 11 12 13
A B C D E F G H J
COPYRIGHT GEORGE PHILIP LTD.

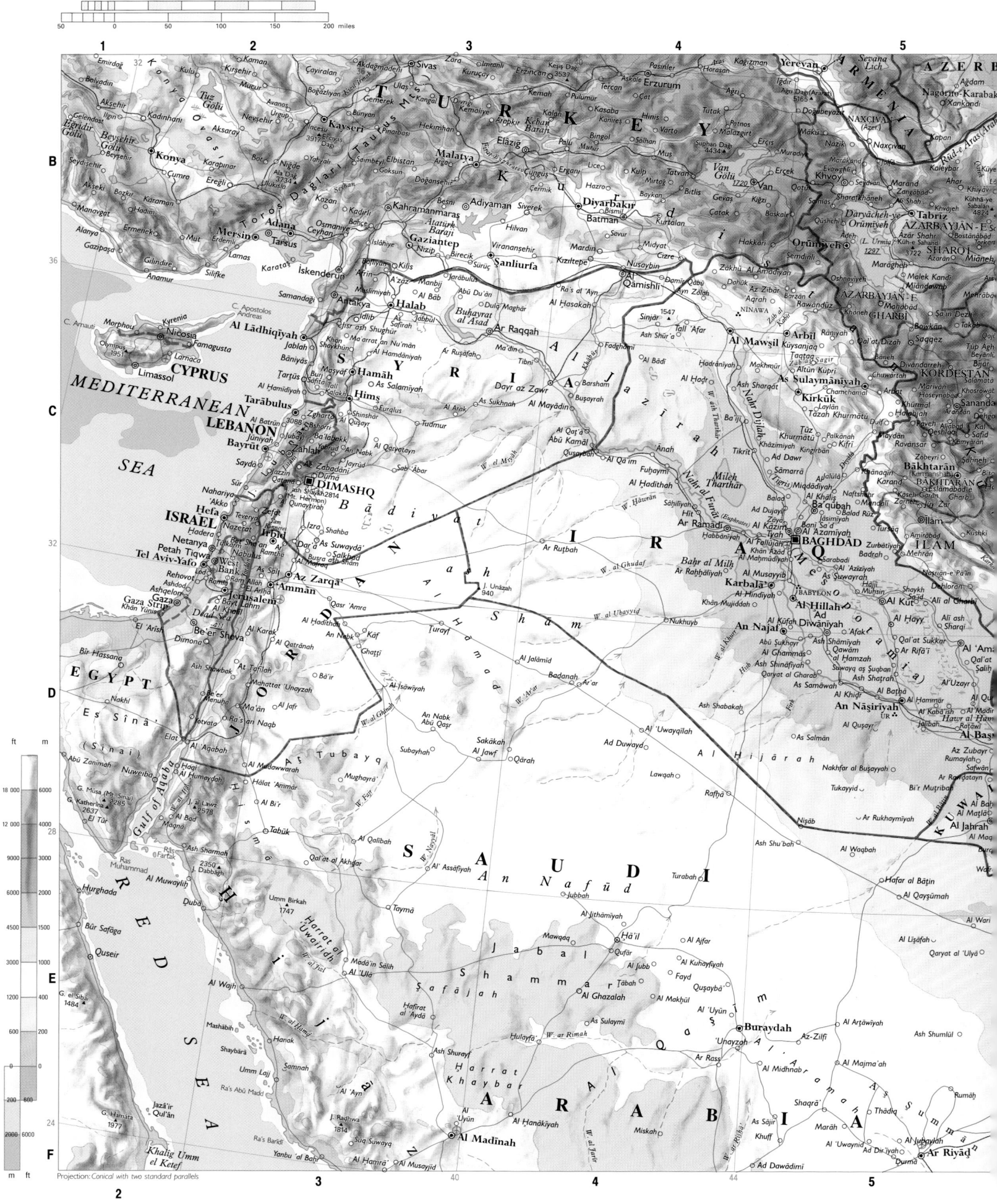

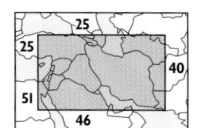

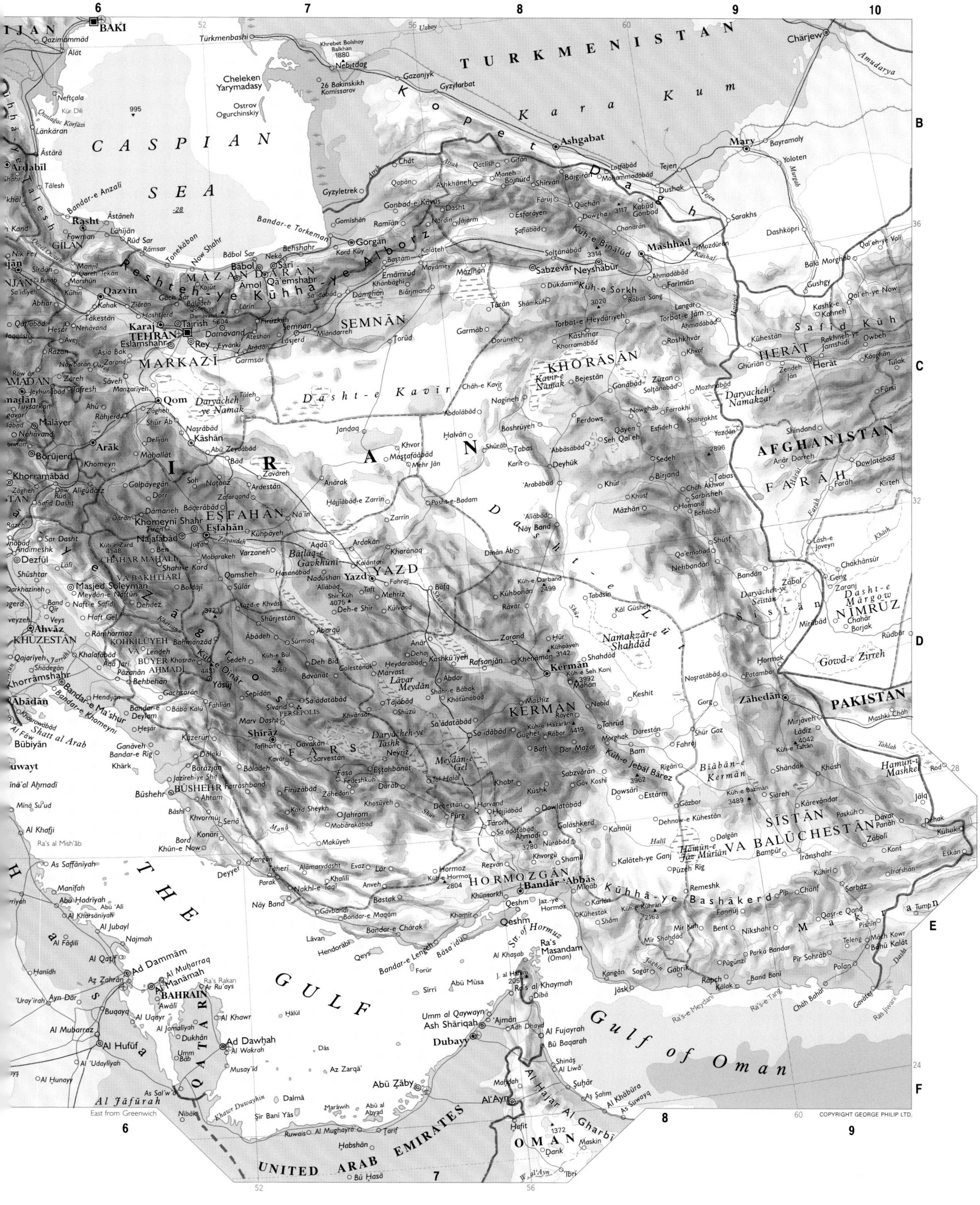

100 0 100 200 300 400 500 600 km
100 0 100 200 300 400 miles

1 2 3 4 5 6 7

LEBANON
BAYRŪT (BEIRUT)
SYRIA
DIMASHQ (DAMASCUS)
Jabal ad Duruz 1801
AFGHANISTAN
Khvor
I R A N
Birjand
Farāh
ISRAEL
Tel Aviv-Yafo
Hefa
AMMĀN
Ar Rutbah
BAGHDĀD
Kūh-ha
EŞFAHĀN
4548
Yazd
Dasht-e Lut
Ashdod
JORDAN
Jabal ad
Karbalā
Al Amarah
Ahvāz
Zābol
Jerusalem
West Bank
An Najaf
Nahr al Furāt
Khorramshahr
Kermān
Daryācheh-ye Seistan
Būr Sa'id (Port Said)
Gaza Strip
Ma'ān
An Nāşiriyah
Al Başrah
Ābādān
Zāgros
Qanā es Suweis
Isma'iliya
El Suweis (Suez)
Elat
Al 'Aqabah
Rafhā
Al-Kuwayt
J. Khārk
Kāzerūn
Shīrāz
PERSEPOLIS
Zāhedān
Bam
Neyriz
Es Sīnā'
G. Mūsa 2637
2578
Tabūk
Hafar al Bāţin
KUWAIT
Būshehr
Deyyer
Jahrom
Bandar 'Abbās
Bampūr
Hurghada
Būr Safāga
Al Muwayliḥ
An Nafūd
Hā'il
Hasa
Khamir
Qeshm
Str. of Hormuz
Ra's al-Khaymah
Ash Shāriqah
Gābrik
EGYPT
Qena
El Uqsur
Al Wajh
Buraydah
'Unayzah
Al Qatīf
Ad Dammām
BAHRAIN
Al Manāmah
QATAR
Ra's al-Khaymah (Oman)
Ra's Musandam
Maţraḥ
Masqat
Idfū
Kōm Ombo
SAUDI
Al Mubarraz
Al Hufūf
Ad Dawhā (Doha)
Dubayy (Dubai)
Abū Zaby (Abu Dhabi)
Şuḥār
Gulf of Oman
Aswān
Sadd el Aali
Ras Bānās
Bīr Shalatein
Al Madīnah
Tropic of Cancer
AR RIYĀD (RIYADH)
Harad
UNITED ARAB EMIRATES
Nazwā
3019
Şūr
Ras al Hadd
Buheirat en Naser
Wadi Halfa
Halaib
Ras Hadarba
Rābigh
ARABIA
Layla
Al 'Ubaylah
Khalūf
Khalīj Maşīrah
Es
Sahrâ
Delgo
3rd Cataract
Kosha
en
Nûbiya
2259
Muhammad Qol
MAKKAH (Mecca)
Aţ Ţā'if
2565
Al Lith
Turabah
As Sulayyil
Rub' al Khālī
(Empty Quarter)
Zufār
OMAN
Maşirah
Dongola
4th Cataract
Abu Hamed
JIDDAH (JEDDA)
RED
SEA
Asīr
Ra's al Madrakah
Kareima
Berber
5th Cataract
Nahr en Nil
Sinkat
Trinkitat
Karora
2180
Abhā
Jīzan
Farasān
Khamir
Shibām
Hadramawt
Salālah
Mirbāţ
J. Khuriyā Muriyā
Ed Debba
Atbara
Būr Sûdân
Suakin
Haiya
Wad Hamid
6th Cataract
Shendi
Adarama
Nakfa
Al Luhayyah
Khamir
2469
Sayḥūt
Rās Fartak
Kosti
Omdurmân
El Khartûm (Khartoum)
Kassalâ
Khashm el Girba
Akordat
Adigrat
Adwa
Massawa
Zula
Dahlak Kebir
Al Hudaydah
Kamaran
Sana'
Nişāb
Al Mukallā
YEMEN
SUDAN
El Gezira
Wad Medanî
Gedaref
Aksum
Mekele
Ras Dashen 4620
ERITREA
Hanīsh
Ta'izz
3360 Djebel Manar
Shaqrā
Ahwar
Ed Dueim
Umm Ruwaba
Singa
Gonder
Lalibela 4190
Danakil Desert
Aseb
Bab el Mandeb
Al Mukhā
Al' Adan (Aden)
Gulf of Aden
Abd al Kūri
Hadiboh
Socotra (Yemen)
Ed Damazin
Nil el Abyad
1830
Debre Tabor
Dese
Tendaho
Dikhil
Zeila
Karin
Bosaso
Ras Asir
Bereda
Ras Hafun
L. Tana
Bahir Dar
Bure
Debre Markos
L. Abbé
DJIBOUTI
Tadjoura
Djibouti
Berbera
Erigavo
2406
El Gal
Dante
Nekemte
ADDIS ABEBA
Debre Zevit
Awash
Dire Dawa
Hārer
Jijiga
Hargeisa
Burao
Gardo
Bender Beila
Malakâl
Sobat
Dembidolo
Metu
Gore
ETHIOPIA
Nazret
3381
Las Anod
Garoe
Eil
Sûdd
Bahr el Jebel
3202
L. Zwai
Asela
Ginir
Ogaden
Kebri Dehar
Galcaio
Obbia
Pibor Post
Jima
3686
Omo
Awasa
Yirga Alem
Shashemene
Goba
Mt. Batu 4307
Imi
Scebeli
Sinadogo
Bôr
Arba Minch
L. Abaya
Dila
Kibre Mengist
Negele
Genale
Ferfer
Belet Uen
El Dere
INDIAN
Juba
Tali Post
Mongalla
Kapoeta
Chew Bahir
Mega
Dolo
Lugh Ganana
Bur Acaba
Baidoa
OCEAN
Yei
Kajo Kaji
3187
Lokitaung
L. Turkana
Moyale
El Wak
Bardera
UGANDA
Arua
Gulu
Lira
Moroto
3084
Lodwar
South Horn
Marsabit
Wajir
Dif
SOMALI REP.
MUQDISHO (MOGADISHO)
Merca
Pakwach
Murchison Falls
L. Albert
Masindi
L. Kyoga
4321
Soroti
Mbale
Kitale
KENYA

Projection: Sanson-Flamsteed's Sinusoidal
East from Greenwich
COPYRIGHT GEORGE PHILIP LTD.

ft m
12 000 4000
9000 3000
6000 2000
4500 1500
3000 1000
1200 400
600 200
0 0
200 600
1000 3000
2000 6000
4000 12 000
m ft

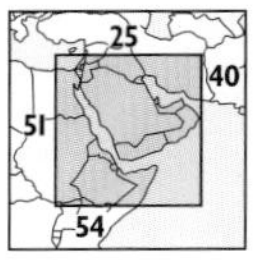

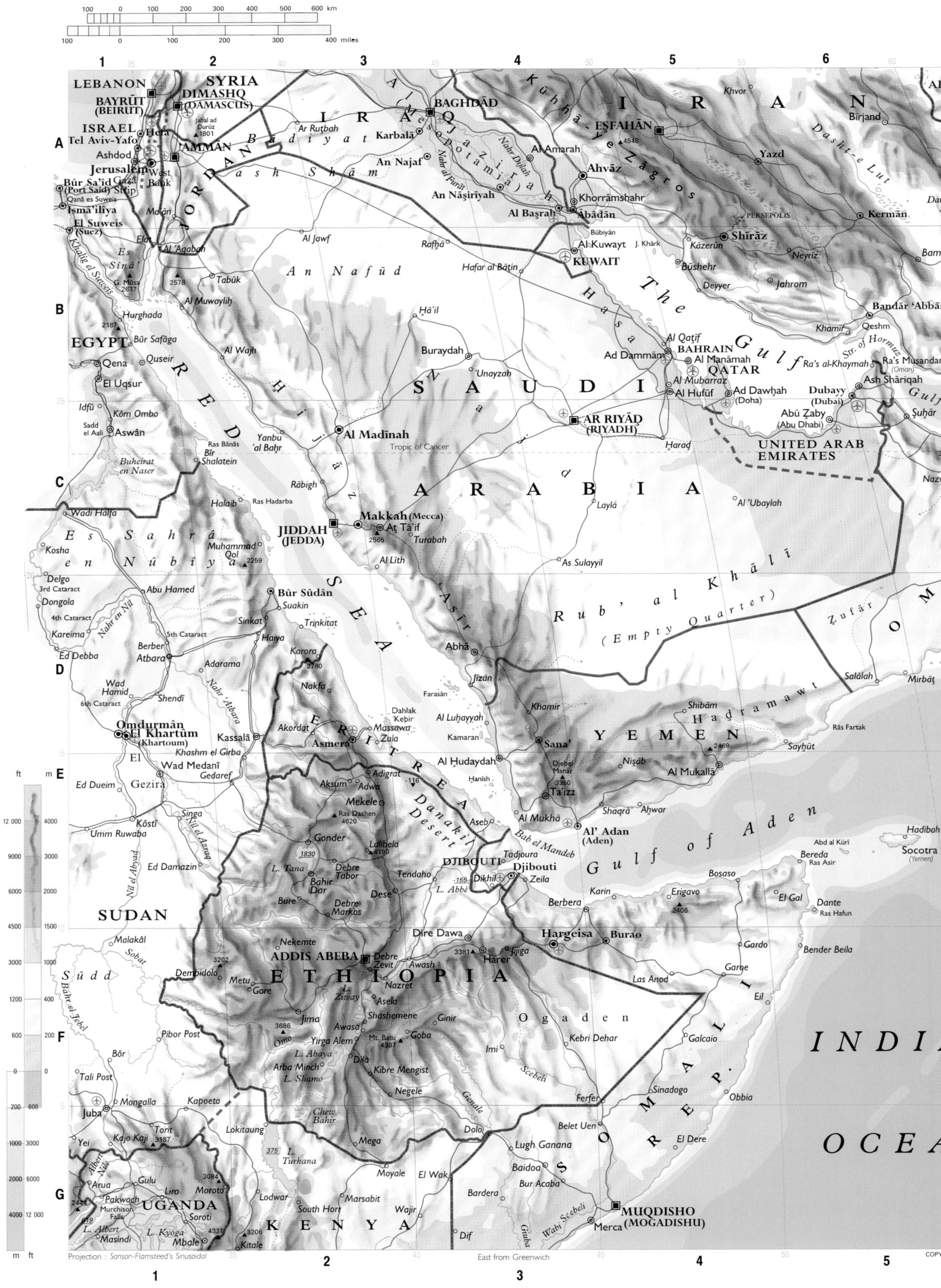

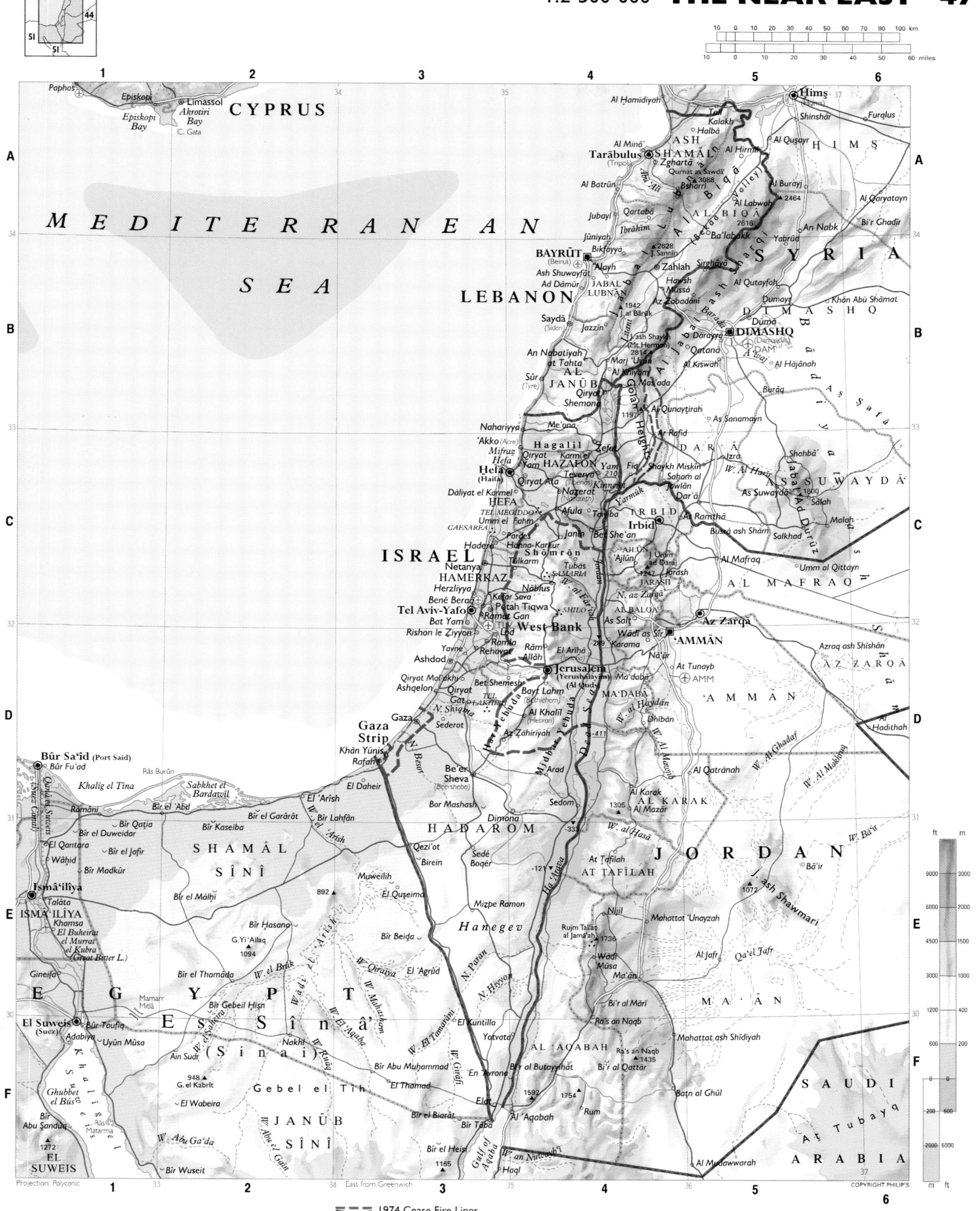

10 0 10 20 30 40 50 60 70 80 100 km

10 0 10 20 30 40 50 60 miles

CYPRUS

Paphos
Episkopi
Limassol
Akrotiri
Episkopi Bay
Bay
C. Gata

M E D I T E R R A N E A N

S E A

Al Ḥamidīyah
Ḥimṣ
Tall
Kalakh
Shinshār
Furqlus
ASH
Al Mīnā'
Halbā
Al Hirmil
Al Quṣayr
H I M Ṣ
Tarābulus
SHAMĀL
Zgharta
Qurnat as Sawdā
(Tripoli)
Bsharri
3088
Al Burayj
2464
Al Qaryatayn
Al Batrūn
Qartabā
Al Labwah
Bī'r Ghadīr
Jubayl
Ibrāhīm
Ba'labakk
Yabrūd
An Nabk
Jūniyah
Bikfayyā
2628
J. Sannīn
BAYRŪT
Zahlah
Sirghāyā
SYRIA
(Beirut)
Alayh
Dumayr
Khān Abū Shāmat
Ash Shuwayfāt
JABAL
Hawsh
Az Zabadānī
Ad Dāmūr
LUBNĀN
Mūssā
Al Qutayfah
DIMASHQ
1942
Dumā
LEBANON
J. al Bārūk
ash Shaykh
Darayyā
DAM
DIMASHQ
(Damascus)
Saydā
Jazzīn
Qaṭanā
Al Hājānah
(Sidon)
2814
Al Kiswah
Burāq
An Nabatīyah
(Mt. Hermon)
at Taḥta
Marj 'Uyūn
Al Khiyām
As Sanamayn
AL
1197
Al Qunayṭirah
Mas'ada
Sūr
JANŪB
Qiryat
(Tyre)
Shemona
Ar Rafid
DAR'Ā
Nahariyya
Me'ona
Izra
Shahbā
'Akko (Acre)
Zefat
Fiq
Shaykh Miskin
As Suwaydā
Hagalil
Qiryat
Karmi'el
Yam
210
Saham al
JABAL AD DURŪZ
Mifraz
Teverya
Jawlān
Dar'ā
1800
Hefa
HAZAFON
Kinneret
Salah
Qiryat Ata
Nazerat
AS SUWAYDĀ
Hefa
(Nazareth)
Yarmūk
(Haifa)
Afula
IRBID
Malah
Dāliyat el Karmel
Ṭayiba
Bet She'an
Al Ramthā
Salkhad
HEFA
TEL MEGIDDO
Irbid
Busrá ash Shām
CAESAREA
Janīn
AJLŪN
Umm el Fahm
Al Mafraq
Pardes
Ajlūn
Umm al Qiṭṭayn
Hadera
Shōmrōn
Umm
Hanna-Karkur
SAMARIA
ad Dami
Tulkarm
Jarash
AL MAFRAQ
ISRAEL
Nāblus
4247
JARASH
Netanya
Tubas
N. az Zarqā
Herzliyya
HAMERKAZ
Benē Beraq
SHILOH
AL BALQĀ
Kefar Sava
As Salt
Tel Aviv-Yafo
Petaḥ Tiqwa
Wādī as Sīr
'AMMĀN
Ramat Gan
Karama
Az Zarqā
Bat Yam
TIL
Rishon le Ziyyon
West Bank
299
Ma'daba
Yavne
Ramla
Rām
El Arīha
Na'ūr
AZ ZARQĀ
Rehovot
Allāh
(Jericho)
At Tunayb
AMM
Ashdod
Jerusalem
Ma'daba
(Yerushalayim)
Qiryat Mol'akhi
Bet Shemesh
(Al Quds)
MA'DABA
'AMMĀN
Ashqelon
Qiryat
Bayt Laḥm
Al Huydān
Gat
(Bethlehem)
Dhibān
Gaza
N. Shiqma
TEL
Al Khalīl
W. Huydān
Gaza
LAKHISH
(Hebron)
Strip
Sederot
Az Zāhirīyah
411
Khān Yūnis
Arad
Rafah
Be'er
Bûr Sa'îd (Port Said)
Sheva
Al Karak
Bûr Fu'ad
(Beersheba)
AL KARAK
Khalīg el Tîna
Ras Burûn
Bor Mashash
Al Mazar
Ramânî
Sabkhet el
El Daheir
Sedom
Bir el 'Abd
Bardawîl
Dimona
1305
Bir el Garârât
El 'Arîsh
333
Bir Qaṭia
Bir Lahfân
HADAROM
Bir el Duweidar
Bir Kaseiba
J O R D A N
El Qantara
Bir el Jafir
Qezi'ot
At Ṭafîlah
Wâḥid
Bir Madkûr
SHAMĀL
Sedé
AT ṬAFÎLAH
Ismâ'ilîya
SÎNÎ
892
Boqér
Bâ'ir
Talâta
Birein
1072
ISMĀ'ILÎYA
Bir el Mâlḥi
Muweilih
Mizpe Ramon
J. ash Shawmari
Khamsa
El Buheirat
Bir Ḥasana
Mahattat 'Unayzah
el Murrat
H a n e g e v
el Kubra
G.Yi'Allaq
Bir Beiḍa
Rujm Talla'
(Great Bitter L.)
1094
al Jama'ah
1738
Gineifa
Bir el Thamâda
W. el Brûk
Al Jafr
Wâdī
Qa'el Jafr
El Suweis
Bir el Tharnâda
W. Qiraiya
El 'Agrûd
Mûsa
Ma'ân
(Suez)
N. Puran
Ma'ân
Adabiya
Mamarr
Bir Gebeil Hisn
N. Ḥiyyon
M A 'Ā N
Uyûn Mûsa
Mitlâ
E G Y P T
Bi'r al Mârî
El Suweis
Ain Sudr
Nakhl
El Kuntilla
Ra's an Naqb
Gulf of
W. el 'Aqaba
Yotvata
AL 'AQABAH
Mahattat ash Shīdīyah
Khalîg el Suweis
948
W. Ruqá
Bi'r al Butayyiḥāt
G. el Kabrît
En 'Avrona
Bi'r al Qaṭṭar
Ghubbet
E S **S Î N Â**
1435
el Bûs
El Thamad
Bī'r al Mârî
Batn al Ghûl
(Sinai)
1592
1754
S A U D I
Bir
Bir el Biarât
Rum
Abu Sandûq
El Wabeira
Elat
Ras
J A N Û B
Bîr el Heisi
Al Mudawwarah
A R A B I A
Matarma
1272
EL
Bîr Taba
1165
Haql
At Ṭubayq
SUWEIS
SÎNÎ
W. Abu Ga'da
W. el Gain
Bîr Wuseit

ft m

9000 3000

6000 2000

4500 1500

3000 1000

1200 400

600 200

0 0

200 600

2000 6000

m ft

Projection: Polyconic

East from Greenwich

COPYRIGHT PHILIP'S

=== 1974 Cease Fire Lines

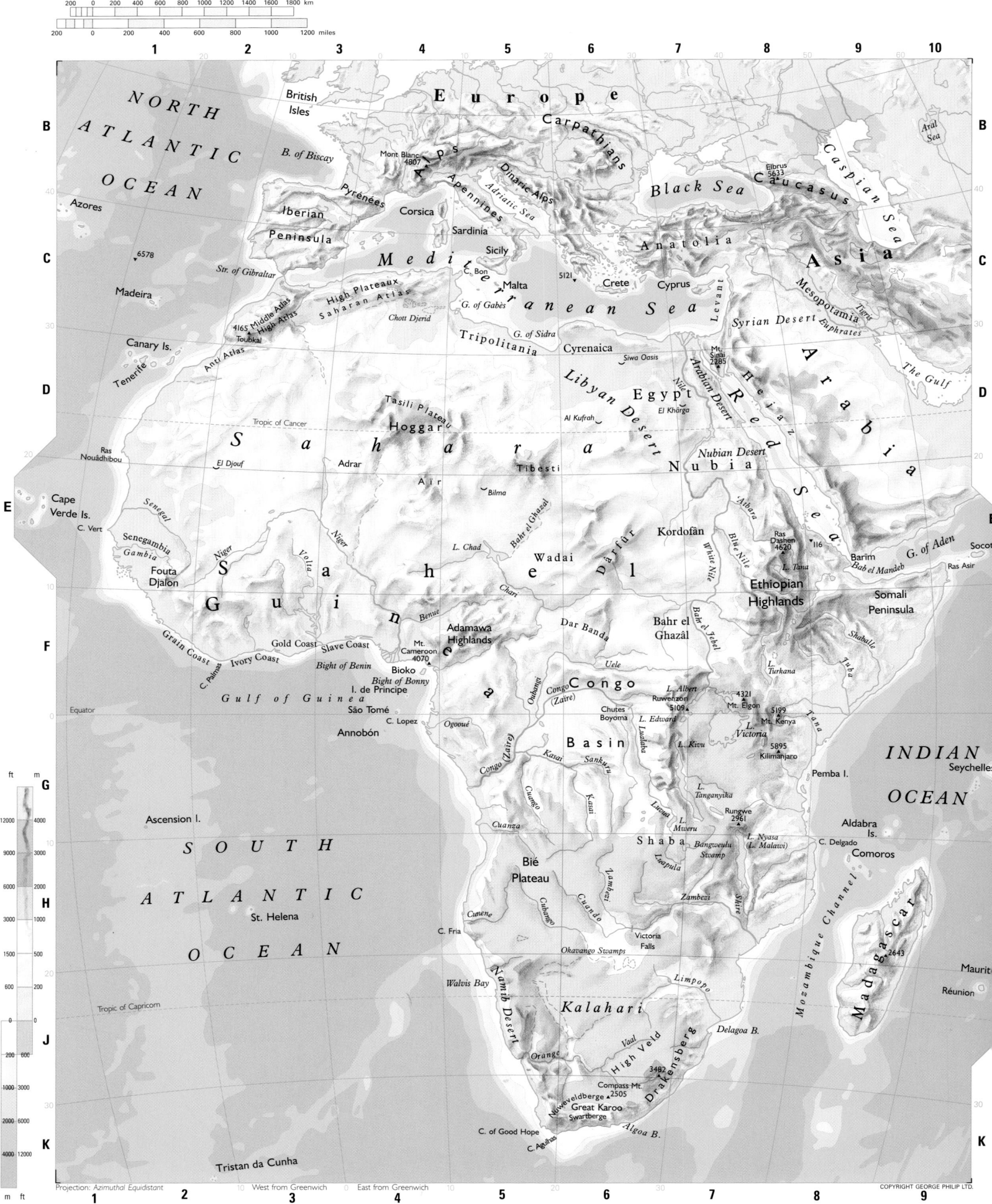

200 0 200 400 600 800 1000 1200 1400 1600 1800 km
200 0 200 400 600 800 1000 1200 miles

NORTH
ATLANTIC
OCEAN

British Isles
Europe
Carpathians
Aral Sea

B. of Biscay
Mont Blanc 4807
ALPS
Elbrus 5633
Caspian Sea
Black Sea
Caucasus

Azores
Pyrénées
Apennines
Dinaric Alps
Adriatic Sea
Anatolia
Asia

Iberian Peninsula
Corsica
Sardinia
Sicily
C. Bon
Malta
5121
Crete
Cyprus
Levant
Mesopotamia
Tigris

6578
Str. of Gibraltar
Mediterranean Sea
Syrian Desert
Euphrates

Madeira
High Plateaux
Saharan Atlas
4165 Middle Atlas
High Atlas
Toubkal
Chott Djerid
G. of Gabès
G. of Sidra
Tripolitania
Cyrenaica
Siwa Oasis
Libyan Desert
Egypt
Arabian Desert
Mt. Sinai 2285
Hejaz
Red Sea
Arabia
The Gulf

Canary Is.
Tenerife
Anti Atlas
Tropic of Cancer
Tasili Plateau
Hoggar
Al Kufrah
El Khârga
Nubian Desert
Nubia

Ras Nouâdhibou
Sahara
El Djouf
Adrar
Aïr
Tibesti
Darfûr
Kordofân
'Atbara
Ras Dashen 4620
116
Barim
Bab el Mandeb
G. of Aden
Ras Asir
Socot

Cape Verde Is.
C. Vert
Senegal
Niger
Bilma
L. Chad
Bahr el Ghazal
Wadai
Sahel
White Nile
Blue Nile
L. Tana
Somali Peninsula

Senegambia
Gambia
Fouta Djalon
Niger
Volta
Sudan
Guinea
Benue
Chari
Dar Banda
Ethiopian Highlands
Shabelle

Grain Coast
Ivory Coast
C. Palmas
Gold Coast
Slave Coast
Bight of Benin
Mt. Cameroon 4070
Adamawa Highlands
Uele
Bahr el Ghazâl
L. Turkana
Juba

Bioko
Bight of Bonny
I. de Principe
São Tomé
C. Lopez
Annobón
Ogooué
Ubangi
Congo (Zaïre)
Congo Basin
Chutes Boyoma
L. Albert
Ruwenzori 5109
Mt. Elgon 4321
5199 Mt. Kenya
Tana

Equator
Kasai
Lualaba
L. Edward
L. Kivu
L. Victoria
5895 Kilimanjaro
Pemba I.
INDIAN OCEAN
Seychelles

Ascension I.
Sankuru
L. Tanganyika
Rungwe 2961
L. Nyasa (L. Malawi)
Aldabra Is.
C. Delgado
Comoros

SOUTH
ATLANTIC
OCEAN
St. Helena
Cuango
Cuanza
Kasai
Bié Plateau
Shaba
Mweru
Luapula
Lualaba
Bangweulu Swamp
Zambezi
Shire
Mozambique Channel
Madagascar 2643
Maurit
Réunion

Cunene
C. Fria
Cubango
Cuando
Zambezi
Victoria Falls
Okavango Swamps
Walvis Bay
Limpopo
Delagoa B.

Tropic of Capricorn
Namib Desert
Kalahari
Orange
Vaal
High Veld
Drakensberg 3482
Compass Mt. 2505
Nieuveldberge
Great Karoo
Swartberge
C. of Good Hope
C. Agulhas
Algoa B.

Tristan da Cunha

ft m
12000 4000
9000 3000
6000 2000
3000 1000
1500 500
600 200
0 0
200 600
1000 3000
2000 6000
4000 12000
m ft

Projection: Azimuthal Equidistant

West from Greenwich   East from Greenwich

⊙ Dakar Capital Cities

COPYRIGHT GEORGE PHILIP LTD.

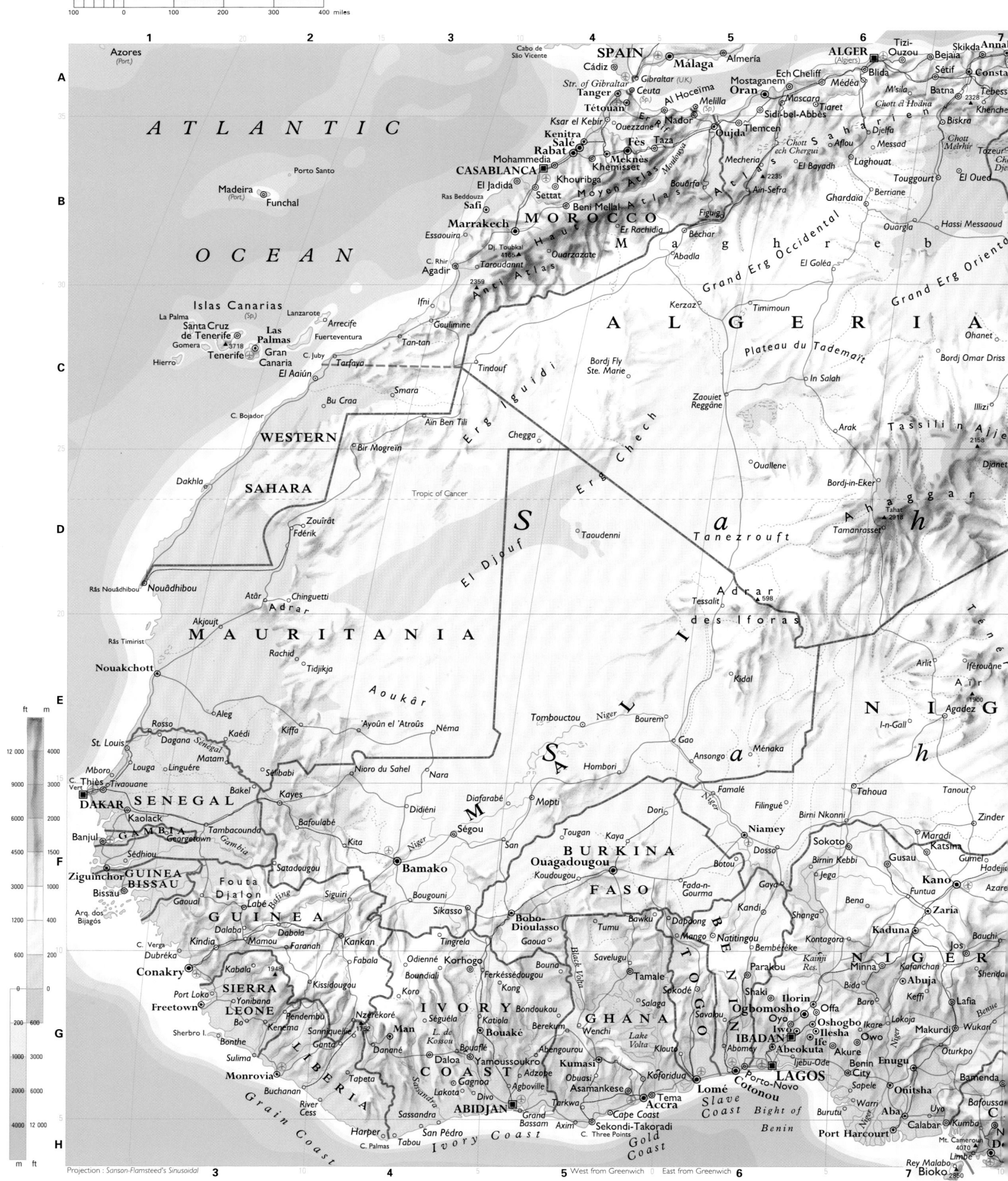

Projection : Sanson-Flamsteed's Sinusoidal
West from Greenwich East from Greenwich Bioko

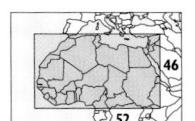

8　　9　　10　　11　　12　　13　　14

Bizerte　Ariana
CARTHAGE
TUNIS　Nabeul
Beja　Sousse
Irouan　Mahdia
Sicilia
GREECE
Ródhos
Kríti
● Antalya　**TURKEY**　● **ADANA**
Al Lādhiqiyah　Antakya　■ **HALAB**
CYPRUS　Nicosia
SYRIA
A

Sfax
Golfe de Gabès　Île de Djerba
Gabès
Médenine　Zarzis
atahouine
Dehibat

M E D I T E R R A N E A N   S E A

Tarābulus　Hims
LEBANON
BAYRŪT　**DIMASHQ**
(Beirut)　(Damascus)
Jabal ad
Durúz
ISRAEL
Tel Aviv-Yafo　Hefa
Ashdod　Jerusalem　**AMMAN**
West
Bank
■ Ar Ruţbah
IRAQ
Bādiyat
ash Shām
B

Zuwārah　**Tarābulus** (Tripoli)
Az Zāwiyah　Al Khums
● Gharyān　Misrātah
968
Mizdah
Daraj
Ghudāmis

Zāwiyat al Baydā　Darnah
Banghāzī　Al Marj
Suluq
Surt　Khalīj
Surt
Ajdābiyā

Tubruq
Bardiyah　Salūm　**EL ISKANDARĪYA**
(Alexandria)
Marsá
Matrūh　El Alamein
Damanhūr
El Mahalla el Kubra
Dumyât　Bûr Sa'id
Tanta
Zagazig　**El Mansûra**
Qanā es Suweis　Ismā'iliya
Ma'ān
Al Jawf

Tripolitania

L I B Y A

Cyrenaica

Al Jaghbūb

Sahrâ'
Sîwa　-133　Munkhafed
el Qattâra
El Faiyûm
El GIZA　● El Suweis
Helwân
Beni Suef
Maghâgha
El Minyâ
Mallawi
Manfalût
Es Sahrâ
Esh Sharqîya
EL QAHIRA (Cairo)

Hün
Zillah
Awjilah

Idehan-
awbārī
Brach
Sabhah
Awbārī
● 1200
Marzūq
Wāw al Kabīr

Fezzan

Sahrâ'
L î b î y a
Qasr Farâfra
El Wâhât
el-Dakhla
Mût
El Khârga
El Wâhât
el-Khârga

E G Y P T
Asyût　2187
Tahta
Sohâg
Girga　Qena
KARNAK
THEBES　**El Uqsur**
Idfû
Kom Ombo
Sadd el Aali
● **Aswân**

Es　Sinâ'
G. Mûsa
2637
2578　● Tabūk
Al Muwayliḥ
Hurghada
Bûr Safâga
Quseir

SAUDI
ARABIA
Al Wajh
C

Al Jawf
Al 'Aqabah
Elat
Khalîg el Suweis
RED

Ghat　Al Qaţrūn
Sahrâ'
Rebiana　Al Jawf
Al Kufrah

a　r
Aozou
Strip
Toummo
Madama
Bardai
Pic Toussidé
3265
Aozou
3150
Târso Emissi
Ma'tan
as Sarra
● 1082
J. Uweinat
1893
ABU SIMBEL
Wadi Halfa
Buheirat
en Naser
Bîr
Shalatein
Ras Bânâs
Halaib
Ras Hadarba
Râbigh
Yanbu
'al Bahr
H i j â z
SEA
D

Chirfa
Tibesti
Zouar
Emi Koussi
3415

El Wâhât
el Selîma

Es　Sahrâ
en　Nûbîya　2259
Muhammad
Qol

Fachi　Bilma
Grand Erg du Bilma
Borkou
Erg du Djourab
Ounianga Sérir
Dépression du Mourdi
Faya-Largeau
Fada　1310
Ennedi
Zagaoua
Oum Chalouba

3rd Cataract
Delgo
Dongola
Bir 'Atrun
Ed Debba
Kareima　4th Cataract
5th Cataract
Abu Hamed
Berber　Adarama
Atbara
Bûr
Sûdân
Suakin
Sinkat
Trinkitat
Haiya
Karora
2180
Nakfa
ERITREA
Akordat
E

E R　e

C H A D

Zigey
Nguigmi
Bosso
Gashua
Iguru　Geidam
Maiduguri
Potiskum
Bama
Bajoga
Kumo
mbe

Lac Tchad
Mao
Massakory
Ati
Ndjamena
Kousseri
Massenya
Maroua
Biu
Mubi
Guider
Bongor

Biltine
Abéché
Oum Hadjer
Mongo
Goz Beida
Am Timan

Al
Junaynah
Zalingei
1954
Kutum
Dârfûr
Jebel
Mara
3088
Nyâlâ
El Fâsher
En Nahud
El Odaiya

Sodiri
Umm
Keddada
Kordofân
El Obeid
Abû
Zabad
Er Rahad
Umm Ruwaba

S U D A N
El Wuz
Malha
Omdurmân
El Khartûm
(Khartoum)
Wad
Hamid
Shendî
6th Cataract
Kassalâ
Khashm el Girba
El
Gezira
Wâd Medanî
Gedaref
Ed Dueim
Kôstî
Singa
Ed Damazin
Kâdugli　1325

Gonder
1830
L. Tana
Bahir
Dar
Bure
Debre
Markos
Nekemte
ETHIOPIA
F

ultoum
Chari

A
Numan
Yola
Garoua
Pala
Moundou
Doba
Laï
Koumra
Sarh
Birao
Songo
1226
Sa'id
Bundas
Bahr el Arab
Bahr el
Jur
Bahr el
Ghazâl
Malakâl
Sobat
Gogriâl
Wâw
Tonj
Raga
Rumbêk
Sûdd
Bahr el Jebel
3202
Dembidolo
Metu
Gore
Jima
3686
Omo
G

Baïbokoum
Ngaoundéré
Paoua
Bossangoa
Bouar
Bozoum
Kaga Bandoro
CENTRAL AFRICAN
REPUBLIC
Yalinga
Ippy
Bakouma
Obo
El　Istiwa'iya
Yâmbiô
Juba
Pibor Post
Bôr
Toinya
Tali Post
Amâdi
Mongalla
Kapoeta
L. Abaya
Arba Minch
L. Shamo
Chew
Bahir

Gashaka
Banyo
assif de
amaoua
Bertoua
Nanga-
Eboko
Abong-Mbang
EROON
Yoko
Yaoundé
Bétaré
Oya
Bouar
Carnot
Berbérati
Mbaïki
Bossembélé
Bozoum
Bambari
Bangassou
Mobaye
Mobayi
Bondo
Uele
Bangui
Zongo
Bosobolo
Libenge
Bomu
Ango
Dungu
Faradje
Yei
Kajo Kaji
Torit
Lokitaung
L. Turkana
375
H

8　　9　　10　　11　　12　　13

COPYRIGHT GEORGE PHILIP LTD.

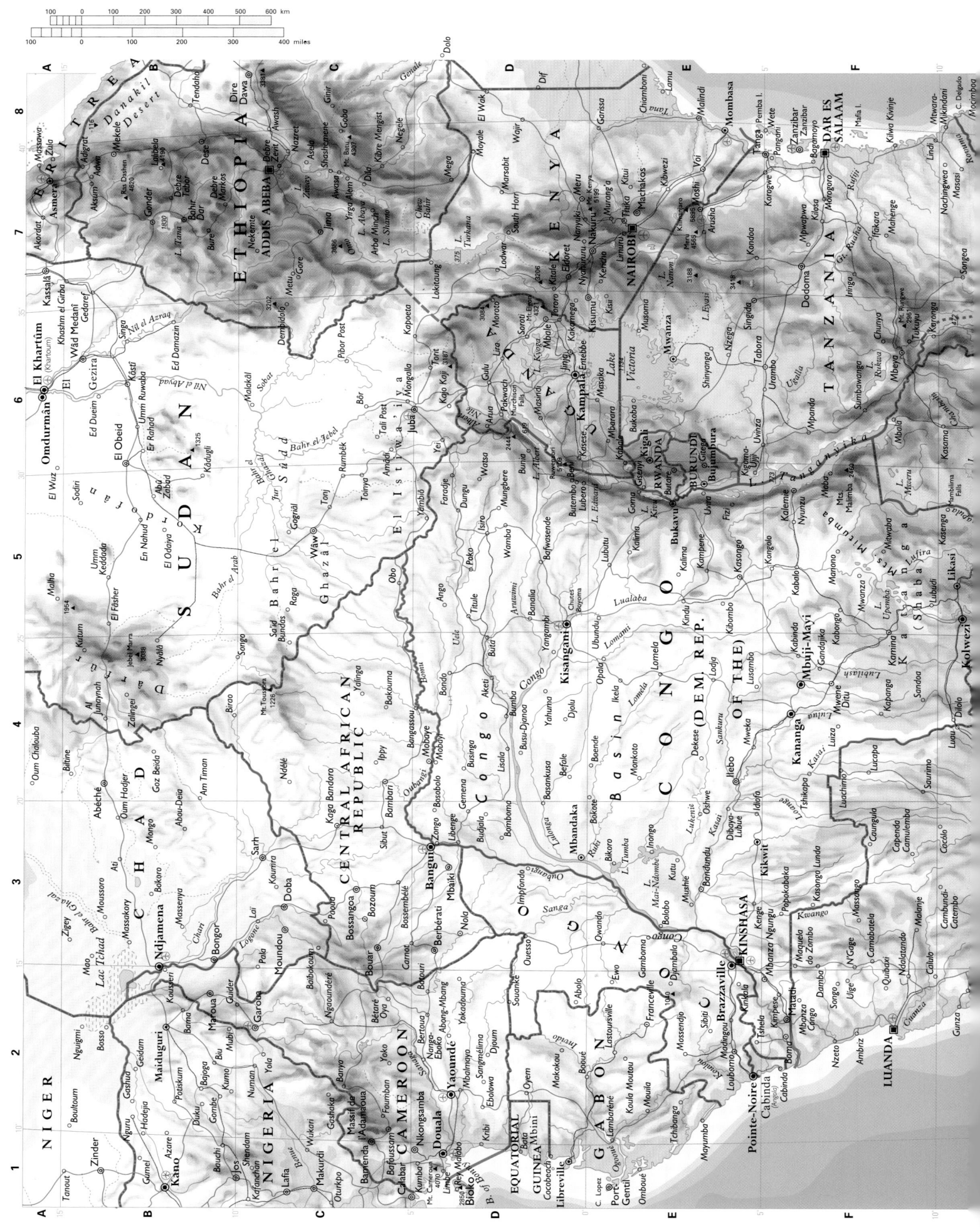

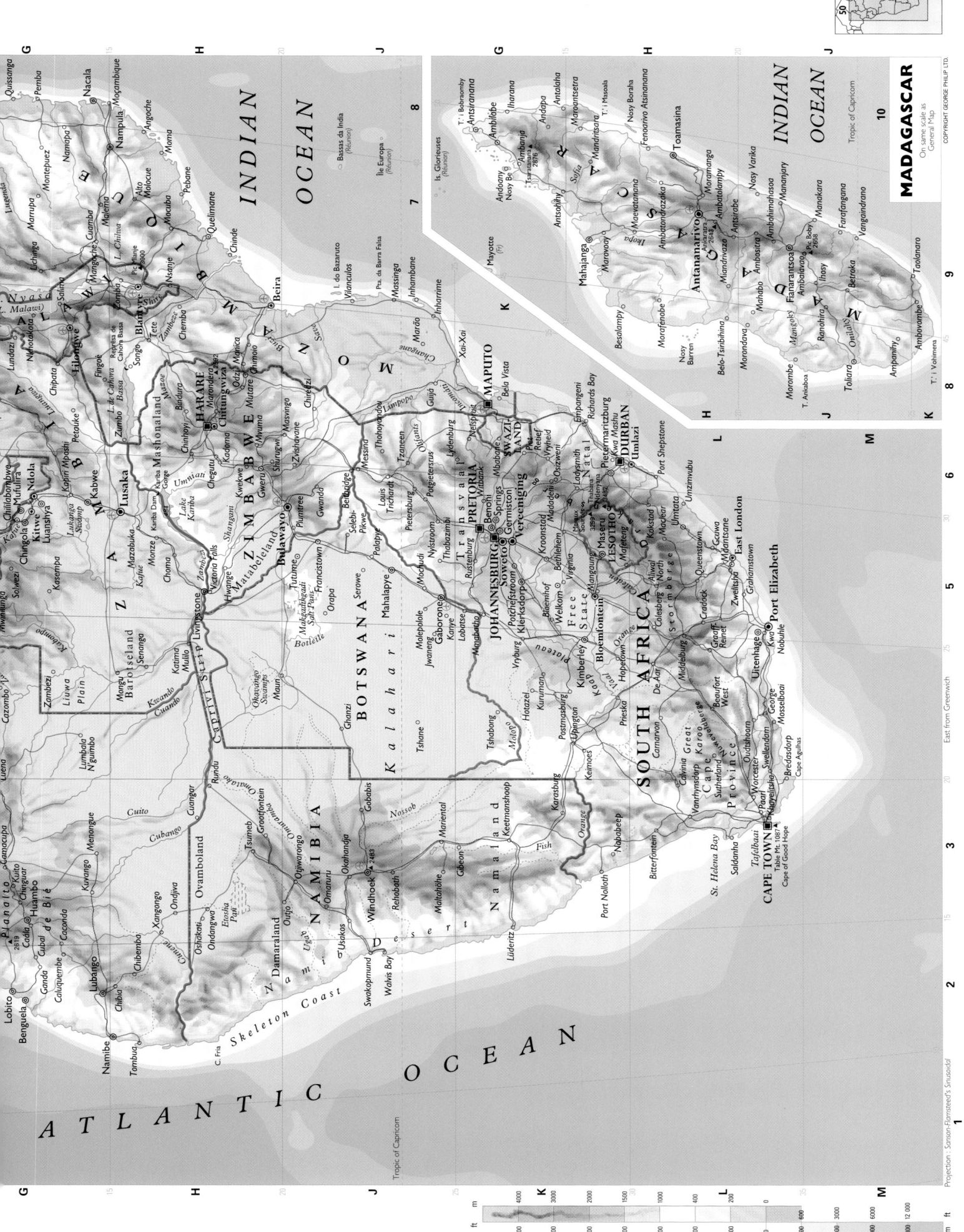

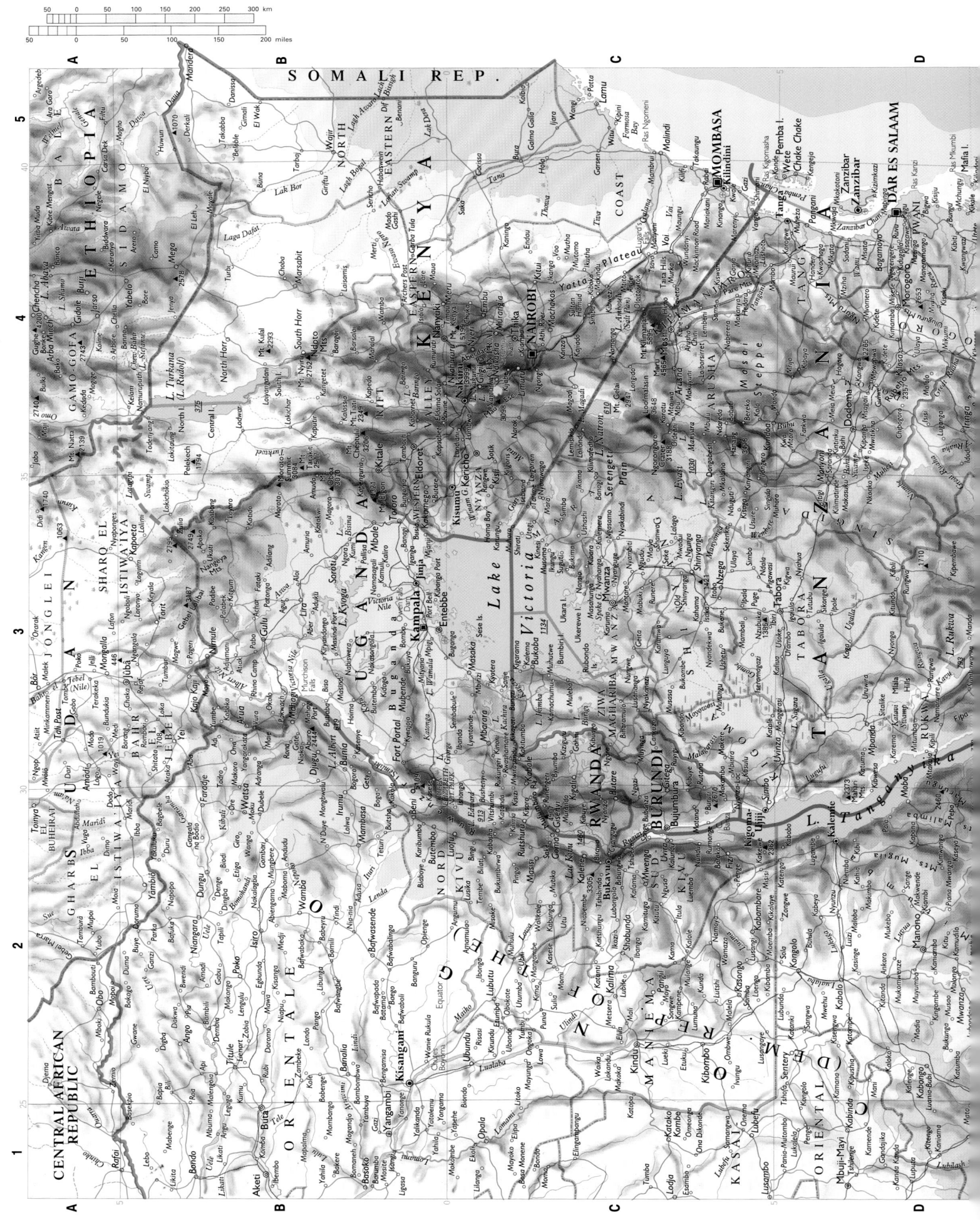

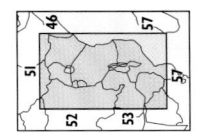

INDIAN OCEAN

L. Nyasa Malawi

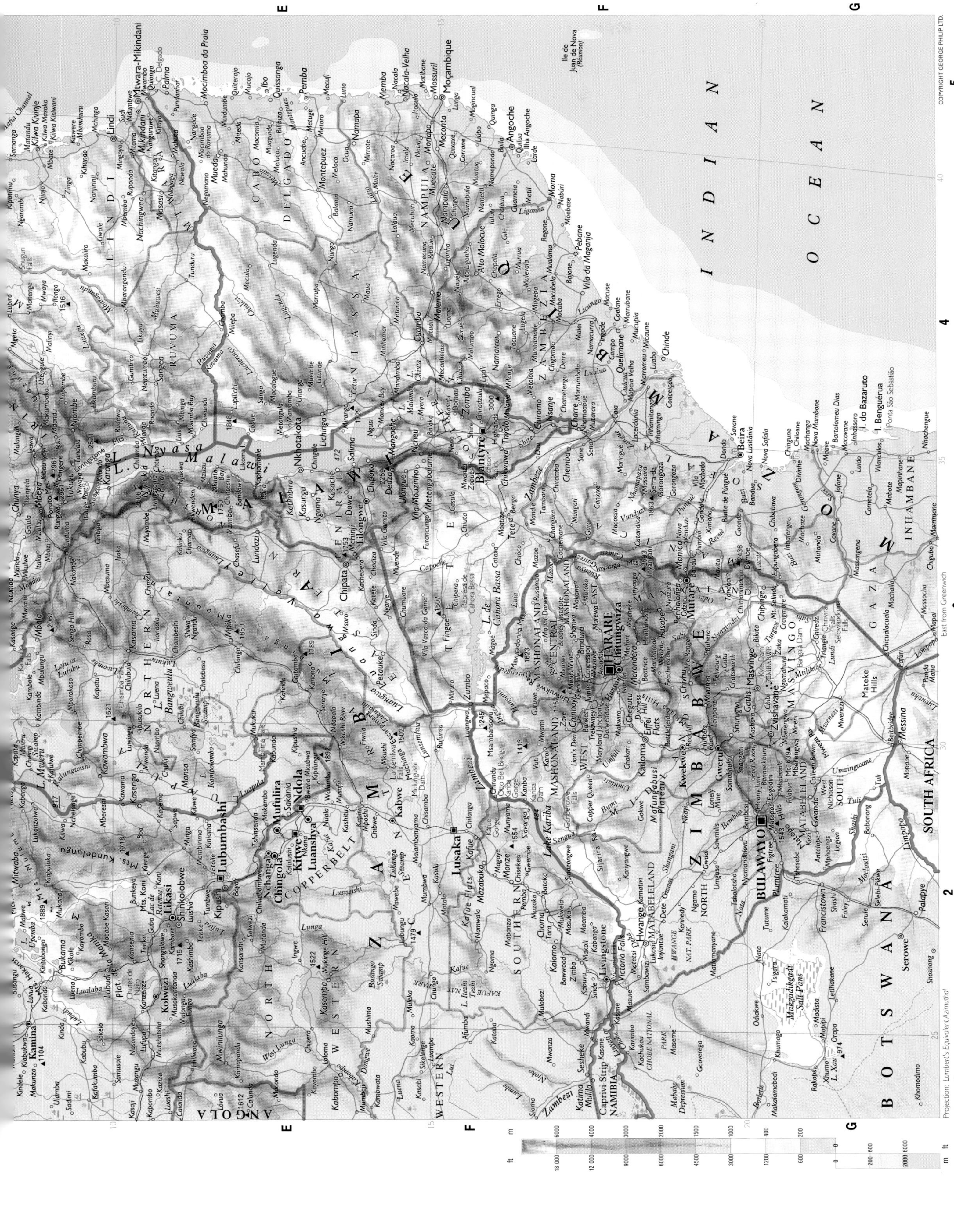

MOZAMBIQUE

ZAMBIA

ZIMBABWE

BOTSWANA

SOUTH AFRICA

ANGOLA

NAMIBIA

MALAWI

TANZANIA

HARARE
BULAWAYO
Lusaka
Lubumbashi
Blantyre
Beira
Lilongwe
Mutare
Livingstone
Victoria Falls
Ndola
Kitwe
Chingola
Likasi
Kolwezi

Projection: Lambert's Equidistant Azimuthal

East from Greenwich

ft   m   m   ft
6000 18 000
      12 000
4000
3000 9000
2000 6000
1500 4500
1000 3000
      1200   400   600
      600   200   200
      0   0   0
                     2000
                     6000

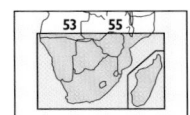

53 55

B

MOZAMBIQUE

CHANNEL

MALAWI

ZAMBEZIA

Ile de Júan de Nova
(Fr.)

TETE

MASHONALAND
WEST

MASHONALAND
CENTRAL

MASHONALAND
EAST

HARARE
Chitungwiza

ZIMBABWE

BELELAND

BULAWAYO

MATABELELAND
SOUTH

MASVINGO

C H A N N E L

Is. Glorieuses
(Fr.)

Antsiranana

ANTSIR-
ANANA

Mahajanga

MADAGASCAR

M O Z A M B I Q U E   C H A N N E L

Beira

NORTHERN

KRUGER
NATIONAL
PARK

Messina

PRETORIA
JOHANNESBURG
Benoni
Springs

MPUMALANGA

SWAZILAND

Maputo

MAPUTO

Vereeniging

ANTANANARIVO

Antananarivo

Antsirabe

Toamasina

KWAZULU
NATAL

Empangeni
Richards Bay

Pietermaritzburg

KwaMashu
DURBAN
Umlazi

EASTERN
CAPE

Fianarantsoa
FIANARANTSOA

ESOTHO

INDIAN

OCEAN

East London

M O Z A M B I Q U E

INDIAN

OCEAN

Toliara

Taolanaro

Tropic of Capricorn

MADAGASCAR

On same scale as General Map

COPYRIGHT GEORGE PHILIP LTD.

East from Greenwich

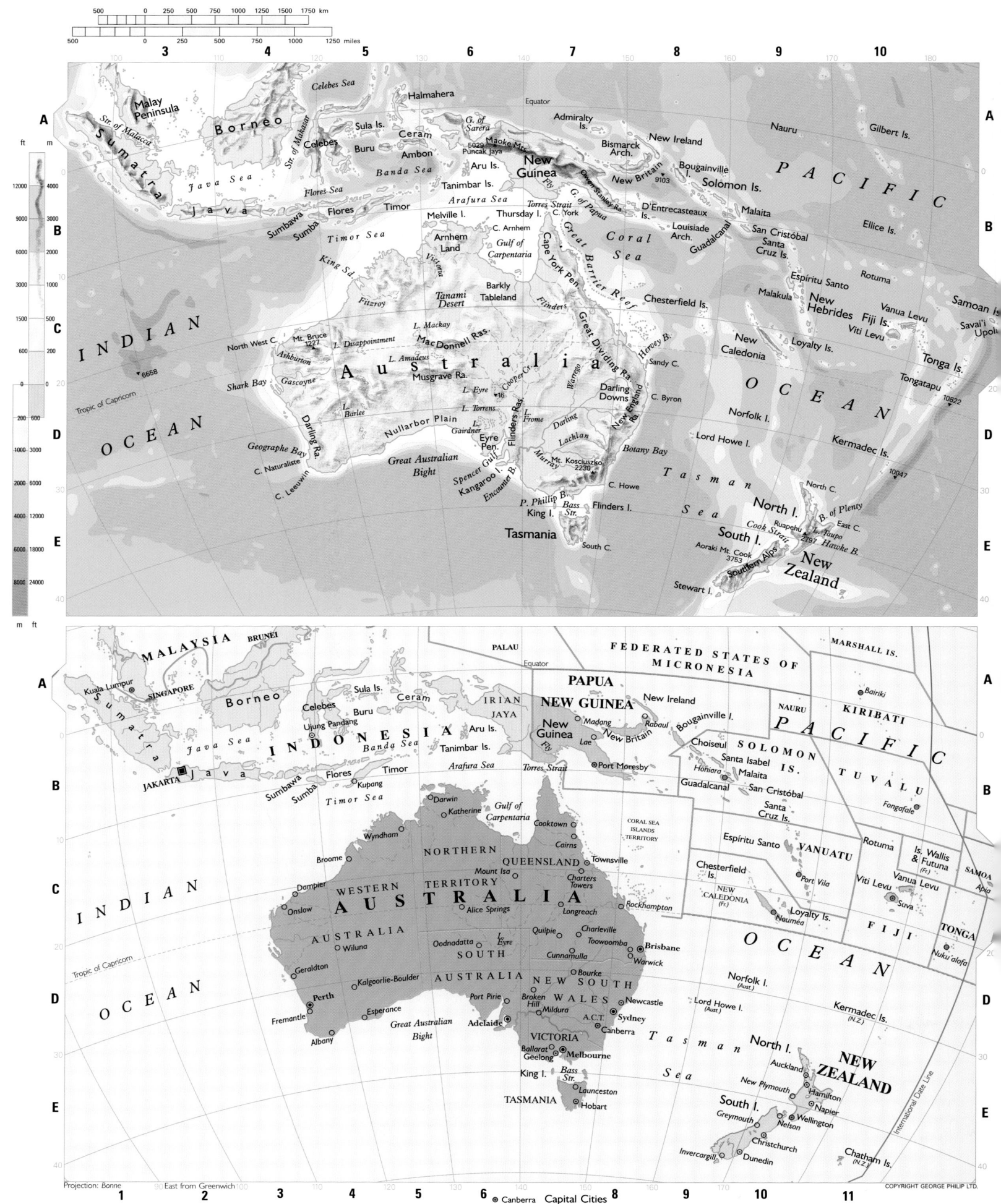

64
64 64
64

50   0   50   100   150   200 km
50   0   50   100   150 miles

PACIFIC OCEAN

C. Reinga
C. Maria
van Diemen
North C.
Houhora Heads
Rangaunu B.
Doubtless B.
Ahipara B.
Kaitaia
Tauroa Pt.
Okaihau
Mangonui
Whangaroa Harb.
B. of Islands
C. Brett
Rawene
Opua
Kaikohe
Hikurangi
Hokianga Harbour
Donnelly's Crossing
Whangarei
Whangarei Harb.
Bream Hd.
Dargaville
Waipu
Bream B.
Little Barrier I.
Great Barrier I.
Warkworth
C. Rodney
C. Colville
Cuvier I.
Kaipara Harbour
Helensville
Hauraki Gulf
Coromandel
Takapuna
Devonport
Whitianga
Manukau
AUCKLAND
Papakura
Thames
Waiuku
Pukekohe
Mercer
Waihi
Mayor I.
Waikato
Paeroa
Tauranga Harb.
Huntly
Te Aroha
Mount Maunganui
White I.
C. Runaway
Morrinsville
Bay of Plenty
East C.
Hamilton
Cambridge
Tauranga
Raglan
Te Awamutu
Whakatane
Hikurangi 1753
Kawhia Harbour
Putaruru
Kawerau
Opotiki
Waipiro
Otorohanga
Tokoroa
Rotorua
Taneatua
Motu
Te Kuiti
Kinleith
L. Rotorua
Murupara
Tolaga Bay
Mokau
Mokau
Mokai
Wairakei
L. Tarawera
Ormond
North Taranaki Bight
Ongarue
Taupo
L. Taupo
Gisborne
Waitara
Taumarunui
Waikaremoana
Poverty Bay
New Plymouth
Whangamomona
Ruapehu 2797
Nuhaka
Waikokopu
Inglewood
Mt. Taranaki (Mt. Egmont)
Turangi
Tarawera
Wairoa
Mahia Pen.
C. Egmont 2518
Stratford
Ohakune
Waiouru
Bay View
Hawke Bay
Opunake
Eltham
Raetihi
Napier
Kapuni
Hawera
Taihape
Mangaweka
Hastings
C. Kidnappers
South Taranaki Bight
Patea
Waverley
Hunterville
Waipawa
Wanganui
Marton
Halcombe
Waipukurau
Balls
Feilding
Danevirke
Palmerston North
Woodville
Foxton
Shannon
Pahiatua
Eketahuna
Levin
C. Turnagain
Otaki
Paraparaumu
Kapiti I.
Masterton
Waikanae
Carterton
Greytown
Martinborough
Upper Hutt
Petone
Lower Hutt
Eastbourne
WELLINGTON

North Island

TASMAN SEA

C. Farewell
Golden B.
D'Urville I.
Collingwood
Takaka
Tasman B.
Tasman Mts.
Motueka
Pelorus Sd.
Karamea
Nelson
Havelock
Picton
Karamea Bight
Richmond
Wakefield
Seddonville
Tadmor
Blenheim
Granity
Murchison
Seddon
Westport
Lyell
Inangahua
Ward
Matiri Ra.
L. Rotoroa
2885 Tapuaenuku
Reefton
Mt. Travers 2338
Blackball
Spenser Mts.
Kaikoura Ra.
Runanga
Lewis Pass
Hanmer Springs
Greymouth
Kaikoura
Kumara
Waiau
Hokitika
Jacksons
Culverden
Ross
Waikari
Hurunui
Arthur's Pass
Waipara
Amberley
Coleridge
Oxford
Rangiora
Pegasus Bay
Springfield
Kaiapoi
Whitecliffs
Christchurch
Methven
Riccarton
New Brighton
Staveley
Lincoln
Lyttelton
Mount Cook
Ellesmere
Little River
Akaroa
Banks Pen.
Southbridge
Rakaia
Ashburton
Ashburton Bight
Aoraki Mt. Cook 3753
Fairlie
Temuka
Mt. Aspiring 3027
Tekapo
Timaru
St. Andrews
Mt. Cook
L. Ohau
Waimate
Kurow
Jackson B.
L. Pukaki
Ngapara
Okuru
Wanaka I.
Tekarahi
Oamaru
Mt. Earnslaw 2818
Wanaka
Maheno
Haast
Duntroon
Hampden
Milford Sd.
Arrowtown
Cromwell
Naseby
Dunback
Sutherland Falls
Milford Sound
Queenstown
Clyde
Palmerston
Bligh Sound
Alexandra
Port Chalmers
George Sound
Wakatipu
Roxburgh
Waikouaiti
Otago Harbour
Secretary I.
Te Anau
Kingston
Waipiata
Mosgiel
Saunders C.
Doubtful Sd.
L. Anau
Ophir
Dunedin
Breaksea Sd.
Manapouri
Edievale
Lawrence
Fairfield
Resolution I.
L. Manapouri
Kelso
Milton
Dusky Sd.
Lumsden
Gore
Tapanui
Balclutha
Pyegrants
Nightcaps
Clinton
Kaitangata
Chalky Inlet
Clifden
Balfour
Mataura
Owaka
Preservation Inlet
Tuatapere
Hedgehope
Wyndham
Nugget Pt.
Te Waewae B.
Orepuki
Winton
Gore
Riverton
South Invercargill
Tokanui
Tahakopa
Invercargill
Bluff
Ruapuke I.
Southwest C.
Foveaux Str.
Halfmoon Bay
Stewart I.
Port Pegasus

South Island
Westland Bight
Southern Alps
Otago
Southland
Eyre Mts.
Garvie Mts.
Umbrella Mts.

SAMOA ISLANDS
1:12 000 000
SAMOA
AMERICAN SAMOA
Savai'i
Apia
Upolu
Pago Pago
Tutuila
West from Greenwich

Futuna
Wallis & Futuna (Fr.)
Niuafo'ou (Tonga)
Thikombia
Labasa
Vanua Levu
FIJI
Yasawa Group
Vanua Balavu
Taveuni
Koro
Lautoka 1323
Levuka
Nandi
Viti Levu
Ovalau
Koro Sea
Lakeba
Lau Group
Suva
Gau
TONGA (Friendly Is.)
Moala
Vava'u
Kandavu
Tofua
Vatoa
Tongatapu
Nuku'alofa

FIJI AND TONGA ISLANDS
1:12 000 000
50   0   50   100   150   200 km
50   0   50   100   150 miles

ft   m
9000   3000
6000   2000
3000   1000
1200   400
600   200
0
200   600
2000   6000
4000   12 000
6000   18 000
m   ft

Projection : Conical with two standard parallels
East from Greenwich
West from Greenwich

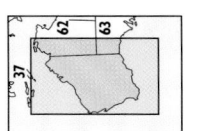

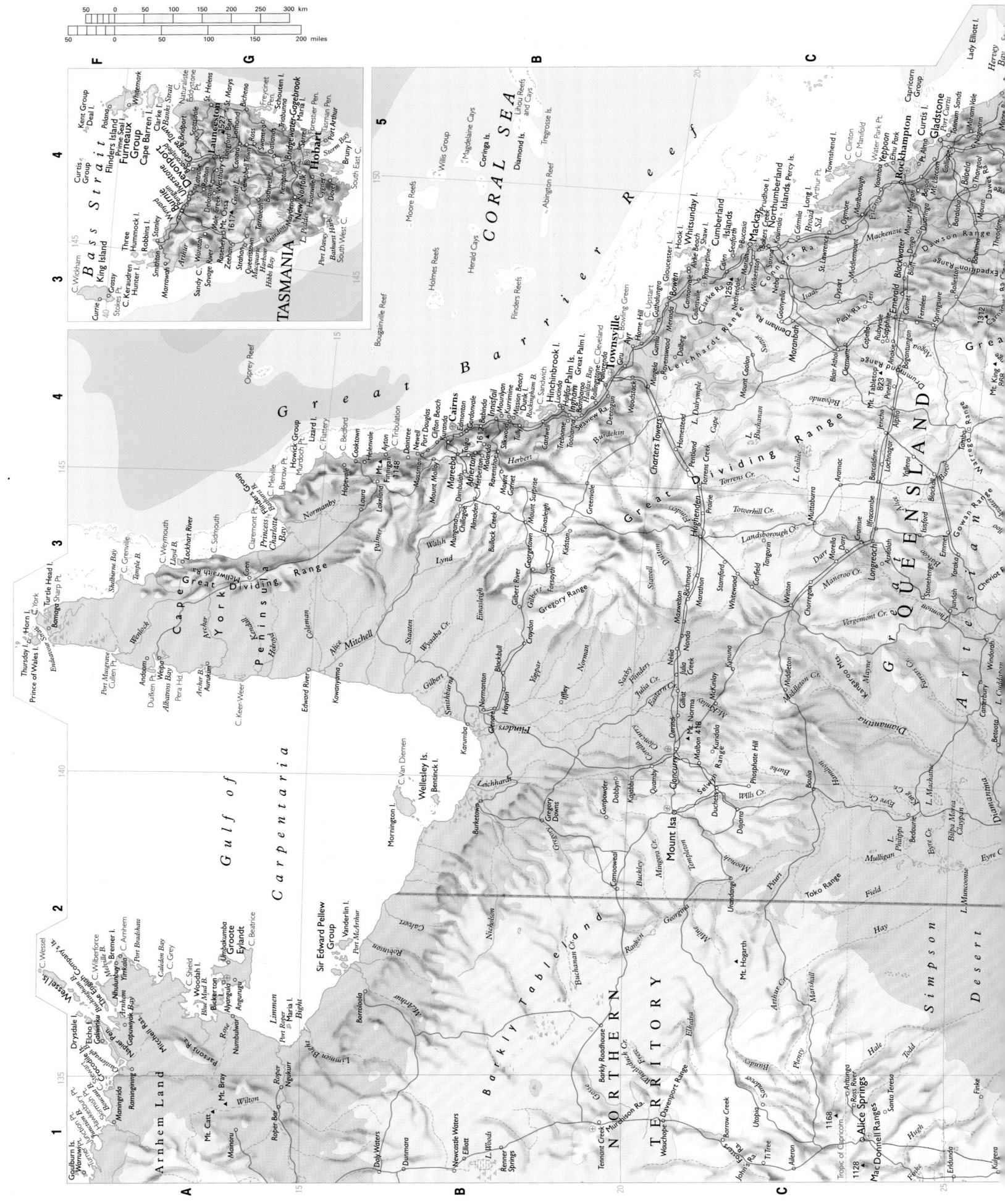

SOUTH AUSTRALIA

NEW SOUTH WALES

V I C T O R I A

BRISBANE

SYDNEY

CANBERRA

ADELAIDE

MELBOURNE

T A S M A N

S E A

S O U T H E R N

O C E A N

Projection: Bonne

East from Greenwich

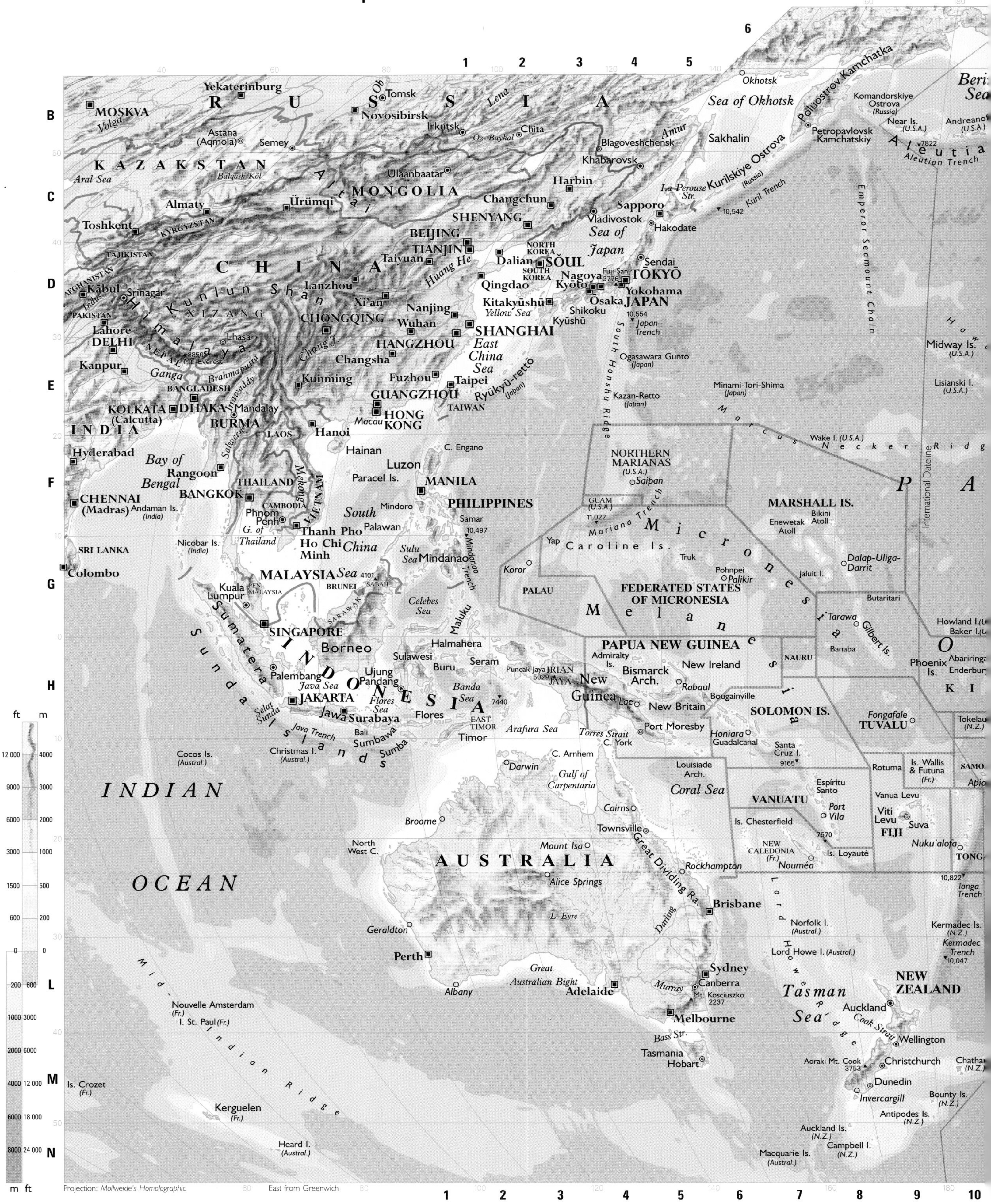

6

7 8 9 10

1 2 3 4 5

Beri
Sea

Okhotsk
Sea of Okhotsk
Poluostrov Kamchatka
Komandorskiye
Ostrova
(Russia)
Petropavlovsk
-Kamchatskiy
Near Is.
(U.S.A.)
Andreanof
(U.S.A.)

B MOSKVA R U S S I A
Yekaterinburg Ob Tomsk
Volga Novosibirsk Lena
Astana Irkutsk Chita
(Aqmola) Oz. Baykal Amur
Semey Blagoveshchensk
K A Z A K S T A N Sakhalin
Aral Sea Balqash Köl Ulaanbaatar Khabarovsk
Altai M O N G O L I A La Pérouse Kuril'skiye Ostrova
Str. (Russia) Aleutian Trench
7822
Aleutia

C Almaty Changchun 10,542 Kuril Trench
Toshkent Ürümqi SHENYANG Vladivostok Sapporo
KYRGYZSTAN BEIJING Hakodate
40 TAJIKISTAN Taiyuan TIANJIN Dalian SÕUL Sea of Emperor Seamount Chain
AFGHANISTAN C H I N A NORTH Japan Sendai
D Kabul Srinagar Lanzhou KOREA Nagoya TOKYO
India Xi'an Qingdao SOUTH Kyõto Fuji-San Yokohama Midway Is.
PAKISTAN Kunlun Shan Nanjing KOREA Osaka JAPAN (U.S.A.)
Lahore XIZANG Wuhan Kitakyūshū Shikoku Lisianski I.
DELHI CHONGQING Yellow Sea Kyūshū (U.S.A.)
Lhasa HANGZHOU SHANGHAI Japan
Kanpur Himalaya Changsha East Trench
8850 Chang J. Fuzhou China Ogasawara Gunto Necker Ridge
E Mt Everest Kunming Taipei Sea (Japan)
KOLKATA NEPAL Ganga TAIWAN Ryūkyū-rettõ Minami-Tori-Shima
(Calcutta) DHAKA Brahmaputra (Japan) (Japan)
I N D I A BANGLADESH Mandalay HONG Kazan-Rettõ
BURMA Macau KONG (Japan) International Dateline
Hyderabad LAOS Hanoi Wake I. (U.S.A.) P A
Bay of Hainan C. Engano NORTHERN Necker
Rangoon Luzon MARIANAS MARSHALL IS.
F Bengal THAILAND Paracel Is. (U.S.A.) Bikini
CHENNAI BANGKOK MANILA Saipan Atoll
(Madras) Andaman Is. Mindoro PHILIPPINES GUAM Enewetak M i c r o n
(India) CAMBODIA Samar (U.S.A.) Atoll
SRI LANKA Phnom South 10,497 11,022 Mariana Trench Yap Caroline Is. Truk Jaluit I. Dalap-Uliga-
Nicobar Is. Penh China Palawan Darrit
(India) Thanh Pho Koror Pohnpei
G Colombo G. of Ho Chi Sulu Mindanao PALAU Palikir Butaritari
Thailand Minh Sea FEDERATED STATES Tarawa
MALAYSIA Sea 4101 Celebes Mindanao Trench OF MICRONESIA M e l Gilbert Is.
Kuala SABAH Sea NAURU Banaba Howland I.(U.
Lumpur PEN. Baker I.(U
MALAYSIA BRUNEI Halmahera PAPUA NEW GUINEA Phoenix Is. Abariringa
SINGAPORE SARAWAK Sulawesi Seram Admiralty Bismarck New Ireland Enderbur
H Sumatera Borneo Buru Banda Is. Arch. N e s i a K I
Palembang I N D O N E S I A Ujung Sea Puncak Jaya IRIAN New Rabaul SOLOMON IS.
Java Sea Pandang 7440 5029 JAYA Guinea New Britain Bougainville
Selat JAKARTA Flores EAST Lae Port Moresby Fongafale
Sunda Jawa Surabaya Flores TIMOR Torres Strait Honiara TUVALU Tokelau
Bali Timor C. York Guadalcanal Santa (N.Z.)
Cocos Is. Sumbawa Arafura Sea Cruz I. Rotuma
(Austral.) Christmas I. Sumba C. Arnhem 9165 Is. Wallis SAMO-
Java Trench (Austral.) Darwin Gulf of Louisiade & Futuna Apia
I N D I A N Carpentaria Arch. Espiritu (Fr.)
Broome Coral Sea VANUATU Santo Vanua Levu
O C E A N Cairns Is. Chesterfield Port Viti Suva
North Vila Levu FIJI Nuku'alofa TONG
West C. Townsville 7570 NEW Noumea Is. Loyauté
L AUSTRALIA Rockhampton CALEDONIA 10,822
Mount Isa Great Dividing Ra. (Fr.) Tonga
Geraldton Alice Springs Brisbane Norfolk I. Trench
L. Eyre Darling (Austral.) Kermadec Is. 10,047
Perth Murray Sydney Lord Howe I. (Austral.) (N.Z.)
Nouvelle Amsterdam Great Canberra NEW Kermadec
(Fr.) Australian Bight Adelaide Mt. Kosciuszko Tasman Auckland ZEALAND Trench
I. St. Paul (Fr.) Albany 2237 Sea 10,047
Melbourne Wellington
Is. Crozet Bass Str. Aoraki Mt. Cook Christchurch Chatham
(Fr.) Tasmania 3753 (N.Z.)
Kerguelen Hobart Dunedin Bounty Is.
(Fr.) Invercargill (N.Z.)
Auckland Is. Antipodes Is.
Heard I. (N.Z.) (N.Z.)
(Austral.) Macquarie I. Campbell I.
(Austral.) (N.Z.)

1 2 3 4 5 6 7 8 9 10

ft m Mid-Indian Ridge
12 000 4000
9000 3000
6000 2000
3000 1000
1500 500
600 200
0 0
200 600
1000 3000
2000 6000
4000 12 000
6000 18 000
8000 24 000
m ft

COPYRIGHT GEORGE PHILIP LTD.

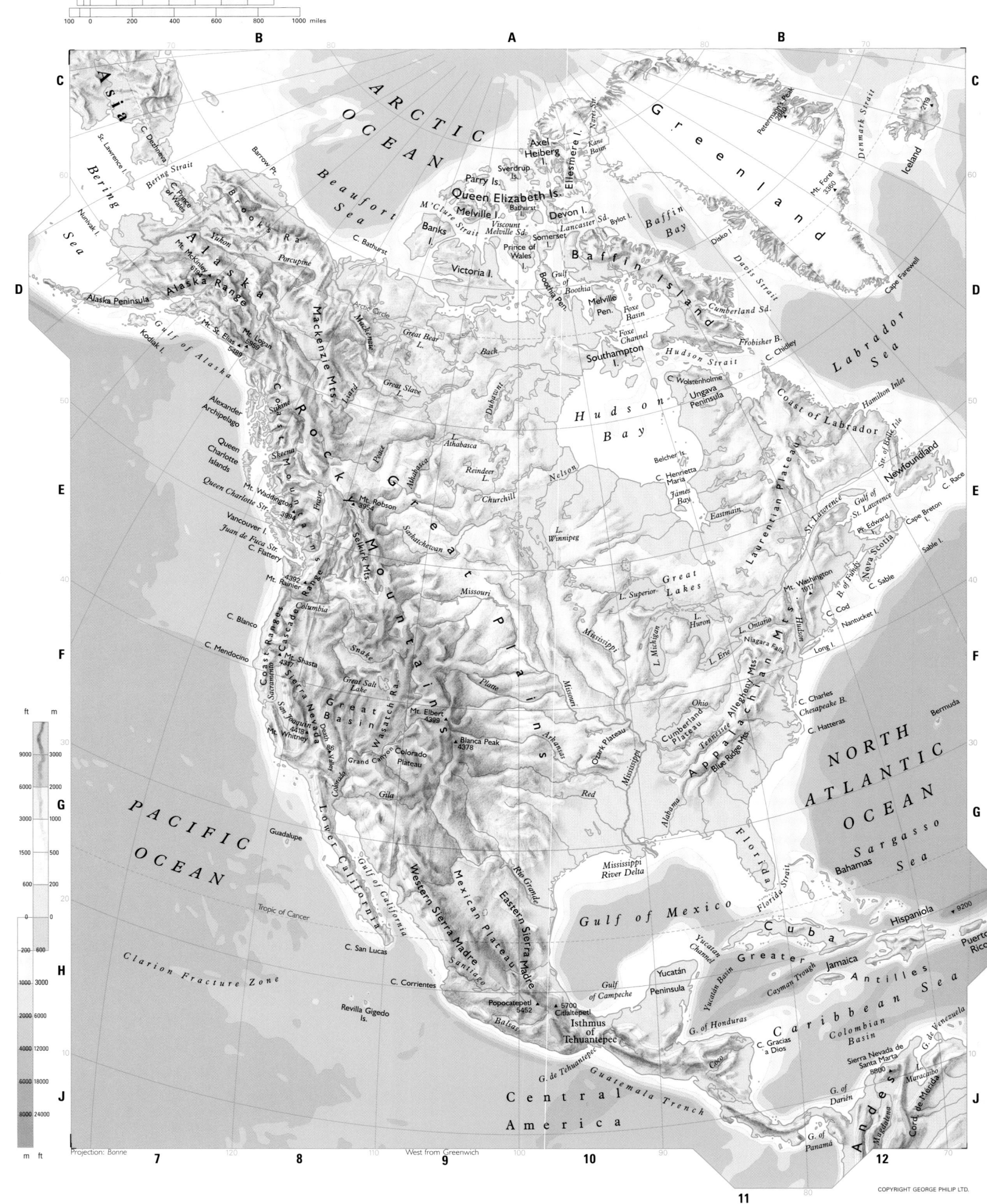

NORTH AMERICA : Physical

100 0 200 400 600 800 1000 1200 1400 km
100 0 200 400 600 800 1000 miles

ft m
9000 3000
6000 2000
3000 1000
1500 500
600 200
0 0
200 600
1000 3000
2000 6000
4000 12000
6000 18000
8000 24000
m ft

Projection: Bonne

Labels on map:

Asia

ARCTIC OCEAN

Greenland

Iceland

Mt. Forel 3360

Petermanns Peak 2940

Denmark Strait

Bering Strait

St. Lawrence I.

C. Dezhneva

Bering Sea

C. Prince of Wales

Numivak I.

Barrow Pt.

Beaufort Sea

C. Bathurst

Banks I.

Victoria I.

Axel Heiberg I.

Sverdrup Is.

Parry Is.

Queen Elizabeth Is.

Melville I.

Bathurst

Viscount Melville Sd.

M'Clure Strait

Somerset I.

Prince of Wales

Devon I.

Ellesmere I.

Kane Basin

Nares Str.

Lancaster Sd.

Bylot I.

Baffin Bay

Baffin Island

Disko I.

Davis Strait

Cape Farewell

Gulf of Boothia

Boothia Pen.

Melville Pen.

Foxe Basin

Foxe Channel

Southampton I.

Hudson Strait

Cumberland Sd.

Frobisher B.

C. Chidley

C. Wolstenholme

Ungava Peninsula

Labrador Sea

Brooks Ra.

Alaska

Yukon

Mt. McKinley 6194

Alaska Range

Mt. Logan 5959

Mt. St. Elias 5489

Kodiak I.

Gulf of Alaska

Alaska Peninsula

Porcupine

Mackenzie Mts.

Liard

Mackenzie

Arctic Circle

Great Bear L.

Back

Great Slave L.

Dubawnt

Athabasca

Peace

Reindeer L.

Churchill

Nelson

L. Winnipeg

Saskatchewan

Hudson Bay

James Bay

Belcher Is.

C. Henrietta Maria

Eastmain

Coast of Labrador

Laurentian Plateau

Hamilton Inlet

Newfoundland

Str. of Belle Isle

C. Race

Cape Breton I.

Nova Scotia

Sable I.

C. Sable

B. of Fundy

St. Lawrence

Gulf of St. Lawrence

Pt. Edward

Alexander Archipelago

Queen Charlotte Islands

Queen Charlotte Str.

Mt. Waddington 3994

Coast Mountains

Skeena

Stikine

Rocky Mountains

Mt. Robson 3954

Peace

Vancouver I.

Juan de Fuca Str.

C. Flattery

Mt. Rainier 4392

Cascade Range

Coast Range

C. Blanco

C. Mendocino

Columbia

Snake

Selkirk Mts.

Great Plains

Missouri

Platte

Great Lakes

L. Superior

L. Michigan

L. Huron

L. Erie

L. Ontario

Niagara Falls

Mississippi

Missouri

Hudson

Long I.

Nantucket I.

C. Cod

Mt. Washington 1917

Allegheny Mts.

Appalachian Mts.

Tennessee

Cumberland Plateau

Ohio

Ozark Plateau

Blue Ridge Mts.

C. Charles

Chesapeake B.

C. Hatteras

Bermuda

Sacramento

San Joaquin

Mt. Shasta 4317

Sierra Nevada

Mt. Whitney 4418

Death Valley 86

Great Basin

Great Salt Lake

Wasatch Ra.

Mt. Elbert 4399

Blanca Peak 4378

Colorado

Grand Canyon

Colorado Plateau

Gila

Arkansas

Red

Alabama

Mississippi

Mississippi River Delta

Florida

Florida Strait

Guadalupe

PACIFIC OCEAN

NORTH ATLANTIC OCEAN

Sargasso Sea

Bahamas

Cuba

Greater Antilles

Jamaica

Cayman Trough

Hispaniola 9200

Puerto Rico

Caribbean Sea

Tropic of Cancer

Lower California

Gulf of California

C. San Lucas

Western Sierra Madre

Eastern Sierra Madre

Mexican Plateau

Santiago

Rio Grande

Balsas

C. Corrientes

Gulf of Mexico

Gulf of Campeche

Yucatán Peninsula

Yucatán

Yucatán Channel

Yucatán Basin

Colombian Basin

Popocatepetl 5452

Citlaltepetl 5700

Isthmus of Tehuantepec

G. de Tehuantepec

Gulf of Honduras

C. Gracias a Dios

Coco

Guatemala Trench

Central America

G. de Darién

G. de Panamá

Andes

Sierra Nevada de Santa Marta 5800

Cord. de Mérida

G. de Venezuela

Magdalena

Maracaibo

Colombian Basin

Clarion Fracture Zone

Revilla Gigedo Is.

Revilla Gigedo Is.

West from Greenwich

100 0   200   400   600   800   1000 1200 1400 km

100 0   200   400   600   800   1000 miles

C   C

RUSSIA

Asia

Bering Strait

St. Lawrence I.

ARCTIC
OCEAN

GREENLAND

(Denmark)

ICELAND

Reykjavík

Denmark Strait

Bering Sea

Yukon

Queen Elizabeth Is.

Ellesmere I.

Baffin Bay

D

ALASKA
(USA)

Fairbanks

Anchorage

Porcupine

Victoria I.

Baffin Island

Davis Strait

Nuuk

Cape Farewell

Kodiak I.

Gulf of Alaska

YUKON
TERRITORY

Arctic Circle

NORTHWEST

Great Bear L.

Mackenzie

NUNAVUT

Hudson Strait

Whitehorse

Juneau

TERRITORIES

Yellowknife

Liard

Back

Great Slave L.

Dubawnt

Hudson

Bay

NEWFOUNDLAND

E

BRITISH
COLUMBIA

Skeena

Peace

ALBERTA

Athabasca

CANADA

Churchill

Nelson

D

Labrador

St. John's

Fraser

Edmonton

SASKATCHEWAN

L. Athabasca

MANITOBA

L. Winnipeg

ONTARIO

QUÉBEC

St-Pierre
Et Miquelon
(Fr.)

Victoria

Vancouver

Calgary

Saskatchewan

Regina

Québec

Fredericton

NEW
BRUNSWICK

PRINCE
EDWARD

Charlottetown

NOVA
SCOTIA

Halifax

F

Olympia

Seattle

WASHINGTON

Portland

Salem

OREGON

Columbia

MONTANA

Helena

IDAHO

Boise

Snake

Missouri

Winnipeg

NORTH
DAKOTA

Bismarck

SOUTH
DAKOTA

MINNESOTA

Minneapolis

WISCONSIN

Madison

L. Superior

Huron

MICHIGAN

Lansing

L. Michigan

Milwaukee

Toronto

L. Ontario

Buffalo

L. Erie

Detroit

Cleveland

Toledo

Montréal

Ottawa

VER.

N.H.

Concord

MAINE

Augusta

C. Sable

MASS.

Boston

Providence

NEW YORK

Hartford

NEW YORK CITY

PHILADELPHIA

G

Sacramento

Carson
City

Salt Lake
City

WYOMING

Cheyenne

NEBRASKA

Lincoln

IOWA

CHICAGO

ILLINOIS

INDIANA

OHIO

Columbus

PA.

Pittsburgh

Baltimore

Washington D.C.

MD.

N.J.

DE.

SAN FRANCISCO

San Jose

CALIFORNIA

NEVADA

UTAH

UNITED STATES

Denver

COLORADO

KANSAS

Kansas City

Topeka

St.
Louis

MISSOURI

Springfield

Indianapolis

Cincinnati

KENTUCKY

Nashville

W.V.

VIRGINIA

Richmond

Raleigh

NORTH
CAROLINA

Bermuda
(U.K.)

LOS ANGELES

Las Vegas

Colorado

ARIZONA

Santa Fe

Albuquerque

NEW MEXICO

OKLAHOMA

Oklahoma
City

ARKANSAS

Little Rock

Mississippi

Memphis

TENNESSEE

Birmingham

GEORGIA

Atlanta

Columbia

SOUTH
CAROLINA

Charlotte

Charleston

NORTH

ATLANTIC

OCEAN

San Diego

Phoenix

Tucson

El Paso

TEXAS

Dallas

MISSISSIPPI

Jackson

ALABAMA

Montgomery

Tallahassee

Jacksonville

H

PACIFIC

OCEAN

Guadalupe
(Mex.)

Hermosillo

MEXICO

Austin

Houston

LOUISIANA

Baton
Rouge

New
Orleans

Rio Grande

Tampa

FLORIDA

Miami

Nassau

BAHAMAS

Turks & Caicos Is.
(U.K.)

Gulf of Mexico

Florida Str.

San Juan

DOMINICAN
REP.

PUERTO
RICO
(U.S.A.)

Tropic of Cancer

Culiacán

Monterrey

Havana

CUBA

Cayman Is.
(U.K.)

HAITI

Port-au-
Prince

Santo
Domingo

Revilla Gigedo Is.
(Mex.)

Guadalajara

MÉXICO

Puebla

Mérida

JAMAICA

Kingston

Caribbean Sea

Acapulco

Belmopan

BELIZE

GUATEMALA

Guatemala

HONDURAS

Tegucigalpa

Maracaibo

VENEZUELA

San Salvador

EL SALVADOR

NICARAGUA

Managua

L. Nicaragua

Barranquilla

J

COSTA
RICA

San José

PANAMA

Panamá

COLOMBIA

Medellín

South

America

Projection: Bonne

7 ■ MÉXICO Capital Cities **8**

West from Greenwich

9   **10**   **12**

11

COPYRIGHT GEORGE PHILIP LTD.

ALASKA
1:30 000 000

Projection : Bonne

West from Greenwich

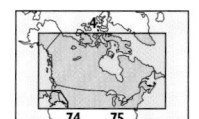

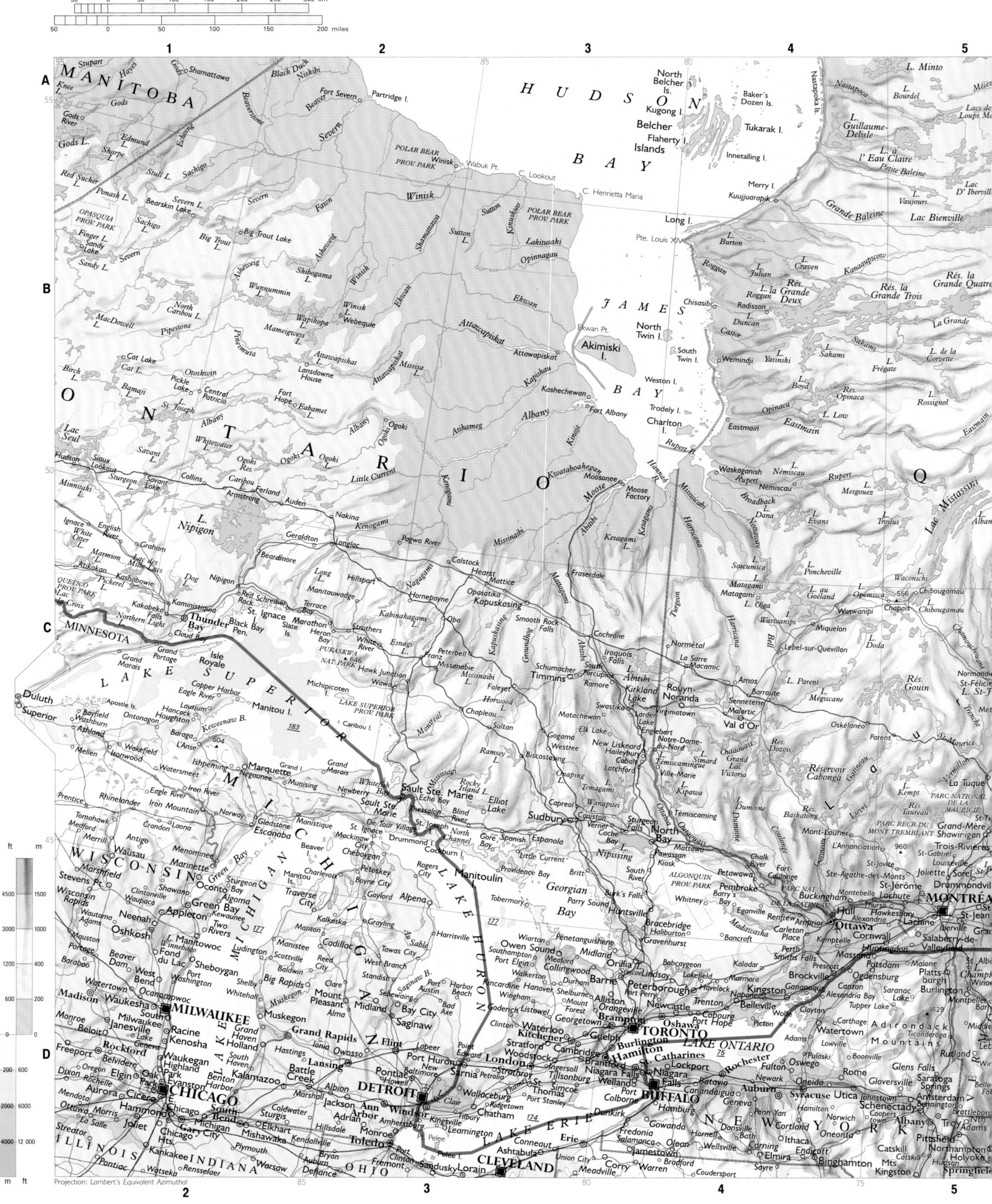

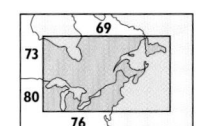

West from Greenwich

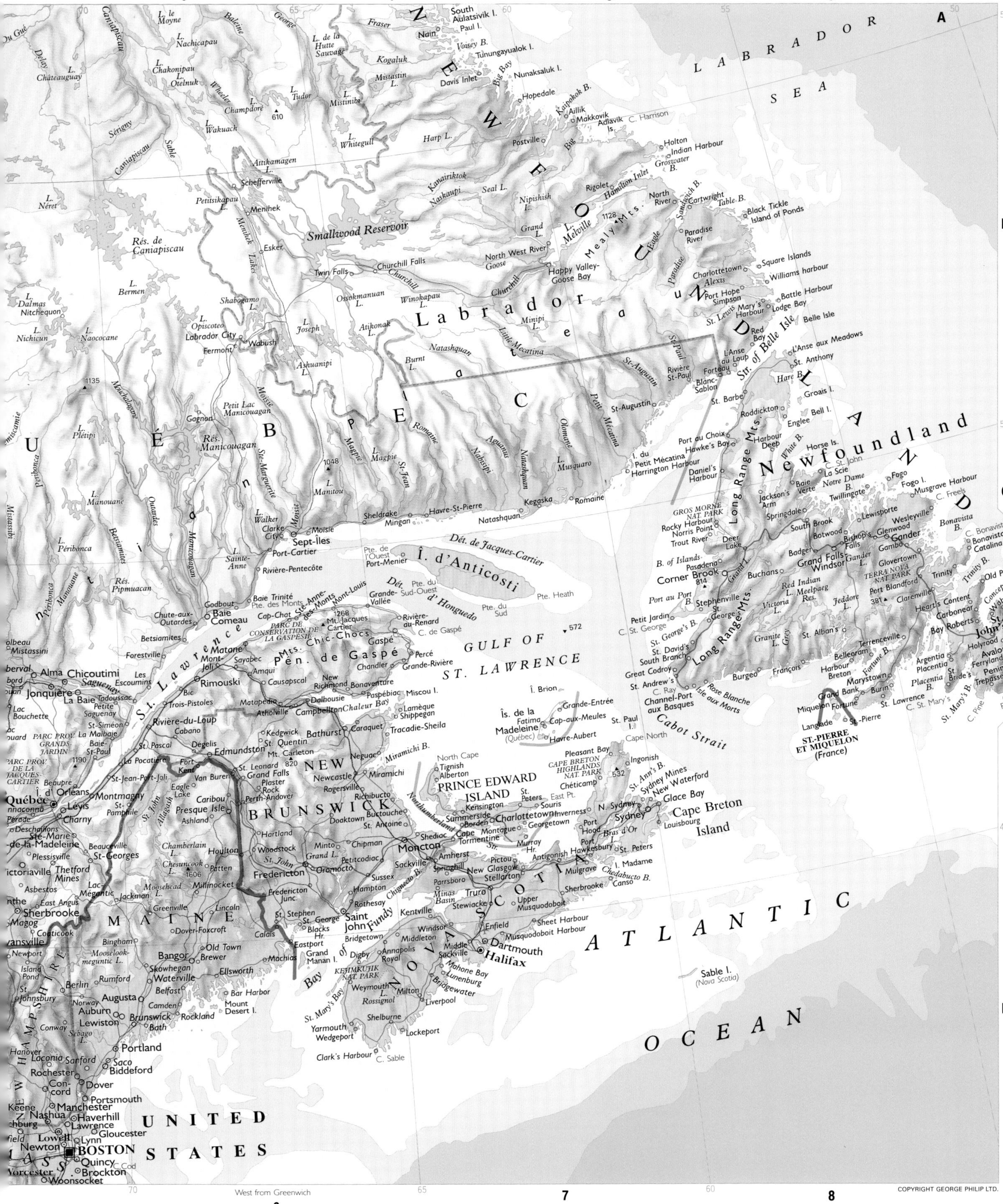

COPYRIGHT GEORGE PHILIP LTD.

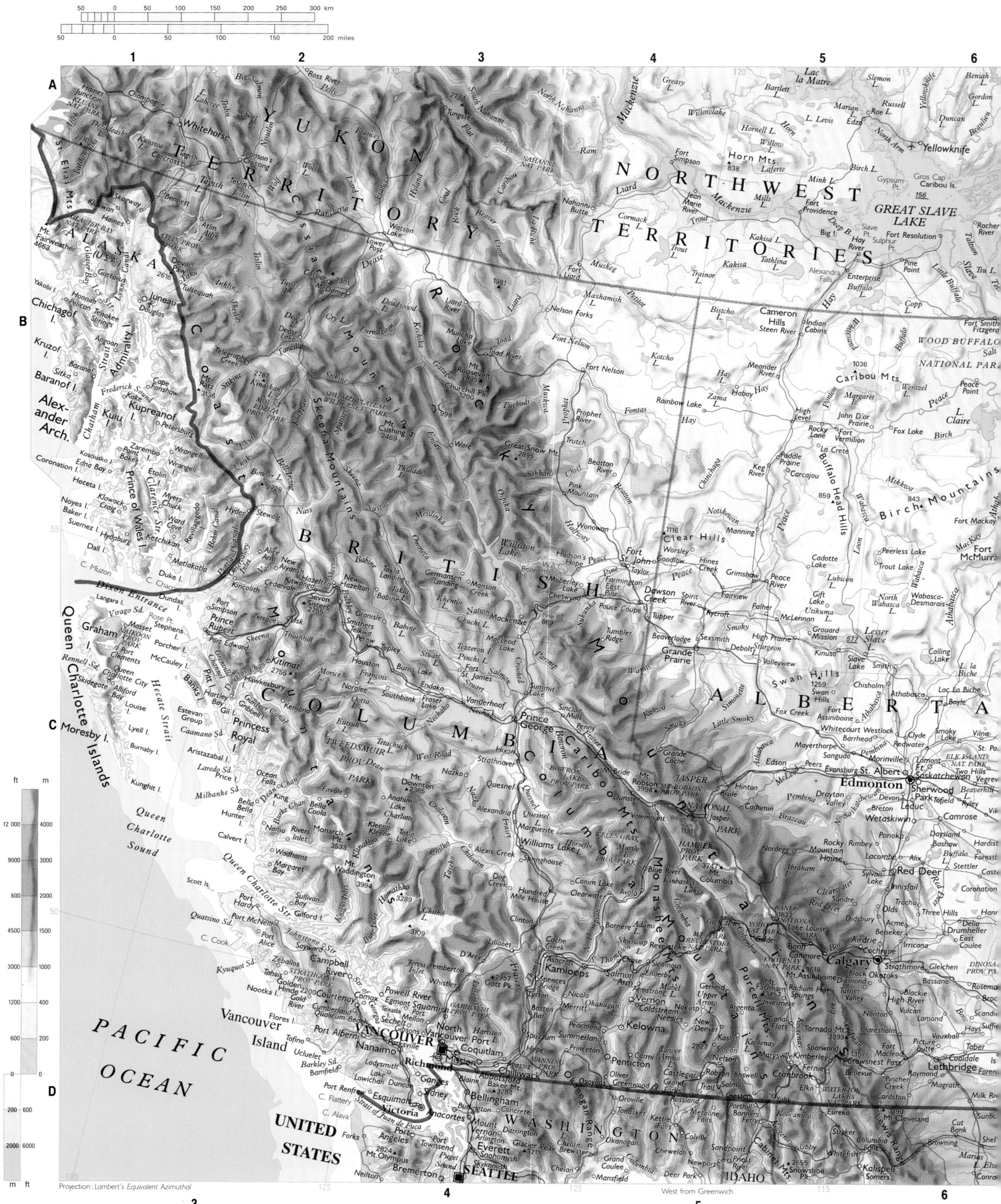

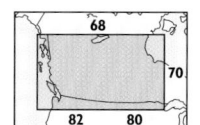

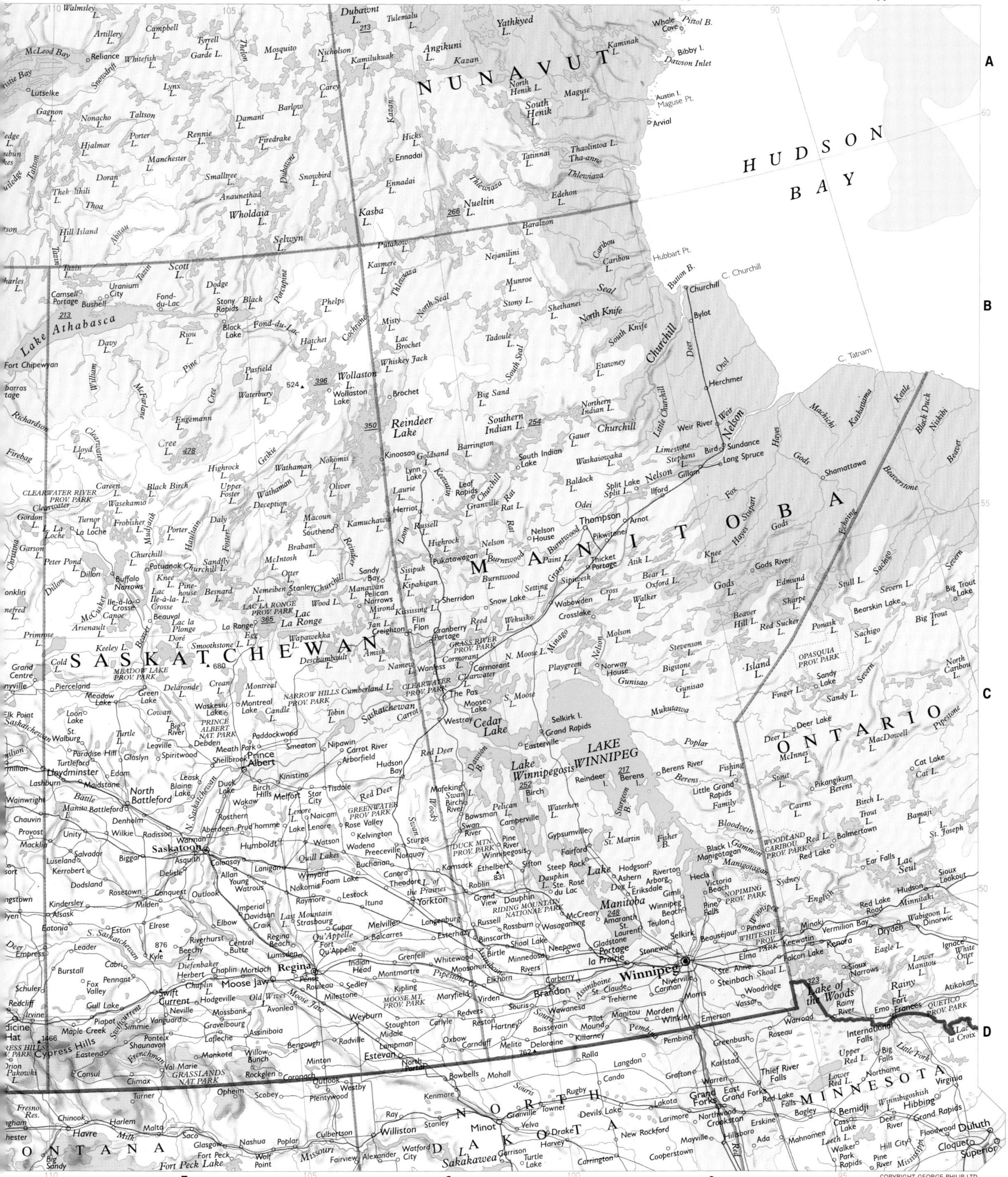

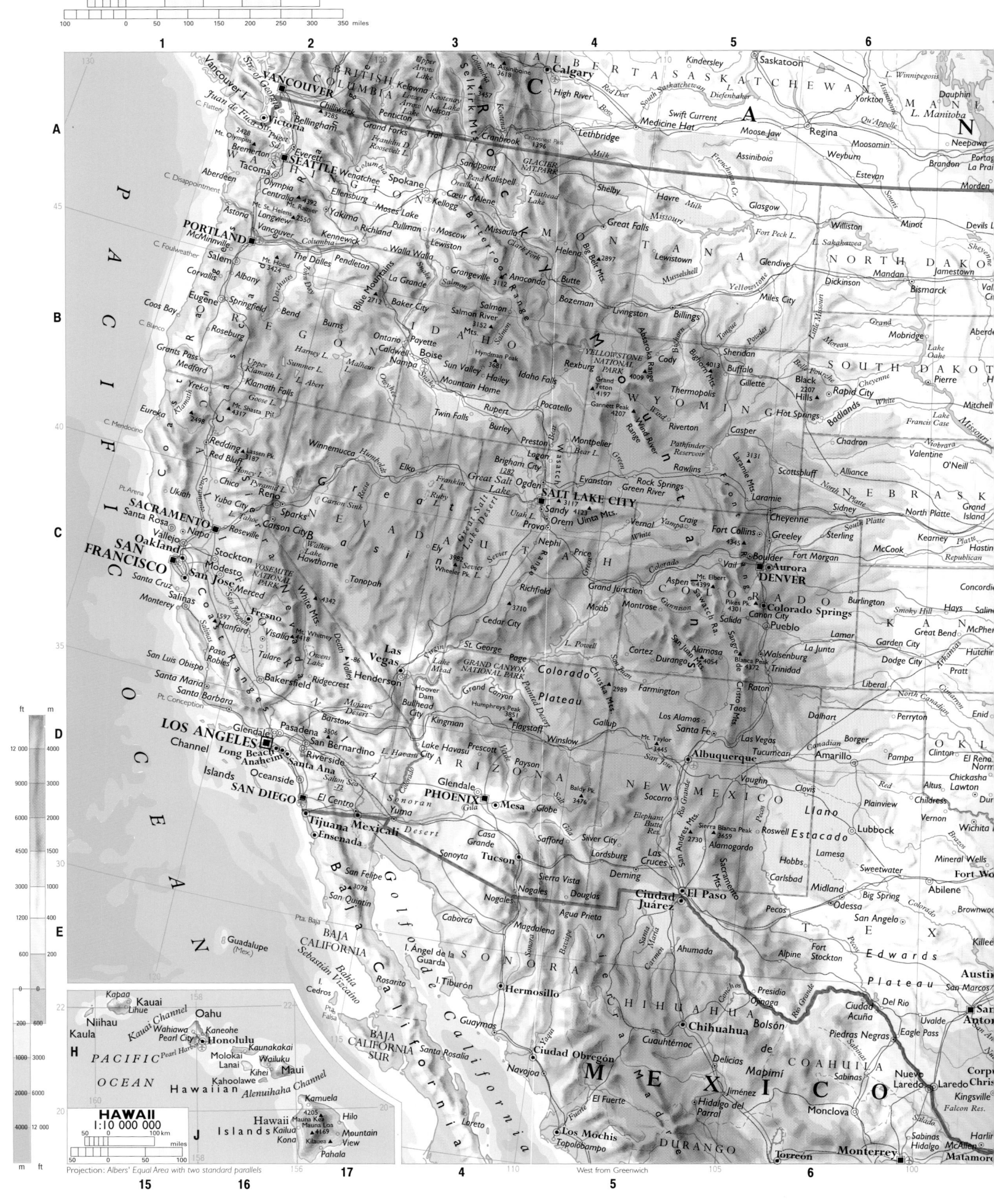

Projection: Albers' Equal Area with two standard parallels

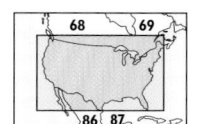

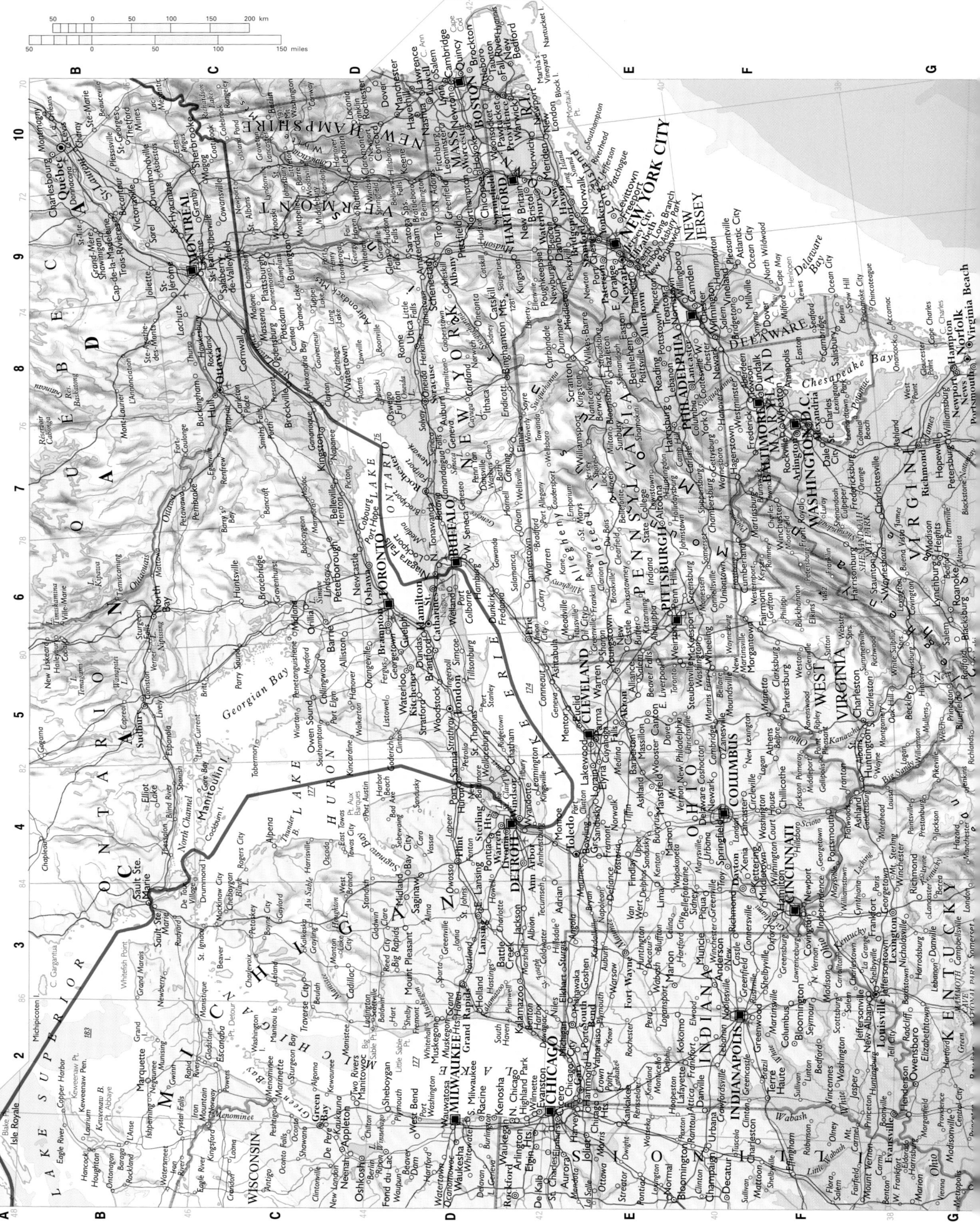

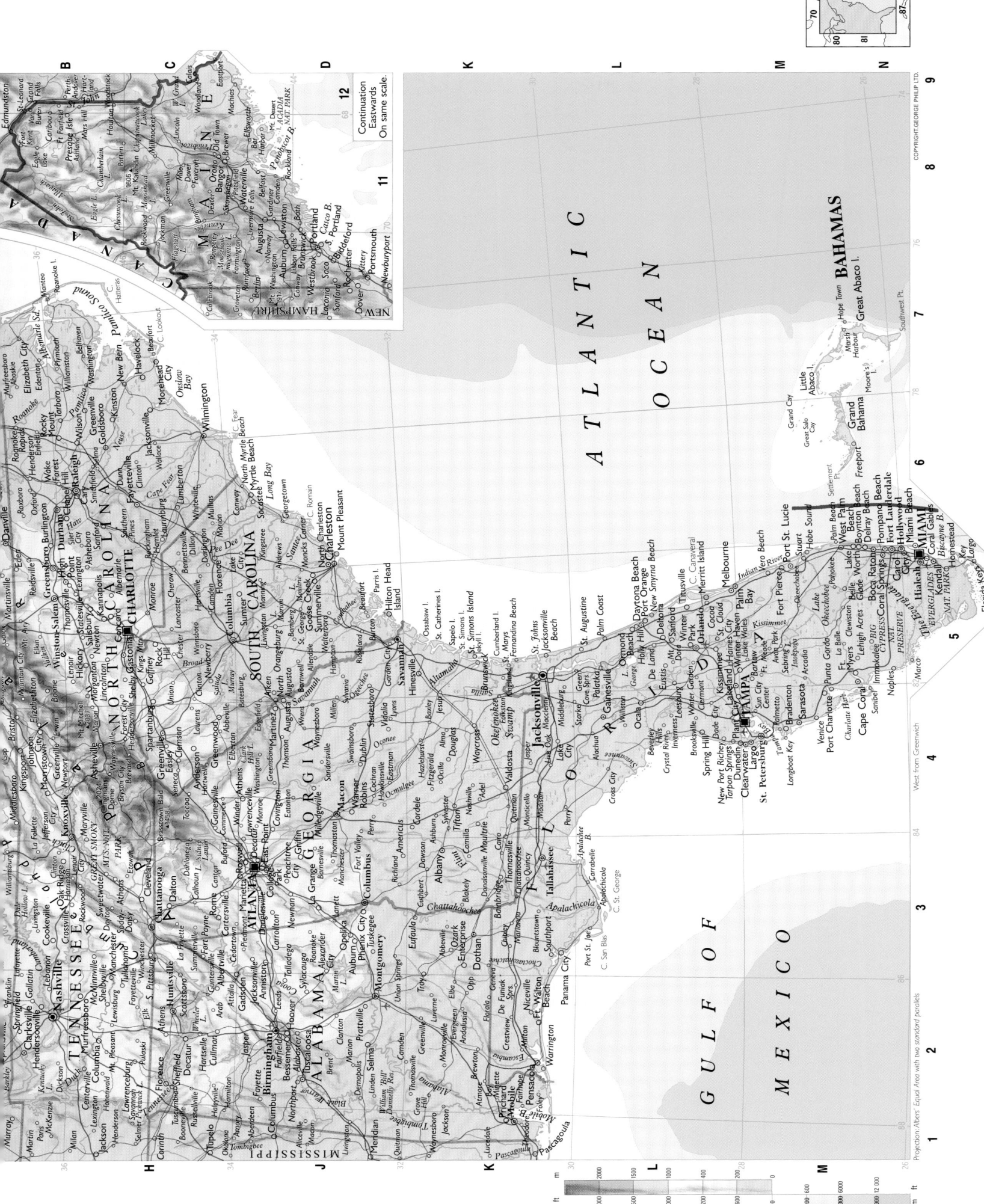

ATLANTIC

OCEAN

GULF OF

MEXICO

BAHAMAS

Projection: Albers' Equal Area with two standard parallels

Continuation
Eastwards
On same scale.

West from Greenwich

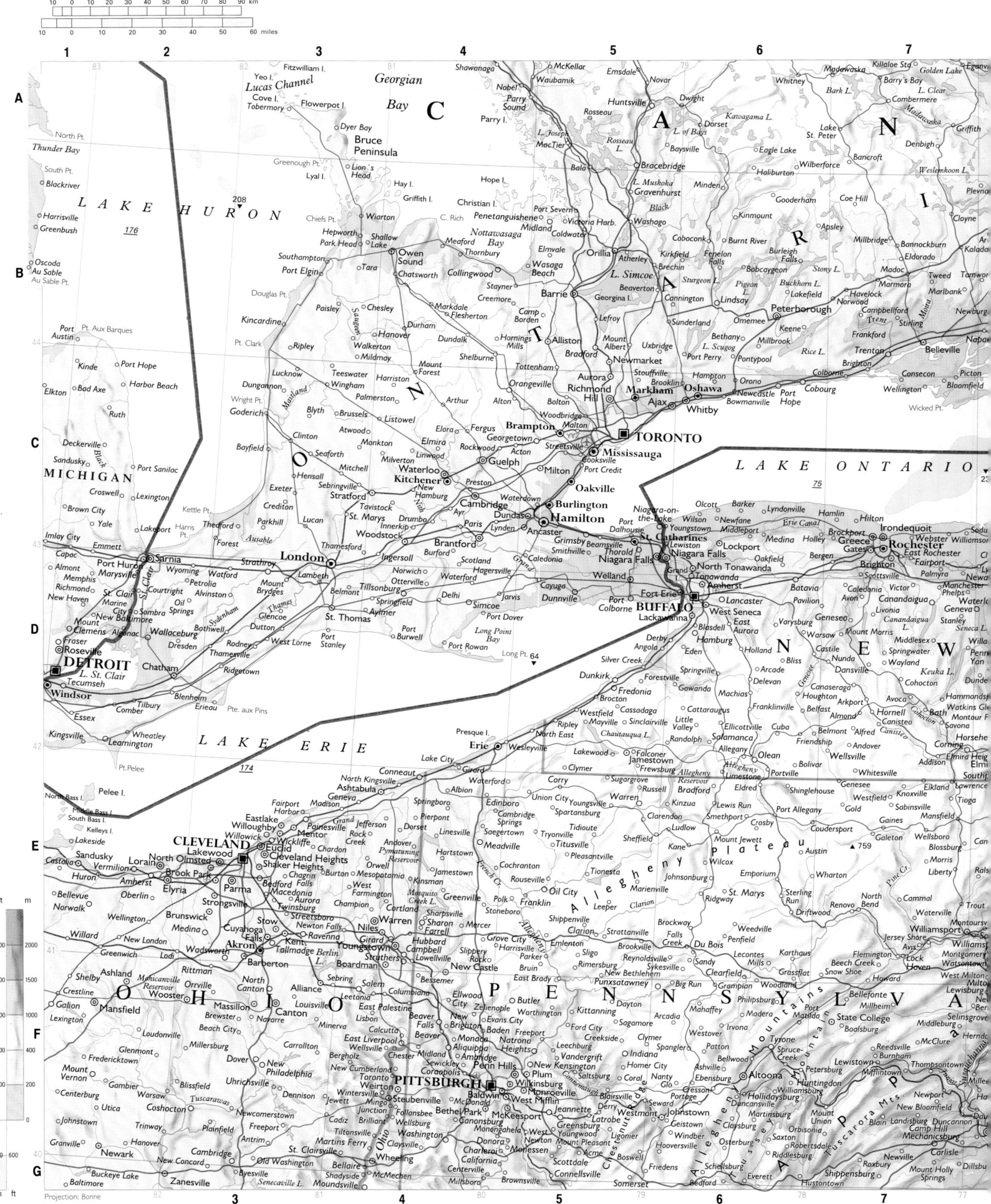

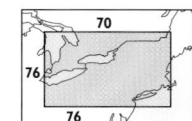

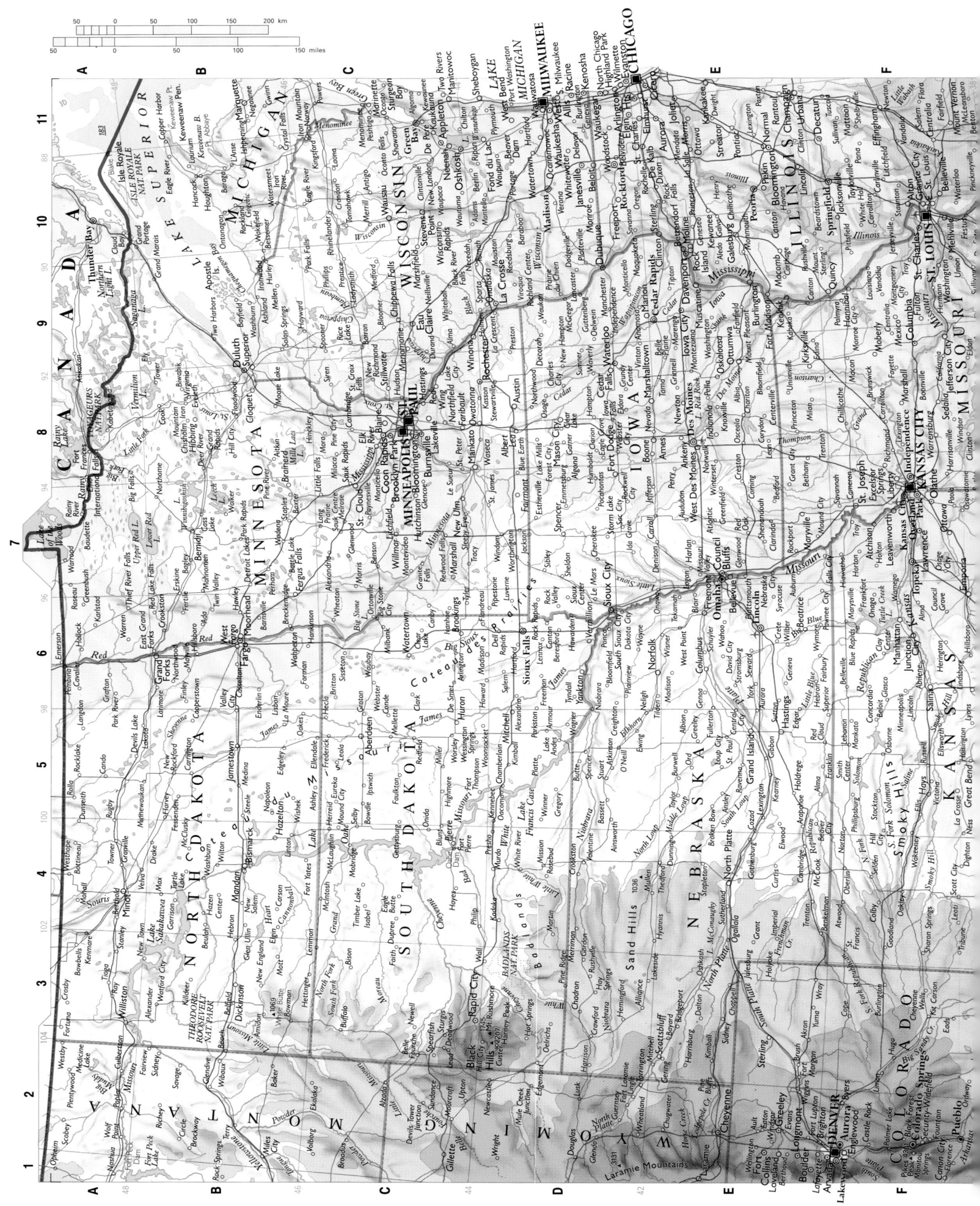

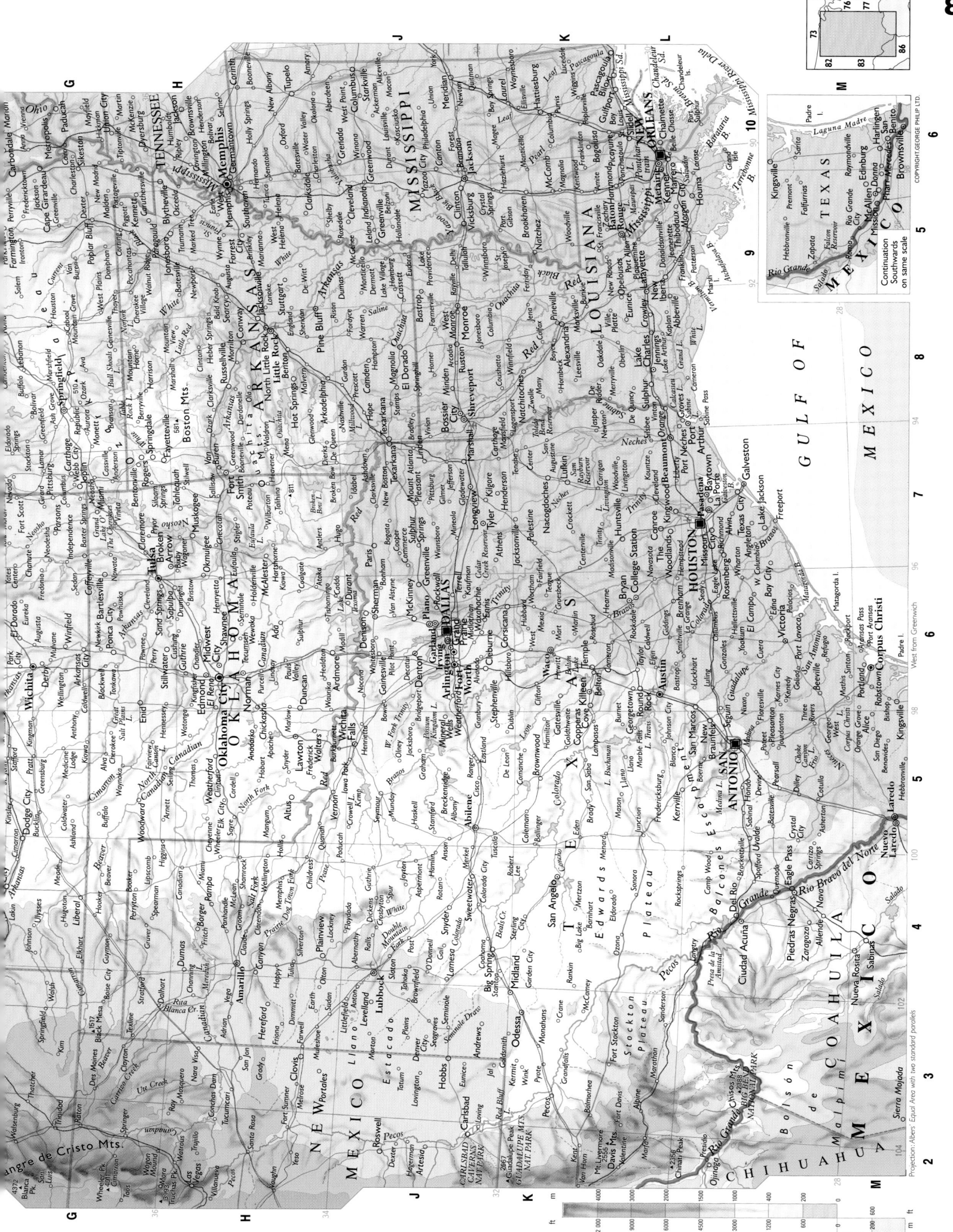

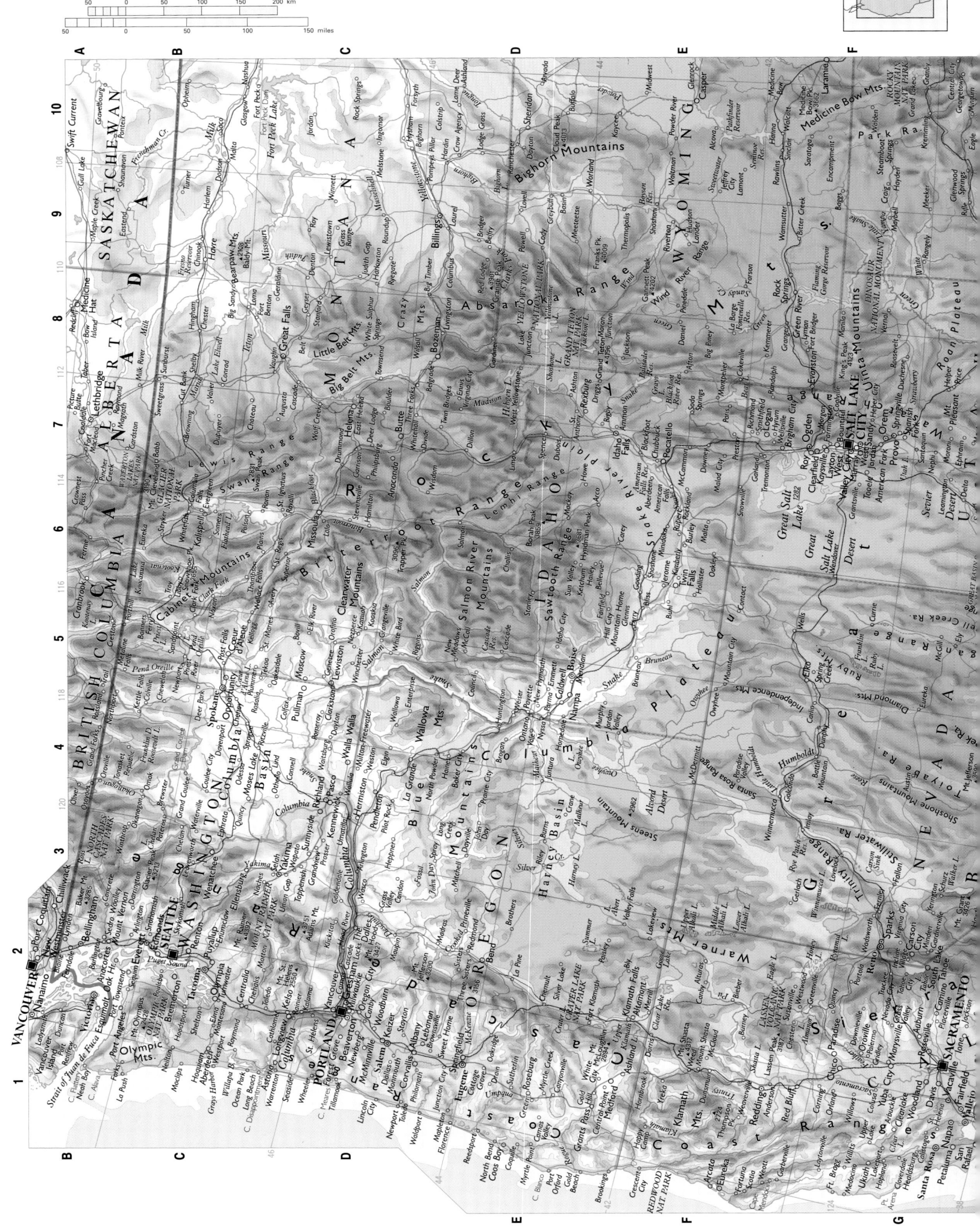

WESTERN WASHINGTON REGION
On same scale

85

Projection: Bonne

COPYRIGHT GEORGE PHILIP LTD

West from Greenwich

PACIFIC OCEAN

Channel Islands

San Pedro Channel

Gulf of Santa Catalina

LOS ANGELES

SAN DIEGO

Tijuana

Mexicali

Yuma

BAJA CALIFORNIA

MEXICO

ARIZONA

NEVADA

Las Vegas

Henderson

Death Valley

Bakersfield

Death Valley National Monument

Sonoran Desert

Mojave Desert

Colorado

Salton Sea

Imperial Valley

Palm Springs

San Bernardino

Riverside

Lake Havasu

Lancaster

Palmdale

Barstow

Victorville

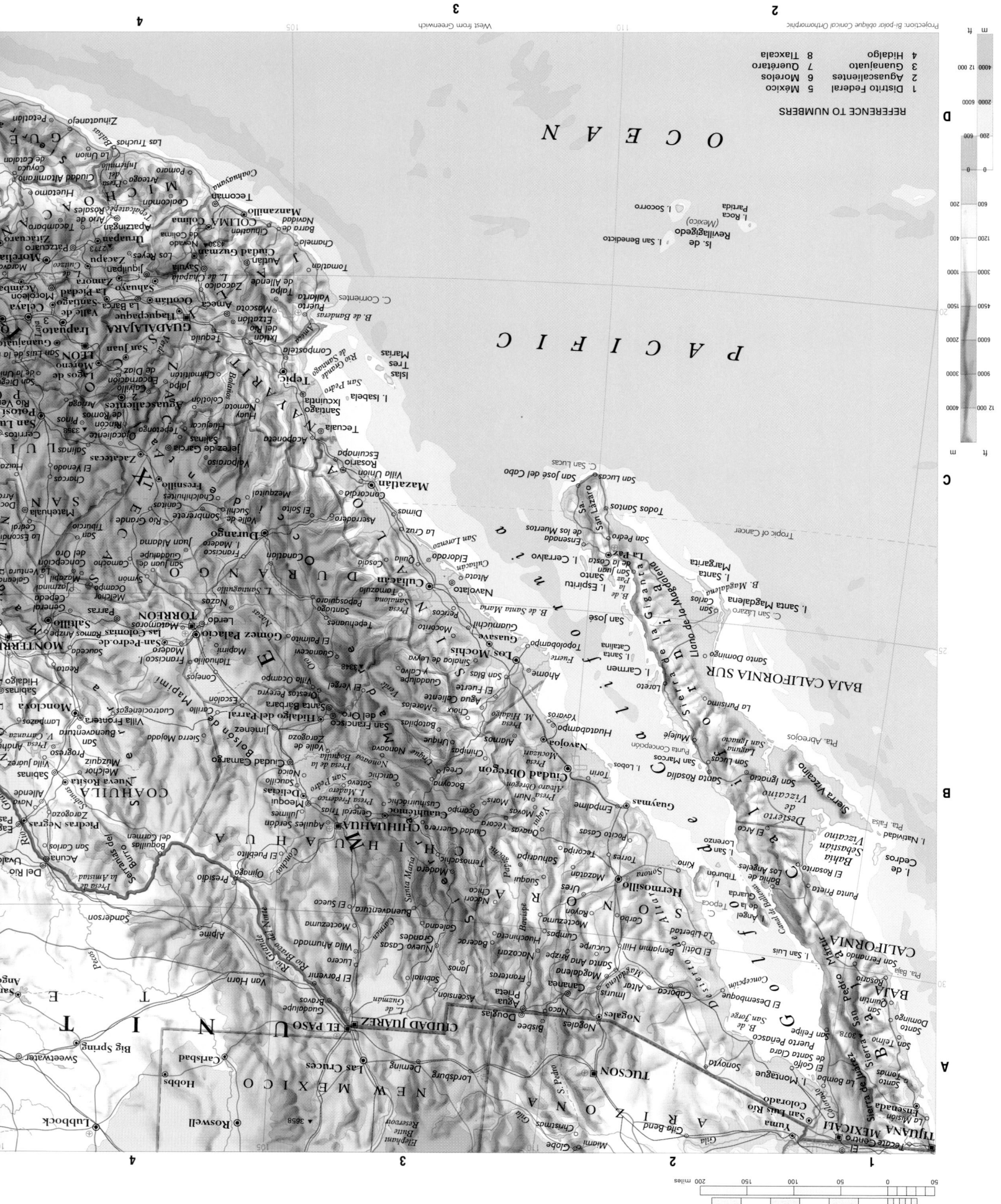

REFERENCE TO NUMBERS

1	Distrito Federal	5	México
2	Aguascalientes	6	Morelos
3	Guanajuato	7	Querétaro
4	Hidalgo	8	Tlaxcala

Projection: Bi-polar oblique Conical Orthomorphic

West from Greenwich

PACIFIC OCEAN

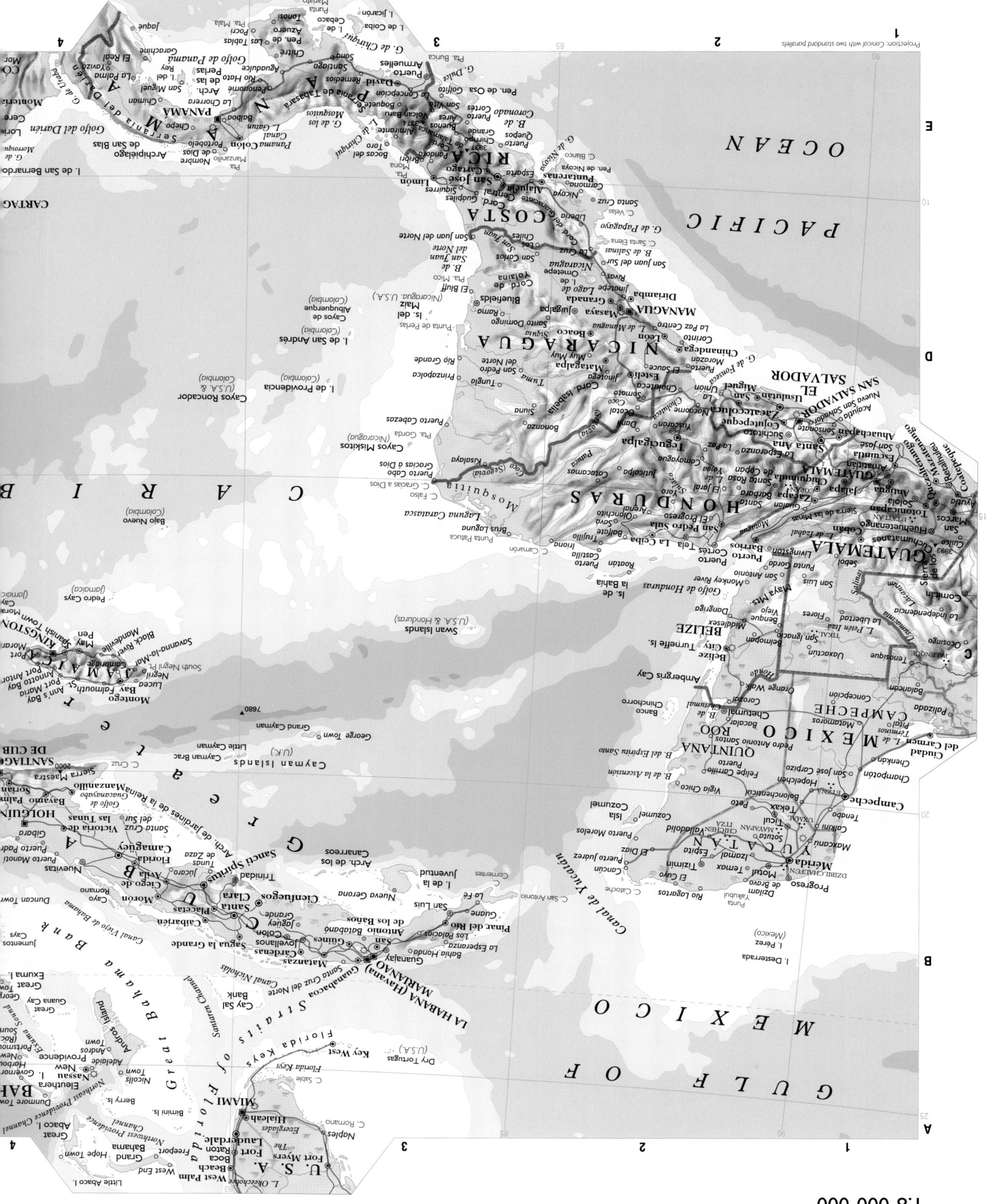

1:8 000 000

Projection: Conical with two standard parallels

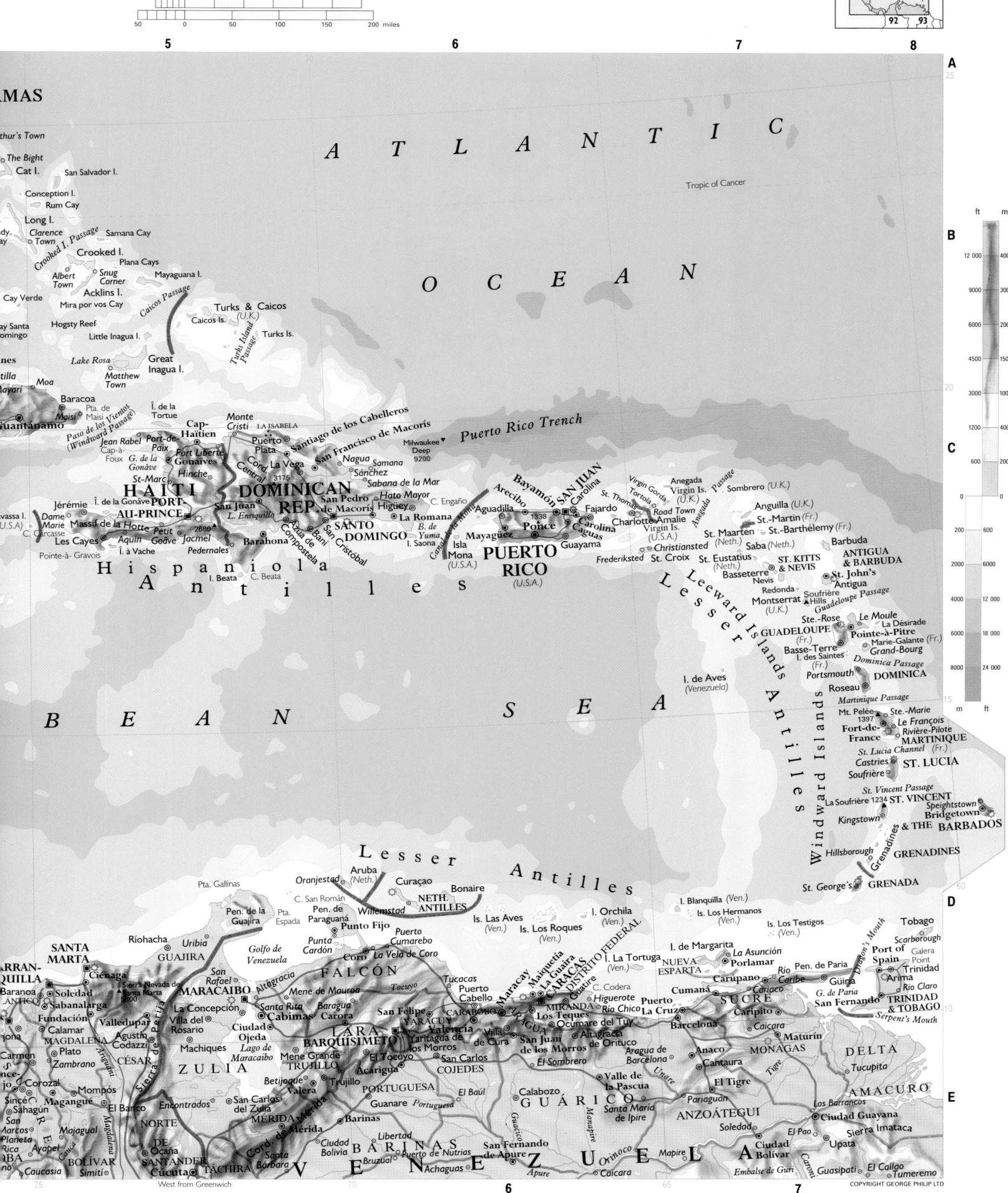

50 0 50 100 150 200 250 300 km

50 0 50 100 150 200 miles

87

92 93

5 **6** **7** **8**

A

25

A T L A N T I C

Tropic of Cancer

B

12 000 4000

O C E A N

9000 3000

6000 2000

4500 1500

3000 1000

1200 400

600 200

C

0

ft m

MAS

rthur's Town

The Bight

Cat I.

San Salvador I.

Conception I.

Rum Cay

Long I.

Clarence
Town

Samana Cay

Crooked I. Passage

Crooked I.

Plana Cays

Albert
Town

Snug
Corner

Mayaguana I.

Cay Verde

Acklins I.

Mira por vos Cay

Caicos Passage

Turks & Caicos
(U.K.)

Caicos Is.

ay Santa
omingo

Hogsty Reef

Little Inagua I.

Turks Island Passage

Turks Is.

nes

tilla

ayari

Lake Rosa

Great
Inagua I.

Moa

Matthew
Town

uantánamo

Baracoa

Maisí

Pta. de
Maisí

Î. de la
Tortue

Monte
Cristi

LA ISABELA

Puerto
Plata

Santiago de los Caballeros

San Francisco de Macorís

*Milwaukee
Deep
9200*

Puerto Rico Trench

Cap-
Haïtien

Jean Rabel

Port-de-
Paix

Cap-à-
Foux

Fort Liberté

Nagua

Samana

Sánchez

Bayamón

SAN JUAN

Anegada

Anegada Passage

Sombrero (U.K.)

Jérémie

Î. de la Gonâve

Gonaïves

Hinche

*Cord.
Central*

La Vega

3175

Sabana de la Mar

Arecibo

Carolina

St. Thomas

Virgin Gorda

Virgin Is.
(U.K.)

Tortola

Anguilla (U.K.)

St.-Martin (Fr.)

St.-Barthélemy (Fr.)

St-Marc

Hato Mayor

San Juan

Aguadilla

Fajardo

Charlotte
Amalie

Road Town

Virgin Is.
(U.S.A.)

avassa I.
(U.S.A.)

Dame
Marie

C. Carcasse

Massif de la Hotte

PORT-
AU-PRINCE

HAITI

DOMINICAN
REP.

San Pedro
de Macorís

Higüey

C. Engaño

Ponce

Caguas

Mayagüez

St.-Croix

St. Eustatius
(Neth.)

St. Maarten
(Neth.)

Saba (Neth.)

Barbuda

ST. KITTS
& NEVIS

ANTIGUA
& BARBUDA

Les Cayes

Aquin

Petit
Goâve

Jacmel

Barahona

Compostela

San Cristóbal

SANTO
DOMINGO

L. Enriquillo

2680

Î. à Vache

Pointe-à- Gravois

Pedernales

*B. de
Yuma*

Isla
Saona

Guayama

Frederiksted

St. Croix

Christiansted

Basseterre

Nevis

Redonda

St. John's

Antigua

Montserrat
(U.K.)

H i s p a n i o l a

Isla
Mona
(U.S.A.)

PUERTO
RICO
(U.S.A.)

Soufrière
Hills

Guadeloupe Passage

Ste.-Rose

Le Moule

La Désirade

A n t i l l e s

I. Beata

C. Beata

GUADELOUPE
(Fr.)

Basse-Terre

Pointe-à-Pitre

Marie-Galante (Fr.)

Grand-Bourg

I. des Saintes
(Fr.)

Dominica Passage

L e e w a r d   I s l a n d s

Portsmouth

DOMINICA

Roseau

Martinique Passage

B E A N S E A

Mt. Pelée
1397

Fort-de-
France

Ste.-Marie

Le François

Rivière-Pilote

MARTINIQUE
(Fr.)

St. Lucia Channel

Castries

Soufrière

ST. LUCIA

St. Vincent Passage

La Soufrière 1234

ST. VINCENT

Speightstown

Bridgetown

BARBADOS

Kingstown

& THE
GRENADINES

Hillsborough

GRENADINES

L e s s e r *A n t i l l e s*

St. George's

GRENADA

Lesser

Aruba
(Neth.)

Curaçao

Bonaire

Antilles

I. Blanquilla (Ven.)

Is. Los Hermanos
(Ven.)

Is. Los Testigos
(Ven.)

Tobago

D

Pta. Gallinas

Oranjestad

NETH.
ANTILLES

Willemstad

I. Orchila
(Ven.)

Scarborough

Port of
Spain

Galera
Point

C. San Román

Pen. de la
Guajira

Pta.
Espada

Pen. de
Paraguaná

Is. Las Aves
(Ven.)

Is. Los Roques
(Ven.)

I. de Margarita

La Asunción

Porlamar

NUEVA
ESPARTA

I. La Tortuga
(Ven.)

Trinidad

Arima

Rio Claro

TRINIDAD
& TOBAGO

SANTA
MARTA

Ríohacha

Uribia

Punto Fijo

*Golfo de
Venezuela*

Puerto
Cumarebo

Coro

La Vela de Coro

FALCÓN

Tucacas

Puerto
Cabello

Maiquetía

La Guaira

CARACAS

DISTRITO FEDERAL

C. Codera

Cumaná

Carúpano

Pen. de Paria

Río
Caribe

Güira

Dragon's Mouth

G. de Paria

San Fernando

Serpent's Mouth

RRAN-
QUILLA

GUAJIRA

San
Rafael

Punta
Cardón

Mene de Mauroa

Tocuyo

Maracay

MIRANDA

Los Teques

Río Chico

Puerto
La Cruz

Barcelona

Caripito

SUCRE

Caicara

Maturín

E

Baranoa

ANTICO

Ciénaga

*Sierra Nevada de
Santa Marta*
5800

Altagracia

Baragua

San Felipe

CARABOBO

Villa
de Cura

YARACUY

Ocumare del Tuy

San Juan
de los Morros

Altagracia de Orituco

Aragua de
Barcelona

Anaco

Cantaura

MONAGAS

DELTA

Soledad

Sabanalarga

MARACAIBO

La Concepción

Santa Rita

Cabimas

Carora

LARA

BARQUISIMETO

Yaritagua

de

San Carlos

Valle de
la Pascua

El Tigre

AMACURO

Tucupita

Fundación

Valledupar

Agustín
Codazzi

Villa del
Rosario

Ciudad
Ojeda

*Lago de
Maracaibo*

Mene Grande

TRUJILLO

Trujillo

COJEDES

GUÁRICO

El Pao

Ciudad Guayana

MAGDALENA

Plato

Zambrano

CÉSAR

Machiques

ZULIA

Betijoque

Valera

PORTUGUESA

El Baúl

Calabozo

Santa María
de Ipire

Pariaguán

El Tigre

Upata

Sierra Imataca

Carmen

Corozal

San Carlos
del Zulia

Anguí

Encontrados

Barinas

Manapire

Unare

Tigre

Los Barrancos

Sincé

Sahagún

El Banco

Mompós

Magangué

NORTE

MÉRIDA

Barinas

Libertad

ANZOÁTEGUI

Ciudad
Bolívar

arcos
Planeta

Rica

BA

Majagual

DE
OCAÑA

Cord. de Mérida

Mérida

BARINAS

San Fernando
de Apure

Ciudad
Bolívar

El Callao

Ayapel

Caucasia

BOLIVAR

Simití

SANTANDER

Cúcuta

TÁCHIRA

Santa
Bárbara

Ciudad
Bolivia

Puerto de Nutrias

V E N E Z U E L A

Apure

Achaguas

Caicara

Orinoco

Embalse de Guri

Guasipati

Tumeremo

West from Greenwich

COPYRIGHT GEORGE PHILIP LTD

5 **6** **7**

75 70 65 60

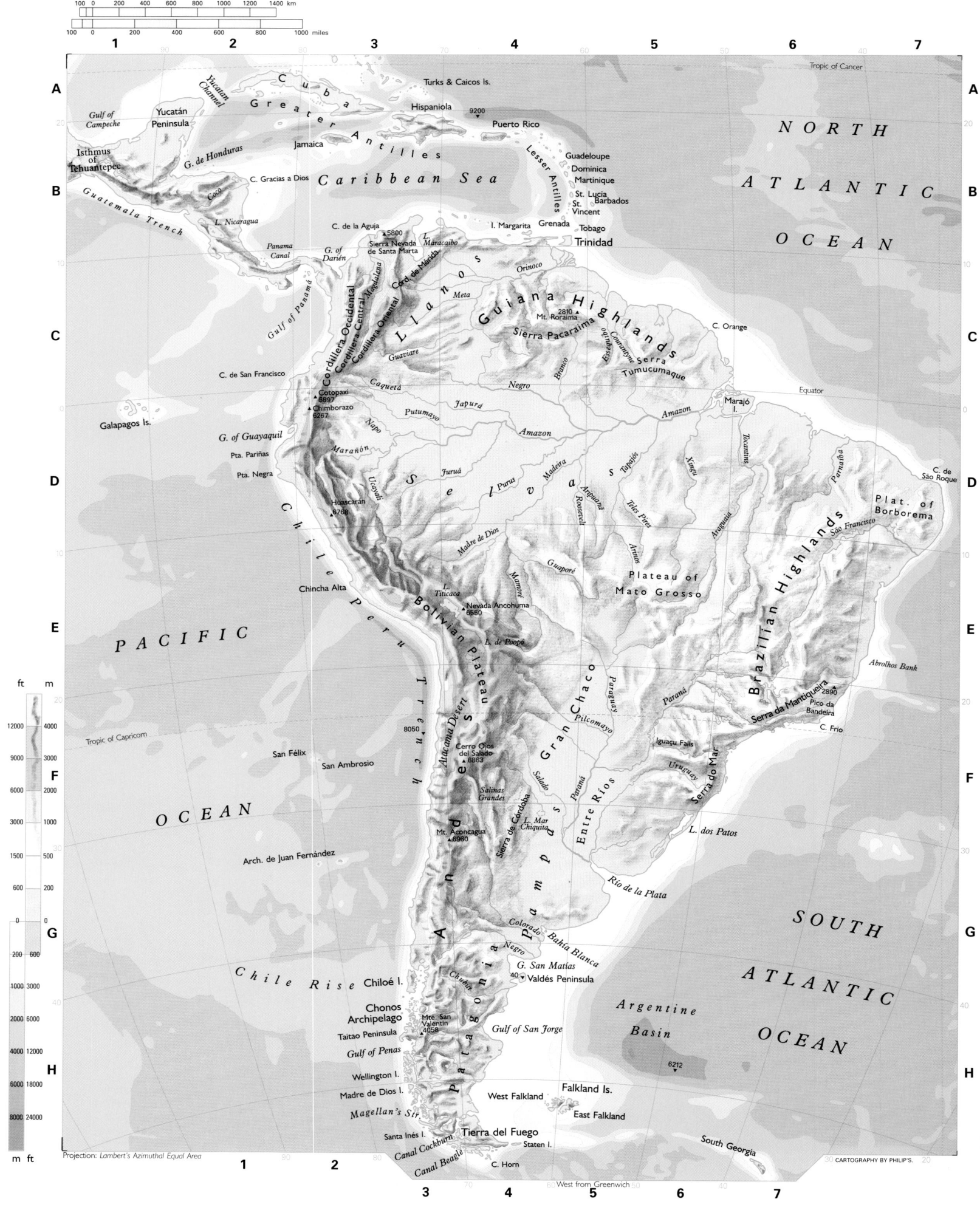

100 0 200 400 600 800 1000 1200 1400 km
100 0 200 400 600 800 1000 miles

1 2 3 4 5 6 7

A
Havana
BAHAMAS
Turks & Caicos Is.
(U.K.)
Tropic of Cancer
C U B A

HAITI **DOMINICAN**
Port-au- **REP.**
Prince San Juan
Virgin Is.
(U.K.)
JAMAICA Kingston PUERTO
RICO
(U.S.A.) ST. KITTS **ANTIGUA &**
& NEVIS **BARBUDA**
Basse-Terre GUADELOUPE
(Fr.)
DOMINICA MARTINIQUE
Caribbean Sea Fort-de-France *(Fr.)*
Castries **ST. LUCIA**
ST. VINCENT
Kingstown **BARBADOS**
GRENADA St. George's Bridgetown
Port of **TRINIDAD &**
Spain **TOBAGO**

MEXICO
BELIZE
GUATEMALA HONDURAS
Guatemala Tegucigalpa
San Salvador **NICARAGUA**
EL SALVADOR
Managua
COSTA San José
RICA Panamá
P A N A M A
Barranquilla
C. de
la Aguja
Cartagena Maracaibo
Barquisimeto Caracas
G. of
Darién
Aruba Curaçao
Cúcuta
Medellín San Cristóbal
Bucaramanga
Cali Bogotá

B

NORTH
ATLANTIC
OCEAN

Gulf of Panama

Ciudad Guayana
Georgetown
Paramaribo
VENEZUELA
Orinoco
Magdalena
GUYANA
Cayenne
SURINAM C. Orange
FRENCH
GUIANA
RORAIMA
Essequibo
COLOMBIA
AMAPÁ
Branco

C

Galapagos Is.
(Ecuador)
Quito
ECUADOR
Equator
Guayaquil
Napo *Putumayo* *Japurá*
Amazon Marajó
I. Belém
Manaus
G. of Guayaquil *Amazon*
Marañón Iquitos Santarém São Luís
AMAZONAS *Madeira*
Chiclayo *Juruá* *Purus* **PARÁ** MARANHÃO Teresina Fortaleza
Ucayali ACRE *Tapajós* *Xingu* *Tocantins* C. de
São Roque
Trujillo Pôrto Velho *Araguaia* CEARÁ RIO G.
Chimbote DO NORTE Natal
PERU RONDÔNIA **B R A Z I L** PIAUÍ *Parnaíba* PARAÍBA
Callao Campina Grande
LIMA *Madre de Dios* TOCANTINS PERNAMBUCO Recife
Cuzco MATO GROSSO ALAGOAS Maceió
Mamoré SERGIPE
Arequipa L. GOIÁS B A H Í A Aracaju
Titicaca *São Francisco*
La Paz **BOLIVIA** Cuiabá DIS. FED Brasília Salvador
Cochabamba Goiânia

D

E

PACIFIC

Iquique
Santa Cruz
Sucre
MATO GROSSO
DO SUL
Paraguay
MINAS GERAIS
Belo
Horizonte ESPÍRITO
Ribeirão SANTO
Prêto Vitória
Juiz R. DE J.
SÃO PAULO de Fora Campos
PARAGUAY Campinas
Pilcomayo SÃO Niterói
PAULO **RIO DE**
Asunción PARANÁ **JANEIRO**
Curitiba

F

Tropic of Capricorn
Antofagasta
Paraná
San Félix
(Chile) San Ambrosio
(Chile) Salta
San Miguel
de Tucumán *Salado*
Resistencia Corrientes
SANTA CATARINA
Uruguay
RIO GRANDE
DO SUL Pôrto Alegre

O C E A N

Arch. de Juan Fernández
(Chile)
Córdoba Santa Fe
San Juan Paraná Pelotas
Viña del Mar Mendoza Rosario **URUGUAY**
Valparaíso **A R G E N T I N A**
SANTIAGO Montevideo
Talca **BUENOS AIRES**
La Plata *Rio de la Plata*
Concepción
Bahía *Colorado*
Blanca Mar del Plata
Valdivia *Negro* Viedma
Puerto Montt

G

SOUTH
ATLANTIC
OCEAN

Comodoro Rivadavia
Gulf of San Jorge
Chubut

H

Gulf of Penas
West Falkland **FALKLAND IS.**
(U.K.)
Stanley
East Falkland
Magellan's Str.
Punta Arenas
Tierra del Fuego
South Georgia
(U.K.)
C. Horn

Projection: *Lambert's Azimuthal Equal Area*
CARTOGRAPHY BY PHILIP'S.

■ LIMA Capital Cities

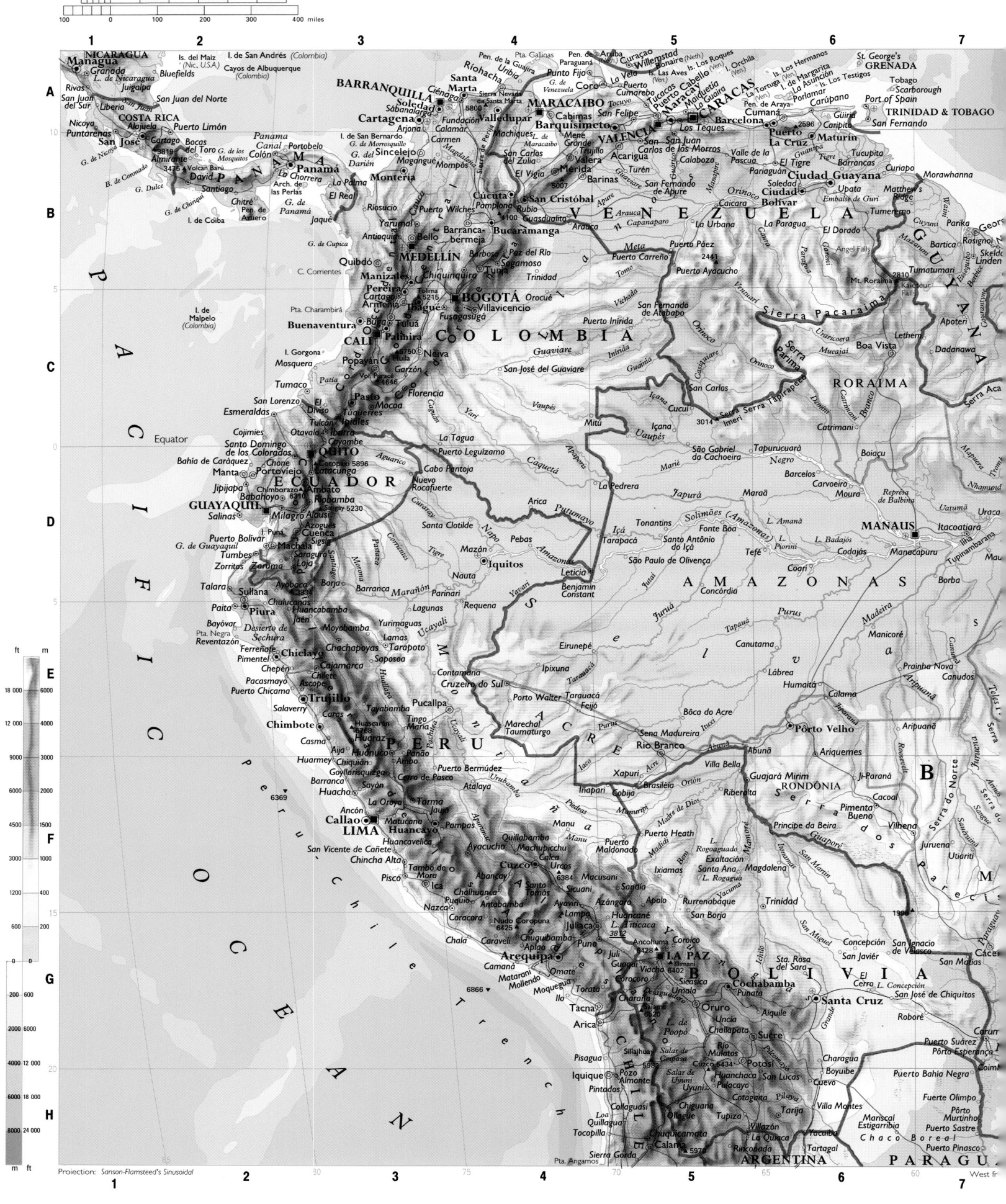

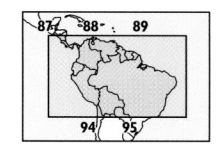

87 88 89
94 95

8 9 10 11 12 13

A

B

A T L A N T I C

O C E A N

C

São Paulo
(Braz.)

Equator

D

Fernando de Noronha
(Braz.)

Rocas

SURINAM
FRENCH GUIANA

Paramaribo
Nieuw Amsterdam
Moengo St-Laurent
Totness Albina Sinnamary
Kwakoegron Kourou
Prof. Van Cayenne
Blommestein- Approuague
meer Kaw
St-Georges
Oiapoque
Camopi

AMAPÁ
Serra do Navio
Macapá
Mazagão
Afuá Chaves
I. Grande Soure Salinópolis
de Gurupá Curuçá
Marajó Vigia Bragança
BELÉM Castanhal Viseu
Abaetetuba Curuçá

Santarém Belterra
Altamira
PARÁ
Tucuruí
Marabá
São João do Araguaia
Carajás
Tocantinópolis
Araguaína
Carolina

São Luís
Rosário
Pinheiro Itapecuru-Mirim
Viana Brejo
Santa Inês Codó Coroatá
Bacabal Caxias
MARANHÃO
Imperatriz Barra do Corda
Grajaú
Pôrto Franco
Estreito
Riachão Loreto
Uruçuí

Parnaíba
Luís Correia
Tutóia
Granja Itapipoca Caucaia
Sobral FORTALEZA
Maranguape Cascavel
Baturité Aracati
Ipu Quixadá Russos
Crateús Areia Branca
Mossoró Macau
RIO GRANDE DO NORTE
Caraúbas Natal
Caicó C. de São Roque
Currais Novos
Patos Campina
PARAÍBA Grande João Pessoa
Cajàzeiras Olinda
Juàzeiro do Norte RECIFE
PERNAMBUCO Caruaru Jaboatão
Salgueiro Garanhuns Palmares
Petrolândia Palmeira Rio Largo
Petrolina Maceió
ALAGOAS Penedo
Propriá
SERGIPE
Aracaju
São Cristóvão
Estância

Teresina
CEARÁ
Piripiri
Campo Maior Oiticica
Amarante
Valença do Piauí
Oeiras Picos
Floriano
Nova Iorque
PIAUÍ
São João do Piauí
Paulistana

TERESINA

5

BRAZIL
TOCANTINS
Palmas
Pôrto Nacional
Gurupi
Peixe
Taguatinga
Paranã
Campos Belos
São Domingos

Parnaguá
Barra
Xique-Xique
Remanso
Juàzeiro
BAHIA
Irecê
Ibotirama
Barreiras
Bom Jesus da Lapa
Caetité
Brumado
Vitória da Conquista

10

Feira de Santana
Alagoinhas
Santo Amaro
SALVADOR
Cachoeira
Valença
Jequié
Itabuna
Ilhéus
Canavieiras
Belmonte
Pôrto Seguro
Prado
Caravelas

6059

MATO GROSSO
Planalto do
Mato Grosso
Santo Antônio
Barra do Garças
Rondonópolis
Coxim
MATO GROSSO DO SUL
Campo Grande
Aquidauana
Miranda

DIST. FED.
Formosa
BRASÍLIA
Taguatinga
Luziânia
Anápolis
GOIÁS
Goiânia
Vianópolis

Januária
São Francisco
Janaúba
Montes Claros
Salinas
Jequitinhonha
Pedra Azul
Itamaraju
Nanuque
Mucuri
Conceição da Barra

15

MINAS GERAIS
Paracatu
Pirapora
Diamantina
Teófilo Otoni
Araçuaí
Governador Valadares
São Mateus
Linhares

Uberlândia
Uberaba
Araxá
Patrocínio
Curvelo
Sete Lagoas
BELO HORIZONTE
Itabira
Colatina
Cariacica
Vitória
Vila Velha

Araguari
Ituiutaba
Frutal
Prata
Divinópolis
Nova Lima
Sabará
Ponte Nova
Ouro Prêto
Barbacena
Juiz de Fora
Cachoeiro de Itapemirim
Campos

G

Trindade
(Braz.)

Campo Grande
Três Lagoas
Rio Prêto
São José do Rio Prêto
Andradina
Araçatuba
Penápolis
Lins
Marília
Bauru
Jaú
São Carlos
Araraquara
Ribeirão Prêto
Franca
Poços de Caldas
São João del Rei
Conselheiro Lafaiete
Três Rios
Nova Friburgo
Petrópolis
Niterói

H

Presidente Prudente
Presidente Epitácio
Dourados
Ponta Porã
SÃO PAULO
Piracicaba
Limeira
Campinas
Jundiaí
Mogi-Mirim
Volta Redonda
Cabo Frio
RIO DE JANEIRO

Greenwich 55

8 9 10 11 12 13

COPYRIGHT GEORGE PHILIP LTD.

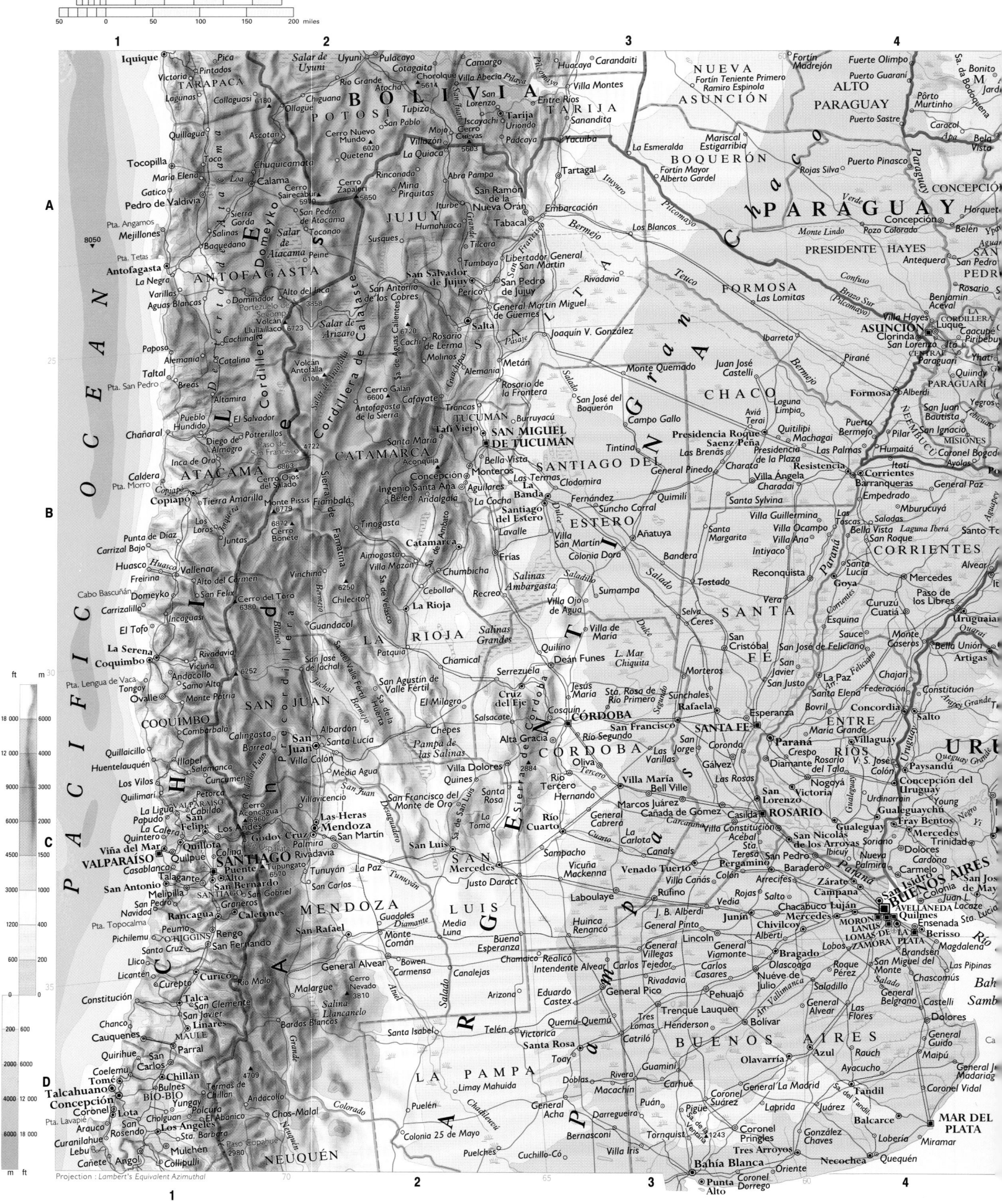

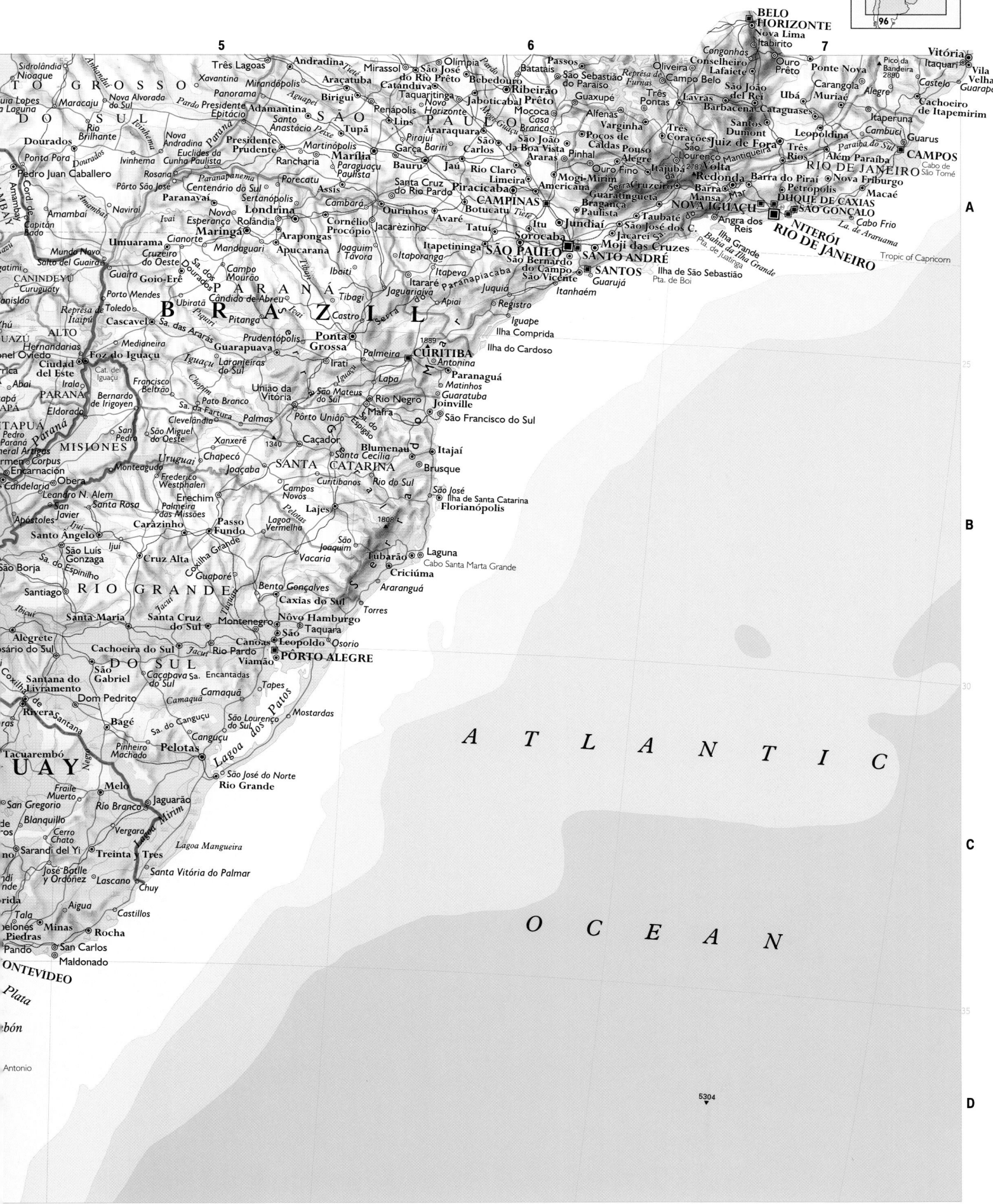

BELO
HORIZONTE
Nova Lima
Itabirito

Vitória
Itaquari
Vila
Velha
Guarapari

Sidrolândia
Nioaque
Congonhas
Conselheiro
Lafaiete
Oliveira
Ouro
Prêto
Ponte Nova
Pico da
Bandeira
2890
Castelo

MATO GROSSO
Três Lagoas
Andradina
Mirassol
São José
do Rio Prêto
Olímpia
Campo Belo
Campo Belo
São João
del Rei
Carangola
Muriaé
Cachoeiro
de Itapemirim

Maracaju
Xavantina
Mirandópolis
Araçatuba
Catanduva
Bebedouro
Ribeirão
Prêto
São Sebastião
do Paraíso
Represa de
Furnas
Três
Pontas
Barbacena
Cataguases
Itaperuna

DO SUL
Panorama
Aguapeí
Penápolis
Taquaritinga
Jaboticabal
Mococa
Casa
Branca
Guaxupé
Alfenas
Varginha
Pouso
Alegre
Lavras
Leopoldina
Cambuci
Guarus

Dourados
Nova
Andradina
Adamantina
Euclides da
Cunha Paulista
Santo
Anastácio
Lins
Araraquara
São
Carlos
Rio Claro
da Boa Vista
Pôços de
Caldas
Três
Corações
São
Lourenço
Juiz de Fora
Três
Rios
Paraíba do Sul
CAMPOS
Cabo de
São Tomé

Ponta Porã
Pedro Juan Caballero
Rio
Brilhante
Presidente
Epitácio
Presidente
Prudente
Martinópolis
Marília
Tupã
Bauru
Jaú
Pirajuí
Bariri
São João
da Boa Vista
Mogi-Mirim
Pinhal
Ouro Fino
Itajubá
Pouso
Alegre
Volta
Redonda
Barra do Pirai
Nova Friburgo
Macaé

RIO DE JANEIRO

Dourados
Ivinhema
Rosana
Pôrto São José
Rancharia
Paraguaçu
Paulista
Garça
Piracicaba
Limeira
Americana
Guaratinguetá
Barra
Mansa
DUQUE DE CAXIAS
SÃO GONÇALO

Mundo Novo
Navirai
Nova
Esperança
Centenário do Sul
Assis
Cambará
Ourinhos
CAMPINAS
Botucatu
Tietê
Bragança
Paulista
Taubaté
Angra dos
Reis
NITERÓI
Cabo Frio
La. de Araruama

Amambai
Amambaí
Cruzeiro
do Oeste
Londrina
Rolândia
Cornélio
Procópio
Jacarèzinho
Avaré
JUNDIAÍ
Jacareí
São José dos C.
Ilha Grande
Bahia da Ilha Grande
RIO DE JANEIRO

Sidrolândia
Salto del Guaíra
Umuarama
Cianorte
Maringá
Mandaguari
Apucarana
Itapetininga
Tatuí
Sorocaba
SÃO PAULO
SANTO ANDRÉ
Moji das Cruzes
Pta. de Juatinga
Tropic of Capricorn

CANINDEYU
Curuguaty
Goio-Erê
Campo
Mourão
Joaquim
Távora
Ibaiti
Itararé
Itapeva
São Bernardo
do Campo
SANTOS
Ilha de São Sebastião

CAGUAZÚ
Hernandarias
Guaíra
Porto Mendes
PARANÁ
Prudentópolis
Tibagi
Jaguariaíva
Paranapiacaba
São Vicente
Guarujá
Pta. de Boi

nel Oviedo
Abaí
Represa de
Toledo
Itaipú
Ubiratã
Pitanga
Castro
Apiaí
Juquiá
Itanhaém

BRAZIL
Cascavel
Sa. das Araras
Ponta
Grossa
Palmeira
1889
Registro
Iguape

Foz do Iguaçu
Medianeira
Guarapuava
Irati
CÚRITIBA
Antonina
Ilha Comprida

Ciudad
del Este
Irala
Cat. del
Iguaçu
Francisco
Beltrão
Laranjeiras
do Sul
União da
Vitória
São Mateus
do Sul
Rio Negro
Paranaguá
Matinhos
Guaratuba
Ilha do Cardoso

APA
Bernardo
de Irigoyen
Sa. do
Chopim
Pato Branco
Palmas
Pôrto Uniáo
Mafra
Joinville
São Francisco do Sul

ITAPUÁ
Pedro
General
Artigas
San
Pedro
São Miguel
do Oeste
Clevelândia
1340
Caçador
Blumenau
Itajaí

Posadas
Corpus
Monteagudo
Xanxerê
Chapecó
Santa Cecília
Brusque

MISIONES
Candelaria
Obera
Frederico
Westphalen
Joaçaba
SANTA CATARINA
Rio do Sul
São José

Encarnación
Leandro N. Alem
Santa Rosa
Palmeira
das Missões
Enechim
Campos
Novos
Curitibanos
Ilha de Santa Catarina
Florianópolis

San
Javier
Carázinho
Lajes
1808

Apóstoles
Ijuí
Passo
Fundo
Lagoa
Vermelha
São
Joaquim
Tubarão
Laguna
Cabo Santa Marta Grande

Santo
Ângelo
Cruz
Alta
Guaporé
Vacaria
Criciúma

São Borja
São Luís
Gonzaga
Bento Gonçalves
Araranguá

RIO GRANDE
Caxias do Sul
Torres

Santiago
Santa Maria
Santa Cruz
do Sul
Montenegro
Nôvo Hamburgo
Taquara

Alegrete
DO SUL
Cachoeira do Sul
Rio Pardo
Canoas
São
Leopoldo
Osorio

Rosário do Sul
São
Gabriel
Caçapava
do Sul
PÔRTO ALEGRE
Viamão

Santana do
Livramento
Dom Pedrito
Encantadas
Sa.
Camaquã
Tapes

Rivera
Santana
Bagé
Sa. do Canguçu
São Lourenço
do Sul
Mostardas

Tacuarembó
Pinheiro
Machado
Pelotas
Canguçu
Lagoa dos Patos

UAY
Melo
Rio Branco
Jaguarão
São José
do Norte
Rio Grande

Fraile
Muerto
Vergara
Lagoa
Mirim

San Gregorio
Blanquillo
Cerro
Chato
Lagoa Mangueira

Sarandi del Yi
Treinta y Tres
Santa Vitória do Palmar

José Batlle
y Ordóñez
Lascano
Chuy

ATLANTIC

Aigua
Castillos

Tala
Minas
Rocha
San Carlos
Maldonado

MONTEVIDEO

Plata

bón

Antonio

OCEAN

5304

West from Greenwich

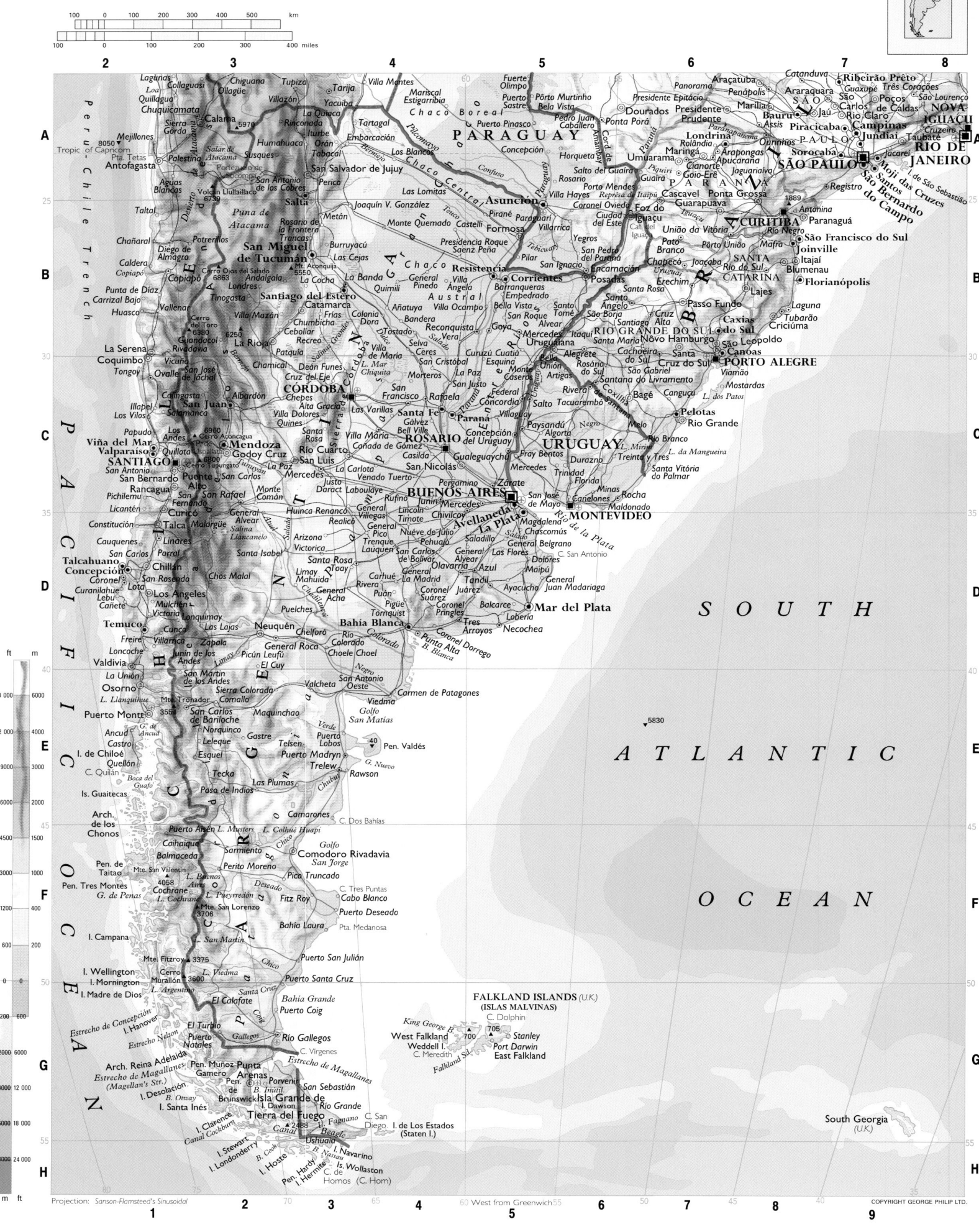

INDEX

The index contains the names of all the principal places and features shown on the World Maps. Each name is followed by an additional entry in italics giving the country or region within which it is located. The alphabetical order of names composed of two or more words is governed primarily by the first word and then by the second. This is an example of the rule:

Mīr Kūh, *Iran*	**45 E8**	26 22N	58 55 E
Mīr Shahdād, *Iran*	**45 E8**	26 15N	58 29 E
Mira, *Italy*	**20 B5**	45 26N	12 8 E
Mira por vos Cay, *Bahamas*	**89 B5**	22 9N	74 30W
Miraj, *India*	**40 L9**	16 50N	74 45 E

Physical features composed of a proper name (Erie) and a description (Lake) are positioned alphabetically by the proper name. The description is positioned after the proper name and is usually abbreviated:

Erie, L., *N. Amer.*	**78 D4**	42 15N	81 0W

Where a description forms part of a settlement or administrative name however, it is always written in full and put in its true alphabetic position:

Mount Morris, *U.S.A.*	**78 D7**	42 44N	77 52W

Names beginning with M' and Mc are indexed as if they were spelled Mac. Names beginning St. are alphabetised under Saint, but Sankt, Sint, Sant', Santa and San are all spelt in full and are alphabetised accordingly. If the same place name occurs two or more times in the index and all are in the same country, each is followed by the name of the administrative subdivision in which it is located. The names are placed in the alphabetical order of the subdivisions. For example:

Jackson, *Ky., U.S.A.*	**76 G4**	37 33N	83 23W
Jackson, *Mich., U.S.A.*	**76 D3**	42 15N	84 24W
Jackson, *Minn., U.S.A.*	**80 D7**	43 37N	95 1W

The number in bold type which follows each name in the index refers to the number of the map page where that feature or place will be found. This is usually the largest scale at which the place or feature appears.

The letter and figure which are in bold type immediately after the page number give the grid square on the map page, within which the feature is situated. The letter represents the latitude and the figure the longitude.

In some cases the feature itself may fall within the specified square, while the name is outside. This is usually the case only with features which are larger than a grid square.

For a more precise location the geographical coordinates which follow the letter/figure references give the latitude and the longitude of each place. The first set of figures represent the latitude which is the distance north or south of the Equator measured as an angle at the centre of the earth. The Equator is latitude 0°, the North Pole is 90°N, and the South Pole 90°S.

The second set of figures represent the longitude, which is the distance East or West of the prime meridian, which runs through Greenwich, England. Longitude is also measured as an angle at the centre of the earth and is given East or West of the prime meridian, from 0° to 180° in either direction.

The unit of measurement for latitude and longitude is the degree, which is subdivided into 60 minutes. Each index entry states the position of a place in degrees and minutes, a space being left between the degrees and the minutes.

The latitude is followed by N(orth) or S(outh) and the longitude by E(ast) or W(est).

Rivers are indexed to their mouths or confluences, and carry the symbol ➜ after their names. A solid square ■ follows the name of a country, while an open square □ refers to a first order administrative area.

Abbreviations used in the index

A.C.T. – Australian Capital Territory
Afghan. – Afghanistan
Ala. – Alabama
Alta. – Alberta
Amer. – America(n)
Arch. – Archipelago
Ariz. – Arizona
Ark. – Arkansas
Atl. Oc. – Atlantic Ocean
B. – Baie, Bahía, Bay, Bucht, Bugt
B.C. – British Columbia
Bangla. – Bangladesh
Barr. – Barrage
Bos.-H. – Bosnia-Herzegovina
C. – Cabo, Cap, Cape, Coast
C.A.R. – Central African Republic
C. Prov. – Cape Province
Calif. – California
Cent. – Central
Chan. – Channel
Colo. – Colorado
Conn. – Connecticut
Cord. – Cordillera
Cr. – Creek
Czech. – Czech Republic
D.C. – District of Columbia
Del. – Delaware
Dep. – Dependency
Des. – Desert
Dist. – District
Dj. – Djebel
Domin. – Dominica
Dom. Rep. – Dominican Republic
E. – East

E. Salv. – El Salvador
Eq. Guin. – Equatorial Guinea
Fla. – Florida
Falk. Is. – Falkland Is.
G. – Golfe, Golfo, Gulf, Guba, Gebel
Ga. – Georgia
Gt. – Great, Greater
Guinea-Biss. – Guinea-Bissau
H.K. – Hong Kong
H.P. – Himachal Pradesh
Hants. – Hampshire
Harb. – Harbor, Harbour
Hd. – Head
Hts. – Heights
I.(s). – Île, Ilha, Insel, Isla, Island, Isle
Ill. – Illinois
Ind. – Indiana
Ind. Oc. – Indian Ocean
Ivory C. – Ivory Coast
J. – Jabal, Jebel, Jazira
Junc. – Junction
K. – Kap, Kapp
Kans. – Kansas
Kep. – Kepulauan
Ky. – Kentucky
L. – Lac, Lacul, Lago, Lagoa, Lake, Limni, Loch, Lough
La. – Louisiana
Liech. – Liechtenstein
Lux. – Luxembourg
Mad. P. – Madhya Pradesh
Madag. – Madagascar
Man. – Manitoba
Mass. – Massachusetts

Md. – Maryland
Me. – Maine
Medit. S. – Mediterranean Sea
Mich. – Michigan
Minn. – Minnesota
Miss. – Mississippi
Mo. – Missouri
Mont. – Montana
Mozam. – Mozambique
Mt.(e) – Mont, Monte, Monti, Montaña, Mountain
N. – Nord, Norte, North, Northern, Nouveau
N.B. – New Brunswick
N.C. – North Carolina
N. Cal. – New Caledonia
N. Dak. – North Dakota
N.H. – New Hampshire
N.I. – North Island
N.J. – New Jersey
N. Mex. – New Mexico
N.S. – Nova Scotia
N.S.W. – New South Wales
N.W.T. – North West Territory
N.Y. – New York
N.Z. – New Zealand
Nebr. – Nebraska
Neths. – Netherlands
Nev. – Nevada
Nfld. – Newfoundland
Nic. – Nicaragua
O. – Oued, Ouadi
Okla. – Oklahoma
Ont. – Ontario
Or. – Orientale

Oreg. – Oregon
Os. – Ostrov
Oz. – Ozero
P. – Pass, Passo, Pasul, Pulau
P.E.I. – Prince Edward Island
Pa. – Pennsylvania
Pac. Oc. – Pacific Ocean
Papua N.G. – Papua New Guinea
Pass. – Passage
Pen. – Peninsula, Péninsule
Phil. – Philippines
Pk. – Park, Peak
Plat. – Plateau
Prov. – Province, Provincial
Pt. – Point
Pta. – Ponta, Punta
Pte. – Pointe
Qué. – Québec
Queens. – Queensland
R. – Rio, River
R.I. – Rhode Island
Ra.(s). – Range(s)
Raj. – Rajasthan
Reg. – Region
Rep. – Republic
Res. – Reserve, Reservoir
S. – San, South, Sea
Si. Arabia – Saudi Arabia
S.C. – South Carolina
S. Dak. – South Dakota
S.I. – South Island
S. Leone – Sierra Leone
Sa. – Serra, Sierra
Sask. – Saskatchewan
Scot. – Scotland
Sd. – Sound

Sev. – Severnaya
Sib. – Siberia
Sprs. – Springs
St. – Saint
Sta. – Santa, Station
Ste. – Sainte
Sto. – Santo
Str. – Strait, Stretto
Switz. – Switzerland
Tas. – Tasmania
Tenn. – Tennessee
Tex. – Texas
Tg. – Tanjung
Trin. & Tob. – Trinidad & Tobago
U.A.E. – United Arab Emirates
U.K. – United Kingdom
U.S.A. – United States of America
Ut. P. – Uttar Pradesh
Va. – Virginia
Vdkhr. – Vodokhranilishche
Vf. – Vîrful
Vic. – Victoria
Vol. – Volcano
Vt. – Vermont
W. – Wadi, West
W. Va. – West Virginia
Wash. – Washington
Wis. – Wisconsin
Wlkp. – Wielkopolski
Wyo. – Wyoming
Yorks. – Yorkshire
Yug. – Yugoslavia

A Coruña

A

A Coruña, Spain 19 A1 43 20N 8 25W
A Estrada, Spain 19 A1 42 43N 8 27W
A Fonsagrada, Spain 19 A2 43 8N 7 4W
Aachen, Germany 16 C4 50 45N 6 6 E
Aalborg = Ålborg, Denmark 9 H13 57 2N 9 54 E
Aalen, Germany 16 D6 48 51N 10 6 E
Aalst, Belgium 15 D4 50 56N 4 2 E
Aalten, Neths. 15 C6 51 56N 6 35 E
Aalter, Belgium 15 C3 51 5N 3 28 E
Äänekoski, Finland 9 E21 62 36N 25 44 E
Aarau, Switz. 18 C8 47 23N 8 4 E
Aare →, Switz. 18 C8 47 33N 8 14 E
Aarhus = Århus, Denmark 9 H14 56 8N 10 11 E
Aarschot, Belgium 15 D4 50 59N 4 49 E
Aba, Dem. Rep. of the Congo 54 B3 3 58N 30 17 E
Aba, Nigeria 50 G7 5 10N 7 19 E
Ābādān, Iran 45 D6 30 22N 48 20 E
Ābādeh, Iran 45 D7 31 8N 52 40 E
Abadla, Algeria 50 B5 31 2N 2 45W
Abaetetuba, Brazil 93 D9 1 40S 48 50W
Abagnar Qi, China 34 C9 43 52N 116 2 E
Abai, Paraguay 95 B4 25 58S 55 54W
Abakan, Russia 27 D10 53 40N 91 10 E
Abancay, Peru 92 F4 13 35S 72 55W
Abariringa, Kiribati 64 H10 2 50S 171 40W
Abarqū, Iran 45 D7 31 10N 53 20 E
Abashiri, Japan 30 B12 44 0N 144 15 E
Abashiri-Wan, Japan 30 C12 44 0N 144 30 E
Ābay = Nîl el Azraq →, Sudan 51 E12 15 38N 32 31 E
Abay, Kazakstan 26 E8 49 38N 72 53 E
Abaya, L., Ethiopia 46 F2 6 30N 37 50 E
Abaza, Russia 26 D9 52 39N 90 6 E
'Abbāsābād, Iran 45 C8 33 34N 58 23 E
Abbay = Nîl el Azraq →, Sudan 51 E12 15 38N 32 31 E
Abbaye, Pt., U.S.A. 76 B1 46 58N 88 8W
Abbé, L., Ethiopia 46 E3 11 8N 41 47 E
Abbeville, France 18 A4 50 6N 1 49 E
Abbeville, Ala., U.S.A. 77 K3 31 34N 85 15W
Abbeville, La., U.S.A. 81 L8 29 58N 92 8W
Abbeville, S.C., U.S.A. 77 H4 34 11N 82 23W
Abbot Ice Shelf, Antarctica 5 D16 73 0S 92 0W
Abbottabad, Pakistan 42 B5 34 10N 73 15 E
Abd al Kūrī, Yemen 46 E5 12 5N 52 20 E
Ābdar, Iran 45 D7 30 16N 55 19 E
'Abdolābād, Iran 45 C8 34 12N 56 30 E
Abdulpur, Bangla. 43 G13 24 15N 88 59 E
Abéché, Chad 51 F10 13 50N 20 35 E
Abengourou, Ivory C. 50 G5 6 42N 3 27W
Åbenrå, Denmark 9 J13 55 3N 9 25 E
Abeokuta, Nigeria 50 G6 7 3N 3 19 E
Aber, Uganda 54 B3 2 12N 32 25 E
Aberaeron, U.K. 11 E3 52 15N 4 15W
Aberayron = Aberaeron, U.K. 11 E3 52 15N 4 15W
Aberchirder, U.K. 12 D6 57 34N 2 37W
Abercorn = Mbala, Zambia 55 D3 8 46S 31 24 E
Abercorn, Australia 63 D5 25 12S 151 5 E
Aberdare, U.K. 11 F4 51 43N 3 27W
Aberdare Ra., Kenya 54 C4 0 15S 36 50 E
Aberdeen, Australia 63 E5 32 9S 150 56 E
Aberdeen, Canada 73 C7 52 20N 106 8W
Aberdeen, S. Africa 56 E3 32 28S 24 2 E
Aberdeen, U.K. 12 D6 57 9N 2 5W
Aberdeen, Ala., U.S.A. 77 J1 33 49N 88 33W
Aberdeen, Idaho, U.S.A. 82 E7 42 57N 112 50W
Aberdeen, Md., U.S.A. 76 F7 39 31N 76 10W
Aberdeen, S. Dak., U.S.A. 80 C5 45 28N 98 29W
Aberdeen, Wash., U.S.A. 84 D3 46 59N 123 50W
Aberdeen, City of □, U.K. 12 D6 57 10N 2 10W
Aberdeenshire □, U.K. 12 D6 57 17N 2 36W
Aberdovey = Aberdyfi, U.K. 11 E3 52 33N 4 3W
Aberdyfi, U.K. 11 E3 52 33N 4 3W
Aberfeldy, U.K. 12 E5 56 37N 3 51W
Abergavenny, U.K. 11 F4 51 49N 3 1W
Abergele, U.K. 10 D4 53 17N 3 35W
Abernathy, U.S.A. 81 J4 33 50N 101 51W
Abert, L., U.S.A. 82 E3 42 38N 120 14W
Aberystwyth, U.K. 11 E3 52 25N 4 5W
Abhā, Si. Arabia 46 D3 18 0N 42 34 E
Abhar, Iran 45 B6 36 9N 49 13 E
Abhayapuri, India 43 F14 26 24N 90 38 E
Abidjan, Ivory C. 50 G5 5 26N 3 58W
Abilene, Kans., U.S.A. 80 F6 38 55N 97 13W
Abilene, Tex., U.S.A. 81 J5 32 28N 99 43W
Abingdon, U.K. 11 F6 51 40N 1 17W
Abingdon, U.S.A. 77 G5 36 43N 81 59W
Abington Reef, Australia 62 B4 18 0S 149 35 E
Abitau →, Canada 73 B7 59 53N 109 3W
Abitibi →, Canada 70 B3 51 3N 80 55W
Abitibi, L., Canada 70 C4 48 40N 79 40W
Abkhaz Republic = Abkhazia □, Georgia 25 F7 43 12N 41 5 E
Abkhazia □, Georgia 25 F7 43 12N 41 5 E
Abminga, Australia 63 D1 26 8S 134 51 E
Åbo = Turku, Finland 9 F20 60 30N 22 19 E
Abohar, India 42 D6 30 10N 74 10 E
Abomey, Benin 50 G6 7 10N 2 5 E
Abong-Mbang, Cameroon 52 D2 4 0N 13 8 E
Abou-Deïa, Chad 51 F9 11 20N 19 20 E
Aboyne, U.K. 12 D6 57 4N 2 47W
Abra Pampa, Argentina 94 A2 22 43S 65 42W
Abraham L., Canada 72 C5 52 15N 116 35W
Abreojos, Pta., Mexico 86 B2 26 50N 113 40W
Abrud, Romania 17 E12 46 19N 23 5 E
Absaroka Range, U.S.A. 82 D9 44 45N 109 50W
Abu, India 42 G5 24 41N 72 50 E
Abū al Abyad, U.A.E. 45 E7 24 11N 53 50 E
Abū al Khaşīb, Iraq 45 D6 30 25N 48 0 E
Abū 'Alī, Si. Arabia 45 E6 27 20N 49 27 E
Abū 'Alī →, Lebanon 47 A4 34 25N 35 50 E
Abu Dhabi = Abū Ẓāby, U.A.E. 46 C5 24 28N 54 22 E
Abū Du'ān, Syria 44 B3 36 25N 38 15 E
Abu el Gairi, W. →, Egypt 47 F2 29 35N 33 30 E
Abu Ga'da, W. →, Egypt 47 F1 29 15N 32 53 E
Abū Ḩadrīyah, Si. Arabia 45 E6 27 20N 48 58 E
Abu Hamed, Sudan 51 E12 19 32N 33 13 E
Abū Kamāl, Syria 44 C4 34 30N 41 0 E
Abū Madd, Ra's, Si. Arabia 44 E3 24 50N 37 7 E
Abū Mūsā, U.A.E. 45 E7 25 52N 55 3 E
Abū Qaşr, Si. Arabia 44 D3 30 21N 38 34 E
Abu Şafāt, W. →, Jordan 47 E5 30 24N 36 7 E
Abu Simbel, Egypt 51 D12 22 18N 31 40 E
Abū Şukhayr, Iraq 44 D5 31 54N 44 30 E
Abu Zabad, Sudan 51 F11 12 25N 29 10 E
Abū Ẓāby, U.A.E. 46 C5 24 28N 54 22 E
Abū Zeydābād, Iran 45 C6 33 54N 51 45 E
Abuja, Nigeria 50 G7 9 5N 7 32 E
Abukuma-Gawa →, Japan 30 E10 38 6N 140 52 E
Abukuma-Sammyaku, Japan 30 F10 37 30N 140 45 E
Abunã, Brazil 92 E5 9 40S 65 20W
Abunã →, Brazil 92 E5 9 41S 65 20W
Aburo, Dem. Rep. of the Congo 54 B3 2 4N 30 53 E
Abut Hd., N.Z. 59 K3 43 7S 170 15 E
Acadia Nat. Park, U.S.A. 77 C11 44 20N 68 13W
Açailândia, Brazil 93 D9 4 57S 47 0W
Acajutla, El Salv. 88 D2 13 36N 89 50W
Acámbaro, Mexico 86 D4 20 0N 100 40W
Acaponeta, Mexico 86 C3 22 30N 105 20W
Acapulco, Mexico 87 D5 16 51N 99 56W
Acarai, Serra, Brazil 92 C7 1 50N 57 50W
Acarigua, Venezuela 92 B5 9 33N 69 12W
Acatlán, Mexico 87 D5 18 10N 98 3W
Acayucan, Mexico 87 D6 17 59N 94 58W
Accomac, U.S.A. 76 G8 37 43N 75 40W
Accra, Ghana 50 G5 5 35N 0 6W
Accrington, U.K. 10 D5 53 45N 2 22W
Acebal, Argentina 94 C3 33 20S 60 50W
Aceh □, Indonesia 36 D1 4 15N 97 30 E
Achalpur, India 40 J10 21 22N 77 32 E
Acheng, China 35 B14 45 30N 126 58 E
Acher, India 42 H5 23 10N 72 32 E
Achill Hd., Ireland 13 C1 53 58N 10 15W
Achill I., Ireland 13 C1 53 58N 10 1W
Achinsk, Russia 27 D10 56 20N 90 20 E
Acireale, Italy 20 F6 37 37N 15 10 E
Ackerman, U.S.A. 81 J10 33 19N 89 11W
Acklins I., Bahamas 89 B5 22 30N 74 0W
Acme, Canada 72 C6 51 33N 113 30W
Acme, U.S.A. 78 F5 40 8N 79 26W
Aconcagua, Cerro, Argentina 94 C2 32 39S 70 0W
Aconquija, Mt., Argentina 94 B2 27 0S 66 0W
Açores, Is. dos, Atl. Oc. 50 A1 38 0N 27 0W
Acornhoek, S. Africa 57 C5 24 37S 31 2 E
Acraman, L., Australia 63 E2 32 2S 135 23 E
Acre = 'Akko, Israel 47 C4 32 55N 35 4 E
Acre □, Brazil 92 E4 9 1S 71 0W
Acre →, Brazil 92 E5 8 45S 67 22W
Acton, Canada 78 C4 43 38N 80 3W
Acuña, Mexico 86 B4 29 18N 100 55W
Ad Dammām, Si. Arabia 45 E6 26 20N 50 5 E
Ad Dāmūr, Lebanon 47 B4 33 44N 35 27 E
Ad Dawādimī, Si. Arabia 44 E5 24 35N 44 15 E
Ad Dawḩah, Qatar 46 B5 25 15N 51 35 E
Ad Dawr, Iraq 44 C4 34 27N 43 47 E
Ad Dir'īyah, Si. Arabia 44 E5 24 44N 46 35 E
Ad Dīwānīyah, Iraq 44 D5 32 0N 45 0 E
Ad Dujayl, Iraq 44 C5 33 51N 44 14 E
Ad Duwayd, Si. Arabia 44 D4 30 15N 42 17 E
Ada, Minn., U.S.A. 80 B6 47 18N 96 31W
Ada, Okla., U.S.A. 81 H6 34 46N 96 41W
Adabiya, Egypt 47 F1 29 53N 32 28 E
Adair, C., Canada 69 A12 71 31N 71 24W
Adaja →, Spain 19 B3 41 32N 4 52W
Adak I., U.S.A. 68 C2 51 45N 176 45W
Adamaoua, Massif de l', Cameroon 51 G7 7 20N 12 20 E
Adamawa Highlands = Adamaoua, Massif de l', Cameroon 51 G7 7 20N 12 20 E
Adamello, Mte., Italy 18 C9 46 9N 10 30 E
Adaminaby, Australia 63 F4 36 0S 148 45 E
Adams, Mass., U.S.A. 79 D11 42 38N 73 7W
Adams, N.Y., U.S.A. 79 C8 43 49N 76 1W
Adams, Wis., U.S.A. 80 D10 43 57N 89 49W
Adam's Bridge, Sri Lanka 40 Q11 9 15N 79 40 E
Adams L., Canada 72 C5 51 10N 119 40W
Adams Mt., U.S.A. 84 D5 46 12N 121 30W
Adam's Peak, Sri Lanka 40 R12 6 48N 80 30 E
Adana, Turkey 25 G6 37 0N 35 16 E
Adapazarı = Sakarya, Turkey 25 F5 40 48N 30 25 E
Adarama, Sudan 51 E12 17 10N 34 52 E
Adare, C., Antarctica 5 D11 71 0S 171 0 E
Adaut, Indonesia 37 F8 8 8S 131 7 E
Adavale, Australia 63 D3 25 52S 144 32 E
Adda →, Italy 18 D8 45 8N 9 53 E
Addis Ababa = Addis Abeba, Ethiopia 46 F2 9 2N 38 42 E
Addis Abeba, Ethiopia 46 F2 9 2N 38 42 E
Addison, U.S.A. 78 D7 42 1N 77 14W
Addo, S. Africa 56 E4 33 32S 25 45 E
Ādeh, Iran 44 B5 37 42N 45 11 E
Adel, U.S.A. 77 K4 31 8N 83 25W
Adelaide, Australia 63 E2 34 52S 138 30 E
Adelaide, Bahamas 88 A4 25 4N 77 31W
Adelaide, S. Africa 56 E4 32 42S 26 20 E
Adelaide I., Antarctica 5 C17 67 15S 68 30W
Adelaide Pen., Canada 68 B10 68 15N 97 30W
Adelaide River, Australia 60 B5 13 15S 131 7 E
Adelanto, U.S.A. 85 L9 34 35N 117 22W
Adele I., Australia 60 C3 15 32S 123 9 E
Adélie, Terre, Antarctica 5 C10 68 0S 140 0 E
Adélie Land = Adélie, Terre, Antarctica 5 C10 68 0S 140 0 E
Aden = Al 'Adan, Yemen 46 E4 12 45N 45 0 E
Aden, G. of, Asia 46 E4 12 30N 47 30 E
Adendorp, S. Africa 56 E3 32 15S 24 30 E
Adh Dhayd, U.A.E. 45 E7 25 17N 55 53 E
Adhoi, India 42 H4 23 26N 70 32 E
Adi, Indonesia 37 E8 4 15S 133 30 E
Adieu, C., Australia 61 F5 32 0S 132 10 E
Adieu Pt., Australia 60 C3 15 14S 124 35 E
Adige →, Italy 20 B5 45 9N 12 20 E
Adigrat, Ethiopia 46 E2 14 20N 39 26 E
Adilabad, India 40 K11 19 33N 78 20 E
Adirondack Mts., U.S.A. 79 C10 44 0N 74 0W
Adjumani, Uganda 54 B3 3 20N 31 50 E
Adlavik Is., Canada 71 B8 55 0N 58 40W
Admiralty G., Australia 60 B4 14 20S 125 55 E
Admiralty I., U.S.A. 72 B2 57 30N 134 30W
Admiralty Is., Papua N. G. 64 H6 2 0S 147 0 E
Adonara, Indonesia 37 F6 8 15S 123 5 E
Adoni, India 40 M10 15 33N 77 18 E
Adour →, France 18 E3 43 32N 1 32W
Adra, India 43 H12 23 30N 86 42 E
Adra, Spain 19 D4 36 43N 3 3W
Adrano, Italy 20 F6 37 40N 14 50 E
Adrar, Mauritania 50 D3 20 30N 7 30 E
Adrar des Iforas, Algeria 50 C5 27 51N 0 11 E
Adrian, Mich., U.S.A. 76 E3 41 54N 84 2W
Adrian, Tex., U.S.A. 81 H3 35 16N 102 40W
Adriatic Sea, Medit. S. 20 C6 43 0N 16 0 E
Adua, Indonesia 37 E7 1 45S 129 50 E
Adwa, Ethiopia 46 E2 14 15N 38 52 E
Adygea □, Russia 25 F7 45 0N 40 0 E
Adzhar Republic = Ajaria □, Georgia 25 F7 41 30N 42 0 E
Adzopé, Ivory C. 50 G5 6 7N 3 49W
Ægean Sea, Medit. S. 21 E11 38 30N 25 0 E
Aerhtai Shan, Mongolia 32 B4 46 40N 92 45 E
'Afak, Iraq 44 C5 32 4N 45 15 E
Afándou, Greece 23 C10 36 18N 28 12 E
Afghanistan ■, Asia 40 C4 33 0N 65 0 E
Aflou, Algeria 50 B6 34 7N 2 3 E
Africa 48 E6 10 0N 20 0 E
'Afrīn, Syria 44 B3 36 32N 36 50 E
Afton, N.Y., U.S.A. 79 D9 42 14N 75 32W
Afton, Wyo., U.S.A. 82 E8 42 44N 110 56W
Afuá, Brazil 93 D8 0 15S 50 20W
'Afula, Israel 47 C4 32 37N 35 17 E
Afyon, Turkey 25 G5 38 45N 30 33 E
Afyonkarahisar = Afyon, Turkey 25 G5 38 45N 30 33 E
Agadès = Agadez, Niger 50 E7 16 58N 7 59 E
Agadez, Niger 50 E7 16 58N 7 59 E
Agadir, Morocco 50 B4 30 28N 9 55W
Agaete, Canary Is. 22 F4 28 6N 15 43W
Agar, India 42 H7 23 40N 76 2 E
Agartala, India 41 H17 23 50N 91 23 E
Agassiz, Canada 72 D4 49 14N 121 46W
Agats, Indonesia 37 F9 5 33S 138 0 E
Agawam, U.S.A. 79 D12 42 5N 72 37W
Agboville, Ivory C. 50 G5 5 55N 4 15W
Ağdam, Azerbaijan 44 B5 40 0N 46 58 E
Agde, France 18 E5 43 19N 3 28 E
Agen, France 18 D4 44 12N 0 38 E
Āgh Kand, Iran 45 B6 37 15N 48 4 E
Aginskoye, Russia 27 D12 51 6N 114 32 E
Agnew, Australia 61 E3 28 1S 120 31 E
Agori, India 43 G10 24 33N 82 57 E
Agra, India 42 F7 27 17N 77 58 E
Ağri, Turkey 25 G7 39 44N 43 3 E
Agri →, Italy 20 D7 40 13N 16 44 E
Ağrı Dağı, Turkey 25 G7 39 50N 44 15 E
Ağri Karakose = Ağri, Turkey 25 G7 39 44N 43 3 E
Agrigento, Italy 20 F5 37 19N 13 34 E
Agrínion, Greece 21 E9 38 37N 21 27 E
Agua Caliente, Baja Calif., Mexico 85 N10 32 29N 116 59W
Agua Caliente, Sinaloa, Mexico 86 B3 26 30N 108 20W
Agua Caliente Springs, U.S.A. 85 N10 32 56N 116 19W
Água Clara, Brazil 93 H8 20 25S 52 45W
Agua Hechicero, Mexico 85 N10 32 26N 116 14W
Agua Prieta, Mexico 86 A3 31 20N 109 32W
Aguadilla, Puerto Rico 89 C6 18 26N 67 10W
Aguadulce, Panama 88 E3 8 15N 80 32W
Aguanga, U.S.A. 85 M10 33 27N 116 51W
Aguanish, Canada 71 B7 50 14N 62 2W
Aguanus →, Canada 71 B7 50 13N 62 5W
Aguapey →, Argentina 94 B4 29 7S 56 36W
Aguaray Guazú →, Paraguay 94 A4 24 47S 57 19W
Aguarico →, Ecuador 92 D3 0 59S 75 11W
Aguas Blancas, Chile 94 A2 24 15S 69 55W
Aguas Calientes, Sierra de, Argentina 94 B2 25 26S 66 40W
Aguascalientes, Mexico 86 C4 21 53N 102 12W
Aguascalientes □, Mexico 86 C4 22 0N 102 20W
Aguilares, Argentina 94 B2 27 26S 65 35W
Aguilas, Spain 19 D5 37 23N 1 35W
Agüimes, Canary Is. 22 G4 27 58N 15 27W
Aguja, C. de la, Colombia 90 B3 11 18N 74 12W
Agulhas, C., S. Africa 56 E3 34 52S 20 0 E
Agulo, Canary Is. 22 F2 28 11N 17 12W
Agung, Gunung, Indonesia 36 F5 8 20S 115 28 E
Agur, Uganda 54 B3 2 28N 32 55 E
Agusan →, Phil. 37 C7 9 0N 125 30 E
Aha Mts., Botswana 56 B3 19 45S 21 0 E
Ahaggar, Algeria 50 D7 23 0N 6 30 E
Ahar, Iran 44 B5 38 35N 47 0 E
Ahipara B., N.Z. 59 F4 35 5S 173 5 E
Ahiri, India 40 K12 19 30N 80 0 E
Ahmad Wal, Pakistan 42 E1 29 18N 65 58 E
Ahmadabad, India 42 H5 23 0N 72 40 E
Aḩmadābād, Khorāsān, Iran 45 C9 35 3N 60 50 E
Aḩmadābād, Khorāsān, Iran 45 C8 35 49N 59 42 E
Aḩmadī, Iran 45 E8 27 56N 56 42 E
Ahmadnagar, India 40 K9 19 7N 74 46 E
Ahmadpur, Pakistan 42 E4 29 12N 71 10 E
Ahmadpur Lamma, Pakistan 42 E4 28 19N 70 3 E
Ahmedabad = Ahmadabad, India 42 H5 23 0N 72 40 E
Ahmednagar = Ahmadnagar, India 40 K9 19 7N 74 46 E
Ahome, Mexico 86 B3 25 55N 109 11W
Ahoskie, U.S.A. 77 G7 36 17N 76 59W
Ahram, Iran 45 D6 28 52N 51 16 E
Ahrax Pt., Malta 23 D1 36 0N 14 22 E
Āhū, Iran 45 C6 34 33N 50 2 E
Ahuachapán, El Salv. 88 D2 13 54N 89 52W
Ahvāz, Iran 45 D6 31 20N 48 40 E
Ahvenanmaa = Åland, Finland 9 F19 60 15N 20 0 E
Aḩwar, Yemen 46 E4 13 30N 46 40 E
Ai →, India 43 F14 26 26N 90 44 E
Ai-Ais, Namibia 56 D2 27 54S 17 59 E
Aichi □, Japan 31 G8 35 0N 137 15 E
Aigua, Uruguay 95 C5 34 13S 54 46W
Aigues-Mortes, France 18 E6 43 35N 4 12 E
Aihui, China 33 A7 50 10N 127 30 E
Aija, Peru 92 E3 9 50S 77 45W
Aikawa, Japan 30 E9 38 2N 138 15 E
Aiken, U.S.A. 77 J5 33 34N 81 43W
Aileron, Australia 62 C1 22 39S 133 20 E
Aillik, Canada 71 A8 55 11N 59 18W
Ailsa Craig, U.K. 12 F3 55 15N 5 6W
'Ailūn, Jordan 47 C4 32 18N 35 47 E
Aim, Russia 27 D14 59 0N 133 55 E
Aimere, Indonesia 37 F6 8 45S 121 3 E
Aimogasta, Argentina 94 B2 28 33S 66 50W
Aïn Ben Tili, Mauritania 50 C4 25 59N 9 27W
Aïn Sefra, Algeria 50 B5 32 47N 0 37W
Ain Sudr, Egypt 47 F2 29 50N 33 6 E
Ainaži, Latvia 9 H21 57 50N 24 24 E
Ainsworth, U.S.A. 80 D5 42 33N 99 52W
Aiquile, Bolivia 92 G5 18 10S 65 10W
Aïr, Niger 50 E7 18 30N 8 0 E
Air Force I., Canada 69 B12 67 58N 74 5W
Air Hitam, Malaysia 39 M4 1 55N 103 11 E
Airdrie, Canada 72 C6 51 18N 114 2W
Airdrie, U.K. 12 F5 55 52N 3 57W
Aire →, U.K. 10 D7 53 43N 0 55W
Aire, I. de l', Spain 22 B11 39 48N 4 16 E
Airlie Beach, Australia 62 C4 20 16S 148 43 E
Aisne →, France 18 B5 49 26N 2 50 E
Ait, India 43 G8 25 54N 79 14 E
Aitkin, U.S.A. 80 B8 46 32N 93 42W
Aiud, Romania 17 E12 46 19N 23 44 E
Aix-en-Provence, France 18 E6 43 32N 5 27 E
Aix-la-Chapelle = Aachen, Germany 16 C4 50 45N 6 6 E
Aix-les-Bains, France 18 D6 45 41N 5 53 E
Aíyion, Greece 21 E10 38 15N 22 5 E
Aizawl, India 41 H18 23 40N 92 44 E
Aizkraukle, Latvia 9 H21 56 36N 25 11 E
Aizpute, Latvia 9 H19 56 43N 21 40 E
Aizuwakamatsu, Japan 30 F9 37 30N 139 56 E
Ajaccio, France 18 F8 41 55N 8 40 E
Ajaigarh, India 43 G9 24 52N 80 16 E
Ajalpan, Mexico 87 D5 18 22N 97 15W
Ajanta Ra., India 40 J9 20 28N 75 50 E
Ajari Rep. = Ajaria □, Georgia 25 F7 41 30N 42 0 E
Ajaria □, Georgia 25 F7 41 30N 42 0 E
Ajax, Canada 78 C5 43 50N 79 1W
Ajdābiyā, Libya 51 B10 30 54N 20 4 E
Ajka, Hungary 17 E9 47 4N 17 31 E
'Ajmān, U.A.E. 45 E7 25 25N 55 30 E
Ajmer, India 42 F6 26 28N 74 37 E
Ajnala, India 42 D6 31 50N 74 48 E
Ajo, U.S.A. 83 K7 32 22N 112 52W
Ajo, C. de, Spain 19 A4 43 31N 3 35W
Akabira, Japan 30 C11 43 33N 142 5 E
Akamas, Cyprus 23 D11 35 3N 32 18 E
Akanthou, Cyprus 23 D12 35 22N 33 45 E
Akaroa, N.Z. 59 K4 43 49S 172 59 E
Akashi, Japan 31 G7 34 45N 134 58 E
Akbarpur, Bihar, India 43 G10 24 39N 83 58 E
Akbarpur, Ut. P., India 43 F10 26 25N 82 32 E
Akelamo, Indonesia 37 D7 1 35N 129 40 E
Aketi, Dem. Rep. of the Congo 52 D4 2 38N 23 47 E
Akharnaí, Greece 21 E10 38 5N 23 44 E
Akhelóös →, Greece 21 E9 38 19N 21 7 E
Akhisar, Turkey 21 E12 38 56N 27 48 E
Akhnur, India 43 C6 32 52N 74 45 E
Akhtyrka = Okhtyrka, Ukraine 25 D5 50 25N 35 0 E
Aki, Japan 31 H6 33 30N 133 54 E
Akimiski I., Canada 70 B3 52 50N 81 30W
Akita, Japan 30 E10 39 45N 140 7 E
Akita □, Japan 30 E10 39 40N 140 30 E
Akjoujt, Mauritania 50 E3 19 45N 14 15W
Akkeshi, Japan 30 C12 43 2N 144 51 E
'Akko, Israel 47 C4 32 55N 35 4 E
Aklavik, Canada 68 B6 68 12N 135 0W
Aklera, India 42 G7 24 26N 76 32 E
Akmolinsk = Astana, Kazakstan 26 D8 51 10N 71 30 E
Akō, Japan 31 G7 34 45N 134 24 E
Akola, India 40 J10 20 42N 77 2 E
Akordat, Eritrea 46 D2 15 30N 37 40 E
Akpatok I., Canada 69 B13 60 25N 68 8W
Åkrahamn, Norway 9 G11 59 15N 5 10 E
Akranes, Iceland 8 D2 64 19N 22 5W
Akron, Colo., U.S.A. 80 E3 40 10N 103 13W
Akron, Ohio, U.S.A. 78 E3 41 5N 81 31W
Akrotiri, Cyprus 23 E11 34 36N 32 57 E
Akrotiri Bay, Cyprus 23 E12 34 35N 33 10 E
Aksai Chin, China 43 B8 35 15N 79 55 E
Aksaray, Turkey 25 G5 38 25N 34 2 E
Aksay, Kazakstan 25 D9 51 11N 53 0 E
Akşehir, Turkey 44 B1 38 18N 31 30 E
Akşehir Gölü, Turkey 25 G5 38 30N 31 25 E
Aksu, China 32 B3 41 5N 80 10 E
Aksum, Ethiopia 46 E2 14 5N 38 40 E
Aktogay, Kazakstan 26 E8 46 57N 79 40 E
Aktsyabrski, Belarus 17 B15 52 38N 28 53 E
Aktyubinsk = Aqtöbe, Kazakstan 25 D10 50 17N 57 10 E
Akure, Nigeria 50 G7 7 15N 5 5 E
Akureyri, Iceland 8 D4 65 40N 18 6W
Akuseki-Shima, Japan 31 K4 29 27N 129 37 E
Akyab = Sittwe, Burma 41 J18 20 18N 92 45 E
Al 'Adan, Yemen 46 E4 12 45N 45 0 E
Al Aḩsā = Hasa □, Si. Arabia 45 E6 25 50N 49 0 E
Al Ajfar, Si. Arabia 44 E4 27 26N 43 0 E
Al Amādīyah, Iraq 44 B4 37 5N 43 30 E
Al 'Amārah, Iraq 44 D5 31 55N 47 15 E
Al 'Aqabah, Jordan 47 F4 29 31N 35 0 E
Al Arak, Syria 44 C3 34 38N 38 35 E
Al 'Aramah, Si. Arabia 44 E5 25 30N 46 0 E
Al Arţāwīyah, Si. Arabia 44 E5 26 31N 45 20 E
Al 'Āşimah = 'Ammān □, Jordan 47 D5 31 40N 36 30 E
Al 'Assāfīyah, Si. Arabia 44 D3 28 17N 38 59 E
Al 'Ayn, Oman 45 E7 24 15N 55 45 E
Al 'Ayn, Si. Arabia 44 E3 25 4N 38 6 E
Al 'Aẓamīyah, Iraq 44 C5 33 22N 44 22 E
Al 'Azīzīyah, Iraq 44 C5 32 54N 45 4 E
Al Bāb, Syria 44 B3 36 23N 37 29 E
Al Bad', Si. Arabia 44 D2 28 28N 35 1 E
Al Bādī, Iraq 44 C4 35 56N 41 32 E
Al Baḩrah, Kuwait 44 D5 29 40N 47 52 E
Al Baḩral Mayyit = Dead Sea, Asia 47 D4 31 30N 35 30 E
Al Balqā' □, Jordan 47 C4 32 5N 35 45 E
Al Bārūk, J., Lebanon 47 B4 33 39N 35 40 E
Al Başrah, Iraq 44 D5 30 30N 47 50 E
Al Baţḩā, Iraq 44 D5 31 6N 45 53 E
Al Batrūn, Lebanon 47 A4 34 15N 35 40 E
Al Bayḑā, Libya 51 B10 32 50N 21 44 E
Al Biqā, Lebanon 47 A5 34 10N 36 10 E
Al Bi'r, Si. Arabia 44 D3 28 51N 36 16 E
Al Burayj, Syria 47 A5 34 15N 36 46 E
Al Faḑilī, Si. Arabia 45 E6 26 58N 49 10 E
Al Fallūjah, Iraq 44 C4 33 20N 43 55 E
Al Fāw, Iraq 45 D6 30 0N 48 30 E
Al Fujayrah, U.A.E. 45 E8 25 7N 56 18 E
Al Ghadaf, W. →, Jordan 47 D5 31 26N 36 43 E
Al Ghammās, Iraq 44 D5 31 45N 44 37 E

Amakusa-Shotō

Al Ghazālah, *Si. Arabia* **44 E4** 26 48N 41 19 E
Al Ḥadīthah, *Iraq* **44 C4** 34 0N 41 13 E
Al Ḥadīthah, *Si. Arabia* **47 D6** 31 28N 37 8 E
Al Ḥaḍr, *Iraq* **44 C4** 35 35N 42 44 E
Al Hājānah, *Syria* **47 B5** 33 20N 36 33 E
Al Ḥajar al Gharbī, *Oman* **45 E8** 24 10N 56 15 E
Al Hāmad, *Si. Arabia* **44 D3** 31 30N 39 30 E
Al Hamdānīyah, *Syria* **44 C3** 35 25N 36 50 E
Al Ḥamīdīyah, *Syria* **47 A4** 34 42N 35 57 E
Al Ḥammār, *Iraq* **44 D5** 30 57N 46 51 E
Al Ḥamrā', *Si. Arabia* **44 E3** 24 2N 38 55 E
Al Ḥanākīyah, *Si. Arabia* **44 E4** 24 51N 40 31 E
Al Ḥarīr, W. →, *Syria* **47 C4** 32 44N 35 59 E
Al Ḥasā, W. →, *Jordan* **47 D4** 31 4N 35 29 E
Al Ḥasakah, *Syria* **44 B4** 36 35N 40 45 E
Al Haydān, W. →, *Jordan* **47 D4** 31 29N 35 34 E
Al Ḥayy, *Iraq* **44 C5** 32 5N 46 5 E
Al Ḥijarah, *Asia* **44 D4** 30 0N 44 0 E
Al Ḥillah, *Iraq* **44 C5** 32 30N 44 25 E
Al Ḥillah, *Si. Arabia* **46 B4** 23 35N 46 50 E
Al Hindīyah, *Iraq* **44 C5** 32 30N 44 10 E
Al Hirmil, *Lebanon* **47 A5** 34 26N 36 24 E
Al Hoceïma, *Morocco* **50 A5** 35 8N 3 58W
Al Ḥudaydah, *Yemen* **46 E3** 14 50N 43 0 E
Al Hufūf, *Si. Arabia* **46 B4** 25 25N 49 45 E
Al Ḥumayḍah, *Si. Arabia* **44 D2** 29 14N 34 56 E
Al Ḥunayy, *Si. Arabia* **45 E6** 25 58N 48 45 E
Al Īsāwīyah, *Si. Arabia* **44 D3** 30 43N 37 59 E
Al Jafr, *Jordan* **47 E5** 30 18N 36 14 E
Al Jāfūrah, *Si. Arabia* **45 E7** 25 0N 50 15 E
Al Jaghbūb, *Libya* **51 C10** 29 42N 24 38 E
Al Jahrah, *Kuwait* **44 D5** 29 25N 47 40 E
Al Jalāmīd, *Si. Arabia* **44 D3** 31 20N 40 6 E
Al Jamalīyah, *Qatar* **45 E6** 25 37N 51 5 E
Al Janūb □, *Lebanon* **47 B4** 33 20N 35 20 E
Al Jawf, *Libya* **51 D10** 24 10N 23 24 E
Al Jawf, *Si. Arabia* **44 D3** 29 55N 39 40 E
Al Jazirah, *Iraq* **44 C5** 33 30N 44 0 E
Al Jithāmīyah, *Si. Arabia* **44 E4** 27 41N 41 43 E
Al Jubayl, *Si. Arabia* **45 E6** 27 0N 49 50 E
Al Jubaylah, *Si. Arabia* **44 E5** 24 55N 46 25 E
Al Jubb, *Si. Arabia* **44 E4** 27 11N 42 17 E
Al Junaynah, *Sudan* **51 F10** 13 27N 22 45 E
Al Kabā'ish, *Iraq* **44 D5** 30 58N 47 0 E
Al Karak, *Jordan* **47 D4** 31 11N 35 42 E
Al Karak □, *Jordan* **47 E5** 31 0N 36 0 E
Al Kāẓim Tyah, *Iraq* **44 C5** 33 22N 44 12 E
Al Khābūra, *Oman* **45 F8** 23 57N 57 5 E
Al Khafji, *Si. Arabia* **45 E6** 28 24N 48 29 E
Al Khalīl, *West Bank* **47 D4** 31 32N 35 6 E
Al Khāliṣ, *Iraq* **44 C5** 33 49N 44 32 E
Al Kharsānīyah, *Si. Arabia* **45 E6** 27 13N 49 18 E
Al Khaṣab, *Oman* **45 E8** 26 14N 56 15 E
Al Khawr, *Qatar* **45 E6** 25 41N 51 30 E
Al Khiḍr, *Iraq* **44 D5** 31 12N 45 33 E
Al Khiyām, *Lebanon* **47 B4** 33 20N 35 36 E
Al Kiswah, *Syria* **47 B5** 33 23N 36 14 E
Al Kūfah, *Iraq* **44 C5** 32 2N 44 24 E
Al Kufrah, *Libya* **51 D10** 24 17N 23 15 E
Al Kuhayfīyah, *Si. Arabia* **44 E4** 27 12N 43 3 E
Al Kūt, *Iraq* **44 C5** 32 30N 46 0 E
Al Kuwayt, *Kuwait* **46 B4** 29 30N 48 0 E
Al Labwah, *Lebanon* **47 A5** 34 11N 36 20 E
Al Lādhiqīyah, *Syria* **44 C2** 35 30N 35 45 E
Al Līth, *Si. Arabia* **46 C3** 20 9N 40 15 E
Al Liwā', *Oman* **45 E8** 24 31N 56 36 E
Al Luḥayyah, *Yemen* **46 D3** 15 45N 42 40 E
Al Madīnah, *Iraq* **44 D5** 30 57N 47 16 E
Al Madīnah, *Si. Arabia* **46 C2** 24 35N 39 52 E
Al Mafraq, *Jordan* **47 C5** 32 17N 36 14 E
Al Maḥmūdīyah, *Iraq* **44 C5** 33 3N 44 21 E
Al Majma'ah, *Si. Arabia* **44 E5** 25 57N 45 22 E
Al Makhruq, W. →, *Jordan* **47 D6** 31 28N 37 0 E
Al Makḥūl, *Si. Arabia* **44 E4** 26 37N 42 39 E
Al Manāmah, *Bahrain* **46 B5** 26 10N 50 30 E
Al Maqwa', *Kuwait* **44 D5** 29 10N 47 59 E
Al Marj, *Libya* **51 B10** 32 25N 20 30 E
Al Maṭlā, *Kuwait* **44 D5** 29 24N 47 40 E
Al Mawjib, W. →, *Jordan* **47 D4** 31 28N 35 36 E
Al Mawṣil, *Iraq* **44 B4** 36 15N 43 5 E
Al Mayādin, *Syria* **44 C4** 35 1N 40 27 E
Al Mazār, *Jordan* **47 D4** 31 4N 35 41 E
Al Midhnab, *Si. Arabia* **44 E5** 25 50N 44 18 E
Al Minā', *Lebanon* **47 A4** 34 24N 35 49 E
Al Miqdādīyah, *Iraq* **44 C5** 34 0N 45 0 E
Al Mubarraz, *Si. Arabia* **45 E6** 25 30N 49 40 E
Al Mudawwarah, *Jordan* **47 F5** 29 19N 36 0 E
Al Mughayrā', *U.A.E.* **45 E7** 24 5N 53 32 E
Al Muḥarraq, *Bahrain* **45 E6** 26 15N 50 40 E
Al Mukallā, *Yemen* **46 E4** 14 33N 49 2 E
Al Mukhā, *Yemen* **46 E3** 13 18N 43 15 E
Al Musayjīd, *Si. Arabia* **44 E3** 24 5N 39 5 E
Al Musayyib, *Iraq* **44 C5** 32 49N 44 20 E
Al Muwayliḥ, *Si. Arabia* **44 E2** 27 40N 35 30 E
Al Qā'im, *Iraq* **44 C4** 34 21N 41 7 E
Al Qalībah, *Si. Arabia* **44 D3** 28 24N 37 42 E
Al Qāmishlī, *Syria* **44 B4** 37 2N 41 14 E
Al Qaryatayn, *Syria* **47 A6** 34 12N 37 13 E
Al Qaṣīm, *Si. Arabia* **44 E4** 26 0N 43 0 E
Al Qaṭ'ā, *Syria* **44 C4** 34 40N 40 48 E
Al Qaṭīf, *Si. Arabia* **45 E6** 26 35N 50 0 E
Al Qatrānah, *Jordan* **47 D5** 31 12N 36 6 E
Al Qaṭrūn, *Libya* **51 D9** 24 56N 15 3 E
Al Qayṣūmah, *Si. Arabia* **44 D5** 28 20N 46 7 E
Al Quds = Jerusalem, *Israel* **47 D4** 31 47N 35 10 E
Al Qunayṭirah, *Syria* **47 C4** 32 55N 35 45 E
Al Qurnah, *Iraq* **44 D5** 31 1N 47 25 E
Al Quṣayr, *Iraq* **44 D5** 30 39N 45 50 E
Al Quṣayr, *Syria* **47 A5** 34 31N 36 34 E
Al Qutayfah, *Syria* **47 B5** 33 44N 36 36 E
Al 'Ubaylah, *Si. Arabia* **46 C5** 21 59N 50 57 E
Al 'Uḍaylīyah, *Si. Arabia* **45 E6** 25 8N 49 18 E
Al 'Ulā, *Si. Arabia* **44 E3** 26 35N 38 0 E
Al 'Uqayr, *Si. Arabia* **45 E6** 25 40N 50 15 E
Al 'Uwaynid, *Si. Arabia* **44 E5** 24 50N 46 0 E
Al 'Uwayqīlah, *Si. Arabia* **44 D4** 30 30N 42 10 E
Al 'Uyūn, *Ḥijāz, Si. Arabia* **44 E3** 24 33N 39 35 E
Al 'Uyūn, *Najd, Si. Arabia* **44 E4** 26 30N 43 50 E
Al 'Uzayr, *Iraq* **44 D5** 31 19N 47 25 E
Al Wajh, *Si. Arabia* **44 E3** 26 10N 36 30 E
Al Wakrah, *Qatar* **45 E6** 25 10N 51 40 E
Al Waqbah, *Si. Arabia* **44 D5** 28 48N 45 33 E
Al Warī'āh, *Si. Arabia* **44 E5** 27 51N 47 25 E
Ala Dağ, *Turkey* **44 B2** 37 44N 35 9 E
Ala Tau Shankou = Dzungarian Gates, *Asia* **32 B3** 45 0N 82 0 E
Alabama □, *U.S.A.* **77 J2** 33 0N 87 0W
Alabama →, *U.S.A.* **77 K2** 31 8N 87 57W
Alabaster, *U.S.A.* **77 J2** 33 15N 86 49W
Alaçam Dağları, *Turkey* **21 E13** 39 18N 28 49 E
Alachua, *U.S.A.* **77 L4** 29 47N 82 30W
Alaérma, *Greece* **23 C9** 36 9N 27 57 E
Alagoa Grande, *Brazil* **93 E11** 7 3S 35 35W
Alagoas □, *Brazil* **93 E11** 9 0S 36 0W
Alagoinhas, *Brazil* **93 F11** 12 7S 38 20W
Alaior, *Spain* **22 B11** 39 57N 4 8 E
Alajero, *Canary Is.* **22 F2** 28 3N 17 13W
Alajuela, *Costa Rica* **88 D3** 10 2N 84 8W
Alakamisy, *Madag.* **57 C8** 21 19S 47 14 E
Alaknanda →, *India* **43 D8** 30 8N 78 36 E
Alakurtti, *Russia* **24 A5** 67 0N 30 30 E
Alamarvdasht, *Iran* **45 E7** 27 37N 52 59 E
Alameda, *Calif., U.S.A.* **84 H4** 37 46N 122 15W
Alameda, *N. Mex., U.S.A.* **83 J10** 35 11N 106 37W
Alamo, *U.S.A.* **85 J11** 37 22N 115 10W
Alamo Crossing, *U.S.A.* **85 L13** 34 16N 113 33W
Alamogordo, *U.S.A.* **83 K11** 32 54N 105 57W
Alamos, *Mexico* **86 B3** 27 0N 109 0W
Alamosa, *U.S.A.* **83 H11** 37 28N 105 52W
Åland, *Finland* **9 F19** 60 15N 20 0 E
Ålands hav, *Sweden* **9 F18** 60 0N 19 30 E
Alania = North Ossetia □, *Russia* **25 F7** 43 30N 44 30 E
Alanya, *Turkey* **25 G5** 36 38N 32 0 E
Alaotra, Farihin', *Madag.* **57 B8** 17 30S 48 30 E
Alapayevsk, *Russia* **24 C11** 57 52N 61 42 E
Alappuzha = Alleppey, *India* **40 Q10** 9 30N 76 28 E
Alarobia-Vohiposa, *Madag.* **57 C8** 20 59S 47 9 E
Alaşehir, *Turkey* **21 E13** 38 23N 28 30 E
Alaska □, *U.S.A.* **68 B5** 64 0N 154 0W
Alaska, G. of, *Pac. Oc.* **68 C5** 58 0N 145 0W
Alaska Peninsula, *U.S.A.* **68 C4** 56 0N 159 0W
Alaska Range, *U.S.A.* **68 B4** 62 50N 151 0W
Älät, *Azerbaijan* **25 G8** 39 58N 49 25 E
Alatyr, *Russia* **24 D8** 54 55N 46 35 E
Alausi, *Ecuador* **92 D3** 2 0S 78 50W
Alava, C., *U.S.A.* **82 B1** 48 10N 124 44W
Alavus, *Finland* **9 E20** 62 35N 23 36 E
Alawoona, *Australia* **63 E3** 34 45S 140 30 E
'Alayh, *Lebanon* **47 B4** 33 46N 35 33 E
Alba, *Italy* **18 D8** 44 42N 8 2 E
Alba-Iulia, *Romania* **17 E12** 46 8N 23 39 E
Albacete, *Spain* **19 C5** 39 0N 1 50W
Albacutya, L., *Australia* **63 F3** 35 45S 141 58 E
Albanel, L., *Canada* **70 B5** 50 55N 73 12W
Albania ■, *Europe* **21 D9** 41 0N 20 0 E
Albany, *Australia* **61 G2** 35 1S 117 58 E
Albany, *Ga., U.S.A.* **77 K3** 31 35N 84 10W
Albany, *N.Y., U.S.A.* **79 D11** 42 39N 73 45W
Albany, *Oreg., U.S.A.* **82 D2** 44 38N 123 6W
Albany, *Tex., U.S.A.* **81 J5** 32 44N 99 18W
Albany →, *Canada* **70 B3** 52 17N 81 31W
Albardón, *Argentina* **94 C2** 31 20S 68 30W
Albatross B., *Australia* **62 A3** 12 45S 141 30 E
Albemarle, *U.S.A.* **77 H5** 35 21N 80 11W
Albemarle Sd., *U.S.A.* **77 H7** 36 5N 76 0W
Alberche →, *Spain* **19 C3** 39 58N 4 46W
Alberdi, *Paraguay* **94 B4** 26 14S 58 20W
Albert, L., *Africa* **54 B3** 1 30N 31 0 E
Albert, L., *Australia* **63 F2** 35 30S 139 10 E
Albert Edward Ra., *Australia* **60 C4** 18 17S 127 57 E
Albert Lea, *U.S.A.* **80 D8** 43 39N 93 22W
Albert Nile →, *Uganda* **54 B3** 3 36N 32 2 E
Albert Town, *Bahamas* **89 B5** 22 37N 74 33W
Alberta □, *Canada* **72 C6** 54 40N 115 0W
Alberti, *Argentina* **94 D3** 35 1S 60 16W
Albertinia, *S. Africa* **56 E3** 34 11S 21 34 E
Alberton, *Canada* **71 C7** 46 50N 64 0W
Albertville = Kalemie, *Dem. Rep. of the Congo* **54 D2** 5 55S 29 9 E
Albertville, *France* **18 D7** 45 40N 6 22 E
Albertville, *U.S.A.* **77 H2** 34 16N 86 13W
Albi, *France* **18 E5** 43 56N 2 9 E
Albia, *U.S.A.* **80 E8** 41 2N 92 48W
Albina, *Surinam* **93 B8** 5 37N 54 15W
Albina, Ponta, *Angola* **56 B1** 15 52S 11 44 E
Albion, *Mich., U.S.A.* **76 D3** 42 15N 84 45W
Albion, *Nebr., U.S.A.* **80 E6** 41 42N 98 0W
Albion, *Pa., U.S.A.* **78 E4** 41 53N 80 22W
Alborán, *Medit. S.* **19 E4** 35 57N 3 0W
Ålborg, *Denmark* **9 H13** 57 2N 9 54 E
Alborz, Reshteh-ye Kūhhā-ye, *Iran* **45 C7** 36 0N 52 0 E
Albuquerque, *U.S.A.* **83 J10** 35 5N 106 39W
Albuquerque, Cayos de, *Caribbean* **88 D3** 12 10N 81 50W
Alburg, *U.S.A.* **79 B11** 44 59N 73 18W
Albury = Albury-Wodonga, *Australia* **63 F4** 36 3S 146 56 E
Albury-Wodonga, *Australia* **63 F4** 36 3S 146 56 E
Alcalá de Henares, *Spain* **19 B4** 40 28N 3 22W
Alcalá la Real, *Spain* **19 D4** 37 27N 3 57W
Álcamo, *Italy* **20 F5** 37 59N 12 55 E
Alcaniz, *Spain* **19 B5** 41 2N 0 8W
Alcântara, *Brazil* **93 D10** 2 20S 44 30W
Alcántara, Embalse de, *Spain* **19 C2** 39 44N 6 50W
Alcantarilla, *Spain* **19 D5** 37 59N 1 12W
Alcaraz, Sierra de, *Spain* **19 C4** 38 40N 2 20W
Alcaudete, *Spain* **19 D3** 37 35N 4 5W
Alcázar de San Juan, *Spain* **19 C4** 39 24N 3 12W
Alchevsk, *Ukraine* **25 E6** 48 30N 38 45 E
Alcira = Alzira, *Spain* **19 C5** 39 9N 0 30W
Alcova, *U.S.A.* **82 E10** 42 34N 106 43W
Alcoy, *Spain* **19 C5** 38 43N 0 30W
Alcúdia, *Spain* **22 B10** 39 51N 3 7 E
Alcúdia, B. d', *Spain* **22 B10** 39 47N 3 15 E
Aldabra Is., *Seychelles* **49 G8** 9 22S 46 28 E
Aldama, *Mexico* **87 C5** 23 0N 98 4W
Aldan, *Russia* **27 D13** 58 40N 125 30 E
Aldan →, *Russia* **27 C13** 63 28N 129 35 E
Aldea, Pta. de la, *Canary Is.* **22 G4** 28 0N 15 50W
Aldeburgh, *U.K.* **11 E9** 52 10N 1 37 E
Alder Pk., *U.S.A.* **84 K5** 35 53N 121 22W
Alderney, *U.K.* **11 H5** 49 42N 2 11W
Aldershot, *U.K.* **11 F7** 51 15N 0 44W
Aledo, *U.S.A.* **80 E9** 41 12N 90 45W
Aleg, *Mauritania* **50 E3** 17 3N 13 55W
Alegranza, *Canary Is.* **22 E6** 29 23N 13 32W
Alegranza, I., *Canary Is.* **22 E6** 29 23N 13 32W
Alegre, *Brazil* **95 A7** 20 50S 41 30W
Alegrete, *Brazil* **95 B4** 29 40S 56 0W
Aleisk, *Russia* **26 D9** 52 40N 83 0 E
Aleksandriya = Oleksandriya, *Ukraine* **17 C14** 50 37N 26 19 E
Aleksandrov Gay, *Russia* **25 D8** 50 9N 48 34 E
Aleksandrovsk-Sakhalinskiy, *Russia* **27 D15** 50 50N 142 20 E
Além Paraíba, *Brazil* **95 A7** 21 52S 42 41W
Alemania, *Argentina* **94 B2** 25 40S 65 30W
Alemania, *Chile* **94 B2** 25 10S 69 55W
Alençon, *France* **18 B4** 48 27N 0 4 E
Alenquer, *Brazil* **93 D8** 1 56S 54 46W
Alenuihaha Channel, *U.S.A.* **74 H17** 20 30N 156 0W
Aleppo = Ḥalab, *Syria* **44 B3** 36 10N 37 15 E
Alès, *France* **18 D6** 44 9N 4 5 E
Alessándria, *Italy* **18 D8** 44 54N 8 37 E
Ålesund, *Norway* **9 E12** 62 28N 6 12 E
Aleutian Is., *Pac. Oc.* **68 C2** 52 0N 175 0W
Aleutian Trench, *Pac. Oc.* **64 C10** 48 0N 180 0 E
Alexander, *U.S.A.* **80 B3** 47 51N 103 39W
Alexander, Mt., *Australia* **61 E3** 28 58S 120 16 E
Alexander Arch., *U.S.A.* **68 C6** 56 0N 136 0W
Alexander Bay, *S. Africa* **56 D2** 28 40S 16 30 E
Alexander City, *U.S.A.* **77 J3** 32 56N 85 58W
Alexander I., *Antarctica* **5 C17** 69 0S 70 0W
Alexandra, *Australia* **63 F4** 37 8S 145 40 E
Alexandra, *N.Z.* **59 L2** 45 14S 169 25 E
Alexandra Falls, *Canada* **72 A5** 60 29N 116 18W
Alexandria = El Iskandarîya, *Egypt* **51 B11** 31 13N 29 58 E
Alexandria, *B.C., Canada* **72 C4** 52 35N 122 27W
Alexandria, *Ont., Canada* **79 A10** 45 19N 74 38W
Alexandria, *Romania* **17 G13** 43 57N 25 24 E
Alexandria, *S. Africa* **56 E4** 33 38S 26 28 E
Alexandria, *U.K.* **12 F4** 55 59N 4 35W
Alexandria, *La., U.S.A.* **81 K8** 31 18N 92 27W
Alexandria, *Minn., U.S.A.* **80 C7** 45 53N 95 22W
Alexandria, *S. Dak., U.S.A.* **80 D6** 43 39N 97 47W
Alexandria, *Va., U.S.A.* **76 F7** 38 48N 77 3W
Alexandria Bay, *U.S.A.* **79 B9** 44 20N 75 55W
Alexandrina, L., *Australia* **63 F2** 35 25S 139 10 E
Alexandroúpolis, *Greece* **21 D11** 40 50N 25 54 E
Alexis →, *Canada* **71 B8** 52 33N 56 8W
Alexis Creek, *Canada* **72 C4** 52 10N 123 20W
Alfabia, *Spain* **22 B9** 39 44N 2 44 E
Alfenas, *Brazil* **95 A6** 21 20S 46 10W
Alford, *Aberds., U.K.* **12 D6** 57 14N 2 41W
Alford, *Lincs., U.K.* **10 D8** 53 15N 0 10 E
Alfred, *Maine, U.S.A.* **79 C14** 43 29N 70 43W
Alfred, *N.Y., U.S.A.* **78 D7** 42 16N 77 48W
Alfreton, *U.K.* **10 D6** 53 6N 1 24W
Alga, *Kazakstan* **25 E10** 49 53N 57 20 E
Algaida, *Spain* **22 B9** 39 33N 2 53 E
Ålgård, *Norway* **9 G11** 58 46N 5 53 E
Algarve, *Portugal* **19 D1** 36 58N 8 20W
Algeciras, *Spain* **19 D3** 36 9N 5 28W
Algemesí, *Spain* **19 C5** 39 11N 0 27W
Alger, *Algeria* **50 A6** 36 42N 3 8 E
Algeria ■, *Africa* **50 C6** 28 30N 2 0 E
Alghero, *Italy* **20 D3** 40 33N 8 19 E
Algiers = Alger, *Algeria* **50 A6** 36 42N 3 8 E
Algoa B., *S. Africa* **56 E4** 33 50S 25 45 E
Algoma, *U.S.A.* **76 C2** 44 36N 87 26W
Algona, *U.S.A.* **80 D7** 43 4N 94 14W
Algonac, *U.S.A.* **78 D2** 42 37N 82 32W
Algonquin Prov. Park, *Canada* **70 C4** 45 50N 78 30W
Algorta, *Uruguay* **96 C5** 32 25S 57 23W
Alhambra, *U.S.A.* **85 L8** 34 8N 118 6W
Alhucemas = Al Hoceïma, *Morocco* **50 A5** 35 8N 3 58W
'Alī al Gharbī, *Iraq* **44 C5** 32 30N 46 45 E
'Alī ash Sharqī, *Iraq* **44 C5** 32 7N 46 44 E
'Alī Khēl, *Afghan.* **42 C3** 33 57N 69 43 E
Alī Shāh, *Iran* **44 B5** 38 9N 45 50 E
'Alīābād, *Khorāsān, Iran* **45 C8** 32 30N 57 30 E
'Alīābād, *Kordestān, Iran* **44 C5** 35 4N 46 58 E
'Alīābād, *Yazd, Iran* **45 D7** 31 41N 53 49 E
Aliağa, *Turkey* **21 E12** 38 47N 26 59 E
Aliákmon →, *Greece* **21 D10** 40 30N 22 36 E
Alicante, *Spain* **19 C5** 38 23N 0 30W
Alice, *S. Africa* **56 E4** 32 48S 26 55 E
Alice, *U.S.A.* **81 M5** 27 45N 98 5W
Alice →, *Queens., Australia* **62 C3** 24 2S 144 50 E
Alice →, *Queens., Australia* **62 B3** 15 35S 142 20 E
Alice Arm, *Canada* **72 B3** 55 29N 129 31W
Alice Springs, *Australia* **62 C1** 23 40S 133 50 E
Alicedale, *S. Africa* **56 E4** 33 15S 26 4 E
Aliceville, *U.S.A.* **77 J1** 33 8N 88 9W
Aliganj, *India* **43 F8** 27 30N 79 10 E
Aligarh, *Raj., India* **42 G7** 25 55N 76 15 E
Aligarh, *Ut. P., India* **42 F8** 27 55N 78 10 E
Alīgūdarz, *Iran* **45 C6** 33 25N 49 45 E
Alimnia, *Greece* **23 C9** 36 16N 27 43 E
Alingsås, *Sweden* **9 H15** 57 56N 12 31 E
Alipur, *Pakistan* **42 E4** 29 25N 70 55 E
Alipur Duar, *India* **41 F16** 26 30N 89 35 E
Aliquippa, *U.S.A.* **78 F4** 40 37N 80 15W
Alitus = Alytus, *Lithuania* **9 J21** 54 24N 24 3 E
Aliwal North, *S. Africa* **56 E4** 30 45S 26 45 E
Alix, *Canada* **72 C6** 52 24N 113 11W
Aljustrel, *Portugal* **19 D1** 37 55N 8 10W
Alkmaar, *Neths.* **15 B4** 52 37N 4 45 E
All American Canal, *U.S.A.* **83 K6** 32 45N 115 15W
Allagash →, *U.S.A.* **77 B11** 47 5N 69 3W
Allah Dad, *Pakistan* **42 G2** 25 38N 67 34 E
Allahabad, *India* **43 G9** 25 25N 81 58 E
Allan, *Canada* **73 C7** 51 53N 106 4W
Allanridge, *S. Africa* **56 D4** 27 45S 26 40 E
Allegany, *U.S.A.* **78 D6** 42 6N 78 30W
Allegheny →, *U.S.A.* **78 F5** 40 27N 80 1W
Allegheny Mts., *U.S.A.* **76 G6** 38 15N 80 10W
Allegheny Reservoir, *U.S.A.* **78 E6** 41 50N 79 0W
Allen, Bog of, *Ireland* **13 C5** 53 15N 7 0W
Allen, L., *Ireland* **13 B3** 54 8N 8 4W
Allendale, *U.S.A.* **77 J5** 33 1N 81 18W
Allende, *Mexico* **86 B4** 28 20N 100 50W
Allentown, *U.S.A.* **79 F9** 40 37N 75 29W
Alleppey, *India* **40 Q10** 9 30N 76 28 E
Aller →, *Germany* **16 B5** 52 56N 9 12 E
Alliance, *Nebr., U.S.A.* **80 D3** 42 6N 102 52W
Alliance, *Ohio, U.S.A.* **78 F3** 40 55N 81 6W
Allier →, *France* **18 C5** 46 57N 3 4 E
Alliford Bay, *Canada* **72 C2** 53 12N 131 58W
Alliston, *Canada* **78 B5** 44 9N 79 52W
Alloa, *U.K.* **12 E5** 56 7N 3 47W
Allora, *Australia* **63 D5** 28 2S 152 0 E
Alluitsup Paa, *Greenland* **4 C5** 60 30N 45 35W
Alma, *Canada* **71 C5** 48 35N 71 40W
Alma, *Ga., U.S.A.* **77 K4** 31 33N 82 28W
Alma, *Kans., U.S.A.* **80 F6** 39 1N 96 17W
Alma, *Mich., U.S.A.* **76 D3** 43 23N 84 39W
Alma, *Nebr., U.S.A.* **80 E5** 40 6N 99 22W
Alma Ata = Almaty, *Kazakstan* **26 E8** 43 15N 76 57 E
Almada, *Portugal* **19 C1** 38 40N 9 9W
Almaden, *Australia* **62 B3** 17 22S 144 40 E
Almadén, *Spain* **19 C3** 38 49N 4 52W
Almanor, L., *U.S.A.* **82 F3** 40 14N 121 9W
Almansa, *Spain* **19 C5** 38 51N 1 5W
Almanzor, Pico, *Spain* **19 B3** 40 15N 5 18W
Almanzora →, *Spain* **19 D5** 37 14N 1 46W
Almaty, *Kazakstan* **26 E8** 43 15N 76 57 E
Almazán, *Spain* **19 B4** 41 30N 2 30W
Almeirim, *Brazil* **93 D8** 1 30S 52 34W
Almelo, *Neths.* **15 B6** 52 22N 6 42 E
Almendralejo, *Spain* **19 C2** 38 41N 6 26W
Almere-Stad, *Neths.* **15 B5** 52 20N 5 15 E
Almería, *Spain* **19 D4** 36 52N 2 27W
Almirante, *Panama* **88 E3** 9 10N 82 30W
Almiroú, Kólpos, *Greece* **23 D6** 35 23N 24 20 E
Almond, *U.S.A.* **78 D7** 42 19N 77 44W
Almont, *U.S.A.* **78 D1** 42 55N 83 3W
Almonte, *Canada* **79 A8** 45 14N 76 12W
Almora, *India* **43 E8** 29 38N 79 40 E
Alness, *U.K.* **12 D4** 57 41N 4 16W
Alnmouth, *U.K.* **10 B6** 55 24N 1 37W
Alnwick, *U.K.* **10 B6** 55 24N 1 42W
Aloi, *Uganda* **54 B3** 2 16N 33 10 E
Alon, *Burma* **41 H19** 22 12N 95 5 E
Alor, *Indonesia* **37 F6** 8 15S 124 30 E
Alor Setar, *Malaysia* **39 J3** 6 7N 100 22 E
Alot, *India* **42 H6** 23 56N 75 40 E
Aloysius, Mt., *Australia* **61 E4** 26 0S 128 38 E
Alpaugh, *U.S.A.* **84 K7** 35 53N 119 29W
Alpena, *U.S.A.* **76 C4** 45 4N 83 27W
Alpha, *Australia* **62 C4** 23 39S 146 37 E
Alphen aan den Rijn, *Neths.* **15 B4** 52 7N 4 40 E
Alpine, *Ariz., U.S.A.* **83 K9** 33 51N 109 9W
Alpine, *Calif., U.S.A.* **85 N10** 32 50N 116 46W
Alpine, *Tex., U.S.A.* **81 K3** 30 22N 103 40W
Alps, *Europe* **18 C8** 46 30N 9 30 E
Alsace, *France* **18 B7** 48 15N 7 25 E
Alsask, *Canada* **73 C7** 51 21N 109 59W
Alsasua, *Spain* **19 A4** 42 54N 2 10W
Alsek →, *U.S.A.* **72 B1** 59 10N 138 12W
Alsten, *Norway* **8 D15** 65 58N 12 40 E
Alston, *U.K.* **10 C5** 54 49N 2 25W
Alta, *Norway* **8 B20** 69 57N 23 10 E
Alta Gracia, *Argentina* **94 C3** 31 40S 64 30W
Alta Sierra, *U.S.A.* **85 K8** 35 42N 118 33W
Altaelva →, *Norway* **8 B20** 69 54N 23 17 E
Altafjorden, *Norway* **8 A20** 70 5N 23 5 E
Altai = Aerhtai Shan, *Mongolia* **32 B4** 46 40N 92 45 E
Altamaha →, *U.S.A.* **77 K5** 31 20N 81 20W
Altamira, *Brazil* **93 D8** 3 12S 52 10W
Altamira, *Chile* **94 B2** 25 47S 69 51W
Altamira, *Mexico* **87 C5** 22 24N 97 55W
Altamont, *U.S.A.* **79 D10** 42 43N 74 3W
Altamura, *Italy* **20 D7** 40 49N 16 33 E
Altanbulag, *Mongolia* **32 A5** 50 16N 106 30 E
Altar, *Mexico* **86 A2** 30 40N 111 50W
Altar, Desierto de, *Mexico* **86 B2** 30 10N 112 0W
Altata, *Mexico* **86 C3** 24 30N 108 0W
Altavista, *U.S.A.* **76 G6** 37 6N 79 17W
Altay, *China* **32 B3** 47 48N 88 10 E
Altea, *Spain* **19 C5** 38 38N 0 2W
Altiplano = Bolivian Plateau, *S. Amer.* **90 E4** 20 0S 67 30W
Alto Araguaia, *Brazil* **93 G8** 17 15S 53 20W
Alto Cuchumatanes = Cuchumatanes, Sierra de los, *Guatemala* **88 C1** 15 35N 91 25W
Alto del Carmen, *Chile* **94 B1** 28 46S 70 30W
Alto del Inca, *Chile* **94 A2** 24 10S 68 10W
Alto Ligonha, *Mozam.* **55 F4** 15 30S 38 11 E
Alto Molocue, *Mozam.* **55 F4** 15 50S 37 35 E
Alto Paraguay □, *Paraguay* **94 A4** 21 0S 58 30W
Alto Paraná □, *Paraguay* **95 B5** 25 30S 54 50W
Alton, *Canada* **78 C4** 43 54N 80 5W
Alton, *U.K.* **11 F7** 51 9N 0 59W
Alton, *Ill., U.S.A.* **80 F9** 38 53N 90 11W
Alton, *N.H., U.S.A.* **79 C13** 43 27N 71 13W
Altoona, *U.S.A.* **78 F6** 40 31N 78 24W
Altūn Kūprī, *Iraq* **44 C5** 35 45N 44 9 E
Altun Shan, *China* **32 C3** 38 30N 88 0 E
Alturas, *U.S.A.* **82 F3** 41 29N 120 32W
Altus, *U.S.A.* **81 H5** 34 38N 99 20W
Alucra, *Turkey* **25 F6** 40 22N 38 47 E
Alūksne, *Latvia* **9 H22** 57 24N 27 3 E
Alunite, *U.S.A.* **85 K12** 35 59N 114 55W
Alusi, *Indonesia* **37 F8** 7 35S 131 40 E
Alva, *U.S.A.* **81 G5** 36 48N 98 40W
Alvarado, *Mexico* **87 D5** 18 40N 95 50W
Alvarado, *U.S.A.* **81 J6** 32 24N 97 13W
Alvaro Obregón, Presa, *Mexico* **86 B3** 27 55N 109 52W
Alvear, *Argentina* **94 B4** 29 5S 56 30W
Alvesta, *Sweden* **9 H16** 56 54N 14 35 E
Alvin, *U.S.A.* **81 L7** 29 26N 95 15W
Alvinston, *Canada* **78 D3** 42 49N 81 52W
Älvkarleby, *Sweden* **9 F17** 60 34N 17 26 E
Alvord Desert, *U.S.A.* **82 E4** 42 30N 118 25W
Älvsbyn, *Sweden* **8 D19** 65 40N 21 0 E
Alwar, *India* **42 F7** 27 38N 76 34 E
Alxa Zuoqi, *China* **34 E3** 38 50N 105 40 E
Alyangula, *Australia* **62 A2** 13 55S 136 30 E
Alyata = Älät, *Azerbaijan* **25 G8** 39 58N 49 25 E
Alyth, *U.K.* **12 E5** 56 38N 3 13W
Alytus, *Lithuania* **9 J21** 54 24N 24 3 E
Alzada, *U.S.A.* **80 C2** 45 2N 104 25W
Alzira, *Spain* **19 C5** 39 9N 0 30W
Am Timan, *Chad* **51 F10** 11 0N 20 10 E
Amadeus, L., *Australia* **61 D5** 24 54S 131 0 E
Amadi, *Dem. Rep. of the Congo* **54 B2** 3 40N 26 40 E
Amâdi, *Sudan* **51 G12** 5 29N 30 25 E
Amadjuak L., *Canada* **69 B12** 65 0N 71 8W
Amagansett, *U.S.A.* **79 F12** 40 59N 72 9W
Amagasaki, *Japan* **31 G7** 34 42N 135 20 E
Amahai, *Indonesia* **37 E7** 3 20S 128 55 E
Amakusa-Shotō, *Japan* **31 H5** 32 15N 130 10 E

Ashkhabad

Antsenavolo, Madag. **57 C8** 21 24S 48 3 E
Antsiafabositra, Madag. **57 B8** 17 18S 46 57 E
Antsirabe, Antananarivo, Madag. **57 B8** 19 55S 47 2 E
Antsirabe, Antsiranana, Madag. **57 A8** 14 0S 49 59 E
Antsirabe, Mahajanga, Madag. **57 B8** 15 57S 48 58 E
Antsiranana, Madag. **57 A8** 12 25S 49 20 E
Antsiranana □, Madag. **57 A8** 12 16S 49 17 E
Antsohihy, Madag. **57 A8** 14 50S 47 59 E
Antsohimbondrona Seranana, Madag. **57 A8** 13 7S 48 48 E
Antu, China **35 C15** 42 30N 128 20 E
Antwerp = Antwerpen, Belgium **15 C4** 51 13N 4 25 E
Antwerp, U.S.A. **79 B9** 44 12N 75 37W
Antwerpen, Belgium **15 C4** 51 13N 4 25 E
Antwerpen □, Belgium **15 C4** 51 15N 4 40 E
Anupgarh, India **42 E5** 29 10N 73 10 E
Anuppur, India **43 H9** 23 6N 81 41 E
Anuradhapura, Sri Lanka **40 Q12** 8 22N 80 28 E
Anveh, Iran **45 E7** 27 23N 54 11 E
Anvers = Antwerpen, Belgium **15 C4** 51 13N 4 25 E
Anvers I., Antarctica **5 C17** 64 30S 63 40W
Anxi, China **32 B4** 40 30N 95 43 E
Anxious B., Australia **63 E1** 33 24S 134 45 E
Anyang, China **34 F8** 36 5N 114 21 E
Anyer-Kidul, Indonesia **37 G11** 6 4S 105 53 E
Anyi, China **34 G6** 35 2N 111 2 E
Anza, U.S.A. **85 M10** 33 35N 116 39W
Anze, China **34 F7** 36 10N 112 12 E
Anzhero-Sudzhensk, Russia **26 D9** 56 10N 86 0 E
Ánzio, Italy **20 D5** 41 27N 12 37 E
Aoga-Shima, Japan **31 H9** 32 28N 139 46 E
Aomen = Macau, China **33 D6** 22 12N 113 33 E
Aomori, Japan **30 D10** 40 45N 140 45 E
Aomori □, Japan **30 D10** 40 45N 140 40 E
Aonla, India **43 E8** 28 16N 79 11 E
Aoraki Mount Cook, N.Z. **59 K3** 43 36S 170 9 E
Aosta, Italy **18 D7** 45 45N 7 20 E
Aoukâr, Mauritania **50 E4** 17 40N 10 0W
Apa →, S. Amer. **94 A4** 22 6S 58 2W
Apache, U.S.A. **81 H5** 34 54N 98 22W
Apache Junction, U.S.A. **83 K8** 33 25N 111 33W
Apalachee B., U.S.A. **77 L4** 30 0N 84 0W
Apalachicola, U.S.A. **77 L3** 29 43N 84 59W
Apalachicola →, U.S.A. **77 L3** 29 43N 84 58W
Apaporis →, Colombia **92 D5** 1 23S 69 25W
Aparri, Phil. **37 A6** 18 22N 121 38 E
Apatity, Russia **24 A5** 67 34N 33 22 E
Apatzingán, Mexico **86 D4** 19 0N 102 20W
Apeldoorn, Neths. **15 B5** 52 13N 5 57 E
Apennines = Appennini, Italy **20 B4** 44 0N 10 0 E
Apia, Samoa **59 A13** 13 50S 171 50W
Apiacás, Serra dos, Brazil **92 E7** 9 50S 57 0W
Apies →, S. Africa **57 D4** 25 15S 28 8 E
Apizaco, Mexico **87 D5** 19 26N 98 9W
Aplao, Peru **92 G4** 16 0S 72 40W
Apo, Mt., Phil. **37 C7** 6 53N 125 14 E
Apolakkiá, Greece **23 C9** 36 5N 27 48 E
Apolakkiá, Órmos, Greece **23 C9** 36 5N 27 45 E
Apolo, Bolivia **92 F5** 14 30S 68 30W
Aporé →, Brazil **93 G8** 19 27S 50 57W
Apostle Is., U.S.A. **80 B9** 47 0N 90 40W
Apóstoles, Argentina **95 B4** 28 0S 56 0W
Apostolos Andreas, C., Cyprus **23 D13** 35 42N 34 35 E
Apoteri, Guyana **92 C7** 4 2N 58 32W
Appalachian Mts., U.S.A. **76 G6** 38 0N 80 0W
Appennini, Italy **20 B4** 44 0N 10 0 E
Apple Hill, Canada **79 A10** 45 13N 74 46W
Apple Valley, U.S.A. **85 L9** 34 32N 117 14W
Appleby-in-Westmorland, U.K. **10 C5** 54 35N 2 29W
Appleton, U.S.A. **76 C1** 44 16N 88 25W
Approuague →, Fr. Guiana **93 C8** 4 30N 51 57W
Aprília, Italy **20 D5** 41 36N 12 39 E
Apsley, Canada **78 B6** 44 45N 78 6W
Apucarana, Brazil **95 A5** 23 55S 51 33W
Apure →, Venezuela **92 B5** 7 37N 66 25W
Apurimac →, Peru **92 F4** 12 17S 73 56W
Āqā Jarī, Iran **45 D6** 30 42N 49 50 E
Aqaba = Al 'Aqabah, Jordan **47 F4** 29 31N 35 0 E
Aqaba, G. of, Red Sea **44 D2** 28 15N 33 20 E
'Aqabah, Khalīj al = Aqaba, G. of, Red Sea **44 D2** 28 15N 33 20 E
'Aqdā, Iran **45 C7** 32 26N 53 37 E
Aqmola = Astana, Kazakstan **26 D8** 51 10N 71 30 E
'Aqrah, Iraq **44 B4** 36 46N 43 45 E
Aqtaū, Kazakstan **26 E6** 43 39N 51 12 E
Aqtöbe, Kazakstan **25 D10** 50 17N 57 10 E
Aquidauana, Brazil **93 H7** 20 30S 55 50W
Aquiles Serdán, Mexico **86 B3** 28 37N 105 54W
Aquin, Haiti **89 C5** 18 16N 73 24W
Aquitain, Bassin, France **18 D3** 44 0N 0 30W
Aqviligjuaq = Pelly Bay, Canada **69 B11** 68 38N 89 50W
Ar Rachidiya = Er Rachidia, Morocco **50 B5** 31 58N 4 20W
Ar Rafīd, Syria **47 C4** 32 57N 35 52 E
Ar Raḩḩālīyah, Iraq **44 C4** 32 44N 43 23 E
Ar Ramādī, Iraq **44 C4** 33 25N 43 20 E
Ar Ramthā, Jordan **47 C5** 32 34N 36 0 E
Ar Raqqah, Syria **44 C3** 35 59N 39 8 E
Ar Rass, Si. Arabia **44 E4** 25 50N 43 40 E
Ar Rifā'ī, Iraq **44 D5** 31 50N 46 10 E
Ar Riyāḑ, Si. Arabia **46 C4** 24 41N 46 42 E
Ar Ru'ays, Qatar **45 E6** 26 8N 51 12 E
Ar Rukhaymīyah, Iraq **44 D5** 29 22N 45 38 E
Ar Ruşāfah, Syria **44 C3** 35 45N 38 49 E
Ar Ruţbah, Iraq **44 C4** 33 0N 40 15 E
Ara, India **43 G11** 25 35N 84 32 E
Arab, U.S.A. **77 H2** 34 19N 86 30W
'Arab, Bahr el →, Sudan **51 G11** 9 0N 29 30 E
Arab, Shatt al →, Asia **45 D6** 30 0N 48 31 E
'Arabābād, Iran **45 C8** 33 2N 57 41 E
Arabia, Asia **28 G8** 25 0N 45 0 E
Arabian Desert = Es Sahrâ' Esh Sharqîya, Egypt **51 C12** 27 30N 32 30 E
Arabian Gulf = Gulf, The, Asia **45 E6** 27 0N 50 0 E
Arabian Sea, Ind. Oc. **29 H10** 16 0N 65 0 E
Aracaju, Brazil **93 F11** 10 55S 37 4W
Aracati, Brazil **93 D11** 4 30S 37 44W
Araçatuba, Brazil **95 A5** 21 10S 50 30W
Aracena, Spain **19 D2** 37 53N 6 38W
Araçuaí, Brazil **93 G10** 16 52S 42 4W
'Arad, Israel **47 D4** 31 15N 35 12 E
Arad, Romania **17 E11** 46 10N 21 20 E
Arādān, Iran **45 C7** 35 21N 52 30 E
Aradhippou, Cyprus **23 E12** 34 57N 33 36 E
Arafura Sea, E. Indies **28 K17** 9 0S 135 0 E
Aragón □, Spain **19 B5** 41 25N 0 40W
Aragón →, Spain **19 A5** 42 13N 1 44W
Araguacema, Brazil **93 E9** 8 50S 49 20W
Araguaia →, Brazil **93 E9** 5 21S 48 41W
Araguaína, Brazil **93 E9** 7 12S 48 12W
Araguari, Brazil **93 G9** 18 38S 48 11W
Araguari →, Brazil **93 C9** 1 15N 49 55W
Arain, India **42 F6** 26 27N 75 2 E
Arak, Algeria **50 C6** 25 20N 3 45 E
Arāk, Iran **45 C6** 34 0N 49 40 E
Arakan Coast, Burma **41 K19** 19 0N 94 0 E
Arakan Yoma, Burma **41 K19** 20 0N 94 40 E
Araks = Aras, Rūd-e →, Asia **44 B5** 40 5N 48 29 E
Aral, Kazakstan **26 E7** 46 41N 61 45 E
Aral Sea, Asia **26 E7** 44 30N 60 0 E
Aral Tengizi = Aral Sea, Asia **26 E7** 44 30N 60 0 E
Aralsk = Aral, Kazakstan **26 E7** 46 41N 61 45 E
Aralskoye More = Aral Sea, Asia **26 E7** 44 30N 60 0 E
Aramac, Australia **62 C4** 22 58S 145 14 E
Aran I., Ireland **13 A3** 55 0N 8 30W
Aran Is., Ireland **13 C2** 53 6N 9 38W
Aranda de Duero, Spain **19 B4** 41 39N 3 42W
Arandān, Iran **44 C5** 35 23N 46 55 E
Aranjuez, Spain **19 B4** 40 1N 3 40W
Aranos, Namibia **56 C2** 24 9S 19 7 E
Aransas Pass, U.S.A. **81 M6** 27 55N 97 9W
Aranyaprathet, Thailand **38 F4** 13 41N 102 30 E
Arapahoe, U.S.A. **80 E5** 40 18N 99 54W
Arapey Grande →, Uruguay **94 C4** 30 55S 57 49W
Arapgir, Turkey **44 B3** 39 5N 38 30 E
Arapiraca, Brazil **93 E11** 9 45S 36 39W
Arapongas, Brazil **95 A5** 23 29S 51 28W
Ar'ar, Si. Arabia **44 D4** 30 59N 41 2 E
Araranguá, Brazil **95 B6** 29 0S 49 30W
Araraquara, Brazil **93 H9** 21 50S 48 0W
Ararás, Serra das, Brazil **95 B5** 25 0S 53 10W
Ararat, Australia **63 F3** 37 16S 143 0 E
Ararat, Mt. = Ağrı Dağı, Turkey **25 G7** 39 50N 44 15 E
Araria, India **43 F12** 26 9N 87 33 E
Araripe, Chapada do, Brazil **93 E11** 7 20S 40 0W
Araruama, L. de, Brazil **95 A7** 22 53S 42 12W
Aras, Rūd-e →, Asia **44 B5** 40 5N 48 29 E
Arauca, Colombia **92 B4** 7 0N 70 40W
Arauca →, Venezuela **92 B5** 7 24N 66 35W
Arauco, Chile **94 D1** 37 16S 73 25W
Araxá, Brazil **93 G9** 19 35S 46 55W
Araya, Pen. de, Venezuela **92 A6** 10 40N 64 0W
Arba Minch, Ethiopia **46 F2** 6 0N 37 30 E
Arbat, Iraq **44 C5** 35 25N 45 35 E
Árbatax, Italy **20 E3** 39 56N 9 42 E
Arbīl, Iraq **44 B5** 36 15N 44 5 E
Arborfield, Canada **73 C8** 53 6N 103 39W
Arborg, Canada **73 C9** 50 54N 97 13W
Arbroath, U.K. **12 E6** 56 34N 2 35W
Arbuckle, U.S.A. **84 F4** 39 1N 122 3W
Arcachon, France **18 D3** 44 40N 1 10W
Arcade, Calif., U.S.A. **85 L8** 34 2N 118 15W
Arcade, N.Y., U.S.A. **78 D6** 42 32N 78 25W
Arcadia, Fla., U.S.A. **77 M5** 27 13N 81 52W
Arcadia, La., U.S.A. **81 J8** 32 33N 92 55W
Arcadia, Pa., U.S.A. **78 F6** 40 47N 78 51W
Arcata, U.S.A. **82 F1** 40 52N 124 5W
Archangel = Arkhangelsk, Russia **24 B7** 64 38N 40 36 E
Archbald, U.S.A. **79 E9** 41 30N 75 32W
Archer →, Australia **62 A3** 13 28S 141 41 E
Archer B., Australia **62 A3** 13 20S 141 30 E
Archers Post, Kenya **54 B4** 0 35N 37 35 E
Arches Nat. Park, U.S.A. **83 G9** 38 45N 109 25W
Arckaringa Cr. →, Australia **63 D2** 28 10S 135 22 E
Arco, U.S.A. **82 E7** 43 38N 113 18W
Arcos de la Frontera, Spain **19 D3** 36 45N 5 49W
Arcot, India **40 N11** 12 53N 79 20 E
Arctic Bay, Canada **69 A11** 73 1N 85 7W
Arctic Ocean, Arctic **4 B18** 78 0N 160 0W
Arctic Red River = Tsiigehtchic, Canada **68 B6** 67 15N 134 0W
Arda →, Bulgaria **21 D12** 41 40N 26 30 E
Ardabīl, Iran **45 B6** 38 15N 48 18 E
Ardakān = Sepīdān, Iran **45 D7** 30 20N 52 5 E
Ardakān, Iran **45 C7** 32 19N 53 59 E
Ardee, Ireland **13 C5** 53 52N 6 33W
Arden, Canada **78 B8** 44 43N 76 56W
Arden, Calif., U.S.A. **84 G5** 38 36N 121 33W
Arden, Nev., U.S.A. **85 J11** 36 1N 115 14W
Ardenne, Belgium **16 D3** 49 50N 5 5 E
Ardennes = Ardenne, Belgium **16 D3** 49 50N 5 5 E
Arderin, Ireland **13 C4** 53 2N 7 39W
Ardestān, Iran **45 C7** 33 20N 52 25 E
Ardivachar Pt., U.K. **12 D1** 57 23N 7 26W
Ardlethan, Australia **63 E4** 34 22S 146 53 E
Ardmore, Okla., U.S.A. **81 H6** 34 10N 97 8W
Ardmore, Pa., U.S.A. **79 G9** 39 58N 75 18W
Ardnamurchan, Pt. of, U.K. **12 E2** 56 43N 6 14W
Ardnave Pt., U.K. **12 F2** 55 53N 6 20W
Ardrossan, Australia **63 E2** 34 26S 137 53 E
Ardrossan, U.K. **12 F4** 55 39N 4 49W
Ards Pen., U.K. **13 B6** 54 33N 5 34W
Arecibo, Puerto Rico **89 C6** 18 29N 66 43W
Areia Branca, Brazil **93 E11** 5 0S 37 0W
Arena, Pt., U.S.A. **84 G3** 38 57N 123 44W
Arenal, Honduras **88 C2** 15 21N 86 50W
Arendal, Norway **9 G13** 58 28N 8 46 E
Arequipa, Peru **92 G4** 16 20S 71 30W
Arévalo, Spain **19 B3** 41 3N 4 43W
Arezzo, Italy **20 C4** 43 25N 11 53 E
Arga, Turkey **44 B3** 38 21N 37 59 E
Arganda, Spain **19 B4** 40 19N 3 26W
Argenta, Canada **72 C5** 50 11N 116 56W
Argentan, France **18 B3** 48 45N 0 1W
Argentário, Mte., Italy **20 C4** 42 24N 11 9 E
Argentia, Canada **71 C9** 47 18N 53 58W
Argentina ■, S. Amer. **96 D3** 35 0S 66 0W
Argentina Is., Antarctica **5 C17** 66 0S 64 0W
Argentino, L., Argentina **96 G2** 50 10S 73 0W
Argeş →, Romania **17 F14** 44 5N 26 38 E
Arghandab →, Afghan. **42 D1** 31 30N 64 15 E
Argolikós Kólpos, Greece **21 F10** 37 20N 22 52 E
Árgos, Greece **21 F10** 37 40N 22 43 E
Argostólion, Greece **21 E9** 38 11N 20 29 E
Arguello, Pt., U.S.A. **85 L6** 34 35N 120 39W
Arguineguín, Canary Is. **22 G4** 27 46N 15 41W
Argun →, Russia **27 D13** 53 20N 121 28 E
Argus Pk., U.S.A. **85 K9** 35 52N 117 26W
Argyle, L., Australia **60 C4** 16 20S 128 40 E
Argyll & Bute □, U.K. **12 E3** 56 13N 5 28W
Århus, Denmark **9 H14** 56 8N 10 11 E
Ariadnoye, Russia **30 B7** 45 8N 134 25 E
Ariamsvlei, Namibia **56 D2** 28 9S 19 51 E
Arica, Chile **92 G4** 18 32S 70 20W
Arica, Colombia **92 D4** 2 0S 71 50W
Arico, Canary Is. **22 F3** 28 9N 16 29W
Arid, C., Australia **61 F3** 34 1S 123 10 E
Arida, Japan **31 G7** 34 5N 135 8 E
Arílla, Ákra, Greece **23 A3** 39 43N 19 39 E
Arima, Trin. & Tob. **89 D7** 10 38N 61 17W
Arinos →, Brazil **92 F7** 10 25S 58 20W
Ario de Rosales, Mexico **86 D4** 19 12N 102 0W
Aripuanã, Brazil **92 E6** 9 25S 60 30W
Aripuanã →, Brazil **92 E6** 5 7S 60 25W
Ariquemes, Brazil **92 E6** 9 55S 63 6W
Arisaig, U.K. **12 E3** 56 55N 5 51W
Aristazabal I., Canada **72 C3** 52 40N 129 10W
Arivonimamo, Madag. **57 B8** 19 1S 47 11 E
Arizaro, Salar de, Argentina **94 A2** 24 40S 67 50W
Arizona, Argentina **94 D2** 35 45S 65 25W
Arizona □, U.S.A. **83 J8** 34 0N 112 0W
Arizpe, Mexico **86 A2** 30 20N 110 11W
Arjeplog, Sweden **8 D18** 66 3N 18 2 E
Arjona, Colombia **92 A3** 10 14N 75 22W
Arjuna, Indonesia **37 G15** 7 49S 112 34 E
Arka, Russia **27 C15** 60 15N 142 0 E
Arkadelphia, U.S.A. **81 H8** 34 7N 93 4W
Arkaig, L., U.K. **12 E3** 56 59N 5 10W
Arkalyk = Arqalyk, Kazakstan **26 D7** 50 13N 66 50 E
Arkansas □, U.S.A. **81 H8** 35 0N 92 30W
Arkansas →, U.S.A. **81 J9** 33 47N 91 4W
Arkansas City, U.S.A. **81 G6** 37 4N 97 2W
Arkaroola, Australia **63 E2** 30 20S 139 22 E
Arkhángelos, Greece **23 C10** 36 13N 28 7 E
Arkhangelsk, Russia **24 B7** 64 38N 40 36 E
Arki, India **42 D7** 31 9N 76 58 E
Arklow, Ireland **13 D5** 52 48N 6 10W
Arkport, U.S.A. **78 D7** 42 24N 77 42W
Arkticheskiy, Mys, Russia **27 A10** 81 10N 95 0 E
Arkville, U.S.A. **79 D10** 42 9N 74 37W
Arlanzón →, Spain **19 A3** 42 3N 4 17W
Arlbergpass, Austria **16 E6** 47 9N 10 12 E
Arles, France **18 E6** 43 41N 4 40 E
Arlington, S. Africa **57 D4** 28 1S 27 53 E
Arlington, N.Y., U.S.A. **79 E11** 41 42N 73 54W
Arlington, Oreg., U.S.A. **82 D3** 45 43N 120 12W
Arlington, S. Dak., U.S.A. **80 C6** 44 22N 97 8W
Arlington, Tex., U.S.A. **81 J6** 32 44N 97 7W
Arlington, Va., U.S.A. **76 F7** 38 53N 77 7W
Arlington, Vt., U.S.A. **79 C11** 43 5N 73 9W
Arlington, Wash., U.S.A. **84 B4** 48 12N 122 8W
Arlington Heights, U.S.A. **76 D2** 42 5N 87 59W
Arlit, Niger **50 E7** 19 0N 7 38 E
Arlon, Belgium **15 E5** 49 42N 5 49 E
Arltunga, Australia **62 C1** 23 26S 134 41 E
Armagh, U.K. **13 B5** 54 21N 6 39W
Armagh □, U.K. **13 B5** 54 18N 6 37W
Armavir, Russia **25 E7** 45 2N 41 7 E
Armenia, Colombia **92 C3** 4 35N 75 45W
Armenia ■, Asia **25 F7** 40 20N 45 0 E
Armenistís, Ákra, Greece **23 C9** 36 8N 27 42 E
Armidale, Australia **63 E5** 30 30S 151 40 E
Armour, U.S.A. **80 D5** 43 19N 98 21W
Armstrong, B.C., Canada **72 C5** 50 25N 119 10W
Armstrong, Ont., Canada **70 B2** 50 18N 89 4W
Arnarfjörður, Iceland **8 D2** 65 48N 23 40W
Arnaud →, Canada **69 B12** 60 0N 70 0W
Arnauti, C., Cyprus **23 D11** 35 6N 32 17 E
Arnett, U.S.A. **81 G5** 36 8N 99 46W
Arnhem, Neths. **15 C5** 51 58N 5 55 E
Arnhem, C., Australia **62 A2** 12 20S 137 30 E
Arnhem B., Australia **62 A2** 12 20S 136 10 E
Arnhem Land, Australia **62 A1** 13 10S 134 30 E
Arno →, Italy **20 C4** 43 41N 10 17 E
Arno Bay, Australia **63 E2** 33 54S 136 34 E
Arnold, U.K. **10 D6** 53 1N 1 7W
Arnold, U.S.A. **84 G6** 38 15N 120 20W
Arnot, Canada **73 B9** 55 56N 96 41W
Arnøy, Norway **8 A19** 70 9N 20 40 E
Arnprior, Canada **79 A8** 45 26N 76 21W
Arnsberg, Germany **16 C5** 51 24N 8 5 E
Aroab, Namibia **56 D2** 26 41S 19 39 E
Aron, India **42 G6** 25 57N 77 56 E
Arqalyk, Kazakstan **26 D7** 50 13N 66 50 E
Arrah = Ara, India **43 G11** 25 35N 84 32 E
Arran, U.K. **12 F3** 55 34N 5 12W
Arras, France **18 A5** 50 17N 2 46 E
Arrecife, Canary Is. **22 F6** 28 57N 13 37W
Arrecifes, Argentina **94 C3** 34 6S 60 9W
Arrée, Mts. d', France **18 B2** 48 26N 3 55W
Arriaga, Chiapas, Mexico **87 D6** 16 15N 93 52W
Arriaga, San Luis Potosí, Mexico **86 C4** 21 55N 101 23W
Arrilalah, Australia **62 C3** 23 43S 143 54 E
Arrino, Australia **61 E2** 29 30S 115 40 E
Arrow, L., Ireland **13 B3** 54 3N 8 19W
Arrowhead, L., U.S.A. **85 L9** 34 16N 117 10W
Arrowtown, N.Z. **59 L2** 44 57S 168 50 E
Arroyo Grande, U.S.A. **85 K6** 35 7N 120 35W
Ars, Iran **44 B5** 37 9N 47 46 E
Arsenault L., Canada **73 B7** 55 6N 108 32W
Arsenev, Russia **30 B6** 44 10N 133 15 E
Árta, Greece **21 E9** 39 8N 21 2 E
Artà, Spain **22 B10** 39 41N 3 21 E
Arteaga, Mexico **86 D4** 18 50N 102 20W
Artem, Russia **30 C6** 43 22N 132 13 E
Artemovsk, Russia **27 D10** 54 45N 93 35 E
Artemovsk, Ukraine **25 E6** 48 35N 38 0 E
Artesia = Mosomane, Botswana **56 C4** 24 2S 26 19 E
Artesia, U.S.A. **81 J2** 32 51N 104 24W
Arthur, Canada **78 C4** 43 50N 80 32W
Arthur →, Australia **62 G3** 41 2S 144 40 E
Arthur Cr. →, Australia **62 C2** 22 30S 136 25 E
Arthur Pt., Australia **62 C5** 22 7S 150 3 E
Arthur River, Australia **61 F2** 33 20S 117 2 E
Arthur's Pass, N.Z. **59 K3** 42 54S 171 35 E
Arthur's Town, Bahamas **89 B4** 24 38N 75 42W
Artigas, Uruguay **94 C4** 30 20S 56 30W
Artillery L., Canada **73 A7** 63 9N 107 52W
Artois, France **18 A5** 50 20N 2 30 E
Artrutx, C. de, Spain **22 B10** 39 55N 3 49 E
Artsyz, Ukraine **17 E15** 46 4N 29 26 E
Artvin, Turkey **25 F7** 41 14N 41 44 E
Aru, Kepulauan, Indonesia **37 F8** 6 0S 134 30 E
Aru Is. = Aru, Kepulauan, Indonesia **37 F8** 6 0S 134 30 E
Arua, Uganda **54 B3** 3 1N 30 58 E
Aruanã, Brazil **93 F8** 14 54S 51 10W
Aruba ■, W. Indies **89 D6** 12 30N 70 0W
Arucas, Canary Is. **22 F4** 28 7N 15 32W
Arun →, Nepal **43 F12** 26 55N 87 10 E
Arun →, U.K. **11 G7** 50 49N 0 33W
Arunachal Pradesh □, India **41 F19** 28 0N 95 0 E
Arusha, Tanzania **54 C4** 3 20S 36 40 E
Arusha □, Tanzania **54 C4** 4 0S 36 30 E
Arusha Chini, Tanzania **54 C4** 3 32S 37 20 E
Aruwimi →, Dem. Rep. of the Congo **54 B1** 1 13N 23 36 E
Arvada, Colo., U.S.A. **80 F2** 39 48N 105 5W
Arvada, Wyo., U.S.A. **82 D10** 44 39N 106 8W
Árvi, Greece **23 E7** 34 59N 25 28 E
Arviat, Canada **73 A10** 61 6N 93 59W
Arvidsjaur, Sweden **8 D18** 65 35N 19 10 E
Arvika, Sweden **9 G15** 59 40N 12 36 E
Arvin, U.S.A. **85 K8** 35 12N 118 50W
Arwal, India **43 G11** 25 15N 84 41 E
Arxan, China **33 B6** 47 11N 119 57 E
Aryirádhes, Greece **23 B3** 39 27N 19 58 E
Aryiroúpolis, Greece **23 D6** 35 17N 24 20 E
Arys, Kazakstan **26 E7** 42 26N 68 48 E
Arzamas, Russia **24 C7** 55 27N 43 55 E
Aş Şafā, Syria **47 B6** 33 10N 37 0 E
As Saffānīyah, Si. Arabia **45 E6** 27 55N 48 50 E
As Safīrah, Syria **44 B3** 36 5N 37 21 E
Aş Şahm, Oman **45 E8** 24 10N 56 53 E
As Sājir, Si. Arabia **44 E5** 25 11N 44 36 E
As Salamīyah, Syria **44 C3** 35 1N 37 2 E
As Salmān, Iraq **44 D5** 30 30N 44 32 E
As Salţ, Jordan **47 C4** 32 2N 35 43 E
As Sal'w'a, Qatar **45 E6** 24 23N 50 50 E
As Samāwah, Iraq **44 D5** 31 15N 45 15 E
As Sanamayn, Syria **47 B5** 33 3N 36 10 E
As Sohar = Şuḩār, Oman **46 C6** 24 20N 56 40 E
As Sukhnah, Syria **44 C3** 34 52N 38 52 E
As Sulaymānīyah, Iraq **44 C5** 35 35N 45 29 E
As Sulaymī, Si. Arabia **44 E4** 26 17N 41 21 E
As Sulayyil, Si. Arabia **46 C4** 20 27N 45 34 E
As Summān, Si. Arabia **44 E5** 25 0N 47 0 E
As Suwaydā', Syria **47 C5** 32 40N 36 30 E
As Suwaydā' □, Syria **47 C5** 32 45N 36 45 E
As Suwayq, Oman **45 F8** 23 51N 57 26 E
As Şuwayrah, Iraq **44 C5** 32 55N 45 0 E
Asab, Namibia **56 D2** 25 30S 18 0 E
Asad, Buḩayrat al, Syria **44 C3** 36 0N 38 15 E
Asahi-Gawa →, Japan **31 G6** 34 36N 133 58 E
Asahigawa, Japan **30 C11** 43 46N 142 22 E
Asamankese, Ghana **50 G5** 5 50N 0 40W
Asan →, India **43 F8** 26 37N 78 24 E
Asansol, India **43 H12** 23 40N 87 1 E
Asbesberge, S. Africa **56 D3** 29 0S 23 0 E
Asbestos, Canada **71 C5** 45 47N 71 58W
Asbury Park, U.S.A. **79 F10** 40 13N 74 1W
Ascensión, Mexico **86 A3** 31 6N 107 59W
Ascensión, B. de la, Mexico **87 D7** 19 50N 87 20W
Ascension I., Atl. Oc. **49 G2** 7 57S 14 23W
Aschaffenburg, Germany **16 D5** 49 58N 9 6 E
Aschersleben, Germany **16 C6** 51 45N 11 29 E
Áscoli Piceno, Italy **20 C5** 42 51N 13 34 E
Ascope, Peru **92 E3** 7 46S 79 8W
Ascotán, Chile **94 A2** 21 45S 68 17W
Aseb, Eritrea **46 E3** 13 0N 42 40 E
Asela, Ethiopia **46 F2** 8 0N 39 0 E
Asenovgrad, Bulgaria **21 C11** 42 1N 24 51 E
Aserradero, Mexico **86 C3** 23 40N 105 43W
Asgata, Cyprus **23 E12** 34 46N 33 15 E
Ash Fork, U.S.A. **83 J7** 35 13N 112 29W
Ash Grove, U.S.A. **81 G8** 37 19N 93 35W
Ash Shabakah, Iraq **44 D4** 30 49N 43 39 E
Ash Shamāl □, Lebanon **47 A5** 34 25N 36 0 E
Ash Shāmīyah, Iraq **44 D5** 31 55N 44 35 E
Ash Shāriqah, U.A.E. **46 B6** 25 23N 55 26 E
Ash Sharmah, Si. Arabia **44 D2** 28 1N 35 16 E
Ash Sharqāt, Iraq **44 C4** 35 27N 43 16 E
Ash Sharqi, Al Jabal, Lebanon **47 B5** 33 40N 36 10 E
Ash Shaţrah, Iraq **44 D5** 31 30N 46 10 E
Ash Shawbak, Jordan **44 D2** 30 32N 35 34 E
Ash Shawmari, J., Jordan **47 E5** 30 35N 36 35 E
Ash Shināfīyah, Iraq **44 D5** 31 35N 44 39 E
Ash Shu'bah, Si. Arabia **44 D5** 28 54N 44 44 E
Ash Shumlūl, Si. Arabia **44 E5** 26 31N 47 20 E
Ash Shūr'a, Iraq **44 C4** 35 58N 43 13 E
Ash Shurayf, Si. Arabia **44 E3** 25 43N 39 14 E
Ash Shuwayfāt, Lebanon **47 B4** 33 45N 35 30 E
Asha, Russia **24 D10** 55 0N 57 16 E
Ashau, Vietnam **38 D6** 16 6N 107 22 E
Ashbourne, U.K. **10 D6** 53 2N 1 43W
Ashburn, U.S.A. **77 K4** 31 43N 83 39W
Ashburton, N.Z. **59 K3** 43 53S 171 48 E
Ashburton →, Australia **60 D1** 21 40S 114 56 E
Ashcroft, Canada **72 C4** 50 40N 121 20W
Ashdod, Israel **47 D3** 31 49N 34 35 E
Ashdown, U.S.A. **81 J7** 33 40N 94 8W
Asheboro, U.S.A. **77 H6** 35 43N 79 49W
Ashern, Canada **73 C9** 51 11N 98 21W
Asherton, U.S.A. **81 L5** 28 27N 99 46W
Asheville, U.S.A. **77 H4** 35 36N 82 33W
Ashewat, Pakistan **42 D3** 31 22N 68 32 E
Asheweig →, Canada **70 B2** 54 17N 87 12W
Ashford, Australia **63 D5** 29 15S 151 3 E
Ashford, U.K. **11 F8** 51 8N 0 53 E
Ashgabat, Turkmenistan **26 F6** 38 0N 57 50 E
Ashibetsu, Japan **30 C11** 43 31N 142 11 E
Ashikaga, Japan **31 F9** 36 28N 139 29 E
Ashington, U.K. **10 B6** 55 11N 1 33W
Ashizuri-Zaki, Japan **31 H6** 32 44N 133 0 E
Ashkarkot, Afghan. **42 C2** 33 3N 67 58 E
Ashkhabad = Ashgabat, Turkmenistan **26 F6** 38 0N 57 50 E

Barakot

Bagamoyo, Tanzania 54 D4 6 28S 38 55 E
Bagan Datoh, Malaysia 39 L3 3 59N 100 47 E
Bagan Serai, Malaysia 39 K3 5 1N 100 32 E
Baganga, Phil. 37 C7 7 34N 126 33 E
Bagani, Namibia 56 B3 18 7S 21 41 E
Bagansiapiapi, Indonesia 36 D2 2 12N 100 50 E
Bagasra, India 42 J4 21 30N 71 0 E
Bagaud, India 42 H6 22 19N 75 53 E
Bagdad, U.S.A. 85 L11 34 35N 115 53W
Bagdarin, Russia 27 D12 54 26N 113 36 E
Bagé, Brazil 95 C5 31 20S 54 15W
Bagenalstown = Muine Bheag, Ireland 13 D5 52 42N 6 58W
Baggs, U.S.A. 82 F10 41 2N 107 39W
Bagh, Pakistan 43 C5 33 59N 73 45 E
Baghain →, India 43 G9 25 32N 81 1 E
Baghdād, Iraq 44 C5 33 20N 44 30 E
Bagheria, Italy 20 E5 38 5N 13 30 E
Baghlān, Afghan. 40 A6 32 12N 68 46 E
Baghlān □, Afghan. 40 B6 36 0N 68 30 E
Bagley, U.S.A. 80 B7 47 32N 95 24W
Bago = Pegu, Burma 41 L20 17 20N 96 29 E
Bagodar, India 43 G11 24 5N 85 52 E
Bagrationovsk, Russia 9 J19 54 23N 20 39 E
Baguio, Phil. 37 A6 16 26N 120 34 E
Bah, India 43 F8 26 53N 78 36 E
Bahadurganj, India 43 F12 26 16N 87 49 E
Bahadurgarh, India 42 E7 28 40N 76 57 E
Bahama, Canal Viejo de, W. Indies 88 B4 22 10N 77 30W
Bahamas ■, N. Amer. 89 B5 24 0N 75 0W
Baharampur, India 43 G13 24 2N 88 27 E
Bahawalnagar, Pakistan 42 E5 30 0N 73 15 E
Bahawalpur, Pakistan 42 E4 29 24N 71 40 E
Baheri, India 43 E8 28 45N 79 34 E
Bahgul →, India 43 F8 27 45N 79 36 E
Bahi, Tanzania 54 D4 5 58S 35 21 E
Bahi Swamp, Tanzania 54 D4 6 10S 35 0 E
Bahía = Salvador, Brazil 93 F11 13 0S 38 30W
Bahía □, Brazil 93 F10 12 0S 42 0W
Bahía, Is. de la, Honduras 88 C2 16 45N 86 15W
Bahía Blanca, Argentina 94 D3 38 35S 62 13W
Bahía de Caráquez, Ecuador 92 D2 0 40S 80 27W
Bahía Honda, Cuba 88 B3 22 54N 83 10W
Bahía Laura, Argentina 96 F3 48 10S 66 30W
Bahía Negra, Paraguay 92 H7 20 5S 58 5W
Bahir Dar, Ethiopia 46 E2 11 37N 37 10 E
Bahmanzād, Iran 45 D6 31 15N 51 47 E
Bahr el Ghazâl □, Sudan 51 G11 7 0N 28 0 E
Bahraich, India 43 F9 27 38N 81 37 E
Bahrain ■, Asia 46 B5 26 0N 50 35 E
Bahror, India 42 F7 27 51N 76 20 E
Bāhū Kalāt, Iran 45 E9 25 43N 61 25 E
Bai Bung, Mui = Ca Mau, Mui, Vietnam 39 H5 8 38N 104 44 E
Bai Duc, Vietnam 38 C5 18 3N 105 49 E
Bai Thuong, Vietnam 38 C5 19 54N 105 23 E
Baia Mare, Romania 17 E12 47 40N 23 35 E
Baião, Brazil 93 D9 2 40S 49 40W
Baïbokoum, Chad 51 G9 7 46N 15 43 E
Baicheng, China 35 B12 45 38N 122 42 E
Baidoa, Somali Rep. 46 G3 3 8N 43 30 E
Baie Comeau, Canada 71 C6 49 12N 68 10W
Baie-St-Paul, Canada 71 C5 47 28N 70 32W
Baie Trinité, Canada 71 C6 49 25N 67 20W
Baie Verte, Canada 71 C8 49 55N 56 12W
Baihar, India 43 H9 22 6N 80 33 E
Baihe, China 34 H6 32 50N 110 5 E
Ba'ījī, Iraq 44 C4 35 0N 43 30 E
Baijnath, India 43 E8 29 55N 79 37 E
Baikal, L. = Baykal, Oz., Russia 27 D11 53 0N 108 0 E
Baikunthpur, India 43 H10 23 15N 82 33 E
Baile Atha Cliath = Dublin, Ireland 13 C5 53 21N 6 15W
Băileşti, Romania 17 F12 44 1N 23 20 E
Bainbridge, Ga., U.S.A. 77 K3 30 55N 84 35W
Bainbridge, N.Y., U.S.A. 79 D9 42 18N 75 29W
Baing, Indonesia 37 F6 10 14S 120 34 E
Bainiu, China 34 H7 32 50N 112 15 E
Bā'ir, Jordan 47 E5 30 45N 36 55 E
Bairin Youqi, China 35 C10 43 30N 118 35 E
Bairin Zuoqi, China 35 C10 43 58N 119 15 E
Bairnsdale, Australia 63 F4 37 48S 147 36 E
Baisha, China 34 G7 34 20N 112 32 E
Baitadi, Nepal 43 E9 29 35N 80 25 E
Baiyin, China 34 F3 36 45N 104 14 E
Baiyu Shan, China 34 F4 37 15N 107 30 E
Baj Baj, India 43 H13 22 30N 88 5 E
Baja, Hungary 17 E10 46 12N 18 59 E
Baja, Pta., Mexico 86 B1 29 50N 116 0W
Baja California, Mexico 86 A1 31 10N 115 12W
Baja California □, Mexico 86 B2 30 0N 115 0W
Baja California Sur □, Mexico 86 B2 25 50N 111 50W
Bajag, India 43 H9 22 40N 81 21 E
Bajamar, Canary Is. 22 F3 28 33N 16 20W
Bajana, India 42 H4 23 7N 71 49 E
Bājgīrān, Iran 45 B8 37 36N 58 24 E
Bajimba, Mt., Australia 63 D5 29 17S 152 6 E
Bajo Nuevo, Caribbean 88 C4 15 40N 78 50W
Bajoga, Nigeria 51 F8 10 57N 11 20 E
Bajool, Australia 62 C5 23 40S 150 35 E
Bakel, Senegal 50 F3 14 56N 12 20W
Baker, Calif., U.S.A. 85 K10 35 16N 116 4W
Baker, Mont., U.S.A. 80 B2 46 22N 104 17W
Baker, L., Canada 68 B10 64 0N 96 0W
Baker City, U.S.A. 82 D5 44 47N 117 50W
Baker I., Pac. Oc. 64 G10 0 10N 176 35W
Baker I., U.S.A. 72 B2 55 20N 133 40W
Baker L., Australia 61 E4 26 54S 126 5 E
Baker Lake, Canada 68 B10 64 20N 96 3W
Baker Mt., U.S.A. 82 B3 48 50N 121 49W
Bakers Creek, Australia 62 C4 21 13S 149 7 E
Baker's Dozen Is., Canada 70 A4 56 45N 78 45W
Bakersfield, Calif., U.S.A. 85 K8 35 23N 119 1W
Bakersfield, Vt., U.S.A. 79 B12 44 45N 72 48W
Bākhtarān, Iran 44 C5 34 23N 47 0 E
Bākhtarān □, Iran 44 C5 34 0N 46 30 E
Bakı, Azerbaijan 25 F8 40 29N 49 56 E
Bakkafjörður, Iceland 8 C6 66 2N 14 48W
Bakony, Hungary 17 E9 47 10N 17 30 E
Bakony Forest = Bakony, Hungary 17 E9 47 10N 17 30 E
Bakouma, C.A.R. 52 C4 5 40N 22 56 E
Bakswaho, India 43 G8 24 15N 79 18 E
Baku = Bakı, Azerbaijan 25 F8 40 29N 49 56 E
Bakutis Coast, Antarctica 5 D15 74 0S 120 0W
Baky = Bakı, Azerbaijan 25 F8 40 29N 49 56 E
Bala, Canada 78 A5 45 1N 79 37W
Bala, U.K. 10 E4 52 54N 3 36W
Bala, L., U.K. 10 E4 52 53N 3 37W
Balabac I., Phil. 36 C5 8 0N 117 0 E
Balabac Str., E. Indies 36 C5 7 53N 117 5 E
Balabagh, Afghan. 42 B4 34 25N 70 12 E
Ba'labakk, Lebanon 47 B5 34 0N 36 10 E
Balabalangan, Kepulauan, Indonesia 36 E5 2 20S 117 30 E
Balad, Iraq 44 C5 34 1N 44 9 E
Balad Rūz, Iraq 44 C5 33 42N 45 5 E
Bālādeh, Fārs, Iran 45 D6 29 17N 51 56 E
Bālādeh, Māzandaran, Iran 45 B6 36 12N 51 48 E
Balaghat, India 40 J12 21 49N 80 12 E
Balaghat Ra., India 40 K10 18 50N 76 30 E
Balaguer, Spain 19 B6 41 50N 0 50 E
Balaklava, Ukraine 25 F5 44 30N 33 30 E
Balakovo, Russia 24 D8 52 4N 47 55 E
Balamau, India 43 F9 27 10N 80 21 E
Balancán, Mexico 87 D6 17 48N 91 32W
Balashov, Russia 25 D7 51 30N 43 10 E
Balasinor, India 42 H5 22 57N 73 23 E
Balasore = Baleshwar, India 41 J15 21 35N 87 3 E
Balaton, Hungary 17 E9 46 50N 17 40 E
Balbina, Reprêsa de, Brazil 92 D7 2 0S 59 30W
Balboa, Panama 88 E4 8 57N 79 34W
Balbriggan, Ireland 13 C5 53 37N 6 11W
Balcarce, Argentina 94 D4 38 0S 58 10W
Balcarres, Canada 73 C8 50 50N 103 35W
Balchik, Bulgaria 21 C13 43 28N 28 11 E
Balclutha, N.Z. 59 M2 46 15S 169 45 E
Balcones Escarpment, U.S.A. 81 L5 29 30N 99 15W
Bald Hd., Australia 61 G2 35 6S 118 1 E
Bald I., Australia 61 F2 34 57S 118 27 E
Bald Knob, U.S.A. 81 H9 35 19N 91 34W
Baldock L., Canada 73 B9 56 33N 97 57W
Baldwin, Mich., U.S.A. 76 D3 43 54N 85 51W
Baldwin, Pa., U.S.A. 78 F5 40 23N 79 59W
Baldwinsville, U.S.A. 79 C8 43 10N 76 20W
Baldy Mt., U.S.A. 82 B9 48 9N 109 39W
Baldy Peak, U.S.A. 83 K9 33 54N 109 34W
Baleares, Is., Spain 22 B10 39 30N 3 0 E
Balearic Is. = Baleares, Is., Spain 22 B10 39 30N 3 0 E
Baleine = Whale →, Canada 71 A6 58 15N 67 40W
Baler, Phil. 37 A6 15 46N 121 34 E
Baleshare, U.K. 12 D1 57 31N 7 22W
Baleshwar, India 41 J15 21 35N 87 3 E
Balfate, Honduras 88 C2 15 48N 86 25W
Bali, Greece 23 D6 35 25N 24 47 E
Bali, India 42 G5 25 11N 73 17 E
Bali, Indonesia 36 F4 8 20S 115 0 E
Bali □, Indonesia 36 F5 8 20S 115 0 E
Bali, Selat, Indonesia 37 H16 8 18S 114 25 E
Baliapal, India 43 J12 21 40N 87 17 E
Balikeşir, Turkey 21 E12 39 39N 27 53 E
Balikpapan, Indonesia 36 E5 1 10S 116 55 E
Balimbing, Phil. 37 C5 5 5N 119 58 E
Baling, Malaysia 39 K3 5 41N 100 55 E
Balipara, India 41 F18 26 50N 92 45 E
Balkan Mts. = Stara Planina, Bulgaria 21 C10 43 15N 23 0 E
Balkhash = Balqash, Kazakstan 26 E8 46 50N 74 50 E
Balkhash, Ozero = Balqash Köl, Kazakstan 26 E8 46 0N 74 50 E
Balla, Bangla. 41 G17 24 10N 91 35 E
Ballachulish, U.K. 12 E3 56 41N 5 8W
Balladonia, Australia 61 F3 32 27S 123 51 E
Ballaghaderreen, Ireland 13 C3 53 55N 8 34W
Ballarat, Australia 63 F3 37 33S 143 50 E
Ballard, L., Australia 61 E3 29 20S 120 40 E
Ballater, U.K. 12 D5 57 3N 3 3W
Ballenas, Canal de, Mexico 86 B2 29 10N 113 45W
Balleny Is., Antarctica 5 C11 66 30S 163 0 E
Ballia, India 43 G11 25 46N 84 12 E
Ballina, Australia 63 D5 28 50S 153 31 E
Ballina, Ireland 13 B2 54 7N 9 9W
Ballinasloe, Ireland 13 C3 53 20N 8 13W
Ballinger, U.S.A. 81 K5 31 45N 99 57W
Ballinrobe, Ireland 13 C2 53 38N 9 13W
Ballinskelligs B., Ireland 13 E1 51 48N 10 13W
Ballston Spa, U.S.A. 79 D11 43 0N 73 51W
Ballycastle, U.K. 13 A5 55 12N 6 15W
Ballyclare, U.K. 13 B5 54 46N 6 0W
Ballyhaunis, Ireland 13 C3 53 46N 8 46W
Ballymena, U.K. 13 B5 54 52N 6 17W
Ballymoney, U.K. 13 A5 55 5N 6 31W
Ballymote, Ireland 13 B3 54 5N 8 31W
Ballynahinch, U.K. 13 B6 54 24N 5 54W
Ballyquintin Pt., U.K. 13 B6 54 20N 5 30W
Ballyshannon, Ireland 13 B3 54 30N 8 11W
Balmaceda, Chile 96 F2 46 0S 71 50W
Balmertown, Canada 73 C10 51 4N 93 41W
Balmoral, Australia 63 F3 37 15S 141 48 E
Balmorhea, U.S.A. 81 K3 30 59N 103 45W
Balochistan = Baluchistan □, Pakistan 40 F4 27 30N 65 0 E
Balonne →, Australia 63 D4 28 47S 147 56 E
Balotra, India 42 G5 25 50N 72 14 E
Balqash, Kazakstan 26 E8 46 50N 74 50 E
Balqash Köl, Kazakstan 26 E8 46 0N 74 50 E
Balrampur, India 43 F10 27 30N 82 20 E
Balranald, Australia 63 E3 34 38S 143 33 E
Balsas, Mexico 87 D5 18 0N 99 40W
Balsas →, Brazil 93 E9 7 15S 44 35W
Balsas →, Mexico 86 D4 17 55N 102 10W
Balston Spa, U.S.A. 79 D11 43 0N 73 52W
Balta, Ukraine 17 D15 48 2N 29 45 E
Bălţi, Moldova 17 E14 47 48N 27 58 E
Baltic Sea, Europe 9 H18 57 0N 19 0 E
Baltimore, Ireland 13 E2 51 29N 9 22W
Baltimore, Md., U.S.A. 76 F7 39 17N 76 37W
Baltimore, Ohio, U.S.A. 78 G2 39 51N 82 36W
Baltit, Pakistan 43 A6 36 15N 74 40 E
Baltiysk, Russia 9 J18 54 41N 19 58 E
Baluchistan □, Pakistan 40 F4 27 30N 65 0 E
Balurghat, India 43 G13 25 15N 88 44 E
Balvi, Latvia 9 H22 57 8N 27 15 E
Balya, Turkey 21 E12 39 44N 27 35 E
Bam, Iran 45 D8 29 7N 58 14 E
Bama, Nigeria 51 F8 11 33N 13 41 E
Bamaga, Australia 62 A3 10 50S 142 25 E
Bamaji L., Canada 70 B1 51 9N 91 25W
Bamako, Mali 50 F4 12 34N 7 55W
Bambari, C.A.R. 52 C4 5 40N 20 35 E
Bambaroo, Australia 62 B4 18 50S 146 10 E
Bamberg, Germany 16 D6 49 54N 10 54 E
Bamberg, U.S.A. 77 J5 33 18N 81 2W
Bambili, Dem. Rep. of the Congo 54 B2 3 40N 26 0 E
Bamfield, Canada 72 D3 48 45N 125 10W
Bāmīān □, Afghan. 40 B5 35 0N 67 0 E
Bamiancheng, China 35 C13 43 15N 124 2 E
Bampūr, Iran 45 E9 27 15N 60 21 E
Ban Ban, Laos 38 C4 19 31N 103 30 E
Ban Bang Hin, Thailand 39 H2 9 32N 98 35 E
Ban Chiang Klang, Thailand 38 C3 19 25N 100 55 E
Ban Chik, Laos 38 D4 17 15N 102 22 E
Ban Choho, Thailand 38 E4 15 2N 102 9 E
Ban Dan Lan Hoi, Thailand 38 D2 17 0N 99 35 E
Ban Don = Surat Thani, Thailand 39 H2 9 6N 99 20 E
Ban Don, Vietnam 38 F6 12 53N 107 48 E
Ban Don, Ao →, Thailand 39 H2 9 20N 99 25 E
Ban Dong, Thailand 38 C3 19 30N 100 59 E
Ban Hong, Thailand 38 C2 18 18N 98 50 E
Ban Kaeng, Thailand 38 D3 17 29N 100 7 E
Ban Kantang, Thailand 39 J2 7 25N 99 31 E
Ban Keun, Laos 38 C4 18 22N 102 35 E
Ban Khai, Thailand 38 F3 12 46N 101 18 E
Ban Kheun, Laos 38 B3 20 13N 101 7 E
Ban Khlong Kua, Thailand 39 J3 6 57N 100 8 E
Ban Khuan Mao, Thailand 39 J2 7 50N 99 37 E
Ban Ko Yai Chim, Thailand 39 G2 11 17N 99 26 E
Ban Kok, Thailand 38 D4 16 40N 103 40 E
Ban Laem, Thailand 38 F2 13 13N 99 59 E
Ban Lao Ngam, Laos 38 E6 15 28N 106 10 E
Ban Le Kathe, Thailand 38 E2 15 49N 98 53 E
Ban Mae Chedi, Thailand 38 C2 19 11N 99 31 E
Ban Mae Laeng, Thailand 38 B2 20 1N 99 17 E
Ban Mae Sariang, Thailand 38 C1 18 10N 97 56 E
Ban Mê Thuôt = Buon Ma Thuot, Vietnam 38 F7 12 40N 108 3 E
Ban Mi, Thailand 38 E3 15 3N 100 32 E
Ban Muong Mo, Laos 38 C4 19 4N 103 58 E
Ban Na Mo, Laos 38 D5 17 7N 105 40 E
Ban Na San, Thailand 39 H2 8 53N 99 52 E
Ban Na Tong, Laos 38 B3 20 56N 101 47 E
Ban Nam Bac, Laos 38 B4 20 38N 102 20 E
Ban Nam Ma, Laos 38 A3 22 2N 101 37 E
Ban Ngang, Laos 38 E6 15 59N 106 11 E
Ban Nong Bok, Laos 38 D5 17 5N 104 48 E
Ban Nong Boua, Laos 38 E6 15 40N 106 33 E
Ban Nong Pling, Thailand 38 E3 15 40N 100 10 E
Ban Pak Chan, Thailand 39 G2 10 32N 98 51 E
Ban Phai, Thailand 38 D4 16 4N 102 44 E
Ban Pong, Thailand 38 F2 13 50N 99 55 E
Ban Ron Phibun, Thailand 39 H2 8 9N 99 51 E
Ban Sanam Chai, Thailand 39 J3 7 33N 100 25 E
Ban Sangkha, Thailand 38 E4 14 37N 103 52 E
Ban Tak, Thailand 38 D2 17 2N 99 4 E
Ban Tako, Thailand 38 E4 14 5N 102 40 E
Ban Tha Dua, Thailand 38 D2 17 59N 98 39 E
Ban Tha Li, Thailand 38 D3 17 37N 101 25 E
Ban Tha Nun, Thailand 39 H2 8 12N 98 18 E
Ban Thahine, Laos 38 E5 14 12N 105 33 E
Ban Xien Kok, Laos 38 B3 20 54N 100 39 E
Ban Yen Nhan, Vietnam 38 B6 20 57N 106 2 E
Banaba, Kiribati 64 H8 0 45S 169 50 E
Banalia, Dem. Rep. of the Congo 54 B2 1 32N 25 5 E
Banam, Cambodia 39 G5 11 20N 105 17 E
Bananal, I. do, Brazil 93 F8 11 30S 50 30W
Banaras = Varanasi, India 43 G10 25 22N 83 0 E
Banas →, Gujarat, India 42 H4 23 45N 71 25 E
Banas →, Mad. P., India 43 G9 24 15N 81 30 E
Bânâs, Ras, Egypt 51 D13 23 57N 35 59 E
Banbridge, U.K. 13 B5 54 22N 6 16W
Banbury, U.K. 11 E6 52 4N 1 20W
Banchory, U.K. 12 D6 57 3N 2 29W
Bancroft, Canada 78 A7 45 3N 77 51W
Band Bonī, Iran 45 E8 25 30N 59 33 E
Band Qīr, Iran 45 D6 31 39N 48 53 E
Banda, Mad. P., India 43 G8 24 3N 78 57 E
Banda, Ut. P., India 43 G9 25 30N 80 26 E
Banda, Kepulauan, Indonesia 37 E7 4 37S 129 50 E
Banda Aceh, Indonesia 36 C1 5 35N 95 20 E
Banda Banda, Mt., Australia 63 E5 31 10S 152 28 E
Banda Elat, Indonesia 37 F8 5 40S 133 5 E
Banda Is. = Banda, Kepulauan, Indonesia 37 E7 4 37S 129 50 E
Banda Sea, Indonesia 37 F7 6 0S 130 0 E
Bandai-San, Japan 30 F10 37 36N 140 4 E
Bandān, Iran 45 D9 31 23N 60 44 E
Bandanaira, Indonesia 37 E7 4 32S 129 54 E
Bandanwara, India 42 F6 26 9N 74 38 E
Bandar = Machilipatnam, India 41 L12 16 12N 81 8 E
Bandār 'Abbās, Iran 45 E8 27 15N 56 15 E
Bandar-e Anzalī, Iran 45 B6 37 30N 49 30 E
Bandar-e Bushehr = Būshehr, Iran 45 D6 28 55N 50 55 E
Bandar-e Chārak, Iran 45 E7 26 45N 54 20 E
Bandar-e Deylam, Iran 45 D6 30 5N 50 10 E
Bandar-e Khomeynı, Iran 45 D6 30 30N 49 5 E
Bandar-e Lengeh, Iran 45 E7 26 35N 54 58 E
Bandar-e Maqām, Iran 45 E7 26 56N 53 29 E
Bandar-e Ma'shur, Iran 45 D6 30 35N 49 10 E
Bandar-e Rīg, Iran 45 D6 29 29N 50 38 E
Bandar-e Torkeman, Iran 45 B7 37 0N 54 10 E
Bandar Maharani = Muar, Malaysia 39 L4 2 3N 102 34 E
Bandar Penggaram = Batu Pahat, Malaysia 39 M4 1 50N 102 56 E
Bandar Seri Begawan, Brunei 36 C4 4 52N 115 0 E
Bandar Sri Aman, Malaysia 36 D4 1 15N 111 32 E
Bandawe, Malawi 55 E3 11 58S 34 5 E
Bandeira, Pico da, Brazil 95 A7 20 26S 41 47W
Bandera, Argentina 94 B3 28 55S 62 20W
Banderas, B. de, Mexico 86 C3 20 40N 105 30W
Bandhogarh, India 43 H9 23 40N 81 2 E
Bandi →, India 42 F6 26 12N 75 47 E
Bandikui, India 42 F7 27 3N 76 34 E
Bandırma, Turkey 21 D13 40 20N 28 0 E
Bandon, Ireland 13 E3 51 44N 8 44W
Bandon →, Ireland 13 E3 51 43N 8 37W
Bandula, Mozam. 55 F3 19 0S 33 7 E
Bandundu, Dem. Rep. of the Congo 52 E3 3 15S 17 22 E
Bandung, Indonesia 36 F3 6 54S 107 36 E
Bāneh, Iran 44 C5 35 59N 45 53 E
Banes, Cuba 89 B4 21 0N 75 42W
Banff, Canada 72 C5 51 10N 115 34W
Banff, U.K. 12 D6 57 40N 2 33W
Banff Nat. Park, Canada 72 C5 51 30N 116 15W
Bang Fai →, Laos 38 D5 16 57N 104 45 E
Bang Hieng →, Laos 38 D5 16 10N 105 10 E
Bang Krathum, Thailand 38 D3 16 34N 100 18 E
Bang Lamung, Thailand 38 F3 13 3N 100 56 E
Bang Mun Nak, Thailand 38 D3 16 2N 100 23 E
Bang Pa In, Thailand 38 E3 14 14N 100 35 E
Bang Rakam, Thailand 38 D3 16 45N 100 7 E
Bang Saphan, Thailand 39 G2 11 14N 99 28 E
Bangaduni I., India 43 J13 21 34N 88 52 E
Bangala Dam, Zimbabwe 55 G3 21 7S 31 25 E
Bangalore, India 40 N10 12 59N 77 40 E
Banganga →, India 42 F6 27 6N 77 25 E
Bangaon, India 43 H13 23 0N 88 47 E
Bangassou, C.A.R. 52 D4 4 55N 23 7 E
Banggai, Indonesia 37 E6 1 34S 123 30 E
Banggai, Kepulauan, Indonesia 37 E6 1 40S 123 30 E
Banggai Arch. = Banggai, Kepulauan, Indonesia 37 E6 1 40S 123 30 E
Banggi, Malaysia 36 C5 7 17N 117 12 E
Banghāzī, Libya 51 B10 32 11N 20 3 E
Bangka, Sulawesi, Indonesia 37 D7 1 50N 125 5 E
Bangka, Sumatera, Indonesia 36 E3 2 0S 105 50 E
Bangka, Selat, Indonesia 36 E3 2 30S 105 30 E
Bangkalan, Indonesia 37 G15 7 2S 112 46 E
Bangkinang, Indonesia 36 D2 0 18N 101 5 E
Bangko, Indonesia 36 E2 2 5S 102 9 E
Bangkok, Thailand 38 F3 13 45N 100 35 E
Bangladesh ■, Asia 41 H17 24 0N 90 0 E
Bangong Co, India 43 B8 35 50N 79 20 E
Bangor, Down, U.K. 13 B6 54 40N 5 40W
Bangor, Gwynedd, U.K. 10 D3 53 14N 4 8W
Bangor, Maine, U.S.A. 69 D13 44 48N 68 46W
Bangor, Pa., U.S.A. 79 F9 40 52N 75 13W
Bangued, Phil. 37 A6 17 40N 120 37 E
Bangui, C.A.R. 52 D3 4 23N 18 35 E
Banguru, Dem. Rep. of the Congo 54 B2 0 30N 27 10 E
Bangweulu, L., Zambia 55 E3 11 0S 30 0 E
Bangweulu Swamp, Zambia 55 E3 11 20S 30 15 E
Bani, Dom. Rep. 89 C5 18 16N 70 22W
Banī Sa'd, Iraq 44 C5 33 34N 44 32 E
Banihal Pass, India 43 C6 33 30N 75 12 E
Bāniyās, Syria 44 C3 35 10N 36 0 E
Banja Luka, Bos.-H. 20 B7 44 49N 17 11 E
Banjar, India 42 D7 31 38N 77 21 E
Banjar →, India 43 H9 22 36N 80 22 E
Banjarmasin, Indonesia 36 E4 3 20S 114 35 E
Banjul, Gambia 50 F2 13 28N 16 40W
Banka, India 43 G12 24 53N 86 55 E
Banket, Zimbabwe 55 F3 17 27S 30 19 E
Bankipore, India 41 G14 25 35N 85 10 E
Banks I., B.C., Canada 72 C3 53 20N 130 0W
Banks I., N.W.T., Canada 68 A7 73 15N 121 30W
Banks Pen., N.Z. 59 K4 43 45S 173 15 E
Banks Str., Australia 62 G4 40 40S 148 10 E
Bankura, India 43 H12 23 11N 87 18 E
Banmankhi, India 43 G12 25 53N 87 11 E
Bann →, Arm., U.K. 13 B5 54 30N 6 31W
Bann →, L'derry., U.K. 13 A5 55 8N 6 41W
Bannang Sata, Thailand 39 J3 6 16N 101 16 E
Banning, U.S.A. 85 M10 33 56N 116 53W
Banningville = Bandundu, Dem. Rep. of the Congo 52 E3 3 15S 17 22 E
Bannockburn, Canada 78 B7 44 39N 77 33W
Bannockburn, U.K. 12 E5 56 5N 3 55W
Bannockburn, Zimbabwe 55 G2 20 17S 29 48 E
Bannu, Pakistan 40 C7 33 0N 70 18 E
Bano, India 43 H11 22 40N 84 55 E
Bansgaon, India 43 F10 26 33N 83 21 E
Banská Bystrica, Slovak Rep. 17 D10 48 46N 19 14 E
Banswara, India 42 H6 23 32N 74 24 E
Bantaeng, Indonesia 37 F5 5 32S 119 56 E
Bantry, Ireland 13 E2 51 41N 9 27W
Bantry B., Ireland 13 E2 51 37N 9 44W
Bantul, Indonesia 37 G14 7 55S 110 19 E
Bantva, India 42 J4 21 29N 70 12 E
Banyak, Kepulauan, Indonesia 36 D1 2 10N 97 10 E
Banyalbufar, Spain 22 B9 39 42N 2 31 E
Banyo, Cameroon 52 C2 6 52N 11 45 E
Banyumas, Indonesia 37 G13 7 32S 109 18 E
Banyuwangi, Indonesia 37 H16 8 13S 114 21 E
Banzare Coast, Antarctica 5 C9 68 0S 125 0 E
Bao Ha, Vietnam 38 A5 22 11N 104 21 E
Bao Lac, Vietnam 38 A5 22 57N 105 40 E
Bao Loc, Vietnam 39 G6 11 32N 107 48 E
Baocheng, China 34 H4 33 12N 106 56 E
Baode, China 34 E6 39 1N 111 5 E
Baodi, China 35 E9 39 38N 117 20 E
Baoding, China 34 E8 38 50N 115 28 E
Baoji, China 34 G4 34 20N 107 5 E
Baoshan, China 32 D4 25 10N 99 5 E
Baotou, China 34 D6 40 32N 110 2 E
Baoying, China 35 H10 33 17N 119 20 E
Bap, India 42 F5 27 23N 72 18 E
Bapatla, India 41 M12 15 55N 80 30 E
Bāqerābād, Iran 45 C6 33 2N 51 58 E
Ba'qūbah, Iraq 44 C5 33 45N 44 50 E
Baquedano, Chile 94 A2 23 20S 69 52W
Bar, Montenegro, Yug. 21 C8 42 8N 19 6 E
Bar, Ukraine 17 D14 49 4N 27 40 E
Bar Bigha, India 43 G11 25 21N 85 47 E
Bar Harbor, U.S.A. 77 C11 44 23N 68 13W
Bar-le-Duc, France 18 B6 48 47N 5 10 E
Bara, India 43 G9 25 16N 81 43 E
Bara Banki, India 43 F9 26 55N 81 12 E
Barabai, Indonesia 36 E5 2 32S 115 34 E
Baraboo, U.S.A. 80 D10 43 28N 89 45W
Baracoa, Cuba 89 B5 20 20N 74 30W
Baradā →, Syria 47 B5 33 33N 36 34 E
Baradero, Argentina 94 C4 33 52S 59 29W
Baraga, U.S.A. 80 B10 46 47N 88 30W
Barah →, India 42 F6 27 42N 77 5 E
Barahona, Dom. Rep. 89 C5 18 13N 71 7W
Barail Range, India 41 G18 25 15N 93 20 E
Barakaldo, Spain 19 A4 43 18N 2 59W
Barakar →, India 43 G12 24 7N 86 14 E
Barakhola, India 41 G18 25 0N 92 45 E
Barakot, India 43 J11 21 33N 84 59 E

Bīārjmand

Bīārjmand, *Iran* 45 B7 36 6N 55 53 E
Biaro, *Indonesia* 37 D7 2 5N 125 26 E
Biarritz, *France* 18 E3 43 29N 1 33W
Bibai, *Japan* 30 C10 43 19N 141 52 E
Bibby I., *Canada* 73 A10 61 55N 93 0W
Biberach, *Germany* 16 D5 48 5N 9 47 E
Bibungwa, *Dem. Rep. of the Congo* 54 C2 2 40S 28 15 E
Bic, *Canada* 71 C6 48 20N 68 41W
Bicester, *U.K.* 11 F6 51 54N 1 9W
Bicheno, *Australia* 62 G4 41 52S 148 18 E
Bichia, *India* 43 H9 22 27N 80 42 E
Bickerton I., *Australia* 62 A2 13 45S 136 10 E
Bida, *Nigeria* 50 G7 9 3N 5 58 E
Bidar, *India* 40 L10 17 55N 77 35 E
Biddeford, *U.S.A.* 77 D10 43 30N 70 28W
Bideford, *U.K.* 11 F3 51 1N 4 13W
Bideford Bay, *U.K.* 11 F3 51 5N 4 20W
Bidhuna, *India* 43 F8 26 49N 79 31 E
Bidor, *Malaysia* 39 K3 4 6N 101 15 E
Bié, Planalto de, *Angola* 53 G3 12 0S 16 0 E
Bieber, *U.S.A.* 82 F3 41 7N 121 8W
Biel, *Switz.* 18 C7 47 8N 7 14 E
Bielefeld, *Germany* 16 B5 52 1N 8 33 E
Biella, *Italy* 18 D8 45 34N 8 3 E
Bielsk Podlaski, *Poland* 17 B12 52 47N 23 12 E
Bielsko-Biała, *Poland* 17 D10 49 50N 19 2 E
Bien Hoa, *Vietnam* 39 G6 10 57N 106 49 E
Bienne = Biel, *Switz.* 18 C7 47 8N 7 14 E
Bienville, L., *Canada* 70 A5 55 5N 72 40W
Biesiesfontein, *S. Africa* 56 E2 30 57S 17 58 E
Big →, *Canada* 71 B8 54 50N 58 55W
Big B., *Canada* 71 A7 55 43N 60 35W
Big Bear City, *U.S.A.* 85 L10 34 16N 116 51W
Big Bear Lake, *U.S.A.* 85 L10 34 15N 116 56W
Big Belt Mts., *U.S.A.* 82 C8 46 30N 111 25W
Big Bend, *Swaziland* 57 D5 26 50S 31 58 E
Big Bend Nat. Park, *U.S.A.* 81 L3 29 20N 103 5W
Big Black →, *U.S.A.* 81 K9 32 3N 91 4W
Big Blue →, *U.S.A.* 80 F6 39 35N 96 34W
Big Creek, *U.S.A.* 84 H7 37 11N 119 14W
Big Cypress Nat. Preserve, *U.S.A.* 77 M5 26 0N 81 10W
Big Cypress Swamp, *U.S.A.* 77 M5 26 15N 81 30W
Big Falls, *U.S.A.* 80 A8 48 12N 93 48W
Big Fork →, *U.S.A.* 80 A8 48 31N 93 43W
Big Horn Mts. = Bighorn Mts., *U.S.A.* 82 D10 44 30N 107 30W
Big I., *Canada* 72 A5 61 7N 116 45W
Big Lake, *U.S.A.* 81 K4 31 12N 101 28W
Big Moose, *U.S.A.* 79 C10 43 49N 74 58W
Big Muddy Cr. →, *U.S.A.* 80 A2 48 8N 104 36W
Big Pine, *U.S.A.* 84 H8 37 10N 118 17W
Big Piney, *U.S.A.* 82 E8 42 32N 110 7W
Big Rapids, *U.S.A.* 76 D3 43 42N 85 29W
Big Rideau L., *Canada* 79 B8 44 40N 76 15W
Big River, *Canada* 73 C7 53 50N 107 0W
Big Run, *U.S.A.* 78 F6 40 57N 78 55W
Big Sable Pt., *U.S.A.* 76 C2 44 3N 86 1W
Big Salmon →, *Canada* 72 A2 61 52N 134 55W
Big Sand L., *Canada* 73 B9 57 45N 99 45W
Big Sandy, *U.S.A.* 82 B8 48 11N 110 7W
Big Sandy →, *U.S.A.* 76 F4 38 25N 82 36W
Big Sandy Cr. →, *U.S.A.* 80 F3 38 7N 102 29W
Big Sioux →, *U.S.A.* 80 D6 42 29N 96 27W
Big Spring, *U.S.A.* 81 J4 32 15N 101 28W
Big Stone City, *U.S.A.* 80 C6 45 18N 96 28W
Big Stone Gap, *U.S.A.* 77 G4 36 52N 82 47W
Big Stone L., *U.S.A.* 80 C6 45 30N 96 35W
Big Sur, *U.S.A.* 84 J5 36 15N 121 48W
Big Timber, *U.S.A.* 82 D9 45 50N 109 57W
Big Trout L., *Canada* 70 B2 53 40N 90 0W
Big Trout Lake, *Canada* 70 B2 53 45N 90 0W
Biğa, *Turkey* 21 D12 40 13N 27 14 E
Bigadiç, *Turkey* 21 E13 39 22N 28 7 E
Biggar, *Canada* 73 C7 52 4N 108 0W
Biggar, *U.K.* 12 F5 55 38N 3 32W
Bigge I., *Australia* 60 B4 14 35S 125 10 E
Biggenden, *Australia* 63 D5 25 31S 152 4 E
Biggleswade, *U.K.* 11 E7 52 5N 0 14W
Biggs, *U.S.A.* 84 F5 39 25N 121 43W
Bighorn, *U.S.A.* 82 C10 46 10N 107 27W
Bighorn →, *U.S.A.* 82 C10 46 10N 107 28W
Bighorn L., *U.S.A.* 82 D9 44 55N 108 15W
Bighorn Mts., *U.S.A.* 82 D10 44 30N 107 30W
Bigstone L., *Canada* 73 C9 53 42N 95 44W
Bigwa, *Tanzania* 54 D4 7 10S 39 10 E
Bihać, *Bos.-H.* 16 F8 44 49N 15 57 E
Bihar, *India* 43 G11 25 5N 85 40 E
Bihar □, *India* 43 G12 25 0N 86 0 E
Biharamulo, *Tanzania* 54 C3 2 25S 31 25 E
Bihariganj, *India* 43 G12 25 44N 86 59 E
Bihor, Munţii, *Romania* 17 E12 46 29N 22 47 E
Bijagós, Arquipélago dos, *Guinea-Biss.* 50 F2 11 15N 16 10W
Bijaipur, *India* 42 F7 26 2N 77 20 E
Bijapur, *Chhattisgarh, India* 41 K12 18 50N 80 50 E
Bijapur, *Karnataka, India* 40 L9 16 50N 75 55 E
Bījār, *Iran* 44 C5 35 52N 47 35 E
Bijawar, *India* 43 G8 24 38N 79 30 E
Bijeljina, *Bos.-H.* 21 B8 44 46N 19 14 E
Bijnor, *India* 42 E8 29 27N 78 11 E
Bikaner, *India* 42 E5 28 2N 73 18 E
Bikapur, *India* 43 F10 26 30N 82 7 E
Bikeqi, *China* 34 D6 40 43N 111 20 E
Bikfayyā, *Lebanon* 47 B4 33 55N 35 41 E
Bikin, *Russia* 27 E14 46 50N 134 20 E
Bikin →, *Russia* 30 A7 46 51N 134 2 E
Bikini Atoll, *Marshall Is.* 64 F8 12 0N 167 30 E
Bikita, *Zimbabwe* 57 C5 20 6S 31 41 E
Bila Tserkva, *Ukraine* 17 D16 49 45N 30 10 E
Bilara, *India* 42 F5 26 14N 73 53 E
Bilaspur, *Chhattisgarh, India* 43 H10 22 2N 82 15 E
Bilaspur, *Punjab, India* 42 D7 31 19N 76 50 E
Bilauk Taungdan, *Thailand* 38 F2 13 0N 99 0 E
Bilbao, *Spain* 19 A4 43 16N 2 56W
Bilbo = Bilbao, *Spain* 19 A4 43 16N 2 56W
Bíldudalur, *Iceland* 8 D2 65 41N 23 36W
Bílé Karpaty, *Europe* 17 D9 49 5N 18 0 E
Bilecik, *Turkey* 25 F5 40 5N 30 5 E
Bilgram, *India* 43 F9 27 11N 80 2 E
Bilhaur, *India* 43 F9 26 51N 80 5 E
Bilhorod-Dnistrovskyy, *Ukraine* 25 E5 46 11N 30 23 E
Bilibino, *Russia* 27 C17 68 3N 166 20 E
Bilibiza, *Mozam.* 55 E5 12 30S 40 20 E
Billabalong Roadhouse, *Australia* 61 E2 27 25S 115 49 E
Billiluna, *Australia* 60 C4 19 37S 127 41 E
Billings, *U.S.A.* 82 D9 45 47N 108 30W
Billiton Is. = Belitung, *Indonesia* 36 E3 3 10S 107 50 E
Bilma, *Niger* 51 E8 18 50N 13 30 E
Biloela, *Australia* 62 C5 24 24S 150 31 E
Biloxi, *U.S.A.* 81 K10 30 24N 88 53W
Bilpa Morea Claypan, *Australia* 62 D3 25 0S 140 0 E
Biltine, *Chad* 51 F10 14 40N 20 50 E
Bima, *Indonesia* 37 F5 8 22S 118 49 E
Bimini Is., *Bahamas* 88 A4 25 42N 79 25W
Bin Xian, *Heilongjiang, China* 35 B14 45 42N 127 32 E
Bin Xian, *Shaanxi, China* 34 G5 35 2N 108 4 E
Bina-Etawah, *India* 42 G8 24 13N 78 14 E
Bīnāb, *Iran* 45 B6 36 35N 48 41 E
Binalbagan, *Phil.* 37 B6 10 12N 122 50 E
Binalong, *Australia* 63 E4 34 40S 148 39 E
Bīnālūd, Kūh-e, *Iran* 45 B8 36 30N 58 30 E
Binatang = Bintangor, *Malaysia* 36 D4 2 10N 111 40 E
Binche, *Belgium* 15 D4 50 26N 4 10 E
Bindki, *India* 43 F9 26 2N 80 36 E
Bindura, *Zimbabwe* 55 F3 17 18S 31 18 E
Bingara, *Australia* 63 D5 29 52S 150 36 E
Bingham, *U.S.A.* 77 C11 45 3N 69 53W
Binghamton, *U.S.A.* 79 D9 42 6N 75 55W
Bingöl, *Turkey* 44 B4 38 53N 40 29 E
Binh Dinh = An Nhon, *Vietnam* 38 F7 13 55N 109 7 E
Binh Khe, *Vietnam* 38 F7 13 57N 108 51 E
Binh Son, *Vietnam* 38 E7 15 20N 108 40 E
Binhai, *China* 35 G10 34 2N 119 49 E
Binisatua, *Spain* 22 B11 39 50N 4 11 E
Binjai, *Indonesia* 36 D3 3 20N 98 30 E
Binnaway, *Australia* 63 E4 31 28S 149 24 E
Binongko, *Indonesia* 37 F6 5 57S 124 2 E
Binscarth, *Canada* 73 C8 50 37N 101 17W
Bintan, *Indonesia* 36 D2 1 0N 104 0 E
Bintangor, *Malaysia* 36 D4 2 10N 111 40 E
Bintulu, *Malaysia* 36 D4 3 10N 113 0 E
Bintuni, *Indonesia* 37 E8 2 7S 133 32 E
Binzert = Bizerte, *Tunisia* 51 A7 37 15N 9 50 E
Binzhou, *China* 35 F10 37 20N 118 2 E
Bío Bío □, *Chile* 94 D1 37 35S 72 0W
Bioko, *Eq. Guin.* 52 D1 3 30N 8 40 E
Bir, *India* 40 K9 19 4N 75 46 E
Bîr Abu Muḥammad, *Egypt* 47 F3 29 44N 34 14 E
Bi'r ad Dabbāghāt, *Jordan* 47 E4 30 26N 35 32 E
Bi'r al Butayyihāt, *Jordan* 47 F4 29 47N 35 20 E
Bi'r al Mārī, *Jordan* 47 E4 30 4N 35 33 E
Bi'r al Qattār, *Jordan* 47 F4 29 47N 35 32 E
Bir Atrun, *Sudan* 51 E11 18 15N 26 40 E
Bîr Beiḍa, *Egypt* 47 E3 30 25N 34 29 E
Bîr el 'Abd, *Egypt* 47 D2 31 2N 33 0 E
Bîr el Biarât, *Egypt* 47 F3 29 30N 34 43 E
Bîr el Duweidar, *Egypt* 47 E1 30 56N 32 32 E
Bîr el Garârât, *Egypt* 47 D2 31 3N 33 34 E
Bîr el Heisi, *Egypt* 47 F3 29 22N 34 36 E
Bîr el Jafir, *Egypt* 47 E1 30 50N 32 41 E
Bîr el Mâlḥi, *Egypt* 47 E2 30 38N 33 19 E
Bîr el Thamâda, *Egypt* 47 E2 30 12N 33 27 E
Bîr Gebeil Ḥiṣn, *Egypt* 47 E2 30 2N 33 18 E
Bi'r Ghadīr, *Syria* 47 A6 34 6N 37 3 E
Bîr Ḥasana, *Egypt* 47 E2 30 29N 33 46 E
Bîr Kaseiba, *Egypt* 47 E2 31 0N 33 17 E
Bîr Lahfân, *Egypt* 47 E2 31 0N 33 51 E
Bîr Madkûr, *Egypt* 47 E1 30 44N 32 33 E
Bîr Mogreïn, *Mauritania* 50 C3 25 10N 11 25W
Bi'r Muṭribah, *Kuwait* 44 D5 29 54N 47 17 E
Bîr Qaṭia, *Egypt* 47 E1 30 58N 32 45 E
Bîr Shalatein, *Egypt* 51 D13 23 5N 35 25 E
Biratnagar, *Nepal* 43 F12 26 27N 87 17 E
Birawa, *Dem. Rep. of the Congo* 54 C2 2 20S 28 48 E
Birch →, *Canada* 72 B6 58 28N 112 17W
Birch Hills, *Canada* 73 C7 52 59N 105 25W
Birch I., *Canada* 73 C9 52 26N 99 54W
Birch L., *N.W.T., Canada* 72 A5 62 4N 116 33W
Birch L., *Ont., Canada* 70 B1 51 23N 92 18W
Birch Mts., *Canada* 72 B6 57 30N 113 10W
Birch River, *Canada* 73 C8 52 24N 101 6W
Birchip, *Australia* 63 F3 35 56S 142 55 E
Bird, *Canada* 73 B10 56 30N 94 13W
Bird I. = Las Aves, Is., *W. Indies* 89 C7 15 45N 63 55W
Birdsville, *Australia* 62 D2 25 51S 139 20 E
Birdum Cr. →, *Australia* 60 C5 15 14S 133 0 E
Birecik, *Turkey* 44 B3 37 2N 38 0 E
Bireuen, *Indonesia* 36 C1 5 14N 96 39 E
Birigui, *Brazil* 95 A5 21 18S 50 16W
Birjand, *Iran* 45 C8 32 53N 59 13 E
Birkenhead, *U.K.* 10 D4 53 23N 3 2W
Bîrlad = Bârlad, *Romania* 17 E14 46 15N 27 38 E
Birmingham, *U.K.* 11 E6 52 29N 1 52W
Birmingham, *U.S.A.* 77 J2 33 31N 86 48W
Birmitrapur, *India* 41 H14 22 24N 84 46 E
Birni Nkonni, *Niger* 50 F7 13 55N 5 15 E
Birnin Kebbi, *Nigeria* 50 F6 12 32N 4 12 E
Birobidzhan, *Russia* 27 E14 48 50N 132 50 E
Birr, *Ireland* 13 C4 53 6N 7 54W
Birrie →, *Australia* 63 D4 29 43S 146 37 E
Birsilpur, *India* 42 E5 28 11N 72 15 E
Birsk, *Russia* 24 C10 55 25N 55 30 E
Birtle, *Canada* 73 C8 50 30N 101 5W
Birur, *India* 40 N9 13 30N 75 55 E
Biržai, *Lithuania* 9 H21 56 11N 24 45 E
Birzebbugga, *Malta* 23 D2 35 50N 14 32 E
Bisa, *Indonesia* 37 E7 1 15S 127 28 E
Bisalpur, *India* 43 E8 28 14N 79 48 E
Bisbee, *U.S.A.* 83 L9 31 27N 109 55W
Biscay, B. of, *Atl. Oc.* 18 D1 45 0N 2 0W
Biscayne B., *U.S.A.* 77 N5 25 40N 80 12W
Biscoe Bay, *Antarctica* 5 D13 77 0S 152 0W
Biscoe Is., *Antarctica* 5 C17 66 0S 67 0W
Biscostasing, *Canada* 70 C3 47 18N 82 9W
Bishkek, *Kyrgyzstan* 26 E8 42 54N 74 46 E
Bishnupur, *India* 43 H12 23 8N 87 20 E
Bisho, *S. Africa* 57 E4 32 50S 27 23 E
Bishop, *Calif., U.S.A.* 84 H8 37 22N 118 24W
Bishop, *Tex., U.S.A.* 81 M6 27 35N 97 48W
Bishop Auckland, *U.K.* 10 C6 54 39N 1 40W
Bishop's Falls, *Canada* 71 C8 49 2N 55 30W
Bishop's Stortford, *U.K.* 11 F8 51 52N 0 10 E
Bisina, L., *Uganda* 54 B3 1 38N 33 56 E
Biskra, *Algeria* 50 B7 34 50N 5 44 E
Bismarck, *U.S.A.* 80 B4 46 48N 100 47W
Bismarck Arch., *Papua N. G.* 64 H7 2 30S 150 0 E
Biso, *Uganda* 54 B3 1 44N 31 26 E
Bison, *U.S.A.* 80 C3 45 31N 102 28W
Bīsotūn, *Iran* 44 C5 34 23N 47 26 E
Bissagos = Bijagós, Arquipélago dos, *Guinea-Biss.* 50 F2 11 15N 16 10W
Bissau, *Guinea-Biss.* 50 F2 11 45N 15 45W
Bistcho L., *Canada* 72 B5 59 45N 118 50W
Bistriţa, *Romania* 17 E13 47 9N 24 35 E
Bistriţa →, *Romania* 17 E14 46 30N 26 57 E
Biswan, *India* 43 F9 27 29N 81 2 E
Bitlis, *Turkey* 44 B4 38 20N 42 3 E
Bitola, *Macedonia* 21 D9 41 1N 21 20 E
Bitolj = Bitola, *Macedonia* 21 D9 41 1N 21 20 E
Bitter Creek, *U.S.A.* 82 F9 41 33N 108 33W
Bitterfontein, *S. Africa* 56 E2 31 1S 18 32 E
Bitterroot →, *U.S.A.* 82 C6 46 52N 114 7W
Bitterroot Range, *U.S.A.* 82 D6 46 0N 114 20W
Bitterwater, *U.S.A.* 84 J6 36 23N 121 0W
Biu, *Nigeria* 51 F8 10 40N 12 3 E
Biwa-Ko, *Japan* 31 G8 35 15N 136 10 E
Biwabik, *U.S.A.* 80 B8 47 32N 92 21W
Bixby, *U.S.A.* 81 H7 35 57N 95 53W
Biyang, *China* 34 H7 32 38N 113 21 E
Biysk, *Russia* 26 D9 52 40N 85 0 E
Bizana, *S. Africa* 57 E4 30 50S 29 52 E
Bizen, *Japan* 31 G7 34 43N 134 8 E
Bizerte, *Tunisia* 51 A7 37 15N 9 50 E
Bjargtangar, *Iceland* 8 D1 65 30N 24 30W
Bjelovar, *Croatia* 20 B7 45 56N 16 49 E
Bjørnevatn, *Norway* 8 B23 69 40N 30 0 E
Bjørnøya, *Arctic* 4 B8 74 30N 19 0 E
Black = Da →, *Vietnam* 38 B5 21 15N 105 20 E
Black →, *Canada* 78 B5 44 42N 79 19W
Black →, *Ariz., U.S.A.* 83 K8 33 44N 110 13W
Black →, *Ark., U.S.A.* 81 H9 35 38N 91 20W
Black →, *Mich., U.S.A.* 78 D2 42 59N 82 27W
Black →, *N.Y., U.S.A.* 79 C8 43 59N 76 4W
Black →, *Wis., U.S.A.* 80 D9 43 57N 91 22W
Black Bay Pen., *Canada* 70 C2 48 38N 88 21W
Black Birch L., *Canada* 73 B7 56 53N 107 45W
Black Diamond, *Canada* 72 C6 50 45N 114 14W
Black Duck →, *Canada* 70 A2 56 51N 89 2W
Black Forest = Schwarzwald, *Germany* 16 D5 48 30N 8 20 E
Black Forest, *U.S.A.* 80 F2 39 0N 104 43W
Black Hd., *Ireland* 13 C2 53 9N 9 16W
Black Hills, *U.S.A.* 80 D3 44 0N 103 45W
Black I., *Canada* 73 C9 51 12N 96 30W
Black L., *Canada* 73 B7 59 12N 105 15W
Black L., *Mich., U.S.A.* 76 C3 45 28N 84 16W
Black L., *N.Y., U.S.A.* 79 B9 44 31N 75 36W
Black Lake, *Canada* 73 B7 59 11N 105 20W
Black Mesa, *U.S.A.* 81 G3 36 58N 102 58W
Black Mt. = Mynydd Du, *U.K.* 11 F4 51 52N 3 50W
Black Mts., *U.K.* 11 F4 51 55N 3 7W
Black Range, *U.S.A.* 83 K10 33 15N 107 50W
Black River, *Jamaica* 88 C4 18 0N 77 50W
Black River Falls, *U.S.A.* 80 C9 44 18N 90 51W
Black Sea, *Eurasia* 25 F6 43 30N 35 0 E
Black Tickle, *Canada* 71 B8 53 28N 55 45W
Black Volta →, *Africa* 50 G5 8 41N 1 33W
Black Warrior →, *U.S.A.* 77 J2 32 32N 87 51W
Blackall, *Australia* 62 C4 24 25S 145 45 E
Blackball, *N.Z.* 59 K3 42 22S 171 26 E
Blackbull, *Australia* 62 B3 17 55S 141 45 E
Blackburn, *U.K.* 10 D5 53 45N 2 29W
Blackburn with Darwen □, *U.K.* 10 D5 53 45N 2 29W
Blackfoot, *U.S.A.* 82 E7 43 11N 112 21W
Blackfoot →, *U.S.A.* 82 C7 46 52N 113 53W
Blackfoot River Reservoir, *U.S.A.* 82 E8 43 0N 111 43W
Blackpool, *U.K.* 10 D4 53 49N 3 3W
Blackpool □, *U.K.* 10 D4 53 49N 3 3W
Blackriver, *U.S.A.* 78 B1 44 46N 83 17W
Blacks Harbour, *Canada* 71 C6 45 3N 66 49W
Blacksburg, *U.S.A.* 76 G5 37 14N 80 25W
Blacksod B., *Ireland* 13 B1 54 6N 10 0W
Blackstone, *U.S.A.* 76 G7 37 4N 78 0W
Blackstone Ra., *Australia* 61 E4 26 0S 128 30 E
Blackwater, *Australia* 62 C4 23 35S 148 53 E
Blackwater →, *Meath, Ireland* 13 C4 53 39N 6 41W
Blackwater →, *Waterford, Ireland* 13 D4 52 4N 7 52W
Blackwater →, *U.K.* 13 B5 54 31N 6 35W
Blackwell, *U.S.A.* 81 G6 36 48N 97 17W
Blackwells Corner, *U.S.A.* 85 K7 35 37N 119 47W
Blaenau Ffestiniog, *U.K.* 10 E4 53 0N 3 56W
Blaenau Gwent □, *U.K.* 11 F4 51 48N 3 12W
Blagodarnoye = Blagodarnyy, *Russia* 25 E7 45 7N 43 37 E
Blagodarnyy, *Russia* 25 E7 45 7N 43 37 E
Blagoevgrad, *Bulgaria* 21 C10 42 2N 23 5 E
Blagoveshchensk, *Russia* 27 D13 50 20N 127 30 E
Blain, *U.S.A.* 78 F7 40 20N 77 31W
Blaine, *Minn., U.S.A.* 80 C8 45 10N 93 13W
Blaine, *Wash., U.S.A.* 84 B4 48 59N 122 45W
Blaine Lake, *Canada* 73 C7 52 51N 106 52W
Blair, *U.S.A.* 80 E6 41 33N 96 8W
Blair Athol, *Australia* 62 C4 22 42S 147 31 E
Blair Atholl, *U.K.* 12 E5 56 46N 3 50W
Blairgowrie, *U.K.* 12 E5 56 35N 3 21W
Blairsden, *U.S.A.* 84 F6 39 47N 120 37W
Blairsville, *U.S.A.* 78 F5 40 26N 79 16W
Blake Pt., *U.S.A.* 80 A10 48 11N 88 25W
Blakely, *Ga., U.S.A.* 77 K3 31 23N 84 56W
Blakely, *Pa., U.S.A.* 79 E9 41 28N 75 37W
Blanc, C., *Spain* 22 B9 39 21N 2 51 E
Blanc, Mont, *Alps* 18 D7 45 48N 6 50 E
Blanc-Sablon, *Canada* 71 B8 51 24N 57 12W
Blanca, B., *Argentina* 96 D4 39 10S 61 30W
Blanca Peak, *U.S.A.* 83 H11 37 35N 105 29W
Blanche, C., *Australia* 63 E1 33 1S 134 9 E
Blanche, L., *S. Austral., Australia* 63 D2 29 15S 139 40 E
Blanche, L., *W. Austral., Australia* 60 D3 22 25S 123 17 E
Blanco, *S. Africa* 56 E3 33 55S 22 23 E
Blanco, *U.S.A.* 81 K5 30 6N 98 25W
Blanco →, *Argentina* 94 C2 30 20S 68 42W
Blanco, C., *Costa Rica* 88 E2 9 34N 85 8W
Blanco, C., *U.S.A.* 82 E1 42 51N 124 34W
Blanda →, *Iceland* 8 D3 65 37N 20 9W
Blandford Forum, *U.K.* 11 G5 50 51N 2 9W
Blanding, *U.S.A.* 83 H9 37 37N 109 29W
Blanes, *Spain* 19 B7 41 40N 2 48 E
Blankenberge, *Belgium* 15 C3 51 20N 3 9 E
Blanquilla, I., *Venezuela* 89 D7 11 51N 64 37W
Blanquillo, *Uruguay* 95 C4 32 53S 55 37W
Blantyre, *Malawi* 55 F4 15 45S 35 0 E
Blarney, *Ireland* 13 E3 51 56N 8 33W
Blasdell, *U.S.A.* 78 D6 42 48N 78 50W
Blåvands Huk, *Denmark* 9 J13 55 33N 8 4 E
Blaydon, *U.K.* 10 C6 54 58N 1 42W
Blayney, *Australia* 63 E4 33 32S 149 14 E
Blaze, Pt., *Australia* 60 B5 12 56S 130 11 E
Blekinge, *Sweden* 9 H16 56 25N 15 20 E
Blenheim, *Canada* 78 D3 42 20N 82 0W
Blenheim, *N.Z.* 59 J4 41 38S 173 57 E
Bletchley, *U.K.* 11 F7 51 59N 0 44W
Blida, *Algeria* 50 A6 36 30N 2 49 E
Bligh Sound, *N.Z.* 59 L1 44 47S 167 32 E
Blind River, *Canada* 70 C3 46 10N 82 58W
Bliss, *Idaho, U.S.A.* 82 E6 42 56N 114 57W
Bliss, *N.Y., U.S.A.* 78 D6 42 34N 78 15W
Blissfield, *U.S.A.* 78 F3 40 24N 81 58W
Blitar, *Indonesia* 37 H15 8 5S 112 11 E
Block I., *U.S.A.* 79 E13 41 11N 71 35W
Block Island Sd., *U.S.A.* 79 E13 41 15N 71 40W
Bloemfontein, *S. Africa* 56 D4 29 6S 26 7 E
Bloemhof, *S. Africa* 56 D4 27 38S 25 32 E
Blois, *France* 18 C4 47 35N 1 20 E
Blönduós, *Iceland* 8 D3 65 40N 20 12W
Bloodvein →, *Canada* 73 C9 51 47N 96 43W
Bloody Foreland, *Ireland* 13 A3 55 10N 8 17W
Bloomer, *U.S.A.* 80 C9 45 6N 91 29W
Bloomfield, *Canada* 78 C7 43 59N 77 14W
Bloomfield, *Iowa, U.S.A.* 80 E8 40 45N 92 25W
Bloomfield, *N. Mex., U.S.A.* 83 H10 36 43N 107 59W
Bloomfield, *Nebr., U.S.A.* 80 D6 42 36N 97 39W
Bloomington, *Ill., U.S.A.* 80 E10 40 28N 89 0W
Bloomington, *Ind., U.S.A.* 76 F2 39 10N 86 32W
Bloomington, *Minn., U.S.A.* 80 C8 44 50N 93 17W
Bloomsburg, *U.S.A.* 79 F8 41 0N 76 27W
Blora, *Indonesia* 37 G14 6 57S 111 25 E
Blossburg, *U.S.A.* 78 E7 41 41N 77 4W
Blouberg, *S. Africa* 57 C4 23 8S 28 59 E
Blountstown, *U.S.A.* 77 K3 30 27N 85 3W
Blue Earth, *U.S.A.* 80 D8 43 38N 94 6W
Blue Mesa Reservoir, *U.S.A.* 83 G10 38 28N 107 20W
Blue Mountain Lake, *U.S.A.* 79 C10 43 52N 74 30W
Blue Mts., *Maine, U.S.A.* 79 B14 44 50N 70 35W
Blue Mts., *Oreg., U.S.A.* 82 D4 45 15N 119 0W
Blue Mts., *Pa., U.S.A.* 79 F8 40 30N 76 30W
Blue Mud B., *Australia* 62 A2 13 30S 136 0 E
Blue Nile = Nîl el Azraq →, *Sudan* 51 E12 15 38N 32 31 E
Blue Rapids, *U.S.A.* 80 F6 39 41N 96 39W
Blue Ridge Mts., *U.S.A.* 77 G5 36 30N 80 15W
Blue River, *Canada* 72 C5 52 6N 119 18W
Bluefield, *U.S.A.* 76 G5 37 15N 81 17W
Bluefields, *Nic.* 88 D3 12 20N 83 50W
Bluff, *Australia* 62 C4 23 35S 149 4 E
Bluff, *N.Z.* 59 M2 46 37S 168 20 E
Bluff, *U.S.A.* 83 H9 37 17N 109 33W
Bluff Knoll, *Australia* 61 F2 34 24S 118 15 E
Bluff Pt., *Australia* 61 E1 27 50S 114 5 E
Bluffton, *U.S.A.* 76 E3 40 44N 85 11W
Blumenau, *Brazil* 95 B6 27 0S 49 0W
Blunt, *U.S.A.* 80 C5 44 31N 99 59W
Bly, *U.S.A.* 82 E3 42 24N 121 3W
Blyth, *Canada* 78 C3 43 44N 81 26W
Blyth, *U.K.* 10 B6 55 8N 1 31W
Blythe, *U.S.A.* 85 M12 33 37N 114 36W
Blytheville, *U.S.A.* 81 H10 35 56N 89 55W
Bo, *S. Leone* 50 G3 7 55N 11 50W
Bo Duc, *Vietnam* 39 G6 11 58N 106 50 E
Bo Hai, *China* 35 E10 39 0N 119 0 E
Bo Xian = Bozhou, *China* 34 H8 33 55N 115 41 E
Boa Vista, *Brazil* 92 C6 2 48N 60 30W
Boaco, *Nic.* 88 D2 12 29N 85 35W
Bo'ai, *China* 34 G7 35 10N 113 3 E
Boalsburg, *U.S.A.* 78 F7 40 46N 77 47W
Boane, *Mozam.* 57 D5 26 6S 32 19 E
Boardman, *U.S.A.* 78 E4 41 2N 80 40W
Bobadah, *Australia* 63 E4 32 19S 146 41 E
Bobbili, *India* 41 K13 18 35N 83 30 E
Bobcaygeon, *Canada* 78 B6 44 33N 78 33W
Bobo-Dioulasso, *Burkina Faso* 50 F5 11 8N 4 13W
Bóbr →, *Poland* 16 B8 52 4N 15 4 E
Bobraomby, Tanjon' i, *Madag.* 57 A8 12 40S 49 10 E
Bobruysk = Babruysk, *Belarus* 17 B15 53 10N 29 15 E
Boby, Pic, *Madag.* 53 J9 22 12S 46 55 E
Bôca do Acre, *Brazil* 92 E5 8 50S 67 27W
Boca Raton, *U.S.A.* 77 M5 26 21N 80 5W
Bocas del Toro, *Panama* 88 E3 9 15N 82 20W
Bochnia, *Poland* 17 D11 49 58N 20 27 E
Bochum, *Germany* 16 C4 51 28N 7 13 E
Bocoyna, *Mexico* 86 B3 27 52N 107 35W
Bodaybo, *Russia* 27 D12 57 50N 114 0 E
Boddam, *U.K.* 12 B7 59 56N 1 17W
Boddington, *Australia* 61 F2 32 50S 116 30 E
Bodega Bay, *U.S.A.* 84 G3 38 20N 123 3W
Boden, *Sweden* 8 D19 65 50N 21 42 E
Bodensee, *Europe* 18 C8 47 35N 9 25 E
Bodhan, *India* 40 K10 18 40N 77 44 E
Bodmin, *U.K.* 11 G3 50 28N 4 43W
Bodmin Moor, *U.K.* 11 G3 50 33N 4 36W
Bodø, *Norway* 8 C16 67 17N 14 24 E
Bodrog →, *Hungary* 17 D11 48 11N 21 22 E
Bodrum, *Turkey* 21 F12 37 3N 27 30 E
Boende, *Dem. Rep. of the Congo* 52 E4 0 24S 21 12 E
Boerne, *U.S.A.* 81 L5 29 47N 98 44W
Boesmans →, *S. Africa* 56 E4 33 42S 26 39 E
Bogalusa, *U.S.A.* 81 K10 30 47N 89 52W
Bogan →, *Australia* 63 D4 29 59S 146 17 E
Bogan Gate, *Australia* 63 E4 33 7S 147 49 E
Bogantungan, *Australia* 62 C4 23 41S 147 17 E
Bogata, *U.S.A.* 81 J7 33 28N 95 13W
Boggabilla, *Australia* 63 D5 28 36S 150 24 E

Brewster

Boggabri, *Australia* **63 E5** 30 45S 150 5 E
Boggeragh Mts., *Ireland* **13 D3** 52 2N 8 55W
Boglan = Solhan, *Turkey* **44 B4** 38 57N 41 3 E
Bognor Regis, *U.K.* **11 G7** 50 47N 0 40W
Bogo, *Phil.* **37 B6** 11 3N 124 0 E
Bogong, Mt., *Australia* **63 F4** 36 47S 147 17 E
Bogor, *Indonesia* **36 F3** 6 36S 106 48 E
Bogotá, *Colombia* **92 C4** 4 34N 74 0W
Bogotol, *Russia* **26 D9** 56 15N 89 50 E
Bogra, *Bangla.* **41 G16** 24 51N 89 22 E
Boguchany, *Russia* **27 D10** 58 40N 97 30 E
Bohemian Forest = Böhmerwald, *Germany* **16 D7** 49 8N 13 14 E
Böhmerwald, *Germany* **16 D7** 49 8N 13 14 E
Bohol □, *Phil.* **37 C6** 9 50N 124 10 E
Bohol Sea, *Phil.* **37 C6** 9 0N 124 0 E
Bohuslän, *Sweden* **9 G14** 58 25N 12 0 E
Boi, Pta. de, *Brazil* **95 A6** 23 55S 45 15W
Boiaçu, *Brazil* **92 D6** 0 27S 61 46W
Boileau, C., *Australia* **60 C3** 17 40S 122 7 E
Boise, *U.S.A.* **82 E5** 43 37N 116 13W
Boise City, *U.S.A.* **81 G3** 36 44N 102 31W
Boissevain, *Canada* **73 D8** 49 15N 100 5W
Bojador, C., *W. Sahara* **50 C3** 26 0N 14 30W
Bojana →, *Albania* **21 D8** 41 52N 19 22 E
Bojnūrd, *Iran* **45 B8** 37 30N 57 20 E
Bojonegoro, *Indonesia* **37 G14** 7 11S 111 54 E
Bokaro, *India* **43 H11** 23 46N 85 55 E
Bokhara →, *Australia* **63 D4** 29 55S 146 42 E
Boknafjorden, *Norway* **9 G11** 59 14N 5 40 E
Bokoro, *Chad* **51 F9** 12 25N 17 14 E
Bokpyin, *Burma* **39 G2** 11 18N 98 42 E
Bolan →, *Pakistan* **42 E2** 28 38N 67 42 E
Bolan Pass, *Pakistan* **40 E5** 29 50N 67 20 E
Bolaños →, *Mexico* **86 C4** 21 14N 104 8W
Bolbec, *France* **18 B4** 49 30N 0 30 E
Boldājī, *Iran* **45 D6** 31 56N 51 3 E
Bole, *China* **32 B3** 45 11N 81 37 E
Bolekhiv, *Ukraine* **17 D12** 49 0N 23 57 E
Bolesławiec, *Poland* **16 C8** 51 17N 15 37 E
Bolgrad = Bolhrad, *Ukraine* **17 F15** 45 40N 28 32 E
Bolhrad, *Ukraine* **17 F15** 45 40N 28 32 E
Bolívar, *Argentina* **94 D3** 36 15S 60 53W
Bolivar, *Mo., U.S.A.* **81 G8** 37 37N 93 25W
Bolivar, *N.Y., U.S.A.* **78 D6** 42 4N 78 10W
Bolivar, *Tenn., U.S.A.* **81 H10** 35 12N 89 0W
Bolivia ■, *S. Amer.* **92 G6** 17 6S 64 0W
Bolivian Plateau, *S. Amer.* **90 E4** 20 0S 67 30W
Bollnäs, *Sweden* **9 F17** 61 21N 16 24 E
Bollon, *Australia* **63 D4** 28 2S 147 29 E
Bolmen, *Sweden* **9 H15** 56 55N 13 40 E
Bolobo, *Dem. Rep. of the Congo* **52 E3** 2 6S 16 20 E
Bologna, *Italy* **20 B4** 44 29N 11 20 E
Bologoye, *Russia* **24 C5** 57 55N 34 5 E
Bolonchenticul, *Mexico* **87 D7** 20 0N 89 49W
Boloven, Cao Nguyen, *Laos* **38 E6** 15 10N 106 30 E
Bolpur, *India* **43 H12** 23 40N 87 45 E
Bolsena, L. di, *Italy* **20 C4** 42 36N 11 56 E
Bolshevik, Ostrov, *Russia* **27 B11** 78 30N 102 0 E
Bolshoi Kavkas = Caucasus Mountains, *Eurasia* **25 F7** 42 50N 44 0 E
Bolshoy Anyuy →, *Russia* **27 C17** 68 30N 160 49 E
Bolshoy Begichev, Ostrov, *Russia* **27 B12** 74 20N 112 30 E
Bolshoy Lyakhovskiy, Ostrov, *Russia* **27 B15** 73 35N 142 0 E
Bolshoy Tyuters, Ostrov, *Russia* **9 G22** 59 51N 27 13 E
Bolsward, *Neths.* **15 A5** 53 3N 5 32 E
Bolt Head, *U.K.* **11 G4** 50 12N 3 48W
Bolton, *Canada* **78 C5** 43 54N 79 45W
Bolton, *U.K.* **10 D5** 53 35N 2 26W
Bolton Landing, *U.S.A.* **79 C11** 43 32N 73 35W
Bolu, *Turkey* **25 F5** 40 45N 31 35 E
Bolungavík, *Iceland* **8 C2** 66 9N 23 15W
Bolvadin, *Turkey* **25 G5** 38 45N 31 4 E
Bolzano, *Italy* **20 A4** 46 31N 11 22 E
Bom Jesus da Lapa, *Brazil* **93 F10** 13 15S 43 25W
Boma, *Dem. Rep. of the Congo* **52 F2** 5 50S 13 4 E
Bombala, *Australia* **63 F4** 36 56S 149 15 E
Bombay = Mumbai, *India* **40 K8** 18 55N 72 50 E
Bomboma, *Dem. Rep. of the Congo* **52 D3** 2 25N 18 55 E
Bombombwa, *Dem. Rep. of the Congo* **54 B2** 1 40N 25 40 E
Bomili, *Dem. Rep. of the Congo* **54 B2** 1 45N 27 5 E
Bømlo, *Norway* **9 G11** 59 37N 5 13 E
Bomokandi →, *Dem. Rep. of the Congo* **54 B2** 3 39N 26 8 E
Bomu →, *C.A.R.* **52 D4** 4 40N 22 30 E
Bon, C., *Tunisia* **48 C5** 37 1N 11 2 E
Bon Sar Pa, *Vietnam* **38 F6** 12 24N 107 35 E
Bonaigarh, *India* **43 J11** 21 50N 84 57 E
Bonaire, *Neth. Ant.* **89 D6** 12 10N 68 15W
Bonang, *Australia* **63 F4** 37 11S 148 41 E
Bonanza, *Nic.* **88 D3** 13 54N 84 35W
Bonaparte Arch., *Australia* **60 B3** 14 0S 124 30 E
Bonaventure, *Canada* **71 C6** 48 5N 65 32W
Bonavista, *Canada* **71 C9** 48 40N 53 5W
Bonavista, C., *Canada* **71 C9** 48 42N 53 5W
Bonavista B., *Canada* **71 C9** 48 45N 53 25W
Bondo, *Dem. Rep. of the Congo* **54 B1** 3 55N 23 53 E
Bondoukou, *Ivory C.* **50 G5** 8 2N 2 47W
Bondowoso, *Indonesia* **37 G15** 7 55S 113 49 E
Bone, Teluk, *Indonesia* **37 E6** 4 10S 120 50 E
Bonerate, *Indonesia* **37 F6** 7 25S 121 5 E
Bonerate, Kepulauan, *Indonesia* **37 F6** 6 30S 121 10 E
Bo'ness, *U.K.* **12 E5** 56 1N 3 37W
Bonete, Cerro, *Argentina* **94 B2** 27 55S 68 40W
Bong Son = Hoai Nhon, *Vietnam* **38 E7** 14 28N 109 1 E
Bongor, *Chad* **51 F9** 10 35N 15 20 E
Bonham, *U.S.A.* **81 J6** 33 35N 96 11W
Bonifacio, *France* **18 F8** 41 24N 9 10 E
Bonifacio, Bouches de, *Medit. S.* **20 D3** 41 12N 9 15 E
Bonin Is. = Ogasawara Gunto, *Pac. Oc.* **28 G18** 27 0N 142 0 E
Bonn, *Germany* **16 C4** 50 46N 7 6 E
Bonne Terre, *U.S.A.* **81 G9** 37 55N 90 33W
Bonners Ferry, *U.S.A.* **82 B5** 48 42N 116 19W
Bonney, L., *Australia* **63 F3** 37 50S 140 20 E
Bonnie Rock, *Australia* **61 F2** 30 29S 118 22 E
Bonny, Bight of, *Africa* **52 D1** 3 30N 9 20 E
Bonnyrigg, *U.K.* **12 F5** 55 53N 3 6W
Bonnyville, *Canada* **73 C6** 54 20N 110 45W
Bonoi, *Indonesia* **37 E9** 1 45S 137 41 E
Bonsall, *U.S.A.* **85 M9** 33 16N 117 14W
Bontang, *Indonesia* **36 D5** 0 10N 117 30 E
Bonthe, *S. Leone* **50 G3** 7 30N 12 33W
Bontoc, *Phil.* **37 A6** 17 7N 120 58 E
Bonython Ra., *Australia* **60 D4** 23 40S 128 45 E
Bookabie, *Australia* **61 F5** 31 50S 132 41 E
Booker, *U.S.A.* **81 G4** 36 27N 100 32W
Boolaboolka L., *Australia* **63 E3** 32 38S 143 10 E
Booligal, *Australia* **63 E3** 33 58S 144 53 E
Boonah, *Australia* **63 D5** 27 58S 152 41 E
Boone, *Iowa, U.S.A.* **80 D8** 42 4N 93 53W
Boone, *N.C., U.S.A.* **77 G5** 36 13N 81 41W
Booneville, *Ark., U.S.A.* **81 H8** 35 8N 93 55W
Booneville, *Miss., U.S.A.* **77 H1** 34 39N 88 34W
Boonville, *Calif., U.S.A.* **84 F3** 39 1N 123 22W
Boonville, *Ind., U.S.A.* **76 F2** 38 3N 87 16W
Boonville, *Mo., U.S.A.* **80 F8** 38 58N 92 44W
Boonville, *N.Y., U.S.A.* **79 C9** 43 29N 75 20W
Boorindal, *Australia* **63 E4** 30 22S 146 11 E
Boorowa, *Australia* **63 E4** 34 28S 148 44 E
Boosaaso = Bosaso, *Somali Rep.* **46 E4** 11 12N 49 18 E
Boothia, Gulf of, *Canada* **69 A11** 71 0N 90 0W
Boothia Pen., *Canada* **68 A10** 71 0N 94 0W
Bootle, *U.K.* **10 D4** 53 28N 3 1W
Booué, *Gabon* **52 E2** 0 5S 11 55 E
Boquete, *Panama* **88 E3** 8 46N 82 27W
Boquilla, Presa de la, *Mexico* **86 B3** 27 40N 105 30W
Boquillas del Carmen, *Mexico* **86 B4** 29 17N 102 53W
Bor, *Serbia, Yug.* **21 B10** 44 5N 22 7 E
Bôr, *Sudan* **51 G12** 6 10N 31 40 E
Bor Mashash, *Israel* **47 D3** 31 7N 34 50 E
Borah Peak, *U.S.A.* **82 D7** 44 8N 113 47W
Borås, *Sweden* **9 H15** 57 43N 12 56 E
Borāzjān, *Iran* **45 D6** 29 22N 51 10 E
Borba, *Brazil* **92 D7** 4 12S 59 34W
Borborema, Planalto da, *Brazil* **90 D7** 7 0S 37 0W
Bord Khūn-e Now, *Iran* **45 D6** 28 3N 51 28 E
Borda, C., *Australia* **63 F2** 35 45S 136 34 E
Bordeaux, *France* **18 D3** 44 50N 0 36W
Borden, *Australia* **61 F2** 34 3S 118 12 E
Borden, *Canada* **71 C7** 46 18N 63 47W
Borden I., *Canada* **4 B2** 78 30N 111 30W
Borden Pen., *Canada* **69 A11** 73 0N 83 0W
Borders = Scottish Borders □, *U.K.* **12 F6** 55 35N 2 50W
Bordertown, *Australia* **63 F3** 36 19S 140 45 E
Borðeyri, *Iceland* **8 D3** 65 12N 21 6W
Bordj Fly Ste. Marie, *Algeria* **50 C5** 27 19N 2 32W
Bordj-in-Eker, *Algeria* **50 D7** 24 9N 5 3 E
Bordj Omar Driss, *Algeria* **50 C7** 28 10N 6 40 E
Borehamwood, *U.K.* **11 F7** 51 40N 0 15W
Borgå = Porvoo, *Finland* **9 F21** 60 24N 25 40 E
Borgarfjörður, *Iceland* **8 D7** 65 31N 13 49W
Borgarnes, *Iceland* **8 D3** 64 32N 21 55W
Børgefjellet, *Norway* **8 D15** 65 20N 13 45 E
Borger, *Neths.* **15 B6** 52 54N 6 44 E
Borger, *U.S.A.* **81 H4** 35 39N 101 24W
Borgholm, *Sweden* **9 H17** 56 52N 16 39 E
Borhoyn Tal, *Mongolia* **34 C6** 43 50N 111 58 E
Borikhane, *Laos* **38 C4** 18 33N 103 43 E
Borisoglebsk, *Russia* **25 D7** 51 27N 42 5 E
Borisov = Barysaw, *Belarus* **17 A15** 54 17N 28 28 E
Borja, *Peru* **92 D3** 4 20S 77 40W
Borkou, *Chad* **51 E9** 18 15N 18 50 E
Borkum, *Germany* **16 B4** 53 34N 6 40 E
Borlänge, *Sweden* **9 F16** 60 29N 15 26 E
Borley, C., *Antarctica* **5 C5** 66 15S 52 30 E
Borneo, *E. Indies* **36 D5** 1 0N 115 0 E
Bornholm, *Denmark* **9 J16** 55 10N 15 0 E
Borogontsy, *Russia* **27 C14** 62 42N 131 8 E
Boron, *U.S.A.* **85 L9** 35 0N 117 39W
Borongan, *Phil.* **37 B7** 11 37N 125 26 E
Borovichi, *Russia* **24 C5** 58 25N 33 55 E
Borrego Springs, *U.S.A.* **85 M10** 33 15N 116 23W
Borroloola, *Australia* **62 B2** 16 4S 136 17 E
Borşa, *Romania* **17 E13** 47 41N 24 50 E
Borsad, *India* **42 H5** 22 25N 72 54 E
Borth, *U.K.* **11 E3** 52 29N 4 2W
Borūjerd, *Iran* **45 C6** 33 55N 48 50 E
Boryslav, *Ukraine* **17 D12** 49 18N 23 28 E
Borzya, *Russia* **27 D12** 50 24N 116 31 E
Bosa, *Italy* **20 D3** 40 18N 8 30 E
Bosanska Gradiška, *Bos.-H.* **20 B7** 45 10N 17 15 E
Bosaso, *Somali Rep.* **46 E4** 11 12N 49 18 E
Boscastle, *U.K.* **11 G3** 50 41N 4 42W
Boshan, *China* **35 F9** 36 28N 117 49 E
Boshof, *S. Africa* **56 D4** 28 31S 25 13 E
Boshrūyeh, *Iran* **45 C8** 33 50N 57 30 E
Bosna →, *Bos.-H.* **21 B8** 45 4N 18 29 E
Bosna i Hercegovina = Bosnia-Herzegovina ■, *Europe* **20 B7** 44 0N 18 0 E
Bosnia-Herzegovina ■, *Europe* **20 B7** 44 0N 18 0 E
Bosnik, *Indonesia* **37 E9** 1 5S 136 10 E
Bosobolo, *Dem. Rep. of the Congo* **52 D3** 4 15N 19 50 E
Bosporus = İstanbul Boğazı, *Turkey* **21 D13** 41 10N 29 10 E
Bosque Farms, *U.S.A.* **83 J10** 34 53N 106 40W
Bossangoa, *C.A.R.* **52 C3** 6 35N 17 30 E
Bossier City, *U.S.A.* **81 J8** 32 31N 93 44W
Bosso, *Niger* **51 F8** 13 43N 13 19 E
Bostan, *Pakistan* **42 D2** 30 26N 67 2 E
Bostānābād, *Iran* **44 B5** 37 50N 46 50 E
Bosten Hu, *China* **32 B3** 41 55N 87 40 E
Boston, *U.K.* **10 E7** 52 59N 0 2W
Boston, *U.S.A.* **79 D13** 42 22N 71 4W
Boston Bar, *Canada* **72 D4** 49 52N 121 30W
Boston Mts., *U.S.A.* **81 H8** 35 42N 93 15W
Boswell, *Canada* **72 D5** 49 28N 116 45W
Boswell, *U.S.A.* **78 F5** 40 10N 79 2W
Botad, *India* **42 H4** 22 15N 71 40 E
Botene, *Laos* **38 D3** 17 35N 101 12 E
Bothaville, *S. Africa* **56 D4** 27 23S 26 34 E
Bothnia, G. of, *Europe* **8 E19** 63 0N 20 15 E
Bothwell, *Australia* **62 G4** 42 20S 147 1 E
Bothwell, *Canada* **78 D3** 42 38N 81 52W
Botletle →, *Botswana* **56 C3** 20 10S 23 15 E
Botoşani, *Romania* **17 E14** 47 42N 26 41 E
Botou, *Burkina Faso* **50 F6** 12 42N 1 59 E
Botswana ■, *Africa* **56 C3** 22 0S 24 0 E
Bottineau, *U.S.A.* **80 A4** 48 50N 100 27W
Bottrop, *Germany* **15 C6** 51 31N 6 58 E
Botucatu, *Brazil* **95 A6** 22 55S 48 30W
Botwood, *Canada* **71 C8** 49 6N 55 23W
Bouaflé, *Ivory C.* **50 G4** 7 1N 5 47W
Bouaké, *Ivory C.* **50 G4** 7 40N 5 2W
Bouar, *C.A.R.* **52 C3** 6 0N 15 40 E
Bouârfa, *Morocco* **50 B5** 32 32N 1 58W
Boucaut B., *Australia* **62 A1** 12 0S 134 25 E
Bougainville, C., *Australia* **60 B4** 13 57S 126 4 E
Bougainville I., *Papua N. G.* **64 H7** 6 0S 155 0 E
Bougainville Reef, *Australia* **62 B4** 15 30S 147 5 E
Bougie = Bejaïa, *Algeria* **50 A7** 36 42N 5 2 E
Bougouni, *Mali* **50 F4** 11 30N 7 20W
Bouillon, *Belgium* **15 E5** 49 44N 5 3 E
Boulder, *Colo., U.S.A.* **80 E2** 40 1N 105 17W
Boulder, *Mont., U.S.A.* **82 C7** 46 14N 112 7W
Boulder City, *U.S.A.* **85 K12** 35 59N 114 50W
Boulder Creek, *U.S.A.* **84 H4** 37 7N 122 7W
Boulder Dam = Hoover Dam, *U.S.A.* **85 K12** 36 1N 114 44W
Boulia, *Australia* **62 C2** 22 52S 139 51 E
Boulogne-sur-Mer, *France* **18 A4** 50 42N 1 36 E
Boultoum, *Niger* **51 F8** 14 45N 10 25 E
Boun Neua, *Laos* **38 B3** 21 38N 101 54 E
Boun Tai, *Laos* **38 B3** 21 23N 101 58 E
Bouna, *Ivory C.* **50 G5** 9 10N 3 0W
Boundary Peak, *U.S.A.* **84 H8** 37 51N 118 21W
Boundiali, *Ivory C.* **50 G4** 9 30N 6 20W
Bountiful, *U.S.A.* **82 F8** 40 53N 111 53W
Bounty Is., *Pac. Oc.* **64 M9** 48 0S 178 30 E
Bourbonnais, *France* **18 C5** 46 28N 3 0 E
Bourdel L., *Canada* **70 A5** 56 43N 74 10W
Bourem, *Mali* **50 E5** 17 0N 0 24W
Bourg-en-Bresse, *France* **18 C6** 46 13N 5 12 E
Bourg-St-Maurice, *France* **18 D7** 45 35N 6 46 E
Bourges, *France* **18 C5** 47 9N 2 25 E
Bourget, *Canada* **79 A9** 45 26N 75 9W
Bourgogne, *France* **18 C6** 47 0N 4 50 E
Bourke, *Australia* **63 E4** 30 8S 145 55 E
Bourne, *U.K.* **10 E7** 52 47N 0 22W
Bournemouth, *U.K.* **11 G6** 50 43N 1 52W
Bournemouth □, *U.K.* **11 G6** 50 43N 1 52W
Bouse, *U.S.A.* **85 M13** 33 56N 114 0W
Bouvet I. = Bouvetøya, *Antarctica* **3 G10** 54 26S 3 24 E
Bouvetøya, *Antarctica* **3 G10** 54 26S 3 24 E
Bovill, *U.S.A.* **82 C5** 46 51N 116 24W
Bovril, *Argentina* **94 C4** 31 21S 59 26W
Bow →, *Canada* **72 C6** 49 57N 111 41W
Bow Island, *Canada* **72 D6** 49 50N 111 23W
Bowbells, *U.S.A.* **80 A3** 48 48N 102 15W
Bowdle, *U.S.A.* **80 C5** 45 27N 99 39W
Bowelling, *Australia* **61 F2** 33 25S 116 30 E
Bowen, *Argentina* **94 D2** 35 0S 67 31W
Bowen, *Australia* **62 C4** 20 0S 148 16 E
Bowen Mts., *Australia* **63 F4** 37 0S 147 50 E
Bowie, *Ariz., U.S.A.* **83 K9** 32 19N 109 29W
Bowie, *Tex., U.S.A.* **81 J6** 33 34N 97 51W
Bowkān, *Iran* **44 B5** 36 31N 46 12 E
Bowland, Forest of, *U.K.* **10 D5** 54 0N 2 30W
Bowling Green, *Ky., U.S.A.* **76 G2** 36 59N 86 27W
Bowling Green, *Ohio, U.S.A.* **76 E4** 41 23N 83 39W
Bowling Green, C., *Australia* **62 B4** 19 19S 147 25 E
Bowman, *U.S.A.* **80 B3** 46 11N 103 24W
Bowman I., *Antarctica* **5 C8** 65 0S 104 0 E
Bowmanville, *Canada* **78 C6** 43 55N 78 41W
Bowmore, *U.K.* **12 F2** 55 45N 6 17W
Bowral, *Australia* **63 E5** 34 26S 150 27 E
Bowraville, *Australia* **63 E5** 30 37S 152 52 E
Bowron →, *Canada* **72 C4** 54 3N 121 50W
Bowron Lake Prov. Park, *Canada* **72 C4** 53 10N 121 5W
Bowser L., *Canada* **72 B3** 56 30N 129 30W
Bowsman, *Canada* **73 C8** 52 14N 101 12W
Bowwood, *Zambia* **55 F2** 17 5S 26 20 E
Box Cr. →, *Australia* **63 E3** 34 10S 143 50 E
Boxmeer, *Neths.* **15 C5** 51 38N 5 56 E
Boxtel, *Neths.* **15 C5** 51 36N 5 20 E
Boyce, *U.S.A.* **81 K8** 31 23N 92 40W
Boyd L., *Canada* **70 B4** 52 46N 76 42W
Boyle, *Canada* **72 C6** 54 35N 112 49W
Boyle, *Ireland* **13 C3** 53 59N 8 18W
Boyne →, *Ireland* **13 C5** 53 43N 6 15W
Boyne City, *U.S.A.* **76 C3** 45 13N 85 1W
Boynton Beach, *U.S.A.* **77 M5** 26 32N 80 4W
Boyolali, *Indonesia* **37 G14** 7 32S 110 35 E
Boyoma, Chutes, *Dem. Rep. of the Congo* **54 B2** 0 35N 25 23 E
Boysen Reservoir, *U.S.A.* **82 E9** 43 25N 108 11W
Boyuibe, *Bolivia* **92 G6** 20 25S 63 17W
Boyup Brook, *Australia* **61 F2** 33 50S 116 23 E
Boz Dağları, *Turkey* **21 E13** 38 20N 28 0 E
Bozburun, *Turkey* **21 F13** 36 43N 28 4 E
Bozcaada, *Turkey* **21 E12** 39 49N 26 3 E
Bozdoğan, *Turkey* **21 F13** 37 40N 28 17 E
Bozeman, *U.S.A.* **82 D8** 45 41N 111 2W
Bozen = Bolzano, *Italy* **20 A4** 46 31N 11 22 E
Bozhou, *China* **34 H8** 33 55N 115 41 E
Bozoum, *C.A.R.* **52 C3** 6 25N 16 35 E
Bra, *Italy* **18 D7** 44 42N 7 51 E
Brabant □, *Belgium* **15 D4** 50 46N 4 30 E
Brabant L., *Canada* **73 B8** 55 58N 103 43W
Brač, *Croatia* **20 C7** 43 20N 16 40 E
Bracadale, L., *U.K.* **12 D2** 57 20N 6 30W
Bracciano, L. di, *Italy* **20 C5** 42 7N 12 14 E
Bracebridge, *Canada* **78 A5** 45 2N 79 19W
Brach, *Libya* **51 C8** 27 31N 14 20 E
Bräcke, *Sweden* **9 E16** 62 45N 15 26 E
Brackettville, *U.S.A.* **81 L4** 29 19N 100 25W
Bracknell, *U.K.* **11 F7** 51 25N 0 43W
Bracknell Forest □, *U.K.* **11 F7** 51 25N 0 44W
Brad, *Romania* **17 E12** 46 10N 22 50 E
Bradenton, *U.S.A.* **77 M4** 27 30N 82 34W
Bradford, *Canada* **78 B5** 44 7N 79 34W
Bradford, *U.K.* **10 D6** 53 47N 1 45W
Bradford, *Pa., U.S.A.* **78 E6** 41 58N 78 38W
Bradford, *Vt., U.S.A.* **79 C12** 43 59N 72 9W
Bradley, *Ark., U.S.A.* **81 J8** 33 6N 93 39W
Bradley, *Calif., U.S.A.* **84 K6** 35 52N 120 48W
Bradley Institute, *Zimbabwe* **55 F3** 17 7S 31 25 E
Brady, *U.S.A.* **81 K5** 31 9N 99 20W
Braeside, *Canada* **79 A8** 45 28N 76 24W
Braga, *Portugal* **19 B1** 41 35N 8 25W
Bragado, *Argentina* **94 D3** 35 2S 60 27W
Bragança, *Brazil* **93 D9** 1 0S 47 2W
Bragança, *Portugal* **19 B2** 41 48N 6 50W
Bragança Paulista, *Brazil* **95 A6** 22 55S 46 32W
Brahmanbaria, *Bangla.* **41 H17** 23 58N 91 15 E
Brahmani →, *India* **41 J15** 20 39N 86 46 E
Brahmapur, *India* **41 K14** 19 15N 84 54 E
Brahmaputra →, *India* **41 F19** 27 48N 95 30 E
Braich-y-pwll, *U.K.* **10 E3** 52 47N 4 46W
Braidwood, *Australia* **63 F4** 35 27S 149 49 E
Brăila, *Romania* **17 F14** 45 19N 27 59 E
Brainerd, *U.S.A.* **80 B7** 46 22N 94 12W
Braintree, *U.K.* **11 F8** 51 53N 0 34 E
Braintree, *U.S.A.* **79 D14** 42 13N 71 0W
Brak →, *S. Africa* **56 D3** 29 35S 22 55 E
Brakwater, *Namibia* **56 C2** 22 28S 17 3 E
Brampton, *Canada* **78 C5** 43 45N 79 45W
Brampton, *U.K.* **10 C5** 54 57N 2 44W
Branco →, *Brazil* **92 D6** 1 20S 61 50W
Brandberg, *Namibia* **56 B2** 21 10S 14 33 E
Brandenburg = Neubrandenburg, *Germany* **16 B7** 53 33N 13 15 E
Brandenburg, *Germany* **16 B7** 52 25N 12 33 E
Brandenburg □, *Germany* **16 B6** 52 50N 13 0 E
Brandfort, *S. Africa* **56 D4** 28 40S 26 30 E
Brandon, *Canada* **73 D9** 49 50N 99 57W
Brandon, *U.S.A.* **79 C11** 43 48N 73 4W
Brandon B., *Ireland* **13 D1** 52 17N 10 8W
Brandon Mt., *Ireland* **13 D1** 52 15N 10 15W
Brandsen, *Argentina* **94 D4** 35 10S 58 15W
Brandvlei, *S. Africa* **56 E3** 30 25S 20 30 E
Branford, *U.S.A.* **79 E12** 41 17N 72 49W
Braniewo, *Poland* **17 A10** 54 25N 19 50 E
Bransfield Str., *Antarctica* **5 C18** 63 0S 59 0W
Branson, *U.S.A.* **81 G8** 36 39N 93 13W
Brantford, *Canada* **78 C4** 43 10N 80 15W
Bras d'Or L., *Canada* **71 C7** 45 50N 60 50W
Brasher Falls, *U.S.A.* **79 B10** 44 49N 74 47W
Brasil, Planalto, *Brazil* **90 E6** 18 0S 46 30W
Brasiléia, *Brazil* **92 F5** 11 0S 68 45W
Brasília, *Brazil* **93 G9** 15 47S 47 55W
Brasília Legal, *Brazil* **93 D7** 3 49S 55 36W
Braslaw, *Belarus* **9 J22** 55 38N 27 0 E
Braşov, *Romania* **17 F13** 45 38N 25 35 E
Brasschaat, *Belgium* **15 C4** 51 19N 4 27 E
Brassey, Banjaran, *Malaysia* **36 D5** 5 0N 117 15 E
Brassey Ra., *Australia* **61 E3** 25 8S 122 15 E
Brasstown Bald, *U.S.A.* **77 H4** 34 53N 83 49W
Brastad, *Sweden* **9 G14** 58 23N 11 30 E
Bratislava, *Slovak Rep.* **17 D9** 48 10N 17 7 E
Bratsk, *Russia* **27 D11** 56 10N 101 30 E
Brattleboro, *U.S.A.* **79 D12** 42 51N 72 34W
Braunau, *Austria* **16 D7** 48 15N 13 3 E
Braunschweig, *Germany* **16 B6** 52 15N 10 31 E
Braunton, *U.K.* **11 F3** 51 7N 4 10W
Bravo del Norte, Rio = Grande, Rio →, *U.S.A.* **81 N6** 25 58N 97 9W
Brawley, *U.S.A.* **85 N11** 32 59N 115 31W
Bray, *Ireland* **13 C5** 53 13N 6 7W
Bray, Mt., *Australia* **62 A1** 14 0S 134 30 E
Bray, Pays de, *France* **18 B4** 49 46N 1 26 E
Brazeau →, *Canada* **72 C5** 52 55N 115 14W
Brazil, *U.S.A.* **76 F2** 39 32N 87 8W
Brazil ■, *S. Amer.* **93 F9** 12 0S 50 0W
Brazilian Highlands = Brasil, Planalto, *Brazil* **90 E6** 18 0S 46 30W
Brazo Sur →, *S. Amer.* **94 B4** 25 21S 57 42W
Brazos →, *U.S.A.* **81 L7** 28 53N 95 23W
Brazzaville, *Congo* **52 E3** 4 9S 15 12 E
Brčko, *Bos.-H.* **21 B8** 44 54N 18 46 E
Breaden, L., *Australia* **61 E4** 25 51S 125 28 E
Breaksea Sd., *N.Z.* **59 L1** 45 35S 166 35 E
Bream B., *N.Z.* **59 F5** 35 56S 174 28 E
Bream Hd., *N.Z.* **59 F5** 35 51S 174 36 E
Breas, *Chile* **94 B1** 25 29S 70 24W
Brebes, *Indonesia* **37 G13** 6 52S 109 3 E
Brechin, *Canada* **78 B5** 44 32N 79 10W
Brechin, *U.K.* **12 E6** 56 44N 2 39W
Brecht, *Belgium* **15 C4** 51 21N 4 38 E
Breckenridge, *Colo., U.S.A.* **82 G10** 39 29N 106 3W
Breckenridge, *Minn., U.S.A.* **80 B6** 46 16N 96 35W
Breckenridge, *Tex., U.S.A.* **81 J5** 32 45N 98 54W
Breckland, *U.K.* **11 E8** 52 30N 0 40 E
Brecon, *U.K.* **11 F4** 51 57N 3 23W
Brecon Beacons, *U.K.* **11 F4** 51 53N 3 26W
Breda, *Neths.* **15 C4** 51 35N 4 45 E
Bredasdorp, *S. Africa* **56 E3** 34 33S 20 2 E
Bree, *Belgium* **15 C5** 51 8N 5 35 E
Bregenz, *Austria* **16 E5** 47 30N 9 45 E
Breiðafjörður, *Iceland* **8 D2** 65 15N 23 15W
Brejo, *Brazil* **93 D10** 3 41S 42 47W
Bremen, *Germany* **16 B5** 53 4N 8 47 E
Bremer Bay, *Australia* **61 F2** 34 21S 119 20 E
Bremer I., *Australia* **62 A2** 12 5S 136 45 E
Bremerhaven, *Germany* **16 B5** 53 33N 8 36 E
Bremerton, *U.S.A.* **84 C4** 47 34N 122 38W
Brenham, *U.S.A.* **81 K6** 30 10N 96 24W
Brennerpass, *Austria* **16 E6** 47 2N 11 30 E
Brent, *U.S.A.* **77 J2** 32 56N 87 10W
Brentwood, *U.K.* **11 F8** 51 37N 0 19 E
Brentwood, *Calif., U.S.A.* **84 H5** 37 56N 121 42W
Brentwood, *N.Y., U.S.A.* **79 F11** 40 47N 73 15W
Bréscia, *Italy* **18 D9** 45 33N 10 15 E
Breskens, *Neths.* **15 C3** 51 23N 3 33 E
Breslau = Wrocław, *Poland* **17 C9** 51 5N 17 5 E
Bressanone, *Italy* **20 A4** 46 43N 11 39 E
Bressay, *U.K.* **12 A7** 60 9N 1 6W
Brest, *Belarus* **17 B12** 52 10N 23 40 E
Brest, *France* **18 B1** 48 24N 4 31W
Brest-Litovsk = Brest, *Belarus* **17 B12** 52 10N 23 40 E
Bretagne, *France* **18 B2** 48 10N 3 0W
Breton, *Canada* **72 C6** 53 7N 114 28W
Breton Sd., *U.S.A.* **81 L10** 29 35N 89 15W
Brett, C., *N.Z.* **59 F5** 35 10S 174 20 E
Brevard, *U.S.A.* **77 H4** 35 14N 82 44W
Breves, *Brazil* **93 D8** 1 40S 50 29W
Brewarrina, *Australia* **63 E4** 30 0S 146 51 E
Brewer, *U.S.A.* **77 C11** 44 48N 68 46W
Brewer, Mt., *U.S.A.* **84 J8** 36 44N 118 28W
Brewster, *N.Y., U.S.A.* **79 E11** 41 23N 73 37W

Brewster

Brewster, Ohio, U.S.A. **78 F3** 40 43N 81 36W
Brewster, Wash., U.S.A. **82 B4** 48 6N 119 47W
Brewster, Kap = Kangikajik, Greenland **4 B6** 70 7N 22 0W
Brewton, U.S.A. **77 K2** 31 7N 87 4W
Breyten, S. Africa **57 D5** 26 16S 30 0 E
Brezhnev = Naberezhnyye Chelny, Russia **24 C9** 55 42N 52 19 E
Briançon, France **18 D7** 44 54N 6 39 E
Bribie I., Australia **63 D5** 27 0S 153 10 E
Bribri, Costa Rica **88 E3** 9 38N 82 50W
Bridgehampton, U.S.A. **79 F12** 40 56N 72 19W
Bridgend, U.K. **11 F4** 51 30N 3 34W
Bridgend □, U.K. **11 F4** 51 36N 3 36W
Bridgeport, Calif., U.S.A. **84 G7** 38 15N 119 14W
Bridgeport, Conn., U.S.A. **79 E11** 41 11N 73 12W
Bridgeport, Nebr., U.S.A. **80 E3** 41 40N 103 6W
Bridgeport, Tex., U.S.A. **81 J6** 33 13N 97 45W
Bridger, U.S.A. **82 D9** 45 18N 108 55W
Bridgeton, U.S.A. **76 F8** 39 26N 75 14W
Bridgetown, Australia **61 F2** 33 58S 116 7 E
Bridgetown, Barbados **89 D8** 13 5N 59 30W
Bridgetown, Canada **71 D6** 44 55N 65 18W
Bridgewater, Canada **71 D7** 44 25N 64 31W
Bridgewater, Mass., U.S.A. **79 E14** 41 59N 70 58W
Bridgewater, N.Y., U.S.A. **79 D9** 42 53N 75 15W
Bridgewater, C., Australia **63 F3** 38 23S 141 23 E
Bridgewater-Gagebrook, Australia **62 G4** 42 44S 147 14 E
Bridgnorth, U.K. **11 E5** 52 32N 2 25W
Bridgton, U.S.A. **79 B14** 44 3N 70 42W
Bridgwater, U.K. **11 F5** 51 8N 2 59W
Bridgwater B., U.K. **11 F4** 51 15N 3 15W
Bridlington, U.K. **10 C7** 54 5N 0 12W
Bridlington B., U.K. **10 C7** 54 4N 0 10W
Bridport, Australia **62 G4** 40 59S 147 23 E
Bridport, U.K. **11 G5** 50 44N 2 45W
Brig, Switz. **18 C7** 46 18N 7 59 E
Brigg, U.K. **10 D7** 53 34N 0 28W
Brigham City, U.S.A. **82 F7** 41 31N 112 1W
Bright, Australia **63 F4** 36 42S 146 56 E
Brighton, Australia **63 F2** 35 5S 138 30 E
Brighton, Canada **78 B7** 44 2N 77 44W
Brighton, U.K. **11 G7** 50 49N 0 7W
Brighton, Colo., U.S.A. **80 F2** 39 59N 104 49W
Brighton, N.Y., U.S.A. **78 C7** 43 8N 77 34W
Brilliant, U.S.A. **78 F4** 40 15N 80 39W
Brindisi, Italy **21 D7** 40 39N 17 55 E
Brinkley, U.S.A. **81 H9** 34 53N 91 12W
Brinnon, U.S.A. **84 C4** 47 41N 122 54W
Brion, I., Canada **71 C7** 47 46N 61 26W
Brisbane, Australia **63 D5** 27 25S 153 2 E
Brisbane →, Australia **63 D5** 27 24S 153 9 E
Bristol, U.K. **11 F5** 51 26N 2 35W
Bristol, Conn., U.S.A. **79 E12** 41 40N 72 57W
Bristol, Pa., U.S.A. **79 F10** 40 6N 74 51W
Bristol, R.I., U.S.A. **79 E13** 41 40N 71 16W
Bristol, Tenn., U.S.A. **77 G4** 36 36N 82 11W
Bristol, City of □, U.K. **11 F5** 51 27N 2 36W
Bristol B., U.S.A. **68 C4** 58 0N 160 0W
Bristol Channel, U.K. **11 F3** 51 18N 4 30W
Bristol I., Antarctica **5 B1** 58 45S 28 0W
Bristol L., U.S.A. **83 J5** 34 23N 116 50W
Bristow, U.S.A. **81 H6** 35 50N 96 23W
Britain = Great Britain, Europe **6 E5** 54 0N 2 15W
British Columbia □, Canada **72 C3** 55 0N 125 15W
British Indian Ocean Terr. = Chagos Arch., Ind. Oc. **29 K11** 6 0S 72 0 E
British Isles, Europe **6 E5** 54 0N 4 0W
Brits, S. Africa **57 D4** 25 37S 27 48 E
Britstown, S. Africa **56 E3** 30 37S 23 30 E
Britt, Canada **70 C3** 45 46N 80 34W
Brittany = Bretagne, France **18 B2** 48 10N 3 0W
Britton, U.S.A. **80 C6** 45 48N 97 45W
Brive-la-Gaillarde, France **18 D4** 45 10N 1 32 E
Brixen = Bressanone, Italy **20 A4** 46 43N 11 39 E
Brixham, U.K. **11 G4** 50 23N 3 31W
Brno, Czech Rep. **17 D9** 49 10N 16 35 E
Broad →, U.S.A. **77 J5** 34 1N 81 4W
Broad Arrow, Australia **61 F3** 30 23S 121 15 E
Broad B., U.K. **12 C2** 58 14N 6 18W
Broad Haven, Ireland **13 B2** 54 20N 9 55W
Broad Law, U.K. **12 F5** 55 30N 3 21W
Broad Sd., Australia **62 C4** 22 0S 149 45 E
Broadalbin, U.S.A. **79 C10** 43 4N 74 12W
Broadback →, Canada **70 B4** 51 21N 78 52W
Broadhurst Ra., Australia **60 D3** 22 30S 122 30 E
Broads, The, U.K. **10 E9** 52 45N 1 30 E
Broadus, U.S.A. **80 C2** 45 27N 105 25W
Brochet, Canada **73 B8** 57 53N 101 40W
Brochet, L., Canada **73 B8** 58 36N 101 35W
Brocken, Germany **16 C6** 51 47N 10 37 E
Brockport, U.S.A. **78 C7** 43 13N 77 56W
Brockton, U.S.A. **79 D13** 42 5N 71 1W
Brockville, Canada **79 B9** 44 35N 75 41W
Brockway, Mont., U.S.A. **80 B2** 47 18N 105 45W
Brockway, Pa., U.S.A. **78 E6** 41 15N 78 47W
Brocton, U.S.A. **78 D5** 42 23N 79 26W
Brodeur Pen., Canada **69 A11** 72 30N 88 10W
Brodhead, Mt., U.S.A. **78 E7** 41 39N 77 47W
Brodick, U.K. **12 F3** 55 35N 5 9W
Brodnica, Poland **17 B10** 53 15N 19 25 E
Brody, Ukraine **17 C13** 50 5N 25 10 E
Brogan, U.S.A. **82 D5** 44 15N 117 31W
Broken Arrow, U.S.A. **81 G7** 36 3N 95 48W
Broken Bow, Nebr., U.S.A. **80 E5** 41 24N 99 38W
Broken Bow, Okla., U.S.A. **81 H7** 34 2N 94 44W
Broken Bow Lake, U.S.A. **81 H7** 34 9N 94 40W
Broken Hill = Kabwe, Zambia **55 E2** 14 30S 28 29 E
Broken Hill, Australia **63 E3** 31 58S 141 29 E
Bromley □, U.K. **11 F8** 51 24N 0 2 E
Bromsgrove, U.K. **11 E5** 52 21N 2 2W
Brønderslev, Denmark **9 H13** 57 16N 9 57 E
Bronkhorstspruit, S. Africa **57 D4** 25 46S 28 45 E
Brønnøysund, Norway **8 D15** 65 28N 12 14 E
Brook Park, U.S.A. **78 E4** 41 24N 81 51W
Brookhaven, U.S.A. **81 K9** 31 35N 90 26W
Brookings, Oreg., U.S.A. **82 E1** 42 3N 124 17W
Brookings, S. Dak., U.S.A. **80 C6** 44 19N 96 48W
Brooklin, Canada **78 C6** 43 55N 78 55W
Brooklyn Park, U.S.A. **80 C8** 45 6N 93 23W
Brooks, Canada **72 C6** 50 35N 111 55W
Brooks Range, U.S.A. **68 B5** 68 0N 152 0W
Brooksville, U.S.A. **77 L4** 28 33N 82 23W
Brookton, Australia **61 F2** 32 22S 117 0 E
Brookville, U.S.A. **78 E5** 41 10N 79 5W
Broom, L., U.K. **12 D3** 57 55N 5 15W
Broome, Australia **60 C3** 18 0S 122 15 E
Brora, U.K. **12 C5** 58 0N 3 52W
Brora →, U.K. **12 C5** 58 0N 3 51W
Brosna →, Ireland **13 C4** 53 14N 7 58W
Brothers, U.S.A. **82 E3** 43 49N 120 36W
Brough, U.K. **10 C5** 54 32N 2 18W
Brough Hd., U.K. **12 B5** 59 8N 3 20W
Broughton Island = Qikiqtarjuaq, Canada **69 B13** 67 33N 63 0W
Brown, L., Australia **61 F2** 31 5S 118 15 E
Brown, Pt., Australia **63 E1** 32 32S 133 50 E
Brown City, U.S.A. **78 C2** 43 13N 82 59W
Brown Willy, U.K. **11 G3** 50 35N 4 37W
Brownfield, U.S.A. **81 J3** 33 11N 102 17W
Browning, U.S.A. **82 B7** 48 34N 113 1W
Brownsville, Oreg., U.S.A. **82 D2** 44 24N 122 59W
Brownsville, Pa., U.S.A. **78 F5** 40 1N 79 53W
Brownsville, Tenn., U.S.A. **81 H10** 35 36N 89 16W
Brownsville, Tex., U.S.A. **81 N6** 25 54N 97 30W
Brownville, U.S.A. **79 C9** 44 0N 75 59W
Brownwood, U.S.A. **81 K5** 31 43N 98 59W
Browse I., Australia **60 B3** 14 7S 123 33 E
Bruas, Malaysia **39 K3** 4 30N 100 47 E
Bruay-la-Buissière, France **18 A5** 50 29N 2 33 E
Bruce, Mt., Australia **60 D2** 22 37S 118 8 E
Bruce Pen., Canada **78 B3** 45 0N 81 30W
Bruce Rock, Australia **61 F2** 31 52S 118 8 E
Bruck an der Leitha, Austria **17 D9** 48 1N 16 47 E
Bruck an der Mur, Austria **16 E8** 47 24N 15 16 E
Brue →, U.K. **11 F5** 51 13N 2 59W
Bruges = Brugge, Belgium **15 C3** 51 13N 3 13 E
Brugge, Belgium **15 C3** 51 13N 3 13 E
Bruin, U.S.A. **78 E5** 41 3N 79 43W
Brûlé, Canada **72 C5** 53 15N 117 58W
Brumado, Brazil **93 F10** 14 14S 41 40W
Brumunddal, Norway **9 F14** 60 53N 10 56 E
Bruneau, U.S.A. **82 E6** 42 53N 115 48W
Bruneau →, U.S.A. **82 E6** 42 56N 115 57W
Brunei = Bandar Seri Begawan, Brunei **36 C4** 4 52N 115 0 E
Brunei ■, Asia **36 D4** 4 50N 115 0 E
Brunner, L., N.Z. **59 K3** 42 37S 171 27 E
Brunssum, Neths. **15 D5** 50 57N 5 59 E
Brunswick = Braunschweig, Germany **16 B6** 52 15N 10 31 E
Brunswick, Ga., U.S.A. **77 K5** 31 10N 81 30W
Brunswick, Maine, U.S.A. **77 D11** 43 55N 69 58W
Brunswick, Md., U.S.A. **76 F7** 39 19N 77 38W
Brunswick, Mo., U.S.A. **80 F8** 39 26N 93 8W
Brunswick, Ohio, U.S.A. **78 E3** 41 14N 81 51W
Brunswick, Pen. de, Chile **96 G2** 53 30S 71 30W
Brunswick B., Australia **60 C3** 15 15S 124 50 E
Brunswick Junction, Australia **61 F2** 33 15S 115 50 E
Bruny I., Australia **62 G4** 43 20S 147 15 E
Brus Laguna, Honduras **88 C3** 15 47N 84 35W
Brush, U.S.A. **80 E3** 40 15N 103 37W
Brushton, U.S.A. **79 B10** 44 50N 74 31W
Brusque, Brazil **95 B6** 27 5S 49 0W
Brussel, Belgium **15 D4** 50 51N 4 21 E
Brussels = Brussel, Belgium **15 D4** 50 51N 4 21 E
Brussels, Canada **78 C3** 43 44N 81 15W
Bruthen, Australia **63 F4** 37 42S 147 50 E
Bruxelles = Brussel, Belgium **15 D4** 50 51N 4 21 E
Bryan, Ohio, U.S.A. **76 E3** 41 28N 84 33W
Bryan, Tex., U.S.A. **81 K6** 30 40N 96 22W
Bryan, Mt., Australia **63 E2** 33 30S 139 0 E
Bryansk, Russia **24 D4** 53 13N 34 25 E
Bryce Canyon Nat. Park, U.S.A. **83 H7** 37 30N 112 10W
Bryne, Norway **9 G11** 58 44N 5 38 E
Bryson City, U.S.A. **77 H4** 35 26N 83 27W
Bsharri, Lebanon **47 A5** 34 15N 36 0 E
Bū Baqarah, U.A.E. **45 E8** 25 35N 56 25 E
Bu Craa, W. Sahara **50 C3** 26 45N 12 50W
Bū Ḩasā, U.A.E. **45 F7** 23 30N 53 20 E
Bua Yai, Thailand **38 E4** 15 33N 102 26 E
Buapinang, Indonesia **37 E6** 4 40S 121 30 E
Bubanza, Burundi **54 C2** 3 6S 29 23 E
Būbiyān, Kuwait **46 B4** 29 45N 48 15 E
Bucaramanga, Colombia **92 B4** 7 0N 73 0W
Bucasia, Australia **62 C4** 21 2S 149 10 E
Buccaneer Arch., Australia **60 C3** 16 7S 123 20 E
Buchach, Ukraine **17 D13** 49 5N 25 25 E
Buchan, U.K. **12 D6** 57 32N 2 21W
Buchan Ness, U.K. **12 D7** 57 29N 1 46W
Buchanan, Canada **73 C8** 51 40N 102 45W
Buchanan, Liberia **50 G3** 5 57N 10 2W
Buchanan, L., Queens., Australia **62 C4** 21 35S 145 52 E
Buchanan, L., W. Austral., Australia **61 E3** 25 33S 123 2 E
Buchanan, L., U.S.A. **81 K5** 30 45N 98 25W
Buchanan Cr. →, Australia **62 B2** 19 13S 136 33 E
Buchans, Canada **71 C8** 48 50N 56 52W
Bucharest = Bucureşti, Romania **17 F14** 44 27N 26 10 E
Buchon, Pt., U.S.A. **84 K6** 35 15N 120 54W
Buck Hill Falls, U.S.A. **79 E9** 41 11N 75 16W
Buckeye, U.S.A. **83 K7** 33 22N 112 35W
Buckeye Lake, U.S.A. **78 G2** 39 55N 82 29W
Buckhannon, U.S.A. **76 F5** 39 0N 80 8W
Buckhaven, U.K. **12 E5** 56 11N 3 3W
Buckhorn L., Canada **78 B6** 44 29N 78 23W
Buckie, U.K. **12 D6** 57 41N 2 58W
Buckingham, Canada **70 C4** 45 37N 75 24W
Buckingham, U.K. **11 F7** 51 59N 0 57W
Buckingham B., Australia **62 A2** 12 10S 135 40 E
Buckinghamshire □, U.K. **11 F7** 51 53N 0 55W
Buckle Hd., Australia **60 B4** 14 26S 127 52 E
Buckleboo, Australia **63 E2** 32 54S 136 12 E
Buckley, U.K. **10 D4** 53 10N 3 5W
Buckley →, Australia **62 C2** 20 10S 138 49 E
Bucklin, U.S.A. **81 G5** 37 33N 99 38W
Bucks L., U.S.A. **84 F5** 39 54N 121 12W
Buctouche, Canada **71 C7** 46 30N 64 45W
Bucureşti, Romania **17 F14** 44 27N 26 10 E
Bucyrus, U.S.A. **76 E4** 40 48N 82 59W
Budalin, Burma **41 H19** 22 20N 95 10 E
Budapest, Hungary **17 E10** 47 29N 19 5 E
Budaun, India **43 E8** 28 5N 79 10 E
Budd Coast, Antarctica **5 C8** 68 0S 112 0 E
Bude, U.K. **11 G3** 50 49N 4 34W
Budennovsk, Russia **25 F7** 44 50N 44 10 E
Budge Budge = Baj Baj, India **43 H13** 22 30N 88 5 E
Budgewoi, Australia **63 E5** 33 13S 151 34 E
Budjala, Dem. Rep. of the Congo **52 D3** 2 50N 19 40 E
Buellton, U.S.A. **85 L6** 34 37N 120 12W
Buena Esperanza, Argentina **94 C2** 34 45S 65 15W
Buena Park, U.S.A. **85 M9** 33 52N 117 59W
Buena Vista, Colo., U.S.A. **83 G10** 38 51N 106 8W
Buena Vista, Va., U.S.A. **76 G6** 37 44N 79 21W
Buena Vista Lake Bed, U.S.A. **85 K7** 35 12N 119 18W
Buenaventura, Colombia **92 C3** 3 53N 77 4W
Buenaventura, Mexico **86 B3** 29 50N 107 30W
Buenos Aires, Argentina **94 C4** 34 30S 58 20W
Buenos Aires, Costa Rica **88 E3** 9 10N 83 20W
Buenos Aires □, Argentina **94 D4** 36 30S 60 0W
Buenos Aires, L., Chile **96 F2** 46 35S 72 30W
Buffalo, Mo., U.S.A. **81 G8** 37 39N 93 6W
Buffalo, N.Y., U.S.A. **78 D6** 42 53N 78 53W
Buffalo, Okla., U.S.A. **81 G5** 36 50N 99 38W
Buffalo, S. Dak., U.S.A. **80 C3** 45 35N 103 33W
Buffalo, Wyo., U.S.A. **82 D10** 44 21N 106 42W
Buffalo →, Canada **72 A5** 60 5N 115 5W
Buffalo →, S. Africa **57 D5** 28 43S 30 37 E
Buffalo Head Hills, Canada **72 B5** 57 25N 115 55W
Buffalo L., Alta., Canada **72 C6** 52 27N 112 54W
Buffalo L., N.W.T., Canada **72 A5** 60 12N 115 25W
Buffalo Narrows, Canada **73 B7** 55 51N 108 29W
Buffels →, S. Africa **56 D2** 29 36S 17 3 E
Buford, U.S.A. **77 H4** 34 10N 84 0W
Bug = Buh →, Ukraine **25 E5** 46 59N 31 58 E
Bug →, Poland **17 B11** 52 31N 21 5 E
Buga, Colombia **92 C3** 4 0N 76 15W
Bugala I., Uganda **54 C3** 0 40S 32 20 E
Buganda, Uganda **54 C3** 0 0 31 30 E
Buganga, Uganda **54 C3** 0 3S 32 0 E
Bugel, Tanjung, Indonesia **37 G14** 6 26S 111 3 E
Bugibba, Malta **23 D1** 35 57N 14 25 E
Bugsuk, Phil. **36 C5** 8 15N 117 15 E
Bugulma, Russia **24 D9** 54 33N 52 48 E
Bugun Shara, Mongolia **32 B5** 49 0N 104 0 E
Buguruslan, Russia **24 D9** 53 39N 52 26 E
Buh →, Ukraine **25 E5** 46 59N 31 58 E
Buhera, Zimbabwe **57 B5** 19 18S 31 29 E
Buhl, U.S.A. **82 E6** 42 36N 114 46W
Builth Wells, U.K. **11 E4** 52 9N 3 25W
Buir Nur, Mongolia **33 B6** 47 50N 117 42 E
Bujumbura, Burundi **54 C2** 3 16S 29 18 E
Bukachacha, Russia **27 D12** 52 55N 116 50 E
Bukama, Dem. Rep. of the Congo **55 D2** 9 10S 25 50 E
Bukavu, Dem. Rep. of the Congo **54 C2** 2 20S 28 52 E
Bukene, Tanzania **54 C3** 4 15S 32 48 E
Bukhara = Bukhoro, Uzbekistan **26 F7** 39 48N 64 25 E
Bukhoro, Uzbekistan **26 F7** 39 48N 64 25 E
Bukima, Tanzania **54 C3** 1 50S 33 25 E
Bukit Mertajam, Malaysia **39 K3** 5 22N 100 28 E
Bukittinggi, Indonesia **36 E2** 0 20S 100 20 E
Bukoba, Tanzania **54 C3** 1 20S 31 49 E
Bukuya, Uganda **54 B3** 0 40N 31 52 E
Būl, Kuh-e, Iran **45 D7** 30 48N 52 45 E
Bula, Indonesia **37 E8** 3 6S 130 30 E
Bulahdelah, Australia **63 E5** 32 23S 152 13 E
Bulan, Phil. **37 B6** 12 40N 123 52 E
Bulandshahr, India **42 E7** 28 28N 77 51 E
Bulawayo, Zimbabwe **55 G2** 20 7S 28 32 E
Buldan, Turkey **21 E13** 38 2N 28 50 E
Bulgar, Russia **24 D8** 54 57N 49 4 E
Bulgaria ■, Europe **21 C11** 42 35N 25 30 E
Buli, Teluk, Indonesia **37 D7** 0 48N 128 25 E
Buliluyan, C., Phil. **36 C5** 8 20N 117 15 E
Bulkley →, Canada **72 B3** 55 15N 127 40W
Bull Shoals L., U.S.A. **81 G8** 36 22N 92 35W
Bullhead City, U.S.A. **85 K12** 35 8N 114 32W
Büllingen, Belgium **15 D6** 50 25N 6 16 E
Bullock Creek, Australia **62 B3** 17 43S 144 31 E
Bulloo →, Australia **63 D3** 28 43S 142 30 E
Bulloo L., Australia **63 D3** 28 43S 142 25 E
Bulls, N.Z. **59 J5** 40 10S 175 24 E
Bulnes, Chile **94 D1** 36 42S 72 19W
Bulsar = Valsad, India **40 J8** 20 40N 72 58 E
Bultfontein, S. Africa **56 D4** 28 18S 26 10 E
Bulukumba, Indonesia **37 F6** 5 33S 120 11 E
Bulun, Russia **27 B13** 70 37N 127 30 E
Bumba, Dem. Rep. of the Congo **52 D4** 2 13N 22 30 E
Bumbiri I., Tanzania **54 C3** 1 40S 31 55 E
Bumhpa Bum, Burma **41 F20** 26 51N 97 14 E
Bumi →, Zimbabwe **55 F2** 17 0S 28 20 E
Buna, Kenya **54 B4** 2 58N 39 30 E
Bunazi, Tanzania **54 C3** 1 3S 31 23 E
Bunbury, Australia **61 F2** 33 20S 115 35 E
Bunclody, Ireland **13 D5** 52 39N 6 40W
Buncrana, Ireland **13 A4** 55 8N 7 27W
Bundaberg, Australia **63 C5** 24 54S 152 22 E
Bundey →, Australia **62 C2** 21 46S 135 37 E
Bundi, India **42 G6** 25 30N 75 35 E
Bundoran, Ireland **13 B3** 54 28N 8 16W
Bung Kan, Thailand **38 C4** 18 23N 103 37 E
Bungay, U.K. **11 E9** 52 27N 1 28 E
Bungil Cr. →, Australia **63 D4** 27 5S 149 5 E
Bungo-Suidō, Japan **31 H6** 33 0N 132 15 E
Bungoma, Kenya **54 B3** 0 34N 34 34 E
Bungotakada, Japan **31 H5** 33 35N 131 25 E
Bungu, Tanzania **54 D4** 7 35S 39 0 E
Bunia, Dem. Rep. of the Congo **54 B3** 1 35N 30 20 E
Bunji, Pakistan **43 B6** 35 45N 74 40 E
Bunkie, U.S.A. **81 K8** 30 57N 92 11W
Bunnell, U.S.A. **77 L5** 29 28N 81 16W
Buntok, Indonesia **36 E4** 1 40S 114 58 E
Bunyu, Indonesia **36 D5** 3 35N 117 50 E
Buol, Indonesia **37 D6** 1 15N 121 32 E
Buon Brieng, Vietnam **38 F7** 13 9N 108 12 E
Buon Ma Thuot, Vietnam **38 F7** 12 40N 108 3 E
Buong Long, Cambodia **38 F6** 13 44N 106 59 E
Buorkhaya, Mys, Russia **27 B14** 71 50N 132 40 E
Buqayq, Si. Arabia **45 E6** 26 0N 49 45 E
Bur Acaba, Somali Rep. **46 G3** 3 12N 44 20 E
Bûr Safâga, Egypt **44 E2** 26 43N 33 57 E
Bûr Sa'îd, Egypt **51 B12** 31 16N 32 18 E
Bûr Sûdân, Sudan **51 E13** 19 32N 37 9 E
Bura, Kenya **54 C4** 1 4S 39 58 E
Burakin, Australia **61 F2** 30 31S 117 10 E
Burao, Somali Rep. **46 F4** 9 32N 45 32 E
Burāq, Syria **47 B5** 33 11N 36 29 E
Buraydah, Si. Arabia **44 E4** 26 20N 43 59 E
Burbank, U.S.A. **85 L8** 34 11N 118 19W
Burda, India **42 G6** 25 50N 77 35 E
Burdekin →, Australia **62 B4** 19 38S 147 25 E
Burdur, Turkey **25 G5** 37 45N 30 17 E
Burdwan = Barddhaman, India **43 H12** 23 14N 87 39 E
Bure, Ethiopia **46 E2** 10 40N 37 4 E
Bure →, U.K. **10 E9** 52 38N 1 43 E
Bureya →, Russia **27 E13** 49 27N 129 30 E
Burford, Canada **78 C4** 43 7N 80 27W
Burgas, Bulgaria **21 C12** 42 33N 27 29 E
Burgeo, Canada **71 C8** 47 37N 57 38W
Burgersdorp, S. Africa **56 E4** 31 0S 26 20 E
Burges, Mt., Australia **61 F3** 30 50S 121 5 E
Burgos, Spain **19 A4** 42 21N 3 41W
Burgsvik, Sweden **9 H18** 57 3N 18 19 E
Burgundy = Bourgogne, France **18 C6** 47 0N 4 50 E
Burhaniye, Turkey **21 E12** 39 30N 26 58 E
Burhanpur, India **40 J10** 21 18N 76 14 E
Burhi Gandak →, India **43 G12** 25 20N 86 37 E
Burhner →, India **43 H9** 22 43N 80 31 E
Burias I., Phil. **37 B6** 12 55N 123 5 E
Burica, Pta., Costa Rica **88 E3** 8 3N 82 51W
Burien, U.S.A. **84 C4** 47 28N 122 21W
Burigi, L., Tanzania **54 C3** 2 2S 31 22 E
Burin, Canada **71 C8** 47 1N 55 14W
Buriram, Thailand **38 E4** 15 0N 103 0 E
Burj Sāfitā, Syria **44 C3** 34 48N 36 7 E
Burkburnett, U.S.A. **81 H5** 34 6N 98 34W
Burke →, Australia **62 C2** 23 12S 139 33 E
Burke Chan., Canada **72 C3** 52 10N 127 30W
Burketown, Australia **62 B2** 17 45S 139 33 E
Burkina Faso ■, Africa **50 F5** 12 0N 1 0W
Burk's Falls, Canada **70 C4** 45 37N 79 24W
Burleigh Falls, Canada **78 B6** 44 33N 78 12W
Burley, U.S.A. **82 E7** 42 32N 113 48W
Burlingame, U.S.A. **84 H4** 37 35N 122 21W
Burlington, Canada **78 C5** 43 18N 79 45W
Burlington, Colo., U.S.A. **80 F3** 39 18N 102 16W
Burlington, Iowa, U.S.A. **80 E9** 40 49N 91 14W
Burlington, Kans., U.S.A. **80 F7** 38 12N 95 45W
Burlington, N.C., U.S.A. **77 G6** 36 6N 79 26W
Burlington, N.J., U.S.A. **79 F10** 40 4N 74 51W
Burlington, Vt., U.S.A. **79 B11** 44 29N 73 12W
Burlington, Wash., U.S.A. **84 B4** 48 28N 122 20W
Burlington, Wis., U.S.A. **76 D1** 42 41N 88 17W
Burlyu-Tyube, Kazakstan **26 E8** 46 30N 79 10 E
Burma ■, Asia **41 J20** 21 0N 96 30 E
Burnaby I., Canada **72 C2** 52 25N 131 19W
Burnet, U.S.A. **81 K5** 30 45N 98 14W
Burney, U.S.A. **82 F3** 40 53N 121 40W
Burnham, U.S.A. **78 F7** 40 38N 77 34W
Burnham-on-Sea, U.K. **11 F5** 51 14N 3 0W
Burnie, Australia **62 G4** 41 4S 145 56 E
Burnley, U.K. **10 D5** 53 47N 2 14W
Burns, U.S.A. **82 E4** 43 35N 119 3W
Burns Lake, Canada **72 C3** 54 20N 125 45W
Burnside →, Canada **68 B9** 66 51N 108 4W
Burnside, L., Australia **61 E3** 25 22S 123 0 E
Burnsville, U.S.A. **80 C8** 44 47N 93 17W
Burnt L., Canada **71 B7** 53 35N 64 4W
Burnt River, Canada **78 B6** 44 41N 78 42W
Burntwood →, Canada **73 B9** 56 8N 96 34W
Burntwood L., Canada **73 B8** 55 22N 100 26W
Burqān, Kuwait **44 D5** 29 0N 47 57 E
Burra, Australia **63 E2** 33 40S 138 55 E
Burray, U.K. **12 C6** 58 51N 2 54W
Burren Junction, Australia **63 E4** 30 7S 148 59 E
Burrinjuck Res., Australia **63 F4** 35 0S 148 36 E
Burro, Serranías del, Mexico **86 B4** 29 0N 102 0W
Burrow Hd., U.K. **12 G4** 54 41N 4 24W
Burruyacú, Argentina **94 B3** 26 30S 64 40W
Burry Port, U.K. **11 F3** 51 41N 4 15W
Bursa, Turkey **21 D13** 40 15N 29 5 E
Burstall, Canada **73 C7** 50 39N 109 54W
Burton, Ohio, U.S.A. **78 E3** 41 28N 81 8W
Burton, S.C., U.S.A. **77 J5** 32 25N 80 45W
Burton, L., Canada **70 B4** 54 45N 78 20W
Burton upon Trent, U.K. **10 E6** 52 48N 1 38W
Buru, Indonesia **37 E7** 3 30S 126 30 E
Burûn, Râs, Egypt **47 D2** 31 14N 33 7 E
Burundi ■, Africa **54 C3** 3 15S 30 0 E
Bururi, Burundi **54 C2** 3 57S 29 37 E
Burutu, Nigeria **50 G7** 5 20N 5 29 E
Burwell, U.S.A. **80 E5** 41 47N 99 8W
Burwick, U.K. **12 C5** 58 45N 2 58W
Bury, U.K. **10 D5** 53 35N 2 17W
Bury St. Edmunds, U.K. **11 E8** 52 15N 0 43 E
Buryatia □, Russia **27 D11** 53 0N 110 0 E
Busan = Pusan, S. Korea **35 G15** 35 5N 129 0 E
Busango Swamp, Zambia **55 E2** 14 15S 25 45 E
Buşayrah, Syria **44 C4** 35 9N 40 26 E
Būshehr, Iran **45 D6** 28 55N 50 55 E
Būshehr □, Iran **45 D6** 28 20N 51 45 E
Bushell, Canada **73 B7** 59 31N 108 45W
Bushenyi, Uganda **54 C3** 0 35S 30 10 E
Bushire = Būshehr, Iran **45 D6** 28 55N 50 55 E
Businga, Dem. Rep. of the Congo **52 D4** 3 16N 20 59 E
Buşra ash Shām, Syria **47 C5** 32 30N 36 25 E
Busselton, Australia **61 F2** 33 42S 115 15 E
Bussum, Neths. **15 B5** 52 16N 5 10 E
Busto Arsízio, Italy **18 D8** 45 37N 8 51 E
Busu Djanoa, Dem. Rep. of the Congo **52 D4** 1 43N 21 23 E
Busuanga I., Phil. **37 B5** 12 10N 120 0 E
Buta, Dem. Rep. of the Congo **54 B1** 2 50N 24 53 E
Butare, Rwanda **54 C2** 2 31S 29 52 E
Butaritari, Kiribati **64 G9** 3 30N 174 0 E
Bute, U.K. **12 F3** 55 48N 5 2W
Bute Inlet, Canada **72 C4** 50 40N 124 53W
Butemba, Uganda **54 B3** 1 9N 31 37 E
Butembo, Dem. Rep. of the Congo **54 B2** 0 9N 29 18 E
Butha Qi, China **33 B7** 48 0N 122 32 E
Butiaba, Uganda **54 B3** 1 50N 31 20 E
Butler, Mo., U.S.A. **80 F7** 38 16N 94 20W
Butler, Pa., U.S.A. **78 F5** 40 52N 79 54W
Buton, Indonesia **37 E6** 5 0S 122 45 E
Butte, Mont., U.S.A. **82 C7** 46 0N 112 32W
Butte, Nebr., U.S.A. **80 D5** 42 58N 98 51W

Canyonville

Butte Creek →, *U.S.A.* **84 F5** 39 12N 121 56W
Butterworth = Gcuwa, *S. Africa* **57 E4** 32 20S 28 11 E
Butterworth, *Malaysia* **39 K3** 5 24N 100 23 E
Buttevant, *Ireland* **13 D3** 52 14N 8 40W
Buttfield, Mt., *Australia* **61 D4** 24 45S 128 9 E
Button B., *Canada* **73 B10** 58 45N 94 23W
Buttonwillow, *U.S.A.* **85 K7** 35 24N 119 28W
Butty Hd., *Australia* **61 F3** 33 54S 121 39 E
Butuan, *Phil.* **37 C7** 8 57N 125 33 E
Butung = Buton, *Indonesia* **37 E6** 5 0S 122 45 E
Buturlinovka, *Russia* **25 D7** 50 50N 40 35 E
Buur Hakaba = Bur Acaba, *Somali Rep.* **46 G3** 3 12N 44 20 E
Buxa Duar, *India* **43 F13** 27 45N 89 35 E
Buxar, *India* **43 G10** 25 34N 83 58 E
Buxtehude, *Germany* **16 B5** 53 28N 9 39 E
Buxton, *U.K.* **10 D6** 53 16N 1 54W
Buy, *Russia* **24 C7** 58 28N 41 28 E
Büyük Menderes →, *Turkey* **21 F12** 37 28N 27 11 E
Büyükçekmece, *Turkey* **21 D13** 41 2N 28 35 E
Buzău, *Romania* **17 F14** 45 10N 26 50 E
Buzău →, *Romania* **17 F14** 45 26N 27 44 E
Buzen, *Japan* **31 H5** 33 35N 131 5 E
Buzi →, *Mozam.* **55 F3** 19 50S 34 43 E
Buzuluk, *Russia* **24 D9** 52 48N 52 12 E
Buzzards B., *U.S.A.* **79 E14** 41 45N 70 37W
Buzzards Bay, *U.S.A.* **79 E14** 41 44N 70 37W
Bwana Mkubwe, *Dem. Rep. of the Congo* **55 E2** 13 8S 28 38 E
Byarezina →, *Belarus* **17 B16** 52 33N 30 14 E
Byaroza, *Belarus* **17 B13** 52 31N 24 51 E
Bydgoszcz, *Poland* **17 B9** 53 10N 18 0 E
Byelarus = Belarus ■, *Europe* **17 B14** 53 30N 27 0 E
Byelorussia = Belarus ■, *Europe* **17 B14** 53 30N 27 0 E
Byers, *U.S.A.* **80 F2** 39 43N 104 14W
Byesville, *U.S.A.* **78 G3** 39 58N 81 32W
Byford, *Australia* **61 F2** 32 15S 116 0 E
Bykhaw, *Belarus* **17 B16** 53 31N 30 14 E
Bykhov = Bykhaw, *Belarus* **17 B16** 53 31N 30 14 E
Bylas, *U.S.A.* **83 K8** 33 8N 110 7W
Bylot, *Canada* **73 B10** 58 25N 94 8W
Bylot I., *Canada* **69 A12** 73 13N 78 34W
Byrd, C., *Antarctica* **5 C17** 69 38S 76 7W
Byrock, *Australia* **63 E4** 30 40S 146 27 E
Byron Bay, *Australia* **63 D5** 28 43S 153 37 E
Byrranga, Gory, *Russia* **27 B11** 75 0N 100 0 E
Byrranga Mts. = Byrranga, Gory, *Russia* **27 B11** 75 0N 100 0 E
Byske, *Sweden* **8 D19** 64 57N 21 11 E
Byske älv →, *Sweden* **8 D19** 64 57N 21 13 E
Bytom, *Poland* **17 C10** 50 25N 18 54 E
Bytów, *Poland* **17 A9** 54 10N 17 30 E
Byumba, *Rwanda* **54 C3** 1 35S 30 4 E

C

Ca →, *Vietnam* **38 C5** 18 45N 105 45 E
Ca Mau, *Vietnam* **39 H5** 9 7N 105 8 E
Ca Mau, Mui, *Vietnam* **39 H5** 8 38N 104 44 E
Ca Na, *Vietnam* **39 G7** 11 20N 108 54 E
Caacupé, *Paraguay* **94 B4** 25 23S 57 5W
Caála, *Angola* **53 G3** 12 46S 15 30 E
Caamano Sd., *Canada* **72 C3** 52 55N 129 25W
Caazapá, *Paraguay* **94 B4** 26 8S 56 19W
Caazapá □, *Paraguay* **95 B4** 26 10S 56 0W
Caballeria, C. de, *Spain* **22 A11** 40 5N 4 5 E
Cabanatuan, *Phil.* **37 A6** 15 30N 120 58 E
Cabano, *Canada* **71 C6** 47 40N 68 56W
Cabazon, *U.S.A.* **85 M10** 33 55N 116 47W
Cabedelo, *Brazil* **93 E12** 7 0S 34 50W
Cabildo, *Chile* **94 C1** 32 30S 71 5W
Cabimas, *Venezuela* **92 A4** 10 23N 71 25W
Cabinda, *Angola* **52 F2** 5 33S 12 11 E
Cabinda □, *Angola* **52 F2** 5 0S 12 30 E
Cabinet Mts., *U.S.A.* **82 C6** 48 0N 115 30W
Cabo Blanco, *Argentina* **96 F3** 47 15S 65 47W
Cabo Frio, *Brazil* **95 A7** 22 51S 42 3W
Cabo Pantoja, *Peru* **92 D3** 1 0S 75 10W
Cabonga, Réservoir, *Canada* **70 C4** 47 20N 76 40W
Cabool, *U.S.A.* **81 G8** 37 7N 92 6W
Caboolture, *Australia* **63 D5** 27 5S 152 58 E
Cabora Bassa Dam = Cahora Bassa, Représa de, *Mozam.* **55 F3** 15 20S 32 50 E
Caborca, *Mexico* **86 A2** 30 40N 112 10W
Cabot, Mt., *U.S.A.* **79 B13** 44 30N 71 25W
Cabot Hd., *Canada* **78 A3** 45 14N 81 17W
Cabot Str., *Canada* **71 C8** 47 15N 59 40W
Cabra, *Spain* **19 D3** 37 30N 4 28W
Cabrera, *Spain* **22 B9** 39 8N 2 57 E
Cabri, *Canada* **73 C7** 50 35N 108 25W
Cabriel →, *Spain* **19 C5** 39 14N 1 3W
Caçador, *Brazil* **95 B5** 26 47S 51 0W
Čačak, *Serbia, Yug.* **21 C9** 43 54N 20 20 E
Caçapava do Sul, *Brazil* **95 C5** 30 30S 53 30W
Cáceres, *Brazil* **92 G7** 16 5S 57 40W
Cáceres, *Spain* **19 C2** 39 26N 6 23W
Cache Bay, *Canada* **70 C4** 46 22N 80 0W
Cache Cr. →, *U.S.A.* **84 G5** 38 42N 121 42W
Cache Creek, *Canada* **72 C4** 50 48N 121 19W
Cachi, *Argentina* **94 B2** 25 5S 66 10W
Cachimbo, Serra do, *Brazil* **93 E7** 9 30S 55 30W
Cachinal de la Sierra, *Chile* **94 A2** 24 58S 69 32W
Cachoeira, *Brazil* **93 F11** 12 30S 39 0W
Cachoeira do Sul, *Brazil* **95 C5** 30 3S 52 53W
Cachoeiro de Itapemirim, *Brazil* **95 A7** 20 51S 41 7W
Cacoal, *Brazil* **92 F6** 11 32S 61 18W
Cacólo, *Angola* **52 G3** 10 9S 19 21 E
Caconda, *Angola* **53 G3** 13 48S 15 8 E
Caddo, *U.S.A.* **81 H6** 34 7N 96 16W
Cader Idris, *U.K.* **11 E4** 52 42N 3 53W
Cadereyta, *Mexico* **86 B5** 25 36N 100 0W
Cadibarrawirracanna, L., *Australia* **63 D2** 28 52S 135 27 E
Cadillac, *U.S.A.* **76 C3** 44 15N 85 24W
Cadiz, *Phil.* **37 B6** 10 57N 123 15 E
Cádiz, *Spain* **19 D2** 36 30N 6 20W
Cadiz, *Calif., U.S.A.* **85 L11** 34 30N 115 28W
Cadiz, *Ohio, U.S.A.* **78 F4** 40 22N 81 0W
Cádiz, G. de, *Spain* **19 D2** 36 40N 7 0W
Cadiz L., *U.S.A.* **83 J6** 34 18N 115 24W
Cadney Park, *Australia* **63 D1** 27 55S 134 3 E
Cadomin, *Canada* **72 C5** 53 2N 117 20W
Cadotte Lake, *Canada* **72 B5** 56 26N 116 23W
Cadoux, *Australia* **61 F2** 30 46S 117 7 E
Caen, *France* **18 B3** 49 10N 0 22W
Caernarfon, *U.K.* **10 D3** 53 8N 4 16W
Caernarfon B., *U.K.* **10 D3** 53 4N 4 40W
Caernarvon = Caernarfon, *U.K.* **10 D3** 53 8N 4 16W
Caerphilly, *U.K.* **11 F4** 51 35N 3 13W
Caerphilly □, *U.K.* **11 F4** 51 37N 3 12W
Caesarea, *Israel* **47 C3** 32 30N 34 53 E
Caetité, *Brazil* **93 F10** 13 50S 42 32W
Cafayate, *Argentina* **94 B2** 26 2S 66 0W
Cafu, *Angola* **56 B2** 16 30S 15 8 E
Cagayan de Oro, *Phil.* **37 C6** 8 30N 124 40 E
Cagayan Is., *Phil.* **37 C5** 9 40N 121 16 E
Cágliari, *Italy* **20 E3** 39 13N 9 7 E
Cágliari, G. di, *Italy* **20 E3** 39 8N 9 11 E
Caguán →, *Colombia* **92 D4** 0 8S 74 18W
Caguas, *Puerto Rico* **89 C6** 18 14N 66 2W
Caha Mts., *Ireland* **13 E2** 51 45N 9 40W
Cahama, *Angola* **56 B1** 16 17S 14 19 E
Caher, *Ireland* **13 D4** 52 22N 7 56W
Caherciveen, *Ireland* **13 E1** 51 56N 10 14W
Cahora Bassa, L. de, *Mozam.* **55 F3** 15 35S 32 0 E
Cahora Bassa, Représa de, *Mozam.* **55 F3** 15 20S 32 50 E
Cahore Pt., *Ireland* **13 D5** 52 33N 6 12W
Cahors, *France* **18 D4** 44 27N 1 27 E
Cahul, *Moldova* **17 F15** 45 50N 28 15 E
Cai Bau, Dao, *Vietnam* **38 B6** 21 10N 107 27 E
Cai Nuoc, *Vietnam* **39 H5** 8 56N 105 1 E
Caia, *Mozam.* **55 F4** 17 51S 35 24 E
Caianda, *Angola* **55 E1** 11 2S 23 31 E
Caibarién, *Cuba* **88 B4** 22 30N 79 30W
Caicara, *Venezuela* **92 B5** 7 38N 66 10W
Caicó, *Brazil* **93 E11** 6 20S 37 0W
Caicos Is., *Turks & Caicos* **89 B5** 21 40N 71 40W
Caicos Passage, *W. Indies* **89 B5** 22 45N 72 45W
Caird Coast, *Antarctica* **5 D1** 75 0S 25 0W
Cairn Gorm, *U.K.* **12 D5** 57 7N 3 39W
Cairngorm Mts., *U.K.* **12 D5** 57 6N 3 42W
Cairnryan, *U.K.* **12 G3** 54 59N 5 1W
Cairns, *Australia* **62 B4** 16 57S 145 45 E
Cairns L., *Canada* **73 C10** 51 42N 94 30W
Cairo = El Qâhira, *Egypt* **51 B12** 30 1N 31 14 E
Cairo, *Ga., U.S.A.* **77 K3** 30 52N 84 13W
Cairo, *Ill., U.S.A.* **81 G10** 37 0N 89 11W
Cairo, *N.Y., U.S.A.* **79 D11** 42 18N 74 0W
Caithness, Ord of, *U.K.* **12 C5** 58 8N 3 36W
Cajamarca, *Peru* **92 E3** 7 5S 78 28W
Cajàzeiras, *Brazil* **93 E11** 6 52S 38 30W
Cala d'Or, *Spain* **22 B10** 39 23N 3 14 E
Cala en Porter, *Spain* **22 B11** 39 52N 4 8 E
Cala Figuera, C. de, *Spain* **22 B9** 39 27N 2 31 E
Cala Forcat, *Spain* **22 B10** 40 0N 3 47 E
Cala Major, *Spain* **22 B9** 39 33N 2 37 E
Cala Mezquida = Sa Mesquida, *Spain* **22 B11** 39 55N 4 16 E
Cala Millor, *Spain* **22 B10** 39 35N 3 22 E
Cala Ratjada, *Spain* **22 B10** 39 43N 3 27 E
Cala Santa Galdana, *Spain* **22 B10** 39 56N 3 58 E
Calabar, *Nigeria* **50 H7** 4 57N 8 20 E
Calabogie, *Canada* **79 A8** 45 18N 76 43W
Calabozo, *Venezuela* **92 B5** 9 0N 67 28W
Calábria □, *Italy* **20 E7** 39 0N 16 30 E
Calafate, *Argentina* **96 G2** 50 19S 72 15W
Calahorra, *Spain* **19 A5** 42 18N 1 59W
Calais, *France* **18 A4** 50 57N 1 56 E
Calais, *U.S.A.* **77 C12** 45 11N 67 17W
Calalaste, Cord. de, *Argentina* **94 B2** 25 0S 67 0W
Calama, *Brazil* **92 E6** 8 0S 62 50W
Calama, *Chile* **94 A2** 22 30S 68 55W
Calamar, *Colombia* **92 A4** 10 15N 74 55W
Calamian Group, *Phil.* **37 B5** 11 50N 119 55 E
Calamocha, *Spain* **19 B5** 40 50N 1 17W
Calang, *Indonesia* **36 D1** 4 37N 95 37 E
Calapan, *Phil.* **37 B6** 13 25N 121 7 E
Călăraşi, *Romania* **17 F14** 44 12N 27 20 E
Calatayud, *Spain* **19 B5** 41 20N 1 40W
Calauag, *Phil.* **37 B6** 13 55N 122 15 E
Calavite, C., *Phil.* **37 B6** 13 26N 120 20 E
Calbayog, *Phil.* **37 B6** 12 4N 124 38 E
Calca, *Peru* **92 F4** 13 22S 72 0W
Calcasieu L., *U.S.A.* **81 L8** 29 55N 93 18W
Calcutta = Kolkata, *India* **43 H13** 22 36N 88 24 E
Calcutta, *U.S.A.* **78 F4** 40 40N 80 34W
Caldas da Rainha, *Portugal* **19 C1** 39 24N 9 8W
Calder →, *U.K.* **10 D6** 53 44N 1 22W
Caldera, *Chile* **94 B1** 27 5S 70 55W
Caldwell, *Idaho, U.S.A.* **82 E5** 43 40N 116 41W
Caldwell, *Kans., U.S.A.* **81 G6** 37 2N 97 37W
Caldwell, *Tex., U.S.A.* **81 K6** 30 32N 96 42W
Caledon, *S. Africa* **56 E2** 34 14S 19 26 E
Caledon →, *S. Africa* **56 E4** 30 31S 26 5 E
Caledon B., *Australia* **62 A2** 12 45S 137 0 E
Caledonia, *Canada* **78 C5** 43 7N 79 58W
Caledonia, *U.S.A.* **78 D7** 42 58N 77 51W
Calemba, *Angola* **56 B2** 16 0S 15 44 E
Calen, *Australia* **62 C4** 20 56S 148 48 E
Caletones, *Chile* **94 C1** 34 6S 70 27W
Calexico, *U.S.A.* **85 N11** 32 40N 115 30W
Calf of Man, *U.K.* **10 C3** 54 3N 4 48W
Calgary, *Canada* **72 C6** 51 0N 114 10W
Calheta, *Madeira* **22 D2** 32 44N 17 11W
Calhoun, *U.S.A.* **77 H3** 34 30N 84 57W
Cali, *Colombia* **92 C3** 3 25N 76 35W
Calicut, *India* **40 P9** 11 15N 75 43 E
Caliente, *U.S.A.* **83 H6** 37 37N 114 31W
California, *Mo., U.S.A.* **80 F8** 38 38N 92 34W
California, *Pa., U.S.A.* **78 F5** 40 4N 79 54W
California □, *U.S.A.* **84 H7** 37 30N 119 30W
California, Baja, *Mexico* **86 A1** 32 10N 115 12W
California, Baja, T.N. = Baja California □, *Mexico* **86 B2** 30 0N 115 0W
California, Baja, T.S. = Baja California Sur □, *Mexico* **86 B2** 25 50N 111 50W
California, G. de, *Mexico* **86 B2** 27 0N 111 0W
California City, *U.S.A.* **85 K9** 35 10N 117 55W
California Hot Springs, *U.S.A.* **85 K8** 35 51N 118 41W
Calingasta, *Argentina* **94 C2** 31 15S 69 30W
Calipatria, *U.S.A.* **85 M11** 33 8N 115 31W
Calistoga, *U.S.A.* **84 G4** 38 35N 122 35W
Calitzdorp, *S. Africa* **56 E3** 33 33S 21 42 E
Callabonna, L., *Australia* **63 D3** 29 40S 140 5 E
Callan, *Ireland* **13 D4** 52 32N 7 24W
Callander, *U.K.* **12 E4** 56 15N 4 13W
Callao, *Peru* **92 F3** 12 0S 77 0W
Calles, *Mexico* **87 C5** 23 2N 98 42W
Callicoon, *U.S.A.* **79 E9** 41 46N 75 3W
Calling Lake, *Canada* **72 B6** 55 15N 113 12W
Calliope, *Australia* **62 C5** 24 0S 151 16 E
Calne, *U.K.* **11 F6** 51 26N 2 0W
Calola, *Angola* **56 B2** 16 25S 17 48 E
Caloundra, *Australia* **63 D5** 26 45S 153 10 E
Calpella, *U.S.A.* **84 F3** 39 14N 123 12W
Calpine, *U.S.A.* **84 F6** 39 40N 120 27W
Calstock, *Canada* **70 C3** 49 47N 84 9W
Caltagirone, *Italy* **20 F6** 37 14N 14 31 E
Caltanissetta, *Italy* **20 F6** 37 29N 14 4 E
Calulo, *Angola* **52 G2** 10 1S 14 56 E
Calvert →, *Australia* **62 B2** 16 17S 137 44 E
Calvert I., *Canada* **72 C3** 51 30N 128 0W
Calvert Ra., *Australia* **60 D3** 24 0S 122 30 E
Calvi, *France* **18 E8** 42 34N 8 45 E
Calvià, *Spain* **19 C7** 39 34N 2 31 E
Calvillo, *Mexico* **86 C4** 21 51N 102 43W
Calvinia, *S. Africa* **56 E2** 31 28S 19 45 E
Calwa, *U.S.A.* **84 J7** 36 42N 119 46W
Cam →, *U.K.* **11 E8** 52 21N 0 16 E
Cam Lam, *Vietnam* **39 G7** 11 54N 109 10 E
Cam Pha, *Vietnam* **38 B6** 21 7N 107 18 E
Cam Ranh, *Vietnam* **39 G7** 11 54N 109 12 E
Cam Xuyen, *Vietnam* **38 C6** 18 15N 106 0 E
Camabatela, *Angola* **52 F3** 8 20S 15 26 E
Camacha, *Madeira* **22 D3** 32 41N 16 49W
Camacho, *Mexico* **86 C4** 24 25N 102 18W
Camacupa, *Angola* **53 G3** 11 58S 17 22 E
Camagüey, *Cuba* **88 B4** 21 20N 78 0W
Camaná, *Peru* **92 G4** 16 30S 72 50W
Camanche Reservoir, *U.S.A.* **84 G6** 38 14N 121 1W
Camaquã, *Brazil* **95 C5** 30 51S 51 49W
Camaquã →, *Brazil* **95 C5** 31 17S 51 47W
Câmara de Lobos, *Madeira* **22 D3** 32 39N 16 59W
Camargo, *Mexico* **87 B5** 26 19N 98 50W
Camargue, *France* **18 E6** 43 34N 4 34 E
Camarillo, *U.S.A.* **85 L7** 34 13N 119 2W
Camarón, C., *Honduras* **88 C2** 16 0N 85 5W
Camarones, *Argentina* **96 E3** 44 50S 65 40W
Camas, *U.S.A.* **84 E4** 45 35N 122 24W
Camas Valley, *U.S.A.* **82 E2** 43 2N 123 40W
Camballin, *Australia* **60 C3** 17 59S 124 12 E
Cambará, *Brazil* **95 A5** 23 2S 50 5W
Cambay = Khambhat, *India* **42 H5** 22 23N 72 33 E
Cambay, G. of = Khambhat, G. of, *India* **40 J8** 20 45N 72 30 E
Cambodia ■, *Asia* **38 F5** 12 15N 105 0 E
Camborne, *U.K.* **11 G2** 50 12N 5 19W
Cambrai, *France* **18 A5** 50 11N 3 14 E
Cambria, *U.S.A.* **84 K5** 35 34N 121 5W
Cambrian Mts., *U.K.* **11 E4** 52 3N 3 57W
Cambridge, *Canada* **78 C4** 43 23N 80 15W
Cambridge, *Jamaica* **88 C4** 18 18N 77 54W
Cambridge, *N.Z.* **59 G5** 37 54S 175 29 E
Cambridge, *U.K.* **11 E8** 52 12N 0 8 E
Cambridge, *Mass., U.S.A.* **79 D13** 42 22N 71 6W
Cambridge, *Minn., U.S.A.* **80 C8** 45 34N 93 13W
Cambridge, *N.Y., U.S.A.* **79 C11** 43 2N 73 22W
Cambridge, *Nebr., U.S.A.* **80 E4** 40 17N 100 10W
Cambridge, *Ohio, U.S.A.* **78 F3** 40 2N 81 35W
Cambridge Bay = Ikaluktutiak, *Canada* **68 B9** 69 10N 105 0W
Cambridge G., *Australia* **60 B4** 14 55S 128 15 E
Cambridge Springs, *U.S.A.* **78 E4** 41 48N 80 4W
Cambridgeshire □, *U.K.* **11 E7** 52 25N 0 7W
Cambuci, *Brazil* **95 A7** 21 35S 41 55W
Cambundi-Catembo, *Angola* **52 G3** 10 10S 17 35 E
Camden, *Ala., U.S.A.* **77 K2** 31 59N 87 17W
Camden, *Ark., U.S.A.* **81 J8** 33 35N 92 50W
Camden, *Maine, U.S.A.* **77 C11** 44 13N 69 4W
Camden, *N.J., U.S.A.* **79 G9** 39 56N 75 7W
Camden, *N.Y., U.S.A.* **79 C9** 43 20N 75 45W
Camden, *S.C., U.S.A.* **77 H5** 34 16N 80 36W
Camden Sd., *Australia* **60 C3** 15 27S 124 25 E
Camdenton, *U.S.A.* **81 F8** 38 1N 92 45W
Cameron, *Ariz., U.S.A.* **83 J8** 35 53N 111 25W
Cameron, *La., U.S.A.* **81 L8** 29 48N 93 20W
Cameron, *Mo., U.S.A.* **80 F7** 39 44N 94 14W
Cameron, *Tex., U.S.A.* **81 K6** 30 51N 96 59W
Cameron Highlands, *Malaysia* **39 K3** 4 27N 101 22 E
Cameron Hills, *Canada* **72 B5** 59 48N 118 0W
Cameroon ■, *Africa* **52 C2** 6 0N 12 30 E
Cameroun, Mt., *Cameroon* **52 D1** 4 13N 9 10 E
Cametá, *Brazil* **93 D9** 2 12S 49 30W
Camiguin I., *Phil.* **37 C6** 18 56N 121 55 E
Camilla, *U.S.A.* **77 K3** 31 14N 84 12W
Caminha, *Portugal* **19 B1** 41 50N 8 50W
Camino, *U.S.A.* **84 G6** 38 44N 120 41W
Camira Creek, *Australia* **63 D5** 29 15S 152 58 E
Cammal, *U.S.A.* **78 E7** 41 24N 77 28W
Camocim, *Brazil* **93 D10** 2 55S 40 50W
Camooweal, *Australia* **62 B2** 19 56S 138 7 E
Camopi, *Fr. Guiana* **93 C8** 3 12N 52 17W
Camp Borden, *Canada* **78 B5** 44 18N 79 56W
Camp Hill, *U.S.A.* **78 F8** 40 14N 76 55W
Camp Nelson, *U.S.A.* **85 J8** 36 8N 118 39W
Camp Pendleton, *U.S.A.* **85 M9** 33 16N 117 23W
Camp Verde, *U.S.A.* **83 J8** 34 34N 111 51W
Camp Wood, *U.S.A.* **81 L5** 29 40N 100 1W
Campana, *Argentina* **94 C4** 34 10S 58 55W
Campana, I., *Chile* **96 F1** 48 20S 75 20W
Campanário, *Madeira* **22 D2** 32 39N 17 2W
Campánia □, *Italy* **20 D6** 41 0N 14 30 E
Campbell, *S. Africa* **56 D3** 28 48S 23 44 E
Campbell, *Calif., U.S.A.* **84 H5** 37 17N 121 57W
Campbell, *Ohio, U.S.A.* **78 E4** 41 5N 80 37W
Campbell I., *Pac. Oc.* **64 N8** 52 30S 169 0 E
Campbell L., *Canada* **73 A7** 63 14N 106 55W
Campbell River, *Canada* **72 C3** 50 5N 125 20W
Campbell Town, *Australia* **62 G4** 41 52S 147 30 E
Campbellford, *Canada* **78 B7** 44 18N 77 48W
Campbellpur, *Pakistan* **42 C5** 33 46N 72 26 E
Campbellsville, *U.S.A.* **76 G3** 37 21N 85 20W
Campbellton, *Canada* **71 C6** 47 57N 66 43W
Campbelltown, *Australia* **63 E5** 34 4S 150 49 E
Campbeltown, *U.K.* **12 F3** 55 26N 5 36W
Campeche, *Mexico* **87 D6** 19 50N 90 32W
Campeche □, *Mexico* **87 D6** 19 50N 90 32W
Campeche, Golfo de, *Mexico* **87 D6** 19 30N 93 0W
Camperdown, *Australia* **63 F3** 38 14S 143 9 E
Camperville, *Canada* **73 C8** 51 59N 100 9W
Câmpina, *Romania* **17 F13** 45 10N 25 45 E
Campina Grande, *Brazil* **93 E11** 7 20S 35 47W
Campinas, *Brazil* **95 A6** 22 50S 47 0W
Campo Grande, *Brazil* **93 H8** 20 25S 54 40W
Campo Maíor, *Brazil* **93 D10** 4 50S 42 12W
Campo Mourão, *Brazil* **95 A5** 24 3S 52 22W
Campobasso, *Italy* **20 D6** 41 34N 14 39 E
Campos, *Brazil* **95 A7** 21 50S 41 20W
Campos Belos, *Brazil* **93 F9** 13 10S 47 3W
Campos del Port, *Spain* **22 B10** 39 26N 3 1 E
Campos Novos, *Brazil* **95 B5** 27 21S 51 50W
Camptonville, *U.S.A.* **84 F5** 39 27N 121 3W
Camptown, *U.S.A.* **79 E8** 41 44N 76 14W
Câmpulung, *Romania* **17 F13** 45 17N 25 3 E
Camrose, *Canada* **72 C6** 53 0N 112 50W
Camsell Portage, *Canada* **73 B7** 59 37N 109 15W
Çan, *Turkey* **21 D12** 40 2N 27 3 E
Can Clavo, *Spain* **22 C7** 38 57N 1 27 E
Can Creu, *Spain* **22 C7** 38 58N 1 28 E
Can Gio, *Vietnam* **39 G6** 10 25N 106 58 E
Can Tho, *Vietnam* **39 G5** 10 2N 105 46 E
Canaan, *U.S.A.* **79 D11** 42 2N 73 20W
Canada ■, *N. Amer.* **68 C10** 60 0N 100 0W
Cañada de Gómez, *Argentina* **94 C3** 32 40S 61 30W
Canadian, *U.S.A.* **81 H4** 35 55N 100 23W
Canadian →, *U.S.A.* **81 H7** 35 28N 95 3W
Canajoharie, *U.S.A.* **79 D10** 42 54N 74 35W
Çanakkale, *Turkey* **21 D12** 40 8N 26 24 E
Çanakkale Boğazı, *Turkey* **21 D12** 40 17N 26 32 E
Canal Flats, *Canada* **72 C5** 50 10N 115 48W
Canalejas, *Argentina* **94 D2** 35 15S 66 34W
Canals, *Argentina* **94 C3** 33 35S 62 53W
Canandaigua, *U.S.A.* **78 D7** 42 54N 77 17W
Canandaigua L., *U.S.A.* **78 D7** 42 47N 77 19W
Cananea, *Mexico* **86 A2** 31 0N 110 20W
Canarias, Is., *Atl. Oc.* **22 F4** 28 30N 16 0W
Canarreos, Arch. de los, *Cuba* **88 B3** 21 35N 81 40W
Canary Is. = Canarias, Is., *Atl. Oc.* **22 F4** 28 30N 16 0W
Canaseraga, *U.S.A.* **78 D7** 42 27N 77 45W
Canatlán, *Mexico* **86 C4** 24 31N 104 47W
Canaveral, C., *U.S.A.* **77 L5** 28 27N 80 32W
Canavieiras, *Brazil* **93 G11** 15 39S 39 0W
Canberra, *Australia* **63 F4** 35 15S 149 8 E
Canby, *Calif., U.S.A.* **82 F3** 41 27N 120 52W
Canby, *Minn., U.S.A.* **80 C6** 44 43N 96 16W
Canby, *Oreg., U.S.A.* **84 E4** 45 16N 122 42W
Cancún, *Mexico* **87 C7** 21 8N 86 44W
Candelaria, *Argentina* **95 B4** 27 29S 55 44W
Candelaria, *Canary Is.* **22 F3** 28 22N 16 22W
Candelo, *Australia* **63 F4** 36 47S 149 43 E
Candia = Iráklion, *Greece* **23 D7** 35 20N 25 12 E
Candle L., *Canada* **73 C7** 53 50N 105 18W
Candlemas I., *Antarctica* **5 B1** 57 3S 26 40W
Cando, *U.S.A.* **80 A5** 48 32N 99 12W
Canea = Khaniá, *Greece* **23 D6** 35 30N 24 4 E
Canelones, *Uruguay* **95 C4** 34 32S 56 17W
Cañete, *Chile* **94 D1** 37 50S 73 30W
Cañete, *Peru* **92 F3** 13 8S 76 30W
Cangas de Narcea, *Spain* **19 A2** 43 10N 6 32W
Canguaretama, *Brazil* **93 E11** 6 20S 35 5W
Canguçu, *Brazil* **95 C5** 31 22S 52 43W
Canguçu, Serra do, *Brazil* **95 C5** 31 20S 52 40W
Cangzhou, *China* **34 E9** 38 19N 116 52 E
Caniapiscau →, *Canada* **71 A6** 56 40N 69 30W
Caniapiscau, Rés. de, *Canada* **71 B6** 54 10N 69 55W
Canicattì, *Italy* **20 F5** 37 21N 13 51 E
Canim Lake, *Canada* **72 C4** 51 47N 120 54W
Canindeyu □, *Paraguay* **95 A5** 24 10S 55 0W
Canisteo, *U.S.A.* **78 D7** 42 16N 77 36W
Canisteo →, *U.S.A.* **78 D7** 42 7N 77 8W
Cañitas, *Mexico* **86 C4** 23 36N 102 43W
Çankırı, *Turkey* **25 F5** 40 40N 33 37 E
Cankuzo, *Burundi* **54 C3** 3 10S 30 31 E
Canmore, *Canada* **72 C5** 51 7N 115 18W
Cann River, *Australia* **63 F4** 37 35S 149 7 E
Canna, *U.K.* **12 D2** 57 3N 6 33W
Cannanore, *India* **40 P9** 11 53N 75 27 E
Cannes, *France* **18 E7** 43 32N 7 1 E
Canning Town = Port Canning, *India* **43 H13** 22 23N 88 40 E
Cannington, *Canada* **78 B5** 44 20N 79 2W
Cannock, *U.K.* **11 E5** 52 41N 2 1W
Cannon Ball →, *U.S.A.* **80 B4** 46 20N 100 38W
Cannondale Mt., *Australia* **62 D4** 25 13S 148 57 E
Cannonsville Reservoir, *U.S.A.* **79 D9** 42 4N 75 22W
Cannonvale, *Australia* **62 C4** 20 17S 148 43 E
Canoas, *Brazil* **95 B5** 29 56S 51 11W
Canoe L., *Canada* **73 B7** 55 10N 108 15W
Canon City, *U.S.A.* **80 F2** 38 27N 105 14W
Canora, *Canada* **73 C8** 51 40N 102 30W
Canowindra, *Australia* **63 E4** 33 35S 148 38 E
Canso, *Canada* **71 C7** 45 20N 61 0W
Cantabria □, *Spain* **19 A4** 43 10N 4 0W
Cantabrian Mts. = Cantábrica, Cordillera, *Spain* **19 A3** 43 0N 5 10W
Cantábrica, Cordillera, *Spain* **19 A3** 43 0N 5 10W
Cantal, Plomb du, *France* **18 D5** 45 3N 2 45 E
Canterbury, *Australia* **62 D3** 25 23S 141 53 E
Canterbury, *U.K.* **11 F9** 51 16N 1 6 E
Canterbury Bight, *N.Z.* **59 L3** 44 16S 171 55 E
Canterbury Plains, *N.Z.* **59 K3** 43 55S 171 22 E
Cantil, *U.S.A.* **85 K9** 35 18N 117 58W
Canton = Guangzhou, *China* **33 D6** 23 5N 113 10 E
Canton, *Ga., U.S.A.* **77 H3** 34 14N 84 29W
Canton, *Ill., U.S.A.* **80 E9** 40 33N 90 2W
Canton, *Miss., U.S.A.* **81 J9** 32 37N 90 2W
Canton, *Mo., U.S.A.* **80 E9** 40 8N 91 32W
Canton, *N.Y., U.S.A.* **79 B9** 44 36N 75 10W
Canton, *Ohio, U.S.A.* **78 F3** 40 48N 81 23W
Canton, *Pa., U.S.A.* **78 E8** 41 39N 76 51W
Canton, *S. Dak., U.S.A.* **80 D6** 43 18N 96 35W
Canton L., *U.S.A.* **81 G5** 36 6N 98 35W
Canudos, *Brazil* **92 E7** 7 13S 58 5W
Canumã →, *Brazil* **92 D7** 3 55S 59 10W
Canutama, *Brazil* **92 E6** 6 30S 64 20W
Canutillo, *U.S.A.* **83 L10** 31 55N 106 36W
Canvey, *U.K.* **11 F8** 51 31N 0 37 E
Canyon, *U.S.A.* **81 H4** 34 59N 101 55W
Canyonlands Nat. Park, *U.S.A.* **83 G9** 38 15N 110 0W
Canyonville, *U.S.A.* **82 E2** 42 56N 123 17W

Cao Bang

Cao Bang, Vietnam 38 A6 22 40N 106 15 E
Cao He →, China 35 D13 40 10N 124 32 E
Cao Lanh, Vietnam 39 G5 10 27N 105 38 E
Cao Xian, China 34 G8 34 50N 115 35 E
Cap-aux-Meules, Canada 71 C7 47 23N 61 52W
Cap-Chat, Canada 71 C6 49 6N 66 40W
Cap-de-la-Madeleine, Canada 70 C5 46 22N 72 31W
Cap-Haïtien, Haiti 89 C5 19 40N 72 20W
Capac, U.S.A. 78 C2 43 1N 82 56W
Capanaparo →, Venezuela 92 B5 7 1N 67 7W
Cape →, Australia 62 C4 20 59S 146 51 E
Cape Barren I., Australia 62 G4 40 25S 148 15 E
Cape Breton Highlands Nat. Park, Canada 71 C7 46 50N 60 40W
Cape Breton I., Canada 71 C7 46 0N 60 30W
Cape Charles, U.S.A. 76 G8 37 16N 76 1W
Cape Coast, Ghana 50 G5 5 5N 1 15W
Cape Coral, U.S.A. 77 M5 26 33N 81 57W
Cape Dorset, Canada 69 B12 64 14N 76 32W
Cape Fear →, U.S.A. 77 H6 33 53N 78 1W
Cape Girardeau, U.S.A. 81 G10 37 19N 89 32W
Cape May, U.S.A. 76 F8 38 56N 74 56W
Cape May Point, U.S.A. 76 F8 38 56N 74 58W
Cape Province, S. Africa 53 L3 32 0S 23 0 E
Cape Tormentine, Canada 71 C7 46 8N 63 47W
Cape Town, S. Africa 56 E2 33 55S 18 22 E
Cape Verde Is. ■, Atl. Oc. 49 E1 16 0N 24 0W
Cape Vincent, U.S.A. 79 B8 44 8N 76 20W
Cape York Peninsula, Australia 62 A3 12 0S 142 30 E
Capela, Brazil 93 F11 10 30S 37 0W
Capella, Australia 62 C4 23 2S 148 1 E
Capim →, Brazil 93 D9 1 40S 47 47W
Capitan, U.S.A. 83 K11 33 35N 105 35W
Capitol Reef Nat. Park, U.S.A. 83 G8 38 15N 111 10W
Capitola, U.S.A. 84 J5 36 59N 121 57W
Capoche →, Mozam. 55 F3 15 35S 33 0 E
Capraia, Italy 18 E8 43 2N 9 50 E
Capreol, Canada 70 C3 46 43N 80 56W
Capri, Italy 20 D6 40 33N 14 14 E
Capricorn Group, Australia 62 C5 23 30S 151 55 E
Capricorn Ra., Australia 60 D2 23 20S 116 50 E
Caprivi Strip, Namibia 56 B3 18 0S 23 0 E
Captain's Flat, Australia 63 F4 35 35S 149 27 E
Caquetá →, Colombia 92 D5 1 15S 69 15W
Caracal, Romania 17 F13 44 8N 24 22 E
Caracas, Venezuela 92 A5 10 30N 66 55W
Caracol, Mato Grosso do Sul, Brazil 94 A4 22 18S 57 1W
Caracol, Piauí, Brazil 93 E10 9 15S 43 22W
Carajas, Brazil 93 E8 6 5S 50 23W
Carajás, Serra dos, Brazil 93 E8 6 0S 51 30W
Carangola, Brazil 95 A7 20 44S 42 5W
Caransebeş, Romania 17 F12 45 28N 22 18 E
Caraquet, Canada 71 C6 47 48N 64 57W
Caras, Peru 92 E3 9 3S 77 47W
Caratasca, L., Honduras 88 C3 15 20N 83 40W
Caratinga, Brazil 93 G10 19 50S 42 10W
Caraúbas, Brazil 93 E11 5 43S 37 33W
Caravaca = Caravaca de la Cruz, Spain 19 C5 38 8N 1 52W
Caravaca de la Cruz, Spain 19 C5 38 8N 1 52W
Caravelas, Brazil 93 G11 17 45S 39 15W
Caraveli, Peru 92 G4 15 45S 73 25W
Caràzinho, Brazil 95 B5 28 16S 52 46W
Carballo, Spain 19 A1 43 13N 8 41W
Carberry, Canada 73 D9 49 50N 99 25W
Carbó, Mexico 86 B2 29 42N 110 58W
Carbonara, C., Italy 20 E3 39 6N 9 31 E
Carbondale, Colo., U.S.A. 82 G10 39 24N 107 13W
Carbondale, Ill., U.S.A. 81 G10 37 44N 89 13W
Carbondale, Pa., U.S.A. 79 E9 41 35N 75 30W
Carbonear, Canada 71 C9 47 42N 53 13W
Carbónia, Italy 20 E3 39 10N 8 30 E
Carcajou, Canada 72 B5 57 47N 117 6W
Carcarana →, Argentina 94 C3 32 27S 60 48W
Carcasse, C., Haiti 89 C5 18 30N 74 28W
Carcassonne, France 18 E5 43 13N 2 20 E
Carcross, Canada 72 A2 60 13N 134 45W
Cardamon Hills, India 40 Q10 9 30N 77 15 E
Cárdenas, Cuba 88 B3 23 0N 81 30W
Cárdenas, San Luis Potosí, Mexico 87 C5 22 0N 99 41W
Cárdenas, Tabasco, Mexico 87 D6 17 59N 93 21W
Cardiff, U.K. 11 F4 51 29N 3 10W
Cardiff □, U.K. 11 F4 51 31N 3 12W
Cardiff-by-the-Sea, U.S.A. 85 M9 33 1N 117 17W
Cardigan, U.K. 11 E3 52 5N 4 40W
Cardigan B., U.K. 11 E3 52 30N 4 30W
Cardinal, Canada 79 B9 44 47N 75 23W
Cardona, Uruguay 94 C4 33 53S 57 18W
Cardoso, Ilha do, Brazil 95 B5 25 8S 47 58W
Cardston, Canada 72 D6 49 15N 113 20W
Cardwell, Australia 62 B4 18 14S 146 2 E
Careen L., Canada 73 B7 57 0N 108 11W
Carei, Romania 17 E12 47 40N 22 29 E
Careme = Ciremai, Indonesia 37 G13 6 55S 108 27 E
Carey, U.S.A. 82 E7 43 19N 113 57W
Carey, L., Australia 61 E3 29 0S 122 15 E
Carey L., Canada 73 A8 62 12N 102 55W
Carhué, Argentina 94 D3 37 10S 62 50W
Caria, Turkey 21 F13 37 20N 28 10 E
Cariacica, Brazil 93 H10 20 16S 40 25W
Caribbean Sea, W. Indies 89 D5 15 0N 75 0W
Cariboo Mts., Canada 72 C4 53 0N 121 0W
Caribou, U.S.A. 77 B12 46 52N 68 1W
Caribou →, Man., Canada 73 B10 59 20N 94 44W
Caribou →, N.W.T., Canada 72 A3 61 27N 125 45W
Caribou I., Canada 70 C2 47 22N 85 49W
Caribou Is., Canada 72 A6 61 55N 113 15W
Caribou L., Man., Canada 73 B9 59 21N 96 10W
Caribou L., Ont., Canada 70 B2 50 25N 89 5W
Caribou Mts., Canada 72 B5 59 12N 115 40W
Carichic, Mexico 86 B3 27 56N 107 3W
Carillo, Mexico 86 B4 26 50N 103 55W
Carinda, Australia 63 E4 30 28S 147 41 E
Carinhanha, Brazil 93 F10 14 15S 44 46W
Carinhanha →, Brazil 93 F10 14 20S 43 47W
Carinthia = Kärnten □, Austria 16 E8 46 52N 13 30 E
Caripito, Venezuela 92 A6 10 8N 63 6W
Carleton, Mt., Canada 71 C6 47 23N 66 53W
Carleton Place, Canada 79 A8 45 8N 76 9W
Carletonville, S. Africa 56 D4 26 23S 27 22 E
Carlin, U.S.A. 82 F5 40 43N 116 7W
Carlingford L., U.K. 13 B5 54 3N 6 9W
Carlinville, U.S.A. 80 F10 39 17N 89 53W
Carlisle, U.K. 10 C5 54 54N 2 56W
Carlisle, U.S.A. 78 F7 40 12N 77 12W
Carlos Casares, Argentina 94 D3 35 32S 61 20W
Carlos Tejedor, Argentina 94 D3 35 25S 62 25W
Carlow, Ireland 13 D5 52 50N 6 56W
Carlow □, Ireland 13 D5 52 43N 6 50W
Carlsbad, Calif., U.S.A. 85 M9 33 10N 117 21W
Carlsbad, N. Mex., U.S.A. 81 J2 32 25N 104 14W
Carlsbad Caverns Nat. Park, U.S.A. 81 J2 32 10N 104 35W
Carluke, U.K. 12 F5 55 45N 3 50W
Carlyle, Canada 73 D8 49 40N 102 20W
Carmacks, Canada 68 B6 62 5N 136 16W
Carman, Canada 73 D9 49 30N 98 0W
Carmarthen, U.K. 11 F3 51 52N 4 19W
Carmarthen B., U.K. 11 F3 51 40N 4 30W
Carmarthenshire □, U.K. 11 F3 51 55N 4 13W
Carmaux, France 18 D5 44 3N 2 10 E
Carmel, U.S.A. 79 E11 41 26N 73 41W
Carmel-by-the-Sea, U.S.A. 84 J5 36 33N 121 55W
Carmel Valley, U.S.A. 84 J5 36 29N 121 43W
Carmelo, Uruguay 94 C4 34 0S 58 20W
Carmen, Colombia 92 B3 9 43N 75 8W
Carmen, Paraguay 95 B4 27 13S 56 12W
Carmen →, Mexico 86 A3 30 42N 106 29W
Carmen, I., Mexico 86 B2 26 0N 111 20W
Carmen de Patagones, Argentina 96 E4 40 50S 63 0W
Carmensa, Argentina 94 D2 35 15S 67 40W
Carmi, Canada 72 D5 49 36N 119 8W
Carmi, U.S.A. 76 F1 38 5N 88 10W
Carmichael, U.S.A. 84 G5 38 38N 121 19W
Carmila, Australia 62 C4 21 55S 149 24 E
Carmona, Costa Rica 88 E2 10 0N 85 15W
Carmona, Spain 19 D3 37 28N 5 42W
Carn Ban, U.K. 12 D4 57 7N 4 15W
Carn Eige, U.K. 12 D3 57 17N 5 8W
Carnac, France 18 C2 47 35N 3 6W
Carnamah, Australia 61 E2 29 41S 115 53 E
Carnarvon, Australia 61 D1 24 51S 113 42 E
Carnarvon, S. Africa 56 E3 30 56S 22 8 E
Carnarvon Ra., Queens., Australia 62 D4 25 15S 148 30 E
Carnarvon Ra., W. Austral., Australia 61 E3 25 20S 120 45 E
Carnation, U.S.A. 84 C5 47 39N 121 55W
Carndonagh, Ireland 13 A4 55 16N 7 15W
Carnduff, Canada 73 D8 49 10N 101 50W
Carnegie, U.S.A. 78 F4 40 24N 80 5W
Carnegie, L., Australia 61 E3 26 5S 122 30 E
Carnic Alps = Karnische Alpen, Europe 16 E7 46 36N 13 0 E
Carniche Alpi = Karnische Alpen, Europe 16 E7 46 36N 13 0 E
Carnot, C.A.R. 52 D3 4 59N 15 56 E
Carnot, C., Australia 63 E2 34 57S 135 38 E
Carnot B., Australia 60 C3 17 20S 122 15 E
Carnoustie, U.K. 12 E6 56 30N 2 42W
Carnsore Pt., Ireland 13 D5 52 10N 6 22W
Caro, U.S.A. 76 D4 43 29N 83 24W
Carol City, U.S.A. 77 N5 25 56N 80 16W
Carolina, Brazil 93 E9 7 10S 47 30W
Carolina, Puerto Rico 89 C6 18 23N 65 58W
Carolina, S. Africa 57 D5 26 5S 30 6 E
Caroline I., Kiribati 65 H12 9 58S 150 13W
Caroline Is., Micronesia 28 J17 8 0N 150 0 E
Caroni →, Venezuela 92 B6 8 21N 62 43W
Caronie = Nébrodi, Monti, Italy 20 F6 37 54N 14 35 E
Caroona, Australia 63 E5 31 24S 150 26 E
Carpathians, Europe 17 D11 49 30N 21 0 E
Carpaţii Meridionali, Romania 17 F13 45 30N 25 0 E
Carpentaria, G. of, Australia 62 A2 14 0S 139 0 E
Carpentras, France 18 D6 44 3N 5 2 E
Carpi, Italy 20 B4 44 47N 10 53 E
Carpinteria, U.S.A. 85 L7 34 24N 119 31W
Carr Boyd Ra., Australia 60 C4 16 15S 128 35 E
Carrabelle, U.S.A. 77 L3 29 51N 84 40W
Carranza, Presa V., Mexico 86 B4 27 20N 100 50W
Carrara, Italy 18 D9 44 5N 10 6 E
Carrauntoohill, Ireland 13 D2 52 0N 9 45W
Carrick-on-Shannon, Ireland 13 C3 53 57N 8 5W
Carrick-on-Suir, Ireland 13 D4 52 21N 7 24W
Carrickfergus, U.K. 13 B6 54 43N 5 49W
Carrickmacross, Ireland 13 C5 53 59N 6 43W
Carrieton, Australia 63 E2 32 25S 138 31 E
Carrington, U.S.A. 80 B5 47 27N 99 8W
Carrizal Bajo, Chile 94 B1 28 5S 71 20W
Carrizalillo, Chile 94 B1 29 5S 71 30W
Carrizo Cr. →, U.S.A. 81 G3 36 55N 103 55W
Carrizo Springs, U.S.A. 81 L5 28 31N 99 52W
Carrizozo, U.S.A. 83 K11 33 38N 105 53W
Carroll, U.S.A. 80 D7 42 4N 94 52W
Carrollton, Ga., U.S.A. 77 J3 33 35N 85 5W
Carrollton, Ill., U.S.A. 80 F9 39 18N 90 24W
Carrollton, Ky., U.S.A. 76 F3 38 41N 85 11W
Carrollton, Mo., U.S.A. 80 F8 39 22N 93 30W
Carrollton, Ohio, U.S.A. 78 F3 40 34N 81 5W
Carron →, U.K. 12 D4 57 53N 4 22W
Carron, L., U.K. 12 D3 57 22N 5 35W
Carrot →, Canada 73 C8 53 50N 101 17W
Carrot River, Canada 73 C8 53 17N 103 35W
Carruthers, Canada 73 C7 52 52N 109 16W
Carson, Calif., U.S.A. 85 M8 33 48N 118 17W
Carson, N. Dak., U.S.A. 80 B4 46 25N 101 34W
Carson →, U.S.A. 84 F8 39 45N 118 40W
Carson City, U.S.A. 84 F7 39 10N 119 46W
Carson Sink, U.S.A. 82 G4 39 50N 118 25W
Cartagena, Colombia 92 A3 10 25N 75 33W
Cartagena, Spain 19 D5 37 38N 0 59W
Cartago, Colombia 92 C3 4 45N 75 55W
Cartago, Costa Rica 88 E3 9 50N 83 55W
Cartersville, U.S.A. 77 H3 34 10N 84 48W
Carterton, N.Z. 59 J5 41 2S 175 31 E
Carthage, Tunisia 51 A8 36 50N 10 21 E
Carthage, Ill., U.S.A. 80 E9 40 25N 91 8W
Carthage, Mo., U.S.A. 81 G7 37 11N 94 19W
Carthage, N.Y., U.S.A. 76 D8 43 59N 75 37W
Carthage, Tex., U.S.A. 81 J7 32 9N 94 20W
Cartier I., Australia 60 B3 12 31S 123 29 E
Cartwright, Canada 71 B8 53 41N 56 58W
Caruaru, Brazil 93 E11 8 15S 35 55W
Carúpano, Venezuela 92 A6 10 39N 63 15W
Caruthersville, U.S.A. 81 G10 36 11N 89 39W
Carvoeiro, Brazil 92 D6 1 30S 61 59W
Carvoeiro, C., Portugal 19 C1 39 21N 9 24W
Cary, U.S.A. 77 H6 35 47N 78 46W
Casa Grande, U.S.A. 83 K8 32 53N 111 45W
Casablanca, Chile 94 C1 33 20S 71 25W
Casablanca, Morocco 50 B4 33 36N 7 36W
Cascade, Idaho, U.S.A. 82 D5 44 31N 116 2W
Cascade, Mont., U.S.A. 82 C8 47 16N 111 42W
Cascade Locks, U.S.A. 84 E5 45 40N 121 54W
Cascade Ra., U.S.A. 84 D5 47 0N 121 30W
Cascade Reservoir, U.S.A. 82 D5 44 32N 116 3W
Cascais, Portugal 19 C1 38 41N 9 25W
Cascavel, Brazil 95 A5 24 57S 53 28W
Cáscina, Italy 20 C4 43 41N 10 33 E
Casco B., U.S.A. 77 D10 43 45N 70 0W
Caserta, Italy 20 D6 41 4N 14 20 E
Caseyr, Raas = Asir, Ras, Somali Rep. 46 E5 11 55N 51 10 E
Cashel, Ireland 13 D4 52 30N 7 53W
Casiguran, Phil. 37 A6 16 22N 122 7 E
Casilda, Argentina 94 C3 33 10S 61 10W
Casino, Australia 63 D5 28 52S 153 3 E
Casiquiare →, Venezuela 92 C5 2 1N 67 7W
Casma, Peru 92 E3 9 30S 78 20W
Casmalia, U.S.A. 85 L6 34 50N 120 32W
Caspe, Spain 19 B5 41 14N 0 1W
Casper, U.S.A. 82 E10 42 51N 106 19W
Caspian Depression, Eurasia 25 E8 47 0N 48 0 E
Caspian Sea, Eurasia 25 F9 43 0N 50 0 E
Cass Lake, U.S.A. 80 B7 47 23N 94 37W
Cassadaga, U.S.A. 78 D5 42 20N 79 19W
Casselman, Canada 79 A9 45 19N 75 5W
Casselton, U.S.A. 80 B6 46 54N 97 13W
Cassiar, Canada 72 B3 59 16N 129 40W
Cassiar Mts., Canada 72 B2 59 30N 130 30W
Cassino, Italy 20 D5 41 30N 13 49 E
Cassville, U.S.A. 81 G8 36 41N 93 52W
Castaic, U.S.A. 85 L8 34 30N 118 38W
Castalia, U.S.A. 78 E2 41 24N 82 49W
Castanhal, Brazil 93 D9 1 18S 47 55W
Castellammare di Stábia, Italy 20 D6 40 42N 14 29 E
Castelli, Argentina 94 D4 36 7S 57 47W
Castelló de la Plana, Spain 19 C5 39 58N 0 3W
Castelo, Brazil 95 A7 20 33S 41 14W
Castelo Branco, Portugal 19 C2 39 50N 7 31W
Castelsarrasin, France 18 E4 44 2N 1 7 E
Castelvetrano, Italy 20 F5 37 41N 12 47 E
Casterton, Australia 63 F3 37 30S 141 30 E
Castile, U.S.A. 78 D6 42 38N 78 3W
Castilla-La Mancha □, Spain 19 C4 39 30N 3 30W
Castilla y Leon □, Spain 19 B3 42 0N 5 0W
Castillos, Uruguay 95 C5 34 12S 53 52W
Castle Dale, U.S.A. 82 G8 39 13N 111 1W
Castle Douglas, U.K. 12 G5 54 56N 3 56W
Castle Rock, Colo., U.S.A. 80 F2 39 22N 104 51W
Castle Rock, Wash., U.S.A. 84 D4 46 17N 122 54W
Castlebar, Ireland 13 C2 53 52N 9 18W
Castleblaney, Ireland 13 B5 54 7N 6 44W
Castlederg, U.K. 13 B4 54 42N 7 35W
Castleford, U.K. 10 D6 53 43N 1 21W
Castlegar, Canada 72 D5 49 20N 117 40W
Castlemaine, Australia 63 F3 37 2S 144 12 E
Castlepollard, Ireland 13 C4 53 41N 7 19W
Castlerea, Ireland 13 C3 53 46N 8 29W
Castlereagh →, Australia 63 E4 30 12S 147 32 E
Castlereagh B., Australia 62 A2 12 10S 135 10 E
Castleton, U.S.A. 79 C11 43 37N 73 11W
Castletown, U.K. 10 C3 54 5N 4 38W
Castletown Bearhaven, Ireland 13 E2 51 39N 9 55W
Castor, Canada 72 C6 52 15N 111 50W
Castor →, Canada 70 B4 53 24N 78 58W
Castorland, U.S.A. 79 C9 43 53N 75 31W
Castres, France 18 E5 43 37N 2 13 E
Castricum, Neths. 15 B4 52 33N 4 40 E
Castries, St. Lucia 89 D7 14 2N 60 58W
Castro, Brazil 95 A6 24 45S 50 0W
Castro, Chile 96 E2 42 30S 73 50W
Castro Alves, Brazil 93 F11 12 46S 39 33W
Castroville, U.S.A. 84 J5 36 46N 121 45W
Castuera, Spain 19 C3 38 43N 5 37W
Cat Ba, Dao, Vietnam 38 B6 20 50N 107 0 E
Cat I., Bahamas 89 B4 24 30N 75 30W
Cat L., Canada 70 B1 51 40N 91 50W
Cat Lake, Canada 70 B1 51 40N 91 50W
Catacamas, Honduras 88 D2 14 54N 85 56W
Cataguases, Brazil 95 A7 21 23S 42 39W
Catalão, Brazil 93 G9 18 10S 47 57W
Çatalca, Turkey 21 D13 41 8N 28 27 E
Catalina, Canada 71 C9 48 31N 53 4W
Catalina, Chile 94 B2 25 13S 69 43W
Catalina, U.S.A. 83 K8 32 30N 110 50W
Catalonia = Cataluña □, Spain 19 B6 41 40N 1 15 E
Cataluña □, Spain 19 B6 41 40N 1 15 E
Catamarca, Argentina 94 B2 28 30S 65 50W
Catamarca □, Argentina 94 B2 27 0S 65 50W
Catanduanes □, Phil. 37 B6 13 50N 124 20 E
Catanduva, Brazil 95 A6 21 5S 48 58W
Catània, Italy 20 F6 37 30N 15 6 E
Catanzaro, Italy 20 E7 38 54N 16 35 E
Catarman, Phil. 37 B6 12 28N 124 35 E
Cateel, Phil. 37 C7 7 47N 126 24 E
Catembe, Mozam. 57 D5 26 0S 32 33 E
Caterham, U.K. 11 F7 51 15N 0 4W
Cathcart, S. Africa 56 E4 32 18S 27 10 E
Cathlamet, U.S.A. 84 D3 46 12N 123 23W
Catlettsburg, U.S.A. 76 F4 38 25N 82 36W
Catoche, C., Mexico 87 C7 21 40N 87 8W
Catriló, Argentina 94 D3 36 26S 63 24W
Catrimani, Brazil 92 C6 0 27N 61 41W
Catrimani →, Brazil 92 C6 0 28N 61 44W
Catskill, U.S.A. 79 D11 42 14N 73 52W
Catskill Mts., U.S.A. 79 D10 42 10N 74 25W
Catt, Mt., Australia 62 A1 13 49S 134 23 E
Cattaraugus, U.S.A. 78 D6 42 22N 78 52W
Catuala, Angola 56 B2 16 25S 19 2 E
Catuane, Mozam. 57 D5 26 48S 32 18 E
Catur, Mozam. 55 E4 13 45S 35 30 E
Catwick Is., Vietnam 39 G7 10 0N 109 0 E
Cauca →, Colombia 92 B4 8 54N 74 28W
Caucaia, Brazil 93 D11 3 40S 38 35W
Caucasus Mountains, Eurasia 25 F7 42 50N 44 0 E
Caungula, Angola 52 F3 8 26S 18 38 E
Cauquenes, Chile 94 D1 36 0S 72 22W
Caura →, Venezuela 92 B6 7 38N 64 53W
Cauresi →, Mozam. 55 F3 17 8S 33 0 E
Causapscal, Canada 71 C6 48 19N 67 12W
Cauvery →, India 40 P11 11 9N 78 52 E
Caux, Pays de, France 18 B4 49 38N 0 35 E
Cavalier, U.S.A. 80 A6 48 48N 97 37W
Cavan, Ireland 13 B4 54 0N 7 22W
Cavan □, Ireland 13 C4 54 1N 7 16W
Cave Creek, U.S.A. 83 K7 33 50N 111 57W
Cavenagh Ra., Australia 61 E4 26 12S 127 55 E
Cavendish, Australia 63 F3 37 31S 142 2 E
Caviana, I., Brazil 93 C8 0 10N 50 10W
Cavite, Phil. 37 B6 14 29N 120 55 E
Cawndilla L., Australia 63 E3 32 30S 142 15 E
Cawnpore = Kanpur, India 43 F9 26 28N 80 20 E
Caxias, Brazil 93 D10 4 55S 43 20W
Caxias do Sul, Brazil 95 B5 29 10S 51 10W
Cay Sal Bank, Bahamas 88 B4 23 45N 80 0W
Cayambe, Ecuador 92 C3 0 3N 78 8W
Cayenne, Fr. Guiana 93 B8 5 5N 52 18W
Cayman Brac, Cayman Is. 88 C4 19 43N 79 49W
Cayman Is. ■, W. Indies 88 C3 19 40N 80 30W
Cayo Romano, Cuba 88 B4 22 0N 78 0W
Cayuga, Canada 78 D5 42 59N 79 50W
Cayuga, U.S.A. 79 D8 42 54N 76 44W
Cayuga L., U.S.A. 79 D8 42 41N 76 41W
Cazenovia, U.S.A. 79 D9 42 56N 75 51W
Cazombo, Angola 53 G4 11 54S 22 56 E
Ceanannus Mor, Ireland 13 C5 53 44N 6 53W
Ceará = Fortaleza, Brazil 93 D11 3 45S 38 35W
Ceará □, Brazil 93 E11 5 0S 40 0W
Ceará Mirim, Brazil 93 E11 5 38S 35 25W
Cebaco, I. de, Panama 88 E3 7 33N 81 9W
Cebollar, Argentina 94 B2 29 10S 66 35W
Cebu, Phil. 37 B6 10 18N 123 54 E
Cecil Plains, Australia 63 D5 27 30S 151 11 E
Cedar →, U.S.A. 80 E9 41 17N 91 21W
Cedar City, U.S.A. 83 H7 37 41N 113 4W
Cedar Creek Reservoir, U.S.A. 81 J6 32 11N 96 4W
Cedar Falls, Iowa, U.S.A. 80 D8 42 32N 92 27W
Cedar Falls, Wash., U.S.A. 84 C5 47 25N 121 45W
Cedar Key, U.S.A. 77 L4 29 8N 83 2W
Cedar L., Canada 73 C9 53 10N 100 0W
Cedar Rapids, U.S.A. 80 E9 41 59N 91 40W
Cedartown, U.S.A. 77 H3 34 1N 85 15W
Cedarvale, Canada 72 B3 55 1N 128 22W
Cedarville, S. Africa 57 E4 30 23S 29 3 E
Cedral, Mexico 86 C4 23 50N 100 42W
Cedro, Brazil 93 E11 6 34S 39 3W
Cedros, I. de, Mexico 86 B1 28 10N 115 20W
Ceduna, Australia 63 E1 32 7S 133 46 E
Ceerigaabo = Erigavo, Somali Rep. 46 E4 10 35N 47 20 E
Cefalù, Italy 20 E6 38 2N 14 1 E
Cegléd, Hungary 17 E10 47 11N 19 47 E
Celaya, Mexico 86 C4 20 31N 100 37W
Celebes Sea, Indonesia 37 D6 3 0N 123 0 E
Celina, U.S.A. 76 E3 40 33N 84 35W
Celje, Slovenia 16 E8 46 16N 15 18 E
Celle, Germany 16 B6 52 37N 10 4 E
Cenderwasih, Teluk, Indonesia 37 E9 3 0S 135 20 E
Center, N. Dak., U.S.A. 80 B4 47 7N 101 18W
Center, Tex., U.S.A. 81 K7 31 48N 94 11W
Centerburg, U.S.A. 78 F2 40 18N 82 42W
Centerville, Calif., U.S.A. 84 J7 36 44N 119 30W
Centerville, Iowa, U.S.A. 80 E8 40 44N 92 52W
Centerville, Pa., U.S.A. 78 F5 40 3N 79 59W
Centerville, Tenn., U.S.A. 77 H2 35 47N 87 28W
Centerville, Tex., U.S.A. 81 K7 31 16N 95 59W
Central □, Kenya 54 C4 0 30S 37 30 E
Central □, Malawi 55 E3 13 30S 33 30 E
Central □, Zambia 55 E2 14 25S 28 50 E
Central, Cordillera, Colombia 92 C4 5 0N 75 0W
Central, Cordillera, Costa Rica 88 D3 10 10N 84 5W
Central, Cordillera, Dom. Rep. 89 C5 19 15N 71 0W
Central African Rep. ■, Africa 52 C4 7 0N 20 0 E
Central America, America 66 H11 12 0N 85 0W
Central Butte, Canada 73 C7 50 48N 106 31W
Central City, Colo., U.S.A. 82 G11 39 48N 105 31W
Central City, Ky., U.S.A. 76 G2 37 18N 87 7W
Central City, Nebr., U.S.A. 80 E6 41 7N 98 0W
Central I., Kenya 54 B4 3 30N 36 0 E
Central Makran Range, Pakistan 40 F4 26 30N 64 15 E
Central Patricia, Canada 70 B1 51 30N 90 9W
Central Point, U.S.A. 82 E2 42 23N 122 55W
Central Russian Uplands, Europe 6 E13 54 0N 36 0 E
Central Siberian Plateau, Russia 28 C14 65 0N 105 0 E
Central Square, U.S.A. 79 C8 43 17N 76 9W
Centralia, Ill., U.S.A. 80 F10 38 32N 89 8W
Centralia, Mo., U.S.A. 80 F8 39 13N 92 8W
Centralia, Wash., U.S.A. 84 D4 46 43N 122 58W
Cephalonia = Kefallinía, Greece 21 E9 38 15N 20 30 E
Cepu, Indonesia 37 G14 7 9S 111 35 E
Ceram = Seram, Indonesia 37 E7 3 10S 129 0 E
Ceram Sea = Seram Sea, Indonesia 37 E7 2 30S 128 30 E
Ceredigion □, U.K. 11 E3 52 16N 4 15W
Ceres, Argentina 94 B3 29 55S 61 55W
Ceres, S. Africa 56 E2 33 21S 19 18 E
Ceres, U.S.A. 84 H6 37 35N 120 57W
Cerignola, Italy 20 D6 41 17N 15 53 E
Cerigo = Kíthira, Greece 21 F10 36 8N 23 0 E
Çerkezköy, Turkey 21 D12 41 17N 28 0 E
Cerralvo, I., Mexico 86 C3 24 20N 109 45W
Cerritos, Mexico 86 C4 22 27N 100 20W
Cerro Chato, Uruguay 95 C4 33 6S 55 8W
Cervantes, Australia 61 F2 30 31S 115 3 E
Cervera, Spain 19 B6 41 40N 1 16 E
Cesena, Italy 20 B5 44 8N 12 15 E
Cēsis, Latvia 9 H21 57 18N 25 15 E
České Budějovice, Czech Rep. 16 D8 48 55N 14 25 E
Českomoravská Vrchovina, Czech Rep. 16 D8 49 30N 15 40 E
Çeşme, Turkey 21 E12 38 20N 26 23 E
Cessnock, Australia 63 E5 32 50S 151 21 E
Cetinje, Montenegro, Yug. 21 C8 42 23N 18 59 E
Cetraro, Italy 20 E6 39 31N 15 55 E
Ceuta, N. Afr. 19 E3 35 52N 5 18W
Cévennes, France 18 D5 44 10N 3 50 E
Ceyhan, Turkey 44 B2 37 4N 35 47 E
Ceylon = Sri Lanka ■, Asia 40 R12 7 30N 80 50 E

Coral Springs

Coral Springs, *U.S.A.* **77 M5** 26 16N 80 13W
Coraopolis, *U.S.A.* **78 F4** 40 31N 80 10W
Corato, *Italy* **20 D7** 41 9N 16 25 E
Corbin, *U.S.A.* **76 G3** 36 57N 84 6W
Corby, *U.K.* **11 E7** 52 30N 0 41W
Corcaigh = Cork, *Ireland* **13 E3** 51 54N 8 29W
Corcoran, *U.S.A.* **84 J7** 36 6N 119 33W
Corcubión, *Spain* **19 A1** 42 56N 9 12W
Cordele, *U.S.A.* **77 K4** 31 58N 83 47W
Cordell, *U.S.A.* **81 H5** 35 17N 98 59W
Córdoba, *Argentina* **94 C3** 31 20S 64 10W
Córdoba, *Mexico* **87 D5** 18 50N 97 0W
Córdoba, *Spain* **19 D3** 37 50N 4 50W
Córdoba □, *Argentina* **94 C3** 31 22S 64 15W
Córdoba, Sierra de, *Argentina* **94 C3** 31 10S 64 25W
Cordova, *U.S.A.* **68 B5** 60 33N 145 45W
Corella →, *Australia* **62 B3** 19 34S 140 47 E
Corfield, *Australia* **62 C3** 21 40S 143 21 E
Corfu = Kérkira, *Greece* **23 A3** 39 38N 19 50 E
Corfu, Str. of, *Greece* **23 A4** 39 34N 20 0 E
Coria, *Spain* **19 C2** 39 58N 6 33W
Corigliano Cálabro, *Italy* **20 E7** 39 36N 16 31 E
Coringa Is., *Australia* **62 B4** 16 58S 149 58 E
Corinth = Kórinthos, *Greece* **21 F10** 37 56N 22 55 E
Corinth, *Miss., U.S.A.* **77 H1** 34 56N 88 31W
Corinth, *N.Y., U.S.A.* **79 C11** 43 15N 73 49W
Corinth, G. of = Korinthiakós Kólpos, *Greece* **21 E10** 38 16N 22 30 E
Corinto, *Brazil* **93 G10** 18 20S 44 30W
Corinto, *Nic.* **88 D2** 12 30N 87 10W
Cork, *Ireland* **13 E3** 51 54N 8 29W
Cork □, *Ireland* **13 E3** 51 57N 8 40W
Cork Harbour, *Ireland* **13 E3** 51 47N 8 16W
Çorlu, *Turkey* **21 D12** 41 11N 27 49 E
Cormack L., *Canada* **72 A4** 60 56N 121 37W
Cormorant, *Canada* **73 C8** 54 14N 100 35W
Cormorant L., *Canada* **73 C8** 54 15N 100 50W
Corn Is. = Maíz, Is. del, *Nic.* **88 D3** 12 15N 83 4W
Cornélio Procópio, *Brazil* **95 A5** 23 7S 50 40W
Corner Brook, *Canada* **71 C8** 48 57N 57 58W
Corneşti, *Moldova* **17 E15** 47 21N 28 1 E
Corning, *Ark., U.S.A.* **81 G9** 36 25N 90 35W
Corning, *Calif., U.S.A.* **82 G2** 39 56N 122 11W
Corning, *Iowa, U.S.A.* **80 E7** 40 59N 94 44W
Corning, *N.Y., U.S.A.* **78 D7** 42 9N 77 3W
Cornwall, *Canada* **79 A10** 45 2N 74 44W
Cornwall, *U.S.A.* **79 F8** 40 17N 76 25W
Cornwall □, *U.K.* **11 G3** 50 26N 4 40W
Corny Pt., *Australia* **63 E2** 34 55S 137 0 E
Coro, *Venezuela* **92 A5** 11 25N 69 41W
Coroatá, *Brazil* **93 D10** 4 8S 44 0W
Corocoro, *Bolivia* **92 G5** 17 15S 68 28W
Coroico, *Bolivia* **92 G5** 16 0S 67 50W
Coromandel, *N.Z.* **59 G5** 36 45S 175 31 E
Coromandel Coast, *India* **40 N12** 12 30N 81 0 E
Corona, *Calif., U.S.A.* **85 M9** 33 53N 117 34W
Corona, *N. Mex., U.S.A.* **83 J11** 34 15N 105 36W
Coronach, *Canada* **73 D7** 49 7N 105 31W
Coronado, *U.S.A.* **85 N9** 32 41N 117 11W
Coronado, B. de, *Costa Rica* **88 E3** 9 0N 83 40W
Coronados, Is. los, *U.S.A.* **85 N9** 32 25N 117 15W
Coronation, *Canada* **72 C6** 52 5N 111 27W
Coronation Gulf, *Canada* **68 B8** 68 25N 110 0W
Coronation I., *Antarctica* **5 C18** 60 45S 46 0W
Coronation Is., *Australia* **60 B3** 14 57S 124 55 E
Coronda, *Argentina* **94 C3** 31 58S 60 56W
Coronel, *Chile* **94 D1** 37 0S 73 10W
Coronel Bogado, *Paraguay* **94 B4** 27 11S 56 18W
Coronel Dorrego, *Argentina* **94 D3** 38 40S 61 10W
Coronel Oviedo, *Paraguay* **94 B4** 25 24S 56 30W
Coronel Pringles, *Argentina* **94 D3** 38 0S 61 30W
Coronel Suárez, *Argentina* **94 D3** 37 30S 61 52W
Coronel Vidal, *Argentina* **94 D4** 37 28S 57 45W
Coropuna, Nevado, *Peru* **92 G4** 15 30S 72 41W
Corowa, *Australia* **63 F4** 35 58S 146 21 E
Corozal, *Belize* **87 D7** 18 23N 88 23W
Corpus, *Argentina* **95 B4** 27 10S 55 30W
Corpus Christi, *U.S.A.* **81 M6** 27 47N 97 24W
Corpus Christi, L., *U.S.A.* **81 L6** 28 2N 97 52W
Corralejo, *Canary Is.* **22 F6** 28 43N 13 53W
Corraun Pen., *Ireland* **13 C2** 53 54N 9 54W
Correntes, C. das, *Mozam.* **57 C6** 24 6S 35 34 E
Corrib, L., *Ireland* **13 C2** 53 27N 9 16W
Corrientes, *Argentina* **94 B4** 27 30S 58 45W
Corrientes □, *Argentina* **94 B4** 28 0S 57 0W
Corrientes →, *Argentina* **94 C4** 30 42S 59 38W
Corrientes →, *Peru* **92 D4** 3 43S 74 35W
Corrientes, C., *Colombia* **92 B3** 5 30N 77 34W
Corrientes, C., *Cuba* **88 B3** 21 43N 84 30W
Corrientes, C., *Mexico* **86 C3** 20 25N 105 42W
Corrigan, *U.S.A.* **81 K7** 31 0N 94 52W
Corrigin, *Australia* **61 F2** 32 20S 117 53 E
Corry, *U.S.A.* **78 E5** 41 55N 79 39W
Corse, *France* **18 F8** 42 0N 9 0 E
Corse, C., *France* **18 E8** 43 1N 9 25 E
Corsica = Corse, *France* **18 F8** 42 0N 9 0 E
Corsicana, *U.S.A.* **81 J6** 32 6N 96 28W
Corte, *France* **18 E8** 42 19N 9 11 E
Cortez, *U.S.A.* **83 H9** 37 21N 108 35W
Cortland, *N.Y., U.S.A.* **79 D8** 42 36N 76 11W
Cortland, *Ohio, U.S.A.* **78 E4** 41 20N 80 44W
Çorum, *Turkey* **25 F5** 40 30N 34 57 E
Corumbá, *Brazil* **92 G7** 19 0S 57 30W
Corunna = A Coruña, *Spain* **19 A1** 43 20N 8 25W
Corvallis, *U.S.A.* **82 D2** 44 34N 123 16W
Corvette, L. de la, *Canada* **70 B5** 53 25N 74 3W
Corydon, *U.S.A.* **80 E8** 40 46N 93 19W
Cosalá, *Mexico* **86 C3** 24 28N 106 40W
Cosamaloapan, *Mexico* **87 D5** 18 23N 95 50W
Cosenza, *Italy* **20 E7** 39 18N 16 15 E
Coshocton, *U.S.A.* **78 F3** 40 16N 81 51W
Cosmo Newberry, *Australia* **61 E3** 28 0S 122 54 E
Coso Junction, *U.S.A.* **85 J9** 36 3N 117 57W
Coso Pk., *U.S.A.* **85 J9** 36 13N 117 44W
Cosquín, *Argentina* **94 C3** 31 15S 64 30W
Costa Blanca, *Spain* **19 C5** 38 25N 0 10W
Costa Brava, *Spain* **19 B7** 41 30N 3 0 E
Costa del Sol, *Spain* **19 D3** 36 30N 4 30W
Costa Dorada, *Spain* **19 B6** 41 12N 1 15 E
Costa Mesa, *U.S.A.* **85 M9** 33 38N 117 55W
Costa Rica ■, *Cent. Amer.* **88 E3** 10 0N 84 0W
Cosumnes →, *U.S.A.* **84 G5** 38 16N 121 26W
Cotabato, *Phil.* **37 C6** 7 14N 124 15 E
Cotagaita, *Bolivia* **94 A2** 20 45S 65 40W
Côte d'Azur, *France* **18 E7** 43 25N 7 10 E
Côte-d'Ivoire = Ivory Coast ■, *Africa* **50 G4** 7 30N 5 0W
Coteau des Prairies, *U.S.A.* **80 C6** 45 20N 97 50W
Coteau du Missouri, *U.S.A.* **80 B4** 47 0N 100 0W
Coteau Landing, *Canada* **79 A10** 45 15N 74 13W
Cotentin, *France* **18 B3** 49 15N 1 30W
Cotillo, *Canary Is.* **22 F5** 28 41N 14 1W
Cotonou, *Benin* **50 G6** 6 20N 2 25 E
Cotopaxi, *Ecuador* **92 D3** 0 40S 78 30W
Cotswold Hills, *U.K.* **11 F5** 51 42N 2 10W
Cottage Grove, *U.S.A.* **82 E2** 43 48N 123 3W
Cottbus, *Germany* **16 C8** 51 45N 14 20 E
Cottonwood, *U.S.A.* **83 J7** 34 45N 112 1W
Cotulla, *U.S.A.* **81 L5** 28 26N 99 14W
Coudersport, *U.S.A.* **78 E6** 41 46N 78 1W
Couedic, C. du, *Australia* **63 F2** 36 5S 136 40 E
Coulee City, *U.S.A.* **82 C4** 47 37N 119 17W
Coulman I., *Antarctica* **5 D11** 73 35S 170 0 E
Coulonge →, *Canada* **70 C4** 45 52N 76 46W
Coulterville, *U.S.A.* **84 H6** 37 43N 120 12W
Council, *U.S.A.* **82 D5** 44 44N 116 26W
Council Bluffs, *U.S.A.* **80 E7** 41 16N 95 52W
Council Grove, *U.S.A.* **80 F6** 38 40N 96 29W
Coupeville, *U.S.A.* **84 B4** 48 13N 122 41W
Courantyne →, *S. Amer.* **92 B7** 5 55N 57 5W
Courcelles, *Belgium* **15 D4** 50 28N 4 22 E
Courtenay, *Canada* **72 D4** 49 45N 125 0W
Courtland, *U.S.A.* **84 G5** 38 20N 121 34W
Courtrai = Kortrijk, *Belgium* **15 D3** 50 50N 3 17 E
Courtright, *Canada* **78 D2** 42 49N 82 28W
Coushatta, *U.S.A.* **81 J8** 32 1N 93 21W
Coutts Crossing, *Australia* **63 D5** 29 49S 152 55 E
Couvin, *Belgium* **15 D4** 50 3N 4 29 E
Cove I., *Canada* **78 A3** 45 17N 81 44W
Coventry, *U.K.* **11 E6** 52 25N 1 28W
Covilhã, *Portugal* **19 B2** 40 17N 7 31W
Covington, *Ga., U.S.A.* **77 J4** 33 36N 83 51W
Covington, *Ky., U.S.A.* **76 F3** 39 5N 84 31W
Covington, *Okla., U.S.A.* **81 G6** 36 18N 97 35W
Covington, *Tenn., U.S.A.* **81 H10** 35 34N 89 39W
Covington, *Va., U.S.A.* **76 G5** 37 47N 79 59W
Cowal, L., *Australia* **63 E4** 33 40S 147 25 E
Cowan, L., *Australia* **61 F3** 31 45S 121 45 E
Cowan L., *Canada* **73 C7** 54 0N 107 15W
Cowangie, *Australia* **63 F3** 35 12S 141 26 E
Cowansville, *Canada* **79 A12** 45 14N 72 46W
Coward Springs, *Australia* **63 D2** 29 24S 136 49 E
Cowcowing Lakes, *Australia* **61 F2** 30 55S 117 20 E
Cowdenbeath, *U.K.* **12 E5** 56 7N 3 21W
Cowell, *Australia* **63 E2** 33 39S 136 56 E
Cowes, *U.K.* **11 G6** 50 45N 1 18W
Cowichan L., *Canada* **84 B2** 48 53N 124 17W
Cowlitz →, *U.S.A.* **84 D4** 46 6N 122 55W
Cowra, *Australia* **63 E4** 33 49S 148 42 E
Coxilha Grande, *Brazil* **95 B5** 28 18S 51 30W
Coxim, *Brazil* **93 G8** 18 30S 54 55W
Cox's Bazar, *Bangla.* **41 J17** 21 26N 91 59 E
Coyote Wells, *U.S.A.* **85 N11** 32 44N 115 58W
Coyuca de Benítez, *Mexico* **87 D4** 17 1N 100 8W
Coyuca de Catalan, *Mexico* **86 D4** 18 18N 100 41W
Cozad, *U.S.A.* **80 E5** 40 52N 99 59W
Cozumel, *Mexico* **87 C7** 20 31N 86 55W
Cozumel, Isla, *Mexico* **87 C7** 20 30N 86 40W
Cracow = Kraków, *Poland* **17 C10** 50 4N 19 57 E
Cracow, *Australia* **63 D5** 25 17S 150 17 E
Cradock, *Australia* **63 E2** 32 6S 138 31 E
Cradock, *S. Africa* **56 E4** 32 8S 25 36 E
Craig, *U.S.A.* **82 F10** 40 31N 107 33W
Craigavon, *U.K.* **13 B5** 54 27N 6 23W
Craigmore, *Zimbabwe* **55 G3** 20 28S 32 50 E
Craik, *Canada* **73 C7** 51 3N 105 49W
Crailsheim, *Germany* **16 D6** 49 8N 10 5 E
Craiova, *Romania* **17 F12** 44 21N 23 48 E
Cramsie, *Australia* **62 C3** 23 20S 144 15 E
Cranberry L., *U.S.A.* **79 B10** 44 11N 74 50W
Cranberry Portage, *Canada* **73 C8** 54 35N 101 23W
Cranbrook, *Australia* **61 F2** 34 18S 117 33 E
Cranbrook, *Canada* **72 D5** 49 30N 115 46W
Crandon, *U.S.A.* **80 C10** 45 34N 88 54W
Crane, *Oreg., U.S.A.* **82 E4** 43 25N 118 35W
Crane, *Tex., U.S.A.* **81 K3** 31 24N 102 21W
Cranston, *U.S.A.* **79 E13** 41 47N 71 26W
Crater L., *U.S.A.* **82 E2** 42 56N 122 6W
Crater Lake Nat. Park, *U.S.A.* **82 E2** 42 55N 122 10W
Crateús, *Brazil* **93 E10** 5 10S 40 39W
Crato, *Brazil* **93 E11** 7 10S 39 25W
Craven, L., *Canada* **70 B4** 54 20N 76 56W
Crawford, *U.S.A.* **80 D3** 42 41N 103 25W
Crawfordsville, *U.S.A.* **76 E2** 40 2N 86 54W
Crawley, *U.K.* **11 F7** 51 7N 0 11W
Crazy Mts., *U.S.A.* **82 C8** 46 12N 110 20W
Crean L., *Canada* **73 C7** 54 5N 106 9W
Crediton, *Canada* **78 C3** 43 17N 81 33W
Cree →, *Canada* **73 B7** 58 57N 105 47W
Cree →, *U.K.* **12 G4** 54 55N 4 25W
Cree L., *Canada* **73 B7** 57 30N 106 30W
Creede, *U.S.A.* **83 H10** 37 51N 106 56W
Creekside, *U.S.A.* **78 F5** 40 40N 79 11W
Creel, *Mexico* **86 B3** 27 45N 107 38W
Creemore, *Canada* **78 B4** 44 19N 80 6W
Creighton, *Canada* **73 C8** 54 45N 101 54W
Creighton, *U.S.A.* **80 D6** 42 28N 97 54W
Crema, *Italy* **18 D8** 45 22N 9 41 E
Cremona, *Italy* **18 D9** 45 7N 10 2 E
Cres, *Croatia* **16 F8** 44 58N 14 25 E
Crescent City, *U.S.A.* **82 F1** 41 45N 124 12W
Crespo, *Argentina* **94 C3** 32 2S 60 19W
Cresson, *U.S.A.* **78 F6** 40 28N 78 36W
Crestline, *Calif., U.S.A.* **85 L9** 34 14N 117 18W
Crestline, *Ohio, U.S.A.* **78 F2** 40 47N 82 44W
Creston, *Canada* **72 D5** 49 10N 116 31W
Creston, *Calif., U.S.A.* **84 K6** 35 32N 120 33W
Creston, *Iowa, U.S.A.* **80 E7** 41 4N 94 22W
Crestview, *Calif., U.S.A.* **84 H8** 37 46N 118 58W
Crestview, *Fla., U.S.A.* **77 K2** 30 46N 86 34W
Crete = Kríti, *Greece* **23 D7** 35 15N 25 0 E
Crete, *U.S.A.* **80 E6** 40 38N 96 58W
Créteil, *France* **18 B5** 48 47N 2 28 E
Creus, C. de, *Spain* **19 A7** 42 20N 3 19 E
Creuse →, *France* **18 C4** 47 0N 0 34 E
Crewe, *U.K.* **10 D5** 53 6N 2 26W
Crewkerne, *U.K.* **11 G5** 50 53N 2 48W
Criciúma, *Brazil* **95 B6** 28 40S 49 23W
Crieff, *U.K.* **12 E5** 56 22N 3 50W
Crimea □, *Ukraine* **25 E5** 45 30N 33 10 E
Crimean Pen. = Krymskyy Pivostriv, *Ukraine* **25 F5** 45 0N 34 0 E
Crişul Alb →, *Romania* **17 E11** 46 42N 21 17 E
Crişul Negru →, *Romania* **17 E11** 46 42N 21 16 E
Crna →, *Macedonia* **21 D9** 41 33N 21 59 E
Crna Gora = Montenegro □, *Yugoslavia* **21 C8** 42 40N 19 20 E
Crna Gora, *Macedonia* **21 C9** 42 10N 21 30 E
Crna Reka = Crna →, *Macedonia* **21 D9** 41 33N 21 59 E
Croagh Patrick, *Ireland* **13 C2** 53 46N 9 40W
Croatia ■, *Europe* **16 F9** 45 20N 16 0 E
Crocker, Banjaran, *Malaysia* **36 C5** 5 40N 116 30 E
Crockett, *U.S.A.* **81 K7** 31 19N 95 27W
Crocodile = Krokodil →, *Mozam.* **57 D5** 25 14S 32 18 E
Crocodile Is., *Australia* **62 A1** 12 3S 134 58 E
Crohy Hd., *Ireland* **13 B3** 54 55N 8 26W
Croix, L. La, *Canada* **70 C1** 48 20N 92 15W
Croker, C., *Australia* **60 B5** 10 58S 132 35 E
Croker, C., *Canada* **78 B4** 44 58N 80 59W
Croker I., *Australia* **60 B5** 11 12S 132 32 E
Cromarty, *U.K.* **12 D4** 57 40N 4 2W
Cromer, *U.K.* **10 E9** 52 56N 1 17 E
Cromwell, *N.Z.* **59 L2** 45 3S 169 14 E
Cromwell, *U.S.A.* **79 E12** 41 36N 72 39W
Crook, *U.K.* **10 C6** 54 43N 1 45W
Crooked →, *Canada* **72 C4** 54 50N 122 54W
Crooked →, *U.S.A.* **82 D3** 44 32N 121 16W
Crooked I., *Bahamas* **89 B5** 22 50N 74 10W
Crooked Island Passage, *Bahamas* **89 B5** 23 0N 74 30W
Crookston, *Minn., U.S.A.* **80 B6** 47 47N 96 37W
Crookston, *Nebr., U.S.A.* **80 D4** 42 56N 100 45W
Crookwell, *Australia* **63 E4** 34 28S 149 24 E
Crosby, *U.K.* **10 D4** 53 30N 3 3W
Crosby, *N. Dak., U.S.A.* **80 A3** 48 55N 103 18W
Crosby, *Pa., U.S.A.* **78 E6** 41 45N 78 23W
Crosbyton, *U.S.A.* **81 J4** 33 40N 101 14W
Cross City, *U.S.A.* **77 L4** 29 38N 83 7W
Cross Fell, *U.K.* **10 C5** 54 43N 2 28W
Cross L., *Canada* **73 C9** 54 45N 97 30W
Cross Lake, *Canada* **73 C9** 54 37N 97 47W
Cross Sound, *U.S.A.* **68 C6** 58 0N 135 0W
Crossett, *U.S.A.* **81 J9** 33 8N 91 58W
Crosshaven, *Ireland* **13 E3** 51 47N 8 17W
Crossville, *U.S.A.* **77 G3** 35 57N 85 2W
Croswell, *U.S.A.* **78 C2** 43 16N 82 37W
Croton-on-Hudson, *U.S.A.* **79 E11** 41 12N 73 55W
Crotone, *Italy* **20 E7** 39 5N 17 8 E
Crow →, *Canada* **72 B4** 59 41N 124 20W
Crow Agency, *U.S.A.* **82 D10** 45 36N 107 28W
Crow Hd., *Ireland* **13 E1** 51 35N 10 9W
Crowell, *U.S.A.* **81 J5** 33 59N 99 43W
Crowley, *U.S.A.* **81 K8** 30 13N 92 22W
Crowley, L., *U.S.A.* **84 H8** 37 35N 118 42W
Crown Point, *Ind., U.S.A.* **76 E2** 41 25N 87 22W
Crown Point, *N.Y., U.S.A.* **79 C11** 43 57N 73 26W
Crownpoint, *U.S.A.* **83 J9** 35 41N 108 9W
Crows Landing, *U.S.A.* **84 H5** 37 23N 121 6W
Crows Nest, *Australia* **63 D5** 27 16S 152 4 E
Crowsnest Pass, *Canada* **72 D6** 49 40N 114 40W
Croydon, *Australia* **62 B3** 18 13S 142 14 E
Croydon □, *U.K.* **11 F7** 51 22N 0 5W
Crozet, Is., *Ind. Oc.* **3 G12** 46 27S 52 0 E
Cruz, C., *Cuba* **88 C4** 19 50N 77 50W
Cruz Alta, *Brazil* **95 B5** 28 45S 53 40W
Cruz del Eje, *Argentina* **94 C3** 30 45S 64 50W
Cruzeiro, *Brazil* **95 A7** 22 33S 45 0W
Cruzeiro do Oeste, *Brazil* **95 A5** 23 46S 53 4W
Cruzeiro do Sul, *Brazil* **92 E4** 7 35S 72 35W
Cry L., *Canada* **72 B3** 58 45N 129 0W
Crystal Bay, *U.S.A.* **84 F7** 39 15N 120 0W
Crystal Brook, *Australia* **63 E2** 33 21S 138 12 E
Crystal City, *U.S.A.* **81 L5** 28 41N 99 50W
Crystal Falls, *U.S.A.* **76 B1** 46 5N 88 20W
Crystal River, *U.S.A.* **77 L4** 28 54N 82 35W
Crystal Springs, *U.S.A.* **81 K9** 31 59N 90 21W
Csongrád, *Hungary* **17 E11** 46 43N 20 12 E
Cu Lao Hon, *Vietnam* **39 G7** 10 54N 108 18 E
Cua Rao, *Vietnam* **38 C5** 19 16N 104 27 E
Cuácua →, *Mozam.* **55 F4** 17 54S 37 0 E
Cuamato, *Angola* **56 B2** 17 2S 15 7 E
Cuamba, *Mozam.* **55 E4** 14 45S 36 22 E
Cuando →, *Angola* **53 H4** 17 30S 23 15 E
Cuando Cubango □, *Angola* **56 B3** 16 25S 20 0 E
Cuangar, *Angola* **56 B2** 17 36S 18 39 E
Cuango = Kwango →, *Dem. Rep. of the Congo* **52 E3** 3 14S 17 22 E
Cuanza →, *Angola* **52 F2** 9 21S 13 9 E
Cuarto →, *Argentina* **94 C3** 33 25S 63 2W
Cuatrociénegas, *Mexico* **86 B4** 26 59N 102 5W
Cuauhtémoc, *Mexico* **86 B3** 28 25N 106 52W
Cuba, *N. Mex., U.S.A.* **83 J10** 36 1N 107 4W
Cuba, *N.Y., U.S.A.* **78 D6** 42 13N 78 17W
Cuba ■, *W. Indies* **88 B4** 22 0N 79 0W
Cubango →, *Africa* **56 B3** 18 50S 22 25 E
Cuchumatanes, Sierra de los, *Guatemala* **88 C1** 15 35N 91 25W
Cuckfield, *U.K.* **11 F7** 51 1N 0 8W
Cucuí, *Brazil* **92 C5** 1 12N 66 50W
Cucurpe, *Mexico* **86 A2** 30 20N 110 43W
Cúcuta, *Colombia* **92 B4** 7 54N 72 31W
Cuddalore, *India* **40 P11** 11 46N 79 45 E
Cuddapah, *India* **40 M11** 14 30N 78 47 E
Cuddapan, L., *Australia* **62 D3** 25 45S 141 26 E
Cue, *Australia* **61 E2** 27 25S 117 54 E
Cuenca, *Ecuador* **92 D3** 2 50S 79 9W
Cuenca, *Spain* **19 B4** 40 5N 2 10W
Cuenca, Serranía de, *Spain* **19 C5** 39 55N 1 50W
Cuernavaca, *Mexico* **87 D5** 18 55N 99 15W
Cuero, *U.S.A.* **81 L6** 29 6N 97 17W
Cuevas del Almanzora, *Spain* **19 D5** 37 18N 1 58W
Cuevo, *Bolivia* **92 H6** 20 15S 63 30W
Cuiabá, *Brazil* **93 G7** 15 30S 56 0W
Cuiabá →, *Brazil* **93 G7** 17 5S 56 36W
Cuijk, *Neths.* **15 C5** 51 44N 5 50 E
Cuilco, *Guatemala* **88 C1** 15 24N 91 58W
Cuillin Hills, *U.K.* **12 D2** 57 13N 6 15W
Cuillin Sd., *U.K.* **12 D2** 57 4N 6 20W
Cuito →, *Angola* **56 B3** 18 1S 20 48 E
Cuitzeo, L. de, *Mexico* **86 D4** 19 55N 101 5W
Cukai, *Malaysia* **39 K4** 4 13N 103 25 E
Culbertson, *U.S.A.* **80 A2** 48 9N 104 31W
Culcairn, *Australia* **63 F4** 35 41S 147 3 E
Culgoa →, *Australia* **63 D4** 29 56S 146 20 E
Culiacán, *Mexico* **86 C3** 24 50N 107 23W
Culiacán →, *Mexico* **86 C3** 24 30N 107 42W
Culion, *Phil.* **37 B6** 11 54N 119 58 E
Cullarin Ra., *Australia* **63 E4** 34 30S 149 30 E
Cullen, *U.K.* **12 D6** 57 42N 2 49W
Cullen Pt., *Australia* **62 A3** 11 57S 141 54 E
Cullera, *Spain* **19 C5** 39 9N 0 17W
Cullman, *U.S.A.* **77 H2** 34 11N 86 51W
Culpeper, *U.S.A.* **76 F7** 38 30N 78 0W
Culuene →, *Brazil* **93 F8** 12 56S 52 51W
Culver, Pt., *Australia* **61 F3** 32 54S 124 43 E
Culverden, *N.Z.* **59 K4** 42 47S 172 49 E
Cumaná, *Venezuela* **92 A6** 10 30N 64 5W
Cumberland, *B.C., Canada* **72 D4** 49 40N 125 0W
Cumberland, *Ont., Canada* **79 A9** 45 29N 75 24W
Cumberland, *U.S.A.* **76 F6** 39 39N 78 46W
Cumberland →, *U.S.A.* **77 G2** 36 15N 87 0W
Cumberland, L., *U.S.A.* **77 G3** 36 57N 84 55W
Cumberland I., *U.S.A.* **77 K5** 30 50N 81 25W
Cumberland Is., *Australia* **62 C4** 20 35S 149 10 E
Cumberland L., *Canada* **73 C8** 54 3N 102 18W
Cumberland Pen., *Canada* **69 B13** 67 0N 64 0W
Cumberland Plateau, *U.S.A.* **77 H3** 36 0N 85 0W
Cumberland Sd., *Canada* **69 B13** 65 30N 66 0W
Cumbernauld, *U.K.* **12 F5** 55 57N 3 58W
Cumborah, *Australia* **63 D4** 29 40S 147 45 E
Cumbria □, *U.K.* **10 C5** 54 42N 2 52W
Cumbrian Mts., *U.K.* **10 C5** 54 30N 3 0W
Cumbum, *India* **40 M11** 15 40N 79 10 E
Cuminá →, *Brazil* **93 D7** 1 30S 56 0W
Cummings Mt., *U.S.A.* **85 K8** 35 2N 118 34W
Cummins, *Australia* **63 E2** 34 16S 135 43 E
Cumnock, *Australia* **63 E4** 32 59S 148 46 E
Cumnock, *U.K.* **12 F4** 55 28N 4 17W
Cumpas, *Mexico* **86 B3** 30 0N 109 48W
Cumplida, Pta., *Canary Is.* **22 F2** 28 50N 17 48W
Cunco, *Chile* **96 D2** 38 55S 72 2W
Cuncumén, *Chile* **94 C1** 31 53S 70 38W
Cunderdin, *Australia* **61 F2** 31 37S 117 12 E
Cunene →, *Angola* **56 B1** 17 20S 11 50 E
Cúneo, *Italy* **18 D7** 44 23N 7 32 E
Çüngüş, *Turkey* **44 B3** 38 13N 39 17 E
Cunillera, I. = Sa Conillera, *Spain* **22 C7** 38 59N 1 13 E
Cunnamulla, *Australia* **63 D4** 28 2S 145 38 E
Cupar, *Canada* **73 C8** 50 57N 104 10W
Cupar, *U.K.* **12 E5** 56 19N 3 1W
Cupica, G. de, *Colombia* **92 B3** 6 25N 77 30W
Curaçao, *Neth. Ant.* **89 D6** 12 10N 69 0W
Curanilahue, *Chile* **94 D1** 37 29S 73 28W
Curaray →, *Peru* **92 D4** 2 20S 74 5W
Curepto, *Chile* **94 D1** 35 8S 72 1W
Curiapo, *Venezuela* **92 B6** 8 33N 61 5W
Curicó, *Chile* **94 C1** 34 55S 71 20W
Curitiba, *Brazil* **95 B6** 25 20S 49 10W
Curitibanos, *Brazil* **95 B5** 27 18S 50 36W
Currabubula, *Australia* **63 E5** 31 16S 150 44 E
Currais Novos, *Brazil* **93 E11** 6 13S 36 30W
Curralinho, *Brazil* **93 D9** 1 45S 49 46W
Currant, *U.S.A.* **82 G6** 38 51N 115 32W
Current →, *U.S.A.* **81 G9** 36 15N 90 55W
Currie, *Australia* **62 F3** 39 56S 143 53 E
Currie, *U.S.A.* **82 F6** 40 16N 114 45W
Curtea de Argeş, *Romania* **17 F13** 45 12N 24 42 E
Curtis, *U.S.A.* **80 E4** 40 38N 100 31W
Curtis Group, *Australia* **62 F4** 39 30S 146 37 E
Curtis I., *Australia* **62 C5** 23 35S 151 10 E
Curuápanema →, *Brazil* **93 D7** 2 25S 55 2W
Curuçá, *Brazil* **93 D9** 0 43S 47 50W
Curuguaty, *Paraguay* **95 A4** 24 31S 55 42W
Curup, *Indonesia* **36 E2** 4 26S 102 13 E
Cururupu, *Brazil* **93 D10** 1 50S 44 50W
Curuzú Cuatiá, *Argentina* **94 B4** 29 50S 58 5W
Curvelo, *Brazil* **93 G10** 18 45S 44 27W
Cushing, *U.S.A.* **81 H6** 35 59N 96 46W
Cushing, Mt., *Canada* **72 B3** 57 35N 126 57W
Cusihuiriáchic, *Mexico* **86 B3** 28 10N 106 50W
Custer, *U.S.A.* **80 D3** 43 46N 103 36W
Cut Bank, *U.S.A.* **82 B7** 48 38N 112 20W
Cutchogue, *U.S.A.* **79 E12** 41 1N 72 30W
Cuthbert, *U.S.A.* **77 K3** 31 46N 84 48W
Cutler, *U.S.A.* **84 J7** 36 31N 119 17W
Cuttaburra →, *Australia* **63 D3** 29 43S 144 22 E
Cuttack, *India* **41 J14** 20 25N 85 57 E
Cuvier, C., *Australia* **61 D1** 23 14S 113 22 E
Cuvier I., *N.Z.* **59 G5** 36 27S 175 50 E
Cuxhaven, *Germany* **16 B5** 53 51N 8 41 E
Cuyahoga Falls, *U.S.A.* **78 E3** 41 8N 81 29W
Cuyo, *Phil.* **37 B6** 10 50N 121 5 E
Cuyuni →, *Guyana* **92 B7** 6 23N 58 41W
Cuzco, *Bolivia* **92 H5** 20 0S 66 50W
Cuzco, *Peru* **92 F4** 13 32S 72 0W
Cwmbran, *U.K.* **11 F4** 51 39N 3 2W
Cyangugu, *Rwanda* **54 C2** 2 29S 28 54 E
Cyclades = Kikládhes, *Greece* **21 F11** 37 0N 24 30 E
Cygnet, *Australia* **62 G4** 43 8S 147 1 E
Cynthiana, *U.S.A.* **76 F3** 38 23N 84 18W
Cypress Hills, *Canada* **73 D7** 49 40N 109 30W
Cypress Hills Prov. Park, *Canada* **73 D7** 49 40N 109 30W
Cyprus ■, *Asia* **23 E12** 35 0N 33 0 E
Cyrenaica, *Libya* **51 C10** 27 0N 23 0 E
Czar, *Canada* **73 C6** 52 27N 110 50W
Czech Rep. ■, *Europe* **16 D8** 50 0N 15 0 E
Częstochowa, *Poland* **17 C10** 50 49N 19 7 E

D

Da →, *Vietnam* **38 B5** 21 15N 105 20 E
Da Hinggan Ling, *China* **33 B7** 48 0N 121 0 E
Da Lat, *Vietnam* **39 G7** 11 56N 108 25 E
Da Nang, *Vietnam* **38 D7** 16 4N 108 13 E
Da Qaidam, *China* **32 C4** 37 50N 95 15 E
Da Yunhe →, *China* **35 G11** 34 25N 120 5 E
Da'an, *China* **35 B13** 45 30N 124 7 E
Daba Shan, *China* **33 C5** 32 0N 109 0 E
Dabbagh, Jabal, *Si. Arabia* **44 E2** 27 52N 35 45 E
Dabhoi, *India* **42 H5** 22 10N 73 20 E
Dabo = Pasirkuning, *Indonesia* **36 E2** 0 30S 104 33 E
Dabola, *Guinea* **50 F3** 10 50N 11 5W
Dabung, *Malaysia* **39 K4** 5 23N 102 1 E

Denbigh

Denbigh, *Canada* **78 A7** 45 8N 77 15W
Denbigh, *U.K.* **10 D4** 53 12N 3 25W
Denbighshire □, *U.K.* **10 D4** 53 8N 3 22W
Dendang, *Indonesia* **36 E3** 3 7S 107 56 E
Dendermonde, *Belgium* **15 C4** 51 2N 4 5 E
Dengfeng, *China* **34 G7** 34 25N 113 2 E
Dengkou, *China* **34 D4** 40 18N 106 55 E
Denham, *Australia* **61 E1** 25 56S 113 31 E
Denham Ra., *Australia* **62 C4** 21 55S 147 46 E
Denham Sd., *Australia* **61 E1** 25 45S 113 15 E
Denholm, *Canada* **73 C7** 52 39N 108 1W
Denia, *Spain* **19 C6** 38 49N 0 8 E
Denial B., *Australia* **63 E1** 32 14S 133 32 E
Deniliquin, *Australia* **63 F3** 35 30S 144 58 E
Denison, *Iowa, U.S.A.* **80 E7** 42 1N 95 21W
Denison, *Tex., U.S.A.* **81 J6** 33 45N 96 33W
Denison Plains, *Australia* **60 C4** 18 35S 128 0 E
Denizli, *Turkey* **25 G4** 37 42N 29 2 E
Denman Glacier, *Antarctica* **5 C7** 66 45S 99 25 E
Denmark, *Australia* **61 F2** 34 59S 117 25 E
Denmark ■, *Europe* **9 J13** 55 45N 10 0 E
Denmark Str., *Atl. Oc.* **4 C6** 66 0N 30 0W
Dennison, *U.S.A.* **78 F3** 40 24N 81 19W
Denny, *U.K.* **12 E5** 56 1N 3 55W
Denpasar, *Indonesia* **36 F5** 8 39S 115 13 E
Denton, *Mont., U.S.A.* **82 C9** 47 19N 109 57W
Denton, *Tex., U.S.A.* **81 J6** 33 13N 97 8W
D'Entrecasteaux, Pt., *Australia* **61 F2** 34 50S 115 57 E
Denver, *Colo., U.S.A.* **80 F2** 39 44N 104 59W
Denver, *Pa., U.S.A.* **79 F8** 40 14N 76 8W
Denver City, *U.S.A.* **81 J3** 32 58N 102 50W
Deoband, *India* **42 E7** 29 42N 77 43 E
Deogarh, *India* **42 G5** 25 32N 73 54 E
Deoghar, *India* **43 G12** 24 30N 86 42 E
Deolali, *India* **40 K8** 19 58N 73 50 E
Deoli = Devli, *India* **42 G6** 25 50N 75 20 E
Deora, *India* **42 F4** 26 22N 70 55 E
Deori, *India* **43 H8** 23 24N 79 1 E
Deoria, *India* **43 F10** 26 31N 83 48 E
Deosai Mts., *Pakistan* **43 B6** 35 40N 75 0 E
Deosri, *India* **43 F14** 26 46N 90 29 E
Depalpur, *India* **42 H6** 22 51N 75 33 E
Deping, *China* **35 F9** 37 25N 116 58 E
Deposit, *U.S.A.* **79 D9** 42 4N 75 25W
Depuch I., *Australia* **60 D2** 20 37S 117 44 E
Deputatskiy, *Russia* **27 C14** 69 18N 139 54 E
Dera Ghazi Khan, *Pakistan* **42 D4** 30 5N 70 43 E
Dera Ismail Khan, *Pakistan* **42 D4** 31 50N 70 50 E
Derabugti, *Pakistan* **42 E3** 29 2N 69 9 E
Derawar Fort, *Pakistan* **42 E4** 28 46N 71 20 E
Derbent, *Russia* **25 F8** 42 5N 48 15 E
Derby, *Australia* **60 C3** 17 18S 123 38 E
Derby, *U.K.* **10 E6** 52 56N 1 28W
Derby, *Conn., U.S.A.* **79 E11** 41 19N 73 5W
Derby, *Kans., U.S.A.* **81 G6** 37 33N 97 16W
Derby, *N.Y., U.S.A.* **78 D6** 42 41N 78 58W
Derby City □, *U.K.* **10 E6** 52 56N 1 28W
Derby Line, *U.S.A.* **79 B12** 45 0N 72 6W
Derbyshire □, *U.K.* **10 D6** 53 11N 1 38W
Derg →, *U.K.* **13 B4** 54 44N 7 26W
Derg, L., *Ireland* **13 D3** 53 0N 8 20W
Dergaon, *India* **41 F19** 26 45N 94 0 E
Dermott, *U.S.A.* **81 J9** 33 32N 91 26W
Derry = Londonderry, *U.K.* **13 B4** 55 0N 7 20W
Derry = Londonderry □, *U.K.* **13 B4** 55 0N 7 20W
Derry, *N.H., U.S.A.* **79 D13** 42 53N 71 19W
Derry, *Pa., U.S.A.* **78 F5** 40 20N 79 18W
Derryveagh Mts., *Ireland* **13 B3** 54 56N 8 11W
Derwent →, *Cumb., U.K.* **10 C4** 54 39N 3 33W
Derwent →, *Derby, U.K.* **10 E6** 52 57N 1 28W
Derwent →, *N. Yorks., U.K.* **10 D7** 53 45N 0 58W
Derwent Water, *U.K.* **10 C4** 54 35N 3 9W
Des Moines, *Iowa, U.S.A.* **80 E8** 41 35N 93 37W
Des Moines, *N. Mex., U.S.A.* **81 G3** 36 46N 103 50W
Des Moines →, *U.S.A.* **80 E9** 40 23N 91 25W
Desaguadero →, *Argentina* **94 C2** 34 30S 66 46W
Desaguadero →, *Bolivia* **92 G5** 16 35S 69 5W
Descanso, Pta., *Mexico* **85 N9** 32 21N 117 3W
Deschaillons, *Canada* **71 C5** 46 32N 72 7W
Deschambault L., *Canada* **73 C8** 54 50N 103 30W
Deschutes →, *U.S.A.* **82 D3** 45 38N 120 55W
Dese, *Ethiopia* **46 E2** 11 5N 39 40 E
Deseado →, *Argentina* **96 F3** 47 45S 65 54W
Desert Center, *U.S.A.* **85 M11** 33 43N 115 24W
Desert Hot Springs, *U.S.A.* **85 M10** 33 58N 116 30W
Deshnok, *India* **42 F5** 27 48N 73 21 E
Desna →, *Ukraine* **17 C16** 50 33N 30 32 E
Desolación, I., *Chile* **96 G2** 53 0S 74 0W
Despeñaperros, Paso, *Spain* **19 C4** 38 24N 3 30W
Dessau, *Germany* **16 C7** 51 51N 12 14 E
Dessye = Dese, *Ethiopia* **46 E2** 11 5N 39 40 E
D'Estrees B., *Australia* **63 F2** 35 55S 137 45 E
Desuri, *India* **42 G5** 25 18N 73 35 E
Det Udom, *Thailand* **38 E5** 14 54N 105 5 E
Dete, *Zimbabwe* **56 B4** 18 38S 26 50 E
Detmold, *Germany* **16 C5** 51 56N 8 52 E
Detour, Pt., *U.S.A.* **76 C2** 45 40N 86 40W
Detroit, *U.S.A.* **78 D1** 42 20N 83 3W
Detroit Lakes, *U.S.A.* **80 B7** 46 49N 95 51W
Deurne, *Neths.* **15 C5** 51 27N 5 49 E
Deutsche Bucht, *Germany* **16 A5** 54 15N 8 0 E
Deva, *Romania* **17 F12** 45 53N 22 55 E
Devakottai, *India* **40 Q11** 9 55N 78 45 E
Devaprayag, *India* **43 D8** 30 13N 78 35 E
Deventer, *Neths.* **15 B6** 52 15N 6 10 E
Deveron →, *U.K.* **12 D6** 57 41N 2 32W
Devgadh Bariya, *India* **42 H5** 22 40N 73 55 E
Devikot, *India* **42 F4** 26 42N 71 12 E
Devils Den, *U.S.A.* **84 K7** 35 46N 119 58W
Devils Lake, *U.S.A.* **80 A5** 48 7N 98 52W
Devils Paw, *Canada* **72 B2** 58 47N 134 0W
Devils Tower Junction, *U.S.A.* **80 C2** 44 31N 104 57W
Devine, *U.S.A.* **81 L5** 29 8N 98 54W
Devizes, *U.K.* **11 F6** 51 22N 1 58W
Devli, *India* **42 G6** 25 50N 75 20 E
Devon, *Canada* **72 C6** 53 24N 113 44W
Devon □, *U.K.* **11 G4** 50 50N 3 40W
Devon I., *Canada* **4 B3** 75 10N 85 0W
Devonport, *Australia* **62 G4** 41 10S 146 22 E
Devonport, *N.Z.* **59 G5** 36 49S 174 49 E
Dewas, *India* **42 H7** 22 59N 76 3 E
Dewetsdorp, *S. Africa* **56 D4** 29 33S 26 39 E
Dexter, *Maine, U.S.A.* **77 C11** 45 1N 69 18W
Dexter, *Mo., U.S.A.* **81 G10** 36 48N 89 57W
Dexter, *N. Mex., U.S.A.* **81 J2** 33 12N 104 22W
Dey-Dey, L., *Australia* **61 E5** 29 12S 131 4 E
Deyhūk, *Iran* **45 C8** 33 15N 57 30 E
Deyyer, *Iran* **45 E6** 27 55N 51 55 E
Dezadeash L., *Canada* **72 A1** 60 28N 136 58W
Dezfūl, *Iran* **45 C6** 32 20N 48 30 E
Dezhneva, Mys, *Russia* **27 C19** 66 5N 169 40W
Dezhou, *China* **34 F9** 37 26N 116 18 E
Dhadhar →, *India* **43 G11** 24 56N 85 24 E
Dháfni, *Greece* **23 D7** 35 13N 25 3 E
Dhahiriya = Az̧ Z̧āhirīyah, *West Bank* **47 D3** 31 25N 34 58 E
Dhahran = Az̧ Z̧ahrān, *Si. Arabia* **45 E6** 26 10N 50 7 E
Dhak, *Pakistan* **42 C5** 32 25N 72 33 E
Dhaka, *Bangla.* **43 H14** 23 43N 90 26 E
Dhaka □, *Bangla.* **43 G14** 24 25N 90 25 E
Dhali, *Cyprus* **23 D12** 35 1N 33 25 E
Dhampur, *India* **43 E8** 29 19N 78 33 E
Dhamtari, *India* **41 J12** 20 42N 81 35 E
Dhanbad, *India* **43 H12** 23 50N 86 30 E
Dhangarhi, *Nepal* **41 E12** 28 55N 80 40 E
Dhankuta, *Nepal* **43 F12** 26 55N 87 40 E
Dhar, *India* **42 H6** 22 35N 75 26 E
Dharampur, *India* **42 H6** 22 13N 75 18 E
Dharamsala = Dharmsala, *India* **42 C7** 32 16N 76 23 E
Dhariwal, *India* **42 D6** 31 57N 75 19 E
Dharla →, *Bangla.* **43 G13** 25 46N 89 42 E
Dharmapuri, *India* **40 N11** 12 10N 78 10 E
Dharmjaygarh, *India* **43 H10** 22 28N 83 13 E
Dharmsala, *India* **42 C7** 32 16N 76 23 E
Dharni, *India* **42 J7** 21 33N 76 53 E
Dharwad, *India* **40 M9** 15 30N 75 4 E
Dhasan →, *India* **43 G8** 25 48N 79 24 E
Dhaulagiri, *Nepal* **43 E10** 28 39N 83 28 E
Dhebar, L., *India* **42 G6** 24 10N 74 0 E
Dheftera, *Cyprus* **23 D12** 35 5N 33 16 E
Dhenkanal, *India* **41 J14** 20 45N 85 35 E
Dherinia, *Cyprus* **23 D12** 35 3N 33 57 E
Dhiarrizos →, *Cyprus* **23 E11** 34 41N 32 34 E
Dhībān, *Jordan* **47 D4** 31 30N 35 46 E
Dhíkti Óros, *Greece* **23 D7** 35 8N 25 30 E
Dhilwan, *India* **42 D6** 31 31N 75 21 E
Dhimarkhera, *India* **43 H9** 23 28N 80 22 E
Dhírfis Óros, *Greece* **21 E10** 38 40N 23 54 E
Dhodhekánisos, *Greece* **21 F12** 36 35N 27 0 E
Dholka, *India* **42 H5** 22 44N 72 29 E
Dhoraji, *India* **42 J4** 21 45N 70 37 E
Dhráhstis, Ákra, *Greece* **23 A3** 39 48N 19 40 E
Dhrangadhra, *India* **42 H4** 22 59N 71 31 E
Dhrápanon, Ákra, *Greece* **23 D6** 35 28N 24 14 E
Dhrol, *India* **42 H4** 22 33N 70 25 E
Dhuburi, *India* **41 F16** 26 2N 89 59 E
Dhule, *India* **40 J9** 20 58N 74 50 E
Di Linh, *Vietnam* **39 G7** 11 35N 108 4 E
Di Linh, Cao Nguyen, *Vietnam* **39 G7** 11 30N 108 0 E
Día, *Greece* **23 D7** 35 28N 25 14 E
Diablo, Mt., *U.S.A.* **84 H5** 37 53N 121 56W
Diablo Range, *U.S.A.* **84 J5** 37 20N 121 25W
Diafarabé, *Mali* **50 F5** 14 9N 4 57W
Diamante, *Argentina* **94 C3** 32 5S 60 40W
Diamante →, *Argentina* **94 C2** 34 30S 66 46W
Diamantina, *Brazil* **93 G10** 18 17S 43 40W
Diamantina →, *Australia* **63 D2** 26 45S 139 10 E
Diamantino, *Brazil* **93 F7** 14 30S 56 30W
Diamond Bar, *U.S.A.* **85 L9** 34 1N 117 48W
Diamond Harbour, *India* **43 H13** 22 11N 88 14 E
Diamond Is., *Australia* **62 B5** 17 25S 151 5 E
Diamond Mts., *U.S.A.* **82 G6** 39 50N 115 30W
Diamond Springs, *U.S.A.* **84 G6** 38 42N 120 49W
Dībā, *Oman* **45 E8** 25 45N 56 16 E
Dibai, *India* **42 E8** 28 13N 78 15 E
Dibaya-Lubue, *Dem. Rep. of the Congo* **52 E3** 4 12S 19 54 E
Dibete, *Botswana* **56 C4** 23 45S 26 32 E
Dibrugarh, *India* **41 F19** 27 29N 94 55 E
Dickens, *U.S.A.* **81 J4** 33 37N 100 50W
Dickinson, *U.S.A.* **80 B3** 46 53N 102 47W
Dickson = Dikson, *Russia* **26 B9** 73 40N 80 5 E
Dickson, *U.S.A.* **77 G2** 36 5N 87 23W
Dickson City, *U.S.A.* **79 E9** 41 29N 75 40W
Didiéni, *Mali* **50 F4** 13 53N 8 6W
Didsbury, *Canada* **72 C6** 51 35N 114 10W
Didwana, *India* **42 F6** 27 23N 74 36 E
Diefenbaker, L., *Canada* **73 C7** 51 0N 106 55W
Diego de Almagro, *Chile* **94 B1** 26 22S 70 3W
Diego Garcia, *Ind. Oc.* **3 E13** 7 50S 72 50 E
Diekirch, *Lux.* **15 E6** 49 52N 6 10 E
Dien Ban, *Vietnam* **38 E7** 15 53N 108 16 E
Dien Bien, *Vietnam* **38 B4** 21 20N 103 0 E
Dien Khanh, *Vietnam* **39 F7** 12 15N 109 6 E
Dieppe, *France* **18 B4** 49 54N 1 4 E
Dierks, *U.S.A.* **81 H8** 34 7N 94 1W
Diest, *Belgium* **15 D5** 50 58N 5 4 E
Dif, *Somali Rep.* **46 G3** 0 59N 0 56 E
Differdange, *Lux.* **15 E5** 49 31N 5 54 E
Dig, *India* **42 F7** 27 28N 77 20 E
Digba, *Dem. Rep. of the Congo* **54 B2** 4 25N 25 48 E
Digby, *Canada* **71 D6** 44 38N 65 50W
Diggi, *India* **42 F6** 26 22N 75 26 E
Dighinala, *Bangla.* **41 H18** 23 15N 92 5 E
Dighton, *U.S.A.* **80 F4** 38 29N 100 28W
Digne-les-Bains, *France* **18 D7** 44 5N 6 12 E
Digos, *Phil.* **37 C7** 6 45N 125 20 E
Digranes, *Iceland* **8 C6** 66 4N 14 44W
Digul →, *Indonesia* **37 F9** 7 7S 138 42 E
Dihang = Brahmaputra →, *India* **41 F19** 27 48N 95 30 E
Dijlah, Nahr →, *Asia* **44 D5** 31 0N 47 25 E
Dijon, *France* **18 C6** 47 20N 5 3 E
Dikhil, *Djibouti* **46 E3** 11 8N 42 20 E
Dikkil = Dikhil, *Djibouti* **46 E3** 11 8N 42 20 E
Diksmuide, *Belgium* **15 C2** 51 2N 2 52 E
Dikson, *Russia* **26 B9** 73 40N 80 5 E
Dila, *Ethiopia* **46 F2** 6 21N 38 22 E
Dili, *E. Timor* **37 F7** 8 39S 125 34 E
Dilley, *U.S.A.* **81 L5** 28 40N 99 10W
Dillingham, *U.S.A.* **68 C4** 59 3N 158 28W
Dillon, *Canada* **73 B7** 55 56N 108 35W
Dillon, *Mont., U.S.A.* **82 D7** 45 13N 112 38W
Dillon, *S.C., U.S.A.* **77 H6** 34 25N 79 22W
Dillon →, *Canada* **73 B7** 55 56N 108 56W
Dillsburg, *U.S.A.* **78 F7** 40 7N 77 2W
Dilolo, *Dem. Rep. of the Congo* **52 G4** 10 28S 22 18 E
Dimas, *Mexico* **86 C3** 23 43N 106 47W
Dimashq, *Syria* **47 B5** 33 30N 36 18 E
Dimashq □, *Syria* **47 B5** 33 30N 36 30 E
Dimbaza, *S. Africa* **57 E4** 32 50S 27 14 E
Dimboola, *Australia* **63 F3** 36 28S 142 7 E
Dîmboviţa = Dâmboviţa →, *Romania* **17 F14** 44 12N 26 26 E
Dimbulah, *Australia* **62 B4** 17 8S 145 4 E
Dimitrovgrad, *Bulgaria* **21 C11** 42 5N 25 35 E
Dimitrovgrad, *Russia* **24 D8** 54 14N 49 39 E
Dimitrovo = Pernik, *Bulgaria* **21 C10** 42 35N 23 2 E
Dimmitt, *U.S.A.* **81 H3** 34 33N 102 19W
Dimona, *Israel* **47 D4** 31 2N 35 1 E
Dinagat, *Phil.* **37 B7** 10 10N 125 40 E
Dinajpur, *Bangla.* **41 G16** 25 33N 88 43 E
Dinan, *France* **18 B2** 48 28N 2 2W
Dīnān Āb, *Iran* **45 C8** 32 4N 56 49 E
Dinant, *Belgium* **15 D4** 50 16N 4 55 E
Dinapur, *India* **43 G11** 25 38N 85 5 E
Dīnār, Kūh-e, *Iran* **45 D6** 30 42N 51 46 E
Dinara Planina, *Croatia* **20 C7** 44 0N 16 30 E
Dinard, *France* **18 B2** 48 38N 2 6W
Dinaric Alps = Dinara Planina, *Croatia* **20 C7** 44 0N 16 30 E
Dindigul, *India* **40 P11** 10 25N 78 0 E
Dindori, *India* **43 H9** 22 57N 81 5 E
Ding Xian = Dingzhou, *China* **34 E8** 38 30N 114 59 E
Dinga, *Pakistan* **42 G2** 25 26N 67 10 E
Dingbian, *China* **34 F4** 37 35N 107 32 E
Dingle, *Ireland* **13 D1** 52 9N 10 17W
Dingle B., *Ireland* **13 D1** 52 3N 10 20W
Dingmans Ferry, *U.S.A.* **79 E10** 41 13N 74 55W
Dingo, *Australia* **62 C4** 23 38S 149 19 E
Dingtao, *China* **34 G8** 35 5N 115 35 E
Dingwall, *U.K.* **12 D4** 57 36N 4 26W
Dingxi, *China* **34 G3** 35 30N 104 33 E
Dingxiang, *China* **34 E7** 38 30N 112 58 E
Dingzhou, *China* **34 E8** 38 30N 114 59 E
Dinh, Mui, *Vietnam* **39 G7** 11 22N 109 1 E
Dinh Lap, *Vietnam* **38 B6** 21 33N 107 6 E
Dinokwe, *Botswana* **56 C4** 23 29S 26 37 E
Dinorwic, *Canada* **73 D10** 49 41N 92 30W
Dinosaur Nat. Monument, *U.S.A.* **82 F9** 40 30N 108 45W
Dinosaur Prov. Park, *Canada* **72 C6** 50 47N 111 30W
Dinuba, *U.S.A.* **84 J7** 36 32N 119 23W
Dipalpur, *Pakistan* **42 D5** 30 40N 73 39 E
Diplo, *Pakistan* **42 G3** 24 35N 69 35 E
Dipolog, *Phil.* **37 C6** 8 36N 123 20 E
Dir, *Pakistan* **40 B7** 35 8N 71 59 E
Dire Dawa, *Ethiopia* **46 F3** 9 35N 41 45 E
Diriamba, *Nic.* **88 D2** 11 51N 86 19W
Dirk Hartog I., *Australia* **61 E1** 25 50S 113 5 E
Dirranbandi, *Australia* **63 D4** 28 33S 148 17 E
Disa, *India* **42 G5** 24 18N 72 10 E
Disappointment, C., *U.S.A.* **82 C2** 46 18N 124 5W
Disappointment, L., *Australia* **60 D3** 23 20S 122 40 E
Disaster B., *Australia* **63 F4** 37 15S 149 58 E
Discovery B., *Australia* **63 F3** 38 10S 140 40 E
Disko = Qeqertarsuaq, *Greenland* **69 B5** 69 45N 53 30W
Disko Bugt, *Greenland* **4 C5** 69 10N 52 0W
Diss, *U.K.* **11 E9** 52 23N 1 7 E
Disteghil Sar, *Pakistan* **43 A6** 36 20N 75 12 E
Distrito Federal □, *Brazil* **93 G9** 15 45S 47 45W
Distrito Federal □, *Mexico* **87 D5** 19 15N 99 10W
Diu, *India* **42 J4** 20 45N 70 58 E
Dīvāndarreh, *Iran* **44 C5** 35 55N 47 2 E
Divide, *U.S.A.* **82 D7** 45 45N 112 45W
Dividing Ra., *Australia* **61 E2** 27 45S 116 0 E
Divinópolis, *Brazil* **93 H10** 20 10S 44 54W
Divnoye, *Russia* **25 E7** 45 55N 43 21 E
Divo, *Ivory C.* **50 G4** 5 48N 5 15W
Dīwāl Kol, *Afghan.* **42 B2** 34 23N 67 52 E
Dixie Mt., *U.S.A.* **84 F6** 39 55N 120 16W
Dixon, *Calif., U.S.A.* **84 G5** 38 27N 121 49W
Dixon, *Ill., U.S.A.* **80 E10** 41 50N 89 29W
Dixon Entrance, *U.S.A.* **68 C6** 54 30N 132 0W
Dixville, *Canada* **79 A13** 45 4N 71 46W
Diyālā →, *Iraq* **44 C5** 33 14N 44 31 E
Diyarbakır, *Turkey* **25 G7** 37 55N 40 18 E
Diyodar, *India* **42 G4** 24 8N 71 50 E
Djakarta = Jakarta, *Indonesia* **36 F3** 6 9S 106 49 E
Djamba, *Angola* **56 B1** 16 45S 13 58 E
Djambala, *Congo* **52 E2** 2 32S 14 30 E
Djanet, *Algeria* **50 D7** 24 35N 9 32 E
Djawa = Jawa, *Indonesia* **36 F3** 7 0S 110 0 E
Djelfa, *Algeria* **50 B6** 34 40N 3 15 E
Djema, *C.A.R.* **54 A2** 6 3N 25 15 E
Djerba, I. de, *Tunisia* **51 B8** 33 50N 10 48 E
Djerid, Chott, *Tunisia* **50 B7** 33 42N 8 30 E
Djibouti, *Djibouti* **46 E3** 11 30N 43 5 E
Djibouti ■, *Africa* **46 E3** 12 0N 43 0 E
Djolu, *Dem. Rep. of the Congo* **52 D4** 0 35N 22 5 E
Djoum, *Cameroon* **52 D2** 2 41N 12 35 E
Djourab, Erg du, *Chad* **51 E9** 16 40N 18 50 E
Djugu, *Dem. Rep. of the Congo* **54 B3** 1 55N 30 35 E
Djúpivogur, *Iceland* **8 D6** 64 39N 14 17W
Dmitriya Lapteva, Proliv, *Russia* **27 B15** 73 0N 140 0 E
Dnepr → = Dnipro →, *Ukraine* **25 E5** 46 30N 32 18 E
Dneprodzerzhinsk = Dniprodzerzhynsk, *Ukraine* **25 E5** 48 32N 34 37 E
Dnepropetrovsk = Dnipropetrovsk, *Ukraine* **25 E6** 48 30N 35 0 E
Dnestr → = Dnister →, *Europe* **17 E16** 46 18N 30 17 E
Dnestrovski = Belgorod, *Russia* **25 D6** 50 35N 36 35 E
Dnieper = Dnipro →, *Ukraine* **25 E5** 46 30N 32 18 E
Dniester = Dnister →, *Europe* **17 E16** 46 18N 30 17 E
Dnipro →, *Ukraine* **25 E5** 46 30N 32 18 E
Dniprodzerzhynsk, *Ukraine* **25 E5** 48 32N 34 37 E
Dnipropetrovsk, *Ukraine* **25 E6** 48 30N 35 0 E
Dnister →, *Europe* **17 E16** 46 18N 30 17 E
Dnistrovskyy Lyman, *Ukraine* **17 E16** 46 15N 30 17 E
Dno, *Russia* **24 C4** 57 50N 29 58 E
Dnyapro = Dnipro →, *Ukraine* **25 E5** 46 30N 32 18 E
Doaktown, *Canada* **71 C6** 46 33N 66 8W
Doan Hung, *Vietnam* **38 B5** 21 30N 105 10 E
Doany, *Madag.* **57 A8** 14 21S 49 30 E
Doba, *Chad* **51 G9** 8 40N 16 50 E
Dobandi, *Pakistan* **42 D2** 31 13N 66 50 E
Dobbyn, *Australia* **62 B3** 19 44S 140 2 E
Dobele, *Latvia* **9 H20** 56 37N 23 16 E
Doberai, Jazirah, *Indonesia* **37 E8** 1 25S 133 0 E
Doblas, *Argentina* **94 D3** 37 5S 64 0W
Dobo, *Indonesia* **37 F8** 5 45S 134 15 E
Doboj, *Bos.-H.* **21 B8** 44 46N 18 4 E
Dobrich, *Bulgaria* **21 C12** 43 37N 27 49 E
Dobruja, *Europe* **17 F15** 44 30N 28 15 E
Dobrush, *Belarus* **17 B16** 52 25N 31 22 E
Doc, Mui, *Vietnam* **38 D6** 17 58N 106 30 E
Docker River, *Australia* **61 D4** 24 52S 129 5 E
Doctor Arroyo, *Mexico* **86 C4** 23 40N 100 11W
Doda, *India* **43 C6** 33 10N 75 34 E
Doda, L., *Canada* **70 C4** 49 25N 75 13W
Dodecanese = Dhodhekánisos, *Greece* **21 F12** 36 35N 27 0 E
Dodge City, *U.S.A.* **81 G5** 37 45N 100 1W
Dodge L., *Canada* **73 B7** 59 50N 105 36W
Dodgeville, *U.S.A.* **80 D9** 42 58N 90 8W
Dodoma, *Tanzania* **54 D4** 6 8S 35 45 E
Dodoma □, *Tanzania* **54 D4** 6 0S 36 0 E
Dodsland, *Canada* **73 C7** 51 50N 108 45W
Dodson, *U.S.A.* **82 B9** 48 24N 108 15W
Doesburg, *Neths.* **15 B6** 52 1N 6 9 E
Doetinchem, *Neths.* **15 C6** 51 59N 6 18 E
Dog Creek, *Canada* **72 C4** 51 35N 122 14W
Dog L., *Man., Canada* **73 C9** 51 2N 98 31W
Dog L., *Ont., Canada* **70 C2** 48 48N 89 30W
Dogran, *Pakistan* **42 D5** 31 48N 73 35 E
Doğubayazıt, *Turkey* **44 B5** 39 31N 44 5 E
Doha = Ad Dawḩah, *Qatar* **46 B5** 25 15N 51 35 E
Dohazari, *Bangla.* **41 H18** 22 10N 92 5 E
Dohrighat, *India* **43 F10** 26 16N 83 31 E
Doi, *Indonesia* **37 D7** 2 14N 127 49 E
Doi Luang, *Thailand* **38 C3** 18 30N 101 0 E
Doi Saket, *Thailand* **38 C2** 18 52N 99 9 E
Dois Irmãos, Sa., *Brazil* **93 E10** 9 0S 42 30W
Dokkum, *Neths.* **15 A5** 53 20N 5 59 E
Dokri, *Pakistan* **42 F3** 27 25N 68 7 E
Dolak, Pulau, *Indonesia* **37 F9** 8 0S 138 30 E
Dolbeau, *Canada* **71 C5** 48 53N 72 18W
Dole, *France* **18 C6** 47 7N 5 31 E
Dolgellau, *U.K.* **10 E4** 52 45N 3 53W
Dolgelley = Dolgellau, *U.K.* **10 E4** 52 45N 3 53W
Dollard, *Neths.* **15 A7** 53 20N 7 10 E
Dolo, *Ethiopia* **46 G3** 4 11N 42 3 E
Dolomites = Dolomiti, *Italy* **20 A4** 46 23N 11 51 E
Dolomiti, *Italy* **20 A4** 46 23N 11 51 E
Dolores, *Argentina* **94 D4** 36 20S 57 40W
Dolores, *Uruguay* **94 C4** 33 34S 58 15W
Dolores, *U.S.A.* **83 H9** 37 28N 108 30W
Dolores →, *U.S.A.* **83 G9** 38 49N 109 17W
Dolphin, C., *Falk. Is.* **96 G5** 51 10S 59 0W
Dolphin and Union Str., *Canada* **68 B8** 69 5N 114 45W
Dom Pedrito, *Brazil* **95 C5** 31 0S 54 40W
Domariaganj →, *India* **43 F10** 26 17N 83 44 E
Domasi, *Malawi* **55 F4** 15 15S 35 22 E
Dombarovskiy, *Russia* **26 D6** 50 46N 59 32 E
Dombås, *Norway* **9 E13** 62 4N 9 8 E
Domel I. = Letsôk-aw Kyun, *Burma* **39 G2** 11 30N 98 25 E
Domeyko, *Chile* **94 B1** 29 0S 71 0W
Domeyko, Cordillera, *Chile* **94 A2** 24 30S 69 0W
Dominador, *Chile* **94 A2** 24 21S 69 20W
Dominica ■, *W. Indies* **89 C7** 15 20N 61 20W
Dominica Passage, *W. Indies* **89 C7** 15 10N 61 20W
Dominican Rep. ■, *W. Indies* **89 C5** 19 0N 70 30W
Domodóssola, *Italy* **18 C8** 46 7N 8 17 E
Domville, Mt., *Australia* **63 D5** 28 1S 151 15 E
Don →, *Russia* **25 E6** 47 4N 39 18 E
Don →, *Aberds., U.K.* **12 D6** 57 11N 2 5W
Don →, *S. Yorks., U.K.* **10 D7** 53 41N 0 52W
Don, C., *Australia* **60 B5** 11 18S 131 46 E
Don Benito, *Spain* **19 C3** 38 53N 5 51W
Dona Ana = Nhamaabué, *Mozam.* **55 F4** 17 25S 35 5 E
Donaghadee, *U.K.* **13 B6** 54 39N 5 33W
Donald, *Australia* **63 F3** 36 23S 143 0 E
Donaldsonville, *U.S.A.* **81 K9** 30 6N 90 59W
Donalsonville, *U.S.A.* **77 K3** 31 3N 84 53W
Donau = Dunărea →, *Europe* **17 F15** 45 20N 29 40 E
Donau →, *Austria* **15 D3** 48 10N 17 0 E
Donauwörth, *Germany* **16 D6** 48 43N 10 47 E
Doncaster, *U.K.* **10 D6** 53 32N 1 6W
Dondo, *Mozam.* **55 F3** 19 33S 34 46 E
Dondo, Teluk, *Indonesia* **37 D6** 0 50N 120 30 E
Dondra Head, *Sri Lanka* **40 S12** 5 55N 80 40 E
Donegal, *Ireland* **13 B3** 54 39N 8 5W
Donegal □, *Ireland* **13 B4** 54 53N 8 0W
Donegal B., *Ireland* **13 B3** 54 31N 8 49W
Donets →, *Russia* **25 E7** 47 33N 40 55 E
Donetsk, *Ukraine* **25 E6** 48 0N 37 45 E
Dong Ba Thin, *Vietnam* **39 F7** 12 8N 109 13 E
Dong Dang, *Vietnam* **38 B6** 21 54N 106 42 E
Dong Giam, *Vietnam* **38 C5** 19 25N 105 31 E
Dong Ha, *Vietnam* **38 D6** 16 55N 107 8 E
Dong Hene, *Laos* **38 D5** 16 40N 105 18 E
Dong Hoi, *Vietnam* **38 D6** 17 29N 106 36 E
Dong Khe, *Vietnam* **38 A6** 22 26N 106 27 E
Dong Ujimqin Qi, *China* **34 B9** 45 32N 116 55 E
Dong Van, *Vietnam* **38 A5** 23 16N 105 22 E
Dong Xoai, *Vietnam* **39 G6** 11 32N 106 55 E
Dongara, *Australia* **61 E1** 29 14S 114 57 E
Dongbei, *China* **35 D13** 45 0N 125 0 E
Dongchuan, *China* **32 D5** 26 8N 103 1 E
Dongfang, *China* **38 C7** 18 50N 108 33 E
Dongfeng, *China* **35 C13** 42 40N 125 34 E
Donggala, *Indonesia* **37 E5** 0 30S 119 40 E
Donggou, *China* **35 E13** 39 52N 124 10 E
Dongguang, *China* **34 F9** 37 50N 116 30 E
Dongjingcheng, *China* **35 B15** 44 5N 129 10 E
Dongning, *China* **35 B16** 44 2N 131 5 E
Dongola, *Sudan* **51 E12** 19 9N 30 22 E
Dongping, *China* **34 G9** 35 55N 116 20 E
Dongsheng, *China* **34 E6** 39 50N 110 0 E
Dongtai, *China* **35 H11** 32 51N 120 21 E
Dongting Hu, *China* **33 D6** 29 18N 112 45 E
Donington, C., *Australia* **63 E2** 34 45S 136 0 E
Doniphan, *U.S.A.* **81 G9** 36 37N 90 50W
Dønna, *Norway* **8 C15** 66 6N 12 30 E
Donna, *U.S.A.* **81 M5** 26 9N 98 4W
Donnaconna, *Canada* **71 C5** 46 41N 71 41W
Donnelly's Crossing, *N.Z.* **59 F4** 35 42S 173 38 E

East Providence

Donnybrook, *Australia* 61 F2 33 34S 115 48 E
Donnybrook, *S. Africa* 57 D4 29 59S 29 48 E
Donora, *U.S.A.* 78 F5 40 11N 79 52W
Donostia = Donostia-San Sebastián, *Spain* 19 A5 43 17N 1 58W
Donostia-San Sebastián, *Spain* 19 A5 43 17N 1 58W
Doon →, *U.K.* 12 F4 55 27N 4 39W
Dora, L., *Australia* 60 D3 22 0S 123 0 E
Dora Báltea →, *Italy* 18 D8 45 11N 8 3 E
Doran L., *Canada* 73 A7 61 13N 108 6W
Dorchester, *U.K.* 11 G5 50 42N 2 27W
Dorchester, C., *Canada* 69 B12 65 27N 77 27W
Dordabis, *Namibia* 56 C2 22 52S 17 38 E
Dordogne →, *France* 18 D3 45 2N 0 36W
Dordrecht, *Neths.* 15 C4 51 48N 4 39 E
Dordrecht, *S. Africa* 56 E4 31 20S 27 3 E
Doré L., *Canada* 73 C7 54 46N 107 17W
Doré Lake, *Canada* 73 C7 54 38N 107 36W
Dori, *Burkina Faso* 50 F5 14 3N 0 2W
Doring →, *S. Africa* 56 E2 31 54S 18 39 E
Doringbos, *S. Africa* 56 E2 31 59S 19 16 E
Dorion, *Canada* 79 A10 45 23N 74 3W
Dornbirn, *Austria* 16 E5 47 25N 9 45 E
Dornie, *U.K.* 12 D3 57 17N 5 31W
Dornoch, *U.K.* 12 D4 57 53N 4 2W
Dornoch Firth, *U.K.* 12 D4 57 51N 4 4W
Dornogovĭ □, *Mongolia* 34 C6 44 0N 110 0 E
Dorohoi, *Romania* 17 E14 47 56N 26 23 E
Döröö Nuur, *Mongolia* 32 B4 48 0N 93 0 E
Dorr, *Iran* 45 C6 33 17N 50 38 E
Dorre I., *Australia* 61 E1 25 13S 113 12 E
Dorrigo, *Australia* 63 E5 30 20S 152 44 E
Dorris, *U.S.A.* 82 F3 41 58N 121 55W
Dorset, *Canada* 78 A6 45 14N 78 54W
Dorset, *U.S.A.* 78 E4 41 40N 80 40W
Dorset □, *U.K.* 11 G5 50 45N 2 26W
Dortmund, *Germany* 16 C4 51 30N 7 28 E
Doruma, *Dem. Rep. of the Congo* 54 B2 4 42N 27 33 E
Dorūneh, *Iran* 45 C8 35 10N 57 18 E
Dos Bahías, C., *Argentina* 96 E3 44 58S 65 32W
Dos Hermanas, *Spain* 19 D3 37 16N 5 55W
Dos Palos, *U.S.A.* 84 J6 36 59N 120 37W
Dosso, *Niger* 50 F6 13 0N 3 13 E
Dothan, *U.S.A.* 77 K3 31 13N 85 24W
Doty, *U.S.A.* 84 D3 46 38N 123 17W
Douai, *France* 18 A5 50 21N 3 4 E
Douala, *Cameroon* 52 D1 4 0N 9 45 E
Douarnenez, *France* 18 B1 48 6N 4 21W
Double Island Pt., *Australia* 63 D5 25 56S 153 11 E
Double Mountain Fork →, *U.S.A.* 81 J4 33 16N 100 0W
Doubs →, *France* 18 C6 46 53N 5 1 E
Doubtful Sd., *N.Z.* 59 L1 45 20S 166 49 E
Doubtless B., *N.Z.* 59 F4 34 55S 173 26 E
Douglas, *S. Africa* 56 D3 29 4S 23 46 E
Douglas, *U.K.* 10 C3 54 10N 4 28W
Douglas, *Ariz., U.S.A.* 83 L9 31 21N 109 33W
Douglas, *Ga., U.S.A.* 77 K4 31 31N 82 51W
Douglas, *Wyo., U.S.A.* 80 D2 42 45N 105 24W
Douglas Chan., *Canada* 72 C3 53 40N 129 20W
Douglas Pt., *Canada* 78 B3 44 19N 81 37W
Douglasville, *U.S.A.* 77 J3 33 45N 84 45W
Dounreay, *U.K.* 12 C5 58 35N 3 44W
Dourada, Serra, *Brazil* 93 F9 13 10S 48 45W
Dourados, *Brazil* 95 A5 22 9S 54 50W
Dourados →, *Brazil* 95 A5 21 58S 54 18W
Dourados, Serra dos, *Brazil* 95 A5 23 30S 53 30W
Douro →, *Europe* 19 B1 41 8N 8 40W
Dove →, *U.K.* 10 E6 52 51N 1 36W
Dove Creek, *U.S.A.* 83 H9 37 46N 108 54W
Dover, *Australia* 62 G4 43 18S 147 2 E
Dover, *U.K.* 11 F9 51 7N 1 19 E
Dover, *Del., U.S.A.* 76 F8 39 10N 75 32W
Dover, *N.H., U.S.A.* 79 C14 43 12N 70 56W
Dover, *N.J., U.S.A.* 79 F10 40 53N 74 34W
Dover, *Ohio, U.S.A.* 78 F3 40 32N 81 29W
Dover, Pt., *Australia* 61 F4 32 32S 125 32 E
Dover, Str. of, *Europe* 11 G9 51 0N 1 30 E
Dover-Foxcroft, *U.S.A.* 77 C11 45 11N 69 13W
Dover Plains, *U.S.A.* 79 E11 41 43N 73 35W
Dovey = Dyfi →, *U.K.* 11 E3 52 32N 4 3W
Dovrefjell, *Norway* 9 E13 62 15N 9 33 E
Dow Rūd, *Iran* 45 C6 33 28N 49 4 E
Dowa, *Malawi* 55 E3 13 38S 33 58 E
Dowagiac, *U.S.A.* 76 E2 41 59N 86 6W
Dowerin, *Australia* 61 F2 31 12S 117 2 E
Dowgha'i, *Iran* 45 B8 36 54N 58 32 E
Dowlatābād, *Iran* 45 D8 28 20N 56 40 E
Down □, *U.K.* 13 B5 54 23N 6 2W
Downey, *Calif., U.S.A.* 85 M8 33 56N 118 7W
Downey, *Idaho, U.S.A.* 82 E7 42 26N 112 7W
Downham Market, *U.K.* 11 E8 52 37N 0 23 E
Downieville, *U.S.A.* 84 F6 39 34N 120 50W
Downpatrick, *U.K.* 13 B6 54 20N 5 43W
Downpatrick Hd., *Ireland* 13 B2 54 20N 9 21W
Downsville, *U.S.A.* 79 D10 42 5N 74 50W
Downton, Mt., *Canada* 72 C4 52 42N 124 52W
Dowsārī, *Iran* 45 D8 28 25N 57 59 E
Doyle, *U.S.A.* 84 E6 40 2N 120 6W
Doylestown, *U.S.A.* 79 F9 40 21N 75 10W
Dozois, Rés., *Canada* 70 C4 47 30N 77 5W
Dra Khel, *Pakistan* 42 F2 27 58N 66 45 E
Drachten, *Neths.* 15 A6 53 7N 6 5 E
Drăgăşani, *Romania* 17 F13 44 39N 24 17 E
Dragichyn, *Belarus* 17 B13 52 15N 25 8 E
Dragoman, Prokhod, *Bulgaria* 21 C10 42 58N 22 53 E
Draguignan, *France* 18 E7 43 32N 6 27 E
Drain, *U.S.A.* 82 E2 43 40N 123 19W
Drake, *U.S.A.* 80 B4 47 55N 100 23W
Drake Passage, *S. Ocean* 5 B17 58 0S 68 0W
Drakensberg, *S. Africa* 57 D4 31 0S 28 0 E
Dráma, *Greece* 21 D11 41 9N 24 10 E
Drammen, *Norway* 9 G14 59 42N 10 12 E
Drangajökull, *Iceland* 8 C2 66 9N 22 15W
Dras, *India* 43 B6 34 25N 75 48 E
Drau = Drava →, *Croatia* 21 B8 45 33N 18 55 E
Drava →, *Croatia* 21 B8 45 33N 18 55 E
Drayton Valley, *Canada* 72 C6 53 12N 114 58W
Drenthe □, *Neths.* 15 B6 52 52N 6 40 E
Drepanum, C., *Cyprus* 23 E11 34 54N 32 19 E
Dresden, *Canada* 78 D2 42 35N 82 11W
Dresden, *Germany* 16 C7 51 3N 13 44 E
Dreux, *France* 18 B4 48 44N 1 23 E
Driffield, *U.K.* 10 C7 54 0N 0 26W
Driftwood, *U.S.A.* 78 E6 41 20N 78 8W
Driggs, *U.S.A.* 82 E8 43 44N 111 6W
Drin →, *Albania* 21 C8 42 1N 19 38 E
Drina →, *Bos.-H.* 21 B8 44 53N 19 21 E
Drøbak, *Norway* 9 G14 59 39N 10 39 E
Drobeta-Turnu Severin, *Romania* 17 F12 44 39N 22 41 E
Drochia, *Moldova* 17 D14 48 2N 27 48 E
Drogheda, *Ireland* 13 C5 53 43N 6 22W
Drogichin = Dragichyn, *Belarus* 17 B13 52 15N 25 8 E
Drogobych = Drohobych, *Ukraine* 17 D12 49 20N 23 30 E
Drohobych, *Ukraine* 17 D12 49 20N 23 30 E
Droichead Atha = Drogheda, *Ireland* 13 C5 53 43N 6 22W
Droichead Nua, *Ireland* 13 C5 53 11N 6 48W
Droitwich, *U.K.* 11 E5 52 16N 2 8W
Dromedary, C., *Australia* 63 F5 36 17S 150 10 E
Dromore, *U.K.* 13 B4 54 31N 7 28W
Dromore West, *Ireland* 13 B3 54 15N 8 52W
Dronfield, *U.K.* 10 D6 53 19N 1 27W
Dronten, *Neths.* 15 B5 52 32N 5 43 E
Drumbo, *Canada* 78 C4 43 16N 80 35W
Drumheller, *Canada* 72 C6 51 25N 112 40W
Drummond, *U.S.A.* 82 C7 46 40N 113 9W
Drummond I., *U.S.A.* 76 C4 46 1N 83 39W
Drummond Pt., *Australia* 63 E2 34 9S 135 16 E
Drummond Ra., *Australia* 62 C4 23 45S 147 10 E
Drummondville, *Canada* 70 C5 45 55N 72 25W
Drumright, *U.S.A.* 81 H6 35 59N 96 36W
Druskininkai, *Lithuania* 9 J20 54 3N 23 58 E
Drut →, *Belarus* 17 B16 53 8N 30 5 E
Druzhina, *Russia* 27 C15 68 14N 145 18 E
Dry Tortugas, *U.S.A.* 88 B3 24 38N 82 55W
Dryden, *Canada* 73 D10 49 47N 92 50W
Dryden, *U.S.A.* 79 D8 42 30N 76 18W
Drygalski I., *Antarctica* 5 C7 66 0S 92 0 E
Drysdale →, *Australia* 60 B4 13 59S 126 51 E
Drysdale I., *Australia* 62 A2 11 41S 136 0 E
Du Bois, *U.S.A.* 78 E6 41 8N 78 46W
Du Gué →, *Canada* 70 A5 57 21N 70 45W
Du Quoin, *U.S.A.* 80 G10 38 1N 89 14W
Duanesburg, *U.S.A.* 79 D10 42 45N 74 11W
Duaringa, *Australia* 62 C4 23 42S 149 42 E
Ḍubā, *Si. Arabia* 44 E2 27 10N 35 40 E
Dubai = Dubayy, *U.A.E.* 46 B6 25 18N 55 20 E
Dubăsari, *Moldova* 17 E15 47 15N 29 10 E
Dubăsari Vdkhr., *Moldova* 17 E15 47 30N 29 0 E
Dubawnt →, *Canada* 73 A8 64 33N 100 6W
Dubawnt, L., *Canada* 73 A8 63 4N 101 42W
Dubayy, *U.A.E.* 46 B6 25 18N 55 20 E
Dubbo, *Australia* 63 E4 32 11S 148 35 E
Dubele, *Dem. Rep. of the Congo* 54 B2 2 56N 29 35 E
Dublin, *Ireland* 13 C5 53 21N 6 15W
Dublin, *Ga., U.S.A.* 77 J4 32 32N 82 54W
Dublin, *Tex., U.S.A.* 81 J5 32 5N 98 21W
Dublin □, *Ireland* 13 C5 53 24N 6 20W
Dubno, *Ukraine* 17 C13 50 25N 25 45 E
Dubois, *U.S.A.* 82 D7 44 10N 112 14W
Dubossary = Dubăsari, *Moldova* 17 E15 47 15N 29 10 E
Dubossary Vdkhr. = Dubăsari Vdkhr., *Moldova* 17 E15 47 30N 29 0 E
Dubovka, *Russia* 25 E7 49 5N 44 50 E
Dubrajpur, *India* 43 H12 23 48N 87 25 E
Dubréka, *Guinea* 50 G3 9 46N 13 31W
Dubrovitsa = Dubrovytsya, *Ukraine* 17 C14 51 31N 26 35 E
Dubrovnik, *Croatia* 21 C8 42 39N 18 6 E
Dubrovytsya, *Ukraine* 17 C14 51 31N 26 35 E
Dubuque, *U.S.A.* 80 D9 42 30N 90 41W
Duchesne, *U.S.A.* 82 F8 40 10N 110 24W
Duchess, *Australia* 62 C2 21 20S 139 50 E
Ducie I., *Pac. Oc.* 65 K15 24 40S 124 48W
Duck →, *U.S.A.* 77 G2 36 2N 87 52W
Duck Cr. →, *Australia* 60 D2 22 37S 116 53 E
Duck Lake, *Canada* 73 C7 52 50N 106 16W
Duck Mountain Prov. Park, *Canada* 73 C8 51 45N 101 0W
Duckwall, Mt., *U.S.A.* 84 H6 37 58N 120 7W
Dudhi, *India* 41 G13 24 15N 83 10 E
Dudinka, *Russia* 27 C9 69 30N 86 13 E
Dudley, *U.K.* 11 E5 52 31N 2 5W
Dudwa, *India* 43 E9 28 30N 80 41 E
Duero = Douro →, *Europe* 19 B1 41 8N 8 40W
Dufftown, *U.K.* 12 D5 57 27N 3 8W
Dūghī Kalā, *Afghan.* 40 C3 32 20N 62 50 E
Dugi Otok, *Croatia* 16 G8 44 0N 15 3 E
Duifken Pt., *Australia* 62 A3 12 33S 141 38 E
Duisburg, *Germany* 16 C4 51 26N 6 45 E
Duiwelskloof, *S. Africa* 57 C5 23 42S 30 10 E
Dūkdamīn, *Iran* 45 C8 35 59N 57 43 E
Dukelský Průsmyk, *Slovak Rep.* 17 D11 49 25N 21 42 E
Dukhān, *Qatar* 45 E6 25 25N 50 50 E
Duki, *Pakistan* 40 D6 30 14N 68 25 E
Duku, *Nigeria* 51 F8 10 43N 10 43 E
Dulce, *U.S.A.* 83 H10 36 56N 107 0W
Dulce →, *Argentina* 94 C3 30 32S 62 33W
Dulce, G., *Costa Rica* 88 E3 8 40N 83 20W
Dulf, *Iraq* 44 C5 35 7N 45 51 E
Dulit, Banjaran, *Malaysia* 36 D4 3 15N 114 30 E
Duliu, *China* 34 E9 39 2N 116 55 E
Dullewala, *Pakistan* 42 D4 31 50N 71 25 E
Dullstroom, *S. Africa* 57 D5 25 27S 30 7 E
Dulq Maghār, *Syria* 44 B3 36 22N 38 39 E
Duluth, *U.S.A.* 80 B8 46 47N 92 6W
Dum Dum, *India* 43 H13 22 39N 88 33 E
Dum Duma, *India* 41 F19 27 40N 95 40 E
Dūmā, *Syria* 47 B5 33 34N 36 24 E
Dumaguete, *Phil.* 37 C6 9 17N 123 15 E
Dumai, *Indonesia* 36 D2 1 35N 101 28 E
Dumaran, *Phil.* 37 B5 10 33N 119 50 E
Dumas, *Ark., U.S.A.* 81 J9 33 53N 91 29W
Dumas, *Tex., U.S.A.* 81 H4 35 52N 101 58W
Ḍumayr, *Syria* 47 B5 33 39N 36 42 E
Dumbarton, *U.K.* 12 F4 55 57N 4 33W
Dumbleyung, *Australia* 61 F2 33 17S 117 42 E
Dumfries, *U.K.* 12 F5 55 4N 3 37W
Dumfries & Galloway □, *U.K.* 12 F5 55 9N 3 58W
Dumka, *India* 43 G12 24 12N 87 15 E
Dumoine →, *Canada* 70 C4 46 13N 77 51W
Dumoine, L., *Canada* 70 C4 46 55N 77 55W
Dumraon, *India* 43 G11 25 33N 84 8 E
Dumyât, *Egypt* 51 B12 31 24N 31 48 E
Dún Dealgan = Dundalk, *Ireland* 13 B5 54 1N 6 24W
Dun Laoghaire, *Ireland* 13 C5 53 17N 6 8W
Duna = Dunărea →, *Europe* 17 F15 45 20N 29 40 E
Dunagiri, *India* 43 D8 30 31N 79 52 E
Dunaj = Dunărea →, *Europe* 17 F15 45 20N 29 40 E
Dunakeszi, *Hungary* 17 E10 47 37N 19 8 E
Dunărea →, *Europe* 17 F15 45 20N 29 40 E
Dunaújváros, *Hungary* 17 E10 46 58N 18 57 E
Dunav = Dunărea →, *Europe* 17 F15 45 20N 29 40 E
Dunay, *Russia* 30 C6 42 52N 132 22 E
Dunback, *N.Z.* 59 L3 45 23S 170 36 E
Dunbar, *U.K.* 12 E6 56 0N 2 31W
Dunblane, *U.K.* 12 E5 56 11N 3 58W
Duncan, *Canada* 72 D4 48 45N 123 40W
Duncan, *Ariz., U.S.A.* 83 K9 32 43N 109 6W
Duncan, *Okla., U.S.A.* 81 H6 34 30N 97 57W
Duncan, L., *Canada* 70 B4 53 29N 77 58W
Duncan L., *Canada* 72 A6 62 51N 113 58W
Duncan Town, *Bahamas* 88 B4 22 15N 75 45W
Duncannon, *U.S.A.* 78 F7 40 23N 77 2W
Duncansby Head, *U.K.* 12 C5 58 38N 3 1W
Duncansville, *U.S.A.* 78 F6 40 25N 78 26W
Dundalk, *Canada* 78 B4 44 10N 80 24W
Dundalk, *Ireland* 13 B5 54 1N 6 24W
Dundalk, *U.S.A.* 76 F7 39 16N 76 32W
Dundalk Bay, *Ireland* 13 C5 53 55N 6 15W
Dundas, *Canada* 78 C5 43 17N 79 59W
Dundas, L., *Australia* 61 F3 32 35S 121 50 E
Dundas I., *Canada* 72 C2 54 30N 130 50W
Dundas Str., *Australia* 60 B5 11 15S 131 35 E
Dundee, *S. Africa* 57 D5 28 11S 30 15 E
Dundee, *U.K.* 12 E6 56 28N 2 59W
Dundee, *U.S.A.* 78 D8 42 32N 76 59W
Dundee City □, *U.K.* 12 E6 56 30N 2 58W
Dundgovĭ □, *Mongolia* 34 B4 45 10N 106 0 E
Dundrum, *U.K.* 13 B6 54 16N 5 52W
Dundrum B., *U.K.* 13 B6 54 13N 5 47W
Dunedin, *N.Z.* 59 L3 45 50S 170 33 E
Dunedin, *U.S.A.* 77 L4 28 1N 82 47W
Dunfermline, *U.K.* 12 E5 56 5N 3 27W
Dungannon, *Canada* 78 C3 43 51N 81 36W
Dungannon, *U.K.* 13 B5 54 31N 6 46W
Dungarpur, *India* 42 H5 23 52N 73 45 E
Dungarvan, *Ireland* 13 D4 52 5N 7 37W
Dungarvan Harbour, *Ireland* 13 D4 52 4N 7 35W
Dungeness, *U.K.* 11 G8 50 54N 0 59 E
Dungo, L. do, *Angola* 56 B2 17 15S 19 0 E
Dungog, *Australia* 63 E5 32 22S 151 46 E
Dungu, *Dem. Rep. of the Congo* 54 B2 3 40N 28 32 E
Dungun, *Malaysia* 39 K4 4 45N 103 25 E
Dunhua, *China* 35 C15 43 20N 128 14 E
Dunhuang, *China* 32 B4 40 8N 94 36 E
Dunk I., *Australia* 62 B4 17 59S 146 29 E
Dunkeld, *Australia* 63 E4 33 25S 149 29 E
Dunkeld, *U.K.* 12 E5 56 34N 3 35W
Dunkerque, *France* 18 A5 51 2N 2 20 E
Dunkery Beacon, *U.K.* 11 F4 51 9N 3 36W
Dunkirk = Dunkerque, *France* 18 A5 51 2N 2 20 E
Dunkirk, *U.S.A.* 78 D5 42 29N 79 20W
Dúnleary = Dun Laoghaire, *Ireland* 13 C5 53 17N 6 8W
Dunleer, *Ireland* 13 C5 53 50N 6 24W
Dunmanus B., *Ireland* 13 E2 51 31N 9 50W
Dunmanway, *Ireland* 13 E2 51 43N 9 6W
Dunmara, *Australia* 62 B1 16 42S 133 25 E
Dunmore, *U.S.A.* 79 E9 41 25N 75 38W
Dunmore Hd., *Ireland* 13 D1 52 10N 10 35W
Dunmore Town, *Bahamas* 88 A4 25 30N 76 39W
Dunn, *U.S.A.* 77 H6 35 19N 78 37W
Dunnellon, *U.S.A.* 77 L4 29 3N 82 28W
Dunnet Hd., *U.K.* 12 C5 58 40N 3 21W
Dunning, *U.S.A.* 80 E4 41 50N 100 6W
Dunnville, *Canada* 78 D5 42 54N 79 36W
Dunolly, *Australia* 63 F3 36 51S 143 44 E
Dunoon, *U.K.* 12 F4 55 57N 4 56W
Dunphy, *U.S.A.* 82 F5 40 42N 116 31W
Duns, *U.K.* 12 F6 55 47N 2 20W
Dunseith, *U.S.A.* 80 A4 48 50N 100 3W
Dunsmuir, *U.S.A.* 82 F2 41 13N 122 16W
Dunstable, *U.K.* 11 F7 51 53N 0 32W
Dunstan Mts., *N.Z.* 59 L2 44 53S 169 35 E
Dunster, *Canada* 72 C5 53 8N 119 50W
Dunvegan L., *Canada* 73 A7 60 8N 107 10W
Duolun, *China* 34 C9 42 12N 116 28 E
Duong Dong, *Vietnam* 39 G4 10 13N 103 58 E
Dupree, *U.S.A.* 80 C4 45 4N 101 35W
Dupuyer, *U.S.A.* 82 B7 48 13N 112 30W
Duque de Caxias, *Brazil* 95 A7 22 45S 43 19W
Durack →, *Australia* 60 C4 15 33S 127 52 E
Durack Ra., *Australia* 60 C4 16 50S 127 40 E
Durance →, *France* 18 E6 43 55N 4 45 E
Durand, *U.S.A.* 80 C9 44 38N 91 58W
Durango, *Mexico* 86 C4 24 3N 104 39W
Durango, *U.S.A.* 83 H10 37 16N 107 53W
Durango □, *Mexico* 86 C4 25 0N 105 0W
Durant, *Miss., U.S.A.* 81 J10 33 4N 89 51W
Durant, *Okla., U.S.A.* 81 J6 33 59N 96 25W
Durazno, *Uruguay* 94 C4 33 25S 56 31W
Durazzo = Durrës, *Albania* 21 D8 41 19N 19 28 E
Durban, *S. Africa* 57 D5 29 49S 31 1 E
Durbuy, *Belgium* 15 D5 50 21N 5 28 E
Düren, *Germany* 16 C4 50 48N 6 29 E
Durg, *India* 41 J12 21 15N 81 22 E
Durgapur, *India* 43 H12 23 30N 87 20 E
Durham, *Canada* 78 B4 44 10N 80 49W
Durham, *U.K.* 10 C6 54 47N 1 34W
Durham, *Calif., U.S.A.* 84 F5 39 39N 121 48W
Durham, *N.C., U.S.A.* 77 H6 35 59N 78 54W
Durham, *N.H., U.S.A.* 79 C14 43 8N 70 56W
Durham □, *U.K.* 10 C6 54 42N 1 45W
Ḍurmā, *Si. Arabia* 44 E5 24 37N 46 8 E
Durmitor, *Montenegro, Yug.* 21 C8 43 10N 19 0 E
Durness, *U.K.* 12 C4 58 34N 4 45W
Durrës, *Albania* 21 D8 41 19N 19 28 E
Durrow, *Ireland* 13 D4 52 51N 7 24W
Dursey I., *Ireland* 13 E1 51 36N 10 12W
Dursunbey, *Turkey* 21 E13 39 35N 28 37 E
Duru, *Dem. Rep. of the Congo* 54 B2 4 14N 28 50 E
Durūz, Jabal ad, *Jordan* 47 C5 32 35N 36 40 E
D'Urville, Tanjung, *Indonesia* 37 E9 1 28S 137 54 E
D'Urville I., *N.Z.* 59 J4 40 50S 173 55 E
Duryea, *U.S.A.* 79 E9 41 20N 75 45W
Dushak, *Turkmenistan* 26 F7 37 13N 60 1 E
Dushanbe, *Tajikistan* 26 F7 38 33N 68 48 E
Dushore, *U.S.A.* 79 E8 41 31N 76 24W
Dusky Sd., *N.Z.* 59 L1 45 47S 166 30 E
Dussejour, C., *Australia* 60 B4 14 45S 128 13 E
Düsseldorf, *Germany* 16 C4 51 14N 6 47 E
Dutch Harbor, *U.S.A.* 68 C3 53 53N 166 32W
Dutlwe, *Botswana* 56 C3 23 58S 23 46 E
Dutton, *Canada* 78 D3 42 39N 81 30W
Dutton →, *Australia* 62 C3 20 44S 143 10 E
Duwayhin, Khawr, *U.A.E.* 45 E6 24 20N 51 25 E
Duyun, *China* 32 D5 26 18N 107 29 E
Duzdab = Zāhedān, *Iran* 45 D9 29 30N 60 50 E
Dvina, Severnaya →, *Russia* 24 B7 64 32N 40 30 E
Dvinsk = Daugavpils, *Latvia* 9 J22 55 53N 26 32 E
Dvinskaya Guba, *Russia* 24 B6 65 0N 39 0 E
Dwarka, *India* 42 H3 22 18N 69 8 E
Dwellingup, *Australia* 61 F2 32 43S 116 4 E
Dwight, *Canada* 78 A5 45 20N 79 1W
Dwight, *U.S.A.* 76 E1 41 5N 88 26W
Dyatlovo = Dzyatlava, *Belarus* 17 B13 53 28N 25 28 E
Dyce, *U.K.* 12 D6 57 13N 2 12W
Dyer, C., *Canada* 69 B13 66 40N 61 0W
Dyer Bay, *Canada* 78 A3 45 10N 81 20W
Dyer Plateau, *Antarctica* 5 D17 70 45S 65 30W
Dyersburg, *U.S.A.* 81 G10 36 3N 89 23W
Dyfi →, *U.K.* 11 E3 52 32N 4 3W
Dymer, *Ukraine* 17 C16 50 47N 30 18 E
Dysart, *Australia* 62 C4 22 32S 148 23 E
Dzamin Üüd = Borhoyn Tal, *Mongolia* 34 C6 43 50N 111 58 E
Dzerzhinsk, *Russia* 24 C7 56 14N 43 30 E
Dzhalinda, *Russia* 27 D13 53 26N 124 0 E
Dzhambul = Taraz, *Kazakstan* 26 E8 42 54N 71 22 E
Dzhankoy, *Ukraine* 25 E5 45 40N 34 20 E
Dzhezkazgan = Zhezqazghan, *Kazakstan* 26 E7 47 44N 67 40 E
Dzhizak = Jizzakh, *Uzbekistan* 26 E7 40 6N 67 50 E
Dzhugdzur, Khrebet, *Russia* 27 D14 57 30N 138 0 E
Dzhungarskiye Vorota = Dzungarian Gates, *Asia* 32 B3 45 0N 82 0 E
Działdowo, *Poland* 17 B11 53 15N 20 15 E
Dzibilchaltun, *Mexico* 87 C7 21 5N 89 36W
Dzierżoniów, *Poland* 17 C9 50 45N 16 39 E
Dzilam de Bravo, *Mexico* 87 C7 21 24N 88 53W
Dzungaria = Junggar Pendi, *China* 32 B3 44 30N 86 0 E
Dzungarian Gates, *Asia* 32 B3 45 0N 82 0 E
Dzuumod, *Mongolia* 32 B5 47 45N 106 58 E
Dzyarzhynsk, *Belarus* 17 B14 53 40N 27 1 E
Dzyatlava, *Belarus* 17 B13 53 28N 25 28 E

E

Eabamet L., *Canada* 70 B2 51 30N 87 46W
Eads, *U.S.A.* 80 F3 38 29N 102 47W
Eagar, *U.S.A.* 83 J9 34 6N 109 17W
Eagle, *Alaska, U.S.A.* 68 B5 64 47N 141 12W
Eagle, *Colo., U.S.A.* 82 G10 39 39N 106 50W
Eagle →, *Canada* 71 B8 53 36N 57 26W
Eagle Butte, *U.S.A.* 80 C4 45 0N 101 10W
Eagle Grove, *U.S.A.* 80 D8 42 40N 93 54W
Eagle L., *Canada* 73 D10 49 42N 93 13W
Eagle L., *Calif., U.S.A.* 82 F3 40 39N 120 45W
Eagle L., *Maine, U.S.A.* 77 B11 46 20N 69 22W
Eagle Lake, *Canada* 78 A6 45 8N 78 29W
Eagle Lake, *Maine, U.S.A.* 77 B11 47 3N 68 36W
Eagle Lake, *Tex., U.S.A.* 81 L6 29 35N 96 20W
Eagle Mountain, *U.S.A.* 85 M11 33 49N 115 27W
Eagle Nest, *U.S.A.* 83 H11 36 33N 105 16W
Eagle Pass, *U.S.A.* 81 L4 28 43N 100 30W
Eagle Pk., *U.S.A.* 84 G7 38 10N 119 25W
Eagle Pt., *Australia* 60 C3 16 11S 124 23 E
Eagle River, *Mich., U.S.A.* 76 B1 47 24N 88 18W
Eagle River, *Wis., U.S.A.* 80 C10 45 55N 89 15W
Eaglehawk, *Australia* 63 F3 36 44S 144 15 E
Eagles Mere, *U.S.A.* 79 E8 41 25N 76 33W
Ealing □, *U.K.* 11 F7 51 31N 0 20W
Ear Falls, *Canada* 73 C10 50 38N 93 13W
Earle, *U.S.A.* 81 H9 35 16N 90 28W
Earlimart, *U.S.A.* 85 K7 35 53N 119 16W
Earn →, *U.K.* 12 E5 56 21N 3 18W
Earn, L., *U.K.* 12 E4 56 23N 4 13W
Earnslaw, Mt., *N.Z.* 59 L2 44 32S 168 27 E
Earth, *U.S.A.* 81 H3 34 14N 102 24W
Easley, *U.S.A.* 77 H4 34 50N 82 36W
East Anglia, *U.K.* 10 E9 52 30N 1 0 E
East Angus, *Canada* 71 C5 45 30N 71 40W
East Aurora, *U.S.A.* 78 D6 42 46N 78 37W
East Ayrshire □, *U.K.* 12 F4 55 26N 4 11W
East Bengal, *Bangla.* 41 H17 24 0N 90 0 E
East Beskids = Vychodné Beskydy, *Europe* 17 D11 49 20N 22 0 E
East Brady, *U.S.A.* 78 F5 40 59N 79 36W
East C., *N.Z.* 59 G7 37 42S 178 35 E
East Chicago, *U.S.A.* 76 E2 41 38N 87 27W
East China Sea, *Asia* 33 D7 30 0N 126 0 E
East Coulee, *Canada* 72 C6 51 23N 112 27W
East Dereham, *U.K.* 11 E8 52 41N 0 57 E
East Dunbartonshire □, *U.K.* 12 F4 55 57N 4 13W
East Falkland, *Falk. Is.* 96 G5 51 30S 58 30W
East Grand Forks, *U.S.A.* 80 B6 47 56N 97 1W
East Greenwich, *U.S.A.* 79 E13 41 40N 71 27W
East Grinstead, *U.K.* 11 F8 51 7N 0 0W
East Hartford, *U.S.A.* 79 E12 41 46N 72 39W
East Helena, *U.S.A.* 82 C8 46 35N 111 56W
East Indies, *Asia* 28 K15 0 0 120 0 E
East Kilbride, *U.K.* 12 F4 55 47N 4 11W
East Lansing, *U.S.A.* 76 D3 42 44N 84 29W
East Liverpool, *U.S.A.* 78 F4 40 37N 80 35W
East London, *S. Africa* 57 E4 33 0S 27 55 E
East Lothian □, *U.K.* 12 F6 55 58N 2 44W
East Main = Eastmain, *Canada* 70 B4 52 10N 78 30W
East Northport, *U.S.A.* 79 F11 40 53N 73 20W
East Orange, *U.S.A.* 79 F10 40 46N 74 13W
East Pacific Ridge, *Pac. Oc.* 65 J17 15 0S 110 0W
East Palestine, *U.S.A.* 78 F4 40 50N 80 33W
East Pine, *Canada* 72 B4 55 48N 120 12W
East Point, *U.S.A.* 77 J3 33 41N 84 27W
East Providence, *U.S.A.* 79 E13 41 49N 71 23W

East Pt.

East Pt., Canada 71 C7 46 27N 61 58W
East Renfrewshire □, U.K. . 12 F4 55 46N 4 21W
East Retford = Retford, U.K. . 10 D7 53 19N 0 56W
East Riding of Yorkshire □, U.K. ... 10 D7 53 55N 0 30W
East Rochester, U.S.A. . 78 C7 43 7N 77 29W
East St. Louis, U.S.A. . 80 F9 38 37N 90 9W
East Schelde = Oosterschelde →, Neths. . 15 C4 51 33N 4 0 E
East Sea = Japan, Sea of, Asia 30 E7 40 0N 135 0 E
East Siberian Sea, Russia . 27 B17 73 0N 160 0 E
East Stroudsburg, U.S.A. . 79 E9 41 1N 75 11W
East Sussex □, U.K. . 11 G8 50 56N 0 19 E
East Tawas, U.S.A. . 76 C4 44 17N 83 29W
East Timor ■, Asia . 37 F7 8 50S 126 0 E
East Toorale, Australia . 63 E4 30 27S 145 28 E
East Walker →, U.S.A. . 84 G7 38 52N 119 10W
East Windsor, U.S.A. . 79 F10 40 17N 74 34W
Eastbourne, N.Z. . 59 J5 41 19S 174 55 E
Eastbourne, U.K. . 11 G8 50 46N 0 18 E
Eastend, Canada . 73 D7 49 32N 108 50W
Easter I. = Pascua, I. de, Chile 65 K17 27 7S 109 23W
Eastern □, Kenya . 54 C4 0 0 38 30 E
Eastern Cape □, S. Africa . 56 E4 32 0S 26 0 E
Eastern Cr. →, Australia . 62 C3 20 40S 141 35 E
Eastern Ghats, India . 40 N11 14 0N 78 50 E
Eastern Group = Lau Group, Fiji . 59 C9 17 0S 178 30W
Eastern Group, Australia . 61 F3 33 30S 124 30 E
Eastern Transvaal = Mpumalanga □, S. Africa . 57 B5 26 0S 30 0 E
Easterville, Canada . 73 C9 53 8N 99 49W
Easthampton, U.S.A. . 79 D12 42 16N 72 40W
Eastlake, U.S.A. . 78 E3 41 40N 81 26W
Eastland, U.S.A. . 81 J5 32 24N 98 49W
Eastleigh, U.K. . 11 G6 50 58N 1 21W
Eastmain, Canada . 70 B4 52 10N 78 30W
Eastmain →, Canada . 70 B4 52 27N 78 26W
Eastman, Canada . 79 A12 45 18N 72 19W
Eastman, U.S.A. . 77 J4 32 12N 83 11W
Easton, Md., U.S.A. . 76 F7 38 47N 76 5W
Easton, Pa., U.S.A. . 79 F9 40 41N 75 13W
Easton, Wash., U.S.A. . 84 C5 47 14N 121 11W
Eastpointe, U.S.A. . 78 D2 42 27N 82 56W
Eastport, U.S.A. . 77 C12 44 56N 67 0W
Eastsound, U.S.A. . 84 B4 48 42N 122 55W
Eaton, U.S.A. . 80 E2 40 32N 104 42W
Eatonia, Canada . 73 C7 51 13N 109 25W
Eatonton, U.S.A. . 77 J4 33 20N 83 23W
Eatontown, U.S.A. . 79 F10 40 19N 74 4W
Eatonville, U.S.A. . 84 D4 46 52N 122 16W
Eau Claire, U.S.A. . 80 C9 44 49N 91 30W
Eau Claire, L. à l', Canada . 70 A5 56 10N 74 25W
Ebbw Vale, U.K. . 11 F4 51 46N 3 12W
Ebeltoft, Denmark . 9 H14 56 12N 10 41 E
Ebensburg, U.S.A. . 78 F6 40 29N 78 44W
Eberswalde-Finow, Germany . 16 B7 52 50N 13 49 E
Ebetsu, Japan . 30 C10 43 7N 141 34 E
Ebolowa, Cameroon . 52 D2 2 55N 11 10 E
Ebro →, Spain . 19 B6 40 43N 0 54 E
Eceabat, Turkey . 21 D12 40 11N 26 21 E
Ech Chéliff, Algeria . 50 A6 36 10N 1 20 E
Echigo-Sammyaku, Japan . 31 F9 36 50N 139 50 E
Echizen-Misaki, Japan . 31 G7 35 59N 135 57 E
Echo Bay, N.W.T., Canada . 68 B8 66 5N 117 55W
Echo Bay, Ont., Canada . 70 C3 46 29N 84 4W
Echoing →, Canada . 70 B1 55 51N 92 5W
Echternach, Lux. . 15 E6 49 49N 6 25 E
Echuca, Australia . 63 F3 36 10S 144 45 E
Ecija, Spain . 19 D3 37 30N 5 10W
Eclipse Is., Australia . 60 B4 13 54S 126 19 E
Eclipse Sd., Canada . 69 A11 72 38N 79 0W
Ecuador ■, S. Amer. . 92 D3 2 0S 78 0W
Ed Damazin, Sudan . 51 F12 11 46N 34 21 E
Ed Debba, Sudan . 51 E12 18 0N 30 51 E
Ed Dueim, Sudan . 51 F12 14 0N 32 10 E
Edam, Canada . 73 C7 53 11N 108 46W
Edam, Neths. . 15 B5 52 31N 5 3 E
Eday, U.K. . 12 B6 59 11N 2 47W
Eddrachillis B., U.K. . 12 C3 58 17N 5 14W
Eddystone, U.K. . 11 G3 50 11N 4 16W
Eddystone Pt., Australia . 62 G4 40 59S 148 20 E
Ede, Neths. . 15 B5 52 4N 5 40 E
Edehon L., Canada . 73 A9 60 25N 97 15W
Eden, Australia . 63 F4 37 3S 149 55 E
Eden, N.C., U.S.A. . 77 G6 36 29N 79 53W
Eden, N.Y., U.S.A. . 78 D6 42 39N 78 55W
Eden, Tex., U.S.A. . 81 K5 31 13N 99 51W
Eden →, U.K. . 10 C4 54 57N 3 1W
Edenburg, S. Africa . 56 D4 29 43S 25 58 E
Edendale, S. Africa . 57 D5 29 39S 30 18 E
Edenderry, Ireland . 13 C4 53 21N 7 4W
Edenton, U.S.A. . 77 G7 36 4N 76 39W
Edenville, S. Africa . 57 D4 27 37S 27 34 E
Eder →, Germany . 16 C5 51 12N 9 28 E
Edgar, U.S.A. . 80 E6 40 22N 97 58W
Edge Hill, U.K. . 11 E6 52 8N 1 26W
Edgefield, U.S.A. . 77 J5 33 47N 81 56W
Edgeley, U.S.A. . 80 B5 46 22N 98 43W
Edgemont, U.S.A. . 80 D3 43 18N 103 50W
Edgeøya, Svalbard . 4 B9 77 45N 22 30 E
Édhessa, Greece . 21 D10 40 48N 22 5 E
Edievale, N.Z. . 59 L2 45 49S 169 22 E
Edina, U.S.A. . 80 E8 40 10N 92 11W
Edinboro, U.S.A. . 78 E4 41 52N 80 8W
Edinburg, U.S.A. . 81 M5 26 18N 98 10W
Edinburgh, U.K. . 12 F5 55 57N 3 13W
Edinburgh, City of □, U.K. . 12 F5 55 57N 3 17W
Edineț, Moldova . 17 D14 48 9N 27 18 E
Edirne, Turkey . 21 D12 41 40N 26 34 E
Edison, U.S.A. . 84 B4 48 33N 122 27W
Edithburgh, Australia . 63 F2 35 5S 137 43 E
Edmeston, U.S.A. . 79 D9 42 42N 75 15W
Edmond, U.S.A. . 81 H6 35 39N 97 29W
Edmonds, U.S.A. . 84 C4 47 48N 122 23W
Edmonton, Australia . 62 B4 17 2S 145 46 E
Edmonton, Canada . 72 C6 53 30N 113 30W
Edmund L., Canada . 70 B1 54 45N 93 17W
Edmundston, Canada . 71 C6 47 23N 68 20W
Edna, U.S.A. . 81 L6 28 59N 96 39W
Edremit, Turkey . 21 E12 39 34N 27 0 E
Edremit Körfezi, Turkey . 21 E12 39 30N 26 45 E
Edson, Canada . 72 C5 53 35N 116 28W
Eduardo Castex, Argentina . 94 D3 35 50S 64 18W
Edward →, Australia . 63 F3 35 5S 143 30 E

Edward, L., Africa . 54 C2 0 25S 29 40 E
Edward River, Australia . 62 A3 14 59S 141 26 E
Edward VII Land, Antarctica . 5 E13 80 0S 150 0W
Edwards, Calif., U.S.A. . 85 L9 34 55N 117 51W
Edwards, N.Y., U.S.A. . 79 B9 44 20N 75 15W
Edwards Air Force Base, U.S.A. . 85 L9 34 50N 117 40W
Edwards Plateau, U.S.A. . 81 K4 30 45N 101 20W
Edwardsville, U.S.A. . 79 E9 41 15N 75 56W
Edzo, Canada . 72 A5 62 49N 116 4W
Eeklo, Belgium . 15 C3 51 11N 3 33 E
Effingham, U.S.A. . 76 F1 39 7N 88 33W
Égadi, Ísole, Italy . 20 F5 37 55N 12 16 E
Egan Range, U.S.A. . 82 G6 39 35N 114 55W
Eganville, Canada . 78 A7 45 32N 77 5W
Eger = Cheb, Czech Rep. . 16 C7 50 9N 12 28 E
Eger, Hungary . 17 E11 47 53N 20 27 E
Egersund, Norway . 9 G12 58 26N 6 1 E
Egg L., Canada . 73 B7 55 5N 105 30W
Éghezée, Belgium . 15 D4 50 35N 4 55 E
Egmont, Canada . 72 D4 49 45N 123 56W
Egmont, C., N.Z. . 59 H4 39 16S 173 45 E
Egmont, Mt. = Taranaki, Mt., N.Z. . 59 H5 39 17S 174 5 E
Egra, India . 43 J12 21 54N 87 32 E
Eğridir, Turkey . 25 G5 37 52N 30 51 E
Eğridir Gölü, Turkey . 25 G5 37 53N 30 50 E
Egvekinot, Russia . 27 C19 66 19N 179 50W
Egypt ■, Africa . 51 C12 28 0N 31 0 E
Ehime □, Japan . 31 H6 33 30N 132 40 E
Ehrenberg, U.S.A. . 85 M12 33 36N 114 31W
Eibar, Spain . 19 A4 43 11N 2 28W
Eidsvold, Australia . 63 D5 25 25S 151 12 E
Eidsvoll, Norway . 9 F14 60 19N 11 14 E
Eifel, Germany . 16 C4 50 15N 6 50 E
Eiffel Flats, Zimbabwe . 55 F3 18 20S 30 0 E
Eigg, U.K. . 12 E2 56 54N 6 10W
Eighty Mile Beach, Australia . 60 C3 19 30S 120 40 E
Eil, Somali Rep. . 46 F4 8 0N 49 50 E
Eil, L., U.K. . 12 E3 56 51N 5 16W
Eildon, L., Australia . 63 F4 37 10S 146 0 E
Einasleigh, Australia . 62 B3 18 32S 144 5 E
Einasleigh →, Australia . 62 B3 17 30S 142 17 E
Eindhoven, Neths. . 15 C5 51 26N 5 28 E
Eire = Ireland ■, Europe . 13 C4 53 50N 7 52W
Eiriksjökull, Iceland . 8 D3 64 46N 20 24W
Eirunepé, Brazil . 92 E5 6 35S 69 53W
Eiseb →, Namibia . 56 C2 20 33S 20 59 E
Eisenach, Germany . 16 C6 50 58N 10 19 E
Eisenerz, Austria . 16 E8 47 32N 14 54 E
Eivissa, Spain . 22 C7 38 54N 1 26 E
Ejeda, Madag. . 57 C7 24 46S 44 20 E
Ejutla, Mexico . 87 D5 16 34N 96 44W
Ekalaka, U.S.A. . 80 C2 45 53N 104 33W
Eketahuna, N.Z. . 59 J5 40 38S 175 43 E
Ekibastuz, Kazakstan . 26 D8 51 50N 75 10 E
Ekoli, Dem. Rep. of the Congo 54 C1 0 23S 24 13 E
Ekuma →, Namibia . 56 B2 18 40S 16 2 E
Ekwan →, Canada . 70 B3 53 12N 82 15W
Ekwan Pt., Canada . 70 B3 53 16N 82 7W
El Aaiún, W. Sahara . 50 C3 27 9N 13 12W
El Abanico, Chile . 94 D1 37 20S 71 31W
El 'Agrûd, Egypt . 47 E3 30 14N 34 24 E
El Alamein, Egypt . 51 B11 30 48N 28 58 E
El 'Aqaba, W. →, Egypt . 47 E2 30 7N 33 54 E
El Ariha, West Bank . 47 D4 31 52N 35 27 E
El 'Arîsh, Egypt . 47 D2 31 8N 33 50 E
El 'Arîsh, W. →, Egypt . 47 D2 31 8N 33 47 E
El Asnam = Ech Chéliff, Algeria . 50 A6 36 10N 1 20 E
El Bayadh, Algeria . 50 B6 33 40N 1 1 E
El Bluff, Nic. . 88 D3 11 59N 83 40W
El Brûk, W. →, Egypt . 47 E2 30 15N 33 50 E
El Cajon, U.S.A. . 85 N10 32 48N 116 58W
El Campo, U.S.A. . 81 L6 29 12N 96 16W
El Centro, U.S.A. . 85 N11 32 48N 115 34W
El Cerro, Bolivia . 92 G6 17 30S 61 40W
El Compadre, Mexico . 85 N10 32 20N 116 14W
El Cuy, Argentina . 96 D3 39 55S 68 25W
El Cuyo, Mexico . 87 C7 21 30N 87 40W
El Daheir, Egypt . 47 D3 31 13N 34 10 E
El Dátil, Mexico . 86 B2 30 7N 112 15W
El Dere, Somali Rep. . 46 G4 3 50N 47 8 E
El Descanso, Mexico . 85 N10 32 12N 116 58W
El Desemboque, Mexico . 86 A2 30 30N 112 57W
El Diviso, Colombia . 92 C3 1 22N 78 14W
El Djouf, Mauritania . 50 D4 20 0N 9 0W
El Dorado, Ark., U.S.A. . 81 J8 33 12N 92 40W
El Dorado, Kans., U.S.A. . 81 G6 37 49N 96 52W
El Dorado, Venezuela . 92 B6 6 55N 61 37W
El Escorial, Spain . 19 B3 40 35N 4 7W
El Faiyûm, Egypt . 51 C12 29 19N 30 50 E
El Fâsher, Sudan . 51 F11 13 33N 25 26 E
El Ferrol = Ferrol, Spain . 19 A1 43 29N 8 15W
El Fuerte, Mexico . 86 B3 26 30N 108 40W
El Gal, Somali Rep. . 46 E5 10 58N 50 20 E
El Geneina = Al Junaynah, Sudan . 51 F10 13 27N 22 45 E
El Gîza, Egypt . 51 C12 30 0N 31 10 E
El Goléa, Algeria . 50 B6 30 30N 2 50 E
El Iskandarîya, Egypt . 51 B11 31 13N 29 58 E
El Istiwa'iya, Sudan . 51 G11 5 0N 28 0 E
El Jadida, Morocco . 50 B4 33 11N 8 17W
El Jardal, Honduras . 88 D2 14 54N 88 50W
El Kabrît, G., Egypt . 47 F2 29 42N 33 16 E
El Khârga, Egypt . 51 C12 25 30N 30 33 E
El Khartûm, Sudan . 51 E12 15 31N 32 35 E
El Kuntilla, Egypt . 47 E3 30 1N 34 45 E
El Maestrazgo, Spain . 19 B5 40 30N 0 25W
El Mahalla el Kubra, Egypt . 51 B12 31 0N 31 0 E
El Mansûra, Egypt . 51 B12 31 0N 31 19 E
El Medano, Canary Is. . 22 F3 28 3N 16 32W
El Milagro, Argentina . 94 C2 30 59S 65 59W
El Minyâ, Egypt . 51 C12 28 7N 30 33 E
El Monte, U.S.A. . 85 L8 34 4N 118 1W
El Obeid, Sudan . 51 F12 13 8N 30 10 E
El Odaiya, Sudan . 51 F11 12 8N 28 12 E
El Oro, Mexico . 87 D4 19 48N 100 8W
El Oued, Algeria . 50 B7 33 20N 6 58 E
El Palmito, Presa, Mexico . 86 B3 25 40N 105 30W
El Paso, U.S.A. . 83 L10 31 45N 106 29W
El Paso Robles, U.S.A. . 84 K6 35 38N 120 41W
El Portal, U.S.A. . 84 H7 37 41N 119 47W
El Porvenir, Mexico . 86 A3 31 15N 105 51W

El Prat de Llobregat, Spain . 19 B7 41 18N 2 3 E
El Progreso, Honduras . 88 C2 15 26N 87 51W
El Pueblito, Mexico . 86 B3 29 3N 105 4W
El Pueblo, Canary Is. . 22 F2 28 36N 17 47W
El Puerto de Santa María, Spain . 19 D2 36 36N 6 13W
El Qâhira, Egypt . 51 B12 30 1N 31 14 E
El Qantara, Egypt . 47 E1 30 51N 32 20 E
El Quseima, Egypt . 47 E3 30 40N 34 15 E
El Real, Panama . 92 B3 8 0N 77 40W
El Reno, U.S.A. . 81 H6 35 32N 97 57W
El Rio, U.S.A. . 85 L7 34 14N 119 10W
El Roque, Pta., Canary Is. . 22 F4 28 10N 15 25W
El Rosarito, Mexico . 86 B2 28 38N 114 4W
El Saheira, W. →, Egypt . 47 E2 30 5N 33 25 E
El Salto, Mexico . 86 C3 23 47N 105 22W
El Salvador ■, Cent. Amer. . 88 D2 13 50N 89 0W
El Sauce, Nic. . 88 D2 13 0N 86 40W
El Sueco, Mexico . 86 B3 29 54N 106 24W
El Suweis, Egypt . 51 C12 29 58N 32 31 E
El Tamarâni, W. →, Egypt . 47 E3 30 7N 34 43 E
El Thamad, Egypt . 47 F3 29 40N 34 28 E
El Tigre, Venezuela . 92 B6 8 44N 64 15W
El Tîh, Gebal, Egypt . 47 F2 29 40N 33 50 E
El Tina, Khalîg, Egypt . 47 D1 31 10N 32 40 E
El Tofo, Chile . 94 B1 29 22S 71 18W
El Tránsito, Chile . 94 B1 28 52S 70 17W
El Tûr, Egypt . 44 D2 28 14N 33 36 E
El Turbio, Argentina . 96 G2 51 45S 72 5W
El Uqsur, Egypt . 51 C12 25 41N 32 38 E
El Venado, Mexico . 86 C4 22 56N 101 10W
El Vergel, Mexico . 86 B3 26 28N 106 22W
El Vigia, Venezuela . 92 B4 8 38N 71 39W
El Wabeira, Egypt . 47 F2 29 34N 33 6 E
El Wak, Kenya . 54 B5 2 49N 40 56 E
El Wuz, Sudan . 51 E12 15 5N 30 7 E
Elat, Israel . 47 F3 29 30N 34 56 E
Eláziğ, Turkey . 25 G6 38 37N 39 14 E
Elba, Italy . 20 C4 42 46N 10 17 E
Elba, U.S.A. . 77 K2 31 25N 86 4W
Elbasan, Albania . 21 D9 41 9N 20 9 E
Elbe →, Europe . 16 B5 53 50N 9 0 E
Elbert, Mt., U.S.A. . 83 G10 39 7N 106 27W
Elberton, U.S.A. . 77 H4 34 7N 82 52W
Elbeuf, France . 18 B4 49 17N 1 2 E
Elbidtan, Turkey . 44 B3 38 13N 37 12 E
Elbing = Elblag, Poland . 17 A10 54 10N 19 25 E
Elblag, Poland . 17 A10 54 10N 19 25 E
Elbow, Canada . 73 C7 51 7N 106 35W
Elbrus, Asia . 25 F7 43 21N 42 30 E
Elburz Mts. = Alborz, Reshteh-ye Kühhâ-ye, Iran . 45 C7 36 0N 52 0 E
Elche, Spain . 19 C5 38 15N 0 42W
Elcho I., Australia . 62 A2 11 55S 135 45 E
Elda, Spain . 19 C5 38 29N 0 47W
Elde →, Germany . 16 B6 53 7N 11 15 E
Eldon, Mo., U.S.A. . 80 F8 38 21N 92 35W
Eldon, Wash., U.S.A. . 84 C3 47 33N 123 3W
Eldora, U.S.A. . 80 D8 42 22N 93 5W
Eldorado, Argentina . 95 B5 26 28S 54 43W
Eldorado, Canada . 78 B7 44 35N 77 31W
Eldorado, Mexico . 86 C3 24 20N 107 22W
Eldorado, Ill., U.S.A. . 76 G1 37 49N 88 26W
Eldorado, Tex., U.S.A. . 81 K4 30 52N 100 36W
Eldorado Springs, U.S.A. . 81 G8 37 52N 94 1W
Eldoret, Kenya . 54 B4 0 30N 35 17 E
Eldred, U.S.A. . 78 E6 41 58N 78 23W
Elea, C., Cyprus . 23 D13 35 19N 34 4 E
Eleanora, Pk., Australia . 61 F3 32 57S 121 9 E
Elefantes →, Mozam. . 57 C5 24 10S 32 40 E
Elektrostal, Russia . 24 C6 55 41N 38 32 E
Elephant Butte Reservoir, U.S.A. . 83 K10 33 9N 107 11W
Elephant I., Antarctica . 5 C18 61 0S 55 0W
Eleuthera, Bahamas . 88 B4 25 0N 76 20W
Elgin, Canada . 79 B8 44 36N 76 13W
Elgin, U.K. . 12 D5 57 39N 3 19W
Elgin, Ill., U.S.A. . 76 D1 42 2N 88 17W
Elgin, N. Dak., U.S.A. . 80 B4 46 24N 101 51W
Elgin, Oreg., U.S.A. . 82 D5 45 34N 117 55W
Elgin, Tex., U.S.A. . 81 K6 30 21N 97 22W
Elgon, Mt., Africa . 54 B3 1 10N 34 30 E
Eliase, Indonesia . 37 F8 8 21S 130 48 E
Elim, Namibia . 56 B2 17 48S 15 31 E
Elim, S. Africa . 56 E2 34 35S 19 45 E
Elista, Russia . 25 E7 46 16N 44 14 E
Elizabeth, Australia . 63 E2 34 42S 138 41 E
Elizabeth, N.J., U.S.A. . 79 F10 40 40N 74 13W
Elizabeth City, U.S.A. . 77 G7 36 18N 76 14W
Elizabethton, U.S.A. . 77 G4 36 21N 82 13W
Elizabethtown, Ky., U.S.A. . 76 G3 37 42N 85 52W
Elizabethtown, N.Y., U.S.A. . 79 B11 44 13N 73 36W
Elizabethtown, Pa., U.S.A. . 79 F8 40 9N 76 36W
Elk, Poland . 17 B12 53 50N 22 21 E
Elk →, Canada . 72 C5 49 11N 115 14W
Elk →, U.S.A. . 77 H2 34 46N 87 16W
Elk City, U.S.A. . 81 H5 35 25N 99 25W
Elk Creek, U.S.A. . 84 F4 39 36N 122 32W
Elk Grove, U.S.A. . 84 G5 38 25N 121 22W
Elk Island Nat. Park, Canada . 72 C6 53 35N 112 59W
Elk Lake, Canada . 70 C3 47 40N 80 25W
Elk Point, Canada . 73 C6 53 54N 110 55W
Elk River, Idaho, U.S.A. . 82 C5 46 47N 116 11W
Elk River, Minn., U.S.A. . 80 C8 45 18N 93 35W
Elkedra →, Australia . 62 C2 21 8S 136 22 E
Elkhart, Ind., U.S.A. . 76 E3 41 41N 85 58W
Elkhart, Kans., U.S.A. . 81 G4 37 0N 101 54W
Elkhorn, Canada . 73 D8 49 59N 101 14W
Elkhorn →, U.S.A. . 80 E6 41 8N 96 19W
Elkhovo, Bulgaria . 21 C12 42 10N 26 35 E
Elkin, U.S.A. . 77 G5 36 15N 80 51W
Elkins, U.S.A. . 76 F6 38 55N 79 51W
Elko, Canada . 72 D5 49 20N 115 10W
Elko, U.S.A. . 82 F6 40 50N 115 46W
Elkton, U.S.A. . 78 C1 43 49N 83 11W
Ell, L., Australia . 61 E4 29 13S 127 46 E
Ellef Ringnes I., Canada . 4 B2 78 30N 102 2W
Ellen, Mt., U.S.A. . 79 B12 44 9N 72 56W
Ellenburg, U.S.A. . 79 B11 44 54N 73 48W
Ellendale, U.S.A. . 80 B5 46 0N 98 32W
Ellensburg, U.S.A. . 82 C3 46 59N 120 34W
Ellenville, U.S.A. . 79 E10 41 43N 74 24W

Ellery, Mt., Australia . 63 F4 37 28S 148 47 E
Ellesmere, L., N.Z. . 59 M4 43 47S 172 28 E
Ellesmere I., Canada . 4 B4 79 30N 80 0W
Ellesmere Port, U.K. . 10 D5 53 17N 2 54W
Ellice Is. = Tuvalu ■, Pac. Oc. . 64 H9 8 0S 178 0 E
Ellicottville, U.S.A. . 78 D6 42 17N 78 40W
Elliot, Australia . 62 B1 17 33S 133 32 E
Elliot, S. Africa . 57 E4 31 22S 27 48 E
Elliot Lake, Canada . 70 C3 46 25N 82 35W
Elliotdale = Xhora, S. Africa . 57 E4 31 55S 28 38 E
Ellis, U.S.A. . 80 F5 38 56N 99 34W
Elliston, Australia . 63 E1 33 39S 134 53 E
Ellisville, U.S.A. . 81 K10 31 36N 89 12W
Ellon, U.K. . 12 D6 57 22N 2 4W
Ellore = Eluru, India . 41 L12 16 48N 81 8 E
Ellsworth, Kans., U.S.A. . 80 F5 38 44N 98 14W
Ellsworth, Maine, U.S.A. . 77 C11 44 33N 68 25W
Ellsworth Land, Antarctica . 5 D16 76 0S 89 0W
Ellsworth Mts., Antarctica . 5 D16 78 30S 85 0W
Ellwood City, U.S.A. . 78 F4 40 52N 80 17W
Elma, Canada . 73 D9 49 52N 95 55W
Elma, U.S.A. . 84 D3 47 0N 123 25W
Elmalı, Turkey . 25 G4 36 44N 29 56 E
Elmhurst, U.S.A. . 76 E2 41 53N 87 56W
Elmira, Canada . 78 C4 43 36N 80 33W
Elmira, U.S.A. . 78 D8 42 6N 76 48W
Elmira Heights, U.S.A. . 78 D8 42 8N 76 50W
Elmore, Australia . 63 F3 36 30S 144 37 E
Elmore, U.S.A. . 85 M11 33 7N 115 49W
Elmshorn, Germany . 16 B5 53 43N 9 40 E
Elmvale, Canada . 78 B5 44 35N 79 52W
Elora, Canada . 78 C4 43 41N 80 26W
Eloúnda, Greece . 23 D7 35 16N 25 42 E
Eloy, U.S.A. . 83 K8 32 45N 111 33W
Elrose, Canada . 73 C7 51 12N 108 0W
Elsie, U.S.A. . 84 E3 45 52N 123 36W
Elsinore = Helsingør, Denmark . 9 H15 56 2N 12 35 E
Eltham, N.Z. . 59 H5 39 26S 174 19 E
Eluru, India . 41 L12 16 48N 81 8 E
Elvas, Portugal . 19 C2 38 50N 7 10W
Elverum, Norway . 9 F14 60 53N 11 34 E
Elvire →, Australia . 60 C4 17 51S 128 11 E
Elvire, Mt., Australia . 61 E2 29 22S 119 36 E
Elwell, L., U.S.A. . 82 B8 48 22N 111 17W
Elwood, Ind., U.S.A. . 76 E3 40 17N 85 50W
Elwood, Nebr., U.S.A. . 80 E5 40 36N 99 52W
Elx = Elche, Spain . 19 C5 38 15N 0 42W
Ely, U.K. . 11 E8 52 24N 0 16 E
Ely, Minn., U.S.A. . 80 B9 47 55N 91 51W
Ely, Nev., U.S.A. . 82 G6 39 15N 114 54W
Elyria, U.S.A. . 78 E2 41 22N 82 7W
Emämrüd, Iran . 45 B7 36 30N 55 0 E
Emba, Kazakstan . 26 E6 48 50N 58 8 E
Emba →, Kazakstan . 25 E9 46 55N 53 28 E
Embarcación, Argentina . 94 A3 23 10S 64 0W
Embarras Portage, Canada . 73 B6 58 27N 111 28W
Embetsu, Japan . 30 B10 44 44N 141 47 E
Embi = Emba, Kazakstan . 26 E6 48 50N 58 8 E
Embi = Emba →, Kazakstan . 25 E9 46 55N 53 28 E
Embóna, Greece . 23 C9 36 13N 27 51 E
Embrun, France . 18 D7 44 34N 6 30 E
Embu, Kenya . 54 C4 0 32S 37 38 E
Emden, Germany . 16 B4 53 21N 7 12 E
Emerald, Australia . 62 C4 23 32S 148 10 E
Emerson, Canada . 73 D9 49 0N 97 10W
Emet, Turkey . 21 E13 39 20N 29 15 E
Emi Koussi, Chad . 51 E9 19 45N 18 55 E
Eminabad, Pakistan . 42 C6 32 2N 74 8 E
Emine, Nos, Bulgaria . 21 C12 42 40N 27 56 E
Emissi, Tarso, Chad . 51 D9 21 27N 18 36 E
Emlenton, U.S.A. . 78 E5 41 11N 79 43W
Emmaus, S. Africa . 56 D4 29 2S 25 15 E
Emmaus, U.S.A. . 79 F9 40 32N 75 30W
Emmeloord, Neths. . 15 B5 52 44N 5 46 E
Emmen, Neths. . 15 B6 52 48N 6 57 E
Emmet, Australia . 62 C3 24 45S 144 30 E
Emmetsburg, U.S.A. . 80 D7 43 7N 94 41W
Emmett, Idaho, U.S.A. . 82 E5 43 52N 116 30W
Emmett, Mich., U.S.A. . 78 D2 42 59N 82 46W
Emmonak, U.S.A. . 68 B3 62 46N 164 30W
Emo, Canada . 73 D10 48 38N 93 50W
Empalme, Mexico . 86 B2 28 1N 110 49W
Empangeni, S. Africa . 57 D5 28 50S 31 52 E
Empedrado, Argentina . 94 B4 28 0S 58 46W
Emperor Seamount Chain, Pac. Oc. . 64 D9 40 0N 170 0 E
Emporia, Kans., U.S.A. . 80 F6 38 25N 96 11W
Emporia, Va., U.S.A. . 77 G7 36 42N 77 32W
Emporium, U.S.A. . 78 E6 41 31N 78 14W
Empress, Canada . 73 C7 50 57N 110 0W
Empty Quarter = Rub' al Khâlî, Si. Arabia . 46 D4 19 0N 48 0 E
Ems →, Germany . 16 B4 53 20N 7 12 E
Emsdale, Canada . 78 A5 45 32N 79 19W
Emu, China . 35 C15 43 40N 128 6 E
Emu Park, Australia . 62 C5 23 13S 150 50 E
'En 'Avrona, Israel . 47 F4 29 43N 35 0 E
En Nahud, Sudan . 51 F11 12 45N 28 25 E
Ena, Japan . 31 G8 35 25N 137 25 E
Enana, Namibia . 56 B2 17 30S 16 23 E
Enard B., U.K. . 12 C3 58 5N 5 20W
Enare = Inarijärvi, Finland . 8 B22 69 0N 28 0 E
Enarotali, Indonesia . 37 E9 3 55S 136 21 E
Encampment, U.S.A. . 82 F10 41 12N 106 47W
Encantadas, Serra, Brazil . 95 C5 30 40S 53 0W
Encarnación, Paraguay . 95 B4 27 15S 55 50W
Encarnación de Díaz, Mexico 86 C4 21 30N 102 13W
Encinitas, U.S.A. . 85 M9 33 3N 117 17W
Encino, U.S.A. . 83 J11 34 39N 105 28W
Encounter B., Australia . 63 F2 35 45S 138 45 E
Endako, Canada . 72 C3 54 6N 125 2W
Ende, Indonesia . 37 F6 8 45S 121 40 E
Endeavour Str., Australia . 62 A3 10 45S 142 0 E
Enderbury, I., Kiribati . 64 H10 3 8S 171 5W
Enderby, Canada . 72 C5 50 35N 119 10W
Enderby I., Australia . 60 D2 20 35S 116 30 E
Enderby Land, Antarctica . 5 C5 66 0S 53 0 E
Enderlin, U.S.A. . 80 B6 46 38N 97 36W
Endicott, U.S.A. . 79 D8 42 6N 76 4W
Endwell, U.S.A. . 79 D8 42 6N 76 1W
Endyalgout I., Australia . 60 B5 11 40S 132 35 E
Eneabba, Australia . 61 E2 29 49S 115 16 E
Enewetak Atoll, Marshall Is. . 64 F8 11 30N 162 15 E
Enez, Turkey . 21 D12 40 45N 26 5 E

Garden City

Fort Yukon, *U.S.A.* **68 B5** 66 34N 145 16W
Fortaleza, *Brazil* **93 D11** 3 45S 38 35W
Forteau, *Canada* **71 B8** 51 28N 56 58W
Fortescue →, *Australia* **60 D2** 21 0S 116 4 E
Forth →, *U.K.* **12 E5** 56 9N 3 50W
Forth, Firth of, *U.K.* **12 E5** 56 5N 2 55W
Fortrose, *U.K.* **12 D4** 57 35N 4 9W
Fortuna, *Calif., U.S.A.* **82 F1** 40 36N 124 9W
Fortuna, *N. Dak., U.S.A.* **80 A3** 48 55N 103 47W
Fortune, *Canada* **71 C8** 47 4N 55 50W
Fortune B., *Canada* **71 C8** 47 30N 55 22W
Forūr, *Iran* **45 E7** 26 17N 54 32 E
Foshan, *China* **33 D6** 23 4N 113 5 E
Fosna, *Norway* **8 E14** 63 50N 10 20 E
Fosnavåg, *Norway* **9 E11** 62 22N 5 38 E
Fossano, *Italy* **18 D7** 44 33N 7 43 E
Fossil, *U.S.A.* **82 D3** 45 0N 120 9W
Foster, *Canada* **79 A12** 45 17N 72 30W
Foster →, *Canada* **73 B7** 55 47N 105 49W
Fosters Ra., *Australia* **62 C1** 21 35S 133 48 E
Fostoria, *U.S.A.* **76 E4** 41 10N 83 25W
Fotadrevo, *Madag.* **57 C8** 24 3S 45 1 E
Fougères, *France* **18 B3** 48 21N 1 14W
Foul Pt., *Sri Lanka* **40 Q12** 8 35N 81 18 E
Foula, *U.K.* **12 A6** 60 10N 2 5W
Foulness I., *U.K.* **11 F8** 51 36N 0 55 E
Foulpointe, *Madag.* **57 B8** 17 41S 49 31 E
Foulweather, C., *U.S.A.* **74 B2** 44 50N 124 5W
Foumban, *Cameroon* **52 C2** 5 45N 10 50 E
Fountain, *U.S.A.* **80 F2** 38 41N 104 42W
Fountain Springs, *U.S.A.* **85 K8** 35 54N 118 51W
Fouriesburg, *S. Africa* **56 D4** 28 38S 28 14 E
Foúrnoi, *Greece* **21 F12** 37 36N 26 32 E
Fourth Cataract, *Sudan* **51 E12** 18 47N 32 3 E
Fouta Djalon, *Guinea* **50 F3** 11 20N 12 10W
Foux, Cap-à-, *Haiti* **89 C5** 19 43N 73 27W
Foveaux Str., *N.Z.* **59 M2** 46 42S 168 10 E
Fowey, *U.K.* **11 G3** 50 20N 4 39W
Fowler, *Calif., U.S.A.* **84 J7** 36 38N 119 41W
Fowler, *Colo., U.S.A.* **80 F3** 38 8N 104 2W
Fowlers B., *Australia* **61 F5** 31 59S 132 34 E
Fowman, *Iran* **45 B6** 37 13N 49 19 E
Fox →, *Canada* **73 B10** 56 3N 93 18W
Fox Creek, *Canada* **72 C5** 54 24N 116 48W
Fox Lake, *Canada* **72 B6** 58 28N 114 31W
Fox Valley, *Canada* **73 C7** 50 30N 109 25W
Foxboro, *U.S.A.* **79 D13** 42 4N 71 16W
Foxe Basin, *Canada* **69 B12** 66 0N 77 0W
Foxe Chan., *Canada* **69 B11** 65 0N 80 0W
Foxe Pen., *Canada* **69 B12** 65 0N 76 0W
Foxton, *N.Z.* **59 J5** 40 29S 175 18 E
Foyle, Lough, *U.K.* **13 A4** 55 7N 7 4W
Foynes, *Ireland* **13 D2** 52 37N 9 7W
Foz do Cunene, *Angola* **56 B1** 17 15S 11 48 E
Foz do Iguaçu, *Brazil* **95 B5** 25 30S 54 30W
Frackville, *U.S.A.* **79 F8** 40 47N 76 14W
Fraile Muerto, *Uruguay* **95 C5** 32 31S 54 32W
Framingham, *U.S.A.* **79 D13** 42 17N 71 25W
Franca, *Brazil* **93 H9** 20 33S 47 30W
Francavilla Fontana, *Italy* **21 D7** 40 32N 17 35 E
France ■, *Europe* **18 C5** 47 0N 3 0 E
Frances, *Australia* **63 F3** 36 41S 140 55 E
Frances →, *Canada* **72 A3** 60 16N 129 10W
Frances L., *Canada* **72 A3** 61 23N 129 30W
Franceville, *Gabon* **52 E2** 1 40S 13 32 E
Franche-Comté, *France* **18 C6** 46 50N 5 55 E
Francis Case, L., *U.S.A.* **80 D5** 43 4N 98 34W
Francisco Beltrão, *Brazil* **95 B5** 26 5S 53 4W
Francisco I. Madero, *Coahuila, Mexico* **86 B4** 25 48N 103 18W
Francisco I. Madero, *Durango, Mexico* **86 C4** 24 32N 104 22W
Francistown, *Botswana* **57 C4** 21 7S 27 33 E
François, *Canada* **71 C8** 47 35N 56 45W
François L., *Canada* **72 C3** 54 0N 125 30W
Franeker, *Neths.* **15 A5** 53 12N 5 33 E
Frankford, *Canada* **78 B7** 44 12N 77 36W
Frankfort, *S. Africa* **57 D4** 27 17S 28 30 E
Frankfort, *Ind., U.S.A.* **76 E2** 40 17N 86 31W
Frankfort, *Kans., U.S.A.* **80 F6** 39 42N 96 25W
Frankfort, *Ky., U.S.A.* **76 F3** 38 12N 84 52W
Frankfort, *N.Y., U.S.A.* **79 C9** 43 2N 75 4W
Frankfurt, *Brandenburg, Germany* **16 B8** 52 20N 14 32 E
Frankfurt, *Hessen, Germany* **16 C5** 50 7N 8 41 E
Fränkische Alb, *Germany* **16 D6** 49 10N 11 23 E
Frankland →, *Australia* **61 G2** 35 0S 116 48 E
Franklin, *Ky., U.S.A.* **77 G2** 36 43N 86 35W
Franklin, *La., U.S.A.* **81 L9** 29 48N 91 30W
Franklin, *Mass., U.S.A.* **79 D13** 42 5N 71 24W
Franklin, *N.H., U.S.A.* **79 C13** 43 27N 71 39W
Franklin, *Nebr., U.S.A.* **80 E5** 40 6N 98 57W
Franklin, *Pa., U.S.A.* **78 E5** 41 24N 79 50W
Franklin, *Va., U.S.A.* **77 G7** 36 41N 76 56W
Franklin, *W. Va., U.S.A.* **76 F6** 38 39N 79 20W
Franklin B., *Canada* **68 B7** 69 45N 126 0W
Franklin D. Roosevelt L., *U.S.A.* **82 B4** 48 18N 118 9W
Franklin I., *Antarctica* **5 D11** 76 10S 168 30 E
Franklin L., *U.S.A.* **82 F6** 40 25N 115 22W
Franklin Mts., *Canada* **68 B7** 65 0N 125 0W
Franklin Str., *Canada* **68 A10** 72 0N 96 0W
Franklinton, *U.S.A.* **81 K9** 30 51N 90 9W
Franklinville, *U.S.A.* **78 D6** 42 20N 78 27W
Franks Pk., *U.S.A.* **82 E9** 43 58N 109 18W
Frankston, *Australia* **63 F4** 38 8S 145 8 E
Fransfontein, *Namibia* **56 C2** 20 12S 15 1 E
Frantsa Iosifa, Zemlya, *Russia* **26 A6** 82 0N 55 0 E
Franz, *Canada* **70 C3** 48 25N 84 30W
Franz Josef Land = Frantsa Iosifa, Zemlya, *Russia* **26 A6** 82 0N 55 0 E
Fraser, *U.S.A.* **78 D2** 42 32N 82 57W
Fraser →, *B.C., Canada* **72 D4** 49 7N 123 11W
Fraser →, *Nfld., Canada* **71 A7** 56 39N 62 10W
Fraser, Mt., *Australia* **61 E2** 25 35S 118 20 E
Fraser I., *Australia* **63 D5** 25 15S 153 10 E
Fraser Lake, *Canada* **72 C4** 54 0N 124 50W
Fraserburg, *S. Africa* **56 E3** 31 55S 21 30 E
Fraserburgh, *U.K.* **12 D6** 57 42N 2 1W
Fraserdale, *Canada* **70 C3** 49 55N 81 37W
Fray Bentos, *Uruguay* **94 C4** 33 10S 58 15W
Fredericia, *Denmark* **9 J13** 55 34N 9 45 E
Frederick, *Md., U.S.A.* **76 F7** 39 25N 77 25W
Frederick, *Okla., U.S.A.* **81 H5** 34 23N 99 1W
Frederick, *S. Dak., U.S.A.* **80 C5** 45 50N 98 31W
Fredericksburg, *Pa., U.S.A.* **79 F8** 40 27N 76 26W
Fredericksburg, *Tex., U.S.A.* **81 K5** 30 16N 98 52W
Fredericksburg, *Va., U.S.A.* **76 F7** 38 18N 77 28W
Fredericktown, *Mo., U.S.A.* **81 G9** 37 34N 90 18W
Fredericktown, *Ohio, U.S.A.* **78 F2** 40 29N 82 33W
Frederico I. Madero, Presa, *Mexico* **86 B3** 28 7N 105 40W
Frederico Westphalen, *Brazil* **95 B5** 27 22S 53 24W
Fredericton, *Canada* **71 C6** 45 57N 66 40W
Fredericton Junction, *Canada* **71 C6** 45 41N 66 40W
Frederikshåb = Paamiut, *Greenland* **4 C5** 62 0N 49 43W
Frederikshavn, *Denmark* **9 H14** 57 28N 10 31 E
Frederiksted, *U.S. Virgin Is.* **89 C7** 17 43N 64 53W
Fredonia, *Ariz., U.S.A.* **83 H7** 36 57N 112 32W
Fredonia, *Kans., U.S.A.* **81 G7** 37 32N 95 49W
Fredonia, *N.Y., U.S.A.* **78 D5** 42 26N 79 20W
Fredrikstad, *Norway* **9 G14** 59 13N 10 57 E
Free State □, *S. Africa* **56 D4** 28 30S 27 0 E
Freehold, *U.S.A.* **79 F10** 40 16N 74 17W
Freel Peak, *U.S.A.* **84 G7** 38 52N 119 54W
Freeland, *U.S.A.* **79 E9** 41 1N 75 54W
Freels, C., *Canada* **71 C9** 49 15N 53 30W
Freeman, *Calif., U.S.A.* **85 K9** 35 35N 117 53W
Freeman, *S. Dak., U.S.A.* **80 D6** 43 21N 97 26W
Freeport, *Bahamas* **88 A4** 26 30N 78 47W
Freeport, *Ill., U.S.A.* **80 D10** 42 17N 89 36W
Freeport, *N.Y., U.S.A.* **79 F11** 40 39N 73 35W
Freeport, *Ohio, U.S.A.* **78 F3** 40 12N 81 15W
Freeport, *Pa., U.S.A.* **78 F5** 40 41N 79 41W
Freeport, *Tex., U.S.A.* **81 L7** 28 57N 95 21W
Freetown, *S. Leone* **50 G3** 8 30N 13 17W
Frégate, L., *Canada* **70 B5** 53 15N 74 45W
Fregenal de la Sierra, *Spain* **19 C2** 38 10N 6 39W
Freiburg = Fribourg, *Switz.* **18 C7** 46 49N 7 9 E
Freiburg, *Germany* **16 E4** 47 59N 7 51 E
Freire, *Chile* **96 D2** 38 54S 72 38W
Freirina, *Chile* **94 B1** 28 30S 71 10W
Freising, *Germany* **16 D6** 48 24N 11 45 E
Freistadt, *Austria* **16 D8** 48 30N 14 30 E
Fréjus, *France* **18 E7** 43 25N 6 44 E
Fremantle, *Australia* **61 F2** 32 7S 115 47 E
Fremont, *Calif., U.S.A.* **84 H4** 37 32N 121 57W
Fremont, *Mich., U.S.A.* **76 D3** 43 28N 85 57W
Fremont, *Nebr., U.S.A.* **80 E6** 41 26N 96 30W
Fremont, *Ohio, U.S.A.* **76 E4** 41 21N 83 7W
Fremont →, *U.S.A.* **83 G8** 38 24N 110 42W
French Camp, *U.S.A.* **84 H5** 37 53N 121 16W
French Creek →, *U.S.A.* **78 E5** 41 24N 79 50W
French Guiana ■, *S. Amer.* **93 C8** 4 0N 53 0W
French Polynesia ■, *Pac. Oc.* **65 K13** 20 0S 145 0W
Frenchman Cr. →, *N. Amer.* **82 B10** 48 31N 107 10W
Frenchman Cr. →, *U.S.A.* **80 E4** 40 14N 100 50W
Fresco →, *Brazil* **93 E8** 7 15S 51 30W
Freshfield, C., *Antarctica* **5 C10** 68 25S 151 10 E
Fresnillo, *Mexico* **86 C4** 23 10N 103 0W
Fresno, *U.S.A.* **84 J7** 36 44N 119 47W
Fresno Reservoir, *U.S.A.* **82 B9** 48 36N 109 57W
Frew →, *Australia* **62 C2** 20 0S 135 38 E
Frewsburg, *U.S.A.* **78 D5** 42 3N 79 10W
Freycinet Pen., *Australia* **62 G4** 42 10S 148 25 E
Fria, C., *Namibia* **56 B1** 18 0S 12 0 E
Friant, *U.S.A.* **84 J7** 36 59N 119 43W
Frías, *Argentina* **94 B2** 28 40S 65 5W
Fribourg, *Switz.* **18 C7** 46 49N 7 9 E
Friday Harbor, *U.S.A.* **84 B3** 48 32N 123 1W
Friedens, *U.S.A.* **78 F6** 40 3N 78 59W
Friedrichshafen, *Germany* **16 E5** 47 39N 9 30 E
Friendly Is. = Tonga ■, *Pac. Oc.* **59 D11** 19 50S 174 30W
Friendship, *U.S.A.* **78 D6** 42 12N 78 8W
Friesland □, *Neths.* **15 A5** 53 5N 5 50 E
Frio →, *U.S.A.* **81 L5** 28 26N 98 11W
Frio, C., *Brazil* **90 F6** 22 50S 41 50W
Friona, *U.S.A.* **81 H3** 34 38N 102 43W
Fritch, *U.S.A.* **81 H4** 35 38N 101 36W
Frobisher B., *Canada* **69 B13** 62 30N 66 0W
Frobisher Bay = Iqaluit, *Canada* **69 B13** 63 44N 68 31W
Frobisher L., *Canada* **73 B7** 56 20N 108 15W
Frohavet, *Norway* **8 E13** 64 0N 9 30 E
Frome, *U.K.* **11 F5** 51 14N 2 19W
Frome →, *U.K.* **11 G5** 50 41N 2 6W
Frome, L., *Australia* **63 E2** 30 45S 139 45 E
Front Range, *U.S.A.* **74 C5** 40 25N 105 45W
Front Royal, *U.S.A.* **76 F6** 38 55N 78 12W
Frontera, *Canary Is.* **22 G2** 27 47N 17 59W
Frontera, *Mexico* **87 D6** 18 30N 92 40W
Fronteras, *Mexico* **86 A3** 30 56N 109 31W
Frosinone, *Italy* **20 D5** 41 38N 13 19 E
Frostburg, *U.S.A.* **76 F6** 39 39N 78 56W
Frostisen, *Norway* **8 B17** 68 14N 17 10 E
Frøya, *Norway* **8 E13** 63 43N 8 40 E
Frunze = Bishkek, *Kyrgyzstan* **26 E8** 42 54N 74 46 E
Frutal, *Brazil* **93 H9** 20 0S 49 0W
Frýdek-Místek, *Czech Rep.* **17 D10** 49 40N 18 20 E
Fryeburg, *U.S.A.* **79 B14** 44 1N 70 59W
Fu Xian = Wafangdian, *China* **35 E11** 39 38N 121 58 E
Fu Xian, *China* **34 G5** 36 0N 109 20 E
Fucheng, *China* **34 F9** 37 50N 116 10 E
Fuchou = Fuzhou, *China* **33 D6** 26 5N 119 16 E
Fuchū, *Japan* **31 G6** 34 34N 133 14 E
Fuencaliente, *Canary Is.* **22 F2** 28 28N 17 50W
Fuencaliente, Pta., *Canary Is.* **22 F2** 28 27N 17 51W
Fuengirola, *Spain* **19 D3** 36 32N 4 41W
Fuentes de Oñoro, *Spain* **19 B2** 40 33N 6 52W
Fuerte →, *Mexico* **86 B3** 25 50N 109 25W
Fuerte Olimpo, *Paraguay* **94 A4** 21 0S 57 51W
Fuerteventura, *Canary Is.* **22 F6** 28 30N 14 0W
Fufeng, *China* **34 G5** 34 22N 108 0 E
Fugou, *China* **34 G8** 34 3N 114 25 E
Fugu, *China* **34 E6** 39 2N 111 3 E
Fuhai, *China* **32 B3** 47 2N 87 25 E
Fuḩaymī, *Iraq* **44 C4** 34 16N 42 10 E
Fuji, *Japan* **31 G9** 35 9N 138 39 E
Fuji-San, *Japan* **31 G9** 35 22N 138 44 E
Fuji-Yoshida, *Japan* **31 G9** 35 30N 138 46 E
Fujian □, *China* **33 D6** 26 0N 118 0 E
Fujinomiya, *Japan* **31 G9** 35 10N 138 40 E
Fujisawa, *Japan* **31 G9** 35 22N 139 29 E
Fujiyama, Mt. = Fuji-San, *Japan* **31 G9** 35 22N 138 44 E
Fukien = Fujian □, *China* **33 D6** 26 0N 118 0 E
Fukuchiyama, *Japan* **31 G7** 35 19N 135 9 E
Fukue-Shima, *Japan* **31 H4** 32 40N 128 45 E
Fukui, *Japan* **31 F8** 36 5N 136 10 E
Fukui □, *Japan* **31 G8** 36 0N 136 12 E
Fukuoka, *Japan* **31 H5** 33 39N 130 21 E
Fukuoka □, *Japan* **31 H5** 33 30N 131 0 E
Fukushima, *Japan* **30 F10** 37 44N 140 28 E
Fukushima □, *Japan* **30 F10** 37 30N 140 15 E
Fukuyama, *Japan* **31 G6** 34 35N 133 20 E
Fulda, *Germany* **16 C5** 50 32N 9 40 E
Fulda →, *Germany* **16 C5** 51 25N 9 39 E
Fulford Harbour, *Canada* **84 B3** 48 47N 123 27W
Fullerton, *Calif., U.S.A.* **85 M9** 33 53N 117 56W
Fullerton, *Nebr., U.S.A.* **80 E6** 41 22N 97 58W
Fulongquan, *China* **35 B13** 44 20N 124 42 E
Fulton, *Mo., U.S.A.* **80 F9** 38 52N 91 57W
Fulton, *N.Y., U.S.A.* **79 C8** 43 19N 76 25W
Funabashi, *Japan* **31 G10** 35 45N 140 0 E
Funafuti = Fongafale, *Tuvalu* **64 H9** 8 31S 179 13 E
Funchal, *Madeira* **22 D3** 32 38N 16 54W
Fundación, *Colombia* **92 A4** 10 31N 74 11W
Fundão, *Portugal* **19 B2** 40 8N 7 30W
Fundy, B. of, *Canada* **71 D6** 45 0N 66 0W
Funhalouro, *Mozam.* **57 C5** 23 3S 34 25 E
Funing, *Hebei, China* **35 E10** 39 53N 119 12 E
Funing, *Jiangsu, China* **35 H10** 33 45N 119 50 E
Funiu Shan, *China* **34 H7** 33 30N 112 20 E
Funtua, *Nigeria* **50 F7** 11 30N 7 18 E
Fuping, *Hebei, China* **34 E8** 38 48N 114 12 E
Fuping, *Shaanxi, China* **34 G5** 34 42N 109 10 E
Furano, *Japan* **30 C11** 43 21N 142 23 E
Furāt, Nahr al →, *Asia* **44 D5** 31 0N 47 25 E
Fūrg, *Iran* **45 D7** 28 18N 55 13 E
Furnás, *Spain* **22 B8** 39 3N 1 32 E
Furnas, Reprêsa de, *Brazil* **95 A6** 20 50S 45 30W
Furneaux Group, *Australia* **62 G4** 40 10S 147 50 E
Furqlus, *Syria* **47 A6** 34 36N 37 8 E
Fürstenwalde, *Germany* **16 B8** 52 22N 14 3 E
Fürth, *Germany* **16 D6** 49 28N 10 59 E
Furukawa, *Japan* **30 E10** 38 34N 140 58 E
Fury and Hecla Str., *Canada* **69 B11** 69 56N 84 0W
Fusagasuga, *Colombia* **92 C4** 4 21N 74 22W
Fushan, *Shandong, China* **35 F11** 37 30N 121 15 E
Fushan, *Shanxi, China* **34 G6** 35 58N 111 51 E
Fushun, *China* **35 D12** 41 50N 123 56 E
Fusong, *China* **35 C14** 42 20N 127 15 E
Futuna, *Wall. & F. Is.* **59 B8** 14 25S 178 20W
Fuxin, *China* **35 C11** 42 5N 121 48 E
Fuyang, *China* **34 H8** 33 0N 115 48 E
Fuyang He →, *China* **34 E9** 38 12N 117 0 E
Fuyu, *China* **35 B13** 45 12N 124 43 E
Fuzhou, *China* **33 D6** 26 5N 119 16 E
Fylde, *U.K.* **10 D5** 53 50N 2 58W
Fyn, *Denmark* **9 J14** 55 20N 10 30 E
Fyne, L., *U.K.* **12 F3** 55 59N 5 23W

G

Gabela, *Angola* **52 G2** 11 0S 14 24 E
Gabès, *Tunisia* **51 B8** 33 53N 10 2 E
Gabès, G. de, *Tunisia* **51 B8** 34 0N 10 30 E
Gabon ■, *Africa* **52 E2** 0 10S 10 0 E
Gaborone, *Botswana* **56 C4** 24 45S 25 57 E
Gabriels, *U.S.A.* **79 B10** 44 26N 74 12W
Gābrīk, *Iran* **45 E8** 25 44N 58 28 E
Gabrovo, *Bulgaria* **21 C11** 42 52N 25 19 E
Gāch Sār, *Iran* **45 B6** 36 7N 51 19 E
Gachsārān, *Iran* **45 D6** 30 15N 50 45 E
Gadag, *India* **40 M9** 15 30N 75 45 E
Gadap, *Pakistan* **42 G2** 25 5N 67 28 E
Gadarwara, *India* **43 H8** 22 50N 78 50 E
Gadhada, *India* **42 J4** 22 0N 71 35 E
Gadra, *Pakistan* **42 G4** 25 40N 70 38 E
Gadsden, *U.S.A.* **77 H3** 34 1N 86 1W
Gadwal, *India* **40 L10** 16 10N 77 50 E
Gaffney, *U.S.A.* **77 H5** 35 5N 81 39W
Gafsa, *Tunisia* **50 B7** 34 24N 8 43 E
Gagaria, *India* **42 G4** 25 43N 70 46 E
Gagnoa, *Ivory C.* **50 G4** 6 56N 5 16W
Gagnon, *Canada* **71 B6** 51 50N 68 5W
Gagnon, L., *Canada* **73 A6** 62 3N 110 27W
Gahini, *Rwanda* **54 C3** 1 50S 30 30 E
Gahmar, *India* **43 G10** 25 27N 83 49 E
Gai Xian = Gaizhou, *China* **35 D12** 40 22N 122 20 E
Gaïdhouronisi, *Greece* **23 E7** 34 53N 25 41 E
Gail, *U.S.A.* **81 J4** 32 46N 101 27W
Gaillimh = Galway, *Ireland* **13 C2** 53 17N 9 3W
Gaines, *U.S.A.* **78 E7** 41 46N 77 35W
Gainesville, *Fla., U.S.A.* **77 L4** 29 40N 82 20W
Gainesville, *Ga., U.S.A.* **77 H4** 34 18N 83 50W
Gainesville, *Mo., U.S.A.* **81 G8** 36 36N 92 26W
Gainesville, *Tex., U.S.A.* **81 J6** 33 38N 97 8W
Gainsborough, *U.K.* **10 D7** 53 24N 0 46W
Gairdner, L., *Australia* **63 E2** 31 30S 136 0 E
Gairloch, L., *U.K.* **12 D3** 57 43N 5 45W
Gaizhou, *China* **35 D12** 40 22N 122 20 E
Gaj →, *Pakistan* **42 F2** 26 26N 67 21 E
Gakuch, *Pakistan* **43 A5** 36 7N 73 45 E
Galán, Cerro, *Argentina* **94 B2** 25 55S 66 52W
Galana →, *Kenya* **54 C5** 3 9S 40 8 E
Galápagos, *Pac. Oc.* **90 D1** 0 0 91 0W
Galashiels, *U.K.* **12 F6** 55 37N 2 49W
Galaţi, *Romania* **17 F15** 45 27N 28 2 E
Galatina, *Italy* **21 D8** 40 10N 18 10 E
Galax, *U.S.A.* **77 G5** 36 40N 80 56W
Galcaio, *Somali Rep.* **46 F4** 6 30N 47 30 E
Galdhøpiggen, *Norway* **9 F12** 61 38N 8 18 E
Galeana, *Chihuahua, Mexico* **86 A3** 30 7N 107 38W
Galeana, *Nuevo León, Mexico* **86 A3** 24 50N 100 4W
Galela, *Indonesia* **37 D7** 1 50N 127 49 E
Galena, *U.S.A.* **68 B4** 64 44N 156 56W
Galera Pt., *Trin. & Tob.* **89 D7** 10 49N 60 54W
Galesburg, *U.S.A.* **80 E9** 40 57N 90 22W
Galeton, *U.S.A.* **78 E7** 41 44N 77 39W
Galich, *Russia* **24 C7** 58 22N 42 24 E
Galicia □, *Spain* **19 A2** 42 43N 7 45W
Galilee = Hagalil, *Israel* **47 C4** 32 53N 35 18 E
Galilee, L., *Australia* **62 C4** 22 20S 145 50 E
Galilee, Sea of = Yam Kinneret, *Israel* **47 C4** 32 45N 35 35 E
Galinoporni, *Cyprus* **23 D13** 35 31N 34 18 E
Galion, *U.S.A.* **78 F2** 40 44N 82 47W
Galiuro Mts., *U.S.A.* **83 K8** 32 30N 110 20W
Galiwinku, *Australia* **62 A2** 12 2S 135 34 E
Gallan Hd., *U.K.* **12 C1** 58 15N 7 2W
Gallatin, *U.S.A.* **77 G2** 36 24N 86 27W
Galle, *Sri Lanka* **40 R12** 6 5N 80 10 E
Gállego →, *Spain* **19 B5** 41 39N 0 51W
Gallegos →, *Argentina* **96 G3** 51 35S 69 0W
Galley Hd., *Ireland* **13 E3** 51 32N 8 55W
Gallinas, Pta., *Colombia* **92 A4** 12 28N 71 40W
Gallipoli = Gelibolu, *Turkey* **21 D12** 40 28N 26 43 E
Gallípoli, *Italy* **21 D8** 40 3N 17 58 E
Gallipolis, *U.S.A.* **76 F4** 38 49N 82 12W
Gällivare, *Sweden* **8 C19** 67 9N 20 40 E
Galloo I., *U.S.A.* **79 C8** 43 55N 76 25W
Galloway, *U.K.* **12 F4** 55 1N 4 29W
Galloway, Mull of, *U.K.* **12 G4** 54 39N 4 52W
Gallup, *U.S.A.* **83 J9** 35 32N 108 45W
Galoya, *Sri Lanka* **40 Q12** 8 10N 80 55 E
Galt, *U.S.A.* **84 G5** 38 15N 121 18W
Galty Mts., *Ireland* **13 D3** 52 22N 8 10W
Galtymore, *Ireland* **13 D3** 52 21N 8 11W
Galva, *U.S.A.* **80 E9** 41 10N 90 3W
Galveston, *U.S.A.* **81 L7** 29 18N 94 48W
Galveston B., *U.S.A.* **81 L7** 29 36N 94 50W
Gálvez, *Argentina* **94 C3** 32 0S 61 14W
Galway, *Ireland* **13 C2** 53 17N 9 3W
Galway □, *Ireland* **13 C2** 53 22N 9 1W
Galway B., *Ireland* **13 C2** 53 13N 9 10W
Gam →, *Vietnam* **38 B5** 21 55N 105 12 E
Gamagōri, *Japan* **31 G8** 34 50N 137 14 E
Gambat, *Pakistan* **42 F3** 27 17N 68 26 E
Gambhir →, *India* **42 F6** 26 58N 77 27 E
Gambia ■, *W. Afr.* **50 F2** 13 25N 16 0W
Gambia →, *W. Afr.* **50 F2** 13 28N 16 34W
Gambier, *U.S.A.* **78 F2** 40 22N 82 23W
Gambier, C., *Australia* **60 B5** 11 56S 130 57 E
Gambier Is., *Australia* **63 F2** 35 3S 136 30 E
Gambo, *Canada* **71 C9** 48 47N 54 13W
Gamboli, *Pakistan* **42 E3** 29 53N 68 24 E
Gamboma, *Congo* **52 E3** 1 55S 15 52 E
Gamka →, *S. Africa* **56 E3** 33 18S 21 39 E
Gamkab →, *Namibia* **56 D2** 28 4S 17 54 E
Gamlakarleby = Kokkola, *Finland* **8 E20** 63 50N 23 8 E
Gammon →, *Canada* **73 C9** 51 24N 95 44W
Gamtoos →, *S. Africa* **56 E4** 33 58S 25 1 E
Gan Jiang →, *China* **33 D6** 29 15N 116 0 E
Ganado, *U.S.A.* **83 J9** 35 43N 109 33W
Gananoque, *Canada* **79 B8** 44 20N 76 10W
Ganāveh, *Iran* **45 D6** 29 35N 50 35 E
Gäncä, *Azerbaijan* **25 F8** 40 45N 46 20 E
Gancheng, *China* **38 C7** 18 51N 108 37 E
Gand = Gent, *Belgium* **15 C3** 51 2N 3 42 E
Ganda, *Angola* **53 G2** 13 3S 14 35 E
Gandajika, *Dem. Rep. of the Congo* **52 F4** 6 45S 23 57 E
Gandak →, *India* **43 G11** 25 39N 85 13 E
Gandava, *Pakistan* **42 E2** 28 32N 67 32 E
Gander, *Canada* **71 C9** 48 58N 54 35W
Gander L., *Canada* **71 C9** 48 58N 54 35W
Ganderowe Falls, *Zimbabwe* **55 F2** 17 20S 29 10 E
Gandhi Sagar, *India* **42 G6** 24 40N 75 40 E
Gandhinagar, *India* **42 H5** 23 15N 72 45 E
Gandía, *Spain* **19 C5** 38 58N 0 9W
Gando, Pta., *Canary Is.* **22 G4** 27 55N 15 22W
Ganedidalem = Gani, *Indonesia* **37 E7** 0 48S 128 14 E
Ganga →, *India* **43 H14** 23 20N 90 30 E
Ganga Sagar, *India* **43 J13** 21 38N 88 5 E
Gangan →, *India* **43 E8** 28 38N 78 58 E
Ganganagar, *India* **42 E5** 29 56N 73 56 E
Gangapur, *India* **42 F7** 26 32N 76 49 E
Gangaw, *Burma* **41 H19** 22 5N 94 5 E
Gangdisê Shan, *China* **41 D12** 31 20N 81 0 E
Ganges = Ganga →, *India* **43 H14** 23 20N 90 30 E
Ganges, *Canada* **72 D4** 48 51N 123 31W
Ganges, Mouths of the, *India* **43 J14** 21 30N 90 0 E
Gangoh, *India* **42 E7** 29 46N 77 18 E
Gangroti, *India* **43 D8** 30 50N 79 10 E
Gangtok, *India* **41 F16** 27 20N 88 37 E
Gangu, *China* **34 G3** 34 40N 105 15 E
Gangyao, *China* **35 B14** 44 12N 126 37 E
Gani, *Indonesia* **37 E7** 0 48S 128 14 E
Ganj, *India* **43 F8** 27 45N 78 57 E
Gannett Peak, *U.S.A.* **82 E9** 43 11N 109 39W
Ganquan, *China* **34 F5** 36 20N 109 20 E
Gansu □, *China* **34 G3** 36 0N 104 0 E
Ganta, *Liberia* **50 G4** 7 15N 8 59W
Gantheaume, C., *Australia* **63 F2** 36 4S 137 32 E
Gantheaume B., *Australia* **61 E1** 27 40S 114 10 E
Gantsevichi = Hantsavichy, *Belarus* **17 B14** 52 49N 26 30 E
Ganyem = Genyem, *Indonesia* **37 E10** 2 46S 140 12 E
Ganyu, *China* **35 G10** 34 50N 119 8 E
Ganzhou, *China* **33 D6** 25 51N 114 56 E
Gao, *Mali* **50 E5** 16 15N 0 5W
Gaomi, *China* **35 F10** 36 20N 119 42 E
Gaoping, *China* **34 G7** 35 45N 112 55 E
Gaotang, *China* **34 F9** 36 50N 116 15 E
Gaoua, *Burkina Faso* **50 F5** 10 20N 3 8W
Gaoual, *Guinea* **50 F3** 11 45N 13 25W
Gaoxiong = Kaohsiung, *Taiwan* **33 D7** 22 35N 120 16 E
Gaoyang, *China* **34 E8** 38 40N 115 45 E
Gaoyou Hu, *China* **35 H10** 32 45N 119 20 E
Gaoyuan, *China* **35 F9** 37 8N 117 58 E
Gap, *France* **18 D7** 44 33N 6 5 E
Gapat →, *India* **43 G10** 24 30N 82 28 E
Gapuwiyak, *Australia* **62 A2** 12 25S 135 43 E
Gar, *China* **32 C2** 32 10N 79 58 E
Garabogazköl Aylagy, *Turkmenistan* **25 F9** 41 0N 53 30 E
Garachico, *Canary Is.* **22 F3** 28 22N 16 46W
Garachiné, *Panama* **88 E4** 8 0N 78 12W
Garafia, *Canary Is.* **22 F2** 28 48N 17 57W
Garah, *Australia* **63 D4** 29 5S 149 38 E
Garajonay, *Canary Is.* **22 F2** 28 7N 17 14W
Garanhuns, *Brazil* **93 E11** 8 50S 36 30W
Garautha, *India* **43 G8** 25 34N 79 18 E
Garba Tula, *Kenya* **54 B4** 0 30N 38 32 E
Garberville, *U.S.A.* **82 F2** 40 6N 123 48W
Garbiyang, *India* **43 D9** 30 8N 80 54 E
Garda, L. di, *Italy* **20 B4** 45 40N 10 41 E
Garde L., *Canada* **73 A7** 62 50N 106 13W
Garden City, *Ga., U.S.A.* **77 J5** 32 6N 81 9W
Garden City, *Kans., U.S.A.* **81 G4** 37 58N 100 53W
Garden City, *Tex., U.S.A.* **81 K4** 31 52N 101 29W

Green River

Gloucester, *Australia* **63 E5** 32 0S 151 59 E
Gloucester, *U.K.* **11 F5** 51 53N 2 15W
Gloucester, *U.S.A.* **79 D14** 42 37N 70 40W
Gloucester I., *Australia* **62 C4** 20 0S 148 30 E
Gloucester Point, *U.S.A.* **76 G7** 37 15N 76 29W
Gloucestershire □, *U.K.* **11 F5** 51 46N 2 15W
Gloversville, *U.S.A.* **79 C10** 43 3N 74 21W
Glovertown, *Canada* **71 C9** 48 40N 54 3W
Glusk, *Belarus* **17 B15** 52 53N 28 41 E
Gmünd, *Austria* **16 D8** 48 45N 15 0 E
Gmunden, *Austria* **16 E7** 47 55N 13 48 E
Gniezno, *Poland* **17 B9** 52 30N 17 35 E
Gnowangerup, *Australia* **61 F2** 33 58S 117 59 E
Go Cong, *Vietnam* **39 G6** 10 22N 106 40 E
Gō-no-ura, *Japan* **31 H4** 33 44N 129 40 E
Goa, *India* **40 M8** 15 33N 73 59 E
Goa □, *India* **40 M8** 15 33N 73 59 E
Goalen Hd., *Australia* **63 F5** 36 33S 150 4 E
Goalpara, *India* **41 F17** 26 10N 90 40 E
Goaltor, *India* **43 H12** 22 43N 87 10 E
Goalundo Ghat, *Bangla.* **43 H13** 23 50N 89 47 E
Goat Fell, *U.K.* **12 F3** 55 38N 5 11W
Goba, *Ethiopia* **46 F2** 7 1N 39 59 E
Goba, *Mozam.* **57 D5** 26 15S 32 13 E
Gobabis, *Namibia* **56 C2** 22 30S 19 0 E
Gobi, *Asia* **34 C6** 44 0N 110 0 E
Gobō, *Japan* **31 H7** 33 53N 135 10 E
Gochas, *Namibia* **56 C2** 24 59S 18 55 E
Godavari →, *India* **41 L13** 16 25N 82 18 E
Godavari Pt., *India* **41 L13** 17 0N 82 20 E
Godbout, *Canada* **71 C6** 49 20N 67 38W
Godda, *India* **43 G12** 24 50N 87 13 E
Goderich, *Canada* **78 C3** 43 45N 81 41W
Godfrey Ra., *Australia* **61 D2** 24 0S 117 0 E
Godhavn = Qeqertarsuaq, *Greenland* **4 C5** 69 15N 53 38W
Godhra, *India* **42 H5** 22 49N 73 40 E
Godoy Cruz, *Argentina* **94 C2** 32 56S 68 52W
Gods →, *Canada* **70 A1** 56 22N 92 51W
Gods L., *Canada* **70 B1** 54 40N 94 15W
Gods River, *Canada* **73 C10** 54 50N 94 5W
Godthåb = Nuuk, *Greenland* **69 B14** 64 10N 51 35W
Godwin Austen = K2, *Pakistan* **43 B7** 35 58N 76 32 E
Goeie Hoop, Kaap die = Good Hope, C. of, *S. Africa* **56 E2** 34 24S 18 30 E
Goéland, L. au, *Canada* **70 C4** 49 50N 76 48W
Goeree, *Neths.* **15 C3** 51 50N 4 0 E
Goes, *Neths.* **15 C3** 51 30N 3 55 E
Goffstown, *U.S.A.* **79 C13** 43 1N 71 36W
Gogama, *Canada* **70 C3** 47 35N 81 43W
Gogebic, L., *U.S.A.* **80 B10** 46 30N 89 35W
Gogra = Ghaghara →, *India* **43 G11** 25 45N 84 40 E
Gogriâl, *Sudan* **51 G11** 8 30N 28 8 E
Gohana, *India* **42 E7** 29 8N 76 42 E
Goharganj, *India* **42 H7** 23 1N 77 41 E
Goi →, *India* **42 H6** 22 4N 74 46 E
Goiânia, *Brazil* **93 G9** 16 43S 49 20W
Goiás, *Brazil* **93 G8** 15 55S 50 10W
Goiás □, *Brazil* **93 F9** 12 10S 48 0W
Goio-Erê, *Brazil* **95 A5** 24 12S 53 1W
Gojō, *Japan* **31 G7** 34 21N 135 42 E
Gojra, *Pakistan* **42 D5** 31 10N 72 40 E
Gökçeada, *Turkey* **21 D11** 40 10N 25 50 E
Gökova Körfezi, *Turkey* **21 F12** 36 55N 27 50 E
Gokteik, *Burma* **41 H20** 22 26N 97 0 E
Gokurt, *Pakistan* **42 E2** 29 40N 67 26 E
Gokwe, *Zimbabwe* **57 B4** 18 7S 28 58 E
Gola, *India* **43 E9** 28 3N 80 32 E
Golakganj, *India* **43 F13** 26 8N 89 52 E
Golan Heights = Hagolan, *Syria* **47 C4** 33 0N 35 45 E
Golāshkerd, *Iran* **45 E8** 27 59N 57 16 E
Golchikha, *Russia* **4 B12** 71 45N 83 30 E
Golconda, *U.S.A.* **82 F5** 40 58N 117 30W
Gold, *U.S.A.* **78 E7** 41 52N 77 50W
Gold Beach, *U.S.A.* **82 E1** 42 25N 124 25W
Gold Coast, *W. Afr.* **50 H5** 4 0N 1 40W
Gold Hill, *U.S.A.* **82 E2** 42 26N 123 3W
Gold River, *Canada* **72 D3** 49 46N 126 3W
Golden, *Canada* **72 C5** 51 20N 116 59W
Golden B., *N.Z.* **59 J4** 40 40S 172 50 E
Golden Gate, *U.S.A.* **82 H2** 37 54N 122 30W
Golden Hinde, *Canada* **72 D3** 49 40N 125 44W
Golden Lake, *Canada* **78 A7** 45 34N 77 21W
Golden Vale, *Ireland* **13 D3** 52 33N 8 17W
Goldendale, *U.S.A.* **82 D3** 45 49N 120 50W
Goldfield, *U.S.A.* **83 H5** 37 42N 117 14W
Goldsand L., *Canada* **73 B8** 57 2N 101 8W
Goldsboro, *U.S.A.* **77 H7** 35 23N 77 59W
Goldsmith, *U.S.A.* **81 K3** 31 59N 102 37W
Goldsworthy, *Australia* **60 D2** 20 21S 119 30 E
Goldthwaite, *U.S.A.* **81 K5** 31 27N 98 34W
Goleniów, *Poland* **16 B8** 53 35N 14 50 E
Golestānak, *Iran* **45 D7** 30 36N 54 14 E
Goleta, *U.S.A.* **85 L7** 34 27N 119 50W
Golfito, *Costa Rica* **88 E3** 8 41N 83 5W
Golfo Aranci, *Italy* **20 D3** 40 59N 9 38 E
Goliad, *U.S.A.* **81 L6** 28 40N 97 23W
Golpāyegān, *Iran* **45 C6** 33 27N 50 18 E
Golra, *Pakistan* **42 C5** 33 37N 72 56 E
Golspie, *U.K.* **12 D5** 57 58N 3 59W
Goma, *Dem. Rep. of the Congo* **54 C2** 1 37S 29 10 E
Gomal Pass, *Pakistan* **42 D3** 31 56N 69 20 E
Gomati →, *India* **43 G10** 25 32N 83 11 E
Gombari, *Dem. Rep. of the Congo* **54 B2** 2 45N 29 3 E
Gombe, *Nigeria* **51 F8** 10 19N 11 2 E
Gombe →, *Tanzania* **54 C3** 4 38S 31 40 E
Gomel = Homyel, *Belarus* **17 B16** 52 28N 31 0 E
Gomera, *Canary Is.* **22 F2** 28 7N 17 14W
Gómez Palacio, *Mexico* **86 B4** 25 40N 104 0W
Gomishān, *Iran* **45 B7** 37 4N 54 6 E
Gomogomo, *Indonesia* **37 F8** 6 39S 134 43 E
Gomoh, *India* **41 H15** 23 52N 86 10 E
Gompa = Ganta, *Liberia* **50 G4** 7 15N 8 59W
Gonābād, *Iran* **45 C8** 34 15N 58 45 E
Gonaïves, *Haiti* **89 C5** 19 20N 72 42W
Gonâve, G. de la, *Haiti* **89 C5** 19 29N 72 42W
Gonâve, I. de la, *Haiti* **89 C5** 18 45N 73 0W
Gonbad-e Kāvūs, *Iran* **45 B7** 37 20N 55 25 E
Gonda, *India* **43 F9** 27 9N 81 58 E
Gondal, *India* **42 J4** 21 58N 70 52 E
Gonder, *Ethiopia* **46 E2** 12 39N 37 30 E
Gondia, *India* **40 J12** 21 23N 80 10 E
Gondola, *Mozam.* **55 F3** 19 10S 33 37 E
Gönen, *Turkey* **21 D12** 40 6N 27 39 E
Gonghe, *China* **32 C5** 36 18N 100 32 E
Gongolgon, *Australia* **63 E4** 30 21S 146 54 E
Gongzhuling, *China* **35 C13** 43 30N 124 40 E
Gonzales, *Calif., U.S.A.* **84 J5** 36 30N 121 26W
Gonzales, *Tex., U.S.A.* **81 L6** 29 30N 97 27W
González Chaves, *Argentina* **94 D3** 38 2S 60 5W
Good Hope, C. of, *S. Africa* **56 E2** 34 24S 18 30 E
Gooderham, *Canada* **78 B6** 44 54N 78 21W
Goodhouse, *S. Africa* **56 D2** 28 57S 18 13 E
Gooding, *U.S.A.* **82 E6** 42 56N 114 43W
Goodland, *U.S.A.* **80 F4** 39 21N 101 43W
Goodlow, *Canada* **72 B4** 56 20N 120 8W
Goodooga, *Australia* **63 D4** 29 3S 147 28 E
Goodsprings, *U.S.A.* **85 K11** 35 49N 115 27W
Goole, *U.K.* **10 D7** 53 42N 0 53W
Goolgowi, *Australia* **63 E4** 33 58S 145 41 E
Goomalling, *Australia* **61 F2** 31 15S 116 49 E
Goomeri, *Australia* **63 D5** 26 12S 152 6 E
Goonda, *Mozam.* **55 F3** 19 48S 33 57 E
Goondiwindi, *Australia* **63 D5** 28 30S 150 21 E
Goongarrie, L., *Australia* **61 F3** 30 3S 121 9 E
Goonyella, *Australia* **62 C4** 21 47S 147 58 E
Goose →, *Canada* **71 B7** 53 20N 60 35W
Goose Creek, *U.S.A.* **77 J5** 32 59N 80 2W
Goose L., *U.S.A.* **82 F3** 41 56N 120 26W
Gop, *India* **40 H6** 22 5N 69 50 E
Gopalganj, *India* **43 F11** 26 28N 84 30 E
Göppingen, *Germany* **16 D5** 48 42N 9 39 E
Gorakhpur, *India* **43 F10** 26 47N 83 23 E
Goražde, *Bos.-H.* **21 C8** 43 38N 18 58 E
Gorda, *U.S.A.* **84 K5** 35 53N 121 26W
Gorda, Pta., *Canary Is.* **22 F2** 28 45N 18 0W
Gorda, Pta., *Nic.* **88 D3** 14 20N 83 10W
Gordan B., *Australia* **60 B5** 11 35S 130 10 E
Gordon, *U.S.A.* **80 D3** 42 48N 102 12W
Gordon →, *Australia* **62 G4** 42 27S 145 30 E
Gordon L., *Alta., Canada* **73 B6** 56 30N 110 25W
Gordon L., *N.W.T., Canada* **72 A6** 63 5N 113 11W
Gordonvale, *Australia* **62 B4** 17 5S 145 50 E
Gore, *Ethiopia* **46 F2** 8 12N 35 32 E
Gore, *N.Z.* **59 M2** 46 5S 168 58 E
Gore Bay, *Canada* **70 C3** 45 57N 82 28W
Gorey, *Ireland* **13 D5** 52 41N 6 18W
Gorg, *Iran* **45 D8** 29 29N 59 43 E
Gorgān, *Iran* **45 B7** 36 50N 54 29 E
Gorgona, I., *Colombia* **92 C3** 3 0N 78 10W
Gorham, *U.S.A.* **79 B13** 44 23N 71 10W
Goriganga →, *India* **43 E9** 29 45N 80 23 E
Gorinchem, *Neths.* **15 C4** 51 50N 4 59 E
Goris, *Armenia* **25 G8** 39 31N 46 22 E
Gorízia, *Italy* **20 B5** 45 56N 13 37 E
Gorki = Nizhniy Novgorod, *Russia* **24 C7** 56 20N 44 0 E
Gorkiy = Nizhniy Novgorod, *Russia* **24 C7** 56 20N 44 0 E
Gorkovskoye Vdkhr., *Russia* **24 C7** 57 2N 43 4 E
Görlitz, *Germany* **16 C8** 51 9N 14 58 E
Gorlovka = Horlivka, *Ukraine* **25 E6** 48 19N 38 5 E
Gorman, *U.S.A.* **85 L8** 34 47N 118 51W
Gorna Dzhumayo = Blagoevgrad, *Bulgaria* **21 C10** 42 2N 23 5 E
Gorna Oryakhovitsa, *Bulgaria* **21 C11** 43 7N 25 40 E
Gorno-Altay □, *Russia* **26 D9** 51 0N 86 0 E
Gorno-Altaysk, *Russia* **26 D9** 51 50N 86 5 E
Gornyatski, *Russia* **24 A11** 67 32N 64 3 E
Gornyy, *Russia* **30 B6** 44 57N 133 59 E
Gorodenka = Horodenka, *Ukraine* **17 D13** 48 41N 25 29 E
Gorodok = Horodok, *Ukraine* **17 D12** 49 46N 23 32 E
Gorokhov = Horokhiv, *Ukraine* **17 C13** 50 30N 24 45 E
Goromonzi, *Zimbabwe* **55 F3** 17 52S 31 22 E
Gorong, Kepulauan, *Indonesia* **37 E8** 3 59S 131 25 E
Gorongose →, *Mozam.* **57 C5** 20 30S 34 40 E
Gorongoza, *Mozam.* **55 F3** 18 44S 34 2 E
Gorongoza, Sa. da, *Mozam.* **55 F3** 18 27S 34 2 E
Gorontalo, *Indonesia* **37 D6** 0 35N 123 5 E
Gort, *Ireland* **13 C3** 53 3N 8 49W
Gortis, *Greece* **23 D6** 35 4N 24 58 E
Gorzów Wielkopolski, *Poland* **16 B8** 52 43N 15 15 E
Gosford, *Australia* **63 E5** 33 23S 151 18 E
Goshen, *Calif., U.S.A.* **84 J7** 36 21N 119 25W
Goshen, *Ind., U.S.A.* **76 E3** 41 35N 85 50W
Goshen, *N.Y., U.S.A.* **79 E10** 41 24N 74 20W
Goshogawara, *Japan* **30 D10** 40 48N 140 27 E
Goslar, *Germany* **16 C6** 51 54N 10 25 E
Gospič, *Croatia* **16 F8** 44 35N 15 23 E
Gosport, *U.K.* **11 G6** 50 48N 1 9W
Gosse →, *Australia* **62 B1** 19 32S 134 37 E
Göta älv →, *Sweden* **9 H14** 57 42N 11 54 E
Göta kanal, *Sweden* **9 G16** 58 30N 15 58 E
Götaland, *Sweden* **9 G15** 57 30N 14 30 E
Göteborg, *Sweden* **9 H14** 57 43N 11 59 E
Gotha, *Germany* **16 C6** 50 56N 10 42 E
Gothenburg = Göteborg, *Sweden* **9 H14** 57 43N 11 59 E
Gothenburg, *U.S.A.* **80 E4** 40 56N 100 10W
Gotland, *Sweden* **9 H18** 57 30N 18 33 E
Gotō-Rettō, *Japan* **31 H4** 32 55N 129 5 E
Gotska Sandön, *Sweden* **9 G18** 58 24N 19 15 E
Gōtsu, *Japan* **31 G6** 35 0N 132 14 E
Gott Pk., *Canada* **72 C4** 50 18N 122 16W
Göttingen, *Germany* **16 C5** 51 31N 9 55 E
Gottwaldov = Zlín, *Czech Rep.* **17 D9** 49 14N 17 40 E
Goubangzi, *China* **35 D11** 41 20N 121 52 E
Gouda, *Neths.* **15 B4** 52 1N 4 42 E
Goúdhoura, Ákra, *Greece* **23 E8** 34 59N 26 6 E
Gough I., *Atl. Oc.* **2 G9** 40 10S 9 45W
Gouin, Rés., *Canada* **70 C5** 48 35N 74 40W
Goulburn, *Australia* **63 E4** 34 44S 149 44 E
Goulburn Is., *Australia* **62 A1** 11 40S 133 20 E
Goulimine, *Morocco* **50 C3** 28 56N 10 0W
Gourits →, *S. Africa* **56 E3** 34 21S 21 52 E
Goúrnais, *Greece* **23 D7** 35 19N 25 16 E
Gouverneur, *U.S.A.* **79 B9** 44 20N 75 28W
Gouviá, *Greece* **23 A3** 39 39N 19 50 E
Governador Valadares, *Brazil* **93 G10** 18 15S 41 57W
Governor's Harbour, *Bahamas* **88 A4** 25 10N 76 14W
Govindgarh, *India* **43 G9** 24 23N 81 18 E
Gowan Ra., *Australia* **62 D4** 25 0S 145 0 E
Gowanda, *U.S.A.* **78 D6** 42 28N 78 56W
Gower, *U.K.* **11 F3** 51 35N 4 10W
Gowna, L., *Ireland* **13 C4** 53 51N 7 34W
Goya, *Argentina* **94 B4** 29 10S 59 10W
Goyder Lagoon, *Australia* **63 D2** 27 3S 138 58 E
Goyllarisquisga, *Peru* **92 F3** 10 31S 76 24W
Goz Beïda, *Chad* **51 F10** 12 10N 21 20 E
Gozo, *Malta* **23 C1** 36 3N 14 15 E
Graaff-Reinet, *S. Africa* **56 E3** 32 13S 24 32 E
Gračac, *Croatia* **16 F8** 44 18N 15 57 E
Gracias a Dios, C., *Honduras* **88 D3** 15 0N 83 10W
Graciosa, I., *Canary Is.* **22 E6** 29 15N 13 32W
Grado, *Spain* **19 A2** 43 23N 6 4W
Grady, *U.S.A.* **81 H3** 34 49N 103 19W
Grafham Water, *U.K.* **11 E7** 52 19N 0 18W
Grafton, *Australia* **63 D5** 29 38S 152 58 E
Grafton, *N. Dak., U.S.A.* **80 A6** 48 25N 97 25W
Grafton, *W. Va., U.S.A.* **76 F5** 39 21N 80 2W
Graham, *Canada* **70 C1** 49 20N 90 30W
Graham, *U.S.A.* **81 J5** 33 6N 98 35W
Graham, Mt., *U.S.A.* **83 K9** 32 42N 109 52W
Graham Bell, Ostrov = Greem-Bell, Ostrov, *Russia* **26 A7** 81 0N 62 0 E
Graham I., *Canada* **72 C2** 53 40N 132 30W
Graham Land, *Antarctica* **5 C17** 65 0S 64 0W
Grahamstown, *S. Africa* **56 E4** 33 19S 26 31 E
Grahamsville, *U.S.A.* **79 E10** 41 51N 74 33W
Grain Coast, *W. Afr.* **50 H3** 4 20N 10 0W
Grajaú, *Brazil* **93 E9** 5 50S 46 4W
Grajaú →, *Brazil* **93 D10** 3 41S 44 48W
Grampian, *U.S.A.* **78 F6** 40 58N 78 37W
Grampian Highlands = Grampian Mts., *U.K.* **12 E5** 56 50N 4 0W
Grampian Mts., *U.K.* **12 E5** 56 50N 4 0W
Grampians, The, *Australia* **63 F3** 37 0S 142 20 E
Gran Canaria, *Canary Is.* **22 G4** 27 55N 15 35W
Gran Chaco, *S. Amer.* **94 B3** 25 0S 61 0W
Gran Paradiso, *Italy* **18 D7** 45 33N 7 17 E
Gran Sasso d'Itália, *Italy* **20 C5** 42 27N 13 42 E
Granada, *Nic.* **88 D2** 11 58N 86 0W
Granada, *Spain* **19 D4** 37 10N 3 35W
Granada, *U.S.A.* **81 F3** 38 4N 102 19W
Granadilla de Abona, *Canary Is.* **22 F3** 28 7N 16 33W
Granard, *Ireland* **13 C4** 53 47N 7 30W
Granbury, *U.S.A.* **81 J6** 32 27N 97 47W
Granby, *Canada* **79 A12** 45 25N 72 45W
Granby, *U.S.A.* **82 F11** 40 5N 105 56W
Grand →, *Canada* **78 D5** 42 51N 79 34W
Grand →, *Mo., U.S.A.* **80 F8** 39 23N 93 7W
Grand →, *S. Dak., U.S.A.* **80 C4** 45 40N 100 45W
Grand Bahama, *Bahamas* **88 A4** 26 40N 78 30W
Grand Bank, *Canada* **71 C8** 47 6N 55 48W
Grand Bassam, *Ivory C.* **50 G5** 5 10N 3 49W
Grand-Bourg, *Guadeloupe* **89 C7** 15 53N 61 19W
Grand Canal = Yun Ho →, *China* **35 E9** 39 10N 117 10 E
Grand Canyon, *U.S.A.* **83 H7** 36 3N 112 9W
Grand Canyon Nat. Park, *U.S.A.* **83 H7** 36 15N 112 30W
Grand Cayman, *Cayman Is.* **88 C3** 19 20N 81 20W
Grand Centre, *Canada* **73 C6** 54 25N 110 13W
Grand Coulee, *U.S.A.* **82 C4** 47 57N 119 0W
Grand Coulee Dam, *U.S.A.* **82 C4** 47 57N 118 59W
Grand Falls, *Canada* **71 C6** 47 3N 67 44W
Grand Falls-Windsor, *Canada* **71 C8** 48 56N 55 40W
Grand Forks, *Canada* **72 D5** 49 0N 118 30W
Grand Forks, *U.S.A.* **80 B6** 47 55N 97 3W
Grand Gorge, *U.S.A.* **79 D10** 42 21N 74 29W
Grand Haven, *U.S.A.* **76 D2** 43 4N 86 13W
Grand I., *Mich., U.S.A.* **76 B2** 46 31N 86 40W
Grand I., *N.Y., U.S.A.* **78 D6** 43 0N 78 58W
Grand Island, *U.S.A.* **80 E5** 40 55N 98 21W
Grand Isle, *La., U.S.A.* **81 L9** 29 14N 90 0W
Grand Isle, *Vt., U.S.A.* **79 B11** 44 43N 73 18W
Grand Junction, *U.S.A.* **83 G9** 39 4N 108 33W
Grand L., *N.B., Canada* **71 C6** 45 57N 66 7W
Grand L., *Nfld., Canada* **71 C8** 49 0N 57 30W
Grand L., *Nfld., Canada* **71 B7** 53 40N 60 30W
Grand L., *U.S.A.* **81 L8** 29 55N 92 47W
Grand Lake, *U.S.A.* **82 F11** 40 15N 105 49W
Grand Manan I., *Canada* **71 D6** 44 45N 66 52W
Grand Marais, *Canada* **80 B9** 47 45N 90 25W
Grand Marais, *U.S.A.* **76 B3** 46 40N 85 59W
Grand-Mère, *Canada* **70 C5** 46 36N 72 40W
Grand Portage, *U.S.A.* **80 B10** 47 58N 89 41W
Grand Prairie, *U.S.A.* **81 J6** 32 47N 97 0W
Grand Rapids, *Canada* **73 C9** 53 12N 99 19W
Grand Rapids, *Mich., U.S.A.* **76 D2** 42 58N 85 40W
Grand Rapids, *Minn., U.S.A.* **80 B8** 47 14N 93 31W
Grand St-Bernard, Col du, *Europe* **18 D7** 45 50N 7 10 E
Grand Teton, *U.S.A.* **82 E8** 43 54N 111 50W
Grand Teton Nat. Park, *U.S.A.* **82 D8** 43 50N 110 50W
Grand Union Canal, *U.K.* **11 E7** 52 7N 0 53W
Grand View, *Canada* **73 C8** 51 10N 100 42W
Grande →, *Jujuy, Argentina* **94 A2** 24 20S 65 2W
Grande →, *Mendoza, Argentina* **94 D2** 36 52S 69 45W
Grande →, *Bolivia* **92 G6** 15 51S 64 39W
Grande →, *Bahia, Brazil* **93 F10** 11 30S 44 30W
Grande →, *Minas Gerais, Brazil* **93 H8** 20 6S 51 4W
Grande, B., *Argentina* **96 G3** 50 30S 68 20W
Grande, Rio →, *U.S.A.* **81 N6** 25 58N 97 9W
Grande Baleine, R. de la →, *Canada* **70 A4** 55 16N 77 47W
Grande Cache, *Canada* **72 C5** 53 53N 119 8W
Grande-Entrée, *Canada* **71 C7** 47 30N 61 40W
Grande Prairie, *Canada* **72 B5** 55 10N 118 50W
Grande-Rivière, *Canada* **71 C7** 48 26N 64 30W
Grande-Vallée, *Canada* **71 C6** 49 14N 65 8W
Grandfalls, *U.S.A.* **81 K3** 31 20N 102 51W
Grandview, *U.S.A.* **82 C4** 46 15N 119 54W
Graneros, *Chile* **94 C1** 34 5S 70 45W
Grangemouth, *U.K.* **12 E5** 56 1N 3 42W
Granger, *U.S.A.* **82 F9** 41 35N 109 58W
Grangeville, *U.S.A.* **82 D5** 45 56N 116 7W
Granisle, *Canada* **72 C3** 54 53N 126 13W
Granite City, *U.S.A.* **80 F9** 38 42N 90 9W
Granite Falls, *U.S.A.* **80 C7** 44 49N 95 33W
Granite L., *Canada* **71 C8** 48 8N 57 5W
Granite Mt., *U.S.A.* **85 M10** 33 5N 116 28W
Granite Pk., *U.S.A.* **82 D9** 45 10N 109 48W
Graniteville, *U.S.A.* **79 B12** 44 8N 72 29W
Granity, *N.Z.* **59 J3** 41 39S 171 51 E
Granja, *Brazil* **93 D10** 3 7S 40 50W
Granollers, *Spain* **19 B7** 41 39N 2 18 E
Grant, *U.S.A.* **80 E4** 40 53N 101 42W
Grant, Mt., *U.S.A.* **82 G4** 38 34N 118 48W
Grant City, *U.S.A.* **80 E7** 40 29N 94 25W
Grant I., *Australia* **60 B5** 11 10S 132 52 E
Grant Range, *U.S.A.* **83 G6** 38 30N 115 25W
Grantham, *U.K.* **10 E7** 52 55N 0 38W
Grantown-on-Spey, *U.K.* **12 D5** 57 20N 3 36W
Grants, *U.S.A.* **83 J10** 35 9N 107 52W
Grants Pass, *U.S.A.* **82 E2** 42 26N 123 19W
Grantsville, *U.S.A.* **82 F7** 40 36N 112 28W
Granville, *France* **18 B3** 48 50N 1 35W
Granville, *N. Dak., U.S.A.* **80 A4** 48 16N 100 47W
Granville, *N.Y., U.S.A.* **79 C11** 43 24N 73 16W
Granville, *Ohio, U.S.A.* **78 F2** 40 4N 82 31W
Granville L., *Canada* **73 B8** 56 18N 100 30W
Graskop, *S. Africa* **57 C5** 24 56S 30 49 E
Grass →, *Canada* **73 B9** 56 3N 96 33W
Grass Range, *U.S.A.* **82 C9** 47 0N 109 0W
Grass River Prov. Park, *Canada* **73 C8** 54 40N 100 50W
Grass Valley, *Calif., U.S.A.* **84 F6** 39 13N 121 4W
Grass Valley, *Oreg., U.S.A.* **82 D3** 45 22N 120 47W
Grasse, *France* **18 E7** 43 38N 6 56 E
Grassflat, *U.S.A.* **78 F6** 41 0N 78 6W
Grasslands Nat. Park, *Canada* **73 D7** 49 11N 107 38W
Grassy, *Australia* **62 G3** 40 3S 144 5 E
Graulhet, *France* **18 E4** 43 45N 1 59 E
Gravelbourg, *Canada* **73 D7** 49 50N 106 35W
's-Gravenhage, *Neths.* **15 B4** 52 7N 4 17 E
Gravenhurst, *Canada* **78 B5** 44 52N 79 20W
Gravesend, *Australia* **63 D5** 29 35S 150 20 E
Gravesend, *U.K.* **11 F8** 51 26N 0 22 E
Gravois, Pointe-à-, *Haiti* **89 C5** 18 15N 73 56W
Grayling, *U.S.A.* **76 C3** 44 40N 84 43W
Grays Harbor, *U.S.A.* **82 C1** 46 59N 124 1W
Grays L., *U.S.A.* **82 E8** 43 4N 111 26W
Grays River, *U.S.A.* **84 D3** 46 21N 123 37W
Graz, *Austria* **16 E8** 47 4N 15 27 E
Greasy L., *Canada* **72 A4** 62 55N 122 12W
Great Abaco I., *Bahamas* **88 A4** 26 25N 77 10W
Great Artesian Basin, *Australia* **62 C3** 23 0S 144 0 E
Great Australian Bight, *Australia* **61 F5** 33 30S 130 0 E
Great Bahama Bank, *Bahamas* **88 B4** 23 15N 78 0W
Great Barrier I., *N.Z.* **59 G5** 36 11S 175 25 E
Great Barrier Reef, *Australia* **62 B4** 18 0S 146 50 E
Great Barrington, *U.S.A.* **79 D11** 42 12N 73 22W
Great Basin, *U.S.A.* **82 G5** 40 0N 117 0W
Great Basin Nat. Park, *U.S.A.* **82 G6** 38 55N 114 14W
Great Bear →, *Canada* **68 B7** 65 0N 124 0W
Great Bear L., *Canada* **68 B7** 65 30N 120 0W
Great Belt = Store Bælt, *Denmark* **9 J14** 55 20N 11 0 E
Great Bend, *Kans., U.S.A.* **80 F5** 38 22N 98 46W
Great Bend, *Pa., U.S.A.* **79 E9** 41 58N 75 45W
Great Blasket I., *Ireland* **13 D1** 52 6N 10 32W
Great Britain, *Europe* **6 E5** 54 0N 2 15W
Great Codroy, *Canada* **71 C8** 47 51N 59 16W
Great Dividing Ra., *Australia* **62 C4** 23 0S 146 0 E
Great Driffield = Driffield, *U.K.* **10 C7** 54 0N 0 26W
Great Exuma I., *Bahamas* **88 B4** 23 30N 75 50W
Great Falls, *U.S.A.* **82 C8** 47 30N 111 17W
Great Fish = Groot Vis →, *S. Africa* **56 E4** 33 28S 27 5 E
Great Guana Cay, *Bahamas* **88 B4** 24 0N 76 20W
Great Inagua I., *Bahamas* **89 B5** 21 0N 73 20W
Great Indian Desert = Thar Desert, *India* **42 F5** 28 0N 72 0 E
Great Karoo, *S. Africa* **56 E3** 31 55S 21 0 E
Great Lake, *Australia* **62 G4** 41 50S 146 40 E
Great Lakes, *N. Amer.* **66 E11** 46 0N 84 0W
Great Malvern, *U.K.* **11 E5** 52 7N 2 18W
Great Miami →, *U.S.A.* **76 F3** 39 20N 84 40W
Great Ormes Head, *U.K.* **10 D4** 53 20N 3 52W
Great Ouse →, *U.K.* **10 E8** 52 48N 0 21 E
Great Palm I., *Australia* **62 B4** 18 45S 146 40 E
Great Plains, *N. Amer.* **74 A6** 47 0N 105 0W
Great Ruaha →, *Tanzania* **54 D4** 7 56S 37 52 E
Great Sacandaga Res., *U.S.A.* **79 C10** 43 6N 74 16W
Great Saint Bernard Pass = Grand St-Bernard, Col du, *Europe* **18 D7** 45 50N 7 10 E
Great Salt L., *U.S.A.* **82 F7** 41 15N 112 40W
Great Salt Lake Desert, *U.S.A.* **82 F7** 40 50N 113 30W
Great Salt Plains L., *U.S.A.* **81 G5** 36 45N 98 8W
Great Sandy Desert, *Australia* **60 D3** 21 0S 124 0 E
Great Sangi = Sangihe, Pulau, *Indonesia* **37 D7** 3 35N 125 30 E
Great Skellig, *Ireland* **13 E1** 51 47N 10 33W
Great Slave L., *Canada* **72 A5** 61 23N 115 38W
Great Smoky Mts. Nat. Park, *U.S.A.* **77 H4** 35 40N 83 40W
Great Snow Mt., *Canada* **72 B4** 57 26N 124 0W
Great Stour = Stour →, *U.K.* **11 F9** 51 18N 1 22 E
Great Victoria Desert, *Australia* **61 E4** 29 30S 126 30 E
Great Wall, *China* **34 E5** 38 30N 109 30 E
Great Whernside, *U.K.* **10 C6** 54 10N 1 58W
Great Yarmouth, *U.K.* **11 E9** 52 37N 1 44 E
Greater Antilles, *W. Indies* **89 C5** 17 40N 74 0W
Greater London □, *U.K.* **11 F7** 51 31N 0 6W
Greater Manchester □, *U.K.* **10 D5** 53 30N 2 15W
Greater Sunda Is., *Indonesia* **36 F4** 7 0S 112 0 E
Greco, C., *Cyprus* **23 E13** 34 57N 34 5 E
Gredos, Sierra de, *Spain* **19 B3** 40 20N 5 0W
Greece, *U.S.A.* **78 C7** 43 13N 77 41W
Greece ■, *Europe* **21 E9** 40 0N 23 0 E
Greeley, *Colo., U.S.A.* **80 E2** 40 25N 104 42W
Greeley, *Nebr., U.S.A.* **80 E5** 41 33N 98 32W
Green-Bell, Ostrov, *Russia* **26 A7** 81 0N 62 0 E
Green, *U.S.A.* **82 E2** 43 9N 123 22W
Green →, *Ky., U.S.A.* **76 G2** 37 54N 87 30W
Green →, *Utah, U.S.A.* **83 G9** 38 11N 109 53W
Green B., *U.S.A.* **76 C2** 45 0N 87 30W
Green Bay, *U.S.A.* **76 C2** 44 31N 88 0W
Green C., *Australia* **63 F5** 37 13S 150 1 E
Green Cove Springs, *U.S.A.* **77 L5** 29 59N 81 42W
Green Lake, *Canada* **73 C7** 54 17N 107 47W
Green Mts., *U.S.A.* **79 C12** 43 45N 72 45W
Green River, *Utah, U.S.A.* **83 G8** 38 59N 110 10W
Green River, *Wyo., U.S.A.* **82 F9** 41 32N 109 28W

J

Keene

Keene, *N.Y., U.S.A.* **79 B11** 44 16N 73 46W
Keeper Hill, *Ireland* **13 D3** 52 45N 8 16W
Keer-Weer, C., *Australia* **62 A3** 14 0S 141 32 E
Keeseville, *U.S.A.* **79 B11** 44 29N 73 30W
Keetmanshoop, *Namibia* **56 D2** 26 35S 18 8 E
Keewatin, *Canada* **73 D10** 49 46N 94 34W
Keewatin →, *Canada* **73 B8** 56 29N 100 46W
Kefallinía, *Greece* **21 E9** 38 15N 20 30 E
Kefamenanu, *Indonesia* **37 F6** 9 28S 124 29 E
Kefar Sava, *Israel* **47 C3** 32 11N 34 54 E
Keffi, *Nigeria* **50 G7** 8 55N 7 43 E
Keflavík, *Iceland* **8 D2** 64 2N 22 35W
Keg River, *Canada* **72 B5** 57 54N 117 55W
Kegaska, *Canada* **71 B7** 50 9N 61 18W
Keighley, *U.K.* **10 D6** 53 52N 1 54W
Keila, *Estonia* **9 G21** 59 18N 24 25 E
Keimoes, *S. Africa* **56 D3** 28 41S 20 59 E
Keitele, *Finland* **8 E22** 63 10N 26 20 E
Keith, *Australia* **63 F3** 36 6S 140 20 E
Keith, *U.K.* **12 D6** 57 32N 2 57W
Keizer, *U.S.A.* **82 D2** 44 57N 123 1W
Kejimkujik Nat. Park, *Canada* **71 D6** 44 25N 65 25W
Kejserr Franz Joseph Fd., *Greenland* **4 B6** 73 30N 24 30W
Kekri, *India* **42 G6** 26 0N 75 10 E
Kelan, *China* **34 E6** 38 43N 111 31 E
Kelang, *Malaysia* **39 L3** 3 2N 101 26 E
Kelantan →, *Malaysia* **39 J4** 6 13N 102 14 E
Kelkit →, *Turkey* **25 F6** 40 45N 36 32 E
Kellerberrin, *Australia* **61 F2** 31 36S 117 38 E
Kellett, C., *Canada* **4 B1** 72 0N 126 0W
Kelleys I., *U.S.A.* **78 E2** 41 36N 82 42W
Kellogg, *U.S.A.* **82 C5** 47 32N 116 7W
Kells = Ceanannus Mor, *Ireland* **13 C5** 53 44N 6 53W
Kelokedhara, *Cyprus* **23 E11** 34 48N 32 39 E
Kelowna, *Canada* **72 D5** 49 50N 119 25W
Kelseyville, *U.S.A.* **84 G4** 38 59N 122 50W
Kelso, *N.Z.* **59 L2** 45 54S 169 15 E
Kelso, *U.K.* **12 F6** 55 36N 2 26W
Kelso, *U.S.A.* **84 D4** 46 9N 122 54W
Keluang, *Malaysia* **39 L4** 2 3N 103 18 E
Kelvington, *Canada* **73 C8** 52 10N 103 30W
Kem, *Russia* **24 B5** 65 0N 34 38 E
Kem →, *Russia* **24 B5** 64 57N 34 41 E
Kema, *Indonesia* **37 D7** 1 22N 125 8 E
Kemah, *Turkey* **44 B3** 39 32N 39 5 E
Kemaman, *Malaysia* **36 D2** 4 12N 103 18 E
Kemano, *Canada* **72 C3** 53 35N 128 0W
Kemasik, *Malaysia* **39 K4** 4 25N 103 27 E
Kemerovo, *Russia* **26 D9** 55 20N 86 5 E
Kemi, *Finland* **8 D21** 65 44N 24 34 E
Kemi älv = Kemijoki →, *Finland* **8 D21** 65 47N 24 32 E
Kemijärvi, *Finland* **8 C22** 66 43N 27 22 E
Kemijoki →, *Finland* **8 D21** 65 47N 24 32 E
Kemmerer, *U.S.A.* **82 F8** 41 48N 110 32W
Kemmuna = Comino, *Malta* **23 C1** 36 1N 14 20 E
Kemp, L., *U.S.A.* **81 J5** 33 46N 99 9W
Kemp Land, *Antarctica* **5 C5** 69 0S 55 0 E
Kempsey, *Australia* **63 E5** 31 1S 152 50 E
Kempt, L., *Canada* **70 C5** 47 25N 74 22W
Kempten, *Germany* **16 E6** 47 45N 10 17 E
Kempton, *Australia* **62 G4** 42 31S 147 12 E
Kemptville, *Canada* **79 B9** 45 0N 75 38W
Ken →, *India* **43 G9** 25 13N 80 27 E
Kenai, *U.S.A.* **68 B4** 60 33N 151 16W
Kendai, *India* **43 H10** 22 45N 82 37 E
Kendal, *Indonesia* **37 G14** 6 56S 110 14 E
Kendal, *U.K.* **10 C5** 54 20N 2 44W
Kendall, *Australia* **63 E5** 31 35S 152 44 E
Kendall, *U.S.A.* **77 N5** 25 41N 80 19W
Kendall →, *Australia* **62 A3** 14 4S 141 35 E
Kendallville, *U.S.A.* **76 E3** 41 27N 85 16W
Kendari, *Indonesia* **37 E6** 3 50S 122 30 E
Kendawangan, *Indonesia* **36 E4** 2 32S 110 17 E
Kendrapara, *India* **41 J15** 20 35N 86 30 E
Kendrew, *S. Africa* **56 E3** 32 32S 24 30 E
Kene Thao, *Laos* **38 D3** 17 44N 101 10 E
Kenedy, *U.S.A.* **81 L6** 28 49N 97 51W
Kenema, *S. Leone* **50 G3** 7 50N 11 14W
Keng Kok, *Laos* **38 D5** 16 26N 105 12 E
Keng Tawng, *Burma* **41 J21** 20 45N 98 18 E
Keng Tung, *Burma* **41 J21** 21 0N 99 30 E
Kengeja, *Tanzania* **54 D4** 5 26S 39 45 E
Kenhardt, *S. Africa* **56 D3** 29 19S 21 12 E
Kenitra, *Morocco* **50 B4** 34 15N 6 40W
Kenli, *China* **35 F10** 37 30N 118 20 E
Kenmare, *Ireland* **13 E2** 51 53N 9 36W
Kenmare, *U.S.A.* **80 A3** 48 41N 102 5W
Kenmare River, *Ireland* **13 E2** 51 48N 9 51W
Kennebago Lake, *U.S.A.* **79 A14** 45 4N 70 40W
Kennebec, *U.S.A.* **80 D5** 43 54N 99 52W
Kennebec →, *U.S.A.* **77 D11** 43 45N 69 46W
Kennebunk, *U.S.A.* **79 C14** 43 23N 70 33W
Kennedy, *Zimbabwe* **56 B4** 18 52S 27 10 E
Kennedy Ra., *Australia* **61 D2** 24 45S 115 10 E
Kennedy Taungdeik, *Burma* **41 H18** 23 15N 93 45 E
Kenner, *U.S.A.* **81 L9** 29 59N 90 15W
Kennet →, *U.K.* **11 F7** 51 27N 0 57W
Kenneth Ra., *Australia* **61 D2** 23 50S 117 8 E
Kennett, *U.S.A.* **81 G9** 36 14N 90 3W
Kennewick, *U.S.A.* **82 C4** 46 12N 119 7W
Kenogami →, *Canada* **70 B3** 51 6N 84 28W
Kenora, *Canada* **73 D10** 49 47N 94 29W
Kenosha, *U.S.A.* **76 D2** 42 35N 87 49W
Kensington, *Canada* **71 C7** 46 28N 63 34W
Kent, *Ohio, U.S.A.* **78 E3** 41 9N 81 22W
Kent, *Tex., U.S.A.* **81 K2** 31 4N 104 13W
Kent, *Wash., U.S.A.* **84 C4** 47 23N 122 14W
Kent □, *U.K.* **11 F8** 51 12N 0 40 E
Kent Group, *Australia* **62 F4** 39 30S 147 20 E
Kent Pen., *Canada* **68 B9** 68 30N 107 0W
Kentaū, *Kazakstan* **26 E7** 43 32N 68 36 E
Kentland, *U.S.A.* **76 E2** 40 46N 87 27W
Kenton, *U.S.A.* **76 E4** 40 39N 83 37W
Kentucky □, *U.S.A.* **76 G3** 37 0N 84 0W
Kentucky →, *U.S.A.* **76 F3** 38 41N 85 11W
Kentucky L., *U.S.A.* **77 G2** 37 1N 88 16W
Kentville, *Canada* **71 C7** 45 6N 64 29W
Kentwood, *U.S.A.* **81 K9** 30 56N 90 31W
Kenya ■, *Africa* **54 B4** 1 0N 38 0 E
Kenya, Mt., *Kenya* **54 C4** 0 10S 37 18 E
Keo Neua, Deo, *Vietnam* **38 C5** 18 23N 105 10 E
Keokuk, *U.S.A.* **80 E9** 40 24N 91 24W
Keonjhargarh, *India* **43 J11** 21 28N 85 35 E
Kep, *Cambodia* **39 G5** 10 29N 104 19 E
Kep, *Vietnam* **38 B6** 21 24N 106 16 E
Kepi, *Indonesia* **37 F9** 6 32S 139 19 E
Kerala □, *India* **40 P10** 11 0N 76 15 E
Kerama-Rettō, *Japan* **31 L3** 26 5N 127 15 E
Keran, *Pakistan* **43 B5** 34 35N 73 59 E
Kerang, *Australia* **63 F3** 35 40S 143 55 E
Keraudren, C., *Australia* **60 C2** 19 58S 119 45 E
Kerava, *Finland* **9 F21** 60 25N 25 5 E
Kerch, *Ukraine* **25 E6** 45 20N 36 20 E
Kerguelen, *Ind. Oc.* **3 G13** 49 15S 69 10 E
Kericho, *Kenya* **54 C4** 0 22S 35 15 E
Kerinci, *Indonesia* **36 E2** 1 40S 101 15 E
Kerki, *Turkmenistan* **26 F7** 37 50N 65 12 E
Kérkira, *Greece* **23 A3** 39 38N 19 50 E
Kerkrade, *Neths.* **15 D6** 50 53N 6 4 E
Kermadec Is., *Pac. Oc.* **64 L10** 30 0S 178 15W
Kermadec Trench, *Pac. Oc.* **64 L10** 30 30S 176 0W
Kermān, *Iran* **45 D8** 30 15N 57 1 E
Kerman, *U.S.A.* **84 J6** 36 43N 120 4W
Kermān □, *Iran* **45 D8** 30 0N 57 0 E
Kermān, Bīābān-e, *Iran* **45 D8** 28 45N 59 45 E
Kermānshāh = Bākhtarān, *Iran* **44 C5** 34 23N 47 0 E
Kermit, *U.S.A.* **81 K3** 31 52N 103 6W
Kern →, *U.S.A.* **85 K7** 35 16N 119 18W
Kernow = Cornwall □, *U.K.* **11 G3** 50 26N 4 40W
Kernville, *U.S.A.* **85 K8** 35 45N 118 26W
Keroh, *Malaysia* **39 K3** 5 43N 101 1 E
Kerrera, *U.K.* **12 E3** 56 24N 5 33W
Kerrobert, *Canada* **73 C7** 51 56N 109 8W
Kerrville, *U.S.A.* **81 K5** 30 3N 99 8W
Kerry □, *Ireland* **13 D2** 52 7N 9 35W
Kerry Hd., *Ireland* **13 D2** 52 25N 9 56W
Kerulen →, *Asia* **33 B6** 48 48N 117 0 E
Kerzaz, *Algeria* **50 C5** 29 29N 1 37W
Kesagami →, *Canada* **70 B4** 51 40N 79 45W
Kesagami L., *Canada* **70 B3** 50 23N 80 15W
Keşan, *Turkey* **21 D12** 40 49N 26 38 E
Kesennuma, *Japan* **30 E10** 38 54N 141 35 E
Keshit, *Iran* **45 D8** 29 43N 58 17 E
Kestell, *S. Africa* **57 D4** 28 17S 28 42 E
Kestenga, *Russia* **24 A5** 65 50N 31 45 E
Keswick, *U.K.* **10 C4** 54 36N 3 8W
Ket →, *Russia* **26 D9** 58 55N 81 32 E
Ketapang, *Indonesia* **36 E4** 1 55S 110 0 E
Ketchikan, *U.S.A.* **72 B2** 55 21N 131 39W
Ketchum, *U.S.A.* **82 E6** 43 41N 114 22W
Ketef, Khalîg Umm el, *Egypt* **44 F2** 23 40N 35 35 E
Keti Bandar, *Pakistan* **42 G2** 24 8N 67 27 E
Ketri, *India* **42 E6** 28 1N 75 50 E
Kętrzyn, *Poland* **17 A11** 54 7N 21 22 E
Kettering, *U.K.* **11 E7** 52 24N 0 43W
Kettering, *U.S.A.* **76 F3** 39 41N 84 10W
Kettle →, *Canada* **73 B11** 56 40N 89 34W
Kettle Falls, *U.S.A.* **82 B4** 48 37N 118 3W
Kettle Pt., *Canada* **78 C2** 43 13N 82 1W
Kettleman City, *U.S.A.* **84 J7** 36 1N 119 58W
Keuka L., *U.S.A.* **78 D7** 42 30N 77 9W
Keuruu, *Finland* **9 E21** 62 16N 24 41 E
Kewanee, *U.S.A.* **80 E10** 41 14N 89 56W
Kewaunee, *U.S.A.* **76 C2** 44 27N 87 31W
Keweenaw B., *U.S.A.* **76 B1** 47 0N 88 15W
Keweenaw Pen., *U.S.A.* **76 B2** 47 30N 88 0W
Keweenaw Pt., *U.S.A.* **76 B2** 47 25N 87 43W
Key Largo, *U.S.A.* **77 N5** 25 5N 80 27W
Key West, *U.S.A.* **75 F10** 24 33N 81 48W
Keynsham, *U.K.* **11 F5** 51 24N 2 29W
Keyser, *U.S.A.* **76 F6** 39 26N 78 59W
Kezhma, *Russia* **27 D11** 58 59N 101 9 E
Kezi, *Zimbabwe* **57 C4** 20 58S 28 32 E
Khabarovsk, *Russia* **27 E14** 48 30N 135 5 E
Khabr, *Iran* **45 D8** 28 51N 56 22 E
Khābūr →, *Syria* **44 C4** 35 17N 40 35 E
Khachmas = Xaçmaz, *Azerbaijan* **25 F8** 41 31N 48 42 E
Khachrod, *India* **42 H6** 23 25N 75 20 E
Khadro, *Pakistan* **42 F3** 26 11N 68 50 E
Khadzhilyangar, *China* **43 B8** 35 45N 79 20 E
Khaga, *India* **43 G9** 25 47N 81 7 E
Khagaria, *India* **43 G12** 25 30N 86 32 E
Khaipur, *Pakistan* **42 E5** 29 34N 72 17 E
Khair, *India* **42 F7** 27 57N 77 46 E
Khairabad, *India* **43 F9** 27 33N 80 47 E
Khairagarh, *India* **43 J9** 21 27N 81 2 E
Khairpur, *Pakistan* **42 F3** 27 32N 68 49 E
Khairpur Nathan Shah, *Pakistan* **42 F2** 27 6N 67 44 E
Khairwara, *India* **42 H5** 23 58N 73 38 E
Khaisor →, *Pakistan* **42 D3** 31 17N 68 59 E
Khajuri Kach, *Pakistan* **42 C3** 32 4N 69 51 E
Khakassia □, *Russia* **26 D9** 53 0N 90 0 E
Khakhea, *Botswana* **56 C3** 24 48S 23 22 E
Khalafābād, *Iran* **45 D6** 30 54N 49 24 E
Khalilabad, *India* **43 F10** 26 48N 83 5 E
Khalīlī, *Iran* **45 E7** 27 38N 53 17 E
Khalkhāl, *Iran* **45 B6** 37 37N 48 32 E
Khalkís, *Greece* **21 E10** 38 27N 23 42 E
Khalmer-Sede = Tazovskiy, *Russia* **26 C8** 67 30N 78 44 E
Khalmer Yu, *Russia* **26 C7** 67 58N 65 1 E
Khalturin, *Russia* **24 C8** 58 40N 48 50 E
Khalūf, *Oman* **46 C6** 20 30N 58 13 E
Kham Keut, *Laos* **38 C5** 18 15N 104 43 E
Khamaria, *India* **43 H9** 23 5N 80 48 E
Khambhaliya, *India* **42 H3** 22 14N 69 41 E
Khambhat, *India* **42 H5** 22 23N 72 33 E
Khambhat, G. of, *India* **40 J8** 20 45N 72 30 E
Khamīr, *Iran* **45 E7** 26 57N 55 36 E
Khamir, *Yemen* **46 D3** 16 2N 44 0 E
Khamsa, *Egypt* **47 E1** 30 27N 32 23 E
Khan →, *Namibia* **56 C2** 22 37S 14 56 E
Khān Abū Shāmat, *Syria* **47 B5** 33 39N 36 53 E
Khān Azād, *Iraq* **44 C5** 33 7N 44 22 E
Khān Mujiddah, *Iraq* **44 C4** 32 21N 43 48 E
Khān Shaykhūn, *Syria* **44 C3** 35 26N 36 38 E
Khān Yūnis, *Gaza Strip* **47 D3** 31 21N 34 18 E
Khanai, *Pakistan* **42 D2** 30 30N 67 8 E
Khānaqīn, *Iraq* **44 C5** 34 23N 45 25 E
Khānbāghī, *Iran* **45 B7** 36 10N 55 25 E
Khandwa, *India* **40 J10** 21 49N 76 22 E
Khandyga, *Russia* **27 C14** 62 42N 135 35 E
Khāneh, *Iran* **44 B5** 36 41N 45 8 E
Khanewal, *Pakistan* **42 D4** 30 20N 71 55 E
Khangah Dogran, *Pakistan* **42 D5** 31 50N 73 37 E
Khanh Duong, *Vietnam* **38 F7** 12 44N 108 44 E
Khaniá, *Greece* **23 D6** 35 30N 24 4 E
Khaniá □, *Greece* **23 D6** 35 30N 24 0 E
Khaniadhana, *India* **42 G8** 25 1N 78 8 E
Khaníon, Kólpos, *Greece* **23 D5** 35 33N 23 55 E
Khanka, L., *Asia* **27 E14** 45 0N 132 24 E
Khankendy = Xankändi, *Azerbaijan* **25 G8** 39 52N 46 49 E
Khanna, *India* **42 D7** 30 42N 76 16 E
Khanozai, *Pakistan* **42 D2** 30 37N 67 19 E
Khanpur, *Pakistan* **42 E4** 28 42N 70 35 E
Khanty-Mansiysk, *Russia* **26 C7** 61 0N 69 0 E
Khapalu, *Pakistan* **43 B7** 35 10N 76 20 E
Khapcheranga, *Russia* **27 E12** 49 42N 112 24 E
Kharaghoda, *India* **42 H4** 23 11N 71 46 E
Kharagpur, *India* **43 H12** 22 20N 87 25 E
Khárakas, *Greece* **23 D7** 35 1N 25 7 E
Kharan Kalat, *Pakistan* **40 E4** 28 34N 65 21 E
Kharānaq, *Iran* **45 C7** 32 20N 54 45 E
Kharda, *India* **40 K9** 18 40N 75 34 E
Khardung La, *India* **43 B7** 34 20N 77 43 E
Khârga, El Wâhât-el, *Egypt* **51 C12** 25 10N 30 35 E
Khargon, *India* **40 J9** 21 45N 75 40 E
Khari →, *India* **42 G6** 25 54N 74 31 E
Kharian, *Pakistan* **42 C5** 32 49N 73 52 E
Khārk, Jazīreh-ye, *Iran* **45 D6** 29 15N 50 28 E
Kharkiv, *Ukraine* **25 E6** 49 58N 36 20 E
Kharkov = Kharkiv, *Ukraine* **25 E6** 49 58N 36 20 E
Kharovsk, *Russia* **24 C7** 59 56N 40 13 E
Kharsawangarh, *India* **43 H11** 22 48N 85 50 E
Kharta, *Turkey* **21 D13** 40 55N 29 7 E
Khartoum = El Khartûm, *Sudan* **51 E12** 15 31N 32 35 E
Khasan, *Russia* **30 C5** 42 25N 130 40 E
Khāsh, *Iran* **40 E2** 28 15N 61 15 E
Khashm el Girba, *Sudan* **51 F13** 14 59N 35 58 E
Khaskovo, *Bulgaria* **21 D11** 41 56N 25 30 E
Khatanga, *Russia* **27 B11** 72 0N 102 20 E
Khatanga →, *Russia* **27 B11** 72 55N 106 0 E
Khatauli, *India* **42 E7** 29 17N 77 43 E
Khatra, *India* **43 H12** 22 59N 86 51 E
Khātūnābād, *Iran* **45 D7** 30 1N 55 25 E
Khatyrka, *Russia* **27 C18** 62 3N 175 15 E
Khavda, *India* **42 H3** 23 51N 69 43 E
Khaybar, Ḥarrat, *Si. Arabia* **44 E4** 25 45N 40 0 E
Khayelitsha, *S. Africa* **53 L3** 34 5S 18 42 E
Khāzimiyah, *Iraq* **44 C4** 34 46N 43 37 E
Khe Bo, *Vietnam* **38 C5** 19 8N 104 41 E
Khe Long, *Vietnam* **38 B5** 21 29N 104 46 E
Khed Brahma, *India* **40 G8** 24 7N 73 5 E
Khekra, *India* **42 E7** 28 52N 77 20 E
Khemarak Phouminville, *Cambodia* **39 G4** 11 37N 102 59 E
Khemisset, *Morocco* **50 B4** 33 50N 6 1W
Khemmarat, *Thailand* **38 D5** 16 10N 105 15 E
Khenāmān, *Iran* **45 D8** 30 27N 56 29 E
Khenchela, *Algeria* **50 A7** 35 28N 7 11 E
Khersān →, *Iran* **45 D6** 31 33N 50 22 E
Kherson, *Ukraine* **25 E5** 46 35N 32 35 E
Khersónisos Akrotíri, *Greece* **23 D6** 35 30N 24 10 E
Kheta →, *Russia* **27 B11** 71 54N 102 6 E
Khewari, *Pakistan* **42 F3** 26 36N 68 52 E
Khilchipur, *India* **42 G7** 24 2N 76 34 E
Khilok, *Russia* **27 D12** 51 30N 110 45 E
Khíos, *Greece* **21 E12** 38 27N 26 9 E
Khirsadoh, *India* **43 H8** 22 11N 78 47 E
Khiuma = Hiiumaa, *Estonia* **9 G20** 58 50N 22 45 E
Khiva, *Uzbekistan* **26 E7** 41 30N 60 18 E
Khīyāv, *Iran* **44 B5** 38 30N 47 45 E
Khlong Khlung, *Thailand* **38 D2** 16 12N 99 43 E
Khmelnik, *Ukraine* **17 D14** 49 33N 27 58 E
Khmelnitskiy = Khmelnytskyy, *Ukraine* **17 D14** 49 23N 27 0 E
Khmelnytskyy, *Ukraine* **17 D14** 49 23N 27 0 E
Khmer Rep. = Cambodia ■, *Asia* **38 F5** 12 15N 105 0 E
Khoai, Hon, *Vietnam* **39 H5** 8 26N 104 50 E
Khodoriv, *Ukraine* **17 D13** 49 24N 24 19 E
Khodzent = Khūjand, *Tajikistan* **26 E7** 40 17N 69 37 E
Khojak Pass, *Afghan.* **42 D2** 30 51N 66 34 E
Khok Kloi, *Thailand* **39 H2** 8 17N 98 19 E
Khok Pho, *Thailand* **39 J3** 6 43N 101 6 E
Kholm, *Russia* **24 C5** 57 10N 31 15 E
Kholmsk, *Russia* **27 E15** 47 40N 142 5 E
Khomas Hochland, *Namibia* **56 C2** 22 40S 16 0 E
Khomeyn, *Iran* **45 C6** 33 40N 50 7 E
Khomeynī Shahr, *Iran* **45 C6** 32 41N 51 31 E
Khomodino, *Botswana* **56 C3** 22 46S 23 52 E
Khon Kaen, *Thailand* **38 D4** 16 30N 102 47 E
Khong →, *Cambodia* **38 F5** 13 32N 105 58 E
Khong Sedone, *Laos* **38 E5** 15 34N 105 49 E
Khonuu, *Russia* **27 C15** 66 30N 143 12 E
Khoper →, *Russia* **25 D6** 49 30N 42 20 E
Khóra Sfakíon, *Greece* **23 D6** 35 15N 24 9 E
Khorāsān □, *Iran* **45 C8** 34 0N 58 0 E
Khorat = Nakhon Ratchasima, *Thailand* **38 E4** 14 59N 102 12 E
Khorat, Cao Nguyen, *Thailand* **38 E4** 15 30N 102 50 E
Khorixas, *Namibia* **56 C1** 20 16S 14 59 E
Khorramābād, *Khorāsān, Iran* **45 C8** 35 6N 57 57 E
Khorramābād, *Lorestān, Iran* **45 C6** 33 30N 48 25 E
Khorrāmshahr, *Iran* **45 D6** 30 29N 48 15 E
Khorugh, *Tajikistan* **26 F8** 37 30N 71 36 E
Khosravī, *Iran* **45 D6** 30 48N 51 28 E
Khosrowābād, *Khuzestān, Iran* **45 D6** 30 10N 48 25 E
Khosrowābād, *Kordestān, Iran* **44 C5** 35 31N 47 38 E
Khost, *Pakistan* **42 D2** 30 13N 67 35 E
Khosūyeh, *Iran* **45 D7** 28 32N 54 26 E
Khotyn, *Ukraine* **17 D14** 48 31N 26 27 E
Khouribga, *Morocco* **50 B4** 32 58N 6 57W
Khowst, *Afghan.* **42 C3** 33 22N 69 58 E
Khowst □, *Afghan.* **40 C6** 33 20N 70 0 E
Khoyniki, *Belarus* **17 C15** 51 54N 29 55 E
Khrysokhou B., *Cyprus* **23 D11** 35 6N 32 25 E
Khu Khan, *Thailand* **38 E5** 14 42N 104 12 E
Khudzhand = Khūjand, *Tajikistan* **26 E7** 40 17N 69 37 E
Khuff, *Si. Arabia* **44 E5** 24 55N 44 53 E
Khūgīānī, *Afghan.* **42 D2** 31 37N 65 4 E
Khuis, *Botswana* **56 D3** 26 40S 21 49 E
Khuiyala, *India* **42 F4** 27 9N 70 25 E
Khūjand, *Tajikistan* **26 E7** 40 17N 69 37 E
Khujner, *India* **42 H7** 23 47N 76 36 E
Khulna, *Bangla.* **41 H16** 22 45N 89 34 E
Khulna □, *Bangla.* **41 H16** 22 25N 89 35 E
Khumago, *Botswana* **56 C3** 20 26S 24 32 E
Khūnsorkh, *Iran* **45 E8** 27 9N 56 7 E
Khunti, *India* **43 H11** 23 5N 85 17 E
Khūr, *Iran* **45 C8** 32 55N 58 18 E
Khurai, *India* **42 G8** 24 3N 78 23 E
Khurayṣ, *Si. Arabia* **45 E6** 25 6N 48 2 E
Khurīyā Murīyā, Jazā'ir, *Oman* **46 D6** 17 30N 55 58 E
Khurja, *India* **42 E7** 28 15N 77 58 E
Khūrmāl, *Iraq* **44 C5** 35 18N 46 2 E
Khurr, Wādī al, *Iraq* **44 C4** 32 3N 43 52 E
Khūsf, *Iran* **45 C8** 32 46N 58 53 E
Khush, *Afghan.* **40 C3** 32 55N 62 10 E
Khushab, *Pakistan* **42 C5** 32 20N 72 20 E
Khust, *Ukraine* **17 D12** 48 10N 23 18 E
Khuzdar, *Pakistan* **42 F2** 27 52N 66 30 E
Khūzestān □, *Iran* **45 D6** 31 0N 49 0 E
Khvāf, *Iran* **45 C9** 34 33N 60 8 E
Khvājeh, *Iran* **44 B5** 38 9N 46 35 E
Khvānsār, *Iran* **45 D7** 29 56N 54 8 E
Khvor, *Iran* **45 C7** 33 45N 55 0 E
Khvorgū, *Iran* **45 E8** 27 34N 56 27 E
Khvormūj, *Iran* **45 D6** 28 40N 51 30 E
Khvoy, *Iran* **44 B5** 38 35N 45 0 E
Khyber Pass, *Afghan.* **42 B4** 34 10N 71 8 E
Kiabukwa, *Dem. Rep. of the Congo* **55 D1** 8 40S 24 48 E
Kiama, *Australia* **63 E5** 34 40S 150 50 E
Kiamba, *Phil.* **37 C6** 6 2N 124 46 E
Kiambi, *Dem. Rep. of the Congo* **54 D2** 7 15S 28 0 E
Kiambu, *Kenya* **54 C4** 1 8S 36 50 E
Kiangara, *Madag.* **57 B8** 17 58S 47 2 E
Kiangsi = Jiangxi □, *China* **33 D6** 27 30N 116 0 E
Kiangsu = Jiangsu □, *China* **35 H11** 33 0N 120 0 E
Kibanga Port, *Uganda* **54 B3** 0 10N 32 58 E
Kibara, *Tanzania* **54 C3** 2 8S 33 30 E
Kibare, Mts., *Dem. Rep. of the Congo* **54 D2** 8 25S 27 10 E
Kibombo, *Dem. Rep. of the Congo* **54 C2** 3 57S 25 53 E
Kibondo, *Tanzania* **54 C3** 3 35S 30 45 E
Kibre Mengist, *Ethiopia* **46 F2** 5 54N 38 59 E
Kibumbu, *Burundi* **54 C2** 3 32S 29 45 E
Kibungo, *Rwanda* **54 C3** 2 10S 30 32 E
Kibuye, *Burundi* **54 C2** 3 39S 29 59 E
Kibuye, *Rwanda* **54 C2** 2 3S 29 21 E
Kibwesa, *Tanzania* **54 D2** 6 30S 29 58 E
Kibwezi, *Kenya* **54 C4** 2 27S 37 57 E
Kichha, *India* **43 E8** 28 53N 79 30 E
Kichha →, *India* **43 E8** 28 41N 79 18 E
Kichmengskiy Gorodok, *Russia* **24 B8** 59 59N 45 48 E
Kicking Horse Pass, *Canada* **72 C5** 51 28N 116 16W
Kidal, *Mali* **50 E6** 18 26N 1 22 E
Kidderminster, *U.K.* **11 E5** 52 24N 2 15W
Kidete, *Tanzania* **54 D4** 6 25S 37 17 E
Kidnappers, C., *N.Z.* **59 H6** 39 38S 177 5 E
Kidsgrove, *U.K.* **10 D5** 53 5N 2 14W
Kidston, *Australia* **62 B3** 18 52S 144 8 E
Kidugallo, *Tanzania* **54 D4** 6 49S 38 15 E
Kiel, *Germany* **16 A6** 54 19N 10 8 E
Kiel Canal = Nord-Ostsee-Kanal, *Germany* **16 A5** 54 12N 9 32 E
Kielce, *Poland* **17 C11** 50 52N 20 42 E
Kielder Water, *U.K.* **10 B5** 55 11N 2 31W
Kieler Bucht, *Germany* **16 A6** 54 35N 10 25 E
Kien Binh, *Vietnam* **39 H5** 9 55N 105 19 E
Kien Tan, *Vietnam* **39 G5** 10 7N 105 17 E
Kienge, *Dem. Rep. of the Congo* **55 E2** 10 30S 27 30 E
Kiev = Kyyiv, *Ukraine* **17 C16** 50 30N 30 28 E
Kiffa, *Mauritania* **50 E3** 16 37N 11 24W
Kifrī, *Iraq* **44 C5** 34 45N 45 0 E
Kigali, *Rwanda* **54 C3** 1 59S 30 4 E
Kigarama, *Tanzania* **54 C3** 1 1S 31 50 E
Kigoma □, *Tanzania* **54 D3** 5 0S 30 0 E
Kigoma-Ujiji, *Tanzania* **54 C2** 4 55S 29 36 E
Kigomasha, Ras, *Tanzania* **54 C4** 4 58S 38 58 E
Kığzı, *Turkey* **44 B4** 38 18N 43 25 E
Kihei, *U.S.A.* **74 H16** 20 47N 156 28W
Kihnu, *Estonia* **9 G21** 58 9N 24 1 E
Kii-Sanchi, *Japan* **31 G8** 34 20N 136 0 E
Kii-Suidō, *Japan* **31 H7** 33 40N 134 45 E
Kikaiga-Shima, *Japan* **31 K4** 28 19N 129 59 E
Kikinda, *Serbia, Yug.* **21 B9** 45 50N 20 30 E
Kikládhes, *Greece* **21 F11** 37 0N 24 30 E
Kikwit, *Dem. Rep. of the Congo* **52 E3** 5 0S 18 45 E
Kilar, *India* **42 C7** 33 6N 76 25 E
Kilauea Crater, *U.S.A.* **74 J17** 19 25N 155 17W
Kilbrannan Sd., *U.K.* **12 F3** 55 37N 5 26W
Kilchu, *N. Korea* **35 D15** 40 57N 129 25 E
Kilcoy, *Australia* **63 D5** 26 59S 152 30 E
Kildare, *Ireland* **13 C5** 53 9N 6 55W
Kildare □, *Ireland* **13 C5** 53 10N 6 50W
Kilfinnane, *Ireland* **13 D3** 52 21N 8 28W
Kilgore, *U.S.A.* **81 J7** 32 23N 94 53W
Kilifi, *Kenya* **54 C4** 3 40S 39 48 E
Kilimanjaro, *Tanzania* **54 C4** 3 7S 37 20 E
Kilimanjaro □, *Tanzania* **54 C4** 4 0S 38 0 E
Kilindini, *Kenya* **54 C4** 4 4S 39 40 E
Kilis, *Turkey* **44 B3** 36 42N 37 6 E
Kiliya, *Ukraine* **17 F15** 45 28N 29 16 E
Kilkee, *Ireland* **13 D2** 52 41N 9 39W
Kilkeel, *U.K.* **13 B5** 54 4N 6 0W
Kilkenny, *Ireland* **13 D4** 52 39N 7 15W
Kilkenny □, *Ireland* **13 D4** 52 35N 7 15W
Kilkieran B., *Ireland* **13 C2** 53 20N 9 41W
Kilkís, *Greece* **21 D10** 40 58N 22 57 E
Killala, *Ireland* **13 B2** 54 13N 9 12W
Killala B., *Ireland* **13 B2** 54 16N 9 8W
Killaloe, *Ireland* **13 D3** 52 48N 8 28W
Killaloe Station, *Canada* **78 A7** 45 33N 77 25W
Killarney, *Australia* **63 D5** 28 20S 152 18 E
Killarney, *Canada* **73 D9** 49 10N 99 40W
Killarney, *Ireland* **13 D2** 52 4N 9 30W
Killary Harbour, *Ireland* **13 C2** 53 38N 9 52W
Killdeer, *U.S.A.* **80 B3** 47 26N 102 48W
Killeen, *U.S.A.* **81 K6** 31 7N 97 44W
Killin, *U.K.* **12 E4** 56 28N 4 19W
Killíni, *Greece* **21 F10** 37 54N 22 25 E
Killorglin, *Ireland* **13 D2** 52 6N 9 47W
Killybegs, *Ireland* **13 B3** 54 38N 8 26W
Kilmarnock, *U.K.* **12 F4** 55 37N 4 29W
Kilmore, *Australia* **63 F3** 37 25S 144 53 E

Kondratyevo

Kilondo, *Tanzania* **55 D3** 9 45S 34 20 E
Kilosa, *Tanzania* **54 D4** 6 48S 37 0 E
Kilrush, *Ireland* **13 D2** 52 38N 9 29W
Kilwa Kisiwani, *Tanzania* **55 D4** 8 58S 39 32 E
Kilwa Kivinje, *Tanzania* **55 D4** 8 45S 39 25 E
Kilwa Masoko, *Tanzania* **55 D4** 8 55S 39 30 E
Kilwinning, *U.K.* **12 F4** 55 39N 4 43W
Kim, *U.S.A.* **81 G3** 37 15N 103 21W
Kimaam, *Indonesia* **37 F9** 7 58S 138 53 E
Kimamba, *Tanzania* **54 D4** 6 45S 37 10 E
Kimba, *Australia* **63 E2** 33 8S 136 23 E
Kimball, *Nebr., U.S.A.* **80 E3** 41 14N 103 40W
Kimball, *S. Dak., U.S.A.* **80 D5** 43 45N 98 57W
Kimberley, *Australia* **60 C4** 16 20S 127 0 E
Kimberley, *Canada* **72 D5** 49 40N 115 59W
Kimberley, *S. Africa* **56 D3** 28 43S 24 46 E
Kimberly, *U.S.A.* **82 E6** 42 32N 114 22W
Kimch'aek, *N. Korea* **35 D15** 40 40N 129 10 E
Kimch'ŏn, *S. Korea* **35 F15** 36 11N 128 4 E
Kimje, *S. Korea* **35 G14** 35 48N 126 45 E
Kimmirut, *Canada* **69 B13** 62 50N 69 50W
Kimpese, *Dem. Rep. of the Congo* **52 F2** 5 35S 14 26 E
Kimry, *Russia* **24 C6** 56 55N 37 15 E
Kinabalu, Gunong, *Malaysia* **36 C5** 6 3N 116 14 E
Kinaskan L., *Canada* **72 B2** 57 38N 130 8W
Kinbasket L., *Canada* **72 C5** 52 0N 118 10W
Kincardine, *Canada* **78 B3** 44 10N 81 40W
Kincolith, *Canada* **72 B3** 55 0N 129 57W
Kinda, *Dem. Rep. of the Congo* **55 D2** 9 18S 25 4 E
Kinde, *U.S.A.* **78 C2** 43 56N 83 0W
Kinder Scout, *U.K.* **10 D6** 53 24N 1 52W
Kindersley, *Canada* **73 C7** 51 30N 109 10W
Kindia, *Guinea* **50 F3** 10 0N 12 52W
Kindu, *Dem. Rep. of the Congo* **54 C2** 2 55S 25 50 E
Kineshma, *Russia* **24 C7** 57 30N 42 5 E
Kinesi, *Tanzania* **54 C3** 1 25S 33 50 E
King, L., *Australia* **61 F2** 33 10S 119 35 E
King, Mt., *Australia* **62 D4** 25 10S 147 30 E
King City, *U.S.A.* **84 J5** 36 13N 121 8W
King Cr. →, *Australia* **62 C2** 24 35S 139 30 E
King Edward →, *Australia* **60 B4** 14 14S 126 35 E
King Frederick VI Land = Kong Frederik VI Kyst, *Greenland* **4 C5** 63 0N 43 0W
King George B., *Falk. Is.* **96 G4** 51 30S 60 30W
King George I., *Antarctica* **5 C18** 60 0S 60 0W
King George Is., *Canada* **69 C11** 57 20N 80 30W
King I. = Kadan Kyun, *Burma* **38 F2** 12 30N 98 20 E
King I., *Australia* **62 F3** 39 50S 144 0 E
King I., *Canada* **72 C3** 52 10N 127 40W
King Leopold Ranges, *Australia* **60 C4** 17 30S 125 45 E
King of Prussia, *U.S.A.* **79 F9** 40 5N 75 23W
King Sd., *Australia* **60 C3** 16 50S 123 20 E
King William I., *Canada* **68 B10** 69 10N 97 25W
King William's Town, *S. Africa* **56 E4** 32 51S 27 22 E
Kingaok = Bathurst Inlet, *Canada* **68 B9** 66 50N 108 1W
Kingaroy, *Australia* **63 D5** 26 32S 151 51 E
Kingfisher, *U.S.A.* **81 H6** 35 52N 97 56W
Kingirbān, *Iraq* **44 C5** 34 40N 44 54 E
Kingisepp = Kuressaare, *Estonia* **9 G20** 58 15N 22 30 E
Kingman, *Ariz., U.S.A.* **85 K12** 35 12N 114 4W
Kingman, *Kans., U.S.A.* **81 G5** 37 39N 98 7W
Kingoonya, *Australia* **63 E2** 30 55S 135 19 E
Kingri, *Pakistan* **42 D3** 30 27N 69 49 E
Kings →, *U.S.A.* **84 J7** 36 3N 119 50W
Kings Canyon Nat. Park, *U.S.A.* **84 J8** 36 50N 118 40W
King's Lynn, *U.K.* **10 E8** 52 45N 0 24 E
Kings Mountain, *U.S.A.* **77 H5** 35 15N 81 20W
Kings Park, *U.S.A.* **79 F11** 40 53N 73 16W
King's Peak, *U.S.A.* **82 F8** 40 46N 110 27W
Kingsbridge, *U.K.* **11 G4** 50 17N 3 47W
Kingsburg, *U.S.A.* **84 J7** 36 31N 119 33W
Kingscote, *Australia* **63 F2** 35 40S 137 38 E
Kingscourt, *Ireland* **13 C5** 53 55N 6 48W
Kingsford, *U.S.A.* **76 C1** 45 48N 88 4W
Kingsland, *U.S.A.* **77 K5** 30 48N 81 41W
Kingsley, *U.S.A.* **80 D7** 42 35N 95 58W
Kingsport, *U.S.A.* **77 G4** 36 33N 82 33W
Kingston, *Canada* **79 B8** 44 14N 76 30W
Kingston, *Jamaica* **88 C4** 18 0N 76 50W
Kingston, *N.Z.* **59 L2** 45 20S 168 43 E
Kingston, *N.H., U.S.A.* **79 D13** 42 56N 71 3W
Kingston, *N.Y., U.S.A.* **79 E11** 41 56N 73 59W
Kingston, *Pa., U.S.A.* **79 E9** 41 16N 75 54W
Kingston, *R.I., U.S.A.* **79 E13** 41 29N 71 30W
Kingston Pk., *U.S.A.* **85 K11** 35 45N 115 54W
Kingston South East, *Australia* **63 F2** 36 51S 139 55 E
Kingston upon Hull, *U.K.* **10 D7** 53 45N 0 21W
Kingston upon Hull □, *U.K.* **10 D7** 53 45N 0 21W
Kingston-upon-Thames □, *U.K.* **11 F7** 51 24N 0 17W
Kingstown, *St. Vincent* **89 D7** 13 10N 61 10W
Kingstree, *U.S.A.* **77 J6** 33 40N 79 50W
Kingsville, *Canada* **78 D2** 42 2N 82 45W
Kingsville, *U.S.A.* **81 M6** 27 31N 97 52W
Kingussie, *U.K.* **12 D4** 57 6N 4 2W
Kingwood, *U.S.A.* **81 K7** 29 54N 95 18W
Kınık, *Turkey* **21 E12** 39 6N 27 24 E
Kinistino, *Canada* **73 C7** 52 57N 105 2W
Kinkala, *Congo* **52 E2** 4 18S 14 49 E
Kinki □, *Japan* **31 H8** 33 45N 136 0 E
Kinleith, *N.Z.* **59 H5** 38 20S 175 56 E
Kinmount, *Canada* **78 B6** 44 48N 78 45W
Kinna, *Sweden* **9 H15** 57 32N 12 42 E
Kinnairds Hd., *U.K.* **12 D6** 57 43N 2 1W
Kinnarodden, *Norway* **6 A11** 71 8N 27 40 E
Kinngait = Cape Dorset, *Canada* **69 B12** 64 14N 76 32W
Kino, *Mexico* **86 B2** 28 45N 111 59W
Kinoje →, *Canada* **70 B3** 52 8N 81 25W
Kinomoto, *Japan* **31 G8** 35 30N 136 13 E
Kinoni, *Uganda* **54 C3** 0 41S 30 28 E
Kinoosao, *Canada* **73 B8** 57 5N 102 1W
Kinross, *U.K.* **12 E5** 56 13N 3 25W
Kinsale, *Ireland* **13 E3** 51 42N 8 31W
Kinsale, Old Hd. of, *Ireland* **13 E3** 51 37N 8 33W
Kinsha = Chang Jiang →, *China* **33 C7** 31 48N 121 10 E
Kinshasa, *Dem. Rep. of the Congo* **52 E3** 4 20S 15 15 E
Kinsley, *U.S.A.* **81 G5** 37 55N 99 25W
Kinsman, *U.S.A.* **78 E4** 41 26N 80 35W
Kinston, *U.S.A.* **77 H7** 35 16N 77 35W
Kintore Ra., *Australia* **60 D4** 23 15S 128 47 E
Kintyre, *U.K.* **12 F3** 55 30N 5 35W
Kintyre, Mull of, *U.K.* **12 F3** 55 17N 5 47W
Kinushseo →, *Canada* **70 A3** 55 15N 83 45W
Kinuso, *Canada* **72 B5** 55 20N 115 25W
Kinyangiri, *Tanzania* **54 C3** 4 25S 34 37 E
Kinzua, *U.S.A.* **78 E6** 41 52N 78 58W
Kinzua Dam, *U.S.A.* **78 E6** 41 53N 79 0W
Kiosk, *Canada* **70 C4** 46 6N 78 53W
Kiowa, *Kans., U.S.A.* **81 G5** 37 1N 98 29W
Kiowa, *Okla., U.S.A.* **81 H7** 34 43N 95 54W
Kipahigan L., *Canada* **73 B8** 55 20N 101 55W
Kipanga, *Tanzania* **54 D4** 6 15S 35 20 E
Kiparissía, *Greece* **21 F9** 37 15N 21 40 E
Kiparissiakós Kólpos, *Greece* **21 F9** 37 25N 21 25 E
Kipawa, L., *Canada* **70 C4** 46 50N 79 0W
Kipembawe, *Tanzania* **54 D3** 7 38S 33 27 E
Kipengere Ra., *Tanzania* **55 D3** 9 12S 34 15 E
Kipili, *Tanzania* **54 D3** 7 28S 30 32 E
Kipini, *Kenya* **54 C5** 2 30S 40 32 E
Kipling, *Canada* **73 C8** 50 6N 102 38W
Kippure, *Ireland* **13 C5** 53 11N 6 21W
Kipushi, *Dem. Rep. of the Congo* **55 E2** 11 48S 27 12 E
Kiranomena, *Madag.* **57 B8** 18 17S 46 2 E
Kirensk, *Russia* **27 D11** 57 50N 107 55 E
Kirghizia = Kyrgyzstan ■, *Asia* **26 E8** 42 0N 75 0 E
Kirghizstan = Kyrgyzstan ■, *Asia* **26 E8** 42 0N 75 0 E
Kirgiziya Steppe, *Eurasia* **25 E10** 50 0N 55 0 E
Kiribati ■, *Pac. Oc.* **64 H10** 5 0S 180 0 E
Kırıkkale, *Turkey* **25 G5** 39 51N 33 32 E
Kirillov, *Russia* **24 C6** 59 49N 38 24 E
Kirin = Jilin, *China* **35 C14** 43 44N 126 30 E
Kirinyaga = Kenya, Mt., *Kenya* **54 C4** 0 10S 37 18 E
Kiritimati, *Kiribati* **65 G12** 1 58N 157 27W
Kirkby, *U.K.* **10 D5** 53 30N 2 54W
Kirkby Lonsdale, *U.K.* **10 C5** 54 12N 2 36W
Kirkcaldy, *U.K.* **12 E5** 56 7N 3 9W
Kirkcudbright, *U.K.* **12 G4** 54 50N 4 2W
Kirkee, *India* **40 K8** 18 34N 73 56 E
Kirkenes, *Norway* **8 B23** 69 40N 30 5 E
Kirkfield, *Canada* **78 B6** 44 34N 78 59W
Kirkjubæjarklaustur, *Iceland* **8 E4** 63 47N 18 4W
Kirkkonummi, *Finland* **9 F21** 60 8N 24 26 E
Kirkland Lake, *Canada* **70 C3** 48 9N 80 2W
Kırklareli, *Turkey* **21 D12** 41 44N 27 15 E
Kirksville, *U.S.A.* **80 E8** 40 12N 92 35W
Kirkūk, *Iraq* **44 C5** 35 30N 44 21 E
Kirkwall, *U.K.* **12 C6** 58 59N 2 58W
Kirkwood, *S. Africa* **56 E4** 33 22S 25 15 E
Kirov, *Russia* **24 C8** 58 35N 49 40 E
Kirovabad = Gäncä, *Azerbaijan* **25 F8** 40 45N 46 20 E
Kirovakan = Vanadzor, *Armenia* **25 F7** 40 48N 44 30 E
Kirovograd = Kirovohrad, *Ukraine* **25 E5** 48 35N 32 20 E
Kirovohrad, *Ukraine* **25 E5** 48 35N 32 20 E
Kirovsk = Babadayhan, *Turkmenistan* **26 F7** 37 42N 60 23 E
Kirovsk, *Russia* **24 A5** 67 32N 33 41 E
Kirovskiy, *Kamchatka, Russia* **27 D16** 54 27N 155 42 E
Kirovskiy, *Primorsk, Russia* **30 B6** 45 7N 133 30 E
Kirriemuir, *U.K.* **12 E5** 56 41N 3 1W
Kirsanov, *Russia* **24 D7** 52 35N 42 40 E
Kırşehir, *Turkey* **25 G5** 39 14N 34 5 E
Kirthar Range, *Pakistan* **42 F2** 27 0N 67 0 E
Kirtland, *U.S.A.* **83 H9** 36 44N 108 21W
Kiruna, *Sweden* **8 C19** 67 52N 20 15 E
Kirundu, *Dem. Rep. of the Congo* **54 C2** 0 50S 25 35 E
Kiryū, *Japan* **31 F9** 36 24N 139 20 E
Kisaga, *Tanzania* **54 C3** 4 30S 34 23 E
Kisalaya, *Nic.* **88 D3** 14 40N 84 3W
Kisámou, Kólpos, *Greece* **23 D5** 35 30N 23 38 E
Kisanga, *Dem. Rep. of the Congo* **54 B2** 2 30N 26 35 E
Kisangani, *Dem. Rep. of the Congo* **54 B2** 0 35N 25 15 E
Kisar, *Indonesia* **37 F7** 8 5S 127 10 E
Kisarawe, *Tanzania* **54 D4** 6 53S 39 0 E
Kisarazu, *Japan* **31 G9** 35 23N 139 55 E
Kishanganga →, *Pakistan* **43 B5** 34 18N 73 28 E
Kishanganj, *India* **43 F13** 26 3N 88 14 E
Kishangarh, *Raj., India* **42 F6** 26 34N 74 52 E
Kishangarh, *Raj., India* **42 F4** 27 50N 70 30 E
Kishinev = Chişinău, *Moldova* **17 E15** 47 2N 28 50 E
Kishiwada, *Japan* **31 G7** 34 28N 135 22 E
Kishtwar, *India* **43 C6** 33 20N 75 48 E
Kisii, *Kenya* **54 C3** 0 40S 34 45 E
Kisiju, *Tanzania* **54 D4** 7 23S 39 19 E
Kisizi, *Uganda* **54 C2** 1 0S 29 58 E
Kiskőrös, *Hungary* **17 E10** 46 37N 19 20 E
Kiskunfélegyháza, *Hungary* **17 E10** 46 42N 19 53 E
Kiskunhalas, *Hungary* **17 E10** 46 28N 19 37 E
Kislovodsk, *Russia* **25 F7** 43 50N 42 45 E
Kismayu = Chisimaio, *Somali Rep.* **49 G8** 0 22S 42 32 E
Kiso-Gawa →, *Japan* **31 G8** 35 20N 136 45 E
Kiso-Sammyaku, *Japan* **31 G8** 35 45N 137 45 E
Kisofukushima, *Japan* **31 G8** 35 52N 137 43 E
Kisoro, *Uganda* **54 C2** 1 17S 29 48 E
Kissidougou, *Guinea* **50 G3** 9 5N 10 5W
Kissimmee, *U.S.A.* **77 L5** 28 18N 81 24W
Kissimmee →, *U.S.A.* **77 M5** 27 9N 80 52W
Kississing L., *Canada* **73 B8** 55 10N 101 20W
Kissónerga, *Cyprus* **23 E11** 34 49N 32 24 E
Kisumu, *Kenya* **54 C3** 0 3S 34 45 E
Kiswani, *Tanzania* **54 C4** 4 5S 37 57 E
Kiswere, *Tanzania* **55 D4** 9 27S 39 30 E
Kit Carson, *U.S.A.* **80 F3** 38 46N 102 48W
Kita, *Mali* **50 F4** 13 5N 9 25W
Kitaibaraki, *Japan* **31 F10** 36 50N 140 45 E
Kitakami, *Japan* **30 E10** 39 20N 141 10 E
Kitakami-Gawa →, *Japan* **30 E10** 38 25N 141 19 E
Kitakami-Sammyaku, *Japan* **30 E10** 39 30N 141 30 E
Kitakata, *Japan* **30 F9** 37 39N 139 52 E
Kitakyūshū, *Japan* **31 H5** 33 50N 130 50 E
Kitale, *Kenya* **54 B4** 1 0N 35 0 E
Kitami, *Japan* **30 C11** 43 48N 143 54 E
Kitami-Sammyaku, *Japan* **30 B11** 44 22N 142 43 E
Kitangiri, L., *Tanzania* **54 C3** 4 5S 34 20 E
Kitaya, *Tanzania* **55 E5** 10 38S 40 8 E
Kitchener, *Canada* **78 C4** 43 27N 80 29W
Kitega = Gitega, *Burundi* **54 C2** 3 26S 29 56 E
Kitengo, *Dem. Rep. of the Congo* **54 D1** 7 26S 24 8 E
Kitgum, *Uganda* **54 B3** 3 17N 32 52 E
Kíthira, *Greece* **21 F10** 36 8N 23 0 E
Kíthnos, *Greece* **21 F11** 37 26N 24 27 E
Kiti, *Cyprus* **23 E12** 34 50N 33 34 E
Kiti, C., *Cyprus* **23 E12** 34 48N 33 36 E
Kitimat, *Canada* **72 C3** 54 3N 128 38W
Kitinen →, *Finland* **8 C22** 67 14N 27 27 E
Kitsuki, *Japan* **31 H5** 33 25N 131 37 E
Kittakittaooloo, L., *Australia* **63 D2** 28 3S 138 14 E
Kittanning, *U.S.A.* **78 F5** 40 49N 79 31W
Kittatinny Mts., *U.S.A.* **79 F10** 41 0N 75 0W
Kittery, *U.S.A.* **77 D10** 43 5N 70 45W
Kittilä, *Finland* **8 C21** 67 40N 24 51 E
Kitui, *Kenya* **54 C4** 1 17S 38 0 E
Kitwanga, *Canada* **72 B3** 55 6N 128 4W
Kitwe, *Zambia* **55 E2** 12 54S 28 13 E
Kivarli, *India* **42 G5** 24 33N 72 46 E
Kivertsi, *Ukraine* **17 C13** 50 50N 25 28 E
Kividhes, *Cyprus* **23 E11** 34 46N 32 51 E
Kivu, L., *Dem. Rep. of the Congo* **54 C2** 1 48S 29 0 E
Kiyev = Kyyiv, *Ukraine* **17 C16** 50 30N 30 28 E
Kiyevskoye Vdkhr. = Kyyivske Vdskh., *Ukraine* **17 C16** 51 0N 30 25 E
Kizel, *Russia* **24 C10** 59 3N 57 40 E
Kiziguru, *Rwanda* **54 C3** 1 46S 30 23 E
Kızıl Irmak →, *Turkey* **25 F6** 41 44N 35 58 E
Kizil Jilga, *China* **43 B8** 35 26N 78 50 E
Kızıltepe, *Turkey* **44 B4** 37 12N 40 35 E
Kizimkazi, *Tanzania* **54 D4** 6 28S 39 30 E
Kizlyar, *Russia* **25 F8** 43 51N 46 40 E
Kizyl-Arvat = Gyzylarbat, *Turkmenistan* **26 F6** 39 4N 56 23 E
Kjölur, *Iceland* **8 D4** 64 50N 19 25W
Kladno, *Czech Rep.* **16 C8** 50 10N 14 7 E
Klaeng, *Thailand* **38 F3** 12 47N 101 39 E
Klagenfurt, *Austria* **16 E8** 46 38N 14 20 E
Klaipėda, *Lithuania* **9 J19** 55 43N 21 10 E
Klaksvík, *Færoe Is.* **8 E9** 62 14N 6 35W
Klamath →, *U.S.A.* **82 F1** 41 33N 124 5W
Klamath Falls, *U.S.A.* **82 E3** 42 13N 121 46W
Klamath Mts., *U.S.A.* **82 F2** 41 20N 123 0W
Klamono, *Indonesia* **37 E8** 1 8S 131 30 E
Klappan →, *Canada* **72 B3** 58 0N 129 43W
Klarälven →, *Sweden* **9 G15** 59 23N 13 32 E
Klatovy, *Czech Rep.* **16 D7** 49 23N 13 18 E
Klawer, *S. Africa* **56 E2** 31 44S 18 36 E
Klazienaveen, *Neths.* **15 B6** 52 44N 7 0 E
Kleena Kleene, *Canada* **72 C4** 52 0N 124 59W
Klein-Karas, *Namibia* **56 D2** 27 33S 18 7 E
Klerksdorp, *S. Africa* **56 D4** 26 53S 26 38 E
Kletsk = Klyetsk, *Belarus* **17 B14** 53 5N 26 45 E
Kletskiy, *Russia* **25 E7** 49 16N 43 11 E
Klickitat, *U.S.A.* **82 D3** 45 49N 121 9W
Klickitat →, *U.S.A.* **84 E5** 45 42N 121 17W
Klidhes, *Cyprus* **23 D13** 35 42N 34 36 E
Klinaklini →, *Canada* **72 C3** 51 21N 125 40W
Klip →, *S. Africa* **57 D4** 27 3S 29 3 E
Klipdale, *S. Africa* **56 E2** 34 19S 19 57 E
Klipplaat, *S. Africa* **56 E3** 33 1S 24 22 E
Kłodzko, *Poland* **17 C9** 50 28N 16 38 E
Klouto, *Togo* **50 G6** 6 57N 0 44 E
Kluane L., *Canada* **68 B6** 61 15N 138 40W
Kluane Nat. Park, *Canada* **72 A1** 60 45N 139 30W
Kluczbork, *Poland* **17 C10** 50 58N 18 12 E
Klukwan, *U.S.A.* **72 B1** 59 24N 135 54W
Klyetsk, *Belarus* **17 B14** 53 5N 26 45 E
Klyuchevskaya, Gora, *Russia* **27 D17** 55 50N 160 30 E
Knaresborough, *U.K.* **10 C6** 54 1N 1 28W
Knee L., *Man., Canada* **70 A1** 55 3N 94 45W
Knee L., *Sask., Canada* **73 B7** 55 51N 107 0W
Knight Inlet, *Canada* **72 C3** 50 45N 125 40W
Knighton, *U.K.* **11 E4** 52 21N 3 3W
Knights Ferry, *U.S.A.* **84 H6** 37 50N 120 40W
Knights Landing, *U.S.A.* **84 G5** 38 48N 121 43W
Knob, C., *Australia* **61 F2** 34 32S 119 16 E
Knock, *Ireland* **13 C3** 53 48N 8 55W
Knockmealdown Mts., *Ireland* **13 D4** 52 14N 7 56W
Knokke-Heist, *Belgium* **15 C3** 51 21N 3 17 E
Knossós, *Greece* **23 D7** 35 16N 25 10 E
Knowlton, *Canada* **79 A12** 45 13N 72 31W
Knox, *U.S.A.* **76 E2** 41 18N 86 37W
Knox Coast, *Antarctica* **5 C8** 66 30S 108 0 E
Knoxville, *Iowa, U.S.A.* **80 E8** 41 19N 93 6W
Knoxville, *Pa., U.S.A.* **78 E7** 41 57N 77 27W
Knoxville, *Tenn., U.S.A.* **77 H4** 35 58N 83 55W
Knysna, *S. Africa* **56 E3** 34 2S 23 2 E
Ko Kha, *Thailand* **38 C2** 18 11N 99 24 E
Koartac = Quaqtaq, *Canada* **69 B13** 60 55N 69 40W
Koba, *Indonesia* **37 F8** 6 37S 134 37 E
Kobarid, *Slovenia* **16 E7** 46 15N 13 30 E
Kobayashi, *Japan* **31 J5** 31 56N 130 59 E
Kobdo = Hovd, *Mongolia* **32 B4** 48 2N 91 37 E
Kōbe, *Japan* **31 G7** 34 45N 135 10 E
København, *Denmark* **9 J15** 55 41N 12 34 E
Kōbi-Sho, *Japan* **31 M1** 25 56N 123 41 E
Koblenz, *Germany* **16 C4** 50 21N 7 36 E
Kobryn, *Belarus* **17 B13** 52 15N 24 22 E
Kocaeli, *Turkey* **25 F4** 40 45N 29 50 E
Kočani, *Macedonia* **21 D10** 41 55N 22 25 E
Koch Bihar, *India* **41 F16** 26 22N 89 29 E
Kochang, *S. Korea* **35 G14** 35 41N 127 55 E
Kochas, *India* **43 G10** 25 15N 83 56 E
Kochi = Cochin, *India* **40 Q10** 9 58N 76 20 E
Kōchi, *Japan* **31 H6** 33 30N 133 35 E
Kōchi □, *Japan* **31 H6** 33 40N 133 30 E
Kochiu = Gejiu, *China* **32 D5** 23 20N 103 10 E
Kodarma, *India* **43 G11** 24 28N 85 36 E
Kodiak, *U.S.A.* **68 C4** 57 47N 152 24W
Kodiak I., *U.S.A.* **68 C4** 57 30N 152 45W
Kodinar, *India* **42 J4** 20 46N 70 46 E
Koedoesberge, *S. Africa* **56 E3** 32 40S 20 11 E
Koes, *Namibia* **56 D2** 26 0S 19 15 E
Koffiefontein, *S. Africa* **56 D4** 29 30S 25 0 E
Kofiau, *Indonesia* **37 E7** 1 11S 129 50 E
Koforidua, *Ghana* **50 G5** 6 3N 0 17W
Kōfu, *Japan* **31 G9** 35 40N 138 30 E
Koga, *Japan* **31 F9** 36 11N 139 43 E
Kogaluk →, *Canada* **71 A7** 56 12N 61 44W
Køge, *Denmark* **9 J15** 55 27N 12 11 E
Koh-i-Khurd, *Afghan.* **42 C1** 33 30N 65 59 E
Koh-i-Maran, *Pakistan* **42 E2** 29 18N 66 50 E
Kohat, *Pakistan* **42 C4** 33 40N 71 29 E
Kohima, *India* **41 G19** 25 35N 94 10 E
Kohkīlūyeh va Būyer Aḥmadi □, *Iran* **45 D6** 31 30N 50 30 E
Kohler Ra., *Antarctica* **5 D15** 77 0S 110 0W
Kohlu, *Pakistan* **42 E3** 29 54N 69 15 E
Kohtla-Järve, *Estonia* **9 G22** 59 20N 27 20 E
Koillismaa, *Finland* **8 D23** 65 44N 28 36 E
Koin-dong, *N. Korea* **35 D14** 40 28N 126 18 E
Kojŏ, *N. Korea* **35 E14** 38 58N 127 58 E
Kojonup, *Australia* **61 F2** 33 48S 117 10 E
Kojūr, *Iran* **45 B6** 36 23N 51 43 E
Kokand = Qŭqon, *Uzbekistan* **26 E8** 40 30N 70 57 E
Kokas, *Indonesia* **37 E8** 2 42S 132 26 E
Kokchetav = Kökshetaū, *Kazakstan* **26 D7** 53 20N 69 25 E
Kokemäenjoki →, *Finland* **9 F19** 61 32N 21 44 E
Kokkola, *Finland* **8 E20** 63 50N 23 8 E
Koko Kyunzu, *Burma* **41 M18** 14 10N 93 25 E
Kokomo, *U.S.A.* **76 E2** 40 29N 86 8W
Koksan, *N. Korea* **35 E14** 38 46N 126 40 E
Kökshetaū, *Kazakstan* **26 D7** 53 20N 69 25 E
Koksoak →, *Canada* **69 C13** 58 30N 68 10W
Kokstad, *S. Africa* **57 E4** 30 32S 29 29 E
Kokubu, *Japan* **31 J5** 31 44N 130 46 E
Kola, *Indonesia* **37 F8** 5 35S 134 30 E
Kola, *Russia* **24 A5** 68 45N 33 8 E
Kola Pen. = Kolskiy Poluostrov, *Russia* **24 A6** 67 30N 38 0 E
Kolachi →, *Pakistan* **42 F2** 27 8N 67 2 E
Kolahoi, *India* **43 B6** 34 12N 75 22 E
Kolaka, *Indonesia* **37 E6** 4 3S 121 46 E
Kolar, *India* **40 N11** 13 12N 78 15 E
Kolar Gold Fields, *India* **40 N11** 12 58N 78 16 E
Kolaras, *India* **42 G6** 25 14N 77 36 E
Kolari, *Finland* **8 C20** 67 20N 23 48 E
Kolayat, *India* **40 F8** 27 50N 72 50 E
Kolchugino = Leninsk-Kuznetskiy, *Russia* **26 D9** 54 44N 86 10 E
Kolding, *Denmark* **9 J13** 55 30N 9 29 E
Kolepom = Dolak, Pulau, *Indonesia* **37 F9** 8 0S 138 30 E
Kolguyev, Ostrov, *Russia* **24 A8** 69 20N 48 30 E
Kolhapur, *India* **40 L9** 16 43N 74 15 E
Kolín, *Czech Rep.* **16 C8** 50 2N 15 9 E
Kolkas rags, *Latvia* **9 H20** 57 46N 22 37 E
Kolkata, *India* **43 H13** 22 36N 88 24 E
Kollam = Quilon, *India* **40 Q10** 8 50N 76 38 E
Kollum, *Neths.* **15 A6** 53 17N 6 10 E
Kolmanskop, *Namibia* **56 D2** 26 45S 15 14 E
Köln, *Germany* **16 C4** 50 56N 6 57 E
Koło, *Poland* **17 B10** 52 14N 18 40 E
Kołobrzeg, *Poland* **16 A8** 54 10N 15 35 E
Kolomna, *Russia* **24 C6** 55 8N 38 45 E
Kolomyya, *Ukraine* **17 D13** 48 31N 25 2 E
Kolonodale, *Indonesia* **37 E6** 2 0S 121 19 E
Kolosib, *India* **41 G18** 24 15N 92 45 E
Kolpashevo, *Russia* **26 D9** 58 20N 83 5 E
Kolpino, *Russia* **24 C5** 59 44N 30 39 E
Kolskiy Poluostrov, *Russia* **24 A6** 67 30N 38 0 E
Kolskiy Zaliv, *Russia* **24 A5** 69 23N 34 0 E
Kolwezi, *Dem. Rep. of the Congo* **55 E2** 10 40S 25 25 E
Kolyma →, *Russia* **27 C17** 69 30N 161 0 E
Kolymskoye Nagorye, *Russia* **27 C16** 63 0N 157 0 E
Kôm Ombo, *Egypt* **51 D12** 24 25N 32 52 E
Komandorskiye Is. = Komandorskiye Ostrova, *Russia* **27 D17** 55 0N 167 0 E
Komandorskiye Ostrova, *Russia* **27 D17** 55 0N 167 0 E
Komárno, *Slovak Rep.* **17 E10** 47 49N 18 5 E
Komatipoort, *S. Africa* **57 D5** 25 25S 31 55 E
Komatou Yialou, *Cyprus* **23 D13** 35 25N 34 8 E
Komatsu, *Japan* **31 F8** 36 25N 136 30 E
Komatsushima, *Japan* **31 H7** 34 0N 134 35 E
Komi □, *Russia* **24 B10** 64 0N 55 0 E
Kommunarsk = Alchevsk, *Ukraine* **25 E6** 48 30N 38 45 E
Kommunizma, Pik, *Tajikistan* **26 F8** 39 0N 72 2 E
Komodo, *Indonesia* **37 F5** 8 37S 119 20 E
Komoran, Pulau, *Indonesia* **37 F9** 8 18S 138 45 E
Komoro, *Japan* **31 F9** 36 19N 138 26 E
Komotini, *Greece* **21 D11** 41 9N 25 26 E
Kompasberg, *S. Africa* **56 E3** 31 45S 24 32 E
Kompong Bang, *Cambodia* **39 F5** 12 24N 104 40 E
Kompong Cham, *Cambodia* **39 F5** 12 0N 105 30 E
Kompong Chhnang = Kampang Chhnang, *Cambodia* **39 F5** 12 20N 104 35 E
Kompong Chikreng, *Cambodia* **38 F5** 13 5N 104 18 E
Kompong Kleang, *Cambodia* **38 F5** 13 6N 104 8 E
Kompong Luong, *Cambodia* **39 G5** 11 49N 104 48 E
Kompong Pranak, *Cambodia* **38 F5** 13 35N 104 55 E
Kompong Som = Kampong Saom, *Cambodia* **39 G4** 10 38N 103 30 E
Kompong Som, Chhung = Kampong Saom, Chaak, *Cambodia* **39 G4** 10 50N 103 32 E
Kompong Speu, *Cambodia* **39 G5** 11 26N 104 32 E
Kompong Sralao, *Cambodia* **38 E5** 14 5N 105 46 E
Kompong Thom, *Cambodia* **38 F5** 12 35N 104 51 E
Kompong Trabeck, *Cambodia* **38 F5** 13 6N 105 14 E
Kompong Trabeck, *Cambodia* **39 G5** 11 9N 105 28 E
Kompong Trach, *Cambodia* **39 G5** 11 25N 105 48 E
Kompong Tralach, *Cambodia* **39 G5** 11 54N 104 47 E
Komrat = Comrat, *Moldova* **17 E15** 46 18N 28 40 E
Komsberg, *S. Africa* **56 E3** 32 40S 20 45 E
Komsomolets, Ostrov, *Russia* **27 A10** 80 30N 95 0 E
Komsomolsk, *Russia* **27 D14** 50 30N 137 0 E
Kon Tum, *Vietnam* **38 E7** 14 24N 108 0 E
Kon Tum, Plateau du, *Vietnam* **38 E7** 14 30N 108 30 E
Konarhā □, *Afghan.* **40 B7** 34 30N 71 3 E
Konārī, *Iran* **45 D6** 28 13N 51 36 E
Konch, *India* **43 G8** 26 0N 79 10 E
Konde, *Tanzania* **54 C4** 4 57S 39 45 E
Kondinin, *Australia* **61 F2** 32 34S 118 8 E
Kondoa, *Tanzania* **54 C4** 4 55S 35 50 E
Kondókali, *Greece* **23 A3** 39 38N 19 51 E
Kondopaga, *Russia* **24 B5** 62 12N 34 17 E
Kondratyevo, *Russia* **27 D10** 57 22N 98 15 E

Köneürgench

134

Makwiro

Lynden, *U.S.A.* **84 B4** 48 57N 122 27W
Lyndhurst, *Australia* **63 E2** 30 15S 138 18 E
Lyndon →, *Australia* **61 D1** 23 29S 114 6 E
Lyndonville, *N.Y., U.S.A.* **78 C6** 43 20N 78 23W
Lyndonville, *Vt., U.S.A.* **79 B12** 44 31N 72 1W
Lyngen, *Norway* **8 B19** 69 45N 20 30 E
Lynher Reef, *Australia* **60 C3** 15 27S 121 55 E
Lynn, *U.S.A.* **79 D14** 42 28N 70 57W
Lynn Lake, *Canada* **73 B8** 56 51N 101 3W
Lynnwood, *U.S.A.* **84 C4** 47 49N 122 19W
Lynton, *U.K.* **11 F4** 51 13N 3 50W
Lyntupy, *Belarus* **9 J22** 55 4N 26 23 E
Lynx L., *Canada* **73 A7** 62 25N 106 15W
Lyon, *France* **18 D6** 45 46N 4 50 E
Lyonnais, *France* **18 D6** 45 45N 4 15 E
Lyons = Lyon, *France* **18 D6** 45 46N 4 50 E
Lyons, *Ga., U.S.A.* **77 J4** 32 12N 82 19W
Lyons, *Kans., U.S.A.* **80 F5** 38 21N 98 12W
Lyons, *N.Y., U.S.A.* **78 C8** 43 5N 77 0W
Lyons →, *Australia* **61 E2** 25 2S 115 9 E
Lyons Falls, *U.S.A.* **79 C9** 43 37N 75 22W
Lys = Leie →, *Belgium* **15 C3** 51 2N 3 45 E
Lysva, *Russia* **24 C10** 58 7N 57 49 E
Lysychansk, *Ukraine* **25 E6** 48 55N 38 30 E
Lytham St. Anne's, *U.K.* **10 D4** 53 45N 3 0W
Lyttelton, *N.Z.* **59 K4** 43 35S 172 44 E
Lytton, *Canada* **72 C4** 50 13N 121 31W
Lyubertsy, *Russia* **24 C6** 55 39N 37 50 E
Lyuboml, *Ukraine* **17 C13** 51 11N 24 4 E

M

M.R. Gomez, Presa, *Mexico* **87 B5** 26 10N 99 0W
Ma →, *Vietnam* **38 C5** 19 47N 105 56 E
Ma'adaba, *Jordan* **47 E4** 30 43N 35 47 E
Maamba, *Zambia* **56 B4** 17 17S 26 28 E
Ma'ān, *Jordan* **47 E4** 30 12N 35 44 E
Ma'ān □, *Jordan* **47 F5** 30 0N 36 0 E
Maanselkä, *Finland* **8 C23** 63 52N 28 32 E
Ma'anshan, *China* **33 C6** 31 44N 118 29 E
Maarianhamina, *Finland* **9 F18** 60 5N 19 55 E
Ma'arrat an Nu'mān, *Syria* **44 C3** 35 43N 36 43 E
Maas →, *Neths.* **15 C4** 51 45N 4 32 E
Maaseik, *Belgium* **15 C5** 51 6N 5 45 E
Maasin, *Phil.* **37 B6** 10 8N 124 50 E
Maastricht, *Neths.* **18 A6** 50 50N 5 40 E
Maave, *Mozam.* **57 C5** 21 4S 34 47 E
Mababe Depression, *Botswana* **56 B3** 18 50S 24 15 E
Mabalane, *Mozam.* **57 C5** 23 37S 32 31 E
Mabel L., *Canada* **72 C5** 50 35N 118 43W
Mabenge, *Dem. Rep. of the Congo* **54 B1** 4 15N 24 12 E
Maberly, *Canada* **79 B8** 44 50N 76 32W
Mablethorpe, *U.K.* **10 D8** 53 20N 0 15 E
Maboma, *Dem. Rep. of the Congo* **54 B2** 2 30N 28 10 E
Mac Bac, *Vietnam* **39 H6** 9 46N 106 7 E
Macachín, *Argentina* **94 D3** 37 10S 63 43W
Macaé, *Brazil* **95 A7** 22 20S 41 43W
McAlester, *U.S.A.* **81 H7** 34 56N 95 46W
McAllen, *U.S.A.* **81 M5** 26 12N 98 14W
MacAlpine L., *Canada* **68 B9** 66 40N 102 50W
Macamic, *Canada* **70 C4** 48 45N 79 0W
Macao = Macau, *China* **33 D6** 22 12N 113 33 E
Macapá, *Brazil* **93 C8** 0 5N 51 4W
McArthur →, *Australia* **62 B2** 15 54S 136 40 E
McArthur, Port, *Australia* **62 B2** 16 4S 136 23 E
Macau, *Brazil* **93 E11** 5 15S 36 40W
Macau, *China* **33 D6** 22 12N 113 33 E
McBride, *Canada* **72 C4** 53 20N 120 19W
McCall, *U.S.A.* **82 D5** 44 55N 116 6W
McCamey, *U.S.A.* **81 K3** 31 8N 102 14W
McCammon, *U.S.A.* **82 E7** 42 39N 112 12W
McCauley I., *Canada* **72 C2** 53 40N 130 15W
McCleary, *U.S.A.* **84 C3** 47 3N 123 16W
Macclenny, *U.S.A.* **77 K4** 30 17N 82 7W
Macclesfield, *U.K.* **10 D5** 53 15N 2 8W
M'Clintock Chan., *Canada* **68 A9** 72 0N 102 0W
McClintock Ra., *Australia* **60 C4** 18 44S 127 38 E
McCloud, *U.S.A.* **82 F2** 41 15N 122 8W
McCluer I., *Australia* **60 B5** 11 5S 133 0 E
McClure, *U.S.A.* **78 F7** 40 42N 77 19W
McClure, L., *U.S.A.* **84 H6** 37 35N 120 16W
M'Clure Str., *Canada* **4 B2** 75 0N 119 0W
McClusky, *U.S.A.* **80 B4** 47 29N 100 27W
McComb, *U.S.A.* **81 K9** 31 15N 90 27W
McConaughy, L., *U.S.A.* **80 E4** 41 14N 101 40W
McCook, *U.S.A.* **80 E4** 40 12N 100 38W
McCreary, *Canada* **73 C9** 50 47N 99 29W
McCullough Mt., *U.S.A.* **85 K11** 35 35N 115 13W
McCusker →, *Canada* **73 B7** 55 32N 108 39W
McDame, *Canada* **72 B3** 59 44N 128 59W
McDermitt, *U.S.A.* **82 F5** 41 59N 117 43W
McDonald, *U.S.A.* **78 F4** 40 22N 80 14W
Macdonald, L., *Australia* **60 D4** 23 30S 129 0 E
McDonald Is., *Ind. Oc.* **3 G13** 53 0S 73 0 E
MacDonnell Ranges, *Australia* **60 D5** 23 40S 133 0 E
MacDowell L., *Canada* **70 B1** 52 15N 92 45W
Macduff, *U.K.* **12 D6** 57 40N 2 31W
Macedonia = Makedhonía □, *Greece* **21 D10** 40 39N 22 0 E
Macedonia, *U.S.A.* **78 E3** 41 19N 81 31W
Macedonia ■, *Europe* **21 D9** 41 53N 21 40 E
Maceió, *Brazil* **93 E11** 9 40S 35 41W
Macerata, *Italy* **20 C5** 43 18N 13 27 E
McFarland, *U.S.A.* **85 K7** 35 41N 119 14W
McFarlane →, *Canada* **73 B7** 59 12N 107 58W
Macfarlane, L., *Australia* **63 E2** 32 0S 136 40 E
McGehee, *U.S.A.* **81 J9** 33 38N 91 24W
McGill, *U.S.A.* **82 G6** 39 23N 114 47W
Macgillycuddy's Reeks, *Ireland* **13 E2** 51 58N 9 45W
McGraw, *U.S.A.* **79 D8** 42 36N 76 8W
McGregor, *U.S.A.* **80 D9** 43 1N 91 11W
McGregor Ra., *Australia* **63 D3** 27 0S 142 45 E
Mach, *Pakistan* **40 E5** 29 50N 67 20 E
Māch Kowr, *Iran* **45 E9** 25 48N 61 28 E
Machado = Jiparaná →, *Brazil* **92 E6** 8 3S 62 52W
Machagai, *Argentina* **94 B3** 26 56S 60 2W
Machakos, *Kenya* **54 C4** 1 30S 37 15 E
Machala, *Ecuador* **92 D3** 3 20S 79 57W
Machanga, *Mozam.* **57 C6** 20 59S 35 0 E
Machattie, L., *Australia* **62 C2** 24 50S 139 48 E
Machava, *Mozam.* **57 D5** 25 54S 32 28 E
Machece, *Mozam.* **55 F4** 19 15S 35 32 E
Macheke, *Zimbabwe* **57 B5** 18 5S 31 51 E
Machhu →, *India* **42 H4** 23 6N 70 46 E
Machias, *Maine, U.S.A.* **77 C12** 44 43N 67 28W
Machias, *N.Y., U.S.A.* **78 D6** 42 25N 78 30W
Machichi →, *Canada* **73 B10** 57 3N 92 6W
Machico, *Madeira* **22 D3** 32 43N 16 44W
Machilipatnam, *India* **41 L12** 16 12N 81 8 E
Machiques, *Venezuela* **92 A4** 10 4N 72 34W
Machupicchu, *Peru* **92 F4** 13 8S 72 30W
Machynlleth, *U.K.* **11 E4** 52 35N 3 50W
Macia, *Mozam.* **57 D5** 25 2S 33 8 E
McIlwraith Ra., *Australia* **62 A3** 13 50S 143 20 E
McInnes L., *Canada* **73 C10** 52 13N 93 45W
McIntosh, *U.S.A.* **80 C4** 45 55N 101 21W
McIntosh L., *Canada* **73 B8** 55 45N 105 0W
Macintosh Ra., *Australia* **61 E4** 27 39S 125 32 E
Macintyre →, *Australia* **63 D5** 28 37S 150 47 E
Mackay, *Australia* **62 C4** 21 8S 149 11 E
Mackay, *U.S.A.* **82 E7** 43 55N 113 37W
MacKay →, *Canada* **72 B6** 57 10N 111 38W
Mackay, L., *Australia* **60 D4** 22 30S 129 0 E
McKay Ra., *Australia* **60 D3** 23 0S 122 30 E
McKeesport, *U.S.A.* **78 F5** 40 21N 79 52W
McKellar, *Canada* **78 A5** 45 30N 79 55W
McKenna, *U.S.A.* **84 D4** 46 56N 122 33W
Mackenzie, *Canada* **72 B4** 55 20N 123 5W
McKenzie, *U.S.A.* **77 G1** 36 8N 88 31W
Mackenzie →, *Australia* **62 C4** 23 38S 149 46 E
Mackenzie →, *Canada* **68 B6** 69 10N 134 20W
McKenzie →, *U.S.A.* **82 D2** 44 7N 123 6W
Mackenzie Bay, *Canada* **4 B1** 69 0N 137 30W
Mackenzie City = Linden, *Guyana* **92 B7** 6 0N 58 10W
Mackenzie Mts., *Canada* **68 B6** 64 0N 130 0W
Mackinaw City, *U.S.A.* **76 C3** 45 47N 84 44W
McKinlay, *Australia* **62 C3** 21 16S 141 18 E
McKinlay →, *Australia* **62 C3** 20 50S 141 28 E
McKinley, Mt., *U.S.A.* **68 B4** 63 4N 151 0W
McKinley Sea, *Arctic* **4 A7** 82 0N 0 0W
McKinney, *U.S.A.* **81 J6** 33 12N 96 37W
Mackinnon Road, *Kenya* **54 C4** 3 40S 39 1 E
McKittrick, *U.S.A.* **85 K7** 35 18N 119 37W
Macklin, *Canada* **73 C7** 52 20N 109 56W
Macksville, *Australia* **63 E5** 30 40S 152 56 E
McLaughlin, *U.S.A.* **80 C4** 45 49N 100 49W
Maclean, *Australia* **63 D5** 29 26S 153 16 E
McLean, *U.S.A.* **81 H4** 35 14N 100 36W
McLeansboro, *U.S.A.* **80 F10** 38 6N 88 32W
Maclear, *S. Africa* **57 E4** 31 2S 28 23 E
Macleay →, *Australia* **63 E5** 30 56S 153 0 E
McLennan, *Canada* **72 B5** 55 42N 116 50W
McLeod →, *Canada* **72 C5** 54 9N 115 44W
MacLeod, B., *Canada* **73 A7** 62 53N 110 0W
McLeod, L., *Australia* **61 D1** 24 9S 113 47 E
MacLeod Lake, *Canada* **72 C4** 54 58N 123 0W
McLoughlin, Mt., *U.S.A.* **82 E2** 42 27N 122 19W
McMechen, *U.S.A.* **78 G4** 39 57N 80 44W
McMinnville, *Oreg., U.S.A.* **82 D2** 45 13N 123 12W
McMinnville, *Tenn., U.S.A.* **77 H3** 35 41N 85 46W
McMurdo Sd., *Antarctica* **5 D11** 77 0S 170 0 E
McMurray = Fort McMurray, *Canada* **72 B6** 56 44N 111 7W
McMurray, *U.S.A.* **84 B4** 48 19N 122 14W
Macodoene, *Mozam.* **57 C6** 23 32S 35 5 E
Macomb, *U.S.A.* **80 E9** 40 27N 90 40W
Mâcon, *France* **18 C6** 46 19N 4 50 E
Macon, *Ga., U.S.A.* **77 J4** 32 51N 83 38W
Macon, *Miss., U.S.A.* **77 J1** 33 7N 88 34W
Macon, *Mo., U.S.A.* **80 F8** 39 44N 92 28W
Macossa, *Mozam.* **55 F3** 17 55S 33 56 E
Macoun L., *Canada* **73 B8** 56 32N 103 40W
Macovane, *Mozam.* **57 C6** 21 30S 35 2 E
McPherson, *U.S.A.* **80 F6** 38 22N 97 40W
McPherson Pk., *U.S.A.* **85 L7** 34 53N 119 53W
McPherson Ra., *Australia* **63 D5** 28 15S 153 15 E
Macquarie →, *Australia* **63 E4** 30 5S 147 30 E
Macquarie Harbour, *Australia* **62 G4** 42 15S 145 23 E
Macquarie Is., *Pac. Oc.* **64 N7** 54 36S 158 55 E
MacRobertson Land, *Antarctica* **5 D6** 71 0S 64 0 E
Macroom, *Ireland* **13 E3** 51 54N 8 57W
MacTier, *Canada* **78 A5** 45 9N 79 46W
Macubela, *Mozam.* **55 F4** 16 53S 37 49 E
Macuiza, *Mozam.* **55 F3** 18 7S 34 29 E
Macusani, *Peru* **92 F4** 14 4S 70 29W
Macuse, *Mozam.* **55 F4** 17 45S 37 10 E
Macuspana, *Mexico* **87 D6** 17 46N 92 36W
Macusse, *Angola* **56 B3** 17 48S 20 23 E
Madadeni, *S. Africa* **57 D5** 27 43S 30 3 E
Madagascar ■, *Africa* **57 C8** 20 0S 47 0 E
Madā'in Sālih, *Si. Arabia* **44 E3** 26 46N 37 57 E
Madama, *Niger* **51 D8** 22 0N 13 40 E
Madame I., *Canada* **71 C7** 45 30N 60 58W
Madaripur, *Bangla.* **41 H17** 23 19N 90 15 E
Madauk, *Burma* **41 L20** 17 56N 96 52 E
Madawaska, *Canada* **78 A7** 45 30N 78 0W
Madawaska →, *Canada* **78 A8** 45 27N 76 21W
Madaya, *Burma* **41 H20** 22 12N 96 10 E
Maddalena, *Italy* **20 D3** 41 16N 9 23 E
Madeira, *Atl. Oc.* **22 D3** 32 50N 17 0W
Madeira →, *Brazil* **92 D7** 3 22S 58 45W
Madeleine, Îs. de la, *Canada* **71 C7** 47 30N 61 40W
Madera, *Mexico* **86 B3** 29 12N 108 7W
Madera, *Calif., U.S.A.* **84 J6** 36 57N 120 3W
Madera, *Pa., U.S.A.* **78 F6** 40 49N 78 26W
Madha, *India* **40 L9** 18 0N 75 30 E
Madhavpur, *India* **42 J3** 21 15N 69 58 E
Madhepura, *India* **43 F12** 26 11N 86 23 E
Madhubani, *India* **43 F12** 26 21N 86 7 E
Madhupur, *India* **43 G12** 24 16N 86 39 E
Madhya Pradesh □, *India* **42 J8** 22 50N 78 0 E
Madidi →, *Bolivia* **92 F5** 12 32S 66 52W
Madikeri, *India* **40 N9** 12 30N 75 45 E
Madill, *U.S.A.* **81 H6** 34 6N 96 46W
Madimba, *Dem. Rep. of the Congo* **52 E3** 4 58S 15 5 E
Ma'din, *Syria* **44 C3** 35 45N 39 36 E
Madingou, *Congo* **52 E2** 4 10S 13 33 E
Madirovalo, *Madag.* **57 B8** 16 26S 46 32 E
Madison, *Calif., U.S.A.* **84 G5** 38 41N 121 59W
Madison, *Fla., U.S.A.* **77 K4** 30 28N 83 25W
Madison, *Ind., U.S.A.* **76 F3** 38 44N 85 23W
Madison, *Nebr., U.S.A.* **80 E6** 41 50N 97 27W
Madison, *Ohio, U.S.A.* **78 E3** 41 46N 81 3W
Madison, *S. Dak., U.S.A.* **80 D6** 44 0N 97 7W
Madison, *Wis., U.S.A.* **80 D10** 43 4N 89 24W
Madison →, *U.S.A.* **82 D8** 45 56N 111 31W
Madison Heights, *U.S.A.* **76 G6** 37 25N 79 8W
Madisonville, *Ky., U.S.A.* **76 G2** 37 20N 87 30W
Madisonville, *Tex., U.S.A.* **81 K7** 30 57N 95 55W
Madista, *Botswana* **56 C4** 21 15S 25 6 E
Madiun, *Indonesia* **36 F4** 7 38S 111 32 E
Madoc, *Canada* **78 B7** 44 30N 77 28W
Madona, *Latvia* **9 H22** 56 53N 26 5 E
Madrakah, Ra's al, *Oman* **46 D6** 19 0N 57 50 E
Madras = Chennai, *India* **40 N12** 13 8N 80 19 E
Madras = Tamil Nadu □, *India* **40 P10** 11 0N 77 0 E
Madras, *U.S.A.* **82 D3** 44 38N 121 8W
Madre, Laguna, *U.S.A.* **81 M6** 27 0N 97 30W
Madre, Sierra, *Phil.* **37 A6** 17 0N 122 0 E
Madre de Dios →, *Bolivia* **92 F5** 10 59S 66 8W
Madre de Dios, I., *Chile* **96 G1** 50 20S 75 10W
Madre del Sur, Sierra, *Mexico* **87 D5** 17 30N 100 0W
Madre Occidental, Sierra, *Mexico* **86 B3** 27 0N 107 0W
Madre Oriental, Sierra, *Mexico* **86 C5** 25 0N 100 0W
Madri, *India* **42 G5** 24 16N 73 32 E
Madrid, *Spain* **19 B4** 40 25N 3 45W
Madrid, *U.S.A.* **79 B9** 44 45N 75 8W
Madura, *Australia* **61 F4** 31 55S 127 0 E
Madura, *Indonesia* **37 G15** 7 30S 114 0 E
Madura, Selat, *Indonesia* **37 G15** 7 30S 113 20 E
Madurai, *India* **40 Q11** 9 55N 78 10 E
Madurantakam, *India* **40 N11** 12 30N 79 50 E
Mae Chan, *Thailand* **38 B2** 20 9N 99 52 E
Mae Hong Son, *Thailand* **38 C2** 19 16N 97 56 E
Mae Khlong →, *Thailand* **38 F3** 13 24N 100 0 E
Mae Phrik, *Thailand* **38 D2** 17 27N 99 7 E
Mae Ramat, *Thailand* **38 D2** 16 58N 98 31 E
Mae Rim, *Thailand* **38 C2** 18 54N 98 57 E
Mae Sot, *Thailand* **38 D2** 16 43N 98 34 E
Mae Suai, *Thailand* **38 C2** 19 39N 99 33 E
Mae Tha, *Thailand* **38 C2** 18 28N 99 8 E
Maebashi, *Japan* **31 F9** 36 24N 139 4 E
Maesteg, *U.K.* **11 F4** 51 36N 3 40W
Maestra, Sierra, *Cuba* **88 B4** 20 15N 77 0W
Maevatanana, *Madag.* **57 B8** 16 56S 46 49 E
Mafeking = Mafikeng, *S. Africa* **56 D4** 25 50S 25 38 E
Mafeking, *Canada* **73 C8** 52 40N 101 10W
Mafeteng, *Lesotho* **56 D4** 29 51S 27 15 E
Maffra, *Australia* **63 F4** 37 53S 146 58 E
Mafia I., *Tanzania* **54 D4** 7 45S 39 50 E
Mafikeng, *S. Africa* **56 D4** 25 50S 25 38 E
Mafra, *Brazil* **95 B6** 26 10S 49 55W
Mafra, *Portugal* **19 C1** 38 55N 9 20W
Mafungabusi Plateau, *Zimbabwe* **55 F2** 18 30S 29 8 E
Magadan, *Russia* **27 D16** 59 38N 150 50 E
Magadi, *Kenya* **54 C4** 1 54S 36 19 E
Magadi, L., *Kenya* **54 C4** 1 54S 36 19 E
Magaliesburg, *S. Africa* **57 D4** 26 0S 27 32 E
Magallanes, Estrecho de, *Chile* **96 G2** 52 30S 75 0W
Magangué, *Colombia* **92 B4** 9 14N 74 45W
Magdalen Is. = Madeleine, Îs. de la, *Canada* **71 C7** 47 30N 61 40W
Magdalena, *Argentina* **94 D4** 35 5S 57 30W
Magdalena, *Bolivia* **92 F6** 13 13S 63 57W
Magdalena, *Mexico* **86 A2** 30 50N 112 0W
Magdalena, *U.S.A.* **83 J10** 34 7N 107 15W
Magdalena →, *Colombia* **92 A4** 11 6N 74 51W
Magdalena →, *Mexico* **86 A2** 30 40N 112 25W
Magdalena, B., *Mexico* **86 C2** 24 30N 112 10W
Magdalena, Llano de la, *Mexico* **86 C2** 25 0N 111 30W
Magdeburg, *Germany* **16 B6** 52 7N 11 38 E
Magdelaine Cays, *Australia* **62 B5** 16 33S 150 18 E
Magee, *U.S.A.* **81 K10** 31 52N 89 44W
Magelang, *Indonesia* **36 F4** 7 29S 110 13 E
Magellan's Str. = Magallanes, Estrecho de, *Chile* **96 G2** 52 30S 75 0W
Magenta, L., *Australia* **61 F2** 33 30S 119 2 E
Magerøya, *Norway* **8 A21** 71 3N 25 40 E
Maggiore, Lago, *Italy* **18 D8** 45 57N 8 39 E
Maghâgha, *Egypt* **51 C12** 28 38N 30 50 E
Magherafelt, *U.K.* **13 B5** 54 45N 6 37W
Maghreb, *N. Afr.* **50 B5** 32 0N 4 0W
Magistralnyy, *Russia* **27 D11** 56 16N 107 36 E
Magnetic Pole (North) = North Magnetic Pole, *Canada* **4 B2** 77 58N 102 8W
Magnetic Pole (South) = South Magnetic Pole, *Antarctica* **5 C9** 64 8S 138 8 E
Magnitogorsk, *Russia* **24 D10** 53 27N 59 4 E
Magnolia, *Ark., U.S.A.* **81 J8** 33 16N 93 14W
Magnolia, *Miss., U.S.A.* **81 K9** 31 9N 90 28W
Magog, *Canada* **79 A12** 45 18N 72 9W
Magoro, *Uganda* **54 B3** 1 45N 34 12 E
Magosa = Famagusta, *Cyprus* **23 D12** 35 8N 33 55 E
Magouládhes, *Greece* **23 A3** 39 45N 19 42 E
Magoye, *Zambia* **55 F2** 16 1S 27 30 E
Magozal, *Mexico* **87 C5** 21 34N 97 59W
Magpie, L., *Canada* **71 B7** 51 0N 64 41W
Magrath, *Canada* **72 D6** 49 25N 112 50W
Maguarinho, C., *Brazil* **93 D9** 0 15S 48 30W
Mague, *Mozam.* **57 D5** 25 2S 32 40 E
Mağusa = Famagusta, *Cyprus* **23 D12** 35 8N 33 55 E
Maguse L., *Canada* **73 A9** 61 40N 95 10W
Maguse Pt., *Canada* **73 A10** 61 20N 93 50W
Magvana, *India* **42 H3** 23 13N 69 22 E
Magwe, *Burma* **41 J19** 20 10N 95 0 E
Maha Sarakham, *Thailand* **38 D4** 16 12N 103 16 E
Mahābād, *Iran* **44 B5** 36 50N 45 45 E
Mahabharat Lekh, *Nepal* **43 E10** 28 30N 82 0 E
Mahabo, *Madag.* **57 C7** 20 23S 44 40 E
Mahadeo Hills, *India* **43 H8** 22 20N 78 30 E
Mahaffey, *U.S.A.* **78 F6** 40 53N 78 44W
Mahagi, *Dem. Rep. of the Congo* **54 B3** 2 20N 31 0 E
Mahajamba →, *Madag.* **57 B8** 15 33S 47 8 E
Mahajamba, Helodranon' i, *Madag.* **57 B8** 15 24S 47 5 E
Mahajan, *India* **42 E5** 28 48N 73 56 E
Mahajanga, *Madag.* **57 B8** 15 40S 46 25 E
Mahajanga □, *Madag.* **57 B8** 17 0S 47 0 E
Mahajilo →, *Madag.* **57 B8** 19 42S 45 22 E
Mahakam →, *Indonesia* **36 E5** 0 35S 117 17 E
Mahalapye, *Botswana* **56 C4** 23 1S 26 51 E
Maḩallāt, *Iran* **45 C6** 33 55N 50 30 E
Māhān, *Iran* **45 D8** 30 5N 57 18 E
Mahan →, *India* **43 H10** 23 30N 82 50 E
Mahanadi →, *India* **41 J15** 20 20N 86 25 E
Mahananda →, *India* **43 G12** 25 12N 87 52 E
Mahanoro, *Madag.* **57 B8** 19 54S 48 48 E
Mahanoy City, *U.S.A.* **79 F8** 40 49N 76 9W
Maharashtra □, *India* **40 J9** 20 30N 75 30 E
Mahari Mts., *Tanzania* **54 D3** 6 20S 30 0 E
Mahasham, W. →, *Egypt* **47 E3** 30 15N 34 10 E
Mahasoa, *Madag.* **57 C8** 22 12S 46 6 E
Mahasolo, *Madag.* **57 B8** 19 7S 46 22 E
Mahattat ash Shīdīyah, *Jordan* **47 F4** 29 55N 35 55 E
Mahattat 'Unayzah, *Jordan* **47 E4** 30 30N 35 47 E
Mahavavy →, *Madag.* **57 B8** 15 57S 45 54 E
Mahaxay, *Laos* **38 D5** 17 22N 105 12 E
Mahbubnagar, *India* **40 L10** 16 45N 77 59 E
Maḩḑah, *Oman* **45 E7** 24 24N 55 59 E
Mahdia, *Tunisia* **51 A8** 35 28N 11 0 E
Mahe, *India* **43 C8** 33 10N 78 32 E
Mahendragarh, *India* **42 E7** 28 17N 76 14 E
Mahenge, *Tanzania* **55 D4** 8 45S 36 41 E
Maheno, *N.Z.* **59 L3** 45 10S 170 50 E
Mahesana, *India* **42 H5** 23 39N 72 26 E
Maheshwar, *India* **42 H6** 22 11N 75 35 E
Mahgawan, *India* **43 F8** 26 29N 78 37 E
Mahi →, *India* **42 H5** 22 15N 72 55 E
Mahia Pen., *N.Z.* **59 H6** 39 9S 177 55 E
Mahilyow, *Belarus* **17 B16** 53 55N 30 18 E
Mahmud Kot, *Pakistan* **42 D4** 30 16N 71 0 E
Mahnomen, *U.S.A.* **80 B7** 47 19N 95 58W
Mahoba, *India* **43 G8** 25 15N 79 55 E
Mahón = Maó, *Spain* **22 B11** 39 53N 4 16 E
Mahone Bay, *Canada* **71 D7** 44 30N 64 20W
Mahopac, *U.S.A.* **79 E11** 41 22N 73 45W
Mahuva, *India* **42 J4** 21 5N 71 48 E
Mai-Ndombe, L., *Dem. Rep. of the Congo* **52 E3** 2 0S 18 20 E
Mai-Sai, *Thailand* **38 B2** 20 20N 99 55 E
Maicurú →, *Brazil* **93 D8** 2 14S 54 17W
Maidan Khula, *Afghan.* **42 C3** 33 36N 69 50 E
Maidenhead, *U.K.* **11 F7** 51 31N 0 42W
Maidstone, *Canada* **73 C7** 53 5N 109 20W
Maidstone, *U.K.* **11 F8** 51 16N 0 32 E
Maiduguri, *Nigeria* **51 F8** 12 0N 13 20 E
Maihar, *India* **43 G9** 24 16N 80 45 E
Maijdi, *Bangla.* **41 H17** 22 48N 91 10 E
Maikala Ra., *India* **41 J12** 22 0N 81 0 E
Mailani, *India* **43 E9** 28 17N 80 21 E
Mailsi, *Pakistan* **42 E5** 29 48N 72 15 E
Main →, *Germany* **16 C5** 50 0N 8 18 E
Main →, *U.K.* **13 B5** 54 48N 6 18W
Maine, *France* **18 C3** 48 20N 0 15W
Maine □, *U.S.A.* **77 C11** 45 20N 69 0W
Maine →, *Ireland* **13 D2** 52 9N 9 45W
Maingkwan, *Burma* **41 F20** 26 15N 96 37 E
Mainit, L., *Phil.* **37 C7** 9 31N 125 30 E
Mainland, *Orkney, U.K.* **12 C5** 58 59N 3 8W
Mainland, *Shet., U.K.* **12 A7** 60 15N 1 22W
Mainoru, *Australia* **62 A1** 14 0S 134 6 E
Mainpuri, *India* **43 F8** 27 18N 79 4 E
Maintirano, *Madag.* **57 B7** 18 3S 44 1 E
Mainz, *Germany* **16 C5** 50 1N 8 14 E
Maipú, *Argentina* **94 D4** 36 52S 57 50W
Maiquetía, *Venezuela* **92 A5** 10 36N 66 57W
Mairabari, *India* **41 F18** 26 30N 92 22 E
Maisí, *Cuba* **89 B5** 20 17N 74 9W
Maisí, Pta. de, *Cuba* **89 B5** 20 10N 74 10W
Maitland, *N.S.W., Australia* **63 E5** 32 33S 151 36 E
Maitland, *S. Austral., Australia* **63 E2** 34 23S 137 40 E
Maitland →, *Canada* **78 C3** 43 45N 81 43W
Maiz, Is. del, *Nic.* **88 D3** 12 15N 83 4W
Maizuru, *Japan* **31 G7** 35 25N 135 22 E
Majalengka, *Indonesia* **37 G13** 6 50S 108 13 E
Majene, *Indonesia* **37 E5** 3 38S 118 57 E
Majorca = Mallorca, *Spain* **22 B10** 39 30N 3 0 E
Makaha, *Zimbabwe* **57 B5** 17 20S 32 39 E
Makalamabedi, *Botswana* **56 C3** 20 19S 23 51 E
Makale, *Indonesia* **37 E5** 3 6S 119 51 E
Makamba, *Burundi* **54 C2** 4 8S 29 49 E
Makarikari = Makgadikgadi Salt Pans, *Botswana* **56 C4** 20 40S 25 45 E
Makarovo, *Russia* **27 D11** 57 40N 107 45 E
Makasar = Ujung Pandang, *Indonesia* **37 F5** 5 10S 119 20 E
Makasar, Selat, *Indonesia* **37 E5** 1 0S 118 20 E
Makasar, Str. of = Makasar, Selat, *Indonesia* **37 E5** 1 0S 118 20 E
Makat, *Kazakstan* **25 E9** 47 39N 53 19 E
Makedhonía □, *Greece* **21 D10** 40 39N 22 0 E
Makedonija = Macedonia ■, *Europe* **21 D9** 41 53N 21 40 E
Makeyevka = Makiyivka, *Ukraine* **25 E6** 48 0N 38 0 E
Makgadikgadi Salt Pans, *Botswana* **56 C4** 20 40S 25 45 E
Makhachkala, *Russia* **25 F8** 43 0N 47 30 E
Makhmūr, *Iraq* **44 C4** 35 46N 43 35 E
Makian, *Indonesia* **37 D7** 0 20N 127 20 E
Makindu, *Kenya* **54 C4** 2 18S 37 50 E
Makinsk, *Kazakstan* **26 D8** 52 37N 70 26 E
Makiyivka, *Ukraine* **25 E6** 48 0N 38 0 E
Makkah, *Si. Arabia* **46 C2** 21 30N 39 54 E
Makkovik, *Canada* **71 A8** 55 10N 59 10W
Makó, *Hungary* **17 E11** 46 14N 20 33 E
Makokou, *Gabon* **52 D2** 0 40N 12 50 E
Makongo, *Dem. Rep. of the Congo* **54 B2** 3 25N 26 17 E
Makoro, *Dem. Rep. of the Congo* **54 B2** 3 10N 29 59 E
Makrai, *India* **40 H10** 22 2N 77 0 E
Makran Coast Range, *Pakistan* **40 G4** 25 40N 64 0 E
Makrana, *India* **42 F6** 27 2N 74 46 E
Makriyialos, *Greece* **23 D7** 35 2N 25 59 E
Mākū, *Iran* **44 B5** 39 15N 44 31 E
Makunda, *Botswana* **56 C3** 22 30S 20 7 E
Makurazaki, *Japan* **31 J5** 31 15N 130 20 E
Makurdi, *Nigeria* **50 G7** 7 43N 8 35 E
Makūyeh, *Iran* **45 D7** 28 7N 53 9 E
Makwassie, *S. Africa* **56 D4** 27 17S 26 0 E
Makwiro, *Zimbabwe* **57 B5** 17 58S 30 25 E

Mbala

Margaret L., Canada 72 B5 58 56N 115 25W
Margaret River, Australia 61 F2 33 57S 115 4 E
Margarita, I. de, Venezuela 92 A6 11 0N 64 0W
Margaritovo, Russia 30 C7 43 25N 134 45 E
Margate, S. Africa 57 E5 30 50S 30 20 E
Margate, U.K. 11 F9 51 23N 1 23 E
Mārgow, Dasht-e, Afghan. 40 D3 30 40N 62 30 E
Marguerite, Canada 72 C4 52 30N 122 25W
Mari El □, Russia 24 C8 56 30N 48 0 E
Mari Indus, Pakistan 42 C4 32 57N 71 34 E
Mari Republic = Mari El □, Russia 24 C8 56 30N 48 0 E
María Elena, Chile 94 A2 22 18S 69 40W
María Grande, Argentina 94 C4 31 45S 59 55W
Maria I., N. Terr., Australia 62 A2 14 52S 135 45 E
Maria I., Tas., Australia 62 G4 42 35S 148 0 E
Maria van Diemen, C., N.Z. 59 F4 34 29S 172 40 E
Mariakani, Kenya 54 C4 3 50S 39 27 E
Marian, Australia 62 C4 21 9S 148 57 E
Marian L., Canada 72 A5 63 0N 116 15W
Mariana Trench, Pac. Oc. 28 H18 13 0N 145 0 E
Marianao, Cuba 88 B3 23 8N 82 24W
Marianna, Ark., U.S.A. 81 H9 34 46N 90 46W
Marianna, Fla., U.S.A. 77 K3 30 46N 85 14W
Marias →, U.S.A. 82 C8 47 56N 110 30W
Mariato, Punta, Panama 88 E3 7 12N 80 52W
Maribor, Slovenia 16 E8 46 36N 15 40 E
Marico →, Africa 56 C4 23 35S 26 57 E
Maricopa, Ariz., U.S.A. 83 K7 33 4N 112 3W
Maricopa, Calif., U.S.A. 85 K7 35 4N 119 24W
Marié →, Brazil 92 D5 0 27S 66 26W
Marie Byrd Land, Antarctica 5 D14 79 30S 125 0W
Marie-Galante, Guadeloupe 89 C7 15 56N 61 16W
Mariecourt = Kangiqsujuaq, Canada 69 B12 61 30N 72 0W
Mariembourg, Belgium 15 D4 50 6N 4 31 E
Mariental, Namibia 56 C2 24 36S 18 0 E
Marienville, U.S.A. 78 E5 41 28N 79 8W
Mariestad, Sweden 9 G15 58 43N 13 50 E
Marietta, Ga., U.S.A. 77 J3 33 57N 84 33W
Marietta, Ohio, U.S.A. 76 F5 39 25N 81 27W
Marieville, Canada 79 A11 45 26N 73 10W
Mariinsk, Russia 26 D9 56 10N 87 20 E
Marijampolė, Lithuania 9 J20 54 33N 23 19 E
Marília, Brazil 95 A6 22 13S 50 0W
Marín, Spain 19 A1 42 23N 8 42W
Marina, U.S.A. 84 J5 36 41N 121 48W
Marinduque, Phil. 37 B6 13 25N 122 0 E
Marine City, U.S.A. 78 D2 42 43N 82 30W
Marinette, U.S.A. 76 C2 45 6N 87 38W
Maringá, Brazil 95 A5 23 26S 52 2W
Marion, Ala., U.S.A. 77 J2 32 38N 87 19W
Marion, Ill., U.S.A. 81 G10 37 44N 88 56W
Marion, Ind., U.S.A. 76 E3 40 32N 85 40W
Marion, Iowa, U.S.A. 80 D9 42 2N 91 36W
Marion, Kans., U.S.A. 80 F6 38 21N 97 1W
Marion, N.C., U.S.A. 77 H5 35 41N 82 1W
Marion, Ohio, U.S.A. 76 E4 40 35N 83 8W
Marion, S.C., U.S.A. 77 H6 34 11N 79 24W
Marion, Va., U.S.A. 77 G5 36 50N 81 31W
Marion, L., U.S.A. 77 J5 33 28N 80 10W
Mariposa, U.S.A. 84 H7 37 29N 119 58W
Mariscal Estigarribia, Paraguay 94 A3 22 3S 60 40W
Maritime Alps = Maritimes, Alpes, Europe 18 D7 44 10N 7 10 E
Maritimes, Alpes, Europe 18 D7 44 10N 7 10 E
Maritsa = Évros →, Greece 21 D12 41 40N 26 34 E
Maritsá, Greece 23 C10 36 22N 28 8 E
Mariupol, Ukraine 25 E6 47 5N 37 31 E
Marīvān, Iran 44 C5 35 30N 46 25 E
Marj 'Uyūn, Lebanon 47 B4 33 20N 35 35 E
Marka = Merca, Somali Rep. 46 G3 1 48N 44 50 E
Markazī □, Iran 45 C6 35 0N 49 30 E
Markdale, Canada 78 B4 44 19N 80 39W
Marked Tree, U.S.A. 81 H9 35 32N 90 25W
Market Drayton, U.K. 10 E5 52 54N 2 29W
Market Harborough, U.K. 11 E7 52 29N 0 55W
Market Rasen, U.K. 10 D7 53 24N 0 20W
Markham, Canada 78 C5 43 52N 79 16W
Markham, Mt., Antarctica 5 E11 83 0S 164 0 E
Markleeville, U.S.A. 84 G7 38 42N 119 47W
Markovo, Russia 27 C17 64 40N 170 24 E
Marks, Russia 24 D8 51 45N 46 50 E
Marksville, U.S.A. 81 K8 31 8N 92 4W
Marla, Australia 63 D1 27 19S 133 33 E
Marlbank, Canada 78 B7 44 26N 77 6W
Marlboro, Mass., U.S.A. 79 D13 42 19N 71 33W
Marlboro, N.Y., U.S.A. 79 E11 41 36N 73 59W
Marlborough, Australia 62 C4 22 46S 149 52 E
Marlborough, U.K. 11 F6 51 25N 1 43W
Marlborough Downs, U.K. 11 F6 51 27N 1 53W
Marlin, U.S.A. 81 K6 31 18N 96 54W
Marlow, U.S.A. 81 H6 34 39N 97 58W
Marmagao, India 40 M8 15 25N 73 56 E
Marmara, Turkey 21 D12 40 35N 27 34 E
Marmara, Sea of = Marmara Denizi, Turkey 21 D13 40 45N 28 15 E
Marmara Denizi, Turkey 21 D13 40 45N 28 15 E
Marmaris, Turkey 21 F13 36 50N 28 14 E
Marmion, Mt., Australia 61 E2 29 16S 119 50 E
Marmion L., Canada 70 C1 48 55N 91 20W
Marmolada, Mte., Italy 20 A4 46 26N 11 51 E
Marmora, Canada 78 B7 44 28N 77 41W
Marne →, France 18 B5 48 48N 2 24 E
Maroala, Madag. 57 B8 15 23S 47 59 E
Maroantsetra, Madag. 57 B8 15 26S 49 44 E
Maroelaboom, Namibia 56 B2 19 15S 18 53 E
Marofandilia, Madag. 57 C7 20 7S 44 34 E
Marolambo, Madag. 57 C8 20 2S 48 7 E
Maromandia, Madag. 57 A8 14 13S 48 5 E
Marondera, Zimbabwe 55 F3 18 5S 31 42 E
Maroni →, Fr. Guiana 93 B8 5 30N 54 0W
Maroochydore, Australia 63 D5 26 29S 153 5 E
Maroona, Australia 63 F3 37 27S 142 54 E
Marosakoa, Madag. 57 B8 15 26S 46 38 E
Maroseranana, Madag. 57 B8 18 32S 48 51 E
Marotandrano, Madag. 57 B8 16 10S 48 50 E
Marotaolano, Madag. 57 A8 12 47S 49 15 E
Maroua, Cameroon 51 F8 10 40N 14 20 E
Marovato, Madag. 57 B8 15 48S 48 5 E
Marovoay, Madag. 57 B8 16 6S 46 39 E
Marquard, S. Africa 56 D4 28 40S 27 28 E
Marquesas Is. = Marquises, Is., Pac. Oc. 65 H14 9 30S 140 0W
Marquette, U.S.A. 76 B2 46 33N 87 24W
Marquises, Is., Pac. Oc. 65 H14 9 30S 140 0W
Marra, Djebel, Sudan 51 F10 13 10N 24 22 E
Marracuene, Mozam. 57 D5 25 45S 32 35 E
Marrakech, Morocco 50 B4 31 9N 8 0W
Marrawah, Australia 62 G3 40 55S 144 42 E
Marree, Australia 63 D2 29 39S 138 1 E
Marrero, U.S.A. 81 L9 29 54N 90 6W
Marrimane, Mozam. 57 C5 22 58S 33 34 E
Marromeu, Mozam. 57 B6 18 15S 36 25 E
Marrowie Cr. →, Australia 63 E4 33 23S 145 40 E
Marrubane, Mozam. 55 F4 18 0S 37 0 E
Marrupa, Mozam. 55 E4 13 8S 37 30 E
Mars Hill, U.S.A. 77 B12 46 31N 67 52W
Marsá Matrûh, Egypt 51 B11 31 19N 27 9 E
Marsabit, Kenya 54 B4 2 18N 38 0 E
Marsala, Italy 20 F5 37 48N 12 26 E
Marsalforn, Malta 23 C1 36 4N 14 16 E
Marsden, Australia 63 E4 33 47S 147 32 E
Marseille, France 18 E6 43 18N 5 23 E
Marseilles = Marseille, France 18 E6 43 18N 5 23 E
Marsh I., U.S.A. 81 L9 29 34N 91 53W
Marshall, Ark., U.S.A. 81 H8 35 55N 92 38W
Marshall, Mich., U.S.A. 76 D3 42 16N 84 58W
Marshall, Minn., U.S.A. 80 C7 44 25N 95 45W
Marshall, Mo., U.S.A. 80 F8 39 7N 93 12W
Marshall, Tex., U.S.A. 81 J7 32 33N 94 23W
Marshall →, Australia 62 C2 22 59S 136 59 E
Marshall Is. ■, Pac. Oc. 64 G9 9 0N 171 0 E
Marshalltown, U.S.A. 80 D8 42 3N 92 55W
Marshbrook, Zimbabwe 57 B5 18 33S 31 9 E
Marshfield, Mo., U.S.A. 81 G8 37 15N 92 54W
Marshfield, Vt., U.S.A. 79 B12 44 20N 72 20W
Marshfield, Wis., U.S.A. 80 C9 44 40N 90 10W
Marshūn, Iran 45 B6 36 19N 49 23 E
Märsta, Sweden 9 G17 59 37N 17 52 E
Mart, U.S.A. 81 K6 31 33N 96 50W
Martaban, Burma 41 L20 16 30N 97 35 E
Martaban, G. of, Burma 41 L20 16 5N 96 30 E
Martapura, Kalimantan, Indonesia 36 E4 3 22S 114 47 E
Martapura, Sumatera, Indonesia 36 E2 4 19S 104 22 E
Martelange, Belgium 15 E5 49 49N 5 43 E
Martha's Vineyard, U.S.A. 79 E14 41 25N 70 38W
Martigny, Switz. 18 C7 46 6N 7 3 E
Martigues, France 18 E6 43 24N 5 4 E
Martin, Slovak Rep. 17 D10 49 6N 18 58 E
Martin, S. Dak., U.S.A. 80 D4 43 11N 101 44W
Martin, Tenn., U.S.A. 81 G10 36 21N 88 51W
Martin, L., U.S.A. 77 J3 32 41N 85 55W
Martina Franca, Italy 20 D7 40 42N 17 20 E
Martinborough, N.Z. 59 J5 41 14S 175 29 E
Martinez, Calif., U.S.A. 84 G4 38 1N 122 8W
Martinez, Ga., U.S.A. 77 J4 33 31N 82 4W
Martinique ■, W. Indies 89 D7 14 40N 61 0W
Martinique Passage, W. Indies 89 C7 15 15N 61 0W
Martinópolis, Brazil 95 A5 22 11S 51 12W
Martins Ferry, U.S.A. 78 F4 40 6N 80 44W
Martinsburg, Pa., U.S.A. 78 F6 40 19N 78 20W
Martinsburg, W. Va., U.S.A. 76 F7 39 27N 77 58W
Martinsville, Ind., U.S.A. 76 F2 39 26N 86 25W
Martinsville, Va., U.S.A. 77 G6 36 41N 79 52W
Marton, N.Z. 59 J5 40 4S 175 23 E
Martos, Spain 19 D4 37 44N 3 58W
Marudi, Malaysia 36 D4 4 11N 114 19 E
Maruf, Afghan. 40 D5 31 30N 67 6 E
Marugame, Japan 31 G6 34 15N 133 40 E
Marunga, Angola 56 B3 17 28S 20 2 E
Marungu, Mts., Dem. Rep. of the Congo 54 D3 7 30S 30 0 E
Marv Dasht, Iran 45 D7 29 50N 52 40 E
Marvast, Iran 45 D7 30 30N 54 15 E
Marvel Loch, Australia 61 F2 31 28S 119 29 E
Marwar, India 42 G5 25 43N 73 45 E
Mary, Turkmenistan 26 F7 37 40N 61 50 E
Maryborough = Port Laoise, Ireland 13 C4 53 2N 7 18W
Maryborough, Queens., Australia 63 D5 25 31S 152 37 E
Maryborough, Vic., Australia 63 F3 37 0S 143 44 E
Maryfield, Canada 73 D8 49 50N 101 35W
Maryland □, U.S.A. 76 F7 39 0N 76 30W
Maryland Junction, Zimbabwe 55 F3 17 45S 30 31 E
Maryport, U.K. 10 C4 54 44N 3 28W
Mary's Harbour, Canada 71 B8 52 18N 55 51W
Marystown, Canada 71 C8 47 10N 55 10W
Marysville, Canada 72 D5 49 35N 116 0W
Marysville, Calif., U.S.A. 84 F5 39 9N 121 35W
Marysville, Kans., U.S.A. 80 F6 39 51N 96 39W
Marysville, Mich., U.S.A. 78 D2 42 54N 82 29W
Marysville, Ohio, U.S.A. 76 E4 40 14N 83 22W
Marysville, Wash., U.S.A. 84 B4 48 3N 122 11W
Maryville, Mo., U.S.A. 80 E7 40 21N 94 52W
Maryville, Tenn., U.S.A. 77 H4 35 46N 83 58W
Marzūq, Libya 51 C8 25 53N 13 57 E
Masahunga, Tanzania 54 C3 2 6S 33 18 E
Masai Steppe, Tanzania 54 C4 4 30S 36 30 E
Masaka, Uganda 54 C3 0 21S 31 45 E
Masalembo, Kepulauan, Indonesia 36 F4 5 35S 114 30 E
Masalima, Kepulauan, Indonesia 36 F5 5 4S 117 5 E
Masamba, Indonesia 37 E6 2 30S 120 15 E
Masan, S. Korea 35 G15 35 11N 128 32 E
Masandam, Ra's, Oman 46 B6 26 30N 56 30 E
Masasi, Tanzania 55 E4 10 45S 38 52 E
Masaya, Nic. 88 D2 12 0N 86 7W
Masbate, Phil. 37 B6 12 21N 123 36 E
Mascara, Algeria 50 A6 35 26N 0 6 E
Mascota, Mexico 86 C4 20 30N 104 50W
Masela, Indonesia 37 F7 8 9S 129 51 E
Maseru, Lesotho 56 D4 29 18S 27 30 E
Mashaba, Zimbabwe 55 G3 20 2S 30 29 E
Mashābih, Si. Arabia 44 E3 25 35N 36 30 E
Masherbrum, Pakistan 43 B7 35 38N 76 18 E
Mashhad, Iran 45 B8 36 20N 59 35 E
Mashīz, Iran 45 D8 29 56N 56 37 E
Māshkel, Hāmūn-i-, Pakistan 40 E3 28 20N 62 56 E
Mashki Chāh, Pakistan 40 E3 29 5N 62 30 E
Mashonaland, Zimbabwe 53 H6 16 30S 31 0 E
Mashonaland Central □, Zimbabwe 57 B5 17 30S 31 0 E
Mashonaland East □, Zimbabwe 57 B5 18 0S 32 0 E
Mashonaland West □, Zimbabwe 57 B4 17 30S 29 30 E
Mashrakh, India 43 F11 26 7N 84 48 E
Masindi, Uganda 54 B3 1 40N 31 43 E
Masindi Port, Uganda 54 B3 1 43N 32 2 E
Maṣīrah, Oman 46 C6 21 0N 58 50 E
Maṣīrah, Khalīj, Oman 46 C6 20 10N 58 10 E
Masisi, Dem. Rep. of the Congo 54 C2 1 23S 28 49 E
Masjed Soleyman, Iran 45 D6 31 55N 49 18 E
Mask, L., Ireland 13 C2 53 36N 9 22W
Maskin, Oman 45 F8 23 30N 56 50 E
Masoala, Tanjon' i, Madag. 57 B9 15 59S 50 13 E
Masoarivo, Madag. 57 B7 19 3S 44 19 E
Masohi = Amahai, Indonesia 37 E7 3 20S 128 55 E
Masomeloka, Madag. 57 C8 20 17S 48 37 E
Mason, Nev., U.S.A. 84 G7 38 56N 119 8W
Mason, Tex., U.S.A. 81 K5 30 45N 99 14W
Mason City, U.S.A. 80 D8 43 9N 93 12W
Maspalomas, Canary Is. 22 G4 27 46N 15 35W
Maspalomas, Pta., Canary Is. 22 G4 27 43N 15 36W
Masqat, Oman 46 C6 23 37N 58 36 E
Massa, Italy 18 D9 44 1N 10 9 E
Massachusetts □, U.S.A. 79 D13 42 30N 72 0W
Massachusetts B., U.S.A. 79 D14 42 20N 70 50W
Massakory, Chad 51 F9 13 0N 15 49 E
Massanella, Spain 22 B9 39 48N 2 51 E
Massangena, Mozam. 57 C5 21 34S 33 0 E
Massango, Angola 52 F3 8 2S 16 21 E
Massawa = Mitsiwa, Eritrea 46 D2 15 35N 39 25 E
Massena, U.S.A. 79 B10 44 56N 74 54W
Massénya, Chad 51 F9 11 21N 16 9 E
Masset, Canada 72 C2 54 2N 132 10W
Massif Central, France 18 D5 44 55N 3 0 E
Massillon, U.S.A. 78 F3 40 48N 81 32W
Massinga, Mozam. 57 C6 23 15S 35 22 E
Massingir, Mozam. 57 C5 23 51S 32 4 E
Masson, Canada 79 A9 45 32N 75 25W
Masson I., Antarctica 5 C7 66 10S 93 20 E
Mastanli = Momchilgrad, Bulgaria 21 D11 41 33N 25 23 E
Masterton, N.Z. 59 J5 40 56S 175 39 E
Mastic, U.S.A. 79 F12 40 47N 72 54W
Mastuj, Pakistan 43 A5 36 20N 72 36 E
Mastung, Pakistan 40 E5 29 50N 66 56 E
Masty, Belarus 17 B13 53 27N 24 38 E
Masuda, Japan 31 G5 34 40N 131 51 E
Masvingo, Zimbabwe 55 G3 20 8S 30 49 E
Masvingo □, Zimbabwe 55 G3 21 0S 31 30 E
Maṣyāf, Syria 44 C3 35 4N 36 20 E
Matabeleland, Zimbabwe 53 H5 18 0S 27 0 E
Matabeleland North □, Zimbabwe 55 F2 19 0S 28 0 E
Matabeleland South □, Zimbabwe 55 G2 21 0S 29 0 E
Matachewan, Canada 70 C3 47 56N 80 39W
Matadi, Dem. Rep. of the Congo 52 F2 5 52S 13 31 E
Matagalpa, Nic. 88 D2 13 0N 85 58W
Matagami, Canada 70 C4 49 45N 77 34W
Matagami, L., Canada 70 C4 49 50N 77 40W
Matagorda B., U.S.A. 81 L6 28 40N 96 0W
Matagorda I., U.S.A. 81 L6 28 15N 96 30W
Matak, Indonesia 39 L6 3 18N 106 16 E
Mátala, Greece 23 E6 34 59N 24 45 E
Matam, Senegal 50 E3 15 34N 13 17W
Matamoros, Campeche, Mexico 87 D6 18 50N 90 50W
Matamoros, Coahuila, Mexico 86 B4 25 33N 103 15W
Matamoros, Tamaulipas, Mexico 87 B5 25 50N 97 30W
Ma'ṭan as Sarra, Libya 51 D10 21 45N 22 0 E
Matandu →, Tanzania 55 D3 8 45S 34 19 E
Matane, Canada 71 C6 48 50N 67 33W
Matanomadh, India 42 H3 23 33N 68 57 E
Matanzas, Cuba 88 B3 23 0N 81 40W
Matapa, Botswana 56 C3 23 11S 24 39 E
Matapan, C. = Taínaron, Ákra, Greece 21 F10 36 22N 22 27 E
Matapédia, Canada 71 C6 48 0N 66 59W
Matara, Sri Lanka 40 S12 5 58N 80 30 E
Mataram, Indonesia 36 F5 8 35S 116 7 E
Matarani, Peru 92 G4 17 0S 72 10W
Mataranka, Australia 60 B5 14 55S 133 4 E
Matarma, Râs, Egypt 47 E1 30 27N 32 44 E
Mataró, Spain 19 B7 41 32N 2 29 E
Matatiele, S. Africa 57 E4 30 20S 28 49 E
Mataura, N.Z. 59 M2 46 11S 168 51 E
Matehuala, Mexico 86 C4 23 40N 100 40W
Mateke Hills, Zimbabwe 55 G3 21 48S 31 0 E
Matera, Italy 20 D7 40 40N 16 36 E
Matetsi, Zimbabwe 55 F2 18 12S 26 0 E
Mathis, U.S.A. 81 L6 28 6N 97 50W
Mathráki, Greece 23 A3 39 48N 19 31 E
Mathura, India 42 F7 27 30N 77 40 E
Mati, Phil. 37 C7 6 55N 126 15 E
Matiali, India 43 F13 26 56N 88 49 E
Matías Romero, Mexico 87 D5 16 53N 95 2W
Matibane, Mozam. 55 E5 14 49S 40 45 E
Matima, Botswana 56 C3 20 15S 24 26 E
Matiri Ra., N.Z. 59 J4 41 38S 172 20 E
Matjiesfontein, S. Africa 56 E3 33 14S 20 35 E
Matla →, India 43 J13 21 40N 88 40 E
Matlamanyane, Botswana 56 B4 19 33S 25 57 E
Matli, Pakistan 42 G3 25 2N 68 39 E
Matlock, U.K. 10 D6 53 9N 1 33W
Mato Grosso □, Brazil 93 F8 14 0S 55 0W
Mato Grosso, Planalto do, Brazil 93 G8 15 0S 55 0W
Mato Grosso do Sul □, Brazil 93 G8 18 0S 55 0W
Matochkin Shar, Russia 26 B6 73 10N 56 40 E
Matopo Hills, Zimbabwe 55 G2 20 36S 28 20 E
Matopos, Zimbabwe 55 G2 20 20S 28 29 E
Matosinhos, Portugal 19 B1 41 11N 8 42W
Matroosberg, S. Africa 56 E2 33 23S 19 40 E
Maṭruḥ, Oman 46 C6 23 37N 58 30 E
Matsue, Japan 31 G6 35 25N 133 10 E
Matsumae, Japan 30 D10 41 26N 140 7 E
Matsumoto, Japan 31 F9 36 15N 138 0 E
Matsusaka, Japan 31 G8 34 34N 136 32 E
Matsuura, Japan 31 H4 33 20N 129 49 E
Matsuyama, Japan 31 H6 33 45N 132 45 E
Mattagami →, Canada 70 B3 50 43N 81 29W
Mattancheri, India 40 Q10 9 50N 76 15 E
Mattawa, Canada 70 C4 46 20N 78 45W
Matterhorn, Switz. 18 D7 45 58N 7 39 E
Matthew Town, Bahamas 89 B5 20 57N 73 40W
Matthew's Ridge, Guyana 92 B6 7 37N 60 10W
Mattice, Canada 70 C3 49 40N 83 20W
Mattituck, U.S.A. 79 F12 40 59N 72 32W
Mattō, Japan 31 F8 36 31N 136 34 E
Mattoon, U.S.A. 76 F1 39 29N 88 23W
Matuba, Mozam. 57 C5 24 28S 32 49 E
Matucana, Peru 92 F3 11 55S 76 25W
Matūn = Khowst, Afghan. 42 C3 33 22N 69 58 E
Maturín, Venezuela 92 B6 9 45N 63 11W
Mau, Mad. P., India 43 F8 26 17N 78 41 E
Mau, Ut. P., India 43 G10 25 56N 83 33 E
Mau, Ut. P., India 43 G9 25 17N 81 23 E
Mau Escarpment, Kenya 54 C4 0 40S 36 0 E
Mau Ranipur, India 43 G8 25 16N 79 8 E
Maubeuge, France 18 A6 50 17N 3 57 E
Maud, Pt., Australia 60 D1 23 6S 113 45 E
Maude, Australia 63 E3 34 29S 144 18 E
Maudin Sun, Burma 41 M19 16 0N 94 30 E
Maués, Brazil 92 D7 3 20S 57 45W
Mauganj, India 41 G12 24 50N 81 55 E
Maughold Hd., U.K. 10 C3 54 18N 4 18W
Maui, U.S.A. 74 H16 20 48N 156 20W
Maulamyaing = Moulmein, Burma 41 L20 16 30N 97 40 E
Maule □, Chile 94 D1 36 5S 72 30W
Maumee, U.S.A. 76 E4 41 34N 83 39W
Maumee →, U.S.A. 76 E4 41 42N 83 28W
Maumere, Indonesia 37 F6 8 38S 122 13 E
Maun, Botswana 56 C3 20 0S 23 26 E
Mauna Kea, U.S.A. 74 J17 19 50N 155 28W
Mauna Loa, U.S.A. 74 J17 19 30N 155 35W
Maungmagan Kyunzu, Burma 38 E1 14 0N 97 48 E
Maupin, U.S.A. 82 D3 45 11N 121 5W
Maurepas, L., U.S.A. 81 K9 30 15N 90 30W
Maurice, L., Australia 61 E5 29 30S 131 0 E
Mauricie, Parc Nat. de la, Canada 70 C5 46 45N 73 0W
Mauritania ■, Africa 50 E3 20 50N 10 0W
Mauritius ■, Ind. Oc. 49 J9 20 0S 57 0 E
Mauston, U.S.A. 80 D9 43 48N 90 5W
Mavli, India 42 G5 24 45N 73 55 E
Mavuradonha Mts., Zimbabwe 55 F3 16 30S 31 30 E
Mawa, Dem. Rep. of the Congo 54 B2 2 45N 26 40 E
Mawai, India 43 H9 22 30N 81 4 E
Mawana, India 42 E7 29 6N 77 58 E
Mawand, Pakistan 42 E3 29 33N 68 38 E
Mawk Mai, Burma 41 J20 20 14N 97 37 E
Mawlaik, Burma 41 H19 23 40N 94 26 E
Mawlamyine = Moulmein, Burma 41 L20 16 30N 97 40 E
Mawqaq, Si. Arabia 44 E4 27 25N 41 8 E
Mawson Coast, Antarctica 5 C6 68 30S 63 0 E
Max, U.S.A. 80 B4 47 49N 101 18W
Maxcanú, Mexico 87 C6 20 40N 92 0W
Maxesibeni, S. Africa 57 E4 30 49S 29 23 E
Maxhamish L., Canada 72 B4 59 50N 123 17W
Maxixe, Mozam. 57 C6 23 54S 35 17 E
Maxville, Canada 79 A10 45 17N 74 51W
Maxwell, U.S.A. 84 F4 39 17N 122 11W
Maxwelton, Australia 62 C3 20 43S 142 41 E
May, C., U.S.A. 76 F8 38 56N 74 58W
May Pen, Jamaica 88 C4 17 58N 77 15W
Maya →, Russia 27 D14 60 28N 134 28 E
Maya Mts., Belize 87 D7 16 30N 89 0W
Mayaguana, Bahamas 89 B5 22 30N 72 44W
Mayagüez, Puerto Rico 89 C6 18 12N 67 9W
Mayāmey, Iran 45 B7 36 24N 55 42 E
Mayanup, Australia 61 F2 33 57S 116 27 E
Mayapan, Mexico 87 C7 20 30N 89 25W
Mayarí, Cuba 89 B4 20 40N 75 41W
Maybell, U.S.A. 82 F9 40 31N 108 5W
Maybole, U.K. 12 F4 55 21N 4 42W
Maydān, Iraq 44 C5 34 55N 45 37 E
Maydena, Australia 62 G4 42 45S 146 30 E
Mayenne →, France 18 C3 47 30N 0 32W
Mayer, U.S.A. 83 J7 34 24N 112 14W
Mayerthorpe, Canada 72 C5 53 57N 115 8W
Mayfield, Ky., U.S.A. 77 G1 36 44N 88 38W
Mayfield, N.Y., U.S.A. 79 C10 43 6N 74 16W
Mayhill, U.S.A. 83 K11 32 53N 105 29W
Maykop, Russia 25 F7 44 35N 40 10 E
Maymyo, Burma 38 A1 22 2N 96 28 E
Maynard, Mass., U.S.A. 79 D13 42 26N 71 27W
Maynard, Wash., U.S.A. 84 C4 47 59N 122 55W
Maynard Hills, Australia 61 E2 28 28S 119 49 E
Mayne →, Australia 62 C3 23 40S 141 55 E
Maynooth, Ireland 13 C5 53 23N 6 34W
Mayo, Canada 68 B6 63 38N 135 57W
Mayo □, Ireland 13 C2 53 53N 9 3W
Mayon Volcano, Phil. 37 B6 13 15N 123 41 E
Mayor I., N.Z. 59 G6 37 16S 176 17 E
Mayotte, Ind. Oc. 53 G9 12 50S 45 10 E
Maysville, U.S.A. 76 F4 38 39N 83 46W
Mayu, Indonesia 37 D7 1 30N 126 30 E
Mayville, N. Dak., U.S.A. 80 B6 47 30N 97 20W
Mayville, N.Y., U.S.A. 78 D5 42 15N 79 30W
Mayya, Russia 27 C14 61 44N 130 18 E
Mazabuka, Zambia 55 F2 15 52S 27 44 E
Mazagán = El Jadida, Morocco 50 B4 33 11N 8 17W
Mazagão, Brazil 93 D8 0 7S 51 16W
Mazán, Peru 92 D4 3 30S 73 0W
Māzandarān □, Iran 45 B7 36 30N 52 0 E
Mazapil, Mexico 86 C4 24 38N 101 34W
Mazara del Vallo, Italy 20 F5 37 39N 12 35 E
Mazarrón, Spain 19 D5 37 38N 1 19W
Mazaruni →, Guyana 92 B7 6 25N 58 35W
Mazatán, Mexico 86 B2 29 0N 110 8W
Mazatenango, Guatemala 88 D1 14 35N 91 30W
Mazatlán, Mexico 86 C3 23 13N 106 25W
Mažeikiai, Lithuania 9 H20 56 20N 22 20 E
Māzhān, Iran 45 C8 32 30N 59 0 E
Mazīnān, Iran 45 B8 36 19N 56 56 E
Mazoe, Mozam. 55 F3 16 42S 33 7 E
Mazoe →, Mozam. 55 F3 16 20S 33 30 E
Mazowe, Zimbabwe 55 F3 17 28S 30 58 E
Mazurian Lakes = Mazurski, Pojezierze, Poland 17 B11 53 50N 21 0 E
Mazurski, Pojezierze, Poland 17 B11 53 50N 21 0 E
Mazyr, Belarus 17 B15 51 59N 29 15 E
Mbabane, Swaziland 57 D5 26 18S 31 6 E
Mbaïki, C.A.R. 52 D3 3 53N 18 1 E
Mbala, Zambia 55 D3 8 46S 31 24 E

Mbalabala

Mbalabala, Zimbabwe 57 C4 20 27S 29 3 E
Mbale, Uganda 54 B3 1 8N 34 12 E
Mbalmayo, Cameroon 52 D2 3 33N 11 33 E
Mbamba Bay, Tanzania 55 E3 11 13S 34 49 E
Mbandaka, Dem. Rep. of the Congo 52 D3 0 1N 18 18 E
Mbanza Congo, Angola 52 F2 6 18S 14 16 E
Mbanza Ngungu, Dem. Rep. of the Congo 52 F2 5 12S 14 53 E
Mbarangandu, Tanzania 55 D4 10 11S 36 48 E
Mbarara, Uganda 54 C3 0 35S 30 40 E
Mbashe →, S. Africa 57 E4 32 15S 28 54 E
Mbenkuru →, Tanzania 55 D4 9 25S 39 50 E
Mberengwa, Zimbabwe 55 G2 20 29S 29 57 E
Mberengwa, Mt., Zimbabwe 55 G2 20 37S 29 55 E
Mbesuma, Zambia 55 E3 10 0S 32 2 E
Mbeya, Tanzania 55 D3 8 54S 33 29 E
Mbeya □, Tanzania 54 D3 8 15S 33 30 E
Mbinga, Tanzania 55 E4 10 50S 35 0 E
Mbini = Río Muni □, Eq. Guin. 52 D2 1 30N 10 0 E
Mbour, Senegal 50 F2 14 22N 16 54W
Mbuji-Mayi, Dem. Rep. of the Congo 54 D1 6 9S 23 40 E
Mbulu, Tanzania 54 C4 3 45S 35 30 E
Mburucuyá, Argentina 94 B4 28 1S 58 14W
Mchinja, Tanzania 55 D4 9 44S 39 45 E
Mchinji, Malawi 55 E3 13 47S 32 58 E
Mdantsane, S. Africa 53 L5 32 56S 27 46 E
Mead, L., U.S.A. 85 J12 36 1N 114 44W
Meade, U.S.A. 81 G4 37 17N 100 20W
Meadow Lake, Canada 73 C7 54 10N 108 26W
Meadow Lake Prov. Park, Canada 73 C7 54 27N 109 0W
Meadow Valley Wash →, U.S.A. 85 J12 36 40N 114 34W
Meadville, U.S.A. 78 E4 41 39N 80 9W
Meaford, Canada 78 B4 44 36N 80 35W
Mealy Mts., Canada 71 B8 53 10N 58 0W
Meander River, Canada 72 B5 59 2N 117 42W
Meares, C., U.S.A. 82 D2 45 37N 124 0W
Mearim →, Brazil 93 D10 3 4S 44 35W
Meath □, Ireland 13 C5 53 40N 6 57W
Meath Park, Canada 73 C7 53 27N 105 22W
Meaux, France 18 B5 48 58N 2 50 E
Mebechi-Gawa →, Japan 30 D10 40 31N 141 31 E
Mecanhelas, Mozam. 55 F4 15 12S 35 54 E
Mecca = Makkah, Si. Arabia 46 C2 21 30N 39 54 E
Mecca, U.S.A. 85 M10 33 34N 116 5W
Mechanicsburg, U.S.A. 78 F8 40 13N 77 1W
Mechanicville, U.S.A. 79 D11 42 54N 73 41W
Mechelen, Belgium 15 C4 51 2N 4 29 E
Mecheria, Algeria 50 B5 33 35N 0 18W
Mecklenburg, Germany 16 B6 53 33N 11 40 E
Mecklenburger Bucht, Germany 16 A6 54 20N 11 40 E
Meconta, Mozam. 55 E4 14 59S 39 50 E
Medan, Indonesia 36 D1 3 40N 98 38 E
Medanosa, Pta., Argentina 96 F3 48 8S 66 0W
Médéa, Algeria 50 A6 36 12N 2 50 E
Medellín, Colombia 92 B3 6 15N 75 35W
Medelpad, Sweden 9 E17 62 33N 16 30 E
Medemblik, Neths. 15 B5 52 46N 5 8 E
Medford, Mass., U.S.A. 79 D13 42 25N 71 7W
Medford, Oreg., U.S.A. 82 E2 42 19N 122 52W
Medford, Wis., U.S.A. 80 C9 45 9N 90 20W
Medgidia, Romania 17 F15 44 15N 28 19 E
Media Agua, Argentina 94 C2 31 58S 68 25W
Media Luna, Argentina 94 C2 34 45S 66 44W
Medianeira, Brazil 95 B5 25 17S 54 5W
Mediaş, Romania 17 E13 46 9N 24 22 E
Medicine Bow, U.S.A. 82 F10 41 54N 106 12W
Medicine Bow Pk., U.S.A. 82 F10 41 21N 106 19W
Medicine Bow Ra., U.S.A. 82 F10 41 10N 106 25W
Medicine Hat, Canada 73 D6 50 0N 110 45W
Medicine Lake, U.S.A. 80 A2 48 30N 104 30W
Medicine Lodge, U.S.A. 81 G5 37 17N 98 35W
Medina = Al Madīnah, Si. Arabia 46 C2 24 35N 39 52 E
Medina, N. Dak., U.S.A. 80 B5 46 54N 99 18W
Medina, N.Y., U.S.A. 78 C6 43 13N 78 23W
Medina, Ohio, U.S.A. 78 E3 41 8N 81 52W
Medina →, U.S.A. 81 L5 29 16N 98 29W
Medina del Campo, Spain 19 B3 41 18N 4 55W
Medina L., U.S.A. 81 L5 29 32N 98 56W
Medina Sidonia, Spain 19 D3 36 28N 5 57W
Medinipur, India 43 H12 22 25N 87 21 E
Mediterranean Sea, Europe 49 C5 35 0N 15 0 E
Médoc, France 18 D3 45 10N 0 50W
Medveditsa →, Russia 25 E7 49 35N 42 41 E
Medvezhi, Ostrava, Russia 27 B17 71 0N 161 0 E
Medvezhyegorsk, Russia 24 B5 63 0N 34 25 E
Medway □, U.K. 11 F8 51 25N 0 32 E
Medway →, U.K. 11 F8 51 27N 0 46 E
Meekatharra, Australia 61 E2 26 32S 118 29 E
Meeker, U.S.A. 82 F10 40 2N 107 55W
Meelpaeg Res., Canada 71 C8 48 15N 56 33W
Meerut, India 42 E7 29 1N 77 42 E
Meeteetse, U.S.A. 82 D9 44 9N 108 52W
Mega, Ethiopia 46 G2 3 57N 38 19 E
Mégara, Greece 21 F10 37 58N 23 22 E
Megasini, India 43 J12 21 38N 86 21 E
Meghalaya □, India 41 G17 25 50N 91 0 E
Mégiscane, L., Canada 70 C4 48 35N 75 55W
Meharry, Mt., Australia 60 D2 22 59S 118 35 E
Mehlville, U.S.A. 80 F9 38 30N 90 19W
Mehndawal, India 43 F10 26 58N 83 5 E
Mehr Jān, Iran 45 C7 33 50N 55 6 E
Mehrābād, Iran 44 B5 36 53N 47 55 E
Mehrān, Iran 44 C5 33 7N 46 10 E
Mehrīz, Iran 45 D7 31 35N 54 28 E
Mei Xian, China 34 G4 34 18N 107 55 E
Meiktila, Burma 41 J19 20 53N 95 54 E
Meissen, Germany 16 C7 51 9N 13 29 E
Meizhou, China 33 D6 24 16N 116 6 E
Meja, India 43 G10 25 9N 82 7 E
Mejillones, Chile 94 A1 23 10S 70 30W
Mekele, Ethiopia 46 E2 13 33N 39 30 E
Mekhtar, Pakistan 40 D6 30 30N 69 15 E
Meknès, Morocco 50 B4 33 57N 5 33W
Mekong →, Asia 39 H6 9 30N 106 15 E
Mekongga, Indonesia 37 E6 3 39S 121 15 E
Mekvari = Kür →, Azerbaijan 25 G8 39 29N 49 15 E
Melagiri Hills, India 40 N10 12 20N 77 30 E
Melaka, Malaysia 39 L4 2 15N 102 15 E
Melalap, Malaysia 36 C5 5 10N 116 5 E
Mélambes, Greece 23 D6 35 8N 24 40 E
Melanesia, Pac. Oc. 64 H7 4 0S 155 0 E
Melbourne, Australia 63 F4 37 50S 145 0 E
Melbourne, U.S.A. 77 L5 28 5N 80 37W
Melchor Múzquiz, Mexico 86 B4 27 50N 101 30W
Melchor Ocampo, Mexico 86 C4 24 52N 101 40W
Mélèzes →, Canada 70 A5 57 40N 69 29W
Melfort, Canada 73 C8 52 50N 104 37W
Melfort, Zimbabwe 55 F3 18 0S 31 25 E
Melhus, Norway 8 E14 63 17N 10 18 E
Melilla, N. Afr. 19 E4 35 21N 2 57W
Melipilla, Chile 94 C1 33 42S 71 15W
Mélissa, Ákra, Greece 23 D6 35 6N 24 33 E
Melita, Canada 73 D8 49 15N 101 0W
Melitopol, Ukraine 25 E6 46 50N 35 22 E
Melk, Austria 16 D8 48 13N 15 20 E
Mellansel, Sweden 8 E18 63 25N 18 17 E
Mellen, U.S.A. 80 B9 46 20N 90 40W
Mellerud, Sweden 9 G15 58 41N 12 28 E
Mellette, U.S.A. 80 C5 45 9N 98 30W
Mellieha, Malta 23 D1 35 57N 14 22 E
Melo, Uruguay 95 C5 32 20S 54 10W
Melolo, Indonesia 37 F6 9 53S 120 40 E
Melouprey, Cambodia 38 F5 13 48N 105 16 E
Melrose, Australia 63 E4 32 42S 146 57 E
Melrose, U.K. 12 F6 55 36N 2 43W
Melrose, Minn., U.S.A. 80 C7 45 40N 94 49W
Melrose, N. Mex., U.S.A. 81 H3 34 26N 103 38W
Melstone, U.S.A. 82 C10 46 36N 107 52W
Melton Mowbray, U.K. 10 E7 52 47N 0 54W
Melun, France 18 B5 48 32N 2 39 E
Melville, Canada 73 C8 50 55N 102 50W
Melville, C., Australia 62 A3 14 11S 144 30 E
Melville, L., Canada 71 B8 53 30N 60 0W
Melville B., Australia 62 A2 12 0S 136 45 E
Melville I., Australia 60 B5 11 30S 131 0 E
Melville I., Canada 4 B2 75 30N 112 0W
Melville Pen., Canada 69 B11 68 0N 84 0W
Memba, Mozam. 55 E5 14 11S 40 30 E
Memboro, Indonesia 37 F5 9 30S 119 30 E
Memel = Klaipėda, Lithuania 9 J19 55 43N 21 10 E
Memel, S. Africa 57 D4 27 38S 29 36 E
Memmingen, Germany 16 E6 47 58N 10 10 E
Mempawah, Indonesia 36 D3 0 30N 109 5 E
Memphis, Mich., U.S.A. 78 D2 42 54N 82 46W
Memphis, Tenn., U.S.A. 81 H10 35 8N 90 3W
Memphis, Tex., U.S.A. 81 H4 34 44N 100 33W
Memphremagog, L., U.S.A. 79 B12 45 0N 72 12W
Mena, U.S.A. 81 H7 34 35N 94 15W
Menai Strait, U.K. 10 D3 53 11N 4 13W
Ménaka, Mali 50 E6 15 59N 2 18 E
Menan = Chao Phraya →, Thailand 38 F3 13 32N 100 36 E
Menarandra →, Madag. 57 D7 25 17S 44 30 E
Menard, U.S.A. 81 K5 30 55N 99 47W
Mendawai →, Indonesia 36 E4 3 30S 113 0 E
Mende, France 18 D5 44 31N 3 30 E
Mendez, Mexico 87 B5 25 7N 98 34W
Mendhar, India 43 C6 33 35N 74 10 E
Mendip Hills, U.K. 11 F5 51 17N 2 40W
Mendocino, U.S.A. 82 G2 39 19N 123 48W
Mendocino, C., U.S.A. 82 F1 40 26N 124 25W
Mendota, Calif., U.S.A. 84 J6 36 45N 120 23W
Mendota, Ill., U.S.A. 80 E10 41 33N 89 7W
Mendoza, Argentina 94 C2 32 50S 68 52W
Mendoza □, Argentina 94 C2 33 0S 69 0W
Mene Grande, Venezuela 92 B4 9 49N 70 56W
Menemen, Turkey 21 E12 38 34N 27 3 E
Menen, Belgium 15 D3 50 47N 3 7 E
Menggala, Indonesia 36 E3 4 30S 105 15 E
Mengjin, China 34 G7 34 55N 112 45 E
Mengyin, China 35 G9 35 40N 117 58 E
Mengzi, China 32 D5 23 20N 103 22 E
Menihek, Canada 71 B6 54 28N 56 36W
Menihek L., Canada 71 B6 54 0N 67 0W
Menin = Menen, Belgium 15 D3 50 47N 3 7 E
Menindee, Australia 63 E3 32 20S 142 25 E
Menindee L., Australia 63 E3 32 20S 142 25 E
Meningie, Australia 63 F2 35 50S 139 18 E
Menlo Park, U.S.A. 84 H4 37 27N 122 12W
Menominee, U.S.A. 76 C2 45 6N 87 37W
Menominee →, U.S.A. 76 C2 45 6N 87 36W
Menomonie, U.S.A. 80 C9 44 53N 91 55W
Menongue, Angola 53 G3 14 48S 17 52 E
Menorca, Spain 22 B11 40 0N 4 0 E
Mentakab, Malaysia 39 L4 3 29N 102 21 E
Mentawai, Kepulauan, Indonesia 36 E1 2 0S 99 0 E
Menton, France 18 E7 43 50N 7 29 E
Mentor, U.S.A. 78 E3 41 40N 81 21W
Menzelinsk, Russia 24 C9 55 47N 53 11 E
Menzies, Australia 61 E3 29 40S 121 2 E
Meob B., Namibia 56 B2 24 25S 14 34 E
Me'ona, Israel 47 B4 33 1N 35 15 E
Meoqui, Mexico 86 B3 28 17N 105 29W
Mepaco, Mozam. 55 F3 15 57S 30 48 E
Meppel, Neths. 15 B6 52 42N 6 12 E
Merabéllou, Kólpos, Greece 23 D7 35 10N 25 50 E
Merak, Indonesia 37 F12 6 10N 106 26 E
Meramangye, L., Australia 61 E5 28 25S 132 13 E
Meran = Merano, Italy 20 A4 46 40N 11 9 E
Merano, Italy 20 A4 46 40N 11 9 E
Merauke, Indonesia 37 F10 8 29S 140 24 E
Merbein, Australia 63 E3 34 10S 142 2 E
Merca, Somali Rep. 46 G3 1 48N 44 50 E
Merced, U.S.A. 84 H6 37 18N 120 29W
Merced →, U.S.A. 84 H6 37 21N 120 59W
Merced Pk., U.S.A. 84 H7 37 36N 119 24W
Mercedes, Buenos Aires, Argentina 94 C4 34 40S 59 30W
Mercedes, Corrientes, Argentina 94 B4 29 10S 58 5W
Mercedes, San Luis, Argentina 94 C2 33 40S 65 21W
Mercedes, Uruguay 94 C4 33 12S 58 0W
Mercedes, U.S.A. 81 M6 26 9N 97 55W
Merceditas, Chile 94 B1 28 20S 70 35W
Mercer, N.Z. 59 G5 37 16S 175 5 E
Mercer, U.S.A. 78 E4 41 14N 80 15W
Mercer Island, U.S.A. 84 C4 47 35N 122 15W
Mercury, U.S.A. 85 J11 36 40N 115 58W
Mercy C., Canada 69 B13 65 0N 63 30W
Mere, U.K. 11 F5 51 6N 2 16W
Meredith, C., Falk. Is. 96 G4 52 15S 60 40W
Meredith, L., U.S.A. 81 H4 35 43N 101 33W
Mergui, Burma 38 F2 12 26N 98 34 E
Mergui Arch. = Myeik Kyunzu, Burma 39 G1 11 30N 97 30 E
Mérida, Mexico 87 C7 20 58N 89 37W
Mérida, Spain 19 C2 38 55N 6 25W
Mérida, Venezuela 92 B4 8 24N 71 8W
Mérida, Cord. de, Venezuela 92 B4 9 0N 71 0W
Meriden, U.K. 11 E6 52 26N 1 38W
Meriden, U.S.A. 79 E12 41 32N 72 48W
Meridian, Calif., U.S.A. 84 F5 39 9N 121 55W
Meridian, Idaho, U.S.A. 82 E5 43 37N 116 24W
Meridian, Miss., U.S.A. 77 J1 32 22N 88 42W
Merinda, Australia 62 C4 20 2S 148 11 E
Merir, Pac. Oc. 37 D8 4 10N 132 30 E
Merirumã, Brazil 93 C8 1 15N 54 50W
Merkel, U.S.A. 81 J5 32 28N 100 1W
Mermaid Reef, Australia 60 C2 17 6S 119 36 E
Merredin, Australia 61 F2 31 28S 118 18 E
Merrick, U.K. 12 F4 55 8N 4 28W
Merrickville, Canada 79 B9 44 55N 75 50W
Merrill, Oreg., U.S.A. 82 E3 42 1N 121 36W
Merrill, Wis., U.S.A. 80 C10 45 11N 89 41W
Merrimack →, U.S.A. 79 D14 42 49N 70 49W
Merriman, U.S.A. 80 D4 42 55N 101 42W
Merritt, Canada 72 C4 50 10N 120 45W
Merritt Island, U.S.A. 77 L5 28 21N 80 42W
Merriwa, Australia 63 E5 32 6S 150 22 E
Merry I., Canada 70 A4 55 29N 77 31W
Merryville, U.S.A. 81 K8 30 45N 93 33W
Mersch, Lux. 15 E6 49 44N 6 7 E
Mersea I., U.K. 11 F8 51 47N 0 58 E
Merseburg, Germany 16 C6 51 22N 11 59 E
Mersey →, U.K. 10 D4 53 25N 3 1W
Merseyside □, U.K. 10 D4 53 31N 3 2W
Mersin, Turkey 25 G5 36 51N 34 36 E
Mersing, Malaysia 39 L4 2 25N 103 50 E
Merta, India 42 F6 26 39N 74 4 E
Merta Road, India 42 F5 26 43N 73 55 E
Merthyr Tydfil, U.K. 11 F4 51 45N 3 22W
Merthyr Tydfil □, U.K. 11 F4 51 46N 3 21W
Mértola, Portugal 19 D2 37 40N 7 40W
Mertzon, U.S.A. 81 K4 31 16N 100 49W
Meru, Kenya 54 B4 0 3N 37 40 E
Meru, Tanzania 54 C4 3 15S 36 46 E
Mesa, U.S.A. 83 K8 33 25N 111 50W
Mesa Verde Nat. Park, U.S.A. 83 H9 37 11N 108 29W
Mesanagrós, Greece 23 C9 36 1N 27 49 E
Mesaoría, Cyprus 23 D12 35 12N 33 14 E
Mesarás, Kólpos, Greece 23 D6 35 6N 24 47 E
Mesgouez, L., Canada 70 B5 51 20N 75 0W
Meshed = Mashhad, Iran 45 B8 36 20N 59 35 E
Meshoppen, U.S.A. 79 E8 41 36N 76 3W
Mesilinka →, Canada 72 B4 56 6N 124 30W
Mesilla, U.S.A. 83 K10 32 16N 106 48W
Mesolóngion, Greece 21 E9 38 21N 21 28 E
Mesopotamia = Al Jazirah, Iraq 44 C5 33 30N 44 0 E
Mesopotamia, U.S.A. 78 E4 41 27N 80 57W
Mesquite, U.S.A. 83 H6 36 47N 114 6W
Messaad, Algeria 50 B6 34 8N 3 30 E
Messalo →, Mozam. 55 E4 12 25S 39 15 E
Messina, Italy 20 E6 38 11N 15 34 E
Messina, S. Africa 57 C5 22 20S 30 5 E
Messina, Str. di, Italy 20 F6 38 15N 15 35 E
Messíni, Greece 21 F10 37 4N 22 1 E
Messiniakós Kólpos, Greece 21 F10 36 45N 22 5 E
Messonghi, Greece 23 B3 39 29N 19 56 E
Mesta →, Bulgaria 21 D11 40 54N 24 49 E
Meta →, S. Amer. 92 B5 6 12N 67 28W
Meta Incognita Peninsula, Canada 69 B13 62 40N 68 0W
Metabetchouan, Canada 71 C5 48 26N 71 52W
Metairie, U.S.A. 81 L9 29 58N 90 10W
Metaline Falls, U.S.A. 82 B5 48 52N 117 22W
Metán, Argentina 94 B3 25 30S 65 0W
Metangula, Mozam. 55 E3 12 40S 34 50 E
Metengobalame, Mozam. 55 E3 14 49S 34 30 E
Methven, N.Z. 59 K3 43 38S 171 40 E
Metil, Mozam. 55 F4 16 24S 39 0 E
Metlakatla, U.S.A. 68 C6 55 8N 131 35W
Metropolis, U.S.A. 81 G10 37 9N 88 44W
Metu, Ethiopia 46 F2 8 18N 35 35 E
Metz, France 18 B7 49 8N 6 10 E
Meulaboh, Indonesia 36 D1 4 11N 96 3 E
Meureudu, Indonesia 36 C1 5 19N 96 10 E
Meuse →, Europe 18 A6 50 45N 5 41 E
Mexia, U.S.A. 81 K6 31 41N 96 29W
Mexiana, I., Brazil 93 D9 0 0 49 30W
Mexicali, Mexico 85 N11 32 40N 115 30W
Mexican Plateau, Mexico 66 G9 25 0N 104 0W
Mexican Water, U.S.A. 83 H9 36 57N 109 32W
México, Mexico 87 D5 19 20N 99 10W
Mexico, Maine, U.S.A. 79 B14 44 34N 70 33W
Mexico, Mo., U.S.A. 80 F9 39 10N 91 53W
Mexico, N.Y., U.S.A. 79 C8 43 28N 76 18W
México □, Mexico 87 D5 19 20N 99 10W
Mexico ■, Cent. Amer. 86 C4 25 0N 105 0W
Mexico, G. of, Cent. Amer. 87 C7 25 0N 90 0W
Mexico B., U.S.A. 79 C8 43 35N 76 20W
Meydān-e Naftūn, Iran 45 D6 31 56N 49 18 E
Meydani, Ra's-e, Iran 45 E8 25 24N 59 6 E
Meymaneh, Afghan. 40 B4 35 53N 64 38 E
Mezen, Russia 24 A7 65 50N 44 20 E
Mezen →, Russia 24 A7 65 44N 44 22 E
Mézenc, Mt., France 18 D6 44 54N 4 11 E
Mezhdurechenskiy, Russia 26 D7 59 36N 65 56 E
Mezőkövesd, Hungary 17 E11 47 49N 20 35 E
Mezőtúr, Hungary 17 E11 47 1N 20 41 E
Mezquital, Mexico 86 C4 23 29N 104 23W
Mfolozi →, S. Africa 57 D5 28 25S 32 26 E
Mgeta, Tanzania 55 D4 8 22S 36 6 E
Mhlaba Hills, Zimbabwe 55 F3 18 30S 30 30 E
Mhow, India 42 H6 22 33N 75 50 E
Miahuatlán, Mexico 87 D5 16 21N 96 36W
Miami, Fla., U.S.A. 77 N5 25 47N 80 11W
Miami, Okla., U.S.A. 81 G7 36 53N 94 53W
Miami, Tex., U.S.A. 81 H4 35 42N 100 38W
Miami Beach, U.S.A. 77 N5 25 47N 80 8W
Mian Xian, China 34 H4 33 10N 106 32 E
Mianchi, China 34 G6 34 48N 111 48 E
Miāndarreh, Iran 45 C7 35 37N 53 39 E
Miāndowāb, Iran 44 B5 37 0N 46 5 E
Miandrivazo, Madag. 57 B8 19 31S 45 29 E
Miāneh, Iran 44 B5 37 30N 47 40 E
Mianwali, Pakistan 42 C4 32 38N 71 28 E
Miarinarivo, Antananarivo, Madag. 57 B8 18 57S 46 55 E
Miarinarivo, Toamasina, Madag. 57 B8 16 38S 48 15 E
Miariravaratra, Madag. 57 C8 20 13S 47 31 E
Miass, Russia 24 D11 54 59N 60 6 E
Mica, S. Africa 57 C5 24 10S 30 48 E
Michalovce, Slovak Rep. 17 D11 48 47N 21 58 E
Michigan □, U.S.A. 76 C3 44 0N 85 0W
Michigan, L., U.S.A. 76 D2 44 0N 87 0W
Michigan City, U.S.A. 76 E2 41 43N 86 54W
Michipicoten I., Canada 70 C2 47 40N 85 40W
Michoacan □, Mexico 86 D4 19 0N 102 0W
Michurin, Bulgaria 21 C12 42 9N 27 51 E
Michurinsk, Russia 24 D7 52 58N 40 27 E
Mico, Pta., Nic. 88 D3 12 0N 83 30W
Micronesia, Pac. Oc. 64 G7 11 0N 160 0 E
Micronesia, Federated States of ■, Pac. Oc. 64 G7 9 0N 150 0 E
Midai, Indonesia 39 L6 3 0N 107 47 E
Midale, Canada 73 D8 49 25N 103 20W
Middelburg, Neths. 15 C3 51 30N 3 36 E
Middelburg, Eastern Cape, S. Africa 56 E4 31 30S 25 0 E
Middelburg, Mpumalanga, S. Africa 57 D4 25 49S 29 28 E
Middelpos, S. Africa 56 E3 31 55S 20 13 E
Middelwit, S. Africa 56 C4 24 51S 27 3 E
Middle Alkali L., U.S.A. 82 F3 41 27N 120 5W
Middle Bass I., U.S.A. 78 E2 41 41N 82 49W
Middle East, Asia 28 F7 38 0N 40 0 E
Middle Fork Feather →, U.S.A. 84 F5 38 33N 121 30W
Middle I., Australia 61 F3 34 6S 123 11 E
Middle Loup →, U.S.A. 80 E5 41 17N 98 24W
Middle Sackville, Canada 71 D7 44 47N 63 42W
Middleboro, U.S.A. 79 E14 41 54N 70 55W
Middleburg, Fla., U.S.A. 77 K5 30 4N 81 52W
Middleburg, N.Y., U.S.A. 79 D10 42 36N 74 20W
Middleburg, Pa., U.S.A. 78 F7 40 47N 77 3W
Middlebury, U.S.A. 79 B11 44 1N 73 10W
Middlemount, Australia 62 C4 22 50S 148 40 E
Middleport, N.Y., U.S.A. 78 C6 43 13N 78 29W
Middleport, Ohio, U.S.A. 76 F4 39 0N 82 3W
Middlesboro, U.S.A. 77 G4 36 36N 83 43W
Middlesbrough, U.K. 10 C6 54 35N 1 13W
Middlesbrough □, U.K. 10 C6 54 28N 1 13W
Middlesex, Belize 88 C2 17 2N 88 31W
Middlesex, N.J., U.S.A. 79 F10 40 36N 74 30W
Middlesex, N.Y., U.S.A. 78 D7 42 42N 77 16W
Middleton, Australia 62 C3 22 22S 141 32 E
Middleton, Canada 71 D6 44 57N 65 4W
Middleton Cr. →, Australia 62 C3 22 35S 141 51 E
Middletown, U.K. 13 B5 54 17N 6 51W
Middletown, Calif., U.S.A. 84 G4 38 45N 122 37W
Middletown, Conn., U.S.A. 79 E12 41 34N 72 39W
Middletown, N.Y., U.S.A. 79 E10 41 27N 74 25W
Middletown, Ohio, U.S.A. 76 F3 39 31N 84 24W
Middletown, Pa., U.S.A. 79 F8 40 12N 76 44W
Midhurst, U.K. 11 G7 50 59N 0 44W
Midi, Canal du →, France 18 E4 43 45N 1 21 E
Midland, Canada 78 B5 44 45N 79 50W
Midland, Calif., U.S.A. 85 M12 33 52N 114 48W
Midland, Mich., U.S.A. 76 D3 43 37N 84 14W
Midland, Pa., U.S.A. 78 F4 40 39N 80 27W
Midland, Tex., U.S.A. 81 K3 32 0N 102 3W
Midlands □, Zimbabwe 55 F2 19 40S 29 0 E
Midleton, Ireland 13 E3 51 55N 8 10W
Midlothian, U.S.A. 81 J6 32 30N 97 0W
Midlothian □, U.K. 12 F5 55 51N 3 5W
Midongy, Tangorombohitr' i, Madag. 57 C8 23 30S 47 0 E
Midongy Atsimo, Madag. 57 C8 23 35S 47 1 E
Midway Is., Pac. Oc. 64 E10 28 13N 177 22W
Midway Wells, U.S.A. 85 N11 32 41N 115 7W
Midwest, U.S.A. 82 E10 43 25N 106 16W
Midwest City, U.S.A. 81 H6 35 27N 97 24W
Midyat, Turkey 44 B4 37 25N 41 23 E
Midzŏr, Bulgaria 21 C10 43 24N 22 40 E
Mie □, Japan 31 G8 34 30N 136 10 E
Międzychód, Poland 16 B8 52 35N 15 53 E
Międzyrzec Podlaski, Poland 17 C12 51 58N 22 45 E
Mielec, Poland 17 C11 50 15N 21 25 E
Mienga, Angola 56 B2 17 12S 19 48 E
Miercurea-Ciuc, Romania 17 E13 46 21N 25 48 E
Mieres, Spain 19 A3 43 18N 5 48W
Mifflintown, U.S.A. 78 F7 40 34N 77 24W
Mifraz Hefa, Israel 47 C4 32 52N 35 0 E
Miguel Alemán, Presa, Mexico 87 D5 18 15N 96 40W
Mihara, Japan 31 G6 34 24N 133 5 E
Mikese, Tanzania 54 D4 6 48S 37 55 E
Mikhaylovgrad = Montana, Bulgaria 21 C10 43 27N 23 16 E
Mikhaylovka, Russia 25 D7 50 3N 43 5 E
Mikkeli, Finland 9 F22 61 43N 27 15 E
Mikkwa →, Canada 72 B6 58 25N 114 46W
Míkonos, Greece 21 F11 37 30N 25 25 E
Mikumi, Tanzania 54 D4 7 26S 37 0 E
Mikun, Russia 24 B9 62 20N 50 0 E
Milaca, U.S.A. 80 C8 45 45N 93 39W
Milagro, Ecuador 92 D3 2 11S 79 36W
Milan = Milano, Italy 18 D8 45 28N 9 12 E
Milan, Mo., U.S.A. 80 E8 40 12N 93 7W
Milan, Tenn., U.S.A. 77 H1 35 55N 88 46W
Milange, Mozam. 55 F4 16 3S 35 45 E
Milano, Italy 18 D8 45 28N 9 12 E
Milanoa, Madag. 57 A8 13 35S 49 47 E
Milâs, Turkey 21 F12 37 20N 27 50 E
Mílatos, Greece 23 D7 35 18N 25 34 E
Milazzo, Italy 20 E6 38 13N 15 15 E
Milbank, U.S.A. 80 C6 45 13N 96 38W
Milbanke Sd., Canada 72 C3 52 15N 128 35W
Milden, Canada 73 C7 51 29N 107 32W
Mildenhall, U.K. 11 E8 52 21N 0 32 E
Mildmay, Canada 78 B3 44 3N 81 7W
Mildura, Australia 63 E3 34 13S 142 9 E
Miles, Australia 63 D5 26 40S 150 9 E
Miles City, U.S.A. 80 B2 46 25N 105 51W
Milestone, Canada 73 D8 49 59N 104 31W
Miletus, Turkey 21 F12 37 30N 27 18 E
Milford, Calif., U.S.A. 84 E6 40 10N 120 22W
Milford, Conn., U.S.A. 79 E11 41 14N 73 3W
Milford, Del., U.S.A. 76 F8 38 55N 75 26W
Milford, Mass., U.S.A. 79 D13 42 8N 71 31W
Milford, N.H., U.S.A. 79 D13 42 50N 71 39W
Milford, Pa., U.S.A. 79 E10 41 19N 74 48W
Milford, Utah, U.S.A. 83 G7 38 24N 113 1W

Mono L.

Milford Haven, U.K. 11 F2 51 42N 5 7W
Milford Sd., N.Z. 59 L1 44 41S 167 47 E
Milḩ, Baḩr al, Iraq 44 C4 32 40N 43 35 E
Milikapiti, Australia 60 B5 11 26S 130 40 E
Miling, Australia 61 F2 30 30S 116 17 E
Milk →, U.S.A. 82 B10 48 4N 106 19W
Milk River, Canada 72 D6 49 10N 112 5W
Mill I., Antarctica 5 C8 66 0S 101 30 E
Mill Valley, U.S.A. 84 H4 37 54N 122 32W
Millau, France 18 D5 44 8N 3 4 E
Millbridge, Canada 78 B7 44 41N 77 36W
Millbrook, Canada 78 B6 44 10N 78 29W
Millbrook, U.S.A. 79 E11 41 47N 73 42W
Mille Lacs, L. des, Canada 70 C1 48 45N 90 35W
Mille Lacs L., U.S.A. 80 B8 46 15N 93 39W
Milledgeville, U.S.A. 77 J4 33 5N 83 14W
Millen, U.S.A. 77 J5 32 48N 81 57W
Millennium I. = Caroline I., Kiribati 65 H12 9 58S 150 13W
Miller, U.S.A. 80 C5 44 31N 98 59W
Millersburg, Ohio, U.S.A. 78 F3 40 33N 81 55W
Millersburg, Pa., U.S.A. 78 F8 40 32N 76 58W
Millerton, U.S.A. 79 E11 41 57N 73 31W
Millerton L., U.S.A. 84 J7 37 1N 119 41W
Millheim, U.S.A. 78 F7 40 54N 77 29W
Millicent, Australia 63 F3 37 34S 140 21 E
Millington, U.S.A. 81 H10 35 20N 89 53W
Millinocket, U.S.A. 77 C11 45 39N 68 43W
Millmerran, Australia 63 D5 27 53S 151 16 E
Millom, U.K. 10 C4 54 13N 3 16W
Mills L., Canada 72 A5 61 30N 118 20W
Millsboro, U.S.A. 78 G5 40 0N 80 0W
Milltown Malbay, Ireland 13 D2 52 52N 9 24W
Millville, N.J., U.S.A. 76 F8 39 24N 75 2W
Millville, Pa., U.S.A. 79 E8 41 7N 76 32W
Millwood L., U.S.A. 81 J8 33 42N 93 58W
Milne →, Australia 62 C2 21 10S 137 33 E
Milo, U.S.A. 77 C11 45 15N 68 59W
Milos, Greece 21 F11 36 44N 24 25 E
Milparinka, Australia 63 D3 29 46S 141 57 E
Milton, N.S., Canada 71 D7 44 4N 64 45W
Milton, Ont., Canada 78 C5 43 31N 79 53W
Milton, N.Z. 59 M2 46 7S 169 59 E
Milton, Calif., U.S.A. 84 G6 38 3N 120 51W
Milton, Fla., U.S.A. 77 K2 30 38N 87 3W
Milton, Pa., U.S.A. 78 F8 41 1N 76 51W
Milton, Vt., U.S.A. 79 B11 44 38N 73 7W
Milton-Freewater, U.S.A. 82 D4 45 56N 118 23W
Milton Keynes, U.K. 11 E7 52 1N 0 44W
Milton Keynes □, U.K. 11 E7 52 1N 0 44W
Milverton, Canada 78 C4 43 34N 80 55W
Milwaukee, U.S.A. 76 D2 43 2N 87 55W
Milwaukee Deep, Atl. Oc. 89 C6 19 50N 68 0W
Milwaukie, U.S.A. 84 E4 45 27N 122 38W
Min Jiang →, Fujian, China 33 D6 26 0N 119 35 E
Min Jiang →, Sichuan, China 32 D5 28 45N 104 40 E
Min Xian, China 34 G3 34 25N 104 5 E
Mina Pirquitas, Argentina 94 A2 22 40S 66 30W
Mīnā Su'ud, Si. Arabia 45 D6 28 45N 48 28 E
Mīnā'al Aḩmadī, Kuwait 45 D6 29 5N 48 10 E
Minago →, Canada 73 C9 54 33N 98 59W
Minaki, Canada 73 D10 49 59N 94 40W
Minamata, Japan 31 H5 32 10N 130 30 E
Minami-Tori-Shima, Pac. Oc. 64 E7 24 20N 153 58 E
Minas, Uruguay 95 C4 34 20S 55 10W
Minas, Sierra de las, Guatemala 88 C2 15 9N 89 31W
Minas Basin, Canada 71 C7 45 20N 64 12W
Minas Gerais □, Brazil 93 G9 18 50S 46 0W
Minatitlán, Mexico 87 D6 17 59N 94 31W
Minbu, Burma 41 J19 20 10N 94 52 E
Minchinabad, Pakistan 42 D5 30 10N 73 34 E
Mindanao, Phil. 37 C6 8 0N 125 0 E
Mindanao Sea = Bohol Sea, Phil. 37 C6 9 0N 124 0 E
Mindanao Trench, Pac. Oc. 37 B7 12 0N 126 6 E
Minden, Canada 78 B6 44 55N 78 43W
Minden, Germany 16 B5 52 17N 8 55 E
Minden, La., U.S.A. 81 J8 32 37N 93 17W
Minden, Nev., U.S.A. 84 G7 38 57N 119 46W
Mindiptana, Indonesia 37 F10 5 55S 140 22 E
Mindoro, Phil. 37 B6 13 0N 121 0 E
Mindoro Str., Phil. 37 B6 12 30N 120 30 E
Mine, Japan 31 G5 34 12N 131 7 E
Minehead, U.K. 11 F4 51 12N 3 29W
Mineola, N.Y., U.S.A. 79 F11 40 45N 73 39W
Mineola, Tex., U.S.A. 81 J7 32 40N 95 29W
Mineral King, U.S.A. 84 J8 36 27N 118 36W
Mineral Wells, U.S.A. 81 J5 32 48N 98 7W
Minersville, U.S.A. 79 F8 40 41N 76 16W
Minerva, U.S.A. 78 F3 40 44N 81 6W
Minetto, U.S.A. 79 C8 43 24N 76 28W
Mingäçevir Su Anbarı, Azerbaijan 25 F8 40 57N 46 50 E
Mingan, Canada 71 B7 50 20N 64 0W
Mingechaurskoye Vdkhr. = Mingäçevir Su Anbarı, Azerbaijan 25 F8 40 57N 46 50 E
Mingela, Australia 62 B4 19 52S 146 38 E
Mingenew, Australia 61 E2 29 12S 115 21 E
Mingera Cr. →, Australia 62 C2 20 38S 137 45 E
Mingin, Burma 41 H19 22 50N 94 30 E
Mingo Junction, U.S.A. 78 F4 40 19N 80 37W
Mingteke Daban = Mintaka Pass, Pakistan 43 A6 37 0N 74 58 E
Mingyuegue, China 35 C15 43 2N 128 50 E
Minho = Miño →, Spain 19 A2 41 52N 8 40W
Minho, Portugal 19 B1 41 25N 8 20W
Minidoka, U.S.A. 82 E7 42 45N 113 29W
Minigwal, L., Australia 61 E3 29 31S 123 14 E
Minilya →, Australia 61 D1 23 45S 114 0 E
Minilya Roadhouse, Australia 61 D1 23 55S 114 0 E
Minipi L., Canada 71 B7 52 25N 60 45W
Mink L., Canada 72 A5 61 54N 117 40W
Minna, Nigeria 50 G7 9 37N 6 30 E
Minneapolis, Kans., U.S.A. 80 F6 39 8N 97 42W
Minneapolis, Minn., U.S.A. 80 C8 44 59N 93 16W
Minnedosa, Canada 73 C9 50 14N 99 50W
Minnesota □, U.S.A. 80 B8 46 0N 94 15W
Minnesota →, U.S.A. 80 C8 44 54N 93 9W
Minnewaukan, U.S.A. 80 A5 48 4N 99 15W
Minnipa, Australia 63 E2 32 51S 135 9 E
Minnitaki L., Canada 70 C1 49 57N 92 10W
Mino, Japan 31 G8 35 32N 136 55 E
Miño →, Spain 19 A2 41 52N 8 40W
Minorca = Menorca, Spain 22 B11 40 0N 4 0 E
Minot, U.S.A. 80 A4 48 14N 101 18W
Minqin, China 34 E2 38 38N 103 20 E
Minsk, Belarus 17 B14 53 52N 27 30 E
Mińsk Mazowiecki, Poland 17 B11 52 10N 21 33 E
Mintabie, Australia 63 D1 27 15S 133 7 E
Mintaka Pass, Pakistan 43 A6 37 0N 74 58 E
Minto, Canada 71 C6 46 5N 66 5W
Minto, L., Canada 70 A5 57 13N 75 0W
Minton, Canada 73 D8 49 10N 104 35W
Minturn, U.S.A. 82 G10 39 35N 106 26W
Minusinsk, Russia 27 D10 53 43N 91 20 E
Minutang, India 41 E20 28 15N 96 30 E
Miquelon, Canada 70 C4 49 25N 76 27W
Miquelon, St- P. & M. 71 C8 47 8N 56 22W
Mīr Kūh, Iran 45 E8 26 22N 58 55 E
Mīr Shahdād, Iran 45 E8 26 15N 58 29 E
Mira, Italy 20 B5 45 26N 12 8 E
Mira por vos Cay, Bahamas 89 B5 22 9N 74 30W
Miraj, India 40 L9 16 50N 74 45 E
Miram Shah, Pakistan 42 C4 33 0N 70 2 E
Miramar, Argentina 94 D4 38 15S 57 50W
Miramar, Mozam. 57 C6 23 50S 35 35 E
Miramichi, Canada 71 C6 47 2N 65 28W
Miramichi B., Canada 71 C7 47 15N 65 0W
Miranda, Brazil 93 H7 20 10S 56 15W
Miranda →, Brazil 92 G7 19 25S 57 20W
Miranda de Ebro, Spain 19 A4 42 41N 2 57W
Miranda do Douro, Portugal 19 B2 41 30N 6 16W
Mirandópolis, Brazil 95 A5 21 9S 51 6W
Mirango, Malawi 55 E3 13 32S 34 58 E
Mirassol, Brazil 95 A6 20 46S 49 28W
Mirbāţ, Oman 46 D5 17 0N 54 45 E
Miri, Malaysia 36 D4 4 23N 113 59 E
Miriam Vale, Australia 62 C5 24 20S 151 33 E
Mirim, L., S. Amer. 95 C5 32 45S 52 50W
Mirnyy, Russia 27 C12 62 33N 113 53 E
Mirokhan, Pakistan 42 F3 27 46N 68 6 E
Mirond L., Canada 73 B8 55 6N 102 47W
Mirpur, Pakistan 43 C5 33 32N 73 56 E
Mirpur Batoro, Pakistan 42 G3 24 44N 68 16 E
Mirpur Bibiwari, Pakistan 42 E2 28 33N 67 44 E
Mirpur Khas, Pakistan 42 G3 25 30N 69 0 E
Mirpur Sakro, Pakistan 42 G2 24 33N 67 41 E
Mirtağ, Turkey 44 B4 38 23N 41 56 E
Miryang, S. Korea 35 G15 35 31N 128 44 E
Mirzapur, India 43 G10 25 10N 82 34 E
Mirzapur-cum-Vindhyachal = Mirzapur, India 43 G10 25 10N 82 34 E
Misantla, Mexico 87 D5 19 56N 96 50W
Misawa, Japan 30 D10 40 41N 141 24 E
Miscou I., Canada 71 C7 47 57N 64 31W
Mish'āb, Ra's al, Si. Arabia 45 D6 28 15N 48 43 E
Mishan, China 33 B8 45 37N 131 48 E
Mishawaka, U.S.A. 76 E2 41 40N 86 11W
Mishima, Japan 31 G9 35 10N 138 52 E
Misión, Mexico 85 N10 32 6N 116 53W
Misiones □, Argentina 95 B5 27 0S 55 0W
Misiones □, Paraguay 94 B4 27 0S 56 0W
Miskah, Si. Arabia 44 E4 24 49N 42 56 E
Miskitos, Cayos, Nic. 88 D3 14 26N 82 50W
Miskolc, Hungary 17 D11 48 7N 20 50 E
Misoke, Dem. Rep. of the Congo 54 C2 0 42S 28 2 E
Misool, Indonesia 37 E8 1 52S 130 10 E
Mişrātah, Libya 51 B9 32 24N 15 3 E
Missanabie, Canada 70 C3 48 20N 84 6W
Missinaibi →, Canada 70 B3 50 43N 81 29W
Missinaibi L., Canada 70 C3 48 23N 83 40W
Mission, Canada 72 D4 49 10N 122 15W
Mission, S. Dak., U.S.A. 80 D4 43 18N 100 39W
Mission, Tex., U.S.A. 81 M5 26 13N 98 20W
Mission Beach, Australia 62 B4 17 53S 146 6 E
Mission Viejo, U.S.A. 85 M9 33 36N 117 40W
Missisa L., Canada 70 B2 52 20N 85 7W
Missisicabi →, Canada 70 B4 51 14N 79 31W
Mississagi →, Canada 70 C3 46 15N 83 9W
Mississauga, Canada 78 C5 43 32N 79 35W
Mississippi □, U.S.A. 81 J10 33 0N 90 0W
Mississippi →, U.S.A. 81 L10 29 9N 89 15W
Mississippi L., Canada 79 A8 45 5N 76 10W
Mississippi River Delta, U.S.A. 81 L9 29 10N 89 15W
Mississippi Sd., U.S.A. 81 K10 30 20N 89 0W
Missoula, U.S.A. 82 C7 46 52N 114 1W
Missouri □, U.S.A. 80 F8 38 25N 92 30W
Missouri →, U.S.A. 80 F9 38 49N 90 7W
Missouri City, U.S.A. 81 L7 29 37N 95 32W
Missouri Valley, U.S.A. 80 E7 41 34N 95 53W
Mist, U.S.A. 84 E3 45 59N 123 15W
Mistassibi →, Canada 71 B5 48 53N 72 13W
Mistassini, Canada 71 C5 48 53N 72 12W
Mistassini →, Canada 71 C5 48 42N 72 20W
Mistassini, L., Canada 70 B5 51 0N 73 30W
Mistastin L., Canada 71 A7 55 57N 63 20W
Mistinibi, L., Canada 71 A7 55 56N 64 17W
Misty L., Canada 73 B8 58 53N 101 40W
Misurata = Mişrātah, Libya 51 B9 32 24N 15 3 E
Mitchell, Australia 63 D4 26 29S 147 58 E
Mitchell, Canada 78 C3 43 28N 81 12W
Mitchell, Nebr., U.S.A. 80 E3 41 57N 103 49W
Mitchell, Oreg., U.S.A. 82 D3 44 34N 120 9W
Mitchell, S. Dak., U.S.A. 80 D6 43 43N 98 2W
Mitchell →, Australia 62 B3 15 12S 141 35 E
Mitchell, Mt., U.S.A. 77 H4 35 46N 82 16W
Mitchell Ranges, Australia 62 A2 12 49S 135 36 E
Mitchelstown, Ireland 13 D3 52 15N 8 16W
Mitha Tiwana, Pakistan 42 C5 32 13N 72 6 E
Mithi, Pakistan 42 G3 24 44N 69 48 E
Mithrao, Pakistan 42 F3 27 28N 69 40 E
Mitilíni, Greece 21 E12 39 6N 26 35 E
Mito, Japan 31 F10 36 20N 140 30 E
Mitrovica = Kosovska Mitrovica, Kosovo, Yug. 21 C9 42 54N 20 52 E
Mitsinjo, Madag. 57 B8 16 1S 45 52 E
Mitsiwa, Eritrea 46 D2 15 35N 39 25 E
Mitsukaidō, Japan 31 F9 36 1N 139 59 E
Mittagong, Australia 63 E5 34 28S 150 29 E
Mittimatalik = Pond Inlet, Canada 69 A12 72 40N 77 0W
Mitú, Colombia 92 C4 1 15N 70 13W
Mitumba, Tanzania 54 D3 7 8S 31 2 E
Mitumba, Mts., Dem. Rep. of the Congo 54 D2 7 0S 27 30 E
Mitwaba, Dem. Rep. of the Congo 55 D2 8 2S 27 17 E
Mityana, Uganda 54 B3 0 23N 32 2 E
Mixteco →, Mexico 87 D5 18 11N 98 30W
Miyagi □, Japan 30 E10 38 15N 140 45 E
Miyāh, W. el →, Syria 44 C3 34 44N 39 57 E
Miyake-Jima, Japan 31 G9 34 5N 139 30 E
Miyako, Japan 30 E10 39 40N 141 59 E
Miyako-Jima, Japan 31 M2 24 45N 125 20 E
Miyako-Rettō, Japan 31 M2 24 24N 125 0 E
Miyakonojō, Japan 31 J5 31 40N 131 5 E
Miyani, India 42 J3 21 50N 69 26 E
Miyanoura-Dake, Japan 31 J5 30 20N 130 31 E
Miyazaki, Japan 31 J5 31 56N 131 30 E
Miyazaki □, Japan 31 H5 32 30N 131 30 E
Miyazu, Japan 31 G7 35 35N 135 10 E
Miyet, Bahr el = Dead Sea, Asia 47 D4 31 30N 35 30 E
Miyoshi, Japan 31 G6 34 48N 132 51 E
Miyun, China 34 D9 40 28N 116 50 E
Miyun Shuiku, China 35 D9 40 30N 117 0 E
Mizdah, Libya 51 B8 31 30N 13 0 E
Mizen Hd., Cork, Ireland 13 E2 51 27N 9 50W
Mizen Hd., Wick., Ireland 13 D5 52 51N 6 4W
Mizhi, China 34 F6 37 47N 110 12 E
Mizoram □, India 41 H18 23 30N 92 40 E
Mizpe Ramon, Israel 47 E3 30 34N 34 49 E
Mizusawa, Japan 30 E10 39 8N 141 8 E
Mjölby, Sweden 9 G16 58 20N 15 10 E
Mjøsa, Norway 9 F14 60 40N 11 0 E
Mkata, Tanzania 54 D4 5 45S 38 20 E
Mkokotoni, Tanzania 54 D4 5 55S 39 15 E
Mkomazi, Tanzania 54 C4 4 40S 38 7 E
Mkomazi →, S. Africa 57 E5 30 12S 30 50 E
Mkulwe, Tanzania 55 D3 8 37S 32 20 E
Mkumbi, Ras, Tanzania 54 D4 7 38S 39 55 E
Mkushi, Zambia 55 E2 14 25S 29 15 E
Mkushi River, Zambia 55 E2 13 32S 29 45 E
Mkuze, S. Africa 57 D5 27 10S 32 0 E
Mladá Boleslav, Czech Rep. 16 C8 50 27N 14 53 E
Mlala Hills, Tanzania 54 D3 6 50S 31 40 E
Mlange = Mulanje, Malawi 55 F4 16 2S 35 33 E
Mlanje, Pic, Malawi 53 H7 15 57S 35 38 E
Mława, Poland 17 B11 53 9N 20 25 E
Mljet, Croatia 20 C7 42 43N 17 30 E
Mmabatho, S. Africa 56 D4 25 49S 25 30 E
Mo i Rana, Norway 8 C16 66 20N 14 7 E
Moa, Cuba 89 B4 20 40N 74 56W
Moa, Indonesia 37 F7 8 0S 128 0 E
Moab, U.S.A. 83 G9 38 35N 109 33W
Moala, Fiji 59 D8 18 36S 179 53 E
Moama, Australia 63 F3 36 7S 144 46 E
Moamba, Mozam. 57 D5 25 36S 32 15 E
Moapa, U.S.A. 85 J12 36 40N 114 37W
Moate, Ireland 13 C4 53 24N 7 44W
Moba, Dem. Rep. of the Congo 54 D2 7 0S 29 48 E
Mobārakābād, Iran 45 D7 28 24N 53 20 E
Mobaye, C.A.R. 52 D4 4 25N 21 5 E
Mobayi, Dem. Rep. of the Congo 52 D4 4 15N 21 8 E
Moberley Lake, Canada 72 B4 55 50N 121 44W
Moberly, U.S.A. 80 F8 39 25N 92 26W
Mobile, U.S.A. 77 K1 30 41N 88 3W
Mobile B., U.S.A. 77 K2 30 30N 88 0W
Mobridge, U.S.A. 80 C4 45 32N 100 26W
Mobutu Sese Seko, L. = Albert, L., Africa 54 B3 1 30N 31 0 E
Moc Chau, Vietnam 38 B5 20 50N 104 38 E
Moc Hoa, Vietnam 39 G5 10 46N 105 56 E
Mocabe Kasari, Dem. Rep. of the Congo 55 D2 9 58S 26 12 E
Moçambique, Mozam. 55 F5 15 3S 40 42 E
Moçâmedes = Namibe, Angola 53 H2 15 7S 12 11 E
Mocanaqua, U.S.A. 79 E8 41 9N 76 8W
Mochudi, Botswana 56 C4 24 27S 26 7 E
Mocimboa da Praia, Mozam. 55 E5 11 25S 40 20 E
Moclips, U.S.A. 84 C2 47 14N 124 13W
Mocoa, Colombia 92 C3 1 7N 76 35W
Mococa, Brazil 95 A6 21 28S 47 0W
Mocorito, Mexico 86 B3 25 30N 107 53W
Moctezuma, Mexico 86 B3 29 50N 109 0W
Moctezuma →, Mexico 87 C5 21 59N 98 34W
Mocuba, Mozam. 55 F4 16 54S 36 57 E
Mocúzari, Presa, Mexico 86 B3 27 10N 109 10W
Modane, France 18 D7 45 12N 6 40 E
Modasa, India 42 H5 23 30N 73 21 E
Modder →, S. Africa 56 D3 29 2S 24 37 E
Modderrivier, S. Africa 56 D3 29 2S 24 38 E
Módena, Italy 20 B4 44 40N 10 55 E
Modena, U.S.A. 83 H7 37 48N 113 56W
Modesto, U.S.A. 84 H6 37 39N 121 0W
Módica, Italy 20 F6 36 52N 14 46 E
Moe, Australia 63 F4 38 12S 146 19 E
Moebase, Mozam. 55 F4 17 3S 38 41 E
Moengo, Surinam 93 B8 5 45N 54 20W
Moffat, U.K. 12 F5 55 21N 3 27W
Moga, India 42 D6 30 48N 75 8 E
Mogadishu = Muqdisho, Somali Rep. 46 G4 2 2N 45 25 E
Mogador = Essaouira, Morocco 50 B4 31 32N 9 42W
Mogalakwena →, S. Africa 57 C4 22 38S 28 40 E
Mogami-Gawa →, Japan 30 E10 38 45N 140 0 E
Mogán, Canary Is. 22 G4 27 53N 15 43W
Mogaung, Burma 41 G20 25 20N 97 0 E
Mogi das Cruzes, Brazil 95 A6 23 31S 46 11W
Mogi-Guaçu →, Brazil 95 A6 20 53S 48 10W
Mogi-Mirim, Brazil 95 A6 22 29S 47 0W
Mogilev = Mahilyow, Belarus 17 B16 53 55N 30 18 E
Mogilev-Podolskiy = Mohyliv-Podilskyy, Ukraine 17 D14 48 26N 27 48 E
Mogincual, Mozam. 55 F5 15 35S 40 25 E
Mogocha, Russia 27 D12 53 40N 119 50 E
Mogok, Burma 41 H20 23 0N 96 40 E
Mogollon Rim, U.S.A. 83 J8 34 10N 110 50W
Mogumber, Australia 61 F2 31 2S 116 3 E
Mohács, Hungary 17 F10 45 58N 18 41 E
Mohales Hoek, Lesotho 56 E4 30 7S 27 26 E
Mohall, U.S.A. 80 A4 48 46N 101 31W
Moḩammadābād, Iran 45 B8 37 52N 59 5 E
Mohammedia, Morocco 50 B4 33 44N 7 21W
Mohana →, India 43 G11 24 43N 85 0 E
Mohanlalganj, India 43 F9 26 41N 80 58 E
Mohave, L., U.S.A. 85 K12 35 12N 114 34W
Mohawk →, U.S.A. 79 D11 42 47N 73 41W
Mohenjodaro, Pakistan 42 F3 27 19N 68 7 E
Mohicanville Reservoir, U.S.A. 78 F3 40 45N 82 0W
Mohoro, Tanzania 54 D4 8 6S 39 8 E
Mohyliv-Podilskyy, Ukraine 17 D14 48 26N 27 48 E
Moidart, L., U.K. 12 E3 56 47N 5 52W
Moira →, Canada 78 B7 44 21N 77 24W
Moires, Greece 23 D6 35 4N 24 56 E
Moisaküla, Estonia 9 G21 58 3N 25 12 E
Moisie, Canada 71 B6 50 12N 66 1W
Moisie →, Canada 71 B6 50 14N 66 5W
Mojave, U.S.A. 85 K8 35 3N 118 10W
Mojave Desert, U.S.A. 85 L10 35 0N 116 30W
Mojo, Bolivia 94 A2 21 48S 65 33W
Mojokerto, Indonesia 37 G15 7 28S 112 26 E
Mokai, N.Z. 59 H5 38 32S 175 56 E
Mokambo, Dem. Rep. of the Congo 55 E2 12 25S 28 20 E
Mokameh, India 43 G11 25 24N 85 55 E
Mokau, N.Z. 59 H5 38 42S 174 39 E
Mokelumne →, U.S.A. 84 G5 38 13N 121 28W
Mokelumne Hill, U.S.A. 84 G6 38 18N 120 43W
Mokhós, Greece 23 D7 35 16N 25 27 E
Mokhotlong, Lesotho 57 D4 29 22S 29 2 E
Mokokchung, India 41 F19 26 15N 94 30 E
Mokolo →, S. Africa 57 C4 23 14S 27 43 E
Mokp'o, S. Korea 35 G14 34 50N 126 25 E
Mokra Gora, Yugoslavia 21 C9 42 50N 20 30 E
Mol, Belgium 15 C5 51 11N 5 5 E
Molchanovo, Russia 26 D9 57 40N 83 50 E
Mold, U.K. 10 D4 53 9N 3 8W
Moldavia = Moldova ■, Europe 17 E15 47 0N 28 0 E
Molde, Norway 8 E12 62 45N 7 9 E
Moldova ■, Europe 17 E15 47 0N 28 0 E
Moldoveanu, Vf., Romania 17 F13 45 36N 24 45 E
Mole →, U.K. 11 F7 51 24N 0 21W
Mole Creek, Australia 62 G4 41 34S 146 24 E
Molepolole, Botswana 56 C4 24 28S 25 28 E
Molfetta, Italy 20 D7 41 12N 16 36 E
Moline, U.S.A. 80 E9 41 30N 90 31W
Molinos, Argentina 94 B2 25 28S 66 15W
Moliro, Dem. Rep. of the Congo 54 D3 8 12S 30 30 E
Mollendo, Peru 92 G4 17 0S 72 0W
Mollerin, L., Australia 61 F2 30 30S 117 35 E
Molodechno = Maladzyechna, Belarus 17 A14 54 20N 26 50 E
Molokai, U.S.A. 74 H16 21 8N 157 0W
Molong, Australia 63 E4 33 5S 148 54 E
Molopo →, Africa 56 D3 27 30S 20 13 E
Molotov = Perm, Russia 24 C10 58 0N 56 10 E
Molson L., Canada 73 C9 54 22N 96 40W
Molteno, S. Africa 56 E4 31 22S 26 22 E
Molu, Indonesia 37 F8 6 45S 131 40 E
Molucca Sea, Indonesia 37 E6 0 0 125 0 E
Moluccas = Maluku, Indonesia 37 E7 1 0S 127 0 E
Moma, Dem. Rep. of the Congo 54 C1 1 35S 23 52 E
Moma, Mozam. 55 F4 16 47S 39 4 E
Mombasa, Kenya 54 C4 4 2S 39 43 E
Mombetsu, Japan 30 B11 44 21N 143 22 E
Momchilgrad, Bulgaria 21 D11 41 33N 25 23 E
Momi, Dem. Rep. of the Congo 54 C2 1 42S 27 0 E
Mompós, Colombia 92 B4 9 14N 74 26W
Møn, Denmark 9 J15 54 57N 12 20 E
Mon □, Burma 41 L20 16 0N 97 30 E
Mona, Canal de la, W. Indies 89 C6 18 30N 67 45W
Mona, Isla, Puerto Rico 89 C6 18 5N 67 54W
Mona, Pta., Costa Rica 88 E3 9 37N 82 36W
Monaca, U.S.A. 78 F4 40 41N 80 17W
Monaco ■, Europe 18 E7 43 46N 7 23 E
Monadhliath Mts., U.K. 12 D4 57 10N 4 4W
Monadnock, Mt., U.S.A. 79 D12 42 52N 72 7W
Monaghan, Ireland 13 B5 54 15N 6 57W
Monaghan □, Ireland 13 B5 54 11N 6 56W
Monahans, U.S.A. 81 K3 31 36N 102 54W
Monapo, Mozam. 55 E5 14 56S 40 19 E
Monar, L., U.K. 12 D3 57 26N 5 8W
Monarch Mt., Canada 72 C3 51 55N 125 57W
Monashee Mts., Canada 72 C5 51 0N 118 43W
Monasterevin, Ireland 13 C4 53 8N 7 4W
Monastir = Bitola, Macedonia 21 D9 41 1N 21 20 E
Moncayo, Sierra del, Spain 19 B5 41 48N 1 50W
Monchegorsk, Russia 24 A5 67 54N 32 58 E
Mönchengladbach, Germany 16 C4 51 11N 6 27 E
Monchique, Portugal 19 D1 37 19N 8 38W
Moncks Corner, U.S.A. 77 J5 33 12N 80 1W
Monclova, Mexico 86 B4 26 50N 101 30W
Moncton, Canada 71 C7 46 7N 64 51W
Mondego →, Portugal 19 B1 40 9N 8 52W
Mondeodo, Indonesia 37 E6 3 34S 122 9 E
Mondovì, Italy 18 D7 44 23N 7 49 E
Mondrain I., Australia 61 F3 34 9S 122 14 E
Monessen, U.S.A. 78 F5 40 9N 79 54W
Monett, U.S.A. 81 G8 36 55N 93 55W
Moneymore, U.K. 13 B5 54 41N 6 40W
Monforte de Lemos, Spain 19 A2 42 31N 7 33W
Mong Hsu, Burma 41 J21 21 54N 98 30 E
Mong Kung, Burma 41 J20 21 35N 97 35 E
Mong Nai, Burma 41 J20 20 32N 97 46 E
Mong Pawk, Burma 41 H21 22 4N 99 16 E
Mong Ton, Burma 41 J21 20 17N 98 45 E
Mong Wa, Burma 41 J22 21 26N 100 27 E
Mong Yai, Burma 41 H21 22 21N 98 3 E
Mongalla, Sudan 51 G12 5 8N 31 42 E
Mongers, L., Australia 61 E2 29 25S 117 5 E
Monghyr = Munger, India 43 G12 25 23N 86 30 E
Mongibello = Etna, Italy 20 F6 37 50N 14 55 E
Mongo, Chad 51 F9 12 14N 18 43 E
Mongolia ■, Asia 27 E10 47 0N 103 0 E
Mongu, Zambia 53 H4 15 16S 23 12 E
Môngua, Angola 56 B2 16 43S 15 20 E
Monifieth, U.K. 12 E6 56 30N 2 48W
Monkey Bay, Malawi 55 E4 14 7S 35 1 E
Monkey Mia, Australia 61 E1 25 48S 113 43 E
Monkey River, Belize 87 D7 16 22N 88 29W
Monkoto, Dem. Rep. of the Congo 52 E4 1 38S 20 35 E
Monkton, Canada 78 C3 43 35N 81 5W
Monmouth, U.K. 11 F5 51 48N 2 42W
Monmouth, Ill., U.S.A. 80 E9 40 55N 90 39W
Monmouth, Oreg., U.S.A. 82 D2 44 51N 123 14W
Monmouthshire □, U.K. 11 F5 51 48N 2 54W
Mono L., U.S.A. 84 H7 38 1N 119 1W

Monolith

144

N

Norderstedt

Neuquén □, *Argentina* 94 D2 38 0S 69 50W
Neuruppin, *Germany* 16 B7 52 55N 12 48 E
Neuse →, *U.S.A.* 77 H7 35 6N 76 29W
Neusiedler See, *Austria* 17 E9 47 50N 16 47 E
Neustrelitz, *Germany* 16 B7 53 21N 13 4 E
Neva →, *Russia* 24 C5 59 50N 30 30 E
Nevada, *Iowa, U.S.A.* 80 D8 42 1N 93 27W
Nevada, *Mo., U.S.A.* 81 G7 37 51N 94 22W
Nevada □, *U.S.A.* 82 G5 39 0N 117 0W
Nevada City, *U.S.A.* 84 F6 39 16N 121 1W
Nevado, Cerro, *Argentina* 94 D2 35 30S 68 32W
Nevel, *Russia* 24 C4 56 0N 29 55 E
Nevers, *France* 18 C5 47 0N 3 9 E
Nevertire, *Australia* 63 E4 31 50S 147 44 E
Neville, *Canada* 73 D7 49 58N 107 39W
Nevinnomyssk, *Russia* 25 F7 44 40N 42 0 E
Nevis, *St. Kitts & Nevis* 89 C7 17 0N 62 30W
Nevşehir, *Turkey* 44 B2 38 33N 34 40 E
Nevyansk, *Russia* 24 C11 57 30N 60 13 E
New →, *U.S.A.* 76 F5 38 10N 81 12W
New Aiyansh, *Canada* 72 B3 55 12N 129 4W
New Albany, *Ind., U.S.A.* 76 F3 38 18N 85 49W
New Albany, *Miss., U.S.A.* 81 H10 34 29N 89 0W
New Albany, *Pa., U.S.A.* 79 E8 41 36N 76 27W
New Amsterdam, *Guyana* 92 B7 6 15N 57 36W
New Angledool, *Australia* 63 D4 29 5S 147 55 E
New Baltimore, *U.S.A.* 78 D2 42 41N 82 44W
New Bedford, *U.S.A.* 79 E14 41 38N 70 56W
New Berlin, *N.Y., U.S.A.* 79 D9 42 37N 75 20W
New Berlin, *Pa., U.S.A.* 78 F8 40 50N 76 57W
New Bern, *U.S.A.* 77 H7 35 7N 77 3W
New Bethlehem, *U.S.A.* 78 F5 41 0N 79 20W
New Bloomfield, *U.S.A.* 78 F7 40 25N 77 11W
New Boston, *U.S.A.* 81 J7 33 28N 94 25W
New Braunfels, *U.S.A.* 81 L5 29 42N 98 8W
New Brighton, *N.Z.* 59 K4 43 29S 172 43 E
New Brighton, *U.S.A.* 78 F4 40 42N 80 19W
New Britain, *Papua N. G.* 64 H7 5 50S 150 20 E
New Britain, *U.S.A.* 79 E12 41 40N 72 47W
New Brunswick, *U.S.A.* 79 F10 40 30N 74 27W
New Brunswick □, *Canada* 71 C6 46 50N 66 30W
New Caledonia ■, *Pac. Oc.* 64 K8 21 0S 165 0 E
New Castile = Castilla-La Mancha □, *Spain* 19 C4 39 30N 3 30W
New Castle, *Ind., U.S.A.* 76 F3 39 55N 85 22W
New Castle, *Pa., U.S.A.* 78 F4 41 0N 80 21W
New City, *U.S.A.* 79 E11 41 9N 73 59W
New Concord, *U.S.A.* 78 G3 39 59N 81 54W
New Cumberland, *U.S.A.* 78 F4 40 30N 80 36W
New Cuyama, *U.S.A.* 85 L7 34 57N 119 38W
New Delhi, *India* 42 E7 28 37N 77 13 E
New Denver, *Canada* 72 D5 50 0N 117 25W
New Don Pedro Reservoir, *U.S.A.* 84 H6 37 43N 120 24W
New England, *U.S.A.* 80 B3 46 32N 102 52W
New England Ra., *Australia* 63 E5 30 20S 151 45 E
New Forest, *U.K.* 11 G6 50 53N 1 34W
New Galloway, *U.K.* 12 F4 55 5N 4 9W
New Glasgow, *Canada* 71 C7 45 35N 62 36W
New Guinea, *Oceania* 28 K17 4 0S 136 0 E
New Hamburg, *Canada* 78 C4 43 23N 80 42W
New Hampshire □, *U.S.A.* 79 C13 44 0N 71 30W
New Hampton, *U.S.A.* 80 D8 43 3N 92 19W
New Hanover, *S. Africa* 57 D5 29 22S 30 31 E
New Hartford, *U.S.A.* 79 C9 43 4N 75 18W
New Haven, *Conn., U.S.A.* 79 E12 41 18N 72 55W
New Haven, *Mich., U.S.A.* 78 D2 42 44N 82 48W
New Hazelton, *Canada* 72 B3 55 20N 127 30W
New Hebrides = Vanuatu ■, *Pac. Oc.* 64 J8 15 0S 168 0 E
New Holland, *U.S.A.* 79 F8 40 6N 76 5W
New Iberia, *U.S.A.* 81 K9 30 1N 91 49W
New Ireland, *Papua N. G.* 64 H7 3 20S 151 50 E
New Jersey □, *U.S.A.* 76 E8 40 0N 74 30W
New Kensington, *U.S.A.* 78 F5 40 34N 79 46W
New Lexington, *U.S.A.* 76 F4 39 43N 82 13W
New Liskeard, *Canada* 70 C4 47 31N 79 41W
New London, *Conn., U.S.A.* 79 E12 41 22N 72 6W
New London, *Ohio, U.S.A.* 78 E2 41 5N 82 24W
New London, *Wis., U.S.A.* 80 C10 44 23N 88 45W
New Madrid, *U.S.A.* 81 G10 36 36N 89 32W
New Martinsville, *U.S.A.* 76 F5 39 39N 80 52W
New Meadows, *U.S.A.* 82 D5 44 58N 116 18W
New Melones L., *U.S.A.* 84 H6 37 57N 120 31W
New Mexico □, *U.S.A.* 83 J10 34 30N 106 0W
New Milford, *Conn., U.S.A.* 79 E11 41 35N 73 25W
New Milford, *Pa., U.S.A.* 79 E9 41 52N 75 44W
New Norcia, *Australia* 61 F2 30 57S 116 13 E
New Norfolk, *Australia* 62 G4 42 46S 147 2 E
New Orleans, *U.S.A.* 81 L9 29 58N 90 4W
New Philadelphia, *U.S.A.* 78 F3 40 30N 81 27W
New Plymouth, *N.Z.* 59 H5 39 4S 174 5 E
New Plymouth, *U.S.A.* 82 E5 43 58N 116 49W
New Port Richey, *U.S.A.* 77 L4 28 16N 82 43W
New Providence, *Bahamas* 88 A4 25 25N 78 35W
New Quay, *U.K.* 11 E3 52 13N 4 21W
New Radnor, *U.K.* 11 E4 52 15N 3 9W
New Richmond, *Canada* 71 C6 48 15N 65 45W
New Richmond, *U.S.A.* 80 C8 45 7N 92 32W
New Roads, *U.S.A.* 81 K9 30 42N 91 26W
New Rochelle, *U.S.A.* 79 F11 40 55N 73 47W
New Rockford, *U.S.A.* 80 B5 47 41N 99 8W
New Romney, *U.K.* 11 G8 50 59N 0 57 E
New Ross, *Ireland* 13 D5 52 23N 6 57W
New Salem, *U.S.A.* 80 B4 46 51N 101 25W
New Scone, *U.K.* 12 E5 56 25N 3 24W
New Siberian I. = Novaya Sibir, Ostrov, *Russia* 27 B16 75 10N 150 0 E
New Siberian Is. = Novosibirskiye Ostrova, *Russia* 27 B15 75 0N 142 0 E
New Smyrna Beach, *U.S.A.* 77 L5 29 1N 80 56W
New South Wales □, *Australia* 63 E4 33 0S 146 0 E
New Town, *U.S.A.* 80 B3 47 59N 102 30W
New Tredegar, *U.K.* 11 F4 51 44N 3 16W
New Ulm, *U.S.A.* 80 C7 44 19N 94 28W
New Waterford, *Canada* 71 C7 46 13N 60 4W
New Westminster, *Canada* 84 A4 49 13N 122 55W
New York, *U.S.A.* 79 F11 40 45N 74 0W
New York □, *U.S.A.* 79 D9 43 0N 75 0W
New York Mts., *U.S.A.* 83 J6 35 0N 115 20W
New Zealand ■, *Oceania* 59 J6 40 0S 176 0 E
Newaj →, *India* 42 G7 24 24N 76 49 E
Newala, *Tanzania* 55 E4 10 58S 39 18 E
Newark, *Del., U.S.A.* 76 F8 39 41N 75 46W
Newark, *N.J., U.S.A.* 79 F10 40 44N 74 10W
Newark, *N.Y., U.S.A.* 78 C7 43 3N 77 6W
Newark, *Ohio, U.S.A.* 78 F2 40 3N 82 24W
Newark-on-Trent, *U.K.* 10 D7 53 5N 0 48W
Newark Valley, *U.S.A.* 79 D8 42 14N 76 11W
Newberg, *U.S.A.* 82 D2 45 18N 122 58W
Newberry, *Mich., U.S.A.* 76 B3 46 21N 85 30W
Newberry, *S.C., U.S.A.* 77 H5 34 17N 81 37W
Newberry Springs, *U.S.A.* 85 L10 34 50N 116 41W
Newboro L., *Canada* 79 B8 44 38N 76 20W
Newbridge = Droichead Nua, *Ireland* 13 C5 53 11N 6 48W
Newburgh, *Canada* 78 B8 44 19N 76 52W
Newburgh, *U.S.A.* 79 E10 41 30N 74 1W
Newbury, *U.K.* 11 F6 51 24N 1 20W
Newbury, *N.H., U.S.A.* 79 B12 43 19N 72 3W
Newbury, *Vt., U.S.A.* 79 B12 44 5N 72 4W
Newburyport, *U.S.A.* 77 D10 42 49N 70 53W
Newcastle, *Australia* 63 E5 33 0S 151 46 E
Newcastle, *N.B., Canada* 71 C6 47 1N 65 38W
Newcastle, *Ont., Canada* 70 D4 43 55N 78 35W
Newcastle, *S. Africa* 57 D4 27 45S 29 58 E
Newcastle, *U.K.* 13 B6 54 13N 5 54W
Newcastle, *Calif., U.S.A.* 84 G5 38 53N 121 8W
Newcastle, *Wyo., U.S.A.* 80 D2 43 50N 104 11W
Newcastle Emlyn, *U.K.* 11 E3 52 2N 4 28W
Newcastle Ra., *Australia* 60 C5 15 45S 130 15 E
Newcastle-under-Lyme, *U.K.* 10 D5 53 1N 2 14W
Newcastle-upon-Tyne, *U.K.* 10 C6 54 58N 1 36W
Newcastle Waters, *Australia* 62 B1 17 30S 133 28 E
Newcastle West, *Ireland* 13 D2 52 27N 9 3W
Newcomb, *U.S.A.* 79 C10 43 58N 74 10W
Newcomerstown, *U.S.A.* 78 F3 40 16N 81 36W
Newdegate, *Australia* 61 F2 33 6S 119 0 E
Newell, *Australia* 62 B4 16 20S 145 16 E
Newell, *U.S.A.* 80 C3 44 43N 103 25W
Newfane, *U.S.A.* 78 C6 43 17N 78 43W
Newfield, *U.S.A.* 79 D8 42 18N 76 33W
Newfound L., *U.S.A.* 79 C13 43 40N 71 47W
Newfoundland, *Canada* 66 E14 49 0N 55 0W
Newfoundland, *U.S.A.* 79 E9 41 18N 75 19W
Newfoundland □, *Canada* 71 B8 53 0N 58 0W
Newhall, *U.S.A.* 85 L8 34 23N 118 32W
Newhaven, *U.K.* 11 G8 50 47N 0 3 E
Newkirk, *U.S.A.* 81 G6 36 53N 97 3W
Newlyn, *U.K.* 11 G2 50 6N 5 34W
Newman, *Australia* 60 D2 23 18S 119 45 E
Newman, *U.S.A.* 84 H5 37 19N 121 1W
Newmarket, *Canada* 78 B5 44 3N 79 28W
Newmarket, *Ireland* 13 D2 52 13N 9 0W
Newmarket, *U.K.* 11 E8 52 15N 0 25 E
Newmarket, *U.S.A.* 79 C14 43 4N 70 56W
Newnan, *U.S.A.* 77 J3 33 23N 84 48W
Newport, *Ireland* 13 C2 53 53N 9 33W
Newport, *I. of W., U.K.* 11 G6 50 42N 1 17W
Newport, *Newp., U.K.* 11 F5 51 35N 3 0W
Newport, *Ark., U.S.A.* 81 H9 35 37N 91 16W
Newport, *Ky., U.S.A.* 76 F3 39 5N 84 30W
Newport, *N.H., U.S.A.* 79 C12 43 22N 72 10W
Newport, *N.Y., U.S.A.* 79 C9 43 11N 75 1W
Newport, *Oreg., U.S.A.* 82 D1 44 39N 124 3W
Newport, *Pa., U.S.A.* 78 F7 40 29N 77 8W
Newport, *R.I., U.S.A.* 79 E13 41 29N 71 19W
Newport, *Tenn., U.S.A.* 77 H4 35 58N 83 11W
Newport, *Vt., U.S.A.* 79 B12 44 56N 72 13W
Newport, *Wash., U.S.A.* 82 B5 48 11N 117 3W
Newport □, *U.K.* 11 F4 51 33N 3 1W
Newport Beach, *U.S.A.* 85 M9 33 37N 117 56W
Newport News, *U.S.A.* 76 G7 36 59N 76 25W
Newport Pagnell, *U.K.* 11 E7 52 5N 0 43W
Newquay, *U.K.* 11 G2 50 25N 5 6W
Newry, *U.K.* 13 B5 54 11N 6 21W
Newton, *Ill., U.S.A.* 80 F10 38 59N 88 10W
Newton, *Iowa, U.S.A.* 80 E8 41 42N 93 3W
Newton, *Kans., U.S.A.* 81 F6 38 3N 97 21W
Newton, *Mass., U.S.A.* 79 D13 42 21N 71 12W
Newton, *Miss., U.S.A.* 81 J10 32 19N 89 10W
Newton, *N.C., U.S.A.* 77 H5 35 40N 81 13W
Newton, *N.J., U.S.A.* 79 E10 41 3N 74 45W
Newton, *Tex., U.S.A.* 81 K8 30 51N 93 46W
Newton Abbot, *U.K.* 11 G4 50 32N 3 37W
Newton Aycliffe, *U.K.* 10 C6 54 37N 1 34W
Newton Falls, *U.S.A.* 78 E4 41 11N 80 59W
Newton Stewart, *U.K.* 12 G4 54 57N 4 30W
Newtonmore, *U.K.* 12 D4 57 4N 4 8W
Newtown, *U.K.* 11 E4 52 31N 3 19W
Newtownabbey, *U.K.* 13 B6 54 40N 5 56W
Newtownards, *U.K.* 13 B6 54 36N 5 42W
Newtownbarry = Bunclody, *Ireland* 13 D5 52 39N 6 40W
Newtownstewart, *U.K.* 13 B4 54 43N 7 23W
Newville, *U.S.A.* 78 F7 40 10N 77 24W
Neya, *Russia* 24 C7 58 21N 43 49 E
Neyrīz, *Iran* 45 D7 29 15N 54 19 E
Neyshābūr, *Iran* 45 B8 36 10N 58 50 E
Nezhin = Nizhyn, *Ukraine* 25 D5 51 5N 31 55 E
Nezperce, *U.S.A.* 82 C5 46 14N 116 14W
Ngabang, *Indonesia* 36 D3 0 23N 109 55 E
Ngabordamlu, Tanjung, *Indonesia* 37 F8 6 56S 134 11 E
N'Gage, *Angola* 52 F3 7 46S 15 16 E
Ngami Depression, *Botswana* 56 C3 20 30S 22 46 E
Ngamo, *Zimbabwe* 55 F2 19 3S 27 32 E
Nganglong Kangri, *China* 41 C12 33 0N 81 0 E
Ngao, *Thailand* 38 C2 18 46N 99 59 E
Ngaoundéré, *Cameroon* 52 C2 7 15N 13 35 E
Ngapara, *N.Z.* 59 L3 44 57S 170 46 E
Ngara, *Tanzania* 54 C3 2 29S 30 40 E
Ngawi, *Indonesia* 37 G14 7 24S 111 26 E
Nghia Lo, *Vietnam* 38 B5 21 33N 104 28 E
Ngoma, *Malawi* 55 E3 13 8S 33 45 E
Ngomahura, *Zimbabwe* 55 G3 20 26S 30 43 E
Ngomba, *Tanzania* 55 D3 8 20S 32 53 E
Ngoring Hu, *China* 32 C4 34 55N 97 5 E
Ngorongoro, *Tanzania* 54 C4 3 11S 35 32 E
Ngozi, *Burundi* 54 C2 2 54S 29 50 E
Ngudu, *Tanzania* 54 C3 2 58S 33 25 E
Nguigmi, *Niger* 51 F8 14 20N 13 20 E
Nguiu, *Australia* 60 B5 11 46S 130 38 E
Ngukurr, *Australia* 62 A1 14 44S 134 44 E
Ngunga, *Tanzania* 54 C3 3 37S 33 37 E
Nguru, *Nigeria* 51 F8 12 56N 10 29 E
Nguru Mts., *Tanzania* 54 D4 6 0S 37 30 E
Ngusi, *Malawi* 55 E3 14 0S 34 50 E
Nguyen Binh, *Vietnam* 38 A5 22 39N 105 56 E
Nha Trang, *Vietnam* 39 F7 12 16N 109 10 E
Nhacoongo, *Mozam.* 57 C6 24 18S 35 14 E
Nhamaabué, *Mozam.* 55 F4 17 25S 35 5 E
Nhamundá →, *Brazil* 93 D7 2 12S 56 41W
Nhangulaze, L., *Mozam.* 57 C5 24 0S 34 30 E
Nhill, *Australia* 63 F3 36 18S 141 40 E
Nho Quan, *Vietnam* 38 B5 20 18N 105 45 E
Nhulunbuy, *Australia* 62 A2 12 10S 137 20 E
Nia-nia, *Dem. Rep. of the Congo* 54 B2 1 30N 27 40 E
Niagara Falls, *Canada* 78 C5 43 7N 79 5W
Niagara Falls, *U.S.A.* 78 C6 43 5N 79 4W
Niagara-on-the-Lake, *Canada* 78 C5 43 15N 79 4W
Niah, *Malaysia* 36 D4 3 58N 113 46 E
Niamey, *Niger* 50 F6 13 27N 2 6 E
Niangara, *Dem. Rep. of the Congo* 54 B2 3 42N 27 50 E
Niantic, *U.S.A.* 79 E12 41 20N 72 11W
Nias, *Indonesia* 36 D1 1 0N 97 30 E
Niassa □, *Mozam.* 55 E4 13 30S 36 0 E
Nibāk, *Si. Arabia* 45 E7 24 25N 50 50 E
Nicaragua ■, *Cent. Amer.* 88 D2 11 40N 85 30W
Nicaragua, L. de, *Nic.* 88 D2 12 0N 85 30W
Nicastro, *Italy* 20 E7 38 59N 16 19 E
Nice, *France* 18 E7 43 42N 7 14 E
Niceville, *U.S.A.* 77 K2 30 31N 86 30W
Nichicun, L., *Canada* 71 B5 53 5N 71 0W
Nichinan, *Japan* 31 J5 31 38N 131 23 E
Nicholás, Canal, *W. Indies* 88 B3 23 30N 80 5W
Nicholasville, *U.S.A.* 76 G3 37 53N 84 34W
Nichols, *U.S.A.* 79 D8 42 1N 76 22W
Nicholson, *Australia* 60 C4 18 2S 128 54 E
Nicholson, *U.S.A.* 79 E9 41 37N 75 47W
Nicholson →, *Australia* 62 B2 17 31S 139 36 E
Nicholson L., *Canada* 73 A8 62 40N 102 40W
Nicholson Ra., *Australia* 61 E2 27 15S 116 45 E
Nicholville, *U.S.A.* 79 B10 44 41N 74 39W
Nicobar Is., *Ind. Oc.* 29 J13 8 0N 93 30 E
Nicola, *Canada* 72 C4 50 12N 120 40W
Nicolls Town, *Bahamas* 88 A4 25 8N 78 0W
Nicosia, *Cyprus* 23 D12 35 10N 33 25 E
Nicoya, *Costa Rica* 88 D2 10 9N 85 27W
Nicoya, G. de, *Costa Rica* 88 E3 10 0N 85 0W
Nicoya, Pen. de, *Costa Rica* 88 E2 9 45N 85 40W
Nidd →, *U.K.* 10 D6 53 59N 1 23W
Niedersachsen □, *Germany* 16 B5 52 50N 9 0 E
Niekerkshoop, *S. Africa* 56 D3 29 19S 22 51 E
Niemba, *Dem. Rep. of the Congo* 54 D2 5 58S 28 24 E
Niemen = Neman →, *Lithuania* 9 J19 55 25N 21 10 E
Nienburg, *Germany* 16 B5 52 39N 9 13 E
Nieu Bethesda, *S. Africa* 56 E3 31 51S 24 34 E
Nieuw Amsterdam, *Surinam* 93 B7 5 53N 55 5W
Nieuw Nickerie, *Surinam* 93 B7 6 0N 56 59W
Nieuwoudtville, *S. Africa* 56 E2 31 23S 19 7 E
Nieuwpoort, *Belgium* 15 C2 51 8N 2 45 E
Nieves, Pico de las, *Canary Is.* 22 G4 27 57N 15 35W
Niğde, *Turkey* 25 G5 37 58N 34 40 E
Nigel, *S. Africa* 57 D4 26 27S 28 25 E
Niger ■, *W. Afr.* 50 E7 17 30N 10 0 E
Niger →, *W. Afr.* 50 G7 5 33N 6 33 E
Nigeria ■, *W. Afr.* 50 G7 8 30N 8 0 E
Nighasin, *India* 43 E9 28 14N 80 52 E
Nightcaps, *N.Z.* 59 L2 45 57S 168 2 E
Nii-Jima, *Japan* 31 G9 34 20N 139 15 E
Niigata, *Japan* 30 F9 37 58N 139 0 E
Niigata □, *Japan* 31 F9 37 15N 138 45 E
Niihama, *Japan* 31 H6 33 55N 133 16 E
Niihau, *U.S.A.* 74 H14 21 54N 160 9W
Niimi, *Japan* 31 G6 34 59N 133 28 E
Niitsu, *Japan* 30 F9 37 48N 139 7 E
Nijil, *Jordan* 47 E4 30 32N 35 33 E
Nijkerk, *Neths.* 15 B5 52 13N 5 30 E
Nijmegen, *Neths.* 15 C5 51 50N 5 52 E
Nijverdal, *Neths.* 15 B6 52 22N 6 28 E
Nīk Pey, *Iran* 45 B6 36 50N 48 10 E
Nikiniki, *Indonesia* 37 F6 9 49S 124 30 E
Nikkō, *Japan* 31 F9 36 45N 139 35 E
Nikolayev = Mykolayiv, *Ukraine* 25 E5 46 58N 32 0 E
Nikolayevsk, *Russia* 25 E8 50 0N 45 35 E
Nikolayevsk-na-Amur, *Russia* 27 D15 53 8N 140 44 E
Nikolskoye, *Russia* 27 D17 55 12N 166 0 E
Nikopol, *Ukraine* 25 E5 47 35N 34 25 E
Nīkshahr, *Iran* 45 E9 26 15N 60 10 E
Nikšić, *Montenegro, Yug.* 21 C8 42 50N 18 57 E
Nîl, Nahr en →, *Africa* 51 B12 30 10N 31 6 E
Nîl el Abyad →, *Sudan* 51 E12 15 38N 32 31 E
Nîl el Azraq →, *Sudan* 51 E12 15 38N 32 31 E
Nila, *Indonesia* 37 F7 6 44S 129 31 E
Niland, *U.S.A.* 85 M11 33 14N 115 31W
Nile = Nîl, Nahr en →, *Africa* 51 B12 30 10N 31 6 E
Niles, *Mich., U.S.A.* 76 E2 41 50N 86 15W
Niles, *Ohio, U.S.A.* 78 E4 41 11N 80 46W
Nim Ka Thana, *India* 42 F6 27 44N 75 48 E
Nimach, *India* 42 G6 24 30N 74 56 E
Nimbahera, *India* 42 G6 24 37N 74 45 E
Nîmes, *France* 18 E6 43 50N 4 23 E
Nimfaíon, Ákra = Pínnes, Ákra, *Greece* 21 D11 40 5N 24 20 E
Nimmitabel, *Australia* 63 F4 36 29S 149 15 E
Nīnawá, *Iraq* 44 B4 36 25N 43 10 E
Nindigully, *Australia* 63 D4 28 21S 148 50 E
Nineveh = Nīnawá, *Iraq* 44 B4 36 25N 43 10 E
Ning Xian, *China* 34 G4 35 30N 107 58 E
Ning'an, *China* 35 B15 44 22N 129 20 E
Ningbo, *China* 33 D7 29 51N 121 28 E
Ningcheng, *China* 35 D10 41 32N 119 53 E
Ningjin, *China* 34 F8 37 35N 114 57 E
Ningjing Shan, *China* 32 D4 30 0N 98 20 E
Ningling, *China* 34 G8 34 25N 115 22 E
Ningpo = Ningbo, *China* 33 D7 29 51N 121 28 E
Ningqiang, *China* 34 H4 32 47N 106 15 E
Ningshan, *China* 34 H5 33 21N 108 21 E
Ningsia Hui A.R. = Ningxia Huizu Zizhiqu □, *China* 34 F4 38 0N 106 0 E
Ningwu, *China* 34 E7 39 0N 112 18 E
Ningxia Huizu Zizhiqu □, *China* 34 F4 38 0N 106 0 E
Ningyang, *China* 34 G9 35 47N 116 45 E
Ninh Binh, *Vietnam* 38 B5 20 15N 105 55 E
Ninh Giang, *Vietnam* 38 B6 20 44N 106 24 E
Ninh Hoa, *Vietnam* 38 F7 12 48N 109 7 E
Ninh Ma, *Vietnam* 38 F7 12 48N 109 21 E
Ninove, *Belgium* 15 D4 50 51N 4 2 E
Nioaque, *Brazil* 95 A4 21 5S 55 50W
Niobrara, *U.S.A.* 80 D6 42 45N 98 2W
Niobrara →, *U.S.A.* 80 D6 42 46N 98 3W
Nioro du Sahel, *Mali* 50 E4 15 15N 9 30W
Niort, *France* 18 C3 46 19N 0 29W
Nipawin, *Canada* 73 C8 53 20N 104 0W
Nipigon, *Canada* 70 C2 49 0N 88 17W
Nipigon, L., *Canada* 70 C2 49 50N 88 30W
Nipishish L., *Canada* 71 B7 54 12N 60 45W
Nipissing, L., *Canada* 70 C4 46 20N 80 0W
Nipomo, *U.S.A.* 85 K6 35 3N 120 29W
Nipton, *U.S.A.* 85 K11 35 28N 115 16W
Niquelândia, *Brazil* 93 F9 14 33S 48 23W
Nīr, *Iran* 44 B5 38 2N 47 59 E
Nirasaki, *Japan* 31 G9 35 42N 138 27 E
Nirmal, *India* 40 K11 19 3N 78 20 E
Nirmali, *India* 43 F12 26 20N 86 35 E
Niš, *Serbia, Yug.* 21 C9 43 19N 21 58 E
Nişāb, *Si. Arabia* 44 D5 29 11N 44 43 E
Nişāb, *Yemen* 46 E4 14 25N 46 29 E
Nishinomiya, *Japan* 31 G7 34 45N 135 20 E
Nishino'omote, *Japan* 31 J5 30 43N 130 59 E
Nishiwaki, *Japan* 31 G7 34 59N 134 58 E
Niskibi →, *Canada* 70 A2 56 29N 88 9W
Nisqually →, *U.S.A.* 84 C4 47 6N 122 42W
Nissáki, *Greece* 23 A3 39 43N 19 52 E
Nissum Bredning, *Denmark* 9 H13 56 40N 8 20 E
Nistru = Dnister →, *Europe* 17 E16 46 18N 30 17 E
Nisutlin →, *Canada* 72 A2 60 14N 132 34W
Nitchequon, *Canada* 71 B5 53 10N 70 58W
Niterói, *Brazil* 95 A7 22 52S 43 0W
Nith →, *Canada* 78 C4 43 12N 80 23W
Nith →, *U.K.* 12 F5 55 14N 3 33W
Nitra, *Slovak Rep.* 17 D10 48 19N 18 4 E
Nitra →, *Slovak Rep.* 17 E10 47 46N 18 10 E
Niuafo'ou, *Tonga* 59 B11 15 30S 175 58W
Niue, *Cook Is.* 65 J11 19 2S 169 54W
Niut, *Indonesia* 36 D4 0 55N 110 6 E
Niuzhuang, *China* 35 D12 40 58N 122 28 E
Nivala, *Finland* 8 E21 63 56N 24 57 E
Nivelles, *Belgium* 15 D4 50 35N 4 20 E
Nivernais, *France* 18 C5 47 15N 3 30 E
Niwas, *India* 43 H9 23 3N 80 26 E
Nixon, *U.S.A.* 81 L6 29 16N 97 46W
Nizamabad, *India* 40 K11 18 45N 78 7 E
Nizamghat, *India* 41 E19 28 20N 95 45 E
Nizhne Kolymsk, *Russia* 27 C17 68 34N 160 55 E
Nizhnekamsk, *Russia* 24 C9 55 38N 51 49 E
Nizhneudinsk, *Russia* 27 D10 54 54N 99 3 E
Nizhnevartovsk, *Russia* 26 C8 60 56N 76 38 E
Nizhniy Novgorod, *Russia* 24 C7 56 20N 44 0 E
Nizhniy Tagil, *Russia* 24 C10 57 55N 59 57 E
Nizhyn, *Ukraine* 25 D5 51 5N 31 55 E
Nizip, *Turkey* 44 B3 37 5N 37 50 E
Nízké Tatry, *Slovak Rep.* 17 D10 48 55N 19 30 E
Njakwa, *Malawi* 55 E3 11 1S 33 56 E
Njanji, *Zambia* 55 E3 14 25S 31 46 E
Njinjo, *Tanzania* 55 D4 8 48S 38 54 E
Njombe, *Tanzania* 55 D3 9 20S 34 50 E
Njombe →, *Tanzania* 54 D4 6 56S 35 6 E
Nkana, *Zambia* 55 E2 12 50S 28 8 E
Nkandla, *S. Africa* 57 D5 28 37S 31 5 E
Nkayi, *Zimbabwe* 55 F2 19 41S 29 20 E
Nkhotakota, *Malawi* 55 E3 12 56S 34 15 E
Nkongsamba, *Cameroon* 52 D1 4 55N 9 55 E
Nkurenkuru, *Namibia* 56 B2 17 42S 18 32 E
Nmai →, *Burma* 41 G20 25 30N 97 25 E
Noakhali = Maijdi, *Bangla.* 41 H17 22 48N 91 10 E
Nobel, *Canada* 78 A4 45 25N 80 6W
Nobeoka, *Japan* 31 H5 32 36N 131 41 E
Noblesville, *U.S.A.* 76 E3 40 3N 86 1W
Nocera Inferiore, *Italy* 20 D6 40 44N 14 38 E
Nocona, *U.S.A.* 81 J6 33 47N 97 44W
Noda, *Japan* 31 G9 35 56N 139 52 E
Nogales, *Mexico* 86 A2 31 20N 110 56W
Nogales, *U.S.A.* 83 L8 31 20N 110 56W
Nōgata, *Japan* 31 H5 33 48N 130 44 E
Noggerup, *Australia* 61 F2 33 32S 116 5 E
Noginsk, *Russia* 27 C10 64 30N 90 50 E
Nogoa →, *Australia* 62 C4 23 40S 147 55 E
Nogoyá, *Argentina* 94 C4 32 24S 59 48W
Nohar, *India* 42 E6 29 11N 74 49 E
Nohta, *India* 43 H8 23 40N 79 34 E
Noires, Mts., *France* 18 B2 48 11N 3 40W
Noirmoutier, Î. de, *France* 18 C2 46 58N 2 10W
Nojane, *Botswana* 56 C3 23 15S 20 14 E
Nojima-Zaki, *Japan* 31 G9 34 54N 139 53 E
Nok Kundi, *Pakistan* 40 E3 28 50N 62 45 E
Nokaneng, *Botswana* 56 B3 19 40S 22 17 E
Nokia, *Finland* 9 F20 61 30N 23 30 E
Nokomis, *Canada* 73 C8 51 35N 105 0W
Nokomis L., *Canada* 73 B8 57 0N 103 0W
Nola, *C.A.R.* 52 D3 3 35N 16 4 E
Noma Omuramba →, *Namibia* 56 B3 18 52S 20 53 E
Nombre de Dios, *Panama* 88 E4 9 34N 79 28W
Nome, *U.S.A.* 68 B3 64 30N 165 25W
Nomo-Zaki, *Japan* 31 H4 32 35N 129 44 E
Nonacho L., *Canada* 73 A7 61 42N 109 40W
Nonda, *Australia* 62 C3 20 40S 142 28 E
Nong Chang, *Thailand* 38 E2 15 23N 99 51 E
Nong Het, *Laos* 38 C4 19 29N 103 59 E
Nong Khai, *Thailand* 38 D4 17 50N 102 46 E
Nong'an, *China* 35 B13 44 25N 125 5 E
Nongoma, *S. Africa* 57 D5 27 58S 31 35 E
Nonoava, *Mexico* 86 B3 27 28N 106 44W
Nonoava →, *Mexico* 86 B3 27 29N 106 45W
Nonthaburi, *Thailand* 38 F3 13 51N 100 34 E
Noonamah, *Australia* 60 B5 12 40S 131 4 E
Noord Brabant □, *Neths.* 15 C5 51 40N 5 0 E
Noord Holland □, *Neths.* 15 B4 52 30N 4 45 E
Noordbeveland, *Neths.* 15 C3 51 35N 3 50 E
Noordoostpolder, *Neths.* 15 B5 52 45N 5 45 E
Noordwijk, *Neths.* 15 B4 52 14N 4 26 E
Nootka I., *Canada* 72 D3 49 32N 126 42W
Nopiming Prov. Park, *Canada* 73 C9 50 30N 95 37W
Noralee, *Canada* 72 C3 53 59N 126 26W
Noranda = Rouyn-Noranda, *Canada* 70 C4 48 20N 79 0W
Norco, *U.S.A.* 85 M9 33 56N 117 33W
Nord-Kivu □, *Dem. Rep. of the Congo* 54 C2 1 0S 29 0 E
Nord-Ostsee-Kanal, *Germany* 16 A5 54 12N 9 32 E
Nordaustlandet, *Svalbard* 4 B9 79 14N 23 0 E
Nordegg, *Canada* 72 C5 52 29N 116 5W
Norderney, *Germany* 16 B4 53 42N 7 9 E
Norderstedt, *Germany* 16 B5 53 42N 10 1 E

O

Orford Ness

Oakhurst, U.S.A. 84 H7 37 19N 119 40W
Oakland, U.S.A. 84 H4 37 49N 122 16W
Oakley, Idaho, U.S.A. 82 E7 42 15N 113 53W
Oakley, Kans., U.S.A. 80 F4 39 8N 100 51W
Oakover →, Australia 60 D3 21 0S 120 40 E
Oakridge, U.S.A. 82 E2 43 45N 122 28W
Oakville, Canada 78 C5 43 27N 79 41W
Oakville, U.S.A. 84 D3 46 51N 123 14W
Oamaru, N.Z. 59 L3 45 5S 170 59 E
Oasis, Calif., U.S.A. 85 M10 33 28N 116 6W
Oasis, Nev., U.S.A. 84 H9 37 29N 117 55W
Oates Land, Antarctica 5 C11 69 0S 160 0 E
Oatlands, Australia 62 G4 42 17S 147 21 E
Oatman, U.S.A. 85 K12 35 1N 114 19W
Oaxaca, Mexico 87 D5 17 2N 96 40W
Oaxaca □, Mexico 87 D5 17 0N 97 0W
Ob →, Russia 26 C7 66 45N 69 30 E
Oba, Canada 70 C3 49 4N 84 7W
Obama, Japan 31 G7 35 30N 135 45 E
Oban, U.K. 12 E3 56 25N 5 29W
Obbia, Somali Rep. 46 F4 5 25N 48 30 E
Obera, Argentina 95 B4 27 21S 55 2W
Oberhausen, Germany 16 C4 51 28N 6 51 E
Oberlin, Kans., U.S.A. 80 F4 39 49N 100 32W
Oberlin, La., U.S.A. 81 K8 30 37N 92 46W
Oberlin, Ohio, U.S.A. 78 E2 41 18N 82 13W
Oberon, Australia 63 E4 33 45S 149 52 E
Obi, Indonesia 37 E7 1 23S 127 45 E
Óbidos, Brazil 93 D7 1 50S 55 30W
Obihiro, Japan 30 C11 42 56N 143 12 E
Obilatu, Indonesia 37 E7 1 25S 127 20 E
Obluchye, Russia 27 E14 49 1N 131 4 E
Obo, C.A.R. 54 A2 5 20N 26 32 E
Oboa, Mt., Uganda 54 B3 1 45N 34 45 E
Oboyan, Russia 26 D4 51 15N 36 21 E
Obozerskaya = Obozerskiy, Russia 24 B7 63 34N 40 21 E
Obozerskiy, Russia 24 B7 63 34N 40 21 E
Observatory Inlet, Canada 72 B3 55 10N 129 54W
Obshchi Syrt, Russia 6 E16 52 0N 53 0 E
Obskaya Guba, Russia 26 C8 69 0N 73 0 E
Obuasi, Ghana 50 G5 6 17N 1 40W
Ocala, U.S.A. 77 L4 29 11N 82 8W
Ocampo, Chihuahua, Mexico 86 B3 28 9N 108 24W
Ocampo, Tamaulipas, Mexico 87 C5 22 50N 99 20W
Ocaña, Spain 19 C4 39 55N 3 30W
Ocanomowoc, U.S.A. 80 D10 43 7N 88 30W
Occidental, Cordillera, Colombia 92 C3 5 0N 76 0W
Occidental, Grand Erg, Algeria 50 B6 30 20N 1 0 E
Ocean City, Md., U.S.A. 76 F8 38 20N 75 5W
Ocean City, N.J., U.S.A. 76 F8 39 17N 74 35W
Ocean City, Wash., U.S.A. 84 C2 47 4N 124 10W
Ocean Falls, Canada 72 C3 52 18N 127 48W
Ocean I. = Banaba, Kiribati 64 H8 0 45S 169 50 E
Ocean Park, U.S.A. 84 D2 46 30N 124 3W
Oceano, U.S.A. 85 K6 35 6N 120 37W
Oceanport, U.S.A. 79 F10 40 19N 74 3W
Oceanside, U.S.A. 85 M9 33 12N 117 23W
Ochil Hills, U.K. 12 E5 56 14N 3 40W
Ocilla, U.S.A. 77 K4 31 36N 83 15W
Ocmulgee →, U.S.A. 77 K4 31 58N 82 33W
Ocniţa, Moldova 17 D14 48 25N 27 30 E
Oconee →, U.S.A. 77 K4 31 58N 82 33W
Oconto, U.S.A. 76 C2 44 53N 87 52W
Oconto Falls, U.S.A. 76 C1 44 52N 88 9W
Ocosingo, Mexico 87 D6 17 10N 92 15W
Ocotal, Nic. 88 D2 13 41N 86 31W
Ocotlán, Mexico 86 C4 20 21N 102 42W
Ocotlán de Morelos, Mexico 87 D5 16 48N 96 40W
Ōda, Japan 31 G6 35 11N 132 30 E
Ódáðahraun, Iceland 8 D5 65 5N 17 0W
Odate, Japan 30 D10 40 16N 140 34 E
Odawara, Japan 31 G9 35 20N 139 6 E
Odda, Norway 9 F12 60 3N 6 35 E
Odei →, Canada 73 B9 56 6N 96 54W
Ödemiş, Turkey 21 E13 38 15N 28 0 E
Odendaalsrus, S. Africa 56 D4 27 48S 26 45 E
Odense, Denmark 9 J14 55 22N 10 23 E
Oder →, Europe 16 B8 53 33N 14 38 E
Odesa, Ukraine 25 E5 46 30N 30 45 E
Odessa = Odesa, Ukraine 25 E5 46 30N 30 45 E
Odessa, Canada 79 B8 44 17N 76 43W
Odessa, Tex., U.S.A. 81 K3 31 52N 102 23W
Odessa, Wash., U.S.A. 82 C4 47 20N 118 41W
Odiakwe, Botswana 56 C4 20 12S 25 17 E
Odienné, Ivory C. 50 G4 9 30N 7 34W
Odintsovo, Russia 24 C6 55 39N 37 15 E
O'Donnell, U.S.A. 81 J4 32 58N 101 50W
Odorheiu Secuiesc, Romania 17 E13 46 21N 25 21 E
Odra = Oder →, Europe 16 B8 53 33N 14 38 E
Odzi, Zimbabwe 57 B5 19 0S 32 20 E
Odzi →, Zimbabwe 57 B5 19 45S 32 23 E
Oeiras, Brazil 93 E10 7 0S 42 8W
Oelrichs, U.S.A. 80 D3 43 11N 103 14W
Oelwein, U.S.A. 80 D9 42 41N 91 55W
Oenpelli, Australia 60 B5 12 20S 133 4 E
Ofanto →, Italy 20 D7 41 22N 16 13 E
Offa, Nigeria 50 G6 8 13N 4 42 E
Offaly □, Ireland 13 C4 53 15N 7 30W
Offenbach, Germany 16 C5 50 6N 8 44 E
Offenburg, Germany 16 D4 48 28N 7 56 E
Ofotfjorden, Norway 8 B17 68 27N 17 0 E
Ōfunato, Japan 30 E10 39 4N 141 43 E
Oga, Japan 30 E9 39 55N 139 50 E
Oga-Hantō, Japan 30 E9 39 58N 139 47 E
Ogaden, Ethiopia 46 F3 7 30N 45 30 E
Ōgaki, Japan 31 G8 35 21N 136 37 E
Ogallala, U.S.A. 80 E4 41 8N 101 43W
Ogasawara Gunto, Pac. Oc. 28 G18 27 0N 142 0 E
Ogbomosho, Nigeria 50 G6 8 1N 4 11 E
Ogden, U.S.A. 82 F7 41 13N 111 58W
Ogdensburg, U.S.A. 79 B9 44 42N 75 30W
Ogeechee →, U.S.A. 77 K5 31 50N 81 3W
Ogilby, U.S.A. 85 N12 32 49N 114 50W
Oglio →, Italy 20 B4 45 2N 10 39 E
Ogmore, Australia 62 C4 22 37S 149 35 E
Ogoki, Canada 70 B2 51 38N 85 58W
Ogoki →, Canada 70 B2 51 38N 85 57W
Ogoki L., Canada 70 B2 50 50N 87 10W
Ogoki Res., Canada 70 B2 50 45N 88 15W
Ogooué →, Gabon 52 E1 1 0S 9 0 E
Ogowe = Ogooué →, Gabon 52 E1 1 0S 9 0 E
Ogre, Latvia 9 H21 56 49N 24 36 E
Ogurchinskiy, Ostrov, Turkmenistan 45 B7 38 55N 53 2 E
Ohai, N.Z. 59 L2 45 55S 168 0 E
Ohakune, N.Z. 59 H5 39 24S 175 24 E
Ohata, Japan 30 D10 41 24N 141 10 E
Ohau, L., N.Z. 59 L2 44 15S 169 53 E
Ohio □, U.S.A. 78 F2 40 15N 82 45W
Ohio →, U.S.A. 76 G1 36 59N 89 8W
Ohře →, Czech Rep. 16 C8 50 30N 14 10 E
Ohrid, Macedonia 21 D9 41 8N 20 52 E
Ohridsko Jezero, Macedonia 21 D9 41 8N 20 52 E
Ohrigstad, S. Africa 57 C5 24 39S 30 36 E
Oiapoque, Brazil 93 3 50N 51 50W
Oikou, China 35 E9 38 35N 117 42 E
Oil City, U.S.A. 78 E5 41 26N 79 42W
Oil Springs, Canada 78 D2 42 47N 82 7W
Oildale, U.S.A. 85 K7 35 25N 119 1W
Oise →, France 18 B5 49 0N 2 4 E
Ōita, Japan 31 H5 33 14N 131 36 E
Ōita □, Japan 31 H5 33 15N 131 30 E
Oiticica, Brazil 93 E10 5 3S 41 5W
Ojacaliente, Mexico 86 C4 22 34N 102 15W
Ojai, U.S.A. 85 L7 34 27N 119 15W
Ojinaga, Mexico 86 B4 29 34N 104 25W
Ojiya, Japan 31 F9 37 18N 138 48 E
Ojos del Salado, Cerro, Argentina 94 B2 27 0S 68 40W
Oka →, Russia 24 C7 56 20N 43 59 E
Okaba, Indonesia 37 F9 8 6S 139 42 E
Okahandja, Namibia 56 C2 22 0S 16 59 E
Okanagan L., Canada 72 D5 50 0N 119 30W
Okanogan, U.S.A. 82 B4 48 22N 119 35W
Okanogan →, U.S.A. 82 B4 48 6N 119 44W
Okaputa, Namibia 56 C2 20 5S 17 0 E
Okara, Pakistan 42 D5 30 50N 73 31 E
Okaukuejo, Namibia 56 B2 19 10S 16 0 E
Okavango Delta, Botswana 56 B3 18 45S 22 45 E
Okavango Swamp = Okavango Delta, Botswana 56 B3 18 45S 22 45 E
Okaya, Japan 31 F9 36 5N 138 10 E
Okayama, Japan 31 G6 34 40N 133 54 E
Okayama □, Japan 31 G6 35 0N 133 50 E
Okazaki, Japan 31 G8 34 57N 137 10 E
Okeechobee, U.S.A. 77 M5 27 15N 80 50W
Okeechobee, L., U.S.A. 77 M5 27 0N 80 50W
Okefenokee Swamp, U.S.A. 77 K4 30 40N 82 20W
Okehampton, U.K. 11 G4 50 44N 4 0W
Okha, India 42 H3 22 27N 69 4 E
Okha, Russia 27 D15 53 40N 143 0 E
Okhotsk, Russia 27 D15 59 20N 143 10 E
Okhotsk, Sea of, Asia 27 D15 55 0N 145 0 E
Okhotskiy Perevoz, Russia 27 C14 61 52N 135 35 E
Okhtyrka, Ukraine 25 D5 50 25N 35 0 E
Oki-Shotō, Japan 31 F6 36 5N 133 15 E
Okiep, S. Africa 56 D2 29 39S 17 53 E
Okinawa □, Japan 31 L4 26 40N 128 0 E
Okinawa-Guntō, Japan 31 L4 26 40N 128 0 E
Okinawa-Jima, Japan 31 L4 26 32N 128 0 E
Okino-erabu-Shima, Japan 31 L4 27 21N 128 33 E
Oklahoma □, U.S.A. 81 H6 35 20N 97 30W
Oklahoma City, U.S.A. 81 H6 35 30N 97 30W
Okmulgee, U.S.A. 81 H7 35 37N 95 58W
Oknitsa = Ocniţa, Moldova 17 D14 48 25N 27 30 E
Okolo, Uganda 54 B3 2 37N 31 8 E
Okolona, U.S.A. 81 J10 34 0N 88 45W
Okombahe, Namibia 56 C2 21 23S 15 22 E
Okotoks, Canada 72 C6 50 43N 113 58W
Oksibil, Indonesia 37 E10 4 59S 140 35 E
Oksovskiy, Russia 24 B6 62 33N 39 57 E
Oktabrsk = Oktyabrsk, Kazakstan 25 E10 49 28N 57 25 E
Oktyabrsk, Kazakstan 25 E10 49 28N 57 25 E
Oktyabrskiy = Aktsyabrski, Belarus 17 B15 52 38N 28 53 E
Oktyabrskiy, Russia 24 D9 54 28N 53 28 E
Oktyabrskoy Revolyutsii, Ostrov, Russia 27 B10 79 30N 97 0 E
Okuru, N.Z. 59 K2 43 55S 168 55 E
Okushiri-Tō, Japan 30 C9 42 15N 139 30 E
Okwa →, Botswana 56 C3 22 30S 23 0 E
Ola, U.S.A. 81 H8 35 2N 93 13W
Ólafsfjörður, Iceland 8 C4 66 4N 18 39W
Ólafsvík, Iceland 8 D2 64 53N 23 43W
Olancha, U.S.A. 85 J8 36 17N 118 1W
Olancha Pk., U.S.A. 85 J8 36 15N 118 7W
Olanchito, Honduras 88 C2 15 30N 86 30W
Öland, Sweden 9 H17 56 45N 16 38 E
Olary, Australia 63 E3 32 18S 140 19 E
Olascoaga, Argentina 94 D3 35 15S 60 39W
Olathe, U.S.A. 80 F7 38 53N 94 49W
Olavarría, Argentina 94 D3 36 55S 60 20W
Oława, Poland 17 C9 50 57N 17 20 E
Ólbia, Italy 20 D3 40 55N 9 31 E
Olcott, U.S.A. 78 C6 43 20N 78 42W
Old Bahama Chan. = Bahama, Canal Viejo de, W. Indies 88 B4 22 10N 77 30W
Old Baldy Pk. = San Antonio, Mt., U.S.A. 85 L9 34 17N 117 38W
Old Castile = Castilla y Leon □, Spain 19 B3 42 0N 5 0W
Old Crow, Canada 68 B6 67 30N 139 55W
Old Dale, U.S.A. 85 L11 34 8N 115 47W
Old Forge, N.Y., U.S.A. 79 C10 43 43N 74 58W
Old Forge, Pa., U.S.A. 79 E9 41 22N 75 45W
Old Perlican, Canada 71 C9 48 5N 53 1W
Old Shinyanga, Tanzania 54 C3 3 33S 33 27 E
Old Speck Mt., U.S.A. 79 B14 44 34N 70 57W
Old Town, U.S.A. 77 C11 44 56N 68 39W
Old Washington, U.S.A. 78 F3 40 2N 81 27W
Old Wives L., Canada 73 C7 50 5N 106 0W
Oldbury, U.K. 11 F5 51 38N 2 33W
Oldcastle, Ireland 13 C4 53 46N 7 10W
Oldeani, Tanzania 54 C4 3 22S 35 35 E
Oldenburg, Germany 16 B5 53 9N 8 13 E
Oldenzaal, Neths. 15 B6 52 19N 6 53 E
Oldham, U.K. 10 D5 53 33N 2 7W
Oldman →, Canada 72 D6 49 57N 111 42W
Oldmeldrum, U.K. 12 D6 57 20N 2 19W
Olds, Canada 72 C6 51 50N 114 10W
Oldziyt, Mongolia 34 B5 44 40N 109 1 E
Olean, U.S.A. 78 D6 42 5N 78 26W
Olekma →, Russia 27 C13 60 22N 120 42 E
Olekminsk, Russia 27 C13 60 25N 120 30 E
Oleksandriya, Ukraine 17 C14 50 37N 26 19 E
Olema, U.S.A. 84 G4 38 3N 122 47W
Olenegorsk, Russia 24 A5 68 9N 33 18 E
Olenek, Russia 27 C12 68 28N 112 18 E
Olenek →, Russia 27 B13 73 0N 120 10 E
Oléron, Î. d', France 18 D3 45 55N 1 15W
Oleśnica, Poland 17 C9 51 13N 17 22 E
Olevsk, Ukraine 17 C14 51 12N 27 39 E
Olga, Russia 27 E14 43 50N 135 14 E
Olga, L., Canada 70 C4 49 47N 77 15W
Olga, Mt., Australia 61 E5 25 20S 130 50 E
Olhão, Portugal 19 D2 37 3N 7 48W
Olifants →, Africa 57 C5 23 57S 31 58 E
Olifants →, Namibia 56 C2 25 30S 19 30 E
Olifantshoek, S. Africa 56 D3 27 57S 22 42 E
Ólimbos, Óros, Greece 21 D10 40 6N 22 23 E
Olímpia, Brazil 95 A6 20 44S 48 54W
Olinda, Brazil 93 E12 8 1S 34 51W
Oliva, Argentina 94 C3 32 0S 63 38W
Olivehurst, U.S.A. 84 F5 39 6N 121 34W
Olivenza, Spain 19 C2 38 41N 7 9W
Oliver, Canada 72 D5 49 13N 119 37W
Oliver L., Canada 73 B8 56 56N 103 22W
Ollagüe, Chile 94 A2 21 15S 68 10W
Olney, Ill., U.S.A. 76 F1 38 44N 88 5W
Olney, Tex., U.S.A. 81 J5 33 22N 98 45W
Olomane →, Canada 71 B7 50 14N 60 37W
Olomouc, Czech Rep. 17 D9 49 38N 17 12 E
Olonets, Russia 24 B5 61 0N 32 54 E
Olongapo, Phil. 37 B6 14 50N 120 18 E
Olot, Spain 19 A7 42 11N 2 30 E
Olovyannaya, Russia 27 D12 50 58N 115 35 E
Oloy →, Russia 27 C16 66 29N 159 29 E
Olsztyn, Poland 17 B11 53 48N 20 29 E
Olt →, Romania 17 G13 43 43N 24 51 E
Olteniţa, Romania 17 F14 44 7N 26 42 E
Olton, U.S.A. 81 H3 34 11N 102 8W
Olymbos, Cyprus 23 D12 35 21N 33 45 E
Olympia, Greece 21 F9 37 39N 21 39 E
Olympia, U.S.A. 84 D4 47 3N 122 53W
Olympic Dam, Australia 63 E2 30 30S 136 55 E
Olympic Mts., U.S.A. 84 C3 47 55N 123 45W
Olympic Nat. Park, U.S.A. 84 C3 47 48N 123 30W
Olympus, Cyprus 23 E11 34 56N 32 52 E
Olympus, Mt. = Ólimbos, Óros, Greece 21 D10 40 6N 22 23 E
Olympus, Mt. = Uludağ, Turkey 21 D13 40 4N 29 13 E
Olympus, Mt., U.S.A. 84 C3 47 48N 123 43W
Olyphant, U.S.A. 79 E9 41 27N 75 36W
Om →, Russia 26 D8 54 59N 73 22 E
Om Koi, Thailand 38 D2 17 48N 98 22 E
Ōma, Japan 30 D10 41 45N 141 5 E
Ōmachi, Japan 31 F8 36 30N 137 50 E
Omae-Zaki, Japan 31 G9 34 36N 138 14 E
Ōmagari, Japan 30 E10 39 27N 140 29 E
Omagh, U.K. 13 B4 54 36N 7 19W
Omagh □, U.K. 13 B4 54 35N 7 15W
Omaha, U.S.A. 80 E7 41 17N 95 58W
Omak, U.S.A. 82 B4 48 25N 119 31W
Omalos, Greece 23 D5 35 19N 23 55 E
Oman ■, Asia 46 C6 23 0N 58 0 E
Oman, G. of, Asia 45 E8 24 30N 58 30 E
Omaruru, Namibia 56 C2 21 26S 16 0 E
Omaruru →, Namibia 56 C1 22 7S 14 15 E
Omate, Peru 92 G4 16 45S 71 0W
Ombai, Selat, Indonesia 37 F6 8 30S 124 50 E
Omboué, Gabon 52 E1 1 35S 9 15 E
Ombrone →, Italy 20 C4 42 42N 11 5 E
Omdurmân, Sudan 51 E12 15 40N 32 28 E
Omemee, Canada 78 B6 44 18N 78 33W
Omeonga, Dem. Rep. of the Congo 54 C1 3 40S 24 22 E
Ometepe, I. de, Nic. 88 D2 11 32N 85 35W
Ometepec, Mexico 87 D5 16 39N 98 23W
Ominato, Japan 30 D10 41 17N 141 10 E
Omineca →, Canada 72 B4 56 3N 124 16W
Omitara, Namibia 56 C2 22 16S 18 2 E
Ōmiya, Japan 31 G9 35 54N 139 38 E
Ommen, Neths. 15 B6 52 31N 6 26 E
Ömnögovĭ □, Mongolia 34 C3 43 15N 104 0 E
Omo →, Ethiopia 46 F2 6 25N 36 10 E
Omodhos, Cyprus 23 E11 34 51N 32 48 E
Omolon →, Russia 27 C16 68 42N 158 36 E
Omono-Gawa →, Japan 30 E10 39 46N 140 3 E
Omsk, Russia 26 D8 55 0N 73 12 E
Omsukchan, Russia 27 C16 62 32N 155 48 E
Ōmu, Japan 30 B11 44 34N 142 58 E
Omul, Vf., Romania 17 F13 45 27N 25 29 E
Ōmura, Japan 31 H4 32 56N 129 57 E
Omuramba Omatako →, Namibia 56 B2 17 45S 20 25 E
Omuramba Ovambo →, Namibia 56 B2 18 45S 16 59 E
Ōmuta, Japan 31 H5 33 5N 130 26 E
Onaga, U.S.A. 80 F6 39 29N 96 10W
Onalaska, U.S.A. 80 D9 43 53N 91 14W
Onancock, U.S.A. 76 G8 37 43N 75 45W
Onang, Indonesia 37 E5 3 2S 118 49 E
Onaping L., Canada 70 C3 47 3N 81 30W
Onavas, Mexico 86 B3 28 28N 109 30W
Onawa, U.S.A. 80 D6 42 2N 96 6W
Oncócua, Angola 56 B1 16 30S 13 25 E
Onda, Spain 19 C5 39 55N 0 17W
Ondaejin, N. Korea 35 D15 41 34N 129 40 E
Ondangwa, Namibia 56 B2 17 57S 16 4 E
Ondjiva, Angola 56 B2 16 48S 15 50 E
Ōndörshil, Mongolia 34 B5 45 13N 108 5 E
Öndverðarnes, Iceland 8 D1 64 52N 24 0W
One Tree, Australia 63 E3 34 11S 144 43 E
Onega, Russia 24 B6 64 0N 38 10 E
Onega →, Russia 24 B6 63 58N 38 2 E
Onega, G. of = Onezhskaya Guba, Russia 24 B6 64 24N 36 38 E
Onega, L. = Onezhskoye Ozero, Russia 24 B6 61 44N 35 22 E
Oneida, U.S.A. 79 C9 43 6N 75 39W
Oneida L., U.S.A. 79 C9 43 12N 75 54W
O'Neill, U.S.A. 80 D5 42 27N 98 39W
Onekotan, Ostrov, Russia 27 E16 49 25N 154 45 E
Onema, Dem. Rep. of the Congo 54 C1 4 35S 24 30 E
Oneonta, U.S.A. 79 D9 42 27N 75 4W
Oneşti, Romania 17 E14 46 17N 26 47 E
Onezhskaya Guba, Russia 24 B6 64 24N 36 38 E
Onezhskoye Ozero, Russia 24 B6 61 44N 35 22 E
Ongarue, N.Z. 59 H5 38 42S 175 19 E
Ongers →, S. Africa 56 E3 31 4S 23 13 E
Ongerup, Australia 61 F2 33 58S 118 28 E
Ongjin, N. Korea 35 F13 37 56N 125 21 E
Ongkharak, Thailand 38 E3 14 8N 101 1 E
Ongniud Qi, China 35 C10 43 0N 118 38 E
Ongoka, Dem. Rep. of the Congo 54 C2 1 20S 26 0 E
Ongole, India 40 M12 15 33N 80 2 E
Ongon = Havirga, Mongolia 34 B7 45 41N 113 5 E
Onida, U.S.A. 80 C4 44 42N 100 4W
Onilahy →, Madag. 57 C7 23 34S 43 45 E
Onitsha, Nigeria 50 G7 6 6N 6 42 E
Onoda, Japan 31 G5 33 59N 131 11 E
Onpyŏng-ni, S. Korea 35 H14 33 25N 126 55 E
Onslow, Australia 60 D2 21 40S 115 12 E
Onslow B., U.S.A. 77 H7 34 20N 77 15W
Ontake-San, Japan 31 G8 35 53N 137 29 E
Ontario, Calif., U.S.A. 85 L9 34 4N 117 39W
Ontario, Oreg., U.S.A. 82 D5 44 2N 116 58W
Ontario □, Canada 70 B2 48 0N 83 0W
Ontario, L., N. Amer. 78 C7 43 20N 78 0W
Ontonagon, U.S.A. 80 B10 46 52N 89 19W
Onyx, U.S.A. 85 K8 35 41N 118 14W
Oodnadatta, Australia 63 D2 27 33S 135 30 E
Ooldea, Australia 61 F5 30 27S 131 50 E
Oombulgurri, Australia 60 C4 15 15S 127 45 E
Oorindi, Australia 62 C3 20 40S 141 1 E
Oost-Vlaanderen □, Belgium 15 C3 51 5N 3 50 E
Oostende, Belgium 15 C2 51 15N 2 54 E
Oosterhout, Neths. 15 C4 51 39N 4 47 E
Oosterschelde →, Neths. 15 C4 51 33N 4 0 E
Oosterwolde, Neths. 15 B6 53 0N 6 17 E
Ootacamund = Udagamandalam, India 40 P10 11 30N 76 44 E
Ootsa L., Canada 72 C3 53 50N 126 2W
Opala, Dem. Rep. of the Congo 54 C1 0 40S 24 20 E
Opanake, Sri Lanka 40 R12 6 35N 80 40 E
Opasatika, Canada 70 C3 49 30N 82 50W
Opasquia Prov. Park, Canada 70 B1 53 33N 93 5W
Opava, Czech Rep. 17 D9 49 57N 17 58 E
Opelika, U.S.A. 77 J3 32 39N 85 23W
Opelousas, U.S.A. 81 K8 30 32N 92 5W
Opémisca, L., Canada 70 C5 49 56N 74 52W
Opheim, U.S.A. 82 B10 48 51N 106 24W
Ophthalmia Ra., Australia 60 D2 23 15S 119 30 E
Opinaca →, Canada 70 B4 52 15N 78 2W
Opinaca, Rés., Canada 70 B4 52 39N 76 20W
Opinnagau →, Canada 70 B3 54 12N 82 25W
Opiscoteo, L., Canada 71 B6 53 10N 68 10W
Opole, Poland 17 C9 50 42N 17 58 E
Opononо L., Namibia 56 B2 18 8S 15 45 E
Oporto = Porto, Portugal 19 B1 41 8N 8 40W
Opotiki, N.Z. 59 H6 38 1S 177 19 E
Opp, U.S.A. 77 K2 31 17N 86 16W
Oppdal, Norway 9 E13 62 35N 9 41 E
Opportunity, U.S.A. 82 C5 47 39N 117 15W
Opua, N.Z. 59 F5 35 19S 174 9 E
Opunake, N.Z. 59 H4 39 26S 173 52 E
Opuwo, Namibia 56 B1 18 3S 13 45 E
Ora, Cyprus 23 E12 34 51N 33 12 E
Oracle, U.S.A. 83 K8 32 37N 110 46W
Oradea, Romania 17 E11 47 2N 21 58 E
Öræfajökull, Iceland 8 D5 64 2N 16 39W
Orai, India 43 G8 25 58N 79 30 E
Oral = Zhayyq →, Kazakstan 25 E9 47 0N 51 48 E
Oral, Kazakstan 25 D9 51 20N 51 20 E
Oran, Algeria 50 A5 35 45N 0 39W
Orange, Australia 63 E4 33 15S 149 7 E
Orange, France 18 D6 44 8N 4 47 E
Orange, Calif., U.S.A. 85 M9 33 47N 117 51W
Orange, Mass., U.S.A. 79 D12 42 35N 72 19W
Orange, Tex., U.S.A. 81 K8 30 6N 93 44W
Orange, Va., U.S.A. 76 F6 38 15N 78 7W
Orange →, S. Africa 56 D2 28 41S 16 28 E
Orange, C., Brazil 93 C8 4 20N 51 30W
Orange Cove, U.S.A. 84 J7 36 38N 119 19W
Orange Free State = Free State □, S. Africa 56 D4 28 30S 27 0 E
Orange Grove, U.S.A. 81 M6 27 58N 97 56W
Orange Walk, Belize 87 D7 18 6N 88 33W
Orangeburg, U.S.A. 77 J5 33 30N 80 52W
Orangeville, Canada 78 C4 43 55N 80 5W
Oranienburg, Germany 16 B7 52 45N 13 14 E
Oranje = Orange →, S. Africa 56 D2 28 41S 16 28 E
Oranje Vrystaat = Free State □, S. Africa 56 D4 28 30S 27 0 E
Oranjemund, Namibia 56 D2 28 38S 16 29 E
Oranjerivier, S. Africa 56 D3 29 40S 24 12 E
Oranjestad, Aruba 89 D5 12 32N 70 2W
Orapa, Botswana 53 J5 21 15S 25 30 E
Oras, Phil. 37 B7 12 9N 125 28 E
Oraşul Stalin = Braşov, Romania 17 F13 45 38N 25 35 E
Orbetello, Italy 20 C4 42 27N 11 13 E
Orbisonia, U.S.A. 78 F7 40 15N 77 54W
Orbost, Australia 63 F4 37 40S 148 29 E
Orcas I., U.S.A. 84 B4 48 42N 122 56W
Orchard City, U.S.A. 83 G10 38 50N 107 58W
Orchila, I., Venezuela 89 D6 11 48N 66 10W
Orcutt, U.S.A. 85 L6 34 52N 120 27W
Ord, U.S.A. 80 E5 41 36N 98 56W
Ord →, Australia 60 C4 15 33S 128 15 E
Ord, Mt., Australia 60 C4 17 20S 125 34 E
Orderville, U.S.A. 83 H7 37 17N 112 38W
Ordos = Mu Us Shamo, China 34 E5 39 0N 109 0 E
Ordu, Turkey 25 F6 40 55N 37 53 E
Ordway, U.S.A. 80 F3 38 13N 103 46W
Ordzhonikidze = Vladikavkaz, Russia 25 F7 43 0N 44 35 E
Ore, Dem. Rep. of the Congo 54 B2 3 17N 29 30 E
Ore Mts. = Erzgebirge, Germany 16 C7 50 27N 12 55 E
Örebro, Sweden 9 G16 59 20N 15 18 E
Oregon, U.S.A. 80 D10 42 1N 89 20W
Oregon □, U.S.A. 82 E3 44 0N 121 0W
Oregon City, U.S.A. 84 E4 45 21N 122 36W
Orekhovo-Zuyevo, Russia 24 C6 55 50N 38 55 E
Orel, Russia 24 D6 52 57N 36 3 E
Orem, U.S.A. 82 F8 40 19N 111 42W
Ören, Turkey 21 F12 37 3N 27 57 E
Orenburg, Russia 24 D10 51 45N 55 6 E
Orense = Ourense, Spain 19 A2 42 19N 7 55W
Orepuki, N.Z. 59 M1 46 19S 167 46 E
Orestiás, Greece 21 D12 41 30N 26 33 E
Orestos Pereyra, Mexico 86 B3 26 31N 105 40W
Orford Ness, U.K. 11 E9 52 5N 1 35 E

153

Randers

Randers, *Denmark* 9 H14 56 29N 10 1 E
Randfontein, *S. Africa* 57 D4 26 8S 27 45 E
Randle, *U.S.A.* 84 D5 46 32N 121 57W
Randolph, *Mass., U.S.A.* 79 D13 42 10N 71 2W
Randolph, *N.Y., U.S.A.* 78 D6 42 10N 78 59W
Randolph, *Utah, U.S.A.* 82 F8 41 40N 111 11W
Randolph, *Vt., U.S.A.* 79 C12 43 55N 72 40W
Randsburg, *U.S.A.* 85 K9 35 22N 117 39W
Råne älv →, *Sweden* 8 D20 65 50N 22 20 E
Rangae, *Thailand* 39 J3 6 19N 101 44 E
Rangaunu B., *N.Z.* 59 F4 34 51S 173 15 E
Rangeley, *U.S.A.* 79 B14 44 58N 70 39W
Rangeley L., *U.S.A.* 79 B14 44 55N 70 43W
Rangely, *U.S.A.* 82 F9 40 5N 108 48W
Ranger, *U.S.A.* 81 J5 32 28N 98 41W
Rangia, *India* 41 F17 26 28N 91 38 E
Rangiora, *N.Z.* 59 K4 43 19S 172 36 E
Rangitaiki →, *N.Z.* 59 G6 37 54S 176 49 E
Rangitata →, *N.Z.* 59 K3 43 45S 171 15 E
Rangkasbitung, *Indonesia* 37 G12 6 21S 106 15 E
Rangon →, *Burma* 41 L20 16 28N 96 40 E
Rangoon, *Burma* 41 L20 16 45N 96 20 E
Rangpur, *Bangla.* 41 G16 25 42N 89 22 E
Rangsit, *Thailand* 38 F3 13 59N 100 37 E
Ranibennur, *India* 40 M9 14 35N 75 30 E
Raniganj, *Ut. P., India* 43 F9 27 3N 82 13 E
Raniganj, *W. Bengal, India* 41 H15 23 40N 87 5 E
Ranikhet, *India* 43 E8 29 39N 79 25 E
Raniwara, *India* 40 G8 24 50N 72 10 E
Rāniyah, *Iraq* 44 B5 36 15N 44 53 E
Ranka, *India* 43 H10 23 59N 83 47 E
Ranken →, *Australia* 62 C2 20 31S 137 36 E
Rankin, *U.S.A.* 81 K4 31 13N 101 56W
Rankin Inlet, *Canada* 68 B10 62 30N 93 0W
Rankins Springs, *Australia* 63 E4 33 49S 146 14 E
Rannoch, L., *U.K.* 12 E4 56 41N 4 20W
Rannoch Moor, *U.K.* 12 E4 56 38N 4 48W
Ranobe, Helodranon' i, *Madag.* 57 C7 23 3S 43 33 E
Ranohira, *Madag.* 57 C8 22 29S 45 24 E
Ranomafana, *Toamasina, Madag.* 57 B8 18 57S 48 50 E
Ranomafana, *Toliara, Madag.* 57 C8 24 34S 47 0 E
Ranomena, *Madag.* 57 C8 23 25S 47 17 E
Ranong, *Thailand* 39 H2 9 56N 98 40 E
Ranotsara Nord, *Madag.* 57 C8 22 48S 46 36 E
Rānsa, *Iran* 45 C6 33 39N 48 18 E
Ransiki, *Indonesia* 37 E8 1 30S 134 10 E
Rantabe, *Madag.* 57 B8 15 42S 49 39 E
Rantauprapat, *Indonesia* 36 D1 2 15N 99 50 E
Rantemario, *Indonesia* 37 E5 3 15S 119 57 E
Rantoul, *U.S.A.* 76 E1 40 19N 88 9W
Raoyang, *China* 34 E8 38 15N 115 45 E
Rapa, *Pac. Oc.* 65 K13 27 35S 144 20W
Rapa Nui = Pascua, I. de, *Chile* 65 K17 27 7S 109 23W
Rapallo, *Italy* 18 D8 44 21N 9 14 E
Rapar, *India* 42 H4 23 34N 70 38 E
Rāpch, *Iran* 45 E8 25 40N 59 15 E
Raper, C., *Canada* 69 B13 69 44N 67 6W
Rapid City, *U.S.A.* 80 D3 44 5N 103 14W
Rapid River, *U.S.A.* 76 C2 45 55N 86 58W
Rapla, *Estonia* 9 G21 59 1N 24 52 E
Rapti →, *India* 43 F10 26 18N 83 41 E
Raquette →, *U.S.A.* 79 B10 45 0N 74 42W
Raquette Lake, *U.S.A.* 79 C10 43 49N 74 40W
Rarotonga, *Cook Is.* 65 K12 21 30S 160 0W
Ra's al 'Ayn, *Syria* 44 B4 36 45N 40 12 E
Ra's al Khaymah, *U.A.E.* 46 B6 25 50N 55 59 E
Rasca, Pta. de la, *Canary Is.* 22 G3 27 59N 16 41W
Raseiniai, *Lithuania* 9 J20 55 25N 23 5 E
Rashmi, *India* 42 G6 25 4N 74 22 E
Rasht, *Iran* 45 B6 37 20N 49 40 E
Rasi Salai, *Thailand* 38 E5 15 20N 104 9 E
Rason L., *Australia* 61 E3 28 45S 124 25 E
Rasra, *India* 43 G10 25 50N 83 50 E
Rasul, *Pakistan* 42 C5 32 42N 73 34 E
Rat Buri, *Thailand* 38 F2 13 30N 99 54 E
Rat Islands, *U.S.A.* 68 C1 52 0N 178 0 E
Rat L., *Canada* 73 B9 56 10N 99 40W
Ratangarh, *India* 42 E6 28 5N 74 35 E
Raṭāwī, *Iraq* 44 D5 30 38N 47 13 E
Rath, *India* 43 G8 25 36N 79 37 E
Rath Luirc, *Ireland* 13 D3 52 21N 8 40W
Rathdrum, *Ireland* 13 D5 52 56N 6 14W
Rathenow, *Germany* 16 B7 52 37N 12 19 E
Rathkeale, *Ireland* 13 D3 52 32N 8 56W
Rathlin I., *U.K.* 13 A5 55 18N 6 14W
Rathmelton, *Ireland* 13 A4 55 2N 7 38W
Ratibor = Racibórz, *Poland* 17 C10 50 7N 18 18 E
Ratlam, *India* 42 H6 23 20N 75 0 E
Ratnagiri, *India* 40 L8 16 57N 73 18 E
Ratodero, *Pakistan* 42 F3 27 48N 68 18 E
Raton, *U.S.A.* 81 G2 36 54N 104 24W
Rattaphum, *Thailand* 39 J3 7 8N 100 16 E
Rattray Hd., *U.K.* 12 D7 57 38N 1 50W
Ratz, Mt., *Canada* 72 B2 57 23N 132 12W
Raub, *Malaysia* 39 L3 3 47N 101 52 E
Rauch, *Argentina* 94 D4 36 45S 59 5W
Raudales de Malpaso, *Mexico* 87 D6 17 30N 23 30W
Raufarhöfn, *Iceland* 8 C6 66 27N 15 57W
Raufoss, *Norway* 9 F14 60 44N 10 37 E
Raukumara Ra., *N.Z.* 59 H6 38 5S 177 55 E
Rauma, *Finland* 9 F19 61 10N 21 30 E
Raurkela, *India* 43 H11 22 14N 84 50 E
Rausu-Dake, *Japan* 30 B12 44 4N 145 7 E
Rava-Ruska, *Poland* 17 C12 50 15N 23 42 E
Rava Russkaya = Rava-Ruska, *Poland* 17 C12 50 15N 23 42 E
Ravalli, *U.S.A.* 82 C6 47 17N 114 11W
Ravānsar, *Iran* 44 C5 34 43N 46 40 E
Rāvar, *Iran* 45 D8 31 20N 56 51 E
Ravena, *U.S.A.* 79 D11 42 28N 73 49W
Ravenna, *Italy* 20 B5 44 25N 12 12 E
Ravenna, *Nebr., U.S.A.* 80 E5 41 1N 98 55W
Ravenna, *Ohio, U.S.A.* 78 E3 41 9N 81 15W
Ravensburg, *Germany* 16 E5 47 46N 9 36 E
Ravenshoe, *Australia* 62 B4 17 37S 145 29 E
Ravensthorpe, *Australia* 61 F3 33 35S 120 2 E
Ravenswood, *Australia* 62 C4 20 6S 146 54 E
Ravenswood, *U.S.A.* 76 F5 38 57N 81 46W
Ravi →, *Pakistan* 42 D4 30 35N 71 49 E
Rawalpindi, *Pakistan* 42 C5 33 38N 73 8 E
Rawāndūz, *Iraq* 44 B5 36 40N 44 30 E
Rawang, *Malaysia* 39 L3 3 20N 101 35 E
Rawene, *N.Z.* 59 F4 35 25S 173 32 E
Rawlinna, *Australia* 61 F4 30 58S 125 28 E
Rawlins, *U.S.A.* 82 F10 41 47N 107 14W
Rawlinson Ra., *Australia* 61 D4 24 40S 128 30 E
Rawson, *Argentina* 96 E3 43 15S 65 5W
Raxaul, *India* 43 F11 26 59N 84 51 E
Ray, *U.S.A.* 80 A3 48 21N 103 10W
Ray, C., *Canada* 71 C8 47 33N 59 15W
Rayadurg, *India* 40 M10 14 40N 76 50 E
Rayagada, *India* 41 K13 19 15N 83 20 E
Raychikhinsk, *Russia* 27 E13 49 46N 129 25 E
Rāyen, *Iran* 45 D8 29 34N 57 26 E
Rayleigh, *U.K.* 11 F8 51 36N 0 37 E
Raymond, *Canada* 72 D6 49 30N 112 35W
Raymond, *Calif., U.S.A.* 84 H7 37 13N 119 54W
Raymond, *N.H., U.S.A.* 79 C13 43 2N 71 11W
Raymond, *Wash., U.S.A.* 84 D3 46 41N 123 44W
Raymondville, *U.S.A.* 81 M6 26 29N 97 47W
Raymore, *Canada* 73 C8 51 25N 104 31W
Rayón, *Mexico* 86 B2 29 43N 110 35W
Rayong, *Thailand* 38 F3 12 40N 101 20 E
Rayville, *U.S.A.* 81 J9 32 29N 91 46W
Raz, Pte. du, *France* 18 C1 48 2N 4 47W
Razan, *Iran* 45 C6 35 23N 49 2 E
Razdel'naya = Rozdilna, *Ukraine* 17 E16 46 50N 30 2 E
Razdolnoye, *Russia* 30 C5 43 30N 131 52 E
Razeh, *Iran* 45 C6 32 47N 48 9 E
Razgrad, *Bulgaria* 21 C12 43 33N 26 34 E
Razim, Lacul, *Romania* 17 F15 44 50N 29 0 E
Razmak, *Pakistan* 42 C3 32 45N 69 50 E
Ré, Î. de, *France* 18 C3 46 12N 1 30W
Reading, *U.K.* 11 F7 51 27N 0 58W
Reading, *U.S.A.* 79 F9 40 20N 75 56W
Reading □, *U.K.* 11 F7 51 27N 0 58W
Realicó, *Argentina* 94 D3 35 0S 64 15W
Ream, *Cambodia* 39 G4 10 34N 103 39 E
Reata, *Mexico* 86 B4 26 8N 101 5W
Reay Forest, *U.K.* 12 C4 58 22N 4 55W
Rebi, *Indonesia* 37 F8 6 23S 134 7 E
Rebiana, *Libya* 51 D10 24 12N 22 10 E
Rebun-Tō, *Japan* 30 B10 45 23N 141 2 E
Recherche, Arch. of the, *Australia* 61 F3 34 15S 122 50 E
Rechna Doab, *Pakistan* 42 D5 31 35N 73 30 E
Rechytsa, *Belarus* 17 B16 52 21N 30 24 E
Recife, *Brazil* 93 E12 8 0S 35 0W
Recklinghausen, *Germany* 15 C7 51 37N 7 12 E
Reconquista, *Argentina* 94 B4 29 10S 59 45W
Recreo, *Argentina* 94 B2 29 25S 65 10W
Red →, *La., U.S.A.* 81 K9 31 1N 91 45W
Red →, *N. Dak., U.S.A.* 68 C10 49 0N 97 15W
Red Bank, *U.S.A.* 79 F10 40 21N 74 5W
Red Bay, *Canada* 71 B8 51 44N 56 25W
Red Bluff, *U.S.A.* 82 F2 40 11N 122 15W
Red Bluff L., *U.S.A.* 81 K3 31 54N 103 55W
Red Cliffs, *Australia* 63 E3 34 19S 142 11 E
Red Cloud, *U.S.A.* 80 E5 40 5N 98 32W
Red Creek, *U.S.A.* 79 C8 43 14N 76 45W
Red Deer, *Canada* 72 C6 52 20N 113 50W
Red Deer →, *Alta., Canada* 73 C7 50 58N 110 0W
Red Deer →, *Man., Canada* 73 C8 52 53N 101 1W
Red Deer L., *Canada* 73 C8 52 55N 101 20W
Red Hook, *U.S.A.* 79 E11 41 55N 73 53W
Red Indian L., *Canada* 71 C8 48 35N 57 0W
Red L., *Canada* 73 C10 51 3N 93 49W
Red Lake, *Canada* 73 C10 51 3N 93 49W
Red Lake Falls, *U.S.A.* 80 B6 47 53N 96 16W
Red Lake Road, *Canada* 73 C10 49 59N 93 25W
Red Lodge, *U.S.A.* 82 D9 45 11N 109 15W
Red Mountain, *U.S.A.* 85 K9 35 37N 117 38W
Red Oak, *U.S.A.* 80 E7 41 1N 95 14W
Red Rock, *Canada* 70 C2 48 55N 88 15W
Red Rock, L., *U.S.A.* 80 E8 41 22N 92 59W
Red Rocks Pt., *Australia* 61 F4 32 13S 127 32 E
Red Sea, *Asia* 46 C2 25 0N 36 0 E
Red Slate Mt., *U.S.A.* 84 H8 37 31N 118 52W
Red Sucker L., *Canada* 70 B1 54 9N 93 40W
Red Tower Pass = Turnu Roşu, P., *Romania* 17 F13 45 33N 24 17 E
Red Wing, *U.S.A.* 80 C8 44 34N 92 31W
Redang, *Malaysia* 36 C2 5 49N 103 2 E
Redange, *Lux.* 15 E5 49 46N 5 52 E
Redcar, *U.K.* 10 C6 54 37N 1 4W
Redcar & Cleveland □, *U.K.* 10 C7 54 29N 1 0W
Redcliff, *Canada* 73 C6 50 10N 110 50W
Redcliffe, *Australia* 63 D5 27 12S 153 0 E
Redcliffe, Mt., *Australia* 61 E3 28 30S 121 30 E
Reddersburg, *S. Africa* 56 D4 29 41S 26 10 E
Redding, *U.S.A.* 82 F2 40 35N 122 24W
Redditch, *U.K.* 11 E6 52 18N 1 55W
Redfield, *U.S.A.* 80 C5 44 53N 98 31W
Redford, *U.S.A.* 79 B11 44 38N 73 48W
Redlands, *U.S.A.* 85 M9 34 4N 117 11W
Redmond, *Oreg., U.S.A.* 82 D3 44 17N 121 11W
Redmond, *Wash., U.S.A.* 84 C4 47 41N 122 7W
Redon, *France* 18 C2 47 40N 2 6W
Redonda, *Antigua* 89 C7 16 58N 62 19W
Redondela, *Spain* 19 A1 42 15N 8 38W
Redondo Beach, *U.S.A.* 85 M8 33 50N 118 23W
Redruth, *U.K.* 11 G2 50 14N 5 14W
Redvers, *Canada* 73 D8 49 35N 101 40W
Redwater, *Canada* 72 C6 53 55N 113 6W
Redwood, *U.S.A.* 79 B9 44 18N 75 48W
Redwood City, *U.S.A.* 84 H4 37 30N 122 15W
Redwood Falls, *U.S.A.* 80 C7 44 32N 95 7W
Redwood Nat. Park, *U.S.A.* 82 F1 41 40N 124 5W
Ree, L., *Ireland* 13 C3 53 35N 8 0W
Reed, L., *Canada* 73 C8 54 38N 100 30W
Reed City, *U.S.A.* 76 D3 43 53N 85 31W
Reedley, *U.S.A.* 84 J7 36 36N 119 27W
Reedsburg, *U.S.A.* 80 D9 43 32N 90 0W
Reedsport, *U.S.A.* 82 E1 43 42N 124 6W
Reedsville, *U.S.A.* 78 F7 40 39N 77 35W
Reefton, *N.Z.* 59 K3 42 6S 171 51 E
Reese →, *U.S.A.* 82 F5 40 48N 117 4W
Refugio, *U.S.A.* 81 L6 28 18N 97 17W
Regensburg, *Germany* 16 D7 49 1N 12 6 E
Reggâne = Zaouiet Reggâne, *Algeria* 50 C6 26 32N 0 3 E
Réggio di Calábria, *Italy* 20 E6 38 6N 15 39 E
Réggio nell'Emilia, *Italy* 20 B4 44 43N 10 36 E
Reghin, *Romania* 17 E13 46 46N 24 42 E
Regina, *Canada* 73 C8 50 27N 104 35W
Regina Beach, *Canada* 73 C8 50 47N 105 0W
Registro, *Brazil* 95 A6 24 29S 47 49W
Rehar →, *India* 43 H10 23 55N 82 40 E
Rehli, *India* 43 H8 23 38N 79 5 E
Rehoboth, *Namibia* 56 C2 23 15S 17 4 E
Rehovot, *Israel* 47 D3 31 54N 34 48 E
Reichenbach, *Germany* 16 C7 50 37N 12 17 E
Reid, *Australia* 61 F4 30 49S 128 26 E
Reidsville, *U.S.A.* 77 G6 36 21N 79 40W
Reigate, *U.K.* 11 F7 51 14N 0 12W
Reims, *France* 18 B6 49 15N 4 1 E
Reina Adelaida, Arch., *Chile* 96 G2 52 20S 74 0W
Reindeer →, *Canada* 73 B8 55 36N 103 11W
Reindeer I., *Canada* 73 C9 52 30N 98 0W
Reindeer L., *Canada* 73 B8 57 15N 102 15W
Reinga, C., *N.Z.* 59 F4 34 25S 172 43 E
Reinosa, *Spain* 19 A3 43 2N 4 15W
Reitz, *S. Africa* 57 D4 27 48S 28 29 E
Reivilo, *S. Africa* 56 D3 27 36S 24 8 E
Reliance, *Canada* 73 A7 63 0N 109 20W
Remarkable, Mt., *Australia* 63 E2 32 48S 138 10 E
Rembang, *Indonesia* 37 G14 6 42S 111 21 E
Remedios, *Panama* 88 E3 8 15N 81 50W
Remeshk, *Iran* 45 E8 26 55N 58 50 E
Remich, *Lux.* 15 E6 49 32N 6 22 E
Remscheid, *Germany* 15 C7 51 11N 7 12 E
Ren Xian, *China* 34 F8 37 8N 114 40 E
Rendsburg, *Germany* 16 A5 54 17N 9 39 E
Renfrew, *Canada* 79 A8 45 30N 76 40W
Renfrewshire □, *U.K.* 12 F4 55 49N 4 38W
Rengat, *Indonesia* 36 E2 0 30S 102 45 E
Rengo, *Chile* 94 C1 34 24S 70 50W
Reni, *Ukraine* 17 F15 45 28N 28 15 E
Renmark, *Australia* 63 E3 34 11S 140 43 E
Rennell Sd., *Canada* 72 C2 53 23N 132 35W
Renner Springs, *Australia* 62 B1 18 20S 133 47 E
Rennes, *France* 18 B3 48 7N 1 41W
Rennie L., *Canada* 73 A7 61 32N 105 35W
Reno, *U.S.A.* 84 F7 39 31N 119 48W
Reno →, *Italy* 20 B5 44 38N 12 16 E
Renovo, *U.S.A.* 78 E7 41 20N 77 45W
Renqiu, *China* 34 E9 38 43N 116 5 E
Rensselaer, *Ind., U.S.A.* 76 E2 40 57N 87 9W
Rensselaer, *N.Y., U.S.A.* 79 D11 42 38N 73 45W
Rentería, *Spain* 19 A5 43 19N 1 54W
Renton, *U.S.A.* 84 C4 47 29N 122 12W
Reotipur, *India* 43 G10 25 33N 83 45 E
Republic, *Mo., U.S.A.* 81 G8 37 7N 93 29W
Republic, *Wash., U.S.A.* 82 B4 48 39N 118 44W
Republican →, *U.S.A.* 80 F6 39 4N 96 48W
Repulse Bay, *Canada* 69 B11 66 30N 86 30W
Requena, *Peru* 92 E4 5 5S 73 52W
Requena, *Spain* 19 C5 39 30N 1 4W
Reşadiye = Datça, *Turkey* 21 F12 36 46N 27 40 E
Reserve, *U.S.A.* 83 K9 33 43N 108 45W
Resht = Rasht, *Iran* 45 B6 37 20N 49 40 E
Resistencia, *Argentina* 94 B4 27 30S 59 0W
Reşiţa, *Romania* 17 F11 45 18N 21 53 E
Resolution I., *Canada* 69 B13 61 30N 65 0W
Resolution I., *N.Z.* 59 L1 45 40S 166 40 E
Ressano Garcia, *Mozam.* 57 D5 25 25S 32 0 E
Reston, *Canada* 73 D8 49 33N 101 6W
Retalhuleu, *Guatemala* 88 D1 14 33N 91 46W
Retenue, L. de, *Dem. Rep. of the Congo* 55 E2 11 0S 27 0 E
Retford, *U.K.* 10 D7 53 19N 0 56W
Réthímnon, *Greece* 23 D6 35 18N 24 30 E
Réthímnon □, *Greece* 23 D6 35 23N 24 28 E
Reti, *Pakistan* 42 E3 28 5N 69 48 E
Réunion ■, *Ind. Oc.* 49 J9 21 0S 56 0 E
Reus, *Spain* 19 B6 41 10N 1 5 E
Reutlingen, *Germany* 16 D5 48 29N 9 12 E
Reval = Tallinn, *Estonia* 9 G21 59 22N 24 48 E
Revda, *Russia* 24 C10 56 48N 59 57 E
Revelganj, *India* 43 G11 25 50N 84 40 E
Revelstoke, *Canada* 72 C5 51 0N 118 10W
Reventazón, *Peru* 92 E2 6 10S 80 58W
Revillagigedo, Is. de, *Pac. Oc.* 86 D2 18 40N 112 0W
Revuè →, *Mozam.* 55 F3 19 50S 34 0 E
Rewa, *India* 43 G9 24 33N 81 25 E
Rewari, *India* 42 E7 28 15N 76 40 E
Rexburg, *U.S.A.* 82 E8 43 49N 111 47W
Rey, *Iran* 45 C6 35 35N 51 25 E
Rey, I. del, *Panama* 88 E4 8 20N 78 30W
Rey Malabo, *Eq. Guin.* 52 D1 3 45N 8 50 E
Reyðarfjörður, *Iceland* 8 D6 65 2N 14 13W
Reyes, Pt., *U.S.A.* 84 H3 38 0N 123 0W
Reykjahlið, *Iceland* 8 D5 65 40N 16 55W
Reykjanes, *Iceland* 8 E2 63 48N 22 40W
Reykjavík, *Iceland* 8 D3 64 10N 21 57W
Reynolds Ra., *Australia* 60 D5 22 30S 133 0 E
Reynoldsville, *U.S.A.* 78 E6 41 5N 78 58W
Reynosa, *Mexico* 87 B5 26 5N 98 18W
Rēzekne, *Latvia* 9 H22 56 30N 27 17 E
Rezvān, *Iran* 45 E8 27 34N 56 6 E
Rhayader, *U.K.* 11 E4 52 18N 3 29W
Rhein →, *Europe* 15 C6 51 52N 6 2 E
Rhein-Main-Donau-Kanal, *Germany* 16 D6 49 1N 11 27 E
Rheine, *Germany* 16 B4 52 17N 7 26 E
Rheinland-Pfalz □, *Germany* 16 C4 50 0N 7 0 E
Rhin = Rhein →, *Europe* 15 C6 51 52N 6 2 E
Rhine = Rhein →, *Europe* 15 C6 51 52N 6 2 E
Rhinebeck, *U.S.A.* 79 E11 41 56N 73 55W
Rhineland-Palatinate = Rheinland-Pfalz □, *Germany* 16 C4 50 0N 7 0 E
Rhinelander, *U.S.A.* 80 C10 45 38N 89 25W
Rhinns Pt., *U.K.* 12 F2 55 40N 6 29W
Rhino Camp, *Uganda* 54 B3 3 0N 31 22 E
Rhir, Cap, *Morocco* 50 B4 30 38N 9 54W
Rhode Island □, *U.S.A.* 79 E13 41 40N 71 30W
Rhodes = Ródhos, *Greece* 23 C10 36 15N 28 10 E
Rhodesia = Zimbabwe ■, *Africa* 55 F3 19 0S 30 0 E
Rhodope Mts. = Rhodopi Planina, *Bulgaria* 21 D11 41 40N 24 20 E
Rhodopi Planina, *Bulgaria* 21 D11 41 40N 24 20 E
Rhön, *Germany* 16 C5 50 24N 9 58 E
Rhondda, *U.K.* 11 F4 51 39N 3 31W
Rhondda Cynon Taff □, *U.K.* 11 F4 51 42N 3 27W
Rhône →, *France* 18 E6 43 28N 4 42 E
Rhum, *U.K.* 12 E2 57 0N 6 20W
Rhyl, *U.K.* 10 D4 53 20N 3 29W
Riachão, *Brazil* 93 E9 7 20S 46 37W
Riasi, *India* 43 C6 33 10N 74 50 E
Riau □, *Indonesia* 36 D2 0 0 102 35 E
Riau, Kepulauan, *Indonesia* 36 D2 0 30N 104 20 E
Riau Arch. = Riau, Kepulauan, *Indonesia* 36 D2 0 30N 104 20 E
Ribadeo, *Spain* 19 A2 43 35N 7 5W
Ribas do Rio Pardo, *Brazil* 93 H8 20 27S 53 46W
Ribauè, *Mozam.* 55 E4 14 57S 38 17 E
Ribble →, *U.K.* 10 D5 53 52N 2 25W
Ribe, *Denmark* 9 J13 55 19N 8 44 E
Ribeira Brava, *Madeira* 22 D2 32 41N 17 4W
Ribeirão Prêto, *Brazil* 95 A6 21 10S 47 50W
Riberalta, *Bolivia* 92 F5 11 0S 66 0W
Riccarton, *N.Z.* 59 K4 43 32S 172 37 E
Rice, *U.S.A.* 85 L12 34 5N 114 51W
Rice L., *Canada* 78 B6 44 12N 78 10W
Rice Lake, *U.S.A.* 80 C9 45 30N 91 44W
Rich, C., *Canada* 78 B4 44 43N 80 38W
Richards Bay, *S. Africa* 57 D5 28 48S 32 6 E
Richardson →, *Canada* 73 B6 58 25N 111 14W
Richardson Lakes, *U.S.A.* 76 C10 44 46N 70 58W
Richardson Springs, *U.S.A.* 84 F5 39 51N 121 46W
Riche, C., *Australia* 61 F2 34 36S 118 47 E
Richey, *U.S.A.* 80 B2 47 39N 105 4W
Richfield, *U.S.A.* 83 G8 38 46N 112 5W
Richfield Springs, *U.S.A.* 79 D10 42 51N 74 59W
Richford, *U.S.A.* 79 B12 45 0N 72 40W
Richibucto, *Canada* 71 C7 46 42N 64 54W
Richland, *Ga., U.S.A.* 77 J3 32 5N 84 40W
Richland, *Wash., U.S.A.* 82 C4 46 17N 119 18W
Richland Center, *U.S.A.* 80 D9 43 21N 90 23W
Richlands, *U.S.A.* 76 G5 37 6N 81 48W
Richmond, *Australia* 62 C3 20 43S 143 8 E
Richmond, *N.Z.* 59 J4 41 20S 173 12 E
Richmond, *U.K.* 10 C6 54 25N 1 43W
Richmond, *Calif., U.S.A.* 84 H4 37 56N 122 21W
Richmond, *Ind., U.S.A.* 76 F3 39 50N 84 53W
Richmond, *Ky., U.S.A.* 76 G3 37 45N 84 18W
Richmond, *Mich., U.S.A.* 78 D2 42 49N 82 45W
Richmond, *Mo., U.S.A.* 80 F8 39 17N 93 58W
Richmond, *Tex., U.S.A.* 81 L7 29 35N 95 46W
Richmond, *Utah, U.S.A.* 82 F8 41 56N 111 48W
Richmond, *Va., U.S.A.* 76 G7 37 33N 77 27W
Richmond, *Vt., U.S.A.* 79 B12 44 24N 72 59W
Richmond Hill, *Canada* 78 C5 43 52N 79 27W
Richmond Ra., *Australia* 63 D5 29 0S 152 45 E
Richwood, *U.S.A.* 76 F5 38 14N 80 32W
Ridder = Leninogorsk, *Kazakstan* 26 D9 50 20N 83 30 E
Riddlesburg, *U.S.A.* 78 F6 40 9N 78 15W
Ridgecrest, *U.S.A.* 85 K9 35 38N 117 40W
Ridgefield, *Conn., U.S.A.* 79 E11 41 17N 73 30W
Ridgefield, *Wash., U.S.A.* 84 E4 45 49N 122 45W
Ridgeland, *U.S.A.* 77 J5 32 29N 80 59W
Ridgetown, *Canada* 78 D3 42 26N 81 52W
Ridgewood, *U.S.A.* 79 F10 40 59N 74 7W
Ridgway, *U.S.A.* 78 E6 41 25N 78 44W
Riding Mountain Nat. Park, *Canada* 73 C9 50 50N 100 0W
Ridley, Mt., *Australia* 61 F3 33 12S 122 7 E
Riebeek-Oos, *S. Africa* 56 E4 33 10S 26 10 E
Ried, *Austria* 16 D7 48 14N 13 30 E
Riesa, *Germany* 16 C7 51 17N 13 17 E
Riet →, *S. Africa* 56 D3 29 0S 23 54 E
Rietbron, *S. Africa* 56 E3 32 54S 23 10 E
Rietfontein, *Namibia* 56 C3 21 58S 20 58 E
Rieti, *Italy* 20 C5 42 24N 12 51 E
Rif, Er = Er Rif, *Morocco* 50 A5 35 1N 4 1W
Riffe L., *U.S.A.* 84 D4 46 32N 122 26W
Rifle, *U.S.A.* 82 G10 39 32N 107 47W
Rift Valley □, *Kenya* 54 B4 0 20N 36 0 E
Rīga, *Latvia* 9 H21 56 53N 24 8 E
Riga, G. of, *Latvia* 9 H20 57 40N 23 45 E
Rīgān, *Iran* 45 D8 28 37N 58 58 E
Rīgas Jūras Līcis = Riga, G. of, *Latvia* 9 H20 57 40N 23 45 E
Rigaud, *Canada* 79 A10 45 29N 74 18W
Rigby, *U.S.A.* 82 E8 43 40N 111 55W
Rīgestān, *Afghan.* 40 D4 30 15N 65 0 E
Riggins, *U.S.A.* 82 D5 45 25N 116 19W
Rigolet, *Canada* 71 B8 54 10N 58 23W
Rihand Dam, *India* 43 G10 24 9N 83 2 E
Riihimäki, *Finland* 9 F21 60 45N 24 48 E
Riiser-Larsen-halvøya, *Antarctica* 5 C4 68 0S 35 0 E
Rijeka, *Croatia* 16 F8 45 20N 14 21 E
Rijssen, *Neths.* 15 B6 52 19N 6 31 E
Rikuzentakada, *Japan* 30 E10 39 0N 141 40 E
Riley, *U.S.A.* 82 E4 43 32N 119 28W
Rimah, Wadi ar →, *Si. Arabia* 44 E4 26 5N 41 30 E
Rimbey, *Canada* 72 C6 52 35N 114 15W
Rimersburg, *U.S.A.* 78 E5 41 3N 79 30W
Rimini, *Italy* 20 B5 44 3N 12 33 E
Rimouski, *Canada* 71 C6 48 27N 68 30W
Rimrock, *U.S.A.* 84 D5 46 38N 121 10W
Rinca, *Indonesia* 37 F5 8 45S 119 35 E
Rincón de Romos, *Mexico* 86 C4 22 14N 102 18W
Rinconada, *Argentina* 94 A2 22 26S 66 10W
Rind →, *India* 43 G9 25 53N 80 33 E
Ringas, *India* 42 F6 27 21N 75 34 E
Ringkøbing, *Denmark* 9 H13 56 5N 8 15 E
Ringvassøy, *Norway* 8 B18 69 56N 19 15 E
Ringwood, *U.S.A.* 79 E10 41 7N 74 15W
Rinjani, *Indonesia* 36 F5 8 24S 116 28 E
Rio Branco, *Brazil* 92 E5 9 58S 67 49W
Río Branco, *Uruguay* 95 C5 32 40S 53 40W
Río Bravo del Norte →, *Mexico* 87 B5 25 57N 97 9W
Rio Brilhante, *Brazil* 95 A5 21 48S 54 33W
Rio Claro, *Brazil* 95 A6 22 19S 47 35W
Rio Claro, *Trin. & Tob.* 89 D7 10 20N 61 25W
Río Colorado, *Argentina* 96 D4 39 0S 64 0W
Río Cuarto, *Argentina* 94 C3 33 10S 64 25W
Rio das Pedras, *Mozam.* 57 C6 23 8S 35 28 E
Rio de Janeiro, *Brazil* 95 A7 23 0S 43 12W
Rio de Janeiro □, *Brazil* 95 A7 22 50S 43 0W
Rio do Sul, *Brazil* 95 B6 27 13S 49 37W
Río Gallegos, *Argentina* 96 G3 51 35S 69 15W
Río Grande = Grande, Rio →, *U.S.A.* 81 N6 25 58N 97 9W
Río Grande, *Argentina* 96 G3 53 50S 67 45W
Rio Grande, *Brazil* 95 C5 32 0S 52 20W
Río Grande, *Mexico* 86 C4 23 50N 103 2W
Río Grande, *Nic.* 88 D3 12 54N 83 33W
Rio Grande City, *U.S.A.* 81 M5 26 23N 98 49W
Río Grande de Santiago →, *Mexico* 86 C3 21 36N 105 26W
Rio Grande do Norte □, *Brazil* 93 E11 5 40S 36 0W
Rio Grande do Sul □, *Brazil* 95 C5 30 0S 53 0W

Russell

Rio Hato, Panama 88 E3 8 22N 80 10W
Rio Lagartos, Mexico 87 C7 21 36N 88 10W
Rio Largo, Brazil 93 E11 9 28S 35 50W
Rio Mulatos, Bolivia 92 G5 19 40S 66 50W
Rio Muni □, Eq. Guin. 52 D2 1 30N 10 0 E
Rio Negro, Brazil 95 B6 26 0S 49 55W
Rio Pardo, Brazil 95 C5 30 0S 52 30W
Rio Rancho, U.S.A. 83 J10 35 14N 106 38W
Rio Segundo, Argentina 94 C3 31 40S 63 59W
Rio Tercero, Argentina 94 C3 32 15S 64 8W
Rio Verde, Brazil 93 G8 17 50S 51 0W
Rio Verde, Mexico 87 C5 21 56N 99 59W
Rio Vista, U.S.A. 84 G5 38 10N 121 42W
Riobamba, Ecuador 92 D3 1 50S 78 45W
Riohacha, Colombia 92 A4 11 33N 72 55W
Riosucio, Colombia 92 B3 7 27N 77 7W
Riou L., Canada 73 B7 59 7N 106 25W
Ripley, Canada 78 B3 44 4N 81 35W
Ripley, Calif., U.S.A. 85 M12 33 32N 114 39W
Ripley, N.Y., U.S.A. 78 D5 42 16N 79 43W
Ripley, Tenn., U.S.A. 81 H10 35 45N 89 32W
Ripley, W. Va., U.S.A. 76 F5 38 49N 81 43W
Ripon, U.K. 10 C6 54 9N 1 31W
Ripon, Calif., U.S.A. 84 H5 37 44N 121 7W
Ripon, Wis., U.S.A. 76 D1 43 51N 88 50W
Rishā', W. ar →, Si. Arabia 44 E5 25 33N 44 5 E
Rishiri-Tō, Japan 30 B10 45 11N 141 15 E
Rishon le Ẓiyyon, Israel 47 D3 31 58N 34 48 E
Rison, U.S.A. 81 J8 33 58N 92 11W
Risør, Norway 9 G13 58 43N 9 13 E
Rita Blanca Cr. →, U.S.A. 81 H3 35 40N 102 29W
Ritter, Mt., U.S.A. 84 H7 37 41N 119 12W
Rittman, U.S.A. 78 F3 40 58N 81 47W
Ritzville, U.S.A. 82 C4 47 8N 118 23W
Riva del Garda, Italy 20 B4 45 53N 10 50 E
Rivadavia, Buenos Aires, Argentina 94 D3 35 29S 62 59W
Rivadavia, Mendoza, Argentina 94 C2 33 13S 68 30W
Rivadavia, Salta, Argentina 94 A3 24 5S 62 54W
Rivadavia, Chile 94 B1 29 57S 70 35W
Rivas, Nic. 88 D2 11 30N 85 50W
River Cess, Liberia 50 G4 5 30N 9 32W
River Jordan, Canada 84 B2 48 26N 124 3W
Rivera, Argentina 94 D3 37 12S 63 14W
Rivera, Uruguay 95 C4 31 0S 55 50W
Riverbank, U.S.A. 84 H6 37 44N 120 56W
Riverdale, U.S.A. 84 J7 36 26N 119 52W
Riverhead, U.S.A. 79 F12 40 55N 72 40W
Riverhurst, Canada 73 C7 50 55N 106 50W
Rivers, Canada 73 C8 50 2N 100 14W
Rivers Inlet, Canada 72 C3 51 42N 127 15W
Riversdale, S. Africa 56 E3 34 7S 21 15 E
Riverside, U.S.A. 85 M9 33 59N 117 22W
Riverton, Australia 63 E2 34 10S 138 46 E
Riverton, Canada 73 C9 51 1N 97 0W
Riverton, N.Z. 59 M2 46 21S 168 0 E
Riverton, U.S.A. 82 E9 43 2N 108 23W
Riverton Heights, U.S.A. 84 C4 47 28N 122 17W
Riviera, U.S.A. 85 K12 35 4N 114 35W
Riviera di Levante, Italy 18 D8 44 15N 9 30 E
Riviera di Ponente, Italy 18 D8 44 10N 8 20 E
Rivière-au-Renard, Canada 71 C7 48 59N 64 23W
Rivière-du-Loup, Canada 71 C6 47 50N 69 30W
Rivière-Pentecôte, Canada 71 C6 49 57N 67 1W
Rivière-Pilote, Martinique 89 D7 14 26N 60 53W
Rivière St. Paul, Canada 71 B8 51 28N 57 45W
Rivne, Ukraine 17 C14 50 40N 26 10 E
Rivoli, Italy 18 D7 45 3N 7 31 E
Rivoli B., Australia 63 F3 37 32S 140 3 E
Riyadh = Ar Riyāḍ, Si. Arabia 46 C4 24 41N 46 42 E
Rize, Turkey 25 F7 41 0N 40 30 E
Rizhao, China 35 G10 35 25N 119 30 E
Rizokarpaso, Cyprus 23 D13 35 36N 34 23 E
Rizzuto, C., Italy 20 E7 38 53N 17 5 E
Rjukan, Norway 9 G13 59 54N 8 33 E
Road Town, Br. Virgin Is. 89 C7 18 27N 64 37W
Roan Plateau, U.S.A. 82 G9 39 20N 109 20W
Roanne, France 18 C6 46 3N 4 4 E
Roanoke, Ala., U.S.A. 77 J3 33 9N 85 22W
Roanoke, Va., U.S.A. 76 G6 37 16N 79 56W
Roanoke →, U.S.A. 77 H7 35 57N 76 42W
Roanoke I., U.S.A. 77 H8 35 55N 75 40W
Roanoke Rapids, U.S.A. 77 G7 36 28N 77 40W
Roatán, Honduras 88 C2 16 18N 86 35W
Robāt Sang, Iran 45 C8 35 35N 59 10 E
Robbins I., Australia 62 G4 40 42S 145 0 E
Robe →, Australia 60 D2 21 42S 116 15 E
Robert Lee, U.S.A. 81 K4 31 54N 100 29W
Robertsdale, U.S.A. 78 F6 40 11N 78 6W
Robertsganj, India 43 G10 24 44N 83 4 E
Robertson, S. Africa 56 E2 33 46S 19 50 E
Robertson I., Antarctica 5 C18 65 15S 59 30W
Robertson Ra., Australia 60 D3 23 15S 121 0 E
Robertstown, Australia 63 E2 33 58S 139 5 E
Roberval, Canada 71 C5 48 32N 72 15W
Robeson Chan., Greenland 4 A4 82 0N 61 30W
Robesonia, U.S.A. 79 F8 40 21N 76 8W
Robinson, U.S.A. 76 F2 39 0N 87 44W
Robinson →, Australia 62 B2 16 3S 137 16 E
Robinson Ra., Australia 61 E2 25 40S 119 0 E
Robinvale, Australia 63 E3 34 40S 142 45 E
Roblin, Canada 73 C8 51 14N 101 21W
Roboré, Bolivia 92 G7 18 10S 59 45W
Robson, Canada 72 D5 49 20N 117 41W
Robson, Mt., Canada 72 C5 53 10N 119 10W
Robstown, U.S.A. 81 M6 27 47N 97 40W
Roca, C. da, Portugal 19 C1 38 40N 9 31W
Roca Partida, I., Mexico 86 D2 19 1N 112 2W
Rocas, I., Brazil 93 D12 4 0S 34 1W
Rocha, Uruguay 95 C5 34 30S 54 25W
Rochdale, U.K. 10 D5 53 38N 2 9W
Rochefort, Belgium 15 D5 50 9N 5 12 E
Rochefort, France 18 D3 45 56N 0 57W
Rochelle, U.S.A. 80 E10 41 56N 89 4W
Rocher River, Canada 72 A6 61 23N 112 44W
Rochester, U.K. 11 F8 51 23N 0 31 E
Rochester, Ind., U.S.A. 76 E2 41 4N 86 13W
Rochester, Minn., U.S.A. 80 C8 44 1N 92 28W
Rochester, N.H., U.S.A. 79 C14 43 18N 70 59W
Rochester, N.Y., U.S.A. 78 C7 43 10N 77 37W
Rock →, Canada 72 A3 60 7N 127 7W
Rock Creek, U.S.A. 78 E4 41 40N 80 52W
Rock Falls, U.S.A. 80 E10 41 47N 89 41W
Rock Hill, U.S.A. 77 H5 34 56N 81 1W
Rock Island, U.S.A. 80 E9 41 30N 90 34W
Rock Rapids, U.S.A. 80 D6 43 26N 96 10W
Rock Sound, Bahamas 88 B4 24 54N 76 12W
Rock Springs, Mont., U.S.A. 82 C10 46 49N 106 15W
Rock Springs, Wyo., U.S.A. 82 F9 41 35N 109 14W
Rock Valley, U.S.A. 80 D6 43 12N 96 18W
Rockall, Atl. Oc. 6 D3 57 37N 13 42W
Rockdale, Tex., U.S.A. 81 K6 30 39N 97 0W
Rockdale, Wash., U.S.A. 84 C5 47 22N 121 28W
Rockefeller Plateau, Antarctica 5 E14 80 0S 140 0W
Rockford, U.S.A. 80 D10 42 16N 89 6W
Rockglen, Canada 73 D7 49 11N 105 57W
Rockhampton, Australia 62 C5 23 22S 150 32 E
Rockingham, Australia 61 F2 32 15S 115 38 E
Rockingham, U.S.A. 77 H6 34 57N 79 46W
Rockingham B., Australia 62 B4 18 5S 146 10 E
Rocklake, U.S.A. 80 A5 48 47N 99 15W
Rockland, Canada 79 A9 45 33N 75 17W
Rockland, Idaho, U.S.A. 82 E7 42 34N 112 53W
Rockland, Maine, U.S.A. 77 C11 44 6N 69 7W
Rockland, Mich., U.S.A. 80 B10 46 44N 89 11W
Rocklin, U.S.A. 84 G5 38 48N 121 14W
Rockmart, U.S.A. 77 H3 34 0N 85 3W
Rockport, Mass., U.S.A. 79 D14 42 39N 70 37W
Rockport, Mo., U.S.A. 80 E7 40 25N 95 31W
Rockport, Tex., U.S.A. 81 L6 28 2N 97 3W
Rocksprings, U.S.A. 81 K4 30 1N 100 13W
Rockville, Conn., U.S.A. 79 E12 41 52N 72 28W
Rockville, Md., U.S.A. 76 F7 39 5N 77 9W
Rockwall, U.S.A. 81 J6 32 56N 96 28W
Rockwell City, U.S.A. 80 D7 42 24N 94 38W
Rockwood, Canada 78 C4 43 37N 80 8W
Rockwood, Maine, U.S.A. 77 C11 45 41N 69 45W
Rockwood, Tenn., U.S.A. 77 H3 35 52N 84 41W
Rocky Ford, U.S.A. 80 F3 38 3N 103 43W
Rocky Gully, Australia 61 F2 34 30S 116 57 E
Rocky Harbour, Canada 71 C8 49 36N 57 55W
Rocky Island L., Canada 70 C3 46 55N 83 0W
Rocky Lane, Canada 72 B5 58 31N 116 22W
Rocky Mount, U.S.A. 77 H7 35 57N 77 48W
Rocky Mountain House, Canada 72 C6 52 22N 114 55W
Rocky Mountain Nat. Park, U.S.A. 82 F11 40 25N 105 45W
Rocky Mts., N. Amer. 82 G10 49 0N 115 0W
Rocky Point, Namibia 56 B2 19 3S 12 30 E
Rod, Pakistan 40 E3 28 10N 63 5 E
Rødbyhavn, Denmark 9 J14 54 39N 11 22 E
Roddickton, Canada 71 B8 50 51N 56 8W
Rodez, France 18 D5 44 21N 2 33 E
Rodhopoú, Greece 23 D5 35 34N 23 45 E
Ródhos, Greece 23 C10 36 15N 28 10 E
Rodney, Canada 78 D3 42 34N 81 41W
Rodney, C., N.Z. 59 G5 36 17S 174 50 E
Rodriguez, Ind. Oc. 3 E13 19 45S 63 20 E
Roe →, U.K. 13 A5 55 6N 6 59W
Roebling, U.S.A. 79 F10 40 7N 74 47W
Roebourne, Australia 60 D2 20 44S 117 9 E
Roebuck B., Australia 60 C3 18 5S 122 20 E
Roermond, Neths. 15 C6 51 12N 6 0 E
Roes Welcome Sd., Canada 69 B11 65 0N 87 0W
Roeselare, Belgium 15 D3 50 57N 3 7 E
Rogachev = Ragachow, Belarus 17 B16 53 8N 30 5 E
Rogagua, L., Bolivia 92 F5 13 43S 66 50W
Rogatyn, Ukraine 17 D13 49 24N 24 36 E
Rogdhia, Greece 23 D7 35 22N 25 1 E
Rogers, U.S.A. 81 G7 36 20N 94 7W
Rogers City, U.S.A. 76 C4 45 25N 83 49W
Rogersville, Canada 71 C6 46 44N 65 26W
Roggan →, Canada 70 B4 54 24N 79 25W
Roggan L., Canada 70 B4 54 8N 77 50W
Roggeveldberge, S. Africa 56 E3 32 10S 20 10 E
Rogoaguado, L., Bolivia 92 F5 13 0S 65 30W
Rogue →, U.S.A. 82 E1 42 26N 124 26W
Róhda, Greece 23 A3 39 48N 19 46 E
Rohnert Park, U.S.A. 84 G4 38 16N 122 40W
Rohri, Pakistan 42 F3 27 45N 68 51 E
Rohri Canal, Pakistan 42 F3 26 15N 68 27 E
Rohtak, India 42 E7 28 55N 76 43 E
Roi Et, Thailand 38 D4 16 4N 103 40 E
Roja, Latvia 9 H20 57 29N 22 43 E
Rojas, Argentina 94 C3 34 10S 60 45W
Rojo, C., Mexico 87 C5 21 33N 97 20W
Rokan →, Indonesia 36 D2 2 0N 100 50 E
Rokiškis, Lithuania 9 J21 55 55N 25 35 E
Rolândia, Brazil 95 A5 23 18S 51 23W
Rolla, U.S.A. 81 G9 37 57N 91 46W
Rolleston, Australia 62 C4 24 28S 148 35 E
Rollingstone, Australia 62 B4 19 2S 146 24 E
Roma, Australia 63 D4 26 32S 148 49 E
Roma, Italy 20 D5 41 54N 12 29 E
Roma, Sweden 9 H18 57 32N 18 26 E
Roma, U.S.A. 81 M5 26 25N 99 1W
Romain C., U.S.A. 77 J6 33 0N 79 22W
Romaine, Canada 71 B7 50 13N 60 40W
Romaine →, Canada 71 B7 50 18N 63 47W
Roman, Romania 17 E14 46 57N 26 55 E
Romang, Indonesia 37 F7 7 30S 127 20 E
Românî, Egypt 47 E1 30 59N 32 38 E
Romania ■, Europe 17 F12 46 0N 25 0 E
Romano, Cayo, Cuba 88 B4 22 0N 77 30W
Romanovka = Basarabeasca, Moldova 17 E15 46 21N 28 58 E
Romans-sur-Isère, France 18 D6 45 3N 5 3 E
Romblon, Phil. 37 B6 12 33N 122 17 E
Rome = Roma, Italy 20 D5 41 54N 12 29 E
Rome, Ga., U.S.A. 77 H3 34 15N 85 10W
Rome, N.Y., U.S.A. 79 C9 43 13N 75 27W
Rome, Pa., U.S.A. 79 E8 41 51N 76 21W
Romney, U.S.A. 76 F6 39 21N 78 45W
Romney Marsh, U.K. 11 F8 51 2N 0 54 E
Rømø, Denmark 9 J13 55 10N 8 30 E
Romorantin-Lanthenay, France 18 C4 47 21N 1 45 E
Romsdalen, Norway 9 E12 62 25N 7 52 E
Romsey, U.K. 11 G6 51 0N 1 29W
Ron, Vietnam 38 D6 17 53N 106 27 E
Rona, U.K. 12 D3 57 34N 5 59W
Ronan, U.S.A. 82 C6 47 32N 114 6W
Roncador, Cayos, Colombia 88 D3 13 32N 80 4W
Roncador, Serra do, Brazil 93 F8 12 30S 52 30W
Ronda, Spain 19 D3 36 46N 5 12W
Rondane, Norway 9 F13 61 57N 9 50 E
Rondônia □, Brazil 92 F6 11 0S 63 0W
Rondonópolis, Brazil 93 G8 16 28S 54 38W
Rong, Koh, Cambodia 39 G4 10 45N 103 15 E
Ronge, L. la, Canada 73 B7 55 6N 105 17W
Rønne, Denmark 9 J16 55 6N 14 43 E
Ronne Ice Shelf, Antarctica 5 D18 78 0S 60 0W
Ronsard, C., Australia 61 D1 24 46S 113 10 E
Ronse, Belgium 15 D3 50 45N 3 35 E
Roodepoort, S. Africa 57 D4 26 11S 27 54 E
Roof Butte, U.S.A. 83 H9 36 28N 109 5W
Rooiboklaagte →, Namibia 56 C3 20 50S 21 0 E
Roorkee, India 42 E7 29 52N 77 59 E
Roosendaal, Neths. 15 C4 51 32N 4 29 E
Roosevelt, U.S.A. 82 F8 40 18N 109 59W
Roosevelt →, Brazil 92 E6 7 35S 60 20W
Roosevelt, Mt., Canada 72 B3 58 26N 125 20W
Roosevelt I., Antarctica 5 D12 79 30S 162 0W
Roper →, Australia 62 A2 14 43S 135 27 E
Roper Bar, Australia 62 A1 14 44S 134 44 E
Roque Pérez, Argentina 94 D4 35 25S 59 24W
Roquetas de Mar, Spain 19 D4 36 46N 2 36W
Roraima □, Brazil 92 C6 2 0N 61 30W
Roraima, Mt., Venezuela 92 B6 5 10N 60 40W
Røros, Norway 9 E14 62 35N 11 23 E
Rosa, Zambia 55 D3 9 33S 31 15 E
Rosa, L., Bahamas 89 B5 21 0N 73 30W
Rosa, Monte, Europe 18 D7 45 57N 7 53 E
Rosalia, U.S.A. 82 C5 47 14N 117 22W
Rosamond, U.S.A. 85 L8 34 52N 118 10W
Rosario, Argentina 94 C3 33 0S 60 40W
Rosário, Brazil 93 D10 3 0S 44 15W
Rosario, Baja Calif., Mexico 86 B1 30 0N 115 50W
Rosario, Sinaloa, Mexico 86 C3 23 0N 105 52W
Rosario, Paraguay 94 A4 24 30S 57 35W
Rosario de la Frontera, Argentina 94 B3 25 50S 65 0W
Rosario de Lerma, Argentina 94 A2 24 59S 65 35W
Rosario del Tala, Argentina 94 C4 32 20S 59 10W
Rosário do Sul, Brazil 95 C5 30 15S 54 55W
Rosarito, Mexico 85 N9 32 18N 117 4W
Roscoe, U.S.A. 79 E10 41 56N 74 55W
Roscommon, Ireland 13 C3 53 38N 8 11W
Roscommon □, Ireland 13 C3 53 49N 8 23W
Roscrea, Ireland 13 D4 52 57N 7 49W
Rose →, Australia 62 A2 14 16S 135 45 E
Rose Blanche, Canada 71 C8 47 38N 58 45W
Rose Pt., Canada 72 C2 54 11N 131 39W
Rose Valley, Canada 73 C8 52 19N 103 49W
Roseau, Domin. 89 C7 15 20N 61 24W
Roseau, U.S.A. 80 A7 48 51N 95 46W
Rosebery, Australia 62 G4 41 46S 145 33 E
Rosebud, S. Dak., U.S.A. 80 D4 43 14N 100 51W
Rosebud, Tex., U.S.A. 81 K6 31 4N 96 59W
Roseburg, U.S.A. 82 E2 43 13N 123 20W
Rosedale, U.S.A. 81 J9 33 51N 91 2W
Roseland, U.S.A. 84 G4 38 25N 122 43W
Rosemary, Canada 72 C6 50 46N 112 5W
Rosenberg, U.S.A. 81 L7 29 34N 95 49W
Rosenheim, Germany 16 E7 47 51N 12 7 E
Roses, G. de, Spain 19 A7 42 10N 3 15 E
Rosetown, Canada 73 C7 51 35N 107 59W
Roseville, Calif., U.S.A. 84 G5 38 45N 121 17W
Roseville, Mich., U.S.A. 78 D2 42 30N 82 56W
Rosewood, Australia 63 D5 27 38S 152 36 E
Roshkhvār, Iran 45 C8 34 58N 59 37 E
Rosignano Marittimo, Italy 20 C4 43 24N 10 28 E
Rosignol, Guyana 92 B7 6 15N 57 30W
Roşiori de Vede, Romania 17 F13 44 9N 25 0 E
Roskilde, Denmark 9 J15 55 38N 12 3 E
Roslavl, Russia 24 D5 53 57N 32 55 E
Rosmead, S. Africa 56 E4 31 29S 25 8 E
Ross, Australia 62 G4 42 2S 147 30 E
Ross, N.Z. 59 K3 42 53S 170 49 E
Ross I., Antarctica 5 D11 77 30S 168 0 E
Ross Ice Shelf, Antarctica 5 E12 80 0S 180 0 E
Ross L., U.S.A. 82 B3 48 44N 121 4W
Ross-on-Wye, U.K. 11 F5 51 54N 2 34W
Ross River, Australia 62 C1 23 44S 134 30 E
Ross River, Canada 72 A2 62 30N 131 30W
Ross Sea, Antarctica 5 D11 74 0S 178 0 E
Rossall Pt., U.K. 10 D4 53 55N 3 3W
Rossan Pt., Ireland 13 B3 54 42N 8 47W
Rossano, Italy 20 E7 39 36N 16 39 E
Rossburn, Canada 73 C8 50 40N 100 49W
Rosseau, Canada 78 A5 45 16N 79 39W
Rosseau L., Canada 78 A5 45 10N 79 35W
Rosses, The, Ireland 13 A3 55 2N 8 20W
Rossignol, L., Canada 70 B5 52 43N 73 40W
Rossignol Res., Canada 71 D6 44 12N 65 10W
Rossland, Canada 72 D5 49 6N 117 50W
Rosslare, Ireland 13 D5 52 17N 6 24W
Rosso, Mauritania 50 E2 16 40N 15 45W
Rossosh, Russia 25 D6 50 15N 39 28 E
Røssvatnet, Norway 8 D16 65 45N 14 5 E
Røst, Norway 8 C15 67 32N 12 0 E
Rosthern, Canada 73 C7 52 40N 106 20W
Rostock, Germany 16 A7 54 5N 12 8 E
Rostov, Don, Russia 25 E6 47 15N 39 45 E
Rostov, Yaroslavl, Russia 24 C6 57 14N 39 25 E
Roswell, Ga., U.S.A. 77 H3 34 2N 84 22W
Roswell, N. Mex., U.S.A. 81 J2 33 24N 104 32W
Rotan, U.S.A. 81 J4 32 51N 100 28W
Rother →, U.K. 11 G8 50 59N 0 45 E
Rotherham, U.K. 10 D6 53 26N 1 20W
Rothes, U.K. 12 D5 57 32N 3 13W
Rothesay, Canada 71 C6 45 23N 66 0W
Rothesay, U.K. 12 F3 55 50N 5 3W
Roti, Indonesia 37 F6 10 50S 123 0 E
Roto, Australia 63 E4 33 0S 145 30 E
Rotondo, Mte., France 18 E8 42 14N 9 8 E
Rotoroa, L., N.Z. 59 J4 41 55S 172 39 E
Rotorua, N.Z. 59 H6 38 9S 176 16 E
Rotorua, L., N.Z. 59 H6 38 5S 176 18 E
Rotterdam, Neths. 15 C4 51 55N 4 30 E
Rotterdam, U.S.A. 79 D10 42 48N 74 1W
Rottnest I., Australia 61 F2 32 0S 115 27 E
Rottumeroog, Neths. 15 A6 53 33N 6 34 E
Rottweil, Germany 16 D5 48 9N 8 37 E
Rotuma, Fiji 64 J9 12 25S 177 5 E
Roubaix, France 18 A5 50 40N 3 10 E
Rouen, France 18 B4 49 27N 1 4 E
Rouleau, Canada 73 C8 50 10N 104 56W
Round Mountain, U.S.A. 82 G5 38 43N 117 4W
Round Mt., Australia 63 E5 30 26S 152 16 E
Round Rock, U.S.A. 81 K6 30 31N 97 41W
Roundup, U.S.A. 82 C9 46 27N 108 33W
Rousay, U.K. 12 B5 59 10N 3 2W
Rouses Point, U.S.A. 79 B11 44 59N 73 22W
Rouseville, U.S.A. 78 E5 41 28N 79 42W
Roussillon, France 18 E5 42 30N 2 35 E
Rouxville, S. Africa 56 E4 30 25S 26 50 E
Rouyn-Noranda, Canada 70 C4 48 20N 79 0W
Rovaniemi, Finland 8 C21 66 29N 25 41 E
Rovereto, Italy 20 B4 45 53N 11 3 E
Rovigo, Italy 20 B4 45 4N 11 47 E
Rovinj, Croatia 16 F7 45 5N 13 40 E
Rovno = Rivne, Ukraine 17 C14 50 40N 26 10 E
Rovuma = Ruvuma →, Tanzania 55 E5 10 29S 40 28 E
Row'ān, Iran 45 C6 35 8N 48 51 E
Rowena, Australia 63 D4 29 48S 148 55 E
Rowley Shoals, Australia 60 C2 17 30S 119 0 E
Roxas, Phil. 37 B6 11 36N 122 49 E
Roxboro, U.S.A. 77 G6 36 24N 78 59W
Roxburgh, N.Z. 59 L2 45 33S 169 19 E
Roxbury, U.S.A. 78 F7 40 6N 77 39W
Roy, Mont., U.S.A. 82 C9 47 20N 108 58W
Roy, N. Mex., U.S.A. 81 H2 35 57N 104 12W
Roy, Utah, U.S.A. 82 F7 41 10N 112 2W
Royal Canal, Ireland 13 C4 53 30N 7 13W
Royal Leamington Spa, U.K. 11 E6 52 18N 1 31W
Royal Tunbridge Wells, U.K. 11 F8 51 7N 0 16 E
Royale, Isle, U.S.A. 80 B10 48 0N 88 54W
Royan, France 18 D3 45 37N 1 2W
Royston, U.K. 11 E7 52 3N 0 0W
Rozdilna, Ukraine 17 E16 46 50N 30 2 E
Rozhyshche, Ukraine 17 C13 50 54N 25 15 E
Rtishchevo, Russia 24 C7 52 18N 43 46 E
Ruacaná, Namibia 56 B1 17 27S 14 21 E
Ruahine Ra., N.Z. 59 H6 39 55S 176 2 E
Ruapehu, N.Z. 59 H5 39 17S 175 35 E
Ruapuke I., N.Z. 59 M2 46 46S 168 31 E
Ruâq, W. →, Egypt 47 F2 30 0N 33 49 E
Rub' al Khālī, Si. Arabia 46 D4 19 0N 48 0 E
Rubeho Mts., Tanzania 54 D4 6 50S 36 25 E
Rubh a' Mhail, U.K. 12 F2 55 56N 6 8W
Rubha Hunish, U.K. 12 D2 57 42N 6 20W
Rubha Robhanais = Lewis, Butt of, U.K. 12 C2 58 31N 6 16W
Rubicon →, U.S.A. 84 G5 38 53N 121 4W
Rubio, Venezuela 92 B4 7 43N 72 22W
Rubtsovsk, Russia 26 D9 51 30N 81 10 E
Ruby L., U.S.A. 82 F6 40 10N 115 28W
Ruby Mts., U.S.A. 82 F6 40 30N 115 20W
Rubyvale, Australia 62 C4 23 25S 147 42 E
Rūd Sar, Iran 45 B6 37 8N 50 18 E
Rudall, Australia 63 E2 33 43S 136 17 E
Rudall →, Australia 60 D3 22 34S 122 13 E
Rudewa, Tanzania 55 E3 10 7S 34 40 E
Rudnyy, Kazakstan 26 D7 52 57N 63 7 E
Rudolfa, Ostrov, Russia 26 A6 81 45N 58 30 E
Rudyard, U.S.A. 76 B3 46 14N 84 36W
Ruenya →, Africa 55 F3 16 24S 33 48 E
Rufiji →, Tanzania 54 D4 7 50S 39 15 E
Rufino, Argentina 94 C3 34 20S 62 50W
Rufunsa, Zambia 55 F2 15 4S 29 34 E
Rugby, U.K. 11 E6 52 23N 1 16W
Rugby, U.S.A. 80 A5 48 22N 100 0W
Rügen, Germany 16 A7 54 22N 13 24 E
Ruhengeri, Rwanda 54 C2 1 30S 29 36 E
Ruhnu, Estonia 9 H20 57 48N 23 15 E
Ruhr →, Germany 16 C4 51 27N 6 43 E
Ruhuhu →, Tanzania 55 E3 10 31S 34 34 E
Ruidoso, U.S.A. 83 K11 33 20N 105 41W
Ruivo, Pico, Madeira 22 D3 32 45N 16 56W
Rujm Tal'at al Jamā'ah, Jordan 47 E4 30 24N 35 30 E
Ruk, Pakistan 42 F3 27 50N 68 42 E
Rukhla, Pakistan 42 C4 32 27N 71 57 E
Ruki →, Dem. Rep. of the Congo 52 E3 0 5N 18 17 E
Rukwa □, Tanzania 54 D3 7 0S 31 30 E
Rukwa, L., Tanzania 54 D3 8 0S 32 20 E
Rulhieres, C., Australia 60 B4 13 56S 127 22 E
Rum = Rhum, U.K. 12 E2 57 0N 6 20W
Rum Cay, Bahamas 89 B5 23 40N 74 58W
Rum Jungle, Australia 60 B5 13 0S 130 59 E
Rumāḥ, Si. Arabia 44 E5 25 29N 47 10 E
Rumania = Romania ■, Europe 17 F12 46 0N 25 0 E
Rumaylah, Iraq 44 D5 30 47N 47 37 E
Rumbêk, Sudan 51 G11 6 54N 29 37 E
Rumford, U.S.A. 77 C10 44 33N 70 33W
Rumia, Poland 17 A10 54 37N 18 25 E
Rumoi, Japan 30 C10 43 56N 141 39 E
Rumonge, Burundi 54 C2 3 59S 29 26 E
Rumson, U.S.A. 79 F11 40 23N 74 0W
Rumuruti, Kenya 54 B4 0 17N 36 32 E
Runan, China 34 H8 33 0N 114 30 E
Runanga, N.Z. 59 K3 42 25S 171 15 E
Runaway, C., N.Z. 59 G6 37 32S 177 59 E
Runcorn, U.K. 10 D5 53 21N 2 44W
Rundu, Namibia 56 B2 17 52S 19 43 E
Rungwa, Tanzania 54 D3 6 55S 33 32 E
Rungwa →, Tanzania 54 D3 7 36S 31 50 E
Rungwe, Tanzania 55 D3 9 11S 33 32 E
Rungwe, Mt., Tanzania 52 F6 9 8S 33 40 E
Runton Ra., Australia 60 D3 23 31S 123 6 E
Ruoqiang, China 32 C3 38 55N 88 10 E
Rupa, India 41 F18 27 15N 92 21 E
Rupar, India 42 D7 31 2N 76 38 E
Rupat, Indonesia 36 D2 1 45N 101 40 E
Rupen →, India 42 H4 23 28N 71 31 E
Rupert, U.S.A. 82 E7 42 37N 113 41W
Rupert →, Canada 70 B4 51 29N 78 45W
Rupert B., Canada 70 B4 51 35N 79 0W
Rupert House = Waskaganish, Canada 70 B4 51 30N 78 40W
Rupsa, India 43 J12 21 37N 87 1 E
Rurrenabaque, Bolivia 92 F5 14 30S 67 32W
Rusambo, Zimbabwe 55 F3 16 30S 32 4 E
Rusape, Zimbabwe 55 F3 18 35S 32 8 E
Ruschuk = Ruse, Bulgaria 21 C12 43 48N 25 59 E
Ruse, Bulgaria 21 C12 43 48N 25 59 E
Rush, Ireland 13 C5 53 31N 6 6W
Rushan, China 35 F11 36 56N 121 30 E
Rushden, U.K. 11 E7 52 18N 0 35W
Rushmore, Mt., U.S.A. 80 D3 43 53N 103 28W
Rushville, Ill., U.S.A. 80 E9 40 7N 90 34W
Rushville, Ind., U.S.A. 76 F3 39 37N 85 27W
Rushville, Nebr., U.S.A. 80 D3 42 43N 102 28W
Russas, Brazil 93 D11 4 55S 37 50W
Russell, Canada 73 C8 50 50N 101 20W
Russell, Kans., U.S.A. 80 F5 38 54N 98 52W

Russell

Russell, *N.Y., U.S.A.* **79 B9** 44 27N 75 9W
Russell, *Pa., U.S.A.* **78 E5** 41 56N 79 8W
Russell L., *Man., Canada* **73 B8** 56 15N 101 30W
Russell L., *N.W.T., Canada* **72 A5** 63 5N 115 44W
Russellkonda, *India* **41 K14** 19 57N 84 42 E
Russellville, *Ala., U.S.A.* **77 H2** 34 30N 87 44W
Russellville, *Ark., U.S.A.* **81 H8** 35 17N 93 8W
Russellville, *Ky., U.S.A.* **77 G2** 36 51N 86 53W
Russia ■, *Eurasia* **27 C11** 62 0N 105 0 E
Russian →, *U.S.A.* **84 G3** 38 27N 123 8W
Russkoye Ustie, *Russia* **4 B15** 71 0N 149 0 E
Rustam, *Pakistan* **42 B5** 34 25N 72 13 E
Rustam Shahr, *Pakistan* **42 F2** 26 58N 66 6 E
Rustavi, *Georgia* **25 F8** 41 30N 45 0 E
Rustenburg, *S. Africa* **56 D4** 25 41S 27 14 E
Ruston, *U.S.A.* **81 J8** 32 32N 92 38W
Rutana, *Burundi* **54 C3** 3 55S 30 0 E
Ruteng, *Indonesia* **37 F6** 8 35S 120 30 E
Ruth, *U.S.A.* **78 C2** 43 42N 82 45W
Rutherford, *U.S.A.* **84 G4** 38 26N 122 24W
Rutland, *U.S.A.* **79 C12** 43 37N 72 58W
Rutland □, *U.K.* **11 E7** 52 38N 0 40W
Rutland Water, *U.K.* **11 E7** 52 39N 0 38W
Rutledge →, *Canada* **73 A6** 61 4N 112 0W
Rutledge L., *Canada* **73 A6** 61 33N 110 47W
Rutshuru, *Dem. Rep. of the Congo* **54 C2** 1 13S 29 25 E
Ruvu, *Tanzania* **54 D4** 6 49S 38 43 E
Ruvu →, *Tanzania* **54 D4** 6 23S 38 52 E
Ruvuma □, *Tanzania* **55 E4** 10 20S 36 0 E
Ruvuma →, *Tanzania* **55 E5** 10 29S 40 28 E
Ruwais, *U.A.E.* **45 E7** 24 5N 52 50 E
Ruwenzori, *Africa* **54 B2** 0 30N 29 55 E
Ruya →, *Zimbabwe* **57 B5** 16 27S 32 5 E
Ruyigi, *Burundi* **54 C3** 3 29S 30 15 E
Ružomberok, *Slovak Rep.* **17 D10** 49 3N 19 17 E
Rwanda ■, *Africa* **54 C3** 2 0S 30 0 E
Ryan, L., *U.K.* **12 G3** 55 0N 5 2W
Ryazan, *Russia* **24 D6** 54 40N 39 40 E
Ryazhsk, *Russia* **24 D7** 53 45N 40 3 E
Rybache = Rybachye, *Kazakstan* **26 E9** 46 40N 81 20 E
Rybachiy Poluostrov, *Russia* **24 A5** 69 43N 32 0 E
Rybachye, *Kazakstan* **26 E9** 46 40N 81 20 E
Rybinsk, *Russia* **24 C6** 58 5N 38 50 E
Rybinskoye Vdkhr., *Russia* **24 C6** 58 30N 38 25 E
Rybnitsa = Râbniţa, *Moldova* **17 E15** 47 45N 29 0 E
Rycroft, *Canada* **72 B5** 55 45N 118 40W
Ryde, *U.K.* **11 G6** 50 43N 1 9W
Ryderwood, *U.S.A.* **84 D3** 46 23N 123 3W
Rye, *U.K.* **11 G8** 50 57N 0 45 E
Rye →, *U.K.* **10 C7** 54 11N 0 44W
Rye Bay, *U.K.* **11 G8** 50 52N 0 49 E
Rye Patch Reservoir, *U.S.A.* **82 F4** 40 28N 118 19W
Ryegate, *U.S.A.* **82 C9** 46 18N 109 15W
Ryley, *Canada* **72 C6** 53 17N 112 26W
Rylstone, *Australia* **63 E4** 32 46S 149 58 E
Ryōtsu, *Japan* **30 E9** 38 5N 138 26 E
Rypin, *Poland* **17 B10** 53 3N 19 25 E
Ryūgasaki, *Japan* **31 G10** 35 54N 140 11 E
Ryūkyū Is. = Ryūkyū-rettō, *Japan* **31 M3** 26 0N 126 0 E
Ryūkyū-rettō, *Japan* **31 M3** 26 0N 126 0 E
Rzeszów, *Poland* **17 C11** 50 5N 21 58 E
Rzhev, *Russia* **24 C5** 56 20N 34 20 E

S

Sa, *Thailand* **38 C3** 18 34N 100 45 E
Sa Canal, *Spain* **22 C7** 38 51N 1 23 E
Sa Conillera, *Spain* **22 C7** 38 59N 1 13 E
Sa Dec, *Vietnam* **39 G5** 10 20N 105 46 E
Sa Dragonera, *Spain* **22 B9** 39 35N 2 19 E
Sa Mesquida, *Spain* **22 B11** 39 55N 4 16 E
Sa Savina, *Spain* **22 C7** 38 44N 1 25 E
Sa'ādatābād, *Fārs, Iran* **45 D7** 30 10N 53 5 E
Sa'ādatābād, *Hormozgān, Iran* **45 D7** 28 3N 55 53 E
Sa'ādatābād, *Kermān, Iran* **45 D7** 29 40N 55 51 E
Saale →, *Germany* **16 C6** 51 56N 11 54 E
Saalfeld, *Germany* **16 C6** 50 38N 11 21 E
Saar →, *Europe* **18 B7** 49 41N 6 32 E
Saarbrücken, *Germany* **16 D4** 49 14N 6 59 E
Saaremaa, *Estonia* **9 G20** 58 30N 22 30 E
Saarijärvi, *Finland* **9 E21** 62 43N 25 16 E
Saariselkä, *Finland* **8 B23** 68 16N 28 15 E
Sab 'Ābar, *Syria* **44 C3** 33 46N 37 41 E
Saba, *W. Indies* **89 C7** 17 42N 63 26W
Šabac, *Serbia, Yug.* **21 B8** 44 48N 19 42 E
Sabadell, *Spain* **19 B7** 41 28N 2 7 E
Sabah □, *Malaysia* **36 C5** 6 0N 117 0 E
Sabak Bernam, *Malaysia* **39 L3** 3 46N 100 58 E
Sabalān, Kūhhā-ye, *Iran* **44 B5** 38 15N 47 45 E
Sabalana, Kepulauan, *Indonesia* **37 F5** 6 45S 118 50 E
Sábana de la Mar, *Dom. Rep.* **89 C6** 19 7N 69 24W
Sábanalarga, *Colombia* **92 A4** 10 38N 74 55W
Sabang, *Indonesia* **36 C1** 5 50N 95 15 E
Sabará, *Brazil* **93 G10** 19 55S 43 46W
Sabarmati →, *India* **42 H5** 22 18N 72 22 E
Sabattis, *U.S.A.* **79 B10** 44 6N 74 40W
Saberania, *Indonesia* **37 E9** 2 5S 138 18 E
Sabhah, *Libya* **51 C8** 27 9N 14 29 E
Sabi →, *India* **42 E7** 28 29N 76 44 E
Sabie, *S. Africa* **57 D5** 25 10S 30 48 E
Sabinal, *Mexico* **86 A3** 30 58N 107 25W
Sabinal, *U.S.A.* **81 L5** 29 19N 99 28W
Sabinas, *Mexico* **86 B4** 27 50N 101 10W
Sabinas →, *Mexico* **86 B4** 27 37N 100 42W
Sabinas Hidalgo, *Mexico* **86 B4** 26 33N 100 10W
Sabine →, *U.S.A.* **81 L8** 29 59N 93 47W
Sabine L., *U.S.A.* **81 L8** 29 53N 93 51W
Sabine Pass, *U.S.A.* **81 L8** 29 44N 93 54W
Sabinsville, *U.S.A.* **78 E7** 41 52N 77 31W
Sablayan, *Phil.* **37 B6** 12 50N 120 50 E
Sable, *Canada* **71 A6** 55 30N 68 21W
Sable, C., *Canada* **71 D6** 43 29N 65 38W
Sable, C., *U.S.A.* **75 E10** 25 9N 81 8W
Sable I., *Canada* **71 D8** 44 0N 60 0W
Sabrina Coast, *Antarctica* **5 C9** 68 0S 120 0 E
Sabulubbek, *Indonesia* **36 E1** 1 36S 98 40 E
Sabzevār, *Iran* **45 B8** 36 15N 57 40 E
Sabzvārān, *Iran* **45 D8** 28 45N 57 50 E
Sac City, *U.S.A.* **80 D7** 42 25N 95 0W
Săcele, *Romania* **17 F13** 45 37N 25 41 E
Sachigo →, *Canada* **70 A2** 55 6N 88 58W
Sachigo, L., *Canada* **70 B1** 53 50N 92 12W
Sachsen □, *Germany* **16 C7** 50 55N 13 10 E
Sachsen-Anhalt □, *Germany* **16 C7** 52 0N 12 0 E
Sackets Harbor, *U.S.A.* **79 C8** 43 57N 76 7W
Sackville, *Canada* **71 C7** 45 54N 64 22W
Saco, *Maine, U.S.A.* **77 D10** 43 30N 70 27W
Saco, *Mont., U.S.A.* **82 B10** 48 28N 107 21W
Sacramento, *U.S.A.* **84 G5** 38 35N 121 29W
Sacramento →, *U.S.A.* **84 G5** 38 3N 121 56W
Sacramento Mts., *U.S.A.* **83 K11** 32 30N 105 30W
Sacramento Valley, *U.S.A.* **84 G5** 39 30N 122 0W
Sada-Misaki, *Japan* **31 H6** 33 20N 132 1 E
Sadabad, *India* **42 F8** 27 27N 78 3 E
Sadani, *Tanzania* **54 D4** 5 58S 38 35 E
Sadao, *Thailand* **39 J3** 6 38N 100 26 E
Sadd el Aali, *Egypt* **51 D12** 23 54N 32 54 E
Saddle Mt., *U.S.A.* **84 E3** 45 58N 123 41W
Sadimi, *Dem. Rep. of the Congo* **55 D1** 9 25S 23 32 E
Sado, *Japan* **30 F9** 38 0N 138 25 E
Sadon, *Burma* **41 G20** 25 28N 97 55 E
Sadra, *India* **42 H5** 23 21N 72 43 E
Sadri, *India* **42 G5** 25 11N 73 26 E
Sæby, *Denmark* **9 H14** 57 21N 10 30 E
Saegertown, *U.S.A.* **78 E4** 41 43N 80 9W
Şafājah, *Si. Arabia* **44 E3** 26 25N 39 0 E
Säffle, *Sweden* **9 G15** 59 8N 12 55 E
Safford, *U.S.A.* **83 K9** 32 50N 109 43W
Saffron Walden, *U.K.* **11 E8** 52 1N 0 16 E
Safi, *Morocco* **50 B4** 32 18N 9 20W
Şafīābād, *Iran* **45 B8** 36 45N 57 58 E
Safīd Dasht, *Iran* **45 C6** 33 27N 48 11 E
Safīd Kūh, *Afghan.* **40 B3** 34 45N 63 0 E
Safīd Rūd →, *Iran* **45 B6** 37 23N 50 11 E
Safipur, *India* **43 F9** 26 44N 80 21 E
Safwān, *Iraq* **44 D5** 30 7N 47 43 E
Sag Harbor, *U.S.A.* **79 F12** 41 0N 72 18W
Saga, *Japan* **31 H5** 33 15N 130 16 E
Saga □, *Japan* **31 H5** 33 15N 130 20 E
Sagae, *Japan* **30 E10** 38 22N 140 17 E
Sagamore, *U.S.A.* **78 F5** 40 46N 79 14W
Sagar, *Karnataka, India* **40 M9** 14 14N 75 6 E
Sagar, *Mad. P., India* **43 H8** 23 50N 78 44 E
Sagara, L., *Tanzania* **54 D3** 5 20S 31 0 E
Saginaw, *U.S.A.* **76 D4** 43 26N 83 56W
Saginaw →, *U.S.A.* **76 D4** 43 39N 83 51W
Saginaw B., *U.S.A.* **76 D4** 43 50N 83 40W
Saglouc = Salluit, *Canada* **69 B12** 62 14N 75 38W
Sagŏ-ri, *S. Korea* **35 G14** 35 25N 126 49 E
Sagua la Grande, *Cuba* **88 B3** 22 50N 80 10W
Saguache, *U.S.A.* **83 G10** 38 5N 106 8W
Saguaro Nat. Park, *U.S.A.* **83 K8** 32 12N 110 38W
Saguenay →, *Canada* **71 C5** 48 22N 71 0W
Sagunt, *Spain* **19 C5** 39 42N 0 18W
Sagunto = Sagunt, *Spain* **19 C5** 39 42N 0 18W
Sagwara, *India* **42 H6** 23 41N 74 1 E
Sahagún, *Spain* **19 A3** 42 18N 5 2W
Saḩam al Jawlān, *Syria* **47 C4** 32 45N 35 55 E
Sahamandrevo, *Madag.* **57 C8** 23 15S 45 35 E
Sahand, Kūh-e, *Iran* **44 B5** 37 44N 46 27 E
Sahara, *Africa* **50 D6** 23 0N 5 0 E
Saharan Atlas = Saharien, Atlas, *Algeria* **50 B6** 33 30N 1 0 E
Saharanpur, *India* **42 E7** 29 58N 77 33 E
Saharien, Atlas, *Algeria* **50 B6** 33 30N 1 0 E
Saharsa, *India* **43 G12** 25 53N 86 36 E
Sahasinaka, *Madag.* **57 C8** 21 49S 47 49 E
Sahaswan, *India* **43 E8** 28 5N 78 45 E
Sahel, *Africa* **50 E5** 16 0N 5 0 E
Sahibganj, *India* **43 G12** 25 12N 87 40 E
Sāḩilīyah, *Iraq* **44 C4** 33 43N 42 42 E
Sahiwal, *Pakistan* **42 D5** 30 45N 73 8 E
Şaḩneh, *Iran* **44 C5** 34 29N 47 41 E
Sahuaripa, *Mexico* **86 B3** 29 0N 109 13W
Sahuarita, *U.S.A.* **83 L8** 31 57N 110 58W
Sahuayo, *Mexico* **86 C4** 20 4N 102 43W
Sai →, *India* **43 G10** 25 39N 82 47 E
Sai Buri, *Thailand* **39 J3** 6 43N 101 45 E
Sa'id Bundas, *Sudan* **51 G10** 8 24N 24 48 E
Sa'īdābād, *Kermān, Iran* **45 D7** 29 30N 55 45 E
Sa'īdābād, *Semnān, Iran* **45 B7** 36 8N 54 11 E
Sa'īdīyeh, *Iran* **45 B6** 36 20N 48 55 E
Saidpur, *Bangla.* **41 G16** 25 48N 89 0 E
Saidpur, *India* **43 G10** 25 33N 83 11 E
Saidu, *Pakistan* **43 B5** 34 43N 72 24 E
Saigon = Thanh Pho Ho Chi Minh, *Vietnam* **39 G6** 10 58N 106 40 E
Saijō, *Japan* **31 H6** 33 55N 133 11 E
Saikanosy Masoala, *Madag.* **57 B9** 15 45S 50 10 E
Saikhoa Ghat, *India* **41 F19** 27 50N 95 40 E
Saiki, *Japan* **31 H5** 32 58N 131 51 E
Sailana, *India* **42 H6** 23 28N 74 55 E
Sailolof, *Indonesia* **37 E8** 1 15S 130 46 E
Saimaa, *Finland* **9 F23** 61 15N 28 15 E
Şa'in Dezh, *Iran* **44 B5** 36 40N 46 25 E
St. Abb's Head, *U.K.* **12 F6** 55 55N 2 8W
St. Alban's, *Canada* **71 C8** 47 51N 55 50W
St. Albans, *U.K.* **11 F7** 51 45N 0 19W
St. Albans, *Vt., U.S.A.* **79 B11** 44 49N 73 5W
St. Albans, *W. Va., U.S.A.* **76 F5** 38 23N 81 50W
St. Alban's Head, *U.K.* **11 G5** 50 34N 2 4W
St. Albert, *Canada* **72 C6** 53 37N 113 32W
St. Andrew's, *Canada* **71 C8** 47 45N 59 15W
St. Andrews, *U.K.* **12 E6** 56 20N 2 47W
St-Anicet, *Canada* **79 A10** 45 8N 74 22W
St. Ann B., *Canada* **71 C7** 46 22N 60 25W
St. Ann's Bay, *Jamaica* **88 C4** 18 26N 77 15W
St. Anthony, *Canada* **71 B8** 51 22N 55 35W
St. Anthony, *U.S.A.* **82 E8** 43 58N 111 41W
St. Antoine, *Canada* **71 C7** 46 22N 64 45W
St. Arnaud, *Australia* **63 F3** 36 40S 143 16 E
St-Augustin →, *Canada* **71 B8** 51 16N 58 40W
St-Augustin-Saguenay, *Canada* **71 B8** 51 13N 58 38W
St. Augustine, *U.S.A.* **77 L5** 29 54N 81 19W
St. Austell, *U.K.* **11 G3** 50 20N 4 47W
St. Barbe, *Canada* **71 B8** 51 12N 56 46W
St-Barthélemy, *W. Indies* **89 C7** 17 50N 62 50W
St. Bees Hd., *U.K.* **10 C4** 54 31N 3 38W
St. Bride's, *Canada* **71 C9** 46 56N 54 10W
St. Brides B., *U.K.* **11 F2** 51 49N 5 9W
St-Brieuc, *France* **18 B2** 48 30N 2 46W
St. Catharines, *Canada* **78 C5** 43 10N 79 15W
St. Catherines I., *U.S.A.* **77 K5** 31 40N 81 10W
St. Catherine's Pt., *U.K.* **11 G6** 50 34N 1 18W
St-Chamond, *France* **18 D6** 45 28N 4 31 E
St. Charles, *Ill., U.S.A.* **76 E1** 41 54N 88 19W
St. Charles, *Mo., U.S.A.* **80 F9** 38 47N 90 29W
St. Charles, *Va., U.S.A.* **76 F7** 36 48N 83 4W
St. Christopher-Nevis = St. Kitts & Nevis ■, *W. Indies* **89 C7** 17 20N 62 40W
St. Clair, *Mich., U.S.A.* **78 D2** 42 50N 82 30W
St. Clair, *Pa., U.S.A.* **79 F8** 40 43N 76 12W
St. Clair →, *U.S.A.* **78 D2** 42 38N 82 31W
St. Clair, L., *Canada* **70 D3** 42 30N 82 45W
St. Clair, L., *U.S.A.* **78 D2** 42 27N 82 39W
St. Clairsville, *U.S.A.* **78 F4** 40 5N 80 54W
St. Claude, *Canada* **73 D9** 49 40N 98 20W
St-Clet, *Canada* **79 A10** 45 21N 74 13W
St. Cloud, *Fla., U.S.A.* **77 L5** 28 15N 81 17W
St. Cloud, *Minn., U.S.A.* **80 C7** 45 34N 94 10W
St. Cricq, C., *Australia* **61 E1** 25 17S 113 6 E
St. Croix, *U.S. Virgin Is.* **89 C7** 17 45N 64 45W
St. Croix →, *U.S.A.* **80 C8** 44 45N 92 48W
St. Croix Falls, *U.S.A.* **80 C8** 45 24N 92 38W
St. David's, *Canada* **71 C8** 48 12N 58 52W
St. David's, *U.K.* **11 F2** 51 53N 5 16W
St. David's Head, *U.K.* **11 F2** 51 54N 5 19W
St-Denis, *France* **18 B5** 48 56N 2 22 E
St-Dizier, *France* **18 B6** 48 38N 4 56 E
St. Elias, Mt., *U.S.A.* **68 B5** 60 18N 140 56W
St. Elias Mts., *Canada* **72 A1** 60 33N 139 28W
St. Elias Mts., *U.S.A.* **68 C6** 60 0N 138 0W
St-Étienne, *France* **18 D6** 45 27N 4 22 E
St. Eugène, *Canada* **79 A10** 45 30N 74 28W
St. Eustatius, *W. Indies* **89 C7** 17 20N 63 0W
St-Félicien, *Canada* **70 C5** 48 40N 72 25W
St-Flour, *France* **18 D5** 45 2N 3 6 E
St. Francis, *U.S.A.* **80 F4** 39 47N 101 48W
St. Francis →, *U.S.A.* **81 H9** 34 38N 90 36W
St. Francis, C., *S. Africa* **56 E3** 34 14S 24 49 E
St. Francisville, *U.S.A.* **81 K9** 30 47N 91 23W
St-François, L., *Canada* **79 A10** 45 10N 74 22W
St-Gabriel, *Canada* **70 C5** 46 17N 73 24W
St. Gallen = Sankt Gallen, *Switz.* **18 C8** 47 26N 9 22 E
St-Gaudens, *France* **18 E4** 43 6N 0 44 E
St. George, *Australia* **63 D4** 28 1S 148 30 E
St. George, *Canada* **71 C6** 45 11N 66 50W
St. George, *S.C., U.S.A.* **77 J5** 33 11N 80 35W
St. George, *Utah, U.S.A.* **83 H7** 37 6N 113 35W
St. George, C., *Canada* **71 C8** 48 30N 59 16W
St. George, C., *U.S.A.* **77 L3** 29 40N 85 5W
St. George Ra., *Australia* **60 C4** 18 40S 125 0 E
St. George's, *Canada* **71 C8** 48 26N 58 31W
St-Georges, *Canada* **71 C5** 46 8N 70 40W
St. George's, *Grenada* **89 D7** 12 5N 61 43W
St. George's B., *Canada* **71 C8** 48 24N 58 53W
St. Georges Basin, *N.S.W., Australia* **63 F5** 35 7S 150 36 E
St. Georges Basin, *W. Austral., Australia* **60 C4** 15 23S 125 2 E
St. George's Channel, *Europe* **13 E6** 52 0N 6 0W
St. Georges Hd., *Australia* **63 F5** 35 12S 150 42 E
St. Gotthard P. = San Gottardo, P. del, *Switz.* **18 C8** 46 33N 8 33 E
St. Helena, *Atl. Oc.* **48 H3** 15 58S 5 42W
St. Helena, *U.S.A.* **82 G2** 38 30N 122 28W
St. Helena, Mt., *U.S.A.* **84 G4** 38 40N 122 36W
St. Helena B., *S. Africa* **56 E2** 32 40S 18 10 E
St. Helens, *Australia* **62 G4** 41 20S 148 15 E
St. Helens, *U.K.* **10 D5** 53 27N 2 44W
St. Helens, *U.S.A.* **84 E4** 45 52N 122 48W
St. Helens, Mt., *U.S.A.* **84 D4** 46 12N 122 12W
St. Helier, *U.K.* **11 H5** 49 10N 2 7W
St-Hubert, *Belgium* **15 D5** 50 2N 5 23 E
St-Hyacinthe, *Canada* **70 C5** 45 40N 72 58W
St. Ignace, *U.S.A.* **76 C3** 45 52N 84 44W
St. Ignace I., *Canada* **70 C2** 48 45N 88 0W
St. Ignatius, *U.S.A.* **82 C6** 47 19N 114 6W
St. Ives, *U.K.* **11 G2** 50 12N 5 30W
St. James, *U.S.A.* **80 D7** 43 59N 94 38W
St-Jean →, *Canada* **71 B7** 50 17N 64 20W
St-Jean, L., *Canada* **71 C5** 48 40N 72 0W
St-Jean-Port-Joli, *Canada* **71 C5** 47 15N 70 13W
St-Jean-sur-Richelieu, *Canada* **79 A11** 45 20N 73 20W
St-Jérôme, *Canada* **70 C5** 45 47N 74 0W
St. John, *Canada* **71 C6** 45 20N 66 8W
St. John, *U.S.A.* **81 G5** 38 0N 98 46W
St. John →, *U.S.A.* **77 C12** 45 12N 66 5W
St. John, C., *Canada* **71 C8** 50 0N 55 32W
St. John's, *Antigua* **89 C7** 17 6N 61 51W
St. John's, *Canada* **71 C9** 47 35N 52 40W
St. Johns, *Ariz., U.S.A.* **83 J9** 34 30N 109 22W
St. Johns, *Mich., U.S.A.* **76 D3** 43 0N 84 33W
St. Johns →, *U.S.A.* **77 K5** 30 24N 81 24W
St. John's Pt., *Ireland* **13 B3** 54 34N 8 27W
St. Johnsbury, *U.S.A.* **79 B12** 44 25N 72 1W
St. Johnsville, *U.S.A.* **79 D10** 43 0N 74 43W
St. Joseph, *La., U.S.A.* **81 K9** 31 55N 91 14W
St. Joseph, *Mo., U.S.A.* **80 F7** 39 46N 94 50W
St. Joseph →, *U.S.A.* **76 D2** 42 7N 86 29W
St. Joseph, I., *Canada* **70 C3** 46 12N 83 58W
St. Joseph, L., *Canada* **70 B1** 51 10N 90 35W
St-Jovite, *Canada* **70 C5** 46 8N 74 38W
St. Kitts & Nevis ■, *W. Indies* **89 C7** 17 20N 62 40W
St. Laurent, *Canada* **73 C9** 50 25N 97 58W
St. Lawrence, *Australia* **62 C4** 22 16S 149 31 E
St. Lawrence, *Canada* **71 C8** 46 54N 55 23W
St. Lawrence →, *Canada* **71 C6** 49 30N 66 0W
St. Lawrence, Gulf of, *Canada* **71 C7** 48 25N 62 0W
St. Lawrence I., *U.S.A.* **68 B3** 63 30N 170 30W
St. Leonard, *Canada* **71 C6** 47 12N 67 58W
St. Lewis →, *Canada* **71 B8** 52 26N 56 11W
St-Lô, *France* **18 B3** 49 7N 1 5W
St. Louis, *Senegal* **50 E2** 16 8N 16 27W
St. Louis, *U.S.A.* **80 F9** 38 37N 90 12W
St. Louis →, *U.S.A.* **80 B8** 47 15N 92 45W
St. Lucia ■, *W. Indies* **89 D7** 14 0N 60 50W
St. Lucia, L., *S. Africa* **57 D5** 28 5S 32 30 E
St. Lucia Channel, *W. Indies* **89 D7** 14 15N 61 0W
St. Maarten, *W. Indies* **89 C7** 18 0N 63 5W
St. Magnus B., *U.K.* **12 A7** 60 25N 1 35W
St-Malo, *France* **18 B2** 48 39N 2 1W
St-Marc, *Haiti* **89 C5** 19 10N 72 41W
St. Maries, *U.S.A.* **82 C5** 47 19N 116 35W
St-Martin, *W. Indies* **89 C7** 18 0N 63 0W
St. Martin, L., *Canada* **73 C9** 51 40N 98 30W
St. Mary Pk., *Australia* **63 E2** 31 32S 138 34 E
St. Marys, *Australia* **62 G4** 41 35S 148 11 E
St. Marys, *Canada* **78 C3** 43 20N 81 10W
St. Mary's, *Corn., U.K.* **11 H1** 49 55N 6 18W
St. Mary's, *Orkney, U.K.* **12 C6** 58 54N 2 54W
St. Marys, *Ga., U.S.A.* **77 K5** 30 44N 81 33W
St. Marys, *Pa., U.S.A.* **78 E6** 41 26N 78 34W
St. Mary's, C., *Canada* **71 C9** 46 50N 54 12W
St. Mary's B., *Canada* **71 C9** 46 50N 53 50W
St. Marys Bay, *Canada* **71 D6** 44 25N 66 10W
St-Mathieu, Pte., *France* **18 B1** 48 20N 4 45W
St. Matthew I., *U.S.A.* **68 B2** 60 24N 172 42W
St. Matthews, I. = Zadetkyi Kyun, *Burma* **39 G1** 10 0N 98 25 E
St-Maurice →, *Canada* **70 C5** 46 21N 72 31W
St-Nazaire, *France* **18 C2** 47 17N 2 12W
St. Neots, *U.K.* **11 E7** 52 14N 0 15W
St-Niklaas, *Belgium* **15 C4** 51 10N 4 8 E
St-Omer, *France* **18 A5** 50 45N 2 15 E
St-Pamphile, *Canada* **71 C6** 46 58N 69 48W
St. Pascal, *Canada* **71 C6** 47 32N 69 48W
St. Paul, *Canada* **72 C6** 54 0N 111 17W
St. Paul, *Minn., U.S.A.* **80 C8** 44 57N 93 6W
St. Paul, *Nebr., U.S.A.* **80 E5** 41 13N 98 27W
St-Paul →, *Canada* **71 B8** 51 27N 57 42W
St. Paul, I., *Ind. Oc.* **3 F13** 38 55S 77 34 E
St. Paul I., *Canada* **71 C7** 47 12N 60 9W
St. Peter, *U.S.A.* **80 C8** 44 20N 93 57W
St. Peter Port, *U.K.* **11 H5** 49 26N 2 33W
St. Peters, *N.S., Canada* **71 C7** 45 40N 60 53W
St. Peters, *P.E.I., Canada* **71 C7** 46 25N 62 35W
St. Petersburg = Sankt-Peterburg, *Russia* **24 C5** 59 55N 30 20 E
St. Petersburg, *U.S.A.* **77 M4** 27 46N 82 39W
St-Pie, *Canada* **79 A12** 45 30N 72 54W
St-Pierre, *St- P. & M.* **71 C8** 46 46N 56 12W
St-Pierre, L., *Canada* **70 C5** 46 12N 72 52W
St-Pierre et Miquelon □, *St- P. & M.* **71 C8** 46 55N 56 10W
St. Quentin, *Canada* **71 C6** 47 30N 67 23W
St-Quentin, *France* **18 B5** 49 50N 3 16 E
St. Regis, *U.S.A.* **82 C6** 47 18N 115 6W
St. Sebastien, Tanjon' i, *Madag.* **57 A8** 12 26S 48 44 E
St-Siméon, *Canada* **71 C6** 47 51N 69 54W
St. Simons I., *U.S.A.* **77 K5** 31 12N 81 15W
St. Simons Island, *U.S.A.* **77 K5** 31 9N 81 22W
St. Stephen, *Canada* **71 C6** 45 16N 67 17W
St. Thomas, *Canada* **78 D3** 42 45N 81 10W
St. Thomas I., *U.S. Virgin Is.* **89 C7** 18 20N 64 55W
St-Tite, *Canada* **70 C5** 46 45N 72 34W
St-Tropez, *France* **18 E7** 43 17N 6 38 E
St. Troud = St. Truiden, *Belgium* **15 D5** 50 48N 5 10 E
St. Truiden, *Belgium* **15 D5** 50 48N 5 10 E
St. Vincent, G., *Australia* **63 F2** 35 0S 138 0 E
St. Vincent & the Grenadines ■, *W. Indies* **89 D7** 13 0N 61 10W
St. Vincent Passage, *W. Indies* **89 D7** 13 30N 61 0W
St-Vith, *Belgium* **15 D6** 50 17N 6 9 E
St. Walburg, *Canada* **73 C7** 53 39N 109 12W
Ste-Agathe-des-Monts, *Canada* **70 C5** 46 3N 74 17W
Ste-Anne, L., *Canada* **71 B6** 50 0N 67 42W
Ste-Anne-des-Monts, *Canada* **71 C6** 49 8N 66 30W
Ste. Genevieve, *U.S.A.* **80 G9** 37 59N 90 2W
Ste-Marguerite →, *Canada* **71 B6** 50 9N 66 36W
Ste-Marie, *Martinique* **89 D7** 14 48N 61 1W
Ste-Marie de la Madeleine, *Canada* **71 C5** 46 26N 71 0W
Ste-Rose, *Guadeloupe* **89 C7** 16 20N 61 45W
Ste. Rose du Lac, *Canada* **73 C9** 51 4N 99 30W
Saintes, *France* **18 D3** 45 45N 0 37W
Saintes, I. des, *Guadeloupe* **89 C7** 15 50N 61 35W
Saintfield, *U.K.* **13 B6** 54 28N 5 49W
Saintonge, *France* **18 D3** 45 40N 0 50W
Saipan, *Pac. Oc.* **64 F6** 15 12N 145 45 E
Sairang, *India* **41 H18** 23 50N 92 45 E
Sairecábur, Cerro, *Bolivia* **94 A2** 22 43S 67 54W
Saitama □, *Japan* **31 F9** 36 25N 139 30 E
Saiyid, *Pakistan* **42 C5** 33 7N 73 2 E
Sajama, *Bolivia* **92 G5** 18 7S 69 0W
Sajószentpéter, *Hungary* **17 D11** 48 12N 20 44 E
Sajum, *India* **43 C8** 33 20N 79 0 E
Sak →, *S. Africa* **56 E3** 30 52S 20 25 E
Sakai, *Japan* **31 G7** 34 30N 135 30 E
Sakaide, *Japan* **31 G6** 34 19N 133 50 E
Sakaiminato, *Japan* **31 G6** 35 38N 133 11 E
Sakākah, *Si. Arabia* **44 D4** 30 0N 40 8 E
Sakakawea, L., *U.S.A.* **80 B4** 47 30N 101 25W
Sakami →, *Canada* **70 B4** 53 40N 76 40W
Sakami, L., *Canada* **70 B4** 53 15N 77 0W
Sakania, *Dem. Rep. of the Congo* **55 E2** 12 43S 28 30 E
Sakaraha, *Madag.* **57 C7** 22 55S 44 32 E
Sakarya, *Turkey* **25 F5** 40 48N 30 25 E
Sakashima-Guntō, *Japan* **31 M2** 24 46N 124 0 E
Sakata, *Japan* **30 E9** 38 55N 139 50 E
Sakchu, *N. Korea* **35 D13** 40 23N 125 2 E
Sakeny →, *Madag.* **57 C8** 20 0S 45 25 E
Sakha □, *Russia* **27 C13** 66 0N 130 0 E
Sakhalin, *Russia* **27 D15** 51 0N 143 0 E
Sakhalinskiy Zaliv, *Russia* **27 D15** 54 0N 141 0 E
Šakiai, *Lithuania* **9 J20** 54 59N 23 2 E
Sakon Nakhon, *Thailand* **38 D5** 17 10N 104 9 E
Sakrand, *Pakistan* **42 F3** 26 10N 68 15 E
Sakri, *India* **43 F12** 26 13N 86 5 E
Sakrivier, *S. Africa* **56 E3** 30 54S 20 28 E
Sakti, *India* **43 H10** 22 2N 82 58 E
Sakuma, *Japan* **31 G8** 35 3N 137 49 E
Sakurai, *Japan* **31 G7** 34 30N 135 51 E
Sala, *Sweden* **9 G17** 59 58N 16 35 E
Sala Consilina, *Italy* **20 D6** 40 23N 15 36 E
Sala-y-Gómez, *Pac. Oc.* **65 K17** 26 28S 105 28W
Salaberry-de-Valleyfield, *Canada* **79 A10** 45 15N 74 8W
Saladas, *Argentina* **94 B4** 28 15S 58 40W
Saladillo, *Argentina* **94 D4** 35 40S 59 55W
Salado →, *Buenos Aires, Argentina* **94 D4** 35 44S 57 22W
Salado →, *La Pampa, Argentina* **96 D3** 37 30S 67 0W
Salado →, *Santa Fe, Argentina* **94 C3** 31 40S 60 41W
Salado →, *Mexico* **81 M5** 26 52N 99 19W
Salaga, *Ghana* **50 G5** 8 31N 0 31W
Sālah, *Syria* **47 C5** 32 40N 36 45 E

San Pedro Ocampo

Sálakhos, Greece 23 C9 36 17N 27 57 E
Salālah, Oman 46 D5 16 56N 53 59 E
Salamanca, Chile 94 C1 31 46S 70 59W
Salamanca, Spain 19 B3 40 58N 5 39W
Salamanca, U.S.A. 78 D6 42 10N 78 43W
Salāmatābād, Iran 44 C5 35 39N 47 50 E
Salamis, Cyprus 23 D12 35 11N 33 54 E
Salamís, Greece 21 F10 37 56N 23 30 E
Salar de Atacama, Chile 94 A2 23 30S 68 25W
Salar de Uyuni, Bolivia 92 H5 20 30S 67 45W
Salatiga, Indonesia 37 G14 7 19S 110 30 E
Salavat, Russia 24 D10 53 21N 55 55 E
Salaverry, Peru 92 E3 8 15S 79 0W
Salawati, Indonesia 37 E8 1 7S 130 52 E
Salaya, India 42 H3 22 19N 69 35 E
Salayar, Indonesia 37 F6 6 7S 120 30 E
Salcombe, U.K. 11 G4 50 14N 3 47W
Saldanha, S. Africa 56 E2 33 0S 17 58 E
Saldanha B., S. Africa 56 E2 33 6S 18 0 E
Saldus, Latvia 9 H20 56 38N 22 30 E
Sale, Australia 63 F4 38 6S 147 6 E
Salé, Morocco 50 B4 34 3N 6 48W
Sale, U.K. 10 D5 53 26N 2 19W
Salekhard, Russia 26 C7 66 30N 66 35 E
Salem, India 40 P11 11 40N 78 11 E
Salem, Ill., U.S.A. 76 F1 38 38N 88 57W
Salem, Ind., U.S.A. 76 F2 38 36N 86 6W
Salem, Mass., U.S.A. 79 D14 42 31N 70 53W
Salem, Mo., U.S.A. 81 G9 37 39N 91 32W
Salem, N.H., U.S.A. 79 D13 42 45N 71 12W
Salem, N.J., U.S.A. 76 F8 39 34N 75 28W
Salem, N.Y., U.S.A. 79 C11 43 10N 73 20W
Salem, Ohio, U.S.A. 78 F4 40 54N 80 52W
Salem, Oreg., U.S.A. 82 D2 44 56N 123 2W
Salem, S. Dak., U.S.A. 80 D6 43 44N 97 23W
Salem, Va., U.S.A. 76 G5 37 18N 80 3W
Salerno, Italy 20 D6 40 41N 14 47 E
Salford, U.K. 10 D5 53 30N 2 18W
Salgótarján, Hungary 17 D10 48 5N 19 47 E
Salgueiro, Brazil 93 E11 8 4S 39 6W
Salibabu, Indonesia 37 D7 3 51N 126 40 E
Salida, U.S.A. 74 C5 38 32N 106 0W
Salihli, Turkey 21 E13 38 28N 28 8 E
Salihorsk, Belarus 17 B14 52 51N 27 27 E
Salima, Malawi 53 G6 13 47S 34 28 E
Salina, Italy 20 E6 38 34N 14 50 E
Salina, Kans., U.S.A. 80 F6 38 50N 97 37W
Salina, Utah, U.S.A. 83 G8 38 58N 111 51W
Salina Cruz, Mexico 87 D5 16 10N 95 10W
Salinas, Brazil 93 G10 16 10S 42 10W
Salinas, Chile 94 A2 23 31S 69 29W
Salinas, Ecuador 92 D2 2 10S 80 58W
Salinas, U.S.A. 84 J5 36 40N 121 39W
Salinas →, Guatemala 87 D6 16 28N 90 31W
Salinas →, U.S.A. 84 J5 36 45N 121 48W
Salinas, B. de, Nic. 88 D2 11 4N 85 45W
Salinas, Pampa de las, Argentina 94 C2 31 58S 66 42W
Salinas Ambargasta, Argentina 94 B3 29 0S 65 0W
Salinas de Hidalgo, Mexico 86 C4 22 30N 101 40W
Salinas Grandes, Argentina 94 C3 30 0S 65 0W
Saline →, Ark., U.S.A. 81 J8 33 10N 92 8W
Saline →, Kans., U.S.A. 80 F6 38 52N 97 30W
Salines, C. de ses, Spain 22 B10 39 16N 3 4 E
Salinópolis, Brazil 93 D9 0 40S 47 20W
Salisbury = Harare, Zimbabwe 55 F3 17 43S 31 2 E
Salisbury, U.K. 11 F6 51 4N 1 47W
Salisbury, Md., U.S.A. 76 F8 38 22N 75 36W
Salisbury, N.C., U.S.A. 77 H5 35 40N 80 29W
Salisbury I., Canada 69 B12 63 30N 77 0W
Salisbury Plain, U.K. 11 F6 51 14N 1 55W
Şalkhad, Syria 47 C5 32 29N 36 43 E
Salla, Finland 8 C23 66 50N 28 49 E
Salliq, Canada 69 B11 64 8N 83 10W
Sallisaw, U.S.A. 81 H7 35 28N 94 47W
Salluit, Canada 69 B12 62 14N 75 38W
Salmās, Iran 44 B5 38 11N 44 47 E
Salmo, Canada 72 D5 49 10N 117 20W
Salmon, U.S.A. 82 D7 45 11N 113 54W
Salmon →, Canada 72 C4 54 3N 122 40W
Salmon →, U.S.A. 82 D5 45 51N 116 47W
Salmon Arm, Canada 72 C5 50 40N 119 15W
Salmon Gums, Australia 61 F3 32 59S 121 38 E
Salmon River Mts., U.S.A. 82 D6 45 0N 114 30W
Salo, Finland 9 F20 60 22N 23 10 E
Salome, U.S.A. 85 M13 33 47N 113 37W
Salon, India 43 F9 26 2N 81 27 E
Salon-de-Provence, France 18 E6 43 39N 5 6 E
Salonica = Thessaloníki, Greece 21 D10 40 38N 22 58 E
Salonta, Romania 17 E11 46 49N 21 42 E
Salpausselkä, Finland 9 F22 61 0N 27 0 E
Salsacate, Argentina 94 C2 31 20S 65 5W
Salsk, Russia 25 E7 46 28N 41 30 E
Salso →, Italy 20 F5 37 6N 13 57 E
Salt →, Canada 72 B6 60 0N 112 25W
Salt →, U.S.A. 83 K7 33 23N 112 19W
Salt Lake City, U.S.A. 82 F8 40 45N 111 53W
Salt Range, Pakistan 42 C5 32 30N 72 25 E
Salta, Argentina 94 A2 24 57S 65 25W
Salta □, Argentina 94 A2 24 48S 65 30W
Saltash, U.K. 11 G3 50 24N 4 14W
Saltburn by the Sea, U.K. 10 C7 54 35N 0 58W
Saltcoats, U.K. 12 F4 55 38N 4 47W
Saltee Is., Ireland 13 D5 52 7N 6 37W
Saltfjellet, Norway 8 C16 66 40N 15 15 E
Saltfjorden, Norway 8 C16 67 15N 14 10 E
Saltillo, Mexico 86 B4 25 25N 101 0W
Salto, Argentina 94 C3 34 20S 60 15W
Salto, Uruguay 94 C4 31 27S 57 50W
Salto →, Italy 20 C5 42 26N 12 25 E
Salto del Guaíra, Paraguay 95 A5 24 3S 54 17W
Salton City, U.S.A. 85 M11 33 29N 115 51W
Salton Sea, U.S.A. 85 M11 33 15N 115 45W
Saltsburg, U.S.A. 78 F5 40 29N 79 27W
Saluda →, U.S.A. 77 J5 34 1N 81 4W
Salûm, Egypt 51 B11 31 31N 25 7 E
Salur, India 41 K13 18 27N 83 18 E
Salvador, Brazil 93 F11 13 0S 38 30W
Salvador, Canada 73 C7 52 10N 109 32W
Salvador, L., U.S.A. 81 L9 29 43N 90 15W
Salween →, Burma 41 L20 16 31N 97 37 E
Salyan, Azerbaijan 25 G8 39 33N 48 59 E
Salzach →, Austria 16 D7 48 12N 12 56 E
Salzburg, Austria 16 E7 47 48N 13 2 E
Salzgitter, Germany 16 B6 52 9N 10 19 E
Salzwedel, Germany 16 B6 52 52N 11 10 E
Sam, India 42 F4 26 50N 70 31 E
Sam Neua, Laos 38 B5 20 29N 104 5 E
Sam Ngao, Thailand 38 D2 17 18N 99 0 E
Sam Rayburn Reservoir, U.S.A. 81 K7 31 4N 94 5W
Sam Son, Vietnam 38 C5 19 44N 105 54 E
Sam Teu, Laos 38 C5 19 59N 104 38 E
Sama de Langreo = Langreo, Spain 19 A3 43 18N 5 40W
Samagaltay, Russia 27 D10 50 36N 95 3 E
Samales Group, Phil. 37 C6 6 0N 122 0 E
Samana, India 42 D7 30 10N 76 13 E
Samana Cay, Bahamas 89 B5 23 3N 73 45W
Samanga, Tanzania 55 D4 8 20S 39 13 E
Samangān □, Afghan. 40 B5 36 15N 68 3 E
Samangwa, Dem. Rep. of the Congo 54 C1 4 23S 24 10 E
Samani, Japan 30 C11 42 7N 142 56 E
Samar, Phil. 37 B7 12 0N 125 0 E
Samara, Russia 24 D9 53 8N 50 6 E
Samaria = Shōmrōn, West Bank 47 C4 32 15N 35 13 E
Samariá, Greece 23 D5 35 17N 23 58 E
Samarinda, Indonesia 36 E5 0 30S 117 9 E
Samarkand = Samarqand, Uzbekistan 26 F7 39 40N 66 55 E
Samarqand, Uzbekistan 26 F7 39 40N 66 55 E
Sāmarrā, Iraq 44 C4 34 12N 43 52 E
Samastipur, India 43 G11 25 50N 85 50 E
Samba, Dem. Rep. of the Congo 54 C2 4 38S 26 22 E
Samba, India 43 C6 32 32N 75 10 E
Sambalpur, India 41 J14 21 28N 84 4 E
Sambar, Tanjung, Indonesia 36 E4 2 59S 110 19 E
Sambas, Indonesia 36 D3 1 20N 109 20 E
Sambava, Madag. 57 A9 14 16S 50 10 E
Sambawizi, Zimbabwe 55 F2 18 24S 26 13 E
Sambhal, India 43 E8 28 35N 78 37 E
Sambhar, India 42 F6 26 52N 75 6 E
Sambhar L., India 42 F6 26 55N 75 12 E
Sambiase, Italy 20 E7 38 58N 16 17 E
Sambir, Ukraine 17 D12 49 30N 23 10 E
Sambor, Cambodia 38 F6 12 46N 106 0 E
Samborombón, B., Argentina 94 D4 36 5S 57 20W
Samch'ŏk, S. Korea 35 F15 37 30N 129 10 E
Samch'onp'o, S. Korea 35 G15 35 0N 128 6 E
Same, Tanzania 54 C4 4 2S 37 38 E
Samfya, Zambia 55 E2 11 22S 29 31 E
Samnah, Si. Arabia 44 E3 25 10N 37 15 E
Samo Alto, Chile 94 C1 30 22S 71 0W
Samoa ■, Pac. Oc. 59 B13 14 0S 172 0W
Samokov, Bulgaria 21 C10 42 18N 23 35 E
Sámos, Greece 21 F12 37 45N 26 50 E
Samothráki = Mathráki, Greece 23 A3 39 48N 19 31 E
Samothráki, Greece 21 D11 40 28N 25 28 E
Sampacho, Argentina 94 C3 33 20S 64 50W
Sampang, Indonesia 37 G15 7 11S 113 13 E
Sampit, Indonesia 36 E4 2 34S 113 0 E
Sampit, Teluk, Indonesia 36 E4 3 5S 113 3 E
Samrong, Cambodia 38 E4 14 15N 103 30 E
Samrong, Thailand 38 E3 15 10N 100 40 E
Samsø, Denmark 9 J14 55 50N 10 35 E
Samsun, Turkey 25 F6 41 15N 36 22 E
Samui, Ko, Thailand 39 H3 9 30N 100 0 E
Samusole, Dem. Rep. of the Congo 55 E1 10 2S 24 0 E
Samut Prakan, Thailand 38 F3 13 32N 100 40 E
Samut Songkhram →, Thailand 36 B1 13 24N 100 1 E
Samwari, Pakistan 42 E2 28 30N 66 46 E
San, Mali 50 F5 13 15N 4 57W
San →, Cambodia 38 F5 13 32N 105 57 E
San →, Poland 17 C11 50 45N 21 51 E
San Agustin, C., Phil. 37 C7 6 20N 126 13 E
San Agustín de Valle Fértil, Argentina 94 C2 30 35S 67 30W
San Ambrosio, Pac. Oc. 90 F3 26 28S 79 53W
San Andreas, U.S.A. 84 G6 38 12N 120 41W
San Andrés, I. de, Caribbean 88 D3 12 42N 81 46W
San Andres Mts., U.S.A. 83 K10 33 0N 106 30W
San Andrés Tuxtla, Mexico 87 D5 18 30N 95 20W
San Angelo, U.S.A. 81 K4 31 28N 100 26W
San Anselmo, U.S.A. 84 H4 37 59N 122 34W
San Antonio, Belize 87 D7 16 15N 89 2W
San Antonio, Chile 94 C1 33 40S 71 40W
San Antonio, N. Mex., U.S.A. 83 K10 33 55N 106 52W
San Antonio, Tex., U.S.A. 81 L5 29 25N 98 30W
San Antonio →, U.S.A. 81 L6 28 30N 96 54W
San Antonio, C., Argentina 94 D4 36 15S 56 40W
San Antonio, C., Cuba 88 B3 21 50N 84 57W
San Antonio, Mt., U.S.A. 85 L9 34 17N 117 38W
San Antonio de los Baños, Cuba 88 B3 22 54N 82 31W
San Antonio de los Cobres, Argentina 94 A2 24 10S 66 17W
San Antonio Oeste, Argentina 96 E4 40 40S 65 0W
San Ardo, U.S.A. 84 J6 36 1N 120 54W
San Augustín, Canary Is. 22 G4 27 47N 15 32W
San Augustine, U.S.A. 81 K7 31 30N 94 7W
San Bartolomé, Canary Is. 22 F6 28 59N 13 37W
San Bartolomé de Tirajana, Canary Is. 22 G4 27 54N 15 34W
San Benedetto del Tronto, Italy 20 C5 42 57N 13 53 E
San Benedicto, I., Mexico 86 D2 19 18N 110 49W
San Benito, U.S.A. 81 M6 26 8N 97 38W
San Benito →, U.S.A. 84 J5 36 53N 121 34W
San Benito Mt., U.S.A. 84 J6 36 22N 120 37W
San Bernardino, U.S.A. 85 L9 34 7N 117 19W
San Bernardino Mts., U.S.A. 85 L10 34 10N 116 45W
San Bernardino Str., Phil. 37 B6 13 0N 125 0 E
San Bernardo, Chile 94 C1 33 40S 70 50W
San Bernardo, I. de, Colombia 92 B3 9 45N 75 50W
San Blas, Mexico 86 B3 26 4N 108 46W
San Blas, Arch. de, Panama 88 E4 9 50N 78 31W
San Blas, C., U.S.A. 77 L3 29 40N 85 21W
San Borja, Bolivia 92 F5 14 50S 66 52W
San Buenaventura, Mexico 86 B4 27 5N 101 32W
San Carlos = Sant Carles, Spain 22 B8 39 3N 1 34 E
San Carlos, Argentina 94 C2 33 50S 69 0W
San Carlos, Chile 94 D1 36 10S 72 0W
San Carlos, Baja Calif. S., Mexico 86 C2 24 47N 112 6W
San Carlos, Coahuila, Mexico 86 B4 29 0N 100 54W
San Carlos, Nic. 88 D3 11 12N 84 50W
San Carlos, Phil. 37 B6 10 29N 123 25 E
San Carlos, Uruguay 95 C5 34 46S 54 58W
San Carlos, U.S.A. 83 K8 33 21N 110 27W
San Carlos, Venezuela 92 B5 9 40N 68 36W
San Carlos de Bariloche, Argentina 96 E2 41 10S 71 25W
San Carlos de Bolívar, Argentina 96 D4 36 15S 61 6W
San Carlos del Zulia, Venezuela 92 B4 9 1N 71 55W
San Carlos L., U.S.A. 83 K8 33 11N 110 32W
San Clemente, Chile 94 D1 35 30S 71 29W
San Clemente, U.S.A. 85 M9 33 26N 117 37W
San Clemente I., U.S.A. 85 N8 32 53N 118 29W
San Cristóbal = Es Migjorn Gran, Spain 22 B11 39 57N 4 3 E
San Cristóbal, Argentina 94 C3 30 20S 61 10W
San Cristóbal, Dom. Rep. 89 C5 18 25N 70 6W
San Cristóbal, Venezuela 92 B4 7 46N 72 14W
San Cristóbal de la Casas, Mexico 87 D6 16 50N 92 33W
San Diego, Calif., U.S.A. 85 N9 32 43N 117 9W
San Diego, Tex., U.S.A. 81 M5 27 46N 98 14W
San Diego, C., Argentina 96 G3 54 40S 65 10W
San Diego de la Unión, Mexico 86 C4 21 28N 100 52W
San Dimitri, Ras, Malta 23 C1 36 4N 14 11 E
San Dimitri Point = San Dimitri, Ras, Malta 23 C1 36 4N 14 11 E
San Estanislao, Paraguay 94 A4 24 39S 56 26W
San Felipe, Chile 94 C1 32 43S 70 42W
San Felipe, Mexico 86 A2 31 0N 114 52W
San Felipe, Venezuela 92 A5 10 20N 68 44W
San Felipe →, U.S.A. 85 M11 33 12N 115 49W
San Félix, Chile 94 B1 28 56S 70 28W
San Félix, Pac. Oc. 90 F2 26 23S 80 0W
San Fernando = Sant Ferran, Spain 22 C7 38 42N 1 28 E
San Fernando, Chile 94 C1 34 30S 71 0W
San Fernando, Baja Calif., Mexico 86 B1 29 55N 115 10W
San Fernando, Tamaulipas, Mexico 87 C5 24 51N 98 10W
San Fernando, La Union, Phil. 37 A6 16 40N 120 23 E
San Fernando, Pampanga, Phil. 37 A6 15 5N 120 37 E
San Fernando, Spain 19 D2 36 28N 6 17W
San Fernando, Trin. & Tob. 89 D7 10 20N 61 30W
San Fernando, U.S.A. 85 L8 34 17N 118 26W
San Fernando de Apure, Venezuela 92 B5 7 54N 67 15W
San Fernando de Atabapo, Venezuela 92 C5 4 3N 67 42W
San Francisco, Argentina 94 C3 31 30S 62 5W
San Francisco, U.S.A. 84 H4 37 47N 122 25W
San Francisco →, U.S.A. 83 K9 32 59N 109 22W
San Francisco, Paso de, S. Amer. 94 B2 27 0S 68 0W
San Francisco de Macorís, Dom. Rep. 89 C5 19 19N 70 15W
San Francisco del Monte de Oro, Argentina 94 C2 32 36S 66 8W
San Francisco del Oro, Mexico 86 B3 26 52N 105 50W
San Francisco Javier = Sant Francesc de Formentera, Spain 22 C7 38 42N 1 26 E
San Francisco Solano, Pta., Colombia 90 C3 6 18N 77 29W
San Gabriel, Chile 94 C1 33 47S 70 15W
San Gabriel Mts., U.S.A. 85 L9 34 20N 118 0W
San Gorgonio Mt., U.S.A. 85 L10 34 7N 116 51W
San Gottardo, P. del, Switz. 18 C8 46 33N 8 33 E
San Gregorio, Uruguay 95 C4 32 37S 55 40W
San Gregorio, U.S.A. 84 H4 37 20N 122 23W
San Ignacio, Belize 87 D7 17 10N 89 0W
San Ignacio, Bolivia 92 G6 16 20S 60 55W
San Ignacio, Mexico 86 B2 27 27N 113 0W
San Ignacio, Paraguay 88 C2 26 52S 57 3W
San Ignacio, L., Mexico 86 B2 26 50N 113 11W
San Ildefonso, C., Phil. 37 A6 16 0N 122 1 E
San Isidro, Argentina 94 C4 34 29S 58 31W
San Jacinto, U.S.A. 85 M10 33 47N 116 57W
San Jaime = Sant Jaume, Spain 22 B11 39 54N 4 4 E
San Javier, Misiones, Argentina 95 B4 27 55S 55 5W
San Javier, Santa Fe, Argentina 94 C4 30 40S 59 55W
San Javier, Bolivia 92 G6 16 18S 62 30W
San Javier, Chile 94 D1 35 40S 71 45W
San Jeronimo Taviche, Mexico 87 D5 16 38N 96 32W
San Joaquin, U.S.A. 84 J6 36 36N 120 11W
San Joaquin →, U.S.A. 84 G5 38 4N 121 51W
San Joaquin Valley, U.S.A. 84 J6 37 20N 121 0W
San Jon, U.S.A. 81 H3 35 6N 103 20W
San Jordi = Sant Jordi, Spain 22 B9 39 33N 2 46 E
San Jorge, Argentina 94 C3 31 54S 61 50W
San Jorge, B. de, Mexico 86 A2 31 20N 113 20W
San Jorge, G., Argentina 96 F3 46 0S 66 0W
San José = San Josep, Spain 22 C7 38 55N 1 18 E
San José, Costa Rica 88 E3 9 55N 84 2W
San José, Guatemala 88 D1 14 0N 90 50W
San José, Mexico 86 C2 25 0N 110 50W
San Jose, Mind. Occ., Phil. 37 B6 12 27N 121 4 E
San Jose, Nueva Ecija, Phil. 37 A6 15 45N 120 55 E
San Jose, U.S.A. 84 H5 37 20N 121 53W
San Jose →, U.S.A. 83 J10 34 25N 106 45W
San Jose de Buenavista, Phil. 37 B6 10 45N 121 56 E
San José de Chiquitos, Bolivia 92 G6 17 53S 60 50W
San José de Feliciano, Argentina 94 C4 30 26S 58 46W
San José de Jáchal, Argentina 94 C2 30 15S 68 46W
San José de Mayo, Uruguay 94 C4 34 27S 56 40W
San José del Cabo, Mexico 86 C3 23 0N 109 40W
San José del Guaviare, Colombia 92 C4 2 35N 72 38W
San Josep, Spain 22 C7 38 55N 1 18 E
San Juan, Argentina 94 C2 31 30S 68 30W
San Juan, Mexico 86 C4 21 20N 102 50W
San Juan, Puerto Rico 89 C6 18 28N 66 7W
San Juan □, Argentina 94 C2 31 9S 69 0W
San Juan →, Argentina 94 C2 32 20S 67 25W
San Juan →, Nic. 88 D3 10 56N 83 42W
San Juan →, U.S.A. 83 H8 37 16N 110 26W
San Juan Bautista = Sant Joan Baptista, Spain 22 B8 39 5N 1 31 E
San Juan Bautista, Paraguay 94 B4 26 37S 57 6W
San Juan Bautista, U.S.A. 84 J5 36 51N 121 32W
San Juan Bautista Valle Nacional, Mexico 87 D5 17 47N 96 19W
San Juan Capistrano, U.S.A. 85 M9 33 30N 117 40W
San Juan Cr. →, U.S.A. 84 J5 35 40N 120 22W
San Juan de Guadalupe, Mexico 86 C4 24 38N 102 44W
San Juan de la Costa, Mexico 86 C2 24 23N 110 45W
San Juan de los Morros, Venezuela 92 B5 9 55N 67 21W
San Juan del Norte, Nic. 88 D3 10 58N 83 40W
San Juan del Norte, B. de, Nic. 88 D3 11 0N 83 40W
San Juan del Río, Mexico 87 C5 20 25N 100 0W
San Juan del Sur, Nic. 88 D2 11 20N 85 51W
San Juan I., U.S.A. 84 B3 48 32N 123 5W
San Juan Mts., U.S.A. 83 H10 37 30N 107 0W
San Justo, Argentina 94 C3 30 47S 60 30W
San Kamphaeng, Thailand 38 C2 18 45N 99 8 E
San Lázaro, C., Mexico 86 C2 24 50N 112 18W
San Lázaro, Sa., Mexico 86 C3 23 25N 110 0W
San Leandro, U.S.A. 84 H4 37 44N 122 9W
San Lorenzo = Sant Llorenç des Cardassar, Spain 22 B10 39 37N 3 17 E
San Lorenzo, Argentina 94 C3 32 45S 60 45W
San Lorenzo, Ecuador 92 C3 1 15N 78 50W
San Lorenzo, Paraguay 94 B4 25 20S 57 32W
San Lorenzo →, Mexico 86 C3 24 15N 107 24W
San Lorenzo, I., Mexico 86 B2 28 35N 112 50W
San Lorenzo, Mte., Argentina 96 F2 47 40S 72 20W
San Lucas, Bolivia 92 H5 20 5S 65 7W
San Lucas, Baja Calif. S., Mexico 86 C3 22 53N 109 54W
San Lucas, Baja Calif. S., Mexico 86 B2 27 10N 112 14W
San Lucas, U.S.A. 84 J5 36 8N 121 1W
San Lucas, C., Mexico 86 C3 22 50N 110 0W
San Luis, Argentina 94 C2 33 20S 66 20W
San Luis, Cuba 88 B3 22 17N 83 46W
San Luis, Guatemala 88 C2 16 14N 89 27W
San Luis, Ariz., U.S.A. 83 K6 32 29N 114 47W
San Luis, Colo., U.S.A. 83 H11 37 12N 105 25W
San Luis □, Argentina 94 C2 34 0S 66 0W
San Luis, I., Mexico 86 B2 29 58N 114 26W
San Luis, Sierra de, Argentina 94 C2 32 30S 66 10W
San Luis de la Paz, Mexico 86 C4 21 19N 100 32W
San Luis Obispo, U.S.A. 85 K6 35 17N 120 40W
San Luis Potosí, Mexico 86 C4 22 9N 100 59W
San Luis Potosí □, Mexico 86 C4 22 10N 101 0W
San Luis Reservoir, U.S.A. 84 H5 37 4N 121 5W
San Luis Río Colorado, Mexico 86 A2 32 29N 114 58W
San Manuel, U.S.A. 83 K8 32 36N 110 38W
San Marcos, Guatemala 88 D1 14 59N 91 52W
San Marcos, Mexico 86 B2 27 13N 112 6W
San Marcos, Calif., U.S.A. 85 M9 33 9N 117 10W
San Marcos, Tex., U.S.A. 81 L6 29 53N 97 56W
San Marino, San Marino 16 G7 43 55N 12 30 E
San Marino ■, Europe 20 C5 43 56N 12 25 E
San Martín, Argentina 94 C2 33 5S 68 28W
San Martín →, Bolivia 92 F6 13 8S 63 43W
San Martín, L., Argentina 96 F2 48 50S 72 50W
San Martín de los Andes, Argentina 96 E2 40 10S 71 20W
San Mateo = Sant Mateu, Spain 22 B7 39 3N 1 23 E
San Mateo, U.S.A. 84 H4 37 34N 122 19W
San Matías, Bolivia 92 G7 16 25S 58 20W
San Matías, G., Argentina 96 E4 41 30S 64 0W
San Miguel = Sant Miguel, Spain 22 B7 39 3N 1 26 E
San Miguel, El Salv. 88 D2 13 30N 88 12W
San Miguel, Panama 88 E4 8 27N 78 55W
San Miguel, U.S.A. 84 K6 35 45N 120 42W
San Miguel →, Bolivia 92 F6 13 52S 63 56W
San Miguel de Tucumán, Argentina 94 B2 26 50S 65 20W
San Miguel del Monte, Argentina 94 D4 35 23S 58 50W
San Miguel I., U.S.A. 85 L6 34 2N 120 23W
San Nicolás, Canary Is. 22 G4 27 58N 15 47W
San Nicolás de los Arroyas, Argentina 94 C3 33 25S 60 10W
San Nicolas I., U.S.A. 85 M7 33 15N 119 30W
San Onofre, U.S.A. 85 M9 33 22N 117 34W
San Pablo, Bolivia 94 A2 21 43S 66 38W
San Pablo, U.S.A. 84 H4 37 58N 122 21W
San Pedro, Buenos Aires, Argentina 94 C4 33 40S 59 40W
San Pedro, Misiones, Argentina 95 B5 26 30S 54 10W
San Pedro, Chile 94 C1 33 54S 71 28W
San Pédro, Ivory C. 50 H4 4 50N 6 33W
San Pedro, Mexico 86 C2 23 55N 110 17W
San Pedro □, Paraguay 94 A4 24 0S 57 0W
San Pedro →, Chihuahua, Mexico 86 B3 28 20N 106 10W
San Pedro →, Nayarit, Mexico 86 C3 21 45N 105 30W
San Pedro →, U.S.A. 83 K8 32 59N 110 47W
San Pedro, Pta., Chile 94 B1 25 30S 70 38W
San Pedro Channel, U.S.A. 85 M8 33 30N 118 25W
San Pedro de Atacama, Chile 94 A2 22 55S 68 15W
San Pedro de Jujuy, Argentina 94 A3 24 12S 64 55W
San Pedro de las Colonias, Mexico 86 B4 25 50N 102 59W
San Pedro de Macorís, Dom. Rep. 89 C6 18 30N 69 18W
San Pedro del Norte, Nic. 88 D3 13 4N 84 33W
San Pedro del Paraná, Paraguay 94 B4 26 43S 56 13W
San Pedro Mártir, Sierra, Mexico 86 A1 31 0N 115 30W
San Pedro Mixtepec, Mexico 87 D5 16 2N 97 7W
San Pedro Ocampo = Melchor Ocampo, Mexico 86 C4 24 52N 101 40W

San Pedro Sula

San Pedro Sula, Honduras 88 C2 15 30N 88 0W
San Pietro, Italy 20 E3 39 8N 8 17 E
San Quintín, Mexico 86 A1 30 29N 115 57W
San Rafael, Argentina 94 C2 34 40S 68 21W
San Rafael, Calif., U.S.A. 84 H4 37 58N 122 32W
San Rafael, N. Mex., U.S.A. 83 J10 35 7N 107 53W
San Rafael Mt., U.S.A. 85 L7 34 41N 119 52W
San Rafael Mts., U.S.A. 85 L7 34 40N 119 50W
San Ramón de la Nueva Orán, Argentina 94 A3 23 10S 64 20W
San Remo, Italy 18 E7 43 49N 7 46 E
San Roque, Argentina 94 B4 28 25S 58 45W
San Roque, Spain 19 D3 36 17N 5 21W
San Rosendo, Chile 94 D1 37 16S 72 43W
San Saba, U.S.A. 81 K5 31 12N 98 43W
San Salvador, El Salv. 88 D2 13 40N 89 10W
San Salvador, Spain 22 B10 39 27N 3 11 E
San Salvador de Jujuy, Argentina 94 A3 24 10S 64 48W
San Salvador I., Bahamas 89 B5 24 0N 74 40W
San Sebastián = Donostia-San Sebastián, Spain 19 A5 43 17N 1 58W
San Sebastián, Argentina 96 G3 53 10S 68 30W
San Sebastián de la Gomera, Canary Is. 22 F2 28 5N 17 7W
San Serra = Son Serra, Spain 22 B10 39 43N 3 13 E
San Severo, Italy 20 D6 41 41N 15 23 E
San Simeon, U.S.A. 84 K5 35 39N 121 11W
San Simon, U.S.A. 83 K9 32 16N 109 14W
San Telmo = Sant Telm, Spain 22 B9 39 35N 2 21 E
San Telmo, Mexico 86 A1 30 58N 116 6W
San Tiburcio, Mexico 86 C4 24 8N 101 32W
San Valentin, Mte., Chile 96 F2 46 30S 73 30W
San Vicente de la Barquera, Spain 19 A3 43 23N 4 29W
San Vito, Costa Rica 88 E3 8 50N 82 58W
Sana', Yemen 46 D3 15 27N 44 12 E
Sana →, Bos.-H. 16 F9 45 3N 16 23 E
Sanaga →, Cameroon 52 D1 3 35N 9 38 E
Sanaloa, Presa, Mexico 86 C3 24 50N 107 20W
Sanana, Indonesia 37 E7 2 4S 125 58 E
Sanand, India 42 H5 22 59N 72 25 E
Sanandaj, Iran 44 C5 35 18N 47 1 E
Sanandita, Bolivia 94 A3 21 40S 63 45W
Sanawad, India 42 H7 22 11N 76 5 E
Sancellas = Sencelles, Spain 22 B9 39 39N 2 54 E
Sanchahe, China 35 B14 44 50N 126 2 E
Sánchez, Dom. Rep. 89 C6 19 15N 69 36W
Sanchor, India 42 G4 24 45N 71 55 E
Sancti Spíritus, Cuba 88 B4 21 52N 79 33W
Sancy, Puy de, France 18 D5 45 32N 2 50 E
Sand →, S. Africa 57 C5 22 25S 30 5 E
Sand Hills, U.S.A. 80 D4 42 10N 101 30W
Sand Springs, U.S.A. 81 G6 36 9N 96 7W
Sanda, Japan 31 G7 34 53N 135 14 E
Sandakan, Malaysia 36 C5 5 53N 118 4 E
Sandan = Sambor, Cambodia 38 F6 12 46N 106 0 E
Sandanski, Bulgaria 21 D10 41 35N 23 16 E
Sanday, U.K. 12 B6 59 16N 2 31W
Sandefjord, Norway 9 G14 59 10N 10 15 E
Sanders, U.S.A. 83 J9 35 13N 109 20W
Sanderson, U.S.A. 81 K3 30 9N 102 24W
Sandersville, U.S.A. 77 J4 32 59N 82 48W
Sandfire Roadhouse, Australia 60 C3 19 45S 121 15 E
Sandfly L., Canada 73 B7 55 43N 106 6W
Sandfontein, Namibia 56 C2 23 48S 29 1 E
Sandía, Peru 92 F5 14 10S 69 30W
Sandila, India 43 F9 27 5N 80 31 E
Sandnes, Norway 9 G11 58 50N 5 45 E
Sandnessjøen, Norway 8 C15 66 2N 12 38 E
Sandoa, Dem. Rep. of the Congo 52 F4 9 41S 23 0 E
Sandomierz, Poland 17 C11 50 40N 21 43 E
Sandover →, Australia 62 C2 21 43S 136 32 E
Sandoway, Burma 41 K19 18 20N 94 30 E
Sandoy, Færoe Is. 8 F9 61 52N 6 46W
Sandpoint, U.S.A. 82 B5 48 17N 116 33W
Sandray, U.K. 12 E1 56 53N 7 31W
Sandringham, U.K. 10 E8 52 51N 0 31 E
Sandstone, Australia 61 E2 27 59S 119 16 E
Sandusky, Mich., U.S.A. 78 C2 43 25N 82 50W
Sandusky, Ohio, U.S.A. 78 E2 41 27N 82 42W
Sandviken, Sweden 9 F17 60 38N 16 46 E
Sandwich, C., Australia 62 B4 18 14S 146 18 E
Sandwich B., Canada 71 B8 53 40N 57 15W
Sandwich B., Namibia 56 C1 23 25S 14 20 E
Sandy, Oreg., U.S.A. 84 E4 45 24N 122 16W
Sandy, Pa., U.S.A. 78 E6 41 6N 78 46W
Sandy, Utah, U.S.A. 82 F8 40 35N 111 50W
Sandy Bay, Canada 73 B8 55 31N 102 19W
Sandy Bight, Australia 61 F3 33 50S 123 20 E
Sandy C., Queens., Australia 62 C5 24 42S 153 15 E
Sandy C., Tas., Australia 62 G3 41 25S 144 45 E
Sandy Cay, Bahamas 89 B4 23 13N 75 18W
Sandy Cr. →, U.S.A. 82 F9 41 51N 109 47W
Sandy L., Canada 70 B1 53 2N 93 0W
Sandy Lake, Canada 70 B1 53 0N 93 15W
Sandy Valley, U.S.A. 85 K11 35 49N 115 36W
Sanford, Fla., U.S.A. 77 L5 28 48N 81 16W
Sanford, Maine, U.S.A. 77 D10 43 27N 70 47W
Sanford, N.C., U.S.A. 77 H6 35 29N 79 10W
Sanford →, Australia 61 E2 27 22S 115 53 E
Sanford, Mt., U.S.A. 68 B5 62 13N 144 8W
Sang-i-Masha, Afghan. 42 C2 33 8N 67 27 E
Sanga, Mozam. 55 E4 12 22S 35 21 E
Sanga →, Congo 52 E3 1 5S 17 0 E
Sangamner, India 40 K9 19 37N 74 15 E
Sangar, Afghan. 42 C1 32 56N 65 30 E
Sangar, Russia 27 C13 64 2N 127 31 E
Sangar Sarai, Afghan. 42 B4 34 27N 70 35 E
Sangarh →, Pakistan 42 D4 30 43N 70 44 E
Sangay, Ecuador 92 D3 2 0S 78 20W
Sange, Dem. Rep. of the Congo 54 D2 6 58S 28 21 E
Sangeang, Indonesia 37 F5 8 12S 119 6 E
Sanger, U.S.A. 84 J7 36 42N 119 33W
Sangerhausen, Germany 16 C6 51 28N 11 18 E
Sanggan He →, China 34 E9 38 12N 117 15 E
Sanggau, Indonesia 36 D4 0 5N 110 30 E
Sanghar, Pakistan 42 F3 26 2N 68 57 E
Sangihe, Kepulauan, Indonesia 37 D7 3 0N 125 30 E
Sangihe, Pulau, Indonesia 37 D7 3 35N 125 30 E
Sangju, S. Korea 35 F15 36 25N 128 10 E
Sangkapura, Indonesia 36 F4 5 52S 112 40 E
Sangkhla, Thailand 38 E2 14 57N 98 28 E
Sangkulirang, Indonesia 36 D5 0 59N 117 58 E
Sangla, Pakistan 42 D5 31 43N 73 23 E
Sangli, India 40 L9 16 55N 74 33 E
Sangmélima, Cameroon 52 D2 2 57N 12 1 E
Sangod, India 42 G7 24 55N 76 17 E
Sangre de Cristo Mts., U.S.A. 81 G2 37 30N 105 20W
Sangrur, India 42 D6 30 14N 75 50 E
Sangudo, Canada 72 C6 53 50N 114 54W
Sangue →, Brazil 92 F7 11 1S 58 39W
Sanibel, U.S.A. 77 M4 26 26N 82 1W
Sanirajak, Canada 69 B11 68 46N 81 12W
Sanjawi, Pakistan 42 D3 30 17N 68 21 E
Sanje, Uganda 54 C3 0 49S 31 30 E
Sanjo, Japan 30 F9 37 37N 138 57 E
Sankh →, India 43 H11 22 15N 84 48 E
Sankt Gallen, Switz. 18 C8 47 26N 9 22 E
Sankt Moritz, Switz. 18 C8 46 30N 9 50 E
Sankt-Peterburg, Russia 24 C5 59 55N 30 20 E
Sankt Pölten, Austria 16 D8 48 12N 15 38 E
Sankuru →, Dem. Rep. of the Congo 52 E4 4 17S 20 25 E
Sanliurfa, Turkey 25 G6 37 12N 38 50 E
Sanlúcar de Barrameda, Spain 19 D2 36 46N 6 21W
Sanmenxia, China 34 G6 34 47N 111 12 E
Sanming, China 33 D6 26 15N 117 40 E
Sannaspos, S. Africa 56 D4 29 6S 26 34 E
Sannicandro Gargánico, Italy 20 D6 41 50N 15 34 E
Sânnicolau Mare, Romania 17 E11 46 5N 20 39 E
Sannieshof, S. Africa 56 D4 26 30S 25 47 E
Sannin, J., Lebanon 47 B4 33 57N 35 52 E
Sanniquellie, Liberia 50 G4 7 19N 8 38W
Sanok, Poland 17 D12 49 35N 22 10 E
Sanquhar, U.K. 12 F5 55 22N 3 54W
Sant Antoni Abat, Spain 22 C7 38 59N 1 19 E
Sant Carles, Spain 22 B8 39 3N 1 34 E
Sant Feliu de Guíxols, Spain 19 B7 41 45N 3 1 E
Sant Ferran, Spain 22 C7 38 42N 1 28 E
Sant Francesc de Formentera, Spain 22 C7 38 42N 1 26 E
Sant Jaume, Spain 22 B11 39 54N 4 4 E
Sant Joan Baptista, Spain 22 B8 39 5N 1 31 E
Sant Jordi, Ibiza, Spain 22 C7 38 53N 1 24 E
Sant Jordi, Mallorca, Spain 22 B9 39 33N 2 46 E
Sant Jordi, G. de, Spain 19 B6 40 53N 1 2 E
Sant Llorenç des Cardassar, Spain 22 B10 39 37N 3 17 E
Sant Mateu, Spain 22 B7 39 3N 1 23 E
Sant Miquel, Spain 22 B7 39 3N 1 26 E
Sant Telm, Spain 22 B9 39 35N 2 21 E
Santa Agnés, Spain 22 B7 39 3N 1 21 E
Santa Ana, Bolivia 92 F5 13 50S 65 40W
Santa Ana, El Salv. 88 D2 14 0N 89 31W
Santa Ana, Mexico 86 A2 30 31N 111 8W
Santa Ana, U.S.A. 85 M9 33 46N 117 52W
Sant' Antíoco, Italy 20 E3 39 4N 8 27 E
Santa Bárbara, Chile 94 D1 37 40S 72 1W
Santa Bárbara, Honduras 88 D2 14 53N 88 14W
Santa Bárbara, Mexico 86 B3 26 48N 105 50W
Santa Barbara, U.S.A. 85 L7 34 25N 119 42W
Santa Barbara Channel, U.S.A. 85 L7 34 15N 120 0W
Santa Barbara I., U.S.A. 85 M7 33 29N 119 2W
Santa Catalina, Gulf of, U.S.A. 85 N9 33 10N 117 50W
Santa Catalina, I., Mexico 86 B2 25 40N 110 50W
Santa Catalina I., U.S.A. 85 M8 33 23N 118 25W
Santa Catarina □, Brazil 95 B6 27 25S 48 30W
Santa Catarina, I. de, Brazil 95 B6 27 30S 48 40W
Santa Cecília, Brazil 95 B5 26 56S 50 18W
Santa Clara, Cuba 88 B4 22 20N 80 0W
Santa Clara, Calif., U.S.A. 84 H5 37 21N 121 57W
Santa Clara, Utah, U.S.A. 83 H7 37 8N 113 39W
Santa Clara, El Golfo de, Mexico 86 A2 31 42N 114 30W
Santa Clara de Olimar, Uruguay 95 C5 32 50S 54 54W
Santa Clarita, U.S.A. 85 L8 34 24N 118 30W
Santa Clotilde, Peru 92 D4 2 33S 73 45W
Santa Coloma de Gramenet, Spain 19 B7 41 27N 2 13 E
Santa Cruz, Argentina 96 G3 50 0S 68 32W
Santa Cruz, Bolivia 92 G6 17 43S 63 10W
Santa Cruz, Chile 94 C1 34 38S 71 27W
Santa Cruz, Costa Rica 88 D2 10 15N 85 35W
Santa Cruz, Madeira 22 D3 32 42N 16 46W
Santa Cruz, Phil. 37 B6 14 20N 121 24 E
Santa Cruz, U.S.A. 84 J4 36 58N 122 1W
Santa Cruz →, Argentina 96 G3 50 10S 68 20W
Santa Cruz de la Palma, Canary Is. 22 F2 28 41N 17 46W
Santa Cruz de Tenerife, Canary Is. 22 F3 28 28N 16 15W
Santa Cruz del Norte, Cuba 88 B3 23 9N 81 55W
Santa Cruz del Sur, Cuba 88 B4 20 44N 78 0W
Santa Cruz do Rio Pardo, Brazil 95 A6 22 54S 49 37W
Santa Cruz do Sul, Brazil 95 B5 29 42S 52 25W
Santa Cruz I., U.S.A. 85 M7 34 1N 119 43W
Santa Cruz Is., Solomon Is. 64 J8 10 30S 166 0 E
Santa Domingo, Cay, Bahamas 88 B4 21 25N 75 15W
Santa Elena, Argentina 94 C4 30 58S 59 47W
Santa Elena, C., Costa Rica 88 D2 10 54N 85 56W
Santa Eulària des Riu, Spain 22 C8 38 59N 1 32 E
Santa Fe, Argentina 94 C3 31 35S 60 41W
Santa Fe, U.S.A. 83 J11 35 41N 105 57W
Santa Fé □, Argentina 94 C3 31 50S 60 55W
Santa Fé do Sul, Brazil 93 H8 20 13S 50 56W
Santa Filomena, Brazil 93 E9 9 6S 45 50W
Santa Gertrudis, Spain 22 C7 39 0N 1 26 E
Santa Inês, Brazil 93 F11 13 17S 39 48W
Santa Inés, I., Chile 96 G2 54 0S 73 0W
Santa Isabel = Rey Malabo, Eq. Guin. 52 D1 3 45N 8 50 E
Santa Isabel, Argentina 94 D2 36 10S 66 54W
Santa Isabel do Morro, Brazil 93 F8 11 34S 50 40W
Santa Lucía, Corrientes, Argentina 94 B4 28 58S 59 5W
Santa Lucía, San Juan, Argentina 94 C2 31 30S 68 30W
Santa Lucía, Uruguay 94 C4 34 27S 56 24W
Santa Lucia Range, U.S.A. 84 K5 36 0N 121 20W
Santa Magdalena, I., Mexico 86 C2 24 40N 112 15W
Santa Margarita, Argentina 94 D3 38 28S 61 35W
Santa Margarita, Spain 22 B10 39 42N 3 6 E
Santa Margarita, U.S.A. 84 K6 35 23N 120 37W
Santa Margarita →, U.S.A. 85 M9 33 13N 117 23W
Santa Margarita, I., Mexico 86 C2 24 30N 111 50W
Santa María, Argentina 94 B2 26 40S 66 0W
Santa Maria, Brazil 95 B5 29 40S 53 48W
Santa Maria, U.S.A. 85 L6 34 57N 120 26W
Santa María →, Mexico 86 A3 31 0N 107 14W
Santa María, B. de, Mexico 86 B3 25 10N 108 40W
Santa Maria da Vitória, Brazil 93 F10 13 24S 44 12W
Santa Maria del Camí, Spain 22 B9 39 38N 2 47 E
Santa Maria di Léuca, C., Italy 21 E8 39 47N 18 22 E
Santa Marta, Colombia 92 A4 11 15N 74 13W
Santa Marta, Sierra Nevada de, Colombia 92 A4 10 55N 73 50W
Santa Marta Grande, C., Brazil 95 B6 28 43S 48 50W
Santa Maura = Levkás, Greece 21 E9 38 40N 20 43 E
Santa Monica, U.S.A. 85 M8 34 1N 118 29W
Santa Paula, U.S.A. 85 L7 34 21N 119 4W
Santa Ponça, Spain 22 B9 39 30N 2 28 E
Santa Rita, U.S.A. 83 K10 32 48N 108 4W
Santa Rosa, La Pampa, Argentina 94 D3 36 40S 64 17W
Santa Rosa, San Luis, Argentina 94 C2 32 21S 65 10W
Santa Rosa, Brazil 95 B5 27 52S 54 29W
Santa Rosa, Calif., U.S.A. 84 G4 38 26N 122 43W
Santa Rosa, N. Mex., U.S.A. 81 H2 34 57N 104 41W
Santa Rosa de Copán, Honduras 88 D2 14 47N 88 46W
Santa Rosa de Río Primero, Argentina 94 C3 31 8S 63 20W
Santa Rosa del Sara, Bolivia 92 G6 17 7S 63 35W
Santa Rosa I., Calif., U.S.A. 85 M6 33 58N 120 6W
Santa Rosa I., Fla., U.S.A. 77 K2 30 20N 86 50W
Santa Rosa Range, U.S.A. 82 F5 41 45N 117 40W
Santa Rosalía, Mexico 86 B2 27 20N 112 20W
Santa Sylvina, Argentina 94 B3 27 50S 61 10W
Santa Tecla = Nueva San Salvador, El Salv. 88 D2 13 40N 89 18W
Santa Teresa, Argentina 94 C3 33 25S 60 47W
Santa Teresa, Australia 62 C1 24 8S 134 22 E
Santa Teresa, Mexico 87 B5 25 17N 97 51W
Santa Vitória do Palmar, Brazil 95 C5 33 32S 53 25W
Santa Ynez →, U.S.A. 85 L6 35 41N 120 36W
Santa Ynez Mts., U.S.A. 85 L6 34 30N 120 0W
Santa Ysabel, U.S.A. 85 M10 33 7N 116 40W
Santai, China 32 C5 31 5N 104 58 E
Santana, Madeira 22 D3 32 48N 16 52W
Santana, Coxilha de, Brazil 95 C4 30 50S 55 35W
Santana do Livramento, Brazil 95 C4 30 55S 55 30W
Santander, Spain 19 A4 43 27N 3 51W
Santander Jiménez, Mexico 87 C5 24 11N 98 29W
Santanilla, Is., Honduras 88 C3 17 22N 83 57W
Santanyí, Spain 22 B10 39 20N 3 5 E
Santaquin, U.S.A. 82 G8 39 59N 111 47W
Santarém, Brazil 93 D8 2 25S 54 42W
Santarém, Portugal 19 C1 39 12N 8 42W
Santaren Channel, W. Indies 88 B4 24 0N 79 30W
Santee, U.S.A. 85 N10 32 50N 116 58W
Santee →, U.S.A. 77 J6 33 7N 79 17W
Santiago, Brazil 95 B5 29 11S 54 52W
Santiago, Chile 94 C1 33 24S 70 40W
Santiago, Panama 88 E3 8 0N 81 0W
Santiago □, Chile 94 C1 33 30S 70 50W
Santiago →, Mexico 66 G9 25 11N 105 26W
Santiago →, Peru 92 D3 4 27S 77 38W
Santiago de Compostela, Spain 19 A1 42 52N 8 37W
Santiago de Cuba, Cuba 88 C4 20 0N 75 49W
Santiago de los Cabelleros, Dom. Rep. 89 C5 19 30N 70 40W
Santiago del Estero, Argentina 94 B3 27 50S 64 15W
Santiago del Estero □, Argentina 94 B3 27 40S 63 15W
Santiago del Teide, Canary Is. 22 F3 28 17N 16 48W
Santiago Ixcuintla, Mexico 86 C3 21 50N 105 11W
Santiago Papasquiaro, Mexico 86 C3 25 0N 105 20W
Santiaguillo, L. de, Mexico 86 C4 24 50N 104 50W
Santo Amaro, Brazil 93 F11 12 30S 38 43W
Santo Anastácio, Brazil 95 A5 21 58S 51 39W
Santo André, Brazil 95 A6 23 39S 46 29W
Santo Ângelo, Brazil 95 B5 28 15S 54 15W
Santo Antônio do Içá, Brazil 92 D5 3 5S 67 57W
Santo Antônio do Leverger, Brazil 93 G7 15 52S 56 5W
Santo Domingo, Dom. Rep. 89 C6 18 30N 69 59W
Santo Domingo, Baja Calif., Mexico 86 A1 30 43N 116 2W
Santo Domingo, Baja Calif. S., Mexico 86 B2 25 32N 112 2W
Santo Domingo, Nic. 88 D3 12 14N 84 59W
Santo Domingo de los Colorados, Ecuador 92 D3 0 15S 79 9W
Santo Domingo Pueblo, U.S.A. 83 J10 35 31N 106 22W
Santo Tomás, Mexico 86 A1 31 33N 116 24W
Santo Tomás, Peru 92 F4 14 26S 72 8W
Santo Tomé, Argentina 95 B4 28 40S 56 5W
Santo Tomé de Guayana = Ciudad Guayana, Venezuela 92 B6 8 0N 62 30W
Santoña, Spain 19 A4 43 29N 3 27W
Santoríni = Thíra, Greece 21 F11 36 23N 25 27 E
Santos, Brazil 95 A6 24 0S 46 20W
Santos Dumont, Brazil 95 A7 22 55S 43 10W
Sanwer, India 42 H6 22 59N 75 50 E
Sanyuan, China 34 G5 34 35N 108 58 E
São Bernardo do Campo, Brazil 95 A6 23 45S 46 34W
São Borja, Brazil 95 B4 28 39S 56 0W
São Carlos, Brazil 95 A6 22 0S 47 50W
São Cristóvão, Brazil 93 F11 11 1S 37 15W
São Domingos, Brazil 93 F9 13 25S 46 19W
São Francisco, Brazil 93 G10 16 0S 44 50W
São Francisco →, Brazil 93 F11 10 30S 36 24W
São Francisco do Sul, Brazil 95 B6 26 15S 48 36W
São Gabriel, Brazil 95 C5 30 20S 54 20W
São Gonçalo, Brazil 95 A7 22 48S 43 5W
Sao Hill, Tanzania 55 D4 8 20S 35 12 E
São João da Boa Vista, Brazil 95 A6 22 0S 46 52W
São João da Madeira, Portugal 19 B1 40 54N 8 30W
São João del Rei, Brazil 95 A7 21 8S 44 15W
São João do Araguaia, Brazil 93 E9 5 23S 48 46W
São João do Piauí, Brazil 93 E10 8 21S 42 15W
São Joaquim, Brazil 95 B6 28 18S 49 56W
São Jorge, Pta. de, Madeira 22 D3 32 50N 16 53W
São José, Brazil 95 B5 27 38S 48 39W
São José do Norte, Brazil 95 C5 32 1S 52 3W
São José do Rio Prêto, Brazil 95 A6 20 50S 49 20W
São José dos Campos, Brazil 95 A6 23 7S 45 52W
São Leopoldo, Brazil 95 B5 29 50S 51 10W
São Lourenço, Brazil 95 A6 22 7S 45 3W
São Lourenço →, Brazil 93 G7 17 53S 57 27W
São Lourenço, Pta. de, Madeira 22 D3 32 44N 16 39W
São Lourenço do Sul, Brazil 95 C5 31 22S 51 58W
São Luís, Brazil 93 D10 2 39S 44 15W
São Luís Gonzaga, Brazil 95 B5 28 25S 55 0W
São Marcos →, Brazil 93 G9 18 15S 47 37W
São Marcos, B. de, Brazil 93 D10 2 0S 44 0W
São Mateus, Brazil 93 G11 18 44S 39 50W
São Mateus do Sul, Brazil 95 B5 25 52S 50 23W
São Miguel do Oeste, Brazil 95 B5 26 45S 53 34W
São Paulo, Brazil 95 A6 23 32S 46 37W
São Paulo □, Brazil 95 A6 22 0S 49 0W
São Paulo, I., Atl. Oc. 2 D8 0 50N 31 40W
São Paulo de Olivença, Brazil 92 D5 3 27S 68 48W
São Roque, Madeira 22 D3 32 46N 16 48W
São Roque, C. de, Brazil 93 E11 5 30S 35 16W
São Sebastião, I. de, Brazil 95 A6 23 50S 45 18W
São Sebastião do Paraíso, Brazil 95 A6 20 54S 46 59W
São Tomé, São Tomé & Principe 48 F4 0 10N 6 39 E
São Tomé, C. de, Brazil 95 A7 22 0S 40 59W
São Tomé & Principe ■, Africa 49 F4 0 12N 6 39 E
São Vicente, Brazil 95 A6 23 57S 46 23W
São Vicente, Madeira 22 D2 32 48N 17 3W
São Vicente, C. de, Portugal 19 D1 37 0N 9 0W
Saona, I., Dom. Rep. 89 C6 18 10N 68 40W
Saône →, France 18 D6 45 44N 4 50 E
Saonek, Indonesia 37 E8 0 22S 130 55 E
Saparua, Indonesia 37 E7 3 33S 128 40 E
Sapele, Nigeria 50 G7 5 50N 5 40 E
Sapelo I., U.S.A. 77 K5 31 25N 81 12W
Saposoa, Peru 92 E3 6 55S 76 45W
Sapphire, Australia 62 C4 23 28S 147 43 E
Sappho, U.S.A. 84 B2 48 4N 124 16W
Sapporo, Japan 30 C10 43 0N 141 21 E
Sapulpa, U.S.A. 81 H6 35 59N 96 5W
Saqqez, Iran 44 B5 36 15N 46 20 E
Sar Dasht, Iran 45 C6 32 32N 48 52 E
Sar-e Pol □, Afghan. 40 B4 36 20N 65 50 E
Sar Gachineh = Yāsūj, Iran 45 D6 30 31N 51 31 E
Sar Planina, Macedonia 21 C9 42 0N 21 0 E
Sara Buri = Saraburi, Thailand 38 E3 14 30N 100 55 E
Sarāb, Iran 44 B5 37 55N 47 40 E
Sarabadi, Iraq 44 C5 33 1N 44 48 E
Saraburi, Thailand 38 E3 14 30N 100 55 E
Saradiya, India 42 J4 21 34N 70 2 E
Saragossa = Zaragoza, Spain 19 B5 41 39N 0 53W
Saraguro, Ecuador 92 D3 3 35S 79 16W
Sarai Naurang, Pakistan 42 C4 32 50N 70 47 E
Saraikela, India 43 H11 22 42N 85 56 E
Sarajevo, Bos.-H. 21 C8 43 52N 18 26 E
Sarakhs, Turkmenistan 45 B9 36 32N 61 13 E
Saran, Gunung, Indonesia 36 E4 0 30S 111 25 E
Saranac L., U.S.A. 79 B10 44 20N 74 10W
Saranac Lake, U.S.A. 79 B10 44 20N 74 8W
Saranda, Tanzania 54 D3 5 45S 34 59 E
Sarandí del Yí, Uruguay 95 C4 33 18S 55 38W
Sarandí Grande, Uruguay 94 C4 33 44S 56 20W
Sarangani B., Phil. 37 C7 6 0N 125 13 E
Sarangani Is., Phil. 37 C7 5 25N 125 25 E
Sarangarh, India 41 J13 21 30N 83 5 E
Saransk, Russia 24 D8 54 10N 45 10 E
Sarapul, Russia 24 C9 56 28N 53 48 E
Sarasota, U.S.A. 77 M4 27 20N 82 32W
Saratoga, Calif., U.S.A. 84 H4 37 16N 122 2W
Saratoga, Wyo., U.S.A. 82 F10 41 27N 106 49W
Saratoga Springs, U.S.A. 79 C11 43 5N 73 47W
Saratok, Malaysia 36 D4 1 55N 111 17 E
Saratov, Russia 25 D8 51 30N 46 2 E
Saravane, Laos 38 E6 15 43N 106 25 E
Sarawak □, Malaysia 36 D4 2 0N 113 0 E
Saray, Turkey 21 D12 41 26N 27 55 E
Sarayköy, Turkey 21 F13 37 55N 28 54 E
Sarbāz, Iran 45 E9 26 38N 61 19 E
Sarbīsheh, Iran 45 C8 32 30N 59 40 E
Sarda →, India 41 F12 27 21N 81 23 E
Sardarshahr, India 42 E6 28 30N 74 29 E
Sardegna □, Italy 20 D3 40 0N 9 0 E
Sardhana, India 42 E7 29 9N 77 39 E
Sardina, Pta., Canary Is. 22 F4 28 9N 15 44W
Sardinia = Sardegna □, Italy 20 D3 40 0N 9 0 E
Sardis, Turkey 21 E12 38 28N 28 2 E
Sardūīyeh = Dar Mazār, Iran 45 D8 29 14N 57 20 E
S'Arenal, Spain 22 B9 39 30N 2 45 E
Sargasso Sea, Atl. Oc. 66 G13 27 0N 72 0W
Sargodha, Pakistan 42 C5 32 10N 72 40 E
Sarh, Chad 51 G9 9 5N 18 23 E
Sārī, Iran 45 B7 36 30N 53 4 E
Saria, India 43 J10 21 38N 83 22 E
Sariab, Pakistan 42 D2 30 6N 66 59 E
Sarıgöl, Turkey 21 E13 38 14N 28 41 E
Sarikei, Malaysia 36 D4 2 8N 111 30 E
Sarila, India 43 G8 25 46N 79 41 E
Sarina, Australia 62 C4 21 22S 149 13 E
Sarita, U.S.A. 81 M6 27 13N 97 47W
Sariwŏn, N. Korea 35 E13 38 31N 125 46 E
Sarju →, India 43 F9 27 21N 81 23 E
Sark, U.K. 11 H5 49 25N 2 22W
Sarkari Tala, India 42 F4 27 39N 70 52 E
Şarköy, Turkey 21 D12 40 36N 27 6 E
Sarlat-la-Canéda, France 18 D4 44 54N 1 13 E
Sarmi, Indonesia 37 E9 1 49S 138 44 E
Sarmiento, Argentina 96 F3 45 35S 69 5W
Särna, Sweden 9 F15 61 41N 13 8 E
Sarnia, Canada 78 D2 42 58N 82 23W
Sarolangun, Indonesia 36 E2 2 19S 102 42 E
Saronikós Kólpos, Greece 21 F10 37 45N 23 45 E
Saros Körfezi, Turkey 21 D12 40 30N 26 15 E
Sarpsborg, Norway 9 G14 59 16N 11 7 E
Sarre = Saar →, Europe 18 B7 49 41N 6 32 E
Sarreguemines, France 18 B7 49 5N 7 4 E
Sarthe →, France 18 C3 47 33N 0 31W
Saruna →, Pakistan 42 F2 26 31N 67 7 E

Sevier Desert

Sarvar, India 42 F6 26 4N 75 0 E
Sarvestān, Iran 45 D7 29 20N 53 10 E
Sary-Tash, Kyrgyzstan 26 F8 39 44N 73 15 E
Saryshagan, Kazakstan 26 E8 46 12N 73 38 E
Sasan Gir, India 42 J4 21 10N 70 36 E
Sasaram, India 43 G11 24 57N 84 5 E
Sasebo, Japan 31 H4 33 10N 129 43 E
Saser, India 43 B7 34 50N 77 50 E
Saskatchewan □, Canada 73 C7 54 40N 106 0W
Saskatchewan →, Canada 73 C8 53 37N 100 40W
Saskatoon, Canada 73 C7 52 10N 106 38W
Saskylakh, Russia 27 B12 71 55N 114 1 E
Sasolburg, S. Africa 57 D4 26 46S 27 49 E
Sasovo, Russia 24 D7 54 25N 41 55 E
Sassandra, Ivory C. 50 H4 4 55N 6 8W
Sassandra →, Ivory C. 50 H4 4 58N 6 5W
Sássari, Italy 20 D3 40 43N 8 34 E
Sassnitz, Germany 16 A7 54 29N 13 39 E
Sassuolo, Italy 20 B4 44 33N 10 47 E
Sasumua Dam, Kenya 54 C4 0 45S 36 40 E
Sasyk, Ozero, Ukraine 17 F15 45 45N 29 20 E
Sata-Misaki, Japan 31 J5 31 0N 130 40 E
Satadougou, Mali 50 F3 12 25N 11 25W
Satakunta, Finland 9 F20 61 45N 23 0 E
Satara, India 40 L8 17 44N 73 58 E
Satara, S. Africa 57 C5 24 29S 31 47 E
Satbarwa, India 43 H11 23 55N 84 16 E
Satevó, Mexico 86 B3 27 57N 106 7W
Satilla →, U.S.A. 77 K5 30 59N 81 29W
Satka, Russia 24 C10 55 3N 59 1 E
Satmala Hills, India 40 J9 20 15N 74 40 E
Satna, India 43 G9 24 35N 80 50 E
Sátoraljaújhely, Hungary 17 D11 48 25N 21 41 E
Satpura Ra., India 40 J10 21 25N 76 10 E
Satsuna-Shotō, Japan 31 K5 30 0N 130 0 E
Sattahip, Thailand 38 F3 12 41N 100 54 E
Satu Mare, Romania 17 E12 47 46N 22 55 E
Satui, Indonesia 36 E5 3 50S 115 27 E
Satun, Thailand 39 J3 6 43N 100 2 E
Saturnina →, Brazil 92 F7 12 15S 58 10W
Sauce, Argentina 94 C4 30 5S 58 46W
Sauceda, Mexico 86 B4 25 55N 101 18W
Saucillo, Mexico 86 B3 28 1N 105 17W
Sauda, Norway 9 G12 59 40N 6 20 E
Sauðarkrókur, Iceland 8 D4 65 45N 19 40W
Saudi Arabia ■, Asia 46 B3 26 0N 44 0 E
Sauerland, Germany 16 C4 51 12N 7 59 E
Saugeen →, Canada 78 B3 44 30N 81 22W
Saugerties, U.S.A. 79 D11 42 5N 73 57W
Saugus, U.S.A. 85 L8 34 25N 118 32W
Sauk Centre, U.S.A. 80 C7 45 44N 94 57W
Sauk Rapids, U.S.A. 80 C7 45 35N 94 10W
Sault Ste. Marie, Canada 70 C3 46 30N 84 20W
Sault Ste. Marie, U.S.A. 69 D11 46 30N 84 21W
Saumlaki, Indonesia 37 F8 7 55S 131 20 E
Saumur, France 18 C3 47 15N 0 5W
Saunders C., N.Z. 59 L3 45 53S 170 45 E
Saunders I., Antarctica 5 B1 57 48S 26 28W
Saunders Point, Australia 61 E4 27 52S 125 38 E
Saurimo, Angola 52 F4 9 40S 20 12 E
Sausalito, U.S.A. 84 H4 37 51N 122 29W
Savá, Honduras 88 C2 15 32N 86 15W
Sava →, Serbia, Yug. 21 B9 44 50N 20 26 E
Savage, U.S.A. 80 B2 47 27N 104 21W
Savage I. = Niue, Cook Is. 65 J11 19 2S 169 54W
Savage River, Australia 62 G4 41 31S 145 14 E
Savai'i, Samoa 59 A12 13 28S 172 24W
Savalou, Benin 50 G6 7 57N 1 58 E
Savane, Mozam. 55 F4 19 37S 35 8 E
Savanna, U.S.A. 80 D9 42 5N 90 8W
Savanna-la-Mar, Jamaica 88 C4 18 10N 78 10W
Savannah, Ga., U.S.A. 77 J5 32 5N 81 6W
Savannah, Mo., U.S.A. 80 F7 39 56N 94 50W
Savannah, Tenn., U.S.A. 77 H1 35 14N 88 15W
Savannah →, U.S.A. 77 J5 32 2N 80 53W
Savannakhet, Laos 38 D5 16 30N 104 49 E
Savant L., Canada 70 B1 50 16N 90 44W
Savant Lake, Canada 70 B1 50 14N 90 40W
Save →, Mozam. 57 C5 21 16S 34 0 E
Sāveh, Iran 45 C6 35 2N 50 20 E
Savelugu, Ghana 50 G5 9 38N 0 54W
Savo, Finland 8 E22 62 45N 27 30 E
Savoie □, France 18 D7 45 26N 6 25 E
Savona, Italy 18 D8 44 17N 8 30 E
Savona, U.S.A. 78 D7 42 17N 77 13W
Savonlinna, Finland 24 B4 61 52N 28 53 E
Savoy = Savoie □, France 18 D7 45 26N 6 25 E
Savur, Turkey 44 B4 37 34N 40 53 E
Sawahlunto, Indonesia 36 E2 0 40S 100 52 E
Sawai, Indonesia 37 E7 3 0S 129 5 E
Sawai Madhopur, India 42 G7 26 0N 76 25 E
Sawang Daen Din, Thailand 38 D4 17 28N 103 28 E
Sawankhalok, Thailand 38 D2 17 19N 99 50 E
Sawara, Japan 31 G10 35 55N 140 30 E
Sawatch Range, U.S.A. 83 G10 38 30N 106 30W
Sawel Mt., U.K. 13 B4 54 50N 7 2W
Sawi, Thailand 39 G2 10 14N 99 5 E
Sawmills, Zimbabwe 55 F2 19 30S 28 2 E
Sawtooth Range, U.S.A. 82 E6 44 3N 114 58W
Sawu, Indonesia 37 F6 10 35S 121 50 E
Sawu Sea, Indonesia 37 F6 9 30S 121 50 E
Saxby →, Australia 62 B3 18 25S 140 53 E
Saxmundham, U.K. 11 E9 52 13N 1 30 E
Saxony = Sachsen □, Germany 16 C7 50 55N 13 10 E
Saxony, Lower = Niedersachsen □, Germany 16 B5 52 50N 9 0 E
Saxton, U.S.A. 78 F6 40 13N 78 15W
Sayabec, Canada 71 C6 48 35N 67 41W
Sayaboury, Laos 38 C3 19 15N 101 45 E
Sayán, Peru 92 F3 11 8S 77 12W
Sayan, Vostochnyy, Russia 27 D10 54 0N 96 0 E
Sayan, Zapadnyy, Russia 27 D10 52 30N 94 0 E
Saydā, Lebanon 47 B4 33 35N 35 25 E
Sayhandulaan = Oldziyt, Mongolia 34 B5 44 40N 109 1 E
Sayḥūt, Yemen 46 D5 15 12N 51 10 E
Saylac = Zeila, Somali Rep. 46 E3 11 21N 43 30 E
Saynshand, Mongolia 33 B6 44 55N 110 11 E
Sayre, Okla., U.S.A. 81 H5 35 18N 99 38W
Sayre, Pa., U.S.A. 79 E8 41 59N 76 32W
Sayreville, U.S.A. 79 F10 40 28N 74 22W
Sayula, Mexico 86 D4 19 50N 103 40W
Sayward, Canada 72 C3 50 21N 125 55W
Sazanit, Albania 21 D8 40 30N 19 20 E
Sázava →, Czech Rep. 16 D8 49 53N 14 24 E
Sazin, Pakistan 43 B5 35 35N 73 30 E
Scafell Pike, U.K. 10 C4 54 27N 3 14W
Scalloway, U.K. 12 A7 60 9N 1 17W
Scalpay, U.K. 12 D3 57 18N 6 0W
Scandia, Canada 72 C6 50 20N 112 0W
Scandicci, Italy 20 C4 43 45N 11 11 E
Scandinavia, Europe 8 E16 64 0N 12 0 E
Scapa Flow, U.K. 12 C5 58 53N 3 3W
Scappoose, U.S.A. 84 E4 45 45N 122 53W
Scarba, U.K. 12 E3 56 11N 5 43W
Scarborough, Trin. & Tob. 89 D7 11 11N 60 42W
Scarborough, U.K. 10 C7 54 17N 0 24W
Scariff I., Ireland 13 E1 51 44N 10 15W
Scarp, U.K. 12 C1 58 1N 7 8W
Scebeli, Wabi →, Somali Rep. 46 G3 2 0N 44 0 E
Schaffhausen, Switz. 18 C8 47 42N 8 39 E
Schagen, Neths. 15 B4 52 49N 4 48 E
Schaghticoke, U.S.A. 79 D11 42 54N 73 35W
Schefferville, Canada 71 B6 54 48N 66 50W
Schelde →, Belgium 15 C4 51 15N 4 16 E
Schell Creek Ra., U.S.A. 82 G6 39 15N 114 30W
Schellsburg, U.S.A. 78 F6 40 3N 78 39W
Schenectady, U.S.A. 79 D11 42 49N 73 57W
Schenevus, U.S.A. 79 D10 42 33N 74 50W
Schiedam, Neths. 15 C4 51 55N 4 25 E
Schiermonnikoog, Neths. 15 A6 53 30N 6 15 E
Schio, Italy 20 B4 45 43N 11 21 E
Schleswig, Germany 16 A5 54 31N 9 34 E
Schleswig-Holstein □, Germany 16 A5 54 30N 9 30 E
Schoharie, U.S.A. 79 D10 42 40N 74 19W
Schoharie →, U.S.A. 79 D10 42 57N 74 18W
Scholls, U.S.A. 84 E4 45 24N 122 56W
Schouten I., Australia 62 G4 42 20S 148 20 E
Schouten Is. = Supiori, Indonesia 37 E9 1 0S 136 0 E
Schouwen, Neths. 15 C3 51 43N 3 45 E
Schreiber, Canada 70 C2 48 45N 87 20W
Schroffenstein, Namibia 56 D2 27 11S 18 42 E
Schroon Lake, U.S.A. 79 C11 43 50N 73 46W
Schuler, Canada 73 C6 50 20N 110 6W
Schumacher, Canada 70 C3 48 30N 81 16W
Schurz, U.S.A. 82 G4 38 57N 118 49W
Schuyler, U.S.A. 80 E6 41 27N 97 4W
Schuylerville, U.S.A. 79 C11 43 6N 73 35W
Schuylkill →, U.S.A. 79 G9 39 53N 75 12W
Schuylkill Haven, U.S.A. 79 F8 40 37N 76 11W
Schwäbische Alb, Germany 16 D5 48 20N 9 30 E
Schwaner, Pegunungan, Indonesia 36 E4 1 0S 112 30 E
Schwarzrand, Namibia 56 D2 25 37S 16 50 E
Schwarzwald, Germany 16 D5 48 30N 8 20 E
Schwedt, Germany 16 B8 53 3N 14 16 E
Schweinfurt, Germany 16 C6 50 3N 10 14 E
Schweizer-Reneke, S. Africa 56 D4 27 11S 25 18 E
Schwenningen = Villingen-Schwenningen, Germany 16 D5 48 3N 8 26 E
Schwerin, Germany 16 B6 53 36N 11 22 E
Schwyz, Switz. 18 C8 47 2N 8 39 E
Sciacca, Italy 20 F5 37 31N 13 3 E
Scilla, Italy 20 E6 38 15N 15 43 E
Scilly, Isles of, U.K. 11 H1 49 56N 6 22W
Scioto →, U.S.A. 76 F4 38 44N 83 1W
Scituate, U.S.A. 79 D14 42 12N 70 44W
Scobey, U.S.A. 80 A2 48 47N 105 25W
Scone, Australia 63 E5 32 5S 150 52 E
Scoresbysund = Ittoqqortoormiit, Greenland 4 B6 70 20N 23 0W
Scotia, Calif., U.S.A. 82 F1 40 29N 124 6W
Scotia, N.Y., U.S.A. 79 D11 42 50N 73 58W
Scotia Sea, Antarctica 5 B18 56 5S 56 0W
Scotland, Canada 78 C4 43 1N 80 22W
Scotland □, U.K. 12 E5 57 0N 4 0W
Scott, C., Australia 60 B4 13 30S 129 49 E
Scott City, U.S.A. 80 F4 38 29N 100 54W
Scott Glacier, Antarctica 5 C8 66 15S 100 5 E
Scott I., Antarctica 5 C11 67 0S 179 0 E
Scott Is., Canada 72 C3 50 48N 128 40W
Scott L., Canada 73 B7 59 55N 106 18W
Scott Reef, Australia 60 B3 14 0S 121 50 E
Scottburgh, S. Africa 57 E5 30 15S 30 47 E
Scottdale, U.S.A. 78 F5 40 6N 79 35W
Scottish Borders □, U.K. 12 F6 55 35N 2 50W
Scottsbluff, U.S.A. 80 E3 41 52N 103 40W
Scottsboro, U.S.A. 77 H3 34 40N 86 2W
Scottsburg, U.S.A. 76 F3 38 41N 85 47W
Scottsdale, Australia 62 G4 41 9S 147 31 E
Scottsdale, U.S.A. 83 K7 33 29N 111 56W
Scottsville, Ky., U.S.A. 77 G2 36 45N 86 11W
Scottsville, N.Y., U.S.A. 78 C7 43 2N 77 47W
Scottville, U.S.A. 76 D2 43 58N 86 17W
Scranton, U.S.A. 79 E9 41 25N 75 40W
Scugog, L., Canada 78 B6 44 10N 78 55W
Scunthorpe, U.K. 10 D7 53 36N 0 39W
Scutari = Shkodër, Albania 21 C8 42 4N 19 32 E
Seabrook, L., Australia 61 F2 30 55S 119 40 E
Seaford, U.K. 11 G8 50 47N 0 7 E
Seaford, U.S.A. 76 F8 38 39N 75 37W
Seaforth, Australia 62 C4 20 55S 148 57 E
Seaforth, Canada 78 C3 43 35N 81 25W
Seaforth, L., U.K. 12 D2 57 52N 6 36W
Seagraves, U.S.A. 81 J3 32 57N 102 34W
Seaham, U.K. 10 C6 54 50N 1 20W
Seal →, Canada 73 B10 59 4N 94 48W
Seal L., Canada 71 B7 54 20N 61 30W
Sealy, U.S.A. 81 L6 29 47N 96 9W
Searchlight, U.S.A. 85 K12 35 28N 114 55W
Searcy, U.S.A. 81 H9 35 15N 91 44W
Searles L., U.S.A. 85 K9 35 44N 117 21W
Seascale, U.K. 10 C4 54 24N 3 29W
Seaside, Calif., U.S.A. 84 J5 36 37N 121 50W
Seaside, Oreg., U.S.A. 84 E3 46 0N 123 56W
Seaspray, Australia 63 F4 38 25S 147 15 E
Seattle, U.S.A. 84 C4 47 36N 122 20W
Seaview Ra., Australia 62 B4 18 40S 145 45 E
Sebago L., U.S.A. 79 C14 43 52N 70 34W
Sebago Lake, U.S.A. 79 C14 43 51N 70 34W
Sebastián Vizcaíno, B., Mexico 86 B2 28 0N 114 30W
Sebastopol = Sevastopol, Ukraine 25 F5 44 35N 33 30 E
Sebastopol, U.S.A. 84 G4 38 24N 122 49W
Sebewaing, U.S.A. 76 D4 43 44N 83 27W
Sebha = Sabhah, Libya 51 C8 27 9N 14 29 E
Şebinkarahisar, Turkey 25 F6 40 22N 38 28 E
Sebring, Fla., U.S.A. 77 M5 27 30N 81 27W
Sebring, Ohio, U.S.A. 78 F3 40 55N 81 2W
Sebringville, Canada 78 C3 43 24N 81 4W
Sebta = Ceuta, N. Afr. 19 E3 35 52N 5 18W
Sebuku, Indonesia 36 E5 3 30S 116 25 E
Sebuku, Teluk, Malaysia 36 D5 4 0N 118 10 E
Sechelt, Canada 72 D4 49 25N 123 42W
Sechura, Desierto de, Peru 92 E2 6 0S 80 30W
Secretary I., N.Z. 59 L1 45 15S 166 56 E
Secunderabad, India 40 L11 17 28N 78 30 E
Security-Widefield, U.S.A. 80 F2 38 45N 104 45W
Sedalia, U.S.A. 80 F8 38 42N 93 14W
Sedan, France 18 B6 49 43N 4 57 E
Sedan, U.S.A. 81 G6 37 8N 96 11W
Seddon, N.Z. 59 J5 41 40S 174 7 E
Seddonville, N.Z. 59 J4 41 33S 172 1 E
Sedé Boqér, Israel 47 E3 30 52N 34 47 E
Sedeh, Fārs, Iran 45 D7 30 45N 52 11 E
Sedeh, Khorāsān, Iran 45 C8 33 20N 59 14 E
Sederot, Israel 47 D3 31 32N 34 37 E
Sédhiou, Senegal 50 F2 12 44N 15 30W
Sedley, Canada 73 C8 50 10N 104 0W
Sedona, U.S.A. 83 J8 34 52N 111 46W
Sedova, Pik, Russia 26 B6 73 29N 54 58 E
Sedro Woolley, U.S.A. 84 B4 48 30N 122 14W
Seeheim, Namibia 56 D2 26 50S 17 45 E
Seeis, Namibia 56 C2 22 29S 17 39 E
Seekoei →, S. Africa 56 E4 30 18S 25 1 E
Seeley's Bay, Canada 79 B8 44 29N 76 14W
Seferihisar, Turkey 21 E12 38 10N 26 50 E
Seg-ozero, Russia 24 B5 63 20N 33 46 E
Segamat, Malaysia 39 L4 2 30N 102 50 E
Segesta, Italy 20 F5 37 56N 12 50 E
Seget, Indonesia 37 E8 1 24S 130 58 E
Segezha, Russia 24 B5 63 44N 34 19 E
Ségou, Mali 50 F4 13 30N 6 16W
Segovia = Coco →, Cent. Amer. 88 D3 15 0N 83 8W
Segovia, Spain 19 B3 40 57N 4 10W
Segre →, Spain 19 B6 41 40N 0 43 E
Séguéla, Ivory C. 50 G4 7 55N 6 40W
Seguin, U.S.A. 81 L6 29 34N 97 58W
Segundo →, Argentina 94 C3 30 53S 62 44W
Segura →, Spain 19 C5 38 3N 0 44W
Seh Konj, Kūh-e, Iran 45 D8 30 6N 57 30 E
Seh Qal'eh, Iran 45 C8 33 40N 58 24 E
Sehitwa, Botswana 56 C3 20 30S 22 30 E
Sehore, India 42 H7 23 10N 77 5 E
Sehwan, Pakistan 42 F2 26 28N 67 53 E
Seil, U.K. 12 E3 56 18N 5 38W
Seiland, Norway 8 A20 70 25N 23 15 E
Seiling, U.S.A. 81 G5 36 9N 98 56W
Seinäjoki, Finland 9 E20 62 40N 22 51 E
Seine →, France 18 B4 49 26N 0 26 E
Seistan = Sīstān, Asia 45 D9 30 50N 61 0 E
Seistan, Daryācheh-ye = Sīstān, Daryācheh-ye, Iran 45 D9 31 0N 61 0 E
Sekayu, Indonesia 36 E2 2 51S 103 51 E
Seke, Tanzania 54 C3 3 20S 33 31 E
Sekenke, Tanzania 54 C3 4 18S 34 11 E
Sekondi-Takoradi, Ghana 50 H5 4 58N 1 45W
Sekuma, Botswana 56 C3 24 36S 23 50 E
Selah, U.S.A. 82 C3 46 39N 120 32W
Selama, Malaysia 39 K3 5 12N 100 42 E
Selaru, Indonesia 37 F8 8 9S 131 0 E
Selby, U.K. 10 D6 53 47N 1 5W
Selby, U.S.A. 80 C4 45 31N 100 2W
Selçuk, Turkey 21 F12 37 56N 27 22 E
Selden, U.S.A. 80 F4 39 33N 100 34W
Sele →, Italy 20 D6 40 29N 14 56 E
Selebi-Pikwe, Botswana 57 C4 21 58S 27 48 E
Selemdzha →, Russia 27 D13 51 42N 128 53 E
Selenga = Selenge Mörön →, Asia 32 A5 52 16N 106 16 E
Selenge Mörön →, Asia 32 A5 52 16N 106 16 E
Seletan, Tanjung, Indonesia 36 E4 4 10S 114 40 E
Sélibabi, Mauritania 50 E3 15 10N 12 15W
Seligman, U.S.A. 83 J7 35 20N 112 53W
Selîma, El Wâhât el, Sudan 51 D11 21 22N 29 19 E
Selinda Spillway →, Botswana 56 B3 18 35S 23 10 E
Selinsgrove, U.S.A. 78 F8 40 48N 76 52W
Selkirk, Canada 73 C9 50 10N 96 55W
Selkirk, U.K. 12 F6 55 33N 2 50W
Selkirk I., Canada 73 C9 53 20N 99 6W
Selkirk Mts., Canada 68 C8 51 15N 117 40W
Selliá, Greece 23 D6 35 12N 24 23 E
Sells, U.S.A. 83 L8 31 55N 111 53W
Selma, Ala., U.S.A. 77 J2 32 25N 87 1W
Selma, Calif., U.S.A. 84 J7 36 34N 119 37W
Selma, N.C., U.S.A. 77 H6 35 32N 78 17W
Selmer, U.S.A. 77 H1 35 10N 88 36W
Selowandoma Falls, Zimbabwe 55 G3 21 15S 31 50 E
Selpele, Indonesia 37 E8 0 1S 130 5 E
Selsey Bill, U.K. 11 G7 50 43N 0 47W
Seltso, Russia 24 D5 53 22N 34 4 E
Selu, Indonesia 37 F8 7 32S 130 55 E
Selva, Argentina 94 B3 29 50S 62 0W
Selvas, Brazil 92 E5 6 30S 67 0W
Selwyn L., Canada 73 B8 60 0N 104 30W
Selwyn Mts., Canada 68 B6 63 0N 130 0W
Selwyn Ra., Australia 62 C3 21 10S 140 0 E
Seman →, Albania 21 D8 40 47N 19 30 E
Semarang, Indonesia 36 F4 7 0S 110 26 E
Sembabule, Uganda 54 C3 0 4S 31 25 E
Semeru, Indonesia 37 H15 8 4S 112 55 E
Semey, Kazakstan 26 D9 50 30N 80 10 E
Seminoe Reservoir, U.S.A. 82 F10 42 9N 106 55W
Seminole, Okla., U.S.A. 81 H6 35 14N 96 41W
Seminole, Tex., U.S.A. 81 J3 32 43N 102 39W
Seminole Draw →, U.S.A. 81 J3 32 27N 102 20W
Semipalatinsk = Semey, Kazakstan 26 D9 50 30N 80 10 E
Semirara Is., Phil. 37 B6 12 0N 121 20 E
Semitau, Indonesia 36 D4 0 29N 111 57 E
Semiyarka, Kazakstan 26 D8 50 55N 78 23 E
Semiyarskoye = Semiyarka, Kazakstan 26 D8 50 55N 78 23 E
Semmering P., Austria 16 E8 47 41N 15 45 E
Semnān, Iran 45 C7 35 40N 53 23 E
Semnān □, Iran 45 C7 36 0N 54 0 E
Semporna, Malaysia 37 D5 4 30N 118 33 E
Semuda, Indonesia 36 E4 2 51S 112 58 E
Sen →, Cambodia 36 B3 13 45N 105 12 E
Senā, Iran 45 D6 28 27N 51 36 E
Sena, Mozam. 55 F4 17 25S 35 0 E
Sena Madureira, Brazil 92 E5 9 5S 68 45W
Senador Pompeu, Brazil 93 E11 5 40S 39 20W
Senanga, Zambia 53 H4 16 7S 23 16 E
Senatobia, U.S.A. 81 H10 34 37N 89 58W
Sencelles, Spain 22 B9 39 39N 2 54 E
Sendai, Kagoshima, Japan 31 J5 31 50N 130 20 E
Sendai, Miyagi, Japan 30 E10 38 15N 140 53 E
Sendai-Wan, Japan 30 E10 38 15N 141 0 E
Sendhwa, India 42 J6 21 41N 75 6 E
Seneca, U.S.A. 77 H4 34 41N 82 57W
Seneca Falls, U.S.A. 79 D8 42 55N 76 48W
Seneca L., U.S.A. 78 D8 42 40N 76 54W
Senecaville L., U.S.A. 78 G3 39 55N 81 25W
Senegal ■, W. Afr. 50 F3 14 30N 14 30W
Sénégal →, W. Afr. 50 E2 15 48N 16 32W
Senegambia, Africa 48 E2 12 45N 12 0W
Senekal, S. Africa 57 D4 28 20S 27 36 E
Senga Hill, Zambia 55 D3 9 19S 31 11 E
Senge Khambab = Indus →, Pakistan 42 G2 24 20N 67 47 E
Sengua →, Zimbabwe 55 F2 17 7S 28 5 E
Senhor-do-Bonfim, Brazil 93 F10 10 30S 40 10W
Senigállia, Italy 20 C5 43 43N 13 13 E
Senj, Croatia 16 F8 45 0N 14 58 E
Senja, Norway 8 B17 69 25N 17 30 E
Senkaku-Shotō, Japan 31 L1 25 45N 124 0 E
Senlis, France 18 B5 49 13N 2 35 E
Senmonorom, Cambodia 38 F6 12 27N 107 12 E
Senneterre, Canada 70 C4 48 25N 77 15W
Seno, Laos 38 D5 16 35N 104 50 E
Sens, France 18 B5 48 11N 3 15 E
Senta, Serbia, Yug. 21 B9 45 55N 20 3 E
Sentani, Indonesia 37 E10 2 36S 140 37 E
Sentery = Lubao, Dem. Rep. of the Congo 54 D2 5 17S 25 42 E
Sentinel, U.S.A. 83 K7 32 52N 113 13W
Seo de Urgel = La Seu d'Urgell, Spain 19 A6 42 22N 1 23 E
Seohara, India 43 E8 29 15N 78 33 E
Seonath →, India 43 J10 21 44N 82 28 E
Seondha, India 43 F8 26 9N 78 48 E
Seoni, India 43 H8 22 5N 79 30 E
Seoni Malwa, India 42 H8 22 27N 77 28 E
Seoul = Sŏul, S. Korea 35 F14 37 31N 126 58 E
Sepīdān, Iran 45 D7 30 20N 52 5 E
Sepo-ri, N. Korea 35 E14 38 57N 127 25 E
Sepone, Laos 38 D6 16 45N 106 13 E
Sept-Îles, Canada 71 B6 50 13N 66 22W
Sequim, U.S.A. 84 B3 48 5N 123 6W
Sequoia Nat. Park, U.S.A. 84 J8 36 30N 118 30W
Seraing, Belgium 15 D5 50 35N 5 32 E
Seraja, Indonesia 39 L7 2 41N 108 35 E
Serakhis →, Cyprus 23 D11 35 13N 32 55 E
Seram, Indonesia 37 E7 3 10S 129 0 E
Seram Sea, Indonesia 37 E7 2 30S 128 30 E
Seranantsara, Madag. 57 B8 18 30S 49 5 E
Serang, Indonesia 37 G12 6 8S 106 10 E
Serasan, Indonesia 39 L7 2 29N 109 4 E
Serbia □, Yugoslavia 21 C9 43 30N 21 0 E
Serdobsk, Russia 24 D7 52 28N 44 10 E
Seremban, Malaysia 39 L3 2 43N 101 53 E
Serengeti Plain, Tanzania 54 C4 2 40S 35 0 E
Serenje, Zambia 55 E3 13 14S 30 15 E
Sereth = Siret →, Romania 17 F14 45 24N 28 1 E
Sergino, Russia 26 C7 62 25N 65 12 E
Sergipe □, Brazil 93 F11 10 30S 37 30W
Sergiyev Posad, Russia 24 C6 56 20N 38 10 E
Seria, Brunei 36 D4 4 37N 114 23 E
Serian, Malaysia 36 D4 1 10N 110 31 E
Seribu, Kepulauan, Indonesia 36 F3 5 36S 106 33 E
Sérifos, Greece 21 F11 37 9N 24 30 E
Sérigny →, Canada 71 A6 56 47N 66 0W
Seringapatam Reef, Australia 60 B3 13 38S 122 5 E
Sermata, Indonesia 37 F7 8 15S 128 50 E
Serov, Russia 24 C11 59 29N 60 35 E
Serowe, Botswana 56 C4 22 25S 26 43 E
Serpentine Lakes, Australia 61 E4 28 30S 129 10 E
Serpukhov, Russia 24 D6 54 55N 37 28 E
Serra do Navio, Brazil 93 C8 0 59N 52 3W
Sérrai, Greece 21 D10 41 5N 23 31 E
Serrezuela, Argentina 94 C2 30 40S 65 20W
Serrinha, Brazil 93 F11 11 39S 39 0W
Sertanópolis, Brazil 95 A5 23 4S 51 2W
Serua, Indonesia 37 F8 6 18S 130 1 E
Serui, Indonesia 37 E9 1 53S 136 10 E
Serule, Botswana 56 C4 21 57S 27 20 E
Ses Salines, Spain 22 B10 39 21N 3 3 E
Sese Is., Uganda 54 C3 0 20S 32 20 E
Sesepe, Indonesia 37 E7 1 30S 127 59 E
Sesfontein, Namibia 56 B1 19 7S 13 39 E
Sesheke, Zambia 56 B3 17 29S 24 13 E
S'Espalmador, Spain 22 C7 38 47N 1 26 E
S'Espardell, Spain 22 C7 38 48N 1 29 E
S'Estanyol, Spain 22 B9 39 22N 2 54 E
Setana, Japan 30 C9 42 26N 139 51 E
Sète, France 18 E5 43 25N 3 42 E
Sete Lagôas, Brazil 93 G10 19 27S 44 16W
Sétif, Algeria 50 A7 36 9N 5 26 E
Seto, Japan 31 G8 35 14N 137 6 E
Setonaikai, Japan 31 G6 34 20N 133 30 E
Settat, Morocco 50 B4 33 0N 7 40W
Setting L., Canada 73 C9 55 0N 98 38W
Settle, U.K. 10 C5 54 5N 2 16W
Settlement Pt., Bahamas 77 M6 26 40N 79 0W
Settlers, S. Africa 57 C4 25 2S 28 30 E
Setúbal, Portugal 19 C1 38 30N 8 58W
Setúbal, B. de, Portugal 19 C1 38 40N 8 56W
Seul, Lac, Canada 70 B1 50 20N 92 30W
Sevan, Ozero = Sevana Lich, Armenia 25 F8 40 30N 45 20 E
Sevana Lich, Armenia 25 F8 40 30N 45 20 E
Sevastopol, Ukraine 25 F5 44 35N 33 30 E
Seven Sisters, Canada 72 C3 54 56N 128 10W
Severn →, Canada 70 A2 56 2N 87 36W
Severn →, U.K. 11 F5 51 35N 2 40W
Severn L., Canada 70 B1 53 54N 90 48W
Severnaya Zemlya, Russia 27 B10 79 0N 100 0 E
Severnyye Uvaly, Russia 24 C8 60 0N 50 0 E
Severo-Kurilsk, Russia 27 D16 50 40N 156 8 E
Severo-Yeniseyskiy, Russia 27 C10 60 22N 93 1 E
Severodvinsk, Russia 24 B6 64 27N 39 58 E
Severomorsk, Russia 24 A5 69 5N 33 27 E
Severouralsk, Russia 24 B10 60 9N 59 57 E
Sevier, U.S.A. 83 G7 38 39N 112 11W
Sevier →, U.S.A. 83 G7 39 4N 113 6W
Sevier Desert, U.S.A. 82 G7 39 40N 112 45W

Söderhamn

Sierra Blanca, *U.S.A.* **83 L11** 31 11N 105 22W
Sierra Blanca Peak, *U.S.A.* **83 K11** 33 23N 105 49W
Sierra City, *U.S.A.* **84 F6** 39 34N 120 38W
Sierra Colorada, *Argentina* **96 E3** 40 35S 67 50W
Sierra Gorda, *Chile* **94 A2** 22 50S 69 15W
Sierra Leone ■, *W. Afr.* **50 G3** 9 0N 12 0W
Sierra Madre, *Mexico* **87 D6** 16 0N 93 0W
Sierra Mojada, *Mexico* **86 B4** 27 19N 103 42W
Sierra Nevada, *Spain* **19 D4** 37 3N 3 15W
Sierra Nevada, *U.S.A.* **84 H8** 39 0N 120 30W
Sierra Vista, *U.S.A.* **83 L8** 31 33N 110 18W
Sierraville, *U.S.A.* **84 F6** 39 36N 120 22W
Sífnos, *Greece* **21 F11** 37 0N 24 45 E
Sifton, *Canada* **73 C8** 51 21N 100 8W
Sifton Pass, *Canada* **72 B3** 57 52N 126 15W
Sighetu-Marmaţiei, *Romania* **17 E12** 47 57N 23 52 E
Sighişoara, *Romania* **17 E13** 46 12N 24 50 E
Sigli, *Indonesia* **36 C1** 5 25N 96 0 E
Siglufjörður, *Iceland* **8 C4** 66 12N 18 55W
Signal, *U.S.A.* **85 L13** 34 30N 113 38W
Signal Pk., *U.S.A.* **85 M12** 33 20N 114 2W
Sigsig, *Ecuador* **92 D3** 3 0S 78 50W
Sigüenza, *Spain* **19 B4** 41 3N 2 40W
Siguiri, *Guinea* **50 F4** 11 31N 9 10W
Sigulda, *Latvia* **9 H21** 57 10N 24 55 E
Sihanoukville = Kampong Saom, *Cambodia* **39 G4** 10 38N 103 30 E
Sihora, *India* **43 H9** 23 29N 80 6 E
Siikajoki →, *Finland* **8 D21** 64 50N 24 43 E
Siilinjärvi, *Finland* **8 E22** 63 4N 27 39 E
Sijarira Ra. = Chizarira, *Zimbabwe* **55 F2** 17 36S 27 45 E
Sika, *India* **42 H3** 22 26N 69 47 E
Sikao, *Thailand* **39 J2** 7 34N 99 21 E
Sikar, *India* **42 F6** 27 33N 75 10 E
Sikasso, *Mali* **50 F4** 11 18N 5 35W
Sikeston, *U.S.A.* **81 G10** 36 53N 89 35W
Sikhote Alin, Khrebet, *Russia* **27 E14** 45 0N 136 0 E
Sikhote Alin Ra. = Sikhote Alin, Khrebet, *Russia* **27 E14** 45 0N 136 0 E
Síkinos, *Greece* **21 F11** 36 40N 25 8 E
Sikkani Chief →, *Canada* **72 B4** 57 47N 122 15W
Sikkim □, *India* **41 F16** 27 50N 88 30 E
Sikotu-Ko, *Japan* **30 C10** 42 45N 141 25 E
Sil →, *Spain* **19 A2** 42 27N 7 43W
Silacayoapan, *Mexico* **87 D5** 17 30N 98 9W
Silawad, *India* **42 J6** 21 54N 74 54 E
Silchar, *India* **41 G18** 24 49N 92 48 E
Siler City, *U.S.A.* **77 H6** 35 44N 79 28W
Silesia = Śląsk, *Poland* **16 C9** 51 0N 16 30 E
Silgarhi Doti, *Nepal* **43 E9** 29 15N 81 0 E
Silghat, *India* **41 F18** 26 35N 93 0 E
Silifke, *Turkey* **25 G5** 36 22N 33 58 E
Siliguri = Shiliguri, *India* **41 F16** 26 45N 88 25 E
Siling Co, *China* **32 C3** 31 50N 89 20 E
Silistra, *Bulgaria* **21 B12** 44 6N 27 19 E
Silivri, *Turkey* **21 D13** 41 4N 28 14 E
Siljan, *Sweden* **9 F16** 60 55N 14 45 E
Silkeborg, *Denmark* **9 H13** 56 10N 9 32 E
Silkwood, *Australia* **62 B4** 17 45S 146 2 E
Sillajhuay, Cordillera, *Chile* **92 G5** 19 46S 68 40W
Sillamäe, *Estonia* **9 G22** 59 24N 27 45 E
Silloth, *U.K.* **10 C4** 54 52N 3 23W
Siloam Springs, *U.S.A.* **81 G7** 36 11N 94 32W
Silsbee, *U.S.A.* **81 K7** 30 21N 94 11W
Šilutė, *Lithuania* **9 J19** 55 21N 21 33 E
Silva Porto = Kuito, *Angola* **53 G3** 12 22S 16 55 E
Silvani, *India* **43 H8** 23 18N 78 25 E
Silver City, *U.S.A.* **83 K9** 32 46N 108 17W
Silver Cr. →, *U.S.A.* **82 E4** 43 16N 119 13W
Silver Creek, *U.S.A.* **78 D5** 42 33N 79 10W
Silver L., *U.S.A.* **84 G6** 38 39N 120 6W
Silver Lake, *Calif., U.S.A.* **85 K10** 35 21N 116 7W
Silver Lake, *Oreg., U.S.A.* **82 E3** 43 8N 121 3W
Silverton, *Colo., U.S.A.* **83 H10** 37 49N 107 40W
Silverton, *Tex., U.S.A.* **81 H4** 34 28N 101 19W
Silvies →, *U.S.A.* **82 E4** 43 34N 119 2W
Simaltala, *India* **43 G12** 24 43N 86 33 E
Simanggang = Bandar Sri Aman, *Malaysia* **36 D4** 1 15N 111 32 E
Simard, L., *Canada* **70 C4** 47 40N 78 40W
Simav, *Turkey* **21 E13** 39 4N 28 58 E
Simba, *Tanzania* **54 C4** 2 10S 37 36 E
Simbirsk, *Russia* **24 D8** 54 20N 48 25 E
Simbo, *Tanzania* **54 C2** 4 51S 29 41 E
Simcoe, *Canada* **78 D4** 42 50N 80 20W
Simcoe, L., *Canada* **78 B5** 44 25N 79 20W
Simdega, *India* **43 H11** 22 37N 84 31 E
Simeria, *Romania* **17 F12** 45 51N 23 1 E
Simeulue, *Indonesia* **36 D1** 2 45N 95 45 E
Simferopol, *Ukraine* **25 F5** 44 55N 34 3 E
Sími, *Greece* **21 F12** 36 35N 27 50 E
Simi Valley, *U.S.A.* **85 L8** 34 16N 118 47W
Simikot, *Nepal* **43 E9** 30 0N 81 50 E
Simla, *India* **42 D7** 31 2N 77 9 E
Simmie, *Canada* **73 D7** 49 56N 108 6W
Simmler, *U.S.A.* **85 K7** 35 21N 119 59W
Simojoki →, *Finland* **8 D21** 65 35N 25 1 E
Simojovel, *Mexico* **87 D6** 17 12N 92 38W
Simonette →, *Canada* **72 B5** 55 9N 118 15W
Simonstown, *S. Africa* **56 E2** 34 14S 18 26 E
Simplonpass, *Switz.* **18 C8** 46 15N 8 3 E
Simpson Desert, *Australia* **62 D2** 25 0S 137 0 E
Simpson Pen., *Canada* **69 B11** 68 34N 88 45W
Simpungdong, *N. Korea* **35 D15** 40 56N 129 29 E
Simrishamn, *Sweden* **9 J16** 55 33N 14 22 E
Simsbury, *U.S.A.* **79 E12** 41 53N 72 48W
Simushir, Ostrov, *Russia* **27 E16** 46 50N 152 30 E
Sin Cowe I., *S. China Sea* **36 C4** 9 53N 114 19 E
Sinabang, *Indonesia* **36 D1** 2 30N 96 24 E
Sinadogo, *Somali Rep.* **46 F4** 5 50N 47 0 E
Sinai = Es Sînâ', *Egypt* **47 F3** 29 0N 34 0 E
Sinai, Mt. = Mûsa, Gebel, *Egypt* **44 D2** 28 33N 33 59 E
Sinai Peninsula, *Egypt* **47 F3** 29 30N 34 0 E
Sinaloa □, *Mexico* **86 C3** 25 0N 107 30W
Sinaloa de Leyva, *Mexico* **86 B3** 25 50N 108 20W
Sinarádhes, *Greece* **23 A3** 39 34N 19 51 E
Sincelejo, *Colombia* **92 B3** 9 18N 75 24W
Sinch'ang, *N. Korea* **35 D15** 40 7N 128 28 E
Sinchang-ni, *N. Korea* **35 E14** 39 24N 126 8 E
Sinclair, *U.S.A.* **82 F10** 41 47N 107 7W
Sinclair Mills, *Canada* **72 C4** 54 5N 121 40W
Sinclair's B., *U.K.* **12 C5** 58 31N 3 5W
Sinclairville, *U.S.A.* **78 D5** 42 16N 79 16W
Sincorá, Serra do, *Brazil* **93 F10** 13 30S 41 0W
Sind, *Pakistan* **42 G3** 26 0N 68 30 E
Sind □, *Pakistan* **42 G3** 26 0N 69 0 E
Sind →, *Jammu & Kashmir, India* **43 B6** 34 18N 74 45 E
Sind →, *Mad. P., India* **43 F8** 26 26N 79 13 E
Sind Sagar Doab, *Pakistan* **42 D4** 32 0N 71 30 E
Sindangan, *Phil.* **37 C6** 8 10N 123 5 E
Sindangbarang, *Indonesia* **37 G12** 7 27S 107 1 E
Sinde, *Zambia* **55 F2** 17 28S 25 51 E
Sindh = Sind □, *Pakistan* **42 G3** 26 0N 69 0 E
Sindri, *India* **43 H12** 23 45N 86 42 E
Sines, *Portugal* **19 D1** 37 56N 8 51W
Sines, C. de, *Portugal* **19 D1** 37 58N 8 53W
Sineu, *Spain* **22 B10** 39 38N 3 1 E
Sing Buri, *Thailand* **38 E3** 14 53N 100 25 E
Singa, *Sudan* **51 F12** 13 10N 33 57 E
Singapore ■, *Asia* **39 M4** 1 17N 103 51 E
Singapore, Straits of, *Asia* **39 M5** 1 15N 104 0 E
Singaraja, *Indonesia* **36 F5** 8 7S 115 6 E
Singida, *Tanzania* **54 C3** 4 49S 34 48 E
Singida □, *Tanzania* **54 D3** 6 0S 34 30 E
Singitikós Kólpos, *Greece* **21 D11** 40 6N 24 0 E
Singkaling Hkamti, *Burma* **41 G19** 26 0N 95 39 E
Singkang, *Indonesia* **37 E6** 4 8S 120 1 E
Singkawang, *Indonesia* **36 D3** 1 0N 108 57 E
Singkep, *Indonesia* **36 E2** 0 30S 104 25 E
Singleton, *Australia* **63 E5** 32 33S 151 0 E
Singleton, Mt., *N. Terr., Australia* **60 D5** 22 0S 130 46 E
Singleton, Mt., *W. Austral., Australia* **61 E2** 29 27S 117 15 E
Singoli, *India* **42 G6** 25 0N 75 22 E
Singora = Songkhla, *Thailand* **39 J3** 7 13N 100 37 E
Singosan, *N. Korea* **35 E14** 38 52N 127 25 E
Sinhung, *N. Korea* **35 D14** 40 11N 127 34 E
Sinjai, *Indonesia* **37 F6** 5 7S 120 20 E
Sinjār, *Iraq* **44 B4** 36 19N 41 52 E
Sinkat, *Sudan* **51 E13** 18 55N 36 49 E
Sinkiang Uighur = Xinjiang Uygur Zizhiqu □, *China* **32 C3** 42 0N 86 0 E
Sinmak, *N. Korea* **35 E14** 38 25N 126 14 E
Sinnamary, *Fr. Guiana* **93 B8** 5 25N 53 0W
Sinni →, *Italy* **20 D7** 40 8N 16 41 E
Sinop, *Turkey* **25 F6** 42 1N 35 11 E
Sinor, *India* **42 J5** 21 55N 73 20 E
Sinp'o, *N. Korea* **35 E15** 40 0N 128 13 E
Sinsk, *Russia* **27 C13** 61 8N 126 48 E
Sintang, *Indonesia* **36 D4** 0 5N 111 35 E
Sinton, *U.S.A.* **81 L6** 28 2N 97 31W
Sintra, *Portugal* **19 C1** 38 47N 9 25W
Sinŭiju, *N. Korea* **35 D13** 40 5N 124 24 E
Siocon, *Phil.* **37 C6** 7 40N 122 10 E
Siófok, *Hungary* **17 E10** 46 54N 18 3 E
Sion, *Switz.* **18 C7** 46 14N 7 20 E
Sion Mills, *U.K.* **13 B4** 54 48N 7 29W
Sioux City, *U.S.A.* **80 D6** 42 30N 96 24W
Sioux Falls, *U.S.A.* **80 D6** 43 33N 96 44W
Sioux Lookout, *Canada* **70 B1** 50 10N 91 50W
Sioux Narrows, *Canada* **73 D10** 49 25N 94 10W
Siping, *China* **35 C13** 43 8N 124 21 E
Sipiwesk L., *Canada* **73 B9** 55 5N 97 35W
Sipra →, *India* **42 H6** 23 55N 75 28 E
Sipura, *Indonesia* **36 E1** 2 18S 99 40 E
Siquia →, *Nic.* **88 D3** 12 10N 84 20W
Siquijor, *Phil.* **37 C6** 9 12N 123 35 E
Siquirres, *Costa Rica* **88 D3** 10 6N 83 30W
Şīr Banī Yās, *U.A.E.* **45 E7** 24 19N 52 37 E
Sir Edward Pellew Group, *Australia* **62 B2** 15 40S 137 10 E
Sir Graham Moore Is., *Australia* **60 B4** 13 53S 126 34 E
Sir James MacBrien, Mt., *Canada* **68 B7** 62 8N 127 40W
Sira →, *Norway* **9 G12** 58 23N 6 34 E
Siracusa, *Italy* **20 F6** 37 4N 15 17 E
Sirajganj, *Bangla.* **43 G13** 24 25N 89 47 E
Sirathu, *India* **43 G9** 25 39N 81 19 E
Sīrdān, *Iran* **45 B6** 36 39N 49 12 E
Sirdaryo = Syrdarya →, *Kazakstan* **26 E7** 46 3N 61 0 E
Siren, *U.S.A.* **80 C8** 45 47N 92 24W
Sirer, *Spain* **22 C7** 38 56N 1 22 E
Siret →, *Romania* **17 F14** 45 24N 28 1 E
Sirghāyā, *Syria* **47 B5** 33 51N 36 8 E
Sirmaur, *India* **43 G9** 24 51N 81 23 E
Sirohi, *India* **42 G5** 24 52N 72 53 E
Sironj, *India* **42 G7** 24 5N 77 39 E
Síros, *Greece* **21 F11** 37 28N 24 57 E
Sirretta Pk., *U.S.A.* **85 K8** 35 56N 118 19W
Sīrrī, *Iran* **45 E7** 25 55N 54 32 E
Sirsa, *India* **42 E6** 29 33N 75 4 E
Sirsa →, *India* **43 F8** 26 51N 79 4 E
Sisak, *Croatia* **16 F9** 45 30N 16 21 E
Sisaket, *Thailand* **38 E5** 15 8N 104 23 E
Sishen, *S. Africa* **56 D3** 27 47S 22 59 E
Sishui, *Henan, China* **34 G7** 34 48N 113 15 E
Sishui, *Shandong, China* **35 G9** 35 42N 117 18 E
Sisipuk L., *Canada* **73 B8** 55 45N 101 50W
Sisophon, *Cambodia* **38 F4** 13 38N 102 59 E
Sisseton, *U.S.A.* **80 C6** 45 40N 97 3W
Sīstān, *Asia* **45 D9** 30 50N 61 0 E
Sīstān, Daryācheh-ye, *Iran* **45 D9** 31 0N 61 0 E
Sīstān va Balūchestān □, *Iran* **45 E9** 27 0N 62 0 E
Sisters, *U.S.A.* **82 D3** 44 18N 121 33W
Siswa Bazar, *India* **43 F10** 27 9N 83 46 E
Sitamarhi, *India* **43 F11** 26 37N 85 30 E
Sitampiky, *Madag.* **57 B8** 16 41S 46 6 E
Sitapur, *India* **43 F9** 27 38N 80 45 E
Siteki, *Swaziland* **57 D5** 26 32S 31 58 E
Sitges, *Spain* **19 B6** 41 17N 1 47 E
Sitia, *Greece* **23 D8** 35 13N 26 6 E
Sitka, *U.S.A.* **72 B1** 57 3N 135 20W
Sitoti, *Botswana* **56 C3** 23 15S 23 40 E
Sittang Myit →, *Burma* **41 L20** 17 20N 96 45 E
Sittard, *Neths.* **15 C5** 51 0N 5 52 E
Sittingbourne, *U.K.* **11 F8** 51 21N 0 45 E
Sittoung = Sittang Myit →, *Burma* **41 L20** 17 20N 96 45 E
Sittwe, *Burma* **41 J18** 20 18N 92 45 E
Situbondo, *Indonesia* **37 G16** 7 42S 114 0 E
Siuna, *Nic.* **88 D3** 13 37N 84 45W
Siuri, *India* **43 H12** 23 50N 87 34 E
Sivand, *Iran* **45 D7** 30 5N 52 55 E
Sivas, *Turkey* **25 G6** 39 43N 36 58 E
Siverek, *Turkey* **44 B3** 37 50N 39 19 E
Sivomaskinskiy, *Russia* **24 A11** 66 40N 62 35 E
Sivrihisar, *Turkey* **25 G5** 39 30N 31 35 E
Sîwa, *Egypt* **51 C11** 29 11N 25 31 E
Sîwa, El Wâhât es, *Egypt* **48 D6** 29 10N 25 30 E
Siwa Oasis = Sîwa, El Wâhât es, *Egypt* **48 D6** 29 10N 25 30 E
Siwalik Range, *Nepal* **43 F10** 28 0N 83 0 E
Siwan, *India* **43 F11** 26 13N 84 21 E
Siwana, *India* **42 G5** 25 38N 72 25 E
Sixmilebridge, *Ireland* **13 D3** 52 44N 8 46W
Sixth Cataract, *Sudan* **51 E12** 16 20N 32 42 E
Siziwang Qi, *China* **34 D6** 41 25N 111 40 E
Sjælland, *Denmark* **9 J14** 55 30N 11 30 E
Sjumen = Shumen, *Bulgaria* **21 C12** 43 18N 26 55 E
Skadarsko Jezero, *Montenegro, Yug.* **21 C8** 42 10N 19 20 E
Skaftafell, *Iceland* **8 D5** 64 1N 17 0W
Skagafjörður, *Iceland* **8 D4** 65 54N 19 35W
Skagastølstindane, *Norway* **9 F12** 61 28N 7 52 E
Skagaströnd, *Iceland* **8 D3** 65 50N 20 19W
Skagen, *Denmark* **9 H14** 57 43N 10 35 E
Skagerrak, *Denmark* **9 H13** 57 30N 9 0 E
Skagit →, *U.S.A.* **84 B4** 48 23N 122 22W
Skagway, *U.S.A.* **68 C6** 59 28N 135 19W
Skala-Podilska, *Ukraine* **17 D14** 48 50N 26 15 E
Skala Podolskaya = Skala-Podilska, *Ukraine* **17 D14** 48 50N 26 15 E
Skalat, *Ukraine* **17 D13** 49 23N 25 55 E
Skåne, *Sweden* **9 J15** 55 59N 13 30 E
Skaneateles, *U.S.A.* **79 D8** 42 57N 76 26W
Skaneateles L., *U.S.A.* **79 D8** 42 51N 76 22W
Skara, *Sweden* **9 G15** 58 25N 13 30 E
Skardu, *Pakistan* **43 B6** 35 20N 75 44 E
Skarżysko-Kamienna, *Poland* **17 C11** 51 7N 20 52 E
Skeena →, *Canada* **72 C2** 54 9N 130 5W
Skeena Mts., *Canada* **72 B3** 56 40N 128 30W
Skegness, *U.K.* **10 D8** 53 9N 0 20 E
Skeldon, *Guyana* **92 B7** 5 55N 57 20W
Skellefte älv →, *Sweden* **8 D19** 64 45N 21 10 E
Skellefteå, *Sweden* **8 D19** 64 45N 20 50 E
Skelleftehamn, *Sweden* **8 D19** 64 40N 21 9 E
Skerries, The, *U.K.* **10 D3** 53 25N 4 36W
Ski, *Norway* **9 G14** 59 43N 10 52 E
Skiathos, *Greece* **21 E10** 39 12N 23 30 E
Skibbereen, *Ireland* **13 E2** 51 33N 9 16W
Skiddaw, *U.K.* **10 C4** 54 39N 3 9W
Skidegate, *Canada* **72 C2** 53 15N 132 1W
Skien, *Norway* **9 G13** 59 12N 9 35 E
Skierniewice, *Poland* **17 C11** 51 58N 20 10 E
Skikda, *Algeria* **50 A7** 36 50N 6 58 E
Skilloura, *Cyprus* **23 D12** 35 14N 33 10 E
Skipton, *U.K.* **10 D5** 53 58N 2 3W
Skirmish Pt., *Australia* **62 A1** 11 59S 134 17 E
Skíros, *Greece* **21 E11** 38 55N 24 34 E
Skive, *Denmark* **9 H13** 56 33N 9 2 E
Skjálfandafljót →, *Iceland* **8 D5** 65 59N 17 25W
Skjálfandi, *Iceland* **8 C5** 66 5N 17 30W
Skoghall, *Sweden* **9 G15** 59 20N 13 30 E
Skole, *Ukraine* **17 D12** 49 3N 23 30 E
Skópelos, *Greece* **21 E10** 39 9N 23 47 E
Skopi, *Greece* **23 D8** 35 11N 26 2 E
Skopje, *Macedonia* **21 C9** 42 1N 21 26 E
Skövde, *Sweden* **9 G15** 58 24N 13 50 E
Skovorodino, *Russia* **27 D13** 54 0N 124 0 E
Skowhegan, *U.S.A.* **77 C11** 44 46N 69 43W
Skull, *Ireland* **13 E2** 51 32N 9 34W
Skunk →, *U.S.A.* **80 E9** 40 42N 91 7W
Skuodas, *Lithuania* **9 H19** 56 16N 21 33 E
Skvyra, *Ukraine* **17 D15** 49 44N 29 40 E
Skye, *U.K.* **12 D2** 57 15N 6 10W
Skykomish, *U.S.A.* **82 C3** 47 42N 121 22W
Skyros = Skíros, *Greece* **21 E11** 38 55N 24 34 E
Slættaratindur, *Færoe Is.* **8 E9** 62 18N 7 1W
Slagelse, *Denmark* **9 J14** 55 23N 11 19 E
Slamet, *Indonesia* **37 G13** 7 16S 109 8 E
Slaney →, *Ireland* **13 D5** 52 26N 6 33W
Slangberge, *S. Africa* **56 E3** 31 32S 20 48 E
Śląsk, *Poland* **16 C9** 51 0N 16 30 E
Slate Is., *Canada* **70 C2** 48 40N 87 0W
Slatina, *Romania* **17 F13** 44 28N 24 22 E
Slatington, *U.S.A.* **79 F9** 40 45N 75 37W
Slaton, *U.S.A.* **81 J4** 33 26N 101 39W
Slave →, *Canada* **72 A6** 61 18N 113 39W
Slave Coast, *W. Afr.* **50 G6** 6 0N 2 30 E
Slave Lake, *Canada* **72 B6** 55 17N 114 43W
Slave Pt., *Canada* **72 A5** 61 11N 115 56W
Slavgorod, *Russia* **26 D8** 53 1N 78 37 E
Slavonski Brod, *Croatia* **21 B8** 45 11N 18 1 E
Slavuta, *Ukraine* **17 C14** 50 15N 27 2 E
Slavyanka, *Russia* **30 C5** 42 53N 131 21 E
Slavyansk = Slovyansk, *Ukraine* **25 E6** 48 55N 37 36 E
Slawharad, *Belarus* **17 B16** 53 27N 31 0 E
Sleaford, *U.K.* **10 D7** 53 0N 0 24W
Sleaford B., *Australia* **63 E2** 34 55S 135 45 E
Sleat, Sd. of, *U.K.* **12 D3** 57 5N 5 47W
Sleeper Is., *Canada* **69 C11** 58 30N 81 0W
Sleepy Eye, *U.S.A.* **80 C7** 44 18N 94 43W
Slemon L., *Canada* **72 A5** 63 13N 116 4W
Slide Mt., *U.S.A.* **79 E10** 42 0N 74 25W
Slidell, *U.S.A.* **81 K10** 30 17N 89 47W
Sliema, *Malta* **23 D2** 35 55N 14 30 E
Slieve Aughty, *Ireland* **13 C3** 53 4N 8 30W
Slieve Bloom, *Ireland* **13 C4** 53 4N 7 40W
Slieve Donard, *U.K.* **13 B6** 54 11N 5 55W
Slieve Gamph, *Ireland* **13 B3** 54 6N 9 0W
Slieve Gullion, *U.K.* **13 B5** 54 7N 6 26W
Slieve Mish, *Ireland* **13 D2** 52 12N 9 50W
Slievenamon, *Ireland* **13 D4** 52 25N 7 34W
Sligeach = Sligo, *Ireland* **13 B3** 54 16N 8 28W
Sligo, *Ireland* **13 B3** 54 16N 8 28W
Sligo, *U.S.A.* **78 E5** 41 6N 79 29W
Sligo □, *Ireland* **13 B3** 54 8N 8 42W
Sligo B., *Ireland* **13 B3** 54 18N 8 40W
Slippery Rock, *U.S.A.* **78 E4** 41 3N 80 3W
Slite, *Sweden* **9 H18** 57 42N 18 48 E
Sliven, *Bulgaria* **21 C12** 42 42N 26 19 E
Sloan, *U.S.A.* **85 K11** 35 57N 115 13W
Sloansville, *U.S.A.* **79 D10** 42 45N 74 22W
Slobodskoy, *Russia* **24 C9** 58 40N 50 6 E
Slobozia, *Romania* **17 F14** 44 34N 27 23 E
Slocan, *Canada* **72 D5** 49 48N 117 28W
Slonim, *Belarus* **17 B13** 53 4N 25 19 E
Slough, *U.K.* **11 F7** 51 30N 0 36W
Slough □, *U.K.* **11 F7** 51 30N 0 36W
Sloughhouse, *U.S.A.* **84 G5** 38 26N 121 12W
Slovak Rep. ■, *Europe* **17 D10** 48 30N 20 0 E
Slovakia = Slovak Rep. ■, *Europe* **17 D10** 48 30N 20 0 E
Slovakian Ore Mts. = Slovenské Rudohorie, *Slovak Rep.* **17 D10** 48 45N 20 0 E
Slovenia ■, *Europe* **16 F8** 45 58N 14 30 E
Slovenija = Slovenia ■, *Europe* **16 F8** 45 58N 14 30 E
Slovenské Rudohorie, *Slovak Rep.* **17 D10** 48 45N 20 0 E
Slovyansk, *Ukraine* **25 E6** 48 55N 37 36 E
Sluch →, *Ukraine* **17 C14** 51 37N 26 38 E
Sluis, *Neths.* **15 C3** 51 18N 3 23 E
Słupsk, *Poland* **17 A9** 54 30N 17 3 E
Slurry, *S. Africa* **56 D4** 25 49S 25 42 E
Slutsk, *Belarus* **17 B14** 53 2N 27 31 E
Slyne Hd., *Ireland* **13 C1** 53 25N 10 10W
Slyudyanka, *Russia* **27 D11** 51 40N 103 40 E
Småland, *Sweden* **9 H16** 57 15N 15 25 E
Smalltree L., *Canada* **73 A8** 61 0N 105 0W
Smallwood Res., *Canada* **71 B7** 54 0N 64 0W
Smarhon, *Belarus* **17 A14** 54 20N 26 24 E
Smartt Syndicate Dam, *S. Africa* **56 E3** 30 45S 23 10 E
Smartville, *U.S.A.* **84 F5** 39 13N 121 18W
Smeaton, *Canada* **73 C8** 53 30N 104 49W
Smederevo, *Serbia, Yug.* **21 B9** 44 40N 20 57 E
Smerwick Harbour, *Ireland* **13 D1** 52 12N 10 23W
Smethport, *U.S.A.* **78 E6** 41 49N 78 27W
Smidovich, *Russia* **27 E14** 48 36N 133 49 E
Smith, *Canada* **72 B6** 55 10N 114 0W
Smith Center, *U.S.A.* **80 F5** 39 47N 98 47W
Smith Sund, *Greenland* **4 B4** 78 25N 74 0W
Smithburne →, *Australia* **62 B3** 17 3S 140 57 E
Smithers, *Canada* **72 C3** 54 45N 127 10W
Smithfield, *S. Africa* **57 E4** 30 9S 26 30 E
Smithfield, *N.C., U.S.A.* **77 H6** 35 31N 78 21W
Smithfield, *Utah, U.S.A.* **82 F8** 41 50N 111 50W
Smiths Falls, *Canada* **79 B9** 44 55N 76 0W
Smithton, *Australia* **62 G4** 40 53S 145 6 E
Smithville, *Canada* **78 C5** 43 6N 79 33W
Smithville, *U.S.A.* **81 K6** 30 1N 97 10W
Smoky →, *Canada* **72 B5** 56 10N 117 21W
Smoky Bay, *Australia* **63 E1** 32 22S 134 13 E
Smoky Hill →, *U.S.A.* **80 F6** 39 4N 96 48W
Smoky Hills, *U.S.A.* **80 F5** 39 15N 99 30W
Smoky Lake, *Canada* **72 C6** 54 10N 112 30W
Smøla, *Norway* **8 E13** 63 23N 8 3 E
Smolensk, *Russia* **24 D5** 54 45N 32 5 E
Smolikas, Óros, *Greece* **21 D9** 40 9N 20 58 E
Smolyan, *Bulgaria* **21 D11** 41 36N 24 38 E
Smooth Rock Falls, *Canada* **70 C3** 49 17N 81 37W
Smoothstone L., *Canada* **73 C7** 54 40N 106 50W
Smorgon = Smarhon, *Belarus* **17 A14** 54 20N 26 24 E
Smyrna = İzmir, *Turkey* **21 E12** 38 25N 27 8 E
Smyrna, *U.S.A.* **76 F8** 39 18N 75 36W
Snæfell, *Iceland* **8 D6** 64 48N 15 34W
Snaefell, *U.K.* **10 C3** 54 16N 4 27W
Snæfellsjökull, *Iceland* **8 D2** 64 49N 23 46W
Snake →, *U.S.A.* **82 C4** 46 12N 119 2W
Snake I., *Australia* **63 F4** 38 47S 146 33 E
Snake Range, *U.S.A.* **82 G6** 39 0N 114 20W
Snake River Plain, *U.S.A.* **82 E7** 42 50N 114 0W
Snåsavatnet, *Norway* **8 D14** 64 12N 12 0 E
Sneek, *Neths.* **15 A5** 53 2N 5 40 E
Sneeuberge, *S. Africa* **56 E3** 31 46S 24 20 E
Snelling, *U.S.A.* **84 H6** 37 31N 120 26W
Sněžka, *Europe* **16 C8** 50 41N 15 50 E
Snizort, L., *U.K.* **12 D2** 57 33N 6 28W
Snøhetta, *Norway* **9 E13** 62 19N 9 16 E
Snohomish, *U.S.A.* **84 C4** 47 55N 122 6W
Snoul, *Cambodia* **39 F6** 12 4N 106 26 E
Snow Hill, *U.S.A.* **76 F8** 38 11N 75 24W
Snow Lake, *Canada* **73 C8** 54 52N 100 3W
Snow Mt., *Calif., U.S.A.* **84 F4** 39 23N 122 45W
Snow Mt., *Maine, U.S.A.* **79 A14** 45 18N 70 48W
Snow Shoe, *U.S.A.* **78 E7** 41 2N 77 57W
Snowbird L., *Canada* **73 A8** 60 45N 103 0W
Snowdon, *U.K.* **10 D3** 53 4N 4 5W
Snowdrift →, *Canada* **73 A6** 62 24N 110 44W
Snowflake, *U.S.A.* **83 J8** 34 30N 110 5W
Snowshoe Pk., *U.S.A.* **82 B6** 48 13N 115 41W
Snowtown, *Australia* **63 E2** 33 46S 138 14 E
Snowville, *U.S.A.* **82 F7** 41 58N 112 43W
Snowy →, *Australia* **63 F4** 37 46S 148 30 E
Snowy Mt., *U.S.A.* **79 C10** 43 42N 74 23W
Snowy Mts., *Australia* **63 F4** 36 30S 148 20 E
Snug Corner, *Bahamas* **89 B5** 22 33N 73 52W
Snyatyn, *Ukraine* **17 D13** 48 27N 25 38 E
Snyder, *Okla., U.S.A.* **81 H5** 34 40N 98 57W
Snyder, *Tex., U.S.A.* **81 J4** 32 44N 100 55W
Soahanina, *Madag.* **57 B7** 18 42S 44 13 E
Soalala, *Madag.* **57 B8** 16 6S 45 20 E
Soaloka, *Madag.* **57 B8** 18 32S 45 15 E
Soamanonga, *Madag.* **57 C7** 23 52S 44 47 E
Soan →, *Pakistan* **42 C4** 33 1N 71 44 E
Soanierana-Ivongo, *Madag.* **57 B8** 16 55S 49 35 E
Soanindrariny, *Madag.* **57 B8** 19 54S 47 14 E
Soavina, *Madag.* **57 C8** 20 23S 46 56 E
Soavinandriana, *Madag.* **57 B8** 19 9S 46 45 E
Sobat, Nahr →, *Sudan* **51 G12** 9 22N 31 33 E
Sobhapur, *India* **42 H8** 22 47N 78 17 E
Sobradinho, Reprêsa de, *Brazil* **93 E10** 9 30S 42 0 E
Sobral, *Brazil* **93 D10** 3 50S 40 20W
Soc Giang, *Vietnam* **38 A6** 22 54N 106 1 E
Soc Trang, *Vietnam* **39 H5** 9 37N 105 50 E
Socastee, *U.S.A.* **77 J6** 33 41N 79 1W
Soch'e = Shache, *China* **32 C2** 38 20N 77 10 E
Sochi, *Russia* **25 F6** 43 35N 39 40 E
Société, Is. de la, *Pac. Oc.* **65 J12** 17 0S 151 0W
Society Is. = Société, Is. de la, *Pac. Oc.* **65 J12** 17 0S 151 0W
Socompa, Portezuelo de, *Chile* **94 A2** 24 27S 68 18W
Socorro, *N. Mex., U.S.A.* **83 J10** 34 4N 106 54W
Socorro, *Tex., U.S.A.* **83 L10** 31 39N 106 18W
Socorro, I., *Mexico* **86 D2** 18 45N 110 58W
Socotra, *Yemen* **46 E5** 12 30N 54 0 E
Soda L., *U.S.A.* **83 J5** 35 10N 116 4W
Soda Plains, *India* **43 B8** 35 30N 79 0 E
Soda Springs, *U.S.A.* **82 E8** 42 39N 111 36W
Sodankylä, *Finland* **8 C22** 67 29N 26 40 E
Soddy-Daisy, *U.S.A.* **77 H3** 35 17N 85 10W
Söderhamn, *Sweden* **9 F17** 61 18N 17 10 E

Suphan Buri

Stanislav = Ivano-Frankivsk, *Ukraine* **17 D13** 48 40N 24 40 E
Stanke Dimitrov, *Bulgaria* **21 C10** 42 17N 23 9 E
Stanley, *Australia* **62 G4** 40 46S 145 19 E
Stanley, *Canada* **73 B8** 55 24N 104 22W
Stanley, *Falk. Is.* **96 G5** 51 40S 59 51W
Stanley, *U.K.* **10 C6** 54 53N 1 41W
Stanley, *Idaho, U.S.A.* **82 D6** 44 13N 114 56W
Stanley, *N. Dak., U.S.A.* **80 A3** 48 19N 102 23W
Stanley, *N.Y., U.S.A.* **78 D7** 42 48N 77 6W
Stanovoy Khrebet, *Russia* **27 D13** 55 0N 130 0 E
Stanovoy Ra. = Stanovoy Khrebet, *Russia* **27 D13** 55 0N 130 0 E
Stansmore Ra., *Australia* **60 D4** 21 23S 128 33 E
Stanthorpe, *Australia* **63 D5** 28 36S 151 59 E
Stanton, *U.S.A.* **81 J4** 32 8N 101 48W
Stanwood, *U.S.A.* **84 B4** 48 15N 122 23W
Staples, *U.S.A.* **80 B7** 46 21N 94 48W
Star City, *Canada* **73 C8** 52 50N 104 20W
Star Lake, *U.S.A.* **79 B9** 44 10N 75 2W
Stara Planina, *Bulgaria* **21 C10** 43 15N 23 0 E
Stara Zagora, *Bulgaria* **21 C11** 42 26N 25 39 E
Starachowice, *Poland* **17 C11** 51 3N 21 2 E
Staraya Russa, *Russia* **24 C5** 57 58N 31 23 E
Starbuck I., *Kiribati* **65 H12** 5 37S 155 55W
Stargard Szczeciński, *Poland* **16 B8** 53 20N 15 0 E
Staritsa, *Russia* **24 C5** 56 33N 34 55 E
Starke, *U.S.A.* **77 L4** 29 57N 82 7W
Starogard Gdański, *Poland* **17 B10** 53 59N 18 30 E
Starokonstantinov = Starokonstyantyniv, *Ukraine* **17 D14** 49 48N 27 10 E
Starokonstyantyniv, *Ukraine* **17 D14** 49 48N 27 10 E
Start Pt., *U.K.* **11 G4** 50 13N 3 39W
Staryy Chartoriysk, *Ukraine* **17 C13** 51 15N 25 54 E
Staryy Oskol, *Russia* **25 D6** 51 19N 37 55 E
State College, *U.S.A.* **78 F7** 40 48N 77 52W
Stateline, *U.S.A.* **84 G7** 38 57N 119 56W
Staten, I. = Estados, I. de Los, *Argentina* **96 G4** 54 40S 64 30W
Staten I., *U.S.A.* **79 F10** 40 35N 74 9W
Statesboro, *U.S.A.* **77 J5** 32 27N 81 47W
Statesville, *U.S.A.* **77 H5** 35 47N 80 53W
Stauffer, *U.S.A.* **85 L7** 34 45N 119 3W
Staunton, *Ill., U.S.A.* **80 F10** 39 1N 89 47W
Staunton, *Va., U.S.A.* **76 F6** 38 9N 79 4W
Stavanger, *Norway* **9 G11** 58 57N 5 40 E
Staveley, *N.Z.* **59 K3** 43 40S 171 32 E
Stavelot, *Belgium* **15 D5** 50 23N 5 55 E
Stavern, *Norway* **9 G14** 59 0N 10 1 E
Stavoren, *Neths.* **15 B5** 52 53N 5 22 E
Stavropol, *Russia* **25 E7** 45 5N 42 0 E
Stavros, *Cyprus* **23 D11** 35 1N 32 38 E
Stavrós, *Greece* **23 D6** 35 12N 24 45 E
Stavrós, Ákra, *Greece* **23 D6** 35 26N 24 58 E
Stawell, *Australia* **63 F3** 37 5S 142 47 E
Stawell →, *Australia* **62 C3** 20 20S 142 55 E
Stayner, *Canada* **78 B4** 44 25N 80 5W
Stayton, *U.S.A.* **82 D2** 44 48N 122 48W
Steamboat Springs, *U.S.A.* **82 F10** 40 29N 106 50W
Steele, *U.S.A.* **80 B5** 46 51N 99 55W
Steelton, *U.S.A.* **78 F8** 40 14N 76 50W
Steen River, *Canada* **72 B5** 59 40N 117 12W
Steenkool = Bintuni, *Indonesia* **37 E8** 2 7S 133 32 E
Steens Mt., *U.S.A.* **82 E4** 42 35N 118 40W
Steenwijk, *Neths.* **15 B6** 52 47N 6 7 E
Steep Pt., *Australia* **61 E1** 26 8S 113 8 E
Steep Rock, *Canada* **73 C9** 51 30N 98 48W
Stefanie L. = Chew Bahir, *Ethiopia* **46 G2** 4 40N 36 50 E
Stefansson Bay, *Antarctica* **5 C5** 67 20S 59 8 E
Steiermark □, *Austria* **16 E8** 47 26N 15 0 E
Steilacoom, *U.S.A.* **84 C4** 47 10N 122 36W
Steilrandberge, *Namibia* **56 B1** 17 45S 13 20 E
Steinbach, *Canada* **73 D9** 49 32N 96 40W
Steinhausen, *Namibia* **56 C2** 21 49S 18 20 E
Steinkjer, *Norway* **8 D14** 64 1N 11 31 E
Steinkopf, *S. Africa* **56 D2** 29 18S 17 43 E
Stellarton, *Canada* **71 C7** 45 32N 62 30W
Stellenbosch, *S. Africa* **56 E2** 33 58S 18 50 E
Stendal, *Germany* **16 B6** 52 36N 11 53 E
Steornabhaigh = Stornoway, *U.K.* **12 C2** 58 13N 6 23W
Stepanakert = Xankändi, *Azerbaijan* **25 G8** 39 52N 46 49 E
Stephens Creek, *Australia* **63 E3** 31 50S 141 30 E
Stephens I., *Canada* **72 C2** 54 10N 130 45W
Stephens L., *Canada* **73 B9** 56 32N 95 0W
Stephenville, *Canada* **71 C8** 48 31N 58 35W
Stephenville, *U.S.A.* **81 J5** 32 13N 98 12W
Stepnoi = Elista, *Russia* **25 E7** 46 16N 44 14 E
Steppe, *Asia* **28 D9** 50 0N 50 0 E
Sterkstroom, *S. Africa* **56 E4** 31 32S 26 32 E
Sterling, *Colo., U.S.A.* **80 E3** 40 37N 103 13W
Sterling, *Ill., U.S.A.* **80 E10** 41 48N 89 42W
Sterling, *Kans., U.S.A.* **80 F5** 38 13N 98 12W
Sterling City, *U.S.A.* **81 K4** 31 51N 101 0W
Sterling Heights, *U.S.A.* **76 D4** 42 35N 83 0W
Sterling Run, *U.S.A.* **78 E6** 41 25N 78 12W
Sterlitamak, *Russia* **24 D10** 53 40N 56 0 E
Stérnes, *Greece* **23 D6** 35 30N 24 9 E
Stettin = Szczecin, *Poland* **16 B8** 53 27N 14 27 E
Stettiner Haff, *Germany* **16 B8** 53 47N 14 15 E
Stettler, *Canada* **72 C6** 52 19N 112 40W
Steubenville, *U.S.A.* **78 F4** 40 22N 80 37W
Stevenage, *U.K.* **11 F7** 51 55N 0 13W
Stevens Point, *U.S.A.* **80 C10** 44 31N 89 34W
Stevenson, *U.S.A.* **84 E5** 45 42N 121 53W
Stevenson L., *Canada* **73 C9** 53 55N 96 0W
Stevensville, *U.S.A.* **82 C6** 46 30N 114 5W
Stewart, *Canada* **72 B3** 55 56N 129 57W
Stewart, *U.S.A.* **84 F7** 39 5N 119 46W
Stewart →, *Canada* **68 B6** 63 19N 139 26W
Stewart, C., *Australia* **62 A1** 11 57S 134 56 E
Stewart, I., *Chile* **96 G2** 54 50S 71 15W
Stewart I., *N.Z.* **59 M1** 46 58S 167 54 E
Stewarts Point, *U.S.A.* **84 G3** 38 39N 123 24W
Stewartville, *U.S.A.* **80 D8** 43 51N 92 29W
Stewiacke, *Canada* **71 C7** 45 9N 63 22W
Steynsburg, *S. Africa* **56 E4** 31 15S 25 49 E
Steyr, *Austria* **16 D8** 48 3N 14 25 E
Steytlerville, *S. Africa* **56 E3** 33 17S 24 19 E
Stigler, *U.S.A.* **81 H7** 35 15N 95 8W
Stikine →, *Canada* **72 B2** 56 40N 132 30W
Stilfontein, *S. Africa* **56 D4** 26 51S 26 50 E
Stillwater, *N.Z.* **59 K3** 42 27S 171 20 E
Stillwater, *Minn., U.S.A.* **80 C8** 45 3N 92 49W
Stillwater, *N.Y., U.S.A.* **79 D11** 42 55N 73 41W
Stillwater, *Okla., U.S.A.* **81 G6** 36 7N 97 4W
Stillwater Range, *U.S.A.* **82 G4** 39 50N 118 5W
Stillwater Reservoir, *U.S.A.* **79 C9** 43 54N 75 3W
Stilwell, *U.S.A.* **81 H7** 35 49N 94 38W
Štip, *Macedonia* **21 D10** 41 42N 22 10 E
Stirling, *Canada* **78 B7** 44 18N 77 33W
Stirling, *U.K.* **12 E5** 56 8N 3 57W
Stirling □, *U.K.* **12 E4** 56 12N 4 18W
Stirling Ra., *Australia* **61 F2** 34 23S 118 0 E
Stittsville, *Canada* **79 A9** 45 15N 75 55W
Stjernøya, *Norway* **8 A20** 70 20N 22 40 E
Stjørdalshalsen, *Norway* **8 E14** 63 29N 10 51 E
Stockerau, *Austria* **16 D9** 48 24N 16 12 E
Stockholm, *Sweden* **9 G18** 59 20N 18 3 E
Stockport, *U.K.* **10 D5** 53 25N 2 9W
Stocksbridge, *U.K.* **10 D6** 53 29N 1 35W
Stockton, *Calif., U.S.A.* **84 H5** 37 58N 121 17W
Stockton, *Kans., U.S.A.* **80 F5** 39 26N 99 16W
Stockton, *Mo., U.S.A.* **81 G8** 37 42N 93 48W
Stockton-on-Tees, *U.K.* **10 C6** 54 35N 1 19W
Stockton-on-Tees □, *U.K.* **10 C6** 54 35N 1 19W
Stockton Plateau, *U.S.A.* **81 K3** 30 30N 102 30W
Stoeng Treng, *Cambodia* **38 F5** 13 31N 105 58 E
Stoer, Pt. of, *U.K.* **12 C3** 58 16N 5 23W
Stoke-on-Trent, *U.K.* **10 D5** 53 1N 2 11W
Stoke-on-Trent □, *U.K.* **10 D5** 53 1N 2 11W
Stokes Pt., *Australia* **62 G3** 40 10S 143 56 E
Stokes Ra., *Australia* **60 C5** 15 50S 130 50 E
Stokksnes, *Iceland* **8 D6** 64 14N 14 58W
Stokmarknes, *Norway* **8 B16** 68 34N 14 54 E
Stolac, *Bos.-H.* **21 C7** 43 5N 17 59 E
Stolbovoy, Ostrov, *Russia* **27 B14** 74 44N 135 14 E
Stolbtsy = Stowbtsy, *Belarus* **17 B14** 53 30N 26 43 E
Stolin, *Belarus* **17 C14** 51 53N 26 50 E
Stomíon, *Greece* **23 D5** 35 21N 23 32 E
Stone, *U.K.* **10 E5** 52 55N 2 9W
Stoneboro, *U.S.A.* **78 E4** 41 20N 80 7W
Stonehaven, *U.K.* **12 E6** 56 59N 2 12W
Stonehenge, *Australia* **62 C3** 24 22S 143 17 E
Stonehenge, *U.K.* **11 F6** 51 9N 1 45W
Stonewall, *Canada* **73 C9** 50 10N 97 19W
Stony L., *Man., Canada* **73 B9** 58 51N 98 40W
Stony L., *Ont., Canada* **78 B6** 44 30N 78 5W
Stony Point, *U.S.A.* **79 E11** 41 14N 73 59W
Stony Pt., *U.S.A.* **79 C8** 43 50N 76 18W
Stony Rapids, *Canada* **73 B7** 59 16N 105 50W
Stony Tunguska = Tunguska, Podkamennaya →, *Russia* **27 C10** 61 50N 90 13 E
Stonyford, *U.S.A.* **84 F4** 39 23N 122 33W
Stora Lulevatten, *Sweden* **8 C18** 67 10N 19 30 E
Storavan, *Sweden* **8 D18** 65 45N 18 10 E
Stord, *Norway* **9 G11** 59 52N 5 23 E
Store Bælt, *Denmark* **9 J14** 55 20N 11 0 E
Storm B., *Australia* **62 G4** 43 10S 147 30 E
Storm Lake, *U.S.A.* **80 D7** 42 39N 95 13W
Stormberge, *S. Africa* **56 E4** 31 16S 26 17 E
Stormsrivier, *S. Africa* **56 E3** 33 59S 23 52 E
Stornoway, *U.K.* **12 C2** 58 13N 6 23W
Storozhinets = Storozhynets, *Ukraine* **17 D13** 48 14N 25 45 E
Storozhynets, *Ukraine* **17 D13** 48 14N 25 45 E
Storrs, *U.S.A.* **79 E12** 41 49N 72 15W
Storsjön, *Sweden* **8 E16** 63 9N 14 30 E
Storuman, *Sweden* **8 D17** 65 5N 17 10 E
Storuman, sjö, *Sweden* **8 D17** 65 13N 16 50 E
Stouffville, *Canada* **78 C5** 43 58N 79 15W
Stoughton, *Canada* **73 D8** 49 40N 103 0W
Stour →, *Dorset, U.K.* **11 G6** 50 43N 1 47W
Stour →, *Kent, U.K.* **11 F9** 51 18N 1 22 E
Stour →, *Suffolk, U.K.* **11 F9** 51 57N 1 4 E
Stourbridge, *U.K.* **11 E5** 52 28N 2 8W
Stout L., *Canada* **73 C10** 52 0N 94 40W
Stove Pipe Wells Village, *U.S.A.* **85 J9** 36 35N 117 11W
Stow, *U.S.A.* **78 E3** 41 10N 81 27W
Stowbtsy, *Belarus* **17 B14** 53 30N 26 43 E
Stowmarket, *U.K.* **11 E9** 52 12N 1 0 E
Strabane, *U.K.* **13 B4** 54 50N 7 27W
Strahan, *Australia* **62 G4** 42 9S 145 20 E
Stralsund, *Germany* **16 A7** 54 18N 13 4 E
Strand, *S. Africa* **56 E2** 34 9S 18 48 E
Stranda, *Møre og Romsdal, Norway* **9 E12** 62 19N 6 58 E
Stranda, *Nord-Trøndelag, Norway* **8 E14** 63 33N 10 14 E
Strangford L., *U.K.* **13 B6** 54 30N 5 37W
Stranraer, *U.K.* **12 G3** 54 54N 5 1W
Strasbourg, *Canada* **73 C8** 51 4N 104 55W
Strasbourg, *France* **18 B7** 48 35N 7 42 E
Stratford, *Canada* **78 C4** 43 23N 81 0W
Stratford, *N.Z.* **59 H5** 39 20S 174 19 E
Stratford, *Calif., U.S.A.* **84 J7** 36 11N 119 49W
Stratford, *Conn., U.S.A.* **79 E11** 41 12N 73 8W
Stratford, *Tex., U.S.A.* **81 G3** 36 20N 102 4W
Stratford-upon-Avon, *U.K.* **11 E6** 52 12N 1 42W
Strath Spey, *U.K.* **12 D5** 57 9N 3 49W
Strathalbyn, *Australia* **63 F2** 35 13S 138 53 E
Strathaven, *U.K.* **12 F4** 55 40N 4 5W
Strathcona Prov. Park, *Canada* **72 D3** 49 38N 125 40W
Strathmore, *Canada* **72 C6** 51 5N 113 18W
Strathmore, *U.K.* **12 E5** 56 37N 3 7W
Strathmore, *U.S.A.* **84 J7** 36 9N 119 4W
Strathnaver, *Canada* **72 C4** 53 20N 122 33W
Strathpeffer, *U.K.* **12 D4** 57 35N 4 32W
Strathroy, *Canada* **78 D3** 42 58N 81 38W
Strathy Pt., *U.K.* **12 C4** 58 36N 4 1W
Strattanville, *U.S.A.* **78 E5** 41 12N 79 19W
Stratton, *U.S.A.* **79 A14** 45 8N 70 26W
Stratton Mt., *U.S.A.* **79 C12** 43 4N 72 55W
Straubing, *Germany* **16 D7** 48 52N 12 34 E
Straumnes, *Iceland* **8 C2** 66 26N 23 8W
Strawberry →, *U.S.A.* **82 F8** 40 10N 110 24W
Streaky B., *Australia* **63 E1** 32 48S 134 13 E
Streaky Bay, *Australia* **63 E1** 32 51S 134 18 E
Streator, *U.S.A.* **80 E10** 41 8N 88 50W
Streetsboro, *U.S.A.* **78 E3** 41 14N 81 21W
Streetsville, *Canada* **78 C5** 43 35N 79 42W
Strelka, *Russia* **27 D10** 58 5N 93 3 E
Streng →, *Cambodia* **38 F4** 13 12N 103 37 E
Streymoy, *Færoe Is.* **8 E9** 62 8N 7 5W
Strezhevoy, *Russia* **26 C8** 60 42N 77 34 E
Strimón →, *Greece* **21 D10** 40 46N 23 51 E
Strimonikós Kólpos, *Greece* **21 D11** 40 33N 24 0 E
Stroma, *U.K.* **12 C5** 58 41N 3 7W
Strómboli, *Italy* **20 E6** 38 47N 15 13 E
Stromeferry, *U.K.* **12 D3** 57 21N 5 33W
Stromness, *U.K.* **12 C5** 58 58N 3 17W
Stromsburg, *U.S.A.* **80 E6** 41 7N 97 36W
Strömstad, *Sweden* **9 G14** 58 56N 11 10 E
Strömsund, *Sweden* **8 E16** 63 51N 15 33 E
Strongsville, *U.S.A.* **78 E3** 41 19N 81 50W
Stronsay, *U.K.* **12 B6** 59 7N 2 35W
Stroud, *U.K.* **11 F5** 51 45N 2 13W
Stroud Road, *Australia* **63 E5** 32 18S 151 57 E
Stroudsburg, *U.S.A.* **79 F9** 40 59N 75 12W
Stroumbi, *Cyprus* **23 E11** 34 53N 32 29 E
Struer, *Denmark* **9 H13** 56 30N 8 35 E
Strumica, *Macedonia* **21 D10** 41 28N 22 41 E
Struthers, *Canada* **70 C2** 48 41N 85 51W
Struthers, *U.S.A.* **78 E4** 41 4N 80 39W
Stryker, *U.S.A.* **82 B6** 48 41N 114 46W
Stryy, *Ukraine* **17 D12** 49 16N 23 48 E
Strzelecki Cr. →, *Australia* **63 D2** 29 37S 139 59 E
Stuart, *Fla., U.S.A.* **77 M5** 27 12N 80 15W
Stuart, *Nebr., U.S.A.* **80 D5** 42 36N 99 8W
Stuart →, *Canada* **72 C4** 54 0N 123 35W
Stuart Bluff Ra., *Australia* **60 D5** 22 50S 131 52 E
Stuart L., *Canada* **72 C4** 54 30N 124 30W
Stuart Ra., *Australia* **63 D1** 29 10S 134 56 E
Stull L., *Canada* **70 B1** 54 24N 92 34W
Stung Treng = Stoeng Treng, *Cambodia* **38 F5** 13 31N 105 58 E
Stupart →, *Canada* **70 A1** 56 0N 93 25W
Sturgeon B., *Canada* **73 C9** 52 0N 97 50W
Sturgeon Bay, *U.S.A.* **76 C2** 44 50N 87 23W
Sturgeon Falls, *Canada* **70 C4** 46 25N 79 57W
Sturgeon L., *Alta., Canada* **72 B5** 55 6N 117 32W
Sturgeon L., *Ont., Canada* **70 C1** 50 0N 90 45W
Sturgeon L., *Ont., Canada* **78 B6** 44 28N 78 43W
Sturgis, *Canada* **73 C8** 51 56N 102 36W
Sturgis, *Mich., U.S.A.* **76 E3** 41 48N 85 25W
Sturgis, *S. Dak., U.S.A.* **80 C3** 44 25N 103 31W
Sturt Cr. →, *Australia* **60 C4** 19 8S 127 50 E
Stutterheim, *S. Africa* **56 E4** 32 33S 27 28 E
Stuttgart, *Germany* **16 D5** 48 48N 9 11 E
Stuttgart, *U.S.A.* **81 H9** 34 30N 91 33W
Stuyvesant, *U.S.A.* **79 D11** 42 23N 73 45W
Stykkishólmur, *Iceland* **8 D2** 65 2N 22 40W
Styria = Steiermark □, *Austria* **16 E8** 47 26N 15 0 E
Su Xian = Suzhou, *China* **34 H9** 33 41N 116 59 E
Suakin, *Sudan* **51 E13** 19 8N 37 20 E
Suan, *N. Korea* **35 E14** 38 42N 126 22 E
Suaqui, *Mexico* **86 B3** 29 12N 109 41W
Suar, *India* **43 E8** 29 2N 79 3 E
Subang, *Indonesia* **37 G12** 6 34S 107 45 E
Subansiri →, *India* **41 F18** 26 48N 93 50 E
Subarnarekha →, *India* **43 H12** 22 34N 87 24 E
Subayhah, *Si. Arabia* **44 D3** 30 2N 38 50 E
Subi, *Indonesia* **39 L7** 2 58N 108 50 E
Subotica, *Serbia, Yug.* **21 A8** 46 6N 19 39 E
Suceava, *Romania* **17 E14** 47 38N 26 16 E
Suchan, *Russia* **30 C6** 43 8N 133 9 E
Suchitoto, *El Salv.* **88 D2** 13 56N 89 0W
Suchou = Suzhou, *China* **33 C7** 31 19N 120 38 E
Süchow = Xuzhou, *China* **35 G9** 34 18N 117 10 E
Suck →, *Ireland* **13 C3** 53 17N 8 3W
Sucre, *Bolivia* **92 G5** 19 0S 65 15W
Sucuriú →, *Brazil* **93 H8** 20 47S 51 38W
Sud, Pte. du, *Canada* **71 C7** 49 3N 62 14W
Sud-Kivu □, *Dem. Rep. of the Congo* **54 C2** 3 0S 28 30 E
Sud-Ouest, Pte. du, *Canada* **71 C7** 49 23N 63 36W
Sudan, *U.S.A.* **81 H3** 34 4N 102 32W
Sudan ■, *Africa* **51 E11** 15 0N 30 0 E
Sudbury, *Canada* **70 C3** 46 30N 81 0W
Sudbury, *U.K.* **11 E8** 52 2N 0 45 E
Sûdd, *Sudan* **51 G12** 8 20N 30 0 E
Sudeten Mts. = Sudety, *Europe* **17 C9** 50 20N 16 45 E
Sudety, *Europe* **17 C9** 50 20N 16 45 E
Suðuroy, *Færoe Is.* **8 F9** 61 32N 6 50W
Sudi, *Tanzania* **55 E4** 10 11S 39 57 E
Sudirman, Pegunungan, *Indonesia* **37 E9** 4 30S 137 0 E
Sueca, *Spain* **19 C5** 39 12N 0 21W
Suemez I., *U.S.A.* **72 B2** 55 15N 133 20W
Suez = El Suweis, *Egypt* **51 C12** 29 58N 32 31 E
Suez, G. of = Suweis, Khalîg el, *Egypt* **51 C12** 28 40N 33 0 E
Suez Canal = Suweis, Qanâ es, *Egypt* **51 B12** 31 0N 32 20 E
Suffield, *Canada* **72 C6** 50 12N 111 10W
Suffolk, *U.S.A.* **76 G7** 36 44N 76 35W
Suffolk □, *U.K.* **11 E9** 52 16N 1 0 E
Sugargrove, *U.S.A.* **78 E5** 41 59N 79 21W
Sugarive →, *India* **43 F12** 26 16N 86 24 E
Sugluk = Salluit, *Canada* **69 B12** 62 14N 75 38W
Şuḥār, *Oman* **46 C6** 24 20N 56 40 E
Sühbaatar □, *Mongolia* **34 B8** 45 30N 114 0 E
Suhl, *Germany* **16 C6** 50 36N 10 42 E
Sui, *Pakistan* **42 E3** 28 37N 69 19 E
Sui Xian, *China* **34 G8** 34 25N 115 2 E
Suide, *China* **34 F6** 37 30N 110 12 E
Suifenhe, *China* **35 B16** 44 25N 131 10 E
Suihua, *China* **33 B7** 46 32N 126 55 E
Suining, *China* **35 H9** 33 56N 117 58 E
Suiping, *China* **34 H7** 33 10N 113 59 E
Suir →, *Ireland* **13 D4** 52 16N 7 9W
Suisun City, *U.S.A.* **84 G4** 38 15N 122 2W
Suiyang, *China* **35 B16** 44 30N 130 56 E
Suizhong, *China* **35 D11** 40 21N 120 20 E
Sujangarh, *India* **42 F6** 27 42N 74 31 E
Sukabumi, *Indonesia* **37 G12** 6 56S 106 50 E
Sukadana, *Indonesia* **36 E3** 1 10S 110 0 E
Sukagawa, *Japan* **31 F10** 37 17N 140 23 E
Sukaraja, *Indonesia* **36 E4** 2 28S 110 25 E
Sukarnapura = Jayapura, *Indonesia* **37 E10** 2 28S 140 38 E
Sukch'ŏn, *N. Korea* **35 E13** 39 22N 125 35 E
Sukhona →, *Russia* **24 C6** 61 15N 46 39 E
Sukhothai, *Thailand* **38 D2** 17 1N 99 49 E
Sukhumi = Sokhumi, *Georgia* **25 F7** 43 0N 41 0 E
Sukkur, *Pakistan* **42 F3** 27 42N 68 54 E
Sukkur Barrage, *Pakistan* **42 F3** 27 40N 68 50 E
Sukri →, *India* **42 G4** 25 4N 71 43 E
Sukumo, *Japan* **31 H6** 32 56N 132 44 E
Sukunka →, *Canada* **72 B4** 55 45N 121 15W
Sula, Kepulauan, *Indonesia* **37 E7** 1 45S 125 0 E
Sulaco →, *Honduras* **88 C2** 15 2N 87 44W
Sulaiman Range, *Pakistan* **42 D3** 30 30N 69 50 E
Sūlār, *Iran* **45 D6** 31 53N 51 54 E
Sulawesi Sea = Celebes Sea, *Indonesia* **37 D6** 3 0N 123 0 E
Sulawesi Selatan □, *Indonesia* **37 E6** 2 30S 120 0 E
Sulawesi Utara □, *Indonesia* **37 D6** 1 0N 122 30 E
Sulima, *S. Leone* **50 G3** 6 58N 11 32W
Sulina, *Romania* **17 F15** 45 10N 29 40 E
Sulitjelma, *Norway* **8 C17** 67 9N 16 3 E
Sullana, *Peru* **92 D2** 4 52S 80 39W
Sullivan, *Ill., U.S.A.* **80 F10** 39 36N 88 37W
Sullivan, *Ind., U.S.A.* **76 F2** 39 6N 87 24W
Sullivan, *Mo., U.S.A.* **80 F9** 38 13N 91 10W
Sullivan Bay, *Canada* **72 C3** 50 55N 126 50W
Sullivan I. = Lanbi Kyun, *Burma* **39 G2** 10 50N 98 20 E
Sulphur, *La., U.S.A.* **81 K8** 30 14N 93 23W
Sulphur, *Okla., U.S.A.* **81 H6** 34 31N 96 58W
Sulphur Pt., *Canada* **72 A6** 60 56N 114 48W
Sulphur Springs, *U.S.A.* **81 J7** 33 8N 95 36W
Sultan, *Canada* **70 C3** 47 36N 82 47W
Sultan, *U.S.A.* **84 C5** 47 52N 121 49W
Sultanpur, *Mad. P., India* **42 H8** 23 9N 77 56 E
Sultanpur, *Punjab, India* **42 D6** 31 13N 75 11 E
Sultanpur, *Ut. P., India* **43 F10** 26 18N 82 4 E
Sulu Arch., *Phil.* **37 C6** 6 0N 121 0 E
Sulu Sea, *E. Indies* **37 C6** 8 0N 120 0 E
Suluq, *Libya* **51 B10** 31 44N 20 14 E
Sulzberger Ice Shelf, *Antarctica* **5 D10** 78 0S 150 0 E
Sumalata, *Indonesia* **37 D6** 1 0N 122 31 E
Sumampa, *Argentina* **94 B3** 29 25S 63 29W
Sumatera □, *Indonesia* **36 D2** 0 40N 100 20 E
Sumatera Barat □, *Indonesia* **36 E2** 1 0S 101 0 E
Sumatera Utara □, *Indonesia* **36 D1** 2 30N 98 0 E
Sumatra = Sumatera □, *Indonesia* **36 D2** 0 40N 100 20 E
Sumba, *Indonesia* **37 F5** 9 45S 119 35 E
Sumba, Selat, *Indonesia* **37 F5** 9 0S 118 40 E
Sumbawa, *Indonesia* **36 F5** 8 26S 117 30 E
Sumbawa Besar, *Indonesia* **36 F5** 8 30S 117 26 E
Sumbawanga □, *Tanzania* **52 F6** 8 0S 31 30 E
Sumbe, *Angola* **52 G2** 11 10S 13 48 E
Sumburgh Hd., *U.K.* **12 B7** 59 52N 1 17W
Sumdeo, *India* **43 D8** 31 26N 78 44 E
Sumdo, *China* **43 B8** 35 6N 78 41 E
Sumedang, *Indonesia* **37 G12** 6 52S 107 55 E
Šumen = Shumen, *Bulgaria* **21 C12** 43 18N 26 55 E
Sumenep, *Indonesia* **37 G15** 7 1S 113 52 E
Sumgait = Sumqayıt, *Azerbaijan* **25 F8** 40 34N 49 38 E
Summer L., *U.S.A.* **82 E3** 42 50N 120 45W
Summerland, *Canada* **72 D5** 49 32N 119 41W
Summerside, *Canada* **71 C7** 46 24N 63 47W
Summersville, *U.S.A.* **76 F5** 38 17N 80 51W
Summerville, *Ga., U.S.A.* **77 H3** 34 29N 85 21W
Summerville, *S.C., U.S.A.* **77 J5** 33 1N 80 11W
Summit Lake, *Canada* **72 C4** 54 20N 122 40W
Summit Peak, *U.S.A.* **83 H10** 37 21N 106 42W
Sumner, *Iowa, U.S.A.* **80 D8** 42 51N 92 6W
Sumner, *Wash., U.S.A.* **84 C4** 47 12N 122 14W
Sumoto, *Japan* **31 G7** 34 21N 134 54 E
Šumperk, *Czech Rep.* **17 D9** 49 59N 16 59 E
Sumqayıt, *Azerbaijan* **25 F8** 40 34N 49 38 E
Sumter, *U.S.A.* **77 J5** 33 55N 80 21W
Sumy, *Ukraine* **25 D5** 50 57N 34 50 E
Sun City, *S. Africa* **56 D4** 25 17S 27 3 E
Sun City, *Ariz., U.S.A.* **83 K7** 33 36N 112 17W
Sun City, *Calif., U.S.A.* **85 M9** 33 42N 117 11W
Sun City Center, *U.S.A.* **77 M4** 27 43N 82 18W
Sun Lakes, *U.S.A.* **83 K8** 33 10N 111 52W
Sun Valley, *U.S.A.* **82 E6** 43 42N 114 21W
Sunagawa, *Japan* **30 C10** 43 29N 141 55 E
Sunan, *N. Korea* **35 E13** 39 15N 125 40 E
Sunart, L., *U.K.* **12 E3** 56 42N 5 43W
Sunburst, *U.S.A.* **82 B8** 48 53N 111 55W
Sunbury, *Australia* **63 F3** 37 35S 144 44 E
Sunbury, *U.S.A.* **79 F8** 40 52N 76 48W
Sunchales, *Argentina* **94 C3** 30 58S 61 35W
Suncho Corral, *Argentina* **94 B3** 27 55S 63 27W
Sunch'ŏn, *S. Korea* **35 G14** 34 52N 127 31 E
Suncook, *U.S.A.* **79 C13** 43 8N 71 27W
Sunda, Selat, *Indonesia* **36 F3** 6 20S 105 30 E
Sunda Is., *Indonesia* **28 K14** 5 0S 105 0 E
Sunda Str. = Sunda, Selat, *Indonesia* **36 F3** 6 20S 105 30 E
Sundance, *Canada* **73 B10** 56 32N 94 4W
Sundance, *U.S.A.* **80 C2** 44 24N 104 23W
Sundar Nagar, *India* **42 D7** 31 32N 76 53 E
Sundarbans, *Asia* **41 J16** 22 0N 89 0 E
Sundargarh, *India* **41 H14** 22 4N 84 5 E
Sundays = Sondags →, *S. Africa* **56 E4** 33 44S 25 51 E
Sunderland, *Canada* **78 B5** 44 16N 79 4W
Sunderland, *U.K.* **10 C6** 54 55N 1 23W
Sundre, *Canada* **72 C6** 51 49N 114 38W
Sundsvall, *Sweden* **9 E17** 62 23N 17 17 E
Sung Hei, *Vietnam* **39 G6** 10 20N 106 2 E
Sungai Kolok, *Thailand* **39 J3** 6 2N 101 58 E
Sungai Lembing, *Malaysia* **39 L4** 3 55N 103 3 E
Sungai Petani, *Malaysia* **39 K3** 5 37N 100 30 E
Sungaigerong, *Indonesia* **36 E2** 2 59S 104 52 E
Sungailiat, *Indonesia* **36 E3** 1 51S 106 8 E
Sungaipenuh, *Indonesia* **36 E2** 2 1S 101 20 E
Sungari = Songhua Jiang →, *China* **33 B8** 47 45N 132 30 E
Sunghua Chiang = Songhua Jiang →, *China* **33 B8** 47 45N 132 30 E
Sunland Park, *U.S.A.* **83 L10** 31 50N 106 40W
Sunndalsøra, *Norway* **9 E13** 62 40N 8 33 E
Sunnyside, *U.S.A.* **82 C3** 46 20N 120 0W
Sunnyvale, *U.S.A.* **84 H4** 37 23N 122 2W
Suntar, *Russia* **27 C12** 62 15N 117 30 E
Suomenselkä, *Finland* **8 E21** 62 52N 24 0 E
Suomussalmi, *Finland* **8 D23** 64 54N 29 10 E
Suoyarvi, *Russia* **24 B5** 62 3N 32 20 E
Supai, *U.S.A.* **83 H7** 36 15N 112 41W
Supaul, *India* **43 F12** 26 10N 86 40 E
Superior, *Ariz., U.S.A.* **83 K8** 33 18N 111 6W
Superior, *Mont., U.S.A.* **82 C6** 47 12N 114 53W
Superior, *Nebr., U.S.A.* **80 E5** 40 1N 98 4W
Superior, *Wis., U.S.A.* **80 B8** 46 44N 92 6W
Superior, L., *N. Amer.* **70 C2** 47 0N 87 0W
Suphan Buri, *Thailand* **38 E3** 14 14N 100 10 E

Suphan Dağı

Suphan Dağı, Turkey 44 B4 38 54N 42 48 E
Supiori, Indonesia 37 E9 1 0S 136 0 E
Supung Shuiku, China 35 D13 40 35N 124 50 E
Sūq Suwayq, Si. Arabia 44 E3 24 23N 38 27 E
Suqian, China 35 H10 33 54N 118 8 E
Sūr, Lebanon 47 B4 33 19N 35 16 E
Şūr, Oman 46 C6 22 34N 59 32 E
Sur, Pt., U.S.A. 84 J5 36 18N 121 54W
Sura →, Russia 24 C8 56 6N 46 0 E
Surab, Pakistan 42 E2 28 25N 66 15 E
Surabaja = Surabaya, Indonesia 36 F4 7 17S 112 45 E
Surabaya, Indonesia 36 F4 7 17S 112 45 E
Surakarta, Indonesia 36 F4 7 35S 110 48 E
Surat, Australia 63 D4 27 10S 149 6 E
Surat, India 40 J8 21 12N 72 55 E
Surat Thani, Thailand 39 H2 9 6N 99 20 E
Suratgarh, India 42 E5 29 18N 73 55 E
Surendranagar, India 42 H4 22 45N 71 40 E
Surf, U.S.A. 85 L6 34 41N 120 36W
Surgut, Russia 26 C8 61 14N 73 20 E
Suriapet, India 40 L11 17 10N 79 40 E
Surigao, Phil. 37 C7 9 47N 125 29 E
Surin, Thailand 38 E4 14 50N 103 34 E
Surin Nua, Ko, Thailand 39 H1 9 30N 97 55 E
Surinam ■, S. Amer. 93 C7 4 0N 56 0W
Suriname = Surinam ■, S. Amer. 93 C7 4 0N 56 0W
Suriname →, Surinam 93 B7 5 50N 55 15W
Sūrmaq, Iran 45 D7 31 3N 52 48 E
Surrey □, U.K. 11 F7 51 15N 0 31W
Sursand, India 43 F11 26 39N 85 43 E
Sursar →, India 43 F12 26 14N 87 3 E
Surt, Libya 51 B9 31 11N 16 39 E
Surt, Khalīj, Libya 51 B9 31 40N 18 30 E
Surtanahu, Pakistan 42 F4 26 22N 70 0 E
Surtsey, Iceland 8 E3 63 20N 20 30W
Suruga-Wan, Japan 31 G9 34 45N 138 30 E
Susaki, Japan 31 H6 33 22N 133 17 E
Sūsangerd, Iran 45 D6 31 35N 48 6 E
Susanville, U.S.A. 82 F3 40 25N 120 39W
Susner, India 42 H7 23 57N 76 5 E
Susquehanna, U.S.A. 79 E9 41 57N 75 36W
Susquehanna →, U.S.A. 79 G8 39 33N 76 5W
Susques, Argentina 94 A2 23 35S 66 25W
Sussex, Canada 71 C6 45 45N 65 37W
Sussex, U.S.A. 79 E10 41 13N 74 37W
Sussex, E. □, U.K. 11 G8 51 0N 0 20 E
Sussex, W. □, U.K. 11 G7 51 0N 0 30W
Sustut →, Canada 72 B3 56 20N 127 30W
Susuman, Russia 27 C15 62 47N 148 10 E
Susunu, Indonesia 37 E8 3 7S 133 39 E
Susurluk, Turkey 21 E13 39 54N 28 8 E
Sutherland, S. Africa 56 E3 32 24S 20 40 E
Sutherland, U.S.A. 80 E4 41 10N 101 8W
Sutherland Falls, N.Z. 59 L1 44 48S 167 46 E
Sutherlin, U.S.A. 82 E2 43 23N 123 19W
Suthri, India 42 H3 23 3N 68 55 E
Sutlej →, Pakistan 42 E4 29 23N 71 3 E
Sutter, U.S.A. 84 F5 39 10N 121 45W
Sutter Creek, U.S.A. 84 G6 38 24N 120 48W
Sutton, Canada 79 A12 45 6N 72 37W
Sutton, Nebr., U.S.A. 80 E6 40 36N 97 52W
Sutton, W. Va., U.S.A. 76 F5 38 40N 80 43W
Sutton →, Canada 70 A3 55 15N 83 45W
Sutton Coldfield, U.K. 11 E6 52 35N 1 49W
Sutton in Ashfield, U.K. 10 D6 53 8N 1 16W
Sutton L., Canada 70 B3 54 15N 84 42W
Suttor →, Australia 62 C4 21 36S 147 2 E
Suttsu, Japan 30 C10 42 48N 140 14 E
Suva, Fiji 59 D8 18 6S 178 30 E
Suva Planina, Serbia, Yug. 21 C10 43 10N 22 5 E
Suvorov Is. = Suwarrow Is., Cook Is. 65 J11 15 0S 163 0W
Suwałki, Poland 17 A12 54 8N 22 59 E
Suwannaphum, Thailand 38 E4 15 33N 103 47 E
Suwannee →, U.S.A. 77 L4 29 17N 83 10W
Suwanose-Jima, Japan 31 K4 29 38N 129 43 E
Suwarrow Is., Cook Is. 65 J11 15 0S 163 0W
Suwayq aş Şuqban, Iraq 44 D5 31 32N 46 7 E
Suweis, Khalîg el, Egypt 51 C12 28 40N 33 0 E
Suweis, Qanâ es, Egypt 51 B12 31 0N 32 20 E
Suwŏn, S. Korea 35 F14 37 17N 127 1 E
Suzdal, Russia 24 C7 56 29N 40 26 E
Suzhou, Anhui, China 34 H9 33 41N 116 59 E
Suzhou, Jiangsu, China 33 C7 31 19N 120 38 E
Suzu, Japan 31 F8 37 25N 137 17 E
Suzu-Misaki, Japan 31 F8 37 31N 137 21 E
Suzuka, Japan 31 G8 34 55N 136 36 E
Svalbard, Arctic 4 B8 78 0N 17 0 E
Svappavaara, Sweden 8 C19 67 40N 21 3 E
Svartisen, Norway 8 C15 66 40N 13 50 E
Svay Chek, Cambodia 38 F4 13 48N 102 58 E
Svay Rieng, Cambodia 39 G5 11 9N 105 45 E
Svealand □, Sweden 9 G16 60 20N 15 0 E
Sveg, Sweden 9 E16 62 2N 14 21 E
Svendborg, Denmark 9 J14 55 4N 10 35 E
Sverdlovsk = Yekaterinburg, Russia 26 D7 56 50N 60 30 E
Sverdrup Is., Canada 4 B3 79 0N 97 0W
Svetlaya, Russia 30 A9 46 33N 138 18 E
Svetlogorsk = Svyetlahorsk, Belarus 17 B15 52 38N 29 46 E
Svir →, Russia 24 B5 60 30N 32 48 E
Svishtov, Bulgaria 21 C11 43 36N 25 23 E
Svislach, Belarus 17 B13 53 3N 24 2 E
Svobodnyy, Russia 27 D13 51 20N 128 0 E
Svolvær, Norway 8 B16 68 15N 14 34 E
Svyetlahorsk, Belarus 17 B15 52 38N 29 46 E
Swabian Alps = Schwäbische Alb, Germany 16 D5 48 20N 9 30 E
Swainsboro, U.S.A. 77 J4 32 36N 82 20W
Swakop →, Namibia 56 C2 22 38S 14 36 E
Swakopmund, Namibia 56 C1 22 37S 14 30 E
Swale →, U.K. 10 C6 54 5N 1 20W
Swan →, Australia 61 F2 32 3S 115 45 E
Swan →, Canada 73 C8 52 30N 100 45W
Swan Hill, Australia 63 F3 35 20S 143 33 E
Swan Hills, Canada 72 C5 54 43N 115 24W
Swan Is. = Santanilla, Is., Honduras 88 C3 17 22N 83 57W
Swan L., Canada 73 C8 52 30N 100 40W
Swan Peak, U.S.A. 82 C7 47 43N 113 38W
Swan Ra., U.S.A. 82 C7 48 0N 113 45W
Swan River, Canada 73 C8 52 10N 101 16W
Swanage, U.K. 11 G6 50 36N 1 58W
Swansea, Australia 62 G4 42 8S 148 4 E
Swansea, Canada 78 C5 43 38N 79 28W
Swansea, U.K. 11 F4 51 37N 3 57W
Swansea □, U.K. 11 F3 51 38N 4 3W
Swar →, Pakistan 43 B5 34 40N 72 5 E
Swartberge, S. Africa 56 E3 33 20S 22 0 E
Swartmodder, S. Africa 56 D3 28 1S 20 32 E
Swartnossob →, Namibia 56 C2 23 8S 18 42 E
Swartruggens, S. Africa 56 D4 25 39S 26 42 E
Swastika, Canada 70 C3 48 7N 80 6W
Swatow = Shantou, China 33 D6 23 18N 116 40 E
Swaziland ■, Africa 57 D5 26 30S 31 30 E
Sweden ■, Europe 9 G16 57 0N 15 0 E
Sweet Home, U.S.A. 82 D2 44 24N 122 44W
Sweetgrass, U.S.A. 82 B8 48 59N 111 58W
Sweetwater, Nev., U.S.A. 84 G7 38 27N 119 9W
Sweetwater, Tenn., U.S.A. 77 H3 35 36N 84 28W
Sweetwater, Tex., U.S.A. 81 J4 32 28N 100 25W
Sweetwater →, U.S.A. 82 E10 42 31N 107 2W
Swellendam, S. Africa 56 E3 34 1S 20 26 E
Świdnica, Poland 17 C9 50 50N 16 30 E
Świdnik, Poland 17 C12 51 13N 22 39 E
Świebodzin, Poland 16 B8 52 15N 15 31 E
Świecie, Poland 17 B10 53 25N 18 30 E
Swift Current, Canada 73 C7 50 20N 107 45W
Swiftcurrent →, Canada 73 C7 50 38N 107 44W
Swilly, L., Ireland 13 A4 55 12N 7 33W
Swindon, U.K. 11 F6 51 34N 1 46W
Swindon □, U.K. 11 F6 51 34N 1 46W
Swinemünde = Świnoujście, Poland 16 B8 53 54N 14 16 E
Swinford, Ireland 13 C3 53 57N 8 58W
Świnoujście, Poland 16 B8 53 54N 14 16 E
Switzerland ■, Europe 18 C8 46 30N 8 0 E
Swords, Ireland 13 C5 53 28N 6 13W
Swoyerville, U.S.A. 79 E9 41 18N 75 53W
Sydenham →, Canada 78 D2 42 33N 82 25W
Sydney, Australia 63 E5 33 53S 151 10 E
Sydney, Canada 71 C7 46 7N 60 7W
Sydney L., Canada 73 C10 50 41N 94 25W
Sydney Mines, Canada 71 C7 46 18N 60 15W
Sydprøven = Alluitsup Paa, Greenland 4 C5 60 30N 45 35W
Sydra, G. of = Surt, Khalīj, Libya 51 B9 31 40N 18 30 E
Sykesville, U.S.A. 78 E6 41 3N 78 50W
Syktyvkar, Russia 24 B9 61 45N 50 40 E
Sylacauga, U.S.A. 77 J2 33 10N 86 15W
Sylarna, Sweden 8 E15 63 2N 12 13 E
Sylhet, Bangla. 41 G17 24 54N 91 52 E
Sylhet □, Bangla. 41 G17 24 50N 91 50 E
Sylt, Germany 16 A5 54 54N 8 22 E
Sylvan Beach, U.S.A. 79 C9 43 12N 75 44W
Sylvan Lake, Canada 72 C6 52 20N 114 3W
Sylvania, U.S.A. 77 J5 32 45N 81 38W
Sylvester, U.S.A. 77 K4 31 32N 83 50W
Sym, Russia 26 C9 60 20N 88 18 E
Symón, Mexico 86 C4 24 42N 102 35W
Synnott Ra., Australia 60 C4 16 30S 125 20 E
Syracuse, Kans., U.S.A. 81 G4 37 59N 101 45W
Syracuse, N.Y., U.S.A. 79 C8 43 3N 76 9W
Syracuse, Nebr., U.S.A. 80 E6 40 39N 96 11W
Syrdarya →, Kazakstan 26 E7 46 3N 61 0 E
Syria ■, Asia 44 C3 35 0N 38 0 E
Syrian Desert = Shām, Bādiyat ash, Asia 44 C3 32 0N 40 0 E
Syzran, Russia 24 D8 53 12N 48 30 E
Szczecin, Poland 16 B8 53 27N 14 27 E
Szczecinek, Poland 17 B9 53 43N 16 41 E
Szczeciński, Zalew = Stettiner Haff, Germany 16 B8 53 47N 14 15 E
Szczytno, Poland 17 B11 53 33N 21 0 E
Szechwan = Sichuan □, China 32 C5 30 30N 103 0 E
Szeged, Hungary 17 E11 46 16N 20 10 E
Székesfehérvár, Hungary 17 E10 47 15N 18 25 E
Szekszárd, Hungary 17 E10 46 22N 18 42 E
Szentes, Hungary 17 E11 46 39N 20 21 E
Szolnok, Hungary 17 E11 47 10N 20 15 E
Szombathely, Hungary 17 E9 47 14N 16 38 E

T

Ta Khli Khok, Thailand 38 E3 15 18N 100 20 E
Ta Lai, Vietnam 39 G6 11 24N 107 23 E
Tabacal, Argentina 94 A3 23 15S 64 15W
Tabaco, Phil. 37 B6 13 22N 123 44 E
Ţābah, Si. Arabia 44 E4 26 55N 42 38 E
Ţabas, Khorāsān, Iran 45 C9 32 48N 60 12 E
Ţabas, Khorāsān, Iran 45 C8 33 35N 56 55 E
Tabasará, Serranía de, Panama 88 E3 8 35N 81 40W
Tabasco □, Mexico 87 D6 17 45N 93 30W
Tabāsīn, Iran 45 D8 31 12N 57 54 E
Tabatinga, Serra da, Brazil 93 F10 10 30S 44 0W
Taber, Canada 72 D6 49 47N 112 8W
Taberg, U.S.A. 79 C9 43 18N 75 37W
Tablas I., Phil. 37 B6 12 25N 122 2 E
Table B. = Tafelbaai, S. Africa 56 E2 33 35S 18 25 E
Table B., Canada 71 B8 53 40N 56 25W
Table Mt., S. Africa 56 E2 34 0S 18 22 E
Table Rock L., U.S.A. 81 G8 36 36N 93 19W
Tabletop, Mt., Australia 62 C4 23 24S 147 11 E
Tábor, Czech Rep. 16 D8 49 25N 14 39 E
Tabora, Tanzania 54 D3 5 2S 32 50 E
Tabora □, Tanzania 54 D3 5 0S 33 0 E
Tabou, Ivory C. 50 H4 4 30N 7 20W
Tabrīz, Iran 44 B5 38 7N 46 20 E
Tabuaeran, Kiribati 65 G12 3 51N 159 22W
Tabūk, Si. Arabia 44 D3 28 23N 36 36 E
Tacámbaro de Codallos, Mexico 86 D4 19 14N 101 28W
Tacheng, China 32 B3 46 40N 82 58 E
Tach'ing Shan = Daqing Shan, China 34 D6 40 40N 111 0 E
Tacloban, Phil. 37 B6 11 15N 124 58 E
Tacna, Peru 92 G4 18 0S 70 20W
Tacoma, U.S.A. 84 C4 47 14N 122 26W
Tacuarembó, Uruguay 95 C4 31 45S 56 0W
Tademaït, Plateau du, Algeria 50 C6 28 30N 2 30 E
Tadjoura, Djibouti 46 E3 11 50N 42 55 E
Tadmor, N.Z. 59 J4 41 27S 172 45 E
Tadoule, L., Canada 73 B9 58 36N 98 20W
Tadoussac, Canada 71 C6 48 11N 69 42W
Tadzhikistan = Tajikistan ■, Asia 26 F8 38 30N 70 0 E
Taechŏn-ni, S. Korea 35 F14 36 21N 126 36 E
Taegu, S. Korea 35 G15 35 50N 128 37 E
Taegwan, N. Korea 35 D13 40 13N 125 12 E
Taejŏn, S. Korea 35 F14 36 20N 127 28 E
Tafalla, Spain 19 A5 42 30N 1 41W
Tafelbaai, S. Africa 56 E2 33 35S 18 25 E
Tafermaar, Indonesia 37 F8 6 47S 134 10 E
Tafí Viejo, Argentina 94 B2 26 43S 65 17W
Tafihān, Iran 45 D7 29 25N 52 39 E
Tafresh, Iran 45 C6 34 45N 49 57 E
Taft, Iran 45 D7 31 45N 54 14 E
Taft, Phil. 37 B7 11 57N 125 30 E
Taft, U.S.A. 85 K7 35 8N 119 28W
Taftān, Kūh-e, Iran 45 D9 28 40N 61 0 E
Taga Dzong, Bhutan 41 F16 27 5N 89 55 E
Taganrog, Russia 25 E6 47 12N 38 50 E
Tagbilaran, Phil. 37 C6 9 39N 123 51 E
Tagish, Canada 72 A2 60 19N 134 16W
Tagish L., Canada 72 A2 60 10N 134 20W
Tagliamento →, Italy 20 B5 45 38N 13 6 E
Tagomago, Spain 22 B8 39 2N 1 39 E
Taguatinga, Brazil 93 F10 12 16S 42 26W
Tagum, Phil. 37 C7 7 33N 125 53 E
Tagus = Tejo →, Europe 19 C1 38 40N 9 24W
Tahakopa, N.Z. 59 M2 46 30S 169 23 E
Tahan, Gunong, Malaysia 39 K4 4 34N 102 17 E
Tahat, Algeria 50 D7 23 18N 5 33 E
Tāherī, Iran 45 E7 27 43N 52 20 E
Tahiti, Pac. Oc. 65 J13 17 37S 149 27W
Tahlequah, U.S.A. 81 H7 35 55N 94 58W
Tahoe, L., U.S.A. 84 G6 39 6N 120 2W
Tahoe City, U.S.A. 84 F6 39 10N 120 9W
Tahoka, U.S.A. 81 J4 33 10N 101 48W
Taholah, U.S.A. 84 C2 47 21N 124 17W
Tahoua, Niger 50 F7 14 57N 5 16 E
Tahrūd, Iran 45 D8 29 26N 57 49 E
Tahsis, Canada 72 D3 49 55N 126 40W
Tahta, Egypt 51 C12 26 44N 31 32 E
Tahulandang, Indonesia 37 D7 2 27N 125 23 E
Tahuna, Indonesia 37 D7 3 38N 125 30 E
Tai Shan, China 35 F9 36 25N 117 20 E
Tai'an, China 35 F9 36 12N 117 8 E
Taibei = T'aipei, Taiwan 33 D7 25 2N 121 30 E
Taibique, Canary Is. 22 G2 27 42N 17 58W
Taibus Qi, China 34 D8 41 54N 115 22 E
T'aichung, Taiwan 33 D7 24 9N 120 37 E
Taieri →, N.Z. 59 M3 46 3S 170 12 E
Taigu, China 34 F7 37 28N 112 30 E
Taihang Shan, China 34 G7 36 0N 113 30 E
Taihape, N.Z. 59 H5 39 41S 175 48 E
Taihe, China 34 H8 33 20N 115 42 E
Taikang, China 34 G8 34 5N 114 50 E
Tailem Bend, Australia 63 F2 35 12S 139 29 E
Taimyr Peninsula = Taymyr, Poluostrov, Russia 27 B11 75 0N 100 0 E
Tain, U.K. 12 D4 57 49N 4 4W
T'ainan, Taiwan 33 D7 23 0N 120 10 E
Taínaron, Ákra, Greece 21 F10 36 22N 22 27 E
T'aipei, Taiwan 33 D7 25 2N 121 30 E
Taiping, Malaysia 39 K3 4 51N 100 44 E
Taipingzhen, China 34 H6 33 35N 111 42 E
Tairbeart = Tarbert, U.K. 12 D2 57 54N 6 49W
Taita Hills, Kenya 54 C4 3 25S 38 15 E
Taitao, Pen. de, Chile 96 F2 46 30S 75 0W
T'aitung, Taiwan 33 D7 22 43N 121 4 E
Taivalkoski, Finland 8 D23 65 33N 28 12 E
Taiwan ■, Asia 33 D7 23 30N 121 0 E
Taïyetos Óros, Greece 21 F10 37 0N 22 23 E
Taiyiba, Israel 47 C4 32 36N 35 27 E
Taiyuan, China 34 F7 37 52N 112 33 E
Taizhong = T'aichung, Taiwan 33 D7 24 9N 120 37 E
Ta'izz, Yemen 46 E3 13 35N 44 2 E
Tājābād, Iran 45 D7 30 2N 54 24 E
Tajikistan ■, Asia 26 F8 38 30N 70 0 E
Tajima, Japan 31 F9 37 12N 139 46 E
Tajo = Tejo →, Europe 19 C1 38 40N 9 24W
Tajrīsh, Iran 45 C6 35 48N 51 25 E
Tak, Thailand 38 D2 16 52N 99 8 E
Takāb, Iran 44 B5 36 24N 47 7 E
Takachiho, Japan 31 H5 32 42N 131 18 E
Takachu, Botswana 56 C3 22 37S 21 58 E
Takada, Japan 31 F9 37 7N 138 15 E
Takahagi, Japan 31 F10 36 43N 140 45 E
Takaka, N.Z. 59 J4 40 51S 172 50 E
Takamatsu, Japan 31 G7 34 20N 134 5 E
Takaoka, Japan 31 F8 36 47N 137 0 E
Takapuna, N.Z. 59 G5 36 47S 174 47 E
Takasaki, Japan 31 F9 36 20N 139 0 E
Takatsuki, Japan 31 G7 34 51N 135 37 E
Takaungu, Kenya 54 C4 3 38S 39 52 E
Takayama, Japan 31 F8 36 18N 137 11 E
Take-Shima, Japan 31 J5 30 49N 130 26 E
Takefu, Japan 31 G8 35 50N 136 10 E
Takengon, Indonesia 36 D1 4 45N 96 50 E
Takeo, Japan 31 H5 33 12N 130 1 E
Tākestān, Iran 45 C6 36 0N 49 40 E
Taketa, Japan 31 H5 32 58N 131 24 E
Takev, Cambodia 39 G5 10 59N 104 47 E
Takh, India 43 C7 33 6N 77 32 E
Takht-Sulaiman, Pakistan 42 D3 31 40N 69 58 E
Takikawa, Japan 30 C10 43 33N 141 54 E
Takla L., Canada 72 B3 55 15N 125 45W
Takla Landing, Canada 72 B3 55 30N 125 50W
Takla Makan = Taklamakan Shamo, China 32 C3 38 0N 83 0 E
Taklamakan Shamo, China 32 C3 38 0N 83 0 E
Taku →, Canada 72 B2 58 30N 133 50W
Tal Halāl, Iran 45 D7 28 54N 55 1 E
Tala, Uruguay 95 C4 34 21S 55 46W
Talagang, Pakistan 42 C5 32 55N 72 25 E
Talagante, Chile 94 C1 33 40S 70 50W
Talamanca, Cordillera de, Cent. Amer. 88 E3 9 20N 83 20W
Talara, Peru 92 D2 4 38S 81 18W
Talas, Kyrgyzstan 26 E8 42 30N 72 13 E
Talâta, Egypt 47 E1 30 36N 32 20 E
Talaud, Kepulauan, Indonesia 37 D7 4 30N 126 50 E
Talaud Is. = Talaud, Kepulauan, Indonesia 37 D7 4 30N 126 50 E
Talavera de la Reina, Spain 19 C3 39 55N 4 46W
Talayan, Phil. 37 C6 6 52N 124 24 E
Talbandh, India 43 H12 22 3N 86 20 E
Talbot, C., Australia 60 B4 13 48S 126 43 E
Talbragar →, Australia 63 E4 32 12S 148 37 E
Talca, Chile 94 D1 35 28S 71 40W
Talcahuano, Chile 94 D1 36 40S 73 10W
Talcher, India 41 J14 21 0N 85 18 E
Taldy Kurgan = Taldyqorghan, Kazakstan 26 E8 45 10N 78 45 E
Taldyqorghan, Kazakstan 26 E8 45 10N 78 45 E
Tālesh, Iran 45 B6 37 58N 48 58 E
Tālesh, Kūhhā-ye, Iran 45 B6 37 42N 48 55 E
Tali Post, Sudan 51 G12 5 55N 30 44 E
Taliabu, Indonesia 37 E6 1 50S 125 0 E
Talibon, Phil. 37 B6 10 9N 124 20 E
Talibong, Ko, Thailand 39 J2 7 15N 99 23 E
Talihina, U.S.A. 81 H7 34 45N 95 3W
Taliwang, Indonesia 36 F5 8 50S 116 55 E
Tall 'Afar, Iraq 44 B4 36 22N 42 27 E
Tall Kalakh, Syria 47 A5 34 41N 36 15 E
Talladega, U.S.A. 77 J2 33 26N 86 6W
Tallahassee, U.S.A. 77 K3 30 27N 84 17W
Tallangatta, Australia 63 F4 36 15S 147 19 E
Tallering Pk., Australia 61 E2 28 6S 115 37 E
Talli, Pakistan 42 E3 29 32N 68 8 E
Tallinn, Estonia 9 G21 59 22N 24 48 E
Tallmadge, U.S.A. 78 E3 41 6N 81 27W
Tallulah, U.S.A. 81 J9 32 25N 91 11W
Taloyoak, Canada 68 B10 69 32N 93 32W
Talpa de Allende, Mexico 86 C4 20 23N 104 51W
Talsi, Latvia 9 H20 57 10N 22 30 E
Taltal, Chile 94 B1 25 23S 70 33W
Taltson →, Canada 72 A6 61 24N 112 46W
Talurqjuak = Taloyoak, Canada 68 B10 69 32N 93 32W
Talwood, Australia 63 D4 28 29S 149 29 E
Talyawalka Cr. →, Australia 63 E3 32 28S 142 22 E
Tam Chau, Vietnam 39 G5 10 48N 105 12 E
Tam Ky, Vietnam 38 E7 15 34N 108 29 E
Tam Quan, Vietnam 38 E7 14 35N 109 3 E
Tama, U.S.A. 80 E8 41 58N 92 35W
Tamale, Ghana 50 G5 9 22N 0 50W
Tamano, Japan 31 G6 34 29N 133 59 E
Tamanrasset, Algeria 50 D7 22 50N 5 30 E
Tamaqua, U.S.A. 79 F9 40 48N 75 58W
Tamar →, U.K. 11 G3 50 27N 4 15W
Tamarinda, Spain 22 B10 39 55N 3 49 E
Tamashima, Japan 31 G6 34 32N 133 40 E
Tamaulipas □, Mexico 87 C5 24 0N 99 0W
Tamaulipas, Sierra de, Mexico 87 C5 23 30N 98 20W
Tamazula, Mexico 86 C3 24 55N 106 58W
Tamazunchale, Mexico 87 C5 21 16N 98 47W
Tambacounda, Senegal 50 F3 13 45N 13 40W
Tambelan, Kepulauan, Indonesia 36 D3 1 0N 107 30 E
Tambellup, Australia 61 F2 34 4S 117 37 E
Tambo, Australia 62 C4 24 54S 146 14 E
Tambo de Mora, Peru 92 F3 13 30S 76 8W
Tambohorano, Madag. 57 B7 17 30S 43 58 E
Tambora, Indonesia 36 F5 8 12S 118 5 E
Tambov, Russia 24 D7 52 45N 41 28 E
Tambuku, Indonesia 37 G15 7 8S 113 40 E
Tâmega →, Portugal 19 B1 41 5N 8 21W
Tamenglong, India 41 G18 25 0N 93 35 E
Tamiahua, L. de, Mexico 87 C5 21 30N 97 30W
Tamil Nadu □, India 40 P10 11 0N 77 0 E
Tamluk, India 43 H12 22 18N 87 58 E
Tammerfors = Tampere, Finland 9 F20 61 30N 23 50 E
Tammisaari, Finland 9 F20 60 0N 23 26 E
Tamo Abu, Pegunungan, Malaysia 36 D5 3 10N 115 5 E
Tampa, U.S.A. 77 M4 27 57N 82 27W
Tampa B., U.S.A. 77 M4 27 50N 82 30W
Tampere, Finland 9 F20 61 30N 23 50 E
Tampico, Mexico 87 C5 22 20N 97 50W
Tampin, Malaysia 39 L4 2 28N 102 13 E
Tamu, Burma 41 G19 24 13N 94 12 E
Tamworth, Australia 63 E5 31 7S 150 58 E
Tamworth, Canada 78 B8 44 29N 77 0W
Tamworth, U.K. 11 E6 52 39N 1 41W
Tamyang, S. Korea 35 G14 35 19N 126 59 E
Tan An, Vietnam 39 G6 10 32N 106 25 E
Tan-Tan, Morocco 50 C3 28 29N 11 1W
Tana →, Kenya 54 C5 2 32S 40 31 E
Tana →, Norway 8 A23 70 30N 28 14 E
Tana, L., Ethiopia 46 E2 13 5N 37 30 E
Tana River, Kenya 54 C4 2 0S 39 30 E
Tanabe, Japan 31 H7 33 44N 135 22 E
Tanafjorden, Norway 8 A23 70 45N 28 25 E
Tanaga, Pta., Canary Is. 22 G1 27 42N 18 10W
Tanahbala, Indonesia 36 E1 0 30S 98 30 E
Tanahgrogot, Indonesia 36 E5 1 55S 116 15 E
Tanahjampea, Indonesia 37 F6 7 10S 120 35 E
Tanahmasa, Indonesia 36 E1 0 12S 98 39 E
Tanahmerah, Indonesia 37 F10 6 5S 140 16 E
Tanakpur, India 43 E9 29 5N 80 7 E
Tanakura, Japan 31 F10 37 10N 140 20 E
Tanami, Australia 60 C4 19 59S 129 43 E
Tanami Desert, Australia 60 C5 18 50S 132 0 E
Tanana →, U.S.A. 68 B4 65 10N 151 58W
Tananarive = Antananarivo, Madag. 57 B8 18 55S 47 31 E
Tánaro →, Italy 18 D8 44 55N 8 40 E
Tancheng, China 35 G10 34 25N 118 20 E
Tanch'ŏn, N. Korea 35 D15 40 27N 128 54 E
Tanda, Ut. P., India 43 F10 26 33N 82 35 E
Tanda, Ut. P., India 43 E8 28 57N 78 56 E
Tandag, Phil. 37 C7 9 4N 126 9 E
Tandaia, Tanzania 55 D3 9 25S 34 15 E
Tandaué, Angola 56 B2 16 58S 18 5 E
Tandil, Argentina 94 D4 37 15S 59 6W
Tandil, Sa. del, Argentina 94 D4 37 30S 59 0W
Tandlianwala, Pakistan 42 D5 31 3N 73 9 E
Tando Adam, Pakistan 42 G3 25 45N 68 40 E
Tando Allahyar, Pakistan 42 G3 25 28N 68 43 E
Tando Bago, Pakistan 42 G3 24 47N 68 58 E
Tando Mohommed Khan, Pakistan 42 G3 25 8N 68 32 E
Tandou L., Australia 63 E3 32 40S 142 5 E
Tandragee, U.K. 13 B5 54 21N 6 24W
Tane-ga-Shima, Japan 31 J5 30 30N 131 0 E
Taneatua, N.Z. 59 H6 38 4S 177 1 E
Tanen Tong Dan = Dawna Ra., Burma 38 D2 16 30N 98 30 E
Tanezrouft, Algeria 50 D6 23 9N 0 11 E
Tang, Koh, Cambodia 39 G4 10 16N 103 7 E
Tang, Ra's-e, Iran 45 E8 25 21N 59 52 E
Tang Krasang, Cambodia 38 F5 12 34N 105 3 E

168

Véroia

Véroia, Greece 21 D10 40 34N 22 12 E
Verona, Canada 79 B8 44 29N 76 42W
Verona, Italy 20 B4 45 27N 10 59 E
Verona, U.S.A. 80 D10 42 59N 89 32W
Versailles, France 18 B5 48 48N 2 8 E
Vert, C., Senegal 50 F2 14 45N 17 30W
Verulam, S. Africa 57 D5 29 38S 31 2 E
Verviers, Belgium 15 D5 50 37N 5 52 E
Veselovskoye Vdkhr., Russia 25 E7 46 58N 41 25 E
Vesoul, France 18 C7 47 40N 6 11 E
Vesterålen, Norway 8 B16 68 45N 15 0 E
Vestfjorden, Norway 8 C15 67 55N 14 0 E
Vestmannaeyjar, Iceland 8 E3 63 27N 20 15W
Vestspitsbergen, Svalbard 4 B8 78 40N 17 0 E
Vestvågøy, Norway 8 B15 68 18N 13 50 E
Vesuvio, Italy 20 D6 40 49N 14 26 E
Vesuvius, Mt. = Vesuvio, Italy 20 D6 40 49N 14 26 E
Veszprém, Hungary 17 E9 47 8N 17 57 E
Vetlanda, Sweden 9 H16 57 24N 15 3 E
Vetlugu →, Russia 24 C8 56 36N 46 4 E
Vettore, Mte., Italy 20 C5 42 49N 13 16 E
Veurne, Belgium 15 C2 51 5N 2 40 E
Veys, Iran 45 D6 31 30N 49 0 E
Vezhen, Bulgaria 21 C11 42 50N 24 20 E
Vi Thanh, Vietnam 39 H5 9 42N 105 26 E
Viacha, Bolivia 92 G5 16 39S 68 18W
Viamão, Brazil 95 C5 30 5S 51 0W
Viana, Brazil 93 D10 3 13S 44 55W
Viana do Alentejo, Portugal 19 C2 38 17N 7 59W
Viana do Castelo, Portugal 19 B1 41 42N 8 50W
Vianden, Lux. 15 E6 49 56N 6 12 E
Viangchan = Vientiane, Laos 38 D4 17 58N 102 36 E
Vianópolis, Brazil 93 G9 16 40S 48 35W
Viaréggio, Italy 20 C4 43 52N 10 14 E
Vibo Valéntia, Italy 20 E7 38 40N 16 6 E
Viborg, Denmark 9 H13 56 27N 9 23 E
Vic, Spain 19 B7 41 58N 2 19 E
Vicenza, Italy 20 B4 45 33N 11 33 E
Vich = Vic, Spain 19 B7 41 58N 2 19 E
Vichada →, Colombia 92 C5 4 55N 67 50W
Vichy, France 18 C5 46 9N 3 26 E
Vicksburg, Ariz., U.S.A. 85 M13 33 45N 113 45W
Vicksburg, Miss., U.S.A. 81 J9 32 21N 90 53W
Victor, India 42 J4 21 0N 71 30 E
Victor, U.S.A. 78 D7 42 58N 77 24W
Victor Harbor, Australia 63 F2 35 30S 138 37 E
Victoria = Labuan, Malaysia 36 C5 5 20N 115 14 E
Victoria, Argentina 94 C3 32 40S 60 10W
Victoria, Canada 72 D4 48 30N 123 25W
Victoria, Chile 96 D2 38 13S 72 20W
Victoria, Malta 23 C1 36 3N 14 14 E
Victoria, Kans., U.S.A. 80 F5 38 52N 99 9W
Victoria, Tex., U.S.A. 81 L6 28 48N 97 0W
Victoria □, Australia 63 F3 37 0S 144 0 E
Victoria →, Australia 60 C4 15 10S 129 40 E
Victoria, Grand L., Canada 70 C4 47 31N 77 30W
Victoria, L., Africa 54 C3 1 0S 33 0 E
Victoria, L., Australia 63 E3 33 57S 141 15 E
Victoria, Mt., Burma 41 J18 21 15N 93 55 E
Victoria Beach, Canada 73 C9 50 40N 96 35W
Victoria de Durango =
Durango, Mexico 86 C4 24 3N 104 39W
Victoria de las Tunas, Cuba 88 B4 20 58N 76 59W
Victoria Falls, Zimbabwe 55 F2 17 58S 25 52 E
Victoria Harbour, Canada 78 B5 44 45N 79 45W
Victoria I., Canada 68 A8 71 0N 111 0W
Victoria L., Canada 71 C8 48 20N 57 27W
Victoria Ld., Antarctica 5 D11 75 0S 160 0 E
Victoria Nile →, Uganda 54 B3 2 14N 31 26 E
Victoria River, Australia 60 C5 16 25S 131 0 E
Victoria Str., Canada 68 B9 69 30N 100 0W
Victoria West, S. Africa 56 E3 31 25S 23 4 E
Victoriaville, Canada 71 C5 46 4N 71 56W
Victorica, Argentina 94 D2 36 20S 65 30W
Victorville, U.S.A. 85 L9 34 32N 117 18W
Vicuña, Chile 94 C1 30 0S 70 50W
Vicuña Mackenna, Argentina 94 C3 33 53S 64 25W
Vidal, U.S.A. 85 L12 34 7N 114 31W
Vidal Junction, U.S.A. 85 L12 34 11N 114 34W
Vidalia, U.S.A. 77 J4 32 13N 82 25W
Vidho, Greece 23 A3 39 38N 19 55 E
Vidin, Bulgaria 21 C10 43 59N 22 50 E
Vidisha, India 42 H7 23 28N 77 53 E
Vidzy, Belarus 9 J22 55 23N 26 37 E
Viedma, Argentina 96 E4 40 50S 63 0W
Viedma, L., Argentina 96 F2 49 30S 72 30W
Vielsalm, Belgium 15 D5 50 17N 5 54 E
Vieng Pou Kha, Laos 38 B3 20 41N 101 4 E
Vienna = Wien, Austria 16 D9 48 12N 16 22 E
Vienna, Ill., U.S.A. 81 G10 37 25N 88 54W
Vienna, Mo., U.S.A. 80 F9 38 11N 91 57W
Vienne, France 18 D6 45 31N 4 53 E
Vienne →, France 18 C4 47 13N 0 5 E
Vientiane, Laos 38 D4 17 58N 102 36 E
Vientos, Paso de los,
Caribbean 89 C5 20 0N 74 0W
Vierzon, France 18 C5 47 13N 2 5 E
Vietnam ■, Asia 38 C6 19 0N 106 0 E
Vigan, Phil. 37 A6 17 35N 120 28 E
Vigévano, Italy 18 D8 45 19N 8 51 E
Vigia, Brazil 93 D9 0 50S 48 5W
Vigía Chico, Mexico 87 D7 19 46N 87 35W
Víglas, Ákra, Greece 23 D9 35 54N 27 51 E
Vigo, Spain 19 A1 42 12N 8 41W
Vihowa, Pakistan 42 D4 31 8N 70 30 E
Vihowa →, Pakistan 42 D4 31 8N 70 41 E
Vijayawada, India 41 L12 16 31N 80 39 E
Vijosë →, Albania 21 D8 40 37N 19 24 E
Vik, Iceland 8 E4 63 25N 19 1W
Vikeke = Viqueque, E. Timor 37 F7 8 52S 126 23 E
Viking, Canada 72 C6 53 7N 111 50W
Vikna, Norway 8 D14 64 55N 10 58 E
Vila da Maganja, Mozam. 55 F4 17 18S 37 30 E
Vila de João Belo = Xai-Xai,
Mozam. 57 D5 25 6S 33 31 E
Vila do Bispo, Portugal 19 D1 37 5N 8 53W
Vila Franca de Xira, Portugal 19 C1 38 57N 8 59W
Vila Gamito, Mozam. 55 E3 14 12S 33 0 E
Vila Gomes da Costa, Mozam. 57 C5 24 20S 33 37 E
Vila Machado, Mozam. 55 F3 19 15S 34 14 E
Vila Mouzinho, Mozam. 55 E3 14 48S 34 25 E
Vila Nova de Gaia, Portugal 19 B1 41 8N 8 37W
Vila Real, Portugal 19 B2 41 17N 7 48W
Vila-real de los Infantes,
Spain 19 C5 39 55N 0 3W
Vila Real de Santo António,
Portugal 19 D2 37 10N 7 28W
Vila Vasco da Gama, Mozam. 55 E3 14 54S 32 14 E
Vila Velha, Brazil 95 A7 20 20S 40 17W
Vilagarcía de Arousa, Spain 19 A1 42 34N 8 46W
Vilaine →, France 18 C2 47 30N 2 27W
Vilanandro, Tanjona, Madag. 57 B7 16 11S 44 27 E
Vilanculos, Mozam. 57 C6 22 1S 35 17 E
Vilanova i la Geltrú, Spain 19 B6 41 13N 1 40 E
Vileyka, Belarus 17 A14 54 30N 26 53 E
Vilhelmina, Sweden 8 D17 64 35N 16 39 E
Vilhena, Brazil 92 F6 12 40S 60 5W
Viliga, Russia 27 C16 61 36N 156 56 E
Viliya →, Lithuania 9 J21 55 8N 24 16 E
Viljandi, Estonia 9 G21 58 28N 25 30 E
Vilkitskogo, Proliv, Russia 27 B11 78 0N 103 0 E
Vilkovo = Vylkove, Ukraine 17 F15 45 28N 29 32 E
Villa Abecia, Bolivia 94 A2 21 0S 68 18W
Villa Ahumada, Mexico 86 A3 30 38N 106 30W
Villa Ana, Argentina 94 B4 28 28S 59 40W
Villa Ángela, Argentina 94 B3 27 34S 60 45W
Villa Bella, Bolivia 92 F5 10 25S 65 22W
Villa Bens = Tarfaya, Morocco 50 C3 27 55N 12 55W
Villa Cañás, Argentina 94 C3 34 0S 61 35W
Villa Cisneros = Dakhla,
W. Sahara 50 D2 23 50N 15 53W
Villa Colón, Argentina 94 C2 31 38S 68 20W
Villa Constitución, Argentina 94 C3 33 15S 60 20W
Villa de María, Argentina 94 B3 29 55S 63 43W
Villa Dolores, Argentina 94 C2 31 58S 65 15W
Villa Frontera, Mexico 86 B4 26 56N 101 27W
Villa Guillermina, Argentina 94 B4 28 15S 59 29W
Villa Hayes, Paraguay 94 B4 25 5S 57 20W
Villa Iris, Argentina 94 D3 38 12S 63 12W
Villa Juárez, Mexico 86 B4 27 37N 100 44W
Villa María, Argentina 94 C3 32 20S 63 10W
Villa Mazán, Argentina 94 B2 28 40S 66 30W
Villa Montes, Bolivia 94 A3 21 10S 63 30W
Villa Ocampo, Argentina 94 B4 28 30S 59 20W
Villa Ocampo, Mexico 86 B3 26 29N 105 30W
Villa Ojo de Agua, Argentina 94 B3 29 30S 63 44W
Villa San José, Argentina 94 C4 32 12S 58 15W
Villa San Martín, Argentina 94 B3 28 15S 64 9W
Villa Unión, Mexico 86 C3 23 12N 106 14W
Villacarlos, Spain 22 B11 39 53N 4 17 E
Villacarrillo, Spain 19 C4 38 7N 3 3W
Villach, Austria 16 E7 46 37N 13 51 E
Villafranca de los Caballeros,
Spain 22 B10 39 34N 3 25 E
Villagrán, Mexico 87 C5 24 29N 99 29W
Villaguay, Argentina 94 C4 32 0S 59 0W
Villahermosa, Mexico 87 D6 17 59N 92 55W
Villajoyosa, Spain 19 C5 38 30N 0 12W
Villalba, Spain 19 A2 43 26N 7 40W
Villanueva, U.S.A. 81 H2 35 16N 105 22W
Villanueva de la Serena,
Spain 19 C3 38 59N 5 50W
Villanueva y Geltrú = Vilanova
i la Geltrú, Spain 19 B6 41 13N 1 40 E
Villarreal = Vila-real de los
Infantes, Spain 19 C5 39 55N 0 3W
Villarrica, Chile 96 D2 39 15S 72 15W
Villarrica, Paraguay 94 B4 25 40S 56 30W
Villarrobledo, Spain 19 C4 39 18N 2 36W
Villavicencio, Argentina 94 C2 32 28S 69 0W
Villavicencio, Colombia 92 C4 4 9N 73 37W
Villaviciosa, Spain 19 A3 43 32N 5 27W
Villazón, Bolivia 94 A2 22 0S 65 35W
Ville-Marie, Canada 70 C4 47 20N 79 30W
Ville Platte, U.S.A. 81 K8 30 41N 92 17W
Villena, Spain 19 C5 38 39N 0 52W
Villeneuve-d'Ascq, France 18 A5 50 38N 3 9 E
Villeneuve-sur-Lot, France 18 D4 44 24N 0 42 E
Villiers, S. Africa 57 D4 27 2S 28 36 E
Villingen-Schwenningen,
Germany 16 D5 48 3N 8 26 E
Vilna, Canada 72 C6 54 7N 111 55W
Vilnius, Lithuania 9 J21 54 38N 25 19 E
Vilvoorde, Belgium 15 D4 50 56N 4 26 E
Vilyuy →, Russia 27 C13 64 24N 126 26 E
Vilyuysk, Russia 27 C13 63 40N 121 35 E
Viña del Mar, Chile 94 C1 33 0S 71 30W
Vinarós, Spain 19 B6 40 30N 0 27 E
Vincennes, U.S.A. 76 F2 38 41N 87 32W
Vincent, U.S.A. 85 L8 34 33N 118 11W
Vinchina, Argentina 94 B2 28 45S 68 15W
Vindelälven →, Sweden 8 E18 63 55N 19 50 E
Vindeln, Sweden 8 D18 64 12N 19 43 E
Vindhya Ra., India 42 H7 22 50N 77 0 E
Vineland, U.S.A. 76 F8 39 29N 75 2W
Vinh, Vietnam 38 C5 18 45N 105 38 E
Vinh Linh, Vietnam 38 D6 17 4N 107 2 E
Vinh Long, Vietnam 39 G5 10 16N 105 57 E
Vinh Yen, Vietnam 38 B5 21 21N 105 35 E
Vinita, U.S.A. 81 G7 36 39N 95 9W
Vinkovci, Croatia 21 B8 45 19N 18 48 E
Vinnitsa = Vinnytsya, Ukraine 17 D15 49 15N 28 30 E
Vinnytsya, Ukraine 17 D15 49 15N 28 30 E
Vinton, Calif., U.S.A. 84 F6 39 48N 120 10W
Vinton, Iowa, U.S.A. 80 D8 42 10N 92 1W
Vinton, La., U.S.A. 81 K8 30 11N 93 35W
Viqueque, E. Timor 37 F7 8 52S 126 23 E
Virac, Phil. 37 B6 13 30N 124 20 E
Virachei, Cambodia 38 F6 13 59N 106 49 E
Virago Sd., Canada 72 C2 54 0N 132 30W
Viramgam, India 42 H5 23 5N 72 0 E
Viranşehir, Turkey 44 B3 37 13N 39 45 E
Virawah, Pakistan 42 G4 24 31N 70 46 E
Virden, Canada 73 D8 49 50N 100 56W
Vire, France 18 B3 48 50N 0 53W
Virgenes, C., Argentina 96 G3 52 19S 68 21W
Virgin →, U.S.A. 83 H6 36 28N 114 21W
Virgin Gorda, Br. Virgin Is. 89 C7 18 30N 64 26W
Virgin Is. (British) ■, W. Indies 89 C7 18 30N 64 30W
Virgin Is. (U.S.) ■, W. Indies 89 C7 18 20N 65 0W
Virginia, S. Africa 56 D4 28 8S 26 55 E
Virginia, U.S.A. 80 B8 47 31N 92 32W
Virginia □, U.S.A. 76 G7 37 30N 78 45W
Virginia Beach, U.S.A. 76 G8 36 51N 75 59W
Virginia City, Mont., U.S.A. 82 D8 45 18N 111 56W
Virginia City, Nev., U.S.A. 84 F7 39 19N 119 39W
Virginia Falls, Canada 72 A3 61 38N 125 42W
Virginiatown, Canada 70 C4 48 9N 79 36W
Viroqua, U.S.A. 80 D9 43 34N 90 53W
Virovitica, Croatia 20 B7 45 51N 17 21 E
Virpur, India 42 J4 21 51N 70 42 E
Virton, Belgium 15 E5 49 35N 5 32 E
Virudunagar, India 40 Q10 9 30N 77 58 E
Vis, Croatia 20 C7 43 4N 16 10 E
Visalia, U.S.A. 84 J7 36 20N 119 18W
Visayan Sea, Phil. 37 B6 11 30N 123 30 E
Visby, Sweden 9 H18 57 37N 18 18 E
Viscount Melville Sd., Canada 4 B2 74 10N 108 0W
Visé, Belgium 15 D5 50 44N 5 41 E
Višegrad, Bos.-H. 21 C8 43 47N 19 17 E
Viseu, Brazil 93 D9 1 10S 46 5W
Viseu, Portugal 19 B2 40 40N 7 55W
Vishakhapatnam, India 41 L13 17 45N 83 20 E
Visnagar, India 42 H5 23 45N 72 32 E
Viso, Mte., Italy 18 D7 44 38N 7 5 E
Visokoi I., Antarctica 5 B1 56 43S 27 15W
Vista, U.S.A. 85 M9 33 12N 117 14W
Vistula = Wisła →, Poland 17 A10 54 22N 18 55 E
Vitebsk = Vitsyebsk, Belarus 24 C5 55 10N 30 15 E
Viterbo, Italy 20 C5 42 25N 12 6 E
Viti Levu, Fiji 59 C7 17 30S 177 30 E
Vitigudino, Spain 19 B2 41 1N 6 26W
Vitim, Russia 27 D12 59 28N 112 35 E
Vitim →, Russia 27 D12 59 26N 112 34 E
Vitória, Brazil 93 H10 20 20S 40 22W
Vitória da Conquista, Brazil 93 F10 14 51S 40 51W
Vitória de São Antão, Brazil 93 E11 8 10S 35 20W
Vitoria-Gasteiz, Spain 19 A4 42 50N 2 41W
Vitsyebsk, Belarus 24 C5 55 10N 30 15 E
Vittória, Italy 20 F6 36 57N 14 32 E
Vittório Véneto, Italy 20 B5 45 59N 12 18 E
Viveiro, Spain 19 A2 43 39N 7 38W
Vivian, U.S.A. 81 J8 32 53N 93 59W
Vizcaíno, Desierto de, Mexico 86 B2 27 40N 113 50W
Vizcaíno, Sierra, Mexico 86 B2 27 30N 114 0W
Vize, Turkey 21 D12 41 34N 27 45 E
Vizianagaram, India 41 K13 18 6N 83 30 E
Vlaardingen, Neths. 15 C4 51 55N 4 21 E
Vladikavkaz, Russia 25 F7 43 0N 44 35 E
Vladimir, Russia 24 C7 56 15N 40 30 E
Vladimir Volynskiy =
Volodymyr-Volynskyy,
Ukraine 17 C13 50 50N 24 18 E
Vladivostok, Russia 27 E14 43 10N 131 53 E
Vlieland, Neths. 15 A4 53 16N 4 55 E
Vlissingen, Neths. 15 C3 51 26N 3 34 E
Vlorë, Albania 21 D8 40 32N 19 28 E
Vltava →, Czech Rep. 16 D8 50 21N 14 30 E
Vo Dat, Vietnam 39 G6 11 9N 107 31 E
Voe, U.K. 12 A7 60 21N 1 16W
Vogelkop = Doberai, Jazirah,
Indonesia 37 E8 1 25S 133 0 E
Vogelsberg, Germany 16 C5 50 31N 9 12 E
Voghera, Italy 18 D8 44 59N 9 1 E
Vohibinany, Madag. 57 B8 18 49S 49 4 E
Vohilava, Madag. 57 C8 21 4S 48 0 E
Vohimarina = Iharana,
Madag. 57 A9 13 25S 50 0 E
Vohimena, Tanjon' i, Madag. 57 D8 25 36S 45 8 E
Vohipeno, Madag. 57 C8 22 22S 47 51 E
Voi, Kenya 54 C4 3 25S 38 32 E
Voiron, France 18 D6 45 22N 5 35 E
Voisey B., Canada 71 A7 56 15N 61 50W
Vojmsjön, Sweden 8 D17 64 55N 16 40 E
Vojvodina □, Serbia, Yug. 21 B9 45 20N 20 0 E
Volborg, U.S.A. 80 C2 45 51N 105 41W
Volcano Is. = Kazan-Rettō,
Pac. Oc. 64 E6 25 0N 141 0 E
Volda, Norway 9 E12 62 9N 6 5 E
Volga →, Russia 25 E8 46 0N 48 30 E
Volga Hts. = Privolzhskaya
Vozvyshennost, Russia 25 D8 51 0N 46 0 E
Volgodonsk, Russia 25 E7 47 33N 42 5 E
Volgograd, Russia 25 E7 48 40N 44 25 E
Volgogradskoye Vdkhr.,
Russia 25 D8 50 0N 45 20 E
Volkhov →, Russia 24 B5 60 8N 32 20 E
Volkovysk = Vawkavysk,
Belarus 17 B13 53 9N 24 30 E
Volksrust, S. Africa 57 D4 27 24S 29 53 E
Volochanka, Russia 27 B10 71 0N 94 28 E
Volodymyr-Volynskyy,
Ukraine 17 C13 50 50N 24 18 E
Vologda, Russia 24 C6 59 10N 39 45 E
Vólos, Greece 21 E10 39 24N 22 59 E
Volovets, Ukraine 17 D12 48 43N 23 11 E
Volozhin = Valozhyn, Belarus 17 A14 54 3N 26 30 E
Volsk, Russia 24 D8 52 5N 47 22 E
Volta →, Ghana 48 F4 5 46N 0 41 E
Volta, L., Ghana 50 G6 7 30N 0 0W
Volta Redonda, Brazil 95 A7 22 31S 44 5W
Voltaire, C., Australia 60 B4 14 16S 125 35 E
Volterra, Italy 20 C4 43 24N 10 51 E
Volturno →, Italy 20 D5 41 1N 13 55 E
Volzhskiy, Russia 25 E7 48 56N 44 46 E
Vondrozo, Madag. 57 C8 22 49S 47 20 E
Vopnafjörður, Iceland 8 D6 65 45N 14 50W
Vóriai Sporádhes, Greece 21 E10 39 15N 23 30 E
Vorkuta, Russia 24 A11 67 48N 64 20 E
Vormsi, Estonia 9 G20 59 1N 23 13 E
Voronezh, Russia 25 D6 51 40N 39 10 E
Voroshilovgrad = Luhansk,
Ukraine 25 E6 48 38N 39 15 E
Voroshilovsk = Alchevsk,
Ukraine 25 E6 48 30N 38 45 E
Võrts Järv, Estonia 9 G22 58 16N 26 3 E
Võru, Estonia 9 H22 57 48N 26 54 E
Vosges, France 18 B7 48 20N 7 10 E
Voss, Norway 9 F12 60 38N 6 26 E
Vostok I., Kiribati 65 J12 10 5S 152 23W
Votkinsk, Russia 24 C9 57 0N 53 55 E
Votkinskoye Vdkhr., Russia 24 C10 57 22N 55 12 E
Votsuri-Shima, Japan 31 M1 25 45N 123 29 E
Vouga →, Portugal 19 B1 40 41N 8 40W
Voúxa, Ákra, Greece 23 D5 35 37N 23 32 E
Vozhe, Ozero, Russia 24 B6 60 45N 39 0 E
Voznesensk, Ukraine 25 E5 47 35N 31 21 E
Voznesenye, Russia 24 B6 61 0N 35 28 E
Vrangelya, Ostrov, Russia 27 B19 71 0N 180 0 E
Vranje, Serbia, Yug. 21 C9 42 34N 21 54 E
Vratsa, Bulgaria 21 C10 43 15N 23 30 E
Vrbas →, Bos.-H. 20 B7 45 8N 17 29 E
Vrede, S. Africa 57 D4 27 24S 29 6 E
Vredefort, S. Africa 56 D4 27 0S 27 22 E
Vredenburg, S. Africa 56 E2 32 56S 18 0 E
Vredendal, S. Africa 56 E2 31 41S 18 35 E
Vrindavan, India 42 F7 27 37N 77 40 E
Vrises, Greece 23 D6 35 23N 24 13 E
Vršac, Serbia, Yug. 21 B9 45 8N 21 20 E
Vryburg, S. Africa 56 D3 26 55S 24 45 E
Vryheid, S. Africa 57 D5 27 45S 30 47 E
Vu Liet, Vietnam 38 C5 18 43N 105 23 E
Vukovar, Croatia 21 B8 45 21N 18 59 E
Vulcan, Canada 72 C6 50 25N 113 15W
Vulcan, Romania 17 F12 45 23N 23 17 E
Vulcaneşti, Moldova 17 F15 45 41N 28 18 E
Vulcano, Italy 20 E6 38 24N 14 58 E
Vulkaneshty = Vulcaneşti,
Moldova 17 F15 45 41N 28 18 E
Vunduzi →, Mozam. 55 F3 18 56S 34 1 E
Vung Tau, Vietnam 39 G6 10 21N 107 4 E
Vyatka = Kirov, Russia 24 C8 58 35N 49 40 E
Vyatka →, Russia 24 C9 55 37N 51 28 E
Vyatskiye Polyany, Russia 24 C9 56 14N 51 5 E
Vyazemskiy, Russia 27 E14 47 32N 134 45 E
Vyazma, Russia 24 C5 55 10N 34 15 E
Vyborg, Russia 24 B4 60 43N 28 47 E
Vychegda →, Russia 24 B8 61 18N 46 36 E
Vychodné Beskydy, Europe 17 D11 49 20N 22 0 E
Vyg-ozero, Russia 24 B5 63 47N 34 29 E
Vylkove, Ukraine 17 F15 45 28N 29 32 E
Vynohradiv, Ukraine 17 D12 48 9N 23 2 E
Vyrnwy, L., U.K. 10 E4 52 48N 3 31W
Vyshniy Volochek, Russia 24 C5 57 30N 34 30 E
Vyshzha = imeni 26
Bakinskikh Komissarov,
Turkmenistan 45 B7 39 22N 54 10 E
Vyškov, Czech Rep. 17 D9 49 17N 17 0 E
Vytegra, Russia 24 B6 61 0N 36 27 E

W

W.A.C. Bennett Dam, Canada 72 B4 56 2N 122 6W
Waal →, Neths. 15 C5 51 37N 5 0 E
Waalwijk, Neths. 15 C5 51 42N 5 4 E
Wabana, Canada 71 C9 47 40N 53 0W
Wabasca →, Canada 72 B5 58 22N 115 20W
Wabasca-Desmarais, Canada 72 B6 55 57N 113 56W
Wabash, U.S.A. 76 E3 40 48N 85 49W
Wabash →, U.S.A. 76 G1 37 48N 88 2W
Wabigoon L., Canada 73 D10 49 44N 92 44W
Wabowden, Canada 73 C9 54 55N 98 38W
Wabuk Pt., Canada 70 A2 55 20N 85 5W
Wabush, Canada 71 B6 52 55N 66 52W
Waco, U.S.A. 81 K6 31 33N 97 9W
Waconichi, L., Canada 70 B5 50 8N 74 0W
Wad Hamid, Sudan 51 E12 16 30N 32 45 E
Wad Medanî, Sudan 51 F12 14 28N 33 30 E
Wad Thana, Pakistan 42 F2 27 22N 66 23 E
Wadai, Africa 48 E5 12 0N 19 0 E
Wadayama, Japan 31 G7 35 19N 134 52 E
Waddeneilanden, Neths. 15 A5 53 20N 5 10 E
Waddenzee, Neths. 15 A5 53 6N 5 10 E
Waddington, U.S.A. 79 B9 44 52N 75 12W
Waddington, Mt., Canada 72 C3 51 23N 125 15W
Waddy Pt., Australia 63 C5 24 58S 153 21 E
Wadebridge, U.K. 11 G3 50 31N 4 51W
Wadena, Canada 73 C8 51 57N 103 47W
Wadena, U.S.A. 80 B7 46 26N 95 8W
Wadeye, Australia 60 B4 14 28S 129 52 E
Wadhams, Canada 72 C3 51 30N 127 30W
Wādī as Sīr, Jordan 47 D4 31 56N 35 49 E
Wadi Halfa, Sudan 51 D12 21 53N 31 19 E
Wadsworth, Nev., U.S.A. 82 G4 39 38N 119 17W
Wadsworth, Ohio, U.S.A. 78 E3 41 2N 81 44W
Waegwan, S. Korea 35 G15 35 59N 128 23 E
Wafangdian, China 35 E11 39 38N 121 58 E
Wafrah, Si. Arabia 44 D5 28 33N 47 56 E
Wageningen, Neths. 15 C5 51 58N 5 40 E
Wager B., Canada 69 B11 65 26N 88 40W
Wagga Wagga, Australia 63 F4 35 7S 147 24 E
Waghete, Indonesia 37 E9 4 10S 135 50 E
Wagin, Australia 61 F2 33 17S 117 25 E
Wagner, U.S.A. 80 D5 43 5N 98 18W
Wagon Mound, U.S.A. 81 G2 36 1N 104 42W
Wagoner, U.S.A. 81 H7 35 58N 95 22W
Wah, Pakistan 42 C5 33 45N 72 40 E
Wahai, Indonesia 37 E7 2 48S 129 35 E
Wahiawa, U.S.A. 74 H15 21 30N 158 2W
Wâḥid, Egypt 47 E1 30 48N 32 21 E
Wahnai, Afghan. 42 C1 32 40N 65 50 E
Wahoo, U.S.A. 80 E6 41 13N 96 37W
Wahpeton, U.S.A. 80 B6 46 16N 96 36W
Waiau →, N.Z. 59 K4 42 47S 173 22 E
Waibeem, Indonesia 37 E8 0 30S 132 59 E
Waigeo, Indonesia 37 E8 0 20S 130 40 E
Waihi, N.Z. 59 G5 37 23S 175 52 E
Waihou →, N.Z. 59 G5 37 15S 175 40 E
Waika, Dem. Rep. of
the Congo 54 C2 2 22S 25 42 E
Waikabubak, Indonesia 37 F5 9 45S 119 25 E
Waikari, N.Z. 59 K4 42 58S 172 41 E
Waikato →, N.Z. 59 G5 37 23S 174 43 E
Waikerie, Australia 63 E3 34 9S 140 0 E
Waikokopu, N.Z. 59 H6 39 3S 177 52 E
Waikouaiti, N.Z. 59 L3 45 36S 170 41 E
Wailuku, U.S.A. 74 H16 20 53N 156 30W
Waimakariri →, N.Z. 59 K4 43 24S 172 42 E
Waimate, N.Z. 59 L3 44 45S 171 3 E
Wainganga →, India 40 K11 18 50N 79 55 E
Waingapu, Indonesia 37 F6 9 35S 120 11 E
Waini →, Guyana 92 B7 8 20N 59 50W
Wainwright, Canada 73 C6 52 50N 110 50W
Waiouru, N.Z. 59 H5 39 28S 175 41 E
Waipara, N.Z. 59 K4 43 3S 172 46 E
Waipawa, N.Z. 59 H6 39 56S 176 38 E
Waipiro, N.Z. 59 H7 38 2S 178 22 E
Waipu, N.Z. 59 F5 35 59S 174 29 E
Waipukurau, N.Z. 59 J6 40 1S 176 33 E
Wairakei, N.Z. 59 H6 38 37S 176 6 E
Wairarapa, L., N.Z. 59 J5 41 14S 175 15 E
Wairoa, N.Z. 59 H6 39 3S 177 25 E
Waitaki →, N.Z. 59 L3 44 56S 171 7 E
Waitara, N.Z. 59 H5 38 59S 174 15 E
Waitsburg, U.S.A. 82 C5 46 16N 118 9W
Waiuku, N.Z. 59 G5 37 15S 174 45 E
Wajima, Japan 31 F8 37 30N 137 0 E

West Helena

Wajir, Kenya 54 B5 1 42N 40 5 E
Wakasa, Japan 31 G7 35 20N 134 24 E
Wakasa-Wan, Japan 31 G7 35 40N 135 30 E
Wakatipu, L., N.Z. 59 L2 45 5S 168 33 E
Wakaw, Canada 73 C7 52 39N 105 44W
Wakayama, Japan 31 G7 34 15N 135 15 E
Wakayama □, Japan 31 H7 33 50N 135 30 E
Wake Forest, U.S.A. 77 H6 35 59N 78 30W
Wake I., Pac. Oc. 64 F8 19 18N 166 36 E
WaKeeney, U.S.A. 80 F5 39 1N 99 53W
Wakefield, N.Z. 59 J4 41 24S 173 5 E
Wakefield, U.K. 10 D6 53 41N 1 29W
Wakefield, Mass., U.S.A. 79 D13 42 30N 71 4W
Wakefield, Mich., U.S.A. 80 B10 46 29N 89 56W
Wakkanai, Japan 30 B10 45 28N 141 35 E
Wakkerstroom, S. Africa 57 D5 27 24S 30 10 E
Wakool, Australia 63 F3 35 28S 144 23 E
Wakool →, Australia 63 F3 35 5S 143 33 E
Wakre, Indonesia 37 E8 0 19S 131 5 E
Wakuach, L., Canada 71 A6 55 34N 67 32W
Walamba, Zambia 55 E2 13 30S 28 42 E
Wałbrzych, Poland 16 C9 50 45N 16 18 E
Walbury Hill, U.K. 11 F6 51 21N 1 28W
Walcha, Australia 63 E5 30 55S 151 31 E
Walcheren, Neths. 15 C3 51 30N 3 35 E
Walcott, U.S.A. 82 F10 41 46N 106 51W
Wałcz, Poland 16 B9 53 17N 16 27 E
Waldburg Ra., Australia 61 D2 24 40S 117 35 E
Walden, Colo., U.S.A. 82 F10 40 44N 106 17W
Walden, N.Y., U.S.A. 79 E10 41 34N 74 11W
Waldport, U.S.A. 82 D1 44 26N 124 4W
Waldron, U.S.A. 81 H7 34 54N 94 5W
Walebing, Australia 61 F2 30 41S 116 13 E
Wales □, U.K. 11 E3 52 19N 4 43W
Walgett, Australia 63 E4 30 0S 148 5 E
Walgreen Coast, Antarctica 5 D15 75 15S 105 0W
Walker, U.S.A. 80 B7 47 6N 94 35W
Walker, L., Canada 71 B6 50 20N 67 11W
Walker L., Canada 73 C9 54 42N 95 57W
Walker L., U.S.A. 82 G4 38 42N 118 43W
Walkerston, Australia 62 C4 21 11S 149 8 E
Walkerton, Canada 78 B3 44 10N 81 10W
Wall, U.S.A. 80 D3 44 0N 102 8W
Walla Walla, U.S.A. 82 C4 46 4N 118 20W
Wallace, Idaho, U.S.A. 82 C6 47 28N 115 56W
Wallace, N.C., U.S.A. 77 H7 34 44N 77 59W
Wallaceburg, Canada 78 D2 42 34N 82 23W
Wallachia = Valahia, Romania 17 F13 44 35N 25 0 E
Wallal, Australia 63 D4 26 32S 146 7 E
Wallam Cr. →, Australia 63 D4 28 40S 147 20 E
Wallambin, L., Australia 61 F2 30 57S 117 35 E
Wallangarra, Australia 63 D5 28 56S 151 58 E
Wallaroo, Australia 63 E2 33 56S 137 39 E
Wallenpaupack, L., U.S.A. 79 E9 41 25N 75 15W
Wallingford, U.S.A. 79 E12 41 27N 72 50W
Wallis & Futuna, Is., Pac. Oc. 64 J10 13 18S 176 10W
Wallowa, U.S.A. 82 D5 45 34N 117 32W
Wallowa Mts., U.S.A. 82 D5 45 20N 117 30W
Walls, U.K. 12 A7 60 14N 1 33W
Wallula, U.S.A. 82 C4 46 5N 118 54W
Wallumbilla, Australia 63 D4 26 33S 149 9 E
Walmsley, L., Canada 73 A7 63 25N 108 36W
Walney, I. of, U.K. 10 C4 54 6N 3 15W
Walnut Creek, U.S.A. 84 H4 37 54N 122 4W
Walnut Ridge, U.S.A. 81 G9 36 4N 90 57W
Walpole, Australia 61 F2 34 58S 116 44 E
Walpole, U.S.A. 79 D13 42 9N 71 15W
Walsall, U.K. 11 E6 52 35N 1 58W
Walsenburg, U.S.A. 81 G2 37 38N 104 47W
Walsh, U.S.A. 81 G3 37 23N 102 17W
Walsh →, Australia 62 B3 16 31S 143 42 E
Walterboro, U.S.A. 77 J5 32 55N 80 40W
Walters, U.S.A. 81 H5 34 22N 98 19W
Waltham, U.S.A. 79 D13 42 23N 71 14W
Waltman, U.S.A. 82 E10 43 4N 107 12W
Walton, U.S.A. 79 D9 42 10N 75 8W
Walton-on-the-Naze, U.K. 11 F9 51 51N 1 17 E
Walvis Bay, Namibia 56 C1 23 0S 14 28 E
Walvisbaai = Walvis Bay, Namibia 56 C1 23 0S 14 28 E
Wamba, Dem. Rep. of the Congo 54 B2 2 10N 27 57 E
Wamba, Kenya 54 B4 0 58N 37 19 E
Wamego, U.S.A. 80 F6 39 12N 96 18W
Wamena, Indonesia 37 E9 4 4S 138 57 E
Wamsutter, U.S.A. 82 F9 41 40N 107 58W
Wamulan, Indonesia 37 E7 3 27S 126 7 E
Wan Xian, China 34 E8 38 47N 115 7 E
Wana, Pakistan 42 C3 32 20N 69 32 E
Wanaaring, Australia 63 D3 29 38S 144 9 E
Wanaka, N.Z. 59 L2 44 42S 169 9 E
Wanaka, L., N.Z. 59 L2 44 33S 169 7 E
Wanapitei L., Canada 70 C3 46 45N 80 40W
Wandel Sea = McKinley Sea, Arctic 4 A7 82 0N 0 0W
Wanderer, Zimbabwe 55 F3 19 36S 30 1 E
Wandhari, Pakistan 42 F2 27 42N 66 48 E
Wandoan, Australia 63 D4 26 5S 149 55 E
Wanfu, China 35 D12 40 8N 122 38 E
Wang →, Thailand 38 D2 17 8N 99 2 E
Wang Noi, Thailand 38 E3 14 13N 100 44 E
Wang Saphung, Thailand 38 D3 17 18N 101 46 E
Wang Thong, Thailand 38 D3 16 50N 100 26 E
Wanga, Dem. Rep. of the Congo 54 B2 2 58N 29 12 E
Wangal, Indonesia 37 F8 6 8S 134 9 E
Wanganella, Australia 63 F3 35 6S 144 49 E
Wanganui, N.Z. 59 H5 39 56S 175 3 E
Wangaratta, Australia 63 F4 36 21S 146 19 E
Wangary, Australia 63 E2 34 35S 135 29 E
Wangdu, China 34 E8 38 40N 115 7 E
Wangerooge, Germany 16 B4 53 47N 7 54 E
Wangi, Kenya 54 C5 1 58S 40 58 E
Wangiwangi, Indonesia 37 F6 5 22S 123 37 E
Wangqing, China 35 C15 43 12N 129 42 E
Wankaner, India 42 H4 22 35N 71 0 E
Wanless, Canada 73 C8 54 11N 101 21W
Wanning, China 38 C8 18 48N 110 22 E
Wanon Niwat, Thailand 38 D4 17 38N 103 46 E
Wanquan, China 34 D8 40 50N 114 40 E
Wanrong, China 34 G6 35 25N 110 50 E
Wantage, U.K. 11 F6 51 35N 1 25W
Wapakoneta, U.S.A. 76 E3 40 34N 84 12W
Wapato, U.S.A. 82 C3 46 27N 120 25W
Wapawekka L., Canada 73 C8 54 55N 104 40W
Wapikopa L., Canada 70 B2 52 56N 87 53W
Wapiti →, Canada 72 B5 55 5N 118 18W
Wappingers Falls, U.S.A. 79 E11 41 36N 73 55W
Wapsipinicon →, U.S.A. 80 E9 41 44N 90 19W
Warangal, India 40 L11 17 58N 79 35 E
Waraseoni, India 43 J9 21 45N 80 2 E
Waratah, Australia 62 G4 41 30S 145 30 E
Waratah B., Australia 63 F4 38 54S 146 5 E
Warburton, Vic., Australia 63 F4 37 47S 145 42 E
Warburton, W. Austral., Australia 61 E4 26 8S 126 35 E
Warburton Ra., Australia 61 E4 25 55S 126 28 E
Ward, N.Z. 59 J5 41 49S 174 11 E
Ward →, Australia 63 D4 26 28S 146 6 E
Ward Mt., U.S.A. 84 H8 37 12N 118 54W
Warden, S. Africa 57 D4 27 50S 29 0 E
Wardha, India 40 J11 20 45N 78 39 E
Wardha →, India 40 K11 19 57N 79 11 E
Ware, Canada 72 B3 57 26N 125 41W
Ware, U.S.A. 79 D12 42 16N 72 14W
Waregem, Belgium 15 D3 50 53N 3 27 E
Wareham, U.S.A. 79 E14 41 46N 70 43W
Waremme, Belgium 15 D5 50 43N 5 15 E
Warialda, Australia 63 D5 29 29S 150 33 E
Wariap, Indonesia 37 E8 1 30S 134 5 E
Warin Chamrap, Thailand 38 E5 15 12N 104 53 E
Warkopi, Indonesia 37 E8 1 12S 134 9 E
Warm Springs, U.S.A. 83 G5 38 10N 116 20W
Warman, Canada 73 C7 52 19N 106 30W
Warmbad, Namibia 56 D2 28 25S 18 42 E
Warmbad, S. Africa 57 C4 24 51S 28 19 E
Warminster, U.K. 11 F5 51 12N 2 10W
Warminster, U.S.A. 79 F9 40 12N 75 6W
Warner Mts., U.S.A. 82 F3 41 40N 120 15W
Warner Robins, U.S.A. 77 J4 32 37N 83 36W
Waroona, Australia 61 F2 32 50S 115 58 E
Warracknabeal, Australia 63 F3 36 9S 142 26 E
Warragul, Australia 63 F4 38 10S 145 58 E
Warrego →, Australia 63 E4 30 24S 145 21 E
Warrego Ra., Australia 62 C4 24 58S 146 0 E
Warren, Australia 63 E4 31 42S 147 51 E
Warren, Ark., U.S.A. 81 J8 33 37N 92 4W
Warren, Mich., U.S.A. 76 D4 42 30N 83 0W
Warren, Minn., U.S.A. 80 A6 48 12N 96 46W
Warren, Ohio, U.S.A. 78 E4 41 14N 80 49W
Warren, Pa., U.S.A. 78 E5 41 51N 79 9W
Warrenpoint, U.K. 13 B5 54 6N 6 15W
Warrensburg, Mo., U.S.A. 80 F8 38 46N 93 44W
Warrensburg, N.Y., U.S.A. 79 C11 43 29N 73 46W
Warrenton, S. Africa 56 D3 28 9S 24 47 E
Warrenton, U.S.A. 84 D3 46 10N 123 56W
Warri, Nigeria 50 G7 5 30N 5 41 E
Warrina, Australia 63 D2 28 12S 135 50 E
Warrington, U.K. 10 D5 53 24N 2 35W
Warrington, U.S.A. 77 K2 30 23N 87 17W
Warrington □, U.K. 10 D5 53 24N 2 35W
Warrnambool, Australia 63 F3 38 25S 142 30 E
Warroad, U.S.A. 80 A7 48 54N 95 19W
Warruwi, Australia 62 A1 11 36S 133 20 E
Warsa, Indonesia 37 E9 0 47S 135 55 E
Warsak Dam, Pakistan 42 B4 34 11N 71 19 E
Warsaw = Warszawa, Poland 17 B11 52 13N 21 0 E
Warsaw, Ind., U.S.A. 76 E3 41 14N 85 51W
Warsaw, N.Y., U.S.A. 78 D6 42 45N 78 8W
Warsaw, Ohio, U.S.A. 78 F3 40 20N 82 0W
Warszawa, Poland 17 B11 52 13N 21 0 E
Warta →, Poland 16 B8 52 35N 14 39 E
Warthe = Warta →, Poland 16 B8 52 35N 14 39 E
Waru, Indonesia 37 E8 3 30S 130 36 E
Warwick, Australia 63 D5 28 10S 152 1 E
Warwick, U.K. 11 E6 52 18N 1 35W
Warwick, N.Y., U.S.A. 79 E10 41 16N 74 22W
Warwick, R.I., U.S.A. 79 E13 41 42N 71 28W
Warwickshire □, U.K. 11 E6 52 14N 1 38W
Wasaga Beach, Canada 78 B4 44 31N 80 1W
Wasagaming, Canada 73 C9 50 39N 99 58W
Wasatch Ra., U.S.A. 82 F8 40 30N 111 15W
Wasbank, S. Africa 57 D5 28 15S 30 9 E
Wasco, Calif., U.S.A. 85 K7 35 36N 119 20W
Wasco, Oreg., U.S.A. 82 D3 45 36N 120 42W
Waseca, U.S.A. 80 C8 44 5N 93 30W
Wasekamio L., Canada 73 B7 56 45N 108 45W
Wash, The, U.K. 10 E8 52 58N 0 20 E
Washago, Canada 78 B5 44 45N 79 20W
Washburn, N. Dak., U.S.A. 80 B4 47 17N 101 2W
Washburn, Wis., U.S.A. 80 B9 46 40N 90 54W
Washim, India 40 J10 20 3N 77 0 E
Washington, U.K. 10 C6 54 55N 1 30W
Washington, D.C., U.S.A. 76 F7 38 54N 77 2W
Washington, Ga., U.S.A. 77 J4 33 44N 82 44W
Washington, Ind., U.S.A. 76 F2 38 40N 87 10W
Washington, Iowa, U.S.A. 80 E9 41 18N 91 42W
Washington, Mo., U.S.A. 80 F9 38 33N 91 1W
Washington, N.C., U.S.A. 77 H7 35 33N 77 3W
Washington, N.J., U.S.A. 79 F10 40 46N 74 59W
Washington, Pa., U.S.A. 78 F4 40 10N 80 15W
Washington, Utah, U.S.A. 83 H7 37 8N 113 31W
Washington □, U.S.A. 82 C3 47 30N 120 30W
Washington, Mt., U.S.A. 79 B13 44 16N 71 18W
Washington Court House, U.S.A. 76 F4 39 32N 83 26W
Washington I., U.S.A. 76 C2 45 23N 86 54W
Washougal, U.S.A. 84 E4 45 35N 122 21W
Wasian, Indonesia 37 E8 1 47S 133 19 E
Wasilla, U.S.A. 68 B5 61 35N 149 26W
Wasior, Indonesia 37 E8 2 43S 134 30 E
Waskaganish, Canada 70 B4 51 30N 78 40W
Waskaiowaka, L., Canada 73 B9 56 33N 96 23W
Waskesiu Lake, Canada 73 C7 53 55N 106 5W
Wasserkuppe, Germany 16 C5 50 29N 9 55 E
Waswanipi, Canada 70 C4 49 40N 76 29W
Waswanipi, L., Canada 70 C4 49 35N 76 40W
Watampone, Indonesia 37 E6 4 29S 120 25 E
Water Park Pt., Australia 62 C5 22 56S 150 47 E
Water Valley, U.S.A. 81 H10 34 10N 89 38W
Waterberge, S. Africa 57 C4 24 10S 28 0 E
Waterbury, Conn., U.S.A. 79 E11 41 33N 73 3W
Waterbury, Vt., U.S.A. 79 B12 44 20N 72 46W
Waterbury L., Canada 73 B8 58 10N 104 22W
Waterdown, Canada 78 C5 43 20N 79 53W
Waterford, Canada 78 D4 42 56N 80 17W
Waterford, Ireland 13 D4 52 15N 7 8W
Waterford, Calif., U.S.A. 84 H6 37 38N 120 46W
Waterford, Pa., U.S.A. 78 E5 41 57N 79 59W
Waterford □, Ireland 13 D4 52 10N 7 40W
Waterford Harbour, Ireland 13 D5 52 8N 6 58W
Waterhen L., Canada 73 C9 52 10N 99 40W
Waterloo, Belgium 15 D4 50 43N 4 25 E
Waterloo, Ont., Canada 78 C4 43 30N 80 32W
Waterloo, Qué., Canada 79 A12 45 22N 72 32W
Waterloo, Ill., U.S.A. 80 F9 38 20N 90 9W
Waterloo, Iowa, U.S.A. 80 D8 42 30N 92 21W
Waterloo, N.Y., U.S.A. 78 D8 42 54N 76 52W
Watersmeet, U.S.A. 80 B10 46 16N 89 11W
Waterton Lakes Nat. Park, U.S.A. 82 B7 48 45N 115 0W
Watertown, Conn., U.S.A. 79 E11 41 36N 73 7W
Watertown, N.Y., U.S.A. 79 C9 43 59N 75 55W
Watertown, S. Dak., U.S.A. 80 C6 44 54N 97 7W
Watertown, Wis., U.S.A. 80 D10 43 12N 88 43W
Waterval-Boven, S. Africa 57 D5 25 40S 30 18 E
Waterville, Canada 79 A13 45 16N 71 54W
Waterville, Maine, U.S.A. 77 C11 44 33N 69 38W
Waterville, N.Y., U.S.A. 79 D9 42 56N 75 23W
Waterville, Pa., U.S.A. 78 E7 41 19N 77 21W
Waterville, Wash., U.S.A. 82 C3 47 39N 120 4W
Watervliet, U.S.A. 79 D11 42 44N 73 42W
Wates, Indonesia 37 G14 7 51S 110 10 E
Watford, Canada 78 D3 42 57N 81 53W
Watford, U.K. 11 F7 51 40N 0 24W
Watford City, U.S.A. 80 B3 47 48N 103 17W
Wathaman →, Canada 73 B8 57 16N 102 59W
Wathaman L., Canada 73 B8 56 58N 103 44W
Watheroo, Australia 61 F2 30 15S 116 0 E
Wating, China 34 G4 35 40N 106 38 E
Watkins Glen, U.S.A. 78 D8 42 23N 76 52W
Watling I. = San Salvador I., Bahamas 89 B5 24 0N 74 40W
Watonga, U.S.A. 81 H5 35 51N 98 25W
Watrous, Canada 73 C7 51 40N 105 25W
Watrous, U.S.A. 81 H2 35 48N 104 59W
Watsa, Dem. Rep. of the Congo 54 B2 3 4N 29 30 E
Watseka, U.S.A. 76 E2 40 47N 87 44W
Watson, Australia 61 F5 30 29S 131 31 E
Watson, Canada 73 C8 52 10N 104 30W
Watson Lake, Canada 72 A3 60 6N 128 49W
Watsontown, U.S.A. 78 E8 41 5N 76 52W
Watsonville, U.S.A. 84 J5 36 55N 121 45W
Wattiwarriganna Cr. →, Australia 63 D2 28 57S 136 10 E
Watuata = Batuata, Indonesia 37 F6 6 12S 122 42 E
Watubela, Kepulauan, Indonesia 37 E8 4 28S 131 35 E
Watubela Is. = Watubela, Kepulauan, Indonesia 37 E8 4 28S 131 35 E
Wau = Wâw, Sudan 51 G11 7 45N 28 1 E
Waubamik, Canada 78 A4 45 27N 80 1W
Waubay, U.S.A. 80 C6 45 20N 97 18W
Wauchope, N.S.W., Australia 63 E5 31 28S 152 45 E
Wauchope, N. Terr., Australia 62 C1 20 36S 134 15 E
Wauchula, U.S.A. 77 M5 27 33N 81 49W
Waukarlycarly, L., Australia 60 D3 21 18S 121 56 E
Waukegan, U.S.A. 76 D2 42 22N 87 50W
Waukesha, U.S.A. 76 D1 43 1N 88 14W
Waukon, U.S.A. 80 D9 43 16N 91 29W
Waupaca, U.S.A. 80 C10 44 21N 89 5W
Waupun, U.S.A. 80 D10 43 38N 88 44W
Waurika, U.S.A. 81 H6 34 10N 98 0W
Wausau, U.S.A. 80 C10 44 58N 89 38W
Wautoma, U.S.A. 80 C10 44 4N 89 18W
Wauwatosa, U.S.A. 76 D2 43 3N 88 0W
Waveney →, U.K. 11 E9 52 35N 1 39 E
Waverley, N.Z. 59 H5 39 46S 174 37 E
Waverly, Iowa, U.S.A. 80 D8 42 44N 92 29W
Waverly, N.Y., U.S.A. 79 E8 42 1N 76 32W
Wavre, Belgium 15 D4 50 43N 4 38 E
Wâw, Sudan 51 G11 7 45N 28 1 E
Wāw al Kabīr, Libya 51 C9 25 20N 16 43 E
Wawa, Canada 70 C3 47 59N 84 47W
Wawanesa, Canada 73 D9 49 36N 99 40W
Wawona, U.S.A. 84 H7 37 32N 119 39W
Waxahachie, U.S.A. 81 J6 32 24N 96 51W
Way, L., Australia 61 E3 26 45S 120 16 E
Waycross, U.S.A. 77 K4 31 13N 82 21W
Wayland, U.S.A. 78 D7 42 34N 77 35W
Wayne, Nebr., U.S.A. 80 D6 42 14N 97 1W
Wayne, W. Va., U.S.A. 76 F4 38 13N 82 27W
Waynesboro, Ga., U.S.A. 77 J4 33 6N 82 1W
Waynesboro, Miss., U.S.A. 77 K1 31 40N 88 39W
Waynesboro, Pa., U.S.A. 76 F7 39 45N 77 35W
Waynesboro, Va., U.S.A. 76 F6 38 4N 78 53W
Waynesburg, U.S.A. 76 F5 39 54N 80 11W
Waynesville, U.S.A. 77 H4 35 28N 82 58W
Waynoka, U.S.A. 81 G5 36 35N 98 53W
Wazirabad, Pakistan 42 C6 32 30N 74 8 E
We, Indonesia 36 C1 5 51N 95 18 E
Weald, The, U.K. 11 F8 51 4N 0 20 E
Wear →, U.K. 10 C6 54 55N 1 23W
Weatherford, Okla., U.S.A. 81 H5 35 32N 98 43W
Weatherford, Tex., U.S.A. 81 J6 32 46N 97 48W
Weaverville, U.S.A. 82 F2 40 44N 122 56W
Webb City, U.S.A. 81 G7 37 9N 94 28W
Webequie, Canada 70 B2 52 59N 87 21W
Webster, Mass., U.S.A. 79 D13 42 3N 71 53W
Webster, N.Y., U.S.A. 78 C7 43 13N 77 26W
Webster, S. Dak., U.S.A. 80 C6 45 20N 97 31W
Webster City, U.S.A. 80 D8 42 28N 93 49W
Webster Springs, U.S.A. 76 F5 38 29N 80 25W
Weda, Indonesia 37 D7 0 21N 127 50 E
Weda, Teluk, Indonesia 37 D7 0 20N 128 0 E
Weddell I., Falk. Is. 96 G4 51 50S 61 0W
Weddell Sea, Antarctica 5 D1 72 30S 40 0W
Wedderburn, Australia 63 F3 36 26S 143 33 E
Wedgeport, Canada 71 D6 43 44N 65 59W
Wedza, Zimbabwe 55 F3 18 40S 31 33 E
Wee Waa, Australia 63 E4 30 11S 149 26 E
Weed, U.S.A. 82 F2 41 25N 122 23W
Weed Heights, U.S.A. 84 G7 38 59N 119 13W
Weedsport, U.S.A. 79 C8 43 3N 76 35W
Weedville, U.S.A. 78 E6 41 17N 78 30W
Weenen, S. Africa 57 D5 28 48S 30 7 E
Weert, Neths. 15 C5 51 15N 5 43 E
Wei He →, Hebei, China 34 F8 36 10N 115 45 E
Wei He →, Shaanxi, China 34 G6 34 38N 110 15 E
Weichang, China 35 D9 41 58N 117 49 E
Weichuan, China 34 G7 34 20N 113 59 E
Weiden, Germany 16 D7 49 41N 12 10 E
Weifang, China 35 F10 36 44N 119 7 E
Weihai, China 35 F12 37 30N 122 6 E
Weimar, Germany 16 C6 50 58N 11 19 E
Weinan, China 34 G5 34 31N 109 29 E
Weipa, Australia 62 A3 12 40S 141 50 E
Weir →, Australia 63 D4 28 20S 149 50 E
Weir →, Canada 73 B10 56 54N 93 21W
Weir River, Canada 73 B10 56 49N 94 6W
Weirton, U.S.A. 78 F4 40 24N 80 35W
Weiser, U.S.A. 82 D5 44 10N 117 0W
Weishan, China 35 G9 34 47N 117 5 E
Weiyuan, China 34 G3 35 7N 104 10 E
Wejherowo, Poland 17 A10 54 35N 18 12 E
Wekusko L., Canada 73 C9 54 40N 99 50W
Welch, U.S.A. 76 G5 37 26N 81 35W
Welkom, S. Africa 56 D4 28 0S 26 46 E
Welland, Canada 78 D5 43 0N 79 15W
Welland →, U.K. 11 E7 52 51N 0 5W
Wellesley Is., Australia 62 B2 16 42S 139 30 E
Wellingborough, U.K. 11 E7 52 19N 0 41W
Wellington, Australia 63 E4 32 35S 148 59 E
Wellington, Canada 78 C7 43 57N 77 20W
Wellington, N.Z. 59 J5 41 19S 174 46 E
Wellington, S. Africa 56 E2 33 38S 19 1 E
Wellington, Somst., U.K. 11 G4 50 58N 3 13W
Wellington, Telford & Wrekin, U.K. 11 E5 52 42N 2 30W
Wellington, Colo., U.S.A. 80 E2 40 42N 105 0W
Wellington, Kans., U.S.A. 81 G6 37 16N 97 24W
Wellington, Nev., U.S.A. 84 G7 38 45N 119 23W
Wellington, Ohio, U.S.A. 78 E2 41 10N 82 13W
Wellington, Tex., U.S.A. 81 H4 34 51N 100 13W
Wellington, I., Chile 96 F2 49 30S 75 0W
Wellington, L., Australia 63 F4 38 6S 147 20 E
Wells, U.K. 11 F5 51 13N 2 39W
Wells, Maine, U.S.A. 79 C14 43 20N 70 35W
Wells, N.Y., U.S.A. 79 C10 43 24N 74 17W
Wells, Nev., U.S.A. 82 F6 41 7N 114 58W
Wells, L., Australia 61 E3 26 44S 123 15 E
Wells, Mt., Australia 60 C4 17 25S 127 8 E
Wells Gray Prov. Park, Canada 72 C4 52 30N 120 15W
Wells-next-the-Sea, U.K. 10 E8 52 57N 0 51 E
Wells River, U.S.A. 79 B12 44 9N 72 4W
Wellsboro, U.S.A. 78 E7 41 45N 77 18W
Wellsburg, U.S.A. 78 F4 40 16N 80 37W
Wellsville, N.Y., U.S.A. 78 D7 42 7N 77 57W
Wellsville, Ohio, U.S.A. 78 F4 40 36N 80 39W
Wellsville, Utah, U.S.A. 82 F8 41 38N 111 56W
Wellton, U.S.A. 83 K6 32 40N 114 8W
Wels, Austria 16 D8 48 9N 14 1 E
Welshpool, U.K. 11 E4 52 39N 3 8W
Welwyn Garden City, U.K. 11 F7 51 48N 0 12W
Wem, U.K. 10 E5 52 52N 2 44W
Wembere →, Tanzania 54 C3 4 10S 34 15 E
Wemindji, Canada 70 B4 53 0N 78 49W
Wen Xian, China 34 G7 34 55N 113 5 E
Wenatchee, U.S.A. 82 C3 47 25N 120 19W
Wenchang, China 38 C8 19 38N 110 42 E
Wenchi, Ghana 50 G5 7 46N 2 8W
Wenchow = Wenzhou, China 33 D7 28 0N 120 38 E
Wenden, U.S.A. 85 M13 33 49N 113 33W
Wendeng, China 35 F12 37 15N 122 5 E
Wendesi, Indonesia 37 E8 2 30S 134 17 E
Wendover, U.S.A. 82 F6 40 44N 114 2W
Wenlock →, Australia 62 A3 12 2S 141 55 E
Wenshan, China 32 D5 23 20N 104 18 E
Wenshang, China 34 G9 35 45N 116 30 E
Wenshui, China 34 F7 37 26N 112 1 E
Wensleydale, U.K. 10 C6 54 17N 2 0W
Wensu, China 32 B3 41 15N 80 10 E
Wensum →, U.K. 10 E8 52 40N 1 15 E
Wentworth, Australia 63 E3 34 2S 141 54 E
Wentzel L., Canada 72 B6 59 2N 114 28W
Wenut, Indonesia 37 E8 3 11S 133 19 E
Wenxi, China 34 G6 35 20N 111 10 E
Wenxian, China 34 H3 32 43N 104 36 E
Wenzhou, China 33 D7 28 0N 120 38 E
Weott, U.S.A. 82 F2 40 20N 123 55W
Wepener, S. Africa 56 D4 29 42S 27 3 E
Werda, Botswana 56 D3 25 24S 23 15 E
Weri, Indonesia 37 E8 3 10S 132 38 E
Werra →, Germany 16 C5 51 24N 9 39 E
Werrimull, Australia 63 E3 34 25S 141 38 E
Werris Creek, Australia 63 E5 31 18S 150 38 E
Weser →, Germany 16 B5 53 36N 8 28 E
Wesiri, Indonesia 37 F7 7 30S 126 30 E
Weslemkoon L., Canada 78 A7 45 2N 77 25W
Wesleyville, Canada 71 C9 49 8N 53 36W
Wesleyville, U.S.A. 78 D4 42 9N 80 0W
Wessel, C., Australia 62 A2 10 59S 136 46 E
Wessel Is., Australia 62 A2 11 10S 136 45 E
Wessington Springs, U.S.A. 80 C5 44 5N 98 34W
West, U.S.A. 81 K6 31 48N 97 6W
West →, U.S.A. 79 D12 42 52N 72 33W
West Baines →, Australia 60 C4 15 38S 129 59 E
West Bank □, Asia 47 C4 32 6N 35 13 E
West Bend, U.S.A. 76 D1 43 25N 88 11W
West Bengal □, India 43 H13 23 0N 88 0 E
West Berkshire □, U.K. 11 F6 51 25N 1 17W
West Beskids = Západné Beskydy, Europe 17 D10 49 30N 19 0 E
West Branch, U.S.A. 76 C3 44 17N 84 14W
West Branch Susquehanna →, U.S.A. 79 F8 40 53N 76 48W
West Bromwich, U.K. 11 E6 52 32N 1 59W
West Burra, U.K. 12 A7 60 5N 1 21W
West Canada Cr. →, U.S.A. 79 C10 43 1N 74 58W
West Cape Howe, Australia 61 G2 35 8S 117 36 E
West Chazy, U.S.A. 79 B11 44 49N 73 28W
West Chester, U.S.A. 76 F8 39 58N 75 36W
West Columbia, U.S.A. 81 L7 29 9N 95 39W
West Covina, U.S.A. 85 L9 34 4N 117 54W
West Des Moines, U.S.A. 80 E8 41 35N 93 43W
West Dunbartonshire □, U.K. 12 F4 55 59N 4 30W
West End, Bahamas 88 A4 26 41N 78 58W
West Falkland, Falk. Is. 96 G5 51 40S 60 0W
West Fargo, U.S.A. 80 B6 46 52N 96 54W
West Farmington, U.S.A. 78 E4 41 23N 80 58W
West Fjord = Vestfjorden, Norway 8 C15 67 55N 14 0 E
West Fork Trinity →, U.S.A. 81 J6 32 48N 96 54W
West Frankfort, U.S.A. 80 G10 37 54N 88 55W
West Hartford, U.S.A. 79 E12 41 45N 72 44W
West Haven, U.S.A. 79 E12 41 17N 72 57W
West Hazleton, U.S.A. 79 F9 40 58N 76 0W
West Helena, U.S.A. 81 H9 34 33N 90 38W

Yetman

Woodend, *Australia* **63 F3** 37 20S 144 33 E
Woodford, *Australia* **63 D5** 26 58S 152 47 E
Woodfords, *U.S.A.* **84 G7** 38 47N 119 50W
Woodlake, *U.S.A.* **84 J7** 36 25N 119 6W
Woodland, *Calif., U.S.A.* **84 G5** 38 41N 121 46W
Woodland, *Maine, U.S.A.* **77 C12** 45 9N 67 25W
Woodland, *Pa., U.S.A.* **78 F6** 40 59N 78 21W
Woodland, *Wash., U.S.A.* **84 E4** 45 54N 122 45W
Woodland Caribou Prov. Park, *Canada* **73 C10** 51 0N 94 45W
Woodridge, *Canada* **73 D9** 49 20N 96 9W
Woodroffe, Mt., *Australia* **61 E5** 26 20S 131 45 E
Woods, L., *Australia* **62 B1** 17 50S 133 30 E
Woods, L. of the, *Canada* **73 D10** 49 15N 94 45W
Woodstock, *Australia* **62 B4** 19 35S 146 50 E
Woodstock, *N.B., Canada* **71 C6** 46 11N 67 37W
Woodstock, *Ont., Canada* **78 C4** 43 10N 80 45W
Woodstock, *U.K.* **11 F6** 51 51N 1 20W
Woodstock, *Ill., U.S.A.* **80 D10** 42 19N 88 27W
Woodstock, *Vt., U.S.A.* **79 C12** 43 37N 72 31W
Woodsville, *U.S.A.* **79 B13** 44 9N 72 2W
Woodville, *N.Z.* **59 J5** 40 20S 175 53 E
Woodville, *Miss., U.S.A.* **81 K9** 31 6N 91 18W
Woodville, *Tex., U.S.A.* **81 K7** 30 47N 94 25W
Woodward, *U.S.A.* **81 G5** 36 26N 99 24W
Woody, *U.S.A.* **85 K8** 35 42N 118 50W
Woody →, *Canada* **73 C8** 52 31N 100 51W
Woolamai, C., *Australia* **63 F4** 38 30S 145 23 E
Wooler, *U.K.* **10 B5** 55 33N 2 1W
Woolgoolga, *Australia* **63 E5** 30 6S 153 11 E
Woomera, *Australia* **63 E2** 31 5S 136 50 E
Woonsocket, *R.I., U.S.A.* **79 E13** 42 0N 71 31W
Woonsocket, *S. Dak., U.S.A.* **80 C5** 44 3N 98 17W
Wooramel →, *Australia* **61 E1** 25 47S 114 10 E
Wooramel Roadhouse, *Australia* **61 E1** 25 45S 114 17 E
Wooster, *U.S.A.* **78 F3** 40 48N 81 56W
Worcester, *S. Africa* **56 E2** 33 39S 19 27 E
Worcester, *U.K.* **11 E5** 52 11N 2 12W
Worcester, *Mass., U.S.A.* **79 D13** 42 16N 71 48W
Worcester, *N.Y., U.S.A.* **79 D10** 42 36N 74 45W
Worcestershire □, *U.K.* **11 E5** 52 13N 2 10W
Workington, *U.K.* **10 C4** 54 39N 3 33W
Worksop, *U.K.* **10 D6** 53 18N 1 7W
Workum, *Neths.* **15 B5** 52 59N 5 26 E
Worland, *U.S.A.* **82 D10** 44 1N 107 57W
Worms, *Germany* **16 D5** 49 37N 8 21 E
Worsley, *Canada* **72 B5** 56 31N 119 8W
Wortham, *U.S.A.* **81 K6** 31 47N 96 28W
Worthing, *U.K.* **11 G7** 50 49N 0 21W
Worthington, *Minn., U.S.A.* **80 D7** 43 37N 95 36W
Worthington, *Pa., U.S.A.* **78 F5** 40 50N 79 38W
Wosi, *Indonesia* **37 E7** 0 15S 128 0 E
Wou-han = Wuhan, *China* **33 C6** 30 31N 114 18 E
Wousi = Wuxi, *China* **33 C7** 31 33N 120 18 E
Wowoni, *Indonesia* **37 E6** 4 5S 123 5 E
Wrangel I. = Vrangelya, Ostrov, *Russia* **27 B19** 71 0N 180 0 E
Wrangell, *U.S.A.* **72 B2** 56 28N 132 23W
Wrangell Mts., *U.S.A.* **68 B5** 61 30N 142 0W
Wrath, C., *U.K.* **12 C3** 58 38N 5 1W
Wray, *U.S.A.* **80 E3** 40 5N 102 13W
Wrekin, The, *U.K.* **11 E5** 52 41N 2 32W
Wrens, *U.S.A.* **77 J4** 33 12N 82 23W
Wrexham, *U.K.* **10 D4** 53 3N 3 0W
Wrexham □, *U.K.* **10 D5** 53 1N 2 58W
Wright, *U.S.A.* **80 D2** 43 47N 105 30W
Wright Pt., *Canada* **78 C3** 43 48N 81 44W
Wrightson Mt., *U.S.A.* **83 L8** 31 42N 110 51W
Wrightwood, *U.S.A.* **85 L9** 34 21N 117 38W
Wrigley, *Canada* **68 B7** 63 16N 123 37W
Wrocław, *Poland* **17 C9** 51 5N 17 5 E
Września, *Poland* **17 B9** 52 21N 17 36 E
Wu Jiang →, *China* **32 D5** 29 40N 107 20 E
Wu'an, *China* **34 F8** 36 40N 114 15 E
Wubin, *Australia* **61 F2** 30 6S 116 37 E
Wubu, *China* **34 F6** 37 28N 110 42 E
Wuchang, *China* **35 B14** 44 55N 127 5 E
Wucheng, *China* **34 F9** 37 12N 116 20 E
Wuchuan, *China* **34 D6** 41 5N 111 28 E
Wudi, *China* **35 F9** 37 40N 117 35 E
Wuding He →, *China* **34 F6** 37 2N 110 23 E
Wudinna, *Australia* **63 E2** 33 0S 135 22 E
Wudu, *China* **34 H3** 33 22N 104 54 E
Wuhan, *China* **33 C6** 30 31N 114 18 E
Wuhe, *China* **35 H9** 33 10N 117 50 E
Wuhsi = Wuxi, *China* **33 C7** 31 33N 120 18 E
Wuhu, *China* **33 C6** 31 22N 118 21 E
Wukari, *Nigeria* **50 G7** 7 51N 9 42 E
Wulajie, *China* **35 B14** 44 6N 126 33 E
Wulanbulang, *China* **34 D6** 41 5N 110 55 E
Wular L., *India* **43 B6** 34 20N 74 30 E
Wulian, *China* **35 G10** 35 40N 119 12 E
Wuliaru, *Indonesia* **37 F8** 7 27S 131 0 E
Wuluk'omushih Ling, *China* **32 C3** 36 25N 87 25 E
Wulumuchi = Ürümqi, *China* **26 E9** 43 45N 87 45 E
Wundowie, *Australia* **61 F2** 31 47S 116 23 E
Wunnummin L., *Canada* **70 B2** 52 55N 89 10W
Wuntho, *Burma* **41 H19** 23 55N 95 45 E
Wuppertal, *Germany* **16 C4** 51 16N 7 12 E
Wuppertal, *S. Africa* **56 E2** 32 13S 19 12 E
Wuqing, *China* **35 E9** 39 23N 117 4 E
Wurtsboro, *U.S.A.* **79 E10** 41 35N 74 29W
Würzburg, *Germany* **16 D5** 49 46N 9 55 E
Wushan, *China* **34 G3** 34 43N 104 53 E
Wusuli Jiang = Ussuri →, *Asia* **30 A7** 48 27N 135 0 E
Wutai, *China* **34 E7** 38 40N 113 12 E
Wuting = Huimin, *China* **35 F9** 37 27N 117 28 E
Wutonghaolai, *China* **35 C11** 42 50N 120 5 E
Wutongqiao, *China* **32 D5** 29 22N 103 50 E
Wuwei, *China* **32 C5** 37 57N 102 34 E
Wuxi, *China* **33 C7** 31 33N 120 18 E
Wuxiang, *China* **34 F7** 36 49N 112 50 E
Wuyang, *China* **34 H7** 33 25N 113 35 E
Wuyi, *China* **34 F8** 37 46N 115 56 E
Wuyi Shan, *China* **33 D6** 27 0N 117 0 E
Wuyuan, *China* **34 D5** 41 2N 108 20 E
Wuzhai, *China* **34 E6** 38 54N 111 48 E
Wuzhi Shan, *China* **38 C7** 18 45N 109 45 E
Wuzhong, *China* **34 E4** 38 2N 106 12 E
Wuzhou, *China* **33 D6** 23 30N 111 18 E
Wyaaba Cr. →, *Australia* **62 B3** 16 27S 141 35 E
Wyalkatchem, *Australia* **61 F2** 31 8S 117 22 E
Wyalusing, *U.S.A.* **79 E8** 41 40N 76 16W
Wyandotte, *U.S.A.* **76 D4** 42 12N 83 9W
Wyandra, *Australia* **63 D4** 27 12S 145 56 E
Wyangala, L., *Australia* **63 E4** 33 54S 149 0 E
Wyara, L., *Australia* **63 D3** 28 42S 144 14 E
Wycheproof, *Australia* **63 F3** 36 5S 143 17 E
Wye →, *U.K.* **11 F5** 51 38N 2 40W
Wyemandoo, *Australia* **61 E2** 28 28S 118 29 E
Wymondham, *U.K.* **11 E9** 52 35N 1 7 E
Wymore, *U.S.A.* **80 E6** 40 7N 96 40W
Wyndham, *Australia* **60 C4** 15 33S 128 3 E
Wyndham, *N.Z.* **59 M2** 46 20S 168 51 E
Wynne, *U.S.A.* **81 H9** 35 14N 90 47W
Wynyard, *Australia* **62 G4** 41 5S 145 44 E
Wynyard, *Canada* **73 C8** 51 45N 104 10W
Wyola L., *Australia* **61 E5** 29 8S 130 17 E
Wyoming, *Canada* **78 D2** 42 57N 82 7W
Wyoming □, *U.S.A.* **82 E10** 43 0N 107 30W
Wyomissing, *U.S.A.* **79 F9** 40 20N 75 59W
Wyong, *Australia* **63 E5** 33 14S 151 24 E
Wytheville, *U.S.A.* **76 G5** 36 57N 81 5W

X

Xaçmaz, *Azerbaijan* **25 F8** 41 31N 48 42 E
Xai-Xai, *Mozam.* **57 D5** 25 6S 33 31 E
Xainza, *China* **32 C3** 30 58N 88 35 E
Xangongo, *Angola* **56 B2** 16 45S 15 5 E
Xankändi, *Azerbaijan* **25 G8** 39 52N 46 49 E
Xánthi, *Greece* **21 D11** 41 10N 24 58 E
Xanxerê, *Brazil* **95 B5** 26 53S 52 23W
Xapuri, *Brazil* **92 F5** 10 35S 68 35W
Xar Moron He →, *China* **35 C11** 43 25N 120 35 E
Xátiva, *Spain* **19 C5** 38 59N 0 32W
Xau, L., *Botswana* **56 C3** 21 15S 24 44 E
Xavantina, *Brazil* **95 A5** 21 15S 52 48W
Xenia, *U.S.A.* **76 F4** 39 41N 83 56W
Xeropotamos →, *Cyprus* **23 E11** 34 42N 32 33 E
Xhora, *S. Africa* **57 E4** 31 55S 28 38 E
Xhumo, *Botswana* **56 C3** 21 7S 24 35 E
Xi Jiang →, *China* **33 D6** 22 5N 113 20 E
Xi Xian, *China* **34 F6** 36 41N 110 58 E
Xia Xian, *China* **34 G6** 35 8N 111 12 E
Xiachengzi, *China* **35 B16** 44 40N 130 18 E
Xiaguan, *China* **32 D5** 25 32N 100 16 E
Xiajin, *China* **34 F9** 36 56N 116 0 E
Xiamen, *China* **33 D6** 24 25N 118 4 E
Xi'an, *China* **34 G5** 34 15N 109 0 E
Xian Xian, *China* **34 E9** 38 12N 116 6 E
Xiang Jiang →, *China* **33 D6** 28 55N 112 50 E
Xiangcheng, *Henan, China* **34 H8** 33 29N 114 52 E
Xiangcheng, *Henan, China* **34 H7** 33 50N 113 27 E
Xiangfan, *China* **33 C6** 32 2N 112 8 E
Xianggang = Hong Kong □, *China* **33 D6** 22 11N 114 14 E
Xianghuang Qi, *China* **34 C7** 42 2N 113 50 E
Xiangning, *China* **34 G6** 35 58N 110 50 E
Xiangquan, *China* **34 F7** 36 30N 113 1 E
Xiangquan He = Sutlej →, *Pakistan* **42 E4** 29 23N 71 3 E
Xiangshui, *China* **35 G10** 34 12N 119 33 E
Xiangtan, *China* **33 D6** 27 51N 112 54 E
Xiangyang, *China* **34 G5** 34 20N 108 40 E
Xiao Hinggan Ling, *China* **33 B7** 49 0N 127 0 E
Xiao Xian, *China* **34 G9** 34 15N 116 55 E
Xiaoyi, *China* **34 F6** 37 8N 111 48 E
Xiawa, *China* **35 C11** 42 35N 120 38 E
Xiayi, *China* **34 G9** 34 15N 116 10 E
Xichang, *China* **32 D5** 27 51N 102 19 E
Xichuan, *China* **34 H6** 33 0N 111 30 E
Xieng Khouang, *Laos* **38 C4** 19 17N 103 25 E
Xifei He →, *China* **34 H9** 32 45N 116 40 E
Xifeng, *Gansu, China* **34 G4** 35 40N 107 40 E
Xifeng, *Liaoning, China* **35 C13** 42 42N 124 45 E
Xifengzhen = Xifeng, *China* **34 G4** 35 40N 107 40 E
Xigazê, *China* **32 D3** 29 5N 88 45 E
Xihe, *China* **34 G3** 34 2N 105 20 E
Xihua, *China* **34 H8** 33 45N 114 30 E
Xiliao He →, *China* **35 C12** 43 32N 123 35 E
Ximana, *Mozam.* **55 F3** 19 24S 33 58 E
Xin Xian = Xinzhou, *China* **34 E7** 38 22N 112 46 E
Xinavane, *Mozam.* **57 D5** 25 2S 32 47 E
Xinbin, *China* **35 D13** 41 40N 125 2 E
Xing Xian, *China* **34 E6** 38 27N 111 7 E
Xing'an, *China* **33 D6** 25 38N 110 40 E
Xingcheng, *China* **35 D11** 40 40N 120 45 E
Xinghe, *China* **34 D7** 40 55N 113 55 E
Xinghua, *China* **35 H10** 32 58N 119 48 E
Xinglong, *China* **35 D9** 40 25N 117 30 E
Xingping, *China* **34 G5** 34 20N 108 28 E
Xingtai, *China* **34 F8** 37 3N 114 32 E
Xingu →, *Brazil* **93 D8** 1 30S 51 53W
Xingyang, *China* **34 G7** 34 45N 112 52 E
Xinhe, *China* **34 F8** 37 30N 115 15 E
Xining, *China* **32 C5** 36 34N 101 40 E
Xinjiang, *China* **34 G6** 35 34N 111 11 E
Xinjiang Uygur Zizhiqu □, *China* **32 C3** 42 0N 86 0 E
Xinjin = Pulandian, *China* **35 E11** 39 25N 121 58 E
Xinkai He →, *China* **35 C12** 43 32N 123 35 E
Xinle, *China* **34 E8** 38 25N 114 40 E
Xinlitun, *China* **35 D12** 42 0N 122 8 E
Xinmin, *China* **35 D12** 41 59N 122 50 E
Xintai, *China* **35 G9** 35 55N 117 45 E
Xinxiang, *China* **34 G7** 35 18N 113 50 E
Xinzhan, *China* **35 C14** 43 50N 127 18 E
Xinzheng, *China* **34 G7** 34 20N 113 45 E
Xinzhou, *China* **34 E7** 38 22N 112 46 E
Xiongyuecheng, *China* **35 D12** 40 12N 122 5 E
Xiping, *Henan, China* **34 H8** 33 22N 114 5 E
Xiping, *Henan, China* **34 H6** 33 25N 111 8 E
Xique-Xique, *Brazil* **93 F10** 10 50S 42 40W
Xisha Qundao = Paracel Is., *S. China Sea* **36 A4** 15 50N 112 0 E
Xiuyan, *China* **35 D12** 40 18N 123 11 E
Xixabangma Feng, *China* **41 E14** 28 20N 85 40 E
Xixia, *China* **34 H6** 33 25N 111 29 E
Xixiang, *China* **34 H4** 33 0N 107 44 E
Xiyang, *China* **34 F7** 37 38N 113 38 E
Xizang Zizhiqu □, *China* **32 C3** 32 0N 88 0 E
Xlendi, *Malta* **23 C1** 36 1N 14 12 E
Xuan Loc, *Vietnam* **39 G6** 10 56N 107 14 E
Xuanhua, *China* **34 D8** 40 40N 115 2 E
Xuchang, *China* **34 G7** 34 2N 113 48 E
Xun Xian, *China* **34 G8** 35 42N 114 33 E
Xunyang, *China* **34 H5** 32 48N 109 22 E
Xunyi, *China* **34 G5** 35 8N 108 20 E
Xúquer →, *Spain* **19 C5** 39 5N 0 10W
Xushui, *China* **34 E8** 39 2N 115 40 E
Xuyen Moc, *Vietnam* **39 G6** 10 34N 107 25 E
Xuzhou, *China* **35 G9** 34 18N 117 10 E
Xylophagou, *Cyprus* **23 E12** 34 54N 33 51 E

Y

Ya Xian, *China* **38 C7** 18 14N 109 29 E
Yaamba, *Australia* **62 C5** 23 8S 150 22 E
Yaapeet, *Australia* **63 F3** 35 45S 142 3 E
Yablonovy Ra. = Yablonovyy Khrebet, *Russia* **27 D12** 53 0N 114 0 E
Yablonovyy Khrebet, *Russia* **27 D12** 53 0N 114 0 E
Yabrai Shan, *China* **34 E2** 39 40N 103 0 E
Yabrūd, *Syria* **47 B5** 33 58N 36 39 E
Yacheng, *China* **33 E5** 18 22N 109 6 E
Yacuiba, *Bolivia* **94 A3** 22 0S 63 43W
Yacuma →, *Bolivia* **92 F5** 13 38S 65 23W
Yadgir, *India* **40 L10** 16 45N 77 5 E
Yadkin →, *U.S.A.* **77 H5** 35 29N 80 9W
Yaeyama-Rettō, *Japan* **31 M1** 24 30N 123 40 E
Yagodnoye, *Russia* **27 C15** 62 33N 149 40 E
Yahila, *Dem. Rep. of the Congo* **54 B1** 0 13N 24 28 E
Yahk, *Canada* **72 D5** 49 6N 116 10W
Yahuma, *Dem. Rep. of the Congo* **52 D4** 1 0N 23 10 E
Yaita, *Japan* **31 F9** 36 48N 139 56 E
Yaiza, *Canary Is.* **22 F6** 28 57N 13 46W
Yakima, *U.S.A.* **82 C3** 46 36N 120 31W
Yakima →, *U.S.A.* **82 C3** 47 0N 120 30W
Yakobi I., *U.S.A.* **72 B1** 58 0N 136 30W
Yakovlevka, *Russia* **30 B6** 44 26N 133 28 E
Yaku-Shima, *Japan* **31 J5** 30 20N 130 30 E
Yakumo, *Japan* **30 C10** 42 15N 140 16 E
Yakutat, *U.S.A.* **68 C6** 59 33N 139 44W
Yakutia = Sakha □, *Russia* **27 C13** 66 0N 130 0 E
Yakutsk, *Russia* **27 C13** 62 5N 129 50 E
Yala, *Thailand* **39 J3** 6 33N 101 18 E
Yale, *U.S.A.* **78 C2** 43 8N 82 48W
Yalgoo, *Australia* **61 E2** 28 16S 116 39 E
Yalinga, *C.A.R.* **52 C4** 6 33N 23 10 E
Yalkubul, Punta, *Mexico* **87 C7** 21 32N 88 37W
Yalleroi, *Australia* **62 C4** 24 3S 145 42 E
Yalobusha →, *U.S.A.* **81 J9** 33 33N 90 10W
Yalong Jiang →, *China* **32 D5** 26 40N 101 55 E
Yalova, *Turkey* **21 D13** 40 41N 29 15 E
Yalta, *Ukraine* **25 F5** 44 30N 34 10 E
Yalu Jiang →, *China* **35 E13** 40 0N 124 22 E
Yam Ha Melaḥ = Dead Sea, *Asia* **47 D4** 31 30N 35 30 E
Yam Kinneret, *Israel* **47 C4** 32 45N 35 35 E
Yamada, *Japan* **31 H5** 33 33N 130 49 E
Yamagata, *Japan* **30 E10** 38 15N 140 15 E
Yamagata □, *Japan* **30 E10** 38 30N 140 0 E
Yamaguchi, *Japan* **31 G5** 34 10N 131 32 E
Yamaguchi □, *Japan* **31 G5** 34 20N 131 40 E
Yamal, Poluostrov, *Russia* **26 B8** 71 0N 70 0 E
Yamal Pen. = Yamal, Poluostrov, *Russia* **26 B8** 71 0N 70 0 E
Yamanashi □, *Japan* **31 G9** 35 40N 138 40 E
Yamantau, Gora, *Russia* **24 D10** 54 15N 58 6 E
Yamba, *Australia* **63 D5** 29 26S 153 23 E
Yambarran Ra., *Australia* **60 C5** 15 10S 130 25 E
Yâmbiô, *Sudan* **51 H11** 4 35N 28 16 E
Yambol, *Bulgaria* **21 C12** 42 30N 26 30 E
Yamdena, *Indonesia* **37 F8** 7 45S 131 20 E
Yame, *Japan* **31 H5** 33 13N 130 35 E
Yamethin, *Burma* **41 J20** 20 29N 96 18 E
Yamma-Yamma, L., *Australia* **63 D3** 26 16S 141 20 E
Yamoussoukro, *Ivory C.* **50 G4** 6 49N 5 17W
Yampa →, *U.S.A.* **82 F9** 40 32N 108 59W
Yampi Sd., *Australia* **60 C3** 16 8S 123 38 E
Yampil, *Moldova* **17 D15** 48 15N 28 15 E
Yampol = Yampil, *Moldova* **17 D15** 48 15N 28 15 E
Yamuna →, *India* **43 G9** 25 30N 81 53 E
Yamunanagar, *India* **42 D7** 30 7N 77 17 E
Yamzho Yumco, *China* **32 D4** 28 48N 90 35 E
Yana →, *Russia* **27 B14** 71 30N 136 0 E
Yanagawa, *Japan* **31 H5** 33 10N 130 24 E
Yanai, *Japan* **31 H6** 33 58N 132 7 E
Yan'an, *China* **34 F5** 36 35N 109 26 E
Yanaul, *Russia* **24 C10** 56 25N 55 0 E
Yanbu 'al Baḥr, *Si. Arabia* **46 C2** 24 0N 38 5 E
Yanchang, *China* **34 F6** 36 43N 110 1 E
Yancheng, *Henan, China* **34 H8** 33 35N 114 0 E
Yancheng, *Jiangsu, China* **35 H11** 33 23N 120 8 E
Yanchep Beach, *Australia* **61 F2** 31 33S 115 37 E
Yanchi, *China* **34 F4** 37 48N 107 20 E
Yanchuan, *China* **34 F6** 36 51N 110 10 E
Yanco Cr. →, *Australia* **63 F4** 35 14S 145 35 E
Yandoon, *Burma* **41 L19** 17 0N 95 40 E
Yang Xian, *China* **34 H4** 33 15N 107 30 E
Yangambi, *Dem. Rep. of the Congo* **54 B1** 0 47N 24 24 E
Yangcheng, *China* **34 G7** 35 28N 112 22 E
Yangch'ü = Taiyuan, *China* **34 F7** 37 52N 112 33 E
Yanggao, *China* **34 D7** 40 21N 113 55 E
Yanggu, *China* **34 F8** 36 8N 115 43 E
Yangliuqing, *China* **35 E9** 39 2N 117 5 E
Yangon = Rangoon, *Burma* **41 L20** 16 45N 96 20 E
Yangpingguan, *China* **34 H4** 32 58N 106 5 E
Yangquan, *China* **34 F7** 37 58N 113 31 E
Yangtse = Chang Jiang →, *China* **33 C7** 31 48N 121 10 E
Yangtze Kiang = Chang Jiang →, *China* **33 C7** 31 48N 121 10 E
Yangyang, *S. Korea* **35 E15** 38 4N 128 38 E
Yangyuan, *China* **34 D8** 40 1N 114 10 E
Yangzhou, *China* **33 C6** 32 21N 119 26 E
Yanji, *China* **35 C15** 42 59N 129 30 E
Yankton, *U.S.A.* **80 D6** 42 53N 97 23W
Yanonge, *Dem. Rep. of the Congo* **54 B1** 0 35N 24 38 E
Yanqi, *China* **32 B3** 42 5N 86 35 E
Yanqing, *China* **34 D8** 40 30N 115 58 E
Yanshan, *China* **35 E9** 38 4N 117 22 E
Yanshou, *China* **35 B15** 45 28N 128 22 E
Yantabulla, *Australia* **63 D4** 29 21S 145 0 E
Yantai, *China* **35 F11** 37 34N 121 22 E
Yanzhou, *China* **34 G9** 35 35N 116 49 E
Yao Xian, *China* **34 G5** 34 55N 108 59 E
Yao Yai, Ko, *Thailand* **39 J2** 8 0N 98 35 E
Yaoundé, *Cameroon* **52 D2** 3 50N 11 35 E
Yaowan, *China* **35 G10** 34 15N 118 3 E
Yap I., *Pac. Oc.* **64 G5** 9 30N 138 10 E
Yapen, *Indonesia* **37 E9** 1 50S 136 0 E
Yapen, Selat, *Indonesia* **37 E9** 1 20S 136 10 E
Yapero, *Indonesia* **37 E9** 4 59S 137 11 E
Yappar →, *Australia* **62 B3** 18 22S 141 16 E
Yaqui →, *Mexico* **86 B2** 27 37N 110 39W
Yar-Sale, *Russia* **26 C8** 66 50N 70 50 E
Yaraka, *Australia* **62 C3** 24 53S 144 3 E
Yaransk, *Russia* **24 C8** 57 22N 47 49 E
Yare →, *U.K.* **11 E9** 52 35N 1 38 E
Yaremcha, *Ukraine* **17 D13** 48 27N 24 33 E
Yarensk, *Russia* **24 B8** 62 11N 49 15 E
Yarí →, *Colombia* **92 D4** 0 20S 72 20W
Yarkand = Shache, *China* **32 C2** 38 20N 77 10 E
Yarker, *Canada* **79 B8** 44 23N 76 46W
Yarkhun →, *Pakistan* **43 A5** 36 17N 72 30 E
Yarmouth, *Canada* **71 D6** 43 50N 66 7W
Yarmūk →, *Syria* **47 C4** 32 42N 35 40 E
Yaroslavl, *Russia* **24 C6** 57 35N 39 55 E
Yarqa, W. →, *Egypt* **47 F2** 30 0N 33 49 E
Yarra Yarra Lakes, *Australia* **61 E2** 29 40S 115 45 E
Yarram, *Australia* **63 F4** 38 29S 146 39 E
Yarraman, *Australia* **63 D5** 26 50S 152 0 E
Yarras, *Australia* **63 E5** 31 25S 152 20 E
Yartsevo, *Russia* **27 C10** 60 20N 90 0 E
Yarumal, *Colombia* **92 B3** 6 58N 75 24W
Yasawa Group, *Fiji* **59 C7** 17 0S 177 23 E
Yaselda, *Belarus* **17 B14** 52 7N 26 28 E
Yasin, *Pakistan* **43 A5** 36 24N 73 23 E
Yasinski, L., *Canada* **70 B4** 53 16N 77 35W
Yasinya, *Ukraine* **17 D13** 48 16N 24 21 E
Yasothon, *Thailand* **38 E5** 15 50N 104 10 E
Yass, *Australia* **63 E4** 34 49S 148 54 E
Yāsūj, *Iran* **45 D6** 30 31N 51 31 E
Yatağan, *Turkey* **21 F13** 37 20N 28 10 E
Yates Center, *U.S.A.* **81 G7** 37 53N 95 44W
Yathkyed L., *Canada* **73 A9** 62 40N 98 0W
Yatsushiro, *Japan* **31 H5** 32 30N 130 40 E
Yatta Plateau, *Kenya* **54 C4** 2 0S 38 0 E
Yavari →, *Peru* **92 D4** 4 21S 70 2W
Yávaros, *Mexico* **86 B3** 26 42N 109 31W
Yavatmal, *India* **40 J11** 20 20N 78 15 E
Yavne, *Israel* **47 D3** 31 52N 34 45 E
Yavoriv, *Ukraine* **17 D12** 49 55N 23 20 E
Yavorov = Yavoriv, *Ukraine* **17 D12** 49 55N 23 20 E
Yawatahama, *Japan* **31 H6** 33 27N 132 24 E
Yazd, *Iran* **45 D7** 31 55N 54 27 E
Yazd □, *Iran* **45 D7** 32 0N 55 0 E
Yazd-e Khvāst, *Iran* **45 D7** 31 31N 52 7 E
Yazman, *Pakistan* **42 E4** 29 8N 71 45 E
Yazoo →, *U.S.A.* **81 J9** 32 22N 90 54W
Yazoo City, *U.S.A.* **81 J9** 32 51N 90 25W
Yding Skovhøj, *Denmark* **9 J13** 55 59N 9 46 E
Ye Xian = Laizhou, *China* **35 F10** 37 8N 119 57 E
Ye Xian, *China* **34 H7** 33 35N 113 25 E
Yebyu, *Burma* **38 E2** 14 15N 98 13 E
Yechŏn, *S. Korea* **35 F15** 36 39N 128 27 E
Yecla, *Spain* **19 C5** 38 35N 1 5W
Yécora, *Mexico* **86 B3** 28 20N 108 58W
Yedintsy = Edineţ, *Moldova* **17 D14** 48 9N 27 18 E
Yegros, *Paraguay* **94 B4** 26 20S 56 25W
Yehuda, Midbar, *Israel* **47 D4** 31 35N 35 15 E
Yei, *Sudan* **51 H12** 4 9N 30 40 E
Yekaterinburg, *Russia* **26 D7** 56 50N 60 30 E
Yekaterinodar = Krasnodar, *Russia* **25 E6** 45 5N 39 0 E
Yelarbon, *Australia* **63 D5** 28 33S 150 38 E
Yelets, *Russia* **24 D6** 52 40N 38 30 E
Yelizavetgrad = Kirovohrad, *Ukraine* **25 E5** 48 35N 32 20 E
Yell, *U.K.* **12 A7** 60 35N 1 5W
Yell Sd., *U.K.* **12 A7** 60 33N 1 15W
Yellow Sea, *China* **35 G12** 35 0N 123 0 E
Yellowhead Pass, *Canada* **72 C5** 52 53N 118 25W
Yellowknife, *Canada* **72 A6** 62 27N 114 29W
Yellowknife →, *Canada* **72 A6** 62 31N 114 19W
Yellowstone →, *U.S.A.* **80 B3** 47 59N 103 59W
Yellowstone L., *U.S.A.* **82 D8** 44 27N 110 22W
Yellowstone Nat. Park, *U.S.A.* **82 D9** 44 40N 110 30W
Yelsk, *Belarus* **17 C15** 51 50N 29 10 E
Yemen ■, *Asia* **46 E3** 15 0N 44 0 E
Yen Bai, *Vietnam* **38 B5** 21 42N 104 52 E
Yenangyaung, *Burma* **41 J19** 20 30N 95 0 E
Yenbo = Yanbu 'al Baḥr, *Si. Arabia* **46 C2** 24 0N 38 5 E
Yenda, *Australia* **63 E4** 34 13S 146 14 E
Yenice, *Turkey* **21 E12** 39 55N 27 17 E
Yenisey →, *Russia* **26 B9** 71 50N 82 40 E
Yeniseysk, *Russia* **27 D10** 58 27N 92 13 E
Yeniseyskiy Zaliv, *Russia* **26 B9** 72 20N 81 0 E
Yennádhi, *Greece* **23 C9** 36 2N 27 56 E
Yenyuka, *Russia* **27 D13** 57 57N 121 15 E
Yeo →, *U.K.* **11 G5** 51 2N 2 49W
Yeo, L., *Australia* **61 E3** 28 0S 124 30 E
Yeo I., *Canada* **78 A3** 45 24N 81 48W
Yeola, *India* **40 J9** 20 2N 74 30 E
Yeoryioúpolis, *Greece* **23 D6** 35 20N 24 15 E
Yeovil, *U.K.* **11 G5** 50 57N 2 38W
Yeppoon, *Australia* **62 C5** 23 5S 150 47 E
Yerbent, *Turkmenistan* **26 F6** 39 30N 58 50 E
Yerbogachen, *Russia* **27 C11** 61 16N 108 0 E
Yerevan, *Armenia* **25 F7** 40 10N 44 31 E
Yerington, *U.S.A.* **82 G4** 38 59N 119 10W
Yermak, *Kazakstan* **26 D8** 52 2N 76 55 E
Yermo, *U.S.A.* **85 L10** 34 54N 116 50W
Yerólakkos, *Cyprus* **23 D12** 35 11N 33 15 E
Yeropol, *Russia* **27 C17** 65 15N 168 40 E
Yeropótamos →, *Greece* **23 D6** 35 3N 24 50 E
Yeroskipos, *Cyprus* **23 E11** 34 46N 32 28 E
Yershov, *Russia* **25 D8** 51 23N 48 27 E
Yerushalayim = Jerusalem, *Israel* **47 D4** 31 47N 35 10 E
Yes Tor, *U.K.* **11 G4** 50 41N 4 0W
Yesan, *S. Korea* **35 F14** 36 41N 126 51 E
Yeso, *U.S.A.* **81 H2** 34 26N 104 37W
Yessey, *Russia* **27 C11** 68 29N 102 10 E
Yetman, *Australia* **63 D5** 28 56S 150 48 E

Z

World: Regions in the News

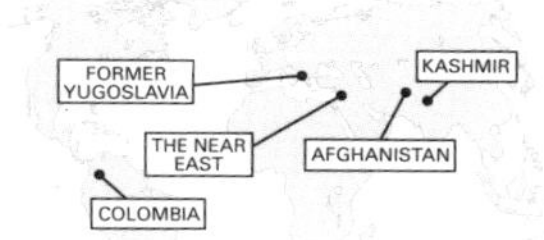

KASHMIR

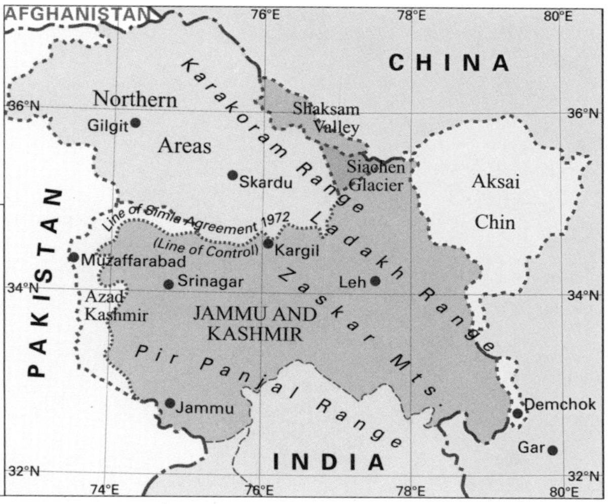

FORMER YUGOSLAVIA

YUGOSLAVIA
POPULATION: 10,677,000
(Serb 62.6%, Albanian 16.5%, Montenegrin 5%, Hungarian 3.3%, Muslim 3.2%)

Serbia POPULATION: 5,799,800
(Serb 87.7%, excluding the provinces of Kosovo and Vojvodina)

Kosovo POPULATION: 2,084,4000
(Albanian 81.6%, Serb 9.9%)

Vojvodena POPULATION: 1,980,800
(Serb 56.8%, Hungarian 16.9%)

Montenegro POPULATION: 635,000
(Montenegrin 61.9%, Muslim 14.6%, Albanian 7%)

CROATIA
POPULATION: 4,334,000
(Croat 78.1%, Serb 12.2%)

SLOVENIA
POPULATION: 1,930,000
(Slovene 88%, Croat 3%, Serb 2%)

MACEDONIA (FYROM)
POPULATION: 2,046,000
(Macedonian 64%, Albanian 21.7%, Turkish 5%, Romanian 3%, Serb 2%)

BOSNIA-HERZEGOVINA
POPULATION: 3,922,000
(Muslim 49%, Serb 31.2%, Croat 17.2%)

COLOMBIA

POPULATION: 40,349,388 (Mestizo 58%, White 20%, Mulatto 14%, Black 4%, Mixed Black-Amerindian 3%, Amerindian 1%)
RELIGIONS: Roman Catholic 90%
FARC MEMBERS: 18,000 (Revolutionary Armed Forces of Colombia)
CIVILIANS IN FARC ZONE: 90,000
AID RECEIVED (US) 2000: US $1.3 billion
AID RECEIVED (US) 2002: US $0.3 billion

THE NEAR EAST

ISRAEL
POPULATION: 5,938,000 (inc. East Jerusalem and Jewish settlers in the areas under Israeli administration. Jewish 82%, Arab Muslim 13.8%, Arab Christian 2.5%, Druze 1.7%)

West Bank
POPULATION: 2,091,000 (Palestinian Arab 97% [of whom Arab Muslim 85%, Jewish 7%, Christian 8%])

Gaza Strip
POPULATION: 1,178,000 (Arab 98%)

JORDAN
POPULATION: 5,153,000 (Arab 99% [of whom about 50% are Palestinian Arab])

LEBANON
POPULATION: 3,628,000 (Arab 93% [of whom 83% are Lebanese Arab and 10% Palestinian Arab])

AFGHANISTAN

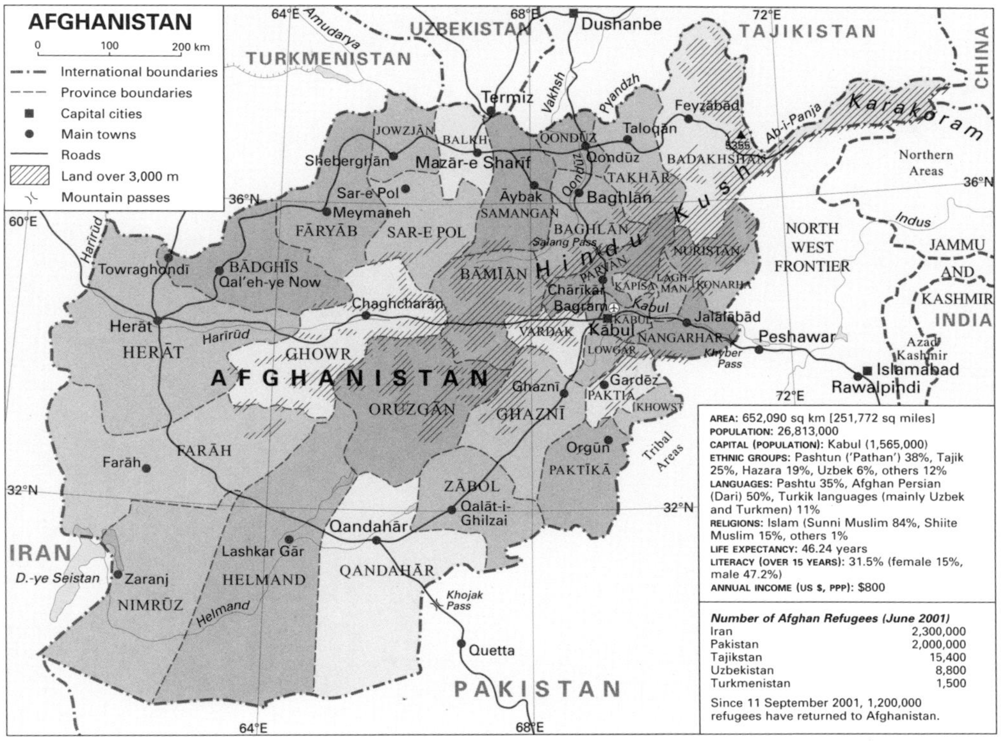

AREA: 652,090 sq km [251,772 sq miles]
POPULATION: 26,813,000
CAPITAL (POPULATION): Kabul (1,565,000)
ETHNIC GROUPS: Pashtun ('Pathan') 38%, Tajik 25%, Hazara 19%, Uzbek 6%, others 12%
LANGUAGES: Pashtu 35%, Afghan Persian (Dari) 50%, Turkik languages (mainly Uzbek and Turkmen) 11%
RELIGIONS: Islam (Sunni Muslim 84%, Shiite Muslim 15%, others 1%
LIFE EXPECTANCY: 46.24 years
LITERACY (OVER 15 YEARS): 31.5% (female 15%, male 47.2%)
ANNUAL INCOME (US $, PPP): $800

Number of Afghan Refugees (June 2001)

Iran	2,300,000
Pakistan	2,000,000
Tajikstan	15,400
Uzbekistan	8,800
Turkmenistan	1,500

Since 11 September 2001, 1,200,000 refugees have returned to Afghanistan.

KEY TO WORLD MAP PAGES

NORTH
AMERICA

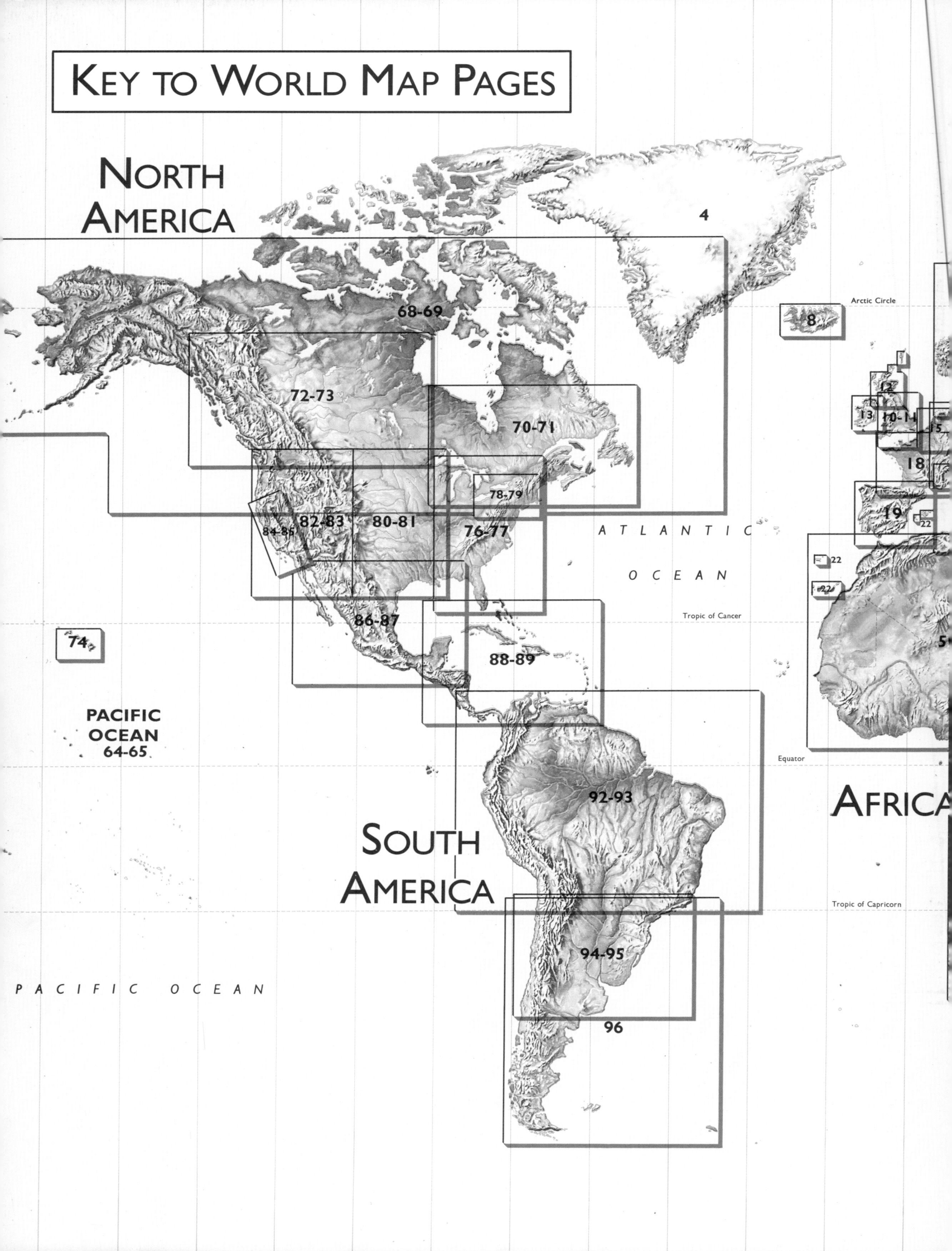

4

Arctic Circle

8

68-69

72-73

70-71

12

13 10-11 15

78-79

18

84-85 82-83 80-81 76-77 19

ATLANTIC

22

OCEAN

22

86-87

22

Tropic of Cancer

74

88-89

5

PACIFIC
OCEAN
64-65

Equator

92-93

AFRICA

SOUTH

AMERICA

94-95

Tropic of Capricorn

PACIFIC   OCEAN

96